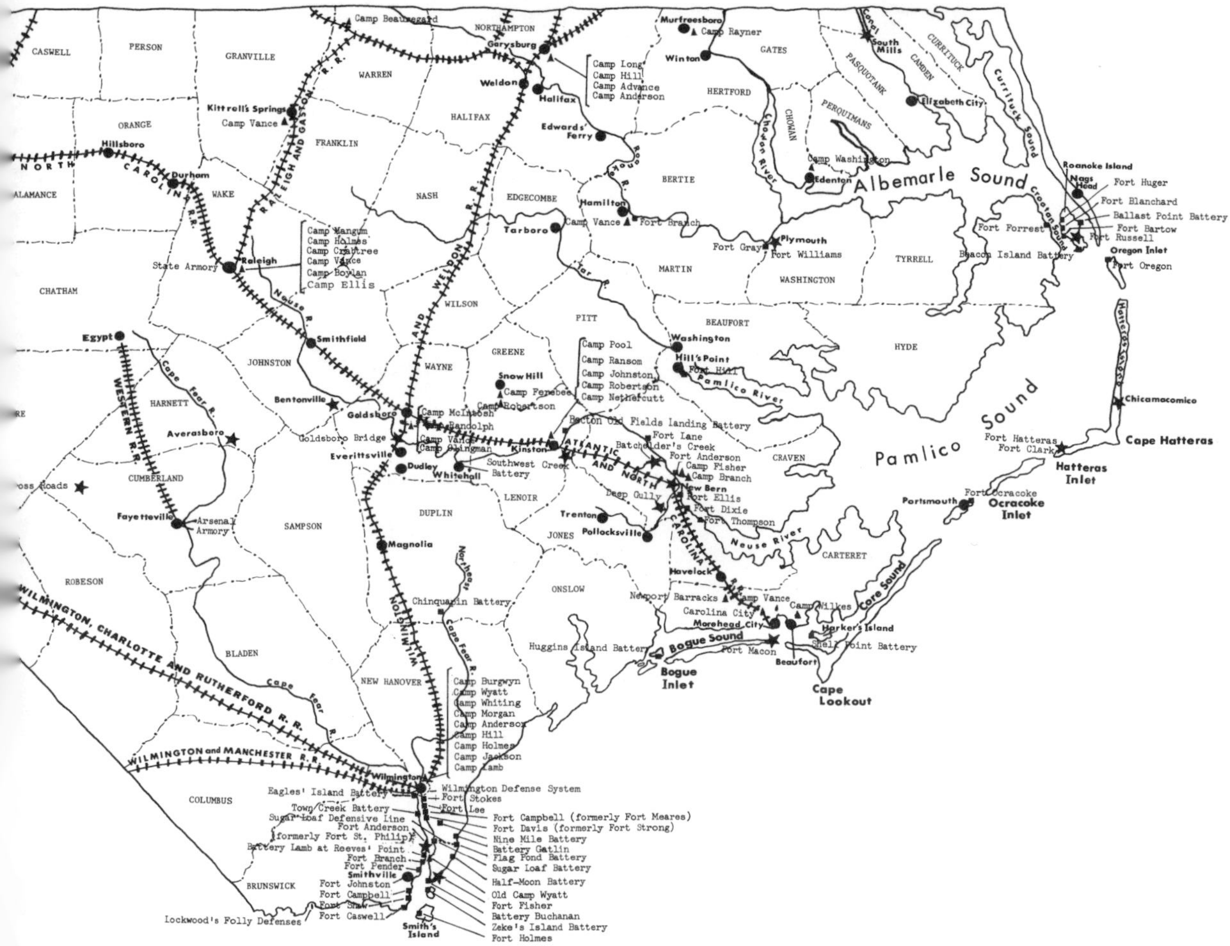
CASWELL
PERSON
GRANVILLE
WARREN
NORTHAMPTON
Camp Beauregard
Garysburg
Murfreesboro
Camp Rayner
Winton
GATES
South Mills
CURRITUCK
CAMDEN
PASQUOTANK
Currituck Sound
Weldon
Halifax
Camp Long
Camp Hill
Camp Advance
Camp Anderson
HERTFORD
Elizabeth City
PERQUIMANS
CHOWAN
Chowan River
Kittrell's Springs
Camp Vance
ORANGE
HALIFAX
Edwards' Ferry
FRANKLIN
RALEIGH AND GASTON R.R.
Hillsboro
NORTH CAROLINA R.R.
Durham
ALAMANCE
WAKE
NASH
EDGECOMBE
Hamilton
Roanoke R.
BERTIE
Camp Washington
Edenton
Albemarle Sound
Roanoke Island
Nags Head
Fort Huger
Fort Blanchard
Ballast Point Battery
Fort Bartow
Fort Russell
Croatan Sound
Camp Vance
Fort Branch
Tarboro
Camp Mangum
Camp Holmes
Camp Crabtree
Camp Vance
Camp Boylan
Camp Ellis
State Armory
Raleigh
Fort Gray
Plymouth
Fort Williams
Fort Forrest
Beacon Island Battery
Oregon Inlet
Fort Oregon
TYRRELL
MARTIN
WASHINGTON
CHATHAM
WILSON
WILMINGTON AND WELDON R.R.
Neuse R.
Smithfield
PITT
BEAUFORT
Washington
Hill's Point
Fort Hill
Pamlico River
HYDE
Egypt
JOHNSTON
GREENE
Camp Pool
Camp Ransom
Camp Johnston
Camp Robertson
Camp Nethercutt
Snow Hill
Camp Ferebee
Camp Robertson
WAYNE
Cape Fear R.
WESTERN R.R.
HARNETT
Bentonville
Goldsboro
Camp McIntosh
Camp Randolph
Camp Vance
Camp Clingman
Goldsboro Bridge
Averasboro
Everittsville
Dudley
Whitehall
Southwest Creek Battery
Kinston
Bacton Old Fields landing Battery
Fort Lane
Batchelder's Creek
ATLANTIC AND NORTH CAROLINA R.R.
Fort Anderson
Camp Fisher
Camp Branch
New Bern
Fort Ellis
Fort Dixie
Fort Thompson
Deep Gully
CRAVEN
Pamlico Sound
Chicamacomico
Hatteras
Fort Hatteras
Fort Clark
Cape Hatteras
Hatteras Inlet
CUMBERLAND
Cross Roads
LENOIR
DUPLIN
Fayetteville
Arsenal Armory
SAMPSON
Trenton
Pollocksville
JONES
Neuse River
Portsmouth
Fort Ocracoke
Ocracoke Inlet
CARTERET
Magnolia
Havelock
Northeast
ROBESON
ONSLOW
Chinquapin Battery
Newport Barracks
Camp Vance
Camp Wilkes
Carolina City
Morehead City
Core Sound
Harker's Island
Shell Point Battery
Bogue Sound
Huggins Island Battery
Fort Macon
Beaufort
Bogue Inlet
Cape Lookout
WILMINGTON, CHARLOTTE AND RUTHERFORD R.R.
BLADEN
Cape Fear R.
NEW HANOVER
Camp Burgwyn
Camp Wyatt
Camp Whiting
Camp Morgan
Camp Anderson
Camp Hill
Camp Holmes
Camp Jackson
Camp Lamb
WILMINGTON and MANCHESTER R.R.
Wilmington
Eagles' Island Battery
Wilmington Defense System
Fort Stokes
Fort Lee
COLUMBUS
Town Creek Battery
Sugar Loaf Defensive Line
Fort Anderson
(formerly Fort St. Philip)
Battery Lamb at Reeves' Point
Fort Branch
Fort Pender
Smithville
Fort Johnston
Fort Campbell
Fort Shaw
Fort Caswell
Lockwood's Folly Defenses
BRUNSWICK
Smith's Island
Fort Campbell (formerly Fort Meares)
Fort Davis (formerly Fort Strong)
Nine Mile Battery
Battery Gatlin
Flag Pond Battery
Sugar Loaf Battery
Half-Moon Battery
Old Camp Wyatt
Fort Fisher
Battery Buchanan
Zeke's Island Battery
Fort Holmes

NORTH CAROLINA TROOPS

1861-1865

A ROSTER

This photograph of William Holland Thomas was taken in 1858, when he was serving as a state senator and chief of the Lufty Cherokees. Image courtesy of the North Carolina State Archives.

North Carolina Troops
1861-1865
A Roster

MATTHEW M. BROWN & MICHAEL W. COFFEY

VOL. XVI

THOMAS'S LEGION

RALEIGH, NORTH CAROLINA
OFFICE OF ARCHIVES AND HISTORY
2008

Printed and Bound by
Edwards Brothers Inc., Ann Arbor, Michigan

ISBN 978-0-86526-336-9 (Volume XVI)
ISBN 978-0-86526-005-4 (Set)

PREFACE

This volume contains the history and roster of a most unorthodox North Carolina Confederate Civil War unit. Thomas's Legion was the creation of William Holland Thomas, an influential businessman and state legislator with strong ties to the Cherokee Indians. He raised a small battalion of Cherokees in April, 1862. He gradually expanded his command with companies of white soldiers raised in western North Carolina, eastern Tennessee, and Virginia. By the end of 1862, Thomas's Legion comprised an infantry regiment and a battalion of infantry and cavalry; an artillery battery was added in April, 1863. The legion was originally stationed in Eastern Tennessee. However, in September, 1863, Thomas and two companies departed for North Carolina and organized a new battalion. The remainder of his legion saw action in eastern Tennessee, southwestern Virginia, and the Shenandoah Valley, before rejoining Thomas in early 1865, for the final military operations in western North Carolina.

This is the first volume of *North Carolina Troops* in twenty-six years not to be edited by Weymouth T. Jordan, Jr. As it would clearly be impossible for any one man to fill Mr. Jordan's shoes, we decided that two men could make a better attempt. This volume was therefore created by the partnership of Matthew M. Brown and Michael W. Coffey. Mr. Brown has worked on the N.C. Troops series since 1994. Dr. Coffey has researched and written on North Carolina Civil War subjects, and received his Ph.D. in history from the University of Southern Mississippi in 2002.

Contributions of others to this book cannot be overestimated. Chief among these is professional researcher Henry Mintz, who, armed with an Archie K. Davis Fellowship from the North Caroliniana Society, delved into the materials at the National Archives to find original records that hold the story of Thomas's Legion.

We are privileged to have in this volume two maps created by Mark A. Moore of the North Carolina Office of Archives and History. Mr. Moore is regarded as the finest Civil War cartographer working today, because of the detail, accuracy and readability of his maps.

Susan M. Trimble at the Historical Publications Section of the North Carolina Office of Archives and History gave her expertise in typesetting this volume.

Mickey Black of Salisbury once again shared his extensive knowledge of uniforms, weapons, accouterments, and Civil War photography, in providing information for the description of the dust cover photograph.

Cemetery historian Charles Purser of Garner provided valuable information about soldiers' places of death, especially those who died in prison camps far from home. Bob High of Whiteville continued his thorough research of 19th-century newspapers, extracting valuable information on soldiers. Tom Broadfoot of Broadfoot Publishing Company, Wilmington, provided valuable access to microfilm records. We are grateful also to the many people who contacted us to provide information concerning their ancestors.

We are thankful as well for the valuable contributions of numerous archivists and other history professionals, especially George Frizzell and the late Priscilla Proctor at Special Collections, Western Carolina University; John E. White at the Southern Historical Collection, University of North Carolina at Chapel Hill; Janie C. Morris, Eleanor A. Mills, and Elizabeth B. Dunn at Special Collections, Perkins Library, Duke University; Kimberly M. Cumber, Doris J. Wilson, A. Christopher Meekins and Larry Odzak at the North Carolina State Archives; Cynthia L. Jones, Pam S. Toms, and Cheryl W. McLean at the North

Carolina State Library, and Donna E. Kelly and William H. Brown at the Historical Publications Section of the North Carolina Office of Archives and History.

Most of all, we are grateful to Weymouth T. Jordan, who in his thirty-four years of work on this series, established the templates and procedures used to create this volume, and amassed our excellent library of reference materials. Mr. Jordan continually strived to improve the quality of the series, making it a more valuable tool for readers, researchers, and descendants. Mr. Jordan began the work on the roster of the Thomas Legion in this volume, even continuing work after his retirement. We are also grateful to Mr. Jordan for developing relationships with volunteers who continue to make important contributions to the series. Mr. Jordan has also lent us his personal Civil War library, saving us many journeys to the State Library. It is a challenge and an honor to carry on his legacy.

Matthew M. Brown
Michael W. Coffey
February 20, 2008

CONTENTS

MAPS

SOME ABBREVIATED CITATIONS USED IN THE HISTORY OF THOMAS'S LEGION

DU: Rare Book, Manuscript, and Special Collections Library, William R. Perkins Library, Duke University, Durham, N.C.

NA: National Archives, Washington, D.C.

NCOAH: State Archives, North Carolina Office of Archives and History, Raleigh, N.C.

O.R.: U.S. War Department, *The War of the Rebellion: A Compilation of the Official Records of the Union and Confederate Armies*, 128 vols. (Washington, D.C.: Government Printing Office, 1880-1901.)

O.R. (Supplement): Janet B. Hewett, et al., eds., *Supplement to the Official Records of the Union and Confederate Armies*, 100 vols. (Wilmington, N.C.: Broadfoot Publishing Company, 1994-2001.)

P.C.: Private Collections, State Archives, North Carolina Office of Archives and History.

RG 109: Record Group 109: War Department Collection of Confederate Records, National Archives.

SHC-UNC: Southern Historical Collection, Manuscripts Department, Wilson Library, University of North Carolina at Chapel Hill, Chapel Hill, N.C.

WCU: Manuscripts, Special Collections, Hunter Library, Western Carolina University, Cullowhee, N.C.

Illustrations appear on pages ii, xv, and xvi.

INTRODUCTION

The service records published in this volume are derived in large part from materials in the North Carolina section of National Archives Record Group 109. That collection, entitled the "Compiled Service Records of Confederate Soldiers Who Served in Organizations from the State of North Carolina," consists of approximately 125,000 envelopes, each of which contains service record information for a soldier who served in a North Carolina unit. Some envelopes contain original documents such as pay vouchers, requisitions, court-martial proceedings, letters of recommendation and resignation, and enlistment and discharge certificates. However, most of the material consists of abstracts from company muster rolls, regimental returns, hospital and prison registers, parole ledgers, appointment books, promotion lists, general and special orders, inspection reports, the North Carolina adjutant general's "Roll of Honor," and other records. The entire North Carolina collection has been reproduced in a 580-reel microfilm edition (M270) that is available at the North Carolina State Archives in Raleigh. That copy was used in preparing this volume.

A second National Archives source used in this volume is the Unfiled Papers and Slips Belonging in Confederate Compiled Service Records (M347). That collection consists of miscellaneous documents collected or abstracted for inclusion in the Compiled Service Records but, for various reasons, never interfiled in specific subgroups. Other National Archives collections of which some use was made are the Compiled Service Records of Confederate Soldiers Who Served in Organizations Raised Directly by the Confederate Government (M258); Register of Confederate Soldiers, Sailors, and Citizens Who Died in Federal Prisons and Military Hospitals in the North, 1861-1865 (M918); Compiled Service Records of Confederate Soldiers Who Served in Organizations from the States of Tennessee (M268), and Virginia (M324); and Compiled Service Records of Volunteer Union Soldiers Who Served in Organizations from the States of North Carolina (M401) and Tennessee (M395). National Archives collections that were utilized primarily in the Thomas Legion history include Letters Received by the Confederate Secretary of War, 1861-1865 (M437); Letters Received by the Confederate Adjutant and Inspector General, 1861-1865 (M474); and Confederate States Army Casualties: Lists and Narrative Reports, 1861-1865 (M836).

Material obtained from the National Archives was supplemented by records in the North Carolina State Archives, primarily in the Adjutant General's Papers and the Civil War Collection. Those include orders and correspondence, muster rolls, bounty payrolls, receipt rolls for clothing, militia records, wartime claims for bounty pay and allowances, postwar registers of claims for artificial limbs, records of the North Carolina Confederate Soldiers' Home, and postwar pension applications filed by Confederate veterans and their widows.

Information was obtained also from the 1860 and 1870 federal censuses of North Carolina, Tennessee, and Virginia; casualty lists and obituaries in newspapers published during and after the Civil War; *The War of the Rebellion: A Compilation of the Official Records of the Union and Confederate Armies*; *Official Records of the Union and Confederate Navies in the War of the Rebellion*; the North Carolina volume of *Confederate Military History*; Walter Clark's *Histories of the Several Regiments and Battalions from North Carolina in the Great War, 1861-'65*; the *Confederate Veteran*; the North Carolina *County Heritage Book* series; published and unpublished genealogies; gravestone indexes; biographical dictionaries; records of the North Carolina division of the United Daughters of the Confederacy; and postwar pension applications filed in the states of

Tennessee and Florida by North Carolina veterans and their widows. Relevant letters, diaries, reminiscences, and other manuscripts in the North Carolina State Archives, the Southern Historical Collection (University of North Carolina-Chapel Hill), and the Duke University Library Special Collections Department, were abstracted. Valuable information concerning Indian soldiers was found in "The Inoli Letters," MS No. 2236, Folder 1, Bureau of American Ethnology, Smithsonian Institute, Washington, D.C., translated and published in Kilpatrick Kilpatrick, translators and editors, *The Shadow of Sequoyah: Social Documents of the Cherokees* (Norman: University of Oklahoma Press, 1965), as well as the *Extra Census Bulletin. Indians. Eastern Band of Cherokees of North Carolina* (Washington, D.C.: 1892). Useful information was received from professional and lay historians, from descendants of Civil War veterans, and from other private individuals. The web site Superpages.com was helpful in determining the common spellings of surnames in different counties. John W. Moore's *Roster of North Carolina Troops in the War Between the States*, although a commendable effort for its day (1882), is outdated and was used only for limited cross-checking and comparison purposes.

The regimental and battalion rosters in this volume are organized as follows:

—Field officers (colonels, lieutenant colonels, and majors), staff officers (adjutants, assistant quartermasters, assistant commissaries of subsistence, surgeons, chaplains, and ensigns), and regimental noncommissioned officers and other ranks (sergeants major, quartermaster sergeants, commissary sergeants, ordnance sergeants, and hospital stewards) are grouped together by rank under a major heading entitled "Field and Staff." Each soldier is listed in the chronological sequence in which he served.

—Rosters of the companies of which each regiment or battalion was composed follow the "Field and Staff" section and are divided into two sections entitled "Officers" and "Noncommissioned Officers and Privates." Within the "Officers" section are separate subsections for "Captains" and "Lieutenants." Captains are listed in chronological order; lieutenants are listed alphabetically. Enlisted men (sergeants, corporals, and privates) are listed alphabetically in the "Noncommissioned Officers and Privates" section.

—Following the last company roster is a "Miscellaneous" section listing soldiers who were members of the regiment or battalion but whose records do not indicate the company to which they belonged.

The procedures adopted in composing the service records in this volume are as follows:

—Spelling of surnames and given names is determined by comparing information in the Compiled Service Records and contemporary military records with information from sources such as Confederate pension applications, the 1860 and 1870 federal censuses of North Carolina, the North Carolina *County Heritage Book* series, gravestone indexes, and Superpages.com. All sources have been utilized with due caution and care, but there is often uncertainty about which version of a name is correct, and errors are inevitable. Some service records therefore conclude with alternate spellings of names, and the index has been cross-referenced to facilitate the location of surnames that may appear in corrupted form.

—Prewar occupations are derived primarily from the Compiled Service Records; the 1860 federal census, the *County Heritage Book* series, and other sources have been utilized also. Age-at-date-of-enlistment information is derived primarily from the Compiled Service Records, the 1860 and 1870 federal censuses, and various genealogical sources. This information is frequently inaccurate or contradictory. If a service record contains any item of misinformation, it is most likely the soldier's age.

—Enlistment dates and places of enlistment are derived primarily from company muster-in rolls or from the first company muster roll on which a soldier's name appears.

—Cities and towns are cited under the names by which they were known in 1861-1865; however, in instances where a name change has occurred, the 1861-1865 designation is followed by the current name in parentheses—for example, Smithville (Southport). North Carolina counties, cities, and towns are not followed by a reference to the state except forclarity (Asheville; but Washington, North Carolina). Counties and localities in other states are followed by the name of the state only the first time that they are mentioned in a service record. West Virginia place names are cited as being in West Virginia if the date of the reference is on or subsequent to June 20, 1863, the date that the state was admitted to the Union. If the reference is prior to that date, the locality is cited as being in [West] Virginia. In a few cases, it has proved impossible to determine the state or county in which a town or geographical feature was located, either because no such place could be identified or because there are two or more places with the same name and no evidence was available as to the one intended. Such place names appear in quotation marks.

—Causes of death and information that reflects negatively upon a soldier is presented in quotation marks to emphasize that it is quoted verbatim from a reliable primary or secondary source. Information that is of doubtful accuracy, ambiguous, contradictory, or unverifiable appears in quotation marks followed by a question mark in brackets.

—"On or about" is used when an event that is not a verified or verifiable historical fact is cited in primary records as having occurred on two or more dates that are more or less consecutive, the date cited being the one that seems most probably correct: "Died at Raleigh on or about August 8, 1864." When there is no reason to favor one date over another, hyphenated dates are cited if the dates are consecutive: "Died at Raleigh on August 8-9, 1864." Hyphenated dates preceded by "during" indicate that a certain condition prevailed *throughout* the period specified: "Hospitalized at Raleigh during March-April, 1864." Hyphenated dates preceded by "in" indicate a *single event* that occurred *during* a specified time frame; for example, "Hospitalized at Raleigh in March-April, 1864," indicates that a soldier was admitted to a Raleigh hospital on an unknown date during March or April, 1864. That system was found necessary because in many instances the exact date of an event could not be determined.

—"Present or accounted for" indicates that a soldier was either present for duty or absent for reasons other than desertion or absence without leave. Desertion and absence without leave are terms that were often employed without distinction by company clerks; hence, a soldier who absented himself without authorization but returned of his own accord sixty days later could be listed during his absence either as a deserter or as absent without leave. The editor has judged it best not to arbitrarily standardize those terms, and references to desertion or absence without leave are, in the overwhelming majority of cases, taken directly from primary sources. In most instances, unauthorized absences of twenty days or less have been excluded.

—"No further records" appears at the end of service records when there is doubt as to the manner in which a soldier's military career terminated: "Company muster rolls indicate that he was discharged at Weldon on May 9, 1864; however, medical records indicate that he died in hospital at Weldon on May 30, 1864. No further records." Use of that phrase does not preclude the existence of additional military records of any description but only of those relative to important aspects of a soldier's service. Additional records pertaining to furloughs, special assignments, issuance of clothing, and other relatively insignificant activities exist, sometimes in quantity, for many of the soldiers whose service records appear in this volume.

—Brackets are utilized at the end of service records to convey information that could not be readily incorporated in the main text. They also enclose interpolations, source citations, cross-references, and editorial comments.

During the forty-six years since the inception of the roster project, rules of capitalization, punctuation, and other matters of style have changed considerably; for example, it is no longer considered appropriate to capitalize an individual's title or rank unless it appears before his name. However, except in those few instances where a new methodology provided greater clarity or otherwise seemed significantly advantageous, stylistic usages employed in earlier volumes have been retained. One particularly noticeable punctuation oddity that should be mentioned involves the use in the possessive case of singular nouns ending in "s." Personal names are rendered "s's" (Jones's Brigade), but, on the theory that the historic spelling of a community or geographical feature should not be altered by modern rules of punctuation, place-names ending in the possessive are rendered without the final "s" (Jones' Mill, Virginia). Thus the legion commanded by Col. William H. Thomas is referred to in this volume as Thomas's Legion, although it was more often referred to as Thomas' Legion in Civil War correspondence.

Matthew M. Brown
Michael W. Coffey
February 20, 2008

This photograph depicts Cherokee veterans of Thomas's Legion who attended a reunion of Confederate veterans in New Orleans in 1903. Among them are Maj. W. W. Stringfield, third man on the back row. To his right is Sgt. Swateh of 2nd Company A, Infantry Regiment. To his right is Pvt. Santoneh of the same company. Image courtesy of *The Carolina Mountaineer* (Waynesville, N.C.).

This photograph depicts Cherokee Indians, some of whom were veterans of 2nd Company A and Company B of the Infantry Regiment of Thomas's Legion, and some of whom were sons of veterans of those companies. They attended a reunion in Louisville, Kentucky, on June 1-3, 1900. They are identified by number: No. 1 is Maj. W. W. Stringfield; No. 2 is "Jno Jason" (probably Jassan of 2nd Company A); No 3 is "Wild Cat" (Cah hah of 2nd Company A); No. 4 is "Se-quo-___" (probably Standing Wolf Sequoyeh of 2nd Company A or Sequoyeh Sellaleeseh of Company B); No. 5 is "Jo Lowen"; No. 6 is "Beat.Slo-Nee-Ta" (probably Bird Sololaneta of 2nd Company A); No. 7 is "Sou-a-tee-Owl" (Swateh of 2nd Company A); No. 8 is "Nick-O-demus" (probably Nickojack Talonusteh or Nickojack Tewyeh of 2nd Company A); No. 9 is "Jno. Jackson" (John Jackson of 2nd Company A); No. 10 is "Jim Keg" (Santoneh of 2nd Company A); No. 11 is "Jno. Greybeard," son of Ezekiel Greybeard of 2nd Company A. Nos. 18 and 20 are unidentified veterans, and the others are sons of veterans. Image courtesy of the North Carolina State Archives.

THOMAS'S LEGION

Any understanding of the record of Thomas's Legion is complicated by both the unit's development and by its treatment in early studies of North Carolina's Civil War record. The Legion evolved from a small battalion into an organization consisting of an infantry regiment, a battalion that at one time included both infantry and cavalry companies, and an artillery battery. Yet the Legion seldom operated together. Throughout much of its service, its companies were scattered defending mountain passes and railroad bridges in eastern Tennessee. In the fall of 1863, two companies of the regiment returned to western North Carolina and formed the nucleus of a second battalion. Meanwhile, the rest of the Legion saw action in eastern Tennessee and the Shenandoah Valley. Furthermore, at different times companies were transferred in or out, or shifted around and redesignated.

The Legion's tangled story was further confused by early historians. When John W. Moore published his pioneering *Roster of North Carolina Troops in the War Between the States* (1882), he was hampered by incomplete records. Whether by accident or design, he imposed a fictitious sense of order on the rather chaotic organization of the state's units. In the process, he rechristened the Infantry Regiment of the Legion as the 69th Regiment N.C. Troops, a designation which during the war belonged to an entirely different unit. Walker's Battalion of infantry and cavalry became a cavalry battalion, while Levi's Battery became Thomas's Light Battery. These errors were compounded in Walter Clark's seminal *Histories of the Several Regiments and Battalions from North Carolina in the Great War 1861-'65* (1901). In that series, William Williams Stringfield also referred to the Infantry Regiment (and, sometimes, the entire Legion) as the 69th Regiment N.C. Troops, while Robert Akin expanded Walker's Battalion into a hitherto unknown regiment, the 80th Regiment N.C. Troops, incorporating the battery and two companies of the second battalion into its organization, and ignoring the fact that other companies transferred out. Both men were veterans of the Legion and surely knew better. Although Vernon H. Crow set much of the record straight in his 1982 book-length study, *Storm in the Mountains: Thomas' Confederate Legion of Cherokee Indians and Mountaineers*, these problems must be kept in mind by anyone interested in researching the Legion or the men who served in its ranks.[1]

1. John W. Moore, *Roster of North Carolina in the War Between the States*, 4 vols. (Raleigh: Ashe & Gatling/Edwards & Broughton, 1882), 1:iv-vi, 3:151, 196, 214 (hereinafter cited as Moore's *Roster*); A. Gordon, "Organization of Troops," in Walter Clark, ed., *Histories of the Several Regiments and Battalions from North Carolina in the Great War 1861-'65. Written By Members of the Respective Commands*, 5 vols. (Goldsboro: Nash Brothers, 1901), 1:15 (hereinafter cited as Clark, *North Carolina Regiments*); W. W. Stringfield, "Sixty-Ninth Regiment," in ibid., 3:729, 733; R. A. Aiken, "Eightieth Regiment," in ibid., 4:119-121; Louis H. Manarin and Weymouth T. Jordan Jr., comps., *North Carolina Troops 1861-1865: A Roster*, 15 vols. to date (Raleigh: Office of Archives and History, 1966-), 2:560-561; Vernon H. Crow, *Storm in the Mountains: Thomas' Confederate Legion of Cherokee Indians and Mountaineers* (Cherokee: Press of the Museum of the Cherokee Indian, 1982), 145-147. See also E. Stanley Godbold and Mattie Russell, *Confederate Colonel and Cherokee Chief: The Life of William Holland Thomas* (Knoxville: University of Tennessee Press, 1990), 107-109. While Godbold and Russell recognize that the term "69th Regiment" was misapplied to the Legion, they also seemed to think that the designation was intended to refer to the entire Legion, not just the regiment, perhaps as a result of Stringfield's interchangeable use of the term in his history. They also thought that the battalion was an all-cavalry unit. Paul A. Thomsen's *Rebel Chief: The Motley Life of Colonel William Holland Thomas, C.S.A.* (New York: Tom Doherty Associates/Forge Press, 2004) presents a confused picture of the Legion's organization and composition (179-181, 183-184). Some postwar materials, including the Clark series, render Robert Akin's last name as "Aiken"; however, other postwar documents and virtually all wartime materials (including those signed by Akin himself) give his name as "Akin," which will be taken in the text as the preferred spelling.

Perhaps more so than other units, Thomas's Legion bore the distinctive stamp of its founder. William Holland Thomas was long a prominent figure in western North Carolina. Born in 1805 near Waynesville, he was raised by his widowed mother, herself a first cousin of the mother of future president Zachary Taylor. Thomas was a classic example of the self-made individual, starting out at the age of thirteen managing a store for another person. From these beginnings, he became a very active businessman, eventually owning a series of stores, shops, and other enterprises stretching throughout the region into eastern Tennessee. He speculated heavily in land, and was a major promoter of railroad development for the western part of the state. In an area where slavery had barely gained a foothold, Thomas was one of the more conspicuous slaveholders, owning over fifty slaves by the 1860s.[2]

With the local prominence gained through his business activities, it is not surprising that Thomas embarked on a career in politics. Elected to the North Carolina Senate in 1848 as the representative of the 50th Senatorial District, he was repeatedly reelected through 1860. A Democrat in an area dominated by Whig politics, Thomas's success as a politician was in part due to his adoption of Whiggish ideas on internal improvements. Much of the road network and consequent trade upon which western North Carolina depended stretched westward into Tennessee and, more importantly, southwards into South Carolina and Georgia. Thomas's plans for local railroad expansion would not only more firmly link the different geographical sections of North Carolina, but would expand his own area's profitable trade with its western and southern neighbors. It was perhaps not coincidental that Thomas's own business dealings would be helped by these efforts, which also influenced his political outlook on the brewing crisis between North and South. Although by no means a militant "fire-eater," Thomas echoed the position of many antebellum Southern Democrats that the region had the right to secede if the Federal government ever attempted to interfere with the "peculiar institution." Like other local politicians, he argued for solidarity between western North Carolina and the plantation South, the focal point of the area's outside trade. As early as February 1851, although still a supporter of the Union, he gave a speech discussing not only the possibility of secession as a last resort, but of a potential war between the sections that might end in a heroic last stand in the mountain passes of North Carolina. When disunion finally came, Thomas put himself more openly in the secessionist camp, writing in February 1861, to the editors of the Raleigh *State Journal* that "[t]he cause of the South is our cause; the safety of the South is our safety; and the destiny of the South is our destiny!" He was chosen a member of the state's secession convention after Fort Sumter.[3]

2. Godbold and Russell, *Confederate Colonel and Cherokee Chief*, 1-16, 28-32, 42, 47-52, 73-77, 86-88; John C. Inscoe, *Mountain Masters: Slavery, and the Sectional Crisis in Western North Carolina* (Knoxville: University of Tennessee Press, 1989), 43, 55, 66; Thomsen, *Rebel Chief*, 29-43, 49-51, 96-98, 108, 117-119, 123-130, 243 n. 94, 244 n. 95.

3. John L. Cheney Jr., ed., *North Carolina Government 1585-1979: A Narrative and Statistical History* (Raleigh: Department of the Secretary of State, 1981), 316-327; Inscoe, *Mountain Masters*, 30-34, 40-53, 132-139, 141-142, 144-150, 152-264 (especially 195-196, 227-228), 295 n. 24; Crow, *Storm in the Mountains*, 3; Godbold and Russell, *Confederate Colonel and Cherokee Chief*, 67-73, 86-96; Thomsen, *Rebel Chief*, 85, 129-130, 137-144; "Remarks of Mr. Thomas, of Haywood," *Semi-Weekly Standard* (Raleigh), February 5, 1851; William Holland Thomas to editors of the *State Journal* (Raleigh), February 18, 1861, William Holland Thomas Papers, Rare Book, Manuscript, and Special Collections Library, William R. Perkins Library, Duke University, Durham, N.C. (hereinafter cited as DU).

What set Thomas apart from other antebellum North Carolina politicians was his long and complex relationship with the Cherokee Indians. Thomas grew up when the Cherokees were still a major part of the population of the western part of the state, and early showed an avid interest in their history and culture. His curiousity led to his adoption into the tribe by Yonaguska, a prominent chief. Thomas's first and main store was located at Quallatown in Haywood County, where he did perhaps as much if not more business with the Indians as he did with neighboring whites. As pressure grew in the 1830s to evict the Cherokees from their lands, a treaty was forcibly negotiated by the federal government which resulted in their removal. Exceptions were made, however, for those Cherokees who under an 1819 treaty had accepted 640 acres of land apiece outside of what was officially considered tribal territory. The new removal treaty provided that those who remained under the 1819 agreement received a share of the federal funds paid in compensation to those evicted. The band led by Yonaguska, known as the Oconaluftee or Lufty Indians, were among the Cherokees who had left their tribal area and settled among adjacent lands now claimed by whites. Treaty or no treaty, Yonaguska's Cherokees were afraid that when the time for removal came that they would be evicted as well. In 1831, they chose Thomas to be their agent in Washington, D.C.[4]

Throughout the 1830s and 1840s, Thomas worked hard to secure the claims of the Lufty Cherokees. He was often opposed in his efforts by the faction led by Chief John Ross, the leader of tribal resistance to the removal treaty, who nevertheless went into the west with most of the Cherokees. Ross sought to get all federal recognition and financial payments granted to the western Cherokees alone. Despite obstacles, Thomas protected not only the Lufty Cherokees and similar groups from removal but others living within the traditional tribal boundaries as well. He also secured promises from the federal government to pay the money owed under the treaty, although actually collecting it proved to be more difficult. Nevertheless, acting as agent for the Lufty Indians collectively and holding power of attorney for many individuals, Thomas disbursed some of the money due to the Indians. Even some of his land speculation was for Cherokee benefit; while he bought thousands of acres for himself, he bought thousands more in trust for the Indians. His position as the representative of the Lufty Cherokees was strengthened when Yonaguska died in 1839. Following their former leader's advice, the tribe elected Thomas to be their new chief, the only white man to have that distinction. After his election to the state senate, Thomas increasingly handed over much of his work on behalf of the Cherokees to business associate James W. Terrell, although he remained close to his adopted people.[5]

Much later in life Thomas said, "If it had not been for the Indians I would not have been in the war," implying that his only motive was to protect them and their culture. In fact,

4. Godbold and Russell, *Confederate Colonel and Cherokee Chief*, 5, 11-16, 18-24; John R. Finger, *The Eastern Band of Cherokees, 1819-1900* (Knoxville: University of Tennessee Press, 1984), 16-17.

5. Godbold and Russell, *Confederate Colonel and Cherokee Chief*, 17-47, 56-63, 85-86; Crow, *Storm in the Mountains*, 2-3; Finger, *Eastern Band of Cherokees*, 18, 31, 41, 44-59. Yonaguska's son-in-law, Flying Squirrel, asserted that he was elected principal chief, not Thomas. His claim was not formally recognized until 1867, however, when he was chosen to replace Thomas, as the latter's mental decline and financial problems threatened the tracts of land that he had bought in trust for the Indians. Finger, *Eastern Band of Cherokees*, 31; Godbold and Russell, *Confederate Colonel and Cherokee Chief*, 40-41, 132-133.

Thomas's motives for taking an active military role were complex, as his political and economic ambitions for himself and western North Carolina played a part. He dreamed that the region would become the economic and educational center for the new Confederate States of America, and might one day be the site of the national capital. His concern for the Indians' well-being was tempered by a willingness to put them into military service for the state and the Confederacy, which would not only expose them to violence, but might carry them far from their homeland. Further, not all Cherokees would share his vision of their role in the war. Some joined the Federals, while others attempted to stay neutral in a conflict which they felt did not concern them. Such divisions mirrored those that on a larger scale divided whites in the region between those supporting the Confederacy, those for the Union, and those who wished the conflict would pass them by.[6]

The genesis of Thomas's Legion was a Cherokee unit organized in May 1861. Following the end of a special session of the legislature to decide on calling a secession convention, Thomas went home to explain the political situation to the Cherokees. Although it was reported that the subchiefs claimed not to understand the sectional crisis, they affirmed their own and the tribe's loyalty to Thomas and to North Carolina. Thomas then mustered some two hundred Cherokees into the "Junaluska Zouaves," apparently a two-company battalion for local use. Outside of reports of its initial organization, it soon lapsed into obscurity. With his concurrent responsibilities to both the senate and the state convention, Thomas was probably too busy to more formally organize the Zouaves. Nevertheless, the defense of western North Carolina remained central to his thinking, as is illustrated by an incident at the convention in June. It was reported that he was called to order for an outburst when his efforts to secure three regiments to guard the mountains failed. It was but one of many clashes during the war between Thomas and those who stood in the way of his plans.[7]

On September 9, Thomas introduced a bill in the North Carolina Senate to authorize the recruitment of his battalion into state service. He then offered the battalion for national service to Pres. Jefferson Davis on September 15. Although not close, Thomas and Davis had a relationship going back many years. Not only did they know each other from Thomas's days in Washington, but they had a more personal link through Thomas's distant kinship to Zachary Taylor, whose late daughter had been Davis's first wife. Davis replied indirectly to Thomas on September 19 through Asst. Adj. Gen. R. H. Chilton. The president authorized the mustering of a Cherokee battalion into Confederate service, accompanied by the rather odd idea that "it can be used advantageously for the defense of the coast and

6. James Mooney, "Myths of the Cherokee," *Nineteenth Annual Report of the Bureau of American Ethnology, 1897-1898* (Washington, D.C.: Government Printing Office, 1900), pt. 1, reprinted in *James Mooney's History, Myths, and Sacred Formulas of the Cherokees* (Asheville: Historical Image, 1992), 169 n. 1 (quote), 170; Inscoe, *Mountain Masters*, 227-228; Jack Frederick Kilpatrick and Anna Gritts Kilpatrick, trans. and eds., *The Shadow of Sequoyah: Social Documents of the Cherokees, 1862-1864* (Norman: University of Oklahoma Press, 1965), 3-4; Godbold and Russell, *Confederate Colonel and Cherokee Chief*, 96; Finger, *Eastern Band of Cherokees*, 98. For others who considered western North Carolina as an ideal spot for the Confederate capital, see John C. Inscoe and Gordon B. McKinney, *The Heart of Confederate Appalachia: Western North Carolina in the Civil War*, Civil War America Series, (Chapel Hill: University of North Carolina Press, 2000), 6.

7. "THE JUNALUSKE ZUAVES," The *State Journal* (Raleigh), undated, reprinted in the *Times* (Greensboro), May 22, 1861; Godbold and Russell, *Confederate Colonel and Cherokee Chief*, 94-96; Crow, *Storm in the Mountains*, 2.

swamps of North Carolina." Meanwhile, although the Senate passed Thomas's bill on September 20, it was rejected in the House of Commons the next day. Regardless, he continued with his plans to organize a battalion under authorization from the Confederate government. It is doubtful that he made much progress, as he not only continued to serve in the senate and the state convention but also ran for a seat in the Confederate Congress.[8]

Thomas's opponent in the congressional race was Allen T. Davidson, an antebellum Unionist and cousin of a not infrequent political foe of Thomas's, popular western North Carolina politician Zebulon Baird Vance. The campaign was vicious, as Thomas was accused of routine absenteeism from the senate and drunkenness while in attendance. Thomas's relationship with the Cherokees quickly became embroiled in the campaign. Among Davidson's supporters was George Hayes, a former employee and friend of Thomas's. A member of the House of Commons and captain of Company A, 19th Regiment N.C. Troops (2nd Regiment N.C. Cavalry), Hayes had earlier led the effort which squashed the Cherokee recruitment bill. He now proclaimed in a speech at Murphy "that he had le[a]ve be catched a voting in the ballet [*sic*] box with a free Negro as an Indian." Meanwhile, with Thomas's assistance two Cherokees in Hayes's company accused the latter of abusing them and unsuccessfully petitioned Gov. Henry Toole Clark to be released from service. Thomas also asked Clark for help in combating what he thought were unfair patronage contracts by some of Davidson's supporters for clothing western North Carolina troops, a service with which Thomas himself was involved as a competitor. Thomas lost his congressional bid, and his efforts to organize the Indians were again stymied. Brig. Gen. Richard C. Gatlin, commander of the Department of North Carolina, was convinced that not enough Cherokees could be successfully recruited and communicated his misgivings to Richmond, which supported him in his decision to abandon the project.[9]

8. North Carolina General Assembly (Senate), *Journal of the Senate of the General Assembly of the State of North Carolina at its Second Extra Session, 1861* (Raleigh: John Spelman, 1861), 104, 211, 217; Thomas to Mercer Fain, October 17, 1861 (typescript), William Holland Thomas Papers, Manuscripts, Special Collections, Hunter Library, Western Carolina University, Cullowhee, N.C. (hereinafter cited as WCU); U.S. War Department, *War of the Rebellion: A Compilation of the Official Records of the Union and Confederate Armies* (hereinafter cited as *O.R.*), 4 ser. in 70 vols. in 127 pts. and index vol. (Washington: Government Printing Office, 1881-1902; all citations to ser. I unless otherwise noted), 51 (pt. 2): 304 (Chilton quote); John Preston Arthur, *Western North Carolina: A History (from 1730 to 1913)* (Raleigh: Edwards & Broughton Printing Co., 1914), 584-585; North Carolina General Assembly (House of Commons), *Journal of the House of Commons of the General Assembly of the State of North Carolina At Its Second Extra Session, 1861* (Raleigh: John Spelman, 1862), 262; Thomas to Gov. Henry Toole Clark, October 8, 1861, Governors' Papers: Henry Toole Clark, State Archives, N.C. Office of Archives and History, Raleigh, N.C. (hereinafter cited as NCOAH); Richard C. Gatlin to Samuel Cooper, January 7, 1862, Letters Received by the Confederate Adjutant and Inspector General's Office, 1861-1865 (M474), reel 20, file 136-G-1862 (hereinafter cited as Letters Received by the Confederate Adjutant and Inspector General's Office [M474]), Record Group 109: War Department Collection of Confederate Records (hereinafter cited as RG 109), National Archives, Washington, D.C. (hereinafter cited as NA); Crow, *Storm in the Mountains*, 2; Godbold and Russell, *Confederate Colonel and Cherokee Chief*, 97, 99.

9. Thomas to Clark, October 8, 17, 1861, A. J. Taylor to James Taylor, October 13, 1861, Jonathan Welch and F. M. Taylor to Clark, October 17, 1861, Governors' Papers: Clark, NCOAH; Manarin and Jordan, *North Carolina Troops*, 2:107, 98, 113; Crow, *Storm in the Mountains*, 2-4; Godbold and Russell, *Confederate Colonel and Cherokee Chief*, 30, 75, 76, 96-99; Inscoe and McKinney, *Heart of Confederate Appalachia*, 146-147, 151; Gordon B. McKinney, "Political Partisans in Western North Carolina: The Rivalry of Zebulon Baird Vance and

Despite his setbacks, Thomas continued to nurture his increasingly elaborate vision for defending western North Carolina. Already he thought in terms of an organization larger than a company or two of Cherokees. In October, he suggested to Clark that he try and secure the return of the 6th Regiment N.C. Volunteers and other mountain units stationed in Virginia. These could then be combined with the 25th Regiment N.C. Troops and Thomas's more-or-less hypothetical Cherokee battalion into an organization which he dubbed "the North Carolina highland Brigade or Legion." Perhaps reflecting both Davis's idea of basing the Cherokees in the eastern swamps and the fact that the 25th N.C. was already on the coast, Thomas asked Clark to "put the Highlanders together so that they can be removed from the seaboard during the sickly season while the Lincolnites are afraid to visit it."[10]

While the combination of units Thomas envisioned did not come to pass, his idea encapsulated the basic concept for Thomas's Legion. Although Thomas suggested putting the mountain units into a brigade, the standard organization into which infantry regiments were grouped, it is significant in the light of future developments that he also mentioned the possibility of a legion. The latter type of unit was designed to operate as a separate small

William Holland Thomas," *The Journal of Cherokee Studies* 24 (2005): 28-34; Thomas to Mercer Fain, October 17, 1861 (typescript), Thomas Papers, WCU; Gatlin to Cooper, January 7, 1862, Letters Received by the Confederate Adjutant and Inspector General's Office (M474), reel 20, file 136-G-1862. Gatlin dispatched 1st Lt. Lynch M. Dillard of Company B, 25th Regiment N.C. Troops, in October to muster Thomas's battalion under authority granted by Samuel Cooper, Confederate adjutant and inspector general. Dillard wrote Gatlin from Webster, "asking for authority to purchase arms and clothing for these Indians." Gatlin recommended to Cooper "that the authority be granted." In December, Dillard wrote from Cashiers Valley (modern Cashiers) that he had met with Thomas, who was quoted as saying that "So soon as the Cherokees could be armed (which would require an ordinance of the Convention) that the Companies would be formed." At this time, Dillard was ordered by his commander, Col. Thomas Clingman, to return to the 25th Regiment N.C. Troops. On December 16, Dillard reported that the Confederate Chief of Ordnance had given permission to arm the Cherokees, and suggested that Clingman might be persuaded to let him complete his mission. Gatlin referred Dillard's letter to Clingman, asking for a statement on the reasons for Dillard's recall. Gatlin forwarded Clingman's response to Cooper on January 7, with a letter summarizing the entire correspondence. Clingman's decision can be inferred from the final sentence of Gatlin's letter: "In conclusion, I respectfully recommend that the whole matter be abandoned and the authority for clothing and arming the Cherokee Battalion be revoked, as there appears to be no prospect of raising a sufficient number to be of any material Service." In an endorsement, Secretary of War Judah P. Benjamin instructed Cooper to "[i]ssue orders in accordance with Genl Gatlin's recommendation."

10. Thomas to Clark, October 8, 1861, Governors' Papers: Clark, NCOAH. Although Thomas opined to Clark in May 1862 that his unit would be "very effective in the swamps of North Carolina," he was probably unhappy with the thought of stationing the Indians permanently in the east; nevertheless, he apparently became taken by the idea of switching troops from the mountains to the coast and back again as circumstances required. In the same month, he wrote newspaper editor William Woods Holden that "[i]n my opinion, our forces ought to be strengthened in East Tennessee during next summer, and, if necessary, a portion of our forces could be removed to Eastern North Carolina upon the coming of frost." Thomas to Clark, May 25, 1862, Governors' Papers: Clark, NCOAH; Thomas to William Woods Holden, May 10, 1862, in Horace Raper and Thornton W. Mitchell, eds., *The Papers of William Woods Holden*, (Raleigh: North Carolina Division of Archives and History, 2000), 1:128. North Carolina adjutant general James G. Martin wrote in April, 1862, that Clark was against the idea of moving men eastwards, due to the already heavy manpower drain on the region, and that the governor had not extended the draft west of the Blue Ridge Mountains for that very reason. Martin added a few days later that Clark had no authority to transfer either the 16th or 25th N.C. from their current stations. Both letters were replies to recent ones from Thomas (no longer extant), and show the persistence of Thomas's thinking on these matters. James G. Martin to Thomas, April 9, 13, 1862, letter book, AG 19: December 10, 1861-April 23, 1862, 576-577, 606-607, N.C. Adjutant General's Papers, microfilm S.1.111, NCOAH.

army, as it contained elements of all three land arms: artillery, cavalry, and infantry. Why Thomas considered the idea is unknown. Legions were relics of an earlier period, particularly the American Revolution, when those of Henry "Light-Horse Harry" Lee on the American side and Banastre Tarleton on the British gained notoriety. They still maintained something of a romantic aura, however, so it is not surprising that several were organized in the amateurish opening phase of the Civil War, perhaps the best-known being that of wealthy South Carolina planter Wade Hampton. They soon proved unsuitable for the large armies organizing in Virginia and Tennessee, and such units as Hampton's Legion were broken up into their component service arms and redistributed accordingly.[11]

As legions were usually organized by wealthy and prominent men whose names were attached to the units, perhaps Thomas sought to share in the glory by creating one himself, although he did not explicitly put his name forward as commander of the proposed unit at this time. His reasons may have been primarily practical, indicating a shrewd understanding of the type of warfare that would be waged over the local geography. While armies might pass through or occupy the mountains, large set-piece open-field battles were impossible. Instead, fighting would involve the struggle for passes and other avenues of communication, and key communities at their junctures. In such warfare, a legion might be very effective, as it would provide flexibility for the different situations that a commander might encounter.[12]

In January 1862, Governor Clark "commissioned one Captain in each of the counties bordering . . . Tennessee, with instructions to raise and equip a company of Rangers, for the protection of our citizens against incursions from abroad." Thomas was assigned to raise the company for Jackson County.[13] He met with the Indians at Quallatown on January 3 and 4, reporting in a notebook that they had "commenced raising a company for [the] local defense of Western North Carolina." The language of his jottings suggests that he was largely starting from scratch. Following the adjournment of the convention at the end of February, Thomas went to South Carolina, winning approval from the governor and his council for a plan to defend the North Carolina mountain passes for the protection of both states and Georgia. He then forwarded his plan to Clark, asking that it be sent to the secretary of war. He also

11. James I. Robertson Jr., "Hampton's Legion," in Richard N. Current, editor-in-chief, *Encyclopedia of the Confederacy* (New York: Simon and Schuster, 1993), 2:733; John R. Elting, "Infantry," in ibid., 816.

12. In discussing the origin and evolution of the Legion's organization, Thomas explained to Samuel Cooper in February 1863 that as he "would be compelled to have Mounted Riflemen to act in concert with the Indians, and also that I would be compelled to have some artillery to defend the bridge at Strawberry Plains, I was advised to assume the Legionary form." On the other hand, Thomas wrote Cooper in 1864 that "I preferred the Legionary organization as the Indians could not be separated and governed as other troops." While it is clear that he did not think the Cherokees would submit to traditional military discipline, it is unclear how placing them in a legion would alleviate the supposed problem. Thomas to Cooper, February 21, 1863, service record file of Samuel L. Love, Records of Confederate Soldiers who Served During the Civil War, Compiled Service Records of Confederate General and Staff Officers, and Non-Regimental Enlisted Men (M331), reel 159, RG 109, NA (hereinafter cited as Compiled Service Records of Confederate General and Staff Officers, and Non-Regimental Enlisted Men [331]); Thomas to "General" (Cooper), July 8, 1864, letter book (unbound), Thomas Papers, DU.

13. "COUNTY RANGERS," *Weekly Standard* (Raleigh), January 8, 1862. Thanks to Alex Christopher Meekins of the North Carolina Office of Archives and History for bringing this item to our attention. In both this and in a piece in the *Asheville News* for June 5, 1862, Thomas was referred to as "Col." If not errors, the designation may indicate that he formerly held that rank in the antebellum militia, although there is no known documentation to corroborate such a supposition.

announced that he would plan the fortification of the pass connecting Jackson County with Sevier County, Tennessee, at the headwaters of the Oconaluftee River, as well as at the place where the Little Tennessee River cut through the Iron (Great Smoky) Mountains. "My Indian Company can perform the duties required at the former with the assistance of some mountaineers which I will supply," he wrote. He continued organizing the company through March. "Your Company being isolated and so far away from here," wrote Brig. Gen. James G. Martin, North Carolina adjutant general, in mid-April, "you must be governed by circumstances, using a good judgment and discretion in every case. When any case arises which you can not dispose of, the necessary direction will be given. The Governor approves of your course in the case of the vigilant committee." It is not clear whether the "cases" involved problems within Thomas's company, or trouble among the locals; however, the reference to a "vigilant committee" suggests his duties as a partisan captain.[14]

Martin's instructions were rendered moot by other developments, as Thomas saw an opportunity for Confederate recognition for the Lufty Indians. The new nation had already ratified a treaty with the western Cherokee, and Davis had urged Congress to reward the eastern Cherokees for their loyalty. In Thomas's past dealings with the Federal government, he had wanted the Eastern Band treated as a separate entity from the Cherokee Nation in order to preserve their autonomy, except in the matter of the monies due them. He now reversed himself and argued that the terms of the treaty between the Confederates and the western Cherokees should apply to the eastern tribesmen as well. Thomas's idea was approved, and the Confederate government accepted the Cherokees for national service.[15]

14. W. H. Thomas Notebook, 1862-1865, January 3 (quote), 4, 1862, [11-12], Colonel W. H. Thomas Paper and Notebook, Private Collection (hereinafter cited as P.C.) 991, NCOAH; Thomas to Clark, March 14, 1862, Governors' Papers: Clark, NCOAH; Martin to Thomas, April 13, 1862, letter book AG19: December 10, 1861-April 23, 1862, 606-607, N.C. Adjutant General's Papers, microfilm S.1.111, NCOAH.

15. Godbold and Russell, *Confederate Colonel and Cherokee Chief*, 99-100. The defeat of Thomas's bill in September 1861 seems to have made him uneasy regarding their enlistment while they held an uncertain status at the state and national levels. He nevertheless argued to Mercer Fain in October that the Cherokees already had citizenship (or the equivalent of it) under the old Federal treaties, and pressed forward a bill as a precaution because they had never been enrolled in the militia. Thomas mentioned three recent bills concerning the Cherokees to Fain: a passed and printed bill authorizing the governor to raise a Cherokee battalion; another one, topic unknown, reported in the state convention's Committee on Military Affairs; and Thomas's bill that was passed in the senate but squelched in the house by George Hayes. Information on the first two bills is lacking outside of Thomas's letter; in particular, there is no known record of the passage of a bill concerning the raising of an Indian battalion. In September, a bill passed in the legislature placing North Carolina Indians on the same level as whites in regards to the rules of evidence in jury trials; this bill by implication solidified their identity as full citizens. The bill was repealed by the convention in November. On the same day, Thomas unsuccessfully attempted to pass a resolution authorizing the formation of a select committee to clarify the status of the North Carolina Cherokees, showing that his claims to Fain were on shakier legal ground than he would have preferred. Thomas to Mercer Fain, October 17, 1861 (typescript), Thomas Papers, WCU; *Public Laws of the State of North Carolina, passed by the General Assembly in Its Second Extra Session, 1861* (Raleigh: John Spelman, 1861), 16; *Journal of the Convention of the People of North Carolina. Second Session Held in November and December, 1861* (Raleigh: John W. Syme, 1862), 14-15, 17. The new national status accorded the Lufty Cherokees by the Confederate government resolved any problems of recruiting them for service. According to Thomas, the authorization for the organization of the battalion came directly from Davis himself. Thomas to Cooper, February 21, 1863, service record file of Samuel L. Love, Compiled Service Records of Confederate General and Staff Officers, and Non-Regimental Enlisted Men (M331), reel 159.

The Cherokees were assigned to the Department of East Tennessee, commanded by Maj. Gen. Edmund Kirby Smith. Tennessee left the United States with a great deal of internal division. The heaviest concentration of Unionist support lay in eastern Tennessee, where two-thirds of the participating voters chose the Union over secession. Both the vote and the subsequent behavior of east Tennesseans is significant when compared with that of their neighbors in western North Carolina. On the surface, the two areas were in many ways alike: mountain country in which slaveholders were distinct minorities. Politically, the two regions were further apart. In western North Carolina, most Unionists temporarily acquiesced to secession following the vote of the Convention, although that situation changed as the war progressed. By contrast, most east Tennesseans, both slaveholders and non-slaveholders alike, supported the United States from the beginning. A number of outspoken Unionists, such as U. S. senator Andrew Johnson and newspaper editor William G. "Parson" Brownlow, provided leadership for local dissent. The Confederate authorities wasted little time in acting, shutting down Brownlow's *Knoxville Whig* in October 1861. A series of attempted bridge burnings in November led to a serious crackdown in the region. In the meantime, unease grew among western North Carolinians about the troubles across the border.[16]

Smith sent Maj. G. Washington Morgan of the 3rd Regiment Tennessee Infantry (Vaughn's), who was himself part Cherokee, to muster in the Indians at Quallatown.[17] Memories of the event became tangled over time. In an account recorded by ethnologist James Mooney in the late nineteenth century, Morgan used his heritage as an enlistment tool, so stirring up "the war spirit among them that a large number declared themselves ready to follow wherever he led." Thomas was not pleased with the turn of events because of Morgan's alleged "reputation for reckless daring" and its possible repercussions for the Indians' well-being. He thus paternalistically enlisted and was elected as company captain, "and proposed to them to enlist in the Confederate legion which he was about to organize." Thomas explained (but not to the Cherokee themselves, "who might not have been satisfied with such an arrangement") that "[h]is object . . . was to keep them out of danger so far as possible by utilizing them as scouts and home guards through the mountains, away from the path of the large armies." Morgan then departed "alone," and the Cherokees joined Thomas.[18]

Morgan's role is supported by a wartime account in the Knoxville *Register*, derived from letters written by Morgan and a "Gen. Mchaffey" who accompanied him. Mchaffey reported that they reached Quallatown on April 7; their "arrival created considerable

16. Crow, *Storm in the Mountains*, 17-19; Inscoe and McKinney, *Heart of Confederate Appalachia,* 45-46, 94-95, 106; W. Todd Groce, *Mountain Rebels: East Tennessee Confederates in the Civil War, 1860-1870* (Knoxville: University of Tennessee Press, 1999), 37 (map showing county breakdown by political sentiment).

17. "MAJ. MORGAN AMONG THE CHEROKEES," *The Daily Register* (Knoxville, Tenn., undated), reprinted in the *Greensborough Patriot*, May 8, 1862; James W. Terrell, Unpublished Reminiscences, 2, 6, James W. Terrell Papers, WCU (microfilm, James Wharrey Terrell Papers, DU); Crow, *Storm in the Mountains*, 4; Mooney, "Myths of the Cherokees," 168-169; Tennessee Civil War Centennial Commission, *Tennesseans in the Civil War: A Military History of Confederate and Union Units with Available Rosters of Personnel* (Nashville: Civil War Centennial Commission, 1964), 1:178; caption accompanying Morgan's picture in *Confederate Veteran* 14 (June 1896): 179.

18. Mooney, "Myths of the Cherokees," 168-169 (quotes). Mooney, who worked for the Smithsonian Institution, interviewed Thomas, Terrell, and others while gathering materials on the Cherokees. Godbold and Russell, *Confederate Colonel and Cherokee Chief*, 147, 149.

excitement among the Indians. . . . Maj. Morgan has thoroughly aroused [them]. . . . Major Morgan is the greatest man I every [ever] saw; the Indians are all well pleased with him, and I think he is the only man who could have got up such an enthusiasm among them."[19] In other ways, however, the contemporary evidence indicates a quite different picture from that depicted by Mooney. Coming so soon after Thomas achieved official recognition for the Cherokees from the Confederate government, Morgan's arrival could not have been coincidental or unexpected; given Thomas's intentions and efforts of almost a year to raise a Cherokee unit, including his attempts to get them into Confederate service, as well as his recent commission from the state, his own decision to enlist was hardly spontaneous, let alone an effort to protect the Cherokees from the command of a "reckless" officer.[20] Further, there is no known evidence indicating that Morgan planned to incorporate the Cherokees into a battalion or regiment of his own, where his leadership might have concerned Thomas. Instead, his task was merely to enroll them and conduct them to their assigned posting.[21] Morgan

19. "MAJ. MORGAN AMONG THE CHEROKEES," *The Daily Register* (Knoxville, Tenn., undated), reprinted in the *Greensborough Patriot*, May 8, 1862. Mchaffey's identity is unclear. He was quoted as if he was well-known in the Knoxville area, although despite his rank he was evidently subordinate to Morgan on this mission, suggesting a retired officer or a member of the Tennessee state militia.

20. Martin to Thomas, April 9, 13, 1862, letter book, AG 19: December 10, 1861-April 23, 1862, 576-577, 606-607, N.C. Adjutant General's Papers, microfilm S.1.111, NCOAH. These letters were in reply to two from Thomas on March 21 and April 5. The earliest message referred to Thomas as "Captain," an indication that he was acting under his commission to form a partisan company. The second letter stated that "[n]o tender of your Company has been received at this Office, although the necessary Muster Rolls for that purpose were given you with your appointment, and also a letter of general instructions at the same time." The documents show that Thomas was well into organizing at least one company prior to Morgan's arrival. Mooney was unaware of this and other information regarding Thomas's efforts to create a Cherokee battalion as far back as 1861.

21. "MAJ. MORGAN AMONG THE CHEROKEES," *The Daily Register* (Knoxville, Tenn., undated), reprinted in the *Greensborough Patriot*, May 8, 1862; Terrell, Unpublished Reminiscences, 1, 6, Terrell Papers, WCU (microfilm, DU). There was an effort to incorporate the Cherokee companies into a proposed unit to be raised and commanded by Thomas's brother-in-law, Lt. Col. Robert G. A. Love of the 16th Regiment N.C. Troops (6th N.C. Volunteers). "I would be pleased if you would allow me to have my regiment composed in part of two Indian Companies[,] that is have the two flanking companies of Indians armed with Rifles as they are from long use expert with that gun," Love wrote Secretary of War George Wythe Randolph on April 3. "I Know from my own personal Knowledge of these Indians that they would make with some training good soldiers, and I Know furthermore that if they are permitted to remain at home the enemies to our cause may induce them to take a stand against us." He added, however, that if he were not allowed to include any Indian companies, that he would like to form a regiment of white soldiers only. Love's brigade commander, Col. Wade Hampton, wrote a letter endorsing the proposal. Letters Received by the Confederate Secretary of War, 1861-1865 (M437), reel 57, file 162-L-1862, RG 109, NA (hereinafter cited as Letters Received by the Confederate Secretary of War [M437]). Love's idea was undoubtedly due at least indirectly to the Thomas's influence and shows a knowledge of his plans, as the timing of the letter and the proposal to recruit specifically two Indian companies demonstrate. Whether the two were acting together is unknown, as it is possible that Love's idea of incorporating the Indians into a regiment of his own might have conflicted with whatever command ambitions Thomas himself was nursing. Love earlier wrote Randolph on March 22 requesting permission to form a legion, another clue that he was aware of Thomas's ideas (although the fact that Hampton was Love's brigade commander might also have been an influence in that regard); he referred to this letter in his April 3 message. Randolph had by that time replied, telling him that "the 'Legion organization' is contrary to the general policy of this department." Love was soon defeated for reelection in the reorganization of th 16th Regiment N.C. Troops, and subsequently raised and commanded the 62nd Regiment N.C. Troops. Manarin and Jordan, *North Carolina Troops*, 6:10, 15:35. The theme of Thomas in conflict with officers who seemed to act entirely independent of any authority or protocol,

also did not leave by himself, thwarted in his ambitions by the wily Thomas; in fact, the two departed together with the Cherokees.[22] The omission from the Knoxville newspaper account of Thomas's role in organizing the Cherokees is not surprising due to the fact that as a Tennessee officer Morgan was an object of local interest, although Thomas was probably not pleased to read that Morgan was considered the only person who could rouse the Indians to action.[23]

The command was made up of over a hundred Cherokees and a few whites, and mustered into Confederate service on April 9, 1862. James W. Terrell, Thomas's longtime assistant in both his business and Indian affairs, was elected 1st lieutenant.[24] Its precise organization is unknown. Some evidence suggests that it was originally a single company that later split into two as recruitment increased; other materials indicate that it was organized into a two-company battalion at a quite early stage, perhaps even on April 9. Certainly there were two companies by May 1 at the latest.[25]

---

like Morgan in Mooney's account, is a persistent element of the legend of Thomas's Legion, most prominent in regards to his protracted feud with Brig. Gen. Alfred E. Jackson. While entertaining, such stories ignore the bureaucratic reality in which the military operated. Note that Love, for example, consulted with Richmond for authorization to organize a regiment and include the Cherokees.

22. Among the sources which record Morgan's departure with Thomas is Terrell, Unpublished Reminiscences, 2-5, Terrell Papers, WCU (microfilm, DU).

23. "MAJ. MORGAN AMONG THE CHEROKEES," *The Daily Register* (Knoxville, Tenn., undated), reprinted in the *Greensborough Patriot*, May 8, 1862. While Mchaffey reported that several chiefs attended the muster, he did not mention Thomas.

24. Mchaffey wrote that 102 men had enrolled in Jackson County by April 15, and that he hoped that another hundred would be recruited along the Valley River. Terrell recalled that the number at the time of the departure from Quallatown was "something over 100 Indians and about a dozen white men." Given allowances for cases where there are conflicts in the records, the muster rolls indicate that 167 men, the majority of whom were Cherokee, enlisted on April 9; however, comparing that figure with those of Mchaffey and Terrell, it is probable that around sixty-five were actually recruited on the journey, especially as Terrell confirmed that more enlisted along the way. The muster was misdated April 8 in Terrell's postwar account. "MAJ. MORGAN AMONG THE CHEROKEES," *The Daily Register* (Knoxville, Tenn., undated), reprinted in the *Greensborough Patriot*, May 8, 1862; Terrell, Unpublished Reminiscences, 1, Terrell Papers, WCU (microfilm, DU); service record file of James W. Terrell, Thomas's Legion, Records of Confederate Soldiers Who Served During the Civil War, Compiled Service Records of Confederate Soldiers Who Served in Organizations from the State of North Carolina (M270), reel 573, RG 109, NA (hereinafter cited as Compiled Service Records of Confederate Soldiers from the State of North Carolina [M270]); muster and descriptive rolls, undated: 2nd Company A ("Rec'd A & IGO June 1/63"), and February 12, 1863: Company B, Infantry Regiment, Thomas's Legion, ibid., reel 567; service record files, 2nd Company A and Company B, Infantry Regiment, Thomas's Legion, ibid., reels 567 through 574.

25. Terrell recalled that one company was originally raised; as Thomas continued to recruit, he divided it before the command moved to Strawberry Plains in May. Vernon H. Crow, accepting Terrell's version, dated the split to May 18, based on the service record of Capt. Gideon Hanks of the second company. Hanks's first surviving pay voucher covered a period commencing on that date, as do the earliest extant vouchers for 1st Lt. James Taylor and 2nd Lt. Horry R. Morris, so it would be logical to assume that it was the date of their elections and the company's organization. Terrell, Unpublished Reminiscences, 9, Terrell Papers, WCU (microfilm, DU); pay vouchers dated October 31, 1862, service record files of Gideon M. Hanks, Horry R. Morris, and James Taylor, Thomas's Legion, Compiled Service Records of Confederate Soldiers from the State of North Carolina (M270), reels 569, 571, and 573; Crow, *Storm in the Mountains*, 7; Godbold and Russell, *Confederate Colonel and Cherokee Chief*, 103. Other sources indicate that there were two companies before May 18, however. The muster roll abstracts in Hanks's service record reported that he enlisted in Thomas's command on April 9, although that

Thomas wrote Clark on April 13 about his ideas for the role that the command would play. Having turned over one company to the Confederate government, Thomas explained that the other was intended for local defense only; he thought that the first company "will entitle the State to credit for troops furnished for the war," a rather naive assumption that any additional units that he raised would not go into national service. "I shall want some ammunition for the other local company," he added, "which will be needed very soon, as the people of East Tennessee are more hostile than ever." He also sounded less like an officer with command responsibilities and more like an active politician: "I shall go on with the company to its destination and then to Raleigh if the Convention should not adjourn by that time." He expressed himself "satisfied" concerning "the plan of placing encampments at French Broad, Ocanalufta, the Tennessee and Highwassee. It will cost us but little, and may be of service." He added that South Carolina had dispatched engineers to examine the passes of the river valleys noted. "I will have their report when completed," he concluded. "One thing I know is they are satisfied of its importance."[26]

The command departed Quallatown on April 15, marching through Webster to Franklin. Thomas wrote Clark from the latter place on April 17, returning to his ideas from the previous October of a larger unit for mountain defense. "I have determined to raise a guerilla force of my own selection to be used with my Indians for the local defence of the

---

may reflect the backdating of his commission. The company muster and descriptive roll, not completed until February 12, 1863, indicated an April 9 organization. A piece in the Knoxville *Register* stated that Morgan went "to recruit a battalion among the Cherokee warriors." Thomas referred to "one of my Indian companies" in an April 13 letter to Governor Clark, and that "I have also raised another Company of Indians and whites for local defense," seeming to indicate two companies by that date. Thomas also wrote of "the 1st and 2nd companies of the 'North Carolina Cherokee Battalion'" to William Woods Holden in a May 10 letter. On requisitions for rifles, rifle caps, flints, and accouterments dated May 1, for camp equipment and clothing dated May 6, and for clothing on May 22, Thomas either signed himself as captain of the "1st Co. N.C. C[herokee]. Battalion," or as commander of the "N.C. Cherokee Battalion" or the "Highland Rangers." Another clue comes from Terrell himself. In a wartime letter to Gov. Zebulon Baird Vance, Terrell wrote that "[o]n the 9th April 1862 Col Thomas entered the service with two large companies of Cherokee Indians and reported immediately to Gen Kirby Smith at Knoxville." Against this argument, however, it should be noted that in an April 17 letter to Clark, Thomas mentioned "(m)y Indian company," while two April letters from North Carolina's adjutant general also referred to a single company. "Cherokees to the Rescue," *The Daily Register* (Knoxville, undated), reprinted in the *Asheville News*, April 12, 1862; "Record of Events": muster and descriptive roll, February 12, 1863: Company B, Infantry Regiment, Thomas's Legion, Compiled Service Records of Confederate Soldiers from the State of North Carolina (M270), reel 567; service record files, Company B, Infantry Regiment, Thomas's Legion, ibid., reels 567 through 574; Thomas to Governor Clark, April 13, 17, 1862, Governors' Papers: Clark, NCOAH; Thomas to Holden, May 10, 1862, in Raper and Mitchell, *Papers of William Woods Holden*, 1:127; requisitions for camp equipment and clothing, May 6, 1862, service record file of William H. Thomas, Thomas's Legion, Compiled Service Records of Confederate Soldiers from the State of North Carolina (M270), reel 573; requisitions for flints, rifle caps, rifles, and accouterments, May 1, 1862, and for clothing, May 22, 1862, William H. Thomas, Records of Confederate Soldiers Who Served During the Civil War, Unfiled Papers and Slips Belonging to Confederate Compiled Service Records (M347), reel 391, RG 109, NA (hereinafter cited as Unfiled Papers and Slips Belonging to Confederate Compiled Service Records [M347]); Terrell to Gov. Zebulon Baird Vance, February 22, 1864, Governors' Papers: Zebulon Baird Vance, 1862-1865, NCOAH; Martin to Thomas, April 9, 13, 1862, letter book, AG 19: December 10, 1861-April 23, 1862, 576-577, 606-607, N.C. Adjutant General's Papers, microfilm S.1.111, NCOAH. Perhaps the best solution is to assume that Thomas intended to organize a two-company battalion and that he completed that goal as soon as possible, whatever the actual date. An analagous situation involving Companies F and G, Infantry Regiment, will be discussed below.

26. Thomas to Clark, April 13, 1862, Governors' Papers: Clark, NCOAH.

Carolinas[,] Virginia[,] and East Tennessee," he wrote, claiming that "[t]he President has agreed to arm and equip them. And all I want you to do is to authorize and to raise of Indians and such whites as I may select one Battalion with the priv[i]lege of increasing it to a regiment to serve . . . during the war. To be armed and equipped agreeably to my own selection and to be ready to take the field by the first of August." The statement implies that Thomas thought of himself and his new command as partisan rangers in accord with his January assignment, and that he seemed to have no idea that their enrollment into Confederate service and transfer to east Tennessee might mean that they were intended for other use. He added that "I want Capt [John H.] Turpins Company of Haywood County and Captain Joseph Dobsens Company of Macon with me as two of my selections. Please submit the proposition to your advisers and if necessary submit to the Convention when in secret session and telegraph me at Knoxville."[27] Both units were western companies exemplifying the type of mixed command that Thomas desired: Turpin's company was an infantry unit, while Dobsen's was a cavalry command. In the event, Thomas received neither company.[28]

Thomas's command continued from Franklin towards Valleytown (modern-day Andrews) in Cherokee County, recruiting more Indians along the way. It was already undergoing some drilling as it traveled. "My Indian Company has the reputation of being the most orderly Company [that] ever marched out of the mountains," Thomas bragged to Clark from Franklin, while their instructor told Thomas that "they learn faster than whites."[29] By the

27. Terrell, Unpublished Reminsicences, 2-3, Terrell Papers, WCU (microfilm, DU); Thomas to Clark, April 17, 1862, Governors' Papers: Clark, NCOAH; "MAJ. MORGAN AMONG THE CHEROKEES," *The Daily Register* (Knoxville, Tenn., undated), reprinted in the *Greensborough Patriot*, May 8, 1862. Although Terrell remembered that they started out on the afternoon of the muster, Thomas wrote Governor Clark from Quallatown on April 13 that they would leave on the 15th. Mchaffey, writing on April 15, confirmed that they planned to depart that day. According to Terrell, the Indians spent the first night of the journey in a barn on the property of George Hayes, the former Thomas associate who had defeated the house bill for raising a Cherokee battalion and used anti-Cherokee rhetoric on behalf of Davidson's congressional candidacy. How Hayes reacted to the intrusion, if he was in residence, is unknown.

28. Manarin and Jordan, *North Carolina Troops*, 15:56, 2:530, 494. Thomas also probably referred to Dobsen's company in an April 13 letter to Clark, in which he commented that "[t]he troops from Macon County will also be at Knoxville about the same time [as Thomas's command]. I presume that both Companies will be placed in camps of instruction." Thomas was probably interested in acquiring Dobsen's company from the beginning. Thomas to Clark, April 13, 1862, Governors' Papers: Clark, NCOAH. Turpin's company became Company C of the 62nd Regiment N.C. Troops, while Dobsen's unit served as Company C, 7th Battalion N.C. Cavalry and later as 2nd Company G, 65th Regiment N.C. Troops (6th Regiment N.C. Cavalry).

29. Thomas to Clark, April 17, 1862, Governors' Papers: Clark, NCOAH. Thomas lavished similar praise on the Indians to William Woods Holden. "So far, the Indian companies have set an example worthy of imitation by whites, in sobriety, morality and submission of duty required of soldiers," he wrote. "They bid fair at no distant day, in Tennessee, at least, to prove themselves better friends to the South and the Southern cause, in this our day of trial, then some persons who claim to be of pure white origin—who have no merit of their own, besides, except to stay at home, and speculate on the necessities of the families of the soldiers who are fighting the battles of their country, for the purpose of achieving our liberty and independence." Thomas to Holden, May 10, 1862, in Raper and Mitchell, *Papers of William Woods Holden*, 1:128. The identity of the drill instructor that Thomas quoted is a mystery. In his April 17 letter to Governor Clark, Thomas refered to him as "Major Walker," a hitherto unmentioned member of their party. It is tempting to identify him with William C. Walker, who later commanded Walker's Battalion in Thomas's Legion. Walker at this time was lieutenant colonel (not major) of the the 29th Regiment N.C. Troops, then at Cumberland Gap. Since Walker outranked Morgan and would have

evening of April 19 they reached Valleytown, where they were held up by heavy rains which caused local streams to overflow. When the march resumed on April 24, the flooding caused further delays, particularly at the Hiwassee River. Nevertheless, by the night of April 25, the party encamped at the Unicoi Mountains on the North Carolina-Tennessee line. The next day they journeyed through Madisonville to Sweetwater, where Thomas and Morgan took a passenger train for Knoxville. Terrell followed on April 27 in another train while the Indians rode in box cars. Upon arrival, they marched through town. "We seemed to be the object of a grand curiousity," Terrell recalled, as "a large crowd followed or passed on the side walks all the way from the depot, increasing at every step of the way and when we were halted[,] the crowd pressed us on every side so dense that one could not get through it." The Cherokees stopped on a hill north of the town. They named their camp Ogonastoka.[30]

The command remained at Camp Ogonastoka for about two weeks, where according to Terrell "we were the wonder of all the place and often visited by the elite of the town." Among the visitors was Morgan's sister, who on one occasion harangued the Indians through an interpreter and urged them to bring home many scalps. Thomas broke in and asked her not to mention the subject, as he refused to even allude to the phrase when dealing with the Indians. "While this interruption occur[r]ed before the Interpreter had time to translate the sentence," Terrell recalled, "still enough of them caught on . . . to infuse her meaning among the rest."[31] It was not the only time in the Legion's history that the topic surfaced.

The men were initially not very well equipped, armed in the main with squirrel rifles, bad powder, and varied ammunition. Some were evidently armed with bows and arrows and spears, which Terrell actually preferred to the squirrel rifles. At least they had some weapons; as late as early June, Smith was complaining to the Richmond authorities that he still had some 4,000 unarmed men in his command. Thomas himself requisitioned 150 rifles on May 1. By that date at the latest, the force had received the title of the North Carolina Cherokee Battalion, and was organized into a 1st and 2nd Company. The 1st Company was under the formal command of Thomas himself but for all intents and purposes was under 1st Lieutenant Terrell, as Thomas exercised command of the entire battalion. The 2nd Company was commanded by Capt. Gideon Hanks, nephew to Major Morgan and formerly 1st lieutenant of Company G, 3rd Regiment Tennessee Infantry (Vaughn's).[32]

---

therefore been the actual recruiter and leader of the party, his presence with Thomas is unlikely given the lack of mention of someone with that surname in other accounts. The reference was therefore probably a "slip of the pen" for Morgan, a more likely candidate.

30. Terrell, Unpublished Reminiscences, 2-6, Terrell Papers, WCU (microfilm, DU). Terrell believed that Ogonastoka was Morgan's Indian name. Finger, *Eastern Band of Cherokees*, 84-85, 200 n. 12, thought that the camp (which he rendered in English as Oconostota) was actually named after a famous warrior of that name from earlier generations, not Morgan. Theoretically, it could have been named in honor of both.

31. Terrell, Unpublished Reminiscences, 6-7, Terrell Papers, (microfilm, DU). The text of Terrell's reminiscences are badly damaged at the bottom, and many of the lower lines are often partially or wholly missing. The text reads ". . . and on one occasion gave them through our main Interpreter [damaged] them to bring home with them [damaged—line missing]." The substance of her remarks are clear from the next page, reporting Thomas's reaction ("Thomas interrupted her and requested her not to name scalping to them," etc.).

32. *O.R.* 10 (pt. 2): 584, 590; Terrell, Unpublished Reminiscences, 8-9, Terrell Papers, WCU (microfilm, DU); Thomas to Holden, May 10, 1862, in Raper and Mitchell, *Papers of William Woods Holden*, 1:127; requisitions for camp equipment and clothing, 1st Company, N.C. C[herokee]. Battalion, service record file of William H.

Smith assigned the North Carolina Cherokee Battalion to guard the bridge at Strawberry Plains, Tennessee. Spanning the Holston River, the bridge was part of the East Tennessee & Virginia Railroad line, which linked the area to southwestern Virginia. From Strawberry Plains the railroad ran west to Knoxville, where the line was continued to the southwest by the East Tennessee & Georgia Railroad. The Holston River bridge was thus one of several important crossings and depots spread out along the railroad network. While the Confederates controlled the length of the line, vital military and commercial traffic continued uninterrupted from Virginia to Georgia. On the other hand, if the Federals seized the line, they could put the railroad to their own purposes. Failing to take the railroad, they could at least interdict travel and transport by capturing or destroying important points. Thus locations like Strawberry Plains became centers of contest. Smith rightly feared that the railroad bridges would become targets of raiders or saboteurs, as demonstrated by events of the previous year. A Tennessean named William B. Carter secured permission from the U.S. government to sabotage the railroad bridges in conjunction with a proposed Federal move from Kentucky into east Tennessee. Although the Federal part of the operation was cancelled due to a sudden Confederate movement towards Kentucky, the attack on the bridges proceeded as planned on November 8, 1861. Five bridges were burned, although the effort against the Strawberry Plains bridge failed. A subsequent uprising on the part of eastern Tennessee Unionists was crushed. Unrest continued to simmer after Smith assumed command in 1862. With Smith's manpower resources strained, Thomas's battalion was a welcome addition to the area's defense.[33]

Thomas, Thomas's Legion, Compiled Service Records of Confederate Soldiers from the State of North Carolina (M270), reel 573; requisition for flints, rifle caps, rifles, and accouterments, May 1, 1862, William H. Thomas, Unfiled Papers and Slips Belonging to Confederate Compiled Service Records (M347), reel 391; Crow, *Storm in the Mountains*, 7; Godbold and Russell, *Confederate Colonel and Cherokee Chief*, 103. Members of the Legion with prior service in the 3rd Regiment Tennesee Infantry (Vaughn's) are often listed in various sources as having served in the 3rd Regiment Tennessee Mounted Infantry (Lillard's). This reflects the fact that the National Archives created service packets in which each soldier's unit was noted under its last known name in order to make sense of the confusing morass of changes that many commands underwent throughout the war. The 3rd Tennessee Infantry (Vaughn's) became the 3rd Tennessee Mounted Infantry (Lillard's) in January 1864 (Tennessee Civil War Centennial Commission, *Tennesseans in the Civil War*, 1:178). Thus, soldiers who served in that unit at any time during the war have service record jackets reporting them as members of the 3rd Tennessee Mounted Infantry (Lillard's), regardless as to whether or not that was the actual name of the regiment during their particular time of service. In this account, units will be identified by the names with which they were known at the time of an individual soldier's service, while the name by which the unit is known in the National Archives microfilms will be put either in a footnote, or in parentheses ( ) in the text, as is most appropriate.

33. *The Official Atlas of the Civil War* (New York: Thomas Yoseloff, 1958) has an excellent map of the region in which Thomas's Legion served and provides a clear understanding of the importance of places such as Strawberry Plains; see plate 142. See also Terrell, Unpublished Reminscences, 8-11, Terrell Papers, WCU (microfilm, DU); N. W. Woodfin to Clark, November 12, 1861, Governors' Papers: Clark, NCOAH; "Heroic Deed of James Keelen," *Confederate Veteran*, 3 (June 1895): 187-189; Godbold and Russell, *Confederate Colonel and Cherokee Chief*, 101-103; Crow, *Storm in the Mountains*, 18-20; Noel C. Fisher, *War at Every Door: Partisan Politics and Guerrilla Violence in East Tennessee, 1860-1869* (Chapel Hill: University of North Carolina Press, 1997), 1-2, 34, 50-61. One account of the strike against the Strawberry Plains bridge misdated the incident to 1862 and connected its defense with Thomas's Legion. James Keelin (or Keelen), the sentry who drove off the defenders and was disabled as a result, was a member of the Legion according to this version. Correspondent of the [Louisville, Kentucky] *Courier-Journal*, "A Modern Horatius. Defence of a Bridge by One

Thomas's post was named Camp Junaluska after the famous Cherokee chief. Shortly after arrival, the command was struck by illness and disease, a problem endemic to Civil War camp life, especially when men from varied areas were placed for the first time in close proximity and encountered hitherto unfamiliar illnesses. In the case of Thomas's battalion, the problem was potentially amplified by the fact that the Indians might have no immunity to a variety of ailments common among their white comrades-in-arms. They were first stricken by what Terrell called "camp fever," but passed through it without too much trouble. The one death suffered, the first in the unit's history, was an unnamed Indian who, while recovering from illness, ate some partially ripe cherries; he sickened and died the next day. No sooner had the fever passed, however, than measles broke out. Very few of the Cherokees had ever had the disease before, and some died. As the measles faded, the mumps followed, an ailment so unfamiliar to the Cherokees that according to Terrell they did not have a name for it. Nevertheless, he remembered that they suffered only small losses, and that the survivors remained "remarkably healthy to the end of the war."[34]

In the meantime, the battalion members became accustomed to the rigors and tedium of military life. Guard duty at the Holston River bridge remained their chief task. Alerts seem to have been frequent. During one such scare, tragedy struck while Thomas was away. On the night of June 13, a popular young Indian of Terrell's company named Scacheloskee fell asleep on guard duty, and was run over by a train traveling backwards. He was the first member of the command to die violently, albeit by accident.[35] Another alert was issued on July 1, after Thomas's return, when very specific rumors circulated about threats to the bridges at Strawberry Plains and at Loudon, west of Knoxville. The alleged plot involved Federal soldiers, disguised as civilians and aided by local sympathizers, who would burn the bridges.[36] Neither danger materialized. About this time the battalion finally received muskets, although of what type and effectiveness is not known.[37]

Confederate Against an Attack by Forty Federals. He Kills Three and Wounds Eight of His Assailants After Losing A Hand," *Southern Historical Society Papers* 21 (1893): 294-297 (hereinafter cited as *SHSP*); Thomsen, *Rebel Chief*, 185. According to the *Confederate Veteran* article, at the time of the attack Keelin/Keelen was a civilian employee of the railroad by night and a daytime employee of the brother-in-law of W. W. Stringfield, future major of the Infantry Regiment, Thomas's Legion; because of fears for his life, the former stayed with the regiment for a couple of years. Given the actual date of the events and the nature of his injuries, this seems to be a more likely explanation for his association with the Legion, rather than active service as a soldier.

34. Thomas to Holden, May 10, 1862, in Raper and Mitchell, *Papers of William Woods Holden*, 1:127; Terrell, Unpublished Reminiscences, 8-11 (quote, 11), Terrell Papers, WCU (microfilm, DU). In late June, Thomas noted that three Cherokees had "died of sickness[,] measles etc." while he was on detached service. Thomas to Sarah Love Thomas, June 25, 1862, Thomas Papers, DU. For a brief discussion of Civil War illness, see James I. Robertson Jr., *Soldiers Blue and Gray* (Columbia: University of South Carolina Press, 1988), 145-169.

35. Terrell, Unpublished Reminiscences, 11-15, Terrell Papers, WCU (microfilm, DU); Thomas to Sarah Love Thomas, June 25, 1862, Thomas Papers, DU; *Asheville News*, June 19, 1862, (reporting an item from *The Tri-Weekly Banner* [Greeneville, Tennessee], June 16, 1862); service record file of Scacheloskee, Thomas's Legion, Compiled Service Records of Confederate Soldiers from the State of North Carolina (M270), reel 572. According to Terrell, Scacheloskee (or Scotcheloskee) was also known as John.

36. *O.R.* 16 (pt. 2): 716.

37. Terrell, Unpublished Reminiscences, 15, Terrell Papers, WCU (microfilm, DU). The relevant text reads, "Not longer after this [Scacheloskee's death] our squeril [*sic*] guns were replaced with M[page damaged]." R. H. Chilton, Confederate assistant adjutant general, wrote Kirby Smith on June 5 that 200 rifles and 1,300 muskets

Thomas's absence at the time of Scacheloskee's death was the result of a more concrete threat further west. Federal Maj. Gen. Ormsby Mitchell in Huntsville, Alabama, had dispatched Brig. Gen. James Negley to break up the Confederate defenses shielding Chattanooga. On June 4, Negley routed a small command under Brig. Gen. John Adams at Sweeden's Cove in southern Tennessee. This development left Chattanooga open to attack. Although Smith was already preoccupied with a threat to Cumberland Gap, he rushed to the city's defense with his available forces. Thomas and a portion of his command were among the reinforcements, accompanying the 31st Regiment Alabama Infantry. Arriving on June 7, Smith found that the garrison under Brig. Gen. Daniel Leadbetter was under bombardment, and that Leadbetter had failed to destroy the bridge spanning the Tennessee River. The Federals withdrew, however, partly due to the failure of a promised gunboat to arrive. During the operation, Smith utilized Thomas's men to watch enemy movements. While scouting on the Federal side of the Tennessee River, Thomas was alone except for a fisherman hired to carry him across. He encountered "an intelligent and gentlemanly" Federal from Michigan who was lost. The latter found surrender to Thomas preferable to being accidentally shot by trigger-happy pickets, perhaps with good reason given the scene that ensued upon their arrival in camp. "The men came near to shooting him after he surrendered and it was all I could do to prevent it!" Thomas wrote his wife. "The Indians say as I took the first prisoner each of them must take one to be even with me." Thomas turned the man over to the post commander without further incident. Smith soon ordered Thomas to Shell Mound, some twenty miles west along the river, where the Confederates confronted the withdrawing Federals. Upon arrival, Thomas found that rumors of a battle were false and that Negley was continuing his movement from the area. Thomas sent ten of his men across the Tennessee to watch the enemy, while he retired to Chattanooga to await their report. According to his account, he received word from the scouts that the Federals were moving on Cumberland Gap; in fact, Negley's command was moving northwest towards Shelbyville, while an entirely different force threatened the gap. Following these incidents, Thomas was sent to Knoxville, and proceeded from there to Strawberry Plains, which he reached by June 25. In the meantime, Cumberland Gap was abandoned by the Confederates.[38]

Besides guarding the bridge at Strawberry Plains and the excursion to Chattanooga, the Cherokees were already involved in the growing irregular warfare in the mountains. On June 1,

---

were on the way to equip the troops in his district. *O.R.* 10 (pt. 2): 590. In September, Thomas requested that Davis send 600 Enfield rifles which the president had supposedly "promised" him. Thomas to Jefferson Davis, September 23, 1862, Letters Received by the Confederate Secretary of War (M437), reel 75, file 415-T-1862.

38. *O.R.* 10 (pt. 1): 903-905, 919-922, (pt. 2): 265, 271-272, 275, 282-283, 287-288, 581, 585, 592-601, 603, 16 (pt. 2): 12-13, 18, 24, 677-698; Thomas to Sarah Love Thomas, June 25, 1862, Thomas Papers, DU; Crow, *Storm in the Mountains*, 9; Thomas Lawrence Connelly, *Army of the Heartland: The Army of Tennessee, 1861-1862* (Baton Rouge: Lousiana State University Press, 1967), 189-191. The Cherokees' report that "the enemy was moving towards Cumberland Gap" suggests that they were misled as to the direction Negley was moving, as Shelbyville is not the logical place that one would move to in order to proceed directly from the Chattanooga area to the gap. While Thomas was not necessarily required to lead such a scout himself, it is odd that he would remove himself from the field to a city many miles away to wait for the Cherokees and their information. This recalls his announcement on April 13 that he planned to leave his force in Knoxville to visit the state convention in Raleigh, and suggests a certain detachment from his command responsbilities. It is possible that he was ordered there by Smith, however, as a convenient place to rendezvous with the scouts upon their return.

just before his departure for Chattanooga, Thomas wrote to Samuel Cooper, Confederate adjutant and inspector general. Among many topics covered, he requested that Terrell be appointed quartermaster for the battalion "so as to supply the Indians with provisions while in the mountains chasing the bushwhackers," a promotion which Thomas understood from Kirby Smith had to come from President Davis. "I have nearly cleared all of them [the bushwhackers] out of the Iron Mountain and will make an effort with Genl Smith on the Cumberland Mountain as soon as I can get the Indians armed." Exactly how the bushwhackers in the Iron Mountains had been driven off by the Indians before they were properly armed went unexplained.[39] Regardless, Unionist guerilla activity in the mountains would increasingly occupy Thomas and his command as the war continued.

According to Terrell, shortly after Thomas's return from Chattanooga he was involved in a controversy involving soldiers from another unit. While the details of the incident are obscure, due to the damaged condition of Terrell's manuscript and the lack of corroborative evidence elsewhere, what remains strikingly suggests Thomas's later attitudes towards military discipline and its enforcement. The matter involved members of the 29th Regiment N.C. Troops, commanded by Col. Robert Brank Vance. Vance was the brother of future North Carolina governor Zebulon Baird Vance and cousin to Allen T. Davidson, Thomas's political opponent from the previous fall. Like Thomas and his battalion, Vance and his regiment were mountaineers. The 29th N.C. was stationed at Cumberland Gap until its evacuation in June. Terrell wrote that Vance antagonized about a hundred of his men by denying them an earlier promised furlough when they were ordered to the gap in February. The offended men took it upon themselves to go on leave anyway, with the mutual understanding that they would return after a certain period of time. Evidently, most of them successfully eluded the cavalry patrols sent after them and returned to duty, but a small number were caught at home, tried, and sentenced to be shot. Thomas at this point decided to interfere, even though the men belonged to another officer's command. Throughout the war, he often operated outside of traditional military protocol when he had ends he wanted to achieve. Further, as a commander Thomas exhibited an astonishing laxness towards military discipline. Finally, Thomas still tended to think like a politician; the fact that the 29th N.C. was recruited from the mountain counties, including the area that Thomas once represented in the state legislature, probably played a deciding role in his course of action. Regardless of his motivations, according to Terrell's account Thomas appealed to Smith and President Davis to have the men's life spared. Once he succeeded, Thomas sent Terrell with a band of twenty-five Indians in July to escort the pardoned men back to their unit. Although the outcome of the

39. Thomas to Samuel Cooper, June 1, 1862, Letters Received by the Confederate Adjutant and Inspector General's Office (M474), reel 50, file 419-T-1862. Today, the ranges running from southwest to northeast along the North Carolina-Tennessee border are generally known as the Unicoi Mountains, the Great Smoky Mountains, the Bald Mountains, the Unaka Mountains, and the Stone Mountains. In many early maps, the terms Bald Mountains, Iron Mountains, and Great Smoky Mountains were often interchangeable, while a plate in the *Official Atlas of the Civil War* refers to the Unicoi Mountains as the Unaka Mountains (both derived from the same Cherokee word) and the Unaka Mountains as the Iron Mountains. It is thus not clear whether by "Iron Mountain" Thomas here meant the Unaka Mountains, or the section of the Great Smoky Mountains where the Little Tennessee River flows through the North Carolina mountains (as he did in a March 14 letter to Clark; see pp. 7-8 above). Powell, *North Carolina Gazetteer*, 21, 201-202, 476, 506-507; *Official Atlas of the Civil War*, plate 142.

story is unknown, due to the abrupt end of Terrell's reminiscences in the midst of his account, it was implied that the men were returned to Vance's service.[40]

In the meantime, Thomas's efforts to expand his command began to bear fruit. On June 1, he wrote Adjutant and Inspector General Cooper that he had four more companies ready to organize, and requested President Davis's authority to do so. He also worked to have Companies A and L of the 16th Regiment N.C. Troops (6th Regiment N.C. Volunteers) transferred to him. The regiment had served under Robert E. Lee in western Virginia before moving to northern Virginia. Companies A and L were of special interest to Thomas because they came from western North Carolina and had personal ties to him. Company A was organized at Webster in Jackson County in May 1861. Its second-in-command was James R. Love Jr., cousin to Thomas's wife, Sarah. During the early stages of the war, Thomas took

40. Terrell, Unpublished Reminiscences, 16-23, Terrell Papers, WCU (microfilm, DU). It is not clear whether all of the absentees were caught and put on trial, or only a small number. The surviving fragments suggest that around ninety escaped the cavalry patrols, took their leave, and came back, while the remaining ten or so were captured at home and put on trial. Vance himself played no role in the surviving sections of Terrell's account, and it is difficult to surmise what his reaction might have been to Thomas's supposed interference. A cursory glance through the published rosters of the 29th Regiment N.C. Troops does not support the story as reported by Terrell, although there were several incidents of individual and group desertion in that regiment between February and July 1862. One example involved the desertion of five Cherokee County men from Company A at Cumberland Gap. They were Robert G. Ely, William F. (or Y.) Harris, William Johnson, John W. Murphy, and Samuel Bell. Harris and Bell deserted in April 1862, and the others probably did at or about the same time. Their company commander advertised a reward for their capture and return on May 29. The advertisement was published in the *Asheville News* for June 5, so the timing was about right for the period indicated by Terrell. In all, thirty men deserted, or were reported as discharged for "dishonorable conduct" from the 29th N.C. between February and July, while a number of others with no specific desertion date or reason for discharge may also have left during that time. Even if these questionables are factored in, however, the total number of men falls far below the approximately one hundred or so that Terrell recalled. Only two seem to have returned to the unit, while the various dates of dishonorable discharge or desertion were scattered rather than all at one time, both facts in contradiction with Terrell's account. Terrell was specific in placing the time of the events and certain individuals involved, however. He put his arrival to pick up the pardoned prisoners as being a day or two after a clash at Walden's Ridge, Kentucky, an event which happened on July 5, 1862. Terrell named the place of the prisoners' detention as the camp of a General Stephenson in Tazewell, Virginia. A Colonel Rains, whom Terrell noted was afterwards a general, was also mentioned. Stephenson was probably Brig. Gen. Carter L. Stevenson, Vance's superior and overall commander of Cumberland Gap who, after its evacuation, was in northern Tennessee; at the time of the clash at Walden's Ridge he was in the vicinity of Bean's Station. The latter site, however, is much closer to Tazewell, Tennessee, lying directly southeast of Cumberland Gap, than to Tazewell, Virginia. Rains was probably Col. James E. Rains of the 11th Regiment Tennessee Infantry, another of Stevenson's commanders. *O.R.* 16 (pt. 1): 771, (pt. 2): 721; Ezra J. Warner, *Generals in Gray: Lives of the Confederate Commanders* (Baton Rouge: Louisiana State University Press, 1959), 250, 292-293; Manarin and Jordan, *North Carolina Troops*, 8:232. Another significant point is that several men who deserted from the 29th N.C. around this general time later served in Thomas's Legion, which might lend some credence to Thomas's alleged involvement in the matter. Eight deserters from Company A of the 29th N.C. later served in Company I of the Infantry Regiment, while a ninth served in Company A of Walker's Battalion. Six more deserters from Company F of the 29th N.C. later served in Levi's Battery. Manarin and Jordan, *North Carolina Troops*, 8:238, 239, 240, 241, 242, 244, 283, 285; service record files of Asa L. Adams, Eppie M. Canup, Francis M. Canup, Robert G. Ely, William F. Harris, Francis M. Jenkins, George W. Loudermilk, Madison Loudermilk, Thomas Pack, Martin V. Prince, John F. Shuler, Thomas J. Shuler, William P. Shuler, A. C. Wiggins, and M. L. Wiggins, Thomas's Legion, Compiled Service Records of Confederate Soldiers from the State of North Carolina (M270), reels 567, 568, 569, 570, 572, 573, 574. These details collectively make it unlikely that the story is totally without substance, although it is almost certainly exaggerated in certain features.

special care to see that Love's company was well-provided for. Company L of the 16th N.C. was recruited from Haywood County. It had originally been organized by Sarah Thomas's brother, Robert G. A. Love, who subsequently became the regiment's lieutenant colonel. Thomas somehow arranged to have Companies A and L transferred to his command in May 1862. Their addition would provide him with some veteran, well-trained troops from western North Carolina who would be ideal for his purposes. Unfortunately for Thomas, their arrival was postponed for months. With the onset of major campaigning in Virginia, the companies could not be spared. As a part of Wade Hampton's Brigade in W. H. C. Whiting's Reserve Division, the 16th N.C. fought at the battle of Seven Pines, where James R. Love was wounded. Following Lee's reorganization of the army in June, the regiment became part of William Dorsey Pender's Brigade in A. P. Hill's Light Division. It saw service in the Seven Days' battles, and at Cedar Mountain, Second Bull Run, and Antietam before Companies A and L were finally sent to Thomas in October. Even then, the tenure of Company A was temporary, as it was by then intended for the 39th Regiment N.C. Troops. It was attached to Thomas only until that regiment's organization was completed.[41]

A third company that Thomas added to his command had mustered into service on June 13, 1862, at Locust Field, located on the Pigeon River on the site of modern-day Canton in Haywood County. It was organized by Dr. Elisha G. Johnson, who had succeeded Robert G. A. Love as captain of Company L, 16th Regiment N.C. Troops. Johnson was defeated for reelection in the April 1862 reorganization election of the regiment. Nothing daunted, Johnson started his own company and was elected captain. It operated independently for a while as Capt. Elisha Johnson's Company, Partisan Rangers, in eastern Tennessee before assignment to Thomas in the summer or fall, possibly on or about July 8.[42]

41. "Records of events": muster roll abstracts, September-October 1862: 1st Company A and Company B [E], Infantry Regiment, Thomas's Legion, Compiled Service Records of Confederate Soldiers from the State of North Carolina (M270), reel 567; service record files, 1st Company A and Company E, Thomas's Legion, ibid. reels 567 through 574; Crow, *Storm in the Mountains*, 13; Thomas to Samuel Cooper, June 1, 1862, Letters Received by the Confederate Adjutant and Inspector General's Office (M474), reel 50, file 419-T-1862; Manarin and Jordan, *North Carolina Troops*, 6:1-5, 10, 13, 100. In this and other notes, company letters in [ ] represent the final letter designation of a company (as represented in the National Archives service records) when that letter is different from the one in use at the time of the particular muster or other company record cited due to reorganizations. Company A, 16th Regiment N.C. Troops, became 1st Company A, Infantry Regiment, Thomas's Legion. According to information abstracted from the musters in the service files, it was assigned to the 39th Regiment N.C. Troops on May 20, 1862 and so was only temporarily attached to the Legion through the fall.

42. Manarin and Jordan, *North Carolina Troops*, 6:100; "Record of Events": muster and descriptive roll, June 13, 1862, Company C, Infantry Regiment, Thomas's Legion, Compiled Service Records of Confederate Soldiers from the State of North Carolina (M270), reel 567; Crow, *Storm in the Mountains*, 9, 165. There seems to be no documentation for when Johnson joined Thomas. The National Archives abstract of the company muster and descriptive roll for June 13, 1862, implied that it happened upon organization; however, the same source referred to it as part of the Infantry Regiment, Thomas's Legion, and neither of those terms were in use until fall. The abstract evidently reflects a degree of later emendation on the part of the muster taker; it will become apparent in the following notes that several muster and descriptive rolls for different companies were not completed on the actual dates enrollment. The service files for the individual soldiers, abstracted from the muster rolls, referred to the company as "Capt. Elisha G. Johnson's Col., Partisan Rangers," and reported that it was raised "for the local defense of the Carolinas, East Tennessee, Southwestern Virginia, and the Cumberland Mountains in Kentucky." This implies that the company initially operated independently; however, as the "local defense" idea was very much a part of Thomas's agenda, that in itself does not prove anything. The next extant muster roll is for

Thomas soon added some new companies to his command, which probably included the four alluded to in his June 1 letter to Cooper. Enrolling these units was the task of a young officer who would play a major role in Thomas's Legion and in both illuminating and confusing its history in the postwar era.[43] William Williams Stringfield was born in Nashville in 1837 but grew up in Strawberry Plains, where his father, a prominent Methodist minister and circuit rider, raised his family. Although originally a Unionist, Stringfield became an ardent secessionist after Fort Sumter, serving in the 3rd Battalion Tennessee Cavalry (Brazelton's) in eastern Tennessee and Kentucky through the winter of 1861. While at home on sick leave, Stringfield left the unit under unknown circumstances.[44] In March 1862 he

---

September-October 1862, by which point it was Company E of the Infantry Regiment (it shortly afterwards became Company C). "Record of Events": muster roll abstract, September-October 1862, Company E [C], Infantry Regiment, Thomas's Legion, Compiled Service Records of Confederate Soldiers from the State of North Carolina (M270), reel 567; service record files, Company C, Infantry Regiment, Thomas's Legion, ibid., reels 567 through 574. Johnson's October 1862 payment voucher assigned July 8 rather than June 13 as the date of his captaincy and the beginning of his first pay period, an oversight that was corrected on a later voucher. If July 8 was not a random error, it may have reflected the date that the company formally became a part of Thomas's battalion; however, that interpetation is far from certain. It is possible that Johnson was not assigned to Thomas until the Infantry Regiment was organized in late September. Service record file of Elisha G. Johnson, Thomas's Legion, Compiled Service Records of Confederate Soldiers from the State of North Carolina (M270), reel 570.

43. William Williams Stringfield's writings are essential for any one looking into the history of Thomas's Legion, but they must be treated with caution. There were three major sets of reminiscences or histories penned by Stringfield, which contain some overlapping materials and frequently contradict one another in detail. The first of these are Stringfield's unpublished reminiscences for his family, "War—Mss—Sketches & Stories—Family Matters," begun in 1899 but written over intervals (he was still adding material during the First World War), and found in a ledger book in the William Williams Stringfield Papers, P.C. 109, NCOAH. The second is his article on the Infantry Regiment's history, "Sixty-Ninth Regiment," in Clark, *North Carolina Regiments*, 3:729-761, published in 1901. The third is his "Memoirs of the Civil War," serialized in newspapers sometime after the turn of the century. A typescript version was prepared in 1938, with copies in the McClung Collection, Lawson-McGhee Library, Knoxville, Tennessee (hereinafter cited as L-McGL), and the William Williams Stringfield Papers, WCU. In addition, a volume of Stringfield's original wartime diary is in his papers at the State Archives of North Carolina. He recopied portions into his ledger book to supplement his reminiscences, and included sections that are no longer extant in the original; however, a comparison of those portions in the ledger book that correspond to the 1864 original shows that the ledger book version is rewritten, including later interpolations and contemporary allusions. While the postwar Stringfield materials are invaluable, they are marred by frequent inaccurate dates; a tendency toward ficitionalization (Stringfield not only went along with the myth that Thomas's Legion—or at least the Infantry Regiment—was known during the war as the 69th Regiment N.C. Troops, but also seemed to positively delight in retroactively promoting several members of the Legion to higher rank than the wartime evidence shows actually happened); and a high degree of disorganization, ranging from topic to topic across space and time. Additional materials concerning the Legion, especially letters, are in the Stringfield collections at the State Archives of North Carolina and at Western Carolina University.

44. The North Carolina volume of the series *Confederate Military History* recorded that Stringfield enlisted in June 1861 in Company F, 1st Regiment Tennessee Cavalry. There were two regiments that formally bore that name at different times during the war: the 1st Regiment Tennessee Cavalry (Rogers's), organized in April 1862, which was later reduced to battalion size and subsequently evolved into the 5th Regiment Tennessee Cavalry (McKenzie's); and the 1st Regiment Tennessee Cavalry (Carter's). It appears from a portion of his diary recopied into his ledger book that Stringfield enlisted in July 1861 in a company that was incorporated into the 3rd Battalion Tennessee Cavalry (Brazelton's) when it organized in August. The battalion reorganized in May 1862 as the 14th Battalion Tennessee Cavalry, and became the 1st Regiment Tennessee Cavalry (Carter's) in November. Based on the names of the company officers mentioned in his diary, Stringfield served in Company F of Brazelton's Battalion, which later became Company A of the 14th Battalion and Company K of the 1st

enlisted in the 31st Regiment Tennessee Infantry (W. M. Bradford's), and was elected captain.[45] Defeated for reelection during the regiment's reorganization, he was appointed deputy provost marshal for Carter and Johnson counties. Stringfield found himself in an area that he not only knew well from his youth, but was strongly Unionist as well. Discouraged at having to arrest the male kin of old female acquaintances, he attempted to resign after two months, but his request was denied. He was instead assigned as a mustering and enrolling officer. It was in this capacity that he became officially associated with Thomas, although the two were already acquainted. The Stringfield family still lived in Strawberry Plains, and Thomas, Hanks, and Terrell were boarding with Stringfield's stepmother. Stringfield was now sent to North Carolina by Thomas to muster in the new companies.[46]

Stringfield traveled through Blount and Monroe counties in Tennessee and then along the Hiwassee River.[47] He was probably accompanied part of the way by Thomas and Terrell.

Tennessee Cavalry (Carter's); the actual Company F of the regiment was a different unit altogether. Stringfield never served in the 1st Tennessee Cavalry (Carter's) itself. According to his diary, he went home on sick furlough in November 1861, and never returned to the battalion; the circumstances went unexplained, although he was given permission by the authorities to recruit his own company. Stringfield recorded that while with Brazelton's Battalion he served as 2nd Sergeant in his company and as orderly sergeant of the battalion. None of his service record for this period evidently survives. William Williams Stringfield, "War—Mss—Sketches & Stories—Family Matters (hereinafter cited as War—Mss)" and "Copy of War Diary—1861-1865" (hereinafter cited as War Diary [copy]), ledger book, 30-33, 36-37, 166-175, Stringfield Papers, NCOAH; Tennessee Civil War Centennial Commission, *Tennesseans in the Civil War*, 1:24-25, 48-50; D. H. Hill Jr., *North Carolina*, vol. 5 of *Confederate Military History*, ed. Clement A. Evans (Atlanta: Confederate Publishing House, 1899; reprint, extended edition, Wilmington: Broadfoot, 1987), 757 (hereinafter cited as Hill, *Confederate Military History: North Carolina*); Crow, *Storm in the Mountains*, 9-10.

45. For a while there were two 31st Tennessee Infantry Regiments commanded by officers named Bradford that were operating at the same time. The 31st Regiment Tennessee Infantry (A. H. Bradford's) was a western Tennessee unit. Stringfield served in the 31st Regiment Tennessee Infantry (W. M. Bradford's) from eastern Tennessee, which for clarity was later redesignated as the 39th Regiment Tennessee Infantry. Long after Stringfield's departure, it became the 39th Regiment Tennessee Mounted Infantry, and all of its service records at the National Archives are filed under the latter designation. Just to make things more confusing, there was also the 1st Regiment Alabama, Tennessee, and Mississippi Infantry (4th Regiment Confederate Infantry), which in the *Official Records* is indexed as the 39th Regiment Tennessee Infantry (Avery's). See Tennessee Civil War Centennial Commission, *Tennesseans in the Civil War*, 1:240, 258-260; service record file for W. W. Stringfield, 39th Regiment Tennessee Mounted Infantry, Records of Confederate Soldiers Who Served in Organizations from the State of Tennessee (M268), reel 278, RG 109, NA (hereinafter cited as Compiled Service Records of Confederate Soldiers from the State of Tennessee [M268]).

46. Stringfield, "War—Mss," ledger book, 180, 86, Stringfield Papers, NCOAH; Stringfield, "Sixty-Ninth Regiment," in Clark, *North Carolina Regiments*, 3:732; Crow, *Storm in the Mountains*, 9-10. There are striking and unreconcilable differences between the account of this journey that Stringfield gave in his unpublished reminiscence and the version in his published memoir. In the latter, he was sent to Cherokee County by Kirby Smith "to muster into service five or six men in that section"; there was no mention of Thomas, or the fact that Stringfield mustered entire companies. William Williams Stringfield, "Memoirs of the Civil War," n.d., typescript, McClung Collection, L-McGL (copy in Stringfield Papers, WCU), 14. In this history, the text follows the unpublished reminiscence, which seems more reliable than the published memoir, although even it presents chronological and geographical problems in relation to information in the company muster rolls.

47. Unless otherwise noted, the following sources are cited in the discussion of the company enrollments in July, 1862 (pp. 23-25 and nn. 48-55): Stringfield, "War—Mss," ledger book, 86-88 (including material quoted in the text), Stringfield Papers, NCOAH; "Record of Events": muster roll abstracts, July 19-August 31, 1862: Companies F and G, July 23-October 31, 1862: Company H, and July 24-October 31, 1862: Company I, Infantry

Both of the latter men were recorded as having mustered in members of a company organized at Quallatown on July 19, with James M. McConnell elected captain. The company evidently split into two on September 1 at Strawberry Plains, with 3rd Lt. Daniel G. Fisher promoted to command the new unit.[48] Stringfield enrolled four companies in what was then Cherokee County. The first of these organized at Beaverdam on July 18, with C. C. Berry elected captain. Another organized the following day at an undocumented location. William C. Walker, former lieutenant colonel of the 29th Regiment N.C. Troops, was chosen captain. Thomas J. Cooper was elected captain of a company mustering in on July 23 at Fort

---

Regiment, Thomas's Legion, and July 18-August 31, 1862: Company A, and July 19-August 31, 1862: Company B, Walker's Battalion, Thomas's Legion, Compiled Service Records of Confederate Soldiers from the State of North Carolina (M270), reel 567; service record files for Companies F, G, H, and I, Infantry Regiment, and Companies A and B, Walker's Battalion, Thomas's Legion, ibid., reels 567 through 574.

48. Thomas wrote his wife in late June that he hoped to visit home in early July, and noted that he had received permission to raise a company in Jackson County. He was recorded as enlisting McConnell's men on July 19 on the undated muster and descriptive roll and on the company muster rolls for July 19-August 31 and September-October 1862. Terrell enrolled the men who later served in Fisher's company on July 19; however, later records for McConnell's company reported Terrell as original enrolling officer for his men as well. As the records exist now, a straightforward reading of the evidence seems to indicate that McConnell's and Fisher's companies began as two separate entities on July 19. There are muster rolls for both companies covering the period July 19 through August 31, designating McConnell's unit as Company D and Fisher's as Company E (later Companies F and G, Infantry Regiment). Curiously, however, the records for Fisher's company indicate that the company did not organize until September 1, despite the July-August muster roll. The officer records of both companies, particularly in regards to date of promotion and rank, imply that the two companies were originally one, then divided on the latter date. McConnell was elected captain on July 19, as was 1st Lt. William Thomas Welch; no one was recorded as 2nd or 3rd lieutenant until September 1. Likewise, there was no captain or 1st lieutenant recorded for Fisher's company from July 19 through August 31. The highest ranking officer was 2nd Lt. Dempsey Manuel Raby, while Fisher was junior 2nd lieutenant (3rd lieutenant); both men were elected to these ranks on July 19. It is unlikely that McConnell went without two lieutenants in a newly organized company for a month and a half, while another company that was still organizing was led by officers of the very ranks missing from McConnell's company. Thus, the gaps in the respective officer ranks coincide perfectly, indicating one original company with McConnell as captain, Welch as 1st lieutenant, Raby as 2nd lieutenant, and Fisher as 3rd lieutenant. Furthermore, a payment voucher for Raby dated October 21, 1862, covering the period July 19 through August 31 as a member of Company E, referred to him as a member of Company D on the endorsement, suggesting ties between the two companies. Finally, at the time Fisher became captain of his own company on September 1, a 2nd lieutenant was elected to McConnell's company, Raby became 1st lieutenant and was assigned to Fisher, and 2nd and 3rd lieutenants were elected for Fisher's company. Given that both companies were recruiting men on July 19 at Quallatown; that the personnel of both companies were together at Strawberry Plains throughout this early period; and the comparative evidence in regards to the company officers, it would appear that McConnell's and Fisher's company were originally one company under McConnell's command until September 1. If this theory is correct, however, the reasons why the information was not clearly stated in the records, and for why the organization was handled in this matter, are unknown. Thomas to Sarah Love Thomas, June 25, 1863, Thomas Papers, DU; service record files of Daniel G. Fisher and Demsey M. Raby, 16th Regiment N.C. Troops (6th Regiment N.C. Volunteers), Compiled Service Records of Confederate Soldiers from the State of North Carolina (M270), reels 243 and 246; "Record of Events": muster roll abstracts for July 19-August 31, 1862 and September-October 1862: Companies F and G, and undated muster and descriptive roll abstract: Company F, Infantry Regiment, Thomas's Legion, ibid., reel 567; service record files for Companies F and G, Infantry Regiment, Thomas's Legion (especially those of Daniel J. Allen, Robert T. Conley, Daniel G. Fisher, James M. McConnell, Dempsey Manuel Raby, John B. Raby, William Thomas Welch, and James West), ibid., reels 567 through 574.

Montgomery at Robbinsville, in modern-day Graham County.[49] On the following day, Stringfield rendezvoused below Valleytown with another group of men who were expecting him.[50] When he arrived, Congressman Allen T. Davidson was delivering a stinging speech against Thomas, whom he claimed had no authority to recruit the men present. Stringfield was hesitant to assert himself. Eventually, some Thomas supporters asked him what he planned to do.[51] Apologizing "for interrupting a North Carolina meeting," Stringfield read aloud his orders and showed them to Davidson, who "at once stopped speaking and gave way to me." Stringfield recalled mustering in "four or five companies" of "several hundred men," although he in fact enrolled only Willis Francis Parker's company for Thomas.[52]

49. The muster roll abstracts reported that Berry, Walker, and Cooper enlisted their men themselves; however, in the undated muster and descriptive roll for Berry's company, Stringfield wrote that "I certify that this Company was mustered into the service of the Confederate States by me on July 18, 1862, in Cherokee Co. N.C." Similar statements, dated July 19 and July 23, are in the muster and descriptive rolls for Walker's and Cooper's companies respectively, although curiously the roll for the former company itself was dated October 31. "Records of Events": muster and descriptive roll, July 23, 1862: Company H, Infantry Regiment, and muster and descriptive roll abstracts: undated, Company A, and October 31, 1862, Company B, Walker's Battalion, Thomas's Legion, Compiled Service Records of Confederate Soldiers from the State of North Carolina (M270), reel 567; muster and descriptive roll abstract, October 31, 1862, service record file of William C. Walker, ibid., reel 574. Fort Montgomery was a former U.S. military camp for interning Indians during the Cherokee removal. North Carolina Chapter of the Trail of Tears Foundation, Chapter News, October 23, 1998, http://www.arch.dcr.state.nc.us/tears/102398.htm. Stringfield wrote in his unpublished memoir that he enrolled Cooper (and presumably his company) at Murphy. The muster roll abstract shows Fort Montgomery as the site of the company's enlistment, however. Graham County was organized from northeastern Cherokee County in 1872. William S. Powell, *The North Carolina Gazetteer: A Dictionary of Tar Heel Places* (Chapel Hill: The University of North Carolina Press, 1968), 196; "Record of Events": muster and descriptive roll abstract, July 23, 1862, and muster roll abstract, July 23-October 31, 1862: Company H, Infantry Regiment, Thomas's Legion, Compiled Service Records of Confederate Soldiers from the State of North Carolina (M270), reel 567.

50. In his published memoir Stringfield described the gathering as "a big meeting of a political nature that was going on and I resolved to go to it" because the "five or six men" (see n. 46 above) that he had supposedly been sent from Tennessee to recruit were somehow known to be in attendance. Stringfield, "Memoirs," typescript, McClung Collection, L-McGL (copy in Stringfield Papers, WCU), 14. His unpublished reminiscence is more accurate, wherein he described the site as a camp where the companies (or more properly, company) he was supposed to muster in were waiting.

51. Stringfield stated in his published memoir that when he arrived "Colonel Davidson was speaking and seemed not inclined to give way to me when I told him my business"; it was only then that he consulted some unnamed companions and confronted Davidson, who then allowed Stringfield to muster in the handful of conscripts that he had supposedly been sent over to get. Stringfield, "Memoirs," typescript, McClung Collection, L-McGL (copy in Stringfield Papers, WCU), 14. In his unpublished reminiscence, Stringfield noted the individuals who urged him to take action as "Cooper, Philips, Whitaker, Loudermilk, and others." Cooper was Thomas J. Cooper, who presumably accompanied Stringfield from Fort Montgomery to Valleytown (Crow, *Storm in the Mountains*, 10, interpreted the evidence this way, although Stringfield did not directly mention Cooper's presence on the journey itself, which must therefore be assumed). Philips was probably 2nd Lt. Nathaniel G. Philips of Parker's company. Loudermilk was 3rd Lt. Garner N. Loudermilk of Walker's company, while Whitaker was Stephen Whitaker, who later organized a company for Thomas at Valleytown in the fall. Whether all of these individuals were present is doubtful, given that most of their companies did not organize at Valleytown on that day.

52. In his unpublished account, Stringfield remembered mustering in the companies of Cooper, Kimsey, Loudermilk, Whitaker, and "possibly one other" at Valleytown. Earlier in the same reminiscence (Stringfield, "War—Mss," ledger book, 86, Stringfield Papers, NCOAH), he stated that he mustered in Cooper's company the day before the Valleytown incident, which would accord with the company records. Kimsey's company was in fact Parker's, which Stringfield enrolled on July 24 (Joseph A. Kimsey commanded it later in the war).

Stringfield recalled that on the following day he rode to muster in another company in the northeastern section of the county.[53] Surprisingly, Davidson traveled with Stringfield part of the way. Despite their first meeting, Stringfield found Davidson "a perfect gentleman and [one who] seemed glad to form my acquaintance." However Davidson behaved towards Stringfield personally, he had by no means warmed towards Thomas or his plans. On August 30, he wrote to Confederate secretary of war George W. Randolph in an effort to get Thomas's command disbanded, claiming that "he has greatly transcended his authority to the prejudice of the service in my opinion" by adding white companies to the Cherokee units, and urging that the new companies be sent to the 39th Regiment N.C. Troops. "Thomas['s] Indians are worthless and never will do any good," Davidson added. "Thomas himself is the old Indian agent at Washington who has made a large fortune by keeping all he got from the government for the Indians, and I venture now to say he will get every Dollar of their Monthly pay and commutation for clothing—and my word for it he will never be on hand when the fight comes off."[54]

In the meantime, Thomas continued organizing his command under the title of the Highland Rangers.[55] Due to seemingly unresolvable contradictions in the information provided in the extant company muster rolls and other documents, there is some confusion as to exactly how the unit was organized at this stage. Some materials suggest that Thomas was organizing two battalions during the summer, one of which became the Infantry Regiment, and the other which was already known as Walker's Battalion. Other materials indicate that Thomas expanded his original battalion into a regiment first, and did not create a second battalion until the regiment was completed. Properly assigning the various companies within either organizational scheme leads to further problems.[56] Assuming that Thomas

---

Loudermilk was at that time a member of Walker's company, which he never commanded. He later commanded Company H of Walker's Battalion, but as that was not organized until the following year, Walker's company was almost certainly intended. Whitaker's company did not organize until later in 1862. With the exception of Parker's company, none of these units organized at Valleytown on July 24. Whether Stringfield enrolled additional companies for officers other than Thomas is not known.

53. Stringfield anachronistically referred to his destination as "Graham County." Stringfield, "War—Mss," ledger book, 88, Stringfield Papers, NCOAH. The identity of the new company is not known. Since Fort Montgomery lay in the future area of Graham County, Stringfield in effect was retracing his previous route, raising the question of why the company was not mustered at the same time as Cooper's. Given the chronological and location problems noted earlier in Stringfield's account, it seems likelier that he was beginning his return journey to Tennessee instead.

54. Stringfield, "War—Mss," ledger book, 88, Stringfield Papers, NCOAH; Crow, *Storm in the Mountains*, 11-12; A. T. Davidson to the Secretary of War, August 30, 1862, Letters Received by the Confederate Secretary of War, 1861-1865 (M437), reel 44, file 525-D-1862.

55. Thomas to Jefferson Davis, September 23, 1862, Letters Received by the Confederate of War (M437), Roll 75, Item 415-T-1862. Thomas's first known use of the term "Highland Rangers" was on May 22, in a requisition for clothing. See William H. Thomas, Unfiled Papers and Slips Belonging to Confederate Compiled Service Records (M347), reel 391.

56. In *Storm in the Mountains*, Vernon H. Crow took the position that Thomas was already organizing a second battalion under Walker's command as far back as July; see especially 11, 12, 14-15, 186, 190, 198-228. In support of this interpretation, it should be noted that the National Archives muster abstracts for Berry's and Walker's companies for the summer of 1862 designated them as belonging to Walker's Battalion, Thomas's Legion. Further, a December payment voucher in Parker's service record for the period of July-August referred

had only one battalion at this time, which seems most likely, the following facts are known: James McConnell's company was originally known as Company D, while Daniel Fisher's unit was called Company E after it split off from McConnell's company on September 1; Thomas Cooper's company was Company F. Willis Parker's unit, which kept only one muster roll covering July through October, was Company I by the end of that period. What it was designated before the end of October is not known, although there is a payment voucher in Parker's papers implying that at one point it was known as Company D. Nor is it known how the 1st and 2nd Companies of the North Carolina Cherokee Battalion, Johnson's Partisan Rangers (if it joined Thomas during the summer), or Berry's and Walker's companies were designated.[57] One possible scenario would be the 1st and 2nd Companies of the N.C.

---

to his unit as Company D, Walker's Battalion. There are reasons to doubt Crow's reconstruction, however. Walker remained a captain in command of his company until the end of September, according to a note on its muster and descriptive roll, while the payment voucher is the only record to make any association between Parker's company and Walker's Battalion. Further, it seems likely that the "Walker's Battalion" references represent some form of updating by officers catching up on the muster rolls. It has already been noted that although Walker's company was organized on July 19, the muster and descriptive roll itself was dated October 31 (see n. 49 above), after Walker's Battalion was officially organized on October 1. Likewise, the July 18-August 31 muster roll for Berry's company gave its geographical location as of September 7, indicating that at least some material was added after the supposed completion date. It should be kept in mind that the companies were also recorded on the July-August rolls as being a part of Thomas's Legion, and that term was definitely not used before the fall. It is therefore tempting to think that the July-August rolls were not filled out until the end of October (as was the muster and descriptive roll for Walker's company), as there are no surviving muster rolls for the September-October period for either company. This was certainly the case in regards to Cooper's and Parker's companies, both of which had muster rolls covering the period from their initial enrollments in late July through the end of October. "Record of Events": muster roll abstracts, July 23-October 31, 1862: Company H, and July 24-October 31, 1862: Company I, Infantry Regiment, July 18-August 31, 1862: Company A and July 19-August 31, 1862: Company B, Walker's Battalion, undated company muster and descriptive roll: Company A, and company muster and descriptive roll, October 31, 1862: Company B, Walker's Battalion, Thomas's Legion, Compiled Service Records of Confederate Soldiers from the State of North Carolina, reel 567; payment voucher for Capt. Willis Parker, December 31, 1862 ("Co. D," covering the period July 24-August 31, 1862), service record file of Willis Parker, Thomas's Legion, ibid., reel 572; muster and descriptive roll abstract, October 31, 1862, service record file of William C. Walker, Thomas's Legion, ibid., reel 574. Crow accidentally misdated a September 23 letter to Davis, in which Thomas discussed the progress of his organization, to August 23 (Crow, *Storm in the Mountains*, 12 and 239 nn. 35 and 36); this automatically implied that developments were somewhat more advanced at an earlier date than actually seems to have been the case. For these reasons, it will be assumed in this history that Thomas had only one battalion which he gradually increased into a regiment, after which he organized Walker's Battalion in the fall. Various statements made by Thomas support the idea that this was indeed the process; see his September 23 letter to Davis noted above, in which he wrote that "I have increased the Battalion of Indians and Mountainiers to a Regiment and am progressing with a legion," and his 1864 remarks to Adjutant and Inspector General Cooper: "It [Thomas's command] was organized as a Battalion[,] increased to a regiment and then to a Legion." Thomas's most detailed remarks on how his organization evolved were contained in a February 1863 letter to Cooper. He stated that the regiment was organized from the original battalion first with the permission of Kirby Smith, while the organization of Walker's Battalion was later authorized by Smith's temporary successor, Maj. Gen. John P. McCown. Thomas to "General" (Samuel Cooper), July 8, 1864, Thomas Papers, DU; Thomas to Davis, September 23, 1862, Letters Received by the Confederate Secretary of War (M437), reel 75, item 415-T-1862; Thomas to Cooper, February 21, 1863, service record file of Samuel L. Love, Compiled Service Records of Confederate General and Staff Officers, and Non-Regimental Enlisted Men (M331), reel 159.

57. "Record of Events": muster roll abstracts, July-August 1862: Companies D [F], and E [G], Infantry Regiment and Companies A and B, Walker's Battalion, July-October 1862: Company F [H] and Company I, Infantry

Cherokee Battalion as Companies A and B; Johnson's company as C; McConnell's as D; Fisher's as E; Cooper's as F; Parker's as G; Berry's as H; and Walker's as I. The limits of the evidence at hand, however, relegate this and any other line-up to the realm of speculation. Regardless, Thomas finally had a unit of full battalion strength. He had been promoted to major on July 19, a rank more in keeping with his unit's present size.[58]

Thomas's Highland Rangers did not accompany the bulk of Kirby Smith's command, which departed on August 14 as part of a series of loosely-coordinated Confederate advances into Kentucky. In Smith's absence, the department was left in the charge first of Maj. Gen. John C. McCown and then, in late September, of Maj. Gen. Samuel Jones.[59] The

---

Regiment, and September-October 1862: Companies C [2nd Company A], D [B], E [C], F, G, H and I, Infantry Regiment, Thomas's Legion, Compiled Military Service Records of Confederate Soldiers from the State of North Carolina (M270), reel 567; service record files for 2nd Company A, Companies B, C, F, G, H, and I, Infantry Regiment, and Companies A and B, Walker's Battalion, reels 567 through 574. Contradictions in the muster rolls and other company papers make it difficult to verify the actual letter designations of some companies prior to the end of October. In addition to the cases of Berry's, Walker's, and Parker's companies discussed in n. 56, there are also problems involving Johnson's and Fisher's units. Company muster rolls imply that both Fisher's company and Elisha Johnson's Partisan Rangers were known as Company E through October. A probable solution would be that Fisher's company was Company E only when it initially split off from McConnell's company on September 1, but was redesignated Company G by the time that the regiment was organized on September 27. What Johnson's company was known as before it became Company E is unknown, as it may not have joined Thomas until later (see n. 42 above). Cooper's company was referred to as Company F in early payment vouchers. A possible solution to problems posed by the designation of Parker's unit as "Co. D" in the payment voucher is that the "D" may have been a sloppy, bloated I; alternatively, it may have been known as Company D during July-August (the payment period covered by the voucher), before McConnell's company split into two. Ultimately, however, there seems to be no way to reconcile all of the conflicts within the muster roll abstracts and other documents. Payment vouchers for Capt. Thomas J. Cooper, November 5, 1862 ("Co. F," covering the pay period July 23-August 1, 1862), December 14, 1862 ("Co. F," covering the pay period August 1-31, 1862), and May 13, 1863 (Company H, covering the pay period November 1, 1862-March 14, 1863), service record file of Thomas J. Cooper, Thomas's Legion, Compiled Service Records of Confederate Soldiers from the State of North Carolina (M270), reel 568; "Record of Events": muster roll abstract, July 19-August 31, 1862: Company E [G], company muster and descriptive roll abstract, September 1, 1862: Company G, and muster roll abstract, September-October 1862: Company G, Infantry Regiment, ibid., reel 567; payment voucher for Capt. Willis Parker, December 31, 1862 ("Co. D," covering the period July 24-August 31, 1862), service record file of Willis Parker, ibid., reel 572; "Record of Events": company muster and descriptive roll abstract: July 24, 1862, muster roll abstract: July 24-October 31, 1862, and muster roll abstract: July 24-December 31, 1862: Company I, Infantry Regiment, ibid., reel 567; Crow, *Storm in the Mountains*, 14-15, 165, 182, 186, 190, 259 nn. 29 and 32.

58. Crow, *Storm in the Mountains*, 12; service record file for William H. Thomas, Thomas's Legion, Compiled Service Records of Confederate Soldiers from the State of North Carolina (M270), reel 573. The proposed battalion line-up above was suggested by the fact that McConnell's, Fisher's, and Cooper's companies kept their order in relation to each other when they were changed from D, E, and F to F, G, and H respectively by late September; it seems natural that if Parker's Company I followed Cooper's Company H at that time, then it probably followed it as Company H when Cooper's was Company G during the summer. Likewise, assigning the 1st and 2nd Companies of the N.C. Cherokee Battalion as A and B, and Johnson's company as C, made sense as they filled a natural hole in the line-up before McConnell's Company D; significantly, when McDonnell's D became F in late September, these three companies became C, D, and E. In general, it is observable that Thomas did as little rearranging of company order or letter designation as possible during his command's periodic reorganizations; however, there were occasional exceptions to this, so it should not be assumed as fact that such was the case from the beginning.

59. *O.R.* 16 (pt. 2): 776; Crow, *Storm in the Mountains*, 241 n. 62. For the background of the late summer 1862 Confederate foray into Kentucky, see Connelly, *Army of the Heartland*, 192-211.

companies of Thomas's command were meanwhile scattered at different posts in eastern Tennessee during July through September. Most of them were probably stationed to the east of Knoxville along the vital East Tennessee & Virginia Railroad. McConnell's company was at Strawberry Plains in July and August, where it split into Companies D and E at the beginning of September. Parker's company was also at Strawberry Plains. The whereabouts for Johnson's company are unknown until the end of October, when it was recorded as stationed to the west of Strawberry Plains on the railroad at the Flat Creek bridge. Cooper's Company F was at Camp Cooper at Chilhowee in southeastern Blount County, probably to watch the mountain passes into North Carolina. Berry's and Walker's companies were stationed further south at Coker Creek in Monroe County, probably to guard the approaches into Cherokee County. The locations of the Cherokee companies are unknown, but they were presumably with Thomas at the battalion headquarters at Strawberry Plains throughout much of the period, and were definitely there by the end of October.[60] For at least a brief period, however, one or both of the Indian companies were on detached service in cooperation with elements of Kirby Smith's forces operating in northern Tennessee. In the process, they became the first elements of Thomas's command to undergo a baptism by fire, appropriately enough at a place called Baptist Gap.

As part of Smith's movement into Kentucky, the division of Brig. Gen. Carter L. Stevenson was sent in mid-August to threaten Cumberland Gap from the south.[61] Although the Confederates had now supposedly isolated the enemy garrison, in early September reports reached McCown of Federal activity south of the gap in the Powell River Valley, along the route through which Smith had recently advanced. Brig. Gen. George W. Morgan, Federal commander at Cumberland Gap, had sent out three expeditions and various smaller detachments in late August and early September to round up enemy stragglers, harass the Confederate forces gathering around the gap, and menace Smith's supply routes into Kentucky. Morgan's main targets were Baptist Gap, immediately to the west of Cumberland Gap; Rogers's Gap, still further west; and Big Creek Gap, southwest of Rogers's Gap. By early September, all three gaps were at least partially blockaded, and minor skirmishes had resulted in the loss of some Confederate prisoners. Fearing for the safety of his communication lines with Smith through Big Creek Gap, McCown ordered his available forces on September 8 to watch both Big Creek and Rogers's gaps.[62]

It is not known precisely when the Indians were dispatched to join Stevenson's operations around the Cumberland Gap.[63] They were assigned to act as scouts and pickets for an

60. "Record of events": muster roll abstracts, July-August 1862: Companies D [F] and E [G], Infantry Regiment, and Companies A and B, Walker's Battalion, July-October 1862: Companies H and I, and September-October 1862: Companies C [2nd Company A], D [B], E [C], F, and G, Infantry Regiment, Thomas's Legion, Compiled Service Records of Confederate Soldiers from the State of North Carolina (M270), reel 567.

61. Connelly, *Army of the Heartland*, 210-212.

62. *O.R.* 16 (pt. 1): 892, 953-954, 957, 992, (pt. 2): 792, 802, 810-811, 813; *Official Atlas of the Civil War*, plates 95:3, 118:2. While Morgan mentioned sending expeditions to all three gaps in his reports, he only specifically noted the blockading of Big Creek and Rogers's gaps; however, other evidence shows that Baptist Gap was blocked as well. See the account of the action at Baptist Gap below, and the accompanying notes.

63. Crow, *Storm in the Mountains*, 15, assumed that it was on September 8, citing McCown's dispatch of that date which included the following passage: "I have ordered every available man (Partisan Rangers) to that point

expedition to Baptist Gap consisting of the 29th Regiment N.C. Troops, the 39th Regiment N.C. Troops, and an Alabama regiment.[64] Formerly accessible as a wagon road through the mountains, Baptist Gap was now passable for horseback and foot travel only.[65] From a high point on the eastern side of Baptist Gap, it was possible with a telescope to observe movements through the Cumberland Gap, making it a place of some importance.[66] 1st Lt. John Davidson of Company C of the 39th N.C. recalled later that the Indians "did good picket duty" while on the expedition.[67] The regiments were soon sent away in an effort to entrap Federals blocking a gap further south, leaving the Indians at Baptist Gap.[68]

After a few days, the three regiments marched back to rejoin the Indians. As they approached Baptist Gap on or about September 13, they heard gunfire.[69] The Federals had

---

[i.e., Big Creek Gap] and Rogers's Gap to watch his [Morgan's] movements." *O.R.* 16 (pt 2): 802. However, based on recollections of the operations by members of the 29th and 39th Regiments N.C. Troops, the Indians may have been sent a few days earlier. Robert B. Vance, "Twenty-Ninth Regiment," in Clark, *North Carolina Regiments*, 2:487; John M. Davidson, "Additional Sketch Thirty-Ninth Regiment," ibid., 2:727. An August 24 communique from Col. John Pegram explained to McCown that Stevenson "is authorized to call on the North Carolina regiments at Jonesborough, Greeneville, and Johnson's Depot, and also on the regiments at Knoxville and Loudon, as he may deem their services indispensable." *O.R.* 16 (pt. 2): 776.

64. Vance, "Twenty-Ninth Regiment," in Clark, *North Carolina Regiments*, 2:487; Davidson, "Additional Sketch," in ibid., 2:727. It is uncertain who commanded the Indian contingent. According to Stringfield, "Sixty-Ninth Regiment," in Clark, *North Carolina Regiments*, 3:736, 2nd Lt. Astoogatogeh of Capt. James W. Terrell's company was in command. In many secondary sources, Bvt. 2nd Lt. (i.e., 3rd Lt.) William S. Terrell of the same company is named as the leader, although he is misidentifed as a 1st lieutenant in the process; see Crow, *Storm in the Mountains*, 15; Godbold and Russell, *Confederate Colonel and Cherokee Chief*, 105; Thomsen, *Rebel Chief*, 183; service record file of William S. Terrell, Thomas's Legion, Compiled Service Records of Confederate Soldiers from the State of North Carolina, (M270), reel 573. 1st Lt. John M. Davidson of Company C, 39th Regiment N.C. Troops, wrote that "Captain Terrell was with us, commanding a company of a hundred Cherokee Indians." Davidson, "Additional Sketch," Clark, *North Carolina Regiments*, 2:728. According to one source, however, he was absent recruiting (Crow, *Storm in the Mountains*, 15); if so, then Astoogatogeh would have been in charge, as he outranked William S. Terrell, unless some other ranking officer was assigned.

65. *Official Atlas of the Civil War*, plate 95:3; Davidson, "Additonal Sketch," in Clark, *North Carolina Regiments*, 2:728.

66. Stevenson would do just that a few days following the incident at Baptist Gap, as he prepared to recapture Cumberland Gap from the Federals. George W. Morgan, "Cumberland Gap," in Robert Underwood Johnson and Clarence Clough Buel, eds., *Battles and Leaders of the Civil War*, 4 vols., (New York: The Century Company, 1887-1888; repr., New York: Castle Books, n.d.,), 3:67.

67. Davidson, "Additional Sketch," in Clark, *North Carolina Regiments*, 2:727.

68. The name of the other gap is unknown, but Big Creek Gap is most likely. Col. Robert B. Vance of the 29th Regiment N.C. Troops remembered that they were sent "to cut off a detachment of Federals which had marched in the direction of a gap still nearer to Knoxville" than Baptist Gap. 1st Lt. John M. Davidson of the 39th Regiment N.C. Troops wrote that "[t]he three regiments were ordered to proceed to another gap, below Baptist Gap, where the Federals were expected to pass." Vance, "Twenty-Ninth Regiment," in Clark, *North Carolina Regiments*, 2:487; Davidson, "Additional Sketch," in ibid., 728. Rogers's Gap lay more to the west than to the south, while Big Creek Gap lay south of the Cumberland Gap, Rogers's Gap, and Baptist Gap. For mention of efforts by Stephenson and McCown to cut off the Federals at Rogers's and Big Creek Gaps around September 10, 1862, see *O.R.* 16 (pt. 2): 810-811, 813.

69. 1st Lt. John M. Davidson recalled that after "two or three days" of waiting to catch the Federals, who had evidently already departed or taken another route, they were ordered back to Baptist Gap. Davidson, "Additional Sketch," in Clark, *North Carolina Regiments*, 2:728. There is some dispute as to the date of the skirmish at Baptist Gap, which is not mentioned in the *Official Records*. In the service record of 2nd Lt. Astoogatogeh of

assaulted and driven back the Cherokee picket line, killing or mortally wounding a popular officer, 2nd Lt. Astoogatogeh of James Terrell's company, as he led a charge against the enemy. The regiments quickly deployed into columns of companies and pushed forward through a heavy undergrowth, proceeded by a skirmish line. The skirmishers soon came upon a party bearing Astoogatogeh off the field. At the sight of the heavy reinforcements, the Federals withdrew. It was an unfortunate decision in regard to the well-being of the Federal wounded, however. Angered by the injury to Astoogatogeh, the Cherokees scalped some of the enemy dead and wounded before they could be stopped.[70]

On the following day, elements of the 39th Regiment N.C. Troops pushed up the gap to clear the felled timber that blocked the road, while other companies guarded the heights on either side. Some of the Cherokees were sent ahead as scouts. "We spent an exciting day," remembered Davidson, whose men acted as skirmishers and as guards for the work party, "as the Federals were in the valley only a short distance away. The Indian scouts captured three of their pickets and reported to me with their prisoners, who were the most frightened men I ever saw. Their captors . . . wore feather plumes on their heads, giving them a savage appearance. I ordered the prisoners taken to headquarters, after assuring them that the Indians would not scalp them." The regiments remained in the area until word came that Morgan had evacuated Cumberland Gap, and then set off to join the pursuit. It is not known whether the Indians journeyed with them, remained in the area, or returned immediately to Strawberry Plains, although the latter is probably the case, as they were reported there in the October muster rolls.[71]

Terrell's company, the date is given as September 15 on an undated company muster and descriptive roll, and as September 13 on the muster roll for September-October 1862. Col. Robert Brank Vance, who at the time of skirmish commanded the 29th Regiment N.C. Troops, recalled long after the war that it happened on September 15. Crow accepted September 13. Godbold and Russell, apparently attempting to reconcile the conflicting dates, believed that the skirmish was spread out over a few days, interpreting the intial brush between the Cherokees and the Federals as occurring on September 13 and Astoogatogeh's death on September 15. As William S. Terrell was promoted to 2nd lieutenant on or to rank from September 14, it would seem probable that the skrimish happened either on that day or on September 13. Service record files of Astoogatogeh and William S. Terrell, Thomas's Legion, Compiled Service Records of Confederate Soldiers from North Carolina (270), reels 567 and 573; Vance, "Twenty-Ninth Regiment," in Clark, *North Carolina Regiments*, 2:487; Crow, *Storm in the Mountains*, 15; Godbold and Russell, *Confederate Colonel and Cherokee Chief*, 105.

70. Vance, "Twenty-Ninth Regiment," in Clark, *North Carolina Regiments*, 2:487; Davidson, "Additional Sketch," ibid., 2:728; Stringfield, "Sixty-Ninth Regiment," in ibid., 3:736; Stringfield, "War—Mss," ledger book, 106-107, NCOAH. Neither Vance or Davidson mentioned the scalping, although Davidson broadly hinted at it in his discussion of the aftermath on the next day (see text below). Most accounts imply that Astoogatogeh was killed outright, but Davidson recalled that he was mortally wounded and died in the night. See also service record file of Astoogatogeh, Thomas's Legion, Compiled Service Records of Confederate Soldiers from the State of North Carolina (M270), reel 567. The identity of the Cherokees' opponents is a mystery, although tradition claims they were members of an Indiana regiment; see Crow, *Storm in the Mountains*, 1, 15. There were two Indiana regiments in Morgan's Seventh Division at Cumberland Gap: the 49th Regiment Indiana Infantry, under Col. John W. Ray, and the 33rd Regiment Indiana Infantry, under Col. John Coburn. *O.R.* 16 (pt. 2): 7. Which if either of the two regiments was involved at Baptist Gap is unknown.

71. Davidson, "Additional Sketch," in Clark, *North Carolina Regiments* 2:728; Vance, "Twenty-Ninth Regiment," ibid., 2:487; muster roll abstracts, service record files for Companies C [2nd A] and D [B], Infantry Regiment, Thomas's Legion, Compiled Service Records for Confederate Soldiers from the State of North Carolina (M270), reels 567 through 574. Thomas made the exaggerated claim to Jefferson Davis that the Cherokees' "attacks on

The Indians returned from Baptist Gap with both valuable combat experience and a controversial and stereotypical reputation. Opinion was later divided among survivors of Thomas's Legion as to whether or not the scalpings were an isolated incident or the first of a series of similar acts. Stringfield passionately supported the former interpretation, emphasizing the positive role that the Indians played. "The writer can truthfully declare that in all the Conduct of the Indians towards the Federals—or their families—they Were always humane and generous—no excesses of any Sort—even to those of ordinary white Soldiers." He added that Baptist Gap was the only incident in which these traits broke down, and that was the result of the loss of Astoogatogeh, a grandson of Junaluska. James W. Terrell remembered things very differently. Recalling the incident when Major Morgan's sister had, to the upset of Thomas, urged the Indians to gather many scalps, he claimed "that throughout the war they did scalp every man they killed if they could get to him, which they generally managed to do, about the only thing in which Thomas could not control them, and while they operated where they were but scantily reported at the end of the war they had at least as many scalps as there were survivors among them." Historian Vernon H. Crow favored Terrell, due to the fact that as Thomas's surrogate Indian agent and as commander of a Cherokee company, he had a close acquaintance with them; Stringfield, on the other hand, had no known interaction with them before the war and during the conflict had little chance to see them in action except at the very end. Truthfully, however, the same could be argued for Terrell as far as the war is concerned, since his appointment as assistant quartermaster of the Infantry Regiment in late September 1862 left him little opportunity to see them in action, either.[72] It should also be noted that there are no known surviving protests from the Federals regarding the Baptist Gap incident. In the end, the Baptist Gap scalpings were swallowed up by the larger cycle of military campaigning as well as by the atrocities committed by both sides in the irregular warfare in the region. It was not the last time that such charges would be made against Thomas's command, however.[73]

Shortly after the Baptist Gap incident, Thomas reorganized the structure of his command, splitting the Highland Rangers into an infantry regiment and a battalion. The expanded organization was called Thomas's Legion. The original battalion was increased to an

---

the [Federal] pickets did much to cause the enemy to evacuate the Cumberland gap." Thomas to Davis, September 23, 1862, Letters Received by the Confederate Secretary of War (M437), reel 75, file 415-T-1862.

72. Stringfield, "War—Mss," ledger book, 106-107, 110, 137 (quote, 106), Stringfield Papers, NCOAH; Terrell, Unpublished Reminiscences, 6-7 (quote, 7), Terrell Papers, WCU (microfilm, Terrell Papers, DU); Crow, *Storm in the Mountains*, 16, 240 n. 32. William S. Terrell also strongly defended the reputation of the Cherokees after the war to Stringfield, although he made no mention of Baptist Gap. William S. Terrell to Stringfield, April 10, 1913, Stringfield Papers, WCU. Godbold and Russell followed Stringfield in understanding the Baptist Gap scalpings as an aberration upon the part of the Cherokees, based on Thomas's efforts to portray them as "civilized" in the Western meaning of the word, and due to the lack of Federal reports about such incidents. They were puzzled by James W. Terrell's claims to the contrary, given his many years as a supporter of the Indians. Godbold and Russell, *Confederate Colonel and Cherokee Chief*, 105-107.

73. Finger, *Eastern Band of Cherokees*, 90-93, argued convincingly that if scalping was as frequent as James W. Terrell claimed, then postwar condemnation by Federal veterans would have been stronger and more widespread, although he also cited evidence showing that Thomas himself, despite his reputation to the contrary (see p. 14 and nn. 31 and 72 above), and other Confederates were not above playing up the "savage" stereotype for propaganda purposes.

infantry regiment. Anticipating the imminent arrival of Companies A and L from the 16th Regiment N.C. Troops (6th N.C. Volunteers), Thomas assigned the former to be Company A of the regiment, while the latter became Company B. The 1st Company of the old North Carolina Cherokee Battalion (Terrell's company) became Company C, while the 2nd Company (Hanks's company) became Company D. Elisha Johnson's Partisan Rangers became Company E, while the old Company D (McConnell's company) was now Company F; Fisher's Company E became Company G; and Cooper's Company F became Company H. Parker's company was Company I. A new Tennessee company, organized on September 27 under Thomas A. Butler at Winters's Gap, Tennessee, became Company K.[74]

On the same day that Butler's company was mustered in, the regiment was organized at Knoxville. Thomas was elected colonel. As commander of the Legion his direct leadership of the regiment itself would be nominal. Responsibility for command thus devolved upon its lieutenant colonel. Capt. James R. Love Jr., of the incoming Company A, 16th Regiment N.C. Troops, was elected to that post. He was a fortunate choice, as his time with the 16th N.C. gave him much-needed combat experience, while as cousin to Thomas's wife he had a personal connection with his superior that would, theoretically at least, promote harmonious working relations between the two. Stringfield was elected major, having become very familiar with Thomas's men from his days as a recruiter in the summer. Among others who filled the field and staff positions in the regiment was James W. Terrell, who became assistant quartermaster. The new captain of Company C was Thomas's brother-in-law, Matthew H. Love, who had formerly served as 1st sergeant of Company L of the 16th N.C.[75]

Thomas's new battalion originally consisted of seven companies. Presumably, he intended for it to become a cavalry battalion to represent that arm of service in his new legion. In the event, only Companies D, F, and G were cavalry units, and their tenure with Thomas was short-lived. Company D was recruited in Blount County, Tennessee, by William C. Wallace, who became its captain. It mustered in on September 28. Company F was incorporated around a small unit organized between June 15 and July 4 and known as DeWitt C. Ghormley's Company, Marshal Guards or DeWitt C. Ghormley's Provost Guard. Although organized at Maryville, Tennessee, to defend and police Monroe, Blount, and Sevier counties in the latter state, the company possessed strong ties to Cherokee County, from which many of its members came. By September 24 it recruited to full company strength among counties on both sides of the state line, at which point it was assigned to Thomas. On the

74."Record of Events": muster roll abstracts, July-October 1862: Companies H and I, September-October 1862: 1st Company A, Companies B [E], C [2nd A], D [B], E [C], F, G, and K, Infantry Regiment, Thomas's Legion, Compiled Service Records of Confederate Soldiers from the State of North Carolina (M270), reel 567; and service record files, 1st and 2nd Companies A, Companies B, C, D, E, F, G, H, I, and K, Infantry Regiment, Thomas's Legion, ibid., reels 567 through 574. Kirby Smith had granted Thomas's request to expand the battalion into a regiment before his departure for Kentucky. McCown in turn authorized Thomas's organization of a new battalion, the addition of an artillery battery, and the adoption of the legion structure. Thomas to Samuel Cooper, February 21, 1863, service record file of Samuel L. Love, Compiled Service Records of Confederate General and Staff Officers, and Non-Regimental Enlisted Men (M331), reel 159.

75. Stringfield, "Sixty-Ninth Regiment," Clark, *North Carolina Regiments*, 3:729-730; Crow, *Storm in the Mountains*, 13-14; service record files of Matthew H. Love, William W. Stringfield, James W. Terrell, and William H. Thomas, Thomas's Legion, Compiled Service Records of Confederate Soldiers from the State of North Carolina (M270), reels 570 and 574.

same day, Company G mustered in at Dandridge, Tennessee, captained by David Neff. It consisted mostly of men from Cocke, Jefferson, and Sevier counties in Tennessee.[76]

The remaining companies of the battalion were infantry. Berry's and Walker's companies were A and B, respectively. James A. McKamy was elected to command a company recruited from Blount County, Tennessee, which mustered in on September 29. It was originally authorized by McCown for incorporation into a Tennessee regiment, but as none were organizing at that time, it was assigned to Thomas. Stephen Whitaker reported to Thomas on September 29 with forty men, mostly from Clay and Cherokee Counties. Evidently due to its understrength size it did not elect officers and formally organize as a company until November 29, becoming Company E, with Whitaker as captain. Another company organized in Jefferson County, Tennessee on September 30. William B. Love, brother of James R. Love Jr., and another cousin of Sarah Thomas, was elected captain. Its actual letter designation at this time is unknown. It later became Company D after Wallace's company transferred out of the Legion in November; unfortunately, the surviving records refer to it as Company D from its organization, resulting in the appearance of two D companies in the battalion from September to November. It therefore may be assumed that Love's company was originally designated by a different letter; given what is otherwise known about the battalion's organization, it seems likely that it would have been Company H, although such a designation is purely speculative.[77]

The new battalion formally organized at Knoxville on October 1. William C. Walker, captain of Company B, was elected lieutenant colonel. Like James R. Love, Walker was a man with both personal connections to Thomas and some prior military experience. He was a friend of Thomas's who had served in the House of Commons as representative for Cherokee County in the 1858-1859 session. Earlier in the war, Walker served as captain of

76. "Record of Events": muster and descriptive rolls, September 28, 1862: [1st] Company D, September 24, 1862: Company F, and undated (received by the Confederate Adjutant and Inspector General's Office, June 1, 1863): Company G, Walker's Battalion, Thomas's Legion, Compiled Service Records of Confederate Soldiers from the State of North Carolina (M270), reel 567; service record files, Companies D, F, and G, Walker's Battalion, Thomas's Legion, Compiled Service Records of Confederate Soldiers from the State of North Carolina (M270), reels 567 through 574. Thomas wrote in early 1863 that "[f]inding that it it [*sic*] could be increased by another battalion and that I would be compelled to have Mounted Riflemen to act in concert with the Indians, and also that I would be compelled to have some artillery . . . I was advised to assume the Legionary form." The statement strongly implies that the intention was for Walker's Battalion to be a mounted battalion. Vernon H. Crow was probably correct in his assumption that the rest of the battalion was not mounted due to a lack of horses, although departmental needs for infantry to act as bridge and depot guards may also have played a part. Thomas to Samuel Cooper, February 21, 1863, service record file of Samuel L. Love, Compiled Service Records of Confederate General and Staff Officers, and Non-Regimental Enlisted Men (M331), reel 159; Crow, *Storm in the Mountains*, 15. A list of members of Company F, dated August 1, 1862, and abstracted in the service record files, reported that it was organized on June 15. See the service record file of William Amburn, Walker's Battalion, ibid., reel 567. The earliest recorded enlistment date for any of its members, however, is July 4.

77. "Record of Events": muster roll abstracts, July-August 1862: Companies A and B, September-October 1862: Companies C, [probably 2nd] D [September 30-October 31, station at Strawberry Plains], E, and H, and April 7, 1864: Company C, Walker's Battalion, and company muster-in and descriptive rolls, undated: Company A, and October 31, 1862: Company B, Walker's Battalion, Thomas's Legion, Compiled Service Records of Confederate Soldiers from the State of North Carolina (M270), reel 567; service record files, Company D, Infantry Regiment and Companies A, B, C, and E, Walker's Battalion, ibid., reels 567 through 574; Thomas to Stephen Whitaker, September 8, 1862, Stephen Whitaker Papers, P.C. 36, NCOAH.

Company A, 29th Regiment N.C. Troops, and then as lieutenant colonel of the same regiment, resigning on May 2, 1862 due to ill health and an unwillingness to stand for reelection when it reorganized for the war.[78]

Thomas still did not command a real legion. Only three of Walker's seven companies were mounted, while a battery had not yet been raised or assigned. In the meantime, the various companies were scattered along different points of the railroad line, or near the mountain passes connecting North Carolina to Tennessee. The surviving muster rolls show that most of the Infantry Regiment was concentrated at Strawberry Plains, where the Legion was headquartered; Companies A, B, C, D, F, G, and I were all there when the muster was taken at the end of October. At the end of December, Companies A, B, and I were still there. Company G was also there for much of the November-December period, but was elsewhere on active operations during part of December. Company E was still at the Flat Creek bridge through the end of December. Company H remained at Camp Cooper through at least the end of October. By the end of December, it had moved to a place called Camp Iron Mountain. Company K remained at its place of organization, Winters's Gap in Anderson County, west of Knoxville, through the end of the year.[79]

Evidence for the whereabouts of the companies of Walker's Battalion is scanty for the latter part of 1862. Companies A and B were previously at Coker Creek in Monroe County. As both companies were reported at Coker Creek on the November-December roll, it is likely that they were also there during September and October. Company E remained at Valleytown. Company F was at Maryville at the time of the October muster. Company D was also reported at Maryville on September 28, but was then reported at Strawberry Plains from September 30 to October 31 in a separate roll. It is doubtful, however, that both records for "Company D" refer to the same unit. It is probable that the first report referred to Wallace's cavalry company, and the second to William B. Love's infantry company, which by the end of the year was at Strawberry Plains. The locations of the rest of Walker's companies are unknown.[80]

78. Aiken, "Eightieth Regiment," in Clark, *North Carolina Regiments*, 4:117, 122; Cheney, *North Carolina Government 1585-1979*, 326; Manarin and Jordan, *North Carolina Troops*, 8:238, 235; service record file of William C. Walker, Thomas's Legion, Compiled Service Records of Soldiers from the State of North Carolina, (M270), reel 574. Walker's Battalion would not have a major until Capt. James A. McKamy of Company C was elected on August 15, 1863. See the service record file of James A. McKamy, Thomas's Legion, ibid., reel 571.

79. "Records of events": muster roll abstracts, July-October 1862: Companies H and I, September-October 1862: 1st Company A, B [E], C [2nd A], D [B], E [C], F, G, and H, and September-December 1862: Company K, Infantry Regiment, Thomas's Legion, Compiled Service Records of Confederate Soldiers from the State of North Carolina (M270), reel 567.

80. "Records of events": muster and descriptive roll abstract, undated: Company A, October 31, 1862: Company B, September 28, 1862: Company D [stationed at Maryville], undated [received at the Confederate Adjutant and Inspector General's Office on June 1, 1863]: Company D [stationed at Strawberry Plains], and muster roll abstracts, September 30-October 31, 1862: Company D [stationed at Strawberry Plains], November-December 1862: Companies A, B, and D [stationed at Strawberry Plains], Walker's Battalion, Thomas's Legion, ibid. The October 31, 1862 muster and descriptive roll for Company B indicates its presence at Coker Creek at that time. Given that 1st Company D, Walker's Battalion, was recruited on September 28 in Blount County, where Maryville is located, it seems likely that the September 28 material referred to this company; whereas Love's company (2nd Company D) was organized on September 30, and is known to have been stationed at Strawberry Plains, it is therefore probable that the September 30-October 31 and November-December material referred to it.

The Legion was a part of Brig. Gen. Henry Heth's Division, but was independent of any of the division's four brigades. Heth's Division was formally a part of the Department of East Tennessee, once again under Smith's command following his return from Kentucky. A report on the reorganization of the forces in eastern Tennessee noted a "Regiment North Carolina Volunteers, Col. W. H. Thomas" among the units of Heth's Division on October 31. On November 20, Thomas's "North Carolina Regiment" was reported numbering 500 aggregate present and absent. On December 27, Thomas's "North Carolina Regiment" was noted to be "in the mountains of North Carolina," while Walker's "North Carolina Battalion" was in Monroe County, Tennessee. As Walker's Battalion was not mentioned in either the October and November reports, it is unclear whether the references to Thomas's "Regiment" indeed referred to the regiment only, or the Legion as a whole. The wording of the December 27 report seemed to imply that the regiment and battalion were separate units with no apparent connection to one another. Cumulatively, the reports suggest that the Legion's organization was either not understood very well by Thomas's superiors or not considered to be of particular importance.[81]

Although it had only existed for a short time, Thomas's Legion soon underwent major changes. All three cavalry companies in Walker's Battalion were transferred to various Tennessee regiments. Company D went to the 1st Regiment Tennessee Cavalry (Carter's) on November 14, 1862, where it became Company I of that regiment. In the same month (and probably on the same date), Company G transferred to the same regiment, becoming Company H. Company F became Company K of the 5th Regiment Tennessee Cavalry (McKenzie's) on December 16. The remainder of the battalion stayed dismounted; William B. Love's infantry company became (2nd) Company D.[82]

81. *O.R.* 16 (pt. 2): 985; 20 (pt. 2): 412, 414-415, 466. The low aggregate present and absent for the Infantry Regiment may reflect either only those companies present at Strawberry Plains, or only those that filed reports.

82. Janet B. Hewett, et al., eds., *Supplement to the Official Records of the Union and Confederate Armies*, 2 pts. in 95 vols. with 5-vol. index (Wilmington, N.C.: Broadfoot Publishing Company, 1994-1999), Pt. II: *Record of Events*, 66:18, 92, 111 (hereinafter cited as *O.R. [Supplement]*); service record files, (1st) Company D and Companies F and G, Walker's Battalion, Thomas's Legion, Compiled Service Records of Confederate Soldiers from the State of North Carolina (M270), reels 567 through 574; "Records of events": muster roll abstracts, November-December 1862: (2nd) Company D [stationed at Strawberry Plains], Walker's Battalion, and January-February 1863: Company D, Infantry Regiment, Thomas's Legion, ibid., reel 567; service record files, Companies H and I, 1st Regiment Tennessee Cavalry (Carter's) and Company K, 5th Regiment Tennessee Cavalry (McKenzie's), Compiled Service Records of Confederate Soldiers from the State of Tennessee (M268), reels 2 through 4 and 22 through 26. In his history of Walker's Battalion, Robert Akin claimed that the cavalry companies "were permanently cut off from the battalion as well as the regiment" while cooperating with the Army of Tennessee; that they "did no service in North Carolina" following Burnside's campaign in eastern Tennessee in the fall and winter of 1863, and that they then "were attached" to Brig. Gen. John C. Vaughn's Tennessee cavalry brigade. Read at face value, Akin seems to indicate that the companies always remained part of Walker's Battalion, but were physically separated by circumstances and became "attached" to other units, thus justifying his claim that the battalion later had enough companies to become a full regiment (the "80th North Carolina"). Aiken, "Eightieth Regiment," in Clark, *North Carolina Regiments*, 4:123. There is no mention of the word "transfer" in Akin's account. In fact, the battalion never became a regiment, and the cavalry companies were formally transferred out of its organization. Akin's views seemed to reflect Thomas's own. As late as December 1863, Thomas claimed that the cavalry companies were still part of the Legion and were merely "detached" to other units; he even linked their loss to the separation of the Legion into segments caused by the Federal invasion of eastern Tennessee in September 1863, which occurred eight months after they had already

This was only the beginning of the changes to the Legion's organization. In January 1863 Company A of the Infantry Regiment (formerly Company A of the 16th Regiment N.C. Troops) was transferred to the 39th Regiment North Carolina Troops, where it became Company K.[83] This led to a major shifting of companies within the regiment. Companies C and D (the Indian companies) became (2nd) Company A and Company B respectively. Company E (Johnson's company) became Company C. Company B (formerly Company L of the 16th N.C.) became Company E. The arrangement of the other companies remained the same. The transformation was completed in February when (2nd) Company D of Walker's Battalion was moved over to the Infantry Regiment, becoming its new Company D.[84]

Other changes took place within the overall command structure of the region. To prevent a recurrence of the lack of military coordination and cooperation evident between different departmental commanders in the Kentucky campaign, the Department of the West was created in November 1862 under the command of Gen. Joseph E. Johnston. It embraced all of the territory between the Appalachians and the Mississippi River and from Kentucky to the Gulf coast. The individual departments, such as the Department of East Tennessee, still retained their identity and much of their local authority. Unlike their Federal counterparts, which were created, expanded, or eliminated as military circumstances dictated, Confederate military departments tended to be rigidly defined along strict geographic lines. Cooperation in the face of enemy operations that ignored those boundaries was therefore problematic. The new arrangement was intended to provide a higher authority to override the tendency of individual departmental commanders to focus on their own immediate situations in times of crisis, and to facilitate the shifting of troops and supplies as needed. Whether or not the system would work was open to question.[85]

As for Thomas himself, he spent much of the period offering more unsolicited advice to various officials on issues concerning local and state defense. "Summer is gone, fall has come," he wrote in a philosophical tone to Jefferson Davis on November 8. "During the latter we came near losing East Tennessee. At present we have to look out for the future." He then offered a plan to defend East Tennessee that he had already submitted to Maj. Gen. Samuel Jones "and others, and [have] received their approval." Thomas's plan basically

---

gone. This is more or less in line with Akin's postwar statements, and may have been the original source for his (mis)information. See Thomas to the editors of the *Asheville News*, December 25, 1863, published in the *Asheville News*, January 21, 1864, reprinted in *The Western Democrat* (Charlotte), January 26, 1864.

83. See p. 20 n. 41 above; Manarin and Jordan, *North Carolina Troops*, 10:180-181.

84. "Records of events": muster roll abstracts, July 24-December 31, 1862: Company I, September 27-December 31, 1862: Company K, November-December 1862: (2nd) Company A, Companies B, C, E, G, and H, and January-February 1863: Companies D and F, Infantry Regiment, Thomas's Legion, Compiled Service Records of Confederate Soldiers from the State of North Carolina (M270), reel 567. The precise date of this reorganization is unknown, due to record-keeping problems in the Legion muster rolls. Given the sometimes conflicting information available, the best reconstruction seems to be that most of it was conducted in November and December.

85. *O.R.* 23 (pt. 2): 423-424; Thomas Lawrence Connelly, *Autumn of Glory: The Army of Tennessee, 1862-1865* (Baton Rouge: Lousiana State University Press, 1971), 32-42; Benjamin Franklin Cooling, *Fort Donelson's Legacy: War and Society in Kentucky and Tennessee, 1862-1863* (Knoxville: University of Tennessee Press, 1997), 152; John E. Stanchak, "department," in Patricia L. Faust, ed., *Historical Times Illustrated Encyclopedia of the Civil War* (New York: Harper & Row, 1986), 216; William Glenn Robertson, "Army Departments," in Current, *Encylopedia of the Confederacy*, 1:71-74.

called for improving supply and communication lines within the region. The primary object was to reopen the salt works at Goose Creek in southeastern Kentucky, where there were also nearby coal deposits, and to enable the Confederacy to trade for badly-needed foodstuffs in the region. Thomas had in June suggested a movement on the saltworks to help the citizens of western North Carolina, who were sorely lacking in the substance. He now proposed the construction of a depot on the western side of the railroad bridge at Strawberry Plains, the site of the Legion's headquarters, and urged the completion of a road from there to link up with another running to Blain's Crossroads in the north. "This would complete the opening of the wagon communications between the East Tennessee and Virginia Railroad and Kentucky." He thought that communications would be secured by adopting the old U. S. military system of keeping the route from the Mississippi to California open through a series of posts set fifteen to twenty miles apart at which the supply wagons could stop each night. Of course, Thomas also anticipated the possible role that his legion might play in this arrangement. "To complete this communication with Kentucky, a guard of Indians or other soldiers would be necessary to pass from post to post, and an old-fashioned block-house should be built at such post to protect our troops against sudden emergencies."[86] While an interesting idea, Thomas's plans were already rendered moot by the failure of the Confederate military operations in Kentucky.

Later in the month, Thomas wrote new North Carolina governor Zebulon Baird Vance to outline his latest ideas on improving conditions at home. On the topic of defense, he focused on "what will ensure success not what would be most agreeable to us." According to Thomas, the General Assembly had appropriated $2,000,000 for the defense of both the eastern and western ends of the state. "Both are now in danger," he complained. "The Western Counties are in danger of being over run by deserters and renegades who by the hundred are taking shelter in the smokey mountains." Thomas advised that all men west of the Blue Ridge Mountains between the ages of thirty-five and forty should be armed and "required to aid in guarding their home[s], And the Confederate[s] should be required to place military camps at every pass in the smokey mountain[s] from Ashe to Cherokee." He concluded that "[a]s long as we can hold the Country encircled by the Blue Ridge and Cumberland Mountains and their outside slopes we have the heart of the South, which commands the surrounding plains."[87]

What Vance thought of Thomas's opinions are unknown; his was only one of many letters pouring into the governor's office lecturing him about some special interest or exhorting him to direct his attention towards problems in the writer's locale. As a man from the western counties himself, however, Vance would have noted with concern Thomas's description of conditions in the west. Thomas was one of a growing number of writers to bombard the state government regarding the steady breakdown of order in the mountains. Disgusted by the compulsory nature of the Confederate conscription laws and the relative defenselessness of their home area as more and more were pulled into the war effort, an increasing number of men from the mountain counties chose to desert. The latent Unionism in

86. Thomas to Cooper, June 1, 1862, Letters Received by the Confederate Adjutant and Inspector General's Office (M474), reel 50, item 419-T-1862; *O.R.* 20 (pt. 2): 395 (quotes).

87. Thomas to Governor Vance, November 22, 1862, Governors' Papers: Vance, 1862-1865, NCOAH.

the region played a role, as those who were reluctant Confederates in 1861 now rethought their early acquiescence to secession. The unrest was exacerbated in 1863 when Confederate units from neighboring states marched into the area and impressed local men into their ranks, despite protests from Vance to both Richmond and other governors. Meanwhile, large numbers of deserters, some in organized bands, roamed the region. They included not only men from the mountains, but soldiers from other parts of the state and, indeed, other states as well. They chose refuge there because of the area's relative inaccessibility. Vance sought to have the conscription law temporarily suspended in western North Carolina, and to allow the locals to organize for their self-defense. The Confederate authorities turned down both proposals, however. Fortunately for the Confederates, the Unionists were badly organized, and unable to exercise any real power due to the efforts of both state and national authorities. Meanwhile, Confederate endeavors to deal with the problem reached their nadir in January 1863 with the "Shelton Laurel Massacre," when members of the 64th Regiment N.C. Troops executed without trial several deserters and local Unionist men who may (or may not) have been involved in a recent raid for salt on Marshall in Madison County.[88]

Although Thomas's Legion was not involved in the "Shelton Laurel Massacre," it participated in Heth's overall efforts to suppress the unrest in the mountain counties. It was reported in the December 1862 muster roll for Company G of the Infantry Regiment that during December it had been "with . . . Thomas in suppressing a Tory Rebellion in Cocke Co. Tenn. & Haywood Co. N.C." The company traveled nearly 300 miles in the course of these activities. It is not known if other companies of the Legion participated in this operation, as Company G was the only unit whose extant records report it.[89]

When news of the raid on Marshall was received, Heth again called upon the Legion to help deal with the crisis. "I send Brig. Genl. W. G. M. Davis of Florida with his brigade and [a] portion of Col. Thomas' Indian Battalion and as much Cavalry as can be subsisted to Madison and adjoining Counties in No. Ca. to put down the outbreak," he wrote Vance on January 17, 1863, asking for the governor's cooperation with Davis.[90] Thomas was ordered

88. R. F. Armfield to Governor Vance, February 19, 1863, R. C. Abernethy to Vance, February 26, 1863, Governors' Papers: Vance, 1862-1865, NCOAH; William A. Pierce to Vance, December 7, 1862, J. W. McElroy to Vance, December 26, 1862, in Frontis W. Johnston and Joe A. Mobley, eds., *The Papers of Zebulon Baird Vance*, 2 vols. to date (Raleigh: State Department of Archives and History, 1963), 1:425, 445-446; Inscoe and McKinney, *Heart of Confederate Appalachia*, 113-140, 143-145, 150. The fullest treatment of the Shelton Laurel killings is Philip Shaw Paludan, *Victims: A True Story of the Civil War* (Knoxville: University of Tennessee Press, 1981). See also John G. Barrett, *The Civil War in North Carolina* (Chapel Hill: University of North Carolina Press, 1963), 197-198; William R. Trotter, *Bushwhackers!: The Civil War in North Carolina—The Mountains*, vol. 2 of *The Civil War in North Carolina* (Winston-Salem: John F. Blair, 1988), 209-232; Weymouth T. Jordan Jr., "64th Regiment N.C. Troops," in Manarin and Jordan, *North Carolina Troops*, 15:142-145.

89. "Records of events": muster roll abstract, November-December 1862: Company G, Infantry Regiment, Thomas's Legion, Compiled Service Records of Confederate Soldiers from the State of North Carolina (M270), reel 567. Heth was placed temporarily in command of the Department of East Tennessee by Smith in mid-November 1862 to replace Jones. After Smith resumed direct command of the department on December 23, Heth was charged with overseeing the area stretching from Bristol on the Tennessee-Virginia border to Loudon, and westward along the railroad from the latter point. *O.R.* 20 (pt. 2): 398, 410, 425, 23 (pt. 2): 461.

90. Davis's Brigade consisted of the 1st Regiment Florida Cavalry (Dismounted), the 6th and 7th Regiments Florida Infantry, the 63rd Regiment Tennessee Infantry, and Capt. H. L. W. McClung's Tennessee Battery. *O.R.* 20 (pt. 2): 466.

According to a newspaper account, Thomas's campaign met with a great deal of success. Citing an item from the Petersburg *Express*, the Wilmington *Daily Journal* reported in early March that Thomas was "in reality conciliating the tories" along the North Carolina/Tennessee border. "A notice that Thomas' Indians are in the country brings in the dodgers at once, for they know that hiding out will not avail against the Cherokees." In addition, a detachment of twelve enlisted men from (2nd) Company A and Company B of the Infantry Regiment, under the command of 1st Lt. James Taylor and Sgt. Chuwannaskee of the latter company, were reported in Carter and Johnson Counties in January and February, probably as part of Garrett's parallel operation in Tennessee. They were apparently part of a group that according to a postwar source was led by a Lieutenant Tipton, a native of Carter County, operating under the overall direction of a Captain Walters, a Georgia officer. The force possibly included as many as three companies of cavalry, and was charged with capturing Unionists hiding in the area. By the postwar era, the expedition was the source of more rumors about the alleged cruelty and savagery of the Indians in Thomas's Legion.[93]

Reports accompanying the January-February 1863 muster rolls show that other elements of the Legion were engaged in related activities. Company H, Infantry Regiment was encamped in the Iron Mountains along the northern Tennessee-North Carolina border. 1st

93. *The Daily Journal* (Wilmington), March 2, 1863, quoting an unknown issue of the Petersburg (Virginia) *Express*; service record files of Ahmascosity, Ah To Hee, Ah Tow Eh, Chuwannaskee, Okuniyeh, Nedda Sammih, Oonanooteh Scachee, Bigmeete Segilleh, James Taylor, Tesateskih, Wahyahcahooneh, John Wahyahneete, Edward Welch, and Moses Wolf, Thomas's Legion, Compiled Service Record of Soldiers from the State of North Carolina (M270), reels 567, 568, 571, 572, 573, 574. Mention of Taylor's activities was made in the January-February, 1863 muster rolls. Most of the individual records only noted that the men were on detached service with Taylor, but some added that they were with him in Carter and Johnson counties. This would seem to identify the expedition as the one described in the postwar history of the 13th Regiment Tennessee Cavalry (Union); Tipton and Walters are identified therein as the officers in command. See Samuel W. Scott and Samuel P. Angel, *History of the Thirteenth Regiment Tennessee Volunteer Cavalry U.S.A. . . .* (Philadelphia: P. W. Ziegler, 1903), 321, 323-324, 332, 373-374, 380-382, 385. Scott and Angel placed the size of the Indian force sent to Carter and Johnson counties as company-sized, and dated the expedition to "about the month of May, 1863" (323). While the tentative date may indicate a different operation altogether, it was probably the same as Taylor's. Lieutenant Tipton was identified by Scott and Angel as Lt. Robert P. Tipton. No soldier by that name has been found among the surviving rosters for Tennessee troops; it is possible that the man in question was 1st Lt. Robert J. Tipton of Company B, 19th Regiment Tennessee Infantry. See also pp. 67-68 n. 155 below. Captain Walters remains otherwise unidentified. While the Indians were described in Scott and Angel's account (often in a highly stereotypical and racially denigrating manner) as stirring up strong anti-Confederate sentiment in the region, no specific atrocities were recounted, other than the shooting in the back of a Unionist attempting to escape. This negative perception, amplified by nearly a half-century, appears to have been based on reactions by Unionist whites to the Indians' physical appearance, and to the fear that they struck when they approached private dwellings looking for Unionists and conscripts. Indeed, in a telling passage, Scott and Angel hinted that their reputation was in fact their greatest weapon: "Indians were always noted for cruelty and cunning and for their ability to move stealthily through the woods and come unawares upon an enemy. So many stories had been told of their cruelty and savage character that it was supposed the very name of Indians would strike terror to the conscripts and induce them to come in and give themselves up" (380-381). This echoed, albeit from an unfriendly perspective, the statement from the *Petersburg Express* cited in the text above. William S. Terrell, in reply to a query from Stringfield about Scott and Angel's book, commented wryly that "I must confess that I never heard of any Capt Walters being in Col Thomas Legion or any such man being with us. I guess Col. [John K.] Miller Commander of the 13 Tenn Regiment must have been a little frightened at some time by one of the Indian Companys." Willam S. Terrell to Stringfield, April 10, 1913, Stringfield Papers, WCU.

Lt. James W. Cooper and Sgt. John M. Colvard were detached with four privates to North Carolina from February 6 to 13 to catch deserters, traveling some fifty-five miles. They evidently achieved some success, because upon their return, Cooper and four men escorted an unknown number of prisoners to Knoxville from February 14 to 18. Sgt. Jason S. Hyde was also reported as commanding a small two-man detachment acting as prisoner escort to Knoxville in the same month, while 2nd Lt. Eli Ingram and eleven men traveled sixteen miles to Cades Cove, a Unionist area, to scout. From its base at Winters's Gap, Company K, Infantry Regiment reported that it had "[c]aptured and took one hundred & thirty four prisoners and killed Twenty bush whackers & wounded several others"; it is not known whether these figures represent results for January and February only, or for the entire period of the company's stay at that location beginning with its organization there on September 27. At the time of the March-April muster, taken after the company had shifted to Carter's Depot, it was recorded with satisfaction that the unit had done "good service in Keeping under the Tories & bushwhackers" while stationed at its former post.[94]

What little is known of Walker's Battalion during this period indicates that it was also employed in scouring the mountains. According to Stringfield, Company B operated in January and February along the border from its base at Coker Creek in Monroe County, Tennessee, "to ap[p]rehend Conscripts & Deserters & to suppress disloyalty of E. Ten. Tor[i]es. They constantly have some men out on scouting expeditions & have rendered considerable service in this particular." Company A was also at Coker Creek by the end of February, as was the battalion field and staff; the presence of the latter probably indicates that the bulk of the battalion was at that place and engaged in similar activities. While Company E was still in North Carolina, camped along the Valley River to enlist more men, it was also there "partly for the purpose of defending that Section from the depredations of Tories & Deserters who would soon fill up the Mountains of E. Tenn. & West. N.C. if allowed to do so."[95]

94. "Record of Events": muster roll abstract, January-February 1863: Company H, Infantry Regiment, Thomas's Legion, and service record files of John M. Colvard, James W. Cooper, Jason S. Hyde, and Eli Ingram, Thomas's Legion, Compiled Service Records of Confederate Soldiers from the State of North Carolina (M270), reels 567, 568, and 570; "Record of Events": muster roll abstracts, January-February and March-April 1863: Company K, Infantry Regiment, Thomas's Legion, ibid., reel 567.

95. "Record of Events": muster roll abstracts, January-February 1863: Companies B and E, and March-April 1863: Field and Staff ("Battalion Head Quarters was at Coker Creek, Tenn. at last Muster"), Walker's Battalion, Thomas's Legion, Compiled Service Records of Confederate Soldiers from the State of North Carolina (M270), reel 567. Stringfield wrote his comments as inspecting officer for Company B in the muster roll for January-February 1863. Interestingly, whether out of humanitarian concern, pragmatism, or in an effort to keep the conflict from spreading, Thomas seems to have taken steps to insure that Unionists were protected from mistreatment by Confederate guerrilla bands. 1st Lt. Lafayette George of Company H, Infantry Regiment, wrote in late March that he had been assigned with thirty men to a post in Sevier County, Tennessee, "to guard the country and the Lincolnites together and protect there [*sic*] property." Lafayette George to Rachel George, March 26, 1863 (photocopy), Roster Document No. 1474, Civil War Roster Project (hereinafter cited as CWRP), NCOAH. This idea is supported by a postwar statement from William S. Terrell in relation to the Cherokee companies: "Now the Truth is that where ever we camped with the Indians the strictest orders were given by Col Thomas not to molest any citizen or property and if we captured any prisoners to treat them kindly and give them to eat such as we our selves had to eat." After naming specific Unionists that had been protected, Terrell added that "Col Thomas and we would not for any thing molested a thing any of those people had[.] It was always Col Thoma[s]'s desire to reconsild the people and make friends[. H]e took great delight in reconsiling the union people where ever he went, and told me often that kindness and good treatment would win them over but harsh

In the meantime, Thomas returned with the Indians to eastern Tennessee and a department in a state of flux. Heth was gone, transferred to the Army of Northern Virginia, and Kirby Smith had been sent to take charge of the Trans-Mississippi theater of operations. In his place was Brig. Gen. Daniel S. Donelson, a nephew of Andrew Jackson. On February 20, Thomas was reported in command at Strawberry Plains of a force consisting of the Legion (minus Company C of Walker's Battalion, on detached service in Knoxville), the 6th Regiment Florida Infantry and the 1st Regiment Florida Cavalry (dismounted) of W. G. M. Davis's old brigade, and Martin's Battery (or the Marion Artillery, another Florida unit). The force consisted of 99 officers, with 1,406 men effective present. The aggregate total present and absent was 2,556. How many of these men were members of the Legion is unknown; however, on a requisition for ordnance and ordnance stores dated January 14, Thomas certified that he had 1,329 "Non-Commissioned Officers, Musicians and Privates" in the Legion at that time. Nothing was said as to how many commissioned officers were with the Legion, or how many of the men Thomas recorded were in fact present. The whereabouts of some of the companies are also unknown. Although Company C of the battalion was the only one specifically reported elsewhere, it has already been noted above that some companies were active in the field. In regards to the remainder, company muster rolls show that Companies B, D, E, F, and I of the Infantry Regiment were at Strawberry Plains, while (2nd) Company A was at Gatlinburg and Company C was still at Flat Creek. Other forces besides Thomas's command were similarly scattered to key points in the department.[96] On paper, the February 20 report would seem to indicate that Thomas had achieved the sort of independent command that he had always looked for. The Legion was no longer listed as part of a division, and there was no indication that Thomas was acting in place of a higher-ranking officer in actual command of the Strawberry Plains post. The data in the report may be deceptive in the latter regard, however, and even if accurate, represent at best a transitional phase in a

means would drive them in to the Federal lines." William S. Terrell to Stringfield, April 10, 1913, Stringfield Papers, WCU.

96. *O.R.* 15:948, 972, 1005; 23 (pt. 2): 621, 626, 629, 644-645; Warner, *Generals in Gray*, 280. Heth acted in command of the department in Kirby Smith's absence until his own replacement by Donelson on January 17. *O.R.* 23 (pt. 2): 621, 626, 629. Company C, Walker's Battalion (noted in the report in the *O.R.* only as "Thomas' Legion, Company C") was part of a force commanded by Capt. J. W. Stokes which included the 3rd Battalion of Hilliard's (Alabama) Legion, the City Police Guard, a detachment of Capt. Gustave A. Huwald's Battery Tennessee Artillery, and W. R. Marshall's Battery Confederate Artillery (the Brown Horse Artillery). *O.R.* 23 (pt. 2): 644, 977, 978, 980; "Record of Events": muster roll abstracts, January-Februrary 1863: 2nd Company A, Companies B, C, D, E, F, G, H, I, and K, Infantry Regiment, and Companies A, B, C, and E, Walker's Battalion, Thomas's Legion, Compiled Service Records of Confederate Soldiers from the State of North Carolina (M270), reel 567. According to the report accompanying the January-February muster roll, Company C was "doing guard and other duty" in Knoxville. In inspection reports and field returns, effective total represented all men (exclusive of commissioned officers) who were present and available for field service; depending on how detailed the form of the report or return was, it usually included privates, non-commissioned officers, and musicians present for duty, as well as enlisted men present on extra duty and present under arrest. Enlisted men who were present but sick were added to give the total present. Commissioned officers (field and staff and company officers), both those present for duty and those present sick, on extra duty, or under arrest were added to create the aggregate (total) present. Officers and soldiers who were absent, whether officially (on detached service or on furlough) or illegally (absent without leave) were added to give the aggregate number of soldiers present and absent.

reorganization of the department initiated by Donelson. Thomas was in a situation where both the identity of his unit and his authority over it were increasingly in doubt, as the Legion was assigned to a brigade under the command of another officer.

The reason for this change was the growing disciplinary problem among the troops in east Tennessee, coupled with the desire of the military authorities to put a more traditional command structure in place to effectively meet the defensive problems of the region. The former trouble was particularly acute among units recruited from the area itself, which was blamed by Confederate authorities on Unionist influences among the local population. Smith was the first of several commanders to believe that the solution was to transfer these units away, where they would not be subjected to such pressures, and would be free from the added distractions of being so close to home and family during times of crisis; once this was accomplished, the troops would submit to discipline and become good soldiers. These views were common among both military leaders and many civilian officials, and eventually led to the transfer of east Tennessee regiments from the area to strongly secessionist Mississippi. The issue of influence soon became a moot point, as these units were captured at Vicksburg; following their paroles, many members never returned to the ranks. Furthermore, the problem of desertion and indiscipline in east Tennessee was not confined to local units only. In mid-February, it was reported that three-fourths of the Florida troops stationed there were at home. Donelson was concerned that there were efforts afoot to transfer the entire brigade back to Florida, using the excuse that most of the troops were already there, anyway.[97]

Similar concerns were raised by Governor Vance. Early in 1863, he wrote to President Davis about the situation. Davis, despite his justified reputation as a meddler in military affairs, refused in this case to concern himself with an internal departmental matter. Vance next approached Gen. Braxton Bragg, commander of the Army of Tennessee and of Department No. 2, the area comprising middle and western Tennessee. Singling out several units by name, including Thomas's Legion, Vance wrote that the vicissitudes of guarding passes and bridges and of subduing the locals had led to general indiscipline among the troops. He echoed other critics in his assessment that much of the problem was due to the service of these units in or near their home areas, and that many otherwise potentially good soldiers would do better if sent away and put into more active service. Although Bragg agreed with Vance's views, he pointed out that he had no jurisdiction in the Department of East Tennessee; the proper persons for Vance to approach were Donelson and Johnston. In the meantime, Vance renewed his efforts for Davis's direct intercession.[98]

Much of the unrest among the troops was the result of anger over the Confederate conscription laws. When the war first broke out, both sides had naively thought that victory would be quick. Patriotism and volunteerism were high, and there were many who enthusiastically rushed forward to enlist, often in regiments mustered into service for only six months to a year. Although military reality soon set in, this did not mean that people were willing to face it, and many who volunteered for short terms of service were quite content to drop out when their time was up, considering that their duty was properly fulfilled. Both

97. *O.R.* 23 (pt. 2): 462, 637; Groce, *Mountain Rebels*, 96-97, 102-103.

98. Vance to Bragg, March 9, 1863, Bragg to Vance, April 12, 1863, Vance to Davis, May 13, 1863, in Johnston and Mobley, *Papers of Zebulon Baird Vance*, 2:83-84, 115-116, 150-152.

national governments faced a crisis in army field organization and in overall manpower as a result. The problem was particularly acute in the South, where the smaller size of the overall population, and the limits on the availability of men for combat that were the results of the region's racial caste system, led to a crisis as the spring of 1862 approached.[99]

For these reasons the Confederate Congress passed a conscription act in April 1862, which made all able-bodied white men from ages eighteen to thirty-five liable for a draft into military service, and required all men already in the service to remain in the ranks "for three years from the date of their original enlistment, unless the war shall have been sooner ended." Jefferson Davis hoped that the measure would alleviate the current manpower crisis. To lessen the expected anger over the nullification of their original service expiration dates, those units affected were allowed to reorganize for the war and elect new officers. Davis hoped that the act would help establish a more uniform, centralized military system, and that it would lead to all segments of society equally sharing the burden of the conflict.[100]

In the event, the results were decidedly mixed. The nature of the draft limited the enlistment choices under which those affected by the law could act. While individuals who had not yet been called up were allowed to volunteer into existing units, new all-volunteer units were only accepted under very limited circumstances. The reorganization of older units led to much mischief, with effective officers who practiced proper discipline often defeated in favor of more popular but less talented replacements. Promised enlistment bounties and furloughs were perpetually put off. Finally, various exemptions to the law, either as part of the original measure or added on at a later date, led to anger and undermined the sense of egalitarianism and shared sacrifice that Davis wanted to promote. Those with enough money hired substitutes to take their place in the ranks; many of these substitutes deserted. Those employed in Confederate and state government positions or in certain civilian jobs considered vital were exempted. Perhaps most controversial among less affluent members of the white population was the exemption of one white man per agricultural establishment where twenty or more slaves were employed. Although modified with various restrictions to make the concept more palatable, the result was the perception that the conflict was "a rich man's war and a poor man's fight."[101]

The conscription law produced a strong reaction in eastern Tennessee and western North Carolina. Disaffection was common among civilians, and desertion was widespread among conscripts from the region. Various efforts were therefore made to provide a temporary reprieve from the Conscription Act. In east Tennessee an exemption was granted from May 1862 until fall, possibly in part due to the efforts of Thomas, who opposed the

99. Albert Burton Moore, *Conscription and Conflict in the Confederacy* (New York: Macmillan, 1924), 1-13; Robertson, *Soldiers Blue and Gray*, 3-18, 34, 37; Reid Mitchell, *Civil War Soldiers: Their Expectations and Their Experiences* (New York: Viking, 1988), 1-23; Walter C. Hilderman III, *They Went Into the Fight Cheering!: Confederate Conscription in North Carolina* (Boone: Parkway Publishers, Inc., 2005), 9-10, 19-23.

100. *O.R.* ser. IV, 1:1095 (quote); Moore, *Conscription and Conflict in the Confederacy*, 13-14.

101. The Federal government introduced its own conscription legislation in 1863, which also resulted in much unrest. For general overviews of conscription issues and problems, see Moore, ibid., 14-139; Robertson, *Soldiers Blue and Gray*, 37-40 (quote, 38); Mitchell, *Civil War Soldiers*, 160-162; Emory M. Thomas, *The Confederate Nation: 1861-1865*, New American Nation Series (New York: Harper Torchbooks, 1979), 152-155; Hilderman, *They Went Into the Fight Cheering!*, 23, 30-34, 36-59, 84-99, 103-113.

law; however, it only delayed the inevitable, as the hoped-for conversion of the locals to the cause of the Confederacy that was supposed to result did not materialize. Vance failed to get a similar exemption passed for western North Carolina. Mountain geography and sympathetic Unionists were havens for deserters and draft evaders; it was such men that Thomas was charged to round up following the troubles at Marshall and Shelton Laurel. Some organized into guerrilla bands which struck at military targets or preyed on civilians.[102]

Thomas's Legion proved far from immune to these problems. Three hundred and sixty-seven men left the ranks without permission between the time that the earliest companies were formed and mid-June 1863. One hundred and fifty-eight of these men returned to the ranks at some point, voluntarily or otherwise; in fact, there were many men who deserted and returned multiple times, indicating a high level of resistance to military service and the probability that in at least some cases the reasons for absence had to do with family or other personal problems. Other men simply and suddenly disappeared from the muster rolls without explanation; it is not known whether any or all of these men were deserters as well.[103]

The desertion trouble among forces from or stationed in eastern Tennessee and western North Carolina were indicative of other problems besides unrest over conscription. Many of the troops suffered from poor training and discipline, while the overall command structure was badly disorganized. Monthly reports and other forms of data necessary for the departmental commander's understanding of the condition and needs of his troops were not being turned in. Among Donelson's complaints was the existence of three legions in the department, including Thomas's. "I would respectfully ask that they be organized into regiments and brigaded," he wrote on March 4 to Col. Benjamin S. Ewell, Johnston's assistant adjutant general. "In their present condition they are inefficient, and scattered in various parts of the department.[104] Donelson was granted permission, and soon Thomas's Legion was placed in a brigade commanded by Brig. Gen. Alfred E. Jackson.

Born in 1807, Jackson was a successful Tennessee businessman prior to the war. He originally served as major and quartermaster on the staff of Brig. Gen. Felix Zollicoffer. After the latter's death in January 1862 at the battle of Mills Springs, Kentucky, Jackson served as a quartermaster in Knoxville.[105] In the latter capacity he became acquainted with Thomas's Legion, as his signature is found on pay vouchers and related materials scattered in the service records of its men and officers. Jackson was ordered to Donelson for assignment on February 9, 1863. It is not known when he took command of his brigade or when Thomas's Legion became part of it, but it was prior to a March 19 report on the organization of the department. The brigade represented an expansion of the force Thomas commanded at

102. Inscoe and McKinney, *Heart of Confederate Appalachia*, 113-140, 145; Crow, *Storm in the Mountains*, 20; *O.R.* 16 (pt. 2): 868-869, 954-955; Stringfield, "Sixty-Ninth Regiment," in Clark, *North Carolina Regiments*, 3:735; Stringfield, "War—Mss," ledger book, 51-53, NCOAH. According to Stringfield's article on the Infantry Regiment, Thomas went to Richmond in an unsuccessful attempt to halt the Conscription Act. It is definite that Thomas wrote Davis to extend or renew the suspension in the fall. Thomas to Davis, September 23, 1862, Letters Received by the Confederate Secretary of War (M437), reel 75, file 415-T-1862.

103. Service record files, Thomas's Legion, Compiled Service Records of Confederate Soldiers from the State of North Carolina (M270), reels 567 through 574.

104. *O.R.* 23 (pt. 2): 630-631, 662 (quote).

105. Warner, *Generals in Gray*, 148-149.

Strawberry Plains in late February. Joining the Legion, the 1st Regiment Florida Cavalry, the 6th Regiment Florida Infantry, and the Marion (Florida) Artillery were the 62nd Regiment N.C. Troops (commanded by Thomas's brother-in-law, Col. Robert G. A. Love), the 7th Regiment Florida Infantry, the 7th Battalion N.C. Cavalry, the 12th Battalion Tennessee Cavalry, and Capt. Edmund Winston's Company of Confederate Sappers and Miners.[106]

It was not long before Thomas clashed with his new superior. The personalities involved were surely much to blame, as both had been powerful men before the war who were used to getting their way. Moreover, Thomas was prone to bypass his superiors and communicate directly with authorities in Raleigh and Richmond. While Stringfield later remembered Jackson as "a Splendid old gentleman" and dwelt on his devotion to the Confederate cause, he admitted that he was "a firm and strict disciplinarian." Thomas, as events increasingly demonstrated, was anything *but* a disciplinarian. The stage was set for a series of conflicts that came close to wrecking the Legion and ruining Thomas's military career.[107] Initially, Jackson seems to have shown some respect for the integrity of the Legion's

106. *O.R.* 23 (pt. 2): 711. If Thomas's Legion was assigned to Jackson at or shortly after Jackson's appointment on February 9, then Thomas must have been acting commander at Strawberry Plains during some absence of Jackson when the February report was made out. There was no reference to Jackson in that report, however, or to the Strawberry Plains garrison as a formal brigade. Donelson's March 4 letter to B. S. Ewell, asking permission to have the three legions in his department brigaded, implies that Thomas's Legion was not part of a brigade yet. For this reason, it is possible that Thomas's Legion fell under Jackson's command some time between March 4 and 19. On the other hand, a December 1863 inspection report for the brigade recorded that Jackson accepted assignment to command the brigade on February 9, the date of his appointment. Inspection Report of the 4th Brigade commanded by Lt. Col. J. R. Love (A. E. Jackson's Brigade), undated ("Remarks show dates as late as December 1863"), Inspection Reports and Related Records Received by the Inspection Branch in the Confederate Adjutant and Inspector General's Office (M935), reel 18, file 311, RG 109, NA (hereinafter cited as Inspection Reports, Confederate Adjutant and Inspector General's Office [M935]).

107. *O.R.* 23 (pt. 2): 630-631; Stringfield, "War—Mss," ledger book, 140, NCOAH. Elsewhere, Stringfield wrote that Jackson "was a cultivated gentleman and personally a brave man. He was a good man and always managed the men to the best advantage in so hostile a region. He was personally and scrupulously honest, and demanded the same of his men; but he was a little too strict for the 'old soldier' ideas of those who wanted to prowl." Stringfield, "Sixty-Ninth Regiment," in Clark, *North Carolina Regiments*, 3:743. Stringfield's opinion was definitely a minority position among the officers of the Legion; in fact, such statements do not entirely reflect his own wartime thinking, as he signed an 1864 petition critical of Jackson's relationship with the command. See J. R. Love, W. W. Stringfield, et al. to Governor Vance, February 25, 1864, Governors' Papers: Vance, 1862-1865, NCOAH. According to some sources, Jackson was so disliked that he was given the nickname "Mudwall" in mocking imitation of Thomas "Stonewall" Jackson; see, for example, Crow, *Storm in the Mountains*, 29, 45, 63. Other sources claim that this was a result of postwar confusion in the *Southern Historical Society Papers* between Alfred E. Jackson and Brig. Gen. William Lowther Jackson, a cousin of "Stonewall" Jackson's who was nicknamed "Mudwall" during the war by the Federals for his poor performance. See Warner, *Generals in Gray*, 153-154; John E. Stanchak, "Jackson, Alfred Eugene," in Faust, *Historical Times Illustrated Encyclopedia of the Civil War*, 389; Jeffry D. Wert, "Jackson, William Lowther," ibid., 392. For an example of a wartime Federal reference to William Lowther Jackson as "Mudwall," see *O.R.* 37 (pt. 1): 12. It should be noted, however, that Crow's source of information was the memoir of Daniel Ellis, a Federal scout and guide for escaped POWs and Unionist refugees in eastern Tennessee. See Ellis, *Thrilling Adventures of Daniel Ellis, the Great Union Guide of East Tennessee for a Period of Nearly Four Years During the Great Southern Rebellion, Written By Himself*, Black Heritage Library Collection (New York: Harper & Brothers, 1867; reprt., Fireport, New York: Books for Libraries Press, 1971), 416. Although an often fanciful account of Ellis's activities, his work was issued in 1867, nearly nine years before the *Southern Historical Society Papers* began publishing. Thus, it is not impossible that Alfred Jackson received the "Mudwall" nickname independently of William Lowther Jackson.

organization and for Thomas's authority over it. In the March 19 report alluded to earlier, the Legion was recorded as a single unit under Thomas in Jackson's Brigade. Depending on when Jackson assumed command, he may have even allowed Thomas to continue increasing the size of the Legion. On March 5, a company was organized in Monroe County, Tennessee, with 2nd Lt. Garner N. Loudermilk of Company B, Walker's Battalion elected captain; it became Company H of the battalion. Thomas came closer to having a true legion with the addition of Capt. John T. Levi's Light Artillery Battery, organized on April 1 at Wytheville, Virginia, from disbanded elements of the Virginia State Line and from other recruits, including a number of deserters from Company F, 29th Regiment N.C. Troops. It is possible that these additions were authorized before Jackson's arrival, however.[108]

When the next departmental report was filed on April 25, however, the component elements of the Legion were noted separately. The Infantry Regiment was listed as the Thomas Legion, while Walker's Battalion was listed as the "Thomas Legion (battalion)." These changes represented the fulfillment of Donelson's plans for breaking up the legions in the department, and did not necessarily involve personal animosity by Jackson against Thomas. What is interesting is that Thomas's name was omitted from the report, with James R. Love and William C. Walker noted in command of the regiment and the battalion respectively. It is possible to read too much into the omission given the hostility that developed between Thomas and Jackson over the following months, as the former may have been absent at the time. Indeed, some later reports place Thomas in command—but only of the regiment.[109] There is little doubt that Jackson soon began interfering in Thomas's arrangements, however, in particular with what in later writings became one of the most confused elements in the Legion's history, Thomas's use of some soldiers for road construction and fortification.

In Walter Clark's *Histories of the Several Regiments and Battalions of the State of North Carolina in the Great War 1861-'65*, Stringfield wrote that Thomas recruited two companies of sappers and miners that were part of a second regiment created out of Walker's Battalion. He recalled that Thomas "had some unique ideas" concerning how to defuse Unionism and the opposition to conscription in east Tennessee "and while known to be intensely loyal to the South, he had gained the confidence of this East Tennessee disloyal element and several thousand at various times had agreed to form companies for local defense, and for road and bridge building. Not being allowed to do this, these men went to the Federal army and ever afterwards were troublesome enemies."[110] Stringfield's claims were amplified in Robert Akin's history of Walker's Battalion in the same series. While Akin continued the fiction that the battalion expanded to a regiment, he did not include the sappers and miners among its companies, although he noted their existence:

108. "Record of Events": muster roll abstracts, March 5-7 and March 5-April 30, 1863: Company H, Walker's Battalion, and April 1-June 30, 1863: Captain Levi's Battery Light Artillery, Thomas's Legion, Compiled Service Records of Confederate Soldiers from the State of North Carolina (M270), reel 567. See also p. 19 n. 40 above and the rosters for Levi's Battery in this volume for soldiers who deserted from the 29th Regiment N.C. Troops.

109. Levi's Battery was not included in the report at all. *O.R.* 23 (pt. 2): 792-793; "Record of Events": muster roll abstracts, April 1-June 30, 1863, Captain Levi's Battery Light Artillery, Thomas's Legion, Compiled Service Records of Confederate Soldiers from the State of North Carolina (M270), reel 567. During the early months of its existence, Levi's Battery was frequently omitted from reports of the Department of East Tennessee.

110. Stringfield, "Sixty-Ninth Regiment," in Clark, *North Carolina Regiments*, 3:735.

> There were three or four companies of "sappers and miners," masons, carpenters, blacksmiths, gunsmiths, salt and salt petre and alum makers. Captain R. C. McCalla, a Scotchman, and a most excellent gentleman, is the only officer whose name I recall.
>
> Nearly half of these were from North Carolina, and in their line did faithful service. They were detached from us and taken to Bragg's and Johnston's army, at and below Chattanooga.

Akin then discussed the shooting of twenty soldiers for desertion. "I have been unable to trace those men to any regiment unless perchance they belonged to these companies of sappers and miners, and were the East Tennessee recruits to those companies, and I really fear they were, and though Tennesseeans, belonged to 'Thomas' Legion,'" he wrote. "I fear they were unjustly and cruelly treated—for, to my personal knowledge, many of them joined with the promise that they were not to be taken out of the State except in the North Carolina mountain line of defense."[111]

This in essence is the legend of Thomas's sappers and miners: that in his efforts to circumvent the troubles caused by the draft law and Unionism, he came up with the "unique" idea of enlisting hostile east Tennesseans for construction projects and other labors. In this way, the men would serve the Confederacy without actually fighting for it. Unfortunately, some unnamed villain either prohibited them from serving or transferred them to the Army of Tennessee, resulting in mass desertion. By the time that historian John Preston Arthur repeated the story in 1914, the sappers and miners were a battalion in size, numbering 500 men. According to Arthur, "[Maj. Gen. Edmund Kirby] Smith's successor" ordered them to serve in the ranks. The result was that 500 men supposedly deserted in twenty-four hours—a 100% desertion rate. Wartime records cited by Vernon H. Crow and subsequent historians show that Jackson was the officer responsible for putting the men in the ranks.[112]

Thomas's idea was not necessarily as "unique" as Stringfield claimed. Zollicoffer had authorized the organization of Capt. Edmund Winston's Confederate Company of Sappers and Miners, a unit that was evidently made up in part of Unionists who wished to avoid service in combat units. There were evidently some who accused the company of being a haven for draft evaders and argued for its disbandment. Although Kirby Smith is regarded by some historians as having a hostile attitude towards east Tennesseans, in this case he stepped forward to defend the useful service given by this company. In January 1863 it reorganized, and as noted above was a part of Jackson's Brigade by March.[113]

111. Aiken, "Eightieth Regiment," Clark, *North Carolina Regiments*, 4:119-120.

112. Arthur, *Western North Carolina: A History*, 609; Crow, *Storm in the Mountains*, 30; Godbold and Russell, *Confederate Colonel and Cherokee Chief*, 113.

113. E. Kirby Smith to Samuel Cooper, May 13, 1862, Chapter 2: Military Commands (hereinafter cited as Chapter 2), Vol. 51: Letters and Telegrams Sent, Department of East Tennessee, 1862, 190, RG 109, NA; Fisher, *War at Every Door*, 109; *O.R. (Supplement)* Pt. II, 73:604-605, 608-611. The identification of the company authorized by Zollicoffer is based on Smith's reference in his letter to Cooper to a 1st Lieutenant Margrave as one of its members; 1st Lt. George R. Margrave served in Winston's company. The company later became Company D, 3rd Regiment Confederate Engineers. In *Mountain Rebels*, 83-87, W. Todd Groce argued that Smith was responsible for much of the negative impression of east Tennesseans held by the Confederate government. Fisher contended that Smith was a good administrator who, if lacking Zollicoffer's empathy for the natives, believed that the inhabitants could be won over with time, although even he noted Smith's pessimism about the possibilities of accomplishing this task (Fisher, op. cit, 103-110).

Thomas was certainly in a position to know about the company authorized by Zollicoffer after his own arrival in the department, and it is likely that it inspired him to raise a similar unit for his own purposes. Thomas seems to have first espoused his plan for an engineering unit in a September 23, 1862, letter to President Davis, in which he suggested the idea of using Tennessee Unionists as sappers and miners for building a road across the mountains to Cumberland Gap. He linked the plan to a request for continuing the suspension of the Conscription Act in the area. He put his ideas into action in November. Terrell wrote in 1864 that Thomas recruited the men from "a large class [of east Tennesseans] who were equally averse to resisting the laws of the Confederate States as to bearing arms in their cause." He received "authority from Genl Kirby Smith to enlist over a hundred men as Sappers and Miners. Not having the authority to organize them into Separate companies they were distributed through the various companies of the command and under Lt R C McCaula did good service in the engineer corps." An examination of the surviving Legion muster rolls show numerous men on detached service, building or repairing roads, or constructing fortifications ("stockading") at Strawberry Plains (and possibly other sites) from the fall of 1862 until early 1863 and, in some cases, beyond. Much of their labor seems to have been devoted to road work, including a project in the Smoky Mountains. John Preston Arthur, relying on information apparently originating with Terrell, confirmed that much of their activity was devoted to building a road across the Great Smoky Mountains with the design of connecting Jackson County, North Carolina with Sevier County, Tennessee. Perhaps not coincidentally, before the war Thomas had advocated the building of just such a road with decidedly commercial interests in mind. Regardless, the "sappers and miners" were the ideal candidates to carry out such a scheme, and Thomas could justify the construction of the road for its potential military usefulness. His actions received some favorable public notice. One Virginia newspaper commented that he had "enlisted, without bloodshed, a great many men in his corps of sappers and miners, who have thus been converted from mischevous tories and bushwhackers into useful employees of the Confederate government."[114]

While Thomas was unable to put the engineers into separate companies officially, they had to be organized, however informally, in order to function properly. It may be presumed that they operated in an ad hoc company or battalion; this would have been the source of the postwar memories of a full battalion of sappers and miners.[115] Their commander was 1st Lt.

114. Thomas to President Davis, September 23, 1862, Letters Received by the Confederate Secretary of War (M437), reel 75, item 415-T-1862; Terrell to Governor Vance, February 22, 1864, Governors' Papers: Vance, 1862-1865, NCOAH; service record files, Thomas's Legion, Compiled Service Records of Confederate Soldiers from the State of North Carolina (M270), reels 567 through 574; Arthur, *Western North Carolina: A History*, 609, 627; Crow, *Storm in the Mountains*, 3, 30, 56, 237 n. 17; *The Daily Journal* (Wilmington), March 2, 1863, quoting an unknown issue of the Petersburg (Virginia) *Express*; Thomas to Cooper, February 21, 1863, service record file of Samuel L. Love, Compiled Service Records of Confederate General and Staff Officers, and Non-Regimental Enlisted Men (M331), reel 159.

115. A clue that supports this theory is in Thomas's badly jumbled wartime notebook. One undated item shows the whereabouts of the Legion companies some time prior to the loss of the cavalry companies. The first entry is for "3 Indian Companies A[t] strawberry Plains and working on a military road—Clinch mountain smokey mountains." Thomas Notebook, undated [48-49], NCOAH. There were only two Indian companies at this time, so the third company must have been the engineering unit. Why Thomas chose to refer to it as an "Indian company" is not known, as those assigned to work on the roads were white. Perhaps Thomas at some point

Richard C. McCalla of 2nd Company A, Infantry Regiment, mentioned by Akin and Terrell in the materials quoted above. Formerly an engineer and 2nd lieutenant in Winston's company, McCalla transferred to Thomas during the period of the September-October 1862 muster. By the end of October he was on detached duty at Cumberland Gap. He was promoted to 1st lieutenant on November 3, about the time that, according to Terrell, Thomas began actively recruiting men as engineers.[116]

It is impossible to tell from the surviving records how much of Thomas's project McCalla oversaw.[117] Certainly his involvement with the Legion quickly diminished. Special Order No. 5 of the Engineer's Office, Department of East Tennessee, assigned McCalla on January 16 to "assume direction of the defensive works at the various Bridges on the line of Railroad between Chattanooga and Bristol," an important component of the Confederacy's

---

intended to use the Cherokees in that capacity also; note that 1st Lt. Richard C. McCalla, the engineering officer who commanded Thomas's sappers and miners, was officially a member of one of the Cherokee companies, 2nd Company A of the Infantry Regiment. The Clinch Mountain range in eastern Tennessee is further north and west of Thomas's usual wartime area of operations. Probably his jotting was meant to suggest that the road was supposed to run from the Great Smoky Mountains to or through Clinch Mountain in connection with his plans for a road running to Blain's Crossroads and linking up with the Kentucky saltworks (pp. 36-37 above); Blain's Crossroads lies at the southwestern end of the range. In a February 1863 letter, Thomas described the sappers and miners unit as a company that he had raised with Smith's permission. He claimed, however, that it was not yet subject to his authority, a possible hint that he was already having trouble with his superiors over the status of the unit. Thomas to Cooper, February 21, 1863, service record file of Samuel L. Love, Compiled Service Records of Confederate General and Staff Officers, and Non-Regimental Enlisted Men (M331), reel 159.

116. Service record file of R. C. McCalla, Thomas's Legion, Compiled Service Records of Confederate Soldiers from the State of North Carolina (M270), reel 571; Compiled Military Service Record of Richard C. McCalla, 3rd Regiment Confederate Engineers, Records of Confederate Soldiers Who Served During the Civil War, Compiled Service Records of Confederate Soldiers Who Served in Organizations Raised Directly by the Confederate Government (M258), reel 108, RG 109, NA (hereinafter cited as Compiled Service Records of Confederate Soldiers Who Served in Organizations Raised Directly by the Confederate Government [M258]).

117. Several members of Company I, Infantry Regiment, were listed on October 31, 1862, as working on a road or roads "in [the] charge of R. Collins." According to information abstracted from the July 24-October 31, 1862 muster roll for this company, many of these same men were recorded as having been enlisted on July 24, 1862 by a "Robt. Collins." While at first glance it might be natural to assume that "R. Collins" (despite the "Robt.") was a garbling of "R. McCalla," it seems instead that he was Robert Collins, a native of what is now Swain County. Although by profession a farmer, Collins's knowledge of the Great Smoky Mountains led to his assisting Professor Arnold Guyot of Princeton in the latter's exploration and mapping of the mountains just prior to the Civil War. A historian of Haywood County wrote that Thomas assigned Collins, who was too old to serve in the army, to lead a company of around forty sappers and miners to build a military road across the mountains. Collins contracted pneumonia in east Tennessee while conducting the project, was taken home, and died in late 1862 or in early 1863. Mount Collins and Collins Gap along the Swain County/Sevier County borders are named for him. W. C. Allen, *The Annals of Haywood County North Carolina Historical, Sociological, Biographical, and Genealogical*, with a New Genealogical Index by Lois Smathers Neal (1935; repr., Spartanburg, SC: The Reprint Company, 1977), 453-454; Powell, *North Carolina Gazetteer*, 115, 337-338. See also service record files for James McCarter, Arthur Ogle, Bradford Ogle, C. T. Ogle, Caleb Ogle, E. T. Ogle, Elisha Ogle, Preston Ogle, Samuel Ogle, Silbert Ogle, James Reagan, Henry Rice, Daniel Roberts, John Roberts, William Russell, and William M. Sutton, Thomas's Legion, Compiled Service Records of Confederate Soldiers from the State of North Carolina (M270), reels 571 through 573. Collins was the father of Pvt. Joseph A. Collins of Company B, 25th Regiment N.C. Troops. Reported as absent without leave from the 25th N.C. in early 1864, Joseph A. Collins may have later served with Thomas's Legion as 1st lieutenant of Company A, Indian Battalion, and is said to have commanded the company in the last days of the war (Manarin and Jordan, *North Carolina Troops*, 7:371; Allen, op. cit., 455).

plans to occupy the region and insure safe communication and transportation between the Deep South and southwest Virginia.[118] The men that he utilized probably included some of those whom Thomas recruited as engineers; those reported employed as "stockading" at Strawberry Plains were almost certainly involved with this project.[119] McCalla was listed on detached or detailed duty with the Engineer's Office through April 1863; he then dropped out of the Legion's records. This may have been when Jackson took action regarding Thomas's engineering recruits. As Terrell wrote:

> One of [Jackson's] first acts [upon assuming command] was to order all the Sappers and Miners to take arms in violation of a pledge which had been given them that they would not be called on to bear arms, and at a time when they were actively engaged in putting up defensive works along the lines of the Railroad. On receiving the orders many of them ran off and most of the rest soon followed them. No steps that I know of were taken to bring them back.

McCalla later transferred back to the Confederate Engineers; he afterwards became captain of Company A, 3rd Regiment Confederate Engineers.[120]

Jackson was indeed blamed by Thomas and many of his subordinates for putting the sappers and miners into the ranks and for the alleged resulting desertion fiasco. It would be a mistake, however to reduce the incident to another clichéd case of "colorful" Civil War military personalities feuding. Standard military doctrine on discipline, as well as the evolving Confederate policy towards the problems posed by east Tennessee Unionists, were undoubtedly the driving forces behind the policy change. It is unclear from the surviving records whether Jackson initiated the idea of putting the pioneers into the ranks himself, or whether he was instructed to do so by Donelson. Donelson's comments on the poor and disorganized nature of the legions in his department have already been noted. He was also concerned by

118. Service record file of R. C. McCalla, Thomas's Legion, Compiled Service Records of Confederate Soldiers from the State of North Carolina (M270), reel 571; service record file of Richard C. McCalla, 3rd Regiment Confederate Engineers, Compiled Service Records of Confederate Soldiers Who Served in Organizations Raised Directly by the Confederate Government (M258), reel 108 (including McCalla's copy of Special Order No. 5).

119. Service record files, Thomas's Legion, Compiled Military Service Records of Confederate Soldiers from the State of North Carolina (M270), reels 567 through 574. Winston's Confederate Company of Sappers and Miners was also involved in constructing the railroad defenses; see *O.R. (Supplement)* Pt. II, 73:609-610. The transfer of Winston's company to the Army of Tennessee during the Chickamauga campaign probably lay behind Akin's recollection that Thomas's sappers and miners were sent to Bragg.

120. Service record file of R. C. McCalla, Thomas's Legion, Compiled Military Service Records of Confederate Soldiers from the State of North Carolina, (M270), reel 571; service record file of Richard C. McCalla, 3rd Regiment Confederate Engineers, Compiled Military Service Records of Confederate Soldiers Who Served in Organizations Raised Directly by the Confederate Government, (M258), reel 108; Terrell to Vance, February 22, 1864, Governors' Papers: Vance, 1862-1865, NCOAH; Judy H. Leas, ed., *The Civil War Diary of Absalom Joshua Burum* (Fresno, CA: J. H. Leas, 1965; typescript copy, WCU), March 29, 1864, April 5, 1864; *O.R. (Supplement)*, Pt. II, 73:604, 606-607, 609; *O.R.* 23 (pt. 2): 792, 31 (pt. 1): 537-539, 31 (pt. 3): 808, 889, 32 (pt. 1): 606, 32 (pt. 2): 591, 32 (pt. 3): 873, 38 (pt. 3): 644, 652, 39 (pt. 3): 907, 49 (pt. 1): 1021-1022; Crow, *Storm in the Mountains*, 29-30, 242 nn. 35 and 36. Burum served in Company K, Infantry Regiment. His diary mentioned McCalla commanding a "pioneer co." in late March and early April 1864 in the area in which the Legion was operating. Burum's reference to these men as "[o]ur Sappers & Miners" led Vernon H. Crow to conclude that Thomas convinced Jackson to let him keep an engineer company under McCalla, and that it was known as the Pioneer Company. This unit was actually Company A, 3rd Regiment Confederate Engineers. Materials in the *Official Records* show that the company was considered a part of the Army of Tennessee by early 1864; although often stationed in the Department of Southwest Virginia and East Tennessee, it was never a part of the Legion.

the strong Unionism in the region and previous Confederate policies which contained at least some measure of conciliation; the latter he branded as a failure shortly after his arrival. He proposed that an ample force be placed in the area to insure that the conscription laws were carried out to the fullest and, echoing the ideas of others, that all Unionist conscripts be sent further south for service, to be replaced by troops from outside of the region.[121]

On the other hand, if the idea of ending Thomas's sappers and miners experiment originated with Jackson, there is good reason to suspect that he thought he was acting in accordance with official Richmond policy. On February 27, 1863, Secretary of War James A. Seddon wrote Donelson responding to the latter's criticisms of earlier Confederate policy and his proposed solution. Seddon reported that President Davis concurred with Donelson that tougher measures were needed to pacify east Tennessee. A particular concern was the vital nitre and iron works in the region, critical factors in Confederate supply, and staffed by a "large collection of disaffected workmen." Seddon agreed with Donelson that the workers should be conscripted, and those considered to be troublemakers sent to Tennessee units serving far away from their home area. Given the importance of the works, however, nothing should be done "without supplying their places with more faithful men, conscripts, or even detailed soldiers, if necessary." Seddon added that "Brigadier-General [A. E.] Jackson, of your command, with whom, on his recent visit to this city, I had free conference on the whole subject of the condition of disaffection in East Tennessee, will be enabled to explain to you more fully the views of the department in relation to these workmen, as well as the kindred subjects of your letter."[122] Although the situation involving the employees at the salt and nitre works did not precisely correspond to that involving Thomas's sappers and miners, there were enough points in common to suggest that the solutions proposed for resolving the former may have influenced Jackson in his actions towards the latter. Given that Jackson had discussions with the secretary of war in regards to dealing with disaffected east Tennesseans about the time that Thomas's Legion came under his command, coupled with Donelson's own concerns, it is not difficult to see the thinking behind the decision to force the informally organized pioneers into the ranks, especially as there were organized engineer companies operating in the area that could perform the same tasks. Furthermore, regardless of Thomas's plans or wishes, the Legion was now part of Jackson's command, and Jackson had the right to make whatever dispositions or arrangements of the units and men under him that he wished within the proper bounds of military authority. The desertion of at least some of these men undoubtedly confirmed in the minds of Jackson and his superiors that the idea represented a failed policy to conciliate an inherently hostile population.

An examination of the service records of Thomas's Legion, however, raises other questions about the story as it was handed down, including the claim of mass desertion in reaction to Jackson's orders. Counting McCalla, there were at least ninety-six members of the Legion who at one time or another were recorded as detached for road work, constructing fortifications, or associated with engineering companies. Of these, five with no known prior association with Thomas's projects were attached either to McCalla's company in the 3rd Confederate Engineers or another engineering company well after Jackson's arrival; at least

121. *O.R.* 23 (pt. 2): 631.

122. *O.R.* 23 (pt. 2): 651-652.

one man who earlier worked on roads was later detached to McCalla. This leaves ninety men documented as employed in such labors before or at the time of Jackson's arrival. Although considerably less than the numbers claimed after the war, it is not too far away from the number of "over a hundred men" cited by Terrell; it should also be taken into account that perhaps others reported on detached service in late 1862 and early 1863 may have been employed in this capacity but were not officially recorded as such in their company musters.[123] It does not appear from the surviving evidence, however, that anywhere near a hundred men were involved in engineering projects at any one given time; instead, some were utilized only during the fall of 1862, some only during the winter, and some only in early 1863. Only a handful of men were employed on pioneer work for more than a few months at a time.[124]

As an example, fifteen members of 2nd Company D, Walker's Battalion/Company D, Infantry Regiment were reported as involved in some type of road work in either the September-October or November-December 1862 musters, or in some cases for the entire period covered by both. Most were back in the ranks of their company at the end of February 1863, whether as a result of Jackson's orders or due to some other reason. Seven deserted eventually, but four of them did so before the end of 1862, indicating that their reasons had nothing to do with Jackson; in fact, three of the four deserters enlisted almost immediately with other Confederate units from Tennessee, which means that they were hardly disgruntled Unionists, while the fourth returned to the ranks with an explanation satisfying his superiors, only to desert again later on.[125] Other men were not employed as engineers until after the first of the year; indeed, twenty-four members of Company G, Infantry Regiment, were not assigned to

123. For example, there are a large number of men listed on detached or detailed service at "Smoky Mountain, Tennessee"; it is probable that some or even all of them were assigned to roadwork. On the other hand, they could have been scouting, hunting deserters, etc. Service record files, Thomas's Legion, Compiled Service Records of Confederate Soldiers from the State of North Carolina (M270), reels 567 through 574.

124. Service record files of William Allison, Edward Arms, Samuel Berry, Reuben Black, Royal Black, James Bohanan, Johnson Bryant, John C. S. Burns, Hugh Clark, James Claughbaugh, Samuel Claughbaugh, D. H. Clift, John W. Cline, William R. Cline, John H. Coats, James H. Coker, Andrew Conner, James Cozart, Edward Douglas, E. E. Dyer, William Dyer, Henry Floyd, James Ford, John R. Franklin, Isaac Granstaff, Joseph Gunter, J. N. Harrison, Alfred Haynes, Benjamin J. E. Henderson, John H. Henderson, J. A. Holder, Isaac Husky, James M. Jett, Marvel Jones, William W. Jones, William Kendrick, Nathaniel W. King, Lewis Kirkpatrick, R. C. McCalla, Eli McCarter, G. B. McCarter, James McCarter, James M. McKinney, Eli McMahan, David Maples, John Messer, Reuben Messer, Royal Messer, George W. Miller, Isaac Miller, William Miller, F. M. Nations, Andrew Ogle, Arthur Ogle, Bradford Ogle, C. T. Ogle, Caleb Ogle, Carter Ogle, E. T. Ogle, Elisha Ogle, Henry Ogle, Levi Ogle, Preston Ogle, Samuel Ogle, Silbert Ogle, Thomas Ogle, Joshua Pack, Thomas Pack, James M. Parris, Marion Petty, James Reagan, Henry Rice, John William Ridley, Daniel Roberts, James Roberts, John Roberts, William Russell, William A. Scully, William B. Seaton, Moses L. Sherrell, John F. Shuler, Thomas F. Simmons, Joel Smith, William Stinnett, Robert L. Stubblefield, William M. Sutton, Moses A. Tague, Smith Tague, Reuben W. Tidwell, James Toomey, J. V. Trantham, James Trott, Thomas Underwood, William P. Turner, David Watson, and Valentine Wyrick, Thomas's Legion, Compiled Military Service Records of Confederate Soldiers from the State of North Carolina (M270), reels 567 through 574, and service record file of Richard C. McCalla, 3rd Regiment Confederate Engineers, Compiled Military Service Records of Confederate Soldiers Serving in Organizations Raised by the Confederate Government (M258), reel 108.

125. Service Record files of Edward Arms, D. H. Clift, John H. Coats, James H. Coker, James Cozart, E. E. Dyer, William Dyer, John R. Franklin, Alfred Haynes, Isaac Husky, William Kendrick, Thomas F. Simmons, Robert L. Stubblefield, James Trott, and Valentine Wyrick, Thomas's Legion, Compiled Military Service Records of Confederate Soldiers from the State of North Carolina, (M270), reels 567 through 570, 573, 574.

road work until June 1863, well after Jackson's arrival, and were last reported still working in that capacity in February 1864. Thus, the supposed number of men involved in these projects, at least in regard to those recorded in the musters, seems to have been much less than Terrell's wartime estimate, let alone the 500 of Arthur or the "thousands" of Stringfield.[126]

Furthermore, the extant evidence does not indicate that there was a mass desertion among men on detached service for pioneer work immediately after Jackson's arrival; many never deserted at all. Whatever truth lies behind the story seems to relate to Company I, Infantry Regiment. Forty-one members of that company were assigned to road work by early 1863. Thirty-three were either natives or residents of Sevier County, Tennessee, and most of the remainder enlisted somewhere in Tennessee. Fourteen of the men were members of one extended clan, the Ogles of Sevier County. Five men (all of them Ogles) dropped out of the musters after February 28, 1863, about the time of Jackson's arrival, although they were reported absent without leave at the end of the previous year. Another man dropped out of the records at the end of October 1862, while two others deserted either in late 1862 or at the beginning of 1863, well before Jackson came. One man transferred to the regimental field and staff when the Legion organized in September. The remaining thirty-two were reported on detached service at either Strawberry Plains or Mossy Creek (modern-day Jefferson City) in the May-June 1863 muster. The nature of their work there is not recorded. It is probable that they were working on fortifications at the railway depots, or (as other members of Thomas's Legion on detached service at Strawberry Plains at this time) were assigned to work with the post commissary. There are no extant records for the company for July and August; however, in the September-October muster, thirty of the thirty-two men previously identified as on detached service were reported absent. There was much confusion in the record keeping of the Legion at this time, which coincided with Federal Maj. Gen. Ambrose E. Burnside's movement into eastern Tennessee, Thomas's departure with the Indian companies for western North Carolina, and his subsequent employment of many absentees from the Legion. As will be discussed below, Legion absentees were often identified in the September-October 1863 musters by some variation of the phrase "cut off in the evacuation of East Tennessee, supposed to have reported to Col. W. H. Thomas in North Carolina." Some of these men subsequently returned to the ranks in Tennessee, but others joined Thomas or simply vanished. All thirty of the detached absentees from Company I were reported as possibly being with Thomas in the September-October muster; later, their records were updated to indicate that they had deserted at Mossy Creek on October 1.[127] This seems to be the only example of

126. Service record files of William Allison, Samuel Berry, Reuben Black, Royal Black, John C. S. Burns, Hugh Clark, James Ford, Isaac Granstaff, Joseph Gunter, Benjamin J. E. Henderson, John H. Henderson, J. A. Holder, Marvel Jones, William W. Jackson, Lewis Kirkpatrick, Eli McMahan, John Messer, Reuben Messer, Royal Messer, George W. Miller, Isaac Miller, William Miller, F. M. Nations, James Parris, John William Ridley, James Roberts, Joel Smith, Moses A. Tague, Smith Tague, and William P. Turner, Thomas's Legion, Compiled Military Service Records of Confederate Soldiers from the State of North Carolina (M270), reels 567 through 574.

127. Service record files of James Bohanan, James Claughbaugh, Samuel Claughbaugh, John W. Cline, William R. Cline, Andrew Conner, Edward Douglas, Henry Floyd, J. N. Harrison, Nathaniel W. King, Eli McCarter, G. B. McCarter, James McCarter, David Maples, Andrew Ogle, Arthur Ogle, Bradford Ogle, C. T. Ogle, Caleb Ogle, Carter Ogle, E. T. Ogle, Elisha Ogle, Henry Ogle, Levi Ogle, Preston Ogle, Samuel Ogle, Silbert Ogle, Thomas Ogle, Joshua Pack, Thomas Pack, Marion Petty, James Reagan, Henry Rice, Daniel Roberts, John Roberts,

a large overnight group desertion of men who at some point were employed as sappers and miners, although the records do not reveal if these men had been put into the ranks with expectations to fight, or were still on detached service at the time of their departure. Thus it seems that much of the complaint by Thomas and his subordinates in regards to the results of putting the pioneers into service as combat soldiers was exaggerated, intentionally or otherwise. Regardless of how serious the situation was, the conflict was representative of future relations between Thomas and Jackson. Thomas regarded the Legion as a unified command under him alone, while Jackson considered the different parts of the Legion to be individual components within his brigade. Officially, Jackson had the upper hand. The situation escalated to the point where he placed Thomas under arrest during the summer.[128]

In the meantime, the main body of the Legion was concentrated at one of two points in northeastern Tennessee: Carter's Depot (or Carter's Station, now Watauga), and Union (modern Bluff City), renamed Zollicoffer in honor of the slain Confederate general and the next major depot along the railroad line. The new dispositions represented a major shift for Thomas's Legion away from the central and southern portion of eastern Tennessee and that section of the North Carolina border which Thomas was most anxious to protect. Most of the Infantry Regiment was at Carter's Depot. Companies E, F, G, and I moved there from Strawberry Plains, and were joined by Company C from Flat Creek, Company H from "Iron Mountain," and Company K from Winters's Gap. Company H subsequently moved to Greeneville around May 3, 1863, and then to Zollicoffer on May 22. Company D remained at Strawberry Plains. Company B was shifted from Strawberry Plains to a place called Camp Creek in Tennessee, while (2nd) Company A moved from Gatlinburg to Clark Creek in Washington County, Tennessee, where it was reported "on scouting duty all the time in the mountains between Tenn. & N.C." The field and staff of Walker's Battalion, the only staff within the Legion to record its movements, shifted from Coker Creek to Strawberry Plains on March 6. On April 8 it moved to Zollicoffer, which for the moment became the battalion's point of concentration. Headquarters was joined there on the same day by Company C; prior to this, the latter unit had completed its detached service at Knoxville and had

---

William Russell, William B. Seaton, William Stinnett, William M. Sutton, Reuben W. Tidwell, James Toomey, J. V. Trantham, and David Watson, Thomas's Legion, Compiled Service Records of Confederate Soldiers from the State of North Carolina (M270), reels 568 through 574, or the roster entries in this volume. All five of the Ogles who dropped out of the records of Company I, Infantry Regiment, after February 28, 1863, had previously deserted from Company A, 31st Regiment Tennessee Infantry (W. M. Bradford's) before joining the Legion. At least three of them had apparently returned to the 31st Tennessee by the end of December 1862, despite the indication that they were working on roads for Thomas at the end of February. Service record files of Arthur Ogle, Bradford Ogle, Caswell T. Ogle, Gilbert Ogle, and Thomas Ogle, 39th Regiment Tennessee Mounted Infantry, Compiled Service Records of Confederate Soldiers from the State of Tennessee (M268), reel 277.

128. Terrell to Vance, February 22, 1864, Governors' Papers: Vance, 1862-1865, NCOAH; Stephen Whitaker to parents, August 2, 1863, Whitaker Papers, NCOAH; service record file of William H. Thomas, Thomas's Legion, Compiled Service Records of Soldiers from the State of North Carolina (M270), reel 573. For an example of Thomas's obstinacy regarding the Legion's status, see his December 25, 1863, letter to the *Asheville News*, published on January 21, 1864, and reprinted in the Charlotte *Western Democrat* on January 26. He referred to the Legion as "my command," and stated that it "became divided" during the invasion of east Tennessee in the fall of 1863, with "[t]he larger portion . . . ordered to Abingdon[, Virginia], and the remainder, five companies, three mounted and two Indian companies . . . assigned to other duties." Jackson was not mentioned; the cavalry companies were described as "detached" (see also pp. 35-36 n. 82 above). For Thomas's arrest, see p. 72 below.

been at Strawberry Plains since March 20. Company E finally left its original camp at Valleytown in Cherokee County on March 5 and moved to Strawberry Plains; it, too, was sent to Zollicoffer, arriving on April 28, although by mid-June it had returned to Strawberry Plains. Company H left Coker Creek on March 11 for Strawberry Plains, and from there journeyed to Zollicoffer. Company B also moved from Coker Creek to Zollicoffer at some point before the muster. The whereabouts of Company A are unknown, although it was last reported to be at Coker Creek; it may have initially shifted to Zollicoffer, although by *the* middle part of June it was at Strawberry Plains. The official whereabouts of Levi's Battery for part of this period are also unknown, although about May 12 it was sent to Strawberry Plains. Jackson's own headquarters was at Jonesborough, Tennessee, about midway on the railroad between Carter's Depot and Greeneville. An abstract from a department field return, dated April 30, showed Jackson with 1,830 officers and men present for duty, with an aggregate present and absent of 2,939. It is not known how much of this number represented the men of Thomas's Legion. In an April 25 breakdown of the department's troop organization, the elements of the Legion were again listed separately as the Thomas Legion and the Thomas Legion (battalion). Besides the Legion, Jackson's Brigade (formally known as the Fourth Brigade) consisted of the 62nd Regiment N.C. Troops, Winston's Company of Confederate Sappers and Miners, McClung's Battery Tennessee Light Artillery and Capt. William H. Burrough's Battery Tennessee Light Artillery (the Rhett Artillery).[129]

The new dispositions were the result of growing concerns regarding the safety of the railroad linking eastern Tennessee with Virginia and the Deep South. Donelson had departed in early April on a two-month sick furlough on the recommendation of a surgeon. He left Jackson in charge of the department during his absence. This change of command came at a moment of controversy over the state of the railroad bridge defenses. Work had been going on for some time by engineering companies and by detached men such as Thomas's sappers and miners to insure the safety of the bridges, but Joe Johnston criticized them as "too extensive" and, by implication, requiring too many men to defend. Capt. W. F. Foster, Chief Engineer of the Department of East Tennessee, was thus left to devise defenses that could be

129. "Record of Events": muster roll abstracts, March-April, 1863: 2nd Company A and Companies B, C, D, E, F, G, H, I, and K, Infantry Regiment, and Field & Staff and Companies A, B, C, and E, Walker's Battalion, March 7 and March 5-April 30, 1863: Company H, Infantry Regiment, May-June 1863: Company H, Walker's Battalion, and April 1-June 30, 1863: Captain Levi's Battery Light Artillery, Thomas's Legion, Compiled Service Records of Confederate Soldiers from the State of North Carolina (M270), reel 567; *O.R.* 23 (pt. 2): 792, 806. In a brief itinerary of the early posts of Walker's Battalion's provided in an 1895 letter from Columbus F. Walker, son of William C. Walker and a staff officer in the battalion, part or all of that unit was stationed at a place called Sweetwater in between the time that some elements had been at Coker Creek and the move to Carter's Depot. There were two places known as Sweetwater in eastern Tennessee at the time. One was in Monroe County, southwest of Loudon and on the East Tennessee & Georgia Railroad and within easy distance of Coker Creek. The other was located near the east bank of the Big Pigeon River within the fork caused by the juncture of that stream with the French Broad River, and thus approximately halfway between Coker Creek and Carter's Depot, although away from the main lines of communication and travel. Which of the two Sweetwaters was meant is unknown, although the railroad location seems to be the most likely choice. Columbus F. Walker to Stringfield, September 4, 1895, Stringfield Papers, WCU. A modern historian of Levi's Battery identified Greeneville, Tennessee, as the site of the battery's first post. Jeffrey C. Weaver, *The Nottoway Artillery and Barr's Battery Virginia Light Artillery,* Virginia Regimental History Series (Lynchburg, VA: H. E. Howard, 1994), 104. The first post for the battery mentioned in its earliest muster roll is Strawberry Plains, where it arrived about May 12.

held by as few men as possible. At the same time, the troops had to be dispersed in such a way that key points could be defended while the bulk of the departmental forces could be quickly shifted to any place that the Federals threatened in force. All of this occurred as Donelson's reorganization of the departmental forces into brigades was reaching completion, and matters were still confused as various companies, battalions, and regiments shifted to new positions. For this reason, when Johnston sought information in early April about how many men were stationed in the vicinity of the railroad, Jackson was unable to provide accurate information. He optimistically stated, however, "that the entire infantry force of this department can be thrown to the railroad in three hours' time, with the exceptions of those at Big Creek and Cumberland Gaps, and Brigadier General [Humphrey] Marshall's."[130]

In the meantime, Johnston was dissatisfied with Donelson's assignment of Jackson as acting departmental commander. Jackson was junior in date of rank to Brig. Gen. W. G. M. Davis, and both Johnston and Secretary of War Seddon wanted someone sent from outside with higher rank than either man. Johnston lobbied for Maj. Gen. Richard S. Ewell, brother of Johnston's assistant adjutant general. In the meantime, military protocol demanded that Davis supersede Jackson. Once in charge, Davis advised placing the departmental cavalry to guard the mountain passes and provide an early warning of any Federal advance. The infantry could then be concentrated on the railroad to move rapidly to any threatened point. Davis believed that if the cavalry were placed in the passes, then the department infantry could be shifted to reinforce Bragg if needed.[131]

Davis's tenure as acting departmental commander proved to be every bit as short-lived as Jackson's. The death of Donelson from natural causes on April 17 at Montvale Springs, Tennessee, accentuated the need to provide a more permanent leader. Ewell was out of the question, as President Davis was convinced that he had not sufficiently recovered from his injury at Groveton, Virginia, the previous year to resume active service. Instead, the government tapped Maj. Gen. Dabney H. Maury, then on assignment at Vicksburg, to take over on April 25.[132] Upon his arrival, Maury quickly became convinced that his old West Point friend, Maj. Gen. Ambrose Burnside, commander of the Federal Department of the Ohio, was planning to advance into the area in force. Burnside was in fact desirous of going on the offensive, and was gradually concentrating troops for that purpose; however, his own limited departmental resources and problems, including the need to leave behind sufficient troops to protect Kentucky and act against potentially violent "Copperhead" anti-war unrest north of the Ohio River, meant that action would not be immediate.[133]

Unaware of Burnside's circumstances, Maury and Johnston were convinced that an invasion was imminent. Maury was greatly worried by the obstacles standing in the way of any successful defense of the department. "It is a hard territory to defend, being a mere frontier, with a railroad line of 200 miles or more in extent, parallel to which is the enemy's line

130. *O.R.* 23 (pt. 2): 742-743 (quotes, 742), 744.

131. *O.R.* 23 (pt. 2): 745-747.

132. *O.R.* 23 (pt. 2): 753, 773-774, 787-788, 791; Warner, *Generals in Gray*, 75; John E. Stanchak, "Donelson, Daniel Smith," in Faust, *Historical Times Illustrated Encylopedia of the Civil War*, 224. The Confederate government was unaware of Donelson's death for several days and appointed him major general on April 22.

133. *O.R.* 23 (pt. 2): 258-259, 805, 807, 810; William Marvel, *Burnside* (Chapel Hill, N.C.: The University of North Carolina Press, 1991), 241-243.

of occupation, from which by many routes he can assail us, and, as the whole course of the railroad is in a disaffected country, our ability to use it is uncertain," he wrote Secretary of War Seddon on May 7. "At present there are but about 4,000 or 5,000 infantry available for movement upon any threatened point, and, therefore, it is essential for the security of the territory that a considerable increase of the infantry force should be made at once." Where any available troops would come from was the problem. With Federal Maj. Gen. Ulysses S. Grant moving on Vicksburg, troops were being sent from Bragg's army as reinforcements, and additional troops for eastern Tennessee were unavailable. In the meantime, Maury had to scramble to find some way utilize his scattered forces to their best advantage.[134]

On April 30, after receipt of a telegram from Johnston regarding the Burnside threat, Maury ordered Jackson to assign the mininum number of troops necessary to successfully defend the bridges, and be ready to rush the bulk of his infantry as quickly as possible to whatever point was directed. Jackson replied the following day about the lack of sufficient troops in both his district and the entire department to guard all points against a strong enemy advance. In response, Maury basically repeated his earlier instructions in greater detail. Jackson was to concentrate the majority of his infantry at Greeneville, ready to move wherever necessary to counter any sudden attack. Small garrisons of thirty to forty men would be detached to guard each railroad bridge. Jackson's cavalry should concentrate at some point along the railroad, minus small detachments for picketing and patrol.[135]

Maury also approached the neighboring Department of West Virginia for assistance. On May 4, he wrote its commander, Maj. Gen. Samuel Jones, requesting that he send reinforcements. At the least, he hoped that Jones could put a large enough force on the railroad between Greeneville and Bristol to allow Maury to withdraw Jackson's Brigade from the former place, in case he needed to use it to block an offensive move from Burnside. Jones's reply was noncommittal. Once Burnside's invasion route was clear, then Jones might be able to follow Maury's suggestion to put troops on the railroad. As whatever force that Jones could send would be so small that he was afraid it would not cover the line from Bristol to Greeneville adequately, he wanted Maury to designate the most important points to defend. By this time, Maury's own defensive plans had become moot. On April 27, only thirteen days after his appointment, he was replaced by Maj. Gen. Simon Bolivar Buckner, who had most recently been in command at Mobile. "I feel no little relief in the change which you have made in my command," Maury wrote Seddon on May 7. "General Buckner

134. *O.R.* 23 (pt. 2): 807, 822 (quote). The "4,000 to 5,000 infantry" that Maury referred to did not represent the total infantry strength in his department, but only his estimate of the total effective infantry that could be gathered for operations without exposing the bridges and mountain passes to danger. Abstracts of department field returns for April 10 and April 20 (when Davis was still in command) showed totals of 7,579 and 7,879 effective infantry present respectively. The aggregate number of infantry present and absent numbered 14,243 in both reports. *O.R.* 23 (pt. 2): 749, 780. For a discussion of the overall military situation facing Johnston in the spring of 1863, placing in context the merry-go-round replacement of departmental commanders in eastern Tennessee and their various defensive schemes, see Connelly, *Autumn of Glory*, 93-111.

135. *O.R.* 23 (pt. 2): 805, 807, 810. The April 25 inspection report for Jackson's (Fourth) Brigade included no cavalry, although the previous report for March 19 did. By April 25, the cavalry formerly under Jackson's command were serving with other units. *O.R.* 23 (pt. 2): 711, 792-793. Perhaps Jackson was given temporary command of some cavalry forces for the threatened emergency; the 16th Battalion Georgia Cavalry was known to have been part of his brigade at the end of July (see p. 65 below).

is the man of all others who should be here, and while I do not know that I am peculiarly suited to the command he has been occupying, I shall enter upon its duties with more satisfaction than I feel here, because there is but one enemy to fight there, and he is outside."[136]

Upon his arrival, Buckner made his own troop dispositions to meet the potential threat from Burnside and pursued his own policy of seeking cooperation with Jones and Bragg. Jackson's Brigade, estimated at about 1,200 men, was assigned on May 18 to defend "the public works" (i.e, the railroad bridges and stations). A minimum number of men were to be assigned to each garrison. Thomas's Indian companies and Jackson's cavalry were not to be stationed at a particular base; instead, they were to act as scouts, police the roads, and be ready to reinforce any threatened point. Three other brigades, totalling some 6,000 men, represented Buckner's force for field operations; these units were scattered, but in such a way that they could concentrate along the railroad. Most of these troops were stationed in more or less equal segments at Greeneville, Morristown, Knoxville, Clinton, and Loudon. Another infantry brigade was scattered along the railway in southwestern Virginia and in the mountain passes of southeast Kentucky, in a zone which to some extent overlapped with Jones's department; neither Buckner or Jones thought much of this particular unit, believing it to be badly disorganized. Nor was Buckner impressed with his cavalry. In all, Buckner felt that he could at most field about 4,000 infantry and 2,000 cavalry to counter danger to any one particular point; however, most of these troops had no combat experience. Jones had been instructed to cooperate with Buckner, but the latter estimated that at most he could only expect another 2,000 to 4,000 men from that source. Buckner suggested to Bragg a number of possible defensive lines, depending on circumstances, that might best insure coordination with the Army of Tennessee in the event of a move by Burnside into east Tennessee and/or an advance by Maj. Gen. William S. Rosecrans's Army of the Cumberland into middle Tennessee. Buckner also felt that it would be best if one commander directly oversaw both departments (which, in this case, would mean Bragg).[137]

The threat from Burnside subsided for the moment, as troops who were necessary for his planned offensive were transferred to support Grant.[138] "Another week has passed and no attack has been made by the Yanks on this point," Thomas wrote his wife from Zollicoffer on June 4, "and I am inclined to believe that none will be made soon. The fortifications are nearly completed. [W]hen finished a Cavalry raid can have but little effect on it, unless accompanied by artillery. This cannot be brought on up the mountains." His optimism soon proved to be unwarranted. On June 17, Jackson received word at Jonesborough that trouble was headed in his direction. "A formidable force of bushwhackers is said to threaten Greeneville, the stores there, and the railroad," wrote J. N. Gallaher, Buckner's assistant adjutant general. "Look to it at once, and if you have not force enough to disperse them, telegraph here." The "bushwhackers" were in fact nothing of the sort. Burnside may have not been able to invade eastern Tennessee or fully support Rosecrans, whose summer offensive was about to begin, but he was not going to remain completely idle. He dispatched two raiding parties into Kentucky and Tennessee. The first, under Brig. Gen. Julius White, targeted

136. *O.R.* 15:1055-1056, 23 (pt. 2): 813, 800, 822(quote), 823.

137. Ibid., 23 (pt. 2): 840, 841-843 (quote, 841), 844-846.

138. Marvel, *Burnside*, 244-245.

the salt works located near Prestonburg, Kentucky. It soon bogged down under a combination of White's lackadaisical leadership and the onset of bad weather.[139]

The other force was the one Gallaher warned Jackson about. It was led by Col. William P. Sanders of the 5th Regiment Kentucky Cavalry (Union). He departed Mount Vernon, Kentucky, on June 14, commanding a force consisting of elements of the 2nd Regiment Ohio Cavalry, the 7th Regiment Ohio Cavalry, the 112th Regiment Illinois Mounted Infantry, the 44th Regiment Ohio Mounted Infantry, the 1st Regiment Kentucky Cavalry (Union), the 1st Regiment East Tennessee Mounted Infantry (Union), and the 1st Regiment Ohio Light Artillery. Sanders's target was the East Tennessee & Virginia Railroad. After several early successes along the line, including a probe of Knoxville on June 19, the column headed for Strawberry Plains. Burnside considered the bridge at the latter site to be the most important on the railroad line. Defending the bridge was a small force consisting of Companies A and E of Walker's Battalion, and Levi's Battery. There were also a number of convalescents from the Legion and other units present at the hospital located there.[140]

Sgt. John Hannibal Stewart of Company I, Infantry Regiment, one of the convalescents at the post hospital, was a witness to what happened. Stewart evidently felt well enough on the morning of June 20 to volunteer for some rather dangerous work: along with Sgt. Newton R. McLelland of Company E, Walker's Battalon, he rode an engine in the direction of Knoxville to discern the enemy's movements. They found out all too soon that the Federals were heading their way. Sanders's force followed the line of the railroad northeast, destroying bridges and depots as it advanced. Some three miles below Strawberry Plains, Sanders left the railroad; rather than risking a foolish assault across the bridge, which stretched over 1,600 feet in length, he crossed the river so as to strike on the same side on which the Confederates were concentrated. As soon as the Federals arrived, they came under fire from four guns of Levi's Battery. Sanders dismounted his men and sent the 44th Ohio Mounted Infantry up the river, while the rest were ordered to work around the defensive position. Skirmishing lasted for about an hour, at which point the majority of the Confederates withdrew on the locomotive; however, Sanders captured 2 officers and 137 enlisted men. The majority of these were from Thomas's Legion. They included Ordnance Sgt. Edwin P. McGee of Walker's Battalion, 39 and 31 enlisted men respectively from Companies A and B of Walker's Battalion, and 10 enlisted men of Levi's Battery; the remainder were members of the Infantry Regiment, either convalescents or men on detached duty. In all, 85 members of the Legion were captured on June 20 at Strawberry Plains; in addition, 6 others who were

139. Thomas to Sarah Thomas, June 4, 1863, Thomas Papers, DU; *O.R.* 23 (pt. 1): 13, (pt. 2): 876 (quote); Marvel, *Burnside*, 249-250.

140. *O.R.* 23 (pt. 1): 385, 386-387; "Record of Events": muster roll abstract, April 1-June 30, 1863: Captain Levi's Battery Light Artillery, Thomas's Legion, Compiled Service Records of Confederate Soldiers from the State of North Carolina (M270), reel 567; service record files (especially Companies A and E, Walker's Battalion and Captain Levi's Battery Light Artillery), Thomas's Legion, ibid., reels 567 through 574. The service files for Companies A and E of Walker's Battalion and Levi's Battery, showing the large number of troops captured from those units, are among the few sources identifying their involvement in the fight at Strawberry Plains. The records include material abstracted from a parole list of the prisoners captured by Sanders (List of 455 Prisoners of War C.S.A. captured in Tennessee June 1863 and Paroled. Captured by Col. Sanders in East Tenn., Chapter 8: Miscellaneous Records [hereinafter cited as Chapter 8], Entry 183, Box 80, item 7069, RG 109, NA).

evidently on detached assignment were captured at other sites along the railroad during the raid. Sanders captured and spiked five guns, at least four of which were from Levi's Battery, as well as 600 sacks full of salt and a large number of tents and camp equipment. He also burned the bridge, which Burnside estimated from local sources could not be rebuilt for several months; within days of the attack, however, Buckner was planning to rebuild it quickly. Although a muster roll report for Levi's Battery reported that they had "inflicte[ed] some punishment" on the the raiders, "killing and wounding several" in a fight that lasted "for hours," Sanders reported only 2 killed and 4 wounded for the entire raid.[141]

On the following day, Sanders turned over the parole of the captured prisoners to Col. R. K. Byrd of the 1st Regiment East Tennessee Mounted Infantry (Union). According to Stewart, the men did not sign formal parole papers, but verbally gave their names and units, which were listed down. In the meantime, Sanders proceeded to Mossy Creek and burned the bridge. Becoming aware of Confederate efforts to trap him, he headed for Rogers's Gap, but found it partly blocked and strongly defended. Forced to abandon his artillery, he made it to safety via Smith's Gap to Boston, Kentucky, on June 24. Despite the loss of the guns, the raid was regarded as successful due to the damage done to the railroad.[142]

The effects of Sanders's raid on Thomas's Legion went far beyond the temporary damage done by loss of the paroled men and of Levi's guns. In the weeks following the clash, there was a huge spike in desertion among the Legion's troops, particularly in the units that had participated. Near the end of June, Jackson ordered those captured to ignore their paroles and return to the ranks. Capts. C. C. Berry and Stephen Whitaker of Companies A and E, Walker's Battalion, were ordered to Clay and Cherokee counties to gather up the absentees and parolees from their companies and forward them to Knoxville. Stewart's postwar account of the manner in which the paroles were taken provides the necessary clue for understanding Jackson's decision. The rules of the exchange cartel issued in July of the previous year stipulated that paroled prisoners had to be brought to certain specified locations for a one-on-one exchange; Sanders, on the other hand, had not wished to encumber his cavalry column with a large body of prisoners on foot. Thus Jackson considered the informally issued paroles not to be legitimate. Many of those paroled refused the call to return, however, a practice all-too-common even among prisoners who were exchanged in a more regular fashion. In the case of prisoners who were not exchanged, the consequences if recaptured

141. John H. Stewart to Stringfield, March 9, 1913, Stringfield Papers, WCU; *O.R.* 23 (pt. 1): 385, 387-389; List of 455 Prisoners of War C.S.A. captured in Tennessee June 1863 and Paroled, Chapter 8, Entry 183, Box 80, item 7069, RG 109, NA; "Record of Events": muster roll abstract, April 1-June 30, 1863, Captain Levi's Battery Light Artillery, Thomas's Legion, Compiled Service Records of Confederate Soldiers from the State of North Carolina (M270), reel 567. In addition to his known casualties, Sanders reported 21 others as missing; elsewhere in his correspondence he identified them as stragglers. Regardless of the number, his casualties were light. The exact number of men defending Strawberry Plains is unknown. Stewart recalled that there was only Levi's Battery and 60 healthy infantrymen to defend the bridge, but this seems far too low. Sanders claimed that the bridge had around 400 defenders, which is probably too high a figure. In a letter to Burnside written while the raid was in progress, he claimed to have captured 125 enlisted men at Strawberry Plains; in his official report for July 26, he put the number at 137 enlisted men and 2 officers, as noted in the text. The dead and wounded on the Confederate side are unknown, although Sanders reported that the commanding officer at Strawberry Plains was killed. He did not identify this officer by name. See Stewart to Stringfield, op. cit.; *O.R.* 23 (pt. 1): 386, 388.

142. *O.R.* 23 (pt. 1): 385, 388; Stewart to Stringfield, March 9, 1913, Stringfield Papers, WCU.

could prove to be quite serious, even fatal. Thus, it is not surprising that of the 91 members of Thomas's Legion captured during Sanders's raid, 49 failed to return, over half the number involved.[143] To make matters worse, in the weeks immediately following the raid many more men deserted who had not been captured and paroled. Including men on furlough at the time of the raid who never returned, 106 additional men were reported as absent without leave or deserters by July 19; many of the absentees were reported as deserters by the end of the year or early in 1864. In all, at least 155 members of Thomas's Legion disappeared from the ranks at this time. Twenty-three of them later returned, some forcibly, although some of these deserted again at a later date.[144] Prior to the commencement of the fall campaign in eastern Tennessee, the number of new absentees reported slackened considerably. Outside of the Indian companies, for which there are no extant muster rolls after April 1863, the surviving records show only 68 men leaving the ranks between July 2 and August 19, a handful of whom returned. Taken together with all earlier cases of absence, however, and allowing for multiple absences and uncertainties of date in some cases, the cumulative loss

143. Stewart to Stringfield, March 9, 1913, Stringfield Papers, WCU; *O.R.* ser. II, 4:266-268, ser. IV, 2:732; Mark Mayo Boatner, *The Civil War Dictionary* (New York: David McKay Co., 1959), 270-271, 619-620; Robertson, *Soldiers Blue and Gray*, 191-192; Frank L. Byrne, "Prisoners of War," in Current, *Encylopedia of the Confederacy*, 1256-1258; service record files, Thomas's Legion, Compiled Service Records of Confederate Soldiers from the State of North Carolina, (M270), reels 567 through 574; Stephen Whitaker to wife, June 28, 1863, Alfred E. Jackson to Whitaker, June 29, 1863 (Special Order No. __), and William C. Walker to Whitaker, June 30, 1863, Whitaker Papers, NCOAH. According to Stewart, following the parole "most of the well men part of Capt Whitakers Co & a few others about 60 infantry in all started home most of them to N.C." The number of men sent by Jackson to collect the missing men is not known. In Jackson's and Walker's orders to Whitaker, the instructions seem to imply that Whitaker was solely responsible for gathering up the men of both companies. All three of his lieutenants were assigned specific roles in the operation; the remnant of the company in Tennessee was probably placed under the authority of the captain of another company. A July 16 letter to Walker from 1st Lt. James N. Bryson of Company A, Walker's Battalion, shows that Berry, Bryson, and 2nd Lt. Mathew C. Fowler of Company B of the battalion were sent, also (*O.R.* ser. IV, 2:732). Bryson wrote that "I was not able to bring in any [of the absentees in his company] by simply notifying them to return to camps. Those who were captured by the enemy at Strawberry Plains say they will not return unless they are obliged to until they are exchanged. Then, they say, they are ready and willing to return to duty."

144. Service record files, Thomas's Legion, Compiled Service Records of Confederate Soldiers from the State of North Carolina (M270), reels 567 through 574. Any attempt to arrive at exact figures for casualties, desertions, and other statistics for Thomas's Legion is hampered by the often contradictory materials in the muster rolls, the result of indifferent book-keeping. There are also no muster rolls for 2nd Company A and Company B of the Infantry Regiment after April 1863; no rolls available for any Legion companies in July-August 1863 outside of Levi's Battery, probably due to the onset of active campaigning in eastern Tennessee towards the end of the latter month; and no known surviving rolls for any companies of the Legion later than April 8, 1864, and for most companies after February 29 of that year. Information for the rest of the war comes from such sources as records of the issuance of clothing (not always an accurate indication of actual presence, and spotty at best even when accurate), reports and requisitions from officers' records, Confederate hospital records, Federal provost marshal records for captured prisoners and deserters, and the like. The fragmentary material gleaned from them is nevertheless important for providing some minimal data. In many cases, it is difficult to determine the exact date and circumstances of absence for many of the men involved. For example, a number of men were reported in the fall as having gone absent without leave on June 25; they were subsequently reported as having deserted on July 1 from specific locations such as Strawberry Plains. As these men included not only parolees who did not return and deserters who had not been captured by Sanders, but individuals who were not even present at the time of the raid (such as soldiers on earlier furloughs who failed to return), it is likely that the dates represented efforts on the part of company officers to square their records months after the events concerned.

of manpower in Thomas's Legion between its initial organization and the late summer of 1863 reduced the unit's size considerably, perhaps by as much as one third.[145]

The Legion was not the only command in eastern Tennessee plagued by growing desertion problems. Once again, the preferred solution was to transfer locally recruited units to more strongly secessionist areas. By the end of July 1863 Buckner proposed the idea of sending some of the more troublesome away, an idea suggested to him by Vance:

> I have several regiments in my command composed of men from East Tennessee and the mountains of North Carolina. Their effective strength is about 2,400. Desertions from them are numerous, on account of their proximity to their homes, and arrests are frequent in consequence of the difficult country to which they can retreat. The Governor of North Carolina has suggested that the regiments from that State be sent as far from home as practicable, to prevent desertions. The same principle would apply to the East Tennessee regiments. All these regiments would become effective in the Army of Mississippi or in South Carolina. I respectfully suggest that they be ordered there. I would prefer 1,000 effective men from distant States to the entire effective strength of these regiments.

Bragg concurred with Buckner's basic ideas, and forwarded them to Cooper for consideration. Indorsements of the correspondence by both Cooper and Seddon indicate that they supported the idea, also, although typical of the Confederate bureacracy the latter wanted Buckner himself to work out the details of the transfer with either Bragg or Johnston. It is possible that only the resumption of active campaigning in late August spared the Legion from transfer to a different theater of operations.[146]

Meanwhile, following Sanders's raid the Legion attempted to regroup as additional desertions continued to bleed its ranks dry. The various movements and stations of the Legion's companies for this period are rather hazy; while it is known where many of the companies were by the end of June, it is not clear in most cases whether they were repositioned before or after the raid. It may be said that generally the Legion was spread out along a wide stretch of the East Tennessee & Georgia and the East Tennessee & Virginia railroads, which connected in Knoxville. Tracing the known positions of the Legion along the line of the railroads from southwest to northeast at the time of the June muster, it is known that Company C of the Infantry Regiment was at Charleston, Tennessee, having moved there from Carter's Depot. Company C of Walker's Battalion had at some point subsequent to April 30 moved from Zollicoffer to Greeneville, but on June 30 was at Loudon. While it reported that "(i)ts principal duty was guarding the R. R. Bridge at this place," it was also active "scouting in the counties of Monroe & Roane for Bushwhackers, Deserters & Conscripts." Companies B and H of the battalion were at Loudon as well, having also moved there from Zollicoffer. Although there is no surviving muster roll for Company E of Walker's Battalion, correspondence in the private papers of Captain Whitaker show that the remnants of that command ("a few men that has stuck to me") were at Loudon. Levi's Battery was still at Strawberry Plains; as it evidently still lacked replacements for the lost cannon as late as October 31, it may have functioned as infantry at this time. Company E of the Infantry Regiment had moved from Carter's Depot to the Lick Creek Bridge, about midway between Russellville

145. Service record files, Thomas's Legion, Compiled Service Records of Confederate Soldiers from the State of North Carolina (M270), reels 567 through 574.

146. *O.R.* 23 (pt. 2): 950-952, 964-965 (quote).

and Greeneville. Company G of the regiment had moved from Carter's Depot to Limestone Depot, about midway between Greeneville and Jonesborough. Company B of the regiment was later reported on the march from Jonesborough to Carter's Depot on June 30, where it would join Companies D and F. Company F had previously been reported at Carter's Depot on the April muster, so it was probably there throughout the period. Company D had been at Strawberry Plains in April, but had left there on an unknown date before the raid. Companies H, I, and K of the regiment had moved from Carter's Depot to Zollicoffer. The whereabouts of Company A, Infantry Regiment, and Company A, Walker's Battalion, are unknown; however, it is probable that the former unit was at Zollicoffer, as it is known that 2nd Lt. David Whitaker of that company was there on June 28.[147]

The Legion remained a part of Jackson's (Fourth) Brigade in Buckner's Army of East Tennessee. Headquartered at Zollicoffer, the brigade on July 31 also included the 16th Battalion Georgia Cavalry, McClung's Tennessee Light Artillery Company, and Burrough's Tennessee Light Artillery Company (the Rhett Artillery). Once again, the regiment and battalion were listed separately on the field return, this time as "Thomas' Regiment" (with Thomas commanding) and Walker's Battalion. Levi's Battery was not mentioned. The physical condition of the units engaged at Strawberry Plains was not good, and morale probably suffered. Capt. Stephen Whitaker of Company E, Walker's Battalion, noted on June 28 that "we lost all in the fight," including blankets and cooking utensils, all of which were abandoned as the remnant of the company withdrew from Strawberry Plains.[148]

More administrative changes were in store for eastern Tennessee as the Confederate government continued to experiment with ways to achieve greater unity of command in the western theater. The changes were all the more necessary due to the military crisis which engulfed the state. On June 24, 1863, the same day that Sanders's raiders reached safety in

147. "Record of Events": muster roll abstracts, March-April 1863, May-June 1863: Companies B, C, D, E, F, G, H, I, and K, Infantry Regiment, and Companies B, C, and H, Walker's Battalion, and April 1-June 30, 1863: Captain Levi's Battery Light Artillery, Thomas's Legion, Combined Military Service Records of Confederate Soldiers from the State of North Carolina (M270), reel 567; Stephen Whitaker to wife, June 28, 1863, Whitaker Papers, NCOAH; Weaver, *Nottoway Artillery and Barr's Battery*, 106. The October 31, 1863, field return for the Department of Western Virginia and East Tennessee reported that Levi's Battery had no guns; however, in a September 15 letter from Col. John W. Foster to Burnside, discussing a report from two deserters on Confederate strength in the area, reference was made to "Barr's battery of four guns" as part of a contingent of troops stationed at Jonesborough. Barr could have been 1st Lt. John W. Barr of Levi's Battery. If this identification is correct (and "Barr's battery" was understood to be a reference to Levi's Battery by the indexers of the *Official Records*), then Levi's Battery did indeed both receive and lose new guns between June 21 and October 31, making it the hard-luck unit of Thomas's Legion. *O.R.* 29 (pt. 2): 813, 30 (pt. 3): 661 (quote). It is probable, however, since Barr did not actually take command of Levi's Battery until the following year, that "Barr's battery" was a reference to Burrough's Tennessee Light Artillery Company (the Rhett Artillery), which was a part of the Confederate concentration in eastern Tennessee at the time (*O.R.* 30 [pt. 2]: 644, 645), and which was not mentioned among the troops cited by the deserters. In his report on the East Tennessee campaign of 1863, Maj. Gen. Samuel Jones reported that there were "a field battery, and parts of two dismounted batteries, acting as bridge guards" in the northeastern section of the state in early September (*O.R.* 30 [pt. 2]: 603); it is likely that Levi's Battery was one of the units mentioned, although since Thomas's Legion was noted separately in the same summary of local troop strength, possibly not. Few departmental commanders seem to have considered Levi's Battery a part of the Legion, probably because of the break-up of the legions instituted earlier by Donelson. See also p. 48 n. 109 above about the lack of references to Levi's Battery in many field returns.

148. *O.R.* 23 (pt. 2): 946; Stephen Whitaker to wife, June 28, 1863, Whitaker Papers, NCOAH.

Kentucky, Rosecrans and the Army of the Cumberland moved southward against Bragg in central Tennessee, marking the beginning of a series of interrelated campaigns which would consume the rest of the year and soon involve the eastern part of the state as well. The immediate result was that by July 7, Bragg had been maneuvered out of his position south of Murfreesboro, retreating all the way to Chattanooga. The need for cooperation between Bragg and Buckner was greater than ever, especially as the former might need reinforcements from the latter's department.[149] On July 25, the Confederate government incorporated the Department of East Tennessee into the Department of Tennessee, placing Bragg in overall command of both regions and separating the whole from Johnston's authority. On August 6, the day Bragg formally assumed command of eastern Tennessee, Buckner's men became the Third Corps of the Army of Tennessee. Buckner, however, continued to administer the district and was expected to report to Richmond on matters not directly concerned with military operations. This led to a flurry of communications between Buckner, Bragg, and the government over the limits of the former's authority. Further, the consolidation still did not solve the problems of military cooperation between eastern Tennessee and southwest Virginia, which soon became an issue once again.[150]

Buckner remained dissatisfied with the arrangment and condition of the troops in the department. His plans for redeploying and reorganizing the troops had been slowed by the raids into eastern Tennessee and southwest Virginia, as well as by the transferral of some units to Bragg. The mountain passes needed strong guards, as did the depots and bridges along the railroad, which in Buckner's opinion were in need of better fortifications to prevent a repeat of Sanders's recent success. All of this required more men, not only to guard the necessary critical points and to supply a sufficient number of men to concentrate as needed, but to provide a labor force to improve the fortifications. Buckner doubtless knew that reinforcements were coming, so he notified Bragg's headquarters that much shifting would result from the temporary assignment of "whole regiments" to work on the fortifications until they were truly strong enough to resist assaults with minimal garrisons.[151]

Because military operations in late August disrupted the normal routine, muster rolls were either not taken for most of Thomas's Legion in July and August, or were lost. It is thus once again difficult to ascertain with certainty where the elements of the Legion were stationed and how they were occupied. The impression left by letters and scattered reports is of confusion and a great deal of movement. Lieutenant Colonel Walker wrote to Captain Whitaker on July 10 of his return to Loudon with the battalion from an excursion to a place called "Runny Water 15 Miles Below Chattanooga." Nothing was mentioned about what the battalion was doing so far from the Legion's normal area of operations. Whitaker himself was absent from Loudon at the time. He was probably still trying to gather up his absentees to forward back to battalion headquarters.[152] In mid-July, some elements of Jackson's

149. Connelly, *Autumn of Glory*, 121-134; Steven E. Woodworth, *Six Armies in Tennessee: The Chickamauga and Chattanooga Campaigns* (Lincoln: University of Nebraska Press, 1998), 1-46.

150. *O.R.* 23 (pt. 2): 931, 954, 962-963, 30 (pt. 4): 512; Connelly, *Autumn of Glory*, 156-158.

151. *O.R.* 23 (pt. 2): 929-930 (quote, 929).

152. "I think I will Stay here for Some time. you Come to this place No difference What you have If you Cant Get Ready to come your Self Now Send on the men with one of the leetenants. But Come So Soon As you can.

Brigade were shifted around the railroad in response to Federal movements in northeastern Tennessee and southwestern Virginia. An "infantry bridge guard" from the brigade, numbering 240 men, was reported on the move from Charleston and Loudon to Zollicoffer via Knoxville. Which part of the brigade was involved was not mentioned, but given that the Legion seems to have been the only infantry left in Jackson's command at that point, it is likely that the troops in question belonged to it. The force was probably composed of Company C of the Infantry Regiment, last reported at Charleston at the end of June, and Walker's Battalion, which was at Loudon. This shift may have also reflected Buckner's current ideas for redeploying his forces. In a letter to Bragg's chief of staff dated July 24, he wrote that "Jackson's brigade will guard the railroad east of Knoxville." It is known that Walker's Battalion was assigned to guard the bridge at Carter's Depot by early August.[153]

The rest of the Legion may have been involved with the growing problem of irregular activity behind the Confederate lines. Matters had continued to worsen in the months following the Confederate efforts at suppression during the winter and spring. Shortly before Sanders's raid, Secretary of War Seddon informed Buckner of "marauding bands of deserters from the army collected in several western counties, especially in Henderson County, North Carolina." These deserters were "recruited and sustained in large measure by the disloyal in the contiguous district of East Tennessee." Seddon asked Buckner to "take appropriate measures of repression as early as the circumstances of your command will allow."[154] In late July, Captain Whitaker wrote to his father that he had had to detour on his journey from North Carolina to rejoin his company because the most direct route was infested with bushwhackers. Weeks later, he wrote of continued bushwhacker activity in the area of Carter's Depot. One night, some marauders approached the home of a man named Felton who lived four miles from the depot. Claiming to be Confederates, they called out to Felton's sons, both lieutenants who were visiting home, claiming that the depot had been captured and that the Federals were coming for them. The officers departed with their visitors. The body of one was found by men from Whitaker's company on August 1 and buried. The other was also initially believed to have been killed, but was rescued by a sympathetic Unionist.[155]

---

we get plenty to Eat." Walker to Stephen Whitaker, July 10, 1863, Whitaker Papers, NCOAH. Whitaker wrote to his father in July of a journey to rejoin his company at Knoxville. Given that he had been ordered at the end of June to go to North Carolina to gather up the Strawberry Plains parolees and other absentees, it is likely that he was finally returning from Cherokee and Clay counties. Jackson to Stephen Whitaker, June 29, 1863, Walker to Whitaker, June 30, 1863, and Whitaker to father, July 23, 1863, all in Whitaker Papers, NCOAH.

153. *O.R.* 23 (pt. 2): 905, 915-917 ("infantry bridge guard" quote, 916), 929-930 ("Jackson's brigade. . . ." quote, 930); Stephen Whitaker to parents, August 2, 1863, Stephen Whitaker to James Whitaker, August 25, 1863, Whitaker Papers, NCOAH.

154. *O.R.* 23 (pt. 2): 872.

155. Stephen Whitaker to father, July 23, August 2, 1863, Whitaker Papers, NCOAH. No lieutenants by the name of Felton are reported among the roster lists of Tennessee soldiers. It is possible that they served in units raised by another state or states. Another possibility is that the name was misspelled. The incident bears a striking similarity to a story told about Lt. Robert P. Tipton and his brother, Elbridge, reported in the history of the 13th Regiment Tennessee Cavalry (Union). That event supposedly happened on August 28, several weeks after the abduction of the Feltons, but also involved Unionist bushwhackers claiming that Carter's Depot had been captured, and that the Tiptons would have to flee their father's home in order to escape. Lieutenant Tipton was murdered, but his brother was rescued by friendly Unionists. Scott and Angel, *History of the Thirteenth Regiment*

1st Lt. James N. Bryson of Company A, Walker's Battalion, encountered similar problems during his effort to round up the absentees and parolees of his company. He informed Walker that in Cherokee County "the outlaws are a terror to the citizens, and especially the soldiers' wives who are alone." Homes were looted and livestock were slaughtered. "I learn they have shot several times at Captain [C. C.] Berry since he has been trying to collect his company together. I learned that those outlaws said that neither Lieutenant [Mathew C.] Fowler [of Company B, Walker's Battalion] nor myself should ever return to the command to report how affairs were going on there." Bryson thought "that a few men" would not be enough to take care of the problem. Furthermore, unless the Confederates got all of the marauders, then soldiers from the region risked losing their lives, homes, and property in reprisals. Bryson concluded that the men were mainly deserters and draft evaders.[156]

Similar news continued to reach authorities throughout the summer. Vance in particular received a steady stream of alarming reports. Lieutenant Bryson's mention of destruction in Cherokee County was probably a reference to a raid on Murphy, an event that outraged and alarmed pro-Confederates in the mountains. The strike was led by Goldman Bryson, who before the war was implicated as the ringleader of a gang of toughs who in August 1856 murdered John Timson, a Cherokee from Valleytown. Bryson's relatives provided an alibi for his whereabouts, and the all-white jury refused to convict him. At the time of the Murphy raid he was a captain in the Tennessee National Guard (Union). Walker informed Vance that marauders lurking in the county consisted of deserters from North Carolina and other states, as well as draft evaders and "Some Desparate C[h]aracters." They claimed to be acting as a part of Burnside's army, and were stealing all the weapons they could find from the locals, and openly drilling. They also prevented furloughed or detailed Confederate soldiers from returning to their commands, were picketing the roads, arresting men, and generally doing all they could to drive those loyal to the Confederacy away. They even allegedly challenged the state militia to an open fight. One correspondent reported that Yancey County was overrun by deserters, while another reported between 200 and 300 deserters in Wilkes County. Unionist meetings were held openly in some places. In eastern Tennessee, word was received that some 200 bushwhackers were planning to disrupt elections on August 6 in the 13th Civil District in Cocke County. Jackson was ordered to "have a sufficient force sent secretly, if possible to arrest [such] persons and prevent illegal voting."[157]

Tennessee Volunter Cavalry U.S.A., 323-325. Lieutenant Tipton, it may be recalled, was reported in Scott and Angel's history as having been in charge of a contingent of the Legion's Cherokees sent to round up Unionists in eastern Tennessee in the spring of that year. See p. 41 and n. 93 above. It is possible that "Felton" and "Tipton" were the same person, although which name is correct if such is the case is unknown.

156. *O.R.* ser. IV, 2:732.

157. J. W. McElroy to Governor Vance, July 13, 1863, M. Fain to Vance, July 18, 1863, Petition of Citizens in Henderson County to Vance, July 18, 1863, W. C. McNiel to Vance, July 19, 1863, D. F. Ramsaur to Vance, July 19, 1863, A.S. Davidson, M. Fain, and others to Vance, July 23, 1863, Walker to Vance, July 27, 1863, Petition of Citizens from Webster to Vance, July 28, 1863, Petition of B. M. Edney and other "citizens of western N.C." to Seddon, July 29, 1863, John W. Patton to Vance, August 5, 1863, W. Murdoch to Vance, August 12, 1863, all in Governors' Papers: Vance, 1862-1865, NCOAH; Trotter, *Bushwhackers*, 91; Sean Michael O'Brien, *Mountain Partisans: Guerrilla Warfare in the Southern Appalachians, 1861-1865* (Westport, CT: Praeger, 1999), 16-17; *O.R.* ser. I, 23 (pt. 2): 936, ser. IV, 2:731-734. According to O'Brien, Pvt. James Bryson of Company A, Walker's Battalion, was Goldman's younger brother, and was conscripted specifically to prevent him from joining

Various solutions to the troubles were proposed. All were limited by the manpower shortages in the department and by the efforts to address the problem through the conscript act. "The militia is worth nothing, now that they are conscripted," complained Capt. J. C. McRae, a recruiting officer stationed at Camp Vance near Morganton, suggesting "that a force of cavalry or mounted infantry be stationed somewhere in the district, and be employed for the purpose of arresting deserters."[158] A Cherokee County resident reported that "[n]o steps have been taken as yet by our Col that will result in any thing like permanent organization. The Home Guards [are] scattered over the county & cannot be got to do anything. Col[John W.] Francis [commander of the 115th Regiment N.C. Militia] is at a loss to know what to do under the circumstances. We believe him to be a good man & only wish that he may have special instructions immediately."[159] Buckner suggested to Adjutant and Inspector General Cooper on July 31 that part of the Confederate prisoners paroled in the summer who had not been exchanged might be used to suppress the bushwhackers "if such a disposition of them be proper."[160] Captain McRae thought it impracticable to send troops from Morganton to Cherokee County due to the distance, but hoped that some infantry and cavalry companies might be spared from Jackson's Brigade. His views were endorsed by his superior, Col. Peter Mallett, Commandant of Conscription in the state, who recommended "that a detachment of two companies from Jackson's brigade of Buckner's division be detailed temporarily to protect the enrolling officer and arrest deserters in counties bordering on Tennessee." Mallett's ideas were echoed by at least one local citizen. "[C]ant you call on the proper authorities of East Tensee to send up 2 Companys say Thomas Indeans & we will do all we can to help them," wrote a resident of Murphy following Bryson's raid.[161]

Limited relief was sent to western North Carolina in late July. Capt. Matthew Love of Company A, Infantry Regiment, was dispatched with part of his command to Yancey County to deal with the bushwhackers there. The expedition did not get off to an auspicious start. On July 28, the Cherokees were informed of the presence of a large number of Federals or Unionists in their area of operation. They soon encountered a body of men holed up in

---

Goldman. If so, the tactic did not work, as he disappeared from Thomas's Legion following Sanders's raid. O'Brien identified Private Bryson with another individual of the same name who entered Federal service in 1865 and attained the rank of sergeant in Company H, 7th Regiment Tennessee Mounted Infantry (Union). While O'Brien is probably correct, there are some apparent contradictions between the Confederate and Federal records that leave a degree of uncertainty to this conclusion. Service record file of James Bryson, Thomas's Legion, Combined Military Service Records of Confederate Soldiers from the State of North Carolina (M270), reel 568; service record file of James Bryson, 7th Regiment Tennessee Mounted Infantry (Union), Records of Volunteer Union Soldiers Who Served During the Civil War, Compiled Service Records of Volunteer Union Soldiers Who Served in Organizations From the State of Tennessee (M395), reel 176 (hereinafter cited to as Compiled Service Records of Volunteer Union Soldiers from the State of Tennessee [M395]), Record Group 94: Records of the U.S. Adjutant General's Office, 1780's-1917 (hereinafter cited as RG 94), NA.

158. *O.R.* ser. IV, 2:734.

159. John W. Patton to Vance, August 5, 1863, Governors' Papers: Vance, 1862-1865, NCOAH. Colonel Francis resigned on September 11. Stephen E. Bradley, *North Carolina Confederate Militia Officers Roster As Contained in the Adjutant-General's Officers Roster* (Wilmington: Broadfoot Publishing Company, 1992), 302.

160. *O.R.* 23 (pt. 2): 939.

161. *O.R.* ser. IV, 2:734 (Mallett quote); D. F. Ramsaur to Governor Vance, July 19, 1863 (quote), Walker to Vance, July 27, 1863, both in Governors' Papers: Vance, 1862-1865, NCOAH.

a house, and opened fire on them as they attempted to flee. They were chagrined to find out that they had fired on some of their own men, wounding one. Soon, however, their mission began to bear fruit. One soldier in the company reported that they had captured twenty-nine prisoners by August 3. He casually described the fates of others in vague but rather ominous terms: "Two are resting on the mountain where they were staying. We made them stop their wrong-doing on Monday. On Tuesday another one rested; Thursday another one rested."[162]

While perhaps acceptable as a short-term solution, the idea of using the Legion for such tasks flew against the ideas of Vance and others about the problems of stationing troops in their home areas. In the letter to Cooper in which he suggested using parolees against the bushwhackers, Buckner requested "that other than East Tennessee and North Carolina troops be located here." On the other hand, Captain Whitaker went to see Jackson about having troops from the brigade sent to Cherokee County. Although Jackson promised to do so, no action was taken, probably because he could not get Buckner's permission. A petition sent to Jackson led to another promise. Whitaker concluded that if no troops were sent quickly that "I fe[a]r Walkers Batt will most all go home to defend thar homes in thar own way."[163]

Thus, Confederate officials, commanders, and soldiers in western North Carolina and eastern Tennessee were locked into a never-ending spiral. The authorities wanted troops to defend the region, but did not want to use locally-recruited units for fear of indiscipline and the ease of desertion; the soldiers themselves were willing to desert anyway to protect their families, dwellings, and property. National interest and military necessity clashed continually with the extreme localism of the individual soldier, for whom the immediate needs of the home front represented the real war. Perhaps if the government and the departmental officers had actually implemented a consistent policy, whether by using the units at hand as needed or by transferring the units with local connections elsewhere and sending troops recruited elsewhere to deal with the problem, then matters might have evolved differently. With the Confederacy on the defensive on so many fronts, however, the available manpower to deal with the mountain unrest simply was not there, at least not without stripping troops from other threatened areas.[164] Nevertheless, circumstances would soon lead to a portion of Thomas's Legion returning permanently to western North Carolina.

162. Do:tsule':?hnv to I:no:li, August 3, 1863, in Kilpatrick and Kilpatrick, *Shadow of Sequoyah*, 11-12 (quote, 11). I:no:li (Black Fox, name also transcribed in English variously as Inoli, Inola, or Enola) later commanded Company C of the Indian Battalion in Thomas's Legion. Do:tsule':?hnv is as yet unidentified; he may be one of two soldiers named Oolstooih, or another named Santoola, who served in Company A, Infantry Regiment.

163. *O.R.* 23 (pt. 2): 939; Stephen Whitaker to James Whitaker, August 13, 1863, Whitaker Papers, NCOAH.

164. The initial Confederate strategy of attempting to defend as much territory as possible by widely dispersing troops that could have been concentrated with the field armies was criticized after the war by some former generals as a waste of scarce manpower, a view echoed by some historians. Jefferson Davis came to recognize the problem and proved more flexible as the war went on. The benefits achieved by trading territory for larger armies ran against the reality that most citizens wanted their local areas defended and were not willing to put up with vulnerability to raids or Federal occupation for a temporary period of time in order to achieve victory. East Tennessee and western North Carolina were therefore not the only regions where action was constantly demanded and was constantly disappointed. See Thomas, *The Confederate Nation*, 104-108, 157-158; Herman Hattaway, *Shades of Blue and Gray: An Introductory Military History of the Civil War* (Columbia: University of Missouri Press, 1997), 152-153; Gary W. Gallagher, *The Confederate War: How Popular Will, Nationalism, and Military Strategy Could Not Stave Off Defeat* (Cambridge: Harvard University Press, 1997), 115-118, 147.

In the meantime, the military situation in eastern Tennessee remained tense. Not only was Rosecrans expected to renew his advance against Bragg, but all signs pointed to Burnside's Army of the Ohio moving against Buckner. Captain Whitaker wrote from Carter's Depot that an attack was expected soon and that it would be a "desperate effort," as "we cant afford to do without this RRoad." Jackson evidently felt a bit jumpy. He wrote to Buckner of rumors regarding "stampeders" (probably deserters), and asked for reinforcements. "Your information in reference to stampeders is too uncertain to justify me in stripping more important points on such an uncertainty," Buckner replied on August 13. He recommended that Jackson use his cavalry and scouts to discover the direction in which the party of "stampeders" was moving, and then send word to the cavalry stationed at Cumberland Gap so that they could be cut off. "I cannot keep a battalion for you in every hamlet of your district, but if the cavalry you have do their duty, and you send information in advance to . . . the gap, such a party, if it moves, can be intercepted."[165]

On August 16, Rosecrans began moving again. Burnside, hampered by manpower shortages and supply problems, reached the Cumberland River on the same day; his mission was to screen Rosecrans's left flank. His force consisted of the Twenty-Third Corps, numbering around 15,000 men. Although the Ninth Corps, which had earlier been transferred to Vicksburg, was finally returning in segments, its ranks were too debilitated and its units too scattered to participate at this point, so he reluctantly campaigned without it. Despite a lack of supplies, he resumed his forward movement on August 20.[166]

Buckner's forces were, if concentrated, perhaps barely adequate in size to face Burnside at this point, but once the Ninth Corps arrived they would outnumbered. Much of the departmental strength was scattered to defend the vital railroad crossings and mountain passes. At best, Buckner felt he could gather together some 7,000 to 8,000 men in a body, and even that would mean letting go of some defensive points. There was potential help available, however. Brig. Gen. Nathan Bedford Forrest's cavalry division was at Kingston, near the juncture of the Clinch and Tennessee rivers and thus not far to the west of Knoxville and the East Tennessee & Georgia Railroad. Buckner could also be reinforced by Bragg or Jones via the railroads. There were complications that clouded the possibility of the latter option, however. The continuing tangle over how the Department of East Tennessee fit into Bragg's command came into play, with Adjutant and Inspector General Cooper suggesting to Bragg on August 21 that he allow Buckner to continue administering the Department of East Tennessee while still answering to Bragg in military matters. This probably led to a message that Bragg sent to Buckner that evening conveying the idea that Buckner would have to rely on his own forces to defend the area without any help from Bragg. Jones was also uncooperative, complaining that he did not have enough men to help Buckner without putting his own department at risk. Fortunately for Buckner, the situation between him and Bragg was soon straightened out. By the end of the month, Buckner would receive reinforcements from Bragg in the form of the division of Maj. Gen. Alexander P. Stewart.[167]

165. Stephen Whitaker to James Whitaker, August 13, 1863, Whitaker Papers, NCOAH; *O.R.* 30 (pt. 4): 495.

166. *O.R.* 30 (pt. 2): 545, 548; Woodworth, *Six Armies in Tennessee*, 52-54; Marvel, *Burnside*, 264-271.

167. *O.R.* 29 (pt. 2): 662, 30 (pt. 4): 520-521, 522, 526-527, 540, 562, 578; Connelly, *Autumn of Glory*, 158; Marvel, *Burnside*, 464-465 n. 18.

In the meantime, Buckner decided to concentrate his infantry at Loudon and his cavalry in a position to cooperate with Forrest and Bragg. His plan was to leave east Tennessee more or less open to Burnside with the goal of striking him on the flanks or in the rear, or, alternatively, combine with Bragg against Rosecrans before the latter and Burnside united. A force of some 2,500 men under Brig. Gen. John W. Frazer guarded Cumberland Gap. Jackson was left at Jonesborough to protect the East Tennessee & Virginia Railroad. If Burnside should dispatch forces towards the railroad and Jackson be unable to hold the line, he was to withdraw in the direction of Abingdon, Virginia, and unite with Jones, delaying Burnside as much as possible. Buckner added that "[i]f no other recourse should be left you, you will retire in the direction of North Carolina, holding the passes as well as possible." It was rumored as early as August 25 that the Legion, or at least the Indians, would soon depart for North Carolina. These stories may have been the result of Mallett's August 17 endorsement of McRae's recommendation, sent to Seddon as part of a bundle of papers about the troubles in western North Carolina. On the other hand, perhaps Buckner's instructions to Jackson had leaked out; certainly, the spread of such rumors at this time is interesting.[168]

The new campaign could not have come at a worst time for Thomas's Legion, as the conflict between Thomas and Jackson finally came to a head. As noted earlier, during the summer Jackson placed Thomas under arrest. Terrell wrote to Vance in February of the following year that it was "for some alleged disobedience of orders." Captain Whitaker commented to his parents that "I donst know all the Charges agains[t] him[. T]he principal one is disobedience of orders. . . . thar is great Pregatis [prejudice] against him[.]" Thomas was sent to Knoxville to stand trial; Whitaker wrote optimistically that "Thomas will be smart enough for them." As matters evolved, the trial was either dismissed or suspended for the duration of the campaign; Whitaker noted on August 25 that Thomas had returned to duty. Inspection reports for Jackson's Brigade continued to report him as under arrest, however, dating from August 15. The uncertain situation hung over Thomas and the Legion for months.[169]

The Legion braced for an attack. Levi's Battery was still at Strawberry Plains. All of Walker's Battalion was at Carter's Depot, along with a battery and some cavalry.[170] The

168.*O.R.* 30 (pt. 4): 521, 526-528, 536-537 (quote, 537), 540, 546-547, 554; Marvel, *Burnside*, 272; Stephen Whitaker to James Whitaker Sr., August 25, 1863, Whitaker Papers, NCOAH.

169. Terrell to Vance, February 22, 1864, Governors' Papers: Vance, 1862-1865, NCOAH; Stephen Whitaker to parents, August 2, 1863 (quote), Stephen Whitaker to James Whitaker, August 25, 1863, Whitaker Papers, NCOAH. There is confusion as to the date of Thomas's arrest. Terrell wrote in 1864 that it happened "[i]n June last [year]"; however, Thomas's service record gives the date as August 15. The information regarding the date of the arrest comes from three inspection reports dated November 24, 1863, December 12, 1863, January 12, 1864, and a fourth report that is undated. Service record file of William H. Thomas, Thomas's Legion, Compiled Military Service Records of Confederate Soldiers from the State of North Carolina (M270), reel 573. While there is a possibility that there was an earlier undocumented arrest, Terrell stated that "[t]his trial was interrupted by the Federal invasion," and noted that Thomas was then ordered on duty with the Indian companies; the latter relates to Thomas's activities in September, which ties the result of the trial to Burnside's movement into eastern Tennessee. On the other hand, Whitaker's August 2 letter has Thomas already under arrest at Knoxville. It is thus possible that, as Terrell remembered, Thomas may have been under arrest for some months before he went to trial, but for how long is unknown. Jackson, as will be shown, apparently refused to acknowledge the suspension of Thomas's trial.

170. "Record of Events": muster roll abstract, July-August 1863: Captain Levi's Battery Light Artillery, Thomas's Legion, Compiled Service Records of Confederate Soldiers from the State of North Carolina (M270),

Cherokee companies were sent to Strawberry Plains. The whereabouts of the rest of the Infantry Regiment are unknown; it was either concentrated at Jonesborough with Jackson, or scattered along the railroad in the northeastern part of the department.[171] The troops felt isolated, facing the advance of a large enemy force and surrounded by bushwhackers and Unionists. Whitaker wrote that "[t]he opinion is universal in camp that North Carolina Troops ort to Protect N.C. Soil & you needed not be Suprised if this thing is cared out before long we have all got tired of protecting those that will not protect them selves and if E Tenn is lost it will be E Tenn that will do it." Nevertheless, according to Whitaker morale was generally good and the troops were ready to defend their post.[172]

Rather than following Buckner's suggestion for a mutual strike on Burnside while he was still separated from Rosecrans, Bragg ordered Buckner to pull back that part of his command that was with him further southwest to Charleston, Tennessee, and the line of the Hiwassee River, in order to better cooperate. This move took Buckner out of his department, leaving him with the problem of how to direct its defense in his absence. The closest available commander was Maj. Gen. Samuel Jones in the Department of Western Virginia. Although reluctant to send troops to aid the Department of East Tennessee in the past, like it or not Jones was about to become very involved. Buckner requested on August 31 that Jones temporarily assume command of the section of southwestern Virginia that fell within the boundaries of Buckner's department. He informed Jones that Jackson was at Jonesborough and would contact Jones for orders. Buckner neglected to mention, however, that he was removing himself from virtually all contact with his department and with Jones, and taking the bulk of his command with him. Jones was preoccupied by a recent cavalry raid into his own department, which his forces successfully repulsed at White Sulphur Springs on August

reel 567; Stephen Whitaker to James Whitaker, Sr., August 25, 1863, Whitaker Papers, NCOAH. Whitaker wrote that "thar is 5 parts of co[m]panys her[e] belonging to Walkers Batt," which would seem to indicate that all five remaining companies of the battalion were at the depot. The reference to "parts of co[m]panys" probably reflects the depleted state of the companies in the battalion due to absences and desertions.

171. Stephen Whitaker to James Whitaker Sr., August 25, 1863, Whitaker Papers, NCOAH. Sgt. William J. Smathers of Company C, Infantry Regiment, wrote on August 21 that his company was at a place called "Fredom Tenn." William J. Smathers to G. F. Smathers, August 21, 1863, in Christopher M. Watford, ed., *The Mountains*, vol. 2 of *The Civil War in North Carolina: Soldiers' and Civilians' Letters and Diaries, 1861-1865* (Jefferson, NC: McFarland and Co. 2003), 120 (hereinafter cited as Watford, *The Civil War in North Carolina: The Mountains*).

172. Stephen Whitaker to James Whitaker, Sr., August 13 and 25 (quote), 1863, Whitaker Papers, NCOAH. On August 13, Whitaker wrote of returning eastern Tennessean parolees from Vicksburg that "they were not disheartened in the least & say they will not give up the strugle the negroes being armed has firded them up & more u[n]ited the South than ever." Black troops in the Federal army were much in the news at the time in which Whitaker wrote, due to their performance in the Port Hudson campaign in May and at Milliken's Bend in Louisiana in June, and by the famous attack by the 54th Regiment Massachusetts Infantry on Battery Wagner in the harbor of Charleston, South Carolina, in July. See Robertson, *Soldiers Blue and Gray*, 30-36; Lawrence Lee Hewitt, *Port Hudson: Confederate Bastion on the Mississippi* (1987; reprt., Baton Rouge: Lousiana State University Paperback Edition, 1994), 147-150, 175-179; Joseph T. Glathaar, *Forged in Battle: The Civil War Alliance of Black Soldiers and White Officers* (New York: The Free Press, 1991), 68-70, 123-141, 155-159; Hattaway, *Shades of Blue and Gray*, 158-160. Whitaker's remarks that the Vicksburg parolees from eastern Tennessee were eager to continue fighting do not seem to be supported by the evidence; certainly the units involved never regained their strength, as many soldiers failed to return to the ranks. See Groce, *Mountain Rebels*, 102-103; *O.R.* 30 (pt. 2): 482, (pt. 4): 560.

26-27. He evidently assumed that Buckner was still concentrating in the Knoxville area, and merely wanted him to take over in southwestern Virginia for administrative and operational convenience.[173]

Even before Buckner approached Jones, Jackson was already turning to the latter for assistance. Around August 28, Jackson asked that Jones send reinforcements. He reported Burnside's advance towards Knoxville, and added that "[o]n their return, I apprehend they will come this way [Jonesborough]." Jones declined to part with any of his men, due to the recent cavalry raid; he promised, however, to have Brig. Gen. John S. Williams, the officer in his department nearest to Jackson, placed on alert. It appears, however, that he waited at least two days (August 30) to do so. In the meantime, Buckner ordered Jackson to fall back to Bristol, and report to Jones for further orders. Jackson asked whether he should destroy the Carter's Depot and Strawberry Plains railroad bridges as he withdrew. By this time, Jones had received Buckner's request to assume local command. Jones informed Jackson that he should hold the bridges if possible, and that he was dispatching reinforcements. On September 1, he finally sent Williams to Bristol with whatever forces he could gather to Jackson's aid. Buckner, meanwhile, was gradually shifted even further south by Bragg. He eventually joined the rest of the Army of Tennessee in northern Georgia, where it had retreated after Rosecrans maneuvered Bragg out of Chattanooga on September 8.[174]

On September 2, advance elements of Burnside's forces reached Knoxville. The general himself arrrived the next day, receiving a joyous welcome from much of the local population, which was steadfastly Unionist. The railroad line was now cut, making proposals circulating among the Confederate authorities to reinforce Bragg with elements of Lee's Army of Northern Virginia uncertain.[175] One immediate result of the enemy advance was Thomas's abandonment of Strawberry Plains and eastern Tennessee. On September 1, a small party of Federal troops burned the railroad bridge at Flat Creek, four miles below Strawberry Plains. According to Stringfield's sister Mary, that night "Col Thomas seeing the light and believing the 'Philistines' were soon to be upon him skedaddled with his indians and one company of dismounted cavalry."[176] Thomas's departure was noted by Unionists in

173. *O.R.* 29 (pt. 2): 662-669, 674-675, 677-680 (quote, 680), 30 (pt. 2): 603, (pt. 4): 547, 562, 565-572, 575, 586-587.

174. *O.R.* 29 (pt. 2): 678, 680, 30 (pt. 4): 603; Connelly, *Autumn of Glory*, 149-150, 162-173; Woodworth, *Six Armies in Tennessee*, 54-66.

175. *O.R.* 30 (pt. 2): 548; Connelly, *Autumn of Glory*, 150-152; Crow, *Storm in the Mountains*, 23, 38; Marvel, *Burnside*, 276-277; Woodworth, *Six Armies in Tennessee*, 50-52, 65-66.

176. Mary Stringfield to Stringfield, September 3, November 26 (quote), 1863, Stringfield Papers, NCOAH. Mary Stringfield, evidently not much of an admirer of Thomas, wrote on September 3 of the Federal party at Flat Creek that "[t]here were only 12 men up at the bridge but nobody knew about it." The identity of the dismounted cavalry unit that escaped with Thomas is unknown. The exact date of the burning of the Flat Creek bridge and of Thomas's withdrawal from Strawberry Plains are a bit uncertain, as neither event is mentioned directly in surviving official correspondence. On November 26, Mary Stringfield wrote: "The last Confederate soldier was withdrawn from this place on September second when a small party of Federals approached within four miles below and burnt flat creek bridge." However, in her earlier letter of September 3, she wrote that "Col Thomas left here night before last when the federals burnt flat Creek bridge." This implies that Thomas left Strawberry Plains on the night of September 1-2; if the time of the departure was after midnight (which may have been the case, given that it would take some time to get the command ready to take the road after hearing the news of the bridge

Sevier County, who sent word to Knoxville. "[T]is said a party came in and cut off Col T.s retreat," she added. "I dont know and dont much believe it."[177]

Instead of moving to rejoin Jackson at Bristol, Thomas headed towards the North Carolina mountains and home. Col. Felix W. Graham and several companies of his 5th Regiment Indiana Cavalry followed to the area of Sevierville, but for some reason turned back to Knoxville. On September 6, he started out again. Somewhere in the vicinity of Gatlinburg, he found Thomas's camp; it is possible that the opposing forces skirmished, although the - evidence is murky. Local Unionists failed to block the way out, however, so Thomas escaped with the loss of only one captured. "They won't fight," Graham complained on September 8, "and the country is so mountainous it is almost impossible to capture them." Returning to Sevierville via Fair Garden, Graham decided to reshoe his horses and capture some nearby Confederate supplies before setting out again. While there, he received instructions from Burnside's assistant adjutant general, Col. George B. Drake, dated September 7: if Graham had a "clear or fair prospect" of overtaking Thomas's group, "and a good prospect of success after having overtaken it, you can keep on and do your best to capture and break up the band," but if he could not do either within two to three days, he was to return to Sevierville and thence to Greeneville. Already at Sevierville, Graham pursued the latter course and reached Greeneville on September 10.[178]

Thomas and Companies A and B of the Infantry Regiment eventually reached Quallatown. Exactly why Thomas acted as he did became a matter of fresh controversy

---

burning), it would reconcile her statements as to the dating of the incidents. In Thomas's notebook there is an incomplete draft for a note written at Bryant's Ferry on September 2 to a "Captain Line." Thomas wrote "I came with my troops to this place this morning. I will remain until my supply arrives from the Plains. The Yankees have possesion of Knoxville and up to Flat Creek." Thomas Notebook, September 2 [90-91], NCOAH. Thus, it is likely that Thomas left Strawberry Plains late on the night of September 1-2 rather than that of September 2-3.

177. Mary Stringfield to Stringfield, September 3, 1863, Stringfield Papers, NCOAH.

178. Judging from regimental and company records, Companies B, C, D, E ("Made two trips to the Smoky Mountains after Indians"), F, H, K, and L of the 5th Indiana Cavalry participated in the pursuit. Vernon H. Crow wrote that Graham attacked Thomas's camp and that the Cherokees withdrew after a sharp skirmish. His cited source was Graham's September 8 message from Sevierville, quoted above; Graham did not, however, specifically mention a clash. Thomas implied in December 1863 to the *Asheville News* that there was some sort of fight, but his brief sketch was hyperbolic to say the least. He claimed that the Indians "held two regiments of the enemy in check, and prevented them from passing into Jackson county, and thence to Asheville, as they probably would have done." Thomas of course was not privy to Graham's orders and did not know that his companies were the actual target, nor did he know the size of the opposing force. Stringfield wrote after the war that "[t]he same day that General Burnside occupied Knoxville, Colonel Thomas, with several hundred men, fell back from Strawberry Plains, passing through Sevierville to the North Carolina line, taking all the Indians and many whites. He was closely followed by the Federals and had quite a skirmish near Sevierville, on 7 or 8 September, 1863." In addition to the lack of explicit information concerning combat in Graham's report, none of the company records for the 5th Regiment Indiana Cavalry mentioned a clash, and there are no known references to one in wartime documents or personal papers associated with the Legion other than Thomas's letter. It therefore must be questioned whether Graham actually attacked the camp or if the Indians departed at or prior to his approach. At best, there might have been some skirmishing between the Federal cavalry and Thomas's rear guard. *O.R.* 30 (pt. 3): 437 (Drake quotes), 473-474 (Graham quote, 474), 501; *O.R. (Supplement)*, Pt. II, 27: 304, 309, 315 ("Made two trips" quote), 320, 326, 332, 343, 349; Stringfield, "Sixty-Ninth Regiment," in Clark, *North Carolina Regiments*, 3:738-739; Thomas to the editors of the *Asheville News*, December 25, 1863, published in the *Asheville News*, January 21, 1864, reprinted in the *Western Democrat* (Charlotte), January 26, 1864; Crow, *Storm in the Mountains*, 50, 244 n. 61.

between him and Jackson. According to Thomas, he was acting under orders by either Bragg or Buckner to defend the passes and raise a new battalion using the Indian companies as a nucleus. In a letter written to the *Asheville News* in December and in an unfinished draft to Allen T. Davidson in January of the following year, Thomas claimed that he was ordered by Buckner to take the Indians to western North Carolina and defend the locals. In the newspaper letter, he claimed that Bragg subsequently assigned him to the command of Brig. Gen. Robert Brank Vance, the governor's brother. In the Davidson draft, Thomas mentioned an October 12, 1863 letter that he wrote to Buckner about the defenseless state of western North Carolina, and added that Bragg had ordered him to report to Vance, implying that Bragg's orders were in response to the letter to Buckner. In a January 1864 letter to President Davis, Thomas repeated the claim that he fell back to the mountains under orders, although he did not specify whose, and that Bragg then assigned him to Vance.[179] "By an order from General Bragg while in command of the department of Tenn," Thomas wrote Adjutant and Inspector General Cooper in July 1864, "I was authorized to increase my Indian force as far as practicable 'to defend the passes in the Smoky Mountains extending along a line over one hundred miles in length and for the protection of Western North Carolina.'" In November 1863, Brigadier General Vance received a letter from Thomas containing copies of Bragg's orders permitting Thomas to expand his force.[180] Over time, these different explanations blurred. The March 1864 inspection report for Jackson's Brigade noted the absence of Thomas and Companies A and B "it is claimed under orders of Gnls Bragg & Buckner & Vance." That phrase, "it is claimed," is telling; so far as the records of Jackson's Brigade were concerned, Thomas and the men with him had been "cut off" by Burnside's arrival on the railroad.[181] James W. Terrell also reported to the Charlotte *Western Democrat* in October 1863 that Thomas, the Indian companies "and a few white men" were cut off and rumored to be defending the Smoky Mountain passes.[182] As noted earlier, however, brigade inspection reports listed Thomas as under arrest from August 15 through at least the next few months, overlapping with the period where he was operating in North Carolina on the supposed authority of superiors.

179. Thomas to the editors of the *Asheville News*, December 25, 1863, published in the *Asheville News*, January 21, 1864, reprinted in the *Western Democrat* (Charlotte), January 26, 1864; Thomas to Allen T. Davidson, January 22, 1864 (unfinished draft), Thomas Papers, DU; Thomas to Davis, January 25, 1863, Letters Received by the Confederate Adjutant and Inspector General's Office (M474), reel 146, item 169-T-1864.

180. Thomas to "General" (Samuel Cooper), July 8, 1864, unbound letterbook, Thomas Papers, DU. See also Thomas to William C. Walker, November 8, 1863, Whitaker Papers, NCOAH; Thomas to Governor Vance, January 24, 1864, Governors' Papers: Vance, 1862-1865, NCOAH; Thomas to John C. Breckinridge, April 27, 1864, Thomas Papers, DU.

181. Inspection Report, 4th Brigade (Jackson's Brigade), Buckner's Division, Army of East Tennessee, March 31, 1864, Inspection Reports Received by the Confederate Adjutant and Inspector General's Office (M935), reel 2, file 10-A-1, RG 109, NA. Numerous men reported absent or absent without leave from the Legion during the fall of 1863 were recorded in the rolls with some variation of the phrase "supposed to have reported to Col. Thomas, who was cut off with a portion of the Command in the evacution of E[ast] Tenn[essee]." Service record files, Thomas's Legion, Compiled Service Records of Confederate Soldiers from the State of North Carolina (M270), reels 567 through 574; see also p. 55 above.

182. James W. Terrell to the Editor, October 19, 1863, published in the *Western Democrat* (Charlotte), November 10, 1863.

To say that the official situation in regards to Thomas's presence in western North Carolina was and remains confused is an understatement.[183] No copies of Buckner's orders to Thomas seem to have survived. It is possible that Buckner gave them at the same time that he charged Jackson to fall back to the western North Carolina mountains as a last resort; it is also possible that no orders were given to Thomas personally, but that he acted on his own initiative based on Buckner's instructions to Jackson. In one sense it seems strange that Buckner would issue such orders to Thomas, given his earlier unenthusiastic appraisal of the troops from western North Carolina and eastern Tennessee in his department and his desire to have them transferred to other theaters. Of course, military exigency had to be considered, and given the location of Jackson's Brigade at the time of the invasion, Buckner really had no other choice of troops if that was in fact his goal. The question remains, though: why did not Buckner order Thomas to fall back up the railroad and rejoin the bulk of Jackson's command? It is possible that Buckner considered that the Indians might be more useful at mountain fighting and scouting rather than the more traditional type of warfare which was about to ensue, or that Thomas was sent to North Carolina due to Mallett's recommendation to Seddon to temporarily send two companies from Jackson's Brigade to the mountains to catch deserters and protect conscription officers; the late August rumors of a move by the Indian companies to North Carolina should again be kept in mind. If so, however, why were instructions or explanations seemingly never offered to Jackson by Buckner or Seddon, at least in the period following the immediate crisis? It would have been more usual in such a case for Buckner to issue orders to Jackson, explaining what he wanted Thomas to carry out; certainly if the authorization came through the Secretary of War, some clarification should have been forwarded to the brigadier. Given Thomas's relationship with Jackson, his recent arrest and trial postponement, and his desire to return with the Legion to western North Carolina, the possibility must be considered that Thomas may have taken advantage of circumstances and acted on his own, or at least exceeded the scope and duration of his orders.

As for Bragg, no copies of his orders to Thomas appear to have survived, either. Robert B. Vance received copies of the order from Thomas in November, but why did Thomas only, and not Vance himself, receive copies directly from Bragg?[184] The closest to an

183. Lieutenant Colonel Walker's son, Columbus F. Walker, who was sergeant major of the battalion, perhaps expressed it best when he wrote of the similar confusion regarding his father after he returned home ill to North Carolina in the summer or fall of 1863 and later began to operate with Thomas and his local command: "Father it seems after he got up a squad of men felt himself subject to the orders of Superior officers in Tenn[.] I say this from the fact that at one time during the fall of 1863 he sent Capt R. A. Akin to Missionary Ridge to see Genl Bragg. Capt Akin told me of this only a day or so ago. he said that Bragg sent orders to father to report to Genl R. B. Vance at Asheville N.C. At an other time as you will see from Genl Vaughn's orders that he was expected to join him (Vaughn) at other times it seems that father Co-operated with and was subject to Col. Thomas orders. Yet Col Love as you see expected him to return to Virginia. So as you see the matter is hard to understand." Columbus F. Walker to Stringfield, September 4, 1895, Stringfield Papers, WCU.

184. According to Vernon H. Crow, Bragg later denied issuing the orders. Crow, *Storm in the Mountains*, 52. His citation (245 n. 73) referred to a December 1863 letter from Robert Vance to Thomas regarding the receipt of Bragg's orders. It is possible that Crow was thinking of an endorsement on a letter from Capt. C. C. Berry of Company A, Walker's Battalion, to Adjutant and Inspector General Cooper asking for reinstatment following his having been dropped from the rolls for prolonged absence of leave. Berry had been sent to gather up absentees from his company and was returning to eastern Tennessee when he was ordered by his immediate superior,

official confirmation of Thomas's activities is in a February 1864 letter from Lieutenant Colonel Love, in which he noted that Thomas and the Indian companies "are being reported as being on detached duty."[185] This still does not explain the lack of official recognition in the brigade's inspection reports, or why Thomas was reported as under arrest for the next several months. Furthermore, Capt. James W. Terrell claimed in February 1864 that when Jackson found out that Terrell was heading to western North Carolina to pay the Indian companies, he protested and got a revocation of the order. Fortunately for the Indians, Jackson moved too slowly and Terrell completed his mission. Upon his return, Terrell was questioned by Jackson about whether or not the captains of the Indian companies had not received official instructions to return to the department.[186] The fact that Thomas was not subsequently seized by the authorities and charged with desertion seems to indicate that his actions had some tacit approval, at least after the fact. In the end, the questions over Thomas's movement to western North Carolina reflects the confused command structure in the region, with the attendant difficulties posed by the local geography. The revolving chain of command from Buckner to Jones to James Longstreet in eastern Tennessee, from Vance to John B. Palmer in western North Carolina, and the more distant influences of Bragg and his successors, coupled with the problems of record-keeping posed by the campaign, all may have contributed; it is simply possible that orders were issued directly to no one else but Thomas by Buckner and Bragg. Regardless of the degree that it was officially sanctioned, the movement to western North Carolina afforded Thomas the opportunity to begin building a new version of the Legion away from Jackson's direct interference.

While Thomas withdrew from Strawberry Plains, the rest of the Legion remained with Jackson at Bristol. Jackson's nervousness, already evident before the arrival of Burnside, now began to approach panic. On September 4, he wired Adjutant and Inspector General Cooper directly, reporting the loss of telegraph service west of Jonesborough due to the flight of the operator at Greeneville, and the capture of a train and some grain at Morristown; the railroad, however, seemed to be intact (he was evidently unaware of the burning of the bridge at Flat Creek, as well as the destruction of the bridge at Loudon on

---

Lieutenant Colonel Walker, to remain with his men and defend Cherokee County; Walker (who, although Berry did not mention it, was acting under orders from Thomas), claimed that they were authorized by Bragg to operate under Vance and that all of his men and officers present in western North Carolina were to report to him. Bragg's endorsement of Berry's letter ran as follows: "Having no records of the Dept with me & my memory not serving, cannot say particularly whether such order was given. But I do not believe there was any such authority from my office." Berry's letter and supporting documents only dealt with his orders from Walker and the consequences, and did not directly mention Thomas's orders; Bragg's comments were specifically a denial that he instructed any of Thomas's absentees and their officers to operate in the area in this manner rather than returning to Jackson's Brigade as was originally expected. Thus, the issue of Bragg's authorization to Thomas to remain in North Carolina and raise more Indian companies remains an open question. Bragg, August 24, 1864, endorsement on letter from C. C. Berry to Cooper, June 5, 1864, Letters Received by the Confederate Adjutant and Inspector General's Office (M474), reel 96, item 2167-B-1864. Additional items related to Berry's case, including various orders from Walker, are included in the same file; see especially the contents of the letter from Berry to Cooper cited above; Special Order No. _, Headquarters, Forces of Cherokee, N.C. (extract), paragraph VI, November 19, 1864; William C. Walker to Berry, November 26, 1863; and Walker to Berry, December 4, 1863.

185. Love to Thomas, February 28, 1864, Thomas Papers, DU.

186. Terrell to Thomas, February 5, 1864, Thomas Papers, WCU (microfilm, Thomas Papers, DU).

September 2 by Buckner's rear guard). Jackson sent a cavalry detachment along the railroad west of Greeneville to see how far the telegraph was undamaged, and to burn the railroad bridge at Lick Creek "if necessary" to delay the Federals. "Hope re-inforcments will arrive soon, otherwise Tennessee will be overrun by bushwhackers," he wrote.[187]

Jackson's communication caused consternation in Richmond, which was receiving contradictory reports from a variety of sources about the developing situation. When it arrived on September 5, Jefferson Davis wrote that "[t]he Yankees are not coming by the railroad, and I do not see the necessity for burning the bridge if it be a railroad bridge, of which I am not informed. It would be well to caution General Jackson against anything which will interfere with our use of the railroad." Cooper wired Jackson the same day to "[i]n no event destroy the railroad bridge . . . nor do anything to prevent our use of the railroad."[188] These instructions were beside the point. The Federal presence at Knoxville and surrounding points already interdicted traffic across a crucial segment of the railroad network, and at least two bridges were already destroyed. Moreover, even if Davis was thinking only in terms of that part of the railroad east of Knoxville and its possible use for local operations, he was wrong in another sense: the Yankees *were*, in fact, coming by the railroad, and had done so already between the time that Jackson telegraphed and the arrival of his message in Richmond. On the night of September 4, two trainloads of Federals occupied Jonesborough. The next morning, they continued up the tracks to Carter's Depot. Facing them was a Confederate force under Lieutenant Colonel Love consisting of elements of the Infantry Regiment of Thomas's Legion, McClung's Tennessee Light Artillery Company, a cavalry detachment of some seventy-five men, and possibly some Tennessee Home Guard units. The Federals demanded that the garrison surrender in the name of Burnside, but were refused. Jackson, expecting a fight, promised Cooper that he would hold the bridges.[189] On the same date, Jones arrived at

187. *O.R.* 30 (pt. 1): 577, (pt. 3): 333, (pt. 4): 598 (quotes).

188. *O.R.* 30 (pt. 4): 598-599. Davis's curiosity was now piqued about Jackson. Davis's aide-de-camp, Col. William Preston Johnston, reported on the troop strength and conditions in the department on September 5 and sketched in some brief details of Jackson's antebellum life and prior service. "I make these statements because you were not fully satisfied what General Jackson it was," Johnston wrote in what was not exactly the most ringing of endorsements. "I hear that he has a very complete topographical knowledge of the country, but is a very nervous person under responsibility, although undoubtedly brave and energetic." Ibid., 30 (pt. 4): 602.

189. Stringfield, War Diary (copy), September 5, 1863, ledger book, 177-178, Stringfield Papers, NCOAH; *O.R.* 30 (pt. 3), 358-359, (pt. 4): 604, 607, 617; Crow, *Storm in the Mountains*, 40, 243 n. 17 and 18. As the following text and notes show, there are major difficulties in understanding what elements of Thomas's Legion were active in the operations of the next few days, as well as the identities of other units mentioned in various accounts. In his recopied diary, Stringfield claimed that he came from Zollicoffer to Carter's Depot on the morning of September 5 to take command of the post; however, wartime papers indicate that Lieutenant Colonel Love was present at Carter's Depot by some point in the day. Possibly Stringfield led an advance party to the depot prior to Love's arrival. Stringfield mentioned the presence of Companies F and K of the Infantry Regiment at Carter's Depot. Lt. Col. Milton A. Haynes, who commanded the artillery in Jackson's subsequent movement down the railroad, claimed that "our whole force was at Bristol" on September 6, the day that Jackson departed for Jonesborough (*O.R.* 30 [pt. 2]: 643). This was not totally accurate, as Jackson had forces guarding the various railroad depots and bridges. The only Legion companies to record their activities on the muster rolls for this period were Companies A, B, and C of Walker's Battalion; all three were at Bristol with Jackson prior to his advance. While the battalion was probably concentrated at Bristol, the regiment may have been scattered anywhere between there and Zollicoffer. Exactly how much of the regiment concentrated over the next few days

Dublin, Virginia, and learned that Buckner was gone from the department with most of his troops.[190] Jones scrambled to orchestrate a defense. Without waiting for orders from Richmond, he rushed to Abingdon. He was not impressed by the forces available to him, later describing Frazer's force at Cumberland Gap and Jackson's Brigade as "[t]wo brigades, or what were called brigades." Jones later estimated Jackson's total force, including the remainder of the Legion, as "about 900 men." Jefferson Davis had meanwhile sent his aide-de-camp, Col. William Preston Johnston, to assess the situation. Reaching Dublin before Jones, Johnston gave the brigade's strength as approximately 1,300, although these may well have included men scattered along the railroad and various other posts. By now, orders were on their way confirming Jones as temporary commander of southwestern Virginia and that part of Tennessee east of Knoxville.[191]

---

is uncertain, although Companies C, E, and H evidently took an active role. In addition to the units mentioned in the text, Stringfield noted the presence of "some home guards, under White and McClain," and "Jones, Water and Brown Cavalry" that are otherwise unidentified. This section of Stringfield's diary no longer exists in the original, but was recopied by him into his ledger book. Since it can not be checked against the original entry, it is possible that the references to the units at Carter's Depot are later interpolations. In his history of the Infantry Regiment in Clark, *North Carolina Regiments*, 3:739, Stringfield reported setting out in pursuit of the Federals the next day with a force that included "a battalion of cavalry (McLin) under Captain D. D Anderson." John B. McLin had been colonel of the 1st Regiment East Tennessee Cavalry (Rogers's)/2nd Regiment Tennessee Cavalry (McLin's), later reduced in size to the 2nd Battalion Tennessee Cavalry/13th Battalion Tennessee Cavalry; it had metamorphosed into the 5th Regiment Tennessee Cavalry (McKenzie's) by the time of the East Tennessee campaign. McLin was relieved of command in August of the previous year. Presumably, Stringfield intended some portion of the 5th Tennessee Cavalry in his reference to a battalion under McLin, although there is no record of a D. D. Anderson with that command; furthermore, the regiment was part of the force that had departed with Buckner. Whether the "Jones, Water and Brown Cavalry" reference also related to the 5th Tennessee Cavalry is unclear, as two companies of Rogers's 1st Regiment were commanded by men named Jones and Brown; however, those companies had transferred out when the regiment was reduced to a battalion. Furthermore, another early company had been commanded by a man named White, and McLin (Stringfield's McClain?) had originally been a company commander prior to promotion; the similarity to the names of Stringfield's "home guard" commanders is striking (Tennessee Civil War Centennial Commission, *Tennesseans in the Civil War*, 1:48-49, 64). If the references in the recopied diary are interpolations, then it is possible that Stringfield did not remember the names of the actual units and commanders present, and drew upon dim memories of other units and officers of his acquaintance. That certainly seems to have been the case with the reference to McLin's Battalion, although it is possible that D. D. Anderson was the officer of an obscure independent cavalry company. The matter is far from conclusive, however, and perhaps all of the names mentioned belonged to commanders of units that are simply not identifiable. It should be noted that in his report of the campaign, Jones wrote that the Federals "were checked by the gallantry and good conduct of Capt. H. L. McClung and his small bridge guard of some 150 men," without any reference paid to the role of the Legion. *O.R.* 30 (pt. 2): 604; it is thus also possible that Stringfield's "McClain" was McClung, rather than McLin.

190. That Jones only now learned this important fact is a graphic illustration of the command and communication problems between both the various Confederate commanders within the region and with Richmond.

191. *O.R.* 30 (pt. 2): 603 (quote), (pt. 4): 602-604, 606, 616-617. Jones made similar criticisms of Jackson's Brigade in letters to Seddon and Cooper dated September 12 and September 14 respectively. To the former, he wrote that Frazer's and Jackson's brigades were "represented to me that they are made up of the most inferior troops and cannot be relied on. . . . General Jackson reports his brigade 1,300 strong, but I am informed that it is utterly unreliable." For some reason, Jones wrote, a second, shorter letter to Seddon on the same day, using almost identical language; he repeated the charges to Cooper. Ibid., 30 (pt. 4): 644-645 (quote, 644), 649. Johnston estimated the total troops available to Jones (exclusive of Frazer's command at Cumberland Gap, which he did not list) as 3,361, "many of them being irregular in their organization and loose in their discipline." He felt, however, that they could potentially be of use if properly directed. Ibid., 30 (pt. 4): 603-604.

Meanwhile, the Federals in front of Carter's Depot withdrew during the night of September 5. The Confederate cavalry at the station pursued, possibly supported by a portion of the Infantry Regiment under Stringfield, who claimed later to have commanded the horsemen also. They found no sign of their opponents. By 9 A.M. they reached Jonesborough. Stringfield enjoyed the greeting he received, as he "galloped through the town, midst the Smiles and Cheers of beautiful women & waving of handkerchiefs." Local Confederate loyalists reported that the Federals had rounded up many of their fellows as prisoners and taken them off. Stringfield stayed in Jonesborough and that night picketed the area below town.[192] Jackson departed Bristol on September 6 with a force that included Walker's Battalion, the 4th Regiment Kentucky Cavalry, the 16th Battalion Georgia Cavalry, Burrough's Tennessee Battery, and most or all of the remainder of the Infantry Regiment. He arrived at Jonesborough the following morning. Confederate sympathizers reported that the Federals had promised local Unionists that they would return on September 8.[193]

On the same day that Jackson reached Jonesborough, Lt. Col. Edwin L. Hayes led a detachment of 300 men from the 100th Regiment Ohio Infantry along the railroad from Greeneville for Jonesborough. Jackson, meanwhile, started down the railroad some time early in the morning of September 8. The composition of his force is unknown, beyond the 4th Regiment Kentucky Cavalry, and a six-pounder gun which he ordered to join him at 2 A.M.[194] The two sides collided at Telford's Station. Lt. Col. Milton Haynes, who commanded

192. Stringfield, War Diary (copy), September 6, 1863, ledger book, 178, Stringfield Papers, NCOAH; *O.R.* 30 (pt. 2): 643. In his history of the Infantry Regiment, Stringfield wrote after the war that he was accompanied by 200 men from that unit in his pursuit, although in the rewritten diary entry he mentioned only taking cavalry. Stringfield, "Sixty-Ninth Regiment," in Clark, *North Carolina Regiments*, 3:739. Whether Companies F and K totaled 200 men at that point is doubtful, so if his recollections were accurate it is likely that other companies had arrived by this time, or were simply not mentioned to begin with. Although Stringfield had brief experience as a non-commissioned cavalry officer, his claims here and elsewhere of assuming overall command of the various cavalry units involved in the operations of the next few days seems doubtful, especially as it would take him away from his duties with the Legion. He might well in this instance have been placed in charge of a pursuing force consisting of companies from the regiment in addition to cavalry, however.

193. Stringfield, War Diary (copy), September 7, 1863, ledger book, 178, Stringfield Papers, NCOAH; "Record of Events": muster roll abstracts, September-October 1863: Companies A, B, and C, and January-February 1864: Company A, Walker's Battalion, Thomas's Legion, Compiled Military Service Records of Confederate Soldiers from the State of North Carolina (M270), reel 567. Curiously, Stringfield did not note the arrival of Walker's Battalion or any portion of the Infantry Regiment at Jonesborough, beyond a vague "& c" following his list of units accompanying Jackson. Only the records of Companies A, B, and C, of Walker's Battalion noted their roles in the September-October musters; however, the January-February 1864 roll for Company A mentioned the participation of Companies E and H also. Corp. George W. Loudermilk of Company H was reported killed in action at Limestone Bridge; however, the date given for his death is September 1, which if not a mistake may indicate that he was killed as Jackson withdrew up the railroad at the beginning of the month. None of the companies of the Infantry Regiment recorded their roles. The presence of Companies F and K at Carter's Depot has already been noted (p. 79 n. 189), and Stringfield mentioned the roles of Companies C, E, and H in the action of September 8 in his diary (p. 82 n. 196), but it is unclear whether they came with Jackson or had already arrived. The whereabouts of Companies D, G, and I are unknown; they may have been left behind to guard the railroad, or they may have been present.

194. Lt. Col. Milton Haynes, who commanded Jackson's artillery on the expedition, reported that the 4th Regiment Kentucky Cavalry was already in action when he arrived with the rest of the guns later in the morning. In his recopied diary, Stringfield claimed to have commanded the cavalry during the action. It is unlikely,

the Confederate artillery, had been left in charge at Jonesborough. He soon received word to send two infantry companies to the front; these were probably Companies E and H of the Infantry Regiment.[195]

Around 8 A.M., Haynes received a fresh message from Jackson to bring "all your artillery and all the infantry except one company."[196] Haynes's force proceeded to Telford's,

---

however, that Jackson would supersede Col. H. L. Giltner of the 4th Kentucky Cavalry with a major from another branch of service. Perhaps Stringfield led the small cavalry force from Carter's Depot as an advance party or skirmish line, as he claimed to have done the day before ("I Commanded the Cavalry. I went on Picket to Leesburg at daylight, thence across to Telfords"), although even this seems improbable as it would take him away from his duties with the regiment (see also n. 192 above). *O.R.* 30 (pt. 2): 578, 643; Stringfield, War Diary (copy), September 8, 1863, ledger book, 178-179, Stringfield Papers, NCOAH. Haynes reported Hayes's force as 450. *O.R.* 30 (pt. 2): 644.

195. In his recopied diary entry, Stringfield wrote that "Cooper['s] & Welch['s] Co[s.] did their duty." These were Companies H and E of the Infantry Regiment respectively; as Walker's Battalion seems not to have gone into action until later, it is likely that these were the companies involved (however, see n. 196 for problems in identifying the respective roles of the regiment and the battalion in the day's action). The time that the fighting started is uncertain. Haynes wrote that "early in the morning I heard the sound of artillery and then of small-arms"; it was after this that he received the order to foward the infantry companies. All of this happened before 8 A.M. In his regimental history, Stringfield wrote that it "was ordered up by General Jackson and at 3:00 A.M. on the 8th, we drove them from Telford's Depot"; however, there is no other evidence to support the idea of a night assault, which besides contradicts Stringfield's diary entry that he left at daybreak, and then moved through Leesburg to Telford's Station. Furthermore, Haynes's account seems to indicate that all of the infantry was left with him at Jonesborough until Jackson began to call for it after the fighting started. *O.R.* 30 (pt. 2): 643 (Haynes quote); Stringfield, War Diary (copy), September 8, 1863, ledger book, 179, Stringfield Papers, NCOAH; Stringfield, "Sixty-Ninth Regiment," in Clark, *North Carolina Regiments*, 3:739.

196. Haynes wrote that his artillery was followed by "Lieutenant-Colonel Walker's battalion, North Carolina volunteers, 300 strong." Later in his report, however, he recorded how "Colonel Walker's men" were positioned on one side of the Confederate line as skirmishers, while "McKamy's battalion" was on the right in support of Haynes's artillery. Maj. James A. McKamy was second-in-command of Walker's Battalion; according to Stringfield's diary entry for September 8, he commanded the battalion during the fighting, or at least a portion of it ("Of troops engaged were Major McKamy with 100 of our battalion"). If this was the case, who were the soldiers referred to as "Walker's men" deployed on the opposite side of the road? It seems that Haynes viewed Walker's Battalion and "McKamy's battalion" as two different units. While it is possible that "Walker's men" were one or more detached companies from the battalion, with the 100 men referred to by Stringfield constituting the remainder, it is likelier that the companies acting as skirmishers were from the Infantry Regiment, and that Haynes confused Walker with Love. While Stringfield did not mention Walker's presence in his diary entries for September 8 and 9, he did note McKamy's role in the September 8 entry and those of both Love and McKamy on September 9, when he wrote a bit more about the fight. Love's presence is also suggested by a communication between Jones and Brig. Gen. John S. Williams on September 9 concerning Love's assessment of Federal troop activities at Fullen's Station, west of Limestone Bridge. Further, McKamy's command of the battalion argues for Walker's absence, unless McKamy was placed in charge of one wing while Walker handled the rest. Walker went home due to health problems some time in 1863, but the date of his departure is unknown. He was reported to be on assignment gathering up absentees beginning on September 29; however, long after the war his son remembered that he went home in the summer, so it is unclear if his mission coincided with his departure, or if he was given the task while already on furlough. The lack of mention of the Infantry Regiment by Haynes is striking, as there seems to be no doubt that at least some companies were present. In his diary, Stringfield reported that Companies E and H of the regiment fought well; on September 9, he added Company C to the list of participants as well. Thus, Walker's Battalion and at least three companies from the Infantry Regiment were present on September 8, unless Stringfield's comments were postwar additions when he recopied the diary. In attempting to synthesize the wartime and postwar evidence, Vernon H. Crow concluded that the Infantry Regiment pushed the Federals out of Telford's Station in the morning during Jackson's initial advance, while

where they found only the wounded; the Federals had already retired, and Jackson was now in pursuit. Continuing down the railroad, about 9 A.M. they heard artillery gunfire from the direction of Limestone Bridge, a few miles west of Telford's. Upon arrival, Haynes found the 4th Regiment Kentucky Cavalry under its commander, Col. H. W. Giltner, in action dismounted against the Federals on the opposite side of Limestone Creek. Giltner's men had gotten around to the rear of the Ohioans, effectively blocking them in; to further isolate them, the Confederates destroyed some six miles of the railroad track running westward to prevent easy reinforcement. Hayes's men had taken refuge in a blockhouse and some brick and stone buildings, all of which provided ideal protection. They detached some skirmishers to occupy a patch of woods which lay in front of the blockhouse on the side facing the bulk of Jackson's command, including the Legion, a thousand yards away. The Federals also may have constructed some entrenchments in the area around the buildings.[197]

While Giltner's Kentuckians kept Hayes's Ohioans focused westward, Haynes put his guns into position. Shortly afterwards, the Legion infantry arrived; identified by Haynes as Lieutenant Colonel Walker and his battalion, it may actually have been Lieutenant Colonel Love with the regiment and battalion together. The infantry were worn out after their rapid march, so Haynes suggested that they take a half-hour rest. "As soon as Colonel Walker's men had rested they deployed as skirmishers to the left to clear the woods, and Major McKamy's battalion on the right to sustain the battery," Haynes wrote in a passage that indicates some confusion on his part in regards to the composition of the Legion forces present.[198] Supported by the fire of Haynes's guns, the infantry advanced into the woods about 1:30 P.M., driving back the Federal skirmishers. "With a shout and a hurrah for the Bonnie Blue Flag, the North Carolina boys made the charge, and the enemy fled before them," Haynes reported. They were joined by the dismounted Kentuckians. The Federals were now trapped in the buildings, from which they kept up a heavy fire. Haynes then brought Burrough's Battery and Giltner's horse artillery up to pound the enemy positions from closer range. Eventually, the Ohioans had enough and surrendered about 4 P.M., with only a company that had been earlier detached to Lick Creek and some twenty other men escaping.[199]

Walker's Battalion went into action in the afternoon at Limestone Bridge. This is certainly a viable interpretation to the problems caused by the evidence, but not the only one. *O.R.* 30 (pt. 2): 643-644; Stringfield, War Diary (copy), September 8, September 9, 1863, ledger book, 179, Stringfield Papers, NCOAH; Stringfield, "Sixty-Ninth Regiment," Clark, *North Carolina Regiments*, 3:739; service record file of William C. Walker, Thomas's Legion, Compiled Service Records of Confederate Soldiers from the State of North Carolina (M270), reel 574; Columbus F. Walker to Stringfield, September 4, 1895, Stringfield Papers, WCU; Crow, *Storm in the Mountains*, 41.

197. *O.R.* 30 (pt. 2): 591, 643-644; Stringfield, War Diary (copy), September 8, September 9, 1863, ledger book, 178-179, Stringfield Papers, NCOAH. In his history of the Infantry Regiment, Stringfield wrote that "the enemy were fortifying in and around the old limestone blockhouse and a stone mansion near by." Stringfield, "Sixty-Ninth Regiment," Clark, *North Carolina Regiments*, 3:739.

198. See n. 196.

199. *O.R.* 30 (pt. 2): 590-591, 643-644 (quote, 644). The information on the times of the attack and the surrender and on the men who escaped comes from the report of Col. John W. Foster of the 65th Regiment Indiana Mounted Infantry, commander of a brigade in the Twenty-Third Corps, who mounted an unsuccessful effort to extricate Hayes and his command. In the account which he recopied from his diary, Stringfield wrote that he killed an opponent whom he encountered "in a briar thicket" near the end of the fight. He also claimed to have

Although a minor affair, the capture of Hayes's command must have been a major morale booster for the Confederate participants. According to James W. Terrell, the Legion "was complimented for its gallant bearing" in what was the first combat for the majority of its soldiers. Reports of losses varied. Based on the military service records for members of Thomas's Legion, the unit suffered two casualties. Stringfield noted 6 killed and 15 wounded; however, while it may be assumed that Stringfield intended this number to represent the Legion's losses only, it is possible that he intended to indicate total Confederate losses. Haynes did not report any Confederate casualties, but claimed that 350 out of what he estimated were originally 450 Federal troops had been captured. In the official itinerary of the Twenty-Third Corps for September 7 and 8, compiled from monthly returns, Federal estimates of their losses ranged from 1 killed, 3 wounded, and 17 officers and 263 enlisted men captured, to 1 killed and 2 wounded at Telford's station, to 200 casualties total (the latter may be for Limestone Bridge only). The Federals variously estimated the size of Jackson's forces from 1,000 to 1,500 to 1,800.[200]

Jackson was now faced with the decision either to follow up his victory with a further advance down the tracks, stay put where he was and await developments, or withdraw back up the railroad. A small column had been sent to Hayes's relief under the command of Col. John W. Foster of the 65th Regiment Indiana Mounted Infantry, commanding the Second Brigade, Fourth Division of the Twenty-Third Corps. The force consisted of 375 men of the 103rd Regiment Ohio Infantry. Foster had received a report from Hayes of the fighting at Telford's and the withdrawal to Limestone Bridge, but due to an exceedingly slow train did not arrive at Henderson's Depot, about midway between Greeneville and Limestone, until midnight on September 8, far too late to be of any help. The next morning he continued forward, delayed by the increasingly damaged track until at last he had to abandon the train and proceed on foot. By now he heard rumors of the outcome of the fight on the previous day. Proceeding onwards to the edge of the Confederate picket line, he confirmed what had happened. Estimating Jackson's force to be at least a thousand, he decided that battle was not the most prudent course, and withdrew to Henderson's Depot with the intention of holding it. Foster learned that Confederate cavalry was moving towards his rear and flank, however, probably intending to isolate him like Hayes. Not wishing to share that fate, Foster withdrew to hold the bridges closer to Greeneville while he brought reinforcements down; once his

---

been the first man reach the blockhouse when the Federals raised the white flag, and to have taken Hayes's sword, which he carried with him until it was seized at the time of his arrest in Knoxville in 1865. Haynes reported that he accepted all of the sidearms for both the officers and the men. Stringfield, War Diary (copy), September 8, September 9, 1863, ledger book, 178-179, Stringfield Papers, NCOAH; *O.R.* 30 (pt. 2): 644.

200. Terrell to the editor, October 19, 1863, published in the *Western Democrat* (Charlotte), November 10, 1863; service record files of George W. Loudermilk and Cooper McAnally, Thomas's Legion, Compiled Service Records of Confederate Soldiers from the State of North Carolina (M270), reels 568 and 570; Stringfield, War Diary (copy), September 8, 1863, ledger book, 179, Stringfield Papers, NCOAH; *O.R.* 30 (pt. 2): 578, 590-591, 644. McAnally was bugler for the Infantry Regiment; Loudermilk was a private in Company H, Walker's Battalion. Loudermilk's records indicate that he was killed in battle at Limestone Bridge on September 1, probably an error for September 8 (see also p. 81 n. 193). In his report for the campaign, written in February of the following year, Jones called the fight at Limestone Bridge "a handsome affair" and noted both Jackson and Giltner by name, although he also somewhat disparaged Jackson's Brigade in his general remarks on the troops in the department. *O.R.* 30 (pt. 2): 603-604 (quote, 604); see also p. 80 and n. 191 above and p. 86 and n. 203 below for Jones's comments on Jackson's Brigade at this time.

entire brigade was present, he intended to go on the offensive. In the meantime, Foster's brief appearance in the area provoked a response further up the line. Love reported that the Federals were "re-enforcing at Fullen's Depot," a station between Limestone and Henderson's, with possibly as many as eight guns. This prompted Jones to order Brigadier General Williams to hurry to Jonesborough and assume command of the forces in the area, with Williams's own troops to follow as soon as possible.[201]

In the meantime, a major disaster befell the Confederates. Prior to Buckner's departure, he had ordered Frazer to destroy his supply depot, abandon Cumberland Gap to avoid being cut off, and fall back to Abingdon to join Jones. Frazer was reluctant to comply, insisting that he was well-enough supplied to defend the gap; he was further suspicious that the message was an enemy ruse, as Buckner had initially ordered him to hold the gap no matter what happened. Buckner deferred the issue to Bragg. Frazer's decision to hold on was supported by Jones, who on September 6 instructed Frazer to defend the gap if possible, as reinforcements were on the way. Within hours of sending this message, Jones received a request from Buckner to have Frazer destroy his supplies, evacuate, and move to Abingdon, adding that the orders came from Bragg. Jones decided not to forward the message after consulting the War Department. Jefferson Davis felt that Jones's judgment was paramount, as he was the man on the spot and surely understood the situation better than Bragg or Buckner. As a result, Frazer stayed put, although by the time Jones, Seddon, and Davis sorted out their decisions, it was probably already a moot point. On September 6, the Federals invested both sides of the gap; on September 10, Frazer surrendered.[202]

More bad news came with the occupation of Chattanooga by the Army of the Cumberland on September 9. On the same day, Burnside ordered the Ninth Corps to join him via Cumberland Gap. Its first elements arrived in Knoxville on September 25 after a series of difficult marches. Future strategy depended on the consolidation of Rosecrans's and Burnside's gains, and the linkage of their forces, at least by cavalry; it would then be determined whether the Army of the Ohio should move south in conjunction with the Army of the Cumberland, or operate independently in eastern Tennessee or adjacent regions. Rosecrans, fearing that all of the Confederate forces in the region were massing against him, was anxious for the two Federal armies to unite, but Burnside was more immediately concerned with enemy activities in his own area. Foster reported from Greeneville on September 11 that Confederate pickets and scouts were hovering in the area of Henderson's Depot, six miles away. He sent out his cavalry to drive them off. Williams had arrived at Jonesborough by that date, and was instructed by Jones to test the strength of Foster's forces and, if possible, drive them back at least as far as Morristown, which lay between Greeneville and Strawberry Plains. These opposing plans resulted in three days of skirmishing in the vicinity of Rheatown between Williams's cavalry and Colonel Graham's 5th Indiana Cavalry, fresh from its unsuccessful pursuit of Thomas and the Indian companies. Jones

201. *O.R.* 30 (pt. 2): 578, 590-591, (pt. 3): 524-526, (pt 4): 630 (quote).

202. *O.R.* 30 (pt. 2): 601-604, 607-639, (pt. 4): 568, 571-572, 586-587, 616-617, 618, 623-624, 637; Crow, *Storm in the Mountains*, 38-40; Marvel, *Burrnside*, 272, 277-279; Connelly, *Autumn of Glory,* 192; Weymouth T. Jordan Jr., "62nd Regiment N.C. Troops," in Manarin and Jordan, *North Carolina Troops 1861-1865: A Roster,* 15:10-21.

was to some extent on his own, as communications with Richmond were temporarily cut by another cavalry raid into southwestern Virginia; as this happened as he was forwarding the first rumors of Frazer's surrender, the government was correspondingly anxious. Visiting Jonesborough briefly on September 14 to assess the situation, Jones was not comforted by what he found. Despite the recent success of Jackson's Brigade, he was informed that it was "utterly unreliable." He estimated overall troop strength in the area as less than 2,800, and felt that the cavalry was utterly worn out as a result of the ongoing skirmishes. Reinforcements had been sent in the form of Montgomery D. Corse's Brigade of Pickett's Division from the Army of Northern Virginia, but it was too far away to provide immediate assistance, while the Ninth Corps would soon be in Williams's front. Preoccupied as always by potential threats to Saltville, Jones worried that the terrain in the Jonesborough area was ill-suited for a stand, and noted the potential threat to his supply and communications by the long railroad line and the easily destructible bridges in Williams's rear. Jones thus ordered Williams to withdraw to Carter's Depot, which was accomplished on the night of September 16-17, while Corse's Brigade was halted at Zollicoffer to wait developments.[203]

Burnside was troubled by signs that troops from Lee were reinforcing Jones. He began concentrating at Greeneville to face this potential threat. At the front, Foster soon received a clearer picture of the state of affairs thanks to two Confederate deserters. They identified the units known to be with Williams, revealing that they were scraped together from the railroad defenses and Saltville and estimating their strength at about 4,000. Foster reported the news on September 15 and asked permission to advance. On the following day he passed along word from Graham that the Confederate pickets had pulled back five miles, a prelude to Williams's withdrawal to Carter's Depot that evening, and requested to conduct a reconnaissance in force towards Jonesborough the next day. Burnside thus sent Foster on September 17 to strike the Confederate flank and rear at Kingsport, Bristol, and Blountsville. Burnside himself prepared to advance on Jonesborough if circumstances permitted. He was receiving increasingly frantic messages from General-in-Chief Henry W. Halleck indicating that bulk of the Confederate troops on the move from Virginia were heading not to eastern Tennessee but to Bragg, and instructing him to unite as much of his command as possible with Rosecrans immediately. Burnside could spare little of his force until the Ninth Corps arrived

203. *O.R.* 30 (pt. 2): 575, 604; (pt. 3): 479, 483, 494, 501-502, 523-524, 530, 555, 557, 592, 596, 617-618, (pt. 4): 637-638, 639-640, 649-651, 652-653, 658-659, 668; *O.R. (Supplement)*, Pt. II, 27:292. See also nn. 191 and 200 above for Jones's negative views on Jackson's Brigade. In a September 14 letter to Cooper, Jones estimated the strength of Jackson's Brigade as "less than 800." *O.R.* 30 (pt. 4): 649. It is unknown whether the discrepancy between this number and Colonel Johnston's earlier report of the brigade's strength at about 1,300 represented a sudden surge in desertions, or merely a more accurate assessment based on absences, detachments, and illness. In the recopied portion of his diary, Stringfield wrote that "[f]or next week or ten days [following the fighting at Telford's Depot and Limestone Bridge] we have been holding Enemy in check _ back to Carter's Depot etc. In retreat—by Fullens Depot. We got in rear of Enemy—& had to <u>Slip</u> <u>back</u> <u>out</u>—In that retreat, We marched and <u>ran</u> 62 miles." This undated passage falls between his entries for September 9 and September 20, and seems to refer to the retreat to Carter's Depot. In light of Williams's withdrawal from Carter's Depot towards Zollicoffer on September 23, Stringfield was probably referring to Foster's strike into the Confederate flank and rear on September 17-22; however, these events concluded after the diary entries for September 20 and 21. This may indicate either that the passage dates at least in part to when the diary was recopied in the ledger book, or that Stringfield wrote several entries in the original at one time on or subsequent to September 22. Stringfield, War Diary (copy), undated entry between September 9 and 20, 1863, ledger book, 179, Stringfield Papers, NCOAH.

at Knoxville unless he gave up eastern Tennessee altogether; further, there were physical obstacles in his path which needed to be dealt with in order to insure his supply line. Thus, Burnside decided to deal with Williams and Jones before reinforcing Rosecrans.[204]

Burnside's advance was spearheaded by the Third Brigade of the Twenty-Third Corps cavalry under Col. James P. T. Carter. It arrived at Carter's Depot on September 20. Jackson was in command, as Williams had departed with the 45th Regiment Virginia Infantry and a dismounted cavalry battalion to reinforce Jones at Zollicoffer as the latter prepared to attack Graham at Blountsville. Although Carter intended to press the Confederates in order to prevent them from reinforcing Jones, the Federals wasted the day due to Col. Eugene W. Crittenden of the 12th Regiment Kentucky Cavalry (Union). Crittenden defied Carter's orders to attack and arranged a truce to meet with his brother, George B. Crittenden, in command of the Confederate cavalry. Carter thus had to wait until the truce ended.[205]

On the morning of September 21, there was heavy skirmishing for around three hours between the opposing cavalry.[206] At some point, the Federals brought a battery into action. The Confederate artillery, under Lt. Col. J. Floyd King and Lieutenant Colonel Haynes, did not return fire. Sporadic gunfire continued throughout the day and into the night. The disposition of the Legion in the defensive line is unknown.[207] In the afternoon, Williams and the

204. *O.R.* 30 (pt. 2): 550-551, 579, 591-592, 604-605, (pt. 3): 618, 638-639, 643-644, 655-656, 658-661, 693, 717-718, 731-732, 746, 750, 755, 756, 770, 776, 785, (pt. 4): 672-673, 675-678, 682.

205. *O.R.* 30 (pt. 2): 550, 555, 579, 580, 605, 607, 644, (pt. 3): 756; Stringfield, War Diary (copy), September 20, 1863, ledger book, 180, Stringfield Papers, NCOAH. George B. Crittenden had resigned his commission as major general in October 1862, following his arrest and court martial for drunkenness, but continued to serve in various capacities in western Virginia. Warner, *Generals in Gray*, 65-66; Charles M. Spearman, "Crittenden, George Bibb," in Faust, *Historical Times Illustrated Encyclopedia of the Civil War*, 191-192. Jones's report, although referring to Crittenden as "General," added in parenthesis "colonel, C.S. Army," which clarifies his rank in the campaign. *O.R.* 30 (pt. 2): 607.

206. Much of the information for the Confederate side comes from the report of Lt. Col. Haynes, dated September 22. Even though it was filed just after the action, the dating of the events and, by implication, of the report itself, seem to be off by two days. Thus, when Haynes referred to September 19 he meant September 21; September 20 when he meant September 22; etc. This assessment is based upon a comparison of the events described for each date in Haynes's report with Jones's official report for the campaign, the itinerary of the Twenty-Third Corps, Stringfield's recopied diary, and various wartime messages. The big clue that something is amiss in the dating is Haynes's statement that Carter's Depot was evacuated on the night of September 20-21, when the withdrawal did not occur until the night of September 22-23. This account will therefore add two days to each date in Haynes's report; the action here on September 21 was placed on September 19 by Haynes.

207. *O.R.* 30 (pt. 2): 579, 644-645; Stringfield, War Diary (copy), September 21, 1863, ledger book, 180, Stringfield Papers, NCOAH; "Record of Events": muster roll abstracts, September-October 1863: Companies D and G, Infantry Regiment, and Companies A and C, Walker's Battalion, Thomas's Legion, Compiled Service Records of Confederate Soldiers from the State of North Carolina (M270), reel 567; service record files, Companies E, F, H, I, and K, Infantry Regiment, and Companies B, E, and H, Walker's Battalion, Thomas's Legion, ibid., reels 567 through 574. Stringfield wrote of "forces are fighting all day & part of night, in full view of each other & the Depot." Company D, Infantry Regiment reported that it "was in the piquett fight . . . night of Sept 22"; Company G, Infantry Regiment, skirmished on September 21; Company A, Walker's Battalion, reported skirmishing on September 21-22; while Company C, Walker's Battalion, "skirmished with Enemy night of 21st-night of 22^{d}." Depending on how the evidence is interpreted, the Legion (or those companies present) was engaged throughout the event; on the night of September 21-22 only; or on the night of September 22-23 only. These discrepancies may reflect either hurried record keeping or the different experiences of the individual companies. The muster roll of Company E, Infantry Regiment, recorded the wounding of one soldier, while the

45th Regiment Virginia Infantry returned by train. Williams ordered Haynes to construct a trestle footbridge across the river in order to secure communications with the Confederates still on the opposite bank of the Watauga River. It was completed by 9 that evening.[208]

At about 3 A.M. on September 22, the Federals opened on the depot with their artillery. Although there were three trains parked on the tracks with supplies intended for Jones at Zollicoffer, Williams refused to allow his men to return fire. Later in the morning, Crittenden's cavalry skirmished dismounted for two to three hours with their opponents. Elements of Burnside's infantry were by now arriving. Despite Williams's orders, McClung's Battery south of the river opened fire on two regiments deployed about 500 yards away and drove them under cover. In the afternoon, a Federal battery unlimbered near the Confederate line. This time, Williams permitted the artillery to reply, and under King's direction, Burrough's guns and Lowry's Virginia Light Artillery soon drove the battery out of range.[209] Late in the afternoon, a message arrived from Burnside, warning that due to military necessity he might have to open fire on the villages scattered along the railroad. He urged Jones to warn citizens to leave, and would refrain from opening fire until 5 P.M. Williams, replying in Jones's absence, was not only outraged by the idea, but was understandably annoyed due to the fact that he did not receive the message until 4:30. It did not reach Jones until long past the deadline, by which point a Federal battery had burnt most of Blountsville during an artillery duel (or so claimed Jones; predictably, Foster reported that it was Confederate gunfire which caused the blaze). After dark Williams ordered the seemingly omnipresent Haynes to take three infantry companies across the river, "deploy them as skirmishers, and bring on an action at the setting of the moon." It would appear that Company D, Infantry Regiment and Company C, Walker's Battalion were among the units involved. King was ordered to support Haynes with the 45th Virginia on the right. Haynes was preparing to open fire at 200 yards when the order came to withdraw. Jones had decided that he could not hold both Carter's Depot and Zollicoffer with his limited manpower; further, Federal forces had flanked the Confederate position at fords on either side, and Foster's cavalry still lurked in Williams's rear. The Confederates pulled out in the night and headed for Zollicoffer. The railroad bridge was burned, but the Federals saved it. Muster rolls show that a corporal from the Infantry Regiment was wounded at Carter's Depot, while fourteen other members of the Legion deserted or went absent without leave during the period of September 20-23.[210]

---

rolls of Companies F, K, H, and I, Infantry Regiment and the remaining companies of Walker's Battalion reported the desertion or absence without leave of men at Carter's Depot or neighboring areas from as early as September 11 up through September 23, indicating their presence as well.

208. *O.R.* 30 (pt. 2): 579, 645; Stringfield, War Diary (copy), September 21, 1863, ledger book, Stringfield Papers, NCOAH.

209. *O.R.* 30 (pt. 2): 645. After the war, Stringfield wrote that two Federal assaults were repulsed, but it does not appear that anything quite so dramatic occurred. He probably referred to the two brief artillery actions noted above. Stringfield, "Sixty-Ninth Regiment," Clark, *North Carolina Regiments*, 3:740. The itinerary of the Twenty-Third Corps recorded that the First Brigade, Third Division, "moved to near Carter's Station"; it is probable that the infantry who came under McClung's fire were from this command. A statement that "[a]fter four hours' fight Carter arrived near Carter's Station" likely refers to the crossing of the fords on either side of the depot by the two flanking columns. *O.R.* 30 (pt. 2): 579.

210. *O.R.* 30 (pt. 2): 579, 593, 605, 645-646 (quotes, 645), (pt. 3): 786; Stringfield, War Diary (copy), September 21, 1863, ledger book, 180, Stringfield Papers, NCOAH; Stringfield, "Sixty-Ninth Regiment," in Clark,

The salvage of the railroad bridge gave Burnside an opportunity to crush Jones's command. Instead, the Federals headed back towards Knoxville due to events further west. On September 19 and 20, Bragg and Rosecrans had clashed at Chickamauga Creek in northwest Georgia. Augmented by two divisions from Lt. Gen. James Longstreet's First Corps of the Army of Northern Virginia and additional reinforcements from Johnston, Bragg achieved victory after a hard-fought contest. Rosecrans retreated to Chattanooga, which Bragg put under siege. In Washington, the government had had enough: Lincoln directly ordered Burnside to Rosecrans's relief. Bedeviled by what he considered contradictory orders to simultaneously guard east Tennessee and aid Rosecrans, as well as the realities of the communication, supply, transport, and geographical problems that he faced in getting his scattered forces there, Burnside nevertheless promised to move at once. The reality proved quite different from the promise, however. An examination of the bewildering itineraries of the elements of the Twenty-Third Corps over the next few days tells the real story, as units marched and countermarched along the part of the railroad controlled by the Federals. Further, Burnside was determined to hold east Tennessee, come what may; so, while he proposed three possible plans of action for approval, Rosecrans remained isolated.[211]

The Federal withdrawal convinced Jones that now was the time to strike again. His plans were aided by the arrival of a very competent officer sent to alleviate the problem of having one brigadier (Williams) in command of other men of the same rank. Maj. Gen. Robert Ransom Jr., was a North Carolinian with prior service in the Army of Northern Virginia and in the eastern part of his state. Jones placed Ransom in direct command in eastern Tennessee, subordinate to his own authority, and returned to southwestern Virginia. Even before Ransom's arrival, Jones had concentrated his infantry and artillery at Carter's Depot, and posted Williams forward with the cavalry at Jonesborough. The small force in eastern Tennessee had been already diminished by the loss of Corse's Brigade, recalled by Lee to Virginia, and would be further decreased when Jones ordered Ransom to dispatch Gabriel C. Wharton's Brigade towards Abingdon to cover the lead mines and salt works in southwest Virginia and deceive Burnside that a move against Cumberland Gap was contemplated.

North Carolina Regiments, 3:740; "Record of Events": muster roll abstracts, September-October 1863: Company D, Infantry Regiment, and Company C, Walker's Battalion, Thomas's Legion, Compiled Service Records of Confederate Soldiers from the State of North Carolina (M270), reel 567; service record files for Jerry Chamberlain, Georger Farmer, Spencer Fisher, H. King Foster, James Gooden, Merimon Hall, John Hammock, John Hatchel, Andrew J. Hughes, Thomas J. Hughes, George King, Alexander Payne, Jefferson Payne, Ashford T. Quinn, and John Marshell Quinn, Thomas's Legion, ibid., reels 568, 569, 570, and 572. The reason for Haynes's and King's nighttime excursion with the infantry is unknown. It is puzzling why artillery officers were put in charge of infantry for such a task; based on Haynes's report, Col. William H. Browne, commander of the 45th Regiment Virginia Infantry, was present. Perhaps it was another example of Jones's lack of confidence in many of his troops and their officers.

211. *O.R.* 30 (pt. 2): 551, 579, 605, (pt. 3): 770, 785, 808-810, 904-907, 954-956. Peter Cozzen's *This Terrible Sound: The Battle of Chickamauga* (Urbana: University of Illinois Press, 1992), is the best study of the battle. Shorter accounts of the clash and its aftermath may be found in Connelly, *Autumn of Glory*, 192-234; Woodworth, *Six Armies in Tennessee*, 79-149. For criticisms of Burnside's failure to reinforce Rosecrans, see Cozzens, 522-523; Woodworth, 131, 136-137; Wiley Sword, *Mountains Touched With Fire: Chattanooga Besieged, 1863* (1995; paperback repr., New York: St Martin's Griffin Edition, 1997), 50-51. Marvel's sympathetic account of this period in *Burnside*, 284-291, is revealing in regards to the context and conditions in which that Federal commander made his decisions.

Believing that the bulk of the Army of the Ohio was heading towards Chattanooga, Jones ordered Ransom to "move his infantry and artillery beyond Jonesborough, and push forward the cavalry as far as he could toward Bull's Gap, the chief object being to harass the enemy and break up the organizations of disloyal East Tennesseeans."[212]

Assuming command upon his arrival on October 1, Ransom ordered Williams to occupy Greeneville. Ransom explained that he was planning to march on Cumberland Gap, and that Williams's movement down the railroad was a diversion, a seeming reversal of Jones's intent. Williams was to proceed "as if I was covering the advance of an army, but not to pass beyond Bull's Gap until further orders." He secured Greeneville by October 2, inflicting a few casualties and capturing some prisoners in his drive down the railroad. Jones at this point felt that the command should proceed no further, and reported to Davis that evening that Wharton had been sent on his bluff towards Cumberland Gap. Based on the wording of his message, it seems that he did not know that Ransom had left with Wharton, and assumed that he was at Carter's Depot. Williams, unaware of Jones's concerns, advanced to Blue Springs, some eight miles beyond Greeneville and within distance of Federal infantry at Lick Creek. The latter stream lay a few miles east of his intended target of Bull's Gap.[213]

Williams skirmished with the Federals at Blue Springs on October 3, and remained there the next day. He was visited by Jones's inspector general, who brought word from Ransom that Williams was not supposed to proceed beyond Greeneville, and that Ransom "would be disappointed in learning that I had gone beyond that place." Williams feared that if he withdrew suddenly, not only would his command's relative weakness be exposed to the Federals, but his diversionary efforts on Ransom's behalf would fail. He now received a note from Ransom, stating that "[b]y direction of General Jones, it is necessary for me, with a portion of the troops under my command, to make a move which will be in such a direction as to prevent my communicating with you." He instructed Williams to take command of all troops in the department other than Wharton's Brigade and King's artillery, which were both with Ransom. "This induced me to believe that the expedition to Cumberland Gap was still progressing," Williams wrote. At what point Wharton's "impression" became a full "expedition" against Cumberland Gap itself is not known; as late as October 2, Jones characterized it to Davis in terms of the former idea. Jones also noted, however, that according to his information the gap was only held by some 500 men; perhaps he was tempted to take advantage of this news to actually attempt to recapture the gap, although given the small size of his force and his overriding worries about defending southwest Virginia, this seems unlikely. Perhaps Ransom decided to exploit the situation without fully informing Jones of his intentions; certainly, if Williams's report is to be believed, Ransom's plans involved something more substantial than an "impression." This seems to contradict not only Jones's message of October 2 implying that Ransom was overseeing operations along the railroad and had sent Wharton off on his own, but also his subsequent report of the east Tennessee campaign itself. It is possible also that Williams misunderstood Jones or Ransom; a lack of precision in

212. Warner, *Generals in Gray*, 253-254; Edward G. Longacre, "Ransom, Robert, Jr.," in Faust, *Historical Times Illustrated Encyclopedia of the Civil War*, 614; *O.R.* 29 (pt. 2): 750, 30 (pt. 2): 605-606 (quote, 606), 640; (pt. 4): 695, 702, 706-709, 711-712, 716, 720, 725.

213. *O.R.* (pt. 2): 606, 640-641 (quote, 640), (pt. 4): 725, 731.

language was the bane of more than one Civil War command relationship. Further, Williams may have pretended to have misunderstood the situation in his report to justify his decision in moving beyond Greeneville. The latter seems unlikely, however; Jones wrote in his report that he had sent Ransom to push the Federals back towards Bull's Gap, while Wharton covered Abingdon via a route which would give the impression that he was moving on Cumberland Gap. Finally, Jones sent word to Williams on October 5 that his idea for a halt at Greeneville had been out of concern for the condition of Williams's troops; if possible he should drive the enemy beyond Bull's Gap. Jones felt that Williams could safely accomplish this because the forces at Cumberland Gap were too small to pose a threat; no mention was made of any intention to seize the latter place. Jones dismissed rumors of recent Federal reinforcements from Kentucky as Unionist hearsay.[214]

Regardless of the reasons for the situation, Williams was in a perilous position. The Federal reinforcements were no rumor but the Ninth Corps, which along with the bulk of the Twenty-Third Corps was concentrated in the Knoxville area while Burnside decided what to do about relieving Rosecrans. Following the repulse of an enemy assault on the evening of October 5, Williams remained in the area of Blue Springs for the next few days, "hourly expecting intelligence that Cumberland Gap had fallen into our hands, and congratulating myself on the success of my diversion in detaining so many of the enemy's forces in my front." He was nevertheless beginning to feel isolated without available infantry support. The only troops nearby were Thomas's Legion, described by Williams as "about 400 infantry and home guards under Brig. Gen. A. E. Jackson." Not knowing exactly where Jackson was, Williams sought word of his whereabouts and ordered him to join him at Blue Springs.[215]

Burnside now decided to deal with Williams once and for all.[216] He sent the Ninth Corps to join the Federals already in the area of Bull's Gap, accompanied by most of his

214. *O.R.* (pt. 2): 597-598, 606 ("impression" quote [also (pt. 4): 725]), 640 ("would be disappointed," "[b]y the direction of General Jones," and "This induced me to believe" quotes), (pt. 4): 725, 731.

215. Ibid., (pt. 2): 575, 606, 640 (quotes). Williams probably mixed his chronology in his report somewhat in implying that he did not order Jackson to join him until on or after October 5. According to the records of Company A, Walker's Battalion, the battalion returned to Carter's Depot via the railroad on September 28, the time at which Jones reoccupied the area. On the following day, it marched to Jonesborough, where it would have joined Williams and the cavalry. It remained at Jonesborough after Williams moved forward until October 2, at which point it marched to Fullen's Depot. On October 4 it marched to Greeneville, and was evidently there until the early hours of October 11. This itinerary is paralleled in the record for Company C of the battalion, which noted that it began marching towards Greeneville as early as October 1, arriving at the same time as Company A. "Record of Events": muster roll abstracts, September-October 1863: Companies A and C, Walker's Battalion, Thomas's Legion, Compiled Service Records of Confederate Soldiers from the State of North Carolina (M270), reel 567. Assuming that Jackson's Brigade was concentrated, it would have been within easy call of Williams on October 5. Probably Williams ordered Jackson to move forward on October 2. Alternatively, since he apparently had to discover where Jackson was, he may have expected to find him still at Jonesborough and was thus unaware of the move to Fullen's Depot; once he found him, he then ordered him forward to Greeneville. Since Fullen's Depot is closer to Blue Springs than Jonesborough, however, this seems unlikely, so unless communications between Williams and Jackson had completely broken down, the reasons that the former did not know of the latter's whereabouts (or perhaps wanted to create that impression among his superiors) are unknown.

216. For brief accounts of this phase of the East Tennessee campaign, see Marvel, *Burnside*, 291-294; Sword, *Mountains Touched With Fire*, 74. The part played by Thomas's Legion is placed in context in Crow, *Storm in the Mountains*, 44-46.

cavalry, and joined them on October 9. On the next day, he attacked up the railroad. Neither commander had any idea of what they were actually facing: Williams was convinced that he was fighting against the forces he had previously encountered, while Burnside depicted the former's rag-tag command as "in heavy force." Skirmishing lasted most of the day, while Burnside gradually extended his lines in an effort to flank Williams, forcing the latter to stretch his defense until it extended nearly two miles. Burnside also sent Foster's cavalry brigade around to the vicinity of Rheatown to cut off Williams's retreat. Burnside later wrote that "[i]t was not desirable to press the enemy until Colonel Foster had to time to reach this point"; as a result he allowed the skirmishing to continue while he sent his chief engineer to reconnoiter Williams's position. Finally satisfied, towards 5 P.M. Burnside launched a more serious assault on the Confederate center, which gave way under the superior numbers. Williams waited until the Federals approached to within 250 yards of his batteries before ordering them to open fire with grapeshot and canister. This successfully broke up the assault, and the Federals sought cover in nearby woods and a ravine on the Confederate left. In the process they came under fire from the 4th Regiment Kentucky Cavalry. Under this combined fire, the Federals withdrew to their starting position. By this time, night had fallen, preventing further fighting. Burnside planned to resume the attack the next day; if everything went as planned, Foster would be in position to prevent Williams's withdrawal.[217]

Still not fully aware that he was up against a sizeable portion of the Army of the Ohio, Williams at least sensed that the opposing forces were growing. He also learned of Foster's drive towards his rear. Williams went to Greeneville to contact Jones via the telegraph. Estimating the opposition as "at least 5,000 strong, with re-enforcements coming up," he "first learned that the expedition to Cumberland Gap had been abandoned." Williams now heard from his cavalry commanders that Burnside had sent two strong columns of infantry on either side of the Confederate position. Williams knew that his only option was to smash through Foster before his pursuers caught up. The Confederates left Blue Springs and reached Greeneville late that night, where Jackson's Brigade joined them.[218]

At daybreak on October 11, Adj. Luther C. May of the Infantry Regiment and Capt. H. H. "Tip" Taylor, Jackson's acting adjutant general, blundered into Foster's men near

217. *O.R.* 30 (pt. 2): 547, 551 (quotes), 570, 596, 640-641, 642-643. To be fair to Burnside, his idea was to try to capture Williams's command, not simply defeat it and drive it further up the railroad; nevertheless, a more aggressive probe might have discovered the weakness of the Confederate forces and led to a quicker and more efficient effort to achieve the same result. Burnside's chief engineer, Capt. Orlando M. Poe, reported that "[t]his reconnaissance was made very leisurely" due to his correct understanding that Burnside wanted to give Foster enough time to get in position (ibid., 570). Williams later justified his misinterpretation of the strength of the Federal assaulting force as due to the rolling terrain of the ground, concealing his opponents' true numbers; in his report, Poe mentioned using the terrain to conceal preparations for the assault. Given the debilitated state of the Ninth Corps, however, Williams's initial assessment of the numbers of the attacking troops may have not been too far off, although Burnside's total force present was still greater than his own. Stringfield, "Sixty-Ninth Regiment," Clark, *North Carolina Regiments* 3:740, misdated the Blue Springs clash to October 15.

218. *O.R.* 30 (pt. 2): 641, (pt. 4): 741-742. The records for Company A of Walker's Battalion indicate that that unit left Greeneville at 2 A.M. "Record of Events": muster roll abstracts, September-October 1863: Company A, Walker's Battalion, Thomas's Legion, Compiled Service Records of Confederate Soldiers from the State of North Carolina (M270), reel 567. *O.R.* 30 (pt. 4): 742. Burnside's earliest account suggested that the Confederate withdrawal from Blue Springs was made in a state of near panic, something that the fighting retreat conducted on the next day would seem to belie. Ibid. (pt. 2): 547.

Henderson's Mill and were captured. May escaped and warned his fellows. At about the same time, Williams's wagon train came under fire. The train halted while Jackson's Brigade moved up to the front; the retreat then continued. Almost immediately, they encountered Foster's cavalry, drawn up with six field pieces in support. Williams ordered Jackson into position on the right, and the 1st Regiment Tennessee Cavalry (Carter's) and elements of the 10th Regiment Kentucky Cavalry and the 21st Regiment Virginia Cavalry on the left. The Federals opened fire. James W. Terrell wrote that the Legion returned fire "and followed up by a charge that forced the dastardly Yankees to run like frightened curs." According to Williams, the Federal rout was due more to the cavalry, which charged across fields and through woodlots towards their evidently dismounted foes. Stringfield wrote years later that the Confederate artillery also played a key part, unleashing "a furious . . . fire upon the enemy in corn fields and meadows confronting us . . . bursting shells in their very midst" prior to the Legion's advance. The Confederates were aided by the fact that Foster had just arrived after several delays, and lacked time to ready a serious defense.[219]

So far, Williams had been fortunate; he had driven the enemy from his immediate front, and had not lost any wagons or cattle. Foster's men regrouped, however, and Burnside's pursuit may have put some pressure on Williams's rear.[220] For the next several miles, a series of short fights erupted, in which the Federal cavalry would be driven back, only to regroup and start the whole process over again. Eventually, the Federals were pushed off the road altogether to the Confederate left. The way seemed clear to Jonesborough and

219. Stringfield, "Sixty-Ninth Regiment," in Clark, *North Carolina Regiments*, 3:740-741 (quote, 741); *O.R.* 30 (pt. 2): 641; Terrell to the editor, October 19, 1863, the *Western Democrat* (Charlotte), November 10, 1863, Stringfield, "Memoirs of the Civil War," typescript, L-McGL (copy, Stringfield Papers, WCU), 17. Terrell stated that cavalry and artillery were not sent to the support of the Legion until after the initial rout of the Federals. In his earliest report (October 17), Burnside claimed that "owing to some misunderstanding," Foster's force "withdrew and allowed them [Williams's command] to pass with only a slight check." He subsequently blamed the failure to trap Williams on Foster's inability to get his command properly set defensively because of delays in reaching his assigned position due to bad roads; Poe noted that Foster did not reach the road until daybreak, which would have given him virtually no time to prepare. Evidently the 5th Regiment Indiana Cavalry bore the brunt of the assault alone. According to the records for Company D of that unit, "The Fifth Indiana Cavalry being in the advance and the brigade commander failing to support it with the remainder of the brigade according to promise, the regiment was overpowered by numbers and forced to fall back after three hours' hard fighting." The reference to a three hour clash might refer to the climatic fight east of Rheatown in the afternoon, which Williams put at about three hours; Company D's report placed that action as having taken place at Rheatown. However, the same report noted that the regiment was reinforced and fought the Confederates later in the afternoon, a seeming reference to the Rheatown fight. The record for the 5th Indiana's field and staff stated that the regiment fell back at Henderson's Mill in the morning after it was not reinforced, but fought again later in the day, a claim supported by the records of Companies B, E, and L. Thus, the "three hours' hard fighting" probably referred to the series of running skirmishes between the two forces throughout the morning; it is also possible that the Hoosiers put up a stiffer initial defense than Confederate sources indicated. *O.R.* 30 (pt. 2): 547 (Burnside quote), 551-552, 570. *O.R. (Supplement)*, Pt. II, 27:292, 298, 305, 309 (quote from record for Company D, 5th Regiment Indiana Cavalry), 315, 321, 330, 338, 344, 349.

220. Burnside reported that "we pursued early in the morning, driving him again beyond the Watauga River." *O.R.* 30 (pt. 2): 551. Williams mentioned no problems with Burnside's pursuit in his own report. While there may have possibly been sporadic contact between the Confederate rear guard and the Federal advance, it must not have been too sustained or close, because Burnside would then have been able to put more serious, and possibly fatal, pressure on Williams's command during its long halt at Rheatown, something which Williams would have surely noted in his report for dramatic purposes, if nothing else.

beyond, where Williams could reunite with Jones. At Rheatown, however, the Confederate artillery took the wrong road, separating it from the rest of Williams's command. A halt was ordered to get word to the artillery to return. In the meantime, Foster's men gathered once again. This time, the Confederates were unable to drive them back. Once the artillery returned, their situation improved, although it still took nearly three hours of steady fighting for the Confederates to break through and make their escape, pursued by the cavalry until nightfall. The exhausted Confederates eventually found temporary refuge in Jonesborough; however, the ordeal was not over for Thomas's Legion, as Williams dispatched Jackson's Brigade on foot to Carter's Depot, where it arrived at 9 A.M. on October 12. From there, the Legion traveled by rail to Zollicoffer, reaching it on October 13.[221] Casualties for the Legion were slight, with 1 officer and 2 enlisted men in the Infantry Regiment wounded and another injured in an accident, while Walker's Battalion suffered 2 wounded. In addition, the Legion lost 13 men reported as absent without leave or as deserters, while 2 men from the regiment (including one of the wounded) were captured during the retreat on October 12.[222]

Following the retreat, the members of Thomas's Legion received official compliments from Jackson and Williams regarding their conduct. Through his assistant adjutant general, William B. Reese, Jackson expressed "his high admiration of their valor on the field of battle

221. *O.R.* 30 (pt. 2): 551-552, 570, 641-642; Terrell to the editor, October 19, 1863, published in the *Western Democrat* (Charlotte), November 10, 1863; Lafayette George to Rachel B. George "and friends," October 17, 1863, RD 1474, CWRP; Stringfield, "Sixty-Ninth Regiment," in Clark, *North Carolina Regiments*, 3:741; Stringfield, "Memoirs of the Civil War," typescript, McClung Collection, L-McGL, (copy, Stringfield Papers, WCU), 17; *O.R. (Supplement)*, Pt. II, 27:292, 298, 305, 309, 315, 321, 330, 338, 344, 349; W. B. Reese to James R. Love Jr., October 14, 1863, Edward O. Guerrant to Love, October 14, 1863, service record file for James R. Love, Thomas's Legion, Compiled Service Records of Confederate Soldiers from the State of North Carolina (M270), reel 570 (the Reese letter was later published in the Wilmington *Daily Journal*, December 25, 1874); "Record of Events": muster roll abstracts, September-October 1863: Company G, Infantry Regiment, and Companies A, B, and C, Walker's Battalion, Thomas's Legion, ibid., reel 567. Williams estimated the strength of Jackson's Brigade as around 300, showing the debilitating effect of absences and desertions as well as the continuing absence of Levi's Battery and the Indian companies. According to Stringfield's account in Clark's *Regiments*, the Infantry Regiment alone numbered 600; Williams's contemporary number was probably more accurate. 1st Lt. Lafayatte George of Company H, Infantry Regiment, wrote on October 17 that only 22 men were present in his company, suggesting how shrunken the Legion had become. According to George, most of the confrontations between Williams's column and the Federals after the initial daybreak clash involved the Confederate cavalry. Congratulations to the Infantry Regiment from Jackson and Williams, issued through their assistant adjutant generals (Reese and Guerrant respectively), singled out their service on the morning of October 11th, although the former noted that the Legion made "repeated charges," indicating their engagement beyond the initial fight. The muster roll for Company A, Walker's Battalion recorded that it skirmished on three different occasions. In contrast to George, Stringfield's account in Clark's *Regiments* gave the impression that the Legion (or at least the regiment) played the primary or even sole role throughout the entire day, supported in the morning by the artillery. His later account in his published memoirs, however, included the cavalry as active participants.

222. Service record files of David Sweatman, 1st Regiment N.C. State Troops, and of Wilson Bradley, H. Hassel Burns, D. F. Butler, Benjamin F. Carter, Robert C. Crouch, John Mc. Derreberrey, Isaac Hendrix, Romulous A. Hice, James A. Kirkland, Alexander R. Ledford, Joseph Lequire, Garner L. Loudermilk, David McPeters, Jesse L. Newton, William H. Pearson, John W. Rains, Phidela E. Sherrill, David Sweatman, William Walker Sr., William Thomas Welch, and James M. Whitaker, Thomas's Legion, Compiled Service Records of Confederate Soldiers from the State of North Carolina (M270), reels 102 and 568 through 574; David Sweatman, North Carolina Application for Pension (1901 series), State Auditor's Office Records, NCOAH; D. F. Butler, Tennessee Confederate Pension Application No. 4796, Roster Document No. 1801, CWRP. Part of Sweatman's records were separated and misfiled among the service record files of the 1st Regiment N.C. State Troops.

and their manly endurance without food or rest of the unprecedented march of sixty miles in less than thirty hours. It affords him great pleasure to thus acknowledge their extraordinary gallantry in the repeated charges made by them upon the enemy in the morning of 11th Instant. He hopes they will continue to manifest the same spirit of bravery and endurance of which they have showed themselves so eminently possessed." Williams's message via his assistant adjutant general, Edward O. Guerrant, stated that "it affords him infinite pleasure to express through you to your Command, his unqualified appreciation of the gallant conduct in the charge upon the enemy on the morning of the 11th Inst. Such exhibition of valor and soldierly bearing will receive, as it deserves, the everlasting remembrance of a grateful Country, and ever be an object of pride to their General."[223] These skirmishes, along with those at Telford's Station, Limestone Bridge, and Carter's Depot, provided the soldiers of Thomas's Legion some much-needed field experience.

For the next couple of days, the Legion rested at Zollicoffer. Burnside began to withdraw the Ninth Corps to Knoxville on October 14, leaving an infantry brigade at Jonesborough to keep an eye on Williams while the cavalry continued to probe at the Confederate right and rear. On October 13-14, skirmishes were fought between the Federals and the Confederate cavalry at Blountsville. By this time, Williams had been reinforced by Wharton's Brigade and the cavalry of Brig. Gen. William E. "Grumble" Jones; nevertheless, the threat to Williams's supply and communication line was too great, so he pulled back on October 14 towards Bristol. The retreat continued across the Virginia border, halting at Abingdon on October 15, where the Confederates threw up breastworks. "Let them Come. We are ready," Stringfield confidently recorded in his diary. A not-so-confident Samuel Jones, fearing the invasion of southwest Virginia, concentrated as much of his force as possible at Abindgon while requesting additional troops from Bragg and Lee. Corse's Brigade was returned to Jones, while Bragg dispatched the division of Maj. Gen. Carter L. Stevenson to relieve the pressure by moving towards Knoxville against Burnside's rear.[224]

The Federals withdrew again, as Burnside was evidently satisfied with pushing Jones's forces into Virginia. The Confederates at Abindgon spent the next several days quietly. The Legion (as Jackson's Brigade) was now a part of Ransom's Division. Lt. Col. James R. Love Jr. still commanded the regiment, referred to in the official returns as "Thomas' (North Carolina) Regiment," while Maj. James A. McKamy commanded Walker's Battalion. Levi's Battery, still with no guns, was reported as unattached. The Legion was not in good shape. Absences had shot up during the retreat up the railroad. It was soon rumored that many of

223. Stringfield, "Sixty-Ninth Regiment," in Clark, *North Carolina Regiments*, 3:741; Crow, *Storm in the Mountains*, 141; W. B. Reese to James R. Love Jr., October 14, 1863, Edward O. Guerrant to Love, October 14, 1863, service record file of James R. Love, Infantry Regiment, Thomas's Legion, Compiled Service Records of Confederate Soldiers from the State of North Carolina (M270), reel 570. It is not clear if the compliments were addressed to the regiment only, or were intended for the entire Legion, although based on the wording the former seems most likely; if separate commendations were issued for Walker's Battalion, they evidently do not survive.

224. *O.R.* 30 (pt. 2): 552, 576, 595, 606, 642, (pt. 4): 749-750, 752-754, 756, 758, 760-762; "Record of Events": muster roll abstracts, September-October 1863: Company A, Walker's Battalion, Thomas's Legion, Compiled Records of Confederate Soldiers from the State of North Carolina (M270), reel 567; Stringfield, War Diary (copy), undated entry written on or prior to October 16, 1863, ledger book, 182, Stringfield Papers, NCOAH; Marvel, *Burnside*, 297-298; Sword, *Mountains Touched With Fire*, 74-75.

these men, finding themselves unable to return to their commands while Federal forces occupied the area, had made their way to join Thomas in North Carolina.[225] Some of these soldiers later rejoined their companies; others were later redesignated as deserters. In some cases this assessment was correct, as there are Federal provost marshal records for missing members of the Legion who gave themselves up and took the Oath of Allegiance, a problem which continued through the winter as more men slipped away. Others simply disappeared, and presumably hid out near their homes or joined the roving bands of deserters from both armies that infested areas of the mountains. Determining which soldiers reported to Thomas is problematic, due to the fact that there are no surviving muster rolls for his forces in North Carolina.[226] These absentees became a new source of trouble between Thomas and Jackson.

Writing to Adjutant and Inspector General Cooper in Richmond on November 6, Jones reported that his forces included "fragments of Thomas' Legion, aggregating 399, under Brig. Gen. A. E. Jackson." By the end of the month, Jackson's Brigade consisted of 51 officers and 312 men present for duty, with an aggregate present of 421. The total aggregate present and absent was 1,012, a slight decrease from the previous month's return of 1,049. Some of the 649 absences were legitimate: furloughs home, sick furloughs, hospitalizations and illnesses in camp, and detached or detailed assignments. Furthermore, the Indian companies were probably considered part of the total missing as well. Regardless, over half the personnel of the Legion were either absent or unfit for duty.[227]

All indications are that the condition of the Legion was hardly unique. Jones complained of the exhausted state of his men and horses and of the lack of shoes for both. Although a major offensive was therefore out of the question, the withdrawal of the Federals towards Knoxville meant that the Confederates could return to eastern Tennessee. Jones unrealistically pleaded with Richmond for "a few thousand of General Lee's infantry" to be sent from Virginia. When it became obvious that reinforcements were not coming, he moved cautiously forward anyway. On October 28, Ransom's Division marched and encamped some three to four miles west of Abingdon. On the afternoon of October 31 they shifted southward to Bristol, halting at Blountsville the following day. "I am rejoiced at [the] thought of redeeming my native State from yankee rule," Stringfield wrote in his diary. "I

225. See pp. 57 and 76 and n. 181 above.

226. *O.R.* 30 (pt. 2): 547, 642; Lafayette George to Rachel George "and friend," October 17, 1864, Roster Document No. 1474, CWRP; Stringfield, War Diary (copy), entries for October 19-25 inclusive, ledger book, 182-183, Stringfield Papers, NCOAH; service record files, Thomas's Legion, Compiled Service Records of Confederate Soldiers from the State of North Carolina (M270) reels 567 through 574. The Legion rosters in this volume, which are primarily based on information abstracted from the muster rolls by the National Archives, document the confusing status of many men who dropped out of the ranks at this time. Even determining date and place of desertion is difficult, as in many cases it appears that specific dates and places were retroactively assigned to absentees after a certain point by muster takers. Such is particularly obvious in the cases of men who never returned from furlough, but were later assigned a date and place of desertion associated with men who had directly dropped out of the ranks. The same method was used earlier in the cases of men who deserted around the time of the Strawberry Plains fight in June (see p. 63 n. 144 above). This lack of precision is reflective not only of the problems that record keepers faced in deciding who actually deserted, but of the harried nature of trying to document the whereabouts of large numbers of men during campaigns. In many cases, after months had passed it was probably the only reasonably effective way of trying to update the records.

227. *O.R.* 29 (pt. 2): 824, 31 (pt. 3): 644.

am willing to make any needed Sacrifice to this end. My little property I cheerfully give. My life and all is in the hands of My God In Him do I trust to Him I yield My every interest. Death before dishonor is My Motto."[228]

Stringfield's dreams were doomed to frustration. Citing the lack of additional infantry, Jones would not permit any of his own to pass beyond the Holston River. Outside of minor cavalry clashes, little was accomplished besides the capture of over 800 prisoners at Rogersville by "Grumble" Jones on November 6. The Legion remained in camp a mile south of Blountsville for nearly a month, its time taken up by daily drilling. Seventy-five recruits arrived, a welcome addition to the command's depleted ranks. The long inactivity caused some restiveness. Stringfield complained on November 12 of "[s]ome fool Soldiers" who ripped up the regimental flag during a tussle over which group would be able to drill under it; he placed them under arrest. The more sobering consequences of indiscipline were brought home with the court martial of some soldiers for desertion. On November 13, Stringfield witnessed his first firing squad, as three men were executed.[229]

Samuel Jones's return to Tennessee occurred as the Confederate position at Chattanooga deteriorated. Constant feuding between Bragg and his subordinate officers rendered the Army of Tennessee's command structure ineffective. As a result, no efforts were made to press the victory at Chickamauga and compel Rosecrans to surrender. A relief force for the Army of the Cumberland, consisting of two corps from the Army of the Potomac under Maj. Gen. Joseph Hooker, had arrived at Bridgeport, Alabama. Maj. Gen. Ulysses S. Grant, the victor at Vicksburg, was assigned on October 16 to command the new Military Division of the Mississippi, consisting of his own Department of the Tennessee, Rosecrans's Department of the Cumberland, and Burnside's Department of the Ohio. Grant thus had the authority over the troops and supplies in the region necessary to relieve Chattanooga, defeat Bragg, and oversee other simultaneous operations. One of his first moves was to sack Rosecrans and replace him with Maj. Gen. George H. Thomas. He then sent Hooker to open a supply line into the besieged city. Further Federal reinforcements from the Army of the Tennessee under Grant's favorite lieutenant, Brig. Gen. William T. Sherman, were on the way.[230]

228. *O.R.*, 30 (pt. 2): 606, 31 (pt. 3): 576 (Jones quote), 593-594; "Record of Events": muster roll abstracts, September-October 1863: Companies C, E, I, and K, Infantry Regiment, Companies B, C, and H, Walker's Battalion, and Levi's Battery, November-December 1863: Company K, Infantry Regiment, and Companies A, B, C, E, and H, Walker's Battalion, and November 10, 1863: Levi's Battery, Thomas's Legion, Compiled Service Records of Confederate Soldiers from the State of North Carolina (M270), reel 567; Stringfield, War Diary (copy), October 28, 31 (quote), 1863, ledger book, 183, Stringfield Papers, NCOAH.

229. Sword, *Mountains Touched With Fire*, 75; *O.R.* 31 (pt. 1): 551-566, (pt. 3): 66, 67, 127, 607, 611-612, 670; Stringfield, War Diary (copy), November 3-9, 12 (quote), 13, 1863, ledger book, 183-184, 185, 188, Stringfield Papers, NCOAH; Stringfield, "Sixty-Ninth Regiment," Clark, *North Carolina Regiments*, 3:742. The three men executed were among the prisoners captured by "Grumble" Jones and were deserters who had joined the Federals. Stringfield identified one of the men as a member of Company K, Infantry Regiment. It is almost a certainty that he was Pvt. William R. Silvey of Company K, Infantry Regiment, who deserted in April 1863 and joined Company B of the 2nd Regiment Tennessee Infantry (Union). According to his service records, he was captured and executed on an unknown date. Service record file of William R. Silvey, Thomas's Legion, Compiled Service Records of Confederate Soldiers from the State of North Carolina (M270), reel 573.

230. *O.R.* 30 (pt. 4): 404, 450-451, 455; Connelly, *Autumn of Glory*, 235-265; Woodworth, *Six Armies in Tennessee*, 137-170; James Lee McDonough, *Chattanooga: A Death Grip on the Confederacy* (Knoxville:

Jones's limited actions, along with those of Stevenson at the other end of the department, led Burnside to hunker down in the area of Knoxville. From the perspective of Braxton Bragg, the time now seemed right to take care of two problems at once. Jones had wanted reinforcements from the Army of Northern Virginia. Although no more were forthcoming, there were already some with Bragg: Longstreet and his two divisions. Longstreet had long wanted independent command, and was also involved in the anti-Bragg intrigues among the Army of Tennessee's leading officers. The constant quarreling and personal dislike between Bragg and Longstreet led to the former's adoption of a plan to send the latter on the offensive in eastern Tennessee. The object would be the destruction of the Army of the Ohio, which would ultimately improve prospects for Bragg at Chattanooga; Longstreet would then be in a position either to return to Bragg or to Lee in Virginia as circumstances evolved. Unfortunately for the Confederates, it would also diminsh Bragg's overall strength at a time when Grant's was steadily increasing. Furthermore, Stevenson was already in place with his own division, and had just been reinforced by another. Nevertheless, despite the resulting unnecessary shift of troops, Bragg dispatched Longstreet to deal with Burnside.[231]

Longstreet was sent with his forces to eastern Tennessee on November 4, with virtually no preparation, little knowledge of what he was up against, and not even a particularly clear idea of what his objectives were in relation to Bragg's operations beyond reconquering the region for the Confederacy. Under the best of circumstances, this would have posed a major challenge; the results proved, however, that while Longstreet was a fine corps commander under Lee, he was not as successful acting in an independent role. After gathering enough supplies and wagons to support his movement, Longstreet launched his campaign on November 13. Efforts to trap the Army of the Ohio proved to be a failure, and Burnside's forces reached the defenses of Knoxville. In the resulting siege, Longstreet was unable to force the capitulation of the city or take it by storm, and Burnside outlasted his opponent until the situation at Chattanooga forced a crisis. With Grant's armies having driven the weakened Army of Tennessee off the heights surrounding Chattanooga, and a relief column under Sherman approaching Knoxville, Longstreet withdrew on the night of December 4-5.[232]

In these events, Thomas's Legion played no part. It remained in northeast Tennessee with the rest of Ransom's Division. Both Jones and Ransom felt it unwise to advance any further than Blountsville, due to the smallness of their forces. As the siege of Knoxville progressed, Jones was asked to cooperate with Longstreet as much as possible to help close the trap around Burnside. Ransom was merely advised from Jones's headquarters to "exercise your own judgment upon the information you have." Due to Longstreet's pleas for assistance, Ransom may have decided to move or perhaps received more direct orders to that effect from Jones, because on November 27 he was reported as moving towards Knoxville,

---

University of Tennessee Press, 1984), 20-94; Sword, *Mountains Touched With Fire,* 29-35, 46-69, 112-144.

231. Connelly, *Autumn of Glory*, 261-265; McDonough, *Chattanooga*, 96-101; Jeffry D. Wert, *General James Longstreet: The Confederacy's Most Controversial Soldier—A Biography* (New York: Simon & Schuster, 1993), 338-339; Sword, *Mountains Touched With Fire*, 74-78, 147; Woodworth, *Six Armies in Tennessee*, 175-177.

232. *O.R.* 31 (pt. 1): 258-550; Connelly, *Autumn of Glory*, 264-276; McDonough, *Chattanooga*, 101-205; Marvel, *Burnside*, 302-331; Wert, *General James Longstreet*, 340-354; Sword, *Mountains Touched With Fire*, 78-80, 149-318, 348-349 (especially 78-80, 161-162, 169-170, 348-349); Woodworth, *Six Armies in Tennessee*, 177-212 (especially 177-179, 206-212).

although it is not clear from the evidence that such in fact was the case. Two days later, Longstreet contacted Ransom, asking him to join him. By this time, Longstreet had received word of Bragg's defeat. Although Longstreet sent messages on that day and the next indicating that he would follow Bragg's orders and rejoin him, other messages, including the one to Ransom, paint a different picture. Longstreet argued to Ransom that it was impracticable to join the Army of Tennessee at Dalton, Georgia, where it had retreated, and that the best course would be for Ransom to combine his forces with Longstreet. Together, they would act to draw off as many Federal troops from the Chattanooga area as possible to give Bragg time to regroup. On the following day, Longstreet repeated his request, asking that Ransom come at least as far south as either Blain's Crossroads or Rutledge. The stated goal of their union in this message, however, was the capture of Burnside's army at Knoxville.[233]

Ransom contacted Longstreet on December 1, assuring him that he was on the way and hoped to arrive at Knoxville by the night of December 3. Evidently unbeknownst to Ransom and Jones, Longstreet wired President Davis on December 2, asking that Ransom be placed directly under his command. Davis replied on December 4, vaguely stating that "Ransom advanced to your support several days since." On the following day, Ransom met Longstreet at Blain's Crossroads as the latter withdrew from Knoxville. Apparently, Ransom was informed that he was now under Longstreet's direct command, or at least such can be inferred from Jones's subsequent surviving notes to Ransom. Ransom contacted Jones, who advised him on December 7 to "[a]ct with General Longstreet until further orders." Jones reiterated his orders to cooperate two days later; his messages to Ransom show, however, that he still considered himself Ransom's immediate superior. It soon devolved that Longstreet claimed command of all troops in eastern Tennessee by order of Davis, apparently on the basis of Davis's December 4 note (and, later, on the basis of a December 10 telegram from Davis that does not seem to have survived). Although Jones seems to have doubted the authenticity of this claim, he acquiesced reluctantly nonetheless. Longstreet's assumption of command was probably the only logical solution: he was both the senior officer and the most distinguished general in the region; and, as Buckner had been deposed as departmental commander during the Chattanooga siege, it would be natural for the him to take that role.[234] Thus, while Ransom's Division was still a part of Jones's department, it was now considered

233. *O.R.* 31 (pt. 1): 461-462, (pt. 3): 697, 741, 748, 750 (quote), 752, 758-762, 765, 767-768. 770, 791, 818-819. Although Longstreet was unaware of the fact when he wrote Ransom, Bragg had resigned as commander of the Army of Tennessee. He was temporarily replaced by Lt. Gen. William J. Hardee. Connelly, *Autumn of Glory*, 277.

234. *O.R.* 30 (pt. 2): 605, 31 (pt. 1): 462-463, (pt. 3): 777, 778, 784 (Davis quote), 792, 802, 811, 819, 838, 859, 864, 866, 872, 33:1092, 1093-1094, 1107-1110. By early 1864, Longstreet's command of the Department of East Tennessee was acknowledged as a fait accompli (if nothing else) by the Confederate government; see ibid., 31 (pt. 3): 893, 32 (pt. 2): 602, 33:1130. The assignment was not formally made until January 23. For Buckner's dismissal, see ibid., 31 (pt. 3): 650-668; Connelly, *Autumn of Glory*, 252-253. Buckner's Department of East Tennessee was broken up by Bragg with Davis's complicity and the part adjacent to southwestern Virginia assigned to Jones, although Buckner evidently never received an order to that effect and only found out about it in late October. Thus, Jones's assignment to take over a portion of eastern Tennessee in Buckner's absence was turned into a redefinition of the region's military boundaries (see Cooper's instructions to Jones on September 5 ordering him to take command of the area in *O.R.* 30 [pt. 4]: 606). The fact that the same thing happened to Jones upon Longstreet's arrival shows both a pattern and a lack of attention to detail.

to be on detached service with Longstreet. As a result, Thomas's Legion fell under Longstreet's command.

Following the conjunction of Longstreet's and Ransom's forces at Blain's Crossroads on December 5, Ransom turned about and moved northeastward some four miles to Rutledge, with Longstreet's veterans occupying Ransom's former campsite. They joined Ransom at Rutledge the following day, where the small army rested until December 8, when the march resumed. The Confederates reached Rogersville on December 9, and Yellow Stone on December 10. "I don't like So much retreating," Stringfield wrote in his diary. By this time, the Federals were in pursuit. Longstreet attempted to strike them on both December 14 and 15, but failed due to a lack of cooperation among his subordinates. In truth, the army was really in little shape for even limited offensive operations, lacking in food, shoes, ammunition, and other vital supplies. Thomas's Legion took no part in these minor actions, although it was sent back as possible support. It marched from Yellow Stone towards Bean's Station on December 14, "an extremely disagreeable tramp," complained Stringfield. "Mud—Mud—Mud. . . . I never saw weather or roads So bad." The Legion arrived at Bean's Station the next day, but Stringfield's hopes for action and the dispersal of the Federals from eastern Tennessee were frustrated, as they remained there until December 21. On December 22 the Legion was sent to a place near Rogersville, and settled into what it was thought would be winter quarters. Over the succeeding weeks, however, they moved twice more, marching south to Whitesburg on December 29 and to Bull's Gap on January 7.[235] These maneuvers put Longstreet back on the railroad between Greeneville and Knoxville.

The Legion was inspected during the late fall and winter by 1st Lt. John W. Barr of Levi's Battery, Jackson's assistant inspector general. These inspections occurred at Kingsport on November 24, Yellow Stone on December 12, and at an unknown location probably at the end of December.[236] Major McKamy remained in command of Walker's

235. *O.R.* 31 (pt. 1): 264-265, 271-272, 278-279, 284-287, 325-331, 338-339, 341, 407-422, 462-464, 479-480, 494-495, 513-518, 521-522, 529-530, 533-537, 546-548, 625-641, 646-665, 32 (pt. 1): 41, 44, 48, 49, 54; Stringfield, War Diary (copy), December 5, 6, 9, 10, 14, 15, 16-17, 18, 19-20, [21], 22, 23-24, 25, 29, 1863, ledger book, 188-191, Stringfield Papers, NCOAH; William Williams Stringfield, 1864 diary (original), January 1, 8, 1864, Stringfield Papers, NCOAH (hereinafter cited as Stringfield Diary [1864]); Leas, *Civil War Diary of Absalom J. Burum* (typescript copy, WCU), January 1, 5, 7, 1864, 21-22; "Record of Events": muster roll abstracts, November-December 1863: Companies D, E, F, G, H, I, and K, Infantry Regiment, and Companies A, B, C, E, and H, Walker's Battalion, and January-February 1864: Companies A and B, Walker's Battalion, Thomas's Legion, Compiled Service Records of Confederate Soldiers from the State of North Carolina (M270), reel 567. For correspondence related to Longstreet's and Ransom's movements and the Federal reactions, see *O.R.* 31 (pt 3): 344-542 passim, 790-792, 795-796, 800, 802, 810-812, 817-820, 837-839, 875, 32 (pt. 2): 3-5, 8-9, 19, 21-22, 27-29, 59, 507-509, 518, 528

236. Unless otherwise noted, the material discussed in the next few paragraphs comes from the following sources: Inspection Reports, 4th Brigade, Regiment: Thomas's Legion, Walker's Battalion, and Levi's Battery, December 12, 1863, and Inspection Report of the 4th Brigade commanded by Lt. Col. J. R. Love (A. E. Jackson's Brigade), undated ("Remarks show dates as late as December 1863"), Inspection Reports Received by the Confederate Adjutant and Inspector General's Office (M935), reel 3, files 1-B-83, 2-B-83, and 3-B-83, and reel 18, item 311, RG 109, NA; Inspection Reports, Regiment: Thomas's Legion, and Walker's Battalion, November 24, 1863, and undated, Chapter 1: Confederate Adjutant and Inspector General's Papers (hereinafter cited as Chapter 1): Muster and Pay Rolls, Entry 18, Box 826, Thomas's Legion Battalion Field and Staff File No. 2, RG 109, NA. The latest dates for information concerning individual officers in the undated report comes from the end of December.

Battalion. Jackson was on furlough at the time of the December 12 and undated reports, so Lieutenant Colonel Love acted as brigade commander, with Major Stringfield in command of the regiment. The strength of the units varied slightly throughout the three inspections. The size of the Infantry Regiment averaged 591 enlisted men (minus the members of Companies A and B) and 287 men present, with an average present for duty or effective total of 245. The average number of men present sick for the period was 22, while the average number absent sick was 73. Walker's Battalion averaged 81 men present out of an average total enlisted of 293; the average present for duty or effective total was 79, showing the extreme extent to which the battalion had shrunk. Almost all of its officers were reported absent without leave, including Walker on the undated report. The average number of men present sick for the period was 2, while the average number of men absent sick was 44. Three men were present sick, while another 41 were absent sick. Levi's Battery reported 43 present and 40 total effective out of a total of 60 enlisted on December 12. Both the regiment and the battalion looked after their sick properly. Barr rated the character of both units as "good; with propper Discipline will make good soldiers." A system of punishment duty, police duty, and extra guard duty was maintained; orders were carried out in a timely fashion. Charges against soldiers were processed correctly, and company officers regularly attended roll calls. Barr described both units as well-drilled.

Barr reported that the troops in both infantry units were armed with a mixture of muskets, Enfield rifles, and Mississippi rifles in "good condition," although Walker's Battalion lacked bayonets, and the Infantry Regiment lacked tools necessary for the maintenance of their weapons in November. Ammunition was ample and in good condition, while lost weapons, ammunition, and accouterments were "strictly accounted for." Accouterments were in good condition in the battalion, but only in fair condition in the regiment. Some accouterments and other equipment were lacking. Clothing was in good condition, but more was needed in the regiment for new recruits and returning absentees; both the regiment and the battalion lacked overcoats, which were badly needed with the onset of winter. Barr added in the December 12 report that the regiment that had "recently lost its 'Battle Flag' and are consequently without one. [R]epeated efforts have been made to procure one, but without success. I would respectfully suggest that measures be adopted to procure one for the command." Barr prudently did not mention, or perhaps did not know, the circumstances of the flag's destruction on November 12.[237]

Levi's Battery had finally received guns by the end of 1863, consisting of one twelve-pound bronze howitzer and one three-inch iron rifle, both in good condition. The battery also had plenty of ammunition. The battery had thirty-nine horses "in fair condition" and five horses that were broken down; however, many of the "fair" horses lacked horseshoes, rendering the company ineffective as field battery. For this reason, on January 1 the battery was sent to Bristol, where it evidently was placed as part of a stationary defensive line. From there it was sent to Saltville, Virginia, where it was reported on duty at the end of the month.[238]

237. The quotes from Barr come from the December 12 report, but are similar to his remarks in the others.

238. Inspection Report, 4th Brigade, Levi's Battery, Inspection Reports Received by the Confederate Adjutant and Inspector General's Office (M935), reel 3, file 3-B-83; *O.R.* 29 (pt. 2): 813, 33:1138; Barr to Samuel Cooper,

At the end of December and in early January, field returns were compiled for the Department of Western Virginia and East Tennessee. Jackson's Brigade was still a part of Ransom's Division. Jackson had overstayed his fifteen-day furlough, begun on December 6; Love still commanded the brigade on December 31, with Stringfield in command of the Regiment and McKamy of Walker's Battalion. On the latter date, Jackson's Brigade consisted of 43 officers and 313 men present for duty, with 313 effective total, 402 aggregate present, and 961 aggregate present and absent, down from 1,012 aggregate present on November 6. Levi's Battery, due to its detachment, was not included. On the January 8 field returns Jackson's Brigade was reported with 44 officers and 309 men present for duty, with 309 effective total, 408 aggregate present, and 771 aggregate present and absent.[239]

The general impression given in Barr's reports is that the various elements of Thomas's Legion were in reasonably good physical and material shape, given the rigors of the recent campaign. Discipline was obviously an ongoing concern; it is interesting that even after the Legion had acquitted itself well on at least two different occasions during the past four months, the verdict was that the men *would* become good soldiers with proper discipline. Coupled with the December and January field returns, however, the total numbers of men recorded in Barr's reports, as present, aggregate, and effective were a sign of deeper problems. The shrunken size of the ranks limited the Legion's fighting effectiveness, and probably did as much as anything to contribute to the negative impression. Three hundred and twenty-three men were reported as either absent without leave or as having deserted between August 20 and the end of October. The majority of these men, 216, came from the Infantry Regiment; 91 came from Walker's Battalion, while Levi's Battery lost 16. Sixty-three returned by the end of that period or were subsequently reported as present, indicating absences due to straggling or other problems; however, many of these returnees were reported as absent or deserters again at a later point.[240] The absence and desertion problem loomed heavily over Thomas's Legion and was a subject of much contention between Thomas and Jackson.

Meanwhile, Thomas found that there were enough threats to western North Carolina to keep him and the Indians occupied following their return to the state. In October, some of the Indians were called upon to deal with another excursion by Goldman Bryson, the Tennessee Unionist who had taken Murphy during the summer. With a command numbering between 100 and 200 men, Bryson was sent by Burnside on October 22 to recruit among disaffected inhabitants of the region, with orders to return to Knoxville in a fortnight; however, as he promptly captured Murphy once again, local Confederates assumed that his operation was primarily a raid. Maj. Gen. Carter L. Stevenson believed from reports that Bryson's goal was to get into Stevenson's rear and gather intelligence. There was also concern that the true

---

February 10, 1865, Letters Received by the Confederate States Adjutant and Inspector General's Office, (M474), reel 153, file 279-B-1865.

239. Inspection Report of the 4th Brigade commanded by Lt. Col. J. R. Love (Jackson's Brigade), undated, Inspection Reports Received by the Confederate Adjutant and Inspector General's Office (M935), reel 18, file 311; *O.R.* 29 (pt. 2): 908, 909, 31 (pt. 3): 892, 32 (pt. 2): 535-536. In light of what was to come in the next few months between Jackson and Thomas, there is a certain irony inherent in the former's overstaying his furlough.

240. Service record files (muster roll abstracts), Thomas's Legion, Compiled Military Service Records of Confederate Soldiers from the State of North Carolina (M270), reels 567 through 574.

objective was Athens, Georgia, where assets from a mint branch had been relocated. Stevenson dispatched Brig. Gen. John C. Vaughn with a force of around 100 men to intercept Bryson. Moving quickly across the mountains, Vaughn defeated Bryson in Cherokee County on October 27, killing 2 men and capturing 17 others, as well as 30 horses and some armaments. The rest of the command were dispersed and escaped.[241]

On the following day, a force departed from Murphy in pursuit under the command of Maj. Marcus L. Brittain of the 47th Battalion N.C. Home Guard. Accompanying Brittain's men were nineteen Cherokee Indians led by 2nd Lt. Campbell H. Taylor of Company B of the Infantry Regiment. Brittain soon ordered Taylor to go ahead with the Indians to see if they could track down Bryson. Taylor, who was part Cherokee himself, proceeded until his party discovered a place where the tracks showed that two horses had departed from the main body of Bryson's force, heading off in the direction of the Bryson family home. Taylor followed and found Bryson and a man otherwise identified only as Ledford near Bryson's house. Taylor called for Bryson to halt, but the latter attempted to flee. Taylor then shot Bryson, who kept on running. It took several more shots before Bryson was finally killed; Ledford was captured. Among the papers found on Bryson's body were his company muster roll and Burnside's orders, which Thomas subsequently distorted in a newspaper letter as indicating that Bryson's "robberies and murders had the sanction of the Lincoln Government." Taylor returned to Murphy, the remainder of Bryson's command having meanwhile escaped to Tennessee. Some Cherokees walked about Murphy wearing bits of Bryson's bloody, bullet-ridden clothing, probably as a sign of contempt for the man they held responsible for the murder of John Timson before the war. Brittain professed to find the sight "a musing."[242]

Unionist activity and lurking deserters continued to plague the area. In Wilkes County, an openly Unionist meeting was held, complete with a raising of the United States flag. At a subsequent meeting, resolutions were passed with the object of bringing an end to the

241. *O.R.* 30 (pt. 4): 748, 31 (pt. 1): 9, 235; M. L. Brittain to Governor Vance, November 1, 1863, Governors' Papers: Vance, 1862-1865, NCOAH; O'Brien, *Mounted Partisans*, 17-18. Brittain placed the size of Bryson's force as "from 120 to 150 men"; 2nd Lt. Campbell H. Taylor of Company B, Infantry Regiment, described it as a "company" (*O.R.* 31 [pt. 1]: 235). As rumors spread, the size of the command magnified; Col. M. H. Wright, who sent out the warning of the possibility of a strike on Athens, described it as "a full regiment of Federals" (ibid., 30 [pt. 4], 748). According to O'Brien, the fight between Vaughn and Bryson was near Beaverdam, and the 17 prisoners were taken by Vaughn to eastern Tennessee and executed.

242. *O.R.* 30 (pt. 4); 748, 31 (pt. 1): 9, 235; Brittain to Governor Vance, November 1, 1863, Governors' Papers: Vance, 1862-1865, NCOAH; Thomas to the editors of the *Asheville News*, December 25, 1863, published in the *Asheville News*, January 21, 1864, reprinted in the *Western Democrat* (Charlotte), January 26, 1864 ("robberies and murders" quote); O'Brien, *Mounted Partisans*, 16, 19. Brittain referred to Taylor as "Captain Taylor," and counted the Cherokee as "Some 25 in number." Taylor, whose report is in *O.R.* 31 (pt.1): 235, gave the number as nineteen. Taylor made no mention of Brittain in his report. It is possible that Brittain sent Taylor ahead early, and then returned to Murphy to await results (which would to a large extent explain the escape of the rest of Bryson's company). Brittain's reason for breaking off the pursuit to was that "I could not persue them to advantage with cavalry & got Capt Taylor to take his Indians & learn if posible the direction he went." The text of Burnside's orders to Bryson were included with Taylor's report; issued on October 22 by Maj. Edward M. Neill, Burnside's assistant adjutant general, they simply stated that "Captain G. Bryson, First Tennessee National Guard, is hereby ordered to proceed with his command to North Carolina and vicinity, for the purpose of recruiting, and will return here [to Knoxville] within a fortnight, when he will report in person to these headquarters."

conflict, followed by a march through Wilkesboro which included from 150 to 200 armed men, most of whom were believed to be deserters. Capt. John V. B. Rogers of Company A, 19th Regiment N.C. Troops (2nd Regiment N.C. Cavalry), wrote that both Unionists and deserters were wreaking havoc in Cherokee, Macon, Jackson, Haywood, Buncombe, Madison, Mitchell, and Yancey counties. Many of the deserters were from the Confederate forces in eastern Tennessee. Organized into bands and defying both military and civil authorities, they had the local pro-Confederate populace at their mercy, stealing horses and, on one occasion, driving 230 head of government cattle to Knoxville. He also repeated the story that deserters were preventing Confederate soldiers on furlough from returning to their units, promising to protect them from reprisals if they stayed. In Cherokee County, they drove off the conscription officer. Another source wrote the governor of further troubles in that county, as local Unionists had prevented the courts from operating in Murphy.[243]

In addition to the depredations of Unionists and deserters, other factors added to the chaos. Confederate troops in Tennessee crossed the border to impress horses and cattle.[244] "The[y] follow up every religious meeting and impress horses from men & women for the army they say," wrote one citizen, adding that the impressment issue was doing more than anything else to erode support for the Confederacy. Others criticized the will of the pro-Confederate people to resist through the militia, or the quality of the local forces and their commanders. Brittain openly disparaged some of the governor's appointments of officers in his letter of acceptance of a commission in the Home Guard, claiming that while he himself was not a military man, at least he knew how to fight. As Brittain's own behavior during Bryson's raid demonstrated, such talk was cheap. In Brittain's case, he may have had the excuse of being out of ammunition, as he reported in early October that his men were down to three or four rounds apiece, if even that. Brig. Gen. J. W. McElroy of the 19th Brigade N.C. Home Guards reported that the Home Guard forces in Madison, McDowell, Rutherford, and Henderson counties had no weapons. Lt. Col. John S. McElroy of the 16th Regiment N.C. Troops (6th Regiment N.C. Volunteers) witnessed conditions in his native Yancey County while at home on wounded furlough. He lamented that the mountain citizenry showed little willingness to resist, and claimed that the Yancey County militia was the only one in the region trying to do something.[245]

Various solutions were proposed to alleviate the problems. Most involved the idea of bringing in more troops. Lieutenant Colonel McElroy proposed the transfer of his regiment, which was recruited almost entirely from mountain counties, from the Army of Northern Virginia; it would crush the dissidents and raiders and inspire further resistance. Similarly,

243. W. W. Hampton to Vance, September 7, 1863, J. S. McElroy to Vance, September 10, 1863, with endorsement from J. W. McElroy on the same date, D. Pendency Johnstone to Vance, September 11, 1863, W. Murdoch to Vance, September 16, 1863, J. V. B. Rogers to Seddon, October 3, 1863, all in Governors' Papers: Vance, 1862-1865, NCOAH.

244. Similar problems occurred in eastern Tennessee itself. Jackson confiscated more than a hundred horses that had been taken without payment or receipt by the 21st Regiment Virginia Cavalry when the former recognized that they belonged to Confederate supporters. *O.R.* 32 (pt. 3): 847.

245. J. F. Foreman to Vance, August 28, 1863, J. S. McElroy to Vance, September 10, 1863, with same date endorsement by J. S. McElroy, D. Pendency Johnstone to Vance, September 11, 1863, Brittain to Vance, October 6, 1863, J. W. McElroy to Vance, October 28, 1863, J. W. McElroy to Vance, November 17, 1863, all in Governors' Papers: Vance, 1862-1865, NCOAH.

Captain Rogers thought that his company, a mountain unit, should be brought from Virginia.[246] These proposals, while sincere, were examples of the localist thinking exhibited by Thomas himself. In the cases of McElroy and Roberts, their ideas no doubt fell on deaf ears: not only would Lee not grant such requests if he knew of them, but they ran against the grain of thinking of many others regarding the usefulness of troops stationed near their homes. This was the situation when Thomas and the Indians arrived, quickly demonstrating their potential usefulness in local defense by the pursuit and killing of Bryson.

Following the death of Bryson, Thomas began laying the groundwork for increasing his force in western North Carolina and having the rest of the Legion transferred back to his command. On September 16, Bragg appointed Brig. Gen. Robert Brank Vance to command the Western District of North Carolina, comprising the area west of the Blue Ridge. Vance had authority over all state and Confederate forces in the district.[247] As noted earlier, Thomas fell under Vance's command. The addition of Thomas's men was welcome news for Vance. Besides Bryson's expedition, Vance had recently been preoccupied with a larger and more serious incursion into Madison County by the 2nd Regiment N.C. Mounted Infantry (Union), among whose ranks was Capt. George W. Kirk, a young Tennessee Unionist whose name soon became prominent in the hit-and-run warfare of the region. Replying on November 4, Vance wrote that "I hasten to say that I am much pleased at the authority he [Bragg] gives you to extend your force." Vance promised to write Jones and ask for the return of the rest of the Legion from eastern Tennessee. "In the mean time you can push up operations in your region and give Lt Col Walker orders to operate in Cherokee, to report to you and you to me."[248]

Walker had been at home for some time on furlough due to increasing health problems, possibly since the summer.[249] Thomas now took advantage of the presence in the area of Walker and a number of his other officers. On November 8, he reported to Walker the contents of Brigadier General Vance's letter and provided his own instructions. Walker would assume authority over Capt. James W. Cooper of Company H, Infantry Regiment, and Capt. Garner N. Loudermilk and 1st Lt. Robert A. Akin of Company H of Walker's own battalion. Orders would shortly go out from Walker to Capt. Stephen Whitaker of Company E of the battalion, who was also at home. Whitaker had been sent to western North Carolina by Ransom along with Capt. C. C. Berry of Company A and Capt. William B. Nelson of Company B of the battalion on October 26 to gather up absentees, arrest deserters, and recruit; it will be recalled that Berry's and Whitaker's companies were those that had suffered so heavily from absenteeism in the wake of the Strawberry Plains defeat in June, and that a

246. J. W. McElroy to Vance, September 10, 1863, J. V. B. Rogers to Seddon, October 3, 1863, Governors' Papers: Vance, 1862-1865, NCOAH.

247. *O.R.* 30 (pt. 4): 656.

248. Robert Brank Vance to Thomas, November 4, 1863, Thomas Papers, DU. For the raid and recruiting expedition of the 2nd Regiment N.C. Mounted Infantry (Union), see *O.R.* 30 (pt. 2): 547; Trotter, *Bushwhackers*, 98-99; Matthew Bumgarner, *Kirk's Raiders: A Notorious Band of Scoundrels and Thieves* (Hickory, N.C.: Tarheel Press, 2000), 18-23.

249. Columbus F. Walker to Stringfield, September 4, 1915, Stringfield Papers, WCU; Thomas to William C. Walker, November 14, 1863, Whitaker Papers, NCOAH. See also p. 82 n. 196 above for questions about when Walker returned to western North Carolina.

similar mission had been sent shortly after that time. They were due to return to Tennessee on November 20, and their failure to do so due to Thomas's orders would cause repercussions for their military careers. Cooper failed to return from a fifteen-day furlough begun on August 15, and evidently attempted to resign from the service at that time, as his father Thomas Cooper, his predecessor as company commander, had done earlier in the year. The younger Cooper's resignation was not approved. His absence resulted in frustration and anger among at least one of his subordinates, 1st Lt. Lafayette George, who complained in letters of Cooper's disappearance, and his failures to communicate with his officers and to gather up and return the company's absentees. Akin had been sent on detached service on August 15 and failed to return; he may have been intercepted by Thomas and ordered to remain. Loudermilk simply dropped out of sight at the time of the of the Henderson's Mill and Rheatown fights on October 11, having been left sick at Carter's Depot on October 1; he somehow managed to make his way home. With this mixed lot, Thomas set out to organize a new battalion while he awaited Brigadier General Vance's efforts to get the rest of the Legion transferred to him.[250]

Trying to understand the nature of Thomas's command in western North Carolina is difficult, due to a lack of official reports and records; a number of tantalizing references in the correspondence of Thomas and others associated with the unit; and confusing comments in writings of the postwar era. According to Thomas, he was authorized by Bragg to recruit at least one more Cherokee company; it was lettered Company C, following the company designations of (2nd) Company A and Company B of the Infantry Regiment. The date of its organization is unknown, but it was during the winter of 1863-1864. Another company, known as D, was active by at least February of the following year. This is known from the fact that when several members of the command were captured at Quallatown at that time, they were identified in Federal provost marshal records as belonging to either Companies C or D of Thomas's Legion.[251]

250. Thomas to William C. Walker, November 8, 1863, and Special Order No. 5, District of Southwest Virginia and East Tennessee, October 25,1863 (excerpt only), Whitaker Papers, NCOAH; service record files of Robert A. Akin, C. C. Berry, James W. Cooper, Thomas J. Cooper, Garner N. Loudermilk, William Butler Nelson, and Stephen Whitaker, Thomas's Legion, Compiled Service Records of Confederate Soldiers from the State of North Carolina (M270), reels 567, 568, 570, and 574; J. A. McKamy to Samuel Cooper, February 22, 1864, Letters Received by the Confederate Adjutant and Inspector General's Office, (M474), reel 133, item 124-N-1864; Lafayette George to Rachel George "and friend," October 17, 1863, and to Rachel George, October 26 and November 9, 1863, Roster Document No. 1474, CWRP. Other officers who ended up in western North Carolina were 1st Lt. Dempsey Manuel Raby of Company G, Infantry Regiment, and Bvt. 2nd Lt. William H. Phillips of Company B, 2nd Lt. James A. Paul of Company C and 3rd Lt. John Hibberts of Company H, Walker's Battalion. J. R. Love to "my dear parents," March 4, 1864, and Love to Thomas, March 8, 1864, Thomas Papers, DU; service record files of John Hibberts, James A. Paul, William H. Phillips, and Dempsey Manuel Raby, Thomas's Legion, Compiled Service Records of Confederate Soldiers from the State of North Carolina (M270), reels 570 and 572. Of the latter four men, Phillips failed to return from the earlier July 1863 mission to gather up absentees; the others either overstayed furloughs or otherwise went AWOL. It is not known for certain that these men were with Thomas, although Lieutenant Colonel Love seemed to imply as much in his March 8 letter by lumping them together with the other absentee officers.

251. Robert Brank Vance to Thomas, November 4, 1863, Thomas Papers, DU; Thomas to William C. Walker, November 8, 1863, Whitaker Papers, NCOAH; Crow, *Storm in the Mountains*, 59, 104, 233; service record files, Thomas's Legion, Compiled Service Records of Confederate Soldiers from the State of North Carolina (M270),

The history of Walker's Battalion in Clark's *North Carolina Regiments* further complicates an understanding of the structure and development of Thomas's command. In the process of retroactively "expanding" the battalion to a full regiment by, among other things, including two later Indian companies, it seems that Robert Akin may have intermixed their officer personnel. The first of these companies, which he associated with Cherokee County, was supposedly commanded by Capt. James Welch. His 1st lieutenant was supposed to have been Campbell H. Taylor, the same man who had led the scout against Bryson. According to Akin, two unnamed Indians served as 2nd lieutenant and junior second lieutenant (3rd lieutenant). Akin wrote that the second company was recruited in Jackson County, led by a man named Black Fox, who in various sources is described as both a Methodist preacher and a traditional shaman. Black Fox's lieutenants were not indentified by Akin, although his 1st lieutenant was supposed to have been a Cherokee. Akin "assigned" these companies to Walker's Battalion as Companies I and K respectively, with both units each possessing conveniently round and identical numbers of ninety officers and men apiece. No muster rolls survive for either company.[252]

Recognizing that Akin's inclusion of the Indian companies in Walker's Battalion had no basis in fact, historian Vernon H. Crow concluded that "Company I" was the new Company C, while "Company K" was in reality Company D. This made sense, as there was a June 1864 letter of resignation from Campbell Taylor as captain of "Company C" in Thomas's command. Crow believed that Taylor was the original captain of Company C and was succeeded by Welch, although Taylor was Welch's lieutenant in Akin's text. As Federal parole records relating to Taylor's capture at Hartwell, Georgia, on May 10, 1865, identified him as captain of Company C, Thomas's Legion, it would seem that Thomas refused Taylor's resignation, or that he continued to serve in some other capacity (Taylor asserted a desire to serve in the ranks when he resigned). This makes the idea of Welch as Taylor's successor somewhat problematic. Further complications arise from the identification by Cherokee historians Jack Frederick Kilpatrick and Anna Gritts Kilpatrick of Black Fox (a translation of a Cherokee name rendered variously in English as Inoli, I:no:li, I:no:la, and Enola) as captain of Company C, not D. If correct, this would indicate that, assuming Taylor's resignation was accepted, he was succeeded by Black Fox/Inoli, rather than Welch—unless Inoli was the Cherokee name of either Taylor or Welch, which does not seem to have been the case. In addition, an April 1864 letter indicates that Welch and Taylor were in command of individual

---

reels 567 through 574. Soldiers from the Legion captured on the February 2 raid on Quallatown were identified in their service records as having been captured on that date or on "February 7" in Jackson County, based on Federal provost marshal records; they were confined at Knoxville on the latter date. Unfortunately, the surviving records, and their interpretation by compilers of the service records at the National Archives, have added another layer of confusion in regard to the rosters, including the implication that some of these men were captured on February 7 rather than February 2. Federal provost marshal records identified members of the Legion captured at Quallatown by their company letter (Company B, Thomas Legion; Company C, Thomas Legion; and Company D, Thomas Legion). National Archives compilers were evidently at a loss when they encountered records for men with a company letter only; as a result, all cases of men who were captured while serving with Thomas in western North Carolina have service files incorrectly identifying them as members of a company of the Infantry Regiment. See also the rosters for Companies A, B, C, and D of the Indian Battalion in this volume.

252. Aiken, "Eightieeth Regiment," in Clark, *North Carolina Regiments*, 4:119.

companies at the same time. It would appear that Welch's Cherokee company was either Company E or Company F, most probably the former.[253]

Company D seems to have been commanded by a man named John D. Berry, a private in Company A, 19th Regiment N.C. Troops (2nd Regiment N.C. Cavalry) who dropped out of its records during the summer of 1863. He first appeared in documents related to the Legion in a cryptic reference by Thomas to Walker in November: "I received your note for J D Berry." Subsequently, he was active in some way with Thomas. John Smiley, a musician in the 39th Regiment N.C. Troops, was home on furlough when Federal raiders struck western North Carolina in February 1864. "[B]y the enemy in Vadeing our country So bad a few days before I got home I had no time to rest on my furlough but took up my gun and went to scouting with Capt Berry and his boys and when his (Co) was organized I was put in as first Segt of the company and has been acting as Such every Since," Smiley wrote Thomas in 1865. He signed his letter as 1st Sgt. of Company D. While at first glance this might be a reference to Capt. C. C. Berry of Walker's Battalion, both the latter's departure for eastern Tennessee in early 1864 with his absentees and the continuing service of Smiley with Thomas in a company commanded by a Captain Berry negate this idea. Furthermore, an officer sent by Thomas to inspect his forces at the mouth of the Tuckasegee River reported in April 1864 that "I next proceeded to organize Capt Berry's Company which resulted in the unanimous choice of J. D. Berry for Capt"; this would appear to be the same company in which Smiley served. Exactly what form the unit was in when Smiley originally joined up with it was unknown; it may possibly have been originally a partisan band or a Home Guard unit. Finally, there is a reference in Stringfield's published Civil War memoir that Thomas's force in western North Carolina included "Tidwell's cavalry company." William B. Tidwell commanded John D. Berry's old company in the 19th N.C. at the end of the war; as there is no evidence that Tidwell himself or the entire company was ever with Thomas, Stringfield was probably thinking of Berry's company. Thus, Berry's company was probably the same Company D from which men were captured in February, although given the fact that it was evidently not organized formally until April, there is a possibility that it was a successor company to an earlier unit broken up by the raid.[254]

Besides the new companies and the absentees, Thomas seems to have been joined by one of the three cavalry companies once belonging Walker's Battalion, the former Company

253. Crow, *Storm in the Mountains*, 59, 104, 131, 233; C. H. Taylor to Thomas, June 27, 1864, Thomas Papers, DU; abstract, Roll of Prisoners of War captured by U.S. Forces under Bvt. Brig. Genl. S. B. Brown and paroled at Hartwell, Ga., and Anderson and Greenville, S.C., in service record file of Campbell H. Taylor, Thomas's Legion, Compiled Service Records of Confederate Soldiers from the State of North Carolina (M270), reel 573; Kilpatrick and Kilpatrick, *The Shadow of Sequoyah*, 5 n. 8, 13; W. H. Parker to Thomas, April 16, 1864, Thomas Papers, WCU (microfilm, Thomas Papers, DU). The assignment of "E" to Welch's company is tentative, but makes sense based on the identification of John D. Berry's company as "D," and information provided in Parker's April 16 letter to Thomas about Welch's and A. L. Hicks's companies.

254. Manarin and Jordan, *North Carolina Troops*, 2:106-107, 10:112, 156; Thomas to William C. Walker, November 14, 1863, Whitaker Papers, NCOAH; J. S. Smiley to Thomas, January 10, 1865 [misdated to 1864], Thomas Papers, DU; C. C. Berry to Samuel Cooper, June 5, 1864, Letters Received by the Confederate Adjutant and Inspector General's Office (M474), reel 96, item 2167-B-1864; W. H. Parker to Thomas, April 16, 1864, Thomas Papers, WCU (microfilm, Thomas Papers, DU); Stringfield, "Memoirs of the Civil War," typescript, McClung Collection, L-McGL, 28 (copy, Stringfield Papers, WCU).

F, now Company K in the 5th Regiment Tennessee Cavalry (McKenzie's). Certainly Thomas had never reconciled himself to their transfer. On March 15, 1863, Thomas had written to Secretary of War Seddon requesting their return, asserting that they had been "assigned to other commands without authority." Donelson, who forwarded the message on March 17, included an explanation of his reasons for reorganizing the department's forces, which had included the transfers. The papers were forwarded back and forth among Thomas, Jackson, and the various departmental commanders throughout the spring and summer. Surprisingly, Seddon ordered the return of the companies, possibly due to the connection between Thomas and President Davis; however, the orders were subsequently suspended. In December 1863, Lieutenant Colonel Love, perhaps at Thomas's prompting, examined the copies of the correspondence in the files of Jackson's assistant adjutant general and summarized their contents to Adjutant and Inspector General Cooper, requesting again the return of the companies. In his endorsement of the message, Ransom pointed out that the two companies with the 1st Regiment Tennessee Cavalry (Carter's) had been with it since its formation, and noted that the Legion was now divided between western North Carolina and eastern Tennessee, with the "efficient parts" in the latter. Whether due to Ransom's caveats or to the cumulative evidence in the correspondence, no action was taken to restore the companies to Thomas.[255]

Although Thomas was not able to get back the companies with the 1st Regiment Tennessee Cavalry, it appears that all or part of Ghormley's company were with him in the fall of 1863. The company disappeared from the records of the 5th Regiment Tennessee Cavalry after the March-April 1863 muster roll. While there is no known mention of a transfer or of anything amiss such as a mass desertion, there are no more muster reports or records of events for the company in the regimental record after that point, although they exist for both the field and staff and the other companies. References crop up in Thomas's papers and other sources, however, in such a way as to indicate that Ghormley and at least part of the company were in western North Carolina. It is possible that, initially at least, Ghormley found himself in a situation somewhat similar to Walker, C. C. Berry, and Whitaker: he may have been home gathering absentees and found himself receiving orders from Thomas. On November 8, Thomas mentioned Ghormley and his men in connection with the former's plans to gather his new command at a place called Rocky Point on the Cheoah River. "[S]uch of Capt Gormley's men as are at home will report to him and hold themselves in readiness to serve when called on. I design getting his company permanently attached to the Legion, and fill up the company with such men as want to mount themselves. He and his men as well as the Indians will be ready to report to me I have a use for them."[256]

255. Love to Cooper, December 20, 1863, with endorsements by Ransom, December 26, 1863, and Jones, December 27, 1863, Letters Received by the Confederate Adjutant and Inspector General's Office (M474), reel 8, file 1398-L-1863. The idea that the transfer of the cavalry companies was unauthorized, although clearly nonsense in respect to conventional military practice and authority, perfectly reflects Thomas's long-held ideas that Davis had given him complete carte blanche to run the Legion exactly as he pleased without reference to any higher authority beyond, perhaps, the issuance of operational orders.

256. Thomas to Walker, November 8, 1863, Whitaker Papers, NCOAH. The records of events for the 5th Regiment Tennessee Cavalry and its companies, and the service records of its soldiers, are in Compiled Service Records of Confederate Soldiers from the State of Tennessee (M268), reels 22 through 26; the records of events

In April of the following year, an officer in the Provisional Army of the Confederate States named W. H. Parker was sent by Thomas to the mouths of the Tuckasegee River to inspect his companies stationed there and formally organize those which had not previously done so. Parker wrote that "Capt Gormley has reported. He informs me that he has made an arrangment with Capt Everett to consolidate their commands." The mention of "Captain Everett" and his company adds another layer of mystery to the activities of Thomas and Ghormley. Eppa (or Eppie/Eppy) Everett had formerly served as 2nd lieutenant of Company E, 3rd Regiment Tennessee Infantry (Vaughn's). He resigned in December 1861 for unknown reasons. According to a postwar account, he was reported acting as an enlistment officer in Blount County, Tennessee, in May 1863 with the rank of captain; the same source claimed that he then commanded a company under Thomas from August 1863 until the end of the war. The date is surely wrong, as Thomas did not add any new companies to his command until after he returned to North Carolina in September, unless Everett was in command of the otherwise unknown company of dismounted cavalry which was reported to have evacuated Strawberry Plains with Thomas when he withdrew to the mountains. Regardless, the exact nature of Everett's company is unclear. Legion historian Vernon H. Crow identified it as a company in the 3rd Regiment Tennessee Cavalry. The latter unit was the original cavalry regiment of Nathan Bedford Forrest; there is no evidence that Everett ever served in it, let alone commanded one of its companies. It is likely that Crow was thinking of Everett's former unit, the 3rd Regiment Tennessee Infantry, which following its parole at Vicksburg was redesignated as the 3rd Regiment Tennessee Mounted Infantry (Lillard's) in January 1864, and was subsequently sometimes referred to incorrectly as the 3rd Regiment Tennessee Cavalry. There is also no evidence, however, that Everett ever rejoined his former regiment following his original resignation.[257]

It is possible that Everett's command was made up at least in part of former men from his old company in the 3rd Regiment Tennessee Infantry who had failed to return to duty following their Vicksburg paroles; however, without firm evidence this interpretation remains speculative. There was, however, some form of consolidation with Ghormley's company, as Stringfield referred long after the war to "Ghormley and Everett's Cavalry of the Eightieth North Carolina (Walker's) Regiment" as active in western North Carolina in January 1865. Among many questions that come to mind regarding this mystery unit is how it functioned command-wise with two captains. As far as is known, Ghormley was the senior of the two in terms of rank, and definitely had the more experience; nevertheless, such

are conveniently abstracted in *O.R. (Supplement)*, Pt. II, 66:93-112, while the service records are published in Carl Campbell, transcriber, *McKenzie's Fighting Fifth: Service Records of the 5th Tennessee Cavalry Regiment Confederate States of America*, 2 vols. (Tenn.: Rhea County Historical and Genealogical Society, 1999).

257. W. H. Parker, P.A.C.S., to Thomas, April 17, 1864, Thomas Papers, DU; Service Record File of Eppy Everett, 3rd Regiment Tennessee Mounted Infantry (Lillard's), Service Record Files of Confederate Soldiers From the State of Tennessee (M268), reel 125; *Tennesseans in the Civil War*, 1:55-57, 178-180; Crow, *Storm in the Mountains*, 136, 220; Hill, *Confederate Military History: North Carolina*, 479. The only contemporary records for Everett's service in the 3rd Regiment Tennessee Infantry (Vaughn's) are a regimental return dated June 1861, a company muster roll for September-October 1861, and a regimental roster dated October 24, 1864; the latter document notes his resignation and the date. Thus, he was not recorded as having returned to the regiment between December 1861, and October 1864, the latter date being after he had begun to serve with Thomas.

situations could lead to potential awkwardness. There was a prior connection between the two men, as Ghormley had also served as 2nd lieutenant in the same company of the 3rd Regiment Tennessee Infantry as Everett before the former lost his position in the May 1862 reorganization; this past relationship probably facilitated the consolidation of their companies and their cooperation.[258] It is possible that, originally at least, the consolidation was effected when Ghormley was recuperating from injuries. It is known that some time during the spring of 1864, Ghormley's company passed through the strongly Unionist area of Cades Cove in Blount County while returning from a raid. The local Unionist Home Guard attempted to blockade the route, and in the resulting skirmish Ghormley was wounded; perhaps Everett took over in the meantime. Beyond that point, matters get even murkier. On October 16, 1864, Ghormley requisitioned ten pairs of shoes for his men; the form was signed by Lt. Col. Bryan Gibbs McDowell of the 62nd Regiment N.C. Troops, who at that time was acting commander of the portion of the Legion in western North Carolina during an absence of Thomas. This indicates that Ghormley was still active with Thomas's command; the requisition documents his unit as Company G. Everett, meanwhile, showed up in Stringfield's postwar writings as among a party of men who accompanied the latter on a mission to Knoxville in May 1865; in those accounts, he is referred to by the rank of captain. When Everett and the rest of the party were captured, however, Federal provost marshal records described him as a private in Company A, Thomas's Legion and as a "deserter." The full truth regarding this company, its officers, and its history with Thomas is probably lost forever.[259]

In addition to the old Indian companies, the new companies, the consolidated company of Ghormley and Everett, and the absentees and deserters from the main body of the Legion, Thomas seems to have recruited quite a bit among deserters from other units with ties to the western mountains. According to court-martial charges filed in May 1864 by the headquarters of the 65th Regiment N.C. Troops (6th Regiment N.C. Cavalry), Thomas recruited twenty-two known absentees or deserters from that unit at some point between September 1863 and April 1864. There were undoubtedly many more from other units, such as John Smiley of the 39th Regiment N.C. Troops, mentioned above in connection with John D. Berry's company. Which companies these men served in is unknown, unless some chance record survived to document their service; some, as in the case of Smiley, probably went into Berry's company, Ghormley and Everett's company, or even one of the Cherokee units.

258. It is probable that one of the two was actually a junior 2nd lieutenant (i.e., 3rd lieutenant), as both men were reported as 2nd lieutenants in the September-October 1861 company muster roll. Since Ghormley was also recorded as 2nd lieutenant in subsequent musters, it is most likely that he was the real 2nd lieutenant, although it is also possible that he was Everett's successor in that rank.

259. Stringfield, "Sixty-Ninth Regiment," in Clark, *North Carolina Regiments*, 3:58 (quote), 760; service record file of DeWitt C. Ghormley, 3rd Regiment Tennessee Mounted Infantry (Lillard's), Compiled Service Records of Confederate Soldiers from the State of Tennessee (M268), reel 126; Durwood Dunn, *Cades Cove: The Life and Death of a Southern Appalachian Community 1818-1937* (Knoxville: University of Tennessee Press, 1988), 135-136; special requisition for shoes, October 16, 1864, service record file of D. C. Ghormley, 5th Regiment Tennessee Cavalry (McKenzie's), Compiled Service Records of Confederate Soldiers from the State of Tennessee (M268), reel 23; Stringfield, "Memoirs of the Civil War," typescript, McClung Collection, L-McGL, 34-35 (copy, Stringfield Papers, WCU); service record file of Eppy Everett, Thomas's Legion, Compiled Service Records of Confederate Soldiers from the State of North Carolina (M270), reel 569.

Others were put into a company commanded by Pvt. Albert L. Hicks, one of the deserters from the 65th N.C., who was elected to temporarily command a mixed group of some forty men in April 1864 subject to official recognition. Some materials suggest that it was granted that status, or at least that Thomas used it anyway, and that it was known as Company F.[260]

Whether known by Thomas or not, the practice of enlisting deserters had been going on for quite a while, even among the main body of the Legion in eastern Tennessee. A cursory examination of the rosters of Thomas's Legion show quite a number of men who are either identifiable as absentees from other units or who have very similar names. Many of these men came from other mountain units, such as the 29th and 39th Regiments N.C. Troops. Sometimes the practice involved a degree of connivance on the part of officers of both the Legion and of the units from which the deserters came. A startling example involved the case of one Pvt. Joseph L. Gipson in Whitaker's company (Company E, Walker's Battalion). Gipson deserted and was reported to be with Company E of the 39th Regiment N.C. Troops. Whitaker wrote the commander of that company, Capt. George E. Bristol, demanding Gipson's return. Bristol replied concerning the details of Gipson's case. It seems that Gipson robbed the home of a Mrs. Baker, who evidently lived somewhere in eastern Tennessee or western North Carolina. Somehow he made his way to Dahlonega, Georgia, where he was apparently apprehended by Bristol's company. Bristol had Gipson sent to the provost marshal in Atlanta, with orders to forward him back to Whitaker. Somehow or another, the provost marshal lost all of the relevant paperwork (or so Bristol claimed), and when the former asked Gipson his unit, he claimed to be a member of the 39th N.C. The provost marshal sent Gipson back to the 39th N.C., where he remained in the custody of the brigade provost guard. Eventually, Gipson asked Bristol to release him from the guard in exchange for service as a member of Bristol's company; it appears that Gipson was afraid that Mr. Baker would kill him in retaliation for the robbery. Bristol agreed; "I did so for his accomenadation[. T]hat is how he came to be in my Company," he wrote.[261]

Bristol wrote again a week later in regards to another message from Whitaker. The case now involved Pvt. Joseph L. Perry in Bristol's company, who had deserted in May

260. Headquarters 65th Regiment N.C. Troops, "Charges and specifications against Col William H Thomas of Thomas N C Legion," May 11, 1864, and W. H. Parker to Thomas, April 16, 1864, Thomas Papers, WCU (microfilm, Thomas Papers, DU); Manarin and Jordan, *North Carolina Troops*, 2:496, 532. Field returns for the summer of 1864 show that Thomas had seven captains, implying seven companies; furthermore, if Ghormley's company was Company G in October 1864, then there should have been six other companies. In the service records of Capt. Matthew H. Love of Company A are requisitions for shoes for men from Companies D, F, and G of Thomas's Legion also dating to October 1864, a time when the Infantry Regiment and Walker's Battalion were in the Shenandoah Valley; this would indicate that the companies mentioned in the requisition were part of Thomas's command in western North Carolina. Return of the Troops in the District of Western North Carolina Commanded by Col. John B. Palmer, June 7, 1864, Field Returns of Troops commanded by Col. John B. Palmer, June 1, June 20, and July 1, 1864, Chapter 1: vol. 15, 16: Entry 65, pt. 2, Entry 24, RG 109, NA; special requistion dated October 24, 1864, service record file of Matthew H. Love, Thomas's Legion, Compiled Service Records of Confederate Soldiers from the State of North Carolina (M270), reel 570. As noted in the text, it is not certain which letters were assigned to Welch's and Hicks's companies; when Parker arrived to muster and inspect Thomas's companies, he dealt with Hicks before Welch. From the information in Parker's letter, however, Welch's company was already organized, while Parker had Hicks's men select officers. Thus it is likely that Welch's company was "E," after John D. Berry's "D," while Hicks's company was "F."

261. George E. Bristol to Stephen Whitaker, November 17, 1863, Whitaker Papers, NCOAH.

1863. Perry, a resident of Clay County, was evidently lurking somewhere in the mountains. His father approached Whitaker about "a Swap" between Whitaker and Bristol over Gipson and Perry. How Mr. Perry received word of the situation so quickly is not known, but as Gipson also haled from Clay County and both soldiers had the same given names and middle initials, it is highly likely that they were related in some way. The proposed switch was fine with Bristol, who promised to send the necessary transfer papers. "Capt any man of mine that is at home if you Can get him to go to your Company do so," he added. "I mean men that have deserted my Company and are afraid to go back[. Y]ou and I will not fall out about them I asshure you so [long as] they are in the Searvice of their Country I am satisfyed[.] I have some men here [who] probably would like to go to your Company if they wish to do so take them in and you and I will make that all right." In the case of Gipson, he served in Company E of the 39th Regiment N.C. Troops, where his name was recorded as Joseph L. Gibson. There is no record of a transfer, however. It appears an effort was made to disguise the nature of the transaction, as it was reported that he enrolled in that unit on February 28, 1863, nine days after he actually had enlisted in Company E, Walker's Battalion instead; a note was added in his records for the 39th N.C., claiming that he had not been assigned to service with that unit until October 1, 1863. As for Perry, there is no evidence that he served in the Legion at all; if he did, he must have joined with Thomas in western North Carolina, rather than Whitaker as the agreement seemed to stipulate.[262]

Such behavior opened the floodgates to a whole range of problems involving command and control, discipline, and troop strength. Furthermore, the inevitable blind spots that existed in the military system led to abuses by less than scrupulous individuals. Such is the case involving David and Center Ledford who also served in Whitaker's company. Like Gipson/Gibson and Perry, the Ledfords were from Clay County. Both David and Center enlisted in Company E, Walker's Battalion, on September 25, 1862. It appears, however, that they had already enlisted in other units. A David A. Ledford and an Eli C. Ledford, both of Clay County, had enlisted in Company E, 39th Regiment N.C. Troops, the same company which Gipson later joined, in November 1861. David A. Ledford is readily identifiable as David Ledford in Company E, Walker's Battalion; if Eli C. Ledford's middle name may assumed to be Center, then the full name of Center Ledford of Walker's Battalion was Eli Center Ledford. Both men were initially reported as captured on October 15, 1862, in Kentucky, but their records in the 39th N.C. were later amended to list them as deserters.

If this were all that there was, it would be easy to discount these identifications; after all, relatives frequently had similar names in those days, and the men in Walker's Battalion could have been cousins to those in the 39th N.C. Furthermore, the fact that both men in the 39th N.C. were supposedly with that unit at the time of their desertion would seem to rule out their being the same as those in Walker's Battalion. This is only the beginning, however, of a series of "coincidences" involving Clay County soldiers with similar or identical names. In July 1862, when David A. Ledford and Eli C. Ledford were serving with the 39th N.C., a David Ledford and a Sentre Ledford, both of Clay County, enlisted in Company B, 7th Battalion N.C. Cavalry. There is no evidence that either men served in this unit at that time,

262. Bristol to Stephen Whitaker, November 23, 1863, Whitaker Papers, NCOAH; Manarin and Jordan, *North Carolina Troops* 10:152, 156.

however. This was two months before David A. Ledford and Center Ledford enlisted in Company E, Walker's Battalion; a month after their enlistment in Thomas's Legion, David A. Ledford and Eli C. Ledford deserted from Company E, 39th N.C. Throughout this period, there are no records showing that David and Center Ledford were actually on duty with Walker's Battalion; in fact, outside of their enlistments, they were not mentioned at all until the January-February 1863 muster, when they were reported as absent without leave (this is the same muster period in which David and Eli Ledford's records in the 39th N.C. were updated to report them as deserters). There is a curious notation, "conscript & carried to Ga," in the Walker's Battalion records of David and Center Ledford. The Georgia reference provides another connection. On February 23, three men named David Ledford, Center Ledford, and E. McC. Ledford enlisted in Company A, 16th Battalion Georgia Partisan Rangers (Cavalry, later known as the 13th Regiment Georgia Cavalry); all three deserted the next day. E. McC. Ledford was a new figure in the emerging pattern, but a similar name soon appeared again. On February 28, 1863, David Ledford and Eli C. Ledford were reported as having returned to Company E, 39th N.C., which at that time was located at Shelbyville, Tennessee. Or so it was set down in their records, for on that very same day, David Ledford and Center Ledford were reported as having enlisted in Company B, 7th Battalion N.C. Cavalry, in Clay County. No reference was made of their supposed previous enlistments in the same company in July of the previous year. A day earlier, a man named Elisha McC. Ledford also enlisted in Company B in Clay County; he would appear to be the same individual as E. McC. Ledford of the 16th Battalion Georgia Cavalry. On July 13, 1863, both David Ledford and Center Ledford were reported absent without leave from Company B, 7th Battalion N.C. Cavalry, and were later recorded as deserters after the command became the 65th Regiment N.C. Troops (6th N.C. Cavalry); Elisha McC. Ledford deserted about the same time. Meanwhile, it is recorded that David A. Ledford deserted from the 39th N.C. on August 1, while Eli C. Ledford left on May 13. Both subsequently returned to the latter unit (willingly or otherwise), and were court-martialed in February 1864, at which point they disappeared from the records.[263]

263. Service record files of Center Ledford, David Ledford, and Elisha McC. Ledford, 65th Regiment N.C. Troops (6th Regiment N.C. Cavalry), David Ledford and Sentre Ledford, 7th Battalion N.C. Cavalry, David A. Ledford and Eli C. Ledford, 39th Regiment N.C. Troops, and _ Ledford, Center Ledford, and David Ledford, Thomas's Legion, Compiled Service Records of Confederate Soldiers from the State of North Carolina (M270), reels 41, 43, 417, and 570; service record files of Center Ledford, David Ledford, and E. McC. Ledford, 13th Regiment Georgia Cavalry, Records of Confederate Soldiers Who Served in the Civil War, Compiled Service Records of Confederate Soldiers Who Served in Organizations from the State of Georgia (M266), reel 54, RG 109, NA. David Ledford's records in Thomas's Legion were accidentally separated into two National Archives service files under the names of _ Ledford and David Ledford. The records of David and Center/Sentre Ledford for Company B, 7th Battalion N.C. Cavalry and Company F, 65th Regiment N.C. Troops, are incorrectly listed in 2:489, 526-527 as present or accounted for from July 1862 until they were recorded absent in the fall of 1863; in fact, there are long gaps in their records for which they are not accounted for at all, and each man has separate enlistment dates for July 1862 and February 1863. It is possible that they did not enlist at all until 1863; July 5, 1862, was the date of the company's organization, and the record of their supposed enlistment on that date may be the result of less than exacting paperwork. The court martials of David A. and Eli C. Ledford as members of Company E, 39th N.C. Troops in February 1864 were accidentally omitted from their published service records in 10:154 of this series. There was an Elijah Ledford in Company E, Walker's Battalion; it is not known if he was the same individual as Elisha McC. Ledford.

It appears that the Ledfords were bounty jumpers, men who signed up for units to collect the bounties offered for new enlistees and then quit to move on to another company, a problem that plagued both sides.[264] The sheer number of coincidences involved in names and desertion patterns link these different men together and identify them as the same three individuals. There are apparent geographical contradictions, however, which make it appear as if at particular times they were serving simultaneously in different units at once. It is possible, if not probable, that they received assistance in their activities, intended or otherwise, from friendly company record keepers. It would not be necessary in such a scenario for a helper to be aware of or condone what the Ledfords were doing, as he could have been persuaded to assist them in covering up their absences by any sort of seemingly reasonable excuse explaining why they needed to be away for such-and-such a time. The obliging Captain Bristol of Company E, 39th Regiment N.C. Troops, whose activities have already been noted and who was himself a Clay County resident, is an obvious suspect, but it could have easily been anyone with access to or oversight of the records in that regiment or in the 7th Battalion N.C. Cavalry, or both units.

Together with Thomas's policies regarding the use of absentees from other units, the cases of the Ledfords and Gipson illustrate the problems that indiscipline, localism, and self-interest inflicted on the Confederate war effort. In regards to his own actions, Thomas was in direct violation both of official military policy and the instructions of his immediate superior. "It is very important to arrest every deserter in the country, and you will give special attention to that," Brigadier General Vance wrote Thomas on November 4. "When arrested send them to me at this point. Deserters soon become our worst enemies & they ought to be attended to at once." Thomas seems to have grasped this idea initially, at least in part. He instructed Walker a few day later to gather up absentees. "Those that come in and defend their homes will be favored," he wrote. "Those that fail to come in of their own accord will erelong be Collected and sent to Asheville to be sent where they cannot runaway." Already, however, Thomas reinterpreted Vance's instructions to suit his own purposes, as the reference to showing favor towards "[t]hose that come in and defend their homes" illustrates.[265]

By March 1864 the situation had not improved. "If the whites of your command wont keep in camp, they must be arrested and sent to East Tennessee," warned Vance's successor, Col. John B. Palmer. "The orders are imperative. There May be some hardship involved in this, but this is a hard & terrible war and the only way we can end it is to, every one of us, do his whole duty." Palmer's orders hint that the problem was not just one of deserters joining Thomas to protect their home area, but one of sheer indiscipline. Perhaps Thomas and his men viewed themselves as glorified militia that had the standing of regular service without the responsibilities, or only those responsibilites that they saw fit to observe. Thomas's original appointment to the rank of partisan ranger captain by the state, as well as the often-referenced but undocumented "promise" from President Davis regarding his authority and mission, may have influenced his conduct in handling his men. Other factors may have been at play here; it is known that Thomas was having trouble feeding his

264. Robertson, *Soldiers Blue and Gray*, 37.

265. Robert Brank Vance to Thomas, November 4, 1863, Thomas Papers, DU; Thomas to William C. Walker, November 8, 1863, Whitaker Papers, NCOAH.

command at the time Palmer wrote, which may explain the particular absence problem referred to. Regardless, a situation in which soldiers absented themselves as they pleased would not result in the discipline necessary for conventional service.[266]

It was Thomas's use of absentees from his own legion that perhaps raised the most eyebrows. It provoked a sharp reproof at the end of December from his friend and usually steadfast supporter, Lieutenant Colonel Love. "I hope you will at once send back all men, who belong to Companies here, under existing orders. if they remain where they are, will be dropped from the rolls as deserters, both officers & men. where is Capt Cooper, Lt Col Walker & others? If they do not report at an early day, I will be Compelled to drop them from the rolls as deserters," Love wrote. "Men who have deserted from here are writing back letters to their friends—stating that they have reported to you—that you have furloughed them home & that all is right. You can readily see that this Causes dis[s]atisfaction in the Command." In February 1864 Capt. James W. Terrell wrote Thomas of his concerns that the white soldiers from the Legion in western North Carolina would never receive their pay unless they returned to their companies. "The captains are compelled to report them absent without leave and if they do not return in a limited time they are drop[p]ed as deserters and instead of getting any pay due them they may think themselves fortunate if they are not shot for desertion." Terrell pleaded that Thomas at least send back Pvt. William Pendleton Hyde of Company F, Infantry Regiment, as "he has never deserted nor did anything of the kind that I know of. there is a large amount of money due him here if by the end of the month[.] he can get it but [at] the next muster Capt McConnell will have to drop him[.] then in addition to the incurred Disgrace will be the loss of his honest dues." He reminded Thomas that "Military regulations cannot be bent and they require a soldier to be with his company except in certain Contingencies which do not cover the cases under consideration." Hyde was subsequently listed in his company's records as having deserted on January 15, 1864.[267]

While Thomas's use of absentees and deserters to defend western North Carolina showed a certain practicality, it reinforced discipline problems within the units affected and sapped their strength, rendering them ineffective in fully performing their tasks of service within the often far more militarily vital theaters of operations in which they served.[268] The

266. John B. Palmer to Thomas, March 11, 1864, Thomas Papers, DU. If Thomas saw his new battalion as a partisan band, it would explain the lax discipline in regards to the comings and goings of his men; however, the Legion was never officially designated as a partisan unit.

267. Love to Thomas, December 28, 1863, Thomas Papers, DU; Terrell to Thomas, February 5, 1864, Thomas Papers, WCU (microfilm, Thomas Papers, DU); service record file of William Pendleton Hyde, Thomas's Legion, Compiled Service Records of Confederate Soldiers from the State of North Carolina (M270), reel 570.

268. See also Robert E. Lee's January 13, 1864, message to Davis regarding similar desertion problems and fixation on home defense at the expense of the overall military situation among soldiers serving in western Virginia and elsewhere in *O.R.* 33:1085-1086. No less a person than Governor Vance, who otherwise disagreed with Thomas on so many other issues, saw the wisdom of such a plan. During the summer of 1863, Vance passed along a proposal made by friends of some 1,200 deserters currently lurking in the mountains that they would be willing to serve in the ranks of local units. His idea was endorsed by John A. Campbell, the Confederate assistant secretary of war. Nothing came of the idea, however. Vance's 1863 letter included his own concerns that "[t]he effect on the Army [of enlisting deserters] might be injurious," while noting that this method might be the only way to get them to serve; his admission that they were currently engaged in "plundering and robbing the people" probably did nothing to advance the concept with the Confederate authorities. *O.R.* ser. IV, 2:674.

effectiveness of the part of the Legion under Jackson was impaired most of all, as one Asheville resident commented to Governor Vance: "I think if you would use your influence to have Thomas's legion put under proper & efficient officers you would do an essential Service[.] at present it is a perfect humbug and so will be as long as it is undercut by Call him Bill Thomas a perfect imposition on the Government & people—but you know him yourself."[269] Furthermore, there is an open question about how effective recruited deserters were even in defense of their own homes; as will be shown, the activities of Thomas's band drew mixed reviews from the very people they were supposed to protect.

In the meantime, Thomas set out to follow Brigadier General Vance's instructions, at least as far as they accorded with his own plans. Vance wanted Thomas to not only act in defense of western North Carolina, but to keep in mind the broader regional military concerns involving eastern Tennessee as well, so that they could offer assistance if an operation was mounted to regain the area. He thought in terms of a possible two-pronged advance, with Thomas moving across the Smokies while Vance himself went via Warm Springs through the Bald Mountains; the two columns could then "hook on to the troops either from below or above." Vance also hoped that Thomas would be able to detach some of his Indians to assist local forces in defending the pass of Cataloochee Creek in Haywood County. "Please make reports of your monthly operations," he added.[270]

Thomas contacted Lieutenant Colonel Walker, recuperating in Cherokee County, with a summary of Vance's orders and ideas, at least as far as defending western North Carolina was concerned; significantly, at this point he made no mention of returning to eastern Tennessee. He explained the new chain of command, adding that "you are relieved from duty with Lt Col Jas R Love," although Jackson was of course Walker's actual superior. Walker was to gather the availabile forces to defend Cherokee County, while Thomas would follow Vance's request to guard the passes in Haywood County. "Under the present arrangement we can combine the entire force in western North Carolina," he wrote. "The home guard being under Brig Genl Vance, will act with our troops and care must be taken to prevent any prejudice between them."[271]

For Thomas, the keys to defending Cherokee County were the passes of the Hiwassee and Cheoah Rivers. Captain Cooper was at the pass for the latter stream at Rocky Point, organizing a camp which seems to have been intended as the base of operations for the new command. Although a member of the Infantry Regiment, Cooper was directed to report to Walker, as were Captain Loudermilk, Lieutenants Akin and William Alexander Wiggins, and any other officers from Walker's Battalion who might be home at the moment, as well

269. William Murdock to Governor Vance, November 6, 1863, Governors' Papers: Vance, 1862-1865, NCOAH.

270. Robert Brank Vance to Thomas, November 4, 1863, Thomas Papers, DU. The officer in charge of the forces defending the Cataloochee Creek area was a Major Rhea; he was probably either Maj. Wilson M. Rhea of the 100th Regiment N.C. Militia, a Burke County unit, or William M. Rhea, who in 1861 had been a captain in the 112th Regiment N.C. Militia from Haywood County and who may have been promoted in the interim. Bradley, *North Carolina Confederate Militia Officers Roster*, 270, 296.

271. Thomas to Walker, November 8 (quotes), 14, 1863, Whitaker Papers, NCOAH. Thomas's embracement of joint action between his command and the Home Guard, as well as his concerns for promoting harmony between them, may be another clue that some of the otherwise unknown companies mentioned as serving with him in 1863-1864 may have belonged to the Home Guard.

as all of the soldiers that Walker could collect. Ghormley was also expected to gather up men from his company. The Cherokee companies, or at least a portion of them, were reported to be in Cherokee County under the command of Lieutenant Taylor; they were ordered to prepare three days' rations and report to Rocky Point. For sustaining the troops, Thomas had accumulated salt and corn meal on the Valley River, which Walker was instructed to bring to Cooper, while beef was to be gathered in the countryside. As to the issue of armaments, Thomas added vaguely that "I presume that you can draw arms and ammunition from the officers in command of our troops in Monroe County [Tennessee]."[272]

Walker may have entertained doubts about the propriety or legality of Thomas's orders, as the colonel included the following passage in a subsequent message on November 14, 1863, as a reinforcement of his instructions: "I enclose herewith a copy of Brig. Genl Vances letter, From which you will perceive, that it was contemplated that you should for the present remain in Cherokee Collect in your troops and report to me and I to Brig Genl Vance, Looking however to a forward movement and a reunion of the Legion." Thomas reiterated many of the points in his earlier letter, adding that Walker was to send the Indians in Cherokee County to Rocky Point immediately. After Walker had used his men, the Home Guard, and (if available) the militia to restore order in Cherokee County, he could then perhaps join Thomas with part of his force or move to some other position. He also hinted at the possibility of a need to support Vance in an anticipated move down the French Broad River into East Tennessee. Although Thomas acknowledged that he had received news that Walker was not well enough to assume active service, he did not offer suggestions for a substitute to carry out his orders or provide any alternative scenarios of operation.[273]

Whatever doubts he might have harbored, Walker instructed C. C. Berry and Whitaker on November 19 to gather up all of their officers and men who were in Cherokee County, prepare three days' cooked rations, and rendezvous with him at Murphy on November 23. Once there, they would proceed to the area of Beaverdam. Unlike Thomas, Walker provided specific instructions to Whitaker on gathering supplies which demonstrated his concern for the citizens: Whitaker was to draw upon government cattle only, and was to buy corn from the locals. All sellers were to be presented with receipts showing the exact number of bushels purchased to present to the local quartermaster for reimbursement. Impressment of private property was strictly forbidden, as was absence from camp without orders. Whitaker was also instructed to arrest all absentees and transport them under guard to Murphy. Similar instructions were given to Berry, with the additional order to take eight men with him to Monroe County, Tennessee, and gather up absentees from his company who were there.[274]

Thomas's plans were soon threatened by new orders from Tennessee. On November 18, Bragg relieved Brigadier General Vance and ordered him to report to the Army of Tennessee's headquarters; his replacement as district commander would be Col. John B. Palmer

272. Thomas to Walker, November 8 (quote), 14, 1863, Whitaker Papers, NCOAH.

273. Thomas to Walker, November 14, 1863, Whitaker Papers, NCOAH. For the difficult and confusing chain of command situation in which Walker and his company officers found themselves in for the next few months, see p. 77 n. 183.

274. Walker to Stephen Whitaker, November 19, November 23, 1863, Whitaker Papers, NCOAH; Walker to C. C. Berry, November 19, November 26, 1863, and Berry to Samuel Cooper, June 5, 1864, Letters Received by the Confederate Adjutant and Inspector General's Office (M474), reel 96, file 2167-B-1864.

of the 58th Regiment N.C. Troops. Vance, however, did not comply. Whatever his initial reasons for delay, his decision to stay put was probably influenced by news of the rout of the Army of Tennessee at Missionary Ridge on November 25, its subsequent withdrawal to northern Georgia, and Bragg's relief from command. Longstreet now attempted to assert his own authority over western North Carolina. On November 29, he ordered Thomas and Walker to bring their forces to Ducktown, Tennessee, proceed to Cleveland, and place themselves under Brig. Gen. John C. Vaughn. They were to bring with them any absentees from other units that had been gathered locally. Beef cattle was to be impressed, leaving a "reasonable Supply for family use in all Cases," while horses "not absolutely needed for farming purposes" would be be taken for the artillery and supply wagons. On the same day, Longstreet wrote Vance "that the best service you could possibly render would be to unite your forces with ours at once. I hope that your views in this matter may coincide with my own, and that you may determine to join us at once." Either growing impatient or failing to receive a message that satisfied him, Longstreet telegraphed Davis on December 2 asking that Vance be put under his authority, the same message noted earlier in which he made a similar request regarding Ransom. In the meantime, Longstreet asked Ransom to order Vance to join him, or at least try to influence him to cooperate. On December 4, Adjutant and Inspector General Cooper telegraphed Governor Vance, asking him to wire his brother with direct orders to join Longstreet around Knoxville. Davis, writing on the same day, informed Longstreet that Brigadier General Vance would "co-operate" with him, "and if he can join you, will, of course, be subject to your orders." Cooper, perhaps only now becoming aware of the command change from Vance to Palmer, wired the governor again on December 5, ordering Palmer to proceed with his troops; on the same day, a special order was issued from Cooper's office again ordering Brigadier General Vance to move forward with his men. While the published order of these last two documents in the *Official Records* do not necessarily reflect the chronologies of their actual issuance, they suggest along with the related correspondence that even Richmond was not entirely sure who answered to whom.[275]

Thomas's reaction to these developments are unknown, although any orders which would have resulted in his falling under Jackson's command again could not have been pleasing to him. For his part, Walker reported Longstreet's orders to Whitaker and C. C. Berry on December 4 and instructed them to join him at Persimmon Creek, bringing the cattle and any hides collected with them. No further action was taken, however, and Walker and his absentees were still in Cherokee County on December 21; at that time, he ordered Whitaker to mount some of his men to picket and scout "while the Command stays in the country by order of Col Thomas Comdg Legion." Brigadier General Vance evidently did not move to Longstreet's aid at all, or at least there is no known surviving record of his having done so; probably the whole idea became moot as Longstreet withdrew from Knoxville.[276]

275. *O.R.* 31 (pt. 3): 711, 752, 759 (Longstreet to Vance quotes), 770, 777, 778, 782, 784 (Davis quotes), 786; Special Order No. ?, November 29, 1863 (Longstreet to Thomas quotes), Thomas Papers, DU; Walker to Whitaker, December 4, 1863, Whitaker Papers, NCOAH. It would appear that Palmer was formally the district commander from November 18 on, but had to defer to Vance as senior and ranking officer as long as the latter remained in the area, a situation somewhat analogous to the Longstreet-Jones relationship in eastern Tennessee.

276. Walker to Whitaker, Special Order _, December 4, 1863, Whitaker Papers, NCOAH; Walker to Berry, December 4, 1863, Letters Received by the Confederate Adjutant and Inspector General's Office (M474), reel

Although Thomas did not join Longstreet, he soon made an incursion into eastern Tennessee. Some time after the Bryson expedition, several of Thomas's men were arrested by the Union Home Guard of Sevier County. In December, Thomas descended from the Smoky Mountains with less than two hundred men, including the Indians and possibly some detached men from the 25th Regiment N.C. Troops.[277] After a journey of some forty miles, they reached Sevierville, probably on December 8, at daybreak.[278] Thomas rescued his men from the jail and captured the local provost marshal, six other Federals, and "about sixty" of the Home Guard. Federal sources reported that Thomas's troops "robbed the citizens of considerable property." In addition, a document suggests that he seized at least one Unionist citizen and transported him back to North Carolina.[279] Thomas retired to Gatlinburg, where he

---

96, file 2167-B-1864; Crow, *Storm in the Mountains*, 52-53. Palmer had already gone to Tennessee on November 28 to harry the Federal supply trains moving from the Sevier County area into Knoxville when he received Longstreet's request to unite with him on December 1. He left his cavalry and returned to North Carolina to gather up the available infantry and artillery. Palmer joined Longstreet at Russellville, Tennessee, on December 8; however, due to his description of conditions in western North Carolina, he was almost immediately ordered to return and guard the pass to Warm Springs on the French Broad River in Madison County. He was in place there by December 11. *O.R.* 31 (pt. 2): 811-812. It is possible that similar orders reached Vance, Thomas and Walker instructing them to stay put in North Carolina, although if so there is no known surviving evidence for it.

277. Thomas to the editors of the *Asheville News*, December 25, 1863, published in the *Asheville News*, January 21, 1864, reprinted in the *Western Democrat* (Charlotte), January 26, 1864. Thomas referred to "Capt Boon and his squad" as part of the command. This may have been a Home Guard unit; however, members of the 25th Regiment N.C. Troops had been active on a recruiting mission in the mountains in October, when they skirmished with Unionists in Madison County. Although it appears that the detachment had returned to the regiment at Kinston by November, Capt. Harlen Aurelius Boone of Company B was on detached service through February 1864. Various receipts, requisitions, and vouchers from December 3, 1863 to February 11, 1864, show that he was at Asheville for much of that period and that he was evidently responsible for the provision and equipage of other men besides himself. Cumulatively, this evidence makes it at least a possibility that he was the man mentioned by Thomas and that the troops in question were from the 25th Regiment N.C. Troops. Boone's detached service, however, was the result of a July 1863 request to be taken out of field service and assigned to post duty due to chronic dyspepsia, making his involvement in a campaign unlikely and the identification tenuous. *O.R. (Supplement)*, Pt. II, 48:810; Garland S. Ferguson, "Twenty-Fifth Regiment," in Clark, *North Carolina Regiments*, 2:297; Louis H. Manarin, "25th Regiment N.C. Troops," in Manarin and Jordan, *North Carolina Troops*, 7:353; service record file of Harlen A. Boone, 25th Regiment N.C. Troops, Compiled Service Records of Confederate Soldiers from the State of North Carolina (M270), reel 313.

278. Thomas wrote that he set out on December 8, indicating that he reached Sevierville on the morning of December 9. Accounts by members of the 15th Regiment Pennsylvania Cavalry, as well as company records for the same unit, indicate that they set out in pursuit of Thomas from Knoxville on December 7 or 8, with most versions supporting the latter date. As their orders came directly from Burnside in response to the raid, and it is not known how long it took for the news to get from Sevierville to Knoxville due to the unsettled countryside and the recent collapse of Longstreet's siege, the raid could have been no later than December 8 and possibly a few days sooner. Thomas to the editors of the *Asheville News*, December 25, 1863, published in the *Asheville News*, January 21, 1864, reprinted in the *Western Democrat* (Charlotte), January 26, 1864; *O.R. (Supplement)*, Pt. II, 57:313, 322, 333, 355, 364, 371, 380, 406, 413; Charles B. Lamborn, "First East Tennessee Campaign—December 3, 1863, to February 11, 1864," in Chester H. Kirk, ed. and comp., *History of the Fifteenth Pennsylvania Volunteer Cavalry in the Rebellion of 1861-1865* (N.p: Philadelphia, 1906), 332; Wm. Spang, "The Cherokee Indian Raid," in ibid., 345.

279. Federal Provost Marshal Charles Inman wrote to Thomas from Sevierville on January 4: "The Military Authorities at Knoxville have ordered me to arrest John Mullendore Esqr and hold him prisoner as a hostage for Thommy Baker which I have done accordingly. Mr. Mullendore will receive the same treatment that Mr. Baker does. If you release Mr. Baker and permit him to return home and remain at home a peaceful and quiet citizen,

had established a camp and, according to statements made by his men to the locals, planned to winter there.[280]

News reached Knoxville of the Sevierville raid by December 8. Burnside called out a detachment of the 15th Regiment Pennsylvania Cavalry, which had arrived on December 7 as part of Sherman's relief column, to pursue Thomas. Under the command of Col. William J. Palmer, the Federals set out on the afternoon of December 8. Reaching Sevierville the next day, they learned that Thomas had withdrawn to Gatlinburg. The expedition continued to a place called Chandler's, where Palmer sent back those with horses unfit for the steeper paths that lay ahead to picket the roads from Sevierville and prevent Confederate sympathizers from warning Thomas. "The people everywhere evinced the greatest delight to meet our cavalry," recalled Lt. Col. Charles B. Lamborn, "and attested the sincerity of their loyalty by feeding our command and horses and guiding the command through the difficult and unknown mountain paths." Palmer arrived at Weir's Crossroads by 5 P.M. From there the direct route went to Gatlinburg, the final approach running up a narrow gorge which was easily defendable by the Confederates and making surprise unlikely if not impossible. It was from Gatlinburg that Thomas had escaped the pursuit of the 5th Regiment Indiana Cavalry in September, and he must have had this in mind in choosing the same site for his current base of operations; if the Federals attempted to retaliate for the Sevierville raid, history would hopefully repeat itself and he would be able to get away at the first sign of an approach up the defile. Palmer attempted to prevent that prospect by dividing his force. He took the main body, numbering 150, on a circuitous and steep horse trail across Cove Mountain which would bring him to the rear of Thomas's camp. The remainder, consisting of "about 50 men" under Lamborn, would take the direct route. If all went as planned, both contingents would attack at dawn, capturing or destroying Thomas's force.[281]

Mr. Mullendore will be released and permitted to return home likewise as a peaceful citizen, and enjoy the same privileges he did before the arrest. Otherwise, Mr. Mullendore will be held as long as Mr. Baker is." Charles Inman to Thomas, January 4, 1864, Thomas Papers, DU. The outcome of the exchange and the reasons for the seizure of Baker are unknown. The incident suggests that, for all his efforts to maintain friendly relations with Unionist civilians in eastern Tennessee, Thomas had adopted the practice of seizing pro-Union citizens, similar to the abductions by Unionist bushwhackers of pro-Confederates, at least under certain circumstances.

280. Thomas to the editors of the *Asheville News*, December 25, 1863, printed in the *Asheville News*, January 21, 1864, reprinted in the *Western Democrat* (Charlotte), January 26, 1864 ("about sixty" quote); Lamborn, "First East Tennessee Campaign," in Kirk, *History of the Fifteenth Pennsylvania Volunteer Cavalry*, 332 ("robbed the citizens" quote); James W. Over, "Fighting Cherokee Indians," in ibid., 348; *O.R.* 31 (1): 439. Although Thomas retrospectively emphasized that the object of the expedition was to free the captive men, it is unlikely that this was the sole reason, and even more difficult to believe that Brigadier General Vance would authorize the mission if that were the only goal. It is likely that Thomas planned to use Gatlinburg all along as a winter base for provisioning the Indians and launching raids into eastern Tennessee, and that the captured men were scouts and foragers from the expedition. It is speculated in Crow, *Storm in the Mountains*, 53, that Thomas crossed the border in response to Vance's instructions in November. Thomas may have also decided that the best defense was an offense, setting up a raiding base in eastern Tennessee in order to keep the Federals further away from his beloved North Carolina mountains.

281. Spang, "The Cherokee Indian Raid," in Kirk, *History of the Fifteenth Pennsylvania Volunteer Cavalry*, 345; Lamborn, "First East Tennessee Campaign," in ibid., 332-333; Over, "Fighting Cherokee Indians" in ibid., 348; Wm. M. Palmer, "Left to Die in Rebel Hands," in ibid., 357; *O.R. (Supplement)*, Pt. II, 57:313, 322, 333, 355, 364, 371, 380, 406, 413; *O.R.* 31 (1): 438-439 (quote, 438), (pt. 3): 298.

The Federals advanced to their positions after dark. It appears that Palmer's own segment had the worst of it, as they had the longer and more difficult approach to go, single file up the steep and forested mountain path, leading their horses on foot. In the darkness, his men lost the trail twice; fortunately for them, they had assistance from Unionists who acted as guides. By 1 A.M., Palmer's party stopped to rest and allow the stragglers to catch up. The trek soon resumed, this time down the mountain. The local scouts led the way, bearing pine-wood torches. "I thought the column resembled an immense serpent, with every vertebra in its back in violent action, winding away its way into the darkness of the forest," recalled Corp. William Spang of Company E. Finally reaching the foot of Cove Mountain, the Federals quickly watered their horses in a nearby stream, mounted and prepared to attack.[282]

Lamborn reached his designated position about the same time as Palmer. It was now daybreak on the morning of December 10. How many Confederates were encamped nearby is unknown. In his brief account of the ensuing clash for the *Asheville News*, Thomas reported that the original force that he had taken to Sevierville, which he put at "less than two hundred men. . . . became divided" at Gatlinburg, and those that participated in the fight consisted of "[t]he part that remained"; the rest probably were escorting the prisoners to North Carolina. In his after-action report of December 11, Palmer estimated the number of men as about 200, consisting of around 150 Indians and the rest whites; however, based on his wording, his information seems to have derived from the reports of others, probably the natives of Sevierville, rather than direct observation. Given the rapid and confused nature of the skirmish that followed, he probably had no opportunity to make an accurate estimate of the size of the Confederate command, and it seems likely that the force he encountered consisted entirely of the Cherokee companies (which included some whites, besides the officers).[283]

The Federals surprised and dispersed Thomas's pickets. They were not quite quick enough, however, as the pickets opened fire before they were driven off, alerting the camp. This proved crucial as the Federals reached the camp itself. Thomas had shrewdly chosen a steep hillside for the camp, itself the spur of a wooded ridge which provided an escape route. The hill dominated both Palmer's and Lamborn's routes to the camp and separated them, preventing communication and the coordination of their assaults. Furthermore, a wide and deep creek, recalled by one Pennsylvanian as "about thirty feet across," ran at the base of the hill on Palmer's side. "A direct and open attack . . . could not have carried it or even reached the camp through the narrow and easily defended defile up which the road ran," Lamborn wrote; nevertheless, he reported that the Indians were surprised and completely panicked, as his men were in range of the camp before resistance could be fully organized. Despite Lamborn's triumphal account which makes it seem as if the Indians were routed, the Cherokee position proved to be a tough nut to crack. Palmer himself crossed the creek on horseback to make a quick reconnaissance from a small clearing that lay between it and the hill.

282. *O.R.* 31 (pt. 1): 439; Lamborn, "First East Tennessee Campaign," in Kirk, *History of the Fifteenth Pennsylvania Volunteer Cavalry*, 333; Spang, "The Cherokee Indian Raid," in ibid., 345-346 (quote, 346).

283. *O.R.* 31 (pt. 1): 439; Thomas to the editors of the *Asheville News*, December 25, 1863, published in the *Asheville News*, January 21, 1864, reprinted in the *Western Democrat* (Charlotte), January 26, 1864; Lamborn, "First East Tennessee Campaign," in Kirk, *History of the Fifteenth Pennsylvania Volunteer Cavalry*, 333. The part of the expedition which left the main body was probably "Capt Boon and his squad" (see p. 120 n. 277).

Dodging bullets all the while, he returned, ordered his men to dismount, and sent them forward. The Cherokees fired down upon them, accompanying their shots with war whoops. After about an hour's fight they abandoned their camp, but only after being flanked.[284]

Palmer's men quickly searched the camp. The Cherokees had been interrupted while making breakfast, so the Federals grabbed the corn cakes from the hot frying pans and ate them. Finding no men hiding in the huts, the Pennsylvanians regrouped and moved up the ridge towards the woods. The Indians, who had withdrawn eastward along the ridge to a nearby mountain, opened up a steady if not particularly accurate fire from the timber. The resulting skirmish lasted for some hours before the Confederates withdrew for good. Only two captains and a sergeant among the cavalrymen had been wounded. One Confederate was captured, described by Palmer as "belonging to Wheeler's cavalry," possibly a deserter who had joined Thomas. Lamborn estimated that six Cherokees were killed, but if so, their bodies were taken away, a point made by Palmer in his report, who refused to speculate on whether there were actually any killed or not. Some Indian women who arrived the night before were reported as present in the camp and evidently taken prisoner, another indication that Thomas had planned to spend the winter at Gatlinburg. The Federals also captured "16 horses, 18 muskets, 2 boxes of ammunition, several bushels of salt, meal, dried fruit, & c.," as well as Thomas's hat, abandoned in his quarters at the foot of the hill. At least some of the horses had been stolen from local Unionists, and were subsequently returned to their owners. The Federals destroyed the weapons, ammunition, and supplies that could not be taken with them, burnt the camp and left, mocking their foes with their own war whoops.[285]

284. *O.R.* 31 (pt. 1): 439; Lamborn, "First East Tennessee Campaign," in Kirk, *History of the Fifteenth Pennsylvania Volunteer Cavalry*, 333; Spang, "The Cherokee Indian Raid," in ibid., 346 (including "thirty feet wide" quote); Over, "Fighting Cherokee Indians," in ibid., 348-349; Palmer, "Wounded and Left to Die in Rebel Hands," in ibid., 357. Lamborn claimed that the Indians were "terrified by the suddenness of the attack" and "fled in disorder," although he also admitted that they abandoned their encampment only "after a sharp skirmish." The overall impression given by other witnesses is of a more sustained action.

285. *O.R.* 31 (pt. 1): 439-440 ("16 horses" quote, 439; "belonging to Wheeler's cavalry" quote, 440); *O.R. (Supplement)*, Pt. II, 57:313, 322, 333, 355, 364, 371, 380, 406, 413; Lamborn, "First East Tennessee Campaign," in Kirk, *History of the Fifteenth Pennsylvania Volunteer Cavalry*, 333; Spang, "The Cherokee Indian Raid," in ibid., 346-347; Over, "Fighting Cherokee Indians," in ibid., 349; Palmer, "Wounded and Left to Die in Rebel Hands," in ibid. 357; Thomas to the editors of the *Asheville News*, December 25, 1863, published in the *Asheville News*, January 21, 1864, reprinted in the *Western Democrat* (Charlotte) January 26, 1864. Colonel Palmer reported that the Indians were driven from their camp "in about an hour," and continued skirmishing from an inaccessible position on the mountainside "for several hours" before withdrawing. The records of events from the muster rolls of Companies D and F of the 15th Regiment Pennsylvania Cavalry put the fight at four hours, while those of A, G, L, and M recorded four-and-a-half hours, and that of E noted five hours. Lamborn implied a short fight and precipitous flight by the Cherokees, and Corporal Over's account, taken on its own, could also be read as suggesting the same. Corporal Spang put the fight at about four hours, although his account is worded in such a way as to imply that that was the length of time for the second phase of the fight only. Pvt. William M. Palmer of Company L gave an approximate length of two hours. Although the record of events for the regiment's field and staff, dated December 10, claimed the capture of several prisoners, Colonel Palmer's December 11 report and the record of events for the regiment (also dated December 10) noted only one prisoner; in a followup note dated December 13, Palmer identified him as one of Wheeler's men. Perhaps the number in the field and staff record included the Indian women referred to by Colonel Palmer, or to 6 members of an Arkansas unit captured on December 13. The regimental record stated that the Pennsylvanians killed 2 and wounded 4. Palmer wrote that if there were any casualties, they had been taken away; Lamborn, who asserted that 6 were killed, claimed

On the following day, Companies G and H of the 15th Regiment Pennsylvania Cavalry under Capt. Henry McAllister Jr., and a party of mounted Tennessee Home Guards, followed Thomas to determine whether his command had left Tennessee. The Cherokees were traveling along "an abandoned trail" toward North Carolina. As the narrow path wound through a dense forest, worries grew about an ambush. The party dismounted, formed a skirmish line, and with difficulty pushed through the woods. If the Indians were present, Corp. James W. Over of Company G admitted, they would have been able to hide so well as to escape notice. Fortunately for the Federals, their foes did not pause to make a stand. Around dusk the cavalrymen arrived at a farm at the foot of a mountain range, where they saw the Cherokees moving quickly near the top. They were out of range, however, and a night attack was impossible. Abandoning the chase, Over and other men were sent out to round up stragglers. Nervous of being attacked, he wandered around a short time calling for his comrades. Returning, he found that the main party had left without him to return to their horses. Panicked with the thought of being ambushed and scalped, Over ran through the woods and arrived just as the expedition rode away; he quickly mounted and joined them. Over's feelings, as well as the very hasty withdrawal of his comrades, suggests the fears that the Cherokees' reputation, amplified by white stereotypes about them, could engender.[286]

Colonel Palmer was somewhat disappointed by the results of the skirmish. Although he felt that he and his men had done all that was possible based on how events developed, his later examination of the area convinced him that nearly all of Thomas's command could have been bagged "by making certain dispositions before reaching Gatlinburg." Thomas emphasized his belief in his own overall success, including the Sevierville raid: "The enemy have at least been taught that while we hold the Smoky Mountain[s,] Western N. Carolina and the adjacent portions of East Tennessee are hard to subjugate." The latter claim seems spurious, given that many of the inhabitants of east Tennessee saw the Confederates as *their* subjugators. Lamborn thought that the skirmish "proved very serviceable in protecting the border counties of East Tennessee from further depredation, and so thoroughly was this band so disheartened and routed that the North Carolina Indians did not venture again . . . to make predatory incursions into these Union districts." There is indeed little evidence that Thomas ever launched another major independent incursion into east Tennessee, regardless of the reasons.[287]

Thomas's defeat at Gatlinburg was only the beginning of a series of setbacks.[288] The most personally affecting was the loss of Walker under alarming circumstances. Walker was

that the bodies were carried off. It is possible that the casualty figures were given by the captive. In his December 25 letter to the editors of the *Asheville News*, Thomas claimed only 2 casualties, both with minor wounds.

286. *O.R.* 31 (pt. 1): 439; Over, "Fighting Cherokee Indians," in Kirk, *History of the Fifteenth Pennsylvania Volunteer Cavalry*, 349-350 (quotes, 349).

287. *O.R.* 31 (pt. 1): 439; Thomas to the editors of the *Asheville News*, December 25, 1863, published in the *Asheville News*, January 21, 1864, reprinted in the *Western Democrat* (Charlotte), January 26, 1864; Lamborn, "First East Tennessee Campaign," in Kirk, *History of the Fifteenth Pennsylvania Volunteer Cavalry*, 333. See pp. 215-216 below for possible evidence that Thomas and the Indians raided eastern Tennessee in 1864.

288. A January 24, 1864, newspaper item in the Atlanta *Register* indicated that Thomas and the Indians were involved in the repulse of a Federal raid into Cherokee County and Georgia some time late in 1863: "I presume you have heard of the recent invasion of Western North Carolina and a small portion of Towns county, Ga., by a column of Yankee cavalry 1,500 in number. They came from East Tennessee and entered North Carolina through

ill at home on the night of January 3, 1864, when a Union guerrilla band surrounded the house. Called to the door, he was shot and killed. His son, Sgt. Maj. Columbus F. Walker of Walker's Battalion, was also home on furlough with typhoid fever and was taken prisoner. Carried several miles on horseback, he pretended to be almost dead and was set free. He somehow made it home and buried his father.[289] Lieutenant Akin of Company H, Walker's Battalion, later recalled that in the wake of the murder "there was much apprehension among officers and men" of the Legion who, like him, were in western North Carolina at the time. Thomas was undoubtedly concerned most of all; as Walker's superior, he had to imagine a similar fate awaiting him. It was probably at this time that he organized a personal bodyguard of some twenty Cherokees, who "were constantly with him as protection to his person against robbers" until the end of the war. This "Life Guard" was evidently in Thomas's personal employment, as its members were not paid by the Confederate government.[290]

---

the county of Cherokee. They were stopped by want of subsistence for themselves and horses, and the frequent assaults upon them in their forages by the Carolina Home Guards and a portion of the Indian forces of Thomas's Legion, then scouring the mountains in search of bushwhackers." The article mentioned the robbery of the locals and the murder of two soldiers home on furlough, captured by the Federals and turned over to North Carolina and Tennessee bushwhackers. These incidents occurred before the death of Lieutenant Colonel Walker on January 3; coupled with the description of the incursion as "recent," this implies some time in late December. There are no known reports of Federal raids into western North Carolina in late December 1863, although there were skirmishes at Warm Springs on October 23, October 26, and November 26. The first two were associated with the raid and recruiting drive of the 2nd North Carolina Mounted Infantry (Union) in late October at the time of the Goldman Bryson raid; it is possible that, despite the large size attributed to the Federal force, that the account was based upon Bryson's excursion, the operations of the 2nd N.C. Mounted Infantry (Union), or the two together. Later legends about a series of raids supposedly carried out late in the year by Capt. George W. Kirk of the 2nd N.C. Mounted Infantry (Union) might also be kept in mind. "INVASION OF NORTH GEORGIA AND WESTERN NORTH CAROLINA—Barbarity of the Invaders and Tories," *Atlanta Daily Register*, January 24, 1864, reprinted in the *Western Democrat* (Charlotte), February 9, 1864. *O.R.* 29 (pt. 1): 4, 5; Powell, *North Carolina Gazeteer*, 238; Trotter, *Bushwhackers*, 114-115; Bumgarner, *Kirk's Raiders*, 26.

289. James R. Love Jr., to Samuel Cooper, February 15, 1864, service record file of William C. Walker, Thomas's Legion, Compiled Service Records of Confederate Service from the State of North Carolina (M270), reel 574; James Whitaker Jr., to Governor Vance, January 11, 1864, Governors' Papers: Vance, 1862-1865, NCOAH; Columbus F. Walker to Stringfield, September 4, 1895, Stringfield Papers, WCU; Aiken, "Eightieth Regiment," in Clark, *North Carolina Regiments* 4:122, 126. Another William Walker from Cherokee County was murdered under strikingly similar but not identical circumstances in October 1864 in retaliation for the death of three Unionists. He is confused with Lieutenant Colonel Walker in Inscoe and McKinney, *Heart of Confederate Appalachia*, 196, 238-239. The two men are differentiated in B. T. Morrison, "Sixty-Fourth Regiment," in Clark, op. cit., 3:662, and in Trotter, *Bushwhackers*, 169-170.

290. Aiken, "Eightieth Regiment," in Clark, *North Carolina Regiments*, 4:126; Crow, *Storm in the Mountains*, 56; *O.R.* 49 (pt. 2): 755 ("were constantly with him" and "Life Guard" quotes); Godbold and Russell, *Confederate Colonel and Cherokee Chief*, 118, 121. Crow argued that Walker's murder caused Thomas to focus on defending western North Carolina over the Confederate war effort in general. The evidence presented throughout this history, however, indicates that Thomas always regarded the defense of western North Carolina to be his primary objective; at best, Walker's death and its circumstances only reinforced that goal. Godbold and Russell argued that Thomas was suffering from a lot of mental stress at the time. One of the sources they cited was a letter from Lt. Col. James R. Love Jr., to his parents, in which Love wrote that "Thomas has improved wonderfully both physically & mentally, and is thoroughly impressed with the justice of the cause for which we are contending." Love to parents, March 4, 1864, Thomas Papers, DU. It appears from context, however, that Love was referring to Pvt. Thomas J. Love of Company F, Infantry Regiment, who along with his brother Dallas F. Love was discussed in the sentences immediately before the quoted passage.

Thomas next received a great deal of criticism for his role in an incursion into east Tennessee organized by Brigadier General Vance. By this time, either the command relationships between Longstreet and the District of Western North Carolina had been formally arranged by Richmond, or Vance had agreed to cooperate with Longstreet, at least on paper. Vance offered his services and that of his troops to Longstreet on December 15, 1863. On December 21, Longstreet suggested that he move to Newport, Tennessee, on the French Broad River, where he could cover his district from Federal incursions and scout in the direction of Sevierville. Any information thus uncovered would be passed to Longstreet, while Vance could harry Federal forage parties from Knoxville. By December 23, Longstreet had received no reply. On December 27, Longstreet's assistant adjutant, Lt. Col. Moxley Sorrel, was reduced to writing Col. John B. Palmer to request that he "suggest to General Vance at the earliest opportunity the propriety of establishing his cavalry at Newport, as being a position that offers many advantages." Why Vance was so dilatory in acting or replying is unknown, especially as he had just offered his cooperation to Longstreet. When Vance finally decided to move in January, he evidently did so without informing Longstreet, a decision that proved costly.[291]

On January 8, Brigadier General Vance departed from Asheville with the 14th Battalion N.C. Cavalry, numbering 375 men, and an artillery section. According to Thomas, Vance's goal was basically a supply raid. Thomas claimed later to have advised against the move, probably on the basis of his own recent experiences in the area. Traveling through Waynesville and Quallatown, Vance was joined by Thomas and 100 Cherokees. The expedition crossed the Tennessee border on January 12 and halted at Gatlinburg. Vance went on with 180 of the cavalry and, according to Thomas, sent Lt. Col. James L. Henry of the 14th Battalion N.C. Cavalry with the rest of the cavalry to Weir's Cove to gather supplies. Thomas was left at Gatlinburg. Vance reached Sevierville on the following day, where in the mid-afternoon he captured a wagon train, laden with supplies. From there, he proceeded in the direction of Newport, the place where Longstreet had wanted him to move in December. On January 14, he halted around 2 P.M. for about two-and-a-half hours at a place called Shultz's Mill, on Cosby Creek, to rest and feed his men and horses.[292]

291. *O.R.* 52 (pt. 2): 579, 580, 583 (quote); James Longstreet, *From Manassas to Appomattox*, ed. with an introduction and notes by James I. Robertson Jr., Civil War Centennial Series (Bloomington: Indiana University Press, 1960), 531. In his memoir, Longstreet made no mention of his efforts to get Vance to join him, and wrote as if the incursion was totally spontaneous on Vance's part.

292. *O.R.* 32 (pt. 1): 75-76, (pt. 2): 95; Thomas to Allen T. Davidson, January 22, 1864 (unfinished draft), Thomas Papers, DU; Thomas to Governor Vance, January 24, 1864, Governors' Papers: Vance, 1862-1865, NCOAH. Reports differ as to the size and composition of Vance's force and of the detachment taken with him to Sevierville. Col. John B. Palmer gave the number as 375 cavalry, 100 infantry, and an artillery section; Vance took 180 of the cavalry with him. It is presumed that the 100 infantrymen were the Cherokees, as they are not otherwise identified. In his draft to Davidson, Thomas wrote that Vance took "upwards of a hundred Mounted Men" with him to Sevierville; in his letter to the governor, he wrote that he took "about 150." Vance's assistant adjutant general told Col. William J. Palmer of the 15th Regiment Pennsylvania Cavalry that the contingent which Vance took to Sevierville "was about 300 men," while Thomas's Indians numbered 150. It is possible that the adjutant was speaking of the size of the whole expedition, or that he deliberately exaggerated the numbers of Vance's and Thomas's respective parties for some reason. The size of the captured wagon train is also in dispute; Col. William J. Palmer's figure of 18 wagons is probably accurate.

While at Sevierville or at some point along the line of march, Vance dispatched orders to the remainder of the command; these orders are evidently no longer extant. Col. John B. Palmer reported that Vance ordered Thomas "to fall back with his infantry" but send Henry with the rest of the cavalry and the artillery to rendezvous with Vance at Schultz's Mill. Palmer included a copy of these orders in his own report, although they were later misplaced. Henry declined, however, thinking it best to fall back with Thomas; according to a newspaper account, his excuse was that the terrain was not practicable for artillery.[293]

Why Vance waited so long at Schultz's Mill is unknown; he may have thought that he was out of danger, as Thomas later suggested, or may have tarried to see if Henry would show up. Regardless, the halt proved fatal, as Federal cavalry had set out from Dandridge in pursuit. Numbering less than 200, they were led by Thomas's new acquaintance from the Gatlinburg skirmish, Col. William J. Palmer of the 15th Regiment Pennsylvania Cavalry, and included Companies A, C, D, E, F, G, L, and M of his own regiment, as well as Companies B, H, M and a detachment from Company K of the 10th Regiment Ohio Cavalry. Palmer found Vance and his men preparing to resume the journey to Newport. Evidently, Vance felt so secure that he had neither pickets nor a rearguard in place. As a result, Palmer charged directly into the Confederates and completely routed them. Fifty-two men were captured, including Vance and two members of his staff, as well as 150 saddled horses and a large number of weapons. The wagons seized at Sevierville were recaptured, along with their horses, mules, and drivers, and other supplies which Vance had either brought along with him or acquired on the way were taken. The Federals suffered no losses, while the Confederates lost two wounded. Palmer sent Unionist Home Guard troops to hunt the largely dismounted escapees. He next went to the area of Sevierville. Joined by the 1st Regiment Tennessee Cavalry (Union), the Federals set out again on January 16 in the hopes of bagging the rest of the expedition at Gatlinburg. Thomas, however, had already begun his withdrawal and escaped. Henry did not return with Thomas. He finally moved to Schultz's Mill on January 15; from there he went to Newport, returning to North Carolina along the French Broad River. Palmer proceeded down the same stream, capturing a Confederate wagon train on the south bank which, once again, had not properly set out pickets.[294]

Col. John B. Palmer, Thomas's new commanding officer, did not seem to blame him for the failure to support Vance, based on his own understanding of Vance's orders and Henry's actions. He arrested Henry for disobedience of orders. Rumors were soon flying through the press and the public that Thomas was actually responsible for the fiasco,

293. *O.R.* 32 (pt. 1): 76; "Another Fight on Cosby—Capture of Brigadier General Vance," *Asheville News*, January 21, 1864, reprinted in the *Western Democrat* (Charlotte), January 26, 1864, and as an undated and untitled item in the *Fayetteville Observer Weekly*, January 28, 1864. Palmer's report was dated January 19, 1864. In referring to Vance's orders to Thomas and Henry, Palmer added "(See copy of order marked A)." As to Henry's reply, its contents were evidently derived from information from a member of Vance's staff; Palmer's report included the notation "(See statement marked B, by Lieutenant Davidson, General Vance's acting assistant adjutant-general)" in discussing the reply. Notes accompanying the text of Palmer's report in the *Official Records* indicate that Vance's orders and Davidson's statement were missing at the time of publication.

294. *O.R.* 32 (pt. 1): 75-76, 110-112, (pt. 2): 95; *O.R. (Supplement))*, Pt. II, 50:156, 184, 192, 199, 57:314, 333, 356, 364-365, 372, 380-381, 407, 414, 65:416. The record of events in the muster roll of Company B, 10th Regiment Ohio Cavalry, gives the total Federal force as 110, although it exaggerated the size of Vance's contingent considerably (250 men).

however. The *Fayetteville Observer Weekly*, quoting an item from the Columbia *South Carolinian*, reported that Vance had ordered Thomas to join him at Schultz's Mill. Henry was not mentioned at all, other than noting that he and his men "passed the same place the next day" and arrived at Newport. An account from the *Asheville News* noted Henry's presence as a part of Vance's command, but only mentioned that the troops left at Gatlinburg failed to come up as Vance had ordered. Thomas, meanwhile, wrote to the governor in late January about the operation, and started (but perhaps did not finish) the draft of a letter to Congressman Allen T. Davidson, whose son was a participant. In both cases he gave a bare accounting of the circumstances of Vance's capture. While noting that he took command of the remnants of the expedition after the Federal attack, he did not mention any controversy regarding his actions. Thomas did not criticize Henry, either; in fact, beyond adding the detail (omitted from Colonel Palmer's report) that Vance had sent Henry to Weir's Cove, he did not mention Henry at all, and did not bring up the subject of the orders to move to Schultz's Mill. He was also careful not to criticize Vance, beyond claiming to Davidson that he had advised the brigadier general not to undertake the operation to begin with.[295]

While Thomas probably wrote the governor and Davidson as professional and personal courtesies, he may have also intended to stem the effects of the press criticism. Besides the considerations of military conduct, the potential political fallout was huge, given that the brigadier general was the governor's brother. If Thomas hoped to escape censure from that quarter, then he probably failed. "This sad affair is mainly attributable to that disobedient rascal W H Thomas," wrote one of the governor's correspondents in February. More serious was the disapproval of Gen. Joseph E. Johnston, who now commanded the Army of Tennessee. Col. John B. Palmer furnished an account of the incident to Johnston, together with copies of Brigadier General Vance's orders to Thomas and Henry; as a result, Johnston ordered both men court-martialed. They went to trial at Asheville on February 23; it was reported that there was "some excitement on the subject" among the locals, understandable since the Vances were Buncombe County residents. While the outcome is not known, the fact that Thomas retained his command argues that the charges were dismissed. It would not have helped the prosecution's case that the Confederate secretary of war on February 2 had put at least part of the blame on Vance himself for negligence in not preparing for the possibility of an attack; President Davis, in his endorsement of Palmer's report, added that since Vance was a prisoner of war, "no action is practicable which seems proper."[296]

295. *O.R.* 32 (pt. 1): 76; *Fayetteville Observer Weekly*, January 28, 1864, reprinting undated items from the Columbia *South Carolinian* ("The Capture of General Vance"); "Another Fight on Cosby—Capture of Brigadier General Vance," *Asheville News*, January 21, 1864, reprinted in the *Western Democrat* (Charlotte), January 26, 1864, and (undated and untitled) in the *Fayetteville Observer Weekly*, January 28, 1864; Thomas to Davidson, January 22, 1864, (unfinished draft), Thomas Papers, DU; Thomas to Governor Vance, January 24, 1864, Governors' Papers: Vance, 1862-1865, NCOAH.

296. Godbold and Russell, *Confederate Colonel and Cherokee Chief*, 75, 87-88, 111-114, 119-120; Crow, *Storm in the Mountains*, 56-58, 100, 115-116; Inscoe and McKinney, *Heart of Confederate Appalachia*, 131-132; C. D. Smith to Governor Vance, February 15, 1864 ("disobedient rascal" quote), Joseph E. Johnston to Vance, February 3, 1864, G. W. Herndon to Vance, February 22, 1864 ("Some excitment." quote), Governors' Papers: Vance, 1862-1865, NCOAH; *O.R.* 32 (pt. 1): 77 (Davis quote). It is possible, given the reaction of Johnston to both Palmer's message and the contents of Brigadier General Vance's orders to Thomas and Henry, that some evidence had turned up which caused Palmer to change his mind about Thomas's lack of culpability.

Based on the surviving documents, it appears that Thomas carried little if any responsibility for the capture of Brig. Gen. Vance. Henry disobeyed orders by delaying to go to Schultz's Mill as requested, while Vance himself was negligent in not setting out pickets or a rear guard. The only blame that seems to reside with Thomas was that, as ranking officer, he did not force Henry to comply with Vance's orders to be at Schultz's Mill on January 14, although Legion historian Vernon H. Crow reasonably speculated that Thomas may have been responsible for making sure that Henry started out the next day.[297] Nevertheless, the fact that he did not compel Henry to do so on the day assigned may indicate that Thomas was unable to muster sufficient personal authority to get Henry to act. Thomas was a politician and a businessman, not a professional military officer, and the skills necessary for success in the former two fields may not have translated into those necessary for the latter. It is also possible that he was guilty of reacting too slowly to the unfolding events: he had recently had a bad experience of his own in the general geographical area and may have been hesitant about which choices to make. He had evidently advised Vance not to mount the expedition to begin with; and he may well have been laboring under shock from the death of Walker, whose murder had only been ten days before. Regardless, while Thomas was not truly to blame for the disaster, he nevertheless received a blow to his reputation in the eyes of the governor and at least of some members of the press and public.

Thomas soon received another shock, courtesy of the Federal cavalry, in an action which in some ways recalled the Gatlinburg affair from December. Brig. Gen. Samuel D. Sturgis, who commanded the cavalry in the Department of the Ohio, received intelligence that the Indians were encamped in Jackson County, not far from Quallatown at Deep Creek, which lay amid the fork of the Tuckasegee and the Little Tennessee Rivers. By this time Thomas and the Cherokees had achieved quite a reputation in eastern Tennessee, whether deserved or not, as Sturgis asserted that they "had become a terror to the Union people of East Tennessee and the borders of North Carolina from the atrocities they were daily perpetrating." In hopes of ridding the area of Thomas's force once and for all, Sturgis dispatched Maj. Francis M. Davidson and the 14th Regiment Illinois Cavalry into North Carolina. Accompanied by a three-piece artillery section and some forty to fifty Unionist guides, the Federal cavalry surprised Thomas's camp on February 2.[298]

Accounts of this event are widely disparate. At least two writers, one of them possibly an eyewitness, praised the stiff resistance given by the Cherokees. L. F. Siler wrote to Governor Vance that "[t]he Indians fought nobly, under the surprise, until their ammunition failed," at which point they withdrew after a brief fight. The other account lavished praise while implying that Thomas himself was absent from the fight. "I am told that your men when attacked by the Yankees at Deep Creek," wrote I. Roder, "tho surprised and greatly outnumbered, yet fought gallantly and nearly whipped or routed them from which I think it reasonable to conclude had you been there and apprised of them coming you could have gave them a good drubbing." Newspaper accounts, although also praising Thomas and the Indians, bear little relation to what actually transpired. The *Asheville News* claimed that it was Thomas who surprised the Federals, not the other way around: "Col. Thomas' Indians

297. Crow, *Storm in the Mountains*, 57-58.

298. *O.R.* 32 (pt. 1): 137-138 (Sturgis quote, 137), (pt. 2): 273, 749, 53:314.

bushwhacked them so unmercifully that they turned at that point and hurriedly retreated, having had one Captain, two Lieutenants and a number of privates killed, and a considerable number wounded. The dead they left lying where they fell, but carried off the wounded." Another version published in the same paper stated that the raiders "came off second best" to Thomas and the Indians. At least one letter to Governor Vance was more skeptical and critical. "Col Thomas has been pretending to picket the pass at the Smokey Mountains but to no purpose as recent facts go to prove," wrote C. D. Smith. "He had the Indians and a few whites lying around near his own home. A Regt of Yankees came up the river . . . and pas[s]ed on to Thomas' camp and into the Camp amongst his Indians before they or any one else had any warning of their approach."[299]

Just how badly the encounter went for the Cherokees was the subject of controversy. Federal accounts, which placed Thomas's force at around 250, claimed that nearly the entire command, or "gang" as Maj. Gen. John G. Foster dubbed it, was killed and the rest dispersed or captured. Sturgis asserted that almost 200 had been killed, with 22 Indians and 32 whites captured, and less than 50 escaping. Foster boasted to Grant that 215 of Thomas's men had been killed or wounded, and that 50 had been captured. On February 21, Foster wrote to Maj. Gen. Henry W. Halleck that the group had been annihilated except for 22 prisoners and 50 who had escaped. He reported 2 killed and 6 wounded among the Federals. On the Confederate side, Col. John B. Palmer recorded 2 Indians killed, as did Siler, while Thomas reported to Palmer that his men had killed 8 Federals and captured 1. Thomas, in a letter written to the governor and council of South Carolina at the end of the month, reported 5 dead. Palmer, apparently relying on information from Thomas, reported that the Confederate wounded were carried off the field; interestingly, this is the same claim that the *Asheville News* account of February 11 made in reverse about the Federals, and is a probable indication that actual casualties were light on both sides. Palmer also estimated that 20 to 30 Indians and whites were captured; Siler listed 18. Federal provost marshal records exist for 32 men captured; of these, 17 were definitely identified as Cherokee. It is noticeable that the total number reported captured in the provost records equals the number given by Sturgis for whites captured alone, and perhaps suggests the manner in which the number of prisoners and, by extension, casualties, gradually became exaggerated in the Federal reports. Certainty is hampered by the lack of records for Thomas's command to indicate how many were present and how many killed or wounded. Nevertheless, although Thomas's force had been mauled, it was far from destroyed.[300]

299. L. F. Siler to Governor Vance, February 8, 1864, C. D. Smith to Vance, February 15, 1864, Governors' Papers: Vance, 1862-1865, NCOAH; I. Roder to Thomas, March 21, 1864, Thomas Papers, DU; "THE LATE RAID," the *Asheville News*, February 11, 1864, reprinted in *The Greensborough Patriot*, February 18, 1864; "THE RAID INTO MACON COUNTY, N.C.," letter from an unnamed resident of Franklin to the editors of the *Asheville News*, February 12, 1864, reprinted in the *Western Democrat* (Charlotte), March 1, 1864 ("came off second best" quote). Although Roder implied that Thomas was not present, Thomas referred to the defenders as "the Indians, under my command" in a letter to the governor and council of South Carolina. *O.R.* 53:314.

300. *O.R.* 32 (pt. 1), 46, 137-138, 159 (Foster "gang" quotes, 46, 159), (pt. 2): 749, 53:314; L. F. Siler to Vance, February 8, 1864, Governors' Papers: Vance, 1862-1865, NCOAH; service record files, Thomas's Legion, Compiled Service Records of Confederate Soldiers from the State of North Carolina (M270), reels 567 through 574; Crow, *Storm in the Mountains*, 58-59; Inscoe and McKinney, *Heart of Confederate Appalachia*, 132. The records of the men captured may conveniently be found in the Indian Battalion roster in this volume. The

Following the raid, signs emerged of a loss of morale and of confidence in Thomas among some Cherokees. All of the Cherokees and two of the whites captured at Deep Creek gave the Oath of Allegiance to their captors in March. At least one, and possibly two, of the Indians subsequently enlisted into Federal service in Company D, 3rd Regiment N.C. Mounted Infantry (Union), which Capt. George W. Kirk organized in June 1864.[301] A more ominous sign of trouble emerged towards the end of the month. A second Federal raid was launched on February 17, this time into Cherokee County, consisting of 250 men of the 1st Regiment Wisconsin Cavalry under Maj. Nathan W. Paine. Dividing into detachments, the expedition went up the Hiwassee River as far as Murphy, reporting much of the area deserted (at least as far as friendly Unionists went) and stripped of provisions. "There is no organized armed force in that vicinity," it was reported, suggesting that while Thomas's command was not destroyed, it was so seriously damaged that for the moment it was not capable of offering effective resistance. The Federals took 33 prisoners. Among these were 15 Indians who voluntarily surrendered on February 22. "They report that the rest of Thomas' Indians have laid down their arms and disbanded," although the same report added that "Thomas' force is at Franklin."[302]

Thirteen of the Indians are identifiable from Federal provost marshal records. Three were members of Company A and one of Company B; the companies of the others are

---

prisoners included members of Companies A, B, C, and D. Many of the men were listed as having been captured in Jackson County on February 7, not February 2; however, they were also all reported as having been confined as prisoners of war at Knoxville on February 7. As it would have been a physical impossibility to move the prisoners from Deep Creek to Knoxville on the same date, it would appear that a transcription error was involved; the men were captured on February 2, and incarcerated at Knoxville on February 7.

301. The Cherokees in question are Pvt. Mason Reckley (Mason Ratley/Mason Ratliff) of Company A, and Pvt. Jim Cheoih of Company B, who may have been the same man as Corp. Chio-E-Li of Company D, 3rd Regiment N.C. Mounted Infantry (Union). Service record files of Jim Cheoih and Mason Reckley, Thomas's Legion, Compiled Service Records of Confederate Soldiers from the State of North Carolina (M270), reels 568, 572; service record files of Chio-E-Li and Mason Ratliff, 3rd Regiment N.C. Mounted Infantry (Union), Records of Volunteer Union Soldiers Who Served During the Civil War, Compiled Service Records of Volunteer Union Soldiers Who Served in Organizations from the State of North Carolina (M401), reels 19 and 23, RG 94, NA (hereinafter cited as Compiled Service Records of Union Soldiers from the State of North Carolina [M401]). A useful list of surviving Cherokee soldiers who served in Company D, 3rd Regiment N.C. Mounted Infantry (Union) and other Federal units, along with lists of the widows of others and of survivors of Thomas's Companies A and B, are found in Thomas Donaldson, *Eleventh Census of the United States. Extra Census Bulletin. Eastern Band of Cherokees of North Carolina* (Washington: U.S. Census Printing Office, 1892), 21. For the origins and organization of the 3rd Regiment N.C. Mounted Infantry (Union), see Bumgarner, *Kirk's Raiders*, 24-30.

302. *O.R.* 32 (pt. 1): 37, 404-406 (405, "There is no organized force" quote), (pt. 2): 447 (including "They report that the rest of Thomas' Indians" and "Thomas' force is at Franklin" quotes). 450. Crow, *Storm in the Mountains*, 59, claimed that Capt. Campbell Taylor's Company C of Thomas's force harried the Federal party and contributed to its turning back. The quote that Crow provided to illustrate Taylor's supposed activities, however, was from an article about earlier events published in the Charlotte *Western Democrat* of February 9, 1864, and reprinted from the January 24, 1864, *Atlanta Daily Register* (discussed and quoted in pp. 124-125 n. 288 above), and thus could not have referred to Paine's raid, which began on February 17 (for Crow's citation, see *Storm in the Mountains*, 246 n. 26). Taylor's company was not specifically identified in the article. The idea that it participated may have derived from Akins's postwar identification of Taylor's company as a unit from Cherokee County, the area through which Paine passed. See also Crow, *Storm in the Mountains*, 233; Aiken, "Eightieth Regiment," in Clark's *North Carolina Regiments*, 4:119.

unknown. All took the Oath in March. Rumors swirled around them. According to the *Asheville News*, once they were taken to Knoxville "they were flattered and feasted, big talks held, and magnificent promises made" if they switched sides. "They were promised their liberty and *five thousand dollars in gold* if they would bring in *the scalp of their Chief, Col. Wm. H. Thomas!*," the article continued melodramatically. "The Indians seemed to pause—consult—and finally agreed to the proposition. They were released, returned to their native mountains, sought the camp of their Chief, told him all, and have ever since been on the warpath."[303] Variations of the story developed over the years. Ethnologist James Mooney recorded in 1900 that the men were captured in a skirmish in early 1863. Taken to Knoxville, and "having become dissatisfied with their experience in Confederate service, they were easily persuaded to go over to the Union side. Through the influence of their principal man, Diganeski, several others were induced to desert to the Union army, making about thirty in all." Serving in the 3rd Regiment N.C. Mounted Infantry (Union) until the war's end, "they returned to their homes to find their tribesmen so bitterly incensed against them that for some time their lives were in danger." Mooney reported that eight were still alive. Other accounts claimed that the men were murdered by their tribesmen because they had betrayed Thomas.[304]

In some ways, Mooney's version was closer to the facts than the wartime newspaper account, although he misdated the year and conflated those who surrendered on February 22 with those captured at Deep Creek. At least two of the men who surrendered subsequently served in Company D, 3rd Regiment N.C. Mounted Infantry, the same company one (and perhaps two) of the Cherokee captives at Deep Creek joined. Given the sometimes widely variant renderings of Cherokee names into English script, and the fact that many Cherokee had additional English-language names that bore little or no resemblance to their native names, it is possible that more of the deserters joined the Federals. It is known that five other Cherokees of the Legion who were evidently neither among those captured at Deep Creek nor among those who surrendered on February 22 deserted at some point and served in that unit. Nine Cherokees who served both in Thomas's Legion and in Federal units were alive as late as 1892. Diganeski remains currently unidentified. Whether any of the deserters rejoined Thomas is unknown, due to the lack of surviving muster rolls.[305]

303. "*Cherokee Warriors*," undated item from the *Asheville News*, reprinted in the *Fayetteville Observer* (semi-weekly edition), May 26, 1864. The men were Pvts. Cola Chustee, Kuntiskee (John Igotpa), and Iyantooga Thompson of Company A; Jim Otter of Company B; and Catalani, Dave, Jimmy, Johnny, Schirska, Selola, Takaska, Tistaska, and Willie, companies unknown. Dave was probably David Patridge (Patridge) of Company B, Infantry Regiment, who was reported in a postwar source as having deserted and served with the Federals. The service records of these men are in the Compiled Service Records of Confederate Soldiers from the State of North Carolina (M270), reels 568-570, 572-574. See also Donaldson, *Eleventh Census of the United States. Extra Census Bulletin. Eastern Band of Cherokees of North Carolina*, 21.

304. James Mooney, "Myths of the Cherokee," 171; Crow, *Storm in the Mountains*, 59.

305. The soldiers who surrendered on February 22 and who later served in Company D, 3rd Regiment N.C. Mounted Infantry (Union) were Pvts. Kuntiskee (John Igotpa) of Company A and Jim Otter of Company B; in addition, the Cherokee named Dave who was part of the surrender party may have been David Partridge of Company B. At some unknown date, Privates Howeeneete (James D. Walkingstick), Oolstoih (also known variously as John Wagoola, John Daboo, and John Brown), Oostenacoo (John Taylor), and Noweyouteeh Otter (Tom Otter) of Company A, and Eucheleheh of Company B also deserted and joined the same Federal company.

The defection of several members of the Cherokee companies at this time was probably due in part to conflicts within the Eastern Band over Thomas's leadership and Cherokee participation in the Confederate war effort. It is known that Yonaguska's son-in-law, Flying Squirrel, asserted that he was chosen the principal chief upon the former's death, although his claims were evidently not accepted by the majority of his people until after the war. A more certain factor leading to the desertions was the destitute condition in which western North Carolinians, and in particular the Cherokees, now found themselves. With the majority of the men gone to the war, farming families struggled to raise crops, a problem occurring as early as 1862. More recently, an early frost had affected the crops in Cherokee and Clay Counties. What few frost-bitten bushels of corn were available sold at $10 a barrel. Thomas wrote to the governor of South Carolina in late February that the Indian families were starving, but also noted that it was difficult to feed the locally-based troops. The transportation system had broken down, with rumors that some carriers were charging $30 a day for handling; even if food was available from other than local sources, as one man wrote to Governor Vance, how could they afford to have it brought to them? Those that could get away were moving further south, but for many that was not an option.[306]

The recent military reversals suffered by Thomas, and by the Confederate forces in eastern Tennessee, almost certainly contributed to the desertions. It must have appeared increasingly to many that the Confederate and state governments simply could not defend the region or protect the inhabitants with any degree of efficiency; given the other factors noted, especially the starvation of their families, it is not surprising that some Cherokees chose to exit the war or even join the Federal side.

Such thoughts were certainly present in the minds of many whites living in the region, even among die-hard Confederates. Complaining about the breakdown of local authority under continued pressure from Federal troops and Unionist guerillas and the inability of local officers to accomplish much, one man wrote Governor Vance that "a bold dashing fearless man to inspire courage among our citizens and arouse them to united action" was needed. This was the image to which Thomas undoubtedly aspired, but not everyone saw him as the man to fit the mold. Writing about the need for effective troops in the region, L. F. Siler wrote Governor Vance that "It is true, W H Thomas is in Jackson. But what does he do? No order ever reaches him or if it does, his own way is the best." Despite the criticisms, the colonel still had supporters. "From the knowledge you have of the Geography of that country [the area around the mouth of the Tuckasegee River, where Thomas's forces were concentrated at that time] attained even from your boyhood together with the great influence you have over your men, makes us Come to the conclusion that you are the right man in the right place," wrote one citizen. "And I hope & trust our conclusion will be verified by your

---

Their service records are found in Compiled Service Records of Confederate Soldiers from the State of North Carolina (M270), reels 569 through 571; and service record files, 3rd Regiment N.C. Mounted Infantry (Union), Compiled Service Records of Volunteer Union Soldiers from the State of North Carolina (M401), reels 20 through 22; see also Donaldson, *Eleventh Census of the United States. Extra Census Bulletin. Eastern Band of Cherokees of North Carolina*, 21.

306. *O.R.* 18:772-773, 53:314; James Whitaker Jr., to Governor Vance, January 11, 1864, S. S. Westall to Vance, January 17, 1864, C. D. Smith to Vance, February 15, 1864, all in Governors' Papers: Vance, 1862-1865, NCOAH. For Flying Squirrel, see p. 3 n. 5 above and citations.

successfully keeping back the yankee invaders and pursue on and punish the worse than yankees—Tory Raiders robbers & Bushwhackers." Regardless of Thomas's qualities as a leader, the fact remained that Confederate forces in western North Carolina were too few and spread too thin to deal with the threats to the area.[307]

Thomas tried to alleviate the sufferings of the Indians, approaching Col. John B. Palmer for assistance. In March, Palmer authorized the purchase of 100 bushels of corn from a Macon County citizen by Capt. Matthew H. Love of Company A for the Cherokee families and authorized the impressment of wagons for transporting it. "I trust this will afford you temporary relief," he wrote. "If you will prepare a Memorial on the subject of the destitution of your Indians and another upon the necessity for retaining laboring men in this non slaveholding section and send them to some friend in Richmond to be presented to the Secty of War possibly some remedy for the evils you complain of may be applied. As Commanding officer in this district I will second you in any effort you may make consistent with the public interest."[308]

Thomas also approached Gov. Milledge L. Bonham of South Carolina and his council for support. Recalling the plan he had submitted to Bonham's predecessor two years earlier, Thomas sketched his perspective on the military crisis in the mountains, describing his command as "the principal force" in the area with the exception of Palmer's troops near Asheville. Georgia forces kept an eye on the Hiwassee River pass and blocked Federal movements via that route beyond Cherokee County. It was up to the Carolinas to watch the passes of the French Broad and Little Tennessee Rivers. Left open by Longstreet's withdrawal northeastward, the latter two routes were now open, as the Federal raid to Deep Creek proved. Ignoring mention of the recent uncontested raid by Paine, Thomas with considerable exaggeration boasted that the Cherokees had stopped the Federals in their tracks at Deep Creek. In order to prevent future raids, a substantial force was needed to guard the passes, and subsistence would have to be provided for both it and the starving Indian familes. The source of this subsistence would have to be South Carolina. Thus, Thomas neatly tied together his various objectives to the defense of the mountain passes.[309]

307. W. N. Bilbo to Governor Vance, January 17, 1864 ("bold dashing fearless" quote), L. F. Siler to Vance, February 19, 1864, all in Governors' Papers: Vance, 1862-1865, NCOAH; I. Roder to Thomas, March 21, 1864 ("From the knowledge you have" quote), Thomas Papers, DU.

308. Palmer to Thomas, March 11, 1864, Thomas Papers, DU.

309. *O.R.* 53:313-314. In addition to Thomas, Maj. John Ashmore, chief enrolling officer of the 5th South Carolina Congressional District, submitted to P. G. T. Beauregard on February 15 a plan for defending the North Carolina passes that gave access to South Carolina for Federal raiders. It included a report on Deep Creek from Colonel Palmer addressed to Ashmore. Ashmore requested cavalry and artillery to bolster the forces already assigned to watch those routes. Although Beauregard could not send any cavalry at the present, he wrote that he would rush at least two companies to the area in the event of any future threats. For his part, Palmer expressed to Ashmore his concerns that the region would be more susceptible to future raids if Longstreet's cavalry withdrew from the Sevier County area, and thus urged cooperation between his command and the military authorities in South Carolina. Ashmore's and Palmer's letters probably served to alert Beauregard to the problem and thus laid the groundwork for the favorable reception of Thomas's proposals to the latter and to the South Carolina government. Palmer was urged by Longstreet's headquarters about the same time to operate on the Federal flank in eastern Tennessee. In a letter to Thomas written in late March, Lieutenant Colonel Love also emphasized the importance of the mountain passes for both western North Carolina and South Carolina. *O.R.* 31 (pt. 2): 746-749, 750-751; Love to Thomas, March 28, 1864, Thomas Papers, WCU (microfilm, Thomas Papers, DU).

Thomas requested that Bonham have corn, flour, and other necessities sent to Walhalla for the force (his own command, although he did not directly say so) that would guard the French Broad and Little Tennessee passes. He also asked permission to buy grain in South Carolina for the familes of Confederate soldiers, including the Cherokee families, again using Walhalla as a transportation site. Thomas wanted "a small quantity" of rice, beans, peas, and other foodstuffs sent to him, as well as cotton and cloth to make clothes. Bonham forwarded Thomas's letter on March 4 to Gen. P. G. T. Beauregard, commander of the Department of South Carolina, Georgia, and Florida, reporting that he would forward what he could to assist Thomas. On March 11, a departmental commissary officer wrote to Thomas from Anderson, reporting Beauregard's authorization to transfer by special requisition whatever subsistence stores Thomas required, as well as "to supply in a moderate degree such needy families with subsistence as you may order." Thomas thus successfully established two sources of supply for both his troops and for the needy families in the area that he defended. He lacked an officially appointed quartermaster, however, and was evidently paying for at least some food out of his own pocket.[310]

The troubles in western North Carolina prompted renewed efforts to get the Legion reunited there under Thomas's command. Discontent rumbled among the officers in eastern Tennessee opposed to Jackson. Returning from a mission to pay the Indian companies in early February—a mission that Jackson had unsuccessfully tried to circumvent through Ransom—Capt. James W. Terrell noted that "Gen Jackson is now I believe trying to reinstate himself with me as he is quite friendly. I am chillingly polite and have none but strictly official intercourse with him." Meanwhile, with a true sense of bad timing, Thomas wrote Governor Vance and General Johnston for assistance in the immediate aftermath of the capture of Brigadier General Vance, even including a request for Governor Vance's influence in getting the Legion transferred to western North Carolina in the very same letter in which he wrote to inform him of his brother's capture. He also wrote Johnston to the same effect, unaware that the latter would soon have court-martial charges preferred against him. Their responses are unknown. Thomas also wrote to President Davis, arguing that "[i]f the balance of my Legion of Indians and Highlanders were sent to me to be under my control, as you promised me when I proposed to raise my command of Indians and Highlanders, I am satisfied that I can hold the pas[s]es in the smokey mountain and aid materially in retaking East Tennessee and protecting Western North Carolina." He criticized Jackson, "who never raised a company and never governed any men in his life until he by accident succeeded in getting control over a portion of my Legion, clings to about 300 of my men calling it his Brigade and getting the pay of a Brigadier Genl. There is no use for us both to govern one small Legion." Claiming that "Burnside refused to treat my men as prisoners of war because I have citizinized Indians in my command," Thomas claimed that "if my life and the lives of my men have to be thus jeopardized is it not fair that I should have my command to defend me[?] If this cannot be done and I have to remain without my commission and deprived of

310. *O.R.* 53:314; K. L. Seniors to Thomas, March 9, 1864, Thomas Papers, DU. "As a preparatory measure [to reuniting the Legion in western North Carolina,] could you not get Genl Breckinridge to send me one bonded quarter master, supplied with food I have had to pay my own way for six months." Thomas to Love, April 27, 1864, Thomas Papers, DU.

my command after serving two years then I have but two requests[:] accept my resignation and disband the Indians."[311]

In many ways, the letter was classic Thomas: the references to a supposed past promise by Davis to allow him to run his unit as he saw fit, the odd jumps of logic, and the shaky accuracy of some of Thomas's claims. Thomas wrote again as if Jackson's command of the Legion was some sort of personal, private power grab that the latter somehow got away with in defiance of the rules, despite the fact that Jackson had been placed in command by his superior officer as part of a perfectly legal reorganization of departmental forces. Finally, if Thomas did not have his way, he would resign. Perhaps most startling was Thomas's claim that he needed to have the Legion with him in order to "defend me," an indication of the colonel's agitated state of mind in the wake of Walker's murder and a clear indication that he saw himself as a future target.

In the meantime, the February raids into western North Carolina caused the cold war between Jackson and his officers to heat up. Terrell wrote Governor Vance about the problem on February 22, in a letter that deserves to be quoted at length for its summation of the troubles from the perspective of Thomas and his supporters:

> The misunderstanding between Gen Jackson and Col Thomas is of so serious a nature as to preclude all reconciliation, and it is certain that Col Thomas will never again under any circumstances serve under him. This leaves the command divided, part of it here under Gen Jackson and the rest in the mountains with Col Thomas
>
> Gen Jackson is not popular with the troops, Col Thomas is. Our soldiers thought their homes were in danger and thought that Col Thomas and the Indians were all the protection they had. He was immediately between their homes and the enemy. He was the officer of their choice. Mail facilities were cut off and they could not hear from their families. Of the Sappers and miners who had deserted, none of them had been punished. No vigorous steps had been taken to catch them.[312] Under these circumstances, it is not to be wondered at that some simple minded ignorant men went from this command to Col Thomas. This is the explanation of our present depleted numbers.
>
> Gen. Jackson is certainly prejudiced against us. He certainly underestimates the importance of protecting our homes He could never be made to see the necessity of protecting Western Carolina when it was in his district and his special duty to afford it protection. He has certainly tried to leave the homes of every man in his Brigade . . . exposed by repeatedly calling for the withdrawal of the Indians from the mountains and having them sent to Jonesboro his own home.[313] He has ignored the existence of the men who raised all the men he commands

311. James W. Terrell to Thomas, February 5, 1864, Thomas Papers, WCU (microfilm, Thomas Papers, DU); Thomas to Governor Vance, January 22, 1864, Governors' Papers: Vance, 1862-1865, NCOAH; Thomas to Stephen Whitaker, January 31, 1864, Whitaker Papers, NCOAH; Thomas to Davis, January 25, 1864, Letters Received by the Confederate Adjutant and Inspector General's Office (M474), reel 146, file 169-T-1864. There is no other evidence indicating that Thomas's men were not treated as prisoners of war by Burnside, whether because of the Indians or otherwise. The statement may be in relation to the seizing of mutual hostages referred to in p. 120 n. 279 above, although the latter seems to have involved civilians rather than soldiers. It is also possible that he was referring to the jailing of some of his men at Sevierville which led to Thomas's December 1863 raid to free them, although again this does not quite seem to fit the situation described.

312. The latter statement is an interesting twist on the usual accusations that Jackson ran the sappers and miners off by forcing them back into the ranks; now he was guilty for not attempting to catch and prosecute them.

313. This curious remark is probably related to Thomas's claim in his recent letter to Davis that Jackson "kept one of my Indian Companies for months guarding one of his sons, who happened [to] have the only Negroes [in

> by having orders sent directly to his captains to report to him with their companies. He has tried to destroy our organization by reporting us, not as Thomas Legion, but as Thomas Regiment, Walker's Battalion and Levi's Battery in order to make the show of a brigade without acknowledging his indebtedness to Thomas Legion. We had served almost a whole campaign with Gen Ransom before he knew that the two last named commands belonged to the Legion. He [Jackson] has by arbitrary arrests and ill natured reprimands delivered in [the] presence of the privates offended the officers. They feel that there is no security against disgrace except the very uncertain state of a naturely iritable temper intensified by diseased nerves and aggravated by being in a position for which the man is morally and physically unfit. We hold ourselves to be amongst the truest of the true Southern men. We are proud of the name of North Carolinians we want our command by all means united. We would hail with joy the orders that would send us to the Department of North Carolina. If through the influence of the man whom North Carolina 'delights to honor' we should be sent to defend her soil we would be doubly gratified in getting away from a General who has no sympathies in common with us and in finding ourselves an object of interest to our Governor.[314]

The letter is interesting because it reveals that a good deal of the opposition to Jackson was due not just to loyalty towards Thomas and the desire of members of the Legion from western North Carolina to return to that section, but to Jackson's temper and inability to handle disciplinary matters involving subordinate officers in a discrete manner. Jackson's requirement that company officers report directly to him might indicate that he was trying to bypass and possibly undermine Love, Stringfield, and McKamy, although it is possible that Terrell referred to the tug-of-war regarding the captains who had gone to North Carolina to gather absentees. Terrell attempted to excuse Thomas and the absentees with him by arguing that this was a natural response to Jackson's failure to protect western North Carolina, although despite Terrell's claim the area was never under Jackson's personal charge. Terrell did not take into account that political patronage of the sort which he hoped to find from Vance was negated by military realities; the governor could ask the Richmond government to transfer the Legion, but nothing more. Furthermore, Vance stood by his conviction that assigning troops to defend their native areas was a mistake. "Men seldom do well near their homes," he noted in his endorsement.[315]

Three days after Terrell penned his letter, forty-one officers of Thomas's Legion signed a petition to Vance requesting its reunification. They were probably inspired by the effort of officers in the Army of Tennessee to unseat Braxton Bragg from command the previous October. The Legion officers averred that they wrote "[w]ith a view to rendering our command more efficient to serve the cause for which we are contending, and to render the Circumstances of its Service More agreeable than at present." Summarizing briefly the geographical and command divisions which separated the Legion, they appealed to Vance's

---

the area]. I have not Indian companies to spare for such purposes." Thomas to Davis, January 25, 1864, Letters Received by the Confederate Adjutant and Inspector General's Office (M474), reel 146, file 169-T-1864. Like many of Thomas's claims, this one probably had some partial basis in fact that is now lost, although Thomas might have misinterpreted some quite logical orders from Jackson to station troops at an important railway depot such as Jonesborough or some other post that happened to be near the son's estate.

314. Terrell to Vance, February 22, 1864, Governors' Papers: Vance, 1862-1865, NCOAH. The letter was endorsed by Terrell's counterpart in Walker's Battalion, Capt. and Asst. Quartermaster Thomas D. Johnston.

315. Vance, endorsement on the back of Terrell to Vance, February 22, 1864, ibid.

understanding as a former officer of the negative effects of the situation on the command, adding:

> Between Genl Jackson and this entire command there has for Sometime unfortunately existed an unfriendly feeling which we deplore, but the causes of which we will not here discuss. It is sufficient for evil to our cause that this feeling Seems reciprocal and increasing in intensity. We deem it our duty to make this condition of things Known to those charged with the safety of the country and the welfare of the army, and we beg your excellency's influence to aid us in Soliciting the President to have it So ordered that our entire command May be united and the portion relieved from duty With the Brigadier General who now commands it.
>
> While we believe it due to Suggest that the Numerical Strength of the Command would be Very Much increased by a short tour of duty where Col Thomas is now operating, cheerful obedience on our part awaits any orders that will unite us.[316]

The officers were wise in not insisting that the Legion serve in western North Carolina, although that was doubtless the desire of many of them, or in making personal attacks on Jackson. Instead, they emphasized how the separation of the Legion into parts and the resulting command confusion impacted on its effectiveness as a combat force and on the morale of its men. Despite both the restraint of the letter in comparison with Terrell's angrier missive, and a flowery politeness towards Vance, their effort was only partially successful. In his endorsement, Vance reiterated that he could not support the idea of bringing the Legion to western North Carolina because of his strong conviction that troops did not perform well when serving near their homes; nevertheless, he agreed to write Davis on their behalf.[317]

Jackson's response to his subordinates was tied to the problem of the absentee captains in western North Carolina. The first to feel the axe were the most deserving: Captains Nelson and Loudermilk of Companies B and H, Walker's Battalion. Nelson was one of the officers dispatched in October 1863 to gather up his absentees; Major McKamy, who had replaced Walker as commander of the battalion, had heard by the end of February 1864 that Nelson did not plan to return. Loudermilk cooperated with Thomas for a while before

316. The signing officers were Lieutenant Colonel Love, Major Stringfield, Adj. Luther C. May, Capt. and Asst. Quartemaster Terrell, and Asst. Surgeon John C. Love, with Capt. Elisha G. Johnson and 2nd Lt. John H. Smathers of Company C, Capt. William B. Love and 2nd Lt. William W. Jones of Company D, Capt. Julius M. Welch, 1st Lt. Thomas J. Ferguson, and 2nd Lt. John H. Moody of Company E, Capt. James M. McConnell, 2nd Lt. Robert T. Conley, and "2nd" (3rd) Lt. James West of Company F, Capt. Daniel G. Fisher and 2nd Lt. John B. Raby of Company G, Capt. James Warner Cooper, 1st Lt. Lafayette George, and 2nd Lt. Eli G. Ingram of Company H, 1st Lt. Joseph A. Kimsey and 2nd Lt. Nathaniel Greene Philips of Company I, Capt. Thomas A. Butler, 1st Lt. Lewis Rector, and 2nd Lt. David Houston Gallaher of Company K, all of the Infantry Regiment; Lt. Col. James A. McKamy and Adj. Parley C. Gaston, with 1st Lt. James N. Bryson and 2nd Lt. Elisha F. Burgess of Company A, 1st Lt. William J. McRee and 2nd Lt. Mathew C. Fowler of Company B, Capt. James M. Singleton, 1st Lt. William Ashley, and 2nd Lt. John W. McKamy of Company C, Capt. Stephen Whitaker, 1st Lt. James A. Robinson, and 2nd Lt. William Alexander Wiggins of Company E, and 1st Lt. Robert A. Akin and 2nd Lt. Hiram Leford of Company H, all of Walker's Battalion; and Capt. John T. Levi of Levi's Battery. Love, et al. to Vance, February 25, 1864, Governors' Papers: Vance, 1862-1865, NCOAH. For the rebellion of the Army of Tennessee officer corps against Bragg and its results, see Connelly, *Autumn of Glory*, 235-278; McDonough, *Chattanooga*, 27-40; 95-102; 323-329, 339; Judith Lee Hallock, *Braxton Bragg and Confederate Defeat*, Vol. 2 (Tuscaloosa: The University of Alabama Press, 1991), 88-149; Sword, *Mountains Touched With Fire*, 29-35, 63-67. 76-78; Woodworth, *Six Armies in Tennessee*, 138-141, 155-157, 176-177. Vernon H. Crow drew a parallel between the actions of the anti-Jackson and anti-Bragg officers in *Storm in the Mountains*, 61.

317. Love, et al. to Vance, February 25, 1864, Governors' Papers: Vance, 1862-1865, NCOAH.

returning to his prewar occupation. McKamy wrote Adjutant and Inspector General Cooper on February 22 to drop both men from the rolls, which was done in the spring. Also dropped from service by early March were 1st Lt. Dempsey Manuel Raby of Company G, Infantry Regiment, and 3rd Lt. William H. Phillips of Company B, 3rd Lt. James A. Paul of Company C, and 3rd Lt. John Hibberts of Company H, Walker's Battalion. Later records imply that Phillips eventually returned to duty with his company. The other three seem to be more clear-cut desertion cases.[318] Jackson's handling of the cases of those officers detained by Thomas's orders with the approval of Brigadier General Vance seems to indicate, however, that restoring discipline was not the former's only motive. Captain Cooper of Company H, Infantry Regiment, and Captain Whitaker of Company E and 1st Lieutenant Akin of Company H, Walker's Battalion, had rejoined their companies by the end of February. All three signed the petition against Jackson. Captain Berry of Company A, Walker's Battalion, was still absent at that time, but returned shortly afterwards. Akin evidently accounted satisfactorily for his absence, as there is no evidence that he was dropped from the rolls. Cooper was court-martialed at Greeneville on March 25; he was evidently acquitted, as he subsequently served in command of his company. Both Whitaker and Berry were dismissed from the service, however, despite having copies of the orders from Thomas and Walker directing them to remain in North Carolina and operate under Thomas's command. Both men were restored to their ranks after undergoing boards of inquiry at their own requests, Whitaker on June 21, 1864, and Berry as late as March 30, 1865. Jackson also had Captain Levi court-martialed and cashiered from the army for unknown reasons in late February. Levi was replaced in command of the battery by his own 1st lieutenant, John W. Barr, who perhaps significantly was not only Jackson's assistant inspector general but had not signed the petition against him.[319] Also siding with Jackson according to Captain Cooper was 2nd Lt. Eli Ingram of

318. McKamy to Cooper, February 22, 1864, Letters Received by the Confederate Adjutant and Inspector General's Office (M474), reel 133, file 124-N-1864; service record files of John Hibberts, Garner N. Loudermilk, William B. Nelson, William H. Philips, James A. Paul, and Dempsey M. Raby, Thomas's Legion, Compiled Service Records of Confederate Soldiers from the State of North Carolina (M279), reels 570 through 572; J. R. Love to "my dear parents," March 4, 1864, Love to Thomas, March 8, 1864, and Terrell to Thomas, March 12, 1864, Thomas Papers, DU; Special Orders No. 46, Confederate Adjutant & Inspector General's Office, February 25, 1864, Chapter 1: vol. 16, RG 109, NA. According to Paragraph 21 of Special Orders No. 46, Nelson was ordered dropped from the rolls on February 25, three days after McKamy's message to Cooper; Nelson's service file indicates that he was dropped on April 12. The reasons for the discrepancy are unknown. Loudermilk deserted to the Federals on an unknown date and took the Oath of Allegiance at Chattanooga on February 14, 1864, eight days before McKamy's letter to Cooper. Hospital records show Phillips at Lynchburg, Virginia, in August 1864, indicating that he was with his company in the Shenandoah Valley.

319. Barr's promotion, dated March 22, was probably backdated. He remained Jackson's assistant inspector general at least through April, when in that capacity he compiled a list of AWOL officers from Walker's Battalion. A March 31 brigade inspection report gives the ranking officer in Levi's Battery as a 2nd Lieutenant, indicating that J. M. Shipp commanded until Barr's promotion. Abstract of Report of officers "Absent without leave" in the Battalion, Thomas's Legion, 4th Brigade, Army of East Tennessee, April 20, 1864, in service record file of John W. Barr, Thomas's Legion, Compiled Service Record of Confederate Soldiers from the State of North Carolina (M270), reel 567; J. W. Barr, Report of Officers "Absent without leave" in the Battalion, Thomas Legion, 4th Brigade, A. E. Tenn., April 20, 1864, and Inspection Report, 4th Brigade, Buckner's Division, Army of East Tennessee, March 31, 1864, both in Inspection Reports, Confederate Adjutant and Inspector General's Office (M935), reel 2, files 8-A-1 and 10-A-1.

Company H, although Ingram in fact signed the petition. Major Stringfield, another signer, may have been somewhat ambivalent about the conflict. As an east Tennessean, he seems to have thought better of Jackson after the war than other officers in the Legion; furthermore, there is some evidence indicating that his family wanted him to tread lightly with Jackson in order to protect his military career.[320]

In other ways, Jackson seems to have been more circumspect in dealing with his rebellious subordinates than had Bragg in like circumstances. He does not seem to have tried to move directly against such Thomas supporters as Love and McKamy who had not gone AWOL, although uncertainty surrounds the reasons for Levi's dismissal. Terrell's comments concerning orders for company commanders to report directly to Jackson, however, may indicate a plan to isolate and neutralize the higher-ranking officers. Regardless, Jackson's real target was Thomas, whom he doubtless viewed as the source of his trouble. Love wrote Thomas that upon the return of the absent officers from western North Carolina, Jackson "compelled them to give up all papers received from me. . . . He has recently been to Genl Longstreet, and I am quite certain with no other business than to abuse you, and prejudice you with Genl Longstreet. . . . My impression is that the whole thing is to get after you, & to accomplish that he would be willing to distroy this Command."[321]

Jackson's actions further demoralized that part of the Legion under him, particularly the officers. Frustrated, Love renewed his pleas for Thomas to return the absentees. Citing army regulations and the dropping of some officers who had never returned, he wrote that

320. Service record files of Robert Akin, C. C. Berry, James W. Cooper, John T. Levi, and Stephen Whitaker, Thomas's Legion, Compiled Service Record of Confederate Soldiers from the State of North Carolina (M270), reels 567, 568, 570, and 574; J. R. Love to Thomas, February 28, 1864, Love to Thomas, March 8, 1864, Terrell to Thomas, March 12, 1864, and [James W.] Cooper to Thomas, March _, 1864, all in Thomas Papers, DU; Stephen Whitaker to James Whitaker Sr., March 22, 1863, and April 6 and May 6, 1864, McKamy to J. N. Gallaher, April 19, 1864, McKamy to Stephen Whitaker, May 1, 1864, Elisha C. Johnson, John C. Summer, and Luther C. May to B. S. Mannard, June 18, 1864, and Manard, Special Order No. _, 1st Division, Army of the Valley, June 21, 1864, all in Whitaker Papers, NCOAH; Crow, *Storm in the Mountains*, 63. A reimbursement receipt for Barr's service at a court martial held at Bristol beginning on January 25 has been misinterpreted in some sources to indicate that Levi was tried on the latter date. Levi was present, however, in the Legion's camp at Carter's Depot on February 25, when he signed the anti-Jackson petition as captain of the battery. Lieutenant Colonel Love reported to Thomas on February 28 that "Capt Levi is . . . under arrest and being tried." This would place the court-martial in late February; the court-martial in which Barr was involved either as a witness or as a member of the examining board is probably unrelated. Strangely, Levi was listed as "absent captured" in the battery muster roll for November 1, 1863-February 29, 1864; as there is no record of his having been taken by the enemy, the notation probably refers to his arrest by Jackson. Levi's subsequent disappearance from the Legion records and his replacement as commander by Barr confirm that he was dismissed from the army. For Stringfield's postwar comments on Jackson, see the quote from his history of the Infantry Regiment in Clark, *North Carolina Regiments* cited in p. 47 n. 107 above, and also "War—Mss," ledger book, 140, Stringfield Papers, NCOAH. For evidence of the Stringfield family's efforts to restrain the major from engaging in conflict with Jackson, see [Mary Stringfield?] to Stringfield, "c. December, 1863" (actually subsequent to January 21, 1864), and Mary Stringfield to Stringfield, March 27, 1864, Stringfield Papers, NCOAH. The latter letter is the more detailed in this regard, and involved advice to Stringfield from one of his sisters in regards to his anger concerning tight pass regulations recently authorized by Jackson.

321. Love to Thomas, March 8, 1864, Thomas Papers, DU. Jackson's interest in accessing orders issued by Thomas to the company officers with him in western North Carolina was also noted in Terrell to Thomas, February 5, 1864, Thomas Papers, WCU (microfilm, Thomas Papers, DU); Cooper to Thomas, March _, 1864, Thomas Papers, DU.

> I have fought this matter long enough here, & the evil of these officers Must be remedied. Where is Capt Berry? I have written you regularly but received no answer of late. . . . I go this evening to a Court Martial to look after the interests of my men. . . . Why not send back the men belonging to Companies here. . . . I am satisfied they would come, if you did not encourage them to remain where they are.
>
> You have no authority to retain any one except those belonging to Cos A & B (Indians) the last named & yourself are being reported as being on detached duty, all others as deserters and absent without leave.[322]

Love's exasperation was due not only to the influence that Thomas's policy towards deserters was having on cohesion and discipline, but to its impact on the men themselves. "I have had recently some men who had deserted to voluntarily return & express themselves as having done a great wrong for which they were very sorry," Love wrote his parents. "These men (those who voluntarily return) I shall use my influence to keep from being shot, but men who desert & lie out and have to be arrested & brought back under guard May expect the Law to take its Course. I have no sympathy for such men."[323] Love, with his veteran's experience in the Army of Northern Virginia, understood the realities of the situation far better than the well-meaning but unorthodox Thomas.

Love informed Thomas in early March of the petition in a letter that shows that the two were not in full communication or coordinating their actions. "What efforts are you Making?," Love inquired: "Why not write to the President—giving the divided state of your command, & its peculiar organization; Let us go to Genl Johns[t]on or to Eastern N.C.—or any where so that we can get away from a Genl whose only object seems to be to distroy the Command. Let me hear from you—& let me know your views." The next day, March 9, Love received a letter from Thomas dated February 24. It evidently does not survive, but its contents can be inferred from a reply written on an ailing Love's behalf by Terrell. A paranoid Thomas accused Love of losing interest in the defense and welfare of western North Carolina due to his continual absence. Terrell hastened to reassure Thomas that this was not true, and that Love's devotion towards his home area was paramount in his own thinking and plans. Terrell felt that the misunderstanding must be because Thomas had not received any of the various letters sent from Love, Terrell, and May.[324] Love's comments on deserters had also apparently riled Thomas; Terrell felt obliged to explain tactfully, if not entirely accurately, that Love was only referring to those particular deserters who were skulking at home and doing nothing, thereby taking food from local needy military families, and

322. Love to Thomas, February 28, 1864, Thomas Papers, DU. Love's assertion here is perhaps the clearest evidence that Thomas and the Indian companies had some sort of official sanction to be in western North Carolina with the military authorities in eastern Tennessee although it still does not account for why the matter seemed to be called into doubt in brigade inspection reports and other sources. Captain Cooper also noted Thomas's role in encouraging men to desert and join him, although certainly from the opposite perspective of Love's: "If something is not done soon to relieve your Legion from Jackson they will nearly all come to you, especially if you will give them any encouragement." Cooper to Thomas, March _, 1864, Thomas Papers, DU.

323. Love to "my dear parents," March 4, 1864, Thomas Papers, DU.

324. In fact, at least some of those letters made it through because they are today in Thomas's papers at Duke and Western Carolina University, but they may have not reached him before his February 24 letter; alternatively, Thomas ignored or misread their comments because they did not completely coincide with his own assessments and plans.

causing frustration and discontent among those soldiers who remained in the ranks and refused to leave. "But if we could only get leave we would hail with joy the moment when we could join and aid in defending our homes," he wrote. "We have made and are still making all the efforts we can to get away from the Brigade, consistent with our honor as gentlemen and soldiers."[325]

While Terrell was for reuniting the Legion under Thomas, he raised two objections to the idea of a transferral to western North Carolina. The most interesting was the same basic argument raised by Vance and others: "it is very hard to prevent the demorilization of troops serving near their homes." The second was the concern that the Legion might not be able to receive its food supplies from eastern Tennessee, which would force them to subsist off of the local people. The argument implicit in both of these statements was that the best defense of western North Carolina would be for the Legion to serve in east Tennessee. Terrell's use of the plural in this section ("As for going to the mountains of Western North Carolina we have but two objections" and "we are fearful that we we would fail to get our supplies from Tenn and in that case we would have to draw on the already small stock in North Carolina") indicates that these views were meant to represent those of Love, and possibly the majority of the officers of the Legion, as well as Terrell's own.[326]

Perhaps hoping to reassure Thomas as to his intentions, Love wrote the colonel on March 28, as Longstreet withdrew towards the Tennessee-Virginia border. Love expressed his concerns about the dangers posed to western North Carolina by the abandonment of east Tennessee, and noted the ideal role the Legion could play in protecting the mountain passes and both Carolinas, especially if the Smokies were chosen as the line of defense rather than the Blue Ridge. Even here, however, Love added that "[i]t is immaterial to me on what field I serve—and I know it is the same to you, especially when we are dealing blows to our cruel enemy."[327]

Thus, while Thomas's officers supported his quest to reunify the Legion, some disagreed with him on the circumstances under which it should occur. Thomas would have none of their arguments. Replying on April 27 to a later letter from Love, Thomas wrote that "I entirely agree with you that the Legion ought to be united. And the best way in my opinion to unite the command is to get your part of it at an early day sent to defend western North Carolina, our common land." The successful defense of the passes in Cherokee County had to be established first; then the Legion could advance back into eastern Tennessee, assist in a Confederate effort to retake that region, and participate in its occupation. "If my troops were removed [from western North Carolina] the inhabitants would move too," he maintained. Possibly in an effort to alleviate the concerns raised by Terrell, he noted his efforts to supply the local troops and families through Beauregard. Thomas hoped that "If you could be sent to Genl Beauregards Command and Could soon be united, and Our officers could be together, I could then have you promoted, as I have intended."[328]

325. Love to Thomas, March 8, 1864, and Terrell to Thomas, March 10, 1864, Thomas Papers, DU.

326. Terrell to Thomas, March 10, 1864, Thomas Papers, DU.

327. Love to Thomas, March 28, 1864, Thomas Papers, WCU (microfilm, Thomas Papers, DU).

328. Thomas to Love, April 27, 1864, Thomas Papers, DU.

Not everyone welcomed the idea of a transfer. A kinswoman of Stringfield's (probably his sister Mary) wrote to the major in late January concerning rumors of the Legion's removal to western North Carolina. "I wonder what that's for. I do trust not to obey Col Thomas[']s behests, and hide behind the mountains over there now there's something do in E Tenn[.] If so—'tis an outrage on all manliness thus to be subjected to self interest and cowardice—So I hope there is a better ground for your transfer. My kindest regards to Gen Jackson."[329] Her letter touched on an aspect ignored by the participants in the current controversy, particularly those who wanted to justify the desertion of North Carolina troops to Thomas. Implicit in all of the arguments and counterarguments was the mutual understanding of Thomas, Love, and others that Thomas's Legion was a North Carolina unit, and that questions regarding its role in the Confederate war effort were limited as to whether or not it was best to station it in western North Carolina. This, of course, was not entirely the case in regards to the composition of those in its ranks. Although considered a North Carolina unit because it was organized under the auspices of that state before it went into Confederate service, many of its members came from other states and did not necessarily view the war in terms of the interests of North Carolina. Companies D and K of the Infantry Regiment and Companies C and H of Walker's Battalion had been recruited in eastern Tennessee, while others from that region had enlisted in the North Carolina companies; Levi's Battery included a core contingent of Virginians. In defending his soldiers who deserted in eastern Tennessee to join him, Thomas thought only in terms of those from his own area who wished to defend their homes. Taking his actions and arguments to their (il)logical conclusions, the east Tennesseans would be justified, if Thomas succeeded in uniting the Legion in western North Carolina, to desert him and go and defend their own homes; and what should prevent the Virginians, already serving in an outside area, from doing the same? It is hard to imagine that Thomas would have been pleased by such a turn of events.

For now, the Legion remained divided. The eastern Tennessee contingent marched southward from Whitesburg to Bull's Gap on January 7, where it occupied a former Federal camp. This completed a series of movements begun in mid-December when Longstreet had moved from Yellow Stone following his withdrawal from Knoxville, and now brought him back astride the railroad between Greeneville and New Market. Elements of Longstreet's command were already at work rebuilding the railroad bridges destroyed in the previous year's campaign. In this, Longstreet expected the cooperation of Samuel Jones but, relieved of his responsibilities in eastern Tennessee (and miffed about it, as well), the latter returned to his old practice of hunkering down in southwestern Virginia and refused to offer aid.

329. [Mary Stringfield?] to Stringfield, "c. December, 1863" (actually subsequent to January 21, 1864), Stringfield Papers, NCOAH. The exact date of this long letter, which is missing at least four pages, is unknown; a family member or archivist was responsible for the "c. December, 1863" heading. The letter writer referred to a recent Federal raid and skirmish at Strawberry Plains, and to a General Ferrero occupying the Stringfield home as headquarters. Brig. Gen. Edward Ferrero was sent to Strawberry Plains with the Ninth Corps on January 16, 1864, where he skirmished on January 20-21, and withdrew on the latter evening after destroying the bridge. See *O.R.* 32 (pt. 1): 104-105. See also Stringfield Diary (1864), February 2, 1864, Stringfield Papers, NCOAH. In that entry, Stringfield recorded receiving a letter from his sister "Mollie" regarding Federal depredations at home; it is probably a reference to the letter in question, although the surviving section of the letter has little to say on the topic and had more to do with the dangers posed to the family during the skirmish and the inconveniences of the occupation. Mary Stringfield's apparent antipathy towards Thomas was noted on p.74 and n. 176 above.

Longstreet contacted Richmond in order to try to force Jones to help; meanwhile, Jones continued to complain about the confused regional command situation in the area until Longstreet was formally named head of the Department of East Tennessee on January 23. Jones also made repeated requests for the return of units which had once belonged to his own command that were now under Longstreet. The little army in eastern Tennessee was destitute of both shoes and winter clothing, and obtaining supplies from outside the district was difficult. Confederate offensive operations were nil, due not only to the condition of the troops but to the fact that numerous detachments had to be sent out on foraging expeditions. A letter from Longstreet to Adjutant and Inspector General Cooper on January 4 suggests that it was partly in this context that Longstreet requested Brigadier General Vance to move to Newport, where he would be able to cover Longstreet's left flank and provide protection for the foraging parties in that area; however, as this goal for the expedition was not mentioned in Longstreet's earlier correspondence with Vance, it would appear that it was an addition resulting from the current circumstances. The disaster that befell Vance on January 14 rendered the issue moot.[330]

On January 13, Company K of the Infantry Regiment was dispatched with the wagon train as part of the foraging operations. It was recalled the next day as Ransom's Division, temporarily under the command of Corse, prepared to march again. The company did not receive word on time, and thus the division departed without it on the morning of January 15, leaving the sick behind. Longstreet's objective was Morristown, to the west of Bull's Gap along the railroad. The movement was in response to a Federal advance from Dandridge on the preceding day which had driven back the Confederate pickets. Grant had ordered Maj. Gen. John G. Foster, Burnside's replacement, to drive Longstreet north of Bull's Gap to beyond Red Bridge, pushing him as far away as possible. The advance would take place once Foster's forces, which were suffering logistical problems of their own, were fully resupplied. The movement from Dandridge was one of a number of deployments made in order to allow the Army of the Ohio to forage and resupply preparatory to an actual advance. After three days of inconclusive skirmishing, the Federals withdrew in the direction of New Market and Strawberry Plains, with Longstreet in a tepid pursuit which was soon halted.[331]

330. Leas, *Civil War Diary of Absalom Joshua Burum* (typescript copy, WCU), January 7, 1864; "Record of events": muster roll abstracts, January-February 1864: Company B, Walker's Battalion, Thomas's Legion, Compiled Service Records of Confederate Soldiers from the State of North Carolina (M270), reel 567; *O.R.* 32 (pt. 2): 58-61, 72, 80-81, 508-509, 518, 539, 551, 33:1092, 1093-1094, 1107-1110. Things became so confused that Robert E. Lee, who kept an eye on the Department of Western Virginia because of its relation to his own department, wrote in late January that Ransom's Division, including Jackson's Brigade (which he believed consisted of "Tennessee" troops), could probably be "returned" to Jones's department in the spring. Jackson's Brigade had of course always been a part of the Department of East Tennessee and had only fallen under Jones's command due to the circumstances surrounding Buckner's departure. Similarly, when Corse's Brigade was recalled to Virginia on January 20 to rejoin the rest of Pickett's Division at Petersburg, Adjutant and Inspector General Cooper had to telegraph both Jones and Longstreet because he was unsure exactly under which of the two the brigade was serving. Ibid., 33:1099, 1106, 1107.

331. Leas, *Civil War Diary of Absalom Joshua Burum* (typescript copy, WCU), January 13-15, 1864; *O.R.* 31 (pt. 1): 278-279, 281-287, (pt. 3): 384-385, 32 (pt. 1): 3-5, 27-28, 33-34, 41-51, 54, 78-94, (pt. 2): 27, 54, 63, 72, 80-83, 87, 96, 99-102, 109-111, 116-117, 127-130, 138-141, 148-154, 555-556, 563, 576, 581, 654, 52 (pt. 1): 511; Longstreet, *From Manassas to Appomattox*, 525-531; Wert, *General James Longstreet*, 367-368. Besides Jackson's small brigade, Ransom's Division consisted of Corse's and Wharton's infantry brigades, the cavalry

Although called out as part of Longstreet's response to Foster's new dispositions, the Legion saw no fighting during these maneuvers. It arrived at Morristown on January 16, where it was rejoined by Company K and the wagons. On the following day, it was sent south to Dandridge on the French Broad River. The troops endured a heavy snow which fell on the night of January 18-19. On January 19, it was sent northwards again, and had just settled into camp about two-and-a-half miles from Talbott's Station when it was ordered to move out by 1 P.M. The brigade marched to Sulphur Springs, south of Morristown. By this time it was alone, the rest of the division having been sent elsewhere. On January 20 the brigade reached Bull's Gap, where it reoccupied its old quarters.[332] At noon of the next day it departed, this time heading southward in the direction of the North Carolina mountains. Rumors spread through the ranks as to the purpose of the move; some soldiers in Company K of the Infantry Regiment, an eastern Tennessee unit, thought the Legion was going "to hide" there.[333] The command passed through Springvale and camped that night in some woods. Crossing the Nolichucky River the next day, the Legion's presence was noted by Federal intelligence operatives, who reported its passage through Greene County and estimated its size at around 600. It encamped that night close to the mountains.[334]

Despite the fears of some east Tennesseans, there was no present cause for concern in regards to a transfer of the Legion to western North Carolina. Instead, Jackson had been dispatched to hunt bushwhackers in the mountains. On January 24, the scope of his operations

---

brigades of "Grumble" Jones and Brig. Gen. John S. Williams (the latter under Col. James E. Carter), and J. Floyd King's Battalion Virginia Artillery (13th Battalion Virginia Light Artillery; see Lee A. Wallace Jr., *A Guide to Virginia Military Organizations 1861-1865*, Revised 2nd Edition, Virginia Regimental History Series [Lynchburg: H. E. Howard, 1986], 6). Ransom was on leave at the time. *O.R.* 32 (pt. 2): 535-536; 681. As the Federal foraging parties were covering an area around and to the south of the French Broad, where Longstreet was sending his own foragers, these actions were related to the context of Brigadier General Vance's capture.

332. Leas, *Civil War Diary of Absalom Joshua Burum* (typescript copy, WCU), January 16-20, 1864. On the January-February muster roll of Company A, Walker's Battalion, it was recorded that that unit was on picket duty at Mossy Creek on January 17, and returned to Bull's Gap on January 21. It is possible that the company was detached for picket service on the former date and rejoined the rest of the Legion at Bull's Gap; alternatively, the date intended was January 19, when the Legion was near Mossy Creek at Talbott's Station. "Record of events": muster roll abstract, January-February 1864: Company A, Walker's Battalion, Thomas's Legion, Compiled Service Records of Confederate Soldiers from the State of North Carolina (M270), reel 567.

333. Leas, *Civil War Diary of Absalom Joshua Burum* (typescript copy, WCU), January 21, 1864. The parallel with the comments of Stringfield's sister, made in a private letter about the same time and noted above, is almost certainly not coincidental and probably reflects commonly held opinions among frustrated east Tennesseans regarding Thomas's activities and intentions at this time.

334. Leas, *Civil War Diary of Absalom Joshua Burum* (typescript copy, WCU), January 21-22, 1864; *O.R.* 32 (pt. 2): 312-313. The report from Col. R. A. Crawford, described as "Chief of Police" (and in other documents as "Chief of Secret Police"), and filed from Greene County, is difficult to reconcile with Burum's diary entries in regards to dating. Crawford reported some 1,200 men of Ransom's Divison under Corse as having "passed up the country" in his January 21 entry. The same entry reported that Jackson "passed up the south side of Nola Chucky River"; Burum's diary, however, indicates that the Legion was north of the Nolichucky on that day. Since the next entry in Crawford's report was dated January 24, then either Crawford did not specifically date every item, and his reference was to after the Legion's crossing of the river on January 22, or his information was mistaken, most likely the former. Based on the number of effective men given in the January 8 field report noted earlier (353 effective officers and men) and the January 31 return given below (313 effective officers and men), the figure of about 600 men in the intelligence report is probably inaccurate, doubling the Legion's numbers, even if various support elements (cooks, wagoneers, etc.) were not included in the official returns.

were widened by Longstreet to include protection of his foraging trains south of the French Broad River, although if Jackson received the latter directive he probably did not have the chance to act on it due to the course of events. The men cooked three days' rations on January 24 and set out on the next day, moving into the mountains and the rough terrain surrounding Shelton Laurel. According to Sgt. Absalom J. Burum of Company K, Infantry Regiment, the soldiers spotted only about a half dozen men during the excursion. They fired at three who made their escape, but captured three horses and feasted on green apples before moving on to a new camp at Allen's Stand (Allanstand) in Madison County, where they arrived about 11 P.M. after having marched around twelve miles.[335]

On the following day, the Legion moved out again around 4 A.M., once again scouring the Laurel area. A few men were captured, but otherwise the day was fairly quiet. "Oh what a 'howling wilderness' this!!," griped a homesick Stringfield. "Away from Law & Order, away from civilization, away from all that is refined & delicate noble & humane. These people are next to the aboriginal inhabitants of these Mountains." At one point the troops passed near a high point on the state border (probably Coldspring Mountain in Madison County), from which they could see a great deal of the eastern Tennessee expanse spread out below them. After a roundabout journey of some sixteen miles, they returned to their camp that evening. On the following day they moved back into Tennessee, stopping for the night at Clark Creek, a tributary of the Nolichucky, in Washington County, some twelve miles from Jonesborough.[336]

After Jackson's Brigade was sent south to the mountains, Longstreet continued to spar with Foster along the railroad and in the surrounding district. Rumors soon reached Longstreet's headquarters of a possible Federal move to destroy the railroad bridges in his

335. *O.R.* 32 (pt. 2): 595, 610-611; Leas, *Civil War Diary of Absalom Joshua Burum* (typescript copy, WCU), January 24 and 26, 1864; Stringfield Diary (1864), January 25 and 27, Stringfield Papers, NCDAH; Powell, *The North Carolina Gazetteer*, 7, 235. This part of Stringfield's wartime diary exists in the original, although parts of it were subsequently recopied into his ledger book along with sections of the no longer extant 1863 diary. Unless otherwise noted, references to the 1864 diary pertain to the original. It is difficult to reconcile the diaries of Burum and Stringfield as to the places the Legion visited, possibly due to different segments proceeding along different trails and setting out and arriving at different times. Stringfield wrote that the Legion moved out on the evening of January 25, and marched twelve miles to Allen's Stand, arriving at 11 P.M. Burum reported that the Legion moved into the Shelton Laurel area and encamped at a place called Horse Creek, probably the tributary of Shelton Laurel Creek of that name, lying south of Allen's Stand; his account implied some time spent in that vicinity searching for guerillas.

336. Leas, *Civil War Diary of Absalom Joshua Burum* (typescript copy, WCU), January 26-27, 1864; Stringfield Diary (1864), January 25 and 27, (quote from January 27 entry), Stringfield Papers, NCOAH. Both Burum and Stringfield mentioned the spectacular view of eastern Tennessee from the mountains. The latter identified the viewing site as "'Cold Springs.'" There is a Coldspring Mountain on the Madison County-Greene County (Tennessee) border (Powell, *North Carolina Gazetteer*, 113). The Legion probably marched northeast through the mountains along the border. Burum indicated that it moved up the Nolichucky River from Horse Creek to its destination. Stringfield mentioned Clark Creek in Washington County as the Legion's stopping place on the night of January 27. Clark Creek is a tributary of the Nolichucky running south from Washington into Unicoi County. It is possible that Jackson may have moved back into eastern Tennessee in response to the January 24 orders from Longstreet's headquarters to cover the foraging teams south of the French Broad River, although if so why he then moved eastward away from the French Broad and then into the mountains is unclear. It is more likely that he was making a broad (and very brief) sweep for guerrillas along the border, moving northeast and, perhaps not so coincidentally, staying well away from Thomas's domain in the southwest corner of North Carolina.

rear. Jackson was ordered on January 28 to move to Carter's Depot and protect the bridge there; he would be joined by all or a portion of the 38th Regiment Tennessee Infantry and by the 9th (Leyden's) Battalion Georgia Artillery. Grant, still concerned about Longstreet's presence, had in fact directed Foster to mount just such a raid about this time; however, Brig. Gen. Samuel D. Sturgis was unwilling to make the effort due to the worn-out condition of his horses and the continuing forage problems, so the operation was continually postponed. As the raid did not immediately materialize, orders were sent for Jackson to leave Carter's Depot and resume the anti-guerrilla operation in the mountains. He was almost immediately sent yet another set of orders, this time to return to the old task of guarding the scattered railroad bridges and depots. On February 1, only one day after Jackson was ordered to leave Carter's Depot to return on the bushwhacking mission, Longstreet's headquarters contacted Col. John C. Carter, commander of the 38th Regiment Tennessee Infantry, whose troops were divided between the former post and Zollicoffer. The message noted that Carter would be relieved from guarding those sites by Jackson's Brigade in a few days.[337]

In fact, it seems that the Legion never arrived at Carter's Depot until around February 1, the reason for apparent incongruities in the various messages from Longstreet's headquarters to Jackson and Carter regarding the units involved.[338] The Legion had already moved deeper into the mountains on January 28 before the assignment issued on that date from headquarters could reach Jackson. Its destination was Indian Creek, a tributary of the Nolichucky that ran through a valley known as Greasy Cove, an area rumored to be rife with bushwhackers. The Legion had not gone more than two miles from camp when the advance guard encountered a small band of guerrillas. The Confederates killed one man by the name of Pritchett and dispersed the rest. The Legion then split into two contingents to cover the northern and southern branches of the creek and thus both ends of the cove, with a rendezvous site on the river. As things turned out, the operation was curtailed by both logistics and timing. The men had only prepared rations for two days when they departed camp, and had to wait for more to be brought up to be able to continue their mission. It was apparently on the next day that Longstreet's orders to go to Carter's Depot finally reached Jackson. Around 2 in the morning of January 30, the Legion left camp and began the march to the depot, arriving there by February 1.[339]

337. For general information on military activities in eastern Tennessee at this time, see *O.R.* 32 (pt. 1): 34-35, 42-51, 54-55, 94-97, 104-109, 114-115, 126-127, 130-152, 159-161, (pt. 2): 151-346 passim, 581-654 passim, 52 (pt. 1): 514-515, (pt. 2): 603; *O.R. (Supplement)*, Pt I, 6:218-219. See especially *O.R.* 32 (pt. 2): 627-628, 633-634, 651 for the assignments relative to Jackson. This phase of the operations in eastern Tennessee led to the raid on Thomas's camp at Deep Creek on February 2. Although Sturgis felt unable to mount the raid proposed by Grant, he became aware of the Cherokee camp while passing through Tuckasegee Cove on his way from Fair Garden to Maryville following a series of clashes south of the French Broad River, and decided to destroy it because of Thomas's recent activities in eastern Tennessee. Ibid., 32 (pt. 1): 137, (pt. 2): 273.

338. The confusion was due not only to the difficulties of tracking Jackson's location, but to the fact that there was a transition in command of the division during this time as Corse and his brigade were ordered back to Virginia. Wharton briefly served as Corse's replacement during Ransom's continuing absence. Ibid., 32 (pt. 2): 595, 597, 628, 642.

339. Leas, *Civil War Diary of Absalom Joshua Burum* (typescript copy, WCU), January 28 and 30, 1864; Stringfield Diary (1864), February 1, Stringfield Papers, NCOAH. In his diary, Burum did not mention a march from Clark Creek to Carter's Depot on January 27, but had the regiment moving directly to Greasy Cove on

To the frustration and annoyance of the men and officers, the cavalry raid never materialized and the interruption of their mission was in vain. "Back to our old 'Stomping ground'—guarding bridges[.] Seems to be my fate," groused Stringfield. "I will submit for a while—& in the mean while hunt 'Buffalo' to pass away the time." "Buffalo" was a common term in North Carolina for Southern Unionist, especially on the coast. Thus, Stringfield's diary reference on February 14, "Went 'Buffalo' hunting to day and caught—a 'tartar,'" has a rather violent ring to it.[340] Such incidents seem to have been relatively isolated, despite his claim after the war that the Legion used Carter's Depot "as a base of operations" from which "we could 'swing around' the mountains on several trips after 'renegades,' blockade stills and deserters." Instead, the Legion was divided to cover the posts previously held by the 38th Regiment Tennessee Infantry. The Infantry Regiment was concentrated at Carter's Depot, with the exception of Company F, sent to Limestone Bridge, while Walker's Battalion was sent to Zollicoffer on February 3. Levi's Battery was brought down from Saltville to Carter's Depot by the end of February, although there is no evidence that it was formally reintegrated into Jackson's Brigade at this time. These deployments were still in place when the company muster rolls were taken at the end of February.[341]

Lieutenant Barr inspected the Infantry Regiment and Walker's Battalion again on January 12. The regiment reported the total number of men enlisted as 490, with a total present of 274 and an effective total of 204. The regiment reported 50 present sick and 56 absent sick. Walker's Battalion reported the total number enlisted as 209, with a total present and

January 28. Likewise, Stringfield wrote from Carter's Depot on February 1 that he arrived there after a five-day expedition to Greasy Cove; counting the march to the depot itself, this would neatly cover the period of January 28-February 1 (or January 27-31, if the march to Clark Creek were included and the Legion arrived at the depot on the latter date). Given the distance and time involved, this would rule out the possibility that Jackson received Longstreet's January 28 order, marched to Carter's Depot, returned to the mountains following the January 31 order, and returned to the depot again on February 1, the interpretation taken in Crow, *Storm in the Mountains*, 63. It seems safer to assume that Jackson did not receive the January 28 message until the Legion had gone to Greasy Cove, its eventual arrival prompting the march on the night of January 29-30. The wording on the muster roll for Company A, Walker's Battalion, implies that the Legion arrived at Carter's Depot on January 30, indicating an all-night and all-day march, but perhaps only the starting date of the return march was intended. "Record of events"; muster roll abstract. January-February 1864: Company A, Walker's Battalion, Thomas's Legion, Compiled Service Records of Confederate Soldiers from the State of North Carolina (M270), reel 567.

340. The origins of the pejorative term "Buffalo" are unclear. See Barrett, *The Civil War in North Carolina*, 59, 174-177; Paul D. Escott, "North Carolina," in Current, *Encyclopedia of the Confederacy*, 3:1125; Alex Christopher Meekins, "The Arcane Origin of the Term 'Buffalo': A Civil War Epithet from Eastern North Carolina," unpublished paper delivered at the Annual Meeting of the Historical Society of North Carolina, April 2006. "To catch a Tartar" was an old slang phrase, referring to something caught that proved surprisingly difficult to manage. Philip Babcock Gove, editor-in-chief, *Webster's Third New International Dictionary of the English Language Unabridged* (Springfield: G. & C. Merrian Col. 1969), 2342.

341.Stringfield Diary (1864), February 1, 6, and 11, Stringfield Papers, NCOAH ("'Stomping ground'" quote, February 1); Stringfield, "Sixty-Ninth Regiment," in Clark, *North Carolina Regiments* 3:743 ("as a base of operations" and "we could 'swing around'" quotes); "Record of events": muster roll abstracts, January-February 1864: Companies C, D, E, F, G, H, I, and K, Infantry Regiment, Companies A, B, C, E, and H, Walker's Battalion, and November 11, 1863-February 29, 1864: Capt. Levi's Battery Light Artillery, Thomas's Legion, Compiled Service Records of Confederate Soldiers from the State of North Carolina (M270), reel 567; Terrell to Thomas, February 5, 1864, Thomas Papers, WCU (microfilm, Thomas Papers, DU); Love to Thomas, February 28, 1864, Thomas Papers, DU; Stephen Whitaker to father, March 22, 1864 [misdated 1863], Whitaker Papers, NCOAH.

an effective total of 73. Forty-one were absent sick. These figures represent a decrease in the total number of men enlisted in both units from the individual reports of November and December, probably as the result of absentees being cleared off the rolls. Barr's comments on the overall condition of the troops and their equipment, their drill, discipline, and character echoed those in his reports of the previous year, with minor variations. In general, the elements of the Legion seemed to be in pretty good shape, despite the absence of overcoats and the lack of clothing for new recruits and returning absentees.[342]

Official returns from the end of January show Jackson's Brigade as still a part of Ransom's Division of the Department of West Virginia, but on detached assignment with the Department of East Tennessee. Forty-four officers and 275 men were present for duty, out of 397 aggregate present and 769 aggregate present and absent. The number present for duty was considerably less than the 600 estimated in the earlier Federal intelligence report as the Legion headed towards the mountains; however, the number was not far from the January 8 field return which had given the brigade's strength as 44 officers and 309 men present for duty. The brigade was divided into "Thomas' North Carolina Regiment" (the Infantry Regiment) under Love, and Walker's Battalion under McKamy. Levi's Battery was at the time still unattached at Saltville as part of the Department of West Virginia, with 1 officer and 32 men present for duty out of 34 aggregate present and 64 aggregate present and absent.[343] Returns from the Department of East Tennessee dated February 29 showed Jackson's Brigade and Wharton's Brigade, both formerly parts of Ransom's Division, as separate from any division. By this time, Corse's Brigade had returned to the Army of Northern Virginia, and Ransom was in command of the departmental cavalry. Jackson's Brigade was reported to have 49 officers and 322 men present for duty out of an aggregate 428 present and an aggregate of 786 present and absent. Although Levi's Battery had arrived by that time, it was not noted as a part of the brigade's strength or even reported as part of the department at all.[344]

As the winter continued, a stalemate settled over eastern Tennessee. Foster believed that it was impossible for either army to wage a campaign, given the logistical problems and the condition of troops and roads. Suffering from the effects of old wounds that needed treatment, he was relieved on January 28 and replaced by Maj. Gen. John M. Schofield, who took command of the Army of the Ohio on February 9. Outside of demonstrations, fitful skirmishing, and minor raids, there was no military action. Longstreet's brief advance to Strawberry Plains and subsequent withdrawal up the valley in mid-February was the cause of speculation on both sides that he was preparing to mount a new effort to take Knoxville, or was abandoning Tennessee for Virginia or Georgia. In fact, Longstreet desired to go on

342. Inspection Reports, Regiment: Thomas's Legion, and Walker's Battalion, January 12, 1864, Chapter 1: Muster and Pay Rolls, Box 826, Entry 18, Thomas's Legion Battalion Field and Staff File No. 2, RG 109, NA.

343. *O.R.*, 32 (pt. 2): 640, 33:1136-1138.

344. Ibid., 32 (pt. 2): 595, 632, 642, 654, 681-682, 726, 822. Ransom was assigned to command the departmental cavalry on February 12, 1864. His division had already ceased to exist by that point. In the January-February 1864 muster roll for Company C, Walker's Battalion, it was noted that that unit was a part of Ransom's Division "until about the 1st of February 1864," in other words, about the time that the Legion was dispersed for guard duty along the railroad and just after the January 31 field return. "Record of events": muster roll abstract, January-February 1864: Company C, Walker's Battalion, Thomas's Legion, Compiled Service Records of Confederate Soldiers from the State of North Carolina (M270), reel 567.

the offensive again; however, he was ordered to return the part of the Army of Tennessee's cavalry that was still in eastern Tennessee, and a proposed coordinated diversionary move from Johnston failed to materialize. Although Longstreet so interpreted the orders concerning the cavalry that he only sent one division, the reduction of his force and the lack of assistance from Johnston led to his decision to retreat to the area of Bull's Gap and establish a strong defensible position. Similarly, a Federal offensive which would have included reinforcements from the Army of the Cumberland to destroy Longstreet's command sputtered out before it began, due to supply and transportation problems and Grant's realization (partially on information from Foster) that Longstreet was more of a distraction than a threat.[345]

The military inaction continued through March, while Longstreet attempted to get Lee's support for a plan to invade Kentucky by combining his forces with those of Johnston and Beauregard. The plan was not approved due to a number of logistical and strategic problems posed by the proposed operation. Grant was promoted to lieutenant general and became general-in-chief of all Federal armies, while Sherman assumed command of forces in the western theater. Occasional skirmishes erupted as the opposing forces probed each other's defenses or made minor adjustments in their deployments. Neither side had a particularly clear picture of the other's strength and intentions. Things remained quiet for the members of Thomas's Legion, scattered along the railroad; Stringfield recorded in his diary that he did a lot of visiting and socializing. It was perhaps no accident that this was the period in which the Legion officers submitted their petition against Jackson to Governor Vance, and Jackson prosecuted many of the company commanders, as not only had these matters naturally come to a head, but a stationary position and a lack of combat left everyone with plenty of time to pursue their grievances. In March, Jackson became involved with a problem somewhat analagous to the earlier situation involving Thomas's sappers and miners, in this case involving Federal deserters from eastern Tennessee. He sought direction from Longstreet about what to do with these men, some of whom may have been employed in the Confederate niter works; he was instructed to have them rounded up and sent to Richmond and to supply their names to the Niter and Mining Bureau for security purposes.[346] Despite deep snows on March 22 and March 24-25, indifferent rations, and anger over rumors of widespread destruction to the railroad and civilian property in the direction of Strawberry Plains, the troops were reported in good spirits and enthusiastic about the coming spring campaign. Like other Confederate units at this time, the companies of the Legion reenlisted for the war. Their hopes were soon dashed. Longstreet was forced to send the remaining part of the Army of Tennessee's cavalry that was with him to Johnston, and in consequence decided to withdraw the bulk of his command towards Bristol at the end of the month. The Federals were unable to follow up because the Ninth Corps was transferred to Virginia, limiting Schofield to a defensive posture. The removal of the Ninth Corps had serious

345. *O.R.* 31 (pt. 3): 502-503, 529, 571, 32 (pt. 1): 8-9, 23, 36-37, 42-52, 160-161, 391-393, 404-407, 409-415, 485, (pt. 2): 251, 253, 319-496 passim, 667-818 passim, (pt. 3): 3, 9, 14, 137-138, 576-577, 582-583, 654, 675, 33:1185, 52 (pt. 1): 517-518, 522-527, (pt. 2): 626, 627, 629; Wert, *General James Longstreet*, 368; Leas, *Civil War Diary of Absalom Joshua Burum* (typescript copy, WCU), February 27, 1864.

346. Jackson's behavior reinforces the arguments given earlier that whatever course he took against Thomas's sappers and miners likely proceeded under official direction.

repercussions for the Confederates in eastern Tennessee in turn, as it resulted in the recall of Longstreet and his divisions to Virginia on April 7.[347]

The withdrawal and eventual loss of Longstreet and his troops caused consternation within the ranks of Thomas's Legion. Those who were natives of eastern Tennessee bemoaned the abandonment of their home region, while those from western North Carolina feared that the absence of a major field force in the area opened the door to more raids through the mountain passes. The sense of gloom was probably not helped by the fact that the Legion was in an isolated and exposed position, serving as an advanced outpost for the diminishing eastern Tennessee command. Fortunately, the lack of a strong Federal pursuit of Longstreet spared it from any imminent danger. The Infantry Regiment remained at Carter's Depot, and was probably rejoined by Company F at this time. On April 6, Walker's Battalion was brought up to Carter's Depot from Zollicoffer.[348]

Field returns and inspection reports for the period show a small decline in strength in March from the previous records for February, followed by a precipitous loss of manpower in April. The March 31 field return for the forces in eastern Tennessee showed Jackson's Brigade as a part of Buckner's Division, commanded on that date by Brig. Gen. Bushrod Johnson. The brigade return showed 53 commissioned officers present for duty. Jackson and his staff accounted for 6 of the officers; the remainder consisted of 47 officers from the Legion. Thirteen of these officers represented the field and staff of the Infantry Regiment and Walker's Battalion present for duty (9 and 4 respectively); the remainder were the commissioned company officers of those units, and a lieutenant from Levi's Battery. In addition, 2 officers from the regiment were present but sick, while 1 officer each from the regiment and Levi's Battery were reported under arrest.[349] There were 285 enlisted men present for duty in

347. *O.R.* 32 (pt. 1): 24, 49, 52-53, 490-491, 496-497, (pt. 3): 3-283 passim, 576-599 passim, 613-680 passim, 736-738, 749, 756, 52 (pt. 1): 527, 529-535, (pt. 2): 634-635, 642-644, 648-649; Stringfield Diary (1864), March 31, April 1-2, Stringfield Papers, NCOAH; Wert, *General James Longstreet*, 369-372; Leas, *Civil War Diary of Absalom Joshua Burum* (typescript copy, WCU), February 27, March 22, March 25, 1864; Captain [James W.] Cooper to Thomas, March _, 1864, J. R. Love to parents, March 4, 1864, and Love to Thomas, March 8, 1864, Thomas Papers, DU; Love to Thomas, March 28, 1864 Thomas Papers, WCU (microfilm, Thomas Papers, DU); Stephen Whitaker to father, March 22, 1864 [misdated 1863], and Whitaker to James Whitaker Sr., April 6-7, 1864, Whitaker Papers, NCOAH. Rumors of Longstreet's plan for a move into Kentucky may have leaked out of his headquarters and circulated down to the troops as gossip, as Cooper (March _), Love (March 4), and Whitaker (letter begun April 6 and finished April 7) mention the possibility in correspondence; however, the talk may have just been reflected typical soldier speculation before the commencement of a campaign season.

348. Stringfield Diary (1864), April 1-2, April 26 (sideways scrawl and crosshatch), Stringfield Papers, NCOAH; Leas, *Civil War Diary of Absalom Joshua Burum* (typescript copy, WCU), April 3, 1864; Love to Thomas, March 28, 1864, Thomas Papers, WCU (microfilm, Thomas Papers, DU); Weaver, *Nottoway Battery and Barr's Artillery*, 110. Capt. Stephen Whitaker of Company E, Walker's Battalion, viewed Longstreet's movement as a prelude to a possible offensive, probably in Kentucky. According to Weaver, Levi's Battery was at Abingdon by at least April 7; it probably pulled back with Longstreet's troops and was left there.

349. Field Return, 4th Brigade, Buckner's Division, Army of East Tennessee, March 31, 1864, Inspection Reports, Confederate Adjutant and Inspector General's Office (M935), reel 2, file 10-A-1; *O.R.* 32 (pt. 3): 721-722. The figures reported represent the actual totals derived from adding the numbers for each category; there are some minor errors in the totals on the actual field return. Some of the totals in the abstract published in *O.R.* 32 (pt. 3): 721 are in error. Buckner had participated in the effort to oust Bragg from command of the Army of Tennessee, and as a result one of his two divisions was transferred. His remaining division participated in

Thomas's Legion (privates, non-commissioned officers, and musicians), of which only 196 were privates. In addition, there were 63 men present on extra duty and 3 under arrest, combining with those present for duty for an effective total of 351 men. There were 37 men present sick, combining for a total present of 386. The aggregate present of commissioned officers and enlisted men was 436, with Jackson and his staff making the number 442. Two commissioned officers and 99 men were absent on detached duty, and 6 commissioned officers (including one member of the brigade staff) and 23 men were absent with leave. Two commissioned officers and 106 men were reported absent without leave. Four commissioned officers and 69 men were absent sick. In all, 14 commissioned officers and 297 men were absent, although one of the detached officers was on assignment with the brigade staff and thus double-counted.[350]

The Infantry Regiment was in the best shape of any contingent of the Legion. It had an effective total of 237, of which 142 were privates present for duty. Twenty-eight more enlisted men were present on extra duty. Nine field officers and 19 company officers were present, including 5 of the regiment's 8 captains, and 52 non-commissioned officers. Still, the unit was much diminished in size. One commissioned officer and 80 enlisted men were reported on detached service, a possible reference to Thomas and the Cherokee companies, although a note on the report stated that it did not include any information on those units, adding that Thomas was in western North Carolina "acting it is claimed under orders of Genls. Bragg & Buckner & Vance." One commissioned officer and 51 men were absent without leave; in addition, one officer and three enlisted men were under arrest. Outside of field officers, Walker's Battalion was down to 6 commissioned officers, only one of which was a captain. It is clear that Jackson's purge of the company officers, however justified it may have seemed, had had a devastating effect on the unit's command structure; if there was any consolation, it was that the reduced strength of the battalion made additional officers and even its field and staff superfluous. Only 17 non-commissioned officers and 22 privates were present for duty; adding a musician and 35 enlisted men on detached service, it left an effective total of 75, not even the strength of an ideal full-sized company. While only 16 men were on detached duty, one officer and 50 men were absent without leave.[351]

Levi's Battery was in relatively good shape personnel-wise, although its command structure was weak. 2nd Lt. J. M. Shipp was the only commissioned officer reported present on duty. One officer was reported under arrest (Levi himself), 1 on detached duty (Barr, who was still Jackson's assistant inspector general), and another on sick leave (3rd Lt. R. C. Searcey). Thirty-nine enlisted men were present on duty, including 32 privates. Only 5 men from the battery were absent without leave. In addition, the return noted that Burroughs's

---

Longstreet's siege of Knoxville, and had remained in eastern Tennessee ever since. At the time of the March 31 return it also included Johnson's own Tennessee brigade, Archibald Gracie's Alabama brigade, Evander M. Law's Alabama brigade of Hood's Division, and Wharton's Brigade of Ransom's old division. By the next return, Law's and Wharton's brigades would no longer be part of the division, the former unit returning to the Army of Northern Virginia and the latter shortly to the Department of Western Virginia. See Connelly, *Autumn of Glory*, 252-253; Woodworth, *Six Armies in Tennessee*, 141, 179, 181, 207; *O.R.*, 32 (pt. 3): 721-722, 793, 802, 803, 835.

350. Field Return, 4th Brigade, Buckner's Division, Army of East Tennessee, March 31, 1864, Inspection Reports, Confederate Adjutant and Inspector General's Office (M935), reel 2, file 10-A-1.

351. Ibid.

and McClung's batteries were still considered to be a part of the brigade, but had been detached due to "the excess of Artillery in the Dept" and a lack of horses; they were stationed at Saltville. There were 683 total present and absent enlisted men for the Legion; adding commissioned officers, the aggregate total and absent was 746, with Jackson and his staff adding to a brigade total of 752. This compared favorably with the previous return, where the aggregate brigade total had been 759. Since the last return there had been 1 enlistment, 2 returning deserters, a death, a new desertion, 2 discharges, and 1 resignation.[352]

On April 20, the brigade was inspected at Carter's Depot by Lt. Col. Archer Anderson. Only 22 officers and 162 men from the regiment and the battalion were present for duty; there was no mention of Levi's Battery, which was at Abingdon. Twelve men were reported as absent without leave, although they had "received furloughs of indulgence" evidently due to some extenuating circumstance. Anderson described a state was one of disarray, with virtually no discipline or drilling. "No school of tactics in the battalion," he wrote, although Love had had one in place for the regiment for the past month. "There have been no company or battalion drills since October. The officers & men appear almost entirely ignorant of the simplest evolutions. Not even the facings were correctly executed." The Articles of War had not been read to the men on parade for the past six months, and there were only two roll calls a day. The battalion did not keep morning reports or even possess a morning report book. While Anderson noted that there were not too many men on extra duty, "the staff itself is Sufficient for a brigade of 2000 men," adding that "[t]he brigade organization for so few men is cumbrous." Incredibly, there were no camp guards posted. Weapons were described as "[r]usty," indicating that proper maintenance was not kept. Clothing was described as "[p]assable," with some lacking trousers. Twenty-two men had no shoes and eleven had bad ones, although only four lacked blankets. All-in-all, it was not surprising that Anderson concluded that the "[m]en's bearing is decidedly unmilitary." About the only bright spot was that the general sanitary condition of the men was good. The report emphasized the brigade's role as an outpost unit. While Anderson reported that "[t]he officers say the men are in good spirits" and that "[t]heir local knowledge may be valuable," he concluded that "they will hardly become soldiers till they are put where they can be disciplined and drilled."[353]

Supply problems also plagued the brigade. In addition to the poor condition of the arms (a hodgepodge of different calibers), there were only twenty-five bayonets available. The men were rationed either a quarter pound of bacon or a pound of beef, along with a pound of flour; bacon was issued four days a week. The beef was described as "poor—so poor that the men Sometimes throw it away." Just two weeks previously, a member of the regiment had recorded in his diary that their rations had been reduced to two-thirds of a pound of flour daily, three quarters of a pound of beef five days a week, and around a quarter of a pound of bacon two days a week, occasionally supplemented by a little rice; the report thus indicated quite a deterioration in the quantity of rations in a short period of time. Supplies were drawn from the Bristol depot.[354]

352. Ibid.

353. Inspection Report of Jackson's Brigade, April 20, [1864], Inspection Reports, Confederate Adjutant and Inspector General's Office (M935), reel 2, file 7-A-1.

354. Ibid; Leas, *Civil War Diary of Absalom Joshua Burum* (typescript copy, WCU), April 5, 1864.

While the inspection did not provide much detail, it would appear at first glance that the basic strength of the brigade had stayed the same over the month, except for the number of officers present, which was less than half reported at the end of the previous month. Given the skimpiness of information in Anderson's report, however, the number of men reported present at the inspection could be misleading; for example, it is unclear if the number of "enlisted men" present refers to privates only, or if it includes non-commissioned officers and musicians also, as in the case of the field report. If the latter is true, then the Legion had undergone a serious drop in troop strength: with non-commissioned officers and musicians included, there would be 246 enlisted men from both the regiment and the battalion present for duty on March 31 versus 162 on April 20. The smaller number of officers at the April inspection suggests a decrease as well.

Anderson's report is also revealing in its depiction of the efficiency of the Legion at this time. Once again, even after their previous field experience a report mentioned the *possibility* of its men becoming good soldiers under proper leadership. There seems to be no single explanation for this state of affairs. Discipline problems plagued the armies of both sides.[355] Thomas's Legion seemed to suffer from more than its share, however, with a near total breakdown of responsibility in insuring that it functioned properly, something that was inexcusable during a period when it was not on the march or otherwise involved in a military campaign. Despite the problems caused by Thomas's actions and the absenteeism of many of the men, much of the blame belonged to Jackson, who, for all his reputation as a martinet seemed incapable of imposing his will on the brigade. It was his responsiblity to set the initiative to make sure that drills were properly and frequently conducted, that the Articles of War were read and understood, that weapons were properly maintained. The responsiblity for carrying out those things had to be shared, however; everyone from Jackson's staff down to the company officers had to play their parts, and it would seem that this was not being done. The possible exception was Love, who with his background in the Army of Northern Virginia seems to have been the officer who took his responsibilities the most seriously, and had at least reinstituted a school of tactics for his regiment. Even in Love's case, however, the lack of battalion or company drill is noticeable. Nevertheless, as brigade commander Jackson was ultimately responsible for the shape of his command.

One person who shared that point of view was Braxton Bragg, now Davis's military advisor. After receiving Anderson's report, Bragg disparagingly commented on April 25 that the Legion "is called a brigade, under Brig. Gen. A. E. Jackson. It reports 360 men for duty, but could show but 180 on parade—all in miserable order." The occasion of Bragg's comments was yet another plea from western North Carolina to send more troops to defend that area. Governor Vance had written Secretary of War Seddon on April 18 requesting that "one regiment, at least" be sent to Colonel Palmer at Asheville. Vance enclosed an April 12 message from Brigadier General McElroy of the N.C. Home Guard, complaining of recent depredations by a band of Unionists in Burnsville. Seddon confessed himself "at a loss" as to where he might find the troops, but opined hopefully that when the state reserves were organized that perhaps they might be sent. Davis, perhaps vaguely remembering the requests

355. Gerald F. Linderman, *Embattled Courage: The Experience of Combat in the American Civil War* (New York: The Free Press, 1987), 34-60; Robertson, *Soldiers Blue and Gray*, 122-144.

from Thomas and the Legion officers about a possible reunification, wrote to Bragg, "Have not the companies of Thomas' legion been sent to the section referred to?" It was this message which prompted Bragg's remarks. Bragg explained that it had been intended for the Legion to go to the area, but that they had been delayed to be inspected. "I propose to order the infantry to Western North Carolina, relieving General Jackson"—news which would have warmed Thomas and his subordinates had they known about it. Further impetus for a transfer came from South Carolina, when Governor Bonham expressed his concerns to Seddon on April 22 regarding the safety of the mountain passes in the wake of Longstreet's withdrawal, and the potential threat posed to the region by rumored enemy activity; this message was passed along to Bragg, also. Reiterating many of his earlier points on May 2, Bragg added that "[f]rom the condition of the command, as reported by a recent inspecting officer, General Jackson should be relieved from it and sent to some point where he can be in contact with good and disciplined officers and troops," while the Legion "might well be spared" from eastern Tennessee and sent to Thomas.[356]

Special Order No. 105 of the Confederate Adjutant and Inspector General's Office, issued on May 5, directed the Legion to march under the command of Love to Asheville and report to Palmer for orders.[357] Events had been in motion in the field for some time, however, that would prevent the order from being carried out for seven months. Military affairs in eastern Tennessee and western North Carolina were becoming of less concern to Sherman and Johnston, as the Federals realized that Longstreet was not moving into Kentucky, and preparations continued for a major Federal offensive southward. With the Knoxville area secure, Schofield began shifting the bulk of his forces to join Sherman, and the Confederate forces remaining in the region were drawn into the operations in southwestern Virginia, itself a back door to the military theater of northern Virginia. Buckner reassumed command in eastern Tennessee on April 12, while Johnson remained in command of Buckner's Division. Maj. Gen. John C. Breckinridge was assigned on February 25 to replace Samuel Jones, and took command of the Department of Western Virginia on March 5.[358]

On April 21, 1864, the day after Anderson's inspection, Jackson received a message from Buckner's aide-de-camp of a potential Federal raid in the direction of Saltville, possibly from Pound's Gap in Kentucky. Jackson was ordered to prepare and to place scouts on

356. *O.R.* 32 (pt. 2): 799, 53:325-327 (Vance, Seddon, and Davis quotes, 325; Bragg's April 25 quotes, 326), 327-329 (Bragg's May 2 quotes, 328).

357. Ibid., 36 (pt. 2): 959. Stringfield believed long after the war that the reunification was due to Thomas's lobbying efforts with the government. Stringfield, "Sixty-Ninth Regiment," in Clark, *North Carolina Regiments* 3:745. It is probable that he was thinking of the situation at the end of 1864, when Thomas played a role in getting the decision to reunite the Legion finally enforced following the hiatus caused by the 1864 Shenandoah Valley campaign (see p. 222 below). As far the initial idea itself, however, the efforts that Thomas and his officers had made were not mentioned in the relevant correspondence regarding the order. Instead, the contents of Anderson's report seems to have been the factor that led directly to the decision.

358. *O.R.* 32 (pt. 1): 670, (pt. 2): 805, (pt. 3): 288, 293, 294, 305, 307, 312-314, 332-333, 343-345, 368-369, 377, 385, 410, 413-414, 422-423, 774-775, 795, 33:1085-1086, 1124, 1172-1173, 1198, 1210-1211; *O.R. (Supplement)*, Pt. I, 6:217; Richard R. Duncan, *Lee's Endangered Left: The Civil War in Western Virginia Spring 1864* (Baton Rouge: Lousiana State University Press, 1998), 30-34. Jones was relieved in part due to Lee, who wanted a more reliable commander in charge of that department because of its geographical and supply relations to his own.

both sides of his position at Carter's Depot. If a raid occurred, he was to destroy the railroad bridges, and to cooperate if necessary with Brig. Gen. John C. Vaughn, whose Tennessee cavalry brigade was in Ashe County. Buckner would keep Jackson advised about the progress of the raid. Jackson was evidently already aware of a rumored threat, albeit in the opposite direction from Pound's Gap, as he had dispatched Stringfield with some troops at midnight on April 20 to Elizabethton in the south "to repel a Bushwhackers raid upon that place." The Confederates searched the area but found no sign of their presence. It is possible that they then received fresh orders from Jackson as a result of the warning from headquarters, as instead of moving directly back to Carter's Depot they marched southwest to Jonesborough. After remaining there two days, they returned to Carter's Depot.[359]

Stringfield arrived back at the depot just in time. Although the rumored raid from Kentucky was a false alarm, the warning was in other ways prophetic. Sherman directed Schofield to send his cavalry north to make sure that Longstreet was gone, and destroy the railroad bridges between Bull's Gap and the Watauga River, thus allowing Schofield to turn his back on the Confederate forces in his rear and participate with the bulk of his troops in the coming Georgia campaign. One of the primary targets was the bridge across the Watauga River at Carter's Depot, putting Thomas's Legion in the center of the Federal bull's eye.[360]

The expedition against the railroad was commanded by Brig. Gen. Mahlon Dickerson Manson of the Second Brigade, Third Division, Twenty-Third Corps. The main striking force consisted of the 10th Regiment Michigan Cavalry and elements of the 3rd Regiment Indiana Cavalry under the overall command of Lt. Col. Luther S. Trowbridge of the former unit. At least one infantry regiment from Manson's brigade, wrecking the railroad from Jonesborough back to Bull's Gap, was in supporting distance of the cavalry, as was some artillery.[361] The Federals moved out from Bull's Gap on April 24. First contact between the

359. *O.R.* 32 (pt. 3): 808, Stringfield, Diary (1864), April 21, 24, 1864, Stringfield Papers, NCOAH. Vaughn's Brigade was part of the Cavalry Corps of the Department of East Tennessee; it included the 1st Regiment Tennessee Cavalry (Carter's), to which two of the cavalry companies from Walker's Battalion had transferred in November 1862. The brigade was sent to Ashe County when Ransom dispersed the cavalry due to local foraging problems, and was reported to be in terrible shape on a May 6 inspection report. *O.R.* 32 (pt. 3): 803, 845.

360. *O.R.* 32 (pt. 3): 422-426, 437, 458-459, 468, 474-478, 492-493, 497, 500-501, 52 (pt. 1): 549.

361. *O.R.* 32 (pt. 3): 475-477, John W. Lawing to the editors of the *Western Democrat* (Charlotte), April 28, 1864, published May 10, 1864 (reprinted in *O.R. [Supplement]*, Pt. I, 6:236); *O.R. (Supplement)*, Pt. II, 15:231, 245, 246, 248, 249, 251, 252, 27: 677, 683, 690, 697, 701, 704, 707, 710, 714, 30:227-228, 234-235, 243-244; Stringfield Diary (1864), April 26, Stringfield Papers, NCOAH. Lawing was assistant surgeon of the Infantry Regiment. Stringfield, writing the day after the fight, reported that the Federal units involved were the 3rd Regiment Indiana Cavalry, the 9th Regiment Michigan Cavalry, and the "13th E Tenn," or 13th Regiment Tennessee Cavalry (Union); Lawing wrote on April 28 that the units were the 3rd Indiana Cavalry, "the Tenth Michigan Mounted Infantry," and an infantry battalion with two artillery pieces. Companies G through M of the 3rd Indiana Cavalry were stationed in the Knoxville-Chattanooga areas between January and April; all of them, with the possible exception of Company M, seem to have participated in the raid. The regimental records of the 3rd Indiana Cavalry mentions the participation of 200 men from the 10th Regiment Michigan Cavalry; records of the latter unit show that at least Companies A, B, C, F, G, H, I, and M, and possibly the entire regiment, were involved. The 9th Michigan Cavalry was in eastern Tennessee until the end of March, when with the exception of Company B, it was sent to Kentucky; the latter company rejoined the regiment later. Although Company B was in eastern Tennessee on April 20, where it was reported in the vicinity of Strawberry Plains, it does not appear that it participated in the raid. Stringfield probably confused the 9th Michigan Cavalry with the 10th Michigan Cavalry. The 13th Tennessee Cavalry (Union) seems to have been in the Department of the Cumberland at that

opposing forces came early the next morning at Jonesborough. Finding that Confederates were camped in or near the town, part of the 10th Michigan Cavalry charged directly through Jonesborough. On the opposite side of town, the Confederates counterattacked, only to be driven off in turn. The cavalry then proceeded in the direction of the Watauga River. Trowbridge split the command upon reaching a fork in the road. He took half with him down the main road towards Carter's Depot, while the rest under Maj. Israel C. Smith of the 10th Michigan Cavalry took the parallel fork to the left with a section that included the companies from the 3rd Indiana Cavalry.[362]

The Federals encountered the Confederates defending the Watauga crossings some time between 11 A.M. and 2 P.M. The Confederate forces consisted of the Legion (minus Levi's Battery) and some cavalry, probably the 4th Regiment Kentucky Cavalry.[363] Smith attempted to force a passage below Carter's Depot at a place called DeVault's Ford. His men were fired upon by Confederate pickets as they attempted to cross. The cavalry put the pickets to flight and captured one prisoner. Finding the ford too deep and swift, they then reconcentrated opposite the depot. The approach to the bridge was guarded by entrenchments occupied by three companies under Stringfield. The companies from the 3rd Indiana Cavalry were sent against them; after driving Confederate pickets back to the earthworks, they fell back to their own main body. Both sides settled down to a steady exchange of fire.[364]

Lieutenant Colonel Trowbridge soon arrived on Smith's right. Trowbridge dismounted Companies F, I, C, M, H, G, and B of his own regiment and ordered them to advance towards the earthworks. They halted on a hilltop and opened fire on the Confederates. At this point, Stringfield received an order from Jackson to fall back with his command to the eastern side of the bridge. "I obeyed the order under protest knowing that I would be subjected

---

time. See the regimental and company records for the 9th Michigan Cavalry and the 13th Tennessee Cavalry (Union) in *O.R. (Supplement)*, Pt. II, 30:131, 140, 151-152, 159-160, 170-171, 176, 181-182, 190, 196, 199-200, 207-208, 216, 224, and 65:612, 616-620, and for the latter only, Tennessee Civil War Centennial Commission, *Tennesseans in the Civil War*, I:352.

362. *O.R. (Supplement)*, Pt. II, 30:227-228, 243.

363. Stringfield Diary (1864), April 26, Stringfield Papers, NCOAH; Leas, *Civil War Diary of Absalom Joshua Burum* (typescript copy, WCU), April 26, 1864; Stephen Whitaker to James Whitaker, Sr., April 28, 1864, Whitaker Papers, NCOAH; *O.R. (Supplement)*, Pt. I, 6:236, and Pt. II, 30:243. Stringfield put the beginning of the fight at about 11; Burum at noon; Whitaker at 1; and Lawing at 2. Lawing wrote that only part of the Legion under the command of Love was present, without any artillery. This implies that Love's (and Lawing's) own unit, the Infantry Regiment, was the only portion that participated. In his history of the Infantry Regiment for Clark's *North Carolina Regiments*, Stringfield claimed that "our regiment alone [was] engaged." Stringfield, "Sixty-Ninth Regiment," Clark, *North Carolina Regiments*, 3:743. Whitaker's letter, however, indicated the presence and participation of Walker's Battalion as well. Based on a letter from Stringfield to his sister, three companies of the regiment bore the brunt of the fighting, which was probably the basis for Lawing's and Stringfield's comments (see Stringfield to "Sister Mollie" [Mary Stringfield], April 30, 1864, Stringfield Papers, NCOAH). The record of Company F, 10th Regiment Michigan Cavalry, noted the capture of a prisoner who claimed to be a member of the 4th Regiment Kentucky Cavalry (Confederate). The latter regiment was certainly in the region; however, it was inspected on April 26 by Archer Anderson, who made no reference to its having been engaged the day before. *O.R.* 32 (pt. 3): 844.

364. Stringfield Diary (1864), April 26, and Stringfield to "Sister Mollie" (Mary Stringfield), April 30, 1864, Stringfield Papers, NCOAH; *O.R. (Supplement)* Pt. 2: 30:243; Stephen Whitaker to James Whitaker Sr., April 28, 1864, Whitaker Papers, NCOAH. The account of the attempt to ford the Watauga in the record for Company F, 10th Regiment Michigan Cavalry, referred to DeVault's Ford as Messengale's Ford.

to a galling fire in crossing the bridge," he wrote a few days later. "As soon as I started from my works the Yanks commenced yelling & dashed forward to occupy my place." Joining the Michigan cavalrymen in the charge were the companies of the 3rd Regiment Indiana Cavalry. Caught in a predicament, Stringfield reacted swiftly. He put his men under cover along the western slope of the riverbank, and among the saw and grist mills that were at the river's edge. As the Federals overran the abandoned earthworks and charged towards the bridge, Stringfield's companies opened fire from their new position, killing and wounding several of their foes. The Federal dash was halted. The cavalrymen withdrew, taking cover in the Confederate trenches and behind stumps and trees. The firing continued until dusk. During a lull, Stringfield managed to extricate his party and withdraw it successfully across the bridge. The men slept on their arms, the darkness punctuated by occasional shots.[365]

365. *O.R. (Supplement)* Pt. I, 6:236, Pt. II, 15:231, 30:234-235, 244; Stringfield Diary (1864), April 26, and Stringfield to "Sister Mollie" (Mary Stringfield), April 30, 1864, Stringfield Papers, NCOAH; Leas, *Civil War Diary of Absalom Joshua Burum* (typescript copy, WCU), April 26, 1864; *O.R. (Supplement)*, Pt. I, 6:236; Stephen Whitaker to James Whitaker Sr., April 28, 1864, Whitaker Papers, NCOAH; *O.R.* 32 (pt. 3): 831. The reconstruction of the skirmish is based largely on Stringfield's April 30 letter, supplemented by the Federal regimental and company records and other sources. In his 1901 history of the Infantry Regiment (Stringfield, "Sixty-Ninth Regiment," Clark, *North Carolina Regiments*, 3:743-744), Stringfield gave a rather different version of the fight. Misdating the clash to April 26, he stated in 1901 that he was sent across the river with 250 men to search for the enemy. Leaving the men behind at the bridge under the command of Captain Cooper, Stringfield walked for a quarter of mile accompanied by a lieutenant from Company K of the regiment. Discovering the Federals making a flanking movement on a ridge to the south and west, he ordered the troops into the earthworks with a hand signal. While there is nothing inherently impossible with the idea that Stringfield and his men were sent across to reconnoiter and were caught out in the open and forced into the trenches, it seems more likely that they were put there to defend the bridge and prevent a crossing. In other ways, Stringfield's 1901 account directly contradicted statements made in his 1864 letter and other materials that document the fighting. The number of men that he gave for his detachment, 250, is probably more than the entire Legion was able to muster at that time, based on the information on the Legion's condition in Anderson's report. In his wartime letter, Stringfield mentioned that he had three companies with him, while his postwar account implied more, based on the number of men he claimed were present and the specific officers and their companies noted (officers from E, F, G, H, I, and K in the Infantry Regiment were singled out). In the postwar account, the movement from the earthworks to the riverbank and the saw and grist mills was in response to further Federal flanking movements; the Confederates were then ordered to recross the river after repulsing an assault from the riverbank. In his wartime letter, Stringfield was ordered by Jackson to abandon the earthworks, which he did so reluctantly; these orders led to the withdrawal to the riverbank and the buildings (it is possible, of course that Jackson's order may have been related to a Federal flanking movement; the key point to note is that in Stringfield's 1864 letter the order to withdraw came while the men were in the earthworks, while in 1901 the order came after the men had left the trenches and reached the riverbank). The postwar account depicted desperate hand-to-hand fighting at Stringfield's position along the river bank; Stringfield's wartime letter mentioned no combat of this nature, and instead reported breaking up the Federal charge from his position along the riverbank and among the buildings through firepower. Stringfield claimed in 1901 that the Federals were between his position along the riverbank and the bridge, and that only the Confederate fire from the opposite side of the Watauga permitted his men to escape; in 1864, he stated that they slipped across during a lull in the skirmishing. The Confederates possessed artillery in the postwar version, which were used to help cover Stringfield's withdrawal across the river; both Asst. Surgeon Lawing's letter to the Charlotte *Western Democrat* and Burum's diary specifically mentioned that the Confederates had no artillery. For these reasons, the postwar account must be regarded as generally unreliable, although perhaps including some details that were authentic. Based on comments in Burum's and Stringfield's diaries and an April 26 message from Buckner to Adjutant and Inspector General Cooper, it would appear that the Federal assault and the heaviest fighting occurred around dark.

On the following day, the firing resumed at daybreak. The Federals had to decide whether or not to cross the river, drive off or capture Jackson's command, and destroy the bridge as planned. The task would be difficult; not only was the river still difficult to ford, but the Legion was well-placed behind earthworks at the other end. Manson had by now brought up an infantry battalion and two pieces of artillery. His instructions from Schofield gave him some discretion regarding the destruction of the Watauga bridge; given the loss of life that an assault would take, the timetable he was operating under, and the successful progress of the mission so far in regards to the destruction of much of the railroad, he decided to withdraw. Contact was broken off about 9 A.M. Later in the day, the Legion was reinforced by the 44th Regiment Tennessee Infantry and Levi's Battery, delayed due to a train breakdown. The Confederates expected further attacks through at least the morning of April 28, when their scouts reported the Federals were below Jonesborough. The Federals continued to move back down the partially wrecked track of the railroad, burning each bridge after their passage. A small party of Confederate cavalry pursued them as far as the first destroyed bridge to make sure that a second assault was not contemplated.[366]

Casualties at Carter's Depot were light. Five Confederates were captured; some reports claimed that there were no deaths or woundings, although Stringfield reported 1 Confederate killed and Whitaker claimed 4 wounded. Estimates for the Federals varied. The records for the 3rd Regiment Indiana Cavalry reported 8 wounded and 2 captured, while those for the 10th Regiment Michigan Cavalry reported 1 officer and 2 men killed, 16 wounded, and 4 missing for the entire command; for the 10th Michigan Cavalry alone, 1 officer and 2 men were reported killed, with 8 men wounded and 3 missing. The records for Company F of the 10th Michigan agreed on the numbers killed but instead noted 9 wounded and 6 missing. The jubilant Confederates naturally gave higher figures. Stringfield claimed that the Federals lost 3 killed, 17 wounded, and 3 captured, but acknowledged one report stating that there were 19 Federals killed and 17 wounded; in addition, he wrote that several more drowned in the attempt to ford the river. These figures are similar to those given by Asst. Surgeon John W. Lawing of the Infantry Regiment, and may have derived from him. Lawing wrote the Charlotte *Western Democrat* on April 28 that the Federals had lost 19 killed, 27 wounded, and 3 captured. Burum wrote that "at least" 10 Federals were killed, while Whitaker wrote

366. Leas, *Civil War Diary of Absalom Joshua Burum* (typescript copy, WCU), April 26, 1864; Stephen Whitaker to James Whitaker Sr., April 28, 1864, Whitaker Papers, NCOAH; Stringfield Diary (1864), April 26, and Stringfield to "Sister Mollie," April 30, 1864, Stringfield Papers, NCOAH; *O.R.* 32 (pt. 1): 686, (pt. 3): 475-477, 493, 500, 512; *O.R. (Supplement)* Pt. I, 6:236, Pt. II, 30:228, 244. Unlike the widely different starting times given for the clash on April 24, those sources that note the time of the Federal departure on April 25 (Stringfield, Whitaker, and the records of Company F, 10th Regiment Michigan Cavalry) were consistent about the 9 A.M. withdrawal time. In their diaries, both Burum and Stringfield identified the reinforcing infantry as the 44th Regiment Tennessee Infantry, a regiment in Johnson's Brigade of Buckner's Division; however, the records for that unit indicate that it left Abingdon for Richmond on April 22. It is possible that the date given for the transfer is wrong, or the regiment had not gone far enough away for recall, as both Burum and Stringfield would surely have had the opportunity to speak to the men of the unit in question. Regardless, Johnson did reinforce Carter's Depot with some troops over the next couple of days. See Tennessee Civil War Centennial Commission, *Tennesseans in the Civil War*, 1:272; *O.R.* 32 (pt. 3): 802, 831-832, 835. According to his 1864 letter, Stringfield led the cavalry himself for four miles in pursuit of the Federals, similar to his claims of having commanded a cavalry pursuit following the Federal withdrawal from in front of Carter's Depot on September 5 of the previous year and of commanding cavalry during the actions at Telford's Station and Limestone Bridge.

that 30 Federals were killed or wounded and 3 captured. According to Lawing, 2 of the dead were a major and a captain. The captain was a member of the 10th Michigan Cavalry, according to the records of that regiment. Stringfield identified the major in a wartime letter as belonging to the 3rd Indiana Cavalry; neither the records of the latter unit or of the 10th Michigan Cavalry mention the death of an officer of that rank, however.[367]

The skirmish at Carter's Depot was part of a minor operation designed to secure the Federal hold on eastern Tennessee before the diversion of troops to the critical campaign for Georgia. Although the Confederates were victorious in preventing the Federals from destroying the Watauga River bridge, the latter were able to accomplish the bulk of their mission, wrecking much of the railroad track and returning quickly to Knoxville to begin the shift southward. The bridge at Carter's Depot, while a major objective, had been rendered an optional target in the orders for the operation; furthermore, Federal sources indicate that the Confederates may have helped them out in some respects, as there were reports that they themselves destroyed all or part of the bridge (something that, if true, Confederate accounts failed to mention).[368] The skirmish was a morale booster for the members of the Legion, and showed once again that they were capable of performing well in small-action combat, regardless of the frequent criticism leveled at them over discipline. They would sorely need that boost in the coming months, which would bring them into a more intensive level of fighting than they had ever previously encountered.[369]

367. *O.R. (Supplement)* Pt. II, 15:231, 30:228, 235, 244; Stringfield Diary (1864), April 26, and Stringfield to "Sister Mollie" (Mary Stringfield), April 30, 1864, Stringfield Papers, NCOAH; Leas, *Civil War Diary of Absalom Joshua Burum* (typescript copy, WCU), April 26, 1864; Stephen Whitaker to James Whitaker Sr., April 28, 1864, Whitaker Papers, NCOAH. The five captured soldiers from Thomas's Legion were Pvts. John W. Franklin and Francis Plemmons (Clemmens) of Company C, Infantry Regiment, Pvts. John Henry Harrison Boyd and George W. Franklin of Company E, Infantry Regiment, Pvt. Thomas Whitten of Company A, Walker's Battalion, and Sgt. John H. Kirkland of Company B, Walker's Battalion. See Compiled Service Records of Confederate Soldiers from the State of North Carolina (M270), reels 568 through 570 and 574. The presence of two members of Walker's Battalion among the captured implies a greater role on the part of that unit than Lawing's newspaper letter and Stringfield's 1901 account indicate. A postwar history of the 3rd Regiment Indiana Cavalry did not mention the death of its major; in fact, it did not even record the skirmish (it was heavily reliant on materials published in the *Official Records*, which did not publish a battle report for the unit). It did, however, briefly sketch its operations with the 10th Regiment Michigan Cavalry in relation to the wrecking of the railroad track. W. N. Pickerill, *History of the Third Indiana Cavalry* (Indianapolis: Aetna Printing Co. 1906), 101-105. In his 1901 account for Clark's *Regiments*, Stringfield changed the identity of the dead major's unit to the 9th Regiment Michigan Cavalry (which was not present). Stringfield, "Sixty-Ninth Regiment," in Clark, *North Carolina Regiments* 3:744.

368. *O.R.* 32 (pt. 1): 686, (pt. 3): 512. According to Assistant Surgeon Lawing, the Confederate cavalry pursuit "reported that the enemy had burned a small bridge, torn up a portion of the railroad track, and were still retreating." Perhaps this "small bridge" along a point of the track before Carter's Depot was the one referred to in Federal reports, although certainly the impression given was that the Watauga River bridge itself was the one in question. *O.R. (Supplement)* Pt. I, 6:237.

369. For comments by members of the Legion indicating their exultant mood in the wake of Carter's Depot, see Lawing in *O.R. (Supplement)* Pt. I, 6:237; Stringfield Diary (1864), April 26, and Stringfield to "Sister Mollie" (Mary Stringfield), April 30, 1864, Stringfield Papers, NCOAH; Leas, *Civil War Diary of Absalom Joshua Burum* (typescript copy, WCU), April 26, 1864; Stephen Whitaker to James Whitaker Sr., April 28, 1864, Whitaker Papers, NCOAH. Pvt. Isaac H. Hendrix (Hendricks) of Company I, Infantry Regiment, would later recall the Carter's Depot skirmish as "fun" in comparison with the battle of Piedmont (see I. H. Hendricks to James Whitaker, June 8, 1864, Whitaker Papers, NCOAH).

Due to the possible Federal threats to Saltville and other points in western Virginia, the Confederate response to the strike at Carter's Depot was confused. Johnson was initially ordered by Buckner on April 26 not to reinforce Jackson, but to have the latter withdraw to Zollicoffer, where the bulk of Johnson's force was concentrated; however, Johnson was given some discretion in the matter, and as noted earlier both Levi's Battery and the 44th Regiment Tennessee Infantry arrived at the depot to bolster the defense. On April 29, Johnson was ordered to start back to Abingdon with his infantry and artillery within two days, leaving the cavalry with Jackson and the Legion. Vaughn's cavalry was ordered from North Carolina to cover Jackson's lines of supply and retreat from Carter's Depot to Bristol. In the midst of these preparations, Buckner was relieved of command of the Department of East Tennessee on April 28 and ordered to the Trans-Mississippi theater. His replacment was William E. "Grumble" Jones.[370]

In the days following the skirmish, Stringfield secured a three-day furlough to visit his stepmother and siblings, who had relocated from Strawberry Plains to Emory, Virginia for safety. Traveling by train, he lamented the local conditions, "laid waste & deserted by both armies. My once happy & Comfortable home is totally ruined, but I cheerfully loose all for my country. I am not yet ready to cry 'hold enough,'" he continued defiantly. "I Say never Submit. I am willing & determined to fight on as long as we have an organized army & then bushwhack if necessary." It would be months before he returned to eastern Tennessee, and by that time even bushwhacking was no longer an option. Stringfield did not need to take the train to rejoin the Legion when his furlough expired; instead, he walked to Saltville, where it had been sent the day after his furlough began to defend that vital site against a major enemy expedition.[371]

The looming Federal threat was the result of Grant's strategy to be aggressive in all major theaters of operation at once in order to pressure the beleagured Confederates to the breaking point. In the west, Sherman and the Armies of the Tennessee, the Cumberland, and the Ohio would assault Johnston and the Army of Tennessee. In the east, three campaigns would be mounted in Virginia. Maj. Gen. George G. Meade and the Army of the Potomac, under the personal direction of Grant himself, would cross the Rappahannock River and battle Lee's Army of Northern Virginia. To the southeast, Maj. Gen. Benjamin Butler would attempt to reach Richmond via Bermuda Hundred, while to the west Maj. Gen. Franz Sigel would advance against the militarily and economically strategic Shenandoah Valley and the railroad lines linking western and southwestern Virginia with Richmond.[372]

The rumors of raids against Saltville and western Virginia around the time of the Carter's Depot skirmish were related to preparations for Sigel's operations. While Sigel moved on the Valley, a second prong under the overall command of Brig. Gen. George Crook would aim for the Virginia & Tennessee Railroad, the extension of the East Tennessee & Virginia Railroad beyond Bristol; at Lynchburg, the former line connected with other railroads running to Petersburg and, indirectly, Richmond. Crook's expedition was divided

370. *O.R.* 32 (pt. 3): 830-832, 835-836, 838, 852, 854, 855, 33:1318-1319, 1321-1325, 39 (pt. 2): 565, 567, 576; Stringfield Diary (1864), May 6, Stringfield Papers, NCOAH.

371. Stringfield Diary (1864), May 6-8 (quotes in May 6 entry), Stringfield Papers, NCOAH.

372. *O.R.* 32 (pt. 3): 312-313, 33:794-795, 827-829, 904-905, 36 (pt. 1): 12-17.

into two columns. He would take over 6,000 men via Fayetteville and Princeton, West Virginia, while Brig. Gen. W. W. Averell and some 2,000 cavalry would strike Saltville before moving eastward to Dublin Depot. The destruction of the railroad would sever the link between southwestern Virginia and Richmond, while a successful strike on the salt mines at Saltville would deprive the Confederacy of one of its major sources for that important substance. Another vital target was the lead works at Wytheville.[373]

Crook departed the Kanawha River on May 2.[374] His column proceeded with little opposition until it clashed with the forces of Brig. Gen. Albert Gallatin Jenkins at Cloyd's Mountain on May 9. The Confederates lost the battle and Jenkins was killed. The Federals then burnt the New River Bridge, severing the route of the Virginia & Tennessee Railroad until June.[375] Averell was not so successful. On May 6 he found a strong defense posted at Saltville under the command of "Grumble" Jones and Brig. Gen. John Hunt Morgan. Unwilling to risk an assault, he moved on to Wytheville, where he was repulsed in a sharp skirmish by Morgan. Pursued by Morgan, Averell got his men across the New River. Meanwhile, captured Confederate messages at Dublin inaccurately indicated that Grant was in retreat following the battle of the Wilderness, opening the possibility that Confederate reinforcements might be shifted to the area; coupled with a lack of concrete news from Sigel, Crook was convinced that he had overstayed his welcome. He turned northward, uniting with Averell on May 15. Although the mission was not completely successful, it accomplished the destruction of the New River bridge and several miles of track.[376]

Acting on reports from scouts, Lee warned Breckinridge as early as May 1 that Averell seemed to be on the move. Although Lee was not able to send reinforcements due to Grant's impending offensive, Breckinridge had time to shift his troops and organize his defense, and was instructed on May 4 to report directly to Lee. Jones brought much of his cavalry to assist Breckinridge and protect Saltville. Considerable confusion prevailed, as the Confederates tried to sort out the different threats to the Valley and southwestern Virginia; to add to the chaos, Bragg ordered Jones to head back into Tennessee for a broad mission to harry the rear of Schofield's columns marching on Johnston, and simultaneously guard the passes of western North Carolina from raids. These orders were soon modified, as the immediate circumstances required Jones and Jenkins (prior to the latter's death) to cover southwest Virginia while Breckinridge concentrated the bulk of his forces to face Sigel in the Valley.[377]

Jackson was apprised of the situation on May 1 and 3. He was basically on his own, as Jones would be too far away to issue orders relevant to the situation around Carter's Depot. "You would do well to keep your scouts active in your front and your mounted pickets to

373. Ibid., 33:758, 762-766, 788-793, 798-799, 812-813, 823, 828, 844-846, 858, 874, 893, 900-901, 910-911, 938, 945, 964, 975-976, 978-979, 986, 997-998, 1027-1028, 36 (pt. 1): 17, 37 (pt. 1): 9-10, 368-369; Duncan, *Lee's Endangered Left*, 9-11, 19-41, 44-45, 78-79.

374. For Crook's and Averell's strike on the railroad, see Duncan, *Lee's Endangered Left*, 41-84; *O.R.* 37 (pt. 1): 8-68, and *O.R. (Supplement)* Pt. I, 6:847-848.

375. *O.R.* 37 (pt. 1): 10-12, 13-25, 28-40, 44-58, 59-61, 66-68; Duncan, *Lee's Endangered Left*, 43-65.

376. *O.R.* 37 (pt. 1): 12-13, 25-28, 30-31, 33-35, 37, 41-44, 39 (pt. 2): 575; Duncan, *Lee's Endangered Left*, 65-84.

377. *O.R.* 37 (pt. 1): 707-728, 39 (pt. 2): 576-579, 51 (pt. 2): 887, 889, 905, 915. Some materials are duplicated in both *O.R.* 37 (pt. 1) and 39 (pt. 2).

your front, as you will not probably meet with support west of Glade [Spring] for several days," Jones warned. "If you should be compelled to fall back, you will have to depend on your own judgment, guided by future developments of the enemy, for the control and movements of the troops immediately under you." No reinforcements could be expected until the arrival of Vaughn's Brigade; if a crisis developed that Jackson was unable to handle with the troops at hand, he should fall back to Zollicoffer or Bristol. Circumstances soon altered the situation. On May 6, Jackson's Brigade and other troops in the area were ordered to Virginia, their place taken by Vaughn's Brigade. The movement began on May 7, two days after the issuance of the War Department order sending the Legion back to North Carolina; it had not yet had the chance to arrive. After resting at Bristol, the Legion continued to Glade Spring, arriving before dawn on May 8. That night it was sent to Saltville, where it replaced Morgan's cavalry and the 45th Regiment Virginia Infantry in the defensive works, the former going to Wytheville and the latter to Dublin and Cloyd's Mountain.[378]

The Legion was in line of battle for five days after its arrival at Saltville, until it became clear that the immediate crisis was past.[379] It remained at Saltville for most of May. Levi's Battery, under Barr, was also at Saltville during at least part of the period, the last time that it was together with the rest of the Legion. In the meantime, the armies of Grant and Lee clashed at the Wilderness on May 5-6 and at Spotsylvania Court House on May 9-10 and May 12-13. The casualty figures on both sides were horrible. Although Lee's men blunted the attacks of Grant's, the latter refused to withdraw either time and swung around Lee's right flank, edging ever closer to Richmond. Butler's effort to take Richmond from the rear sputtered out, however. Sigel's movement up the Shenandoah Valley also faltered when Breckinridge defeated him at New Market on May 15, forcing his withdrawal. To the west, Sherman steadily pushed Johnston back towards Atlanta. Relatively isolated at Saltville, some members of the Legion fed on wild and optimistic rumors: Johnston had defeated the Federals near Chattanooga, and the western armies had somehow all moved to Richmond to join in on the big showdown. Stringfield recalled later that "our men were constantly drilled and disciplined," suggesting that Jackson had read the handwriting on the wall in Anderson's inspection report, or perhaps had caught a whiff of Bragg's displeasure emanating from Richmond; if so, it would come too late for the dour brigadier. Rations were poor, as might be expected with the railroad break and the generally dire military situation. Sgt. Absalom J. Burum of Company K, Infantry Regiment, wrote in his diary near the end of the month that the men had only had a pound of corn meal and a third of a pound of bacon per month, while Stringfield remembered a different if equally dire diet of "double rations of rice, salt and water for near three weeks, and nothing else."[380]

378. *O.R.* 37 (pt. 1): 52, 711 (quote), 726, 39 (pt. 2): 565, 576 (quote; Jones's communication is in both volumes), 582, 588; Leas, *Civil War Diary of Absalom Joshua Burum* (typescript copy, WCU), May 7-9, 1864; Stringfield Diary (1864), May 8-9, Stringfield Papers, NCOAH; Stephen Whitaker to James Whitaker Sr., May 19, 1864, Whitaker Papers, NCOAH.

379. Stephen Whitaker to James Whitaker Sr., May 19, 1864, Whitaker Papers, NCOAH. "We've been prepared to give the Yankees a warm reception should they come here," wrote Stringfield, "but they will not come here. Stringfield Diary (1864), May 12, Stringfield Papers, NCOAH.

380. Weaver, *Nottoway Artillery and Barr's Battery*, 111; Barr to Samuel Cooper, February 10, 1865, Letters Received by the Confederate Adjutant and Inspector General's Office (M474), reel 153, file 279-B-1865;

In the meantime, Breckinridge was ordered to join Lee with his infantry, partly on the false assumption that Sigel's troops were going to Grant. Jones, with his own troops and whatever else was available, was left as commander of both Breckinridge's and his own department. Sigel was replaced by Maj. Gen. David Hunter. A fervent abolitionist, Hunter worked quickly to whip Sigel's command back into shape. On May 26, he resumed the offensive, reaching New Market by May 30. Hunter also attempted to squash Confederate partisan activity in the Valley, personified by Lt. Col. John S. Mosby, in order to secure his supply line. The latter was a major concern to Hunter, whose army was so ill-supplied that it went on the march with the bare mininum of subsistence; further, Grant had suggested that Hunter live off the land as much as possible. As a result, although Hunter issued orders against the molestation of civilians or the wanton and unauthorized taking or destruction of their property, his hungry troops readily disobeyed, and the general either failed or refused to impose his will upon them. Coupled with his ordering the deliberate destruction of homes suspected as havens for the guerrillas, as well as the accompanying impressment of supplies typical of Civil War armies on the march, Hunter quickly gained a bad reputation among Confederate sympathizers in the Valley.[381]

In accordance with his instructions from Grant, Hunter's major goal was the capture of Staunton, an important supply hub for Lee's army. Hunter would hopefully unite there with Crook, who had been ordered to raid in that direction by Sigel before his replacement; Hunter would then, depending on the situation, move on to Charlottesville and Lynchburg, wrecking as much of the railroad network as was possible, and either join Grant or return to his starting point. Hunter set out from New Market on June 2. Opposing him was a small force commanded by Brig. Gen. John Imboden. Already, Jones had set out with his available troops to join him. Among them were the Infantry Regiment and Walker's Battalion of Thomas's Legion, which departed Saltville at 5 P.M. on May 29.[382]

Levi's Battery was left behind due to a lack of horses. It would never serve with the rest of the Legion again, at least in its entirety. It remained in the area for the next few

---

Stephen Whitaker to James Whitaker Sr., May 19, 1864, Whitaker Papers, NCOAH; Leas, *Civil War Diary of Absalom Joshua Burum* (typescript copy, WCU), May 27, 1864; Stringfield, "Sixty-Ninth Regiment," in Clark, *North Carolina Regiments* 3:744 (quote). Studies of the spring 1864 campaigns include Gordon C. Rhea, *The Battle of the Wilderness May 5-6, 1864* (Baton Rouge: Louisiana State University Press, 1994); Gordon C. Rhea, *The Battles for Spotsylvania Courthouse and the Road to Yellow Tavern, May 7-12, 1864* (Baton Rouge: Louisiana State University Press, 1997); William Glenn Robertson, *Back Door to Richmond: The Bermuda Hundred Campaign April-June, 1864* (Newark: University of Delaware Press, 1987); Duncan, *Lee's Endangered Left* (see 85-136 for Sigel's phase of the campaign, including New Market); William C. Davis, *The Battle of New Market* (Garden City: Doubleday, 1975); and Albert Castel, *Decision in the West: The Atlanta Campaign of 1864* (Lawrence: University of Kansas Press, 1992). For the reports on Sigel's operations and New Market, see *O.R.* 37 (pt. 1): 5, 73-91; *O.R. (Supplement)* Pt. I, 6:848-878.

381. *O.R.* 36 (pt. 1): 23-24; 37 (pt. 1): 492-493, 508, 516-518, 524-528, 533, 543, 546, 548, 555-556, 735, 737-738, 742-748, 39 (pt. 2): 340, 366, 616-617; Marshall Moore Brice, *Conquest of a Valley* (Charlottesville: University Press of Virginia, 1965), 13-19; Duncan, *Lee's Endangered Left*, 137-155; Scott C. Patchan, *The Forgotten Fury: The Battle of Piedmont, Va.* (Fredericksburg: Sergeant Kirkland's Museum and Historical Society, Inc., 1996), 7-41, 51-56.

382. *O.R.* 37 (pt. 1): 479, 482, 500, 507, 536, 543, 749-751, 39 (pt. 2): 629, 51 (pt. 2): 981; Brice, *Conquest of a Valley*, 4-5, 19-20, 22-33; Duncan, *Lee's Endangered Left*, 11, 143, 155, 171-173, 188-190; Patchan, *The Forgotten Fury*, 6, 29, 57-61; Stringfield Diary (1864), May 30, Stringfield Papers, NCOAH.

months, stationed mostly at Saltville. In August 1864 the battery became formally known as Capt. John W. Barr's Company Virginia Light Artillery, and was no longer officially a part of Thomas's Legion. Efforts were later made to rectify the situation; on December 8, Love would order Barr to report with the battery to Legion headquarters in Asheville. On January 20, 1865, the battery was transferred to Richmond, where it served under Lt. Gen. Richard S. Ewell. Although Barr attempted to have the battery sent to Thomas in February, he failed to convince the Confederate authorties, and it remained in Richmond until the fall of the city. Federal provost marshal records show that the battery was captured with much of the rest of Ewell's command at Sayler's Creek on April 6, 1865.[383]

Also left behind was Jackson. Although Jackson supporters in eastern Tennessee soon complained to Richmond about the supposed injustice of removing him from command of the Legion, the government stood firm, and he received another assignment.[384] Love now commanded the troops from his own regiment and Walker's Battalion; according to Love, they numbered some 390 men at this time. By this time, Special Order No. 105 had finally made its way to "Grumble" Jones through the geographical and administrative maze caused by successive command turnovers and troop shifts in the area. Due to the necessities of the campaign, however, he put off implementing the transfer of the Legion to western North Carolina. He did let Love know of the existence of the order while the command was on the move from Saltville, and promised that the transfer would be carried out as soon as Hunter was defeated.[385]

The Legion arrived at the site of the New River bridge at 9 A.M. on May 30. It did not reach Central Depot on the opposite side of the river until dusk the next day, due to the earlier destruction of the bridge by Crook.[386] The men were ordered to cook two days' rations in preparations for moving to the Valley. Stringfield, at least, was excited about their destination: "Bound for the Valley of Va—good." On the evening of June 1, they passed through Lynchburg and on the following day through Charlottesville and Staunton, arriving at

383. Weaver, *Nottoway Artillery and Barr's Battery*, 111, 119-121, 123, 126-127; *O.R.* 39 (pt. 3): 907-908, ser. IV, 3:858; Barr to Cooper, February 10, 1865 (including as inclosure Love to Barr, December 8, 1864), Letters Received by the Confederate Adjutant and Inspector General's Office (M474), reel 153, item 279-B-1865; service record file of John W. Barr, Captain Barr's Company Virginia Light Artillery, Compiled Service Records of Confederate Soldiers from the State of Virginia (M324), reel 265. "I think this Comp [is] more needed at Richmond [at] this time than with Col Thomas," Lee wrote on March 9 in his endorsement of Barr's letter. For the possibility that some members of the battery may have joined Thomas in western North Carolina before the end of the war, see p. 232 and n. 538 below.

384. In his endorsement of the protest by Jackson's supporters, Seddon wrote that "[t]he representations reaching the Department . . . were that General Jackson had been able to obtain the command of only a few hundred irregular troops, in no wise worthy of the name of a brigade, and that they were ill-disciplined and inefficient. In consequence it was thought better he should be transferred to some more important field of operations, where his services could be more available, and he was accordingly ordered to General Johnston's army, where he is now in command of a brigade. It is doubted whether the exchange asked would be agreeable to General J. himself, while it certainly would not, in my judgment, promote the general service." *O.R.* 37 (pt. 1): 753.

385. James R. Love Jr. to "Dear Genl" (John C. Breckinridge), October 15, 1864 (copy?), Stringfield Papers, WCU.

386. Stringfield Diary (1864), May 30-31, Stringfield Papers, NCOAH; Duncan, *Lee's Endangered Left*, 68; Patchan, *The Forgotten Fury*, 44-45.

Mount Crawford on June 3.[387] Here Imboden's men, numbering between 1,000 and 3,000, had halted to await Jones. Imboden wrote in 1923 that he had understood Jones was coming with 3,000 men, but was upset to find out that, with few exceptions, "no large *organized* body of troops was on its way"; instead, the troops arriving were a motley collection of various units, convalescents gathered from the hospitals between Bristol and Lynchburg, and railroad guards. Imboden estimated that the total reinforcement was less than 2,200; in fact, they were probably closer to 4,000, as he made a major effort to give himself full credit for everything that went right and Jones for everything that went wrong. The reinforcements included at least three regiments of various strengths.[388] Imboden split the force into two small brigades under Cols. William H. Browne of the 45th Regiment Virginia Infantry and Beuhring H. Jones of the 60th Regiment Virginia Infantry. The Legion was placed in Browne's Brigade, along with the 45th Virginia and one or two Virginia battalions.[389]

On June 4, the Confederates marched north to meet Hunter's Army of West Virginia. "Grumble" Jones arrived and by seniority assumed command, although due to his lack of knowledge of the topography, he deferred to Imboden as to troop dispositions. When Hunter took a road on the east that led to Port Republic in his opponents' rear, Imboden suggested

387. Stringfield Diary (1864), May 31-June 3 (quote, June 1), Stringfield Papers, NCOAH.

388. *O.R.* 51 (pt. 2): 981; John D. Imboden, "The Battle of Piedmont," Pt. 1, *Confederate Veteran* 31 (December 1923): 459; Brice, *Conquest of a Valley*, 33-35, 35 n. 28; Patchan, *The Forgotten Fury*, 43-50. Imboden recalled in 1923 that his cavalry numbered 1,000 at the time of his withdrawal to Mount Crawford, and that Jones's reinforcements did not begin arriving until June 3; he wrote Lee on June 2, 1864, however, that he had nearly 3,000 men with him then. Duncan, *Lee's Endangered Left*, 173, understood this to mean that Imboden's own command numbered about 3,000; based on various sources, he believed that Jones's reinforcements began arriving on June 2, not June 3. It is therefore uncertain whether the nearly 3,000 men cited by Imboden to Lee was intended to include some of Jones's reinforcements, or if Imboden either inflated his numbers in 1864 or deflated them in 1923. Based on papers recovered by the Federals, Hunter believed that the total Confederate concentration was somewhere between 6,000 and 7,000; see n. 393 below. Patchan, using various sources for the units involved, believed that Imboden's brigade approximated 1,200 men, the Virginia Reserves 600, and Jones's reinforcements about 3,800; this gave an approximate Confederate strength of 5,800, not too far off from Hunter's figures. Patchan, *The Forgotten Fury*, 226-227.

389. Imboden, "Battle of Piedmont," Pt. 1, *Confederate Veteran* 31 (December 1923): 459; Stringfield Diary (1864), June 3, Stringfield Papers, NCOAH; Stephen Whitaker to James Whitaker, August 5, 1864, Whitaker Papers, NCOAH. Stringfield did not identify the two Virginia battalions, although one of them was possibly the 45th Battalion Virginia Infantry, which according to Brice was a part of Browne's Brigade; Brice did not mention Thomas's Legion at all, however (Brice, *Conquest of a Valley*, 34, 57-59). Patchan, *The Forgotten Fury*, 45-46, 49, 221, identified the units of Browne's Brigade as the Legion, the 45th Regiment Virginia Infantry, and Maj. R. Henry Brewer's Battalion, the latter a thrown-together force made up of dismounted cavalry from "Grumble" Jones's brigade; he placed the 45th Battalion Virginia Infantry in Beuhring Jones's Brigade. Both Stringfield's diary and Whitaker's letter confirm that the Legion was in Browne's Brigade. After the war, however, Stringfield indirectly identified the brigade as Beuhring Jones's, reporting the other units as the 36th, 51st, and 60th Regiments Virginia Infantry (Stringfield, "War—Mss," ledger book, 140, Stringfield Papers, NCOAH) or the 36th, 45th, 51st, and 60th Regiments Virginia Infantry (Stringfield, "Sixty-ninth Regiment," Clark, *North Carolina Regiments*, 3:745). This confusion is due to the fact that after Piedmont the Legion was transferred to what had been Beurhing Jones's Brigade, and thus served with the 36th and 60th Regiments Virginia Infantry. Patchan was skeptical of Imboden's claim that he organized all of the units into brigades himself prior to Jones's arrival, pointing out that many of the troops served together as parts of specific garrisons prior to their movement into the Shenandoah Valley; both the 45th Regiment Virginia Infantry and Thomas's Legion, for example, were part of the Saltville garrison, which Browne had commanded. Patchan, *The Forgotten Fury*, 49-50.

that the Confederates pull back a few miles to a position south and west of the village of New Hope. Located on a hill on the property of George W. Mowry, Imboden believed that the site was a strong enough defensive position to offset the larger Federal numbers. Jones agreed. Imboden's cavalry delayed Hunter while the command moved back.[390]

On the morning of June 5, 1864, Imboden engaged Hunter south of Port Republic. Although instructed not to become entangled in a full-scale fight from which he might be unable to extricate himself, Imboden did so anyway. Reinforcements arrived allowing Imboden to disengage. He then fell back south of the village of Piedmont, where he formed a battle line on a rise "overlooking cleared land for more than a mile in our front." Imboden hoped that the position would compel Hunter to deploy off the march, allowing Imboden time to pull away before Hunter could get his forces back into column. In the meantime, Imboden would withdraw through New Hope and rejoin Jones. Imboden was in the process of sending a request for a battery and 500 infantry to help in his delaying effort when Jones himself arrived with the bulk of the command.[391] Why Jones decided to make a stand there, instead of the better position at Mowry's farm, is unknown. Imboden's version depicted the two arguing over the choice of ground, with Jones supposedly asserting that "I don't want any advantage of ground, for I can whip Hunter *anywhere*." Regardless of the reasons, Hunter's force had by now arrived, so the Confederates would have to fight there and then.[392]

The exact numbers involved on either side are unknown, although Hunter outnumbered Jones significantly.[393] Jones's deployment of his troops is something of a mystery. He

390. Imboden, "Battle of Piedmont," Pt. 1, *Confederate Veteran* 31 (December 1923): 460; Stringfield Diary (1864), June 4, Stringfield Papers, NCOAH; Stephen Whitaker to James Whitaker, August 5, 1864, Whitaker Papers, NCOAH; Brice, *Conquest of a Valley*, 35-36, 39-41; Duncan, *Lee's Endangered Left*, 174-176; Patchan, *The Forgotten Fury*, 62-69.

391. Imboden, "Battle of Piedmont," Pt. 1, *Confederate Veteran* 31 (December 1923): 460-461 (quote, 460). For summaries of the early skirmishing, see Brice, *Conquest of a Valley*, 41-54; Duncan, *Lee's Endangered Left*, 176-177; Patchan, *The Forgotten Fury*, 71-83.

392. Imboden, "Battle of Piedmont," Pt. 2, *Confederate Veteran* 32 (January 1924): 18. It is possible that Jones decided to fight at Piedmont because Hunter could use the road network to avoid the position at Mowry's Hill and strike directly at Staunton (Duncan, *Lee's Endangered Left*, 177). Patchan, *The Forgotten Fury*, 68-69, 84, believed that it was due to overconfidence, combined with a message from Lee received on the night of June 4 instructing Jones to defeat Hunter before he could unite with Crook and Averell. While Imboden may have been accurate in regards to the events that morning as far as his memory allowed, it should be kept in mind in the light of what occurred that he would have been anxious to insure that all of the blame fell on Jones's shoulders. Brice, *Conquest of a Valley*, 50, 50-51 n. 14, was skeptical of an earlier Imboden version of the argument written in 1894, containing a supposedly verbatim recounting of the conversation utilized again for the 1924 article; not only are there memory issues involved in such a detailed account, but Brice pointed out that the irascible Jones would probably have arrested Imboden for a supposed threat to see that Jones would bear the full responsibility for whatever happened as a result of his decision. Brice did not doubt, however, that Imboden protested Jones's deployment in some form. Patchan, *The Forgotten Fury*, 83-84 was also inclined to believe that Imboden indulged in some retrospective hyperbole in his account of events.

393. Hunter's force was estimated to be as much as 8,500 at the time of the expedition's start. If accurate, the figure would have been reduced somewhat by the time of the battle of Piedmont due to straggling, detachment of soldiers for various assignments, etc. Imboden claimed in 1923 that, according to "a trusty scout" who sneaked into Port Republic on the night of June 4, the Federals "very accurately" numbered 9,000 infantry, 2,500 cavalry, and 31 guns. Confederate figures vary even more widely. In 1923, Imboden gave their number as 2,200 infantry, 1,800 cavalry, 200 "'reserve'" (presumably members of the Virginia Reserves), and 14 guns; see also the figures

placed his infantry on the left and his cavalry, under Imboden and Vaughn, on the right, the latter having been brought up with his men (minus their horses) from eastern Tennessee. The infantry covered the ground from the Middle River on the left to the East Road, which ran through Piedmont south to New Hope. It would seem that Beuhring H. Jones's Brigade was on the left, and Browne's, including Thomas's Legion, was on the right; however, several sources related to the Legion place the 60th Regiment Virginia Infantry of Jones's Brigade on the Legion's right. For whatever reason, it would appear that the units of the two brigades became intermixed as the battle progressed.[394] In addition, there was a major gap in the center of the Confederate line, as Vaughn's dismounted cavalry did not connect with the right of the infantry; in fact, Vaughn's and Imboden's men were set back much further than the left wing. Both Vaughn and Imboden were aware of the gap, but regardless of what transpired during the battle, refused to move from their designated deployments to cover it, claiming later that Jones's orders gave them no leeway to shift their troops. This behavior, the result of either a major miscommunication between the cavalry officers and Jones, or sulkiness as a result of the argument over fighting at Piedmont instead of Mowry's Hill, would prove fatal to the Confederate effort.[395] In the meantime, according to Stringfield the

---

in Patchan cited in p. 166 n. 388 above, which gives a total figure of approximately 5,800. Brig. Gen. John C. Vaughn, writing the day after the battle, stated that the Confederates went into action with a 5,600 aggregate; based on papers Hunter found after the battle, the number was between 6,000 and 7,000, with 16 pieces of artillery. It is sufficient to say that Hunter had the edge in both men and guns, although not so much as to render a Confederate chance for victory impossible. *O.R. (Supplement)* Pt. I, 6:881; Imboden, "Battle of Piedmont," Pt. 1, *Confederate Veteran* 31 (December 1923): 461; *O.R.* 37 (pt. 1): 95, 151.

394. For general discussions of the deployments of both armies, see Brice, *Conquest of a Valley*, 55-68, and Patchan, *The Forgotten Fury*, 90-99. For evidence that Vaughn's cavalry fought dismounted at Piedmont, see Patchan, *The Forgotten Fury*, 44, 45 n. 104, 94-95. For a good discussion of the sources regarding the Confederate position at Piedmont and the problems of determining the Legion's place within it, see Crow, *Storm in the Mountains*, 70, 247 n. 21. Brice, *Conquest of a Valley*, 61, placed Browne's Brigade on the left against the river and Beuhring H. Jones's Brigade on the right, with the 60th Regiment Virginia Infantry resting against the road. Information in the report of Capt. James F. Jones of the C.S. Niter and Mining Corps, whose men were ordered by Imboden to join the campaign, indicate that the 36th Regiment Virginia Infantry of Jones's Brigade was on the left; see *O.R.* 51 (pt. 1): 1226. Furthermore, Beuhring H. Jones was ordered by "Grumble" Jones to take the left flank (Duncan, *Lee's Endangered Left*, 178, citing the former's unpublished report in an archival collection). Brice, who was unaware of the materials related to the Legion and in fact does not mention it at all, interpreted the evidence to mean that the 36th Virginia merely formed the left of Jones's Brigade (61 n. 11). Crow argued that Browne must have been on the right, based on Stringfield's description of the Legion's position. It would appear that "Grumble" Jones shifted troops from one section to another as circumstances warranted. The latter explanation is supported by Stringfield in "Sixty-Ninth Regiment," Clark, *North Carolina Regiments*, 3:747, in which he claimed that Jones brought both the 36th and the 60th Regiments Virginia Infantry to the Legion's relief at a critical point in the fighting; however, it should be noted that in his diary he only indicated that the 60th Virginia formed the right flank of the line, without reference to time (Stringfield Diary [1864], June 5, Stringfield Collection, NCOAH). Patchan provided the most detailed reconstruction of the Confederate battle line. His analysis jibed with Crow's—that Beuhring Jones's Brigade was on the left and Browne's on the right, with Thomas's Legion at the angle where the battle line reached the road. Patchan concluded that "Grumble" Jones withdrew the 60th Virginia from the center of Beuhring Jones's section just before the battle started and placed it to the right of Thomas's Legion, extending that portion of the Legion's battleline which ran southward parallel to the road. Patchan, *The Forgotten Fury*, 104.

395. Imboden's explanation as to why he and Vaughn chose to do nothing about the gap when it was threatened during the battle by Federal flanking movements is in Imboden, "Battle of Piedmont," Pt. 2, *Confederate*

Legion was positioned in an angular formation, partially facing northward until it reached the road and then facing eastward as the line bent south parallel with the road, indicating an effort to cover partially the dangling right flank of the infantry; this line was extended further south by the 60th Regiment Virginia Infantry after it was shifted to that sector.[396]

Few details remain to shed light on how the different companies of the Legion were deployed in its angular formation. According to Stringfield, six companies of the Infantry Regiment stretched westward from the road as a part of Jones's main battle line, while two companies ran southward on the eastern face of the angle, parallel to the road. How the five companies of Walker's Battalion fit in is unknown. Finding the Federals already on the field as it arrived, the Legion quickly threw up fence rails as breastworks, as did other units. Hunter, meanwhile, deployed his First Infantry Brigade on his left, opposite Vaughn and Imboden, and his Second Brigade on his right, opposite Browne. Around 9 A.M., the artillery of both sides opened up. The Federals attacked Browne around 10, but were repulsed; this was followed by a Confederate counterattack, which was driven back in turn. By 11:30, the Federal artillery had silenced its opposition, and was hammering the Confederate breastworks. Pvt. Isaac H. Hendrix (Hendricks) of Company I, Infantry Regiment, wrote three days later that "[t]he Yankees poured the grape and canister [and] solid shot and bombs into [us.] They cut the timber all to pieces." Hunter, meanwhile, prepared a second assault on the Confederate infantry. It was launched at 1 P.M., and was also beaten back.[397]

Shortly after the second Federal attack failed, Hunter saw that "Grumble" Jones was shifting the bulk of his forces to the Confederate left wing, as the latter was planning to launch an assault of his own. Among his changes in deployment, Jones withdrew the 60th Regiment Virginia Infantry from its position extending the line of Thomas's Legion southward parallel to the road, thus leaving the central gap undefended. Hunter became aware of

---

Veteran 32 (January 1924): 18-19. Brice, Crow and Duncan all expressed puzzlement over the failure of Imboden and Vaughn to close the gap when necessary or at least counterattack when the Federals moved against it, although Crow hinted that it was due to pique on the part of the cavalry officers over Jones's irascible behavior during the argument over whether or not the army should fight at Piedmont. Given the annoyed tone in Imboden's account, still evident nearly sixty years after the event, it is easy to accept the latter intepretation. Patchan, however, argued that the failure was due to a combination of factors, including the excellent firing positions of the Federal artillery over that section of the field; the size of the area that Imboden and Vaughn had to cover, stretching their lines to the limit; and the transfer of elements of Vaughn's force to other parts of the field at different points in the battle, weakening that section of the line still further and rendering it useless for a counterpunch. Brice, *Conquest of a Valley*, 80-81; Crow, *Storm in the Mountains*, 70, 73; Duncan, *Lee's Endangered Left*, 178, 180-182; Patchan, *The Forgotten Fury*, 94-95, 211, 213-215. For evidence that Jones considered pulling the infantry back to a position parallel to Vaughn's during the first phase of the battle, see Patchan, ibid., 120, 131.

396. Stringfield, "Sixty-Ninth Regiment," Clark, *North Carolina Regiments* 3:746-747; Patchan, *The Forgotten Fury*, 104.

397. Stringfield, "Sixty-Ninth Regiment," Clark, *North Carolina Regiments*, 3:746-747; *O.R.* 37 (pt. 1): 94-95 (Hunter's report); I. H. Hendricks to James Whitaker, June 8, Whitaker Papers, NCOAH. The fullest account of the battle of Piedmont is Patchan, *The Forgotten Fury*; 84-170. For shorter accounts, see Brice, *Conquest of a Valley*, 69-81; Crow, *Storm in the Mountains*, 69-76, and Duncan, *Lee's Endangered Left*, 176-185. The official reports are in *O.R.* 37 (pt. 1): 94-95, 110-111, 117-119, 150-153, 51 (pt. 1): 1225-1227, *O.R. (Supplement)* Pt. I, 6:895-896. The times used here for the different actions are derived from Hunter. Stringfield placed the first attack at 9 A.M., rather than 10. Stringfield Diary (1864), June 5, 1864, Stringfield Papers, NCOAH.

the gap, and instructed his Second Brigade to move towards it. At 2 P.M., the Confederates advanced, but were again driven back with the help of the Federal artillery. After their attack faltered, the Federal First Brigade advanced again. While the Confederates were preoccupied with the foes in their front, the Federal Second Brigade moved into the gap and struck the exposed right flank of the Legion. Realizing the danger to his position in that quarter, Jones returned the 60th Regiment Virginia Infantry to the Legion's support. Advancing beyond its previous position to the east side of the road, it was in the process of deploying when the Federals opened fire. The Virginians broke and fled right through the ranks of the Legion, disrupting its formation and causing it to break in turn as the Federals followed up their fire with a charge. In some places, the fighting was hand-to-hand. The entire right of the Confederate infantry gave way, and "Grumble" Jones was killed trying to rally his men.[398]

Meanwhile, Vaughn and Imboden stayed in position, and although they witnessed the Federal move into the gap and its threat towards the infantry's right, they refused to move without direct authorization from Jones due to his "peremptory" orders earlier. However, once Jones was killed, the Confederate line collapsed, and "the day was lost," they suddenly became flexible again and acted. Command now devolved on Vaughn, who ranked Imboden by reason of seniority. As Jones himself had done, however, Vaughn deferred to Imboden for advice because of his lack of knowledge of the terrain. Imboden immediately urged a withdrawal to his original preferred position, Mowry's Hill, where the Confederates could remake a stand and regroup. In the meantime, the two tried to get as much of the command safely off the field as possible. Imboden found a six-gun battery unlimbering near the road, and searched for infantry to support it. At this point, "a battalion of about eighty Tennessee riflemen, under Maj. W. W. Stringfellow, as I now remember his name, a perfect little game cock, not over five feet six or eight inches in height, and who had escaped from the battle field when poor Jones and so many others were killed, came out of the edge of the woods at a double quick and on up the lane toward me." "Stringfellow" was, of course, Stringfield; the men with him were remnants of the Legion, possibly with some refugees from other

398. *O.R.* 37 (pt. 1): 95, 118-119; Patchan, *The Forgotten Fury*, 131, 147-151; Stringfield Diary (1864), June 5, 1864, Stringfield, War Diary, June 5, 1864, recopied in ledger book, 212-213, and Stringfield, "War—Mss," ledger book, 140-143, all in Stringfield Papers, NCOAH; Imboden, "Battle of Piedmont," Pt. 1, *Confederate Veteran* 31 (December 1923): 460, and Pt. 2, *Confederate Veteran* 32 (January 1924): 19 (quotes); Leas, *Civil War Diary of Absalom Joshua Burum* (typescript copy, WCU), June 5, 1864; I. H. Hendricks to James Whitaker, June 8, 1864, and Stephen Whitaker to James Whitaker, August 5, 1864, Whitaker Papers, NCOAH; Stringfield, "Sixty-Ninth Regiment" in Clark, *North Carolina Regiments*, 3:747. Stringfield's diary entry for June 5, 1864, was fairly brief; when he recopied it into his ledger book years later, he reworked it heavily and added more details, as he did in the account of the battle that formed a part of his unpublished reminiscences. In the rewritten diary account, he claimed that his "Clothes [were] partly Shot off" (213), while in the reminiscence he stated that a Federal "Shot off a lock of My hair—burnt My right ear when I started to retreat"; in the next paragraph, he averred that "I was ordered to Surrender by the Irishman that shot off My beard" (143). Stringfield also stated that Capt. Julius M. Welch of Company E, Infantry Regiment, was killed in Stringfield's arms as the latter was attempting to help the already-wounded officer off the field (143, 213); there seems no reason to doubt the information. According to Pvt. Isaac H. Hendrix of Company I, Infantry Regiment, the 60th Regiment Virginia Infantry broke when the Federals were approximately thirty paces away, at which point the Legion was struck by a crossfire from both front and rear as the 60th Virginia fled through the Legion's ranks. Hendrix added that the Federals were only twenty paces away when the Legion left its barricade, indicating that the collapse must have been relatively sudden in the resulting confusion.

units mixed among them.[399] As Imboden recalled it, he asked "Will your men fight again?" to which the major replied, "Yes, like hell if you give them the chance." Imboden ordered Stringfield to form up on the opposite side of the road from the battery, behind a rail fence running at right angles to the road, and to open fire as soon as the enemy cavalry came into view. "He gave the order," Imboden wrote, "when his men scrambled over the fence with a defiant yell and, stringing themselves along the cross fence, two or three in a corner, were ready for action."[400]

Immediately the Federal cavalry appeared, galloping down the lane in a tight formation. "Just at the entrance to the lane, the battery poured a salvo of all six guns into them, and the Tennesseans a rifle volley." The front of the enemy column suffered heavy casualties; a second volley caused them to withdraw out of range, but they regrouped. Meanwhile, Imboden's own cavalry brigade deployed to the rear and right of Stringfield's men. The Federal cavalry tried another time, but were once again repulsed by the combined fire of the infantry and artillery. Suffering badly once again, the horsemen broke off contact.[401]

Hunter now chose to end the action due to doubts about the effectiveness of his cavalry. His decision probably saved the little Confederate army which was, with the exception

399. Brice, *Conquest of a Valley*, 84, identified Imboden's "Stringfellow" as Maj. Charles S. Stringfellow of Breckinridge's staff, but he was probably with his superior in Lee's army. Crow, *Storm in the Mountains*, 75, 248 n. 41, correctly identified "Stringfellow" as Stringfield.

400. Imboden, "Battle of Piedmont," Pt. 2, *Confederate Veteran* 32 (January 1924): 18-19; Stringfield, "War—Mss," ledger book, 142-143, Stringfield Papers, NCOAH. In his reminiscences, Stringfield did not mention Imboden at all. He stated that he encountered Love "at the river," who "ordered Me to collect all available Men & guard our rear—in the lane." He then gathered up 23 men, and with them repulsed a charge by the 10th Regiment New York Cavalry against his position; in both the unpublished reminiscence and the rewritten version of his June 5 diary entry, he claimed to have killed one Federal and captured another. The 10th New York Cavalry was not at Piedmont, however, but was with Grant. The Federals were probably members of either the 1st Regiment New York (Lincoln) Cavalry or the 1st Regiment New York Veteran Cavalry. Stringfield claimed in his rewritten diary entry that a "Col Key" of the "Ten Cavalry" assisted in his defense; the same officer was also noted in the reminiscence as having been with Love at the river. Vernon H. Crow identified the other officer as Lt. Col. David Key of the 43rd Regiment Tennessee Mounted Infantry, a unit in Vaughn's Brigade. Stringfield, "War—Mss," and Stringfield, War Diary, June 5, 1864 (recopied), both in ledger book, 143, 213, Stringfield Papers, NCOAH; Duncan, *Lee's Endangered Left*, 183; Patchan, *The Forgotten Fury*, 164, 166; Crow, *Storm in the Mountains*, 74, 248 n. 40; Tennessee Civil War Centennial Commission, *Tennesseans in the Civil War*, 1:268-270; for the itinerary of the 10th New York Cavalry at this time, see *O.R. (Supplement)* Pt. II, 41:429, 439, 445, 449, 455, 460, 463, 467, 473, 478, 480, 482, 487, 490. Regardless of Stringfield's imprecision as to many details, it is evident that the incident described by him is the same related by Imboden, although Stringfield seems to have, at least vaguely, given Imboden's role to Love; in his history of the Infantry Regiment he assigned the role to Vaughn (see Stringfield, "Sixty-Ninth Regiment," in Clark, *North Carolina Regiments* 3:748). It is possible that Stringfield did not know Imboden by sight. In his account in Clark's *Regiments*, Stringfield associated hand-to-hand combat with his fight against the cavalry, but he was probably mixing memories of the final moments of the Legion's defense of its original position as the infantry line collapsed. In regards to the cavalryman he killed, Stringfield claimed that "[t]he poor fellow—was a German. I know by his words—when shot: 'Mine Gott I'm kilt' he Said. I instantly thought, 'Mine Gott—I'm glad of it'—glad it wasn't me" (143). Stringfield, a pronounced nativist, had been a member of the American Party or "Know Nothings" before the war; this was not the only occasion in which he called attention to the immigrant character of some Union troops. See "War—Mss," ledger book, 28-29, 145-147, 150-151. Stringfield Papers, NCOAH.

401. Imboden, "Battle of Piedmont," *Confederate Veteran* 32 (January 1924): 18-19.

of isolated bodies of men such as Vaughn's and Imboden's own cavalry and Stringfield's contingent from the Legion, in total disarray. As was often the case when a battle line collapsed under heavy pressure, especially when flanked, the Confederate force at Piedmont had completely broken up in an understandable case of every man for himself. Sgt. Absalom J. Burum of Company K, Infantry Regiment, noted that when the 60th Regiment Virginia Infantry "stampeded right through our regiment" it "compelled us all to take care of ourselves." This was echoed by Private Hendrix of Company I of the Infantry Regiment, who wrote that "I believe every fellow took his own road." Capt. Stephen Whitaker wrote two months after the battle that "it was a miracle that any of us escaped."[402]

Piedmont was the first full-scale battle that Thomas's Legion participated in and, despite the criticisms leveled at it for months by its detractors, it seems to have acquitted itself well under the circumstances. Stringfield's participation in the rearguard effort showed that at least some of its officers and men were able to keep their heads in a difficult situation, and were still remembered with praise by Imboden six decades. The Legion suffered more heavily at Piedmont than at any engagement since Strawberry Plains in June of the previous year. Unlike that skirmish, where the casualties had been almost all prisoners, here there were injuries and deaths as well. Initial reports were confused, as would be expected in the immediate aftermath of a fight. Sergeant Burum reported at the end of the day that 1 was "said to be killed," with 4 wounded and 4 missing, but he probably referred to his own company only. Stringfield recorded 15 killed, 24 wounded, and 21 missing from the regiment in his diary. Pvt. Isaac H. Hendrix of Company I, Infantry Regiment, wrote three days after the battle that the entire Legion lost 13 killed, 21 wounded, and 42 missing. Writing many years after the war, Stringfield claimed that the Infantry Regiment alone lost 20 killed, 30 wounded, and 21 missing.[403] A variety of wartime and postwar records, including company medical records, Federal provost marshal records, and pension records, indicate that the Legion lost at least 6 killed or mortally wounded, 15 wounded, and 42 captured, figures very close to those provided by Hendrix. Of the captured, 27 were paroled in either February or March of the following year. It is not known if any of them were able to return to the ranks, and at least one was captured in hospital at Richmond in April. Four died in captivity, 2 took the Oath of Allegiance while prisoners, and 2 disappeared from the records; the remaining 5 were in prison until after the war, when they took the Oath either in late May or in June 1865.[404]

402. Brice, *Conquest of a Valley*, 83-84; Duncan, *Lee's Endangered Left*, 183-184, 210; Leas, *Civil War Diary of Absalom Joshua Burum* (typescript copy, WCU), June 5, 1864; I. H. Hendricks to James Whitaker, June 8, 1864, and Stephen Whitaker to James Whitaker, August 5, 1864, Whitaker Papers, NCOAH. "So numerous were the captures made of the enemy," wrote Col. Jacob Campbell of the 54th Regiment Pennsylvania Infantry, "that I was compelled to turn them out over the barricade to be taken charge of by the cavalry." *O.R.* 37 (pt. 1): 119.

403. Compare Burum's figures with those of Capt. Stephen Whitaker of Company E, Walker's Battalion, for his command; Whitaker reported on August 5 that his company lost 1 killed and 2 prisoners. Leas, *Civil War Diary of Absalom Joshua Burum* (typescript copy, WCU), June 5, 1864; Stringfield Diary (1864), June 5, Stringfield Papers, NCOAH; I. H. Hendricks to James Whitaker, June 8, 1864, and Stephen Whitaker to James Whitaker, August 5, 1864, Whitaker Papers, NCOAH.

404. This information comes from the records of the individual soldiers in Compiled Service Records of Confederate Soldiers from the State of North Carolina (M270), reels 567 through 574, supplemented by information in North Carolina and Tennessee pension records; I. H. Hendricks to James Whitaker, June 8, 1864,

In the aftermath, the entire Confederate command probably numbered between 2,000 and 2,500 and certainly less than 3,000 effectives. The Legion's brigade commander, Colonel Browne, was mortally wounded. Hunter estimated his opponents' losses as 600 killed and wounded, with between 1,000 and 1,500 prisoners, including some 60 officers. On the positive side for the Confederates, the loss in material appears to have been negligent. Vaughn reported to Seddon late on the night of the battle that the artillery and wagons had been saved, a claim echoed by Stringfield in his diary, while Captain Whitaker wrote two months after the battle that "we saved all our wagons & canons ammunition & co." Hunter, however, claimed that his men captured "3,000 stand of arms, 3 pieces of artillery, and a vast quantity of stores." He estimated his own casualties as under 500 killed and wounded. Confederate estimates of Federal losses were predictably much higher, although as they did not hold the field at the end of the day they were hardly in a position to make any real assessment. In all, Hunter may have suffered around 840 casualties.[405]

Vaughn had to regroup quickly. One major concern involved "Grumble" Jones, whose body had fallen into Federal hands. It was known that he had been in communication with Lee prior to the battle, but the contents of the dispatches were unknown and possibly in possession of the enemy. Once Imboden and his rearguard rejoined the main body, Vaughn dashed off to the nearest telegraph office at Fisherville, leaving Imboden in charge. By the time Imboden arrived with the troops, Lee had replied. The news was not good: Lee, in the midst of a major clash with Grant at Cold Harbor, had telegraphed Jones to let him know that he would not be able to send reinforcements for at least a week. Vaughn and Imboden were worried that Hunter had that information in his possession. Based on what he knew that evening, Vaughn felt that he could not carry out any sort of bluff to keep Hunter at bay. The Confederates thus withdrew to Waynesboro and Rockfish Gap until reinforcements could arrive; in the meantime, they ceded control of the Valley to Hunter.[406]

Whitaker Papers, NCOAH; William J. Smathers to father and mother, June 11, 1864, in Watford, *The Civil War in North Carolina: The Mountains*, 170, 235 n. 59; D. K. Collins to Stringfield, August 17, 1895, Stringfield Papers, WCU; Stringfield, "Sixty-Ninth Regiment," in Clark, *North Carolina Regiments*, 3:747.

405. Brice, *Conquest of a Valley*, 77-79, 87; Duncan, *Lee's Endangered Left*, 184, 187; *O.R.* 37 (pt. 1): 95, 119, 150-151, 606 (Hunter quote), 755; Stringfield Diary (1864), June 5, Stringfield Papers, NCOAH; I. H. Hendricks to James Whitaker, June 8, 1864 and Stephen Whitaker to James Whitaker, August 5, 1864, Whitaker Papers, NCOAH.

406. Imboden, "Battle of Piedmont," Pt. 2, *Confederate Veteran* 32 (January 1924): 20; *O.R.* 37 (pt. 1): 150-151; Stringfield Diary (1864), June 6, Stringfield Papers, NCOAH. While Hunter noted the finding of papers on Jones's body in his report of Piedmont, he did not mention anything about Lee's inability to reinforce Vaughn; the only information that he called attention to related to Jones's pre-battle troop strength (*O.R.* 37 [pt. 1]: 94). It is therefore likely that the paper was not found, or was understood as a ruse, the latter especially likely in light of Breckinridge's return to the Valley shortly afterwards. Information in a postwar report by Hunter's chief-of-staff, Col. David H. Strother, indicates that other correspondence found with Jones was perhaps equally damaging in their revelations regarding the Confederate situation in the Valley and neighboring regions. *O.R. (Supplement)* Pt. I, 6:882-883. It is stated in at least one source (Crow, *Storm in the Mountains*, 77) that Jones's copy of Special Order No. 105 was on his body when it fell into Federal hands, thus explaining why the Legion was not immediately transferred back to North Carolina after the battle as Jones had promised. This, however, cannot be assumed; the idea that Jones would have carried that particular order (and, presumably, all others he had received since that time, regardless of relative importance) on his person for that many days is not tenable. In fact, the necessities brought about by the military crisis would have kept every available unit in the area indefinitely.

Hunter pressed on to Staunton and occupied it on June 6. He soon set about destroying the infrastructure associated with the Confederate war effort, including the railroad depot and track, the telegraph, and factories and shops. Hunter promised the citizens that he would respect private property; however, once again he either proved unable or unwilling to impose order on his troops. While some of the Federal depredations were impressment efforts typical of Civil War armies, widespread looting and vandalism also occurred, and some homes were deliberately set afire. When Crook arrived with his command on June 8, efforts were made to restore order, but by that time things were too far out of control.[407]

Hunter's next objective was determined by Grant. After moving on Charlottesville and Lynchburg and wrecking as much of the railroad as possible, Hunter should march eastward. Hunter's movements would be made in conjunction with a strike westward by Meade's cavalry commander, Maj. Gen. Philip H. Sheridan, whose target was the Virginia Central Railroad; upon completion of the mission, the combined force would move toward Grant, destroying the James & Kanawha Canal. Based on papers found on "Grumble" Jones's body indicating Confederate military weaknesses and concerns for the region, Hunter opted for a direct drive through the Valley via Lexington, rather than a march eastward across the Blue Ridge to Charlottesville and then south to Lynchburg as originally proposed by Grant. Hunter's movement would bypass Vaughn's position at Rockfish Gap, which would be screened by a cavalry brigade; Sheridan's operations would prevent any reinforcements from Lee from arriving. The loss of Lynchburg would be a particular blow for the Confederacy. A major railway terminus with lines linking the Shenandoah Valley to the rest of Virginia and east Tennessee, it was also the site of another important supply depot for the Army of Northern Viriginia. Hunter set out in four columns from Staunton on June 10 after reorganizing his army, which now included the troops of Crook and Averell. What scant resistance they encountered came in the form of the cavalry brigade of Brig. Gen. John McCausland. On June 11 McCausland tried to make a stand inside Lexington itself, infuriating Hunter at what he called an "unsoldierly and inhuman attempt . . . to defend an indefensible position against an overwhelming force by screening himself behind the private dwellings of women and children." Rather than destroying the town with his artillery, Hunter used a flanking force to capture it, forcing McCausland to withdraw. Hunter became even more enraged after he discovered a proclamation issued by former governor John Letcher calling for guerrilla warfare against the Federals. Over the opposition of several of his officers, including Crook, Hunter responded by burning Letcher's home and the Virginia Military Institute.[408]

The Confederates in the Valley scrambled to organize a response to Hunter's new initiative. Due to the urgent need for reinforcements, and concerns over whether Vaughn was capable of handling the responsibilities that had been thrust upon him by Jones's death, Lee dispatched Breckinridge and his infantry back to the Valley on or about June 7. Breckinridge

407. *O.R.* 37 (pt. 1): 95-96, 151-153, 607, 51 (pt. 1): 989-990, 993; Brice, *Conquest of a Valley*, 90-105; Duncan, *Lee's Endangered Left*, 192-198. For the operations of Crook and Averell against the Virginia Central Railroad prior to their junction with Hunter at Staunton, see *O.R.* 37 (pt. 1): 119-120, 122, 124-126, 136, 145, 561, 563-564, 584, 586, 594, 599, 603, 606, 754, 51 (pt. 2): 981; Duncan, *Lee's Endangered Left*, 200-209.

408. *O.R.* 36 (pt. 1): 22, 24, (pt. 3): 628-629, 662, 37 (pt. 1): 96-97 (Hunter quotes, 96), 111, 120, 154-155, 593, 598-599, 612-615, 618-619, 625, 626, 759; *O.R. (Supplement)* Pt. I, 6:882-883; Brice, *Conquest of a Valley*, 101, 105-108, 114-116; Duncan, *Lee's Endangered Left*, 198-200, 209-228, 254-255, 258-260.

could only exercise nominal control over the command, however, as he was recovering from injuries inflicted at Cold Harbor. The main body of the army, including Thomas's Legion, remained at Rockfish Gap through June 11, unsure of the Federals' ultimate intentions: did they plan to move on from Lexington to Lynchburg, or on Saltville? By June 10 Breckinridge had reorganized his infantry into two divisions under Vaughn and Brig. Gen. Gabriel C. Wharton. Thomas's Legion was placed in Wharton's Division in Beuhring Jones's former brigade, now commanded by Col. Thomas Smith of the 36th Regiment Virginia Infantry. Besides the Legion, the brigade included Smith's own regiment, the 60th Regiment Virginia Infantry, and the 45th Battalion Virginia Infantry. Breckinridge counted his effective infantry at 5,023, including dismounted cavalry and some units of the Virginia Reserves. His cavalry, including McCausland's Brigade (not present with the main body) numbered 4,000; Imboden commanded the other mounted brigade. Morale seemed good, despite the setback at Piedmont; Pvt. Isaac H. Hendrix of Company I, Infantry Regiment, wrote that the Confederates were "eager for them [the Federals] to come."[409]

Hunter resumed his march until June 14. He advanced southward by way of Buchanan, planning to follow the path of the James & Kanawha Canal across the Blue Ridge to Lynchburg. Averell's cavalry had departed on the previous day to scout and forward intelligence back to Hunter. Initially, McCausland's cavalry provided the only resistance; he was joined by Imboden as the Federals approached Lynchburg. Breckinridge, unaware that Lexington had fallen, set out from Rockfish Gap with the infantry on June 12, marching through Waynesboro. His object was to turn south in the direction of Greenville and threaten or attack Hunter from behind; Imboden and McCausland would guard the Blue Ridge gaps in the meanwhile. The command marched only part of the way before Breckinridge learned that Lexington was already occupied. Coupled with other intelligence, he was now certain that Hunter was aiming for Lynchburg. He turned the column eastward again, marching it across the mountains to a place within five miles of their previous camp. The following day the command moved south along the Fish River in the direction of Amherst Court House. Thomas's Legion marched through the latter place on June 15, encamping two miles from town. That evening, Breckinridge arrived in Lynchburg with advance elements of the command. The march resumed for the remainder on the following day, with Thomas's Legion reaching the town in the evening. The relieving troops received a huge welcome from the locals. The Legion was marched to the trenches on College Hill on the southwestern outskirts, and with the rest of Breckinridge's troops awaited the approach of Hunter.[410]

409. Duncan, *Lee's Endangered Left*, 203, 249-252; *O.R.* 37 (pt. 1): 754-760, 43 (pt. 2): 884, 51 (pt. 1): 989-990, 992, 993, 1000, 1002, 1005; Douglas Southall Freeman, ed. and annotator, *Lee's Dispatches: Unpublished Letters of General Robert E. Lee, C.S.A., to Jefferson Davis and the War Department of the Confederate States of America 1862-1865, From the Private Collection of Wymberley Jones de Renne of Wormsloe, Georgia* (New York: G. P. Putnam's Sons, 1957; new edition, with Additional Dispatches and Foreward by Grady McWhiney, Baton Rouge: Lousiana State University Press, 1994), 215-219 (hereinafter cited as Freeman and McWhiney, eds., *Lee's Dispatches*); Patchan, *The Forgotten Fury*, 49, 221; Stringfield Diary (1864), June 7-11, Stringfield Papers, NCOAH; I. H. Hendricks to James Whitaker, June 8, 1864, Whitaker Papers, NCOAH.

410. *O.R.* 36 (pt. 1): 24, 37 (pt. 1): 98-99, 111, 154-160, 627, 631-635, 761-762, 764-765, 40 (pt. 2): 658; 51 (pt. 2): 1005, 1007-1008; *O.R. (Supplement)* Pt. I, 6:884-885; Stringfield Diary (1864), June 12-16, Stringfield Papers, NCOAH; Duncan, *Lee's Endangered Left*, 233-244, 252-253.

In the meantime, several developments occurred elsewhere that affected the outcome of the campaign. Lee found out about Sheridan's raid and sent part of his own cavalry after him; the resulting clashes slowed the Federal cavalry's progress. As the armies lay quiescent at Cold Harbor, Lee also decided to send the veteran Second Corps, commanded by the irascible Maj. Gen. Jubal A. Early, to reinforce the Confederates in the Valley and crush Hunter's Army of West Virginia. Early departed on June 13. Grant, meanwhile, slipped away from Cold Harbor with the Army of the Potomac on June 12 in a dash to take the city of Petersburg, a move which if successful would lead to the fall of Richmond; as a result, he was neither aware of Early's departure or in a position to prevent it. Finally, Sheridan received word that Hunter had not advanced via Charlottesville to meet him; facing diminishing supplies and stiff Confederate resistance, he returned to Grant. Early was thus able to reach Lynchburg with the first contigent of his troops without interference on June 17.[411]

Assuming command with the ailing Breckinridge's consent, Early quickly pushed forward to confront Hunter before the latter was in a position to bombard Lynchburg. The division of Maj. Gen. Stephen Dodson Ramseur and part of the division of Maj. Gen. John B. Gordon were the first of Early's troops to arrive; they were rushed to the front, where they joined Imboden's cavalry to contest the advance of Crook and Averell. The two sides engaged in a spirited skirmish which lasted until nightfall. Thomas's Legion did not participate, but remained in the defensive line at College Hill throughout the day.[412]

On the Federal side, Hunter learned as early as June 15 that Lynchburg was not strongly defended, and issued new orders to push forward and capture it as quickly as possible. Hunter himself, however, at this point adopted a lackadaisical attitude towards his own objectives. He frittered away what opportunities he had, spending too much time on the march destroying railroad track. Once he finally arrived at Lynchburg his sense of urgency was still lacking; satisfied at the progress of events on June 17, he opted to await morning before pressing his attack. This allowed Early time to strengthen his defensive line while successfully employing a series of ruses that made the Federals think that more Confederates were present and arriving than was then the case. Under these circumstances the action resumed on June 18. Early's Second Corps veterans occupied the Confederate left, while Breckinridge's men (under Wharton) occupied the right. Little is known of the Legion's role or position, although it was presumably with the rest of Smith's Brigade; other than a few artillery shells landing among its ranks, which hurt no one, it appears not to have been actively engaged during the day.[413] Around 1 P.M., Early probed Hunter's right flank with the

411. *O.R.* 36 (pt. 1): 11-12, 22-23, 25-26, 98, 195, 346, 626, 784-786, 795-797, 1035, 1095-1097, (pt. 3): 888, 897, 37 (pt. 1): 758, 761-765, 51 (pt. 2): 1002-1003, 1009, 1012-1013, 1020; *O.R. (Supplement)* Pt. I, 6:897, 906-907; Freeman and McWhiney, *Lee's Dispatches*, 240-241; Jubal Anderson Early, *Autobiographical Sketch and Narrative of the War Between the States* (Philadelphia: J. B. Lippincott Company, 1912; reprt., Wilmington, N.C.: Broadfoot Publishing Company, 1989), 371-373 (hereinafter cited as Early, *Autobiographical Sketch and Narrative*); Frank E. Vandiver, *Jubal's Raid: General Early's Famous Attack on Washington in 1864* (New York: McGraw-Hill, 1960), 19-36; Duncan, *Lee's Endangered Left*, 255-257, 260-266.

412. *O.R.* 37 (pt. 1): 99, 112, 121, 125-130, 132, 134, 135, 137, 138, 141, 147-148, 645; Early, *Autobiographical Sketch and Narrative*, 373-375; Vandiver, *Jubal's Raid*, 37-40; Duncan, *Lee's Endangered Left*, 270-272.

413. Although Stringfield reported in his diary that there were no injuries from the cannon fire, two members of the Infantry Regiment claimed in their pension applications to have been wounded at Lynchburg. Pvt. Lebo Medford of Company E reported that he suffered an ankle injury, while Pvt. Henry P. Brendle recorded that a

Second Corps troops and was subequently repulsed. In the meantime, to the north Federal Brig. Gen. Alfred Duffie advanced against Wharton and McCausland on the right flank amd slowly drove them back. Around 5 P.M., the Confederates counterattacked and pushed Duffie back in turn. Hunter's army still outnumbered the Confederates by this point—although the rest of Early's men under Gordon and Maj. Gen. Robert Rodes were arriving late in the day, it would have taken some time to properly organize them and move them to the field—but the stiff resistance and Early's efforts at deception paid off. Recognizing that reinforcements from the Army of Northern Virginia were on the field, and convinced that Early's numbers were far greater than they were, Hunter made the decision to withdraw secretly after dark. The Federals encamped that night some seven miles east of Liberty Court House.[414]

Over the next few days the Federals withdrew westward across the mountains along the line of the Virginia & Tennessee Railroad, destroying more track, bridges, and depots as they went. The Army of West Virginia was exhausted and short on ammunition and subsistence. Far from its supply base and forced to live off the land again, its best option was to leave the Shenandoah Valley and move into West Virginia. On June 21 it turned northward at Salem, moving on a route which eventually brought it to Charleston, West Virginia, where it could be resupplied and rested. Early discovered Hunter's withdrawal on June 19, and followed with his worn-out corps, accompanied by Breckinridge's (Wharton's) Division under Maj. Gen. Arnold Elzey, and the cavalry under Maj. Gen. Robert Ransom. Early was hampered by miscommunications, the lack of his own supply train, and the condition of his command; despite some sharp skirmishes, he was unable to prevent Hunter's escape. He gave up the chase at Salem on June 21. After resting his men half a day and allowing his artillery and supply trains to catch up, he turned them northeastwards down the Valley.[415]

"bum shell" injured his right hand (with fingers shot off), his right arm, his right thigh, and the back of his neck. Brendle, however, recalled that his wounding occurred at Lynchburg in "April, 1865." Lebo Medford, North Carolina Application for Pension (1901), State Auditor's Office Records, NCOAH; H. P. Brendle, Tennessee Confederate Pension Application No. 10170, Roster Document No. 1844, CWRP.

414. *O.R.* 37 (pt. 1): 98-100, 111-112, 120-126, 129, 130, 132-138, 141-143, 147-148, 160, 640-642, 644-645, 648-650; *O.R. (Supplement)* Pt. I, 6:884-885; Early, *Autobiographical Sketch and Narrative*, 375; Stringfield Diary (1864), June 18, Stringfield Papers, NCOAH; Vandiver, *Jubal's Raid*, 43-53; Duncan, *Lee's Endangered Left*, 228, 234-246, 266, 273-288. There are only vague clues regarding the Legion's position in the Confederate battle line during the fighting on June 18. Stringfield's diary entry reads as follows: "Carried to the front. left wing. a few shells bursted among us. Nobody hurt. Evening—ordered to the right wing. Enemy repulsed on the left Soon after we left." On the surface, this passage seems to indicate that the Legion was detached from Smith's Brigade and placed somewhere in the left wing of Early's army, consisting of the Second Corps veterans, and then was shifted back to Breckinridge's (Wharton's) men in the right wing, where it presumably rejoined Smith. It is unlikely that so small a unit as the Legion would be moved from Wharton's division to bolster the Second Corps, however, unless it was needed to cover some specific post in support of the main line. Possibly Stringfield meant that the Legion was originally in the left half of Wharton's line, and then shifted towards its right; or that it was placed on the left flank of Smith's Brigade before moving right. A map in the *Official Atlas* shows that Smith's Brigade occupied the center of Wharton's line and thus a move from the left to the right flank of the brigade would also represent a move from the left "wing" to the right "wing" of the division as a whole (see *Official Atlas of the Civil War*, plate 133:7). Stringfield's reference to a Federal assault "on the left Soon after we left" in the evening, could refer to action either against the Second Corps brigades, or an advance by Duffie against Wharton's or Smith's left, and thus does not settle matters about the Legion's position.

415. *O.R.* 37 (pt. 1): 100-102, 112-113, 121, 143-144, 160, 650-654, 657-658, 660-661, 664-666, 670-671, 676-677, 683-686, 760-766, 51 (pt. 2): 1006; *O.R. (Supplement)* Pt. I, 6:885-886; Early, *Autobiographical Sketch*

Early's decision was due not just to the difficulties which a campaign in West Virginia would entail. Instead, it was largely to do with his original instructions from Lee. Once Hunter's army was destroyed, Early was to move down the Valley towards or into Maryland. An aggressive campaign would hopefully bring about the same results as the operations of the late Thomas J. "Stonewall" Jackson in the Valley in the spring of 1862: alarming the Federal government with a potential threat to Washington and causing a diversion of troops from the Army of the Potomac. All sorts of possibilites might then open up for Lee as the pressure in his own front was relieved. At the least, if Early could tie up a large number of Federal troops without suffering any major defeats, and keep his army intact, then the campaign would be a success. Although Hunter's army had not been crushed, its removal from the Valley gave Early a free hand to put Lee's ideas into motion. Impetus had been added by a telegram from Lee to Early while the latter was at Lynchburg, requesting him to undertake the campaign or to come to Petersburg as the circumstances best warranted.[416]

Early moved steadily down the Valley over the next few days. Breckinridge's Division, including Thomas's Legion, brought up the rear of the infantry column. The army reached Lexington at noon on June 25. There, the soldiers paraded silently past Jackson's grave, a morale booster with quasi-religious overtones which evidently achieved its purpose, if Stringfield's rapturous diary entry was any indication: "Oh how grand the Scene, a Nations Soldiery, honoring the Noble dead!!" Continuing northward the next day, Stringfield noted the welcome received by the largely pro-Confederate population in this part of the Valley: "[T]his portion of Va will do." The Confederates reached Staunton on June 27 and rested for a half day. Early then reorganized the army into two informal corps of two divisions each. One corps was placed under Early's senior division commander, Maj. Gen. Robert Rodes, while Breckinridge was given the other. Breckinridge's Corps consisted of his own division, commanded at this time by Vaughn, along with Gordon's veteran Second Corps division. Resuming its trek, the new Army of the Valley soon reached Piedmont. On June 30 it camped on the site of the battle of New Market, and on July 2 reached Winchester.[417]

---

and Narrative, 376-379; Stringfield Diary (1864), June 20-22, Stringfield Papers, NCOAH; Vandiver, *Jubal's Raid*, 53-60; B. F. Cooling, *Jubal Early's Raid on Washington* (Baltimore: The Naval & Aviation Publishing Company of America, 1989), 13-15; Duncan, *Lee's Endangered Left*, 287-301. Ransom was brought up to command the Valley cavalry because of questions regarding Imboden's leadership and the indiscipline among his men. *O.R.* 40 (pt. 2): 658; Early, *Autobiographical Sketch and Narrative*, 375-376; Brice, *Conquest of a Valley*, 23-24; Duncan, *Lee's Endangered Left*, 253-254. For the circumstances of Elzey's assuming command of Breckinridge's Division, see n. 417 below.

416. *O.R.* 37 (pt. 1): 346, 766-767, 769-770; Vandiver, *Jubal's Raid*, 19, 60-61; Cooling, *Jubal Early's Raid on Washington*, 10-11, 14; Duncan, *Lee's Endangered Left*, 301-302.

417. *O.R.* 37 (pt. 1): 766, 768; Early, *Autobiographical Sketch and Narrative*, 381-383; Stringfield Diary (1864), June 22-30, July 3 ("this portion of Va" quote, June 26 entry), Stringfield Papers, NCOAH; Vandiver, *Jubal's Raid*, 61-75; Cooling, *Jubal Early's Raid on Washington*, 15-24. Attempting to follow the succession of commanders of Breckinridge's Division in the summer of 1864 is difficult. Breckinridge was recovering from his Cold Harbor injuries during the Lynchburg campaign and the early stages of the march up the Valley, and his senior brigade commander, John C. Echols, was absent. Breckinridge wanted Maj. Gen. D. H. Hill, who was at Lynchburg without a command, to take over the division; however, Hill was on the outs with Richmond for his participation in the anti-Bragg faction in the Army of Tennessee the previous year, so that idea was scuttled (Early himself also tried to get Hill placed in charge of Breckinridge's infantry following Lynchburg). Instead,

Early had so far been aided by Federal ignorance of his presence and movements, due to Hunter's withdrawal and to Confederate partisan strikes against the local lines of communication. There was uncertainty on Grant's and Hunter's parts as to whether or not Early had returned to Lee; Grant in fact contemplated having Hunter move against the railroad line running from Charlottesville again as soon as the Army of West Virginia refitted. For that matter, the Federal authorities were mystified as to Hunter's own whereabouts, as his route took him out of contact with the war department and Grant for several days. The nearest Federal forces in the lower Valley were the Department of West Virginia's Reserve Division, under Sigel; his main force was concentrated at Martinsburg, a major supply depot. Sigel's responsibilities included the key post of Harper's Ferry, which would need to be captured or isolated in order for Early's advance to continue. Upon his arrival at Winchester, Early had received a telegram from Lee, instructing him to stay in the area until all preparations were complete for a move across the Potomac; in the meantime, he was to inflict as much damage as possible on the Baltimore & Ohio Railroad and the Chesapeake & Ohio Canal, giving him time to replenish his supplies and prevent Federal reinforcements from arriving by train. Early sent the cavalry of McCausland and Brig. Gen. Bradley T. Johnson on sweeping movements to the left and right that would bring them to Hainesville, where they would reunite and cut off Sigel from retreat to Williamsport and the Potomac River. Breckinridge's Corps was sent forward directly against Sigel at Martinsburg, while Early himself took Rodes's Corps in the wake of Johnson to Leetown. Despite growing rumors, Sigel and his superiors were not truly aware that Early was in the area until July 2; even after the first frantic messages from Sigel of the Confederate advance reached Washington on July 3, Grant still believed that Early was with Lee, and was not completely convinced otherwise for two more full days. Meanwhile, faced with a possible encirclement Sigel quickly beat a retreat across the Potomac. Although there was some skirmishing, particularly on Johnson's and Rodes's front, the Federals were able to reach safety. Sigel abandoned many of the stores at Martinsburg without destroying them, including food for a July 4 celebration. Breckinridge allowed his troops a late start on that day in order to enjoy their good fortune. "The Yanks had a great dinner prepared for this day & the Rebels feasted upon it," gloated Stringfield. Breckinridge's men burned the railroad bridges after their repast and marched down the track to Duffield's Depot, where they would be in a position to support Rodes.[418]

Brig. Gen. Arnold Elzey was sent from the Army of Northern Virginia to take command at the time of the fighting at Lynchburg, but he did not arrive until June 18; as a consequence, Wharton commanded the division during much or all of the skirmishing on that day. Following Lynchburg, as Early was now commanding officer of the Valley troops, he removed the cavalry from Breckinridge's control, leaving him his infantry only; however, with Elzey in overall command of the infantry, Breckinridge was rendered superfluous. Nevertheless, once he recovered from his injuries, Breckinridge accompanied Early's movement up the Valley. It was partly due to Breckinridge's anomalous status—and to better utilize his experience—that Early decided to reorganize the army at Staunton. Elzey was relieved at his own request at that time due to health problems; until Echols reported for duty, his place was taken by Vaughn. *O.R.* 37 (pt. 1): 764-766, 768, 51 (pt. 2): 1002, 1020, 52 (pt. 2): 677-678; Early, *Autobiographical Sketch and Narrative*, 375-376, 381, 385; Vandiver, *Jubal's Raid*, 37-38, 40-41; Brice, *Conquest of a Valley*, 110; Crow, *Storm in the Mountains*, 84; Cooling, *Jubal Early's Raid on Washington*, 17-18; Duncan, *Lee's Endangered Left*, 270-271, 286, 288.

418. *O.R.* 37 (pt. 1): 102, 174-176, 181, 350, 357-358, 518-519, 533, 662, 664, 667-668, 671, 673-676, 680, 682-684, 688-689, 691-695, 769-770, (pt. 2): 3-6, 8-13, 15-30, 32-33, 47, 60, 74, 77-79, 95, 367, 591-592; Early,

Early, meanwhile, moved with Rodes's Corps against Harper's Ferry. By the morning of July 5, he realized the post had been reinforced by Sigel and was too strong to take, and confined his activities to a demonstration prior to crossing the Potomac. Breckinridge sent Gordon's Division across Boteler's Ford at Shephardstown, where it was placed in a position to observe Harper's Ferry; Vaughn followed with Breckinridge's own division, which encamped that night near Sharpsburg on the old Antietam battleground. Rodes and Ramseur followed in the early hours of July 6, leaving one of Ramseur's brigades behind to keep the Harper's Ferry garrison occupied. During the day, the Confederates began the destruction of the canal locks and boats in the vicinity, although Imboden's cavalry failed to do much damage to the Baltimore & Ohio Railroad; meanwhile Gordon advanced on Maryland Heights and skirmished with the Federals there to keep up the pressure on Harper's Ferry, while McCausland was sent to Hagerstown to levy cash from the locals. The goal of these efforts would become a hallmark of Early's Valley strategy: to confuse the enemy as much as possible as to his numbers and intentions. Early now received a special dispatch from Lee, informing him of a mysterious plan to rescue Confederate soldiers from the Point Lookout prisoner-of-war camp, south of Baltimore, and asking for Early's cooperation by sending a cavalry force to act as a diversion and to perhaps even participate in the attempt itself. Although details of the plan were lacking, Early decided that within the context of the stalemate at Harper's Ferry it was enough to shift his line of march across the gaps of the South Mountains; once on the other side, he would be able to get a better sense of the Federal response to his presence and send the cavalry out that Lee requested. When a long-awaited supply of shoes arrived on July 7—much to the relief of his men—Early began to move again. Breckinridge's Division, now under the command of Brig. Gen. John C. Echols, supported Gordon's Division in further demonstrations against Maryland Heights. By the end of the day, contact was broken off as the army moved towards the mountains; Breckinridge's Corps and Rodes's Division camped near Rohrersville, while Ramseur halted for the night near Sharpsburg. Early meanwhile had sent Johnson's cavalry across the mountains to Frederick, where he skirmished with Federal forces in an effort to determine their numbers; he was withdrawn by Ransom before he had fully achieved that purpose. On July 8, the rest of the army marched across South Mountain; Breckinridge's Corps, including Thomas's Legion, went by way of Fox's Gap, while Rodes took Crampton's Gap and Ramseur Boonsboro Gap. At the end of the day, Rodes stopped near Jefferson while Ramseur and Breckinridge camped near Middletown.[419]

Gathering to stop them was a small force of some 2,500 Federals under Maj. Gen. Lew Wallace, commander of the Middle District. Wallace's goal was to prevent Early from capturing Washington and Baltimore. Encouraged by the withdrawal of the Confederate cavalry

---

Autobiographical Sketch and Narrative, 382-384; Vandiver, *Jubal's Raid*, 75-82, 85, 90-91; Cooling, *Jubal Early's Raid on Washington*, 25-27, 29-38, 41-42; Stringfield Diary (1864), July 4, Stringfield Papers, NCOAH; Stephen Whitaker to James Whitaker, August 5, 1864, Whitaker Papers, NCOAH.

419. *O.R.* 37 (pt. 1): 176-182, 184-187, 190, 194, 219-220, 223, (pt. 2): 33-60, 62-68, 76-77, 80-81, 85-88, 91, 94-98, 101, 108-111, 116-117, 119-120, 123-131, 133, 135-138, 144, 592, 767-769, 51 (pt. 1): 1172-1173; Early, *Autobiographical Sketch and Narrative*, 384-386; Stephen Whitaker to James Whitaker, August 5, 1864, Whitaker Papers, NCOAH; Vandiver, *Jubal's Raid*, 82-97, 99-103; Cooling, *Jubal Early's Raid on Washington*, 27-29, 37-48.

from Frederick on July 7 and by news that Grant had dispatched part of the veteran Sixth Corps from the Army of the Potomac to Maryland, Wallace determined to make a stand on the southeast bank of the Monocacy River, a tributary of the Potomac, near a spot where the Baltimore & Ohio Railroad bisected the stream.[420]

After pushing the Federal rearguard out of Frederick, the Army of the Valley marched southward on July 9. While Early extorted $200,000 from the citizens of Frederick in exchange for sparing the town, his troops deployed and the artillery of both sides opened up. Upon arriving at the front, Early surveyed the situation. There were two roads running from Frederick that crossed the Monocacy River, the Baltimore Pike to the north and the Washington Pike in the south; in between was the bridge of the Baltimore & Ohio Railroad. Desiring to gain control of the Washington Pike, which was the direct road to the U.S. capital, he decided to make his main effort in that direction. McCausland's cavalry forded the river and engaged the Federal left, followed by Breckinridge's Corps. Gordon led the advance, with Echols in reserve; meanwhile, Rodes skirmished near the Baltimore Pike crossing and Ramseur pressured the Federal center at the railroad crossing. Wallace's line was thus stretched thin, and he was unable to do much shifting to reinforce the critical position on the left; this allowed Gordon to successfully cross the river. Fortunately for Wallace, he had been reinforced on the previous night by two brigades from the Sixth Corps, and they were stationed on the left wing. They adjusted and met the Confederate assault. Gordon, however, flanked the Federal position, and after a hard struggle pushed it back, uncovering the railroad crossing and allowing Ramseur to join in. The Federals retreated by way of the Baltimore Pike, effectively removing them from use in the defense of Washington; regardless, by delaying Early for a day, Wallace's stand at the Monocacy proved crucial for the Federal defense of the capital. Breckinridge's Division, including Thomas's Legion, was brought up as the Federals withdrew, but did not participate in the fighting.[421]

Early marched in the direction of Washington the next day, with Breckinridge's Corps in the lead. It was a hot march, with much straggling. Federal cavalry nipped at Ramseur's Division bringing up the rear, a sign that the enemy were beginning to concentrate in that sector, possibly to cut off Early's line of retreat. Hunter, in fact, was on the way, having been ordered by Grant on July 3 to move with all of his available troops to protect the Baltimore & Ohio Railroad. Although Imboden's cavalry had not caused serious damage to the railroad, it had done just enough to slow Hunter's progress, coupled with the low water level of the Ohio River which delayed Hunter's departure by boat. The Confederates stopped for the night north of Rockville, where Early received word that the only Federal forces between them and Washington were cavalry. Within the fortifications of the city was a rag-tag group of Veteran Reserve troops, state militia units, and whatever else the Federals could gather. The strength of the defenders was much less than it could have been, as a significant body of men had been sent in the direction of Harper's Ferry prior to Monocacy; however, they were

420. *O.R.* 36 (pt. 1): 28, 37 (pt. 1): 193-195, 204-223, 270, 274, (pt. 2): 30-32, 51, 55, 58-60, 72-73, 92-94, 100-101, 108-115, 124-125, 127-129, 138, 144, 372-373; Vandiver, *Jubal's Raid*, 97-101, 122-124; Cooling, *Jubal Early's Raid on Washington*, 55-59.

421. *O.R.* 36 (pt. 1): 28, 37 (pt. 1): 191-192, 195-224, 347-348, 350-352, (pt. 2): 110-115, 127-129, 134-135, 137-139, 142, 144-145, 190, 594, 51 (pt. 2): 1175-1177; Early, *Autobiographical Sketch and Narrative*, 387-388; Vandiver, *Jubal's Raid*, 103-120; Cooling, *Jubal Early's Raid on Washington*, 49-52, 59-81.

SHENANDOAH VALLEY
Virginia and Vicinity

thus in a position to unite with Hunter when he arrived. Further, reinforcements for Washington were on the way in the form of a division and part of another from the Nineteenth Corps of the Army of the Gulf. Fresh from the Red River Campaign, these troops had originally been transferred to the Army of the Potomac, but were diverted on landing to Washington. Grant also decided to send the rest of the Sixth Corps. Although Early was unware of all of this, he knew that the Federals would not leave the capital defenseless, and that he was in a race against time if he hoped to capture and occupy the city, however briefly.[422]

The Confederates resumed their march at 3:30 A.M. on the morning of July 11. McCausland's cavalry was in the lead, followed by the divisions of Rodes, Ramseur, Gordon, and Echols. The army advanced southward through Rockville on another hot, dusty day. The first Confederate infantry reached the Washington fortifications sometime around 1 P.M. Their route was blocked by Fort Stevens, guarding the Seventh Street road into the city. The works seemed lightly armed, and the chances of securing a lodgement within were good. On Early's orders, Rodes formed his exhausted men into a skirmish line to advance on the fort. More Federal units arrived during the day to bolster the defense; although many of these were Veteran Reserve units of invalid soldiers, makeshift units of clerks, and whatever else could be thrown forward, they were enough to man the more important sectors and bolster the Federal skirmish line. After a long day of heavy skirmishing, the tired and dehydrated Confederates did not attempt to storm the works. As Echols remained in reserve, Thomas's Legion did not participate. That night, Early held a council of war at which he decided to launch a full-scale attack the next morning. He changed his plans, however, when he received a report from Bradley Johnson, whom Early had dispatched with his cavalry on July 8 to raid north of Baltimore in support of the attempt to liberate the prisoners at Point Lookout. Johnson reported that two Federal corps were on the way to the relief of the city; indeed, parts of the Sixth and Nineteenth Corps had begun to arrive about the time that the initial skirmishing started, and were in reserve behind the main entrenchments. Deciding that caution was wise, Early postponed the attack until he was able to gain fuller information.[423]

422. *O.R.* 36 (pt. 1): 27-28, 37 (pt. 1): 102-103, 113, 175, 186-188, 231, 236, 239, 248-249, 254-255, 260, 264, 285, 295, 331, 348, (pt. 2): 3-4, 7, 15, 18-19, 23, 29-30, 33-39, 43, 58-64, 67, 69-71, 74-75, 78-91, 94-108, 111, 117-121, 123-127, 129, 132-137, 139-142, 144-145, 155-173, 178, 185, 340; Early, *Autobiographical Sketch and Narrative*, 389; Weymouth T. Jordan Jr., "54th Regiment N.C. Troops," in Manarin and Jordan, *North Carolina Troops*, 13:219 n. 215; Vandiver, *Jubal's Raid*, 120-121, 135-147; Cooling, *Jubal Early's Raid on Washington*, 83-107. Lee became aware of the possibility of Federal reinforcements for Washington as early as July 7, and by July 11 knew that at least one division of the Sixth Corps had been sent. Although he sent messages immediately to warn Early, due to the relative geographical positions of the forces involved they would have been unable to reach him in time to be of benefit. *O.R.* 37 (pt. 2): 593-596.

423. *O.R.* 36 (pt. 1): 28, 37 (pt. 1): 231-232, 236-246, 249, 253, 255, 258-262, 264-265, 270-273, 275-276, 278, 283, 348, (pt. 2): 193-210, 415, 594; *O.R. (Supplement)* Pt. I, 6:887-888; Early, *Autobiographical Sketch and Narrative*, 386, 389-394; Stringfield Diary (1864), July 11, Stringfield Papers, NCOAH; Bradley T. Johnson, "My Ride Around Baltimore In Eighteen Hundred and Sixty-Four," *Journal of the U.S. Cavalry Association* (September, 1889), repr. in *SHSP* 30 (1902): 217-219; Vandiver, *Jubal's Raid*, 102-103, 149-161; Cooling, *Jubal Early's Raid on Washington*, 107-127, 136. Stringfield was not with the Legion, having been left in charge of the division's wagon train on July 6. He was apparently sick, as he reported that he and his fellow guards were "on the invalid order." Although nevertheless well enough on the day of his assignment to get into a fight with Early's quartermaster, whom Stringfield described as "drunk," by July 8 he was "played out," and rode in different conveyances for much of the rest of the trip. He reported that the division wagons were parked outside

On July 12, Early surveyed the defensive line again, and noted that the works were indeed reinforced. Weighing his options, he decided to withdraw that night without an attack. During the day, he again sent forward skirmishers, supported by the rest of the infantry in battle line, in order to make a serious impression of strength on the defenders and give Johnson time to withdraw, as the rescue and safe conveyance of the Point Lookout prisoners to Confederate territory was impossible under the circumstances. Echols's Division, including Thomas's Legion, remained in reserve and again saw no fighting. Skirmishing lasted throughout the day. The most serious moment for the Confederates came about 6 P.M., when the Federals advanced a strong line of battle against Rodes and pushed his men back after a stiff fight. The fighting died down by dark, and Early's command left during the night.[424]

The Army of the Valley marched through the night and into the next morning, passing through Rockville and eventually stopping at Poolsville. When night fell, the retreat resumed. The Federal pursuit was not especially vigorous, nor did Hunter, who had arrived with part of his command at Harper's Ferry, make a strong effort to intercept Early; as a result, the latter was able to get a day's march ahead of his foes. The Confederates crossed the Potomac into Virginia at White's Ford on the morning of July 14 and stopped for the night at Leesburg in the Catoctin Mountains. After a day's rest, the march resumed on July 16. Although the army crossed the Shenandoah River on July 17, Early was not out of trouble yet. Maj. Gen. Horatio G. Wright commanded the pursuing force from Washington, consisting of his own Sixth Corps and the detachment from the Nineteenth Corps. Meanwhile, the advance forces of the Army of West Virginia lumbered eastward under Maj. Gen. Jeremiah Sullivan, replaced by Crook on July 16 when Sullivan missed an opportunity to cut Early off at Leesburg. Crook quickly launched a cavalry strike against Early's supply train as the Army of the Valley marched towards Snicker's Gap. The two Federal columns united on July 17. On July 18, Wright sent Crook to establish a bridgehead across the Shenandoah at Island Ford. The Federals successfully pushed through the Confederate pickets, but soon discovered that Breckinridge's (Echols') Division was only a few miles away while Rodes and Ramseur were to the north. The Confederates counterattacked, spearheaded by Rodes, and after a struggle that proved costly for both sides, the Federals withdrew. A detachment of twenty sharpshooters from Thomas's Legion, under the command of 2nd Lt. Robert T.

---

of Washington about a mile ahead of Echols's position. Like a lot of Confederates, especially those writing years after the campaign, Stringfield claimed that he saw the unfinished capitol dome from his position, assertions that at least one scholar of the campaign doubts due to the local terrain and the smoke from the skirmishing (Cooling, *Jubal Early's Raid on Washington*, 123); however, as Stringfield's account was contemporary, it is possible that the site of the wagon park was of sufficient elevation and distance to view the building. It is probable that Stringfield's diary entry for July 11 was actually written on July 13 (or even later) as a "catch-up", as he mentioned the burning of the home of U.S. Postmaster Gen. Montgomery Blair, which did not occur until the Confederate withdrawal on the evening of July 12. Stringfield Diary (1864), July 6-11, Stringfield Papers, NCOAH; *O.R.* 37 (pt. 2): 259; Early, *Autobiographical Sketch and Narrative*, 395 n. *; Vandiver, *Jubal's Raid*, 172; Cooling, *Jubal Early's Raid on Washington*, 152.

424. *O.R.* 37 (pt. 1): 232-240, 242-244, 246-249, 253, 255-256, 259, 261-263, 276-277, 348-349, (pt. 2): 222-246, 257-258, 415-416; Early, *Autobiographical Sketch and Narrative*, 392-394; Vandiver, *Jubal's Raid*, 161-172; Cooling, *Jubal Early's Raid on Washington*, 135-153. For Johnson's raid and the unsuccessful effort to free the Confederate prisoners at Point Lookout, see *O.R.* 37 (pt. 1): 225, 229-230, 349; (pt. 2): 62, 175-177, 186, 192-193, 212-219, 247-255, 293, 295, 301; Johnson, "My Ride Around Baltimore In Eighteen Hundred and Sixty-Four," *SHSP* 30 (1902): 215-225; Cooling, *Jubal Early's Raid on Washington*, 157-176.

Conley of Company F, Infantry Regiment, were among the troops who participated in the fight. One soldier from Conley's company was reported killed in the clash. Conley was later cited for bravery for his role with the sharpshooters in this and other fights.[425]

Hearing of a strike by Averell from Martinsburg towards Winchester, Early withdrew his main body from the Shenandoah in the direction of Strasburg on the night of July 19. Ramseur was dispatched to block Averell. Ramseur's men were routed at Stephenson's Depot, between Bunker Hill and Winchester, on July 20; Averell, however, did not follow up his victory. On the same day, Wright and Crook crossed the river, but only advanced as far as Berryville before Wright broke off and started the Sixth Corps and the Nineteenth Corps detachment on a grueling return march to Washington, as Grant wanted them at Petersburg. Grant assumed that Early and the Second Corps would soon go to Petersburg themselves, so the Army of West Virginia was left to handle affairs in the Valley. Early pulled back to the area of Middletown on July 21, then withdrew southward across Cedar Creek the next day, covering the roads which led from Winchester. The army rested on July 23; the Legion's Infantry Regiment was sent out about noon on picket duty. Learning of Wright's withdrawal and the presence of Crooks's and Averell's forces at Kernstown, Early marched on the following day to strike them. He planned to pin the Federals in front with Breckinridge's Corps and Rodes's Division, while Ramseur slipped around their right flank and Ransom's cavalry were sent in two flanking columns on either side. If all worked well, the cavalry would unite in the Federal rear, while Ramseur rolled up the Federal right as Breckinridge and Rodes drove forward, entrapping Crook and Averell. According to Stringfield, the fighting began around 11 A.M. Early soon found that the Federal left was exposed to a potential flanking movement. He sent orders to Breckinridge for Echols's Division, now under Wharton again, to advance under cover of a series of ravines and attack. Wharton was successful, and the Federal left doubled up under the surprise assault. Early now ordered his other divisions to attack, and the Federal line collapsed. Unfortunately for Early, the cavalry failed to complete its mission, and the Federals were able to make their escape; nevertheless, the Confederates gobbled up some 200 to 300 prisoners. "Our command under Lt Col Love acted well," exulted Stringfield in his diary; "Breckinridges men all did well, as did all others." Based on the number of casualties, Thomas's Legion was either lightly engaged or was in reserve (although Early himself noted that the overall Confederate loss was "very slight"); only two privates from the Infantry Regiment were reported wounded in hospital the next day.[426]

425. *O.R.* 37 (pt. 1): 103, 113-114, 204-205, 249, 252, 270-275, 282-283, 285, 287-291, 295, 299-300, 319-321, 346, (pt. 2): 171-172, 246-247, 259-264, 266-272, 276-288, 291-295 301-305, 309-320, 322, 330-333, 336-344, 350-351, 354-356, 361, 367-372, 374, 392-393, 396, 400-401, 597; Early, *Autobiographical Sketch and Narrative*, 394-396; Stringfield Diary (1864), July 16, July 18, Stringfield Papers, NCOAH; service record file of John F. Beck, Thomas's Legion, Compiled Service Records of Confederate Soldiers from the State of North Carolina (M270), reel 567; Cooling, *Jubal Early's Raid on Washington*, 177-196, 199-202. "The Genl requests that you return to your officers and men his warm commendations for their patriotic conduct while with us, particularly Lieut R. T. Conley, whose coolness, steadiness, bravery and judgement upon the skirmish line deserves honorable mention." C. A. De Russy to Love, December 8, 1864, service record file of James R. Love, Thomas's Legion, Compiled Service Records of Confederate Soldiers from the State of North Carolina (M270), reel 570.

426. *O.R.* 37 (pt. 1): 249, 269-275, 282, 284-286, 292-296, 299, 300-302, 304-319, 323-324, 326-328, 330-331, 347, 353-354, (pt. 2): 350, 361, 366, 368, 380-381, 392-393, 395-399, 400-414, 417-424, 426, 428-431, 436,

Following their victory, the Confederates marched through Winchester to the acclaim of the pro-Confederate members of the population. Stringfield thought their reception "was the grandest & Most enthusiastic Sight I ever witnessed the entire populace greeted us most kindly. the Ladies beautiful indeed were all Smiles." They halted that night two miles beyond town, waiting for rations to be brought up. On July 25, Crook and the Army of West Virginia retreated through Bunker Hill and Martinsburg. Early rested his exhausted infantry, still without rations, and sent his cavalry in pursuit. By mid-afternoon he put the infantry on the march towards Bunker Hill, where the troops were finally fed. Crook recrossed the Potomac on July 26 and halted. That same day, Early's infantry crossed the Maryland border and moved to the vicinity of Martinsburg. Detachments from the army began wrecking the recently repaired track of the Baltimore & Ohio Railroad, continuing their work through July 27. The rest of the infantry rested through July 30, "enjoying it 'hugely,'", according to Stringfield. "This is the longest rest we've had Since we left 'Rock fish Gap.' this is very well for the Men need it." Others concurred. Capt. Stephen Whitaker of Company E, Walker's Battalion, wrote that the march from Lynchburg to Washington and back "has Kild many good soldiers[. O]ne of my Co[.,] Wm Henry he sank down with fatigue between Salam [Salem] & Staunton & soon dide[.] I saw many a Soldier Boy give out & fall down on the Rode Side[. T]his was coman all the way[.] I dont Know now how I stood it threw. I had to stop & wash the blood out of my socks more than once on the march[.]"[427]

The Federals were engaged in destructive activities of their own. Following his arrival, Hunter received orders from Grant via Halleck, requesting again that he move if possible on Gordonsville and Charlottesville to destroy the railroads there. Otherwise, Hunter "'should make all the valleys south of the Baltimore & Ohio road a desert as high up as possible. I do not mean that houses should be burned,'" Grant warned, "'but every particle of provisions and stock should be removed, and the people notified to move out.'" Hunter's men should "'eat out Virginia clear and clean as far as they go, so that crows flying over it for the balance of the season will have to carry their provender with them.'" Grant's intentions were clear: deny the Confederates their traditional use of the Shenandoah Valley as the breadbasket for Lee's army. Hunter, however, increasingly targeted civilian homes in the lower Valley, West Virginia and Maryland for wanton destruction during the middle and latter parts of July. While some of those whose homes were burnt may have been guilty of harboring

---

597-601; Early, *Autobiographical Sketch and Narrative*, 396-400 (quote, 400); Stringfield Diary (1864), July 19-24 (quote, July 24), Stringfield Papers, NCOAH; service record files of Samuel Ash and Thomas J. Hooper, Thomas's Legion, Compiled Service Records of Confederate Soldiers from the State of North Carolina (M270), reels 567 and 570; Cooling, *Jubal Early's Raid on Washington*, 203-206, 203-211; Gary W. Gallagher, *Stephen Dodson Ramseur: Lee's Gallant General* (Chapel Hill: University of North Carolina Press, 1985), 131-135. The circumstances and times of Echols's departure and Wharton's assumption of command are unknown. Echols was appointed commander of the Department of Western Virginia and East Tennessee during the fall. *O.R.* 43 (pt. 1): 864.

427. *O.R.* 37 (pt. 1): 260, 294-299, 302-304, 307-308, 310, 312-313, 315, 318, 328-329, 331, 347, (pt. 2): 409, 437-442, 451-456, 461-462, 464, 466-473, 476, 484-486, 489, 498-499, 600-601; Early, *Autobiographical Sketch and Narrative*, 400-402; Stringfield Diary (1864), July 25-30 (quotes, July 25 and 30 entries); Stephen Whitaker to James Whitaker, [August, 1864], Whitaker Papers, NCOAH; Cooling, *Jubal Early's Raid on Washington*, 211-213. Whitaker's letter is an undated fragment from a larger one; it is almost certainly a continuation of an August 5, 1864, letter to his father, found in the same collection. For the similarly dire effects on Federal troops of the endless marching and counter-marching, see Cooling, *Jubal Early's Raid on Washington*, 213-214.

Confederate guerrillas at times, many others were not. Coupled with Hunter's activities earlier in the campaign, his depredations aroused a vindictive spirit among the Confederates which contributed to the burning of Chambersburg, Pennsylvania, by McCausland's cavalry on July 30. During McCausland's raid, Breckinridge's Corps remained at Martinsburg while Early moved to Williamsport with Ramseur, Rodes, and Vaughn's cavalry; the horsemen of Imboden and Brig. Gen. William Lowther "Mudwall" Jackson demonstrated towards Harper's Ferry. On July 30, Early fell back with the rest of the infantry on Martinsburg, and on July 31 the army made what Stringfield described as a "leisurely" march to Darksville and Bunker Hill, where they halted for the night. Stringfield was dispatched with a hundred men on picket duty to cover the Leesburg road; they rejoined their command on the next day. Early's retreat was prompted by a sluggish advance by Hunter in the direction of Frederick. He was reinforced by Wright, who had been ordered to return. The Army of the Valley remained in the Bunker Hill-Darksville area through August 3, where Smith's Brigade was formally inspected. Early now prepared to cover McCausland's return. On August 4 he marched to the Potomac, crossing it the next day. Ramseur and Rodes crossed at Williamsport and halted at St. James's College, while Breckinridge moved via Shephardstown to Sharpsburg, where the men encamped on the same site as a month earlier; Vaughn's cavalry went to Hagerstown.[428]

The burning of Chambersburg was the culmination of a steady escalation of destruction of civilian property on both sides; coupled with the vandalism and torching of some homes in the Washington area by Early's men, it prompted an outcry in the North similar to that which Hunter's activities provoked in the South. Early's raids could not have come at a worst time for the Lincoln administration, which faced a grueling reelection campaign in November: with Grant and Lee deadlocked at Petersburg and Sherman's descent on Atlanta moving at a seeming snail's pace, the strikes against Washington and Chambersburg made the Union military effort look weak. The problem in the Valley lay with command and control: four different military departments had been concerned in one form or another with Early's incursion, with overlapping and contradictory responsiblities preventing a unified effort. Wright's presence added another element. There was also the distant role played by Grant, preoccupied with Petersburg, and the interference of Chief of Staff Henry W. Halleck and Secretary of War Edwin M. Stanton. In addition, there was Hunter's disappointing performance, and the general feeling on the part of everyone (except Grant) that there were insufficient troops to defend Washington and other important points in Maryland and Pennsylvania while fielding an army large enough to defeat Early. Finally realizing that Early was not returning to Lee, Grant saw the solution in a unified military command for the area at the operational level. After several suggestions for commander were rejected, Grant decided upon Sheridan. He was formally appointed on August 6, after Hunter asked to be relieved. The four departments were consolidated as the Middle Military Division. Crook was breveted to major general and assumed command of the Army of West Virginia infantry.

428. *O.R.* 37 (pt. 1): 188, 190, 270-275, 279, 281-282, 284-285, 331-337, 354-355, (pt. 2): 300-301 ("eat out Virginia clear" quote, 301 (also 366), 366 ("should make all the valleys" quote), 375, 378, 390, 394, 445-446, 451, 456-459, 474, 478-479, 482-483, 486-487, 489, 501, 506-508, 511-512, 516, 518-519, 523-528, 531-532, 564-565, 576-577, 584-586, 603-606, 43 (pt. 1): 567, 684-687, 1023, 51 (pt. 2): 1178; Early, *Autobiographical Sketch and Narrative*, 401, 404; Cooling, *Jubal Early's Raid on Washington*, 214-220.

Another division of the Nineteenth Corps joined the first, which with the Sixth Corps was retained for the campaign. Two divisions of Sheridan's cavalry from the Army of the Potomac were also added. The new force became known as the Army of the Shenandoah.[429]

Sheridan consolidated and reorganized his forces in preparation for implementing Grant's ideas for a campaign, outlined in a directive originally issued to Hunter on August 5. It brought together the essence of the scattered orders and suggestions that Grant had given over the past few weeks: contact must always be maintained with Early's forces; the Confederates must be driven permanently out of the Valley; and while civilian property must be protected, the Valley must be rendered incapable of subsisting Confederate forces. Even before Sheridan's arrival, Averell was in pursuit of McCausland and Johnson, driving them before him. The Confederate cavalry was defeated by Brig. Gen. Benjamin Franklin Kelley at Cumberland, Maryland, on August 1, and was routed by Averell at Moorefield, West Virginia, on August 7. Grant himself stepped in during the transition period, ordering the infantry forward from the area of Frederick and Monocacy Junction to Halltown, south of Harper's Ferry, in response to Early's latest move across the Potomac. The new Federal concentration prompted an immediate Confederate withdrawal back across the Potomac. Stringfield recorded in his diary how the Legion was rousted out of its camp at Sharpsburg on August 6 and marched in the direction of Hagerstown until about 11 A.M., when they suddenly turned in the direction of Williamsport. After recrossing the river, they camped a mile beyond town on the road to Martinsburg. "[R]ather a Short Stay of <u>two</u> <u>days</u> in Maryland," Stringfield noted with perplexity. "'Old Jube' (Early) knows what he is up to—no one else does." His frustration increased the next day when they returned to their old camp in the vicinity of Darksville "after a <u>four</u> <u>days</u> wild goose chase in Maryland. What next?" The answer to that question was over a month of maneuvering in the lower Valley by both armies. Although Sheridan's objective was to bring Early to battle as soon as possible, he had to exhibit some caution, particularly in the beginning as he awaited the arrival of his remaining troops and confronted rumors of Early's reinforcement by Longstreet's First Corps. For his part, Early had to withdraw in the face of Sheridan's greater strength, while at the same time dispersing his forces in such a way as to blind his opponent to his weaker numbers and his strategic intentions. When Sheridan moved forward, Early moved backward; if Sheridan pulled back in uncertainty over Early's next move, then the latter advanced.[430]

Early's immediate intentions were to cover Winchester from his position in the vicinity of Bunker Hill. The Legion was ordered from Darksville as part of this concentration on August 9, marching "in some haste" and arriving at Bunker Hill well before dark. Sheridan, however, plunged forward to Berryville on August 10, placing himself in a position to move

429. *O.R.* 36 (pt. 1): 29-30, 37 (pt. 1): 284, (pt. 2): 332-333, 337-341, 361, 365-366, 374, 377, 384-385, 400, 408, 413-414, 423-424, 426-427, 433-434, 438-439, 444-446, 458-459, 463, 475, 478, 482, 509-510, 558-559, 572-573, 582-583, 43 (pt. 1): 40, 681, 709, 711, 719, 723, 726; Cooling, *Jubal Early's Raid on Washington*, 183-184, 191-193, 196-199, 202, 205-208, 220-225; Jeffry D. Wert, *From Winchester to Cedar Creek: The Shenandoah Campaign of 1864* (Carlisle, Pa: South Mountain Press, 1987; paperback repr., New York: Touchstone, 1989), 6, 8-13, 16.

430. *O.R.* 36 (pt. 1): 29-30, 37 (pt. 1): 188-190, 329-331, 355-356, (pt. 2): 533-535, 540, 567-572, 577-580, 587-588, 590, 43 (pt. 1): 2-8, 40, 57-58, 551, 567-568, 686-710, 712-716, 720, 724-726, 731, 734-736, 990-991, 994, 1023-1024; Early, *Autobiographical Sketch and Narrative*, 404-405; Cooling, *Jubal Early's Raid on Washington*, 219-220, 224-225; Wert, *From Winchester to Cedar Creek*, 12.

beyond Early's right to Winchester and get into the Confederate rear. In response, Early pulled further back to cover the roads east and south of Winchester. Stringfield noted that the resumption of field operations did not prevent the execution of a deserter from the 22nd Regiment Virginia Infantry in Col. George S. Patton's Brigade in Wharton's Division, a sign that maintaining discipline was much on the minds of the army commanders. The Confederates endured a tense day, remaining in battle line until nightfall and expecting an attack after dark. On the following day, there was much skirmishing. Thomas's Legion was initially put in the line of battle, but then was marched through the fields (probably with other units from Smith's Brigade and Wharton's Division) on a route parallel to the Valley Pike on the east, covering the withdrawal of the army's supply train. They were then placed in battle line again, at a point which Stringfield estimated as about a half mile southeast of where the July 24 fight at Kernstown had begun. That night, the army encamped south of Winchester in the vicinity of Newtown. On August 12, the Legion was placed as part of a battle line about a half mile north of Newtown. Before the day was over, the army withdrew to a new position at Hupp's Hill, between Strasburg and Cedar Creek. The following day it continued its retreat to Fisher's Hill, a steep ridge which bisected the Valley and which, if properly defended from one end to another, would be impossible to capture. Throughout this phase there were sharp skirmishes between Early's forces and the suddenly more aggressive Federal horsemen. By now the Confederates were aware that Sheridan had taken command and that they were facing an enlarged Federal force. Nevertheless, confidence was still high. "[H]ere the Yanks dare not Come," wrote Stringfield. "[W]e are now far enough back."[431]

On August 14, Smith's Brigade, including Thomas's Legion, was out in front of the Army of the Valley as skirmishers. Sheridan kept the bulk of his army north of Cedar Creek as he mulled over reports of Confederate reinforcements. Lee, in fact, had dispatched help to Early under Maj. Gen. Richard H. Anderson, acting commander of the First Corps while Longstreet recuperated from a wound received at the Wilderness. The expedition consisted of Maj. Gen. Joseph B. Kershaw's infantry division, the cavalry division of Maj. Gen. FitzHugh Lee, and an artillery battalion. Sheridan stayed at Cedar Creek through August 16, deciding to withdraw back to Halltown, which he considered to be the most viable place for a defense. As they retreated, the Federals seized livestock and destroyed crops that might be of use to their opponents. The pursuit began August 17. Wharton's Division was in the lead on August 18 when it collided with the Federal rear guard in the vicinity of Kernstown and Winchester, quickly dispersing it and corralling 350 prisoners. Stringfield wrote after the war that the Infantry Regiment led the attack, accompanied by Breckinridge himself on foot. As the firing died down after dark, the Legion became separated from the Confederate line east of the Valley Pike. Following the capture of thirty Federal pickets, the Legion halted to the north of some fortifications, readjusted its line, and fell back, rejoining the army. By August 19 the Army of the Valley reached the Bunker Hill vicinity, where it rested a day while the cavalry skirmished. On August 21 the Confederates marched to Charlestown, West

431. *O.R.* 43 (pt. 1): 17-19, 40-42, 154-155, 360, 421-423, 568-569, 737, 739-741, 743-747, 760-761, 833, 991-997, 1000-1001, 1024; Early, *Autobiographical Sketch and Narrative*, 406-407; Stringfield Diary (1864), August 9-13 ("in some haste quote," August 9; "here the Yanks" quote, August 13), Stringfield Papers, NCOAH; Wert, *From Winchester to Cedar Creek*, 30-31.

Virginia. For the first time in days, Wharton's Division was in reserve, as the two sides skirmished; it is possible, however, that the Legion's sharpshooters under Conley participated. During the night, the Federals slipped away to Halltown. Sheridan's decision to withdraw was understandable given the political realities of the situation, as the Lincoln government could not afford a serious defeat; however, it managed to confuse both his own troops and Early. The latter misjudged Sheridan to be timorous and afterwards acted accordingly.[432]

On August 23, the armies rested; Stringfield had time to visit the site where John Brown was hanged in 1859. Sheridan tested Early's strength with a probe of the Confederate right flank the next day, which was repulsed. On August 25, Early acted on his assumption of Sheridan's mettle by faking another movement northward. Leaving Anderson's troops at Charlestown, he marched towards the Potomac. Wharton was in the lead, followed by Gordon, Rodes, and Ramseur. Near Leetown, the cavalry advance blundered into two divisions of Sheridan's horsemen. Thinking that the Confederate cavalry was all that was in their front, the Federals deployed and charged, pushing their foes back into the ambulance train which in turn threw Wharton's Division into confusion. Stringfield, who was divisional officer of the day, was in the road with Breckinridge, Wharton, and their attendant staffs when the fight suddenly erupted; the first inkling they had of the Federal presence was when an enemy battery suddenly opened up on the lane, causing a stampede among the officers which "would have seemed supremely ludicrous but for the perils of the moment." After being pushed back perhaps as much as a mile, Wharton steadied the division as Early brought up more of his infantry. Wharton deployed astride the road and to its left, with Rodes on his left and Gordon on his right. After a hard skirmish, the Confederates drove the Federals off and pursued them towards the river. The Federals made a stand at Shepherdstown, but the Legion did not participate in that clash. Stringfield recorded in his diary that the Legion lost 5 wounded at Leetown, while the division as a whole lost 20 killed and 75 wounded.[433]

The Army of the Valley remained near Shepherdstown on August 26. Stringfield doubted that it would cross the Potomac again, as Sheridan could easily slip past the

432. *O.R.* 43 (pt.1): 19-20, 42-45, 155-156, 360, 423-425, 516, 569-570, 1024-1025; Stringfield Diary (1864), August 14, August 16, August 18-22, Stringfield Papers, NCOAH; Early, *Autobiographical Sketch and Narrative*, 407-409, 415; *O.R. (Supplement)* Pt. I, 7:566-567; Stringfield, "Sixty-Ninth Regiment," in Clark, *North Carolina Regiments*, 3:751-752; Wert, *From Winchester to Cedar Creek*, 32-38, 45. The nativist Stringfield could not refrain from commenting in 1901 that the picket captured near Winchester on the night of August 18 was "Dutch or Hessian." Stringfield, "Sixty-Ninth Regiment," in Clark, *North Carolina Regiments*, 3:751.

433. Stringfield Diary (1864), August 23-25, Stringfield Papers, NCOAH; *O.R.* 43 (pt. 1): 20-21, 45, 98, 101-102, 425, 440, 473, 488, 517, 570-571, 905-906, 910-912, 1005-1006, 1025; Early, *Autobiographical Narrative and Sketch*, 409-410; Philip H. Sheridan, *Personal Memoirs of P. H. Sheridan, General United States Army*, 2 vols. (New York: Charles L. Webster & Co., 1888), 1: 493-494; Stringfield, "Sixty-Ninth Regiment," in Clark, *North Carolina Regiments*, 3:752 (quote); Wert, *From Winchester to Cedar Creek*, 38. Pvt. George W. Franklin of Company E, Infantry Regiment, is the only identifiable Thomas's Legion casualty from Leetown. According to the *Asheville News* of November 3, 1864, he was mortally wounded there. It is likely that 2nd Lt. Eli G. Ingram of Company H, Infantry Regiment, was also wounded at Leetown, although some of his hospital records indicate that he was wounded on or about August 15. Service record file for Eli G. Ingram, Thomas's Legion, Compiled Service Records of Confederate Soldiers from the State of North Carolina (M270), reel 570. In his 1901 account for Clark's *Regiments*, Stringfield wrote that the Confederates lost 25 men; he was probably referring to Wharton's Division only. According to Brig. Gen. James H. Wilson, commanding the Third Division of Sheridan's cavalry, his men captured 60 prisoners from Breckinridge's Corps. *O.R.* 43 (pt. 1): 517.

Confederates and get into their rear. His assessment was correct, as Early withdrew to Leetown on August 26-27; the Legion departed on the evening of the latter date. By August 28, the Confederates were back at Bunker Hill. Sheridan followed as far as Charlestown, and the armies settled down to occasional skirmishing. On September 2, Early marched towards Berryville, where a Federal presence had been detected. Wharton's Division occupied the middle of the infantry column, between the divisions of Gordon and Ramseur. Averell's cavalry routed Vaughn's horsemen in the rear, capturing several wagons of the supply train. Given the position of Wharton's Division in the column, it is unlikely that Thomas's Legion was involved in this affair, notwithstanding Stringfield's diary entry that the "Yankee cavalry run over us on the pike," probably meant as a comment on the day's action as a whole. The bulk of the Confederates thereafter about-faced and marched to Stephenson's Depot, where they halted for the night; Anderson's infantry and Lee's cavalry proceeded on to Berryville.[434]

Wharton's Division remained at Stephenson's Depot throughout the next day. Early initially decided to return to Bunker Hill, but in the end only Rodes's Division went, encountering Federal troops there. Ramseur deployed to cover the local roads, while Gordon marched to Winchester. Meanwhile, Anderson's men bumped into Crook's well-entrenched infantry at Berryville. The Confederates either drove the Federals from their outer works (according to Stringfield) or were repulsed with some loss to both sides (according to Sheridan). Early set out with Ramseur, Wharton, and Rodes that night, and found that Sheridan had constructed a defensive line stretching some eight miles northward from Berryville to Summit Point, a position roughly paralleling Limestone Ridge, Opequon Creek, and the Valley Pike to the west. Early probed the position and found it too strong, withdrawing across the Opequon to the line of the Valley Pike and concentrating at Stephenson's Depot. One member of the Legion was killed in the day's skirmishing and buried by the road. A stalemate lasted for the next eleven days, punctuated by occasional cavalry clashes and infantry skirmishes. On September 7, pickets from Wharton's Division were covering the Brucetown Road running north from the depot when they were attacked by a brigade of Federal cavalry. The rest of the division was called up and drove them back across Opequon Creek. It does not appear that the Legion was involved in any more actions during that period. It is known that Wharton's Division was moved back to Stephenson's Depot on September 13.[435]

434. Stringfield Diary (1864), August 27-28, August 31-September 2 (quote, September 2), Stringfield Papers, NCOAH; *O.R.* 43 (pt. 1): 21-23, 45-46, 85, 156, 425-426, 497, 571-572, 925, 934, 936-937, 961-962, 1007, 1025-1026, (pt. 2): 12-13, 861-862; Early, *Autobiographical Sketch and Narrative*, 410-411; Wert, *From Winchester to Cedar Creek*, 38. In his 1901 history, Stringfield specified that it was the Confederate cavalry that was routed. Stringfield, "Sixty-Ninth Regiment," in Clark, *North Carolina Regiments*, 3:753.

435. Stringfield Diary (1864), September 3-11, Stringfield Papers, NCOAH; *O.R.* 43 (pt. 1): 23-24, 46, 95, 156, 426-427, 490, 572-574, 1026, (pt. 2): 57, 77, 80, 863-864, 868, 871, 875; Early, *Autobiographical Sketch and Narrative*, 411-413; Wert, *From Winchester to Cedar Creek*, 38-39. According to Stringfield's diary, the soldier killed on September 5 was Pvt. Ephraim S. Connor of Company F, Infantry Regiment. He may have been killed as part of Lieutenant Conley's detachment of sharpshooters on the skirmish line; Stringfield noted that the latter had been deployed in his September 4 entry. Stringfield was absent sick from September 12 through September 28, and as his diary is the primary source for information on Thomas's Legion for this period, it is possible that it might have participated in minor skirmishing that went unrecorded. Federal sources cited in the *Official Records*

At this point, Sheridan's intelligence brought him crucial information: Anderson had departed for Petersburg with Kershaw's Division and the artillery that had come with him. The Federal commander decided to strike for Early's line of communications in the vicinity of Newtown. The timing could not have been more providential for Sheridan: political pressure had been steadily building in Washington over the possible impact on the operations of the Baltimore & Ohio Railroad that the continuing Confederate presence posed. On September 16, the same day that Sheridan received confirmation of Anderson's departure and began drawing up his plans, he heard that Grant wanted to meet with him at Charlestown. Although Grant had supported Sheridan in his hitherto cautious approach to committing to a major battle, he was beginning to lose patience. Sherman's capture of Atlanta on September 2 had greatly boosted morale on the Northern home front, and showed that Grant's overall strategy was beginning to work; however, with the main eastern armies stalemated at Petersburg, there was a need for a victory of some sort in the region. Grant was pleased with Sheridan's decision to act, and authorized him to put his plan into motion. An even better opportunity presented itself when Averell brought fresh news on September 18. Early had moved north with Rodes, Gordon, and Jackson on September 17, leaving Ramseur to cover Winchester and Wharton to guard Bunker Hill. Early's target was Martinsburg, where repair parties were reported at work on the railroad. While the objective was worthwhile, the choice of military arms was not: Early had left half of his infantry to face Sheridan's combined force. This decision was later widely criticized by participants in the campaign and by historians, as the cavalry alone would have been better employed for such a purpose. Early distrusted his horsemen, however. Part of this seems to have lain with his own irascible personality, and part with the dislike and contempt that many infantrymen had for cavalry; furthermore, Early did not really seem to understand how cavalry should be properly used. At the same time, the cavalry units he inherited at the start of the campaign were a mixed lot, poorly disciplined and in many ways poorly led. Ransom was an ineffective cavalry commander, perhaps in part due to illness, and had been replaced by Fitzhugh Lee. The latter had brought with him some cavalry brigades from the Army of Northern Virginia, and these were of better quality; still, Early did not really feel confident in them, either. Furthermore, his growing contempt for Sheridan's abilities probably played a factor in his taking the risk. Regardless, by utilizing half his remaining infantry on a minor mission, Early placed his army in a very vulnerable position.[436]

Sheridan quickly shifted his plans, deciding to strike at Winchester and destroy Ramseur's and Wharton's Divisions on the following day. Early, meanwhile, reached

---

reported a skirmish with pickets from Breckinridge's Corps along Opequon Creek on September 13, in which some Confederates were captured; it would appear that Wharton's Division was involved. Pvt. Elihu Chambers, a drummer from Company C, Infantry Regiment, was captured at Leetown on that date according to Federal provost marshal records; as Leetown lay on the eastern side of the Opequon, however, it is possible that he was captured under different circumstances. Service record file of Elihu Chambers, Thomas's Legion, Compiled Service Records of Confederate Soldiers from the State of North Carolina (M270), reel 568.

436. Sheridan, *Personal Memoirs*, 2:1-10; *O.R.* 36 (pt. 1): 30, 34, 43 (pt. 1): 46, 554, 573, (pt. 2): 83-84, 95, 102, 106, 873-876; *O.R. (Supplement)* Pt. I, 7:570, 604; Early, *Autobiographical Sketch and Narrative*, 414-416, 419; Wert, *From Winchester to Cedar Creek*, 24-25, 39-45; Robert K. Krick, "'The Cause of All My Disasters': Jubal A. Early and the Undisciplined Valley Cavalry," in Gary W. Gallagher, ed., *Struggle for the Shenandoah: Essays on the 1864 Valley Campaign* (Kent, OH: The Kent State University Press), 77-106.

Martinsburg on September 18. At the telegraph office, he learned that Grant had been up to see Sheridan. "Old Jube" realized immediately that the visit indicated an imminent Federal advance, and hurried his troops back. Rodes arrived at Stephenson's Depot that evening, while Gordon reached Bunker Hill. Thus, Early's position was not as bad as it could have been; nevertheless, the hasty circumstances of his return and the lack of knowledge as to Sheridan's exact intentions meant that the Confederates were not concentrated to the best advantage. Given Sheridan's edge in numbers, Early was in a difficult position.[437]

Sheridan's plan called for an advance towards Winchester across Opequon Creek along the Berryville Pike, which ran through a two-mile defile west of the stream called the Berryville Canyon. Brig. Gen. James H. Wilson's Third Cavalry Division would secure the ravine, followed by the Sixth Corps and the Nineteenth Corps under Wright; the Army of West Virginia would be in reserve. If all went well, the Federals would push rapidly across the stream and through the canyon, deploy, rout Ramseur, and wheel northward, destroying Early's remaining divisions as they arrived piecemeal. Averell's Second Cavalry Division, which had followed Early back down the Valley Pike from Martinsburg, was ordered to continue driving southward, while Brig. Gen. Wesley Merritt's First Cavalry Division would cross the Opequon north of Winchester at Locke's and Sevier's Fords, unite with Averell, and strike the Confederate rear.[438] Wilson advanced on schedule and engaged Ramseur's nearest brigade, poorly deployed far from the streambank on the west side of the gorge. The chance for a decisive Federal victory soon bogged down in Berryville Canyon, which proved to narrow for both the Sixth and Nineteenth Corps, together with their ammunition wagons and artillery, to pass through quickly. As a result, Ramseur had time to bring up his other brigades while Early sent Rodes and Gordon to the battlefront. It was not until the late forenoon that the Federal infantry were fully deployed and the main attack began. Both sides suffered heavy casualties; among the slain was Rodes.[439]

Thomas's Legion did not take part in this action. Early had left Wharton's Division and an artillery battalion to support McCausland's cavalry, which was watching the fords. Breckinridge, reduced to a de facto division commander for the action, sent the brigades of Smith and Col. Augustus Forsberg to Locke's Ford, the furthest north of the crossings, to

437. Sheridan, *Personal Memoirs*, 2: 10-11; Early, *Autobiographical Sketch and Narrative*, 419-420; *O.R.* 43 (pt. 1): 149, 454, 573-574, (pt. 2): 119; Wert, *From Winchester to Cedar Creek*, 44-45. The exact numbers of the Army of the Valley at this time are unknown. An inspection report dated August 31 showed 7,684 effective for duty in the divisions of Rodes, Gordon, and Ramseur, as well as 802 artillerymen, for a total effective of 8,486 in the units reported. Wharton's Division showed an aggregate present of 503 for Patton's Brigade and 638 for Forsberg's (Wharton's) Brigade; how many of those were present effective is not known. There were no figures for Smith's Brigade, which included Thomas's Legion, or for the cavalry. As the August 31 figures would not include more recent absences and returns to the ranks, estimates that the infantry numbered somewhere between 8,000 and 12,000, and that the army as whole was about 18,000, are probably accurate, and may be a bit high. *O.R.* 43 (pt. 1): 1011; Roger U. Delauter and Brandon H. Beck, *Early's Valley Campaign: The Third Battle of Winchester*, The Virginia Civil War Battles and Leaders Series (Lynchburg: H. E. Howard, 1997), 11.

438. *O.R.* 43 (pt. 1): 46-47, 361, 443, (pt. 2): 102-107; Sheridan, *Personal Memoirs*, 2:11-14. For secondary accounts, see Wert, *From Winchester to Cedar Creek*, 47-107; Delauter and Beck, *Third Battle of Winchester.*

439. Sheridan, *Personal Memoirs*, 2: 18-19; *O.R.* 43 (pt. 1): 47, 149-150, 279-280, 361, 554-555; Early, *Autobiographical Sketch and Narrative*, 420-423; Wert, *From Winchester to Cedar Creek*, 47-70; Delauter and Beck, *Third Battle of Winchester*, 27-31, 34-47.

protect the route to Brucetown; Patton's Brigade was sent to Sevier's Ford, covering the direct approach to Stephenson's Depot. The Legion went into action under Lieutenant Colonel McKamy of Walker's Battalion, as Love was sick in the hospital. Merritt had already pushed across the fords and was engaged with McCausland by the time Wharton's infantry arrived. Forsberg deployed behind some earthworks about a mile from Locke's Ford and sent skirmishers to support the cavalry, while Patton took position behind a line of works near Sevier's Ford. Smith's Brigade was deployed to the right of Forsberg but some distance back and closer to Brucetown; later in the morning, Breckinridge pulled Forsberg back so that he was more closely aligned with Smith. The Confederates threw up makeshift works for protection. The Federal cavalry made no real effort to drive off Breckinridge, with the exception of Brig. Gen. George Armstrong Custer. At about 11 o'clock, he sent his First Brigade of the First Division against Forsberg and Smith, but was repulsed.[440]

Further south, by the early afternoon Early had committed all of his available infantry against the Sixth and Nineteenth Corps. He decided to pull Wharton's Division to the main battle east of Winchester, leaving his cavalry to hold off their counterparts. Upon arrival about 2:00 P.M., Wharton was placed to the right of Ramseur's Division. Meanwhile, Averell and Merritt had united and driven the Confederate cavalry through Stephenson's Depot. To face this threat, Wharton's Division was shifted north and placed in the rear of the main Confederate line astride the Valley Pike to watch for the cavalry; it is not known for certain where Smith's Brigade was positioned. About this time, Crook attacked the Confederate left flank, held by Gordon, slowly bending it back until it came into line next to Wharton. By 5:00 the Confederate infantry was massed in an inverted "L"-shaped position, with Wharton's and Gordon's Divisions north of Winchester, and Rodes's (under Brig. Gen. Bryan Grimes) and Ramseur's Divisions facing east. The Sixth Corps mounted another attack against Ramseur and Grimes, while Crook drove against Gordon and Wharton again. By now the Federal cavalry had arrived. A massive mounted charged was launched which overlapped and broke Wharton's and Gordon's Divisions. This collapse uncovered the rear of Rodes's and Ramseur's Divisions. Although Grimes managed to change his division's front toward the north to meet the threat, Early's position was untenable. Ramseur's Division, having more time to adjust to the situation due to its position in the line, covered the retreat of the rest of the army. The Confederates halted for the night in the vicinity of Newtown.[441]

440. *O.R.* 43 (pt. 1): 427, 443-444, 454-456, 462, 490, 555, (pt. 2): 112-113; Lafayette George to Rachel George, September 18, 1864, RD 1474, CWRP; Early, *Autobiographical Sketch and Narrative*, 424; Wert, *From Winchester to Cedar Creek*, 71-76; Delauter and Beck, *Third Battle of Winchester*, 31-34.

441. *O.R.* 43 (pt. 1): 47, 150, 280-281, 361-362, 427-428, 444-445, 456-458, 482, 490, 555, (pt. 2): 876; *O.R. (Supplement)* Pt. I, 7:601-602; Early, *Autobiographical Sketch and Narrative*, 424-428; Wert, *From Winchester to Cedar Creek*, 76-98; Delauter and Beck, *Third Battle of Winchester*, 48-70. In Stringfield's history of the Infantry Regiment, he stated that the Legion was on the left flank of Early's army, "holding a large force in check, while most of our division had been sent to repel the final assault upon our centre." Although most of Wharton's Division had been in support of the main Confederate center for a while, it did not play a role in the final fighting in that sector, as it was shifted to to the north. Stringfield may have intended to place the Legion's position at the far left of Early's line, in either the Star Fort, a fortification north of Winchester to the west of the Martinsburg Pike; or in Fort Collier, an earthwork near the end of Wharton's sector. There is no evidence that the Legion was in either position, however, and it is known that dismounted Confederate cavalry occupied the Star Fort while artillery were placed in Fort Collier. In his memoirs, Early specified that Patton's Brigade (not Smith's) was

Although exact figures are impossible to derive, it would appear that the losses of Thomas's Legion at Winchester were almost as severe as at Piedmont, even though it was not fully engaged for much of the day. Hospital records, Federal provost marshal records, and newspaper accounts suggest that the Legion suffered at least 75 casualties: 6 killed or mortally wounded, 16 wounded, and 53 captured, of which 9 of the latter were also wounded. At least one of the wounded was permanently disabled for future service, having an arm amputated. Of the captured, 2 escaped and rejoined their units, while 8 (not counting those who were mortally wounded when they fell into Federal hands) died in captivity. Twenty-six prisoners were exchanged, but in most cases not until February or March 1865, and it is unknown whether any returned to service; regardless, they were lost for the rest of the Valley campaign. In his diary entry for the following day, Stringfield also reported that the Legion lost 75 men. Love, however, wrote at the end of the month that the Legion's entire losses during September, which would have included other actions, were 71. Although the majority of the Legion's casualties were in the Infantry Regiment, the most serious damage was done to Walker's Battalion because of its already-dimished size. Among the captured was McKamy, leaving the Legion leaderless until either Stringfield or Love returned to duty; one of the remaining company captains probably exercised command in the interim.[442]

---

placed on the left, while the remaining brigades of the division were placed "in the centre, in order to be moved to any point that might be attacked"; in his wartime account of the battle (dated October 9, 1864), he stated that he placed Wharton on the right of Ramseur initially before moving it to this position. Early's language in his posthumously published memoir closely echoed that of another account published by him just after the war: "When Wharton's division arrived, Patton's brigade of that division was placed on the left to aid Fitz Lee in guarding the Martinsburg road, against the force of cavalry which was advancing on that road watched by Lomax's two small brigades; and the rest of the division was formed in the rear of Rodes' division in the centre in order to be moved to any point that might be attacked." The parallels between Early's phrasing and Stringfield's are very striking, with the exception of Patton's Brigade on the left instead of the Legion. As Stringfield was absent sick and did not participate in the battle, he likely used Early's account as a model for his own, with the Legion taking the role actually played in the battle by Patton's Brigade. Although the possibility cannot be ruled out that the Legion was detached from Smith's Brigade and sent to the left flank, it is unclear what so small a force could have been expected to accomplish unless it was temporarily assigned to Patton. There is no known wartime evidence to confirm that such was the case, especially as Smith's small brigade would be further diminished. Regardless, Stringfield wrote that when the Federal cavalry charged, the Legion was pushed backward, "losing, however, no wagons and only two cannon. Our men fought like heroes, deploying and fighting as in squad drill and holding the enemy in check till Early could bring back his infantry line; but for this dare-devil spirit shown by our men, and their utter refusal to surrender, great damage would have resulted." The problem with this statement is that, of course, "great damage" *did* result; the evidence from both Federal and Confederate sources is that Wharton's and Gordon's line broke up pretty quickly when the cavalry struck. While Early's memoirs indicated that Breckinridge repulsed the horsemen when he repositioned to the north, and again shortly afterwards, Breckinridge instead was occupied fighting Crook's infantry prior to the cavalry charge. It is possible that Early might have been thinking of Patton's Brigade, which did help slow the Federal horsemen as they approached from the north. Stringfield, "Sixty-Ninth Regiment," in Clark, *North Carolina Regiments*, 3:753-754; Early, *Autobiographical Sketch and Memoir*, 424; *O.R.* 43 (pt. 1): 555; Jubal Early, *A Memoir of the Last Year of the War for Independence in the Confederate States of America Consisting of An Account of the Operations of his Command in the Years 1864 and 1865* (Lynchburg: Charles W. Button, 1867), 88-89; Wert, *From Winchester to Cedar Creek*, 84-96; Delauter and Beck, *Third Battle of Winchester*, 62-66, 69 (who argue without any details that Wharton repulsed the cavalry three times during the final assault).

442. Four of the mortally wounded fell into Federal hands, thus making the total number of captured 57. In addition, the hospital records of Pvt. Calvin Duncan of Company K, Infantry Regiment, who was paralyzed from

Similar losses pervaded the army as a whole. On October 9, Early placed his total losses among the infantry and artillery at 3,611, with 226 killed, 1,567 wounded, and 1,818 missing; many of the latter who were not captured eventually found their way back to the army in the succeeding weeks. In the army's official casualty tally, compiled a few days earlier, Wharton's Division was recorded as losing 23 killed and 194 wounded for a total of 217 casualties, the least loss among any of Early's divisions. This was undoubtedly due to the very limited role that the division played early in the battle. Six regiments of Wharton's Division lost their colors, however, an indication of how suddenly the division fell apart in the face of the cavalry assault. Overall Federal casualties were even heavier. Returns reported 697 men killed, 3,983 wounded, and 338 captured and missing for a total of 5,018 casualties. The Army of the Valley also lost three brigadier generals and two division commanders, Rodes and Fitzhugh Lee, the latter wounded and knocked out of the campaign. In addition, Early lost Breckinridge two days after the battle when orders were received sending him back to his post as commander of the Department of Southwest Virginia. Although Breckinridge was needed to provide leadership and direction in that area, which was soon enlarged to include eastern Tennessee, it could not have come at a worst time for Early.[443]

The retreat continued on the day after the battle. Early organized a defensive line on Fisher's Hill. His forces were greatly weakened, and he did not deploy the troops to their best advantage, stretching his thinned-out infantry the entire length of the ridge, even at steep areas where a Federal assault would be very difficult or impossible. The latter was especially true of the far right, where Early placed Wharton's Division. Next was Gordon's Division, followed by Ramseur's Division, now commanded by Brig. Gen. John Pegram, and Rodes's old division, now commanded by Ramseur, who had formerly served in that division as a brigadier general. The left wing was anchored by a dismounted portion of the cavalry, which had been roughly handled by Sheridan's horsemen at Winchester and were now without the leadership of Fitzhugh Lee. They covered the lowest ground on the ridge,

---

a shot in the back and died later in October, suggests that he might also have been wounded at Third Winchester; however, it also possible that he was injured at Fisher's Hill or in the subsequent skirmishing as Early withdrew up the Valley. The 1902 pension application of Pvt. Jesse Taylor of Company H, Walker's Battalion, reported that he was shot in the right side of his stomach at Winchester; however, it is unclear whether this was supposed to have occurred at Third Winchester or in one of the other clashes in that area during the late summer and early fall. Stringfield did not return to duty until September 28; Love returned to duty by September 30, when he wrote Captain Whitaker of Company E, Walker's Battalion, in relation to the Legion's casualties in the recent fighting. Love specified that his figure of 71 included the "killed, wounded, & captured" at Third Winchester, Fisher's Hill, and New Market (the latter refers to the skirmishing after Fisher's Hill). Service records files, Thomas's Legion, Compiled Service Records of Confederate soldiers from the State of North Carolina (M270), reels 567 through 574; *Western Democrat* (Charlotte), October 25, 1864; *Asheville News*, November 3, 1864; Love to Stephen Whitaker, September 30, 1864, Whitaker Papers, NCOAH; Civil War Pension Application for Jesse Taylor (1902), Applications for Pension after 1901, Records of the North Carolina State Auditor's Office, NCOAH; Stringfield Diary (1864), September 28, Stringfield Papers, NCOAH.

443. *O.R.* 39 (pt. 2): 877, 43 (pt. 1): 555, 557, 574, 590, (pt. 2): 110-111, 864-877, 43 (pt. 1); 25, 59-60, 112-119; Early, *Autobiographical Sketch and Narrative*, 429-430. Separate figures were not reported for the Confederate cavalry's losses at Third Winchester, but instead for the month of September as a whole. Wert, *From Winchester to Cedar Creek*, 103, believed that it was possible that as many as 200 of the 348 reported cavalry casualties may have been lost at Third Winchester, making Early's losses in killed and wounded as between 1,900 and 2,000, approximately 15% of the Army of the Valley's strength.

and therefore the area most vulnerable to attack; their position lay in wooded ground which limited their visibility of the enemy forces in their immediate front.[444]

The Army of the Shenandoah reached the Strasburg area by the end of the day. At a council of war, Sheridan adopted a proposal by Crook to flank the Confederates by crossing Little North Mountain on the northern end of the line; unbeknownst to the Federals, if successful this would bring Crook's infantry down right on top of Early's cavalry at the weakest section of the line. Sheridan also sent part of his cavalry towards Front Royal in an effort to sweep around behind Early and cut off his retreat. During the next day, the infantry skirmished as the Federals sought to get a clearer view of the enemy strength and the terrain.[445]

On September 22, the skirmishing continued as Crook got into position. The authors of at least two Confederate post-battle sources claimed to have seen the Army of West Virginia infantry filing across the mountainside. If true, it would appear that either the news was not properly brought to Early's attention or that he inexcusably failed to act upon it. Regardless, Crook's movement was successful. His men charged into the surprised Confederate cavalry, which quickly mounted and fled. Simultaneously, the Sixth and Nineteenth Corps attacked in front. Although Ramseur redeployed to face Crook, it was too little too late, and the Confederate battle line collapsed. Early's mapmaker, Jedediah Hotchkiss, brought Wharton's Division over from the far right to protect the Valley Turnpike, but the main Confederate battle line had already withdrawn and the division had just gotten into position on the turnpike when it became the focus of Federal artillery. Wharton's Division now broke in turn and joined the rout. As night fell, various officers managed to throw together isolated groups of soldiers and artillery pieces to slow the Federal advance. Wharton managed to rally some of his men and placed them parallel to the pike, where they were able to offer some resistance. A rearguard was assembled from elements of Wharton's Division at Tom's Brook, which repulsed an enemy attack; Hotchkiss specifically mentioned Smith's Brigade in connection with this action. Darkness allowed the remaining Confederates to slip away. Many were captured, and Early also lost much of his artillery, which was overrun before it could be withdrawn. Not everything went the Sheridan's way, however; the Federal cavalry expedition accomplished nothing, and Early was able to retire.[446]

The pursuit continued throughout the night before petering out on the next day. The Federal cavalry vanguard under Averell and Bvt. Brig. Gen. Thomas C. Devin failed to press the Confederate rearguard of Ramseur and Wharton at Mount Jackson, resulting in Averell's sacking by an unforgiving Sheridan. After dark, the Confederates took up position on Rude's Hill. On September 24, the rest of the Federal army straggled up, and found Early drawn up in line of battle. Wharton's and Ramseur's Divisions formed the front line, with

444. *O.R.* 43 (pt. 1): 556, (pt. 2): 877; Early, *Autobiographical Sketch and Narrative*, 429; Wert, *From Winchester to Cedar Creek*, 107-111.

445. *O.R.* 43 (pt. 1): 25-26, 47-48, 152, 282, 428, 574, (pt. 2): 110-114, 118, 121-122, 137-138; Wert, *From Winchester to Cedar Creek*, 107-108, 111-115.

446. *O.R.* 43 (pt. 1): 26-28, 48, 153, 282-283, 363-364, 428, 556-557, 574-575, 611, 1028, (pt. 2): 135-136, 142, 152, 156, 162; Pulaski Cowper, compiler, *Extract of Letters of Major-General Bryan Grimes to His Wife, Written While in Active Service in the Army of Northern Virginia. Together With Some Personal Recollections of the War, Written By Him After Its Close, Etc.*; reprint ed. by Gary W. Gallagher (Raleigh: Alfred Williams & Co., 1884; reprt., Wilmington: Broadfoot Publishing Company, 1986), 69; Wert, *From Winchester to Cedar Creek*, 117-132.

Wharton on the left; Gordon and Pegram were in position behind them. Sheridan sent cavalry columns on either side to flank the position, while his artillery opened up briefly. Early pulled back in the leap-frogging pattern he had used after Third Winchester, with brigades successively alternating between manning the battle line and retreating. This method kept the Federals at bay while the Confederates withdrew through New Market, where they halted in line of battle until after dark. The Confederates then resumed their retreat. Wharton's Division followed Ramseur's and Gordon's in the line of march and preceded Pegram's. At midnight the infantry stopped to rest. On the following day they continued on through Port Republic to Brown's Gap in the Blue Ridge Mountains.[447]

The news of Early's defeats alarmed the Confederate authorities. Lee sent Kershaw's Division back to the Valley, although Anderson continued on to Petersburg. Kershaw linked up with Early on the morning of September 26 at Brown's Gap. During the day, the Confederates and Federals skirmished, Wharton's Division acting in support of Ramseur's. On September 27, the Confederates drove the Federal cavalry back in the vicinity of Port Republic; on this occasion, Wharton's Division was in support of Pegram's. Sheridan, meanwhile, did not press his pursuit further. Halting his infantry at Harrisonburg, he unleashed his troops to fulfill another part of Grant's command: rendering the Shenandoah Valley unfit for the future sustenance of Confederate forces. A nasty side war with local Confederate guerrilla bands erupted in the process. Early, his army in no shape for a full-scale battle, traveled in the opposite direction, hoping to disrupt enemy cavalry operations against the railroad running from Staunton through Waynesboro and Rockfish Gap to Charlottesville. After some delays, the Confederates set out on September 28 in two columns. The supply trains went by way of the South River, with Ramseur in the lead and Pegram and Wharton following the wagons, while Kershaw and Gordon escorted the artillery through Piedmont and New Hope. The army encamped near Waynesboro. On the following day the Confederates moved southwest of Waynesboro and began to repair the damaged railroad bridges, while the Federal cavalry withdrew, burning crops and barns as they went. The Confederates remained near Waynesboro through September 30. On October 1, Early turned northward again to be closer to Sheridan's forces at Harrisonburg. The object of Early's new concentration was Mount Sidney. Wharton's and Ramseur's Divisions marched via New Hope. Early remained in the vicinity of Mount Sidney through October 5.[448]

During this period, the Army of the Valley attempted to recuperate from the blows it had received. In the wake of Third Winchester and Fisher's Hill, Early was widely criticized in the press and by the Confederate public. He in turn placed much of the blame on his cavalry, although not surprisingly he neglected to fault himself for the bad deployment at Fisher's Hill. He promised Lee, however, to do what he could with what he had available. Lee tried to be encouraging, but it was obvious from his messages that he had no real idea of

447. *O.R.* 43 (pt. 1): 27-29, 49, 156-157, 499-500, 505, 556, 576-577, (pt. 2): 158, 163, 170-172, 209; Early, *Autobiographical Sketch and Narrative*, 432-433; Wert, *From Winchester to Cedar Creek*, 129-130, 132-134.

448. *O.R.* 43 (pt. 1): 29-30, 49-50, 157, 556, 576-578, 1028-1029, (pt. 2): 181-182, 197, 200-203, 209-210, 217, 219-220, 249-250, 878, 51 (pt. 2): 1041; *O.R. (Supplement)* Pt. I, 7:571, 604-605; Early, *Autobiographical Sketch and Narrative*, 433-435; Wert, *From Winchester to Cedar Creek*, 134, 157-158. For discussions of Sheridan's conflict with John Mosby and other Confederate partisans and guerrillas, see Wert, *From Winchester to Cedar Creek*, 145-156; Jeffry D. Wert, *Mosby's Rangers* (New York: Simon & Schuster, 1990), 187-272.

the seriousness of Early's setbacks, the condition of the Army of the Valley, or the size of Sheridan's force. Lee blithely averred that all Early needed was just one victory to restore Confederate success to the Valley. In the meantime, he could offer no more infantry, as he was stretched to the limit at Petersburg. To Early's request that Hampton be sent with the Army of Northern Virginia's cavalry, Lee sent instead only one mounted brigade under Brig. Gen. Thomas Rosser, and according to Early it was in a jaded condition.[449]

The Army of the Valley was inspected on September 29 and 30. Smith's Brigade reported the loss of all field officers except for Smith and one lieutenant colonel; this statement was meant to include Thomas's Legion, which as "the command of Lieutenant-Colonel Love" was mentioned (although Stringfield and Love had returned to duty by this point). The brigade was worn out and the company and regimental organizations were in disarray. The strength of the brigade had been reduced to "but little over 400 aggregate effective"; how much of this number belonged to the Legion is unknown. Love noted on September 30 that the Legion had lost 71 killed, wounded, and captured during the month. In mid-October he told Breckinridge that he had entered the campaign with 390 men but had lost 16 commissioned officers and 135 enlisted men at Piedmont and Winchester; as it is uncertain whether the 390 included officers, and Love did not figure in casualties from other engagements or returns to the ranks, it is possible that the Legion had been cut roughly in half before Fisher's Hill, and was now probably much smaller. Besides losses due to combat, desertion further sapped the strength of the Legion and other units in the army. On October 1, the acting Federal provost marshal for the Middle Military Division reported that there were about a thousand Confederate stragglers scattered between Strasburg and Harrisonburg. Some were banding together with or rounding up Federal stragglers (the exact wording is a bit unclear) and organizing into guerrilla bands. The source of the information was described as "a rebel deserter from the Thomas (North Carolina) Legion." Not everyone was willing to give up, however. Love wrote that "the men are again in good spirits, & the hope is entertained that we will soon drive the enemy again from the valley."[450]

449. *O.R.* 43 (pt. 1): 557-559, (pt. 2): 880-881, 893-898; Early, *Autobiographical Sketch and Narrative*, 435; Wert, *From Winchester to Cedar Creek*, 136-140.

450. *O.R.* 43 (pt. 1): 595-596 ("the command of Lieutenant-Colonel Love" quote), (pt. 2): 250 ("rebel deserter" quote); Love to Stephen Whitaker, September 30, 1864, Whitaker Papers, NCOAH; Love to "Dear Genl" (Breckinridge), October 15, 1864, Stringfield Papers, WCU. For a discussion of the Army of the Valley's condition at this time, see Theodore C. Mahr, *Early's Valley Campaign: The Battle of Cedar Creek: Showdown in the Shenandoah October 1-30, 1864*, The Virginia Civil War Battles and Leaders Series (Lynchburg: H. E. Howard, Inc., 1992), 9-20, 79-80. Stringfield wrote after the war that the Legion was reduced "to only 150 men." According to inspection reports for Wharton's Division, on September 29 Smith's Brigade had 416 officers and men present effective for the field out of an aggregate present for duty of 457, an aggregate present of 632, and an aggregate present and absent of 1,494 (prisoners of war not included). The total for Wharton's Division was 1,091 present effective for duty. The totals for the Army of the Valley were 6,291 infantry and artillerymen effective for the field, with 35 artillery pieces; there was no report for the cavalry. Sheridan reported at the end of September that the total strength for the Middle Military Division was 74,233 officers and men present for duty, but only a portion would have been in the field against Early. Mahr estimated that Early's strength at the time of the battle of Cedar Creek on October 19 was approximately 9,500 to 10,000 infantry, around 2,000 cavalry, and 1,091 artillerymen with 34 guns, while Sheridan had around 22,254 infantry, 7,500 cavalry, 1,214 artillerymen with 60 guns, and 642 horse artillerymen with 30 guns. Stringfield, "Sixty-Ninth Regiment," in Clark, *North Carolina Regiments* 3:755; *O.R.* 43 (pt. 2): 248, 882-883; Mahr, *The Battle of Cedar Creek*, 367-372.

On October 5, Sheridan began withdrawing northward from the Harrisonburg front. Grant had wanted Sheridan to implement his old objectives of a march on Charlottesville, followed by the destruction of the Virginia Central Railroad and James & Kanawha Canal as he moved eastward, cutting off Richmond from supply. Sheridan, however, did not want to take that route, much as he had been reluctant in May to follow it in the opposite direction to link up with Hunter. Offering one excuse after another regarding the supply problems of sustaining the Army of the Shenandoah, while arguing that Early's command was finished as an effective fighting force, he prevailed on a reluctant Grant to allow him to complete the devastation of the Confederacy's food supplies in the region; in the meantime, his army would be supplied via the Manassas Gap Railroad through Front Royal. Afterwards, the army could be disbanded and its respective units sent to other theaters of operation as needed. Early followed Sheridan on October 6, although he was unable to prevent the Federals from carrying out the destruction of crops, barns, mills, and other structures and property which might support the Confederate war effort. Although orders forbade the wanton destruction of houses, many soldiers disobeyed and took advantage of the situation to loot or vandalize, as had happened when Hunter was in command. The effects on the livelihood and the sustenance of the locals was severe, and many civilians were forced by necessity to leave their homes and the Valley behind. It would be many years before the area would recover. "It would make your heart sad, and if possible a better Confederate, to witness the vandalism of the enemy in this Valley," Lieutenant Colonel Love wrote to the editors of the *Asheville News*.[451]

Although Early was unable to halt the destruction, his lurking presence was certainly felt by Sheridan. Gordon's Division led the march northward, followed by those of Pegram, Kershaw, and Wharton; the artillery and Ramseur followed. The Army of the Valley camped for the night in the vicinity of Harrisonburg. On the next day, the march continued to New Market, with Pegram's Division in the lead. That evening, Pegram's and Wharton's Divisions encamped on the Timberville Road. Unexpected weather struck on October 8 in the form of a mixture of hail and snow, a day in which Rosser's cavalry attacked and drove off Federal horsemen near Round Hill. On the following day, an annoyed Sheridan counterattacked, routing the forces of Rosser and Brig. Gen. Lunsford Lomax at Tom's Brook and giving Early another excuse to disdain his mounted arm. Although Ramseur and Kershaw were called out when the cavalry fled back into camp, Wharton evidently remained inactive. The Army of the Valley remained in the vicinity of New Market through October 11.[452]

Sheridan meanwhile resumed his march up the Valley, with Early following on October 12. A minor action took place at Hupp's Hill on October 13. Gordon's Division deployed at mid-morning to the left of the Valley Pike in a concealing patch of woods, while

451. *O.R.* 43 (pt. 1): 28, 30-31, 50, 578 (pt. 2): 177, 187, 196, 210, 249, 257-258, 266-267, 292-293, 296-297, 302, 307-308; Sheridan, *Personal Memoirs*, 2:53-56; Wert, *From Winchester to Cedar Creek*, 142-144, 157-160; Mahr, *The Battle of Cedar Creek*, 28-33; Love to the editors, October 15, 1864, published as "FROM THOMAS' LEGION. Correspondence of the Asheville News," the *Asheville News*, November 3, 1864 (hereinafter cited as Love to Asheville *News*, October 15, 1864 [published November 3, 1864]). For a summary of property destroyed by the Army of the Shenandoah between August 10 and November 16, see *O.R.* 43 (pt. 1): 37.

452. *O.R.* 43 (pt. 1): 30-32, 50-51, 559, 578-579, (pt. 2): 320-321, 327, 339; Love to *Asheville News* October 15, 1864 (published November 3, 1864); Early, *Autobiographical Sketch and Narrative*, 436; Sheridan, *Personal Memoirs*, 2:56-59; Wert, *From Winchester to Cedar Creek*, 161-165, 167; Mahr, *The Battle of Cedar Creek*, 35-56.

the other infantry divisions went into line behind the brow of the hill. Early allowed only some cavalry and a few artillery pieces to show themselves. His plan was to develop the strength of the Federals in his front and get some idea as to Sheridan's intentions; the Confederate commander was puzzled as to whether his opposite number planned to remain in the Valley, move east of the mountains, or return to Petersburg. The Federals were camped north of Cedar Creek. The Confederate artillery opened fire on the Nineteenth Corps camp to announce their presence, scattering the surprised soldiers. Col. Joseph Thoburn's First Division of the Army of West Virginia was sent forward to reconnoiter the Confederate position. Crossing Cedar Creek, it deployed and advanced. Early sent forward Kershaw's Division on the right to contest it, supported by Ramseur; Gordon's and Wharton's divisions formed on the left and pushed their skirmishers forward. The Confederates drove the Federals back across the creek in a sharp skirmish whch resulted in the loss of around 200 casualties apiece. Early now knew that Sheridan retained the bulk of his infantry in the lower Valley, while Sheridan realized in turn that Early had not departed the Valley as previously assumed. That evening, the Confederates pulled back to Fisher's Hill, which they occupied for the next few days. Outside of mutual probings on October 14, and a joint raid by Rosser's cavalry and Grimes's infantry brigade on October 17, the armies remained quiet.[453]

Until this time, Sheridan had indeed contemplated dispatching part of his force to Petersburg, but hesitated after receiving word from Grant via Halleck to keep the Nineteenth Corps and to send the Sixth Corps and a cavalry division at his discretion. Now that Early had shown up again, Sheridan began to consider the possibility that he might need to fight another battle. Grant also reiterated his preference for Sheridan to operate eastward against the railroad from Charlottesville. Once again, Sheridan balked. This led to a direct request from Stanton to meet with Sheridan in person before the former went to talk with Grant. Although uneasy about Early, Sheridan agreed to travel to Washington on October 15. Further skirmishing convinced him that for now Early would stay put at Fisher's Hill. Sheridan had reconcentrated his entire army near Middletown behind Cedar Creek, minus two cavalry divisions which he begrudingly planned to send against the Virginia Central Railroad as a sop to Grant. Wright was left in charge of the army during Sheridan's absence. The latter had only reached Front Royal on the first day of his journey when he received an intercepted Confederate signal message. Ascribed to Longstreet, it instructed Early to be ready to unite with the First Corps for an assault on the Federals. Sheridan correctly judged the message as a ruse designed to throw him off as to Early's intentions, probably to prevent him from reinforcing Grant. Nevertheless, although Sheridan thought that Early's army was in no condition to pose a real threat, he ordered the cavalry returned to Wright to play safe.[454]

Although Early did not receive reinforcements, he felt that he either had to act or withdraw up the Valley due to the lack of supplies; he was also still under the pressure of Lee's expectations. Together with Gordon, he hatched a plan to beat the Army of the Shenandoah

453. *O.R.* 43 (pt. 1): 51, 478, 561, 579-580, (pt. 2): 364-365; Early, *Autobiographical Sketch and Narrative*, 437-438; Wert, *From Winchester to Cedar Creek*, 166-170; Mahr, *The Battle of Cedar Creek*, 57-75, 77-79.

454. *O.R.* 43 (pt. 1): 51-52, (pt. 2): 266, 327, 339-341, 345-347, 349, 355-356, 358-359, 363-365, 385-386, 389-390; Sheridan, *Personal Memoirs*, 2:59-65; Wert, *From Winchester to Cedar Creek*, 166-167, 169-170, 172-173; Mahr, *The Battle of Cedar Creek*, 60-61, 69-71, 75-76.

decisively. The three Second Corps divisions and one of Rosser's cavalry brigades would march on the night of October 18 along a narrow path across the face of supposedly impassable Massanutten Mountain, where they would deploy on the Federal left and rear, ford the North Fork of the Shenandoah at Bowman's Ford, and attack. For command and control purposes, Gordon would exercise control on this portion of the field in the opening phases. Kershaw's Division would assault the Federal center to the left of the mountain, where it would cross and join up with the other divisions on their left. Wharton's Division would escort the artillery down the Valley Pike, eventually passing over to the Confederate right to secure the road to Middletown, enveloping the Federal left and blocking any buildup of Federal cavalry from that direction. Rosser's remaining two brigades would cross to the far Confederate left to attack their counterparts as a diversion. Lomax's cavalry division would drive up from Front Royal and get into the Federal rear north of Middletown, cutting off escape. The plan would be aided by Sheridan's faulty troop dispositions, which were made without consideration for a flanking assault from the area of Massanutten Mountain.[455]

Early was successful in getting his troops into position after a difficult night march, and before sunrise on October 19, he attacked.[456] Struck almost simultaneously in front by Kershaw's Division and in the flank and rear by Gordon's (under the command of Brig. Gen. Clement A. Evans), the Army of West Virginia was routed out of its camps. It was pushed back as Ramseur joined up on Evans's right and Kershaw linked up on his left. Wharton also pushed forward down the Valley Pike, with Smith's Brigade in the lead, followed by Patton's former brigade; Wharton's old brigade escorted the artillery further back. The division's first advance was halted by enemy artillery fire from across the creek; however, the Federal guns were soon flanked by Kershaw, forcing them to withdraw and allowing Wharton to move forward again. Wharton was still be unable to cross until Kershaw had pushed beyond the pike on the opposite side of the creek. The pike was finally cleared shortly before 7 A.M.; Early rode in front of Smith's Brigade as Wharton crossed.[457]

As the Confederates swept into the camps of the Nineteenth Corps, pockets of Federal resistance developed which slowed the advance. The assault quickly became disorganized, due in part to fog which covered the battlefield until well after sunrise. Units veered off course or became intermixed. Further, some Confederates fell out of the lines to loot or grab the Federals' abandoned breakfasts, a problem which grew steadily throughout the day. On Gordon's front, Pegram was sent into a gap which had opened up amidst Ramseur's brigades. At this point, Early overrode Gordon's recommendation for an immediate assault on the Sixth Corps, which had formed into line on the opposite side of Meadow Brook, a tributary of Cedar Creek. By the time Wharton was on the field, the Sixth Corps was putting up a stiff fight. Arriving behind the main battle line, Wharton prepared to follow his original

455. *O.R.* 43 (pt. 1): 52, 561, 580, (pt. 2): 891-892; *O.R. (Supplement)* Pt. I, 7:589-590; Early, *Autobiographical Sketch and Narrative*, 438-442, 452; Wert, *From Winchester to Cedar Creek*, 168, 170-175, 240-242; Mahr, *The Battle of Cedar Creek*, 61-63, 71, 73-75, 79-92, 349-350.

456. The most detailed tactical study of the battle is Mahr, *The Battle of Cedar Creek*. For a shorter account, see Wert, *From Winchester to Cedar Creek*, 177-246.

457. *O.R.* 43 (pt. 1): 158, 160, 365-366, 561, 580-581; *O.R. (Supplement)* Pt. I, 7:591; Early, *Autobiographical Sketch and Narrative*, 442-444; Wert, *From Winchester to Cedar Creek*, 175-197; Mahr, *The Battle of Cedar Creek*, 98-103, 105-137, 140-177, 185-189. Patton was killed at Third Winchester.

instructions to move against the Federal far left and control the pike. Receiving requests from both Pegram and Ramseur to come to their assistance instead, he deferred to Early, whom Wharton recalled in 1905 as ordering him to support Pegram. In the event, he went in on the right flank of the Confederate army, next to Grimes's Brigade of Ramseur's Division. Instead of the planned envelopment, however, he was to assault the Federal position directly. Wharton placed Patton's Brigade on the left and Smith's Brigade, including Thomas's Legion, on the right. Their target was Cemetery Hill, the northernmost extension of a steep ridge on the opposite side of Meadow Brook. It was occupied by Brig. Gen. George W. Getty's Second Division of the Sixth Corps. Getty had repulsed Grimes shortly before Wharton arrived. Wharton was getting his men in position when an officer behind the line ordered the charge. "The men, thinking the order was properly given, immediately rushed forward in some disorder and irregularity," recalled Wharton. "I came riding at the head of the lines, and before I could get back to correct the error, the men had gotten so far I could not correct the mistake that had been made, but had to order a general charge." To make matters worse, Wharton's men were "at great disadvantage, having to pass through a thick patch of cane and by a house and across a ditch about ten or twelve feet wide and three or four feet deep, and then up a steep hill with some trees and bushes."[458]

Getty's division took full advantage of the situation and opened a heavy fire on Wharton's struggling men, repulsing them. Wharton reported that the two brigades "lost heavily in killed and wounded." He ordered his men to fall back to the foot of the hill and the brook bed. The latter place proved to be no sanctuary from the Federal fire, so Wharton drew his men back to the Valley Pike. Ordering up his former brigade to join the other two, he reorganized his men and planned to try the earlier flanking movement. Instead, he received fresh orders from Early to march up the Valley Pike through Middletown and to take a position to the east of that community. Joined by Brig. Gen. William T. Wofford's Georgia brigade of Kershaw's Division, Wharton's new task was to keep an eye on a Federal cavalry buildup to the north. The last thing Early needed was for his army to give way to another flanking attack, especially as only one of Rosser's brigades was in that section of the battlefield. Meanwhile, other than an early morning skirmish when he crossed Cedar Creek, Rosser did nothing against the cavalry on the Federal right, allowing the bulk of it to move and concentrate on the Army of the Shenandoah's left; it was this redeployment which concerned Early. Lomax's brigade never came close enough to play any sort of role.[459]

While Wharton and Wofford skirmished with the Federal cavalry, the Sixth Corps pulled back northward. Early took advantage of the opportunity to reorganize the army and gather up stragglers preparatory for a final advance. By the late morning, the Confederate battle line was just above Middletown, facing northeastward. The Federals also regrouped. They were heartened by the return of Sheridan, who had stopped on the previous night at Winchester on his return from Washington and headed for the front when the continuing

458. *O.R.* 43 (pt. 1): 158-161, 194, 215, 220, 284-285, 366, 561, 581, 599; *O.R. (Supplement)*, Pt. I, 7:591-592 (Wharton quotes, 592); Early, *Autobiographical Sketch and Narrative*, 444-445; Wert, *From Winchester to Cedar Creek*, 181-184, 186-194, 197-211; Mahr, *The Battle of Cedar Creek*, 115-117, 121-122, 131, 137-177, 184-228.

459. *O.R.* 43 (pt. 1): 159, 194, 433, 561, 581, 599; *O.R. (Supplement)* Pt. I, 7:592-593 (Wharton quote, 592), 605; Early, *Autobiographical Sketch and Narrative*, 445-446; Wert, *From Winchester to Cedar Creek*, 211-215; Mahr, *The Battle of Cedar Creek*, 104-105, 136, 177-184, 220-221, 228-238, 247-248, 270-274, 324-326.

sound of gunfire in the distance that morning convinced him that all was not well. His presence brought much-needed encouragement to his men and rallied many stragglers. At the same time, the Confederate situation deteriorated. Not only did Early not resume the attack until the afternoon, but fewer Confederates than ever were in the ranks due to straggling and plundering. The soldiers had long lacked decent subsistence and needed supplies, and the temptation was too much; furthermore, Early had lost too many of his field officers during the campaign to insure discipline. To add to his problems, Early was uneasy about the Federal cavalry buildup. When he sent the infantry forward again, he retained Pegram and Wharton at the northern edge of Middletown to watch the cavalry. After advancing a short distance, the other divisions were halted again about 1 P.M. and remained so for the next three hours, giving Sheridan plenty of time to reorganize and prepare a counterattack.[460]

Sheridan shifted Custer's Third Cavalry Division back to the Federal right; in the midafternoon it pushed Rosser's horsemen back towards Cedar Creek. Rosser did not make an effort afterwards to get back into the fight. This left Early's left flank, held by Gordon's infantry, uncovered. An hour later, Sheridan launched his counterattack. Merritt's cavalry attacked Wharton on the Confederate right, while the Sixth Corps advanced on the Confederate center. The Nineteenth Corps struck Gordon's overstretched line and broke it. Kershaw's and Ramseur's Divisions withdrew in good order and attempted to establish a new line further back upon which Gordon could rally. The Nineteenth Corps kept its pressure up and was soon joined by Custer's cavalry, which charged into the faltering line. Once again, Early's left wing was routed by cavalry. Ramseur's Division held for awhile until its commander fell mortally wounded, while Early ordered Pegram and Wharton to withdraw. As they did so, Wharton was attacked by Merritt; Wharton's men kept their poise, however, and repulsed the horsemen. Moving through the southeastern portion of Middletown, Wharton found that Federal troops were already on the Valley Pike and that refugees from other Confederate units were in his front. He pulled his men further southwest to Bowman's Ford. The division arrived back at the Confederate camp at Fisher's Hill around 11 that night; according to Wharton, the division was "in fairly good order" although "tired and dispirited."[461]

460. *O.R.* 43 (pt. 1): 52-53, 159, 433-434, 562, 581; Sheridan, *Personal Memoirs*, 2:68-86; Early, *Autobiographical Sketch and Narrative*, 446-448; Wert, *From Winchester to Cedar Creek*, 215-228; Mahr, *The Battle of Cedar Creek*, 239-258. Early's so-called "fatal halt" or "fatal delay" to continue the advance is a major controversy of the battle of Cedar Creek. It is often framed around an alleged discussion between Early and Gordon, reported by the latter after the war, and used to argue that Early was culpable for the Army of the Valley's defeat and that the Confederate attack ran out of steam quite early in the battle due to his dilatory attitude. Wert, who believed that the conversation occurred (if it happened at all) sometime between 9:30 and 10:30 A.M., discounted the idea of a "fatal halt" at this time, as Early needed to reorganize the troops before they could resume the offensive; his later forfeiture of the offensive in the early afternoon was another matter entirely, however. Mahr placed the conversation at sometime around 7 A.M., just after Early crossed the creek, and related it to Early's reassumption of overall command of the army and Gordon's return to his own division. Mahr argued that the evidence showed that the Confederate attack gradually lost momentum in a series of halts or delays—at least three—culminating in the real "fatal halt" around 12:30 P.M. At least one member of Thomas's Legion supported the claim that looting and straggling at Cedar Creek weakened the Confederate battle lines. See Leas, *Civil War Diary of Absalom Joshua Burum* (typescript copy, WCU), October 19, 1864.

461. *O.R.* 43 (pt. 1): 53-54, 159, 285, 434, 450-451, 562-563, 581, (pt. 2): 170, 218; *O.R. (Supplement)*, Pt. I, 7:593-594 (Wharton quotes, 594); Early, *Autobiographical Sketch and Narrative*, 448-450; Sheridan, *Personal Memoirs*, 2:87-92; Wert, *From Winchester to Cedar Creek*, 224, 227-238; Mahr, *The Battle of Cedar Creek*,

Much of the Army of the Valley was scattered, and most of the wagon train was cut off, abandoned, and captured in the vicinity of Strasburg. Thomas's Legion suffered surprisingly few documented casualties considering the extent to which Smith's Brigade was engaged, but the numbers perhaps reflect the skeletal level to which the Legion had shrunk; further, as there are no extant company muster rolls, the number missing is no longer available. Federal provost marshal records, Confederate hospital records, and other sources indicate that the Legion lost 3 killed or mortally wounded, 3 wounded, and 5 captured; 3 of the latter were also wounded. It is known that 2 of the wounded who were not captured later returned to duty. One of the captured who was not wounded died of illness in prison; another was paroled in November, but it is undocumented whether he returned to service. The remaining three wounded were not paroled until after the war. Two of those reported as killed in action come from a source written many years after the war, and are otherwise undocumented as members of the Legion.[462]

Cedar Creek was a costly contest for both victor and vanquished. Early wrote Lee that "[m]y loss in killed and wounded was not more than 700 or 800, and I think very few prisoners were lost." Claiming that with the exception of the loss of 23 cannon "the enemy has far the worst of it," Early reported that Federal casualties were "very heavy" and that the Army of the Valley had captured some 1,300 prisoners. One source estimated the Confederate losses as about 2,910, with some 320 killed, 1,540 wounded, and 1,051 missing. Early was correct in his estimate of Federal losses. Official figures for the Army of the Shenandoah were 644 killed (52 officers and 592 men), 3,430 (244 officers and 3,186 men), and 1,591 captured or missing (30 officers and 1,561 men), for an aggregate loss of 5,665. Besides the Confederate cannon captured, during the final rout Early embarrasingly lost 20 more cannon captured from the Federals earlier in the battle. Unfortunately for the Confederates, while their overall casualties were less than the Federals, they were also less able to absorb the impact due to the smaller size of their army.[463]

In the following weeks, the Army of the Valley recovered some of its strength as stragglers slowly found their way back to the army and absentees and recovered sick returned to the ranks. The army had lost heavily in material and morale, however. Recriminations sailed back and forth between Early and Gordon over the planning and execution of the battle, while Early's criticism of the straggling that had sapped much of the army during crucial

---

258-269, 272-324, 327-330. Custer had assumed command of the Third Cavalry Division when Wilson was transferred to Sherman's army in September.

462. *O.R.* 43 (pt. 1): 560, 563, 564; service record files, Thomas's Legion, Compiled Service Records of Confederate Soldiers from the State of North Carolina (M270), reels 567 through 574; D. K. Collins to Stringfield, August 17, 1895, Stringfield Papers, WCU. Hotchkiss reported that Early and his subordinates were unable to get any of the troops or fragments of units which arrived at Fisher's Hill to go back to Strasburg to rescue the wagon train. *O.R.* 43 (pt. 1): 582.

463. *O.R.* 43 (pt. 1): 32-34, 57, 137, 560, 564 (Early quotes, 564); Wert, *From Winchester to Cedar Creek*, 246; Mahr, *The Battle of Cedar Creek*, 334-338. The main problem with compiling the Confederate losses with any degree of accuracy is the lack of survivng records; see Mahr, *The Battle of Cedar Creek*, 337-338. See also the figures given by Early in *Autobiographical Sketch and Narrative*, 451-452. The loss in material was a particularly hard blow. For a summary of military equipment captured by Sheridan's forces between August 10 and November 16, see *O.R.* 43 (pt. 1): 37. Among the items captured were 94 guns, 19,230 small arms, 1,061,000 rounds of small arms ammunition, and 40 battle flags.

moments provoked resentment within the ranks (even if the charges were essentially true). Accusations regarding Early's reputation as a poor disciplinarian added to the controversy, while false rumors circulated that he was drunk during the battle. Southern newspapers roundly condemned him. The defeat was a blow to the morale of the Southern populace. The opposite was true in the North: coupled with Sheridan's earlier victories and Sherman's capture of Atlanta, the Battle of Cedar Creek did much to insure Lincoln's reelection.[464]

In the immediate aftermath of the battle, the Army of the Valley had no choice but to continue its withdrawal. On October 20 the infantry followed the remaining wagons to New Market, "most of the men having sorted themselves and order . . . somewhat restored," according to Jedediah Hotchkiss. The army remained there for several days. Other than a cavalry clash at Milford on October 26 there was little military activity; as in the case of Fisher's Hill, Sheridan did not mount an aggressive pursuit to finish Early, resuming his arguments with Grant over the wisdom of moving on the Virginia Central Railroad. In early November, Early decided to move forward again, due to rumors (untrue at that point) that Sheridan was sending elements of his army to Petersburg. At sunrise on November 10, the Confederates departed, the order of march being Kershaw's Division, the artillery, and the divisions of Pegram, Grimes (replacing Ramseur), Gordon, and Wharton (including Thomas's Legion). Rosser's cavalry proceeded to Fairview, while Lomax went to Front Royal. The army camped in the area of Woodstock. The march continued on November 11, with Pegram taking the lead, followed by Grimes, the artillery, Gordon, Wharton, and Kershaw. Reaching the Cedar Creek area, the Confederates found that the Federals had withdrawn in the direction of Kernstown and Bartonsville, with forward entrenchments at Newtown. The Confederates spread out in a battle line, with Wharton's and Kershaw's Divisions on the left. Part of the army stayed in line during the night.[465]

On the following day, there were infantry skirmishes and some minor cavalry clashes. The Federals spent the day improving their entrenchments and gave no indication of advancing to engage Early. Given his recent defeats, Early did not consider attack a viable option. On November 13, the Army of the Valley withdrew, encamping at Pence's Hill. It arrived in New Market on the next day. On November 15, Early suffered the loss of Kershaw's Division, which was returned to Lee. This began the slow dismemberment of the Army of the Valley, a process that lasted until mid-December as Lee took back the Army of Northern Virginia units, leaving Early behind with Wharton's Division. Sheridan likewise began dispatching most of his troops to Grant. One other departure occurred: on November 9, Special Order No. 267 of the Confederate Adjutant and Inspector General's Office ordered Lieutenant Colonel Love and the Legion to return "without delay" to western North Carolina and report to district commander Brig. Gen. James G. Martin.[466]

464. Wert, *From Winchester to Cedar Creek*, 246-249; Mahr, *The Battle of Cedar Creek*, 336-347, 349, 351-355; Early, *Autobiographical Sketch and Narrative*, 452; *O.R.* 43 (pt. 1): 583; *O.R. (Supplement)* Pt. I, 7:575-577.

465. *O.R.* 43 (pt. 1): 33-36, 55, 582-584 (Hotchkiss quote, 582), (pt. 2): 464-466, 475, 520, 553, 563-564, 583-586, 604-605, 611; Early, *Autobiographical Sketch and Narrative*, 451, 453; Wert, *From Winchester to Cedar Creek*, 250; Mahr, *The Battle of Cedar Creek*, 331-334, 338, 347.

466. *O.R.* 43 (pt. 1): 36-37, 55, 584-585, (pt. 2): 611, 624, 630, 919 ("without delay" quote), 921; Early, *Autobiographical Sketch and Narrative*, 454; Wert, *From Winchester to Cedar Creek*, 250; Mahr, *The Battle of Cedar Creek*, 347-348.

Down perhaps to less than a hundred men present for duty, Thomas's Legion departed the Valley on November 17. Their brigade commander, Colonel Smith, saw them off with a brief speech. In December, Wharton's assistant adjutant general addressed to Love a commendation for the Legion's conduct. Citing its "gallant and effective service," Wharton's "personal observations of their efficiency and heroic conduct at Kernstown, Winchester, Leetown and many other hard fought fields enable him to speak accurately of the soldierly bearing, heroic fighting, and admirable steadiness and coolness though confronted by a myriad foe, which you and your brave men ever displayed in action." Adding that "[t]he patience and cheerful endurance of the toilsome march, brief rests and hard fighting which you and your gallant band ever exhibited has won his hearty commendation and leaves each of your patriotic command a record bright and unsullied," Wharton's adjutant revealed that the "[t]he gallant conduct of Your command rendered your effort to rejoin your command in North Carolina abortive, and the constant refusal to your many applications for transfer, is complimentary evidence of the esteem in which you were held, and a grateful acknowledgment of the services you could render."[467] Having been put into the field with an army at last, the Legion demonstrated what had been hinted at in the various small actions it had participated in in Tennessee: that under the right circumstances and leadership, it could function as an effective combat unit. The arguments regarding the transferral of troops away from their immediate home areas for the purposes of efficiency seems to have proven true in the case of the Legion. These ideas were echoed by Love in late September, when he wrote that "[m]en never fought better or acted more gallantly than those of Thomas Legion under me during this Campaign."[468]

The Legion faced a changed situation in western North Carolina. The military and economic situation there had continued to deteriorate. Despite Thomas's efforts, conditions had not improved for local families. Love's mother, Margaret, wrote to Governor Vance in May "that the wives and children of the brave Indians that have kept the enemy back and are now defending our homes are living on weeds and the bark of trees and many of them have left their homes and gone to the South in search of bread." The supplies brought up from Walhalla were "exhausted." Thomas echoed her statements in a strongly-worded letter that came close to accusing Vance of contributing to the problem: "I may as well mention that you are charged with preventing the commissary at Anderson from making sales of provisions for soldiers families and that you had alledged that ample provision had already been made through County Commissaries. I have mentioned this allegation for your benefit to afford you an opportunity to Correct the error." Like Margaret Love, Thomas noted that many families were quitting the area to find subsistence; what alarmed Thomas was that many soldiers were departing with their families. As might be expected, Thomas also called attention to the plight of the Cherokees, whose "families bore the want of bread with patience but since the supply of provisions of their families have stopped they too begin to follow the example of the whites."[469]

467. Crow, *Storm in the Mountains*, 101-102; Stringfield, "Sixty-Ninth Regiment," in Clark, *North Carolina Regiments*, 3:756; C. A. De Russy to Love, December 8, 1864, service record file of James R. Love, Thomas's Legion, Compiled Service Records of Confederate Soldiers from the State of North Carolina (M270), reel 570.

468. Love to Stephen Whitaker, September 30, 1864, Whitaker Papers, NCOAH.

469. Margaret E. Love to Vance, May 10, 1864, Thomas to Vance, May 13, 1864, Governors' Papers: Vance, 1862-1865, NCOAH; Faye Barnes Waldroop and John L. Waldroop, "The Loves of Loves Field," in Jackson

Adding to the crisis was continued resentment towards the conscription laws. Thomas asked Vance again to do something about the problem. As in earlier letters, Thomas emphasized how the absence of widespread slavery in the region made it difficult for local families to subsist when the available able-bodied men were drafted. He feared that the results would lead many to seek shelter with or assistance from the Federals, which would eventually result in a Unionist population. He asked for Vance's aid in getting food for the mountain inhabitants, and wondered why the governor could not "induce" the Secretary of War to allow local conscripts "to make corn and guard their homes." Vance, however, was already well aware of the troubles, and had requested to Seddon in April that the conscription law be suspended for much the reasons that Thomas cited. It all proved in vain, as both Seddon and Bragg recommended against such a course of action and were sustained by Davis.[470]

The situation had also deteriorated in a military sense, as the overstretched Confederate forces could not adequately counter the increasingly effective Federal raids into the region. In June 1864 Schofield sent George W. Kirk with some 130 men of the 2nd Regiment N.C. Mounted Infantry (Union) on a raid from Morristown, Tennessee, to destroy the bridge of the North Carolina Railroad over the Yadkin River near Salisbury. Kirk moved through Bull's Gap to Greeneville before turning southeast, defeating a small Confederate force at Broylesville, Tennessee. Crossing into North Carolina, he proceeded via Crab Orchard before striking Camp Vance, a conscript camp east of Morganton. The camp was occupied by conscripts, many of them unarmed. Kirk lay siege to the camp on the night of June 27; it surrendered the next day. The Federals netted 277 prisoners, as well as a large amount of military material, including 1,200 small arms, ammunition, and 3,000 bushels of grain, as well as a locomotive with three cars. Kirk burned the camp, the depot, the train, and the captured material. A few escapees managed to put out the alert, and Kirk withdrew from the camp, abandoning his plans for a more sweeping raid towards the east. The Confederate response was fairly weak. Hunkering down in his headquarters in Asheville, Col. John B. Palmer offered many excuses for his failure to mount only a tardy pursuit, ranging from the fact that Camp Vance was not in the District of Western North Carolina (which extended only as far as the Blue Ridge) to his lack of cavalry. His most valid reason, however, was that he simply did not have enough men. Kirk had some brushes with the North Carolina Home Guard on June 29-30, the most serious of which occurred at Piedmont Springs on the latter date. Nevertheless, he made it back to Tennessee with 132 prisoners and forty new recruits for his own 3rd Regiment N.C. Mounted Infantry (Union).[471]

Further trouble soon landed in Thomas's backyard. A Confederate guerrilla band raided Athens, Tennessee, on August 1, and then retreated southward through the passes of North Carolina. A detachment from the 1st Regiment Ohio Heavy Artillery was sent to Athens from Loudon, where it impressed enough horses to mount sixty men and set off in pursuit. Crossing the border, the Federals caught up with their quarry at Murphy on August 2 and routed them. The Federals returned to Athens without encountering any other resistance. The absence of a

---

County Genealogical Society, *Jackson County Heritage North Carolina* (Marceline, Mo., and Waynesville, N.C.: Jackson County Genealogical Society in Cooperation with Wadsworth Publishing Company, 1992), 1:324.

470. Thomas to Vance, May 13, 1864, Governors' Papers: Vance, 1862-1865, NCOAH; *O.R.* 53:324-325, 329.

471. *O.R.* 39 (pt. 1): 232-237, (pt. 2): 72-73; Barrett, *Civil War in North Carolina*, 233-237; Crow, *Storm in the Mountains*, 104-106; Trotter, *Bushwhackers*, 116-118; Matthew Bumgarner, *Kirk's Raiders*, 35-46.

response by Thomas's North Carolina command is noteworthy. The incident demonstrated once again the comparative ease with which Federal raiders could penetrate the mountains.[472]

Eastern Tennessee Confederates were similarly bedeviled. The remaining Confederate forces had trouble matching up with their increasingly aggressive Federal counterparts. Indifferent or overburdened departmental leadership did not help. When "Grumble" Jones departed for the Valley, he put Col. George B. Crittenden temporarily in command of both the Departments of East Tennessee and Southwest Virginia. With Jones's death at Piedmont, Crittenden was left with an assignment for which he was not fitted. Command should have passed to Brig. Gen. John Hunt Morgan, but he was absent on a raid. Upon his return, Morgan assumed command of both departments. In late August, Echols was sent from the Valley to take over while Breckinridge was with Early. Leaving Morgan in immediate command of the troops in the field in eastern Tennessee, Echols attempted to bring some organization to the forces in both departments while attending more directly to matters in southwestern Virginia. His task was complicated by Morgan's death in a Federal raid on Greeneville, Tennessee, in early September. Crittenden reassumed immediate command of the troops in eastern Tennessee, until replaced by Vaughn; Echols continued to exercise overall command in both departments. Echols was succeeded by Breckinridge following the battle of Winchester. For all intents and purposes, by that time the two departments now functioned again as one. Throughout this period, each of these commanders were faced with the same problems of trying to defend a long stretch of territory with minimal resources.[473]

There was confusion during the summer as to whether the District of Western North Carolina was still part of the Department of Southwest Virginia and Eastern Tennessee. Acting on that assumption, Morgan attempted in July to get a reluctant Palmer to launch a demonstration as a distraction from other movements he had planned. Possibly as a result of this disagreement, Palmer received instructions in October from Lee "to cooperate with General Breckinridge when notified by him" for a possible movement into Tennessee. Meanwhile, in August Brig. Gen. James G. Martin superseded Palmer, who retained direct command of the troops. As Martin answered directly to Lt. Gen. Theophilus H. Holmes, commander of the North Carolina Reserves, his appointment settled the question of the district's separation from east Tennessee and southwest Virginia, although geography and military necessity still dictated close cooperation between the two administrations.[474]

472. *O.R.* 39 (pt. 1): 367-369. The identity of the unit of Confederate raiders are unknown, at least so far as the band dispersed at Murphy is concerned. While it is tempting to assume that they were part of Thomas's command, that is probably not the case if they were the same men who committed the raid on Athens, as one Federal source identified them (on the basis of prisoners captured) with a unit based in Georgia. If the recipients of the Federal assault were Thomas's men, however, they may have belonged to the company whose commander communicated from Murphy a few days later to Federal authorities that many of Thomas's men were willing to come in as long as the Federals offered them protection; see p. 215 below.

473. *O.R.* 37 (pt. 1): 751-752, 754-756, 758-759, (pt. 2): 593, 601-605, 39 (pt. 1): 369-370, 457, 484-492, 502, 552-567, (pt. 2): 629-630, 632, 635-636, 638-639, 654, 657, 664-665, 667, 673-674, 678-679, 701, 722-723, 727-730, 732-733, 735-736, 738, 740-742, 746-747, 750, 792, 804, 816, 864, 867, 871, 877, 43 (pt. 1): 1005, 1010-1011, 1013, (pt. 2): 864-866, 868-873, 876.

474. *O.R.* 39 (pt. 1): 852 (quote), (pt. 2): 708, 40 (pt. 3): 788, 833; Edward G. Longacre, "Martin, James Green," in Faust, *Historical Times Illustrated Encyclopedia of the Civil War,* 477; Barrett, *The Civil War in North Carolina,* 20-21, 25-27, 129, 211-212, 458 n. 63. Technically, Martin was assigned to command the Reserve

During 1864 Thomas seems to have remained relatively inactive. In August, he tried to organize a company of east Tennessee mounted infantry to act as scouts. John Tillery, a former officer of the 8th Regiment Tennessee Cavalry (Baxter Smith's), was assigned to raise the company behind Federal lines. The outcome of this effort is unknown, although Tillery's capture in September makes it unlikely that the company's organization was ever completed. Thomas also communicated his belief to Cooper that some North Carolinians and east Tennesseans "who have served out their three years in the Confederate army and conscripts that have not been in the service" were "now secreting themselves along the Northern base of the Smoky Mountains" and were resisting pressure and offers of "a bounty of upwards of three hundred dollars" to enter Federal service. "They would come out and join me if they could do so in safety. . . . Would it be advisable to take them in? If they do not join us they will be compelled to join the enemy."[475]

The district return for the month of April showed Thomas's command at the mouths of the Tuckasegee, with three companies of "Indians principally" consisting of 7 commissioned officers and 196 non-commissioned officers and enlisted men on duty, with three men absent on extra duty. Two commissioned officers and 75 men were absent. The aggregate present and absent was given as 283 (9 officers and 274 non-commissioned officers, musicians, and privates).[476] These figures were echoed in returns for May 5 and May 15. The returns for June and July showed a steady growth in the size of the force—or perhaps more accurately, more of its real strength was reported. On June 1, the North Carolina contingent of the Legion reported 22 commissioned officers (including 7 captains), 23 non-commissioned officers, and 195 enlisted men present for duty. One officer and 21 enlisted men were reported present sick, while another officer and 72 enlisted men were present on extra duty. The total aggregate was 335 (24 officers and 311 enlisted men), while 2 officers and 83 enlisted men were absent; the total aggregate present and absent was 420. These figures were repeated in a district return for June 7 and field returns for June 20 and July 1. The July 4 field return showed Thomas with 22 commissioned officers, 44 non-commissioned officers, and 425 enlisted men present for duty. Nine enlisted men were present sick, while 29 enlisted men were present for duty and 1 was under arrest. The aggregate present was 530 (22 commissioned officers and 508 non-commissioned officers and enlisted men), with 1 officer and 109 enlisted men for an aggregate present and absent of 640.[477]

---

troops in western North Carolina; however, Palmer was placed under Martin's authority as well, making him de facto commander of the district.

475. Thomas to Cooper, August 2, 1864, Thomas to John Tellery [Tillery], August 19, 1864, unbound letterbook, Thomas Papers, DU; service record file, John Tillery, 8th Regiment Tennessee Cavalry (Baxter Smith's), Compiled Service Records of Confederate Soldiers from the State of Tennessee (M268), reel 38.

476. Return of the District of Western North Carolina Commanded by Col. John B. Palmer, April 25, 1864, Chapter 1: vol. 15, 16, Entry 65, pt. 2, Entry 24, RG 109, NA (abstracted in *O.R.* 32 [pt. 3]: 865). Other sources place Thomas's command at the mouths of the Tuckasegee at this time; see W. H. Parker to Thomas, April 16, 1864, Thomas Papers, WCU (microfilm, Thomas Papers, DU), Palmer to Thomas, March 11, 1864, I. Rodier to Thomas, March 21, 1864, Thomas Papers, DU.

477. Return of the Troops in the District of Western North Carolina Commanded by Col. John B. Palmer, June 7, 1864, Field Returns of Troops commanded by Col. John B. Palmer, May 5, May 15, June 1, June 20, and July 1, 1864, Field Return of Troops commanded by Col. John B. Palmer, July 4, 1864, Chapter 1: vol. 15, 16, Entry 65, pt. 2, Entry 24, RG 109, NA.

During this time, the western North Carolina contingent of Thomas's Legion made up a substantial portion of Palmer's total strength. Palmer's aggregate of present and absent ranged from 1,122 on April 25 to 1,620 on July 1. On paper, then, Palmer's command, which besides Thomas's force consisted of the 62nd and 64th Regiments N.C. Troops, a small detachment of the 58th Regiment N.C. Troops (in April only), the 14th Battalion N.C. Cavalry, and the MacBeth Light Artillery (from June on) possessed slightly over the ideal approximate strength of a full regiment—not really adequate for the task at hand. When absentees were factored in, Palmer's overall strength ranged from 556 officers and enlisted men present for duty on April 25 to 886 on July 1, with a high of 1,057 on June 20. These forces were dispersed at Asheville, Marshall, and at the mouths of the Ivy and Tuckasegee Rivers. Thus, there was truth in Palmer's claims that he lacked the concentrated strength to pursue Kirk following Camp Vance.[478]

In mid-April, a Confederate officer named W. H. Parker inspected Thomas's troops at the mouth of the Tuckasegee. He found that the arms and equipment of at least one company (Welch's) were "very Deficient, supply of ammunition small." In a subsequent letter written on April 17, Parker reported that "we are sadly in want of" ammunition, while Capt. James Taylor wrote Thomas in August that his men were "in much need of ammunition," hinting at how the shortage affected his men's current hunt for a party of Tennessee bushwhackers. Thomas soon wrote to a "Capt Carnes" of an unidentified Tennessee unit (probably Capt. Elliot E. Carnes of Company B, 39th Regiment Tennessee Mounted Infantry) that the latter had been "authorized" in Thomas's name to go to Walhalla "or further if necessary" to procure ammunition for both Thomas's command and for Carnes's own men, as well.[479]

Subsistence problems continued to trouble Thomas. In July he complained to Maj. R. W. Memminger, assistant adjutant general of the Department of South Carolina, Georgia, and Florida, of having only six wagons to bring provisions from Walhalla to the different places where his companies were stationed. If provided sufficient quartermaster funds, however, which he requested from Memminger, he believed that there was enough beef cattle in the area that he could purchase for his men. In the meantime, he explained that due to the lack of transportation for supplies that "I keep but a small force in Camp at the different stations and the 'present for duty' is not the number actually in Camp but the number which can be collected on a short notice." This highly irregular arrangement may have been the reason for Palmer's comments to Thomas in late March that he could "[p]ossibly . . . supply you with a little bacon for your troops <u>actually</u> <u>in the</u> <u>field</u>, but it must be on your provision return supported by a field return and other reports called for[,] forms which are herewith transmitted." If so, Palmer would have feared the effects of the policy on discipline; already in mid-March he had ordered Thomas to arrest any white soldiers that refused to stay in

478. Return of the District of Western North Carolina Commanded by Col. John B. Palmer, April 25, 1864 (abstracted in *O.R.* 32 [pt. 3]: 865), Return of the Troops in the Dist. West. N.C. Commanded by Col. John B. Palmer, June 7, 1864, Field Returns of Troops Commanded by Col. John B. Palmer, May 5, May 15, June 1, June 20, and July 1, 1864, Chapter 1: vol. 15, 16, Entry 65, pt. 2, Entry 24, RG 109, NA; *O.R.* 39 (pt. 1): 235.

479. W. H. Parker to Thomas, April 16, 1864, Thomas Papers, WCU (microfilm, Thomas Papers, DU); Parker to Thomas, April 17, 1864, Thomas Papers, DU; James Taylor to Thomas, August 10, 1864, Terrell Papers, WCU (microfilm, Terrell Papers, DU); Tennessee Civil War Centennial Commission, *Tennesseans in the Civil War*, 1:259.

camp and send them to eastern Tennessee, where the main body of the Legion was at that time still with Jackson. Palmer's emphasis on tying the provisioning of Thomas's force to properly filled out and submitted returns may have also been related to fears that Thomas might desire to draw more of the scarce supplies than the actual number of his troops dictated. W. H. Parker reported to Thomas in April rumors that Capt. Campbell Taylor of Company C had attempted to draw requisitions for a company that did not exist. As Taylor did in fact command a company, it is not known if these accusations were inaccurate, or if Taylor claimed responsibility for another company as well. Whatever the case, Taylor's actual behavior did nothing to ease Parker's mind. Arriving for the inspection rendezvous without any of his men, Taylor informed Parker that they would be in on the following day, left, and then sent in a request for a leave of absence late that night so he could spend it at his brother's house. A messenger, whom Parker sent to fetch Taylor at Captain Welch's request, returned with Taylor's brother, explaining that Taylor had departed and was en route to Thomas's headquarters. "What this strange conduct means I leave for you to say," Parker added. It is likely that if Taylor was involved in some sort of scheme to requisition extra provisions, with or without Thomas's cooperation, that it probably was not the result of greed but represented another effort to find food for the starving Cherokee families.[480]

Rumors of discipline problems continued to plague Thomas. Palmer complained on March 29 that some of Thomas's men assigned to guard prisoners had allowed their charges to escape. "You are instructed to have the matter investigated and the men punished," he ordered. The case may not have directly involved members of the Legion, however, but a detachment from the 14th Battalion N.C. Cavalry commanded by Capt. Wiley F. Parker, which seems to have been acting under Thomas's command at that time.[481] The most serious charges regarding Thomas and his men during came from a citizen named Will Hicks. "I have just been robbed by some of Thomas' pets (deserters) of about three thousand dollars' worth of goods. He is building up a little Kingdom here, of very bad material—deserters, vagabonds, out-laws and rascals," he wrote Governor Vance in June. "These regard him as the great Mogul of the Confederacy. He is quite popular with them. And this exposes the lives and property of every man that opposes his command. I am sure that every true Southerner can but do this. For God's sake if it can be done, transfer his kingdom to the sea coast and let us have some body here of the true grit. We go up this summer if something is not done for us."[482]

480. W. H. Parker to Thomas, April 16, 1864, Thomas Papers, WCU (microfilm, Thomas Papers, DU); Thomas to Major R. W. Memminger, July 7, 1864, Thomas to "Major," July 8, 1864, Thomas to Sergeant Bassett, July 8, 1864, Thomas to Mr. F. Erwin Rice, August 18, 1864, unbound letterbook, Palmer to Thomas, March 11 and March 29 (quote), 1864, Thomas Papers, DU. Thomas included a report on his command in his letter to Memminger which is evidently now lost.

481. Palmer to Thomas, March 29, 1864, W. H. Parker to Thomas, April 17, 1864, Thomas Papers, DU; W. F. Parker to Thomas, April 15, 1864, Thomas Papers, WCU (original in Thomas Papers, DU). The case involving Captain Parker of the 14th Battalion N.C. Cavalry may not be the same as the one referred to by Palmer, although Parker evidently allowed at least one prisoner (a recaptured deserter) to escape due to negligence; it also appears that troops under his command may have been guilty of theft. Captain Parker was not the same man as W. H. Parker, the inspecting officer sent to examine Thomas's companies at the Tuckasegee, as the latter commented on W. F. Parker's situation in his correspondence.

482. Will Hicks to Vance, June 25, 1864, Governors' Papers: Vance, 1862-1865, NCOAH. In a postscript, Hicks added that "I hate to write about a neighbor as I have about Col. Thomas, but Something must be done, or we

Despite Hicks's caustic assessment, it appears that Thomas was aware of the depredations committed by some of his men and made efforts to rein them in. In August he ordered a Sergeant Brown, operating in the area of Mount Sterling in Haywood County, to "not let your men raid on the citizens of Tennessee Keep them as much as possible in camp or out Scouting, protecting the citizens generally."[483] Nevertheless, local criticism of Thomas remained strong, at least among those who committed their opinions to paper. "Thomas' Legion is just doing as they have always done—virtually no good," complained C. D. Smith of Franklin. "They rather increase desertion than check it."[484]

By the time of Hicks's letter, Thomas's use of deserters from other commands had caught up with him. The headquarters of the 65th Regiment N.C. Troops (6th Regiment N.C. Cavalry) preferred charges against Thomas on May 11 for "[k]nowingly entertaining and receiving into his command" twenty-two deserters from that unit between September 1863 and April 1864; for "[c]onduct unbecoming an officer and a Gentleman" in relation to the first charge; and for "[c]onduct to the prejudice of good order and Military discipline," also in relation to the first charge.[485] The charges led to Thomas's third court-martial, which convened at Goldsboro on October 22. This time, Thomas did not emerge unscathed, although he still got off rather lightly. On the first charge, Thomas was found not guilty of actively recruiting deserters, but was found guilty of "conduct prejudicial to good order and military discipline," a conviction related to the specifications of the third charge. He was

---

lose western North Carolina. I failed to make up a company because I am not willing to co-operate with the refuse of our army. Such, with a few honorable exceptions, are our forces here."

483. Thomas to Sergeant Brown, August 26, 1864, Thomas Papers, DU. Brown's identity is unknown; like a lot of the officers and non-commissioned officers to whom Thomas wrote during this time (see, for example, "Sergeant Bassett" in n. 480), he was probably either a recent recruit to one of Thomas's companies, or perhaps affiliated with a Home Guard unit that was cooperating with Thomas.

484. C. D. Smith to Vance, November 20, 1864, Governors' Papers: Vance, 1862-1865, NCOAH.

485. "Charges and specifications against Col William H Thomas of Thomas[']s N C Legion," May 11, 1864, "Statement of J. T. Siler, formerly of 'A' 65th NC Troops, Commanded by Col. G. N. Folk," September 16, 1864, and Siler to Col. John B. Palmer, September 16, 1864, Thomas Papers, WCU (microfilm, Thomas Papers, DU). Siler was a former officer of the 65th Regiment N.C. Troops. who was called by the prosecution as a witness against Thomas, and evidently proved very indifferent and uncooperative. There is a possibility that the charges may have had some degree of political motivation, related to Thomas's unsuccesful run for Confederate Congress in 1861 against Allen T. Davidson. Leon F. Sensabaugh, the surgeon of the 65th N.C., wrote Governor Vance three days before the charges against Thomas were issued. Sensabaugh was former editor of the *Henderson Times* and a Davidson supporter. He received a letter from the Confederate Surgeon General on the night before he wrote Vance, regarding accusations made by an east Tennessean that Sensabaugh was guilty of editing a newspaper "calculated to increase the disaffection" in North Carolina and that he should be removed from his current post with the 65th N.C. Although Sensabaugh admitted to having been a former supporter of Vance's rival, William Woods Holden, up until almost a year-and-a-half before the governor's reelection, he denied the charges. "I have reason to believe that this letter was written at the instance of Col. W. H. Thomas, who still smarts under the severe castigation I gave him when he and Davidson were candidates for Congress, and who ever since, has sought ever[y] clandestine opportunity to stab at me." Sensabaugh asked for Vance's assistance in clearing his reputation, and noted that the 65th N.C.'s commander, Col. George N. Folk, supported him. Leon F. Sensabaugh to Governor Vance, May 8, 1864, Governors' Papers, 1862-1865, NCOAH. Given the time it would have taken to gather the information about each of the missing soldiers and prepare the charges, it is likely that the timing of their issuance with the recent accusations against Sensabaugh was coincidental; nevertheless, he would have doubtless enjoyed the situation.

found not guilty on twenty-one of the twenty-two individual specifications involving the first charge. The specification on which he was convicted concerned Albert L. Hicks, the deserter from the 7th Battalion N.C. Cavalry (forerunner of the 65th Regiment N.C. Troops) who in April had been elected captain of a company of absentees for service under Thomas. He was cleared on the second charge altogether; on the third charge, he was convicted on two specifications (one of which also involved Hicks) but found not guilty on another. Walter H. Taylor, Lee's assistant adjutant general, wrote in his summation that Thomas was "sentence[d] . . . to be reprimanded in orders from Department Head Quarters," and that "[t]o an officer of military spirit (as the evidence shows Colonel Thomas to be), the censure of his peers is as severe as it can be, without regard to the word by which it is conveyed. The Commanding General can therefore add nothing to the Censure of the Court. Colonel Thomas will resume his sword."[486]

There may have been more to the story. Stringfield wrote in his diary that Thomas "was found guilty of all the Charges . . . but upon his appealing to Pres Davis the whole Matter was revised & he fully exonerated." Stringfield's information, which came directly from Thomas himself in a letter, was not correct on all points; the major wrote of an additional charge of incompetency, and hinted that there was at least another charge besides that. Furthermore, if the verdict as recorded by Taylor was the version following the appeal to Davis, then Thomas was still convicted on three specifications and reprimanded. Either Thomas exaggerated the extent of the original conviction to Stringfield, or the published version was the original verdict and Thomas persuaded Davis to intervene and do away with the minor convictions as well, probably amplifying the extent of his troubles to Stringfield in order to play up his connections to Davis. Regardless, Stringfield had been rather prophetic when he wrote of Thomas prior to the proceedings that "[a]s he is a very Shifty & polite man, he is likely to Come out OK in the end."[487]

Incredibly, at the very time Thomas's trial was impending, he was involved in a troop swap with a company captain from the 65th Regiment N.C. Troops, reminiscent of the earlier ones between Captain Whitaker and the 39th Regiment N.C. Troops. Evidently with the full consent of his lieutenant colonel, Capt. William E. McDowell of Company E, 65th N.C., wrote Thomas on October 9 involving the exchange of two soldiers in his company with two of Thomas's men. "I am willing to exchange any of my men that wants to stay in the mountain district for any of your able[-]bodied men that will report to me well[-]mounted, provided they come with your consent," McDowell wrote. "In fact I would like to be transferred to the Mountains myself[.] We are willing to serve our common country any where but at the same time the mountain district is first in our thoughts and affections. If the time should

486. Paragraph IX, General Order No. 63, October 22, 1864, Orders and Circulars, Department of Northern Virginia, Chapter 2: Entry 68, Box 2, RG 109, NA. Lee's authority over Thomas stems from Special Order No. 139, issued by the Confederate Adjutant and Inspector General's Office on June 15, 1864. Paragraph 20 stated that "[a]ll officers exercising separate commands in the States of Virginia and North Carolina will report to and received orders from General R. E. Lee." *O.R.* 40 (pt. 2): 654. Lee's expanded powers were the result of the military situation in the eastern theater of operations, where events in southeastern Virginia and eastern North Carolina, the Shenandoah Valley, and southwestern Virginia (and, by extension, eastern Tennessee and western North Carolina) all impinged on the ongoing struggle between the Army of Northern Virginia and the Army of the Potomac.

487. Stringfield Diary (1864), October 31, November 13, Stringfield Papers, NCOAH.

come when me and my company should be needed in the defense of our mountain Homes and you can get us transferred to that department We will try and do our whole duty."[488] The exchanges do not appear to be transfers in the traditional sense, as McDowell wrote that Thomas "may consider" one of the men as "belonging to your command," implying that the soldier had already joined Thomas before approval was made. Given that Thomas's concurrent prosecution had been instigated by the headquarters of this same regiment for his having enlisted some of its members as deserters, his trial takes on the appearance of a farce.

In addition to these problems, in mid-August an unnamed captain of one of Thomas's Indian companies communicated from Murphy via his loyalist brother-in-law to the Federal provost marshal of Monroe County, Tennessee, that many of "Major [sic] Thomas' Indians and white soldiers will come in and give themselves up if they can be assured protection." The outcome of this attempted defection is unknown.[489] It is possible that payment issues were involved; Capt. James Taylor complained a few days before the Federals were contacted that "I am in need of some money [and] would like to know whether or not Capt[. James W.] Terrill [*sic*] is prepared to pay any to officers or not." On August 20, Thomas promised Capt. James Welch that "all or a part of the pay due will be paid, at least to the Indians" at an inspection scheduled at the end of the month.[490]

What little military activity that Thomas's command was involved with was mainly confined to the endless conflict with Unionist guerrillas.[491] In mid-April W. H. Parker reported that two Indians from Captain Welch's company were killed by bushwhackers, while Capt. James Taylor noted the murder of two local citizens in August by men from Tennessee, and his efforts to entrap them.[492] There are no surviving reports of any major activities with two exceptions. Ghormley's company passed through Cade's Cove, a Unionist stronghold in Blount County, Tennessee, some time during the spring while returning from a raid. There it skirmished with the local Unionist Home Guard; Ghormley and 1st Lt. John Grant were reported wounded.[493] In late July Federal sources reported "that Thomas was up on Tellico Reiver with a force of Indians and rebs, reported from 100 to 300, about twenty-six miles" from Loudon, Tennessee. Lt. Col. Michael L. Patterson of the 4th Regiment Tennessee Volunteer Infantry (Union) sent a scouting party of an officer and fifteen men out at midnight on July 22-23 to determine the strength and location of the party. The raiders

488. W. E. McDowell to Thomas, October 9, 1864, Thomas Papers, WCU (microfilm, Thomas Papers, DU).

489. *O.R.* 39 (pt. 2): 253. No surviving Federal provost marshal records indicate that any of Thomas's men deserted at this time.

490. James Taylor to Thomas, August 10, 1864, microfilm (original in Terrell Papers, WCU), Terrell Papers, DU; Thomas to James Welch, August 20, 1864, unbound letterbook, Thomas Papers, DU. Thomas ordered Welch to bring the Indians to the inspection, leaving the whites of the company behind under a lieutenant. Noting that some shoes and clothing had arrived, he instructed Welch to have the Cherokees to "bring their blankets & c so that the mustering officer can report all they need."

491. Thomas reported to Palmer that "a large portion of the N.C. Renegades refuse to join the federal army proper," which probably indicated a preference for operating as irregulars or partisans. Thomas to Palmer, August 24, 1864, unbound letterbook, Thomas Papers, DU.

492. Parker to Thomas, April 17, 1864, Thomas Papers, DU; Taylor to Thomas, August 10, 1864, Terrell Papers, WCU, (microfilm, Terrell Papers, DU).

493. Dunn, *Cade's Cove*, 135-136. This incident was alluded to earlier in it possible connection to the circumstances of the consolidation of Ghormley's and Everett's companies (p. 111 above).

burned the house of the Federal provost marshal in Monroe County and then dispersed into small groups. "Their only object seems to be to steal and plunder," Patterson wrote.[494]

Thomas also evidently sent scouts periodically to eastern Tennessee; further, in a letter to Palmer in August he reported information gathered by "[t]wo of my secret agents," apparently civilian informers. One of these men reported that Kirk was planning to mount an operation against Thomas, something which did not happen until the succeeding year. Possibly to watch for this move or prepare an ambush, Thomas ordered Sergeant Brown and his men to "move . . . to some convenient point near the forks of the road on the south side of Mount Starlin [Mount Starling, in Haywood County] And keep out Scouts in the different trails. . . . The Indians are watching a portion of the trail on this Side of the main defile." There were vague records of the comings and going of different units, such as the arrival of Company A in Asheville in late May on an unknown errand.[495] In early October Capt. James Taylor of Company B was captured, either during a Federal raid into Cherokee County or while on an incursion with his own command in Monroe County.[496] In general, though, it seems that Thomas was restrained in mounting operations by the paucity of his command and the ongoing lack of ammunition and subsistence for his men.

Some companies of Thomas's Legion participated in a movement into Tennessee under Palmer in October. Palmer had previously crossed the border with part of his command and operated with Vaughn's cavalry. A Federal advance late in September on Abingdon and Saltville and another on Jonesborough forced Vaughn to fall back towards Virginia and Palmer to Warm Springs. Palmer then moved into Cocke County, Tennessee, to get into the Federal rear. This caused the Federals advancing up the railroad to withdraw back to Bull's Gap. Palmer retired to Asheville, leaving behind a small cavalry force in Cocke County to prevent the Federals from moving into North Carolina from that direction. Keeping in mind his instructions from Lee to cooperate with Breckinridge on a possible drive up the French Broad River, Palmer moved from Asheville to Warm Springs on October 17 and concentrated his forces for the expedition. He crossed Paint Mountain on October 19 with 800 men, consisting of the 62nd and 64th Regiments N.C. Troops, a three-gun battery, and a contingent from Thomas's western North Carolina battalion under the command of Capt. Matthew

494. *O.R.* 39 (pt. 2): 200, 202, 205. Due to the sketchy information, it is possible that this incident involves another unit, as it seems to go against Thomas's long-held policy of conciliation towards east Tennessee Unionists, unless he had changed his mind on the issue by that point in the war. His warning to Sergeant Brown to prevent his troops from raiding into Tennessee in the following month (see p. 213 above) may have been related to this raid, and may indicate that it was done without Thomas 's authority.

495. Thomas to Palmer, August 24, 1864 ("Two of my secret agents" quote), unsigned (possibly unfinished?) letter, Thomas to Sergeant Brown, August 26, 1864, unbound letterbook, Palmer to Thomas, March 11, 1864, Thomas Papers, DU; "Cherokee Warriors," undated item from the *Asheville News*, reprinted in the *Fayetteville Observer* (semi-weekly edition), May 26, 1864.

496. Taylor was captured on October 9. Crow, *Storm in the Mountains*, 131, 255 n. 10; service record file of James Taylor, Thomas's Legion, Compiled Service Records of Confederate Soldiers from the State of North Carolina (M270), reel 573. All but one of the Federal provost marshal records for Taylor reported that he was captured in Cherokee County, implying that he was taken by Federal raiders in North Carolina. The remaining document reported that he was captured in Monroe County. Taylor later wrote Thomas from Johnson's Island Prison in Ohio, requesting that the colonel supply the needs of his family. Taylor to Thomas, December 25, 1864, Thomas Papers, WCU.

H. Love of Company A. Love's force consisted of the white companies of the battalion only: Berry's Company D, Hicks's Company F, and Ghormley and Everett's Company G. Palmer wrote Breckinridge on October 20 that "I have brought no Indians with me, General Martin having prohibited my doing so." The reasons for this stricture are unknown.[497]

Palmer sent the cavalry previously left in Cocke County to strike Mossy Creek, where they destroyed the railroad bridge. This caused the Federals at Bull's Gap to retire to the northwest towards Bean's Station, permitting Palmer to link up with Vaughn at the former site on October 21. That night, Palmer was sent with his command to Russellville, where he destroyed the railroad track. He then returned to Bull's Gap, and remained there for the next few days to keep an eye on the Federals at Bean's Station while Vaughn moved to Morristown and Strawberry Plains further west. Vaughn's force was soon diminished by the loss of Brig. Gen. John S. Williams's cavalry brigade to the Army of Tennessee. Williams's departure led Federal Brig. Gen. Alvan C. Gillem to plan a strike against Vaughn. Palmer was meanwhile ordered by Breckinridge to join Vaughn at Morristown on October 27, where skirmishing was in progress. Upon arrival, Palmer understood from Vaughn's instructions that he was to send back word to Bull's Gap to have his command ready for a possible move on Russellville at 6 A.M. the next morning. Palmer then spent the night at Morristown. He received no further word in the morning; an inquiry to Vaughn via courier brought the reply that Palmer's force had already been ordered to Russellville the previous evening.[498]

Upon reaching Russellville, Palmer found that Vaughn had only sent some 600 of his command there, while the rest had been left at Bull's Gap. Palmer selected a defensive position approximately one mile in front of town on the Morristown road. He was just getting his men into line when a member of Vaughn's staff ordered him to move to a site behind Russellville, on the road back to Bull's Gap. His column was still on the march when Vaughn's cavalry "swept by my men in the wildest disorder"; they had been routed at Morristown, losing four pieces of artillery (including a mountain howitzer which Palmer had loaned at Vaughn's request). Palmer's efforts to halt Vaughn's men failed. The rear of Vaughn's supply and baggage train was passing through Palmer's line when the pursuit appeared. Palmer sent out a skirmish line to contest the enemy, while his remaining artillery opened fire. As Vaughn finally managed to rally a small part of his force in the rear, Palmer's guns halted the Federals, who withdrew back to Morristown.[499]

497. *O.R.* 39 (pt. 1): 852-853, (pt. 3): 819, 833-834 (quote, 834), 852, 871; Jordan, "62nd Regiment N. C. Troops" in Manarin and Jordan, *North Carolina Troops*, 15:25-26; Jordan, "64th Regiment N.C. Troops," in ibid., 15:158-159; service record file of Matthew H. Love, Thomas's Legion, Compiled Service Records of Confederate Soldiers from the State of North Carolina (M270), reel 570. For the operations against Saltville and other points in late September and early October, see *O.R.* 39 (pt. 1): 552-567. Matthew Love's role as leader of the contingent from Thomas's Legion is documented in requisitions and receipts for shoes dated October 17, October 20, and October 24 in his service file; on the latter document, he is listed as "Commdg Thomas Legion." The receipts for shoes are for seven men listed as members of Companies D, F, and G of the Legion; as these company letters correspond to those of the white companies in Thomas's command, they confirm Palmer's comments on Martin's orders as to which companies participated in the expedition.

498. *O.R.* 39 (pt. 1): 844-845, 847, 849-850, 853, (pt. 2): 348, 849, 863, 871, 877-878, (pt. 3): 784, 786, 801-802, 837, 854, 858, 45 (pt. 2): 775-777.

499. *O.R.* 39 (pt. 1): 847, 851, 853-858 (Palmer quote, 853).

Following the debacle, Vaughn and Palmer withdrew to Bull's Gap and then to Greeneville. Palmer went reluctantly and under protest, believing that the Confederates could make a stand. At Greeneville, the commanders parted ways: Vaughn continued down the railroad to Rheatown, while Palmer was ordered back to the District of Western North Carolina, having accomplished nothing concrete. The role played by Matthew Love's contingent from Thomas's command is not documented, including whether or not it was with the main body of Palmer's command at Russellville on October 28 or was part of the force left at Bull's Gap. Referring to the expedition in a statement that seems to bundle it together with some of Thomas's earlier operations in 1863 and 1864, Stringfield (who was not present) wrote in 1901 that "[t]hat part of the regiment with Colonel J. B. Palmer that operated in East Tennessee between Hot Springs, N.C., and Morristown, New Market, Newport and Bull's Gap, etc. and along the foot of the Smoky Mountains by Sevierville, Maryville, etc., is reported to have done faithful service." Palmer specifically singled out the Legion in his own wartime report on the expedition, the only unit to which he in fact directly referred; however, his comments did not exactly jibe with Stringfield's. "Thomas' legion, as at present organized, is of but little if any use, either for local defense or aggressive movements."[500] Possibly for this reason, it does not appear that any part of Thomas's Legion was involved in Breckinridge's subsequent drive into eastern Tennessee in mid-November, an operation in which Palmer participated.

Thomas's command was not the only element of Palmer's command of questionable utility as 1864 drew to a close. Lt. Col. and Confederate Asst. Adj. Gen. David Urquhart wrote to Samuel Cooper on December 8 that the members of the 62nd and 64th Regiments N.C. Troops who had been absent without leave prior to the capture of their regiments at Cumberland Gap "are really deserters and stragglers," and therefore could not be relied upon to hunt down other deserters. Urquhart's assessment was an unfair oversimplification of the status of the men who constituted the reorganized remnants of these regiments; however, as both units had relatively high desertion rates before their surrenders, it is possible that some may have been absentees who, like those in Thomas's ranks, wanted to serve near home. Regardless, Urquhart may have been right about their unreliability for hunting deserters, given the unpopularity of the conscription laws. He noted "the case of a Captain Poor, who has fifty men in his company, all from the Twenty-fifth North Carolina Regiment of the Army of Northern Virginia. He says he is hunting up deserters. Every one of these men are deserters." "Captain" Poor was evidently 2nd Lt. Julius A. Poor of Company A, 25th Regiment N.C. Troops. Urquhart was probably right to suspect that Poor and his "company" were not involved in any legitimate purpose, as Poor had resigned from the service in October. Regardless, the district was beset by two interconnected problems: unreliable, understrength units, and deserters from both armies lurking in the mountains. Urquhart felt that a force was

500. *O.R.* 39 (pt. 1): 854 (Palmer quote), (pt. 3): 857, 865; Stringfield, "Sixty-ninth Regiment," in Clark, *North Carolina Regiments*, 3:756 (quote). In his histories of the 62nd and 64th Regiments N.C. Troops, Weymouth T. Jordan Jr. concluded that those two units were present at Russellville. Given the small size of Love's command, it would seem logical that it was part of the force left behind at Bull's Gap. The matter currently cannot be proven, however. Jordan, "62nd Regiment N.C. Troops" in Manarin and Jordan, *North Carolina Troops*, 15:25-26; Jordan, "64th Regiment N.C. Troops," in ibid., 15:158-159.

needed to drive the deserters out and "mak[e] the mountains untenable for them"; where such a loyal force could be found at that point in the war was the question.[501]

Under the circumstances, the news that Love's battle-hardened section of the Legion was coming to western North Carolina was probably welcome both to local commanders and the civilian population. Once it arrived, however, it would take time for the Legion to regain its strength, and Love's contingent would have to be integrated with Thomas's section. Preparations to address these matters had been going on for some time. Even before Special Order No. 267 were issued on November 9, the groundwork was being laid for the return of the Legion to Thomas in accord with the earlier orders from May. In late September Love ordered Stringfield to proceed to North Carolina to take charge of the elements of the Legion already there. The immediate impetus was the absence of Thomas, due to his impending court martial; in his place, the North Carolina contingent of the Legion was under the temporary command of Lt. Col. Bryan Gibbs McDowell of the 62nd Regiment N.C. Troops.[502]

501. *O.R.* 53:380-381 (quotes, 381). For discussions of desertion problems within the 62nd and 64th Regiments N.C. Tropps and their reorganizations following Cumberland Gap, see Jordan, "62nd Regiment N.C. Troops" in Manarin and Jordan, *North Carolina Troops*, 15:12-23, 27, and Jordan, "64th Regiment N.C. Troops" in ibid., 149-155, 160-161. For Julius A. Poor's service record, see ibid., 7: 357-358.

502. Love to Stephen Whitaker, September 30, 1864, Whitaker Papers, NCOAH; Special Requisition dated October 16, 1864, in which McDowell signed hmself "Lt Col Comdg[.]," service record file of D.C. Ghormley, 5th Regiment Tennessee Cavalry (McKenzie's), Compiled Service Records of Confederate Soldiers from the State of Tennessee (M268), reel 25; Special Requisition dated October 17, 1864, in which McDowell signs himself as "Lt Col Comdg Thomas Legion" with his headquarters in Asheville, service record file of B. G. McDowell, 62nd Regiment N.C. Troops, Compiled Service Records of Confederate Soldiers from the State of North Carolina (M270), reel 552; Palmer to J. W. Riely, January 17, 1865, Chapter 1: Mss. 1225, Entry 183, Box 12, RG 109, NA; McDowell to Stringfield, January 26, 1912, Stringfield Collection, WCU. The date on which McDowell assumed command is unknown. In 1912, McDowell stated to Stringfield that "I was ordered as you no doubt remember (soon after Col Thomas was relieved of his Command) to take charge of his command composed largely of Indians, which I did. I had that portion of his Legion under me for some time, but how long, I dont now remember." Palmer's wartime letter confirms this arrangement, noting that McDowell "was placed by me in command of the Legion while Col Thomas was under arrest." There has been some confusion about the nature of McDowell's assignment and its circumstances in more recent works. In *Storm in the Mountains*, Vernon H. Crow asserted that Palmer put McDowell in command after the return of the main body from Virginia in December, due to an illness suffered by Love; his cited sources were McDowell's letter to Stringfield and William C. Allen's 1935 *The Annals of Haywood County*. Although McDowell noted in 1912 that "[y]ou know Col Jas R Love had command of a portion of the Legion in the Valley of Va. if I am not mistaken," nowhere did he claim that he actually commanded Love's contingent. The page cited from Allen's book by Crow merely quoted Stringfield's 1901 history of the Infantry Regiment in Clark's *Regiments* verbatim. In it, Stringfield wrote that "[t]hat part of the regiment with Colonel J. B. Palmer that operated in East Tennessee between Hot Springs, N.C., and Morristown, New Market, Newport and Bull's Gap, etc., and along the foot of the Smoky Mountains by Sevierville, Maryville, etc., is reported to have done faithful service under Lieutenant-Colonel B. G. McDowell, of the Sixty-second." Although Stringfield placed this comment within a discussion of the situation in western North Carolina following his and the regiment's return near the end of the year, it seems that he was lumping together Palmer's expedition into eastern Tennessee in October 1864 with other actions associated with Thomas's contingent. Allen mentioned that Love took a rest due to health problems following his return to North Carolina on another page of the book, but did not link his absence to McDowell's tenure. The statement in volume 15 of this series that McDowell took over a portion of Love's Infantry Regiment in August 1864 is therefore correct only insofar as two of the Indian companies were formerly part of the regiment. The history of the 62nd Regiment N.C. Troops in volume 15 stated that McDowell assumed command some time about August 25, while his published service file put the date at August 8. An abstract of payments in McDowell's service

Stringfield departed on October 1. Love meanwhile wrote Capt. Stephen Whitaker of Company E, Walker's Battalion, who was at home recuperating from an illness, to gather up all of the men from Walker's Battalion (and, by implication, from the whole Legion) who were in the mountains and have them ready for Stringfield's arrival. Whitaker was informed that other Legion officers present in the mountains should also report to Stringfield. Love had evidently heard rumors about the disciplinary state of Thomas's contingent; praising the conduct of the portion under his own command in the Valley, he stated pointedly that "I shall do all in my power to make the Command efficient," and "with proper discipline All can be brought to the same standards of soldiership."[503]

Stringfield's trek was basically without incident until he reached Emory, Virginia, on October 8, where he stopped to see his relocated family. While there, he visited the local hospital and nearly lost his life. Champ Ferguson, a notorious Confederate guerrilla long associated with John Hunt Morgan, entered the building and killed a Federal lieutenant. Although unarmed, Stringfield assisted a local college professor and members of the hospital staff in confronting Ferguson, who backed down and left without killing any more of the wounded. After the war, Stringfield testified at Ferguson's trial in Nashville, where he was convicted and executed.[504]

After taking time to visit friends in eastern Tennessee, Stringfield departed Emory some time between October 17 and 19. He arrived at Asheville on October 26, where he would have reported for orders. On October 31 he reached Quallatown, which he sardonically described as "the long heard of place of Security where Yankees never come and conscripts find shelter." Referring to his roundabout travels as "a long and tiresome journey of one month," he decided to "rest awhile before I undertake to Straiten out this end of the Legion." His initial assessment was mixed. "I find matters in rather a crude State here, but Most all Seem good Men & glad I am to assume command[.] Col Thomas, in his excess of kindness, goes too far, but he is a true Southerner, which I formerly doubted. Troops are

record file for the month of August was issued on the latter date; however, it represents payment for McDowell's service in the 62nd N.C. for the period of September 1863 through February 1864, and would thus appear to have nothing to do with his service with the Legion. Thomas issued orders at least through August 26, and the date of his relief is unknown. Crow, *Storm in the Mountains*, 112-113, 252 n. 43; Allen, *Annals of Haywood County*, 81, 86; Stringfield, "Sixty-Ninth Regiment," in Clark, *North Carolina Regiments*, 3:756; Manarin and Jordan, *North Carolina Troops*, 15:22, 35; service record file of B. G. McDowell, Compiled Service Records of Confederate Soldiers from the State of North Carolina (M270), reel 552; Thomas to Sergeant Brown, August 26, 1864, unbound letterbook, Thomas Papers, DU.

503. Stringfield Diary (1864), October 1, Stringfield Papers, NCOAH; Love to Whitaker, September 30, 1864, Whitaker Papers, NCOAH.

504. Stringfield Diary (1864), October 1-6, 8, Stringfield Collection, NCOAH; Stringfield, "Memoirs of the Civil War," typescript, McClung Collection, L-McGL (copy, Stringfield Papers, WCU), 19-20, 28-30; *O.R.* 39 (pt. 1): 554-556; F. A. Butler to Stringfield, January 18-19, 1865, Stringfield Collection, NCOAH. The incident seems to have been partly mixed up with (or at least immediately followed) the murder of two black prisoners of war in the hospital on the previous day, although the latter tragedy may have been connected with the killing of some wounded black soldiers following the battle of Saltville on October 3. In his memoirs, Stringfield recounted two different versions of the Ferguson incident, with widely varying details, and misdated Ferguson's visit to October 6, the day of the killing of the black prisoners. According to Frank A. Butler, Stringfield's brother-in-law, Emory was spared the destruction inflicted upon neighboring communities during a December raid by Federal Maj. Gen. George Stoneman due to the actions taken by Stringfield and others on behalf of the wounded prisoners.

Scattered along the Smoky Mts & Tenn line, to Haywood [County and] Murphy in Cherokee Co. I will have to study geography a while & men afterwards." Stringfield eventually decided to make his headquarters at Franklin in Macon County, a more centrally located position than Quallatown, although he recognized that his responsibilities would require him to "be much in the Saddle."[505]

Stringfield had his work cut out for him. "I was here on duty . . . in the Midst of Scattered bands of Scouts—Deserters—Conscript officers—with not half Soldiers enough to protect the people & families of our brave Men in the field," he recalled many years later. "There were daily appeals to Me as commander for protection." An example of Stringfield's efforts were provided after the war by Pleasant Henry, a resident of Blount County, Tennessee, who wrote in support of Stringfield's efforts to receive a pardon. A wartime Unionist, Henry reported that he received permission from Stringfield to move from Cherokee County to the Federal-occupied area of eastern Tennessee, along with an escort under a flag of truce. Before Henry could leave, Confederate soldiers took one of his horses. Henry sent his son to Stringfield, who seized the horse and kept it until Henry was ready to depart, at which point he returned it to him. Henry also reported the case of another former Cherokee County resident, E. A. Deweese, whose oxen and a horse were seized by Captain Whitaker. Deweese asked Stringfield for help. Whitaker justified his actions on the ground that Deweese was supposed to be "a Stray union man." Stringfield told Whitaker that he had no right to take anyone's property "for opinions sake" and ordered him to return the animals.[506]

On one occasion, Stringfield had a run-in with a soldier who was not only fond of drink, but who made the liquid on the side. Stringfield confronted him when he refused to back down: "I stopped him—and he nearly Stopped me."[507] Such incidents doubtless increased as Stringfield used the Legion against alcohol manufacturers in the area. "I was sent to Cherokee county to protect the citizenship from rude attacks by a band of lawless scouts and deserters," he wrote later. "Here I made many friends and some enemies by destroying stills and capturing violators of the law. . . . Nothing ever afforded me greater pleasure than destroying whiskey joints."[508] Other problems Stringfield faced bordered on the bizarre. A few days after the incident with the drinker, he went to Clay County to muster in a company of men and "was astonished and Indignant" when the recruits "came marching into town under the 'Stars and Stripes.'" The captain attempted to explain the incident away as a prank, but when Stringfield checked further, he found that sixty-two of the men were Confederate deserters. As he had gone alone to the muster, there was nothing he could do.[509]

505. Stringfield Diary (1864), October 9-10, 13, 15-17, 19-21, 25-26, 28-31, Stringfield Collection, NCOAH. All quotes in the paragraph above came from the October 31 entry, although given that the next entry is November 13 it is possible that they represent jottings made over several days. Vernon H. Crow, *Storm in the Mountains*, 135, 255 n. 38, pointed out that Franklin lay on a direct route to Walhalla, from where the Legion got most of its supplies.

506. Stringfield, "War—Mss," ledger book, 72-74 (quote, 72), Stringfield Collection, NCOAH; Pleasant Henry to Stringfield, December 24, 1866 (photostat copy of the original from James Mooney, Bureau of American Ethnology, April _, 1917), Stringfield Papers, WCU.

507. Stringfield, "War—Mss," ledger book, 90, NCOAH.

508. Stringfield, "Memoirs of the Civil War," typescript, McClung Collection, L-McGL (copy, Stringfield Papers, WCU), 21.

509. Stringfield, "War—Mss," ledger book, 90, NCOAH.

Even though his court martial was over, Thomas was still absent when Stringfield arrived. The colonel had gone to Richmond, and as noted earlier may have seen Davis in connection with the outcome of the trial. It seems he did quite a bit of politicking, as he was evidently responsible for the November 9 order returning the rest of the Legion to North Carolina.[510] Another document issued on the same day by Lt. Col. Samuel Melton, Confederate assistant adjutant general, strengthened Thomas's position. Thomas was granted

> [a]uthority . . . to recruit companies of the Legion within the enemies lines in East Tennessee and the adjacent counties of North Carolina west of the Blue Ridge where the conscript law cannot be enforced. . . . The Indians and persons not liable to service . . . may at the expiration of their time be re-enlisted for the war with the usual allotment of bounty & co.
>
> Col Thomas is authorized to employ one of his companies as Engineers or Sappers and Miners and such companies as may be necessary as Sharp shooters and as mounted Riflemen. . . . Companies belonging to the Legion will not be detached from Col Thomas command except in emergency and then only temporarily.

Perhaps not surprisingly, Thomas interpreted the final passage to mean that he answered directly to Martin only, a view that Palmer would not share.[511]

All-in-all, when Thomas returned it must have been with an air of triumph, as he could finally structure the Legion as originally intended. Others did not welcome the news. North Carolina's adjutant general, Richard C. Gatlin, who was in favor of recruiting new units for local defense, wrote Martin in December that "I have seen an order from the Secy of War authorizing Col Thomas to fill up his Legion from those counties where conscription cannot be enforced. If he is willing to throw away men in this way, he probably would not object to having them enlisted in such organizations as might have some show of usefulness."[512] More criticism came from those charged with conducting and enforcing conscription in the state. 1st Lt. L. H. Yabb, the conscription officer in Macon, Jackson, and Haywood counties, complained in early December to his commanding officer, Col. Peter Mallett, that all but one of a group of detailed men ordered to report to camp had refused to do so, having joined Thomas instead. Yabb wondered how men assigned to other units had a right to volunteer for the Legion, or if Thomas had been given some special authority to recruit them. Mallett in turn approached Holmes to get the orders rescinded. "This Officer [Thomas] has been on Several occasions reported for direct violation and total disregard of orders from the A. & I.G. Office—and interfering by enlisting and retaining Conscripts without authority." Mallett warned that Thomas's mandate "opens the door wider for abuse, and will cause constant interference with orders from this Department making his Command as already

510. Stringfield Diary (1864), October 31, November 13, Stringfield Collection, NCOAH; Thomas to Sarah Thomas, November 13, 1864, Thomas Papers, WCU. Thomas annoyed the adjutant and inspector general with his meddling, writing his wife that Cooper was "not well pleased with my success" in preventing him from permanently disbanding the Legion, as had been the earlier fate of similar units. According to Thomas, both Davis and Seddon supported him against the adjutant general.

511. Samuel Melton to Thomas, November 9, 1864, and Cooper to Seddon, January 6, 1865 (endorsement on Thomas to Seddon, December 26, 1864), service record file of William H. Thomas, Thomas's Legion, Compiled Service Records of Confederate Soldiers from the State of North Carolina (M270), reel 573; Thomas to Sarah Thomas, November 13, 1864, Thomas Papers, WCU. Thomas told his wife Sarah that the new orders gave him "the privlege of reporting to the commanding genl [Martin] only."

512. Adjutant General [Chilton] to J. Martin, December 7, 1864, Adjutant General's Letter book, 1864-1865 (AG-55), Adjutant General's Papers, NCOAH.

reported an asylum for recusant Conscripts and Deserters." Holmes endorsed Mallett's request and forwarded it and Yabb's message to Adjutant and Inspector General Cooper.[513]

Concerned about the extent of his authority, Thomas wrote Secretary of War Seddon in late December for confirmation regarding both his recruitment powers and his original commission. The documents could not be found in the Adjutant and Inspector General's Office, however; the only description of Thomas's authority was in Melton's November 9 message, which was forwarded to Seddon. Annoyed over Thomas's recent antics in Richmond, Cooper sided firmly with Mallett, writing Seddon in early January that he "regret[ted] that any authority should be given Col. Thomas for raising the Legion," and "earnestly" recommended that the authorization be revoked. "I am fully convinced from what has proceeded in respect to that Legion on a former occasion, that it will be of no possible benefit to the Confederacy under the command of this officer. This authority was granted on the 9th Novbr last, & he has been in this city without authority since that time until the past ten days or a fortnight when he should have been at his post." Echoes of the dispute reached Davis, who wrote Seddon that "[m]y attention has been called to the order authorizing Colonel Thomas to recruit for his Legion men found in the section of country where the enrollment act cannot be enforced. If it has not been done this order should be communicated to [Lieutenant] General [T.] H. Holmes, with instructions to define the country thus generally described, and to fix its geographical limits so as to prevent confusion and conflict with the authority of the enrolling officers in North Carolina." Seddon subsequently ordered Cooper to have Thomas return the men referred to by Yabb "and all other conscripts . . . under penalty of having his powers revoked."[514]

These criticisms of Thomas occurred as the situation in the mountains reached a crisis point. An increasingly desperate Vance wrote Breckinridge in late October of conditions "in certain locations, particularly in Cherokee County and the region bordering," the area occupied by Thomas and his contingent of the Legion, where "the warfare between scattering bodies of irregular troops is conducted by both sides without any regard whatever to the rules of civilized warfare or the dictates of humanity. The murder of prisoners and non-combatants in cold blood has, I learn, become quite common, and, in fact, almost every other horror incident to brutal and unrestrained soldiery." Vance wanted to end these problems once and for all. "The troops on our side are all commissioned and regularly authorized home guards or militia are under my control, and can be made to conform to the usages of war provided a similar control can be exercised over our enemies." He asked Breckinridge to request the Federal authorities in eastern Tennessee to exercise greater control over their own irregular and local units, whom Vance dismissed as "mostly tory renegades from both North Carolina and Tennessee." If things continued as they did, Vance saw nothing but an

513. L. H. Yabb to E. F. Harden, December 6, 1864, with endorsements by Peter Mallett, December 13, 1864, and T. H. Holmes, December 15, 1864, service record file of William H. Thomas, Thomas's Legion, Compiled Service Records of Confederate Soldiers from the State of North Carolina (M270), reel 573.

514. Thomas to Seddon, December 26, 1864, John B. Hoge to Cooper, January 5, 1864 (endorsement of Thomas to Seddon letter), Cooper to Seddon, January 6, 1864 (endorsement of Thomas to Seddon letter), Seddon to Cooper, January 10, 1865 (endorsement of Yabb to Harden, December 6, 1864), service record file of William H. Thomas, Thomas's Legion, Compiled Service Records of Confederate Soldiers from the State of North Carolina (M270), reel 573; *O.R.* 46 (pt. 2): 1006; Crow, *Storm in the Mountains*, 114-115.

increasingly escalating pattern of violence and retaliation, something that he himself felt obliged to authorize in response to certain acts but nevertheless deplored. "I will not stop to show that any acts of violence on our part are more than provoked and justified by the atrocities of the enemy, as I am not seeking to exculpate my own people or inculpate those of the Federals; I desire only, if possible, to check the evil." Vance requested that Breckinridge contact Palmer, "and give him such instructions as you may think best for bringing about the desired end." Vance also wrote Lee on or about the same date in a message discussing these problems alongside other issues related to the state's defense. "I hope that the troops under Colonel Palmer are sufficient for the necessities of that region, especially as he is now co-operating with General Breckinridge so as to prevent the advance of the enemy from East Tennessee," Lee replied, while simultaneously recommending the transfer of troops from the western part of the state to shore up the defenses of Wilmington.[515]

Christopher G. Memminger, former Confederate secretary of the treasury, wrote Davis from Flat Rock in early December, describing western North Carolina as in a "state of anarchy." With most of the loyal Confederate men in the army, there was no one to protect the area from the bands of deserters holed up in the mountains. Memminger believed that the deserters were organized into at least two bands, which had "driven away some of the inhabitants, and they seem to proceed only against the low country people and the families of soldiers who are absent in the army." Memminger claimed that "Yankee officers have been seen among" the deserter bands, which in his interpretation meant that their actions were part of deliberately directed Federal policy "so as to discontent the [Confederate] soldiers and induce them to desert."[516] While Memminger believed that "[i]t would seem a task of no great difficulty to capture or destroy these outlaws," such was not the case, due to the operations which drew Palmer into eastern Tennessee to cooperate with Breckinridge. "On each of these occasions the deserters have taken advantage of his absence to renew their outrages." Memminger also believed that corrruption and inefficiency in the administration of court-martials and punishments for deserters contributed to the problem. The solution to these problems lay in making the District of Western North Carolina into a distinct, separate military jurisdiction. "The region now under the charge of [Lieutenant] General Holmes is so extensive and inaccessible that he cannot possibly conduct its business." On the basis of Palmer's character and his role in salvaging Vaughn's rout at Russellville, Memminger recommended his promotion to brigadier general to command a new department.[517]

In mid-December, Vance reinforced the arguments for a change in the command structure in western North Carolina. "Colonel Thomas is worse than useless; he is a positive injury to that country," the governor wrote in a blistering attack. "His command is a favorite resort for deserters; numbers of them, I learn, are on his rolls, who do no service. He is disobedient of orders, and invariably avoids the enemy when he advances." While Vance described Palmer as "a good bureau officer," the governor thought him "unfitted for field

515. *O.R.* 42 (pt. 3): 1183-1184. The published version of Vance's letter to Breckinridge is dated October 29, but the copy in Vance's letterbook gives October 25 as the date. See Vance to Breckinridge, October 25, 1864, Governors' Letterbook, Zebulon Baird Vance, 1862-1864, GLB 50.1, pp. 601-602, NCOAH. According to Lee, Vance wrote him on October 25.

516. Another possibility is that any Federals seen among these bands may have been deserters themselves.

517. *O.R.* 42 (pt. 3): 1251-1252.

service, especially of the peculiar character required in that country." Vance recommended that English-born Collett Leventhorpe, former colonel of the 11th Regiment N.C. Troops (1st North Carolina Volunteers) and currently a brigadier general in the state service, be promoted to Confederate brigadier general and placed in command of the district. Vance's letter made the rounds and eventually was filed as part of the correspondence related to Memminger's message. When Seddon received the governor's communication, he wrote that "[t]he complaints against Colonel Thomas and Colonel Palmer surprise me, as I had, from all the representations made, supposed them both to be particularly efficient. It may be, however, that the appointment of [a] brigadier to give unity to the command might prove beneficial, and therefore I submit Governor Vance's letter." Davis replied a few days later, with perhaps a touch of asperity, "Is not Brigadier-General Martin in command of the District of Western North Carolina? If so, his experience and tried gallantry should secure good order and public confidence." As to Martin, Seddon acknowledged a bit sheepishly that "Brigadier-General Martin is in such command."[518]

Davis thought that Lee should be consulted. Lee echoed Memminger's recommendations that the District of Western North Carolina be separated from Holmes's jurisdiction because of distance and communication problems; this would also place the district more directly under Lee's own authority, as its commander would answer directly to him. Lee suggested that Martin should be retained in command, but if he did "not succeed, Colonel Palmer, whom I believe to be an excellent officer, can be tried." He added that Leventhorpe should be promoted but ordered to Bragg, who since November 11 commanded the Department of North Carolina, covering the area east of the Blue Ridge.[519] Davis meanwhile responded to Memminger on January 4. "The force of General Martin is the only available one," he wrote. "It consists of troops under Colonel Palmer, Thomas' Legion, and home militia. Thomas' Legion, now being recruited, it is hoped will be able to afford sufficient aid to disperse or capture the bands infesting that district." Davis promised that the South Carolina Reserves would also help "[s]hould circumstances allow," while Lee instructed Breckinridge to help as much as he could, perhaps even detaching a force to cooperate with Martin in eastern Tennessee. "General Lee will give the matter his further attention, and no means will be spared to afford protection to the loyal people of western North Carolina."[520] Unfortunately, Lee was preoccupied with the Petersburg-Richmond front, while Confederate commanders in eastern Tennessee expected the forces in western North Carolina to cooperate with their operations, not the other way around.

518. Ibid., 1253-1254. For Leventhorpe, see Warner, *Generals in Gray*, 185.

519. *O.R.* 42 (pt. 3): 1252-1254. Although Bragg's appointment specifically stated that his department covered North Carolina east of the Blue Ridge, he thought it should be otherwise, and complained in January of Martin's subordination to Holmes, rather than to Bragg himself. *O.R.* 42 (pt. 3): 1209, 1218, 46 (pt. 2): 1019.

520. Ibid. 46 (pt. 2): 1005-1006, 1013. Davis's reply to Memminger was not included in the packet containing the correspondence related to Memminger's and Vance's letters. In a separate letter to Seddon written a day earlier, Davis directed that the understrength companies in the 62nd and 64th Regiments N.C. Troops be recruited in the mountains and then exchanged to Lee for North Carolina units in the Army of Northern Virginia which were understrength and in need of recruiting in turn. Such a process would help rebuild the North Carolina units at the vital Virginia front and doubtless would solve various practical problems of the recruiting process, but would at the same time always insure that such units on duty in western North Carolina were in a weakened state. The Legion was evidently intended to fill the gap in coverage.

Palmer added his own voice to the calls for change. He convinced Bragg and Breckinridge that Thomas and the Indians needed to be separated from the whites, with Love in command of the latter and either Thomas or Capt. James W. Terrell in charge of the former. Breckinridge passed on his recommendations to Lee, who wrote to Secretary of War Seddon on the matter on December 12. "I know nothing of this organization of the Thomas Legion & will be glad to know something about it, how it was raised, its strength, the proportion of Indians to whites," Lee wrote. "You will oblige me much by causing this information to be sent to me from the Department. I am anxious to render Col Palmer's command as effective as possible as it has already done good Service in Co operating with Gen. Breckinridge in East Tennessee." The Adjutant and Inspector General's Office soon wrote Palmer for information on Lee's behalf, and received other materials critical of Thomas and the Legion. Both Palmer's letter and the additional items he mentioned were probably circulated among the Confederate authorities at this time.[521]

In February, after Lee was appointed commander of all Confederate armies, Palmer's and Breckinridge's ideas were referred to Martin. While Palmer's correspondence and reports to Breckinridge appear not to have survived, their contents can be inferred from the final endorsement on Lee's letter to Breckinridge, written by Lee's assistant adjutant general on February 22: "The Gen. In Chief desires that the absent men of the command be required to return and desires General Martin to see that discipline is maintained in the Legion and that every effort be made to render it efficient. If any of the officers are incompetent steps should be taken to have them removed and if orders are not obeyed charges must be preferred and the officers brought to trial." Martin in turn defended Thomas. "Col. Thomas certainly is no Military man, but many allowances are to be made for him," citing the former's lack of a quartermaster and commissary, a supply base, or an adequate transportation system.[522]

It was in the midst of these controversies that Love and the remnant of the main body of the Legion arrived in western North Carolina. Having been held up in Staunton for several days by winter weather, it had finally set out by train on November 21. Traveling via Lynchburg, Bristol, and Jonesborough, the Legion crossed the North Carolina border on December 2. After marching to Warm Springs and through Asheville, it encamped at Alexandria. Palmer estimated its strength upon its return as around 110 men. Upon arrival, Love assumed command of the reunited Legion. One of the first things he did was attempt to get Barr's Battery returned to the Legion, issuing special orders to Barr on December 5 to

521. Palmer to Robert Strange, October 10, 1864, with endorsement by Bragg, October 11, 1864, and Lee to Seddon, December 12, 1864, Letters Received by the Confederate Adjutant & Inspector General's Office (M474), reel 126, file 1662-L-1864; Palmer to J. W. Rieley, January 17, 1865, Chapter 1: Mss 1225, Entry 183, Box 12, RG 109, NA. Major Rieley was an officer in the Adjutant and Inspector General's Office. Among other sources, Palmer cited letters written by Lieutenant Colonel McDowell; Lt. F. F. Davidson, a former officer on Brigadier General Vance's staff, who had inspected the Legion at Palmer's request; and J. H. Wilkes, adjutant of the 62nd Regiment N.C. Troops, who had previously served as adjutant to Donelson and Buckner as department commanders and who according to Palmer was Thomas's adjutant in western North Carolina. The actual letters (many of them barely legible) are found in Letters Received by the Confederate Adjutant and Inspector General's Officer (M474), reel 126, file 1662-L-1864.

522. Endorsements on Lee to Seddon, December 12, 1864, by Walter H. Taylor, February 22, 1865, and Martin, March 11, 1865, Letters Received by the Confederate Adjutant and Inspector General's Officer (M474), reel 126, file 1662-L-1864.

proceed immediately via Lynchburg and Danville to Morganton, bringing both the guns and all baggage. The battery remained in Virginia, however, despite Barr's efforts to carry the orders out.[523] There may have also been an effort to reinstate some of the officers dismissed by Jackson. In a telegram to the governor, Love asked if Vance "had read the communication of former officers of this command[?] If so what action has been taken[?]"[524] Once Thomas himself finally returned from Richmond, one of the problems he faced was how the Legion should be organized. The scanty available information suggests that for the moment, Thomas's western North Carolina command remained under Stringfield, with Love over the combined Infantry Regiment and McKamy's Battalion as in the Valley; however, this arrangement is by no means certain.[525]

Until the Legion reorganized and recruited to greater strength, it was relatively useless for major field operations. As the fighting continued, however, it was inevitable that it would be called up for local operations, regardless of its condition. As noted earlier, it does not seem to have been involved in Breckinridge's movement into eastern Tennessee in November. Following his defeat at Morristown, Vaughn had withdrawn to the east side of the Watauga River at Carter's Depot. The Federals followed, a move which made Breckinridge uneasy for the security of Bristol. He gathered together a little army totaling around 1,800 men, consisting of Vaughn's and Brig. Gen. Basil Duke's cavalry, dismounted men from the commands of Duke, Brig. Gen. George B. Cosby, and Col. Henry L. Giltner, elements of the Tennessee Reserves, and some men from the niter and mining operations, along with six artillery pieces. Breckinridge moved forward in early November, pushing back Gillem's advance forces. Gillem fell back to Greeneville and then to Bull's Gap. After fighting at Bull's Gap from November 11-13, Gillem withdrew as Confederate reinforcements arrived. These were Palmer's forces, estimated at about 600 men and probably consisting of the 62nd and 64th Regiments N.C. Troops. Vaughn and Duke routed Gillem's rearguard on the night of November 14 at Russellville. Breckinridge pursued as far as Strawberry Plains, but found the Federal position there was too strong to attempt to carry. After skirmishing and demonstrating against the Federal rear for several days, Breckinridge withdrew the bulk of

523. Crow, *Storm in the Mountains*, 110-111; Palmer to Rieley, January 17, 1865, Chapter 1: Mss 1225, Entry 183, Box 12, RG 109, NA; Barr to Samuel Cooper, February 10, 1865, and Love to Barr, December 5, 1864 (inclosure), Letters Received by the Confederate Adjutant and Inspector General's Office (M474), reel 153, item 279-B-1865, NA. See also pp. 164-165 and n. 383.

524. Love to Vance, [December] 1864, Governors' Papers: Vance, 1862-1865, NCOAH. It is possible that this message, tentatively dated to December 1864, belongs to an earlier period when the Legion was still with Jackson. Love mentioned that Confederate forces were at Bull's Gap, and that Federal raids into western North Carolina were expected. Since the date of the telegram is unknown, that information is not necessarily helpful, although it probably refers to the situation prior to Stoneman's raid in mid-December 1864, when much of Breckinridge's command was reported at Bull's Gap. See *O.R.* 45 (pt. 1), 1104, 1129. Former captain C. C. Berry of Company A, Walker's Battalion, appeared before a Board of Inquiry in February in regards to Jackson's old charges, which recommended that he be reinstated; it is possible that Love's letter was connected with that upcoming case. Matthew H. Love, Luther C. May, and Robert A. Akin, report on Board of Inquiry Examining the Case of C. C. Berry, February 20, 1865, Letters Received by the Confederate Adjutant and Inspector General (M 474), reel 96, file 2167-B-1864, RG 109, NA.

525. Stringfield, "Sixty-Ninth Regiment," in Clark, *North Carolina Regiments*, 3:757; Stringfield, "Memoirs of the Civil War," typescript, McClung Collection, L-McGL, (copy in Stringfield Papers, WCU), 22.

his force, relying on Vaughn and the onset of winter weather to keep the Federals at bay. "I do not the think he [the enemy] will attempt a campaign this winter in upper East Tennessee," he concluded optimistically.[526]

He was wrong. On December 10, Maj. Gen. George Stoneman launched a major raid from Knoxville towards southwestern Virginia. Prior to setting out, he sent Lt. Col. Michael L. Patterson's 4th Regiment Tennessee Volunteer Infantry (Union) and Kirk's 3rd Regiment N.C. Mounted Infantry (Union) on a subsidiary movement to hold the passes into western North Carolina until the Confederate forces in eastern Tennessee were driven out, at which point Patterson would move down the French Broad to protect Federal forage parties. Kirk would meanwhile sweep the mountains to clear them of Confederates. Stoneman went with the main body, consisting of the cavalry brigades of Gillem and of Bvt. Maj. Gen. Stephen G. Burbridge of the District of Kentucky, to Bean's Station on December 11. The expedition set out for Kingsport on the following day. Although Stoneman exaggerated the subsequent degree of his success, the Confederates were pushed into southwestern Virginia, Saltville was captured, and the salt works destroyed.[527]

As part of his standing orders to cooperate with Breckinridge as much as possible, Palmer was expected to link up with Vaughn and strike at Stoneman's rear. He began his movement relatively late, on December 20, possibly due to tardiness on part of the Legion to reach his point of concentration.[528] Palmer's main body consisted of the 62nd and 64th Regiments N.C. Troops. In order to push forward, Palmer first had to clear Patterson and Kirk out of his path. The role played by the Legion in Palmer's subsequent operation is difficult to entangle, as he was not precise as to dates and other vital information in his report. He wrote that the Federals withdrew as he advanced, with Kirk halting in Washington County, Tennessee. In the meantime, "[a]n unexpected and severe storm so raised the streams that the troops sent to the rear of the enemy did not reach there, and they escaped." By this time, the main action had already passed out of eastern Tennessee and into southwest Virginia. Recognizing that he was unable to comply with his original orders, and surmising that Kirk probably planned to move either against the Watauga and Holston railroad bridges or back into western North Carolina, Palmer decided to go after the pesky Unionist instead. "But for positive disobedience of orders by one of my subordinate officers, I would have surrounded and captured, or at least have effectually routed, Kirk's command," Palmer commented, stating that he drove Kirk back to Knoxville nonetheless. "A portion of my command, temporarily detached in carrying out my plans, returned without authority to North Carolina," he added. With the majority of his men nearly barefoot, he withdrew to western North Carolina

526. *O.R.* 39 (pt. 1): 885-898 (Breckinridge quote, 893). Breckinridge described Palmer's command as "a mixed force" (ibid., 892) but elaborated no further; Palmer's own report (a brief message to Breckinridge dated November 11) is equally unilluminating (ibid., 897-898). Stringfield's diary did not list individual entries between October 31 and November 13; the latter itself is the final surviving entry, and there is nothing to indicate that any part of the Legion went with Palmer (see also p. 218 above). It is therefore most likely that Palmer's contingent consisted of the 62nd and 64th Regiments N.C. Troops; the former was certainly present. Jordan, "62nd Regiment N.C. Troops," in Manarin and Jordan, *North Carolina Troops*, 15:26-27.

527. *O.R.* 45 (pt. 1): 807-839, 841.

528. Ibid., 45 (pt. 1): 841. For his part, Vaughn claimed that he never received his orders to attack Stoneman in the rear (ibid., 45 [pt. 1]: 825).

after a sixteen-day absence, placing his return sometime around January 5. "Want of promptness on the part of Thomas' Legion (only 200 of whom joined me, and most of them not until the 26th) prevented an earlier movement on my part," he wrote. "I am very anxious to do what I can to aid General Breckinridge, but much cannot be expected of me unless I am given the control of Thomas' Legion."[529]

Palmer's oblique style of writing did not work to his advantage in conveying what went wrong, as he did not explicitly link together the failure of part of his command to cut Kirk off due to a storm, the subordinate officer who deliberately disobeyed orders, the unauthorized return of part of his force to western North Carolina, and the tardy arrival of a portion of Thomas's Legion which supposedly delayed his early start. Although he apparently was referring in all four cases to the Legion, in what way is difficult to figure out. Stringfield wrote after the war that Love marched from Asheville to Yancey County in an effort to cut off Kirk, while Stringfield marched with about 300 men into eastern Tennessee to a spot about ten miles below Jonesborough, which in 1901 he estimated to be somewhere in the vicinity of the town of Unicoi. It appears from Stringfield's description that Palmer was attempting a double envelopment of Kirk, with Love and Stringfield sweeping around from opposite sides while Palmer threatened Kirk in front, although it is also possible that Love was part of Palmer's main column, or at least marching to join him. Stringfield wrote that his men were slowed by an eighteen-inch snowfall, the storm referred to by Palmer, and were thus unable to trap Kirk. "Meeting with neither disaster or success" and complaining of the lack of civilian support in that section of eastern Tennessee, Stringfield decided to return to North Carolina, taking a route through Paint Rock, Waynesville, Webster, Quallatown, and eventually following the local streams to Murphy. In his published memoir, however, he wrote that he rejoined Colonel Palmer "on the North side of Paint Mountain" and mentioned no other details of the return journey. Based on the comment in Stringfield's memoir, historian Vernon H. Crow believed that Stringfield's segment was the portion which arrived on December 26; however, that is not necessarily the case, as Palmer indicated that the late arrival of part of the Legion was due to "[w]ant of promptness," not the weather. Further, Palmer's report indicated a second effort to trap Kirk, at which point the "portion of my command, temporarily detached . . . returned without authority to North Carolina"; this would also seem to be the unit whose commander was guilty of "positive disobedience" in failing to cut off Kirk. It would seem that Stringfield was the officer whom Palmer accused of disobeying orders, and that the portion of Thomas's Legion led by Stringfield was the unit that made an unauthorized return to western North Carolina. The lack of chronological referents make the details difficult to determine, as Stringfield's account seemingly compresses the decision to return to North Carolina into a part of the same phase in which he and his men were slowed up by the storm; coupled with the ambiguities in Palmer's own report, this makes it difficult to understand the full reasons and timing for his supposed disobedience.[530] Ironically, Stringfield was anxious to cooperate with Palmer and avoid getting caught up in the conflict between him and Thomas, or at least so he claimed after the war.

529. Ibid., (pt. 1): 841-842 (quotes, 842).

530. Stringfield, "Sixty-Ninth Regiment," in Clark, *North Carolina Regiments*, 3:757; *O.R.* 45 (pt. 1): 842; Crow, *Storm in the Mountains*, 112-113.

Possibly this may have been an effort to deflect Palmer's criticism after the fact, however, as he also went to some pains to claim that Palmer actually supported his decision to retreat.[531]

Federal records shed little light on the incident. They reported that Kirk occupied Newport, Tennessee, on January 6, 1865. Although it was stated that he did not go deeper into North Carolina than Warm Springs, the Federals deemed his mission as "uniformly successful, killing over 100 of Palmer's men and the guerrillas, and wounding a large number." He also brought in 32 prisoners and 56 captured horses. Kirk reported his own losses as 2 killed and 4 wounded (including himself). He arrived back at Knoxville by January 17.[532]

Regardless of what happened, Stringfield reported that upon his return he "left behind me all the troops under Colonel Love." It is unclear if this meant that the former had been temporarily assigned some companies from the latter for the expedition. It is possible that he was making an oblique reference to the reorganization of the Legion, which may not have occurred prior to the expedition. Regardless, the Infantry Regiment went into camp at Locust Field, while Stringfield's force camped near Murphy.[533]

In the aftermath of Stoneman's raid, Lee wanted Palmer to establish a strong presence at Big Creek Gap, east of Rogersville. Palmer had previously put the 62nd and 64th N.C. there either after Breckinridge's November offensive or following Stoneman's countermove in December, but due to Vaughn's withdrawal from the Bull's Gap area to Greeneville, the regiments quickly pulled back to Warm Springs.[534] Palmer reassured Breckinridge's

531. "Palmer and Martin were in Command at Asheville, and I think Palmer had had much trouble with Colonel Thomas all through the year. I felt it my duty to obey the orders of Colonel Palmer and I did so for a month or so. . . . Colonel Palmer also endorsed my action in retreating from Nolly Chucky to Paint Mountain. . . . Finally we reached the springs where Colonel Palmer's forces were, and here it was that Colonel Palmer as commanding officer gave me his endorsement of the way I had conducted the retreat from East Tennessee." Stringfield, "Memoirs of the Civil War," typescript, McClung Collection, L-McGL (copy in Stringfield Papers, WCU), 22. By the time that Stringfield wrote these memoirs, the *Official Records* had been published and Stringfield would have had a chance to read Palmer's report.

532. *O.R.* 45 (pt. 2): 608-609 (quote, 609). According to Bumgarner, *Kirk's Raiders*, 53-56, Kirk ambushed Palmer's column (consisting at that point of the 64th Regiment N.C. Troops only) in the area of Paint Rock on December 13 and captured a few officers and men. The Confederates continued their progress in the ensuing bad weather to Erwin, Tennessee on December 26. This was the same storm which slowed Stringfield, whose men only got as far as Horse Creek before retiring to Warm Springs. Kirk then launched a surprise attack against Palmer early on December 29, in which the Confederates got the worst of the resulting skirmish. The 64th N.C. then pulled back hastily to Warm Springs, where it was joined by the rest of Palmer's command and the Legion and scattered the Federal pursuers in turn. Bumgarner placed Kirk's return to Knoxville at January 14.

533. Stringfield, "Sixty-Ninth Regiment," in Clark, *North Carolina Regiments*, 3:757.

534. There are difficulties in dating Palmer's and Vaughn's deployments due to Palmer's phrasing in his January 12 report. On the surface, it would seem that Palmer left the 62nd and 64th N.C. at Big Gap Creek following Stoneman's December raid, as this is where he discusses the matter chronologically in his report; they withdrew to North Carolina quickly when Vaughn suddenly pulled back "from below Bull's Gap, to Greeneville," either in late December or early January. This is the interpretation assumed in Jordan, "62nd Regiment N.C. Troops" and "64th Regiment N.C. Troops," in Manarin and Jordan, *North Carolina Troops*, 15: 29, 162. A careful reading of Palmer's report, coupled with a look at other Confederate and Federal documents associated with operations in the area from November through January, suggests instead that Palmer sent the regiments to Big Creek Gap following Breckinridge's advance in mid-November. Vaughn, who was left behind to watch the Federals from the vicinity of New Market and Strawberry Plains, withdrew in late November to the area of Morristown and Bull's Gap. By early December he was as far back as Jonesborough, but on December 7 he was at Greeneville, and was

headquarters that he would post both regiments at Spring Creek, with orders to scout as far as Big Creek Gap. He also ordered four companies of the Legion to Jonathan's Creek in Haywood County, to either support the forces at Spring Creek "or move into Tennessee as occasion may require." It is not known which companies of the Legion were referred to.[535]

There is little documentation for the Legion during 1865. Brig. Gen. Jacob Ammen, who commanded the Federal District of East Tennessee, estimated on January 10 that Palmer had around 1,000 men dispersed from Asheville outwards in the direction of Paint Rock. Vaughn was at Jonesborough with a force numbering around 600, while Breckinridge was in southwestern Virginia with an untold number of troops. In early January Palmer reported the Legion's approximate aggregate strength at 610, based on its last field return. He estimated the number of Indians as between 250 and 300, including "old men and small boys." Thomas had not sent in any field returns to either Palmer or Martin since September 1. Palmer gave no clues about the Legion's organization at the time, other than listing the staffs for the regiment, the battalion, and the Legion itself.[536]

In February Martin divided the district into two, one area covering the southwestern counties of the mountains and commanded by Thomas, and another centering on Asheville under Palmer. This made administrative sense geographically, and rather neatly resolved the problem of whom Thomas reported to. Martin also initiated the reorganization of the Legion. Love retained command of the Infantry Regiment, while Stringfield was put in command of McKamy's Battalion. The Indian companies were separated into another battalion, although who commanded it is unknown. A record from the district quartermaster for March 11 shows that the regiment had ten companies, while Stringfield's (McKamy's) Battalion had six; this indicates that the three white companies from Thomas's North Carolina command were distributed between the regiment and the battalion, two going to the former and one to the latter.[537] By this time, Thomas had acquired or been assigned a field piece. A return for March

still there at the start of Stoneman's raid. See especially *O.R.* 39 (pt. 1): 893, 45 (pt. 1): 810-811, 815, 817, 820, 825-828, 830-832, 835-836, 841-842 (quote, 842), 970, 1014, 1030, 1103, 1129, 1164, 1237, 1258, (pt. 2): 15, 632, 643, 646, 649, 657, 664, 671-672, 687, 698, 703-704, 708, 711-714. If this hypothesis is correct, the case illustrates the confusion which can arise from reading one of Palmer's reports, written in a series of isolated and semi-isolated segments which do not easily cohere into an orderly narrative.

535. *O.R.* 45 (pt. 1): 842. One of the companies may have been Company G, Infantry Regiment, as a man who applied for a pension for service in "Company G," Thomas's Legion reported that he was wounded at Jonathan's Creek in 1865. Robert Harrell, North Carolina Application for Pension (1901), State Auditor's Office Records, NCOAH. Companies E and F of the Regiment are also possible candidates due to the fact that they evidently saw action there during a raid by George W. Kirk in early February, as are Companies H and I, which were in Haywood County by late February.

536. *O.R.* 45 (pt.2): 565; Palmer to Rieley, January 17, 1865, Chapter 1: Mss 1225, Entry 183, Box 12, RG 109, NA; "Remarks," Tri-Monthly Field Return of the Troops in the Western District of N.C. Commanded by Brigadier General J. G. Martin, December 18, 1864, January 18, 1865, Chapter 1: vol. 15, 16, Entry 65, pt. 2, Entry 24, RG 109, NA. The last known field return from July gave an aggregate of 640 (see p. 210 above). Perhaps Palmer referred to the August field return, which does not seem to have survived, or perhaps "610" was a "slip of the pen" for 640.

537. Endorsements by Martin, March 11, 1865, on Lee to Seddon, December 12, 1864, Letters Received by the Confederate Adjutant and Inspector General's Officer (M474), reel 126, file 1662-L-1864; Consolidated Estimate of Funds Required for the Pay of the Troops in the Department of Western North Carolina for the Months of March and April 1865, March 11, 1865, Thomas Legion, Battalion Field and Staff File #1, Muster and Pay Rolls,

10 not only noted the gun but made a reference to Barr's Battery as if it was still part of the Legion; no report was included for it, however. The identity of this one-gun "battery" is unknown, although it may have included absentee members of Barr's Battery.[538]

Stringfield was promoted to lieutenant colonel, and Love to full colonel, on unknown dates.[539] Based on the scanty evidence, it seems that Thomas assigned Love and Stringfield

---

Chapter 1: Entry 18, Box 826, RG 109, NA. The number of companies is deduced from the number of positions for captains and 1st lieutenants for each unit in the consolidated estimate. As part of the reorganization, Ghormley's company may have resumed its role as Company F of Walker's old battalion. Pvt. Thomas N. Hurst of Company E, 65th Regiment N.C. Troops (6th N.C. Cavalry) was informed in February 1865 that he had been appointed 3rd lieutenant of Company F of a unit identified as Walker's Battalion. This company was under an otherwise unknown Capt. W. S. Singleton. It is possible, however, that this "Walker's Battalion" may not have been the same unit as the one associated with Thomas's Legion (although it was understood as such by the National Archives compiler of Hurst's record). By that point the battalion would have been referred to as either McKamy's or Stringfield's Battalion; furthermore, Singleton's company was at Clayton, Georgia, a bit far from the Legion's normal range of operations, although not entirely out of the realm of possibility given Thomas's interests in maintaining a supply line to Walhalla, South Carolina. Given the lack of documentation these matters remain speculative. Service record file of Thomas N. Hurst, 65th Regiment N.C. Troops (6th Regiment N.C. Cavalry), Compiled Service Records of Confederate Soldiers from the State of North Carolina (M270), reel 41.

538. *O.R.* 49 (pt. 1): 1048; Tri-Monthly Field Return of the Forces of the District of Western North Carolina, Commanded by Brigadier General J. G. Martin, March 10, 1865, Chapter 1: vol. 15, 16, Entry 65, pt. 2, Entry 24, RG 109, NA. The full unpublished version of the return confirms that there was no report for Barr's Battery. The references to the artillery piece and Barr's Battery in the published version in the *Official Records* led historian Vernon H. Crow to assume that a section of the battery was sent to Thomas, and implied in an endnote that the gun was under the command of Barr himself. Crow, *Storm in the Mountains*, 118, 229, 253 n. 11. Federal provost marshal records, however, show that Barr and twenty-five of his men were captured at Sayler's Creek, Virginia, on April 6, 1865, with another member surrendering at Richmond. Further, Lee's comments on Barr's request for a transfer shows that he had no intention of removing the battery from the Richmond defenses (see pp. 164-165 and n. 383 above). Finally, the absence of a report is a probable indication that the battery was not with the rest of the Legion, and thus the gun with Thomas was unconnected to it. The rosters for Captain Barr's Company Virginia Light Artillery are in Compiled Service Records of Confederate Soldiers from the State of Virginia (M324), reel 265, and are printed in Weaver, *The Nottoway Artillery and Barr's Battery*, 131-140. Weaver believed that the gun with Thomas was manned by absentees from Barr's Battery (Weaver, op. cit., p. 127), a likely conjecture.

539. Love was referred to as a lieutenant colonel in the January 17 letter by Palmer cited above. The Charlotte *Western Democrat* of March 21, 1865, reported the promotion; however, Thomas still addressed Love as lieutenant colonel in a letter dated March 31. There was an unsuccessful effort by members of the General Assembly to get Love promoted to brigadier general in early 1865. An aide to Davis wrote the representatives on March 8 of the decision not to promote Love; in that message, Love was referred as a lieutenant colonel. As for Stringfield, he claimed after the war that he was promoted lieutenant colonel in November 1864, about the time he arrived in western North Carolina, while in *Confederate Military History* the date of the promotion was given as March 6, 1865. He was still signing his correspondence as "Major" in late February, however, and Thomas referred to him by that rank in his March 31 letter to Love. The March 11 quartermaster report shows the Legion broken down into a regiment under Love, a battalion under Stringfield, and an "Indian Battalion"; refers to Love as "Col."; and notes an officer of that rank in regard to the regiment. Likewise, a lieutenant colonel was listed in command of "Stringfield's Battalion." On the same day, however, Martin wrote Lee that "Maj. W. W. Stringfield" was "at present" in command of McKamy's Battalion. Stringfield was described as "Lieutenant Colonel" in Federal provost marshal records related to his capture on May 1, so there seems to be no doubt that the promotion occurred. It is possible that both men were promoted by Thomas on or about March 6, but that the appointments were not confirmed by the Confederate government until later (if at all). Palmer to Rieley, January 17, 1865, Chapter 1: Mss 1225, Entry 183, Box 12, RG 109, NA; Consolidated Estimate of Funds Required for the Pay of the Troops in the Department of Western North Carolina for the Months of March and April, 1865,

to defend specific counties, with the troops divided accordingly. Stringfield's Battalion was responsible for watching Clay, Graham, and Cherokee counties. It is possible that Captain Whitaker of Company E acted as Stringfield's second-in-command. Although postwar claims were made that Whitaker held the rank of major, his own papers show that at the end of the war he was still captain, so his position would have been as acting major at best.[540]

Discipline remained a problem. Stringfield wrote from Franklin in late January that "I find a good many men Strolling about over this County[,] Some of whom belong to various Regts in the Service, and many others of our Command. A man calling himself a Lt Hicks of Caml Taylor Co is in this neighborhood, & Says that he has authority from you to Collect the absentees of his co & retain them here till further order[s.]" Stringfield requested that Thomas "order all Men properly belonging to my District to their cos at once." Thomas himself had issued orders a few days earlier regarding discipline issues, including protecting citizens from abuse and the curtailment of excursions into Tennessee without orders.[541]

By January, the military situation in the western theater of operations had changed drastically. Sherman had cut loose from his base with elements of the Army of the Tennessee and the Army of the Cumberland in November, living off the land as he marched to Savannah, where he opened a new base of supplies and prepared to move north to join Grant. Gen. John Bell Hood's Army of Tennessee did not follow, marching instead into Tennessee, where it faced the Army of the Ohio and the remainder of the Armies of the Cumberland and the Tennessee under the overall command of Maj. Gen. George H. Thomas. Hood was badly beaten at Franklin in November and at Nashville in mid-December. With the Confederate threat in the area vanquished, Schofield and the Twenty-Third Corps were transferred in

March 11, 1865, Thomas Legion Battalion Field and Staff File #1, Muster and Pay Rolls, Chapter 1: Entry 18, Box 826, RG 109, NA; the *Western Democrat* (Charlotte), March 21, 1865; Thomas to Love, March 31, 1865, Thomas Papers, WCU; James L. Carson, et al. to Davis, undated, with endorsements by Davis (February 17, 1865), Cooper (February 17, 1865), Lee (February 22, 1865), Cooper (February 22, 1865), and Davis (February 27, 1865), and F. R. Lubbock to Representatives William H. Brown, James L. Carson, J. J. Erwin, "and other members of the Legislature of the State of North Carolina," March 8, 1865, service record file of James R. Love, Thomas's Legion, Compiled Service Record of Confederate Soldiers from the State of North Carolina (M270), reel 570; service record file of William W. Stringfield, Thomas's Legion, in ibid., reel 573; Cheney, *North Carolina Government*, 330-332; Crow, *Storm in the Mountains*, 254 n. 64; Hill, *Confederate Military History: North Carolina*, 757 (quote); Stringfield to Thomas, February 21, February 22, 1865, Thomas Papers, DU; endorsement by Martin, March 11, 1865, on Lee to Seddon, December 12, 1864, Letters Received by the Confederate Adjutant and Inspector General's Officer (M474), reel 126, file 1662-L-1864.

540. Stringfield, "Sixty-Ninth Regiment," in Clark, *North Carolina Regiments*, 3:758; Aiken, "Eightieth Regiment," in ibid., 4:118; Stringfield to Thomas, February 21, February 22, 1865, Thomas Papers, DU; Hill, *Confederate Military History: North Carolina*, 791; parole for Stephen E. Whitaker, May 12, 1865, and parole roll of S. Whitaker, Company E, 1st Battalion, Thomas's Legion, May 12, 1865, Whitaker Papers, NCOAH. The March 11 quartermaster report cited in n. 539 lists a major for Stringfield's Battalion and another in command of the Indian Battalion, although Martin wrote on the same date that he had not yet found a field officer to command the latter unit. This lends strength to the idea that many of these appointments had not been confirmed. Martin, March 11, 1865, endorsement on Lee to Seddon, December 12, 1864, Letters Received by the Confederate Adjutant and Inspector General's Officer (M474), reel 126, file 1662-L-1864.

541. Stringfield to Thomas, January 21, 1865, Thomas Papers, DU; Crow, *Storm in the Mountains*, 118-119. "Caml Taylor" was Capt. Campbell Taylor of Company C of Thomas's western North Carolina force, although as noted previously he had tried to resign in 1864. Hicks may have been Capt. Albert Hicks of Company F of the same battalion, although if so the circumstances of his demotion and reassignment are unknown.

January to the North Carolina coast, with the Department of the Cumberland absorbing the Department of the Ohio.[542] In this context, on January 21 Sherman imparted to Major General Thomas his general instructions for the spring campaigns. Among other things, the latter "should have a small cavalry force of, say, 2,000 men to operate from Knoxville through the mountain pass along the French Broad into North Carolina, to keep up the belief that it is to be followed by a considerable force of infantry. Stoneman could do this, whilst Gillem merely watches up the Holston."[543] Operations in western North Carolina were thus to be diversionary, designed to induce the Confederates to stretch their military resources further.

Stringfield reported after the war that in January 1865 an Indiana cavalry regiment attacked a small party of his command near Deep Creek, and was pursued by Ghormley's and Everett's consolidated company. There is no known independent confirmation in wartime records of this clash. A somewhat better-documented event occurred in February when Kirk struck again. Kirk's numbers have been estimated from a total of 250 to a combined force of 400 cavalry and 200 infantry. His path took him from Cocke County, Tennessee, into Haywood County, following the Pigeon River, Cataloochee Creek, and Jonathan's Creek before turning eastward towards Waynesville. Kirk brushed aside a Home Guard unit under Capt. Robert Howell, and seized Waynesville on February 4. His men plundered the town; after freeing the prisoners, he also burned the jail and some houses, including the home of Col. Robert Love, a local Revolutionary War hero and grandfather of Lieutenant Colonel Love and Capts. Matthew and William Love of the Legion and Thomas's wife Sarah.[544]

Kirk's next movements are unclear. Modern reconstructions indicate that he proceeded southwestward for Balsam Gap late on the afternoon of February 4, but was ambushed at night in camp by local troops, who were driven off. He then supposedly doubled back to Waynesville, tried to force a passage through Soco Gap to the northwest, and was turned back again, finally crossing Balsam Gap on February 6 and moving northwards towards Quallatown. One contemporary source styling himself "Oseola," however, related to the editors of the Charlotte *Western Democrat* that Kirk "crossed at Soco mountain." This implies that Kirk moved through Soco Gap rather than Balsam Gap, and followed Soco Creek

542. *O.R.* 44: 6-418, 45 (pt. 1): 32-776, (pt. 2): 377, 419-420, 529, 540, 586-587, 603; *O.R. (Supplement)* Pt. I, 7: 629-647, 664-686. Secondary literature includes Connelly, *Autumn of Glory*, 470-514; Anne J. Bailey, *The Chessboard of War: Sherman and Hood in the Autumn Campaigns of 1864*, Great Campaigns of the Civil War (Lincoln: University of Nebraska Press, 2000); Burke Davis, *Sherman's March* (New York: Random House, 1980), 3-119; Joseph T. Glathaar, *The March to the Sea and Beyond: Sherman's Troops in the Savannah and Carolinas Campaigns* (New York: New York University Press, 1985); Wiley Sword, *Embrace an Angry Wind: the Confederacy's Last Hurrah: Spring Hill, Franklin, and Nashville* (New York: HarpersCollins Publishers, 1992); James Lee McDonough and Thomas L. Connelly, *Five Tragic Hours: The Battle of Franklin* (Knoxville: University of Tennessee Press); Stanley F. Horn, *The Decisive Battle of Nashville* (Knoxville: University of Tennessee Press, 1956).

543. *O.R.* 45 (pt. 2): 621.

544. Stringfield, "Sixty-Ninth Regiment," in Clark, *North Carolina Regiments* 3:758; Stringfield, "Memoirs of the Civil War," typescript, McClung Collection, L-McGL, (copy in Stringfield Papers, WCU), 21-23; "Oseola" to the editors, February 20, 1865, published in the *Western Democrat* (Charlotte), March 21, 1865 (hereinafter cited as "Oseola" to the *Western Democrat* [Charlotte], February 20, 1865, [published March 21, 1865]); Allen, *Annals of Haywood County*, 81-82; Crow, *Storm in the Mountains*, 13, 121. In his memoirs, Stringfield gave two separate accounts of Kirk's February raid, dating one correctly but placing the second in March. In each version he gave different details. His account in Clark's *North Carolina Regiments* was also misdated to March.

westward. Haywood County historican W. C. Allen's account seems to support this idea, as he wrote that Kirk tried to "[a]gain . . . force his way across Soco" following his first repulse there. In some ways this is a more logical route given the time limits involved. Stringfield's account in his memoirs could suggest either route. "Pretending to go by Webster, he [Kirk] rapidly returned towards Tennessee, crossed Soco Creek, and went through the Indian reservation," he wrote. Kirk could have either gone directly to or bypassed Webster if he rode west through Balsam Gap. The assertion that Kirk "pretended" to go toward Webster may confirm that Kirk unsuccessfully attempted to cross Balsam Gap earlier, or at least feinted in that direction before turning north; or it could mean that he rode through Balsam Gap in the direction of Webster before turning north towards Quallatown.[545]

Whichever route Kirk took, the Legion was on the alert by the time he crossed the mountain. Stringfield, returning to Franklin from Quallatown, was spending the night of February 4 at a farm on the Little Tennessee River when he was awakened at midnight and informed of the raid. He rushed to Quallatown and found things in a state of confusion. Thomas and Love were absent, and those officers present were in a dither about what should be done. Stringfield decided to send all available forces, which he recalled in his memoirs as numbering about 150 white men and 150 Cherokees, to block a crossing of the Tuckasegee River to the south, concentrating near Wilmot. "Here we fortified the mountain side and blockaded the road below."[546] Other elements of the Legion may have gone into action on

545. The basic idea that Kirk tried both the Balsam Gap and the Soco Gap routes was laid out in W. C. Allen's 1935 history of Haywood County, and was modified by Vernon H. Crow in his 1982 history of Thomas's Legion. Allen's version reflected an effort to reconcile several different accounts into a coherent whole. Although he did not cite his sources, one of them was Stringfield, as he echoed the latter in misdating the raid to March. Allen implied that Kirk headed for Balsam Gap after he left Waynesville, as he placed the site of the night attack on Kirk's camp as "on the Balsam road." He then wrote that Kirk was repulsed in an attempt to cross Soco Gap, but as noted in the text above he implied that Kirk successfully crossed at the same place on the following day. Crow in turn based his account on Allen, "Oseola," and Stringfield's various accounts, and like Allen made an effort to harmonize his sources. He explicitly stated that Kirk headed for Balsam Gap following his departure from Waynesville, but turned back following the night attack. Crow followed Allen in depicting Kirk as then unsuccessfully attempting to cross at Soco Gap, but departed from Allen's version by having Kirk turn back again and crossing at Balsam Gap. Crow's interpretation of the latter route is derived from Stringfield's account in his memoirs, which depicted Kirk advancing towards the Tuckasegee in a direction indicating a passage at Balsam Gap. Kirk's movements might be more properly simplified to either a direct move from Waynesville through Balsam Gap, or one through Soco Gap following a feint towards Balsam Gap, rather than back-and-forth attempts at both. Stringfield, "Memoirs of the Civil War," typescript, McClung Collection, L-McGL (copy in Stringfield Papers, WCU), 21-23 (quote, 21); "Oseola" to the *Western Democrat* (Charlotte), February 20, 1865 (published March 21, 1865); Stringfield, "Sixty-Ninth Regiment," in Clark, *North Carolina Regiments*, 3:758-759; Allen, *Annals of Haywood County*, 82; Crow, *Storm in the Mountains*, 121, 123; Trotter, *Bushwhackers*, 237-238; Bumgarner, *Kirk's Raiders*, 57-58; Powell, *The North Carolina Gazetteer*, 22, 462. Allen stated that the ambushers of Kirk's camp were made up of "about one hundred Haywood County troops augmented by some farmers." The attackers (including the farmers) were probably members of one or more Home Guard or militia units. Allen, op. cit., 82.

546. Crow, *Storm in the Mountains*, 121, 123; Stringfield, "Memoirs of the Civil War," typescript, McClung Collection, L-McGL, (copy in Stringfield Papers, WCU), 22-23; "Oseola" to the *Western Democrat* (Charlotte), February 20, 1865 (published March 21, 1865); Stringfield, "War—Mss," ledger book, 110, Stringfield Collection, NCOAH. In his memoirs, Stringfield mentioned the presence at Quallatown of Thomas's adjutant, Luther C. May, as well as Captain McConnell of Company F, Infantry Regiment, and "Captain" Everett of

the eastern side of Balsam Mountain, as Stringfield recalled that Conley's sharpshooters fought Kirk at Soco Gap.[547] Federal provost marshal records and North Carolina pension applications indicate the capture or wounding of men from Companies E, F, and G, Infantry Regiment at Cataloochee Creek and Jonathan's Creek in Haywood County.[548]

Ghormley's and Everett's consolidated cavalry company. Which Indian company or companies were present is unknown. The assumption would be Company A or Company B, as Stringfield recalled in his unpublished reminiscences that he never had any contact with the two companies organized by Thomas in 1863 and 1864 (although he should have had an opportunity following his return from the Valley); however, the only Indian casualties recorded were members of Company C.

547. Stringfield, "Sixty-Ninth Regiment," in Clark, *North Carolina Regiments* 3:759; Allen, *Annals of Haywood County*, 82. According to Stringfield, "Lieutenant Conley fought and drove them [Kirk's men] across the Balsam Mountains at Soco Gap." This could indicate that Conley repulsed Kirk as he attempted to cross at Soco Gap, the interpretation taken by several modern authors (see Crow, *Storm in the Mountains*, 123; Trotter, *Bushwhackers!*, 238; Bumgarner, *Kirk's Raiders*, 58). It could as easily mean that Conley drove Kirk westward across Balsam Mountain as he moved through Soco Gap, an important point to keep in mind in regards to "Oseola's" account. It is possible, however, that Conley's command was not at Soco Gap at this time; it was there near the end of the war, and it is perhaps this later deployment that Stringfield recalled. If Conley fought near Jonathan's Creek or Cataloochee Creek as Kirk moved towards Waynesville, then perhaps the separate dates and events were conflated by Stringfield in his memory. Conley's supposed presence at Soco Gap was taken by Crow, Trotter, and (to a lesser extent) Bumgarner to indicate that Stringfield was attempting to trap Kirk between two different forces. While this is possible, it is speculative at best, and Stringfield did not mention any specific effort to accomplish such a goal. It is not clear whether the Legion's sharpshooter detachment was maintained as a separate unit following the Valley campaign, or if the men were put back into the ranks of their respective companies. See, however, R. T. Conley, "The Last Gun of the War," *The Atlanta Constitution*, July 13, 1892. Conley recalled that he was "a commandant of the skirmishers of Thomas's Legion" at the end of the war. It is possibile that the sharpshooter company was combined with Company F of the Infantry Regiment, or Company F converted into a sharpshooter company. Conley came from Company F, and Stringfield later identified many of the sharpshooters with members of that unit. See also Crow, *Storm in the Mountains*, 178, 249 n. 2.

548. Service record files of Eunitteni, Newton Francis, David Alex Hogan, Jeremiah A. Liner, Lebo Medford, John L. Morrell, Francis Penton, Henry C. Rice, Selkonie, and Adolphus Welch, Thomas's Legion, Compiled Service Records of Confederate Soldiers from the State of North Carolina (M270), reels 569 through 572, 574; Jeremiah Liner, North Carolina Applicatin for Pension (1901), Sophia A. Sherrill, North Carolina Application for Widow's Pension (1903), Green B. Swanger, North Carolina Application for Pension (1901), State Auditor's Office Records, NCOAH; Stringfield, "Sixty-Ninth Regiment," in Clark, *North Carolina Regiments*, 3:759; "Oseola" to the *Western Democrat* (Charlotte), February 20, 1865 (published March 21, 1865). Francis, Hogan, Liner, Medford, Morell, and Swanger were members of Company E, Infantry Regiment. Federal provost marshal records document the capture of all but Swanger in Haywood County on dates ranging from February 2 to February 5. Liner claimed to have been wounded on the "Cattaloochee River" on February 3, as did Swanger on an unknown date. Sophia Sherrill's husband, W. Judson Sherrill, along with Welch were members of Company F, Infantry Regiment. Her pension application stated that her husband was killed "by Kirk" in February 1865. Welch was captured in Haywood County on February 5. Eunitenni and Selkonie were members of Company C, the third Indian company; the former was captured in Haywood County on February 5, while the latter was wounded and captured in Haywood County on February 4. Penton and Rice were both captured in Haywood County on February 5 and 4 respectively. Penton's company is unknown; Rice was a member of "Company E, Thomas's Legion," so it is probable that he belonged to the Infantry Regiment, also. In addition, the pension application of Robert Harrell, who claimed to be a member of Company G wounded at Jonathan's Creek some time in 1865, may have been another casualty of this raid. Based on the sites and dates of the woundings, whatever actions Companies E, F, and G participated in was before Kirk reached Waynesville, when he was traveling down Cataloochee and Jonathan's Creeks. The fact that the majority of the losses were captured might be an indication that they were taken by surprise, before Kirk's approach was widely known. In his history of the Infantry Regiment, Stringfield stated that it fought Kirk in Haywood County during this raid, a probable

After crossing the mountain, Kirk skirmished with Stringfield on February 6 at Soco Creek. According to Stringfield, the skirmish took place near the home of Black Fox/Inoli, on the site of an old Cherokee lodge where Tecumseh had unsuccessfully tried to persuade the Cherokees to join his coalition of tribes against the United States during the war of 1812.[549] Evidently, Kirk found a way to bypass Stringfield's position at Wilmot, forcing him to rush to meet him at Soco Creek to the north. Stringfield recalled that from his position near Wilmot that he "sent scouts up the river and awaited the approach of the enemy. All manner of reports came to us about Yankee Calvary [*sic*] on Scott's Creek." Scott Creek flows into the Tuckasegee River west of Webster, an indication that Kirk came from Balsam Gap. There is little doubt that the forces clashed at Soco Creek, rather than at Wilmot. The contemporary account by "Oseola" specified that Kirk fought "near the Indian church on Soco creek," and Stringfield noted Soco Creek as the site of the clash in his history of the Infantry Regiment and in a section of his memoirs. Stringfield may have left part of the force behind at Wilmot, as he reported having only "fifty or sixty men" with him at Soco Creek; this is echoed by "Oseola," who noted that the defenders consisted of "about sixty Indians and a few whites."[550]

Stringfield recalled that as Kirk approached "[t]he Indians were spoiling for a fight and I could hardly manage them." "Oseola," who may have been a participant or an eyewitness, reported that the Cherokees "behaved with great coolness and fought well. This brave little band of soldiers, however, was soon overpowered, and with the exception of an occasional shot from the Indians, still eager to pursue, Col. Kirk passed on without being further molested." Stringfield put the matter more bluntly: "If we had had ammunition, we could have almost destroyed the 'Yanks.'" After the fight Kirk rode west along Soco Creek until it merged with the Oconaluftee River, then turned northward and crossed into Tennessee. Stringfield reported that he sent men up the Oconaluftee "to harrass the enemy as much as possible," but without more ammunition little could be accomplished. Both Thomas and Love arrived that evening, but by then it was too late.[551]

---

reference to the actions of these companies. The newspaper account of "Oseola" (who may have been a member of the Legion) mentioned two "squads" of soldiers contesting Kirk; one along "Chatthuchee creek" (Cataloochee Creek), in which "most" of the Confederates were "wounded, and captured" (probably a reference to Captain Howell's Home Guard company); and another group that "bushwhacked" Kirk at Waynesville "for a short while, but with little effect." The latter is a reference to the night attack on Kirk's camp.

549. "Oseola" to the *Western Democrat* (Charlotte), February 20, 1865 (published March 21, 1865); Stringfield, "Memoirs of the Civil War," typescript, McClung Collection, L-McGL (copy in Stringfield Papers, WCU), 21, 23; Stringfield, "Sixty-Ninth Regiment," in Clark, *North Carolina Regiments* 3:759; Allen, *Annals of Haywood County*, 82; Crow, *Storm in the Mountains*, 123. There are two Soco Creeks in western North Carolina. One, rising east of Soco Gap, flows northeastward into Jonathan's Creek. The other, beginning on the opposite side of Soco Gap and running westward to the Oconaluftee River, was the site of the February 6 skirmish. Powell, *The North Carolina Gazetteer*, 462.

550. Stringfield, "Memoirs of the Civil War," typescript, McClung Collection, L-McGL (copy in Stringfield Papers, WCU), 21, 23; "Oseola" to the *Western Democrat* (Charlotte), February 20, 1865 (published March 21, 1865); Stringfield, "Sixty-Ninth Regiment," in Clark, *North Carolina Regiments*, 3:759; Powell, *The North Carolina Gazetteer*, 443.

551. Stringfield, "Memoirs of the Civil War," typescript, McClung Collection, L-McGL (copy in Stringfield Papers, WCU), 21, 23 (quote, 23); "Oseola" to the *Western Democrat* (Charlotte), February 20, 1865 (published March 21, 1865); Crow, *Storm in the Mountains*, 123; Powell, *The North Carolina Gazetteer*, 115, 244. "Oseola" addressed his letter from Quallatown, and his comments demonstrate a direct knowledge of the situation.

Kirk's raid was less damaging than it could have been, but the failure to decisively defeat his band was galling. "[B]ut for the negligence on the part of some one, I think this would have been Kirk's last raid," commented "Oseola." "In this department there are troops enough to have captured him, but they did not concentrate rapidly enough, and the few that did fight had a limited supply of ammunition. I saw several who had only five rounds of cartridges when they went into action. Surely this ought never to happen any more."[552]

Things did not improve in the days ahead. Stringfield was assigned Capt. James W. Cooper's Company H and Capt. Nathaniel G. Philips's Company I from the Infantry Regiment, probably as reinforcements against further strikes following Kirk's foray. On February 18 Thomas ordered them to Franklin in response to another rumored raid. In response, Stringfield wrote from his new headquarters at Valleytown to Thomas on both February 21 and 22, to protest this move and complain of other problems. "Excuse me for so often troubling you with my troubles, but really, I am uneasy about this Country, and my inability to defend it properly," he wrote sarcastically on the former date. "The withdrawal of Coopers & Philips Co[s] from Cherokee will very Sensibly weaken my forces—now little enough, and the want of arms and ammunition render it almost impossible to get along at all, with no enemy threatening, but these frequent raids into Tenn will have the effect to draw a Yankee force upon me. And then how must I act? I can but run and hide." Stringfield complained of a lack of guns, ammo, and accouterments, "the latter most greatly needed, for it is impossible for men to carry the cartridges in Cotton haversack & in their pockets without great loss." The troops also lacked shoes and cooking vessels.[553]

On the following day, Stringfield, complained that Cooper had only 40 men in camp, of whom "only 18 or 20 could be paraded. I was deeply mortified at the conduct of this co. and I am Sorry to know that Capt Cooper is an apologist for those men that so shamefully refused to go to the adjoining co. of Macon." He then warned:

> You will find Some day I fear[,] Col Thomas, a fearful and Shameful want of discipline on the part of a great many men & not a few officers of the Legion. This must be checked —destroyed—or our command is worthless when the hour of trial comes. In an election held in Cooper[']s Co[.] some time Since, a cowardly deserter by the name of Carver was elected Lieut. I now do most earnestly protest against this fellow retaining that place[.] I will not recognize him as an officer unless forced to do So, for I know from experience & observation that this fellow is bad at heart and cowardly by nature. I hope you will refuse to receive this fellow & order a new election[;] it will Save me the unpleasant duty of protesting before a higher tribunal.
>
> We already have Some men as officers who disgrace their uniform and I wish no more such. Col Love knows this man Carver & will coincide with me in protesting against his promotion. I do this all after mature reflection and with the Sincere desire to promote the good of the Service."[554]

552. "Oseola" to the *Western Democrat* (Charlotte), February 20, 1865 (published March 21, 1865).

553. Stringfield to Thomas, February 21, 1865, J. W. Cooper to Thomas, February 22, 1865, Thomas Papers, DU. Stringfield's comments may indicate that Thomas's instructions regarding raids into Tennessee without his orders (see p. 233) were not being obeyed; it is possible, however, that Thomas may have been launching raids himself that are undocumented.

554. Stringfield to Thomas, February 22, 1865, Thomas Papers, DU. There were at least four privates named Carver in Cooper's Company H; the most likely candidates for the man whom Stringfield noted were Pvt. Azor

Cooper wrote Thomas on the same day. Finding that the Federals had departed, he claimed that he was "at a loss to Know what I ought to do with my co. . . . Being of the opinion that the order was intended to be temporary and that we would not remain here but a few days at most we are waiting anxiously to see an order from you for our return to Cherokee Co." Cooper was not just guilty of supporting men who refused to leave Cherokee County, where their company was organized, but fully shared their views. "Col.[,] [i]t is not my place in any wise to ever question your orders, yet I think there is no wrong in giving my views privately on what should be the situation of the troops west of Quallatown." Cooper argued along the lines that the area was basically undefendable, and that it would therefore be best to be stationed in some advanced site, evidently Cherokee County. "I can not see that troops at this place more than a guard would be of much advantage to the border of our County near the Enemy," as Federal raiders could plunder the area with impunity regardless. "[I]f we were Stationed with guns and ammunition at Cheoah or the forks of the [Tuckasegee?] River nothing but an overwhelming force could come up any distance into our lines[.] Then the people could put their stock out of the way." He appealed to Thomas's concerns about the agricultural crisis in the area, but it was clear that he was only focused on his home county. "Col[,] several families have moved back to our County with the expectation that it would be protected . . . but if my Co. are taken from there and none put in its stead they will not feel very safe. I hope you will have my company ordered back as our property will be in constant danger until our Return." Probably well aware of Stringfield's ire and seeking to put the best face on it, he added, "I don't think I can keep any men here if their place [in Cherokee County] is not supplied by other troops. Maj Stringfield says he will not stay there without my co[.]"[555] If Cooper's company was any measure (and such might not have been equally the case for all companies), then whatever positive impact that serving with the Army of the Valley had had on the discipline of Thomas's Legion seems to have unraveled upon its return to North Carolina.[556]

The war would not wait for the situation to be resolved, however, as both sides prepared for the spring campaigns. On March 10, Martin reported his troop strength to Richmond as 130 officers and 1,433 men present for duty; an effective total of 1,535; an aggregate present of 1,745; and an aggregate present and absent of 2,910, along with 7 artillery pieces. Perhaps surprisingly, the largest contingent of Martin's command was Thomas's Legion. Martin reported that the Legion consisted of 70 officers and 906 men, with an effective total of 943, an aggregate present of 1,055, and an aggregate present and absent of 1,473. In

Carver and Pvt. Lawson Carver, who were last reported as having deserted in September 1863. However, it is possible that it might be one of the other two Carvers who could have deserted after the last records, or even another person altogether who joined the company at a later date. Service record files of Azor Carver and Lawson Carver, Thomas's Legion, Compiled Service Records of Confederate Soldiers from the State of North Carolina (M270), reel 570.

555. J. W. Cooper to Thomas, February 22, 1865, Thomas Papers, DU.

556. Thomas may have felt no choice in acquiescing to his troops' misbehavior by this point in the war. An example of how dire things could get in disciplining troops in the region is shown by the fate of Col. George W. Tait, commander of the newly organized 69th Regiment N.C. Troops (7th N.C. Cavalry), expanded from the 14th Battalion N.C. Cavalry. When Tait arrived to take command of the regiment in February, he was knocked out by a rock thrown by one of the soldiers. *O.R.* 47 (pt. 2): 1178; Crow, *Storm in the Mountains*, 117.

addition, as noted earlier there was 1 field piece. A quartermaster's report filed the next day shows a total 1,690 men for the Legion, although obviously not all of these officers and men were present or fit for duty. By contrast, Palmer's Brigade, which consisted of the 62nd Regiment N.C. Troops, the 64th Regiment N.C. Troops, and the 69th Regiment N.C. Troops (7th Regiment N.C. Cavalry) had only 39 officers and 401 men present for duty on March 10. On paper at least, the Legion looked to be stronger than many brigades at that point in the war.[557]

On March 21, Stoneman embarked on another raid. Taking with him 6,000 men consisting of the Cavalry Division of the District of East Tennessee under Gillem, and elements of Brig. Gen. Davis Tillson's Fourth Division of the Army of the Cumberland, Stoneman's target was western North Carolina and southwestern Virginia. Gillem concentrated at Mossy Creek and Tillson at Morristown on March 22. On the following day, Gillem moved to Morristown, while Tillson marched to Bull's Gap. He moved from there to secure the mountain passes into North Carolina; as part of this mission, the 2nd Regiment N.C. Mounted Infantry (Union) and Kirk's 3rd Regiment N.C. Mounted Infantry (Union) were sent to Boone on April 5.[558]

Meanwhile, Stoneman moved with Gillem and the cavalry. Dispatching one brigade to swing around between Jonesborough and Carter's Depot via Bull's Gap, the other two brigades moved on Jonesborough. As the Confederates withdrew before they were cut off, the Federals crossed the North Carolina border in the Stone Mountains. Maj. Miles Keogh took part of the 12th Regiment Kentucky Volunteer Cavalry (Union) to Boone on March 28. He successfully routed the Home Guards there, killing 9 and capturing at least 68. Stoneman then sent the cavalry to Wilkesboro on separate routes. From there the Federals moved deep into southwestern Virginia, striking Christiansburg to the east of Wytheville on April 5. Destroying railroad track and supplies in the area, they turned towards North Carolina again.[559]

As in previous cases, the divided Confederate departmental command worked against a coordinated response, although "cooperation" was as always expected between commanders. In March, Lee instructed Martin to cooperate with Early, even though Lee had already been warned that Martin's and Vaughn's combined forces were not sufficient to halt Stoneman. Martin was expected to cooperate with Brig. Gen. John Echols, who was now commander of the District of Southwestern Virginia and East Tennessee, and both were to cooperate with Beauregard in the defense of the Western North Carolina Railroad.[560] As

557. *O.R.* 49 (pt. 1): 1048; Consolidated Estimate of Funds Required for the Pay of the Troops in the Department of Western North Carolina for the Months of March and April, 1865, March 11, 1865, Thomas Legion Battalion Field and Staff File #1, Muster and Pay Rolls, Chapter 1: Entry 18, Box 826, RG 109, NA. Thomas received authority from the Adjutant and Inspector General's Office to reenlist the two original Indian companies upon the expiration of their terms of service on April 9. According to Thomas's interpretation, he could not formally organize the Indian companies into a separate battalion until the anniversary of that date, although under Martin's direction he had informally done so before then. Thomas to Love, March 31, 1865, Thomas Papers, WCU; Crow, *Storm in the Mountains*, 126, 233.

558. *O.R.* 49 (pt. 1): 325, 337-338; *O.R. (Supplement)* pt. I, 7:967.

559. *O.R.* 49 (pt. 1): 323-324, 326-328, 330-332; *O.R. (Supplement)* pt. I, 7:967.

560. *O.R.* 46 (pt. 1): 475-477, 484-485, 502-503, 505, 508, 516-517 (pt. 2), 1243, (pt. 3): 712, 736-737, 1362-1363, 1366; Early, *Autobiographical Sketch and Narrative*, 460-468. After Breckinridge was appointed to be Confederate secretary of war, Early's duties as commander of the Department of the Valley were expanded in February to include eastern Tennessee and southwestern Virgina. It was probably hoped that the move would

circumstances developed, no one would actually be in a position to cooperate with anyone else. While Stoneman was in southwestern Virginia, Grant finally broke the siege lines at Petersburg, compelling Lee to retreat westward. Outraced by Sheridan's cavalry and hemmed in by the Army of the Potomac and the Army of the James, the Army of Northern Virginia surrendered at Appomattox Courthouse on April 9. Sherman, meanwhile, marched northward from the Savannah River in February. Devastating South Carolina as he passed, he arrived in North Carolina to confront a small, patched-together Confederate army under the command of Joseph E. Johnston. Including elements of the decimated Army of Tennessee, Johnston's force attempted unsuccessfully to halt Sherman at Bentonville on March 18-21. The port of Wilmington fell in February, and Schofield marched from there with the Twenty-Third Corps to join Sherman. A large cavalry raid was launched from the Department of the Cumberland into Alabama, while other Federal troops threatened Mobile.[561] The Confederacy thus faced its worst crisis yet.

At the end of March, Johnston ordered Martin to support the Confederate garrison at Salisbury. Asked to report on his situation, Martin responded that "I regret to say I have nothing to report but disobedience of orders, neglect of duty, demoralization of the people, and desertion of both officers and men. I regret to say that from further appearances there is no prospect of things being any better. The enemy has been able to impress the whole country with the belief that all this part of the State is to be given up by our forces, and in consequence every man is doing as little for our cause as he possibly can, hoping by this course, undoubtedly, to be able to save his property when the enemy takes possession, which they represent will be in a week or two." Unable to protect Salisbury, Martin faced a more immediate threat in his own front. Col. Isaac Kirby, commander of the First Brigade, First Division, Fourth Corps, was sent towards Asheville as a demonstration in support of Stoneman. After skirmishing with Palmer in Asheville's defensive lines on April 6, Kirby broke off further efforts to take the town, convinced that Martin's force exceeded his own (it did not, at least as far as regular Confederate units were concerned). He also received word on April 5 "that there were about 600 men of Thomas' command on the mountain road leading from Waynesville to Warm Springs," and that "a force of the enemy, about 2,000 strong, had been started out from Waynesville with the intention of striking the Knoxville railroad at Loudon, when, hearing of our march into North Carolina, they were halted at Quallatown."[562] The location of the latter troops indicates that they were also members of the Legion, although the numbers were probably exaggerated. An officer accompanying Kirby wrote that "Colonel Thomas' Legion, consisting of 800 infantry, 400 Indians, a four-gun battery of 150 men, and

---

make it easier for the troops throughout the region to be shifted around as needed, but by this time it was a moot point. Ironically, Early was relieved from command on March 29, the day after Lee told him to expect Martin's cooperation. Early's stock as a commander had continued to plummet, due to a fresh defeat from Sheridan at Waynesboro on March 2. The short-lived Department of Western Virginia and East Tennessee was once again separated into the Valley District, now under Maj. Gen. Lunsford L. Lomax, and the District of Southwestern Virginia and East Tennessee under Echols.

561. *O.R.* 46 (pt. 1): 44-59.

562. Ibid., 47 (pt. 3): 724, 730 (Martin quote, 730), 49 (pt. 1): 20, 31-33 (Kirby quotes, 31, 33); J. G. Martin to Cornelia Phillips Spencer, June 11, 1866, Cornelia Phillips Spencer Papers, SHC.

about 450 cavalry stationed at Quallatown, N.C.," were "preparing for a raid on the Knoxville and Chattanooga [East Tennessee & Georgia] Railroad, at Loudon or Charleston."[563]

Whether Thomas had truly been about to embark on a massive raid into eastern Tennessee until the spring campaign disrupted the plan is unknown; if so, it would have been the most ambitious operation that the Legion had ever undertaken under his direct command. Based on the timing of the events, historian Vernon H. Crow concluded that the gathering had more to do with the re-enlistment of the two original Indian companies and the subsequent final reorganization of the Legion. Thomas informed Love at the end of March that "Major Stringfield and others from the troops" were ordered to Locust Field; it is probable that these were the troops Kirby reported between Waynesville and Warm Springs. The increase of Thomas's artillery from one gun to a four-gun battery and the addition of as many as 450 cavalry shows that he at last had all the components of a true legion, although it is possible that both the horsemen and the battery were temporarily assigned to him from other forces in the department.[564] It is not known how many men would actually be available for combat, and it is important to note that the figures given represent Federal estimates only.

As the campaign began, another spate of desertions wracked the Legion, making the number actually available for operations problematic. The actual extent of the damage is unknown; Federal provost marshal records provide most of the available information, but these did not include those who just decided to leave the ranks without taking the Oath of Allegiance. The largest documented case involves twenty-one members of Company C, Infantry Regiment, who turned themselves over to the Federals in two large groups in Haywood County on March 27 and 28.[565]

On April 12, Breckinridge ordered Echols to withdraw from southwestern Virginia and eastern Tennessee to the area of Flat Rock in northwestern South Carolina. Martin was given similar orders, but either never received them, decided not to obey them, or received

563. *O.R.* 49 (pt. 2): 309.

564. Crow, *Storm in the Mountains*, 126; Thomas to Love, March 31, 1865 (quote), Thomas Papers, WCU. One problem with Crow's idea is that when Thomas wrote from Quallatown on March 31, he seemed to be preparing for possibly immediate action against the Federal raiders, while noting he would not be able to do anything towards organizing a battalion out of the Indian companies until the first two reenlisted on April 9. "The Indians are being Collected against [illegible]," he wrote. "I will go on with the troops." The latter statement implies that Thomas was not planning to stay at Quallatown in order to carry out any reorganization, which would have been difficult during an active campaign. Whether the original two companies ever reenlisted in those circumstances is unknown, although Thomas certainly would have made every effort to have ensured that they would do so. The identity of the four-gun battery, and whether or not it was an expansion of the one-gun section previously serving with Thomas, is not known.

565. Service record files of Henson Avery, Taylor Chambers, Isaac C. Clark, John W. Clauts, William R. Clouts, Elias S. Fowler, Rubin T. Franklin, Joseph H. Henson, Wiley Henson, E. E. Johnson, Morgan Meece, L. C. Miller, William W. Pressley, F. B. Riddle, David Allen Sharp, Manson Smathers, James R. Trull, William R. Trull, R. P. Williams, G. W. Wise, and Joseph Young, Compiled Service Records of Confederate Soldiers from the State of North Carolina (M270), reels 567 through 574. Thomas mentioned to Colonel Love that a "Lt Moss and some absentees are said to have gone to the yankees in the last few days," but it is not certain whether these individuals were members of the Legion (possibly the same group of deserters) or of another unit. Thomas to Love, March 31, 1865, Thomas Papers, WCU. Crow, *Storm in the Mountains*, 254 n. 51, believed that "Lt Moss" was "Lt Mays", i.e. 1st Lt. Luther C. May, adjutant of the Infantry Regiment. If so, Crow was also correct that Thomas was guilty of misjudging May, as he was probably with Stringfield and, if not, would be shortly.

countermanding orders to stay where he was. In the meantime, Stoneman returned to North Carolina, capturing a garrison at Germantown on April 10 before moving on to Salisbury, site of a major railway hub, an important military supply depot, and a prisoner-of-war camp. He captured Salisbury on April 12. Finding that most of the prisoners had already been taken away, he destroyed the prison, a tremendous amount of material, and various shops and factories related to the war effort.[566]

Stoneman returned to eastern Tennessee, leaving his forces to continue their operations. After capturing Morganton, Gillem and two brigades headed towards Asheville via Swannanoa Gap on April 19. Martin sent the Infantry Regiment and a four-gun battery to block them. Love reached the gap first. His men cut down trees to blockade the road and waited for the Federals to arrive on April 20. They were able to repulse all efforts to force the gap. After two days, Gillem left one brigade to occupy Love while taking the other on a roundabout route to Asheville via Rutherfordton, Howard's Gap, and Hendersonville.[567] In response, Martin ordered Palmer's Brigade to go Hickory Nut Gap. It was a measure of the state of the Confederate cause that Palmer's men refused to budge. As Gillem went by Howard's Gap instead of Hickory Nut Gap, the departure of Palmer's men would only have left Asheville largely undefended anyway. Martin meanwhile ordered the Infantry Regiment to Asheville. When Gillem arrived on April 24, a truce was arranged. In exchange for giving Gillem's men three-days' worth of rations in order to spare the locals from Federal foraging, Gillem promised to give Martin a forty-eight-hour notice before resuming hostilities. The Federals departed, with two brigades under orders to head directly for Greeneville and the third going by way of Waynesville and Quallatown; as no reports of resistance were noted, evidently the rest of the Legion withdrew as the Federals advanced. Complications soon arose. Instead of making straight for Greeneville as ordered, Col. Simon Brown's Second Brigade returned to Asheville on April 25 and demanded Martin's surrender. The Confederate commander capitulated. In contrast to Gillem, Brown and his men plundered the town. Love and the majority of the Infantry Regiment evidently escaped, jumping the section of the breastworks that they defended and crossing the French Broad River. After moving through Pigeon Gap, they joined up with Thomas at Waynesville. Meanwhile, after Brown's departure Martin sent word to Gillem, protesting the situation. Acting on behalf of his superior, an embarrassed Col. William J. Palmer rescinded the paroles issued by Brown to Martin's men, citing the failure to observe the forty-eight-hour notice of a return to hostilities.[568]

566. *O.R.* 47 (pt. 3): 795; 49 (pt. 1): 324, 328, 332-334.

567. Ibid., 335; Martin to Cornelia Phillips Spencer, June 11, 1865, Spencer Papers, SHC. It is unclear where the regiment was prior to its departure from Asheville; presumably, it was part of the concentration of Thomas's forces at Quallatown noted by members of Kirby's expedition. It apparently arrived at Asheville after Kirby's departure, as Martin did not include it as part of the Asheville garrison in his letter to Cornelia Spencer. Later in the letter, he noted that after the move to the Swannanoa Gap that Love "was ordered back to Asheville," confirming that it was there at some prior point. The battery was possibly the same one earlier reported with Thomas, or a South Carolina battery (Macbeth's Light Artillery) alluded to in Martin's letter in relation to the earlier defense of Asheville; see also *O.R.* 49 (pt. 1): 1048.

568. Martin to Cornelia Phillips Spencer, June 11, 1866, and William J. Palmer to Martin, April 28, 1865, Spencer Papers, SHC; *O.R.* 49 (pt. 1): 335-336; Stringfield, "Memoirs of the Civil War," typescript, McClung Collection, L-McGL (copy in Stringfield Papers, WCU), 40-41. Stringfield's source on Love's escape was John

Although most of Tillson's division went back to Greeneville, Col. William C. Bartlett was ordered out on April 27 with the 2nd and 3rd Regiments N.C. Mounted Infantry (Union) and the 1st U.S. Colored Heavy Artillery. While Col. John K. Miller's Third Brigade of Gillem's Division secured Asheville and opened up communications with Greeneville, Bartlett's troops would fan out to the south and north. The Federals arrived at Asheville on April 30; Martin had departed the day before. Outside of various Home Guard, Local Defense, and partisan units, Thomas's Legion was all that Martin had left. Most of Palmer's Brigade had gone home, many of the men never receiving parole. Because of rumors of Johnston's surrender, Martin decided to send a flag of truce to Stoneman for clarification. Stringfield was chosen to lead the party, consisting of nineteen officers and men.[569]

Stringfield left Franklin on April 28. At Maryville his party encountered Federals who believed Stringfield and his men were bushwhackers. In order to allay their suspicions, Stringfield allowed one of their officers to inspect his men to insure themselves of their intentions. The officer selected, a Tennessee Unionist named Lieutenant Sanderson, accused Eppa Everett of having killed his father and a Captain Love and one John Henderson of being horse thieves. After a period of tension in which the Federals at first demanded to have Everett, Love, and Henderson unconditionally surrendered to them, another officer asked to see Stringfield's papers. It turned out that he had been acquainted with Stringfield's father,

---

S. Rice, said to have been an eyewitness and thus possibly a soldier in the Infantry Regiment. A man by the same name filed a pension for service in "Company F, Thomas's Legion." John S. Rice, North Carolina Application for Pension (1901), State Auditor's Office Records, NCOAH.

569. *O.R.* 49 (pt. 1): 338-339, (pt. 2): 407-08 (Stoneman quote, 408); Martin to Cornelia Phillips Spencer, June 11, 1866, Spencer Papers, SHC; B. G. McDowell, "Sixty-Second Regiment," in Clark, *North Carolina Regiments* 3:527; S. V. Pickens, "Seventy-Ninth Regiment," in ibid., 4:116; Jordan, "62nd Regiment N.C. Troops," in Manarin and Jordan, *North Carolina Troops*, 15:34; Jordan, "64th Regiment N. C. Troops," in ibid., 15:167-168; Stringfield, "Memoirs of the Civil War," typescript, McClung Collection, L-McGL (copy in Stringfield Papers, WCU), 33. In his memoirs, Stringfield recalled that there were twenty-three members of the party besides himself. Based on the Federal provost marshal records, there were nineteen (including Stringfield). The other members were 1st Lt. Luther C. May, adjutant of the Infantry Regiment; Pvt. R. B. Lloyd, Q.M. Sgt., Infantry Regiment; Capt. William B. Love and Pvt. William P. Cobb, Company D, Infantry Regiment; Capt. Thomas A. Butler and Pvts. Samuel C. Crozier, Albert H. Gallaher, William Hedrick, Stephen P. McKinney, J. C. McBee, W. R. McNelly, John W. Martin, and W. Taylor, Company K, Infantry Regiment; "Pvt." (Capt.?) Eppie Everett and Pvts. J. W. Bowman, Noah Earl, J. G. Henderson, Patrick H. May, and S. C. Swann of "Company A." National Archives transcribers designated the latter six men as members of "Co. A, Thomas Legion," and their service jackets were filed among those of the Infantry Regiment. It is possible that one of the white companies from Thomas's North Carolina command became the new Company A of the Infantry Regiment (or Thomas relettered the already existing companies); otherwise, these men served either in Company A, Stringfield's Battalion, or Company A, Indian Battalion. All of the men in this "Co. A, Thomas Legion" are otherwise unknown, with the exception of Everett, whose case and rank has been discussed elsewhere in relation to Ghormley's company. Stringfield referred to Everett as a captain in his memoirs. The service record files of all members of the party can be found in Compiled Service Records of Confederate Soldiers from the State of North Carolina (M270), reels 568 through 571 and 574. In his memoirs Stringfield identified Capt. William B. Reese, adjutant of the Legion, Capt. Matthew H. Love of Company A, Indian Battalion, and an otherwise unknown Lt. John Henderson as members, making twenty-two (not twenty-three) in all; however, there are no Federal provost marshal records for the latter three men. It is possible that "Lieutenant" Henderson was the same man as Pvt. J. G. Henderson of the unidentified "Company A." Why Stringfield chose to make the party so topheavy with officers, who might better have remained with their commands, is unknown; perhaps he thought it would add greater legitimacy to the mission and convince the Federals that it was not a raiding party. If so, he would soon prove mistaken. It is also not known why so many of the participants were members of the regiment rather than Stringfield's own battalion.

and after explaining that there were rumors of Confederate bushwhackers around ordered Stringfield to proceed to Knoxville. Once he arrived there on May 1, however, he ran into further trouble. After conferring with his officers, Stoneman announced that there was really no need to answer Martin, as his troops already had taken western North Carolina. When Stringfield objected and turned down Stoneman's offer to take the Oath of Allegiance, Stoneman had the entire party thrown in jail. There they remained until well in the summer.[570]

Meanwhile, Bartlett and Kirk moved against Martin and Thomas. Love was at Balsam Gap with some 200 men of the Infantry Regiment, while Thomas was at Soco Gap with a force of around 200 that included some Indians, in addition to Conley's sharpshooter company. Conley was ordered to join Love at Balsam Gap. Taking a route that led him to White Sulphur Springs near Waynesville, Conley encountered Bartlett's men on May 6, surprised them and drove them off. This skirmish is frequently referred to as the last clash of the Civil War east of the Mississippi. Martin, who had gone to Franklin for word of Stringfield, was eating that night in the home of Love's father near Webster when the colonel brought news of the clash. Martin decided to move against Bartlett, who had withdrawn to Waynesville. That night, Thomas tried to practice some psychological warfare by having the Cherokees build numerous fires in the hills surrounding Waynesville in an effort to make it look like the Federals were surrounded by a large force; he also had the Indians beat their drums and utter war whoops throughout the night. Bartlett asked for a flag of truce the next morning.[571]

Martin arrived for the meeting with Bartlett along with Love and Thomas, the latter accompanied by twenty Cherokee "stripped to the waist and *painted and feathered in good old style*." According to some sources, Thomas threatened Bartlett and his men with scalping if they did not retreat, but cooler heads prevailed.[572] Martin knew that it was only a matter of

570. Stringfield, "Memoirs of the Civil War," typescript, McClung Collection, L-McGL (copy in Stringfield Papers, WCU), 33-38; Stringfield, "Sixty-Ninth Regiment," in Clark, *North Carolina Regiments*, 3:760. Perhaps the encounter with the hostile Federal officer at Maryville is why Everett gave his rank as "private" to the provost marshal, in order to convince the Federals that he was someone else; the Federal records also referred to him as a "deserter." Stringfield identified the two accused of horse thievery as Capt. Matthew H. Love and Lt. John Henderson. Other than Stringfield's memoir and his history of the Infantry Regiment, there is no evidence that Love went with the party. A secondary source claimed that 2nd Lt. Joseph A. Collins commanded Matthew Love's company at the end of the war, which might have been the case if the latter was part of Stringfield's party; see Allen, *Annals of Haywood County*, 455. It is instead likely that Stringfield confused Matthew Love in his memory with Capt. William B. Love, whom Federal provost marshal records indicate was part of the group. The service record files of the members of the party gives information about the dates of their releases.

571. Conley, "The Last Gun of the War," *The Atlanta Constitution*, July 13, 1892; Stringfield, "Sixty-Ninth Regiment," in Clark, *North Carolina Regiments*, 3:760-761; W. W. Stringfield, "The Last Battle and the Last Surrender," in ibid, 5:653, 655; Crow, *Storm in the Mountains*, 138, 256 n. 54. The skirmish is frequently misdated. Stringfield gave the date of the clash as May 9, Martin's surrender as May 10, and Whitaker's surrender as May 14. In his history of the regiment, Stringfield placed Love in command of the Confederate forces at the skirmish, rather than Conley.

572. Stringfield, "Sixty-Ninth Regiment," in Clark, *North Carolina Regiments* 3:761 (quote); Crow, *Storm in the Mountains*, 138. In his history of the regiment, Stringfield (who was not present) reported that Thomas became unusually worked up in his conversation with Bartlett, evidently upset over the heavy Federal foraging. In another account, Stringfield claimed that Thomas himself was also in war paint and feathers. "Col Thomas—as you probably know—lost his Mind after the war. I think he was a little off at this time, from his actions." Stringfield to James Mooney, September 17, 1900, Stringfield Papers, WCU. Stringfield seems to have derived

time before he would be overwhelmed. After negotiations, Thomas's Legion and the rest of Martin's command surrendered at Waynesville on May 7, almost a full month after Lee's surrender at Appomattox. The members of Thomas's so-called Life Guard, who were not in Confederate service, were allowed to retain their arms, as were some other Cherokees whom Thomas claimed were not involved in the war; arguing that it was necessary for them to keep their weapons to protect their families from the marauder bands in the mountains. Bartlett's decision to allow this got him into trouble with his superiors, as rumors flew that he had exempted an entire battalion from giving up their arms. These stories were exaggerated after the war, when some members of the Legion claimed that everyone walked away with their weapons. While it is probable that many soldiers did slip away, so far as is known the majority turned in their weapons and surrendered.[573] Meanwhile, Kirk advanced to Franklin against Stringfield's Battalion. Acting in Stringfield's absence, Capt. Stephen Whitaker of Company E surrendered the remainder of the Legion at Franklin on May 12.[574]

In the years after the war, Thomas's Legion gained a legendary reputation in the mountains far beyond what it actually accomplished. The desertion and discipline problems which plagued the Legion and hampered its effectiveness were forgotten. Thomas's clashes with his superiors became part of a popular genre of tales of feuding Civil War officers based around the eccentric, larger-than-life personalities involved, and ignored specifics involving military policy. The Legion's history also became confused in postwar writings, and its organizational structure and evolution obscured. Regrettably, many records concerning such matters as Thomas's western North Carolina battalion or details of the guerrilla warfare in the mountains were lost, and veterans of the Legion did nothing to provide a full record of its activities. As much as we owe today to Stringfield's writings, his contradictions, errors, and lack of concrete detail on many things have proved to be as misleading as much as enlightening.

For Thomas himself, the tale ended in tragedy. He was forced to resign his chieftainship of the Eastern Band of Cherokees and was reluctantly sued by them in an effort to disentangle the lands he had bought on their behalf from his creditors' claims against him. Plagued by a tremendous amount of debt and mental instability, he died in an institution in Morganton in 1893.[575] Despite this sad ending to Thomas's life, the history of Thomas's Legion remains one of the more fascinating and unusual chapters in North Carolina's Civil War participation.

---

his information on events in part from the same John S. Rice who also gave the account of Love's escape from Asheville. Stringfield, "Memoirs of the Civil War," typescript, McClung Collection, L-McGL (copy in Stringfield Papers, WCU), 40.

573. *O.R.* 49 (pt. 2): 669, 754-755; Martin to Cornelia Phillips Spencer, June 11, 1866, Spencer papers, SHC; Conley, "The Last Gun of the War," *The Atlanta Constitution*; Crow, *Storm in the Mountains*, 138-139. By the turn of the century, some believed that Bartlett surrendered to Thomas. Arthur, *Western North Carolina*, 581. In the published version of Tillson's report, the date for Martin's surrender is given as May 3. *O.R.* 49 (pt. 1): 339.

574. *O.R.* 49 (pt. 2): 669, 754-755; Conley, "The Last Gun of the War," *The Atlanta Constitution*, July 13, 1892; Crow, *Storm in the Mountains*, 138-140; Parole for Stephen E. Whitaker, May 12, 1865, and Parole Roll of Capt. S. Whitaker, Company E, 1st Batt., Thomas Legion, May 12, 1865, Whitaker Papers, NCOAH. The surviving parole roll in Whitaker's papers cover his company only, not the entire battalion. There were 27 men from Company E who surrendered on May 12: Whitaker himself, 3 lieutenants, 4 sergeants, and 19 privates.

575. For Thomas's later years, see Crow, *Storm in the Mountains*, 142; Godbold and Russell, *Confederate Colonel and Cherokee Chief*, 129-150.

THOMAS'S LEGION FIELD AND STAFF

COLONEL

THOMAS, WILLIAM HOLLAND

Previously served as Major in command of the Infantry Regiment of this legion. Promoted to Colonel in command of this legion, September 27, 1862. Name appears on a pay voucher dated June 8, 1863, for service in January-April, 1863. Signature appears on requisitions for ordnance and ordnance stores dated January 14 and February 17, 1863. Between February 9 and March 19, 1863, Thomas's Legion was incorporated into a brigade commanded by Brig. Gen. Alfred E. Jackson [*Official Records (Army)* Ser. I: 23 (pt. 2): 621, 639-631, 711, 945-946]. During that time, the component parts of this legion (Infantry Regiment, Walker's Battalion, and Levi's Battery) were treated as separate elements of Jackson's Brigade, and Colonel Thomas was officially considered to be Colonel in command of the Infantry Regiment only. He later served as commander of an informal "Indian Battalion" in western North Carolina from September, 1863, through November, 1864, but still considered himself to be the commander of the entire legion. [For Thomas's record as Colonel in command of the Infantry Regiment and of the Indian Battalion, see the entries for him in the Field and Staff sections of those rosters.] The legion was officially restored to Thomas's command in November, 1864; he assumed full command upon the return of the Infantry Regiment and Walker's Battalion to North Carolina from the Shenandoah Valley in December, 1864. Reported present and in command of the reunited Legion in western North Carolina, January 17, 1865 [Col. J. B. Palmer to Maj. J. W. Riely, Manuscript No. 1225, Box 12, Entry 183, Miscellaneous Records, Manuscripts 1861-1865, National Archives]. Paroled at Waynesville, May 9, 1865 [Clark's *Regiments* 3:761; *Official Records (Army)* 49 (pt. 2): 669-670].

ADJUTANT

REESE, WILLIAM B., Captain

Previously served on the staff of Brig. Gen. Felix K. Zollicoffer and as Assistant Adjutant General to Brig. Gen. Alfred E. Jackson. Appointed Adjutant of this legion on an unspecified date. Reported absent in a letter from Col. John B. Palmer to Maj. J. W. Riely of the Adjutant and Inspector General's Office, January 17, 1865 [Manuscript No. 1225, Box 12, Entry 183, Miscellaneous Records, Manuscripts 1861-1865, Record Group 109, National Archives]. [His surname may have been Reece. According to Clark's *Regiments* 3: 760, and William Williams Stringfield, "Memoirs of the Civil War," p. 34, he was part of the flag-of-truce party under Lt. Col. William W. Stringfield of Walker's Battalion which was arrested and imprisoned by the Federals at Knoxville, Tennessee, on May 1, 1865, when they refused to take the Oath of Allegiance. For his prior service, see Robert E. L. Krick, *Staff Officers in Gray*, p. 350.]

QUARTERMASTER

FOLSOM, HENDERSON MITCHELL, Major

Born in Greene County, Tennessee, October 4, 1831. Was by occupation an attorney. Previously served as Quartermaster with the rank of Major in the brigades of Brig. Gen. Alfred E. Jackson and Col. George S. Patton. His name appears as a signature on payment vouchers dated July 5 and August 9, 1864, and a special requisition dated September 1, 1864, in the papers of 2nd Lt. William W. Jones of Company D, Infantry Regiment of this legion. He is referred to as Major and Quartermaster in these documents. His name also appears as a signature on a payment voucher dated August 13, 1863, in the papers of James McKamy of Walker's Battalion, as well as on other official documents scattered in the combined military service records of various members of Thomas's Legion. Reported absent in a letter from Col. John B. Palmer to Maj. J. W. Riely of the Adjutant and Inspector General's Office, January 17, 1865 [Manuscript No. 1225, Box 12, Entry 183, Miscellaneous Records, Manuscripts 1861-1865, RG 109, National Archives]. No further records. [For his previous service, see Krick, *Staff Officers in Gray*, p.130.]

ASSISTANT QUARTERMASTER

TERRELL, JAMES WHARREY

Previously served as Assistant Quartermaster (Captain) of the Infantry Regiment of this legion. Appointed Assistant Quartermaster (Captain) of Thomas's Legion on November 25, 1864, to rank from November 12, 1864. Reported present in a letter from Col. John B. Palmer to Maj. J. W. Riely of the Adjutant and Inspector General's Office, January 17, 1865 [Manuscript No. 1225, January 17, 1865, Box 12, Entry 183, Miscellaneous Records, Manuscripts 1861-1865, Record Group 109, National Archives]. Sent letter confirming acceptance of appointment on March 3, 1865. No further records. Survived the war.

COMMISSARY OF SUBSISTENCE

HENDERSON, FINLEY HOUSTON, Major

Born in Greene County, Tennessee. Previously served as Private in Company B, 2nd Regiment Tennessee Cavalry (Ashby's), Commissary of Subsistence with the rank of Major in the brigade of Brig. Gen. Alfred E. Jackson, Volunteer Aide-de-Camp with the rank of Major to Maj. Gen. John B. Gordon at the battle of Third Winchester; and as Commissary of Subsistence with the rank of Major in the brigade of Brig. Gen. Gabriel S. Wharton. Appointed Commissary of Subsistence of this legion on an unspecified date. Reported absent in a letter from Col. John B. Palmer to Maj. J. W. Riely of the Adjutant and Inspector General's Office, January 17, 1865. No further records. [Manuscript No. 1225, January 17, 1865, Box 12, Entry 183, Miscellaneous Records, Manuscripts 1861-1865, Record Group 109, National Archives. For his earlier service see Krick, *Staff Officers in Gray*, p.156.]

ASSISTANT COMMISSARY OF SUBSISTENCE

JOHNSTON, THOMAS DILLARD, Captain

Previously served as Assistant Quartermaster (Captain) of Walker's Battalion. Appointed Assistant Commissary of Subsistence (Captain) on November 25, 1864, to rank from November 21, 1864. Reported present in a letter from Col. John B. Palmer to Maj. J. W. Riely of the Adjutant and Inspector General's Office, January 17, 1865 [Manuscript No. 1225, Box 12, Entry 183, Miscellaneous Records, Manuscripts 1861-1865, Record Group 109, National Archives]. No further records. Survived the war.

INFANTRY REGIMENT
(COL. J. R. LOVE'S REGIMENT)

FIELD AND STAFF

COLONELS

THOMAS, WILLIAM HOLLAND

Previously served as Captain of 2nd Company A of this regiment. Appointed Major and transferred to the Field and Staff on July 19, 1862. Promoted to Colonel in command of this legion on September 27, 1862. [For his service in that capacity, see the entry for him in the Thomas's Legion Field and Staff roster.] Between February 9 and March 19, 1863, Thomas's Legion was incorporated into a brigade commanded by Brig. Gen. Alfred E. Jackson [*Official Records (Army)* Ser. I: 23 (pt. 2): 621, 639-631, 711, 945-946]. During that time, the component parts of this legion (Infantry Regiment, Walker's Battalion, Capt. John T. Levi's Battery) were treated as separate elements of Jackson's Brigade, and Colonel Thomas was officially considered to be Colonel in command of this regiment only. Reported absent under arrest from August 15, 1863, on three inspection reports dated November 24 and December 12, 1863, and January 12, 1864, as well as a fourth report which is undated. Reason he was under arrest is not reported, but it appears that it was due to "some alleged disobedience of orders." Thomas was then sent to Knoxville, Tennessee, for trial. "This trial was interrupted by the Federal invasion" of eastern Tennessee in the fall of 1863 [James Wharrey Terrell to Gov. Zebulon Baird Vance, February 22, 1864, Governors' Papers: Zebulon Baird Vance, 1862-1865, N.C. State Archives. Terrell misdates the arrest to June.]. According to Capt. Stephen Whitaker of Company E, Walker's Battalion, Thomas had been restored to duty by August 25, 1863 [Stephen Whitaker to James Whitaker, August 25, 1863, Stephen Whitaker Papers, N.C. State Archives]. Why he was still officially considered under arrest for so long is not known, but the charges were originally instituted by General Jackson, and it is possible that he considered Thomas's restoration to command as only a temporary expediency in the face of military necessity. According to Thomas and others, either Maj.Gen. Simon Bolivar Buckner, then commander of the Department of East Tennessee, or Gen. Braxton Bragg, commander of the Department of Tennessee (to whom Buckner at that time answered), or both, officially ordered him at this time to take 2nd Company A and Company B of this regiment to guard the mountain passes running from eastern Tennessee to western North Carolina. Under this arrangement, Thomas was supposed to answer directly to Buckner, rather than Jackson [Terrell to Vance, February 22, 1864, Governors' Papers: Zebulon Baird Vance, near Morganton, N.C. State Archives; William Holland Thomas to "General" (Samuel Cooper), July 8, 1864, unbound letterbook pages, William Holland Thomas Papers, Special Collections, Perkins Library, Duke University; William Holland Thomas, remarks written on Special Requisition No. 40, September 3, 1864, Compiled Service Records for Col. William Holland Thomas, National Archives.]. No official papers directly documenting this assignment have so far surfaced. Thomas is known to have departed with the Indian companies from Strawberry Plains, Tennessee, on September 2, 1863 [Mollie Stringfield to William Williams Stringfield, September 3, 1863, William Williams Stringfield Papers, N.C. State Archives]. Although the companies were still considered officially to be a part of the Infantry Regiment, Thomas soon began organizing other companies which he lettered successively in order after the companies he already had. Companies C and D are documented. This informally marks the beginning of what became known as the Indian Battalion, although it was not officially organized until 1865. From September, 1863, until December, 1864, when the remnants of the legion returned to North Carolina from the Shenandoah Valley, Thomas had direct command only of these companies, although he both claimed and attempted to exercise direct authority over the rest of the Legion.

LOVE, JAMES ROBERT, JR.

Previously served as Captain of Company A, 16th Regiment N.C. Troops (6th Regiment N.C. Volunteers). Elected Lieutenant Colonel of this regiment on September 27, 1862. Signature appears on payment vouchers dated December 19, 1862, for service from August 31 through October 31, 1862, May 31, 1863, March 1 through April 30, 1863, and June, 1863. Name appears on a list to serve on a general court-martial on or about May 4, 1863 [General Orders No. 5, Dept. of East Tennessee, May 1, 1863, Maury Dept. of East Tennessee, General & Special Orders, 1863, Entry 85, Box #1, Record Group 109, National Archives]. Signature appears on a special requisition for writing materials for use on a court-martial board in Jonesborough, Tennessee, August 2, 1863. Name appears as a signature on a petition to Gov. Zebulon B. Vance dated February 25, 1864, requesting his assistance in reuniting Thomas's Legion and removing it from the command of Brig. Gen. Alfred E. Jackson [Love, et al., to Vance, February 25, 1864, Governors' Papers: Zebulon Baird Vance, 1862-1865, N.C. State Archives]. Signature appears on requisitions for horse forage dated August 1 and 20 and September 1, 1864. Reported sick in hospital on September 18, 1864 [Lafayette George to Rachel George, September 18, 1864, Roster Document 1474, Civil War Roster Project, N.C. Office of Archives & History]. Signature appears on a special requisition for clothing for non-commissioned officers in the Legion, September 27(?), 1864. Reported present on January 17, 1865. He was evidently absent ill during part of early 1865 (see Crow, *Storm in the Mountains*, 112-113, 150). Promoted to Colonel between January 17 and March 21, 1865. Numerous documents in the *Official Records*, the private papers of Col. William Holland Thomas, the official state papers of Gov. Zebulon B. Vance, and the Confederate Adjutant & Inspector General's Office, as well as many postwar writings by various members of the Legion, document Love's service throughout the war. As Thomas exercised control over the entire Legion, Love was the direct commander of the Infantry Regiment, a role that he continued under Brig. Gen. Alfred E. Jackson after Thomas departed for the mountains with the two Indian companies of this regiment in September, 1863. Love further acted as commander of those elements of the Legion that participated in the 1864 Shenandoah Valley campaign. Upon the return of the legion from Virginia to western North Carolina in the winter of 1864, Love reverted to direct command of the Infantry Regiment under Thomas. He surrendered with Thomas and the Infantry Regiment and the Indian Battalion at Waynesville on May 9, 1865.

LIEUTENANT COLONEL

McDOWELL, BRYAN GIBBS

Served as Lieutenant Colonel of the 62nd Regiment N.C. Troops. Also served as acting commander of that portion of Thomas's Legion active in western North Carolina in the fall of 1864 (the "Indian Battalion."). After the war, McDowell also claimed to have temporarily commanded this regiment due to the illness of Lt. Col. James R. Love, evidently in early 1865 [Crow, *Storm in the Mountains*, 112-113, 150]. There is no surviving wartime evidence to corroborate this claim. It is unclear whether a mention of

McDowell's service as commander of a portion of Thomas's Legion in Clark's *Regiments*, 3:756, is a reference to his temporary replacement of Love, or his earlier stint as commander of the Indian Battalion.

MAJORS

STRINGFIELD, WILLIAM WILLIAMS

Born in Nashville, Tennessee, March 7, 1837. Previously served as Sergeant in Company F, 3rd Battalion Tennessee Cavalry (Brazelton's), and Captain of Company E, 31st Regiment Tennessee Infantry (W. M. Bradford's). Elected Major of this regiment at age 25, September 27, 1862. Name appears on pay vouchers, requisitions, and inspection reports dated December 22, 1862, and January 31, May 19, July 16, August 1, August 28, November 24, and December 12, 1863. Reported on leave, January 10-12, 1864. Name appears as a signature on a petition dated February 25, 1864, to Gov. Zebulon B. Vance requesting his assistance in reuniting Thomas's Legion and removing it from the command of Brig. Gen. Alfred E. Jackson [Lt. Col. James R. Love, et al. to Vance, February 25, 1864, Governors' Papers: Zebulon Baird Vance, 1862-1865, N.C. State Archives]. Name appears on pay vouchers, requisitions, and receipt rolls for clothing dated July 5, August 1, August 8, and September 1, 1864. Reported sick in hospital, September 18, 1864 [Lafayette George to Rachel George, September 18, 1864, Roster Document 1474, Civil War Roster Project, N.C. Office of Archives & History]. Reported present on January 17, 1865 [see Col. John B. Palmer to Maj. J. W. Riely, Manuscript No. 1225, Letters Received, Confederate Adjutant & Inspector General's Office, Record Group 109, National Archives]. Transferred with the rank of Major to Walker's Battalion prior to February 21, 1865 [Stringfield to Colonel Thomas, February 21, 1865, and February 22, 1865, William Holland Thomas Papers, Special Collection, Perkins Library, Duke University].

JOHNSON, ELISHA G.

Served as Captain of Company C of this regiment from June, 1862. In his history of the "Sixty-Ninth Regiment," in Clark's *Regiments*, 3:732, Lt. Col. William W. Stringfield claimed that Johnson was promoted to Major of the regiment following its return from Virginia in November, 1864, although there is no official wartime evidence to back up that claim. Survived the war.

ADJUTANTS

MAY, LUTHER C.

Born in Virginia. Resided in Albemarle County, Virginia. Appointed Adjutant (1st Lieutenant) of this regiment on September 27, 1862. Name appears on pay vouchers for service from September 27, 1862, through April 30, 1863, and October 1 through 31, 1863. Name appears on inspection reports dated November 24, 1863, December 12, 1863, and January 12, 1864. Name appears as a signature on a petition to Gov. Zebulon B. Vance dated February 25, 1864, requesting his assistance in reuniting Thomas's Legion and removing it from the command of Brig. Gen. Alfred E. Jackson. Name appears on an inspection report dated April 20, 1864. Captured at Knoxville, Tennessee, May 1, 1865. Sent to Chattanooga, Tennessee, May 3, 1865. Sent to Nashville, Tennessee. Confined at Louisville, Kentucky, May 15, 1865. Released at Louisville on July 25, 1865, after taking the Oath of Allegiance. [He probably previously served as Captain of Company A, 3rd Regiment Tennessee Infantry (Vaughn's). A register of appointments, Confederate States Army, indicates that his appointment to this rank and position was made official on March 23, 1863, to rank from September 27, 1862. His capture at Knoxville on May 1, 1865, indicates that he was a member of Lt. Col. William W. Stringfield's flag-of-truce party that was arrested when they refused to take the Oath of Allegiance.]

CARMACK, ALEXANDER R.

Served as Sergeant Major of this regiment. Signed, as Acting Adjutant, forage requisitions for horses dated August 31 and September 30, 1864.

ASSISTANT QUARTERMASTER

TERRELL, JAMES WHARREY

Previously served as Captain of 2nd Company A of this regiment. Appointed Assistant Quartermaster (Captain) on September 27, 1862, and transferred to the Field and Staff. Signature appears on pay vouchers for service from September 28, 1862, through August 31, 1863. Name appears on an inspection report dated November 24, 1863. Reported on leave from December 29, 1863, through January 12, 1864. Name appears on a report of the staff of this regiment dated April 20, 1864. Appointed Assistant Quartermaster of Thomas's entire Legion on November 25, 1864, to rank from November 12, 1864, and transferred to the Legion Field and Staff.

ASSISTANT COMMISSARIES OF SUBSISTENCE

TIDWELL, REUBEN W., Captain

Previously served as Private in Company I of this regiment. Appointed Assistant Commissary of Subsistence (2nd Lieutenant) and transferred to the Field and Staff on or about September 27, 1862. Promoted to Captain subsequent to December 29, 1862, to rank from September 27. Signature appears on payment vouchers dated April 18, 1863, and May 3, 1863, for service from September 27 through April 30, 1863. Appointed Assistant Commissary of Subsistence to Alfred E. Jackson's Brigade, August 12, 1863. Subsequently served as Assistant Commissary of Subsistence in the brigades of William E. Jones and Bradley T. Johnson. [His service record file for Thomas's Legion indicates that he received the rank of Captain with this appointment on September 27, 1862; however, a December 29, 1862 letter from Tidwell to Secretary of War James Seddon in Tidwell's service record in the General and Staff Officer files indicates that he held the rank of 2nd Lieutenant at that time, a claim upheld by supporting documents.]

WELCH, LUCIUS M., Private

Served as Private in Company E of this regiment, and on extra duty as Commissary Sergeant of this regiment. According to Clark's *Regiments*, 3:730, 733, he also served as Assistant Commissary of Subsistence of this regiment.

SURGEONS

LOVE, SAMUEL L.

Previously served as Private in Company E of this regiment. Appointed Surgeon of this regiment on March 14, 1863, to rank from September 27, 1862, but declined the appointment. Survived the war. [He may have served also as Private in Company E, 62nd Regiment N.C. Troops.]

LAWING, JOHN W.

Previously served as Assistant Surgeon of the 10th Regiment N.C. State Troops (1st Regiment N.C. Artillery). Also served previously as Assistant Surgeon in various other staff and non-regimental positions. Appointed Assistant Surgeon of this regiment on July 30, 1863. Signature appears on requisitions for horse forage dated August 1 and September 1, 1864. Promoted to Surgeon on November 4, 1864, to rank from July 30, 1863. Reported present on January 17, 1865. Paroled at Charlotte on May 12, 1865. [Service record omitted in volume 1 of this series. He resided in Lincoln County.]

ASSISTANT SURGEON

LOVE, JOHN C.

Previously served as Assistant Surgeon in the 16th Regiment N.C. Troops (6th Regiment N.C. Volunteers). Appointed Assistant Surgeon of this regiment on July 19, 1862. Signature appears on a pay voucher for service from January 1 through April 30, 1863. Name appears as a signature on a requisition for horse forage dated October 1, 1863. Name appears as a signature on a pay voucher for service in December, 1863. Reported absent with leave, December 29, 1863-January 12, 1864. Name appears as a signature on a petition to Gov. Zebulon B. Vance dated February 25, 1864, requesting his assistance in reuniting Thomas's Legion and removing it from the command of Brig. Gen. Alfred E. Jackson. Name appears as a signature on requistions for horse forage dated August 20 and 26, 1864. Reported present on January 17, 1865. No further records. Survived the war. [Clark's *Regiments* 3:733 states that he "[d]ied soon after the war from its exposures."]

CHAPLAINS

UNAGUSKIE

Cherokee Indian. Reported in John R. Finger, *The Eastern Band of Cherokees, 1819-1900* (Knoxville: University of Tennessee Press, 1984), p. 85, as Chaplain of the "North Carolina Cherokee Battalion" in the spring of 1862.

WEST, HEZEKIAH

Methodist-Episcopal. Resided in Haywood County. Appointed Chaplain on April 10, 1863, to rank from March 21, 1863. Paid on July 10, 1863, for service during May-June, 1863. Resigned on April 26, 1864, because he believed that he could "be more useful in some other field of labor." Captured by the enemy on May 17, 1864, before his resignation had been acted upon. Sent to Knoxville, Tennessee, where he was "reported to be a spy." Apparently cleared of that charge. Released at Knoxville on May 23, 1864, after taking the Oath of Allegiance.

ENSIGNS

JONES, W. W.

Place and date of enlistment and appointment not reported. Wounded in the thigh and captured at Winchester, Virginia, September 19, 1864. Hospitalized at Winchester on September 20, 1864. Treated for ligation of the femoral artery. Died at Winchester on October 6, 1864, of "secondary hemorrhage." [He was 25 years of age at the time of his death.]

LOVE, THOMAS J.

Previously served as Private in Company F of this regiment. Appointed Ensign (1st Lieutenant) to rank from October 31, 1864, and transferred to the Field and Staff. No further records. Survived the war.

SERGEANT MAJORS

CARMACK, ALEXANDER R.

Previously served as Sergeant in Company D of this regiment. Promoted to Sergeant Major and transferred to the Field and Staff on April 1, 1863. Wounded at Strawberry Plains, Tennessee, August 19, 1863. Signed, as Acting Adjutant, forage requisitions for horses dated August 31 and September 30, 1864. Appointed 2nd Lieutenant and transferred back to Company D subsequent to September 27, 1864.

MOORE, DAVID SWAIN

Contrary to 6:12 of this series, he was not transferred from the 16th Regiment N.C. Troops (6th Regiment N.C. Volunteers) to the Infantry Regiment of this legion on October 5, 1862. He was killed in action at Mechanicsville, Virginia, June 26, 1862.

QUARTERMASTER SERGEANT

LLOYD, ROBERT B.

Previously served as Private in Company F of this regiment. Appointed Quartermaster Sergeant subsequent to February 28, 1864. Captured at Knoxville, Tennessee, May 1, 1865. Sent to Chattanooga, Tennessee, May 3, 1865. Transferred to Nashville, Tennessee. Confined at Louisville, Kentucky, May 15, 1865. Released at Louisville on June 16, 1865, after taking the Oath of Allegiance. [His capture at Knoxville on May 1, 1865, indicates that he was a member of Lt. Col. William W. Stringfield's flag-of-truce party that was arrested when they refused to take the Oath of Allegiance.]

COMMISSARY SERGEANT

WELCH, LUCIUS M., Private

Served as Private in Company E of this regiment. Reported on extra duty as Commissary Sergeant of this regiment in September-October, 1863. He probably also served as such in November, 1863-February, 1864. [According to Clark's *Regiments*, 3:730, 733, he also served as Assistant Commissary of Subsistence of this regiment.]

ORDNANCE SERGEANT

BRYSON, GEORGE W.

Served as Private in Company F of this regiment. Assigned to the Field and Staff of this regiment as Acting Ordnance Sergeant, September 1, 1863. Reported present in September-October, 1863. Died near Whitesburg, Tennessee, January 1, 1864. Cause of death not reported.

1st COMPANY A

This company was raised in Jackson County. It served previously as Company A, 16th Regiment N.C. Troops (6th Regiment N.C. Volunteers). It was transferred to this regiment on October 5, 1862. In January, 1863, it was transferred to the 39th Regiment N.C. Troops, where it became Company K.

The following roster was compiled in large part from a company muster roll dated September-December, 1862. This is abstracted in the microfilm edition of the Compiled Service Records of Confederate Soldiers Who Served in Organizations from the State of North Carolina (Record Group 109, M270), National Archives, Washington, D.C. Other valuable information in the Compiled Service Records includes enlistment papers, pay vouchers, requisitions, letters of resignation, discharge certificates, and abstracts of medical and prisoner of war records.

Also utilized in this roster were *The War of the Rebellion: A Compilation of the Official Records of the Union and Confederate Armies*, the North Carolina Adjutant General's papers, state militia records, newspaper casualty lists and obituaries, wartime claims for bounty pay and allowances, postwar registers of claims for artificial limbs, Confederate pension applications filed with the states of North Carolina, Tennessee, and Florida, records of the North Carolina Confederate Soldiers' Home, and the 1860 and 1870 federal censuses of North Carolina. A search was made also for relevant letters, diaries, reminiscences, and other manuscripts in the Southern Historical Collection (University of North Carolina-Chapel Hill) and the Duke University Library Special Collections Department.

Among the secondary sources consulted were records of the North Carolina division of the United Daughters of the Confederacy, postwar rosters, regimental and county histories, marriage bond, will, and cemetery indexes, published and unpublished genealogies, biographical dictionaries, the North Carolina *County Heritage Book* series, the *Confederate Veteran*, Walter Clark's *Histories of the Several Regiments and Battalions from North Carolina in the Great War, 1861-'65*, and the North Carolina volume of the extended edition of *Confederate Military History*.

OFFICERS

CAPTAIN

BRYSON, ANDREW W.

Previously served as 1st Lieutenant of Company A, 16th Regiment N.C. Troops (6th Regiment N.C. Volunteers). Transferred to this company on October 5, 1862, while absent wounded. Promoted to Captain to rank from September 27, 1862. Reported for duty prior to November 1, 1862. Transferred to Company K, 39th Regiment N.C. Troops, in January, 1863.

LIEUTENANTS

BROWN, ROBERT HAMILTON, 3rd Lieutenant

Previously served as Private in Company A, 16th Regiment N.C. Troops (6th Regiment N.C. Volunteers). Transferred to this company on October 5, 1862. Appointed 3rd Lieutenant on November 8, 1862. Reported present through December, 1862. Transferred to Company K, 39th Regiment N.C. Troops, January, 1863. [Contrary to 10:181of this series, he was probably elected 3rd Lieutenant prior to the date of his transfer from this company to the 39th Regiment.]

CATHEY, BENJAMIN HAMILTON, 2nd Lieutenant

Previously served as 2nd Lieutenant of Company A, 16th Regiment N.C. Troops (6th Regiment N.C. Volunteers). Transferred to this company on October 5, 1862. Reported present through December, 1862. Transferred to Company K, 39th Regiment N.C. Troops, January, 1863.

FISHER, JULIUS WILBURN, 1st Lieutenant

Previously served as 1st Lieutenant of Company A, 16th Regiment N.C. Troops (6th Regiment N.C. Volunteers). Transferred to this company on October 5, 1862. Mustered in as 1st Lieutenant. Reported present through December, 1862. Transferred to Company K, 39th Regiment N.C. Troops, January, 1863. [Contrary to 6:13 of this series, he was promoted to 1st Lieutenant on September 27, 1862, prior to his transfer to this company.]

NONCOMMISSIONED OFFICERS AND PRIVATES

ALLEN, WILLIAM J., Private

Previously served as Private in Company A, 16th Regiment N.C. Troops (6th Regiment N.C. Volunteers). Transferred to this company on October 5, 1862. Reported on duty as a nurse in hospital at Richmond, Virginia, October 31, 1862. Rejoined the company prior to December 31, 1862. Transferred to Company K, 39th Regiment N.C. Troops, January, 1863.

ALLISON, BENJAMIN JEFFERSON., Private

Previously served as Private in Company A, 16th Regiment N.C. Troops (6th Regiment N.C. Volunteers). Transferred to this company on October 5, 1862. Reported present through December, 1862. Transferred to Company K, 39th Regiment N.C. Troops, January, 1863.

BALLEW, WILLIAM J., Private

Previously served as Private in Company A, 16th Regiment N.C. Troops (6th Regiment N.C. Volunteers). Wounded at Shepherdstown, Virginia, September 20, 1862, while a member of that unit. Transferred to this company on October 5, 1862, while in hospital at Winchester, Virginia. Discharged on an unspecified date following the amputation of his right leg.

BEARD, DANIEL T., Private

Previously served as Private in Company A, 16th Regiment N.C. Troops (6th Regiment N.C. Volunteers). Transferred to this company on October 5, 1862. Reported present through December, 1862. Transferred to Company K, 39th Regiment N.C. Troops, January, 1863.

BROOKS, SYLVANUS R., Private

Previously served as Private in Company A, 16th Regiment N.C. Troops (6th Regiment N.C. Volunteers). Transferred to this company on October 5, 1862. Reported present through December, 1862. Transferred to Company K, 39th Regiment N.C. Troops, January, 1863.

BROWN, FRANCIS M., Private

Previously served as Private in Company A, 16th Regiment N.C. Troops (6th Regiment N.C. Volunteers). Transferred to this company on October 5, 1862. Reported present through December, 1862. Transferred to Company K, 39th Regiment N.C. Troops, January, 1863.

BROWN, WALTER E., Sergeant

Previously served as Sergeant in Company A, 16th Regiment N.C. Troops (6th Regiment N.C. Volunteers). Transferred to this company on October 5, 1862. Reported present through December, 1862. Transferred to Company K, 39th Regiment N.C. Troops, January, 1863.

BRYANT, JAMES, Private
Served as Private in Company A, 16th Regiment N.C. Troops (6th Regiment N.C. Volunteers). Transferred to this company on October 5, 1862, while listed as a deserter. Never reported for duty with this company. Later served as Private in Company K, 39th Regiment N.C. Troops.

BRYSON, HOUSTON H., Private
Previously served as Private in Company A, 16th Regiment N.C. Troops (6th Regiment N.C. Volunteers). Transferred to this company on October 5, 1862. Reported present through December, 1862. Transferred to Company K, 39th Regiment N.C. Troops, January, 1863.

BRYSON, MARCUS W., Private
Previously served as Private in Company A, 16th Regiment N.C. Troops (6th Regiment N.C. Volunteers). Transferred to this company on October 5, 1862. Reported present through December, 1862. Transferred to Company K, 39th Regiment N.C. Troops, January, 1863.

BRYSON, RICHARD J., Private
Previously served as Private in Company A, 16th Regiment N.C. Troops (6th Regiment N.C. Volunteers). Transferred to this company on October 5, 1862. Reported present through December, 1862. Transferred to Company K, 39th Regiment N.C. Troops, January, 1863.

BRYSON, RUCIUS, Private
Previously served as Private in Company A, 16th Regiment N.C. Troops (6th Regiment N.C. Volunteers). Transferred to this company on October 5, 1862. Reported present or accounted for through December, 1862. Transferred to Company K, 39th Regiment N.C. Troops, January, 1863.

BUMGARNER, JAMES POWELL, Corporal
Previously served as Corporal in Company A, 16th Regiment N.C. Troops (6th Regiment N.C. Volunteers). Transferred to this company on October 5, 1862, while absent wounded. Reported absent wounded through December, 1862. Transferred to Company K, 39th Regiment N.C. Troops, January, 1863.

BURNS, NOAH H. H., Private
Previously served as Private in Company A, 16th Regiment N.C. Troops (6th Regiment N.C. Volunteers). Transferred to this company on October 5, 1862, while absent wounded. Reported for duty in November-December, 1862. Transferred to Company K, 39th Regiment N.C. Troops, January, 1863.

CABE, AMOS, Private
Previously served as Private in Company A, 16th Regiment N.C. Troops (6th Regiment N.C. Volunteers). Transferred to this company on October 5, 1862. Reported present through December, 1862. Transferred to Company K, 39th Regiment N.C. Troops, January, 1863.

CABE, JOEL, Private
Previously served as Private in Company A, 16th Regiment N.C. Troops (6th Regiment N.C. Volunteers). Transferred to this company on October 5, 1862. Reported present or accounted for through December, 1862. Transferred to Company K, 39th Regiment N.C. Troops, January, 1863.

CATHEY, WILLIAM HILMAN, Private
Previously served as Private in Company A, 16th Regiment N.C. Troops (6th Regiment N.C. Volunteers). Transferred to this company on October 5, 1862, while on sick furlough. Reported present or accounted for through December, 1862. Transferred to Company K, 39th Regiment N.C. Troops, January, 1863.

CHASTAIN, EDWARD, Private
Previously served as Private in Company A, 16th Regiment N.C. Troops (6th Regiment N.C. Volunteers). Transferred to this company on October 5, 1862. Reported present or accounted for through December, 1862. Transferred to Company K, 39th Regiment N.C. Troops, January, 1863.

CHASTAIN, ELANDER W., Private
Previously served as Private in Company A, 16th Regiment N.C. Troops (6th Regiment N.C. Volunteers). Transferred to this company on October 5, 1862. Reported in hospital at Winchester, Virginia, in September-October, 1862. Reported absent without leave in November-December, 1862. Transferred to Company K, 39th Regiment N.C. Troops, January, 1863, while absent without leave.

CHILDERS, NIMROD, Private
Previously served as Private in Company A, 16th Regiment N.C. Troops (6th Regiment N.C. Volunteers). Transferred to this company on October 5, 1862. Reported present or accounted for through October 31, 1862. Transferred to Company K, 39th Regiment N.C. Troops, January, 1863.

CLINE, GEORGE W., Private
Previously served as Private in Company A, 16th Regiment N.C. Troops (6th Regiment N.C. Volunteers). Transferred to this company on October 5, 1862. Reported on sick furlough through October 31, 1862. Transferred to Company K, 39th Regiment N.C. Troops, January, 1863.

CONLEY, JESSE F., Private
Previously served as Private in Company A, 16th Regiment N.C. Troops (6th Regiment N.C. Volunteers). Transferred to this company on October 5, 1862, while absent wounded. Died on or about October 14, 1862, of wounds. Place of death not reported.

CONLEY, WILLIAM DEWITT, 1st Sergeant
Previously served as 1st Sergeant in Company A, 16th Regiment N.C. Troops (6th Regiment N.C. Volunteers). Transferred to this company on October 5, 1862. A company muster roll dated September-October, 1862, states that he was a prisoner of war; however, it is more probable that he was a paroled prisoner on the date of his transfer and was unable to report for duty until he was formally exchanged. Reported for duty prior to December 31, 1862. Transferred to Company K, 39th Regiment N.C. Troops, January, 1863.

COOPER, SAMUEL WAVERLY, Private

Previously served as Private in Company A, 16th Regiment N.C. Troops (6th Regiment N.C. Volunteers). Transferred to this company on October 5, 1862. Reported present through October 31, 1862. Reported on detached service as drillmaster for Company H of this regiment, November-December, 1862. Transferred to Company K, 39th Regiment N.C. Troops, January, 1863.

COPE, JOHN, Private

Previously served as Private in Company A, 16th Regiment N.C. Troops (6th Regiment N.C. Volunteers). Transferred to this company on October 5, 1862, while on sick furlough. Reported for duty prior to December 31, 1862. Transferred to Company K, 39th Regiment N.C. Troops, January, 1863.

COPE, WILLIAM, Private

Previously served as Private in Company A, 16th Regiment N.C. Troops (6th Regiment N.C. Volunteers). Transferred to this company on October 5, 1862, while sick in hospital. Reported for duty prior to December 31, 1862. Transferred to Company K, 39th Regiment N.C. Troops, January, 1863.

DAVIS, JOHN L., Private

Previously served as Private in Company A, 16th Regiment N.C. Troops (6th Regiment N.C. Volunteers). Transferred to this company on October 5, 1862, while absent wounded. Reported absent on wounded furlough through October 31, 1862. Reported for duty prior to December 31, 1862. Transferred to Company K, 39th Regiment N.C. Troops, January, 1863.

DAWSON, JOSEPH C., Private

Previously served as Private in Company A, 16th Regiment N.C. Troops (6th Regiment N.C. Volunteers). Transferred to this company on October 5, 1862. Reported present or accounted for through December, 1862. Transferred to Company K, 39th Regiment N.C. Troops, January, 1863.

DILLS, BARTLETT, Private

Previously served as Private in Company A, 16th Regiment N.C. Troops (6th Regiment N.C. Volunteers). Transferred to this company on October 5, 1862, while absent wounded. Reported absent on wounded furlough through October 31, 1862. Reported for duty in November-December, 1862. Transferred to Company K, 39th Regiment N.C. Troops, January, 1863.

ENSLEY, JAMES, Private

Previously served as Private in Company A, 16th Regiment N.C. Troops (6th Regiment N.C. Volunteers). Transferred to this company on October 5, 1862, while absent without leave. Listed as a paroled prisoner on October 31, 1862. Reported absent on sick furlough in November-December, 1862. Transferred to Company K, 39th Regiment N.C. Troops, January, 1863, while on expired furlough.

FORGY, JOHN, Private

Previously served as Private in Company A, 16th Regiment N.C. Troops (6th Regiment N.C. Volunteers). Transferred to this company on October 5, 1862. Reported in hospital at Richmond, Virginia, October 31, 1862. Reported on sick furlough in November-December, 1862. Transferred to Company K, 39th Regiment N.C. Troops, January, 1863.

FORGY, WILLIAM E., Private

Previously served as Private in Company A, 16th Regiment N.C. Troops (6th Regiment N.C. Volunteers). Transferred to this company on October 5, 1862. Reported in hospital at Bristol, Tennessee, October 31, 1862. Reported on sick furlough in November-December, 1862. Transferred to Company K, 39th Regiment N.C. Troops, January, 1863.

FULBRIGHT, DANIEL M., Private

Previously served as Private in Company A, 16th Regiment N.C. Troops (6th Regiment N.C. Volunteers). Transferred to this company on October 5, 1862, while absent wounded. Reported on wounded furlough through October 31, 1862. Reported for duty in November-December, 1862. Transferred to Company K, 39th Regiment N.C. Troops, January, 1863.

FULBRIGHT, DAVID M., Private

Previously served as Private in Company A, 16th Regiment N.C. Troops (6th Regiment N.C. Volunteers). Transferred to this company on October 5, 1862, while absent wounded. Reported on wounded furlough through October 31, 1862. Reported for duty in November-December, 1862. Transferred to Company K, 39th Regiment N.C. Troops, January, 1863.

HENRY, JOHN, Private

Previously served as Private in Company A, 16th Regiment N.C. Troops (6th Regiment N.C. Volunteers). Transferred to this company on October 5, 1862. Reported present through December, 1862. Transferred to Company K, 39th Regiment N.C. Troops, January, 1863.

HOOPER, LEMUEL W., Private

Previously served as Private in Company A, 16th Regiment N.C. Troops (6th Regiment N.C. Volunteers). Transferred to this company on October 5, 1862. Reported present through December, 1862. Transferred to Company K, 39th Regiment N.C. Troops, January, 1863.

HOYLES, JACOB L., Private

Previously served as Private in Company A, 16th Regiment N.C. Troops (6th Regiment N.C. Volunteers). Transferred to this company on October 5, 1862. Reported present through December, 1862. Transferred to Company K, 39th Regiment N.C. Troops, January, 1863.

HUFFMAN, FREDERICK M., Sergeant

Previously served as Sergeant in Company A, 16th Regiment N.C. Troops (6th Regiment N.C. Volunteers). Transferred to this company on October 5, 1862. Reported present through December, 1862. Transferred to Company K, 39th Regiment N.C. Troops, January, 1863.

HUNTER, JOHN N., Sergeant

Previously served as Sergeant in Company A, 16th Regiment N.C. Troops (6th Regiment N.C. Volunteers). Transferred to this company on October 5, 1862. Reported present through December, 1862. Transferred to Company K, 39th Regiment N.C. Troops, January, 1863.

JENKINS, JEREMIAH, Private
Previously served as Private in Company A, 16th Regiment N.C. Troops (6th Regiment N.C. Volunteers). Transferred to this company on October 5, 1862. Reported present in September-October, 1862. Reported absent without leave in November-December, 1862. Transferred to Company K, 39th Regiment N.C. Troops, January, 1863.

JONES, ALFRED L., Private
Previously served as Private in Company A, 16th Regiment N.C. Troops (6th Regiment N.C. Volunteers). Transferred to this company on October 5, 1862. Reported present through December, 1862. Transferred to Company K, 39th Regiment N.C. Troops, January, 1863.

KEENER, JOHN SIMON, Sergeant
Previously served as Sergeant in Company A, 16th Regiment N.C. Troops (6th Regiment N.C. Volunteers). Transferred to this company on October 5, 1862. Reported present through December, 1862. Transferred to Company K, 39th Regiment N.C. Troops, January, 1863.

LONDON, HARVEY R. B., Private
Previously served as Private in Company A, 16th Regiment N.C. Troops (6th Regiment N.C. Volunteers). Transferred to this company on October 5, 1862. Reported present through December, 1862. Transferred to Company K, 39th Regiment N.C. Troops, January, 1863.

LONDON, THADDEUS D., Private
Previously served as Private in Company A, 16th Regiment N.C. Troops (6th Regiment N.C. Volunteers). Transferred to this company on October 5, 1862. Reported in hospital at Staunton, Virginia, October 31, 1863. Returned to duty prior to December 31, 1862. Transferred to Company K, 39th Regiment N.C. Troops, January, 1863.

MASSENGALE, ROBERT, Private
Previously served as Private in Company A, 16th Regiment N.C. Troops (6th Regiment N.C. Volunteers). Transferred to this company on October 5, 1862, while absent wounded. Reported in hospital at Richmond, Virginia, November-December, 1862. Transferred to Company K, 39th Regiment N.C. Troops, January, 1863, while absent wounded.

MILLS, JAMES, Musician
Previously served as Private in Company A, 16th Regiment N.C. Troops (6th Regiment N.C. Volunteers). Transferred to this company on October 5, 1862. Mustered in as Musician (Fifer). Reported present through December, 1862. Transferred to Company K, 39th Regiment N.C. Troops, January, 1863.

MILLSAPS, FRANCIS M., Private
Previously served as Private in Company A, 16th Regiment N.C. Troops (6th Regiment N.C. Volunteers). Transferred to this company on October 5, 1862. Reported present or accounted for through December, 1862. Transferred to Company K, 39th Regiment N.C. Troops, January, 1863.

MORRISON, HOSEA, Private
Previously served as Private in Company A, 16th Regiment N.C. Troops (6th Regiment N.C. Volunteers). Transferred to this company on October 5, 1862. Reported present through December, 1862. Transferred to Company K, 39th Regiment N.C. Troops, January, 1863.

NEWTON, WILLIAM C. T., Private
Previously served as Private in Company A, 16th Regiment N.C. Troops (6th Regiment N.C. Volunteers). Transferred to this company on October 5, 1862. Reported absent on wounded furlough on October 31, 1862. Reported for duty in November-December, 1862. Transferred to Company K, 39th Regiment N.C. Troops, January, 1863.

PAINTER, ROLEN ANDERSON, Private
Previously served as Private in Company A, 16th Regiment N.C. Troops (6th Regiment N.C. Volunteers). Transferred to this company on October 5, 1862. Reported present through December, 1862. Transferred to Company K, 39th Regiment N.C. Troops, January, 1863.

PARRIS, WILLIAM E., Private
Previously served as Private in Company A, 16th Regiment N.C. Troops (6th Regiment N.C. Volunteers). Transferred to this company on October 5, 1862. Reported on detached service through October 31, 1862. Rejoined the company in November-December, 1862. Transferred to Company K, 39th Regiment N.C. Troops, January, 1863.

PATTON, ANDREW J., Corporal
Previously served as Corporal in Company A, 16th Regiment N.C. Troops (6th Regiment N.C. Volunteers). Transferred to this company on October 5, 1862, while absent wounded. Reported absent wounded through October 31, 1862. Reported for duty in November-December, 1862. Transferred to Company K, 39th Regiment N.C. Troops, January, 1863.

RANDOLPH, THOMAS L., Private
Previously served as Private in Company A, 16th Regiment N.C. Troops (6th Regiment N.C. Volunteers). Transferred to this company on October 5, 1862. Reported absent on sick furlough on October 31, 1862. Reported absent without leave in November-December, 1862. Transferred to Company K, 39th Regiment N.C. Troops, January, 1863, while absent without leave.

RHEA, JOHN H., Private
Previously served as Private in Company A, 16th Regiment N.C. Troops (6th Regiment N.C. Volunteers). Transferred to this company on October 5, 1862. Reported absent on sick furlough on October 31, 1862. Reported absent without leave in November-December, 1862. Transferred to Company K, 39th Regiment N.C. Troops, January, 1863, while absent without leave.

RHINEHART, ISAAC M., Musician
Previously served as Musician (Drummer) in Company A, 16th Regiment N.C. Troops (6th Regiment N.C. Volunteers). Transferred to this company on October 5, 1862, while a prisoner of war at Old Capitol Prison, Washington, D.C. Paroled at Old Capitol Prison and transferred to City Point, Virginia, where he was received on

November 18, 1862, for exchange. Returned to duty prior to being transferred to Company K, 39th Regiment N.C. Troops, January, 1863. [Contrary to 10:185 of this series, his surname was probably Rhinehart.]

RHINEHART, THOMAS P., Private
Previously served as Private in Company A, 16th Regiment N.C. Troops (6th Regiment N.C. Volunteers). Transferred to this company on October 5, 1862, while absent without leave. Reported for duty prior to October 31, 1862. Reported present in November-December, 1862. Records of Company K, 39th Regiment N.C. Troops, indicate that he transferred to that company in November-December, 1862, but did not report for duty. Transferred to Company E of this regiment in January, 1863. [Contrary to 10:185 of this series, his surname was probably Rhinehart.]

ROBERTS, D. R, _____
North Carolina pension records appear to indicate that he served in this company. Survived the war.

ROBERTS, ROBERT MONTREVILLE, Private
Previously served as Private in Company A, 16th Regiment N.C. Troops (6th Regiment N.C. Volunteers). Transferred to this company on October 5, 1862. Reported present or accounted for through November-December, 1862. Transferred to Company K, 39th Regiment N.C. Troops, January, 1863.

SAUNDERS, RUFUS R., Private
Previously served as Private in Company A, 16th Regiment N.C. Troops (6th Regiment N.C. Volunteers). Transferred to this company on October 5, 1862. Reported present in November-December, 1862. Transferred to Company K, 39th Regiment N.C. Troops, January, 1863.

SEAY, JAMES, Private
Previously served as Private in Company A, 16th Regiment N.C. Troops (6th Regiment N.C. Volunteers). Transferred to this company on October 5, 1862. Reported present on October 31, 1862. Reported absent without leave in November-December, 1862. Transferred to Company K, 39th Regiment N.C. Troops, January, 1863, while absent without leave.

SHELTON, ELLIOTT W., Private
Previously served as Private in Company A, 16th Regiment N.C. Troops (6th Regiment N.C. Volunteers). Transferred to this company on October 5, 1862. Reported absent on sick furlough in October, 1862. Returned to duty prior to being transferred to Company K, 39th Regiment N.C. Troops, January, 1863. [His first name may have been Elis.]

SHELTON, JAMES WESLEY, Private
Previously served as Private in Company A, 16th Regiment N.C. Troops (6th Regiment N.C. Volunteers). Transferred to this company on October 5, 1862. Reported absent on detached service in October, 1862. Transferred to Company K, 39th Regiment N.C. Troops, January, 1863.

STILLWELL, ALFRED W., Private
Previously served as Private in Company A, 16th Regiment N.C. Troops (6th Regiment N.C. Volunteers). Transferred to this company on October 5, 1862, while absent wounded. Reported absent wounded until being transferred to Company K, 39th Regiment N.C. Troops, January, 1863.

SUTTON, JOHN, Private
Previously served as Private in Company A, 16th Regiment N.C. Troops (6th Regiment N.C. Volunteers). Transferred to this company on October 5, 1862. Reported absent on sick furlough through December 31, 1862. Transferred to Company K, 39th Regiment N.C. Troops, in January, 1863.

SUTTON, JOSEPH M., Corporal
Previously served as Corporal in Company A, 16th Regiment N.C. Troops (6th Regiment N.C. Volunteers). Transferred to this company on October 5, 1862. Reported absent on sick furlough through December, 1862. Transferred to Company K, 39th Regiment N.C. Troops, January, 1863.

TATHAM, THOMAS N., Private
Previously served as Private in Company A, 16th Regiment N.C. Troops (6th Regiment N.C. Volunteers). Transferred to this company on October 5, 1862. Reported present or accounted for through December, 1862. Transferred to Company K, 39th Regiment N.C. Troops, January, 1863.

TRUETT, JOSEPH L., Private
Previously served as Private in Company A, 16th Regiment N.C. Troops (6th Regiment N.C. Volunteers). Transferred to this company on October 5, 1862. Reported present through November-December, 1862. Transferred to Company K, 39th Regiment N.C. Troops, January, 1863. [His surname may have been Truitt.]

TRUETT, SILAS M., Corporal
Previously served as Private in Company A, 16th Regiment N.C. Troops (6th Regiment N.C. Volunteers). Transferred to this company on October 5, 1862, while a prisoner of war at Old Capitol Prison, Washington, D.C. Exchanged on or about November 18, 1862. Reported for duty and promoted to Corporal prior to December 31, 1862. Transferred to Company K, 39th Regiment N.C. Troops, January, 1863. [His surname may have been Truitt.]

TURPIN, HENRY ALLEN, Private
Previously served as Private in Company A, 16th Regiment N.C. Troops (6th Regiment N.C. Volunteers). Transferred to this company on October 5, 1862. Reported present through December, 1862. Transferred to Company K, 39th Regiment N.C. Troops, January, 1863.

WARREN, ANDREW MITCHELL, Private
Previously served as Private in Company A, 16th Regiment N.C. Troops (6th Regiment N.C. Volunteers). Transferred to this company on October 5, 1862, while a prisoner of war. Paroled subsequent to October 31, 1862. Reported sick in hospital at Warrenton, Virginia, November-December, 1862. Transferred to Company K, 39th Regiment N.C. Troops, January, 1863.

WEEKS, DAVID, Private
Previously served as Private in Company A, 16th Regiment N.C. Troops (6th Regiment N.C. Volunteers). Transferred to this company on October 5, 1862. Reported present through December,

1862. Transferred to Company K, 39th Regiment N.C. Troops, January, 1863.

WIKE, NEHEMIAH, Private
Previously served as Private in Company A, 16th Regiment N.C. Troops (6th Regiment N.C. Volunteers). Transferred to this company on October 5, 1862. Reported present through December, 1862. Transferred to Company K, 39th Regiment N.C. Troops, January, 1863.

WILSON, ALFRED H., Private
Previously served as Private in Company A, 16th Regiment N.C. Troops (6th Regiment N.C. Volunteers). Transferred to this company on October 5, 1862. Reported present through December, 1862. Transferred to Company K, 39th Regiment N.C. Troops, January, 1863.

WILSON, ENOS, Private
Previously served as Private in Company A, 16th Regiment N.C. Troops (6th Regiment N.C. Volunteers). Transferred to this company on October 5, 1862. Reported present through December, 1862. Transferred to Company K, 39th Regiment N.C. Troops, January, 1863.

WILSON, THOMAS M., Private
Previously served as Private in Company A, 16th Regiment N.C. Troops (6th Regiment N.C. Volunteers). Transferred to this company on October 5, 1862. Reported absent wounded on October 31, 1862 (probably suffering from a wound received at Frayser's Farm, Virginia, while serving in the 16th Regiment). Returned to duty prior to December 31, 1862. Transferred to Company K, 39th Regiment N.C. Troops, January, 1863.

2nd COMPANY A

This company was raised in Jackson County and was composed primarily of Cherokee Indians. It was organized at Quallatown on April 9, 1862. As of May 1, 1862, it was known as 1st Company, N.C. Cherokee Battalion. It may have been known as Company A as of August 31, 1862. On or about October 5, 1862, it was designated Company C, Infantry Regiment, Thomas's Legion. It was redesignated Company A, probably in January, 1863. In April, 1865, it formally became Company A, Indian Battalion of this Legion. However, the Indian Battalion had been informally organized in late 1863. For the purposes of these rosters, September 2, 1863, will be used for separating materials for members of 2nd Company A, Infantry Regiment from those of Company A, Indian Battalion. It was on that date that Col. William H. Thomas left Strawberry Plains, Tennessee, with this company and Company B of the Infantry Regiment, marched into the Smoky Mountains, and began recruiting a third Indian company. These companies were never reintegrated into the structure of the Infantry Regiment again, even after the Legion was reunited in western North Carolina in December, 1864.

The following roster was compiled in large part from an undated company muster and descriptive roll, and company muster rolls dated September-October, 1862, and January-April, 1863. These are abstracted in the microfilm edition of the Compiled Service Records of Confederate Soldiers Who Served in Organizations from the State of North Carolina (Record Group 109, M270), National Archives, Washington, D.C. Other valuable information in the Compiled Service Records includes enlistment papers, pay vouchers, requisitions, letters of resignation, discharge certificates, and abstracts of medical and prisoner of war records.

Also utilized in this roster were *The War of the Rebellion: A Compilation of the Official Records of the Union and Confederate Armies*, the North Carolina Adjutant General's papers, state militia records, newspaper casualty lists and obituaries, wartime claims for bounty pay and allowances, postwar registers of claims for artificial limbs, Confederate pension applications filed with the states of North Carolina, Tennessee, and Florida, records of the North Carolina Confederate Soldiers' Home, and the 1860 and 1870 federal censuses of North Carolina. A search was made also for relevant letters, diaries, reminiscences, and other manuscripts in the Southern Historical Collection (University of North Carolina-Chapel Hill) and the Duke University Library Special Collections Department.

Among the secondary sources consulted were records of the North Carolina division of the United Daughters of the Confederacy, postwar rosters, regimental and county histories, marriage bond, will, and cemetery indexes, published and unpublished genealogies, biographical dictionaries, the North Carolina *County Heritage Book* series, the *Confederate Veteran*, Walter Clark's *Histories of the Several Regiments and Battalions from North Carolina in the Great War, 1861-'65*, and the North Carolina volume of the extended edition of *Confederate Military History*.

OFFICERS

CAPTAINS

THOMAS, WILLIAM HOLLAND
Born on February 5, 1805, in the part of Buncombe County that later became Haywood County. Resided in Jackson County and was by occupation a merchant and state legislator. Appointed Captain of this company on April 9, 1862, at age 57. Appointed Major of this regiment on July 19, 1862, and transferred to the Field and Staff.

TERRELL, JAMES WHARREY
Born on December 31, 1829, in Rutherford County or in what later became Jackson County. Resided in Jackson County and was by occupation a merchant and tanner prior to enlisting at age 32. Appointed 1st Lieutenant on April 9, 1862. Promoted to Captain on July 19, 1862. Served as Inspecting and Mustering Officer for both 2nd Company A and Company B from their acceptance into service until an unspecified date. Appointed Assistant Quartermaster (Captain) of this regiment on September 27, 1862, and transferred to the Field and Staff.

LOVE, MATTHEW HALE
Previously served as 1st Sergeant of Company L, 16th Regiment N.C. Troops (6th Regiment N.C. Volunteers). Appointed Captain of this company on September 27, 1862. Reported present in January-April, 1863. Signature appears on a payment voucher for service from March 1 through June 30, 1863. Appointed Captain of Company A, Indian Battalion, on an unspecified date.

LIEUTENANTS

ASTOOGATOGEH, JOHN, 2nd Lieutenant
Cherokee Indian. Born in the part of Haywood County that later became Swain County. Resided in Swain County as a farmer prior to enlisting at age 34. Appointed 2nd Lieutenant on or about April 9,

1862. Killed in action at Baptist Gap, Tennessee, September 13-15, 1862. [His surname was also rendered as Sdhu:gado:ga, Sduhu:gado:ga, and Astoo-ga-Sto-ga.]

GRAYBEARD, PETER, 3rd Lieutenant

Cherokee Indian. Previously served as Private in Company F, 39th Regiment N.C. Troops. Illegally enlisted in this company and was appointed 3rd Lieutenant on April 9, 1862, while absent without leave from Company A, 39th Regiment N.C.Troops. Resigned on September 10, 1862. According to a pay voucher dated November 25, 1862, he resigned due to "his ill state of health."

McCALLA, RICHARD C., 1st Lieutenant

Previously served as 2nd Lieutenant of Capt. E. Winston's Company of Sappers and Miners, Engineer Department. Transferred to this company in September-October, 1862. A register of officers states that he was appointed 1st Lieutenant of this company on November 3, 1862, but he is already listed as 1st Lieutenant on a muster roll dated September-October, 1862. Reported on detached service at Cumberland Gap, Tennessee, September-October, 1862. Assigned by Special Order No. 5, Engineers' Office, Department of East Tennessee, January 16, 1863 to "assume direction of the defensive works at the various Bridges on the line of Railroad between Chattanooga and Bristol." Reported as detailed in the Engineer Department in January-April, 1863. Later served as Captain of Company A, 3rd Regiment Confederate Engineer Troops.

TERRELL, WILLIAM STUART, 1st Lieutenant

Previously served as Private in Company C, 25th Regiment N.C. Troops. Transferred to this company on May 13, 1862. Mustered in as Private. Appointed Brevet 2nd Lieutenant on September 10, 1862. Appointed 2nd Lieutenant on September 14, 1862. Reported present in September-October 1862, and in January-February 1863. Reported on detached duty at Gatlinburg, Tennessee, March-April, 1863. According to Clark's *Regiments* 3:730, he was promoted 1st Lieutenant of this company. If he was promoted, it was subsequent to April 1863, and subsequent to 1st Lt. Richard C. McCalla's transfer to Company A, 3rd Regiment Confederate Engineers. Subsequently served as 1st Lieutenant of Company A, Indian Battalion. [Born on October 21, 1836.]

WHITAKER, DAVID LAFAYETTE, 3rd Lieutenant

Previously served as Private in Company A, 19th Regiment N.C. Troops (2nd Regiment N.C. Cavalry). Appointed 3rd Lieutenant of this company on September 14, 1862. Reported present in January-February, 1863. Reported absent wounded in March-April, 1863. Place and date wounded not reported. May have been promoted to 2nd Lieutenant subsequent to April, 1863. No further records. [He may have served later in Company A, Indian Battalion.]

NONCOMMISSIONED OFFICERS AND PRIVATES

AHMACATOGEH, Private

Cherokee Indian. Born in what later became Jackson County. Resided in Jackson County as a farmer prior to enlisting at age 20, April 9, 1862. Died on July 21, 1862. Place and cause of death not reported.

ARMACHAIN, SEVIER, _____

Cherokee Indian. North Carolina pension records appear to indicate that he served in this company. [His name was also rendered as Severe Armachan. He may have served later in Company A, Indian Battalion.]

ARQUETAGE, JR., Private

Cherokee Indian. Born in the part of Haywood County that later became Jackson County. Resided in Jackson County as a farmer prior to enlisting at Quallatown at age 40, April 9, 1862. Reported present in September-October, 1862, and January-April, 1863. No further records. [He may have served later in Company A, Indian Battalion.]

ARQUETAGE, SR., Private

Cherokee Indian. Born in the part of Buncombe County that later became Jackson County. Resided in Jackson County as a farmer prior to enlisting at Quallatown at age 60, April 9, 1862. Reported present in September-October, 1862, and January-April, 1863. No further records. [He may have served later in Company A, Indian Battalion.]

BATTLE, JAMES F., _____

North Carolina pension records appear to indicate that he served in this company. [He may have instead served in Company F of this regiment. He may have served later in Company A, Indian Battalion.]

BIRD, SQUINEY, _____

Cherokee Indian. North Carolina pension records appear to indicate that he served in this company. Survived the war. [His name was also rendered as Squanci Bird. He may have served later in Company A, Indian Battalion.]

BRADLEY, WILLIAM M., _____

North Carolina pension records appear to indicate that he served in this company. Survived the war. [He may have served later in Company A, Indian Battalion.]

BRANNER, JOSEPH A., Private

Born in Jefferson County, Tennessee, where he resided as a farmer prior to enlisting at age 34, September 27, 1862, for the war. No further records. [He may have served later in Company A, Indian Battalion.]

BURNETT, JAMES A., Private

Enlisted either in this company or in Company A, Walker's Battalion, in Grainger County, Tennessee, October 2, 1862, for the war. Transferred to Company C, Walker's Battalion, February 1, 1863. [His SR includes one card for a James M. Burnett of Company C, Infantry Regiment, one for a James H. Burnet, Company H, Infantry Regiment, and one for a J. P. Burnett of Levi's (Barr's) Battery. The precise relationship of these men, if any, is impossible to identify, although they appear to be all different people. It is assumed from the timing that Burnett's October 1862 enlistment date in Grainger County refers to his enrollment into the Legion; however, it is also possible that he originally served in a Tennessee or C.S.A. unit before coming to the Legion.]

CAH HAH, Private

Cherokee Indian. Born in what later became Jackson County. Resided in Jackson County as a farmer prior to enlisting at Quallatown, age 20, April 9, 1862. Reported present in September-October, 1862, and January-April, 1863. No further records. Survived the war. [He was also known as Wild Cat. He may have served later in Company A, Indian Battalion.]

CAHTOQUASKEE, Private

Cherokee Indian. Born in what later became Jackson County. Resided in Jackson County as a farmer prior to enlisting at Quallatown on April 9, 1862. Reported present in September-October, 1862, and January-February, 1863. Died on April 15, 1863. Place and cause of death not reported.

CHAR CHU, Private

Cherokee Indian. Born in what later became Jackson County. Resided in Jackson County as a farmer prior to enlisting at Quallatown at age 30, April 9, 1862. Reported present in September-October, 1862. Reported on detail as a courier in January-February, 1863. Reported absent sick at Quallatown in March-April, 1863. No further records. [His name may have been Charche or Charchee. He may have served later in Company A, Indian Battalion.]

CHELETOOHSKIH, Corporal

Cherokee Indian. Born in what later became Jackson County. Resided in Jackson County as a farmer prior to enlisting at Quallatown at age 26, April 9, 1862. Mustered in as Private. Reported present in September-October, 1862. Promoted to Corporal between October 31, 1862, and February 28, 1863. Reported present in January-April, 1863. Later served in Company A, Indian Battalion. [His name was also rendered as Chee-le-tos-Key, Chee-lee-tos-Key, and Chiltosk.]

CHELLEE, Private

Cherokee Indian. Born in what later became Jackson County. Resided in Jackson County as a farmer prior to enlisting at Quallatown on April 9, 1862. Reported present in September-October, 1862, and January-February, 1863. Reported on detached duty at Gatlinburg, Tennessee, in March-April, 1863. No further records. [He may have served later in Company A, Indian Battalion.]

CHILDERS, GEORGE, Private

Place and date of enlistment not reported; probably enlisted subsequent to April 30, 1863. Later served in Company A, Indian Battalion.

CHONAH, Private

Cherokee Indian. Born in what later became Jackson County. Resided in Jackson County as a farmer prior to enlisting at Quallatown on April 9, 1862. Reported present in September-October, 1862, and January-April, 1863. No further records. [His name was also rendered as Tso:na. He may have served later in Company A, Indian Battalion.]

CHOWISHKEH, Private

Cherokee Indian. Born in what later became Jackson County. Resided in Jackson County as a farmer prior to enlisting at Quallatown on April 9, 1862. Reported present in September-October, 1862, and January-April, 1863. No further record. [He may have served later in Company A, Indian Battalion.]

CHUCHOLETEH, Private

Cherokee Indian. Born in what later became Jackson County. Resided in Jackson County as a farmer prior to enlisting at Quallatown on April 9, 1862. Reported present in September-October, 1862, and January-April, 1863. No further records. [He may have served later in Company A, Indian Battalion.]

CHULOTATAGEH, Private

Cherokee Indian. Born in what later became Jackson County. Resided in Jackson County as a farmer prior to enlisting at Quallatown at age 19, April 9, 1862. Reported present or accounted for in September-October, 1862, and January-April, 1863. No further records. [He may have served later in Company A, Indian Battalion.]

CHUNOILEGAH, Private

Cherokee Indian. Born in what later became Jackson County. Resided in Jackson County as a farmer prior to enlisting at Quallatown at age 50, November 1, 1862, for the war. Reported present in January-April, 1863. No further records. [He may have served later in Company A, Indian Battalion.]

CHUWHALOOKEEH, Private

Cherokee Indian. Born in what later became Jackson County. Resided in Jackson County as a farmer prior to enlisting at Quallatown on April 9, 1862. Reported present in September-October, 1862, and January-April, 1863. No further records. Survived the war. [His name was also rendered as Chu-wa-lookeh. He may have served later in Company A, Indian Battalion.]

CLANTEESTEH, Private

Cherokee Indian. Born in what later became Jackson County. Resided in Jackson County as a farmer prior to enlisting at Quallatown at age 48, April 9, 1862. Reported present in September-October, 1862, and in January-April, 1863. No further records. Survived the war. [His name was also rendered as Chlantees-teh and Clantechee. He was also known as Pheasant. He may have served later in Company A, Indian Battalion.]

CLARK, HUGH L., Private

Probably served in this company. Place and date of enlistment not reported; probably enlisted subsequent to April 30, 1863. Later served in Company A, Indian Battalion.

CLINE, ALFRED, 1st Sergeant

Born in what later became Jackson County. Resided in Jackson County as a merchant prior to enlisting at Quallatown on April 9, 1862. Mustered in as 1st Sergeant. Reported present in September-October, 1862, and January-April, 1863. No further records. [He may have served later in Company A, Indian Battalion.]

CLINE, JOHN W., Private

Born in what later became Jackson County. Resided in Jackson County as a farmer prior to enlisting at Quallatown at age 20,

April 9, 1862. Transferred to Company I of this regiment on July 24, 1862. Transferred back to this company in January-February, 1863. Reported present through April 30, 1863. No further records. Survived the war. [North Carolina pension records appear to indicate that he served later in Company A, Indian Battalion.]

CLINE, WILLIAM R., Private
Born in what later became Jackson County. Resided in Jackson County as a farmer prior to enlisting at Quallatown at age 22, April 9, 1862. Transferred to Company I of this regiment on July 24, 1862. Transferred back to this company in January-February, 1863. Reported absent sick in January-April, 1863. No further records. Survived the war. [He may have served later in Company A, Indian Battalion.]

COHGOH, Private
Cherokee Indian. Born in Cherokee County and resided in Jackson County as a farmer prior to enlisting in Jackson County on April 9, 1862. Reported present in September-October, 1862, and January-April, 1863. No further records. Survived the war. [His name is also rendered as Cohgah. He was also known as Wesley Crow. He may have served later in Company A, Indian Battalion.]

COLA CHUSTEE, Private
Cherokee Indian. Born in what later became Jackson County. Resided in Jackson County as a farmer prior to enlisting at Quallatown on April 9, 1862. Reported present in September-October, 1862, and January-April, 1863. Later served in Company A, Indian Battalion.

COMMONIH, Private
Cherokee Indian. Born in what later became Jackson County. Resided in Jackson County as a farmer prior to enlisting at Quallatown at age 22, April 9, 1862. Mustered in as Private. Reported present in September-October, 1862. Promoted to Corporal prior to November 1, 1862. Reduced to ranks prior to February 28, 1863. Reported present in January-April, 1863. No further records. [His name was also rendered as Com-mnih. He was also known as Ross Cucumber. He may have served later in Company A, Indian Battalion.]

CONNER, J. S., _____
North Carolina pension records indicate that he served in this company. [North Carolina pension records appear to indicate that he served later in Company A, Indian Battalion.]

COWAN, JAMES D., _____
Place and date of enlistment not reported. Reported present in September-October, 1862. Discharged prior to February 28, 1863, after providing Pvt. Ezekiel Greybeard as a substitute.

COWWHEELEH, JOHNSON, Musician
Cherokee Indian. Born in what later became Jackson County. Resided in Jackson County as a farmer prior to enlisting at Quallatown at age 16, April 9, 1862. Mustered in as Musician (Drummer). Reported present in September-October, 1862, and January-April, 1863. No further records. [He may have served later in Company A, Indian Battalion.]

CRAWLEY, WILLIAM, Private
Enlisted either in this company or in Company A, Walker's Battalion, in Blount County, Tennessee, at age 25, September 29, 1862, for the war. Transferred to Company C, Walker's Battalion, February 1, 1863.

CULLANEESKIH, Private
Cherokee Indian. Born in what later became Jackson County. Resided in Jackson County as a farmer prior to enlisting at Quallatown at age 30, April 9, 1862. Reported present in September-October, 1862, and January-April, 1863. No further records. [He may have served later in Company A, Indian Battalion.]

CULLOQUETAGE, JOEY, Private
Cherokee Indian. Born in what later became Jackson County. Resided in Jackson County as a farmer prior to enlisting at Quallatown at age 19, April 9, 1862. Reported present in September-October, 1862, and January-April, 1863. No further records. [He may have served later in Company A, Indian Battalion.]

DAWASEH, Private
Cherokee Indian. Born in what later became Jackson County. Resided in Jackson County as a farmer prior to enlisting at Quallatown at age 24, April 9, 1862. Reported present in September-October, 1862, and January-April, 1863. No further records. [He may have served later in Company A, Indian Battalion.]

DeHART, DALLAS, ______
A North Carolina pension application for S. C. Panther of this company indicates that DeHart may have served in this company and in Company A, Indian Battalion. Later served as 1st Lieutenant of Company D, Indian Battalion.

DeHART, MARTIN, _____
North Carolina pension records appear to indicate that he served in this company. Survived the war. [He may have served later in Company A, Indian Battalion.]

DO:TSULE':HNV, _____
Cherokee Indian. Place and date of enlistment unknown. Served either in this company or in Company B of this regiment. [Tse:gh(i)sini to I:no:li, July 8, 1862, in "The Inoli Letters," MS No. 2236, Folder 1, Bureau of American Ethnology, Smithsonian Institute, Washington, D.C., translated and published in Kilpatrick Kilpatrick, translators and editors, *The Shadow of Sequoyah: Social Documents of the Cherokees* (Norman: University of Oklahoma Press, 1965), 6. If he served in this company, he may have served later in Company A, Indian Battalion.]

DURHAM, HYRAM, Private
Born in Burke County and resided in Jackson County where he was by occupation a farmer prior to enlisting in Jackson County on April 9, 1862. Reported present in September-October, 1862, and January-February, 1863. Discharged on March 8, 1863, because of "extreme old age.

EARL, NOAH, Private
May have served as Private in Company A, Indian Battalion. If so, he may have served previously in this company.

ECOOEH, JOHN, Private

Cherokee Indian. Born in what later became Jackson County. Resided in Jackson County as a farmer prior to enlisting at Quallatown at age 40, April 9, 1862. Reported present in September-October, 1862, and January-April, 1863. No further records. [He may have served later in Company A, Indian Battalion.]

ESSICKEH, GOOTAGEESKIH, Private

Cherokee Indian. Born in what later became Jackson County. Resided in Jackson County as a farmer prior to enlisting at Quallatown at age 18, November 26, 1862, for the war. Reported present in January-April, 1863. No further records. [He may have served later in Company A, Indian Battalion.]

FARLEY, JAMES S., Private

Born in what later became Jackson County. Resided in Jackson County as a farmer prior to enlisting at Quallatown at age 17, April 9, 1862. Transferred to Company G of this regiment in September-October, 1862.

FORD, JAMES, Private

Served in Company A, Indian Battalion of this legion. May have served previously in this company.

GALBREATH, JOSEPH M., Private

Born in Rutherford County and resided in Jackson County where he was by occupation a farmer prior to enlisting at Quallatown at age 40 or 42, April 9, 1862. Reported present in September-October, 1862. Reported sick at home in Jackson County in January-April, 1863. Enlisted in Company F of this regiment, prior to October 31, 1862. [He seems to have been simultaneously enrolled in this company and Company F from October, 1862, through April, 1863. It is not clear from the records whether he formally transferred to Company F, was on detached service, or was illegally enrolled in both companies at the same time.]

GE:DINI, _____

Cherokee Indian. Served either in this company or in Company B of this regiment. [Do:tsule':hnv to I:no:li, August 3, 1863, in "The Inoli Letters," MS No. 2236, Folder 1, Bureau of American Ethnology, Smithsonian Institution, Washington, D.C., translated and published in Kilpatrick and Kilpatrick, translators and editors, *The Shadow of Sequoyah: Social Documents of the Cherokees* (Norman: University of Oklahoma Press, 1965), 12. If he served in this company, he may have served later in Company A, Indian Battalion.

GIBBS, H. F., Private

Resided in Jackson County and was by occupation a farmer prior to enlisted at Strawberry Plains, Tennessee, at age 38, March 5, 1863, for the war. Company muster roll dated March-April, 1863, states that he was "detailed at Smoky Mountain." No further records. [He may have served later in Company A, Indian Battalion.]

GIBSON, JOHN A., Private

Born in what later became Jackson County. Resided in Jackson County as a farmer prior to enlisting at age 22, April 9, 1862. Reported present in September-October, 1862. Transferred to Company F of this regiment, probably in November-December, 1862.

GIBSON, WILLIAM M., Private

Born in what later became Jackson County. Resided in Jackson County as a farmer prior to enlisting in Jackson County at age 21, April 9, 1862. Reported present until transferred to Company F of this regiment on or about July 19, 1862.

GREYBEARD, EZEKIEL, Private

Cherokee Indian. Born in the part of Macon County that later became Cherokee County. Resided in Cherokee County as a farmer prior to enlisting, probably at Quallatown, at age 26, November, 1862-February, 1863, as a substitute for Pvt. James D. Cowan. Reported on detached service from March 8-31, 1863, as a messenger for Brig. Gen. Alfred E. Jackson. Rejoined the company prior to April 30, 1963. Survived the war. [He may have served later in Company A, Indian Battalion. His surname may have been Graybeard.]

HENSON, THOMAS, Private

Previously served as Private in Company A, Walker's Battalion. Transferred to this company in September-December, 1862. Reported absent on expired sick furlough in January-April, 1863. No further records. Survived the war. [He may have served later in Company A, Indian Battalion.]

HOWEENEETE, Private

Cherokee Indian. Born in what later became Jackson County. Resided in Jackson County as a farmer prior to enlisting at Quallatown at age 30, April 9, 1862. Reported present in September-October, 1862, and January-April, 1863. No further records. Survived the war. [His name is also rendered as Howaneete and Howee-neo-ta. He was also known as James D. Walkingstick. He may have served later in Company A, Indian Battalion. Later served in Company D, 3rd N.C. Mounted Infantry (Union).]

HULLIH, Private

Cherokee Indian. Born in what later became Jackson County. Resided in Jackson County as a farmer prior to enlisting at Quallatown at age 45, April 9, 1862. Reported present in September-October, 1862. Died on January 30, 1863. Place and cause of death not reported. [He was also known as John Otter.]

IYAHANEH, Sergeant

Cherokee Indian. Born in what later became Jackson County. Resided in Jackson County as a farmer prior to enlisting at Quallatown on April 9, 1862. Mustered in as Sergeant. Reported present in September-October, 1862, and January-April, 1863. No further records. Survived the war. [His name was also rendered as Iyo-ha-ne. He was also known as Swimmer Fox. He may have served later in Company A, Indian Battalion.]

JACKSON, JOHN, _____

Cherokee Indian. North Carolina pension records seem to indicate that he served in this company. Survived the war. [He may have served later in Company A, Indian Battalion.]

JASSAN, Private

Cherokee Indian. Born in what later became Jackson County. Resided in Jackson County as a farmer prior to enlisting in Jackson County at age 24, April 9, 1862. Reported present in September-October, 1862, and in January-April, 1863. No further records.

Survived the war. [His name was also rendered as Jessan, Jasson, and Jess Ann. He may have served later in Company A, Indian Battalion.]

JENKINS, JOHN _____

North Carolina pension records appear to indicate that he served in this company. Survived the war. [He may have served later in Company A, Indian Battalion.]

JUNALUSKEE, Musician

Cherokee Indian. Born in Cherokee County and resided in Jackson County where he was by occupation a farmer prior to enlisting at Quallatown at age 16, April 9, 1862. Mustered in as Musician (Fifer). Reported present through September-October, 1862. Reported present in January-April, 1863. No further records. [He may have served later in Company A, Indian Battalion.]

KLEPPER, JOHN M., Private

Resided in Hawkins County, Tennessee, and was by occupation a farmer prior to enlisting either in this company or in Company A, Walker's Battalion in Hawkins County, at about age 28, October 4, 1862, for the war. Transferred to Company C, Walker's Battalion, February 1, 1863.

KUNTISKEE, Private

Cherokee Indian. Born in what later became Jackson County. Resided in Jackson County as a farmer prior to enlisting at Quallatown at age 19, April 9, 1862. Reported present in September-October, 1862, and January-April, 1863. Later served in Company A, Indian Battalion. [His name is also rendered as Keen-tis-kee. He was also known as John Igotpa.]

LOSSIH, JOHN, Private

Cherokee Indian. Born in what later became Jackson County. Resided in Jackson County as a farmer prior to enlisting in Jackson County at age 28, April 9, 1862. Reported sick on July 8, 1862. Reported present in September-October, 1862, and January-February, 1863. Reported wounded but present in March-April, 1863. Place and date wounded not reported. No further records. Survived the war. [His name was also rendered as Tsa:n(i)lo:si. His name is rendered, probably erroneously, as Lossih John in the National Archives Compiled Service Records. He may have served later in Company A, Indian Battalion.]

LOWSINNEH, Private

Cherokee Indian. Born in what later became Jackson County. Resided in Jackson County as a farmer prior to enlisting in Jackson County at age 23, April 9, 1862. Reported present in September-October, 1862, and January-February, 1863. Reported sick in camp, March-April, 1863. [His name was also rendered as La:hw(i)sini. He may have served later in Company A, Indian Battalion. Died at Wolftown, probably of smallpox, in October, 1865.]

McBEE, ELI, Private

Enlisted either in this company or in Company A, Walker's Battalion, in Grainger County, Tennessee, at about age 38, October 3, 1862, for the war. Transferred to Company C, Walker's Battalion, February 1, 1863.

McCALL, JOHN M., Private

Enlisted either in this company or in Company A, Walker's Battalion at about age 34, January 20, 1863, for the war. Transferred to Company C, Walker's Battalion, February 1, 1863.

MATOY, LEVI C., Private

Cherokee Indian. Previously served as Private in Company A, Walker's Battalion. Transferred to this company in September-October, 1862. Reported present on October 31, 1862. Reported absent on expired furlough in January-February, 1863. Returned to duty prior to April 30, 1863. No further records. [He may have served later in Company A, Indian Battalion.]

MATOY, WILLIAM R., "Interpreter"

Cherokee Indian. Previously served as Private in Company A, Walker's Battalion. Transferred to this company in September-October, 1862, to serve as an interpreter (presumably spoke the Cherokee Indian language). Reported present on October 31, 1862, and in January-April, 1863. No further records. [He may have served later in Company A, Indian Battalion.]

MILLIGAN, FRANK H., Private

Resided in Blount County, Tennessee, and enlisted either in this company or in Company A, Walker's Battalion, in Blount County at about age 20, January 21, 1863, for the war. Transferred to Company C, Walker's Battalion, February 1, 1863. [His given name may have been H. Frank.]

MORRISON, WILLIAM S., Private

Enlisted at Strawberry Plains, Tennessee, October 5, 1862, for the war. Transferred to the Engineer Corps on December 12, 1862.

NINNETOOYEH, Private

Cherokee Indian. Born in what later became Jackson County. Resided in Jackson County as a farmer prior to enlisting at Quallatown at age 20, April 9, 1862. Reported present in September-October, 1862. Reported absent sick in January-February, 1863. Returned to duty prior to April 30, 1863. No further records. [He may have served later in Company A, Indian Battalion.]

OODAHNEETAHDEE, _____

Cherokee Indian. North Carolina pension records indicate that he served in this company. Survived the war.[He may have served later in Company A, Indian Battalion.]

OOLASTIEH, Private

Cherokee Indian. Born in what later became Jackson County. Resided in Jackson County as a farmer prior to enlisting at Quallatown at age 22, April 9, 1862. Reported present in September-October, 1862, and January-April, 1863. No further records. Survived the war. [His name was also rendered as Oo-lassta-eh. He was also known as Joe Lowin. He may have served later in Company A, Indian Battalion.]

OOLONUSTEESKIH, Corporal

Cherokee Indian. Born in what later became Jackson County. Resided in Jackson County as a farmer prior to enlisting at Quallatown at age 28, April 9, 1862. Mustered in as Corporal. Reported present in September-October, 1862, and January-April,

1863. Later served in Company A, Indian Battalion. [His name was also rendered as Ooloanustiskee.]

OOLSECOGATE, Corporal

Cherokee Indian. Born in what later became Jackson County. Resided in Jackson County as a farmer prior to enlisting at Quallatown on April 9, 1862. Mustered in as Corporal. Reported present in September-October, 1862, and January-April, 1863. No further records. [He may have served later in Company A, Indian Battalion.]

OOLSTOOIH, Private

Cherokee Indian. Born in what later became Jackson County. Resided in Jackson County as a farmer prior to enlisting at Quallatown at age 22, April 9, 1862. Reported present in September-October, 1862, and January-April, 1863. No further records. [He was also known as John Wagoola, John Daboo, and John Brown. He may have served later in Company A, Indian Battalion. Subsequently deserted to the enemy and served in Company D, 3rd Regiment N.C. Mounted Infantry (Union).]

OOLSTOOIH, Private

Cherokee Indian ("Essicheeh's son"). Born in what later became Jackson County. Resided in Jackson County as a farmer prior to enlisting at Quallatown at age 19, April 9, 1862. Reported present in September-October, 1862, and January-April, 1863. No further records. [He may have served later in Company A, Indian Battalion.]

OONOHLEE, Private

Cherokee Indian. Born in what later became Jackson County. Resided in Jackson County as a farmer prior to enlisting at Quallatown at age 30, April 9, 1862. Reported present in September-October, 1862, and January-April, 1863. No further records. [He may have served later in Company A. Indian Battalion.]

OOSOWIH, Private

Cherokee Indian. Born in what later became Jackson County. Resided in Jackson County as a farmer prior to enlisting at Quallatown at age 60, April 9, 1862. Reported present in September-October, 1862, and January-April, 1863. No further records. Survived the war. [His name was also rendered as John Uosowii. He may have served later in Company A, Indian Battalion. He may have been the same man as Tso:wa of this company.]

OOSTENACOO, Private

Cherokee Indian. Born in what later became Jackson County. Resided in Jackson County as a farmer prior to enlisting at Quallatown at age 27, April 9, 1862. Reported present in September-October, 1862, and January-April, 1863. No further records. Survived the war. [His name was also rendered as Oo-ste-na-coo. He was also known as John Taylor. He may have served later in Company A, Indian Battalion. Subsequently deserted to the enemy and served in Company D, 3rd Regiment N.C. Mounted Infantry (Union).]

OOTALKIH, Private

Cherokee Indian. Born in what later became Jackson County. Resided in Jackson County as a farmer prior to enlisting at Quallatown at age 33, April 9, 1862. Reported present in September-October, 1862, and January-April, 1863. No further records. [He may have served later in Company A, Indian Battalion.]

OOTEELTEGEESKIH, WALLESKIH, Private

Cherokee Indian. Born in what later became Jackson County. Resided in Jackson County as a farmer prior to enlisting at Quallatown at age 28, April 9, 1862. Reported present or accounted for in September-October, 1862, and January-February, 1863. Reported present but sick in camp, March-April, 1863. No further records. Survived the war. [His name was also rendered as Oo-teet-geeskih Wallaski. He may have served later in Company A, Indian Battalion.]

OOTEETTIGEESKIH, TECOLUGEESKIH, Private

Cherokee Indian. Born in what later became Jackson County. Resided in Jackson County as a farmer prior to enlisting at Quallatown at age 20, April 9, 1862. Reported present in September-October, 1862, and January-April, 1863. No further records. [He may have served later in Company A, Indian Battalion.]

OOYOSKEE, TOM, Private

Cherokee Indian. Born in what later became Jackson County. Resided in Jackson County as a farmer prior to enlisting at Quallatown at age 55, April 9, 1862. Reported present in September-October, 1862, and January-April, 1863. No further records. [He may have served later in Company A, Indian Battalion.]

OTTER, NOWEYOUTEEH, Private

Cherokee Indian. Born in what later became Jackson County. Resided in Jackson County as a farmer prior to enlisting at Quallatown at age 17, July 21, 1862, for the war. Reported present in September-October, 1862, and January-April, 1863. No further records. [His name was also rendered as Otter Now-eyontieh. He was also known as Thomas Otter and Tom Otter. He may have served later in Company A, Indian Battalion. Later deserted to the enemy and served in Company D, 3rd Regiment N.C. Mounted Infantry (Union).]

OWKWATAGA, _____

Cherokee Indian. Served in Company A, Indian Battalion. May have served previously in this company.

PANTHER, S. C., _____

North Carolina pension records appear to indicate that he served in this company. Survived the war. [He may have served later in Company A, Indian Battalion.]

POWELL, MICHAEL FRANCIS, Private

One-eighth Cherokee Indian. Born in Cherokee County in 1845. Resided in Cherokee County and was by occupation a student and/or farmer prior to enlisting at Quallatown at age 17, April 9, 1862. Reported absent sick with consumption in September-October, 1862, and January-April, 1863. Discharged at Knoxville, Tennessee, June 19, 1863, because of "paralysis of the right arm & hand."

QUENNA IYANTOOGA, Private

Cherokee Indian. Born in what later became Jackson County. Resided in Jackson County as a farmer prior to enlisting at

Quallatown at age 32, July 21, 1862, for the war. Reported present in September-October, 1862, and January-April, 1863. No further records. [He may have served later in Company A, Indian Battalion.]

RALSTON, WILLIAM H., Private

Enlisted either in this company or in Company A, Walker's Battalion, in Blount County, Tennessee, at about age 37, January 21, 1863, for the war. Transferred to Company C, Walker's Battalion on February 1, 1863.

RECKLEY, MASON, Private

Half Cherokee Indian. Born in what later became Jackson County. Resided in Jackson County as a farmer prior to enlisting at Quallatown at age 45, April 9, 1862. Reported present or accounted for in September-October, 1862, and January-February, 1863. Reported on detached service at Gatlinburg, Tennessee, March-April, 1863. Later served in Company A, Indian Battalion. [His surname may have been Ratley or Ratliff.]

REED, JESSE, Private

Three-quarters Cherokee Indian. Born in what later became Jackson County. Resided in Jackson County as a farmer prior to enlisting at Quallatown at age 20, April 9, 1862. Reported present in September-October, 1862, and January-April, 1863. No further records. Survived the war. [He may have served later in Company A, Indian Battalion. He may have been the same man as Pvt. Jesse whose record appears in the miscellaneous section of the Indian Battalion roster.]

RICE, WILLIAM E., Private

Resided in Haywood County where he enlisted on January 1, 1863, for the war. Reported present through April 30, 1863. Later served in Company A, Indian Battalion.

RIDDLE, ISAAC M., Private

Enlisted either in this company or in Company A, Walker's Battalion, in Bradley County, Tennessee, at about age 18, September 25, 1862, for the war. Transferred to Company C, Walker's Battalion on February 1, 1863.

SAMMIH, NEDDA, Private

Cherokee Indian. Born in what later became Jackson County. Resided in Jackson County as a farmer prior to enlisting at Quallatown at age 32, April 9, 1862. Reported present in September-October, 1862. Reported on detail with Lt. James Taylor of Company B of this regiment in Carter and Johnson Counties, Tennessee, January-February, 1863. Rejoined this company prior to April 30, 1863. Later served in Company A, Indian Battalion. [His name may have been Samuel Needa. He may also have been known as Samrrinreth. He may have been the same man as Tsumi of this company.]

SANDERS, JOHN, Private

Cherokee Indian. Born in what later became Jackson County. Resided in Jackson County as a farmer prior to enlisting at Quallatown at age 37, April 9, 1862. Reported present in September-October, 1862. Reported present sick, January-February, 1863. Returned to duty prior to April 30, 1863. No further records. [He may have served later in Company A, Indian Battalion. According to an 1892 U.S. Extra Census Bulletin, he deserted to the enemy and served in a Federal unit.]

SANTONEH, Private

Cherokee Indian. Born in what later became Jackson County. Resided in Jackson County as a farmer prior to enlisting at Quallatown at age 19, April 9, 1862. Reported present in September-October, 1862, and January-April, 1863. No further records. Survived the war. [His name was also rendered as San-to-neh. He was also known as James Kegg. He may have served later in Company A, Indian Battalion.]

SANTOOLA, Private

Cherokee Indian. Born in what later became Jackson County. Resided in Jackson County as a farmer prior to enlisting at Quallatown at age 18, April 9, 1862. Reported present in September-October, 1862. Reported present sick, January-February, 1863. Returned to duty prior to April 30, 1863. No further records. [He may have served later in Company A, Indian Battalion.]

SCACHELOSKEE, Private

Cherokee Indian. Born in what later became Jackson County. Resided in Jackson County as a farmer prior to enlisting in Jackson County at age 21, April 9, 1862. Died at Strawberry Plains, Tennessee, June 13, 1862, when he fell asleep on guard duty at the railroad bridge and was struck by a train running backwards. [His name was also rendered as Scotcheloskee. He was also known as John.]

SCOTT, JAMES M., Private

Born in Blount County, Tennessee, and was by occupation a farmer prior to enlisting either in this company or in Company A, Walker's Battalion, in Blount County on January 21, 1863, for the war. Transferred to Company C, Walker's Battalion, February 1, 1863.

SCULLY, WILLIAM A., Private

Resided in Jefferson County, Tennessee, and was by occupation a cabinet maker prior to enlisting either in this company or in Company A, Walker's Battalion, in Jefferson County, Tennessee, at about age 34, October 6, 1862, for the war. Transferred to Company C, Walker's Battalion, February 1, 1863.

SEGILLEH, HOWETEIYEH, Private

Cherokee Indian. Born in what later became Jackson County. Resided in Jackson County as a farmer prior to enlisting at Quallatown at age 18, April 9, 1862. Reported present in September-October, 1862, and January-April, 1863. No further records. [He may have served later in Company A, Indian Battalion.]

SEQUOYEH, STANDING WOLF, Private

Cherokee Indian. Born in what later became Jackson County. Resided in Jackson County as a farmer prior to enlisting at Quallatown at age 20, April 9, 1862. Reported present in September-October, 1862, and January-June, 1863. No further records. [His name may have been Sequoyeh Standing Wolf. He may have served later in Company A, Indian Battalion.]

SEXTON, JOSEPH W., Private

Born in Wake County and enlisted at Knoxville, Tennessee, at age 36, November 2, 1862, for the war. Transferred from the Camp of

Instruction at Knoxville, Tennessee, either to this company or to Company A, Walker's Battalion, on January 24, 1863. Transferred to Company C, Walker's Battalion, February 1, 1863.

SHULER, JOSEPH, Private

Born in what later became Jackson County. Resided in Jackson County as a farmer prior to enlisting at Quallatown at age 18, April 9, 1862. Reported present in September-October, 1862, and January-April, 1863. No further records. Survived the war. [He may have served later in Company A, Indian Battalion.]

SIHKIH, Private

Cherokee Indian. Born in what later became Jackson County. Resided in Jackson County as a farmer prior to enlisting at Quallatown at age 20, April 9, 1862. Reported present in September-October, 1862, and January-April, 1863. No further records. Survived the war. [He may have served later in Company A, Indian Battalion. He may have been the same man as Selkonie, also known as John Seke, whose record appears in the miscellaneous section of the Indian Battalion roster.]

SKITTEH, MIKEE, Private

Cherokee Indian. Born in what later became Jackson County. Resided in Jackson County as a farmer prior to enlisting in Jackson County at age 18, April 9, 1862. Reported present in September-October, 1862, and January-April, 1863. No further records. Survived the war. [His name was also rendered as Mickee Skittes and Skitteh Mikee. He may have served later in Company A, Indian Battalion, and/or Company D, 3rd Regiment N.C. Mounted Infantry (Union).]

SMITH, ROSS, _____

Cherokee Indian. Born in Tennessee. Place and date of enlistment not reported. Reported present in September-October, 1862. No further records. Survived the war.

SOLOLANETA, BIRD, _____

Cherokee Indian. North Carolina pension records indicate that he served in this company. Survived the war. [His name was also rendered as Bird Solanuta and Sololaneeta Bird. He may have served later in Company A, Indian Battalion.]

SOOQUECHEE, Private

Cherokee Indian. Born in what later became Jackson County. Resided in Jackson County as a farmer prior to enlisting at Quallatown at age 20, April 9, 1862. Reported present in September-October, 1862, and January-April, 1863. No further records. Survived the war. [His name was also rendered as Soo-quechee. He may have served later in Company A, Indian Battalion.]

SQUENSEH, Private

Cherokee Indian. Born in what later became Jackson County. Resided in Jackson County as a farmer prior to enlisting in Jackson County at age 21, April 9, 1862. Reported present in September-October, 1862. Reported on sick furlough in January-April, 1863. No further records. Survived the war. [He may have served later in Company A, Indian Battalion.]

STEAH, WILL, Private

Cherokee Indian. Born in what later became Jackson County. Resided in Jackson County as a farmer prior to enlisting at age 16, November 26, 1862, for the war. No further records. [He may have served later in Company A, Indian Battalion.]

STEE, SKILLE, Private

Cherokee Indian. Born in what later became Jackson County. Resided in Jackson County as a farmer prior to enlisting at Quallatown at age 45, April 9, 1862. Reported present in September-October, 1862, and January-April, 1863. No further records. [He may have served later in Company A, Indian Battalion.]

STUBBLEFIELD, ROBERT L., Private

Born in Hawkins County, Tennessee, where he resided as a carpenter prior to enlisting at Morristown, Tennessee, at age 36, November 28, 1862, for the war. Transferred to 2nd Company D, Walker's Battalion, December 15, 1862.

SUNKEE, _____

Cherokee Indian. North Carolina pension records indicate that he served in this company. Survived the war. [May have served later in Company A, Indian Battalion.]

SUQUEYEH, Private

Cherokee Indian. Born in what later became Jackson County. Resided in Jackson County as a farmer prior to enlisting at Quallatown at age 20, April 9, 1862. Reported present in September-October, 1862, and January-February, 1863. Reported present sick in March-April, 1863. No further records. Survived the war. [His name was also rendered as Suque-yeh. He may have served later in Company A, Indian Battalion.]

SUTAGAH, _____

Cherokee Indian. North Carolina pension records appear to indicate that he served in this company. Survived the war. [He may have served later in Company A, Indian Battalion.]

SWATEH, Sergeant

Cherokee Indian. Born in what later became Jackson County. Resided in Jackson County as a farmer prior to enlisting at Quallatown on April 9, 1862. Mustered in as Sergeant. Reported present in September-October, 1862, and January-February, 1863. Reported "sent after deserters" in March-April, 1863. No further records. Survived the war. [His name was also rendered as Suateh, Swa-tah, Suate Owl, Swatie Owl, Sou Ate, Sou-ate-Owle, and Sui-ate Owl. He may have served later in Company A, Indian Battalion.]

TAHKEHYEH, Private

Cherokee Indian. Born in what later became Jackson County. Resided in Jackson County as a farmer prior to enlisting in Jackson County at age 17, November 26, 1862, for the war. Reported present in January-April, 1863. No further records. [His name was also rendered as Tahguyeh and Tahgeeyeh. He may have served later in Company A, Indian Battalion.]

TAHNOHLEE, Private

Cherokee Indian. Born in what later became Jackson County. Resided in Jackson County as a farmer prior to enlisting at Quallatown at age 22, July 21, 1862, for the war. Reported present in September-October, 1862, and January-April, 1863. No further records. [He may have served later in Company A, Indian Battalion.]

TAHSEKEYAHGEE, ARQUETAGE, Private
Cherokee Indian. Born in what later became Jackson County. Resided in Jackson County as a farmer prior to enlisting at Quallatown at age 20, April 9, 1862. Reported present in September-October, 1862. Died, probably at Quallatown, on January 27, 1863. Cause of death not reported.

TAHSEKEYAHGEE, STOOGATOGEH, Private
Cherokee Indian. Born in what later became Jackson County. Resided in Jackson County as a farmer prior to enlisting at Quallatown at age 18, July 21, 1862, for the war. Reported present in September-October, 1862. Reported present sick in January-February, 1863. No further records. [He may have served later in Company A, Indian Battalion. He may have been the same man as Sdugi:gado:ga of Company C, Indian Battalion.]

TAHSKEEKETEHEE, Private
Cherokee Indian. Born in what later became Jackson County. Resided in Jackson County as a farmer prior to enlisting at age 25, April 9, 1862. Died on June 18, 1862. Place and cause of death not reported. [His name was also rendered as Da:sg:gidi:hi.]

TALAGEESKIH, Sergeant
Cherokee Indian. Born in what later became Jackson County. Resided in Jackson County as a farmer prior to enlisting at Quallatown on April 9, 1862. Mustered in as Sergeant. Reported present in September-October, 1862, and January-April, 1863. No further records. [He may have served later in Company A, Indian Battalion.]

TALANOSTEH, TAGENTEH, Private
Cherokee Indian. Born in what later became Jackson County. Resided in Jackson County as a farmer prior to enlisting at Quallatown at age 19, April 9, 1862. Reported present in September-October, 1862, and January-April, 1863. No further records. [He may have served later in Company A, Indian Battalion.]

TALASKASKEE, Private
Cherokee Indian. Born in what later became Jackson County. Resided in Jackson County as a farmer prior to enlisting at Quallatown at age 19, April 9, 1862. Reported present in September-October, 1862, and January-April, 1863. No further records. [He may have served later in Company A, Indian Battalion.]

TALLEY, JOHN, Private
Enlisted either in this company or in Company A, Walker's Battalion, in Blount County, Tennessee, at about age 16, April 9, 1863, for the war. Transferred to Company C, Walker's Battalion, on the same date.

TALUNOSTEH, NICKOJACK, Private
Cherokee Indian. Born in what later became Jackson County. Resided in Jackson County as a farmer prior to enlisting at Quallatown at age 20, April 9, 1862. Reported present in September-October, 1862, and January-April, 1863. No further records. [He may have served later in Company A, Indian Battalion.]

TAYLOR, LYCURGUS W., Private
Enlisted either in this company or in Company A, Walker's Battalion, at Maryville, Tennessee, at about age 16, April 15, 1863, for the war. Transferred to Company C, Walker's Battalion, on the same date.

TECOLAGEESKIH, Private
Cherokee Indian. Born in what later became Jackson County. Resided in Jackson County as a farmer prior to enlisting at Quallatown at age 40, April 9, 1862. Reported present in September-October, 1862, and January-April, 1863. No further records. [He may have served later in Company A, Indian Battalion.]

TEDFORD, JOSEPH HOWARD, Private
Enlisted in Blount County, Tennessee on October 6, 1862, for the war, and assigned to a camp of conscription. Transferred either to this company or to Company A, Walker's Battalion, January 26, 1863. Transferred to Company C, Walker's Battalion, February 6, 1863. [His given name may have been Howard Joseph.]

TEEGEESKEE, JESS, _____
Cherokee Indian. North Carolina pension records indicate that he served in this company. [He may have served later in Company A, Indian Battalion.]

TEGAHHOOGEESKIH, Private
Cherokee Indian. Born in what later became Jackson County. Resided in Jackson County as a farmer prior to enlisting at Quallatown at age 18, April 9, 1862. Reported present in September-October, 1862, and January-April, 1863. No further records. [He may have served later in Company A, Indian Battalion.]

TEHEE, JONNY, Private
Cherokee Indian. Born in what later became Jackson County. Resided in Jackson County as a farmer prior to enlisting at Quallatown at age 32, July 21, 1862, for the war. Reported present in September-October, 1862, and January-April, 1863. No further records. [He may have served later in Company A, Indian Battalion.]

TELAHLAH, Private
Cherokee Indian. Born in what later became Jackson County. Resided in Jackson County as a farmer prior to enlisting at Quallatown at age 19, April 9, 1862. Reported present in September-October, 1862, and January-April, 1863. No further records. [He may have served later in Company A, Indian Battalion.]

TENEGEESEE, Private
Cherokee Indian. Born in what later became Jackson County. Resided in Jackson County as a farmer prior to enlisting at Quallatown at age 50, April 9, 1862. Reported present in September-October, 1862. Died on December 18, 1862. Place and cause of death not reported.

TEQUEEESKIH, Sergeant
Cherokee Indian. Born in what later became Jackson County. Resided in Jackson County as a farmer prior to enlisting at Quallatown on April 9, 1862. Mustered in as Sergeant. Reported present in September-October, 1862 and in January-April, 1863. Later served in Company A, Indian Battalion. [His name was also rendered as Teque-eeskih and Sequeeeskih. He was also known as John Bigwitch.]

TESEEKEE, Private

Cherokee Indian. Born in what later became Jackson County. Resided in Jackson County as a farmer prior to enlisting at Quallatown at age 20, April 9, 1862. Reported present in September-October, 1862, and January-April, 1863. No further records. [He may have served later in Company A, Indian Battalion.]

TESEEYOGIH, Private

Cherokee Indian. Born in what later became Jackson County. Resided in Jackson County as a farmer prior to enlisting at Quallatown at age 26, April 9, 1862. Reported present in September-October, 1862, and January-April, 1863. No further records. [He may have served later in Company A, Indian Battalion.]

TESESKIH, Private

Cherokee Indian. Born in what later became Jackson County. Resided in Jackson County as a farmer prior to enlisting at age 17, April 26, 1862, for the war. No further records. Survived the war. [His name was also rendered as Te-ses-kih. He may have been the same man as Pvt. Teseteskih of this company. He may have served later in Company A, Indian Battalion.]

TESETESKIH, Private

Cherokee Indian. Enlisted at Quallatown on November 26, 1862, for the war. Reported present in January-April, 1863. No further records. Survived the war. [He may have been the same man as Pvt. Teseskih of this company. He may have served later in Company A, Indian Battalion.]

TEWYEH, NICKOJACK, Private

Cherokee Indian. Born in what later became Jackson County. Resided in Jackson County as a farmer prior to enlisting at Quallatown at age 35, July 21, 1862, for the war. Reported present in September-October, 1862. Reported absent sick ("tree fell on him and crippled him") in January-February, 1863. Reported on detached duty at Gatlinburg, Tennessee, in March-April, 1863. No further records. [He may have served later in Company A, Indian Battalion.]

THOMPSON, IYANTOOGA, Private

Cherokee Indian. Born in what later became Jackson County. Resided in Jackson County as a farmer prior to enlisting at Quallatown at age 34, July 21, 1862, for the war. Reported present in September-October, 1862, and January-April, 1863. Later served in Company A, Indian Battalion.

THOMPSON, OOLIYOIH, Private

Cherokee Indian. Born in what later became Jackson County. Resided in Jackson County as a farmer prior to enlisting at Quallatown at age 18, April 9, 1862. Reported present in September-October, 1862, and January-April, 1863. No further records. [He may have served later in Company A, Indian Battalion.]

TOONIGHYEH, Private

Cherokee Indian. Born in what later became Jackson County. Resided in Jackson County as a farmer prior to enlisting at Quallatown at age 40, April 9, 1862. Reported present in September-October, 1862, and January-April, 1863. No further records. [He may have served later in Company A, Indian Battalion.]

TOYANEETE, Corporal

Cherokee Indian. Born in Jackson County where he resided as a farmer prior to enlisting at Quallatown at age 28, April 9, 1862. Mustered in as Corporal. Reported present in September-October, 1862, and January-April, 1863. No further records. Survived the war. [His name was also rendered Toya Neta, Toy-a-ne-teh and Toi-neeta. He may have served later in Company A, Indian Battalion.]

TSE:GH(I)SINI, _____

Cherokee Indian. Served either in this company or in Company B of this regiment. Reported sick on July 8, 1862. No further records. [Tse:gh(i)sini to I:no:li, July 8, 1862, in "The Inoli Letters," MS No. 2236, Folder 1, Bureau of American Ethnology, Smithsonian Institution, Washington, D.C., translated and published in Kilpatrick and Kilpatrick, translators and editors, *The Shadow of Sequoyah: Social Documents of the Cherokees* (Norman: University of Oklahoma Press, 1965), 6. May have served also in either Company A or B, Indian Battalion.]

TSO:WA, _____

Cherokee Indian. Served either in this company or in Company B of this regiment. Reported sick prior to July 8, 1862, but had recovered by that date. [Tse:gh(i)sini to I:no:li, July 8, 1862, in "The Inoli Letters," MS No. 2236, Folder 1, Bureau of American Ethnology, Smithsonian Institution, Washington, D.C., translated and published in Kilpatrick and Kilpatrick, translators and editors, *The Shadow of Sequoyah: Social Documents of the Cherokees* (Norman: University of Oklahoma Press, 1965), 6. He is probably either the same man as Pvt. Oosowih of this company, or Pvt. Jim Cheoih of Company B of this regiment. May have served later in Company A or B, Indian Battalion.]

TSUMI, _____

Cherokee Indian. Served either in this company or in Company B of this regiment. [Tse:gh(i)sini to I:no:li, July 8, 1862, in "The Inoli Letters," MS No. 2236, Folder 1, Bureau of American Ethnology, Smithsonian Institution, Washington, D.C., translated and published in Kilpatrick and Kilpatrick, translators and editors, *The Shadow of Sequoyah: Social Documents of the Cherokees* (Norman: University of Oklahoma Press, 1965), 6. He may have been the same man as Pvt. Nedda Sammih of this company. He may have later served in Company A, B, or C, Indian Battalion.]

WAHGACOO, Private

Cherokee Indian. Born in what later became Jackson County. Resided in Jackson County as a farmer prior to enlisting at Quallatown at age 28, April 9, 1862. Reported present in September-October, 1862, and January-April, 1863. No further records. Survived the war. [He may have served later in Company A, Indian Battalion.]

WAHHAHOO, MOSES, Private

Cherokee Indian. Born in what later became Jackson County. Resided in Jackson County as a farmer prior to enlisting at Quallatown at age 21, April 9, 1862. Reported present in September-October, 1862. Reported present sick in January-February, 1863. Returned to duty prior to April 30, 1863. Name appears on a receipt roll for clothing dated October 16, 1864. No further records. [He may have served later in Company A, Indian Battalion.]

WAHLANEETEH, Private
Cherokee Indian. Born in what later became Jackson County. Resided in Jackson County as a farmer prior to enlisting at Quallatown on April 9, 1862. Reported present in September-October, 1862, and January-April, 1863. No further records. [He may have served later in Company A, Indian Battalion.]

WAHTASUTTEH, Private
Cherokee Indian. Born in what later became Jackson County. Resided in Jackson County as a farmer prior to enlisting at Quallatown on April 9, 1862. Reported present in September-October, 1862, and January-April, 1863. No further records. [He may have served later in Company A, Indian Battalion.]

WAHWAHSEETEH, Private
Cherokee Indian. Born in what later became Jackson County. Resided in Jackson County as a farmer prior to enlisting at Quallatown on April 9, 1862. Reported present in September-October, 1862. Reported absent on expired sick leave in January-February, 1863. Returned to duty prior to April 30, 1863. No further records. [He may have served later in Company A, Indian Battalion.]

WAHYELOSSIH, Private
Cherokee Indian. Born in what later became Jackson County. Resided in Jackson County as a farmer prior to enlisting at Quallatown at age 20, April 9, 1862. Reported present in September-October, 1862. Reported present but sick in camp in January-February, 1863. Reported on detail at Gatlinburg, Tennessee, in March-April, 1863. No further records. [He may have served later in Company A, Indian Battalion.]

WARD, ALFRED L., Private
Cherokee Indian. Born in what later became Jackson County. Resided in Jackson County as a farmer prior to enlisting at age 20, April 9, 1862. Died on August 11, 1862. Place and cause of death not reported.

WARD, THOMAS W., Private
Born in what later became Jackson County. Resided in Jackson County as a farmer prior to enlisting at Quallatown at age 27, April 9, 1862. Transferred to Company F of this regiment prior to October 31, 1862.

WASHINGTON, JIM, Private
Cherokee Indian. Born in what later became Jackson County. Resided in Jackson County as a farmer prior to enlisting in Jackson County at age 20, April 9, 1862. Mustered in as Private. Reported present in September-October, 1862, and January-April, 1863. No further records. [He may have served later in Company A, Indian Battalion.]

WATKINS, WILLIAM W., Private
Born in Prince Edward County, Virginia, and resided in Jefferson County, Tennessee, where he was by occupation a farmer prior to enlisting at Strawberry Plains, Tennessee, at age 48, December 14, 1862, for the war. Transferred to 2nd Company D, Walker's Battalion, on the same date.

WELCH, JOE, Private
Cherokee Indian ("Willogeeskih's son"). Born in what later became Jackson County. Resided in Jackson County as a farmer prior to enlisting at Quallatown at age 29, April 9, 1862. Reported present in September-October, 1862, and January-April, 1863. No further records. [He may have served later in Company A, Indian Battalion.]

WHEELER, JORDAN, Private
Resided in Blount County and was by occupation a "tenant" prior to enlisting either in this company or in Company A, Walker's Battalion, at Rockford, Tennessee, at about age 30, September 29, 1862, for the war. Transferred to Company C, Walker's Battalion, February 1, 1863.

WILLEGIH, Private
Cherokee Indian. Born in what later became Jackson County. Resided in Jackson County as a farmer prior to enlisting at Quallatown on April 9, 1862. Reported present in September-October, 1862, and January-April, 1863. No further records. [His name was also rendered as Wi:ligi. He may have served later in Company A, Indian Battalion.]

WILLSOEH, Private
Cherokee Indian. Enlisted at Quallatown on November 26, 1862, for the war. Reported present in January-April, 1863. No further records. [He may have served later in Company A, Indian Battalion.]

WILNOTY, LOUTY, _____
Cherokee Indian. North Carolina pension records indicate that he served in this company. Survived the war. [He may have served later in Company A, Indian Battalion.]

WOHHOHTIH, Private
Cherokee Indian. Born in what later became Jackson County. Resided in Jackson County as a farmer prior to enlisting at Quallatown at age 25, April 9, 1862. Reported present in September-October, 1862, and January-April, 1863. No further records. [He may have served later in Company A, Indian Battalion.]

COMPANY B

This company was raised in Jackson and Cherokee Counties, and was composed primarily of Cherokee Indians. It was organized at Quallatown, reportedly on April 9, 1862. As of May 1, 1862, it was known as 2nd Company, N.C. Cherokee Battalion. It may have been known as Company B as of August 31, 1862. On or about October 5, 1862, it was designated Company D, Infantry Regiment, Thomas's Legion. It was redesignated Company B, probably in January, 1863. It formally became Company B, Indian Battalion of this Legion, in April, 1865, although the Indian Battalion had been informally organized in late 1863. For the purposes of these rosters, September 2, 1863, will be used for separating materials for members of Company B, Infantry Regiment, from those of Company B, Indian Battalion. It was on that date that Col. William H. Thomas left Strawberry Plains, Tennessee, with this company and 2nd Company A of the Infantry Regiment, marched into the Smoky Mountains, and began recruiting a third Indian company. These companies were never reintegrated into the structure of the Infantry Regiment again, even after the Legion was reunited in western North Carolina in December, 1864.

The following roster was compiled in large part from a company muster and descriptive roll dated February 12, 1863, and company muster rolls dated September-October, 1862, and January-June, 1863. These are abstracted in the microfilm edition of the Compiled Service Records of Confederate Soldiers Who Served in Organizations from the State of North Carolina (Record Group 109, M270), National Archives, Washington, D.C. Other valuable information in the Compiled Service Records includes enlistment papers, pay vouchers, requisitions, letters of resignation, discharge certificates, and abstracts of medical and prisoner of war records. Some men in this roster are listed as members of Company D in the Compiled Service Records, because their records were created before the company was redesignated Company B.

Also utilized in this roster were *The War of the Rebellion: A Compilation of the Official Records of the Union and Confederate Armies*, the North Carolina Adjutant General's papers, state militia records, newspaper casualty lists and obituaries, wartime claims for bounty pay and allowances, postwar registers of claims for artificial limbs, Confederate pension applications filed with the states of North Carolina, Tennessee, and Florida, records of the North Carolina Confederate Soldiers' Home, and the 1860 and 1870 federal censuses of North Carolina. A search was made also for relevant letters, diaries, reminiscences, and other manuscripts in the Southern Historical Collection (University of North Carolina-Chapel Hill) and the Duke University Library Special Collections Department.

Among the secondary sources consulted were records of the North Carolina division of the United Daughters of the Confederacy, postwar rosters, regimental and county histories, marriage bond, will, and cemetery indexes, published and unpublished genealogies, biographical dictionaries, the North Carolina *County Heritage Book* series, the *Confederate Veteran*, Walter Clark's *Histories of the Several Regiments and Battalions from North Carolina in the Great War, 1861-'65*, and the North Carolina volume of the extended edition of *Confederate Military History*.

OFFICERS

CAPTAIN

HANKS, GIDEON M.

Resided in Monroe County, Tennessee. Previously served as 1st Lieutenant of Company G, 3rd (Vaughn's) Regiment Tennessee Infantry. Appointed Captain of this company on May 18, 1862, to rank from April 9, 1862. Reported present in September-October, 1862. Detailed to muster in Company K of this regiment at Winter's Gap, January-February, 1863. Reported present, March-June, 1863. Later served as Captain of Company B, Indian Battalion.

LIEUTENANTS

BLYTHE, JACKSON, Brevet 2nd Lieutenant

Born in what later became Jackson County. Resided in Jackson County as a farmer prior to enlisting at age 40, April 9, 1862. Promotion record not reported. Resigned on September 10, 1862. Reason he resigned not reported. [He was white, but was father of Rachel Blythe, the half-Cherokee "Indian Princess" buried in Raleigh's Oakwood Cemetery. See *North Carolina Historical Review*, 60 (No. 3), July, 1983, 283-303.]

MORRIS, HORRY R., 2nd Lieutenant

Half Cherokee Indian. Born in the part of Haywood County that later became Macon County, and resided in Cherokee County where he was by occupation a farmer prior to enlisting at Quallatown at age 40. Appointed 2nd Lieutenant on May 18, 1862. Reported on detached service in September-October, 1862. Resigned on December 27, 1862, due to "bad health."

POWELL, MARCUS L., 3rd Lieutenant

Born in Cherokee County in 1841. A company muster roll dated January-February, 1863, states that he had been appointed Brevet 2nd Lieutenant but had not yet reported for duty. Probably appointed 3rd Lieutenant in 1863. Later served as Lieutenant in Company B, Indian Battalion.

TAYLOR, CAMPBELL HARRISON, 2nd Lieutenant

Part Cherokee Indian. Born in Cherokee County, where he resided as a farmer prior to enlisting at Quallatown at age 23, April 9, 1862. Mustered in as 1st Sergeant. Appointed 3rd Lieutenant on September 10, 1862. Reported present in September-October, 1862, and January-June, 1863. Probably promoted to 2nd Lieutenant subsequent to December 27, 1862. Name appears on a payment voucher dated August 10, 1863. Later served as 2nd Lieutenant of Company B, Indian Battalion.

TAYLOR, JAMES MADISON, 1st Lieutenant

Part Cherokee Indian. Previously served as Private in Company A, 39th Regiment N.C. Troops. Appointed 1st Lieutenant of this company on May 18, 1862. Reported present in September-October, 1862. Reported on detail in the recruiting service at Knoxville, and then on a scout with part of this company in January-February, 1863. Rejoined the company prior to April 30, 1863. Reported present in May-June, 1863. Subsequently served as 1st Lieutenant and Captain of Company B, Indian Battalion. [Contrary to 10:119 of this series, he was appointed 1st Lieutenant of this company on May 18, 1862, rather than in April, 1862.]

NONCOMMISSIONED OFFICERS AND PRIVATES

AH LEE CHEE, Private

Cherokee Indian. Born in what later became Jackson County. Resided in Jackson County as a farmer prior to enlisting in Cherokee County at age 22, September 1, 1862, for the war. Reported present in January-February, 1863; however, other records indicate that he was absent sick from November, 1862, through June 30, 1863. No further records. [He may have served later in Company B, Indian Battalion.]

AHMASCOSITY, Private

Cherokee Indian. Born in what later became Jackson County. Resided in Jackson County as a farmer prior to enlisting at Jackson County at age 20, April 9, 1862. Reported present in September-October, 1862. Reported on detail with Lt. James Taylor of this company in Carter and Johnson Counties, Tennessee, January-February, 1863. Reported present in March-June, 1863. No further records. [He may have served later in Company B, Indian Battalion.]

AH TO HEE, Private

Cherokee Indian. Born in Cherokee County where he resided as a farmer prior to enlisting in Cherokee County at age 20, September 1,

1862, for the war. Reported on detail with Lt. James Taylor of this company in Carter and Johnson Counties, Tennessee, January- February, 1863. Reported present in March-June, 1863. No further records. [He may have served later in Company B, Indian Battalion. His name may have been Ground Squirrel Atowhee or Ahtohee Ground Squirrel].

AH TOW EH, Private

Cherokee Indian. Born in what later became Jackson County. Resided in Jackson County as a farmer prior to enlisting at Quallatown at age 18, July 21, 1862, for the war. Reported present in September-October, 1862. Reported on detail with Lt. James Taylor of this company in Carter and Johnson Counties, Tennessee, January-February, 1863. Reported present in March-June, 1863. No further records. [He may have served later in Company B, Indian Battalion. His name was also rendered as Ahtowih, Ahtowee and Ahtowhee.]

ALLENEH, Private

Cherokee Indian. Born in Cherokee County and resided in Macon County where he was by occupation a farmer prior to enlisting in Cherokee County at age 18, September 1, 1862, for the war. Reported present or accounted for in January-June, 1863. Name appears on a pay voucher for service from June 1 through December 31, 1863. [The period covered by the pay voucher appears to indicate that he served later in Company B, Indian Battalion.]

ALLISON, JULIUS J., _____

Confederate gravestone records indicate that he served in this company.

ARCHEE, Musician

Cherokee Indian. Born in what later became Jackson County. Resided in Jackson County as a farmer prior to enlisting at Quallatown at age 28, April 9, 1862. Mustered in as Musician (Fifer). Reported present in September-October, 1862, and January-June, 1863. Reduced to ranks in February, 1863. Reappointed Musician (Fifer) in March-April, 1863. No further records. [He may have served later in Company B, Indian Battalion.]

ARCHEE, JR., Private

Cherokee Indian ("Owl's son"). Born in Cherokee County where he resided as a farmer prior to enlisting in Cherokee County at age 23, September 1, 1862, for the war. Reported present or accounted for in January-June, 1863. No further records. [He may have served later in Company B, Indian Battalion]

ARROWOOD, WILLIAM H., _____

North Carolina pension records indicate that he served in this company. Survived the war. [He may have served later in Company B, Indian Battalion.]

ATAHHEE, Private

Cherokee Indian. Born in the part of Haywood or Macon County that later became Cherokee County. Resided in Jackson County where he was by occupation a farmer prior to enlisting at Quallatown at age 34, April 9, 1862. Reported present in September-October, 1862, and January-June, 1863. No further records. [He may have served later in Company B, Indian Battalion. His name was also rendered as Ahtahhee.]

AX, WILSON, Sergeant

Cherokee Indian. Place and date of enlistment not reported. Promotion record not reported. Name appears on a pay voucher for service from June 1 through December 31, 1863. [The period covered by the pay voucher appears to indicate that he served later in Company B, Indian Battalion.]

BIGMEAT, LACEY, Private

Cherokee Indian. Born in the part of Macon County that later became Cherokee County. Resided in Cherokee County as a farmer prior to enlisting in Jackson County at age 30, April 9, 1862. Reported present in September-October, 1862. Reported absent sick in January-April, 1863. Returned to duty in May-June, 1863. No further records. Survived the war. [His first name may have been Lazy. He may have served later in Company B, Indian Battalion.]

BIGMEAT, SEGILLEH, Private

Cherokee Indian. Born in Cherokee County where he resided as a farmer prior to enlisting at Quallatown at age 23, April 9, 1862. Reported present in September-October, 1862. Reported on detail with Lt. James Taylor of this company in Carter and Johnson Counties, Tennessee, January-February, 1863. Rejoined the company prior to April 30, 1863. Reported present, May-June, 1863. No further records. Survived the war. [He may have served later in Company B, Indian Battalion. His name was also rendered as Sekilla Bigmeat and Bigmeat Segilleh.]

BRADY, JAMES A., Sergeant

Born in Haywood County and resided in Cherokee County where he was by occupation a farmer prior to enlisting at Quallatown on April 9, 1862. Mustered in as Sergeant. Reported present in September-October, 1862. Died on January 30, 1863. Place and cause of death not reported.

BUSHEYHEAD, GEORGE W., Sergeant

Cherokee Indian. Born in what later became Union County, Georgia, and resided in Cherokee County, North Carolina, where he was by occupation a farmer prior to enlisting at Quallatown, at age 36, April 9, 1862. Mustered in as Sergeant. Reported present in September-October, 1862, and in January-February, 1863. Reported on detached duty at Gatlinburg, Tennessee, from March 6 through June 30, 1863. Name appears on a pay voucher for service from July 1, 1863, through September 30, 1863. Pay vouchers indicate that he served later in Company B, Indian Battalion and Company D, Indian Battalion. Survived the war.

CALHOUN, JOHN, Private

Cherokee Indian. Born in what later became Jackson County. Resided in Jackson County as a farmer prior to enlisting at Quallatown at age 18, April 9, 1862. Mustered in as Private. Reported present in September-October, 1862. Promoted to Musician (Drummer) prior to February 28, 1863. Reduced to ranks in March-April, 1863. Reported present in January-June, 1863. No further records. [He may have served later in Company B, Indian Battalion.]

CASSEE, Private

Cherokee Indian. Born in Cherokee County where he resided as a farmer prior to enlisting at Quallatown at age 17, April 9, 1862. Reported present in September-October, 1862, and January-June,

1863. No further records. [He may have served later in Company B, Indian Battalion.]

CHARLESTOWN, Private
Cherokee Indian. Born in Cherokee County where he resided as a farmer prior to enlisting at Quallatown at age 23, April 9, 1862. Reported present in September-October, 1862, and January-June, 1863. No further records. [He may have served later in Company B, Indian Battalion.]

CHARLE TE HEE, Private
Cherokee Indian. Born in what later became Jackson County, and resided in Macon County where he was by occupation a farmer prior to enlisting at Quallatown at age 33, September 1, 1862, for the war. Died at Strawberry Plains, Tennessee, October 25, 1862. Cause of death not reported.

CHEESQUAHKILLEH, Private
Cherokee Indian. Born in Cherokee County where he resided as a farmer prior to enlisting at Quallatown at age 20, April 9, 1862. Died at Strawberry Plains, Tennessee, September 17, October 15, or October 16, 1862. Cause of death not reported.

CHEESQUAHNEETE, Private
Cherokee Indian. Born in what later became Jackson County. Resided in Jackson County as a farmer prior to enlisting at Quallatown at age 28, April 9, 1862. Reported present in September-October, 1862, and January-June, 1863. No further records. [He may have served later in Company B, Indian Battalion.]

CHEOIH, JIM, Private
Cherokee Indian. Born in the part of Haywood County that later became Cherokee County. Resided in Macon County where he was by occupation a farmer prior to enlisting at Quallatown at age 50, April 9, 1862. Reported present in September-October, 1862, and January-June, 1863. Later served in Company B, Indian Battalion. [He may have been the same man as Tso:wa of this company.]

CHESQUANOLLA, Private
Cherokee Indian. Born in Cherokee County where he resided as a farmer prior to enlisting in Cherokee County at age 18, September 1, 1862, for the war. Reported present in January-June, 1863. No further records. [He may have served later in Company B, Indian Battalion.]

CHICK A LE LEE, Private
Cherokee Indian. Born in the part of Haywood County that later became Cherokee County. Resided in Cherokee County as a farmer prior to enlisting at Quallatown at age 40, April 9, 1862. Reported present in September-October, 1862, and January-June, 1863. No further records. Survived the war. [His name was also rendered as Chickalela, Chickalila, and Chigilili. He may have served later in Company B, Indian Battalion.]

CHONOH, Private
Cherokee Indian (son of Da wa seh). Born in what later became Jackson County. Resided in Jackson County as a farmer prior to enlisting in Quallatown at age 18, July 21, 1862, for the war. Reported present, January-February, 1863. Reported sick in camp in March-April, 1863. Reported present, May-June, 1863. No further records. [He may have served later in Company B, Indian Battalion.]

CHUTAH SOCK TEH, Private
Cherokee Indian. Born in the part of Macon County that later became Cherokee County. Resided in Jackson County where he was by occupation a farmer prior to enlisting Quallatown at age 29, April 9, 1862. Reported present or accounted for in September-October, 1862, and January-February, 1863. Reported absent sick, March-April, 1863. Reported present May-June, 1863. No further records. [He may have served later in Company B, Indian Battalion.]

CHUWANNASKEE, Sergeant
Cherokee Indian. Born in the part of Haywood County that later became Cherokee County. Resided in Cherokee County as a farmer prior to enlisting at Quallatown at age 45, April 9, 1862. Mustered in as Corporal. Reported present or accounted for in September-October, 1862. Reported on detail with Lt. James Taylor of this company in Carter and Johnson Counties, Tennessee, January-February, 1863. Promoted to Sergeant in March-April, 1863. Reported present in March-June, 1863. No further records. [He may have served later in Company B, Indian Battalion.]

COLARCHEE, Private
Cherokee Indian. Born in what later became Jackson County. Resided in Jackson County as a farmer prior to enlisting at Quallatown at age 25, April 9, 1862. Reported present in September-October, 1862, and January-June, 1863. No further records. [He may have served later in Company B, Indian Battalion.]

COLLOWAHESKEE, Private
Cherokee Indian. Enlisted at Quallatown on April 9, 1862. A company muster roll dated May-June, 1863, states that he was "absent sick and has been accidently omited on all muster rolls made out heretofore." No further records. [He may have served later in Company B, Indian Battalion.]

CONNOHHALAKAH, Private
Cherokee Indian. Born in the part of Haywood County that later became Cherokee County. Resided in Cherokee County as a farmer prior to enlisting at Quallatown at age 35, April 9, 1862. Reported present in September-October, 1862, and January-June, 1863. No further records. Survived the war. [He was also known as Hunter Reed. He may have served later in Company B, Indian Battalion.]

CONNOSKEESKEE, Private
Cherokee Indian. Born in what later became Jackson County. Resided in Jackson County as a farmer prior to enlisting at Quallatown at age 33, April 9, 1862. Reported present in September-October, 1862, and January-June, 1863. No further records. [His name was also rendered as Connoskeeskih. He may have served later in Company B, Indian Battalion.]

CONNOSKEESKEE, DEVIR, Private
Cherokee Indian. Born in Cherokee County and resided in Jackson County where he was by occupation a farmer prior to enlisting at Quallatown at age 21, April 9, 1862. Reported present or accounted for in September-October, 1862. Reported absent sick in Jackson County, January-February, 1863. Reported present in March-June,

1863. No further records. Survived the war. [His given name was also rendered as Dever. His surname was also rendered as Cannos-kees-kih or Cannos-kees-kit. He was also known as Armstrong Cornsilk. He may have served later in Company B, Indian Battalion.]

CONNOSTEAH, Private

Cherokee Indian. Enlisted at Gatlinburg, Tennessee, January 2, 1863, for the war. Reported present through June 30, 1863. No further records. [He may have served later in Company B, Indian Battalion.]

COOK, ROBERT, Private

Enlisted at Zollicoffer, Tennessee, April 13, 1863, for the war. Reported present in May-June, 1863. No further records. [He may have served later in Company B, Indian Battalion.]

DANELAH, Private

Cherokee Indian. Born in the part of Macon County that later became Cherokee County. Resided in Jackson County where he was by occupation a farmer prior to enlisting at Quallatown at age 30, April 9, 1862. Reported present in September-October, 1862, and January-June, 1863. No further records. Survived the war. [He may have served later in Company B, Indian Battalion.]

DARROW, ROBERT, _____

Enlisted in this company on an unspecified date either before or after it became Company B, Indian Battalion.

DAVASEH, JOHN, Private

Cherokee Indian. Born in Cherokee County where he resided as a farmer prior to enlisting at Quallatown at age 22, April 9, 1862. Died at Strawberry Plains, Tennessee, October 6 or November 30, 1862. Cause of death not reported.

DICKAGEESKIH, JESS, Private

Cherokee Indian. Born in the part of Macon County that later became Cherokee County. Resided in Cherokee County as a farmer prior to enlisting at Quallatown at age 24, April 9, 1862. Reported present or accounted for in September-October, 1862, and January-June, 1863. Reported sick on about July 8, 1862. No further records. Survived the war. [His name was also rendered as Dick-a-geeskee and Di:ghyui:sgi. He may have served later in Company B, Indian Battalion.]

DO:TSULE':HNV, _____

Cherokee Indian. Place and date of enlistment unknown. Served in either this company or 2nd Company A of this regiment. [Tse:gh(i)sini to I:no:li, July 8, 1862, in "The Inoli Letters," MS No. 2236, Folder 1, Bureau of American Ethnology, Smithsonian Institution, Washington, D.C., translated and published in Kilpatrick and Kilpatrick, translators and editors, *The Shadow of Sequoyah: Social Documents of the Cherokees* (Norman: University of Oklahoma Press, 1965), 6.]

ECHULEHAH, Private

Cherokee Indian. Born in what later became Jackson County. Resided in Jackson County as a farmer prior to enlisting at Quallatown at age 25, April 9, 1862. Reported present in September-October, 1862, and January-June, 1863. No further records. Survived the war. [His name was also rendered as Echu-le-hah. He was also known as Steve Johnson. He may have served later in Company B, Indian Battalion. Later deserted to the enemy and served as a Private in Company D, 3rd Regiment N.C. Mounted Infantry (Union).]

ENELOSSIH, Private

Cherokee Indian. Born in what later became Jackson County. Resided in Jackson County as a farmer prior to enlisting at Quallatown at age 33, July 21, 1862, for the war. Reported present in September-October, 1862, and January-June, 1863. No further records. [He may have served later in Company B, Indian Battalion.]

GE:DINI, _____

Cherokee Indian. Served either in this company or in 2nd Company A of this regiment. [Do:tsule':hnv to I:no:li, August 3, 1863, in "The Inoli Letters," MS No. 2236, Folder 1, Bureau of American Ethnology, Smithsonian Institution, Washington, D.C., translated and published in Kilpatrick and Kilpatrick, translators and editors, *The Shadow of Sequoyah: Social Documents of the Cherokees* (Norman: University of Oklahoma Press, 1965), 12.]

GOOLOWIH, Corporal

Cherokee Indian. Born in what later became Jackson County. Resided in Jackson County as a farmer prior to enlisting in Quallatown at age 21, April 9, 1862. Mustered in as Corporal. Reported present in September-October, 1862, and January-June, 1863. No further records. [He may have served later in Company B, Indian Battalion.]

HAWKINS, JOSEPH, Sergeant

Cherokee Indian. Born in the part of Haywood County that later became Cherokee County. Resided in Cherokee County as a farmer prior to enlisting at Quallatown at age 35, April 9, 1862. Mustered in as Sergeant. Reported present in September-October, 1862, and January-June, 1863. No further records. [He may have served later in Company B, Indian Battalion.]

HOWEE, AQUAH, Corporal

Cherokee Indian. Born in the part of Haywood County that later became Cherokee County. Resided in Cherokee County as a farmer prior to enlisting in Jackson County at age 42, April 9, 1862. Mustered in as Corporal. Reported present in September-October, 1862, and January-June, 1863. No further records. [He may have served later in Company B, Indian Battalion.]

JIMMY, Private

Cherokee Indian ("Quenn's son"). Born in what later became Jackson County. Resided in Jackson County as a farmer prior to enlisting in Jackson County at age 18, April 9, 1862. Died at Strawberry Plains, Tennessee, June 20, 1862. Cause of death not reported.

JOHNSON, BLYTHE, Private

Cherokee Indian. Born in what later became Jackson County. Resided in Jackson County as a farmer prior to enlisting at Quallatown County at age 19, April 9, 1862. Reported present in September-October, 1862, and January-June, 1863. No further records. [He may have served later in Company B, Indian Battalion.]

JONAS, JIM, Private
Cherokee Indian. Resided in Jackson County where he was by occupation a farmer prior to enlisting at Quallatown at age 56, July 21, 1862, for the war. Reported present through August 31, 1862, and in January-June, 1863. No further records. [He may have served later in Company B, Indian Battalion.]

JONES, JAMES A., Private
Cherokee Indian. Enlisted in Company A, Walker's Battalion, on or about July 18, 1862, for the war. Reportedly transferred to this company on or about the same date, but there is no other evidence that he served in this company. Reported present with Company A, Walker's Battalion, August 31, 1862.

KALOUXEH, Private
Cherokee Indian. Enlisted at Gatlinburg, Tennessee, January 2, 1863, for the war. Reported present through June 30, 1863. No further records. [He may have served later in Company B, Indian Battalion.]

KANE, SWAGA, Private
Cherokee Indian. Born in what later became Jackson County. Resided in Jackson County as a farmer prior to enlisting at Quallatown at age 36, July 21, 1862, for the war. Reported present in September-October, 1862, and January-June, 1863. Later served in Company B, Indian Battalion.

KANTZ, WILLIAM H., Private
Born in McMinn County, Tennessee, where he resided as a farmer prior to enlisting in McMinn County at age 22, September 1, 1862, for the war. Reported present in January-June, 1863. Later served in Company B, Indian Battalion.

KENETEH, Private
Cherokee Indian. Born in what later became Jackson County. Resided in Jackson County as a farmer prior to enlisting at Quallatown at age 18, April 9, 1862. Reported present in September-October, 1862, and January-June, 1863. No further records. [He may have served later in Company B, Indian Battalion.]

KIANEH, Private
Cherokee Indian. Born in what later became Jackson County. Resided in Jackson County as a farmer prior to enlisting at Quallatown at age 22, April 9, 1862. Reported present in September-October, 1862. Reported absent sick January-February, 1863. Reported dead in March-April, 1863. Place and cause of death not reported.

KILCHULEE, JOHN, Private
Half Cherokee Indian. Born in the part of Macon County that later became Cherokee County. Resided in Cherokee County as a farmer prior to enlisting at Quallatown at age 24, April 9, 1862. Reported present in September-October, 1862, and January-June, 1863. No further records. [He may have served later in Company B, Indian Battalion.]

KOOE, SKOOE, Private
Cherokee Indian. Born in the part of Haywood County that later became Macon County. Resided in Macon County as a farmer prior to enlisting at Cheoah at age 40, September 1, 1862, for the war. Reported present or accounted for in January-June, 1863. No further records. Survived the war. [His name was also rendered as Kooe-Skooe. He was also known as Ross Cochran. He may have served later in Company B, Indian Battalion.]

KYHULEGA, Private
Cherokee Indian. Born in what later became Jackson County. Resided in Jackson County as a farmer prior to enlisting at Quallatown at age 35, July 21, 1862, for the war. Reported present in September-October, 1862, and January-June, 1863. No further records.

LARCHEE, Private
Cherokee Indian. Born in what later became Jackson County. Resided in Jackson County as a farmer prior to enlisting at Quallatown at age 30, July 21, 1862, for the war. Reported present in September-October, 1862, and January-February, 1863. Reported absent sick in March-April, 1863. Returned to duty prior to June 30, 1863. No further records. Survived the war. [He may have served later in Company B, Indian Battalion.]

LAWRENCE, J. CALVIN, Private
Born in Grainger County, Tennessee, where he resided as a farmer prior to enlisting at Quallatown at age 19, April 9, 1862. Reported present in September-October, 1862. Transferred to 2nd Company D, Walker's Battalion, November 1, 1862.

LEWYEH, Private
Cherokee Indian ("Towih's son"). Born in Cherokee County and resided in Jackson County where he was by occupation a farmer prior to enlisting at Quallatown at age 20, April 9, 1862. Died at Strawberry Plains, Tennessee, September 13 or 15, 1862. Cause of death not reported.

LOCUST, ALFRED, Corporal
Cherokee Indian. Previously served as Private in Company F, 39th Regiment N.C. Troops. Enlisted illegally in this company at Quallatown on April 9, 1862, while absent without leave from the 39th Regiment. Mustered in as Corporal. Reported present in September-October, 1862, and January-June, 1863. No further records. [He may have served later in Company B, Indian Battalion.]

LOCUST, JOHNSON, Private
Cherokee Indian. Born in Cherokee County where he resided as a farmer prior to enlisting at Quallatown at age 22, April 9, 1862. Reported present in September-October, 1862, and January-June, 1863. No further records. [He may have served later in Company B, Indian Battalion.]

McCARTY, WILLIAM T., Private
Born in McMinn County, Tennessee, where he resided as a farmer prior to enlisting at Strawberry Plains, Tennessee, at age 21, September 1, 1862, for the war. Reported present in January-February, 1863. Reported on sick furlough in March-April, 1863. Reported present in May-June, 1863. No further records. [He may have served later in Company B, Indian Battalion.]

MARTIN, HENRY C., Private
Born in McMinn County, Tennessee, where he resided as a farmer prior to enlisting at Strawberry Plains, Tennessee, at age 19, on

September 1, 1862, for the war. Reported present in January-February, 1863. Detailed on medical staff as clerk, March-April, 1863. Rejoined the company prior to June 30, 1863. No further records. [He may have served later in Company B, Indian Battalion.]

MAY, PATRICK H., Private
Born in Augusta County, Virginia, and resided in Sullivan County, Tennessee, or Scottsville, Virginia, where he was by occupation a student prior to enlisting at Strawberry Plains, Tennessee, at age 17, December 26, 1862, for the war. Reported through February 28, 1863. Reported on detail with the regimental staff in March-April, 1863. Reported present in May-June, 1863. Transferred to a Company A of this legion, probably of the Indian Battalion, on an unspecified date.

MURPHY, DAVID, Private
Half Cherokee Indian. Previously served as Private in Company A, Walker's Battalion. Transferred to this company on September 1, 1862. Reported present sick in January-February, 1863. Reported absent sick in March-April, 1863. No further records. Survived the war. [He may have served later in Company B, Indian Battalion.]

MURPHY, JOHN, Private
Previously served as Private in Company A, Walker's Battalion. Transferred to this company on April 1, 1863. No further records. [He may have served later in Company B, Indian Battalion.]

MURPHY, LEVI C., Private
Previously served as Private in Company A, Walker's Battalion. Transferred to this company in September-December, 1862. No further records. [He may have served later in Company B, Indian Battalion.]

MURPHY, WILLIAM, Private
Previously served as Private in Company A, Walker's Battalion. Transferred to this company in September-December, 1862. No further records. [He may have served later in Company B, Indian Battalion.]

NEWETOWIH, ISAAC, Corporal
Cherokee Indian. Born in what later became Jackson County. Resided in Jackson County as a farmer prior to enlisting at Quallatown at age 50, April 9, 1862. Mustered in as Private. Reported present in September-October, 1862, and January-June, 1863. Promoted to Corporal in March-April, 1863. No further records. [He may have served later in Company B, Indian Battalion.]

OBEDIAH, Private
Cherokee Indian. Born in the part of Macon County that later became Cherokee County. Resided in Cherokee County as a farmer prior to enlisting at Quallatown at age 30, April 9, 1862. Reported present in September-October, 1862. Reported absent sick from November 18, 1862, through June 30, 1863. No further records. [He may have served later in Company B, Indian Battalion.]

OGATUTLEE, JOE, Private
Cherokee Indian. Born in the part of Macon County that later became Cherokee County. Resided in Jackson County where he was by occupation a farmer prior to enlisting at Quallatown at age 29, April 9, 1862. Reported present in September-October, 1862, and January-June, 1863. No further records. [He may have served later in Company B, Indian Battalion.]

OKUNIYEH, Private
Cherokee Indian. Born in what later became Jackson County. Resided in Jackson County as a farmer prior to enlisting at Quallatown at age 28, July 21, 1862, for the war. Reported present in September-October, 1862, and January-June, 1863. No further records. [His name was also rendered as Okieniyeh and Okunnieh.]

OKUNIYEH, Private
Cherokee Indian ("Kunaseen's son"). Born in Cherokee County where he resided as a farmer prior to enlisting at Cheoah at age 18, September 1, 1862, for the war. Reported on detail with Lt. James Taylor of this company in Carter and Johnson Counties, Tennessee, January-February, 1863. Rejoined the company prior to April 30, 1863. Reported present, May-June, 1863. No further records. [He may have served later in Company B, Indian Battalion.

OLETASTIEH, Private
Cherokee Indian. Born in what later became Jackson County. Resided in Jackson County as a farmer prior to enlisting at Quallatown at age 30, July 21, 1862, for the war. Reported present in September-October, 1862. Reported absent sick with "leg paralyzed" in January-April, 1863. Returned to duty prior to June 30, 1863. No further records. [He may have served later in Company B, Indian Battalion.]

OOCHEECHETEH, Private
Cherokee Indian. Born in Cherokee County where he resided as a farmer prior to enlisting at Quallatown at age 18, April 9, 1862. Reported present in September-October, 1862. Reported absent sick in January-April, 1863. Died at Cheoah on May 10, 1863. Cause of death not reported.

OOCHELOOTEH, Private
Cherokee Indian. Born in Cherokee County where he resided as a farmer prior to enlisting at Cheoah at age 18, September 1, 1862, for the war. Reported absent sick in January-June, 1863. No further records. [He may have served later in Company B, Indian Battalion.]

OOCHUNTEH, Private
Cherokee Indian. Born in what later became Jackson County. Resided in Cherokee County where he was by occupation a farmer prior to enlisting at Cheoah at age 22, September 1, 1862, for the war. Reported absent without leave in January-February, 1863. Returned to duty prior to April 30, 1863. Reported present in May-June, 1863. No further records. Survived the war. [Name also rendered as Oo-chum-teh. He was also known as Comeback Wolf. He may have served later in Company B, Indian Battalion.]

OOCUMMUH, Private
Cherokee Indian. Born in what later became Jackson County. Resided in Jackson County as a farmer prior to enlisting at Quallatown at age 20, April 9, 1862. Reported present in September-October, 1862, and January-June, 1863. No further records. [His name was also rendered as U:gama. He may have served later in Company B, Indian Battalion.]

OOLETASTICH, _____

Cherokee Indian. North Carolina pension records indicate that he served in this company. Survived the war. [He was also known as Jake Consuna. He may have served later in Company B, Indian Battalion.]

OOLTLOHNANEH, Private

Cherokee Indian. Born in what later became Jackson County. Resided in Jackson County as a farmer prior to enlisting at Quallatown at age 16, April 9, 1862. Reported present in September-October, 1862, and January-June, 1863. No further records. [He may have served later in Company B, Indian Battalion.]

OOTELUKEH, Private

Cherokee Indian. Born in what later became Jackson County. Resided in Jackson County as a farmer prior to enlisting at Quallatown at age 27, April 9, 1862. Reported present in September-October, 1862. Reported present sick, January-February, 1863. Reported on detail at Gatlinburg, Tennessee, March-April, 1863. Rejoined the company prior to June 30, 1863. No further records. [He may have served later in Company B, Indian Battalion.]

OSSAKILLEH, Private

Cherokee Indian. Born in the part of Haywood County that later became Macon County. Resided in Jackson County where he was by occupation a farmer prior to enlisting at Quallatown at age 52, April 9, 1862. Reported present in September-October, 1862, and January-February, 1863. Reported on detail at Gatlinburg, Tennessee, March-April, 1863. Rejoined the company on or about June 30, 1863. Later served in Company B, Indian Battalion.

OTTER, JIM, Private

Cherokee Indian. Born in what later became Jackson County. Resided in Jackson County as a farmer prior to enlisting in Jackson County at age 21, July 21, 1862, for the war. Reported present in September-October, 1862, and January-June, 1863. Later served in Company B, Indian Battalion. [He was also known as James Otter.]

PARTRIDGE, DAVID, Private

Cherokee Indian. Born in what later became Jackson County. Resided in Jackson County as a farmer prior to enlisting at Quallatown at age 40, July 21, 1862, for the war. Reported present in September-October, 1862, and January-June, 1863. Deserted to the enemy on an unspecified date. Later served in Company D, 3rd Regiment N.C. Mounted Infantry (Union). [He may have served later in Company B, Indian Battalion. He may have been the same man as Dave, whose record appears in the miscellaneous section of the Indian Battalion roster.]

QUILL, SCACHEE, Private

Cherokee Indian. Born in what later became Jackson County. Resided in Jackson County as a farmer prior to enlisting at Quallatown at age 25, April 9, 1862. Reported present in September-October, 1862, and January-June, 1863. No further records. [He may have served later in Company B, Indian Battalion.]

ROLAND, W. L., _____

Records of Company E, 65th Regiment N.C. Troops (6th Regiment N.C. Cavalry), indicate that he served in this company, then was transferred to the 65th Regiment on September 11, 1864. No other evidence documents his service in this company.

ROSS, JESSE, Private

Cherokee Indian. Born in the part of Macon County that later became Cherokee County. Resided in Jackson County where he was by occupation a farmer prior to enlisting at Quallatown at age 30, April 9, 1862. Reported present in September-October, 1862, and January-June, 1863. No further records. [He may have served later in Company B, Indian Battalion. He may have been the same man as Pvt. Jesse, whose record appears in the miscellaneous section of the Indian Battalion roster.]

ROSS, JOHN, Sergeant

Cherokee Indian. Born in the part of Macon County that later became Cherokee County. Resided in Cherokee County as a farmer prior to enlisting at Quallatown at age 28, April 9, 1862. Mustered in as Sergeant. Reported present in September-October, 1862, and January-June, 1863. No further records. Survived the war. [He may have served later in Company B, Indian Battalion. He may have served also as Chaplain in this legion.]

SAHGEYAH, Private

Cherokee Indian. Born in Cherokee County where he resided as a farmer prior to enlisting at Quallatown at age 22, April 9, 1862. Reported present in September-October, 1862, and January-June, 1863. No further records. [He may have served later in Company B, Indian Battalion.]

SCACHEE, OONANOOTEH, Private

Cherokee Indian. Born in Cherokee County and resided in Jackson County where he was by occupation a farmer prior to enlisting at Quallatown at age 20, April 9, 1862. Reported present in September-October, 1862. Reported on detail with Lt. James Taylor of this company in Carter and Johnson Counties, Tennessee, January-February, 1863. Reported present in March-June, 1863. No further records. [He may have served later in Company B, Indian Battalion.]

SELLALEESEH, NICKEE, Private

Cherokee Indian. Born in what later became Jackson County. Resided in Jackson County as a farmer prior to enlisting at Quallatown at age 34, July 21, 1862, for the war. Reported present in September-October, 1862, and January-June, 1863. No further records. [He may have served later in Company B, Indian Battalion.]

SELLALEESEH, SEQUOYEH, Private

Cherokee Indian. Born in what later became Jackson County. Resided in Jackson County as a farmer prior to enlisting at Quallatown at age 30, July 21, 1862, for the war. Reported present in September-October, 1862, and January-June, 1863. No further records. Survived the war. [His name was also rendered as Se-qua-yah and as Sequo-yo Sell-alle-seh. He may have served later in Company B, Indian Battalion.]

SELLALEESEH, WAHTEH, Private

Cherokee Indian. Born in what later became Jackson County. Resided in Jackson County as a farmer prior to enlisting in Jackson County at age 32, July 21, 1862, for the war. Reported present in September-October, 1862, and January-June, 1863. No further records. Survived the war. [Name also rendered as Wah-tee and as

Watteh Sell-alle-seh. He may have served later in Company B, Indian Battalion.]

SINECOOYEH, Private

Cherokee Indian. Born in what later became Jackson County. Resided in Jackson County as a farmer prior to enlisting at Quallatown at age 30, April 9, 1862. Reported present in September-October, 1862, and January-June, 1863. No further records. [He may have served later in Company B, Indian Battalion.]

SITAWAGEH, Private

Cherokee Indian. Born in what later became Jackson County. Resided in Jackson County as a farmer prior to enlisting at Quallatown at age 35, April 9, 1862. Reported present in September-October, 1862, and January-April, 1863. Died at Camp Creek, Tennessee, June 12, 1863. Cause of death not reported.

SMITH, GEORGE, Private

Enlisted at Quallatown on April 9, 1862. Reported present in September-October, 1862. No further records. [He may have served later in Company B, Indian Battalion.]

SMITH, NIMROD JARETT, 1st Sergeant

Half Cherokee Indian. Previously served as Private in Company A, Walker's Battalion. Transferred to this company on September 1, 1862. Mustered in as Private. Reported present through October 31, 1862. Promoted to 1st Sergeant in November, 1862-February, 1863. Reported present in January-February and May-June, 1863. No further records. Survived the war. [He may have served later in Company B, Indian Battalion. After the war he became principal chief of the Eastern Band of Cherokees. According to Vernon Crow, *Storm in the Mountains*, his Cherokee name was Tsa la di hi.]

TAGENSEH, Private

Cherokee Indian. Born in Cherokee County and resided in Macon County where he was by occupation a farmer prior to enlisting at Quallatown at age 21, April 9, 1862. Died at Strawberry Plains, Tennessee, June 15 or 29, 1862. Cause of death not reported.

TAHGENSEH, Private

Cherokee Indian. Born in what later became Jackson County. Resided in Jackson County as a farmer prior to enlisting at Quallatown at age 28, July 21, 1862, for the war. Reported present in January-June, 1863. No further records. [He may have served later in Company B, Indian Battalion.]

TAHLEE, Private

Cherokee Indian ("Catalstas's son"). Born in what later became Jackson County. Resided in Jackson County as a farmer prior to enlisting at Quallatown at age 25, July 21, 1862, for the war. Reported present in September-October, 1862, and January-June, 1863. No further records. Survived the war. [He was also known as Tah-lee Casabsta, Ca-tol-ster, and Charley Catolster. He may have served later in Company B, Indian Battalion.]

TAHLEE, Private

Cherokee Indian. Born in what later became Jackson County. Resided in Jackson County as a farmer prior to enlisting at Quallatown at age 24, July 21, 1862, for the war. Reported present in September-October, 1862 and in January-June, 1863. No further records. [He may have served later in Company B, Indian Battalion.]

TAHNEENTEH, Private

Cherokee Indian. Born in what later became Jackson County. Resided in Jackson County as a farmer prior to enlisting at Quallatown at age 22, July 21, 1862, for the war. Reported present in September-October, 1862, and January-June, 1863. No further records. [He may have served later in Company B, Indian Battalion.]

TAWASKILLEH, Private

Cherokee Indian. Born in what later became Jackson County. Resided in Jackson County as a farmer prior to enlisting at Quallatown at age 17, July 21, 1862, for the war. Reported present in September-October, 1862, and January-June, 1863. No further records. [His name was also rendered as Tawaskilles. He may have served later in Company B, Indian Battalion.]

TAYLOR, ANDREW J., Private

Previously served as Private in Company A, 39th Regiment N.C. Troops. Enlisted in this company or was transferred to it at Quallatown on April 9, 1862, while absent without leave from the 39th Regiment. Reported absent sick in September-October, 1862. Returned to duty prior to February 28, 1863. Reported present in March-June, 1863. No further records.[He may have served later in Company B, Indian Battalion.]

TESATESKIH, Private

Cherokee Indian. Born in the part of Haywood County that later became Cherokee County. Resided in Cherokee County as a farmer prior to enlisting at Quallatown at age 40, April 9, 1862. Reported absent sick at Strawberry Plains, Tennessee, in September-October, 1862. Reported on detail with Lt. James Taylor of this company in Carter and Johnson Counties, Tennessee, January-February, 1863. Rejoined the company prior to April 30, 1863. Reported present, May-June, 1863. No further records. [He may have served later in Company B, Indian Battalion.]

TESATESKIH, Private

Cherokee Indian ("Owl's son"). Born in the part of Macon County that later became Cherokee County. Resided in Cherokee County as a farmer prior to enlisting at Cheoah at age 30, September 1, 1862, for the war. Reported present in January-June, 1863. No further records. [He may have served later in Company B, Indian Battalion.]

TETALETOGAH, Private

Cherokee Indian. Born in the part of Macon County that later became Cherokee County. Resided in Cherokee County as a farmer prior to enlisting in Cherokee County at age 30, September 1, 1862, for the war. Reported absent sick from November 14, 1862, through February 28, 1863. Reported absent on expired sick leave in March-April, 1863. Reported "unable to return to duty" in May-June, 1863. No further records. [He may have served later in Company B, Indian Battalion.]

TEYULETOHHEE, JIM, Private

Cherokee Indian. Born in what later became Jackson County. Resided in Jackson County as a farmer prior to enlisting in Jackson County at age 21, July 28, 1862, for the war. Reported present in

September-October, 1862, and January-June, 1863. No further records. [He may have served later in Company B, Indian Battalion.]

TICKANEESKEH, JOE, Private
Cherokee Indian. Born in the part of Macon County that later became Cherokee County. Resided in Jackson County as a farmer prior to enlisting at Quallatown at age 30, July 21, 1862, for the war. Reported present in September-October, 1862, and January-June, 1863. No further records. [He may have served later in Company B, Indian Battalion.]

TOHHEESKIH, Private
Cherokee Indian. Born in what later became Jackson County. Resided in Jackson County as a farmer prior to enlisting at Quallatown at age 22, July 21, 1862, for the war. Reported present in September-October, 1862, and January-June, 1863. No further records. Survived the war. [His name was also rendered as Tohesky. He may have served later in Company B, Indian Battalion.]

TOOCHEESTEH, Private
Cherokee Indian. Born in what later became Jackson County. Resided in Jackson County as a farmer prior to enlisting at Quallatown at age 55, July 21, 1862, for the war. Reported present in January-June, 1863. No further records. [He was also known as Aleck Tiyonehala. He may have served later in Company B, Indian Battalion.]

TOONOWIH, Private
Cherokee Indian. Born in what later became Jackson County. Resided in Jackson County as a farmer prior to enlisting at Quallatown at age 25, July 21, 1862, for the war. Reported present in September-October, 1862, and January-June, 1863. No further records. Survived the war. [He may have served later in Company B, Indian Battalion.]

TOOSTOO, Private
Cherokee Indian. Born in what later became Jackson County. Resided in Jackson County as a farmer prior to enlisting at Quallatown at age 19, July 21, 1862, for the war. Reported present in September-October, 1862, and January-June, 1863. No further records. [He may have served later in Company B, Indian Battalion.]

TOWIH, JOHN, Private
Cherokee Indian. Born in the part of Macon County that later became Cherokee County. Resided at Quallatown where he was by occupation a farmer prior to enlisting in Jackson County at age 30, April 9, 1862. Reported present in September-October, 1862, and January-June, 1863. No further records. [He may have served later in Company B, Indian Battalion.]

TSE:GH(I)SINI, _____
Cherokee Indian. Served either in this company or 2nd Company A of this regiment. Reported sick on July 8, 1862. [Tse:gh(i)sini to I:no:li, July 8, 1862, in "The Inoli Letters," MS No. 2236, Folder 1, Bureau of American Ethnology, Smithsonian Institution, Washington, D.C., translated and published in Kilpatrick and Kilpatrick, translators and editors, *The Shadow of Sequoyah: Social Documents of the Cherokees* (Norman: University of Oklahoma Press, 1965), 6. May have served also in either Company A or B, Indian Battalion.]

TSO:WA, _____
Cherokee Indian. Served either in this company or in 2nd Company A of this regiment. Reported sick prior to July 8, 1862, but had recovered by that date. [Tse:gh(i)sini to I:no:li, July 8, 1862, in "The Inoli Letters," MS No. 2236, Folder 1, Bureau of American Ethnology, Smithsonian Institution, Washington, D.C., translated and published in Kilpatrick and Kilpatrick, translators and editors, *The Shadow of Sequoyah: Social Documents of the Cherokees* (Norman: University of Oklahoma Press, 1965), 6. He is probably either the same man as Pvt. Jim Cheoih of this company or Pvt. Oosowih of 2nd Company A of this regiment. May have served later in Company A or B, Indian Battalion.]

TSUMI, _____
Cherokee Indian. Served either in this company or in 2nd Company A of this regiment. [Tse:gh(i)sini to I:no:li, July 8, 1862, in "The Inoli Letters," MS No. 2236, Folder 1, Bureau of American Ethnology, Smithsonian Institution, Washington, D.C., translated and published in Kilpatrick and Kilpatrick, translators and editors, *The Shadow of Sequoyah: Social Documents of the Cherokees* (Norman: University of Oklahoma Press, 1965), 6. May have been the same man as Pvt. Nedda Sammih of 2nd Company A of this regiment. May have later served in Company A, B, or C, Indian Battalion.]

ULLATEESKIH, Private
Cherokee Indian. Born in the part of Macon County that later became Cherokee County. Resided in Cherokee County as a farmer prior to enlisting in Cherokee County at age 25, September 1, 1862, for the war. Reported present in January-June, 1863. No further records. Survived the war. [He was also known as Jesse Leteske. He may have served later in Company B, Indian Battalion.]

WAHHOSSEH, Private
Cherokee Indian. Enlisted at Gatlinburg, Tennessee, September 1, 1862, for the war. Reported present through June 30, 1863. No further records. Survived the war. [His name was also rendered as Wah-has-eh. He was also known as Tom Skitty. He may have served later in Company B, Indian Battalion.]

WAHYACALOONEH, Private
Cherokee Indian. Born in the part of Haywood County that later became Cherokee County. Resided in Cherokee County as a farmer prior to enlisting at Quallatown at age 38, April 9, 1862. Reported present in September-October, 1862. Reported on detail with Lt. James Taylor of this company in Carter and Johnson Counties, Tennessee, January-February, 1863. Rejoined the company prior to April 30, 1863. Reported present in May-June, 1863. No further records. [He may have served later in Company B, Indian Battalion.]

WAHYAHNEETE, JOHN, Musician
Cherokee Indian. Born in Cherokee County and resided in Macon County where he was by occupation a farmer prior to enlisting at Quallatown at age 20, April 9, 1862. Mustered in as Musician (Drummer). Reported present in September-October, 1862. Served briefly as a Fifer in January-February, 1863. Also reported on detail with Lt. James Taylor of this company in Carter and Johnson Counties, Tennessee, January-February, 1863. Rejoined the company prior to April 30, 1863. Reported present, May-June, 1863. No further records. Survived the war. [His surname was also rendered as Wah-ye-neete, Wah-hah-neeta, and Wahhaneeta. He may have served later in Company B, Indian Battalion.]

WAHYANEETE, SICATOWIH, Private

Cherokee Indian. Born in the part of Haywood County that later became Cherokee County. Resided in Jackson County where he was by occupation a farmer prior to enlisting at Quallatown at age 35, July 21, 1862, for the war. Reported present in September-October, 1862, and in January-June, 1863. No further records. [He may have served later in Company B, Indian Battalion.]

WELCH, DAVID, Private

Cherokee Indian. Born in Cherokee County where he resided as a farmer prior to enlisting at Quallatown at age 22, April 9, 1862. Reported absent sick in September-October, 1862, and in January-June, 1863. No further records. Survived the war. [He may have served later in Company B, Indian Battalion.]

WELCH, EDWARD, Private

Born in the part of Haywood County that later became Macon County. Resided in Cherokee County where he was by occupation a farmer prior to enlisting at Quallatown at age 46, April 9, 1862. Reported present in September-October, 1862. Reported on detail with Lt. James Taylor of this company in Carter and Johnson Counties, Tennessee, January-February, 1863. Rejoined the company on an unspecified date. Detailed for recruiting service on April 25, 1863. Rejoined the company prior to June 30, 1863. Served as an interpreter throughout his service in this company. No further records. [He may have served later in Company B, Indian Battalion. On a muster and descriptive roll dated February 12, 1863, in the column headed "complexion" is the notation "one fourth black." While this may have simply indicated a dark complexion, it may have referred to his race. However, "black" was not a term frequently used in this period to indicate African American ancestry.]

WELCH, JOHN E., Private

Cherokee Indian. Enlisted illegally in this company at Quallatown on April 9, 1862, while already a Private in Company A, 39th Regiment N.C. Troops. Reported absent sick in September-October, 1862. "Was claimed and taken" back to Company A, 39th Regiment N. C. Troops, prior to November 11, 1862.

WILLESTE, Private

Cherokee Indian. Enlisted at Gatlinburg, Tennessee, January 2, 1863, for the war. Reported present through June 30, 1863. No further records. [He may have served later in Company B, Indian Battalion.]

WILSONEH, Private

Cherokee Indian. Enlisted at Gatlinburg, Tennessee, January 2, 1863, for the war. Reported present through June 30, 1863. No further records. [He may have served later in Company B, Indian Battalion.]

WOLF, MOSES, Private

Cherokee Indian. Born in Cherokee County where he resided as a farmer prior to enlisting in Jackson County at age 19, April 9, 1862. Reported present in September-October, 1862. Reported on detail with Lt. James Taylor of this company in Carter and Johnson Counties, Tennessee, January-February, 1863. Rejoined the company prior to April 30, 1863. Reported present, May-June, 1863. No further records. Survived the war. [He may have served later in Company, Indian Battalion.]

WOTTEH, OWL, Private

Cherokee Indian. Born in Cherokee County where he resided as a farmer prior to enlisting in Cherokee County at age 20, September 1, 1862, for the war. Reported absent sick, January-April, 1863. Died at Hanging Dog, May 10, 1863. Cause of death not reported.

COMPANY C

This company was raised in Haywood County. It was organized and mustered into Confederate service at Locust Field (present-day Canton) on the Pigeon River on June 13, 1862, as Capt. Elisha G. Johnson's Co., Partisan Rangers, "for the local defense of the Carolinas, East Tennessee, South Western Virginia, and the Cumberland Mountains." It was assigned to Colonel Thomas's N.C. Cherokee Battalion probably on or about July 8, 1862. It may have been known as Company C as of August 31, 1862. On or about October 5, 1862, it was designated Company E, Infantry Regiment, Thomas's Legion. It was redesignated Company C, probably in January, 1863.

The following roster was compiled in large part from a company muster and descriptive roll dated June 13, 1862, and company muster rolls dated September, 1862-June, 1863, and September, 1863-February, 1864. There are two muster rolls for this company dated September-October, 1862. On one, it is called Company E; on the other it is called Company C. Evidence indicates that the latter was misdated, and should have been dated November-December, 1862. In this roster, information on that muster roll is treated as referring to November-December, 1862.

These muster rolls are abstracted in the microfilm edition of the Compiled Service Records of Confederate Soldiers Who Served in Organizations from the State of North Carolina (Record Group 109, M270), National Archives, Washington, D.C. Other valuable information in the Compiled Service Records includes enlistment papers, pay vouchers, requisitions, letters of resignation, discharge certificates, and abstracts of medical and prisoner of war records.

Also utilized in this roster were *The War of the Rebellion: A Compilation of the Official Records of the Union and Confederate Armies*, the North Carolina Adjutant General's papers, state militia records, newspaper casualty lists and obituaries, wartime claims for bounty pay and allowances, postwar registers of claims for artificial limbs, Confederate pension applications filed with the states of North Carolina, Tennessee, and Florida, records of the North Carolina Confederate Soldiers' Home, and the 1860 and 1870 federal censuses of North Carolina. A search was made also for relevant letters, diaries, reminiscences, and other manuscripts in the Southern Historical Collection (University of North Carolina-Chapel Hill) and the Duke University Library Special Collections Department.

Among the secondary sources consulted were records of the North Carolina division of the United Daughters of the Confederacy, postwar rosters, regimental and county histories, marriage bond, will, and cemetery indexes, published and unpublished genealogies, biographical dictionaries, the North Carolina *County Heritage Book* series, the *Confederate Veteran*, Walter Clark's *Histories of the Several Regiments and Battalions from North Carolina in the Great War, 1861-'65*, and the North Carolina volume of the extended edition of *Confederate Military History*.

OFFICERS

CAPTAIN

JOHNSON, ELISHA G.

Previously served as Captain of Company L, 16th Regiment N.C. Troops (6th Regiment N.C. Volunteers). Appointed Captain of this company on June 13, 1862. Reported present in September-October, 1862, and in January-June, 1863; however, payment records indicate that he was on detached service on a court martial board at Jonesborough, Tennessee, from May 1 to July 31, 1863. Reported on detail in Haywood County in September-October, 1863. Reported sick in hospital at Rogersville, Tennessee, December 29-31, 1863. Returned to duty prior to February 25, 1864, when his name appears as a signature on a petition to Gov. Zebulon B. Vance requesting his assistance in reuniting Thomas's Legion and removing it from the command of Brig. Gen. Alfred E. Jackson. Reported in hospital at Harrisonburg, Virginia, October 31, 1864. No further records. Survived the war. [According to Clark's *Regiments* 3:732, he was promoted to Major of this regiment subsequent to November, 1864. However, no surviving wartime evidence supports this claim.]

LIEUTENANTS

HALL, WILLIAM W., 3rd Lieutenant

Born in Haywood County and was by occupation a farmer prior to enlisting in Haywood County at age 28. Appointed 3rd Lieutenant on June 13, 1862. Name appears on a pay voucher for service from June 13 through August 31, 1862. Reported present in September-October, 1862. Reported absent on sick furlough from January 15 through April 30, 1863. Returned to duty in May-June, 1863. Resigned on July 25, 1863, because of disability from an attack of typhoid fever. Resignation accepted on August 15, 1863. [His rank is recorded as 2nd Lieutenant in a register of commissioned officers and on the company muster-in and descriptive roll, but these are evidently errors.]

MOORE, WILLIAM H., 2nd Lieutenant

Born in Haywood County where he resided as a farmer. Listed as 1st Sergeant on a Company Muster-in and Descriptive Roll dated June 13, 1862, with the note that the blanks by his name "will be filled as soon as he has time to come from Col. Rutledge's Regiment." This likely refers to the 25th Regiment N.C. Troops, although Moore does not appear in surviving records for that unit. Reported on a roster of this legion to have been appointed 2nd Lieutenant of this company on June 13, 1862, but this is probably an error. On a pay voucher dated March-April, 1864, Lt. Col. J. R. Love of this regiment states that Moore was "legally and properly promoted on 16th March 1864 is entitled to pay as 2nd Lt from that date." As John H. Smathers was still 2nd Lieutenant at that time, it is likely that Moore was appointed 3rd Lieutenant (Junior 2nd Lieutenant) to replace Elisha W. Morgan, who had died on January 23, 1864. Wounded at Piedmont, Virginia, June 5, 1864. Hospitalized at Lynchburg, Virginia. Returned to duty on July 12, 1864. Wounded in the right side of the head at Winchester, Virginia, September 19, 1864. Reported in hospital at Lynchburg on September 30, 1864. Reported absent wounded on October 31, 1864. No further records. [He may have been the same man as Pvt. William Henry Moore of this company and Company E of this regiment.]

MORGAN, ELISHA WILSON, 3rd Lieutenant

Born in Haywood or Buncombe County on January 16, 1828. Resided in Haywood County and was by occupation a farmer. Probably served previously as 1st Lieutenant in the 109th Regiment N.C. Militia. Enlisted in this company in Haywood County at age 34, June 13, 1862, for the war. Mustered in as Private. Promoted to 1st Sergeant prior to October 31, 1862. Reported present in September-October, 1862, and January-June, 1863. Elected 3rd Lieutenant on August 29, 1863. Reported present in September-December, 1863. Hospitalized at Bristol, Tennessee on an unspecified date. Died "in Virginia" on January 23, 1864. Cause of death not reported.

SMATHERS, JOHN H., 2nd Lieutenant

Born in Haywood County where he resided as a farmer prior to enlisting in Haywood County at age 23. Appointed 2nd Lieutenant on June 13, 1862. Reported present or accounted for in September-October, 1862. Reported on detached service in November-December, 1862. Rejoined the company prior to February 28, 1863. Reported present in March-June, 1863, and September, 1863-February, 1864. Name appears as a signature on a petition to Gov. Zebulon B. Vance dated February 25, 1864, requesting his assistance in reuniting Thomas's Legion and removing it from the command of Brig. Gen. Alfred E. Jackson. Wounded at Piedmont, Virginia, June 5, 1864. No further records. Survived the war. [His first name may have been Jonathan. He may have been promoted to 1st Lieutenant subsequent to March 27, 1865, when 1st Lt. William R. Trull of this company deserted.]

TRULL, WILLIAM R., 1st Lieutenant

Born in Haywood County where he resided as a farmer prior to enlisting in Haywood County at age 22. Appointed 1st Lieutenant on June 13, 1862. Reported present in September-October, 1862. Reported on detached service in January-February, 1863. Rejoined the company prior to April 30, 1863. Reported present in May-June and September-December, 1863. Reported on furlough from February 19 through 29, 1864. Deserted to the enemy in Haywood County on March 27, 1865. Sent to Knoxville, Tennessee, where he arrived on April 16, 1865. Took the Oath of Allegiance at Knoxville on April 17, 1865. Transferred to Chattanooga, Tennessee, on the same date. Hospitalized at Chattanooga on April 22 and again on May 13, 1865, with remittent fever. Survived the war. [According to Clark's *Regiments* 3:730, he was appointed or elected Captain of this company, presumably after Capt. Elisha C. Johnson's supposed promotion to Major; however, wartime records report him as Lieutenant at the time of his desertion.]

NONCOMMISSIONED OFFICERS AND PRIVATES

ABBOTT, JAMES D., Private

Enlisted at Flat Creek, Tennessee, March 1, 1863, for the war. Reported present through June 30, 1863. Reported absent without leave, "supposed to have reported to Col. Thomas in N.C." in September-October, 1863. Listed as a deserter on December 31, 1863.

ABBOTT, STERLING S., Private

Born in Haywood County on August 31, 1838. Was by occupation a farmer prior to enlisting in Haywood County at age 23, June 13, 1862, for the war. Reported present in September-October, 1862. Reported on detached service in November-December, 1862. Rejoined the company prior to February 28, 1863. Reported present in March-June, 1863. Reported absent without leave, "supposed to have reported to Col. Thomas in N.C." in September-October, 1863. Returned to duty prior to December 31, 1863. Reported present in January-February, 1864. Name appears on receipt rolls for clothing dated June 21, September 1, and September 27, 1864. No further records. Survived the war. [See his Tennessee pension application No. 8343.]

ABBOTT, WILLIAM P., Private

Born in Haywood County on January 7, 1838. He was by occupation a farmer prior to enlisting in Haywood County at age 24, June 13, 1862, for the war. Reported present in September-October, 1862. Reported on detached service in November-December, 1862. Reported present in January-June, 1863. Reported absent without leave, "supposed to have reported to Col. Thomas in N.C." in September-October, 1863. Returned to duty prior to December 31, 1863. Reported present in January-February 1864. Name appears on receipt rolls for clothing dated August 18 and September 19, 1864. No further records. Survived the war.

ABEL, GEORGE P., Private

Previously served as Private in Company E of this regiment. Transferred to this company on October 15, 1862. Reported present through October 31, 1862, and in January-June, 1863. Reported "absent without leave, supposed to have reported to Col. Thomas in N.C." in September-October, 1863. Returned to duty prior to December 31, 1863. Reported present in January-February, 1864. Name appears on receipt rolls for clothing dated August 18 and September 26, 1864. No further records. Survived the war. [His surname may have been Able.]

ABEL, JAMES H. R., Private

Born in Haywood County on March 8, 1843. He was by occupation a farmer prior to enlisting in Haywood County at age 19, June 13, 1862, for the war. Reported present in September-October 1862. Reported on detached service in November-December, 1862. Reported present in January-June, 1863. Reported "absent without leave, supposed to have reported to Col. Thomas in N.C.," in September-October, 1863. Returned to duty prior to December 31, 1863. Reported present in January-February, 1864. No further records. Survived the war. [His surname may have been Able.]

ABEL, JOHN H., Private

Born in Haywood County and was by occupation a farmer prior to enlisting in Haywood County at age 23, June 13, 1862, for the war. Reported present in September-October, 1862. Reported absent sick in January-February, 1863. Reported on detached service and on sick leave in March-April, 1863. Reported present in May-June, 1863. Reported "absent without leave, supposed to have reported to Col. Thomas in N.C.," in September-October, 1863. Reported sick at home in November-December, 1863. Reported absent without leave in January-February, 1864. No further records. [His surname may have been Able.]

ABEL, WILLIAM H., Private

Born in Haywood County and was by occupation a farmer prior to enlisting in Haywood County at age 24, June 13, 1862, for the war. Reported on sick furlough in September-October, 1862. Reported present in November-December, 1862. Reported on detached service in January-February, 1863. Reported present in March-June, 1863. Reported absent without leave, "supposed to have reported to Col. Thomas in N.C.," in September-October, 1863. Returned to duty prior to December 31, 1863. Reported present in January-February, 1864. In January, 1865, Capt. Elisha G. Johnson of this company sought a surgeon's certificate in order to have Abel discharged due to epilepsy. No further records. Survived the war. [His surname may have been Able.]

ALLEN, ANDERSON, Private

Resided in Grainger County, Tennessee, and enlisted either in this company or in Company C, Walker's Battalion, probably either at Strawberry Plains, Tennessee, or at Knoxville, Tennessee, January 2, 1863, for the war. Transferred to 2nd Company D, Walker's Battalion, January 10, 1863.

ALLEN, WILLIAM, Private

Records of the United Daughters of the Confederacy and Confederate gravestone records appear to indicate that he served in this company. Survived the war.

AMMONS, GEORGE W., Private

Resided in Macon County. Place and date of enlistment not reported; probably enlisted subsequent to February 29, 1864. Captured by Federal forces on an unspecified date. Confined at Fort Delaware, Delaware. Released on May 3, 1865, after taking the Oath of Allegiance [He may have been a member of either Company C, Walker's Battalion, or Company C, Indian Battalion, rather than this company.]

APPLEY, JACKSON, Private

Previously served as Private in Company L, 16th Regiment N.C. Troops (6th Regiment N.C. Volunteers). Enlisted in this company at Locust Field (present-day Canton) on June 13, 1862, for the war. Reported present in September-October, 1862. Reported on detached service in November-December, 1862. Reported present in January-June, 1863. Reported absent without leave, "supposed to have reported to Col. Thomas in N.C." in September-October, 1863. Returned to duty prior to December, 1863. Reported present but under arrest in January-February, 1864. No further records. [Contrary to 6:100 of this series, his surname was probably Appley rather than Apply.]

BONHAM, NEHEMIAH, Private

Born in Virginia. Resided in Haywood County and was by occupation a "renter" prior to enlisting in Haywood County at age 30, June 13, 1862, for the war. Reported present in September-October, 1862, and January-June, 1863. Reported absent without leave, "supposed to have reported to Col. Thomas in N.C.," in September-October, 1863. Returned to duty prior to December 31, 1863. Reported present in January-February, 1864. Reported on duty as a teamster in western North Carolina from September 9 through December 31, 1864. No further records. Survived the war.

BONHAM, WILLIAM C., _____

Confederate gravestone records appear to indicate that he served in this company.

BRITTAIN, MARK, _____

Confederate gravestone records appear to indicate that he served in this company.

BUGG, JOHN W., Private

Born in Haywood County and was by occupation a farmer prior to enlisting in Haywood County at age 21, June 13, 1862, for the war. Reported present in September-October, 1862. Reported on detached service in November-December, 1862. Reported present in January-June, 1863. Reported absent without leave, "supposed to have reported to Col. Thomas in N.C.," in September-October, 1863. Returned to duty prior to December 31, 1863. Reported present in January-February, 1864. He may have been killed at Piedmont, Virginia on June 5, 1864.

BURNETT, JAMES M., Private

Born in Haywood County and was by occupation a farmer prior to enlisting in Haywood County at age 23, June 13, 1862, for the war. Transferred to Company I, 62nd Regiment N.C. Troops, on the same date.

CATHRAM, JOHN C., Private

Born in Buncombe County and was by occupation a farmer prior to enlisting in Haywood County at age 20, June 13, 1862, for the war. No further records.

CHAMBERS, ELIHU, Musician

Previously served as Musician (Drummer) in Company E of this regiment. Transferred to this company on January 1, 1864. Name appears on receipt rolls for clothing dated June 21 and September 1, 1864. Promoted to Drum Major prior to September 13, 1864, when he was captured at Leetown, Virginia, apparently while acting as a nurse to a wounded comrade, Pvt. George W. Franklin of Company E, Infantry Regiment. Sent to Harpers Ferry, West Virginia. Transferred to Camp Chase, Ohio, where he arrived on September 19, 1864. Released at Camp Chase on June 11, 1865, after taking the Oath of Allegiance.

CHAMBERS, TAYLOR, Private

Resided in Haywood County. Place and date of enlistment not reported; probably enlisted subsequent to February 29, 1864. Deserted to the enemy in Haywood County on March 27, 1865. Sent to Knoxville, Tennessee. Transferred to Chattanooga, Tennessee, and Louisville, Kentucky. Released at Louisville on or about April 18, 1865, after taking the Oath of Allegiance on parole to remain north of the Ohio River until war's end.

CHRISTOPHER, WILLIAM B., Private

Born in Haywood County and was by occupation a farmer prior to enlisting in Haywood County at age 18, June 13, 1862, for the war. Reported present in September-October, 1862. Reported on sick furlough, November, 1862-February, 1863. Returned to duty prior to April 30, 1863. Reported present in May-June, 1863. Reported absent without leave, "supposed to have reported to Col. Thomas in N.C.," in September-October, 1863. Returned to duty in November-December, 1863. Reported present in January-February, 1864. Name appears on a list of deserters dated May 22, 1864, which states that he took the Oath of Allegiance at Knoxville on May 23, 1864.

CLARK, B. A., _____

North Carolina pension records indicate that he served in this company. Survived the war.

CLARK, B. C., _____

North Carolina pension records indicate that he served in this company. Survived the war.

CLARK, ISAAC C., Private

Born in Haywood County where he resided as a farmer prior to enlisting in Haywood County at age 28, June 13, 1862, for the war. Reported on detached service in September-October, 1862. Rejoined the company prior to December 31, 1862. Reported on detached service in January-February, 1863. Rejoined the company prior to April 30, 1863. Sent to hospital at Greeneville, Tennessee, in May-June, 1863. Returned to duty prior to June 30, 1863. Reported absent without leave, "supposed to have reported to Col. Thomas in N.C." in September-October, 1863. Returned to duty prior to December 31, 1863. Reported on extra duty in January-February, 1864. Name appears on a receipt roll for clothing dated June 21, 1864. Deserted to the enemy in Haywood County on March 27, 1865. Sent to Knoxville, Tennessee. Took the Oath of Allegiance at Knoxville on April 17, 1865. Transferred to Louisville, Kentucky, where he arrived on April 27, 1865. Released at Louisville on April 28, 1865, after taking the Oath of Allegiance.

CLARK, ISAAC R., Private

Enlisted in Haywood County on January 1, 1863, for the war. Reported on detached service in January-February, 1863. Reported present in March-June, 1863. Reported absent without leave, "supposed to have reported to Col. Thomas in N.C.," in September-October, 1863. Returned to duty prior December 31, 1863. Reported present in January-February, 1864. Name appears on receipt rolls for clothing dated September 2 and September 19, 1864. No further records.

CLARK, JONATHAN, _____

Confederate gravestone records appear to indicate that he served in this company.

CLAUTS, JOHN W., Private

Born in Haywood County where he resided as a farmer prior to enlisting in Haywood County at age 31, June 13, 1862, for the war. Reported present through October 31, 1862. Reported on detached service in November-December, 1862. Rejoined the company prior to February 28, 1863. Reported present in March-June, 1863. Reported absent without leave, "supposed to have reported to Col. Thomas in N.C." in September-October, 1863. Returned to duty prior to December 31, 1863. Reported present in January-February, 1864. Name appears on receipt rolls for clothing dated June 21, September 1, and September 27, 1864. Deserted to the enemy in Haywood County on March 27, 1865. Sent to Knoxville, Tennessee, where he arrived on April 16, 1865. Took the Oath of Allegiance at Knoxville on April 17, 1865. Transferred to Chattanooga, Tennessee, the same day. Transferred to Louisville, Kentucky, where he arrived on April 27, 1865. Released at Louisville on or about April 28, 1865, after taking the Oath of Allegiance. [His surname may have been Clouts.]

CLOUTS, WILLIAM R., Private

Resided in Haywood County. Place and date of enlistment not reported; probably enlisted subsequent to February 29, 1864. Deserted to the enemy in Haywood County on March 27, 1865. Sent to Knoxville, Tennessee, where he arrived on April 16, 1865. Transferred to Chattanooga, Tennessee on April 17, 1865. Transferred to

Louisville, Kentucky, where he arrived on April 27, 1865. Released at Louisville on or about April 28, 1865, after taking the Oath of Allegiance.

COOK, FRANCIS M., Sergeant
Born in Haywood County and was by occupation a farmer prior to enlisting in Haywood County at age 22, June 13, 1862, for the war. Mustered in as Sergeant. Reported present in September-October, 1862. Reported on detached service in November, 1862-February, 1863. Rejoined the company in March-April, 1863. Reported present through June, 1863. Reported absent without leave, "supposed to have reported to Col. Thomas, who was cut off with a portion of the Command in the evacution of E[ast] Tenn[essee]," September-October, 1863. Returned to duty prior to December 31, 1863. Reported present in January-February, 1864. Name appears on receipt rolls for clothing dated September 2 and September 17, 1864. No further records. Survived the war.

COOK, GEORGE W., Corporal
Born in Haywood County and was by occupation a farmer prior to enlisting in Haywood County at age 33, June 13, 1862, for the war. Mustered in as Private. Reported on detached service prior to October 31, 1862. Promoted to Corporal prior to November 1, 1862. Reported present in November-December, 1862. Reported sick in camp in January-February, 1863. Reported present in March-June, 1863. Reported absent without leave, "supposed to be with Col. Thomas in N.C.," in September-October, 1863. Returned to duty prior to December 31, 1863. Reported present in January-February, 1864. Name appears on a receipt roll for clothing dated June 21, 1864. No further records. Survived the war.

CULBERSON, MARCUS J. L., Private
Born in Haywood County and was by occupation a farmer prior to enlisting in Haywood County at age 17, June 13, 1862, for the war. Reported present in September-October, 1862. Reported sick in hospital at Strawberry Plains, Tennessee, in November-December, 1862. Reported present in January-June, 1863, and September, 1863-February, 1864. Captured at Harrisonburg, Virginia, on or about September 25, 1864. Sent to Harpers Ferry, West Virginia. Transferred to Point Lookout, Maryland, where he arrived on October 12, 1864. Paroled at Point Lookout on March 17, 1865. Received at Boulware's Wharf, James River, Virginia, March 19, 1865, for exchange. No further records.

DUNN, ANDREW J., Private
Born in Washington County, Virginia, and resided in Knox County, Tennessee, where he was by occupation a farmer prior to enlisting at "Thorn Grove" on October 1, 1862, for the war. Transferred from a camp of instruction to this company at Strawberry Plains, Tennessee, November 2, 1862. Transferred to 2nd Company D, Walker's Battalion, December 7, 1862.

EVANS, HOLDEN G., Private
Born in Haywood County and was by occupation a farmer prior to enlisting in Haywood County at age 32, June 13, 1862, for the war. He probably enlisted illegally in this unit after enlisting previously in Company A, 5th Battalion N.C. Cavalry, and was transferred back to the 5th Battalion in the summer of 1862.

FOWLER, ELIAS S., Private
Born in Haywood County where he resided as a farmer prior to enlisting in Haywood County at age 23, June 13, 1862, for the war. Reported absent without leave in September-October, 1862. Returned to duty prior to December 31, 1862. Reported present in January-June, 1863. Reported absent without leave, "supposed to have reported to Col. Thomas in N.C." in September-October, 1863. Returned to duty in November-December, 1863. Reported present in January-February, 1864. Deserted to the enemy in Haywood County on March 28, 1865. Confined at Knoxville, Tennessee, April 15, 1865. Took the Oath of Allegiance at Knoxville on April 17, 1865. Transferred to Chattanooga, Tennessee, the same date. Transferred to Louisville, Kentucky, April 27, 1865. Released at Louisville on April 28, 1865, after affirming the Oath of Allegiance, and ordered "to remain North of the Ohio River during the war."

FOWLER, ROBERT P., Private
Born in Haywood County and was by occupation a farmer prior to enlisting in Haywood County at age 26, June 13, 1862, for the war. Reported present in September-October, 1862. Reported on detached service in November-December, 1862. Rejoined the company prior to February 28, 1863. Reported present in March-June, 1863. Reported absent without leave, "supposed to have reported to Col. Thomas in N.C.," in September-October, 1863. Listed as a deserter in November-December, 1863.

FOWLER, RUBIN T. FRANKLIN, Private
Born in Haywood County where he resided as a farmer prior to enlisting in Haywood County at age 18, June 13, 1862, for the war. Reported on detached service in September-October, 1862. Rejoined the company prior to December 31, 1862. Rejoined the company prior to February 28, 1863. Reported present in March-June, 1863. Reported absent without leave, "supposed to have reported to Col. Thomas in N.C.," in September-October, 1863. Returned to duty prior to December 31, 1863. Reported present in January-February, 1864. Deserted in Haywood County on March 28, 1865. Confined at Knoxville, Tennessee, April 15, 1865. Took the Oath of Allegiance at Knoxville on April 17, 1865. Transferred to Chattanooga, Tennessee, the same date. Confined at Louisville, Kentucky, April 27, 1865. Released at Louisville on April 28, 1865, after taking the Oath of Allegiance, and ordered "to remain North of the Ohio River during the war." [His first name may have been Robert or Reuben.]

FRANKLIN, JOHN W., Private
Born in Haywood County and was by occupation a farmer prior to enlisting in Haywood County at age 28, June 13, 1862, for the war. Reported on detached service in September-October, 1862. Reported present in November-December, 1862. Reported on detached service in January-February, 1863. Reported present in March-June, 1863, and September, 1863-February, 1864. Captured at Carter's Depot, Tennessee, April 25, 1864. Sent to Nashville, Tennessee, and was confined there prior to May 16, 1864. Transferred to Louisville, Kentucky on May 16, 1864, and arrived there on May 17. Transferred to Camp Morton, Indianapolis, Indiana, May 21, 1864. Paroled at Camp Morton on March 4, 1865. Received at Boulware's and Cox's Wharf, James River, Virginia, March 10-11, 1865, for exchange. Hospitalized at Richmond, Virginia, March 11, 1865, with chronic diarrhoea. Furloughed for sixty days on March 23, 1865. Survived the war.

GREEN, THADDEUS M., Sergeant
Served as Private in Company F, 25th Regiment N.C. Troops. Enlisted, probably illegally, in this company as Sergeant at Locust Field (present-day Canton) on June 13, 1862. Failed to report for duty and continued to serve in the 25th Regiment.

HALL, GREEN C., Sergeant

Born in Haywood County and was by occupation a farmer prior to enlisting at Locust Field (present-day Canton) at age 25, June 13, 1862, for the war. Mustered in as Private. Promoted to Sergeant on June 13, 1862. Reported on detached service in September-October, 1862. Died at Strawberry Plains, Tennessee, December 25, 1862, of "measles." [He may have served previously in an unspecified company of the 25th Regiment N.C. Troops.]

HALL, J. T., _____

North Carolina pension records indicate that served in this company. Survived the war.

HALL, JOHN, JR., Private

Born in Haywood County and was by occupation a farmer prior to enlisting in Haywood County at age 40, June 13, 1862, for the war. Reported on detached service in September-October, 1862. Reported present in November-December, 1862. Reported on detached service in January-February, 1863. Rejoined the company prior to April 30, 1863. Reported present in May-June, 1863. Died at home on or about September 1, 1863. Cause of death not reported.

HALL, LAWSON A., Private

Born in Haywood County and was by occupation a farmer prior to enlisting in Haywood County at age 32, June 13, 1862, for the war. Mustered in as Corporal. Reported sick in hospital at Strawberry Plains, Tennessee, in September-October, 1862. Reduced to ranks prior to October 31, 1862. Reported on detached service in January-February, 1863. Rejoined the company in March-April, 1863. Reported present in May-June, 1863. Reported absent without leave, "supposed to have reported to Col. Thomas in N.C.," in September-October, 1863. Reported absent sick in November, 1863-February, 1864. Name appears on a receipt roll for clothing dated September 19, 1864. No further records. Survived the war. [He previously served as 1st Lieutenant, Beaverdam Company, 112th Regiment N.C. Militia]

HALL, LEE W., Private

Previously enlisted as Private in Company E of this regiment. Transferred to this company on April 11, 1863. Reported present through June 30, 1863. Reported absent without leave, "supposed to have reported to Col. Thomas in N.C.," in September-October, 1863. Listed as a deserter in November-December, 1863.

HALL, SAMUEL, Private

Born in Haywood County and was by occupation a farmer prior to enlisting in Haywood County at age 35, June 13, 1862, for the war. Reported on detached service, September-October, 1862. Reported present, November-December, 1862, and January-June, 1863. Reported absent without leave, "supposed to have reported to Col. Thomas in N.C.," in September-October, 1863. Reported on detached service in November-December, 1863. Reported absent without leave in January-February, 1864. No further records. Survived the war.

HALL, WILLIAM H., Private

Born in 1840. Enlisted at Locust Field (present-day Canton) on August 18, 1863, for the war. Reported present in November, 1863-February, 1864. No further records. Survived the war.

HARBIN, OLIVER N., Private

Born in Buncombe County. Resided in Buncombe County where he was by occupation a farmer prior to enlisting at Locust Field (present-day Canton) at age 31, March 1, 1863, for the war. Reported present through June 30, 1863. Reported absent without leave in September-October, 1863. Listed as a deserter in November-December, 1863.

HARKINS, ISAAC, Private

Resided in Bradley County, Tennessee, and enlisted at Flat Creek, Tennessee, October 25, 1862, for the war. Reported present on October 31, 1862, and in January-June, 1863. Reported absent without leave, "supposed to have reported to Col. Thomas in N.C." in September-October, 1863. Listed as a deserter on December 31, 1863. Returned to duty on an unknown date. Deserted in Haywood County on March 27, 1865. Sent to Knoxville, Tennessee, where he arrived on April 16, 1865. Released at Knoxville on April 17, 1865, after taking the Oath of Allegiance.

HEATHERLEY, ANDREW J., Private

Born in Haywood County and was by occupation a farmer prior to enlisting in Haywood County at age 34, June 13, 1862, for the war. Reported on detached service in September-October, 1862. Rejoined the company prior to December 31, 1862. Reported on detached service in January-February, 1863. Rejoined the company prior to April 30, 1863. Reported present, May-June, 1863. Reported absent without leave, "supposed to have reported to Col. Thomas in N.C.," in September-October, 1863. Listed as a deserter in November-December, 1863, and absent without leave in January-February, 1864. Name appears on receipt rolls for clothing dated September 2 and September 17, 1864. No further records.

HENDERSON, JOHN H., Private

Enlisted at Flat Creek, Tennessee, December 1, 1862, for the war. Reported on detached service through December 31, 1862. Rejoined the company prior to February 28, 1863. Reported absent in March-April, 1863. Rejoined the company prior to June 30, 1863. Reported absent without leave, "supposed to have reported to Col. Thomas in N.C." in September-October, 1863. Listed as a deserter in November-December, 1863.

HENSON, AVERY, Private

Born in Haywood County where he resided as a farmer prior to enlisting in Haywood County at age 25, June 13, 1862, for the war. Reported on detached service in September-October, 1862. Reported present in November-December, 1862. Reported sick in hospital at Strawberry Plains, Tennessee, in January-February, 1863. Returned to duty prior to April 30, 1863. Reported sick in hospital at Greeneville, Tennessee, in May-June, 1863. Reported absent without leave, "supposed to have reported to Col. Thomas in N.C." in September-October, 1863. Reported absent sick at home in November-December, 1863. Reported absent without leave in January-February, 1864. Returned to duty on an unknown date. Deserted to the enemy in Haywood County on March 28, 1865. Confined at Knoxville, Tennessee, April 15, 1865. Took the Oath of Allegiance at Knoxville, Tennessee, April 17, 1865, and transferred to Chattanooga, Tennessee on the same date. Transferred to Louisville, Kentucky, and arrived there on or before April 20, 1865. Released on April 28, 1865, with instructions "to remain North of the Ohio River during the war." [His first name may have been Allen.]

HENSON, JASPER H., Private

Born in Haywood County where he resided as a farmer prior to enlisting in Haywood County at age 21, June 13, 1862, for the war. Reported on detached service in September-October, 1862. Rejoined the company prior to December 31, 1862. Reported present in January-June, 1863. Reported absent without leave, "supposed to have reported to Col. Thomas in N.C.," in September-October, 1863. Listed as a deserter in November-December, 1863. Returned to duty on an unknown date. Deserted to the enemy in Haywood County on March 28, 1865. Confined at Knoxville, Tennessee, April 15, 1865. Took the Oath of Allegiance at Knoxville, Tennessee, April 17, 1865, and transferred to Chattanooga, Tennessee, the same date. Transferred to Louisville, Kentucky, and arrived there on or before April 20, 1865. Released on April 28, 1865, with instructions "to remain North of the Ohio River during the war." [His middle initial may have been M.]

HENSON, WILEY, Private

Resided in Haywood County. Place and date of enlistment not reported; probably enlisted subsequent to February 29, 1864. Deserted to the enemy in Haywood County on March 28, 1865. Confined at Knoxville, Tennessee, April 15, 1865. Took the Oath of Allegiance at Knoxville, Tennessee, April 17, 1865, and transferred to Chattanooga, Tennessee, on the same date. Transferred to Louisville, Kentucky, and arrived there on or before April 20, 1865. Released on April 28, 1865, with instructions "to remain North of the Ohio River during the war."

HERREN, LESTER H., Private

Born in Haywood County and was by occupation a farmer prior to enlisting in Haywood County on June 13, 1862, for the war. Reported on detached service in September-October, 1862. Rejoined the company prior to December 31, 1862. Reported present in January-June, 1863. Reported absent without leave, "supposed to have reported to Col. Thomas in N.C." in September-October, 1863. Listed as a deserter in November-December, 1863.

HOWELL, JAMES K., Private

Enlisted at Knoxville, Tennessee, March 20, 1863, for the war. Detailed to the government shoe shop at Knoxville, Tennessee, April 3-30, 1863. Reported on detached service in May-June, 1863. Listed as a deserter in November-December, 1863. [His middle initial may have been R.

HOWELL, JOHN L., Private

Enlisted at Knoxville, Tennessee, March 20, 1863, for the war. Reported on detached duty April 3-June 30, 1863, and in September, 1863-February, 1864. Was assigned to the government shoe shop at Knoxville during most of that period. No further records. [His correct middle initial may have been M.]

HOWELL, W. H., _____

Name appears on a company muster roll dated September-October, 1862, stating that his name was canceled.

JOHNSON, E. E., Private

Resided in Haywood County. Place and date of enlistment not reported; probably enlisted subsequent to February 29, 1864. Name appears on receipt rolls for clothing dated September 2 and 19, 1864. Deserted to the enemy in Haywood County on March 27, 1865. Confined at Knoxville, Tennessee, April 16, 1865. Transferred to Chattanooga, Tennessee, after taking the Oath of Allegiance at Knoxville on April 17, 1865. Transferred to Louisville, Kentucky, and arrived there on April 27, 1865. Released on April 28, 1865, "to remain North of the Ohio River during the war."

JOHNSON, WILEY M., Private

Born on April 19, 1844. Enlisted in Haywood County at age 18, January 1, 1863, for the war. Reported present in January-June, 1863, and in September, 1863-February, 1864. Name appears on receipt rolls for clothing dated June 21, September 1, and October 16, 1864. No further records. Survived the war. [He may have served later in either Company H, Infantry Regiment of this legion, or Company H, Walker's Battalion.]

JUSTICE, JAMES D., Private

Enlisted at Flat Creek, Tennessee, on March 1, 1863, for the war. Reported present through June 30, 1863. Reported absent without leave, "supposed to have reported to Colonel Thomas in N.C." in September-October, 1863. Returned to duty prior to December 31, 1863. Reported present but on extra duty in January-February, 1864. Name appears on a receipt roll for clothing dated December 14, 1864. No further records.

JUSTICE, WILLIAM T., 1st Sergeant

Previously served as Private in Company E, 60th Regiment N.C. Troops. Transferred to this company on April 1, 1863. Mustered in as Musician (Drummer). Reported on duty as Fifer in May-June, 1863. Promoted to 1st Sergeant prior to October 31, 1863. Reported present in September-October, 1863. Reported sick in hospital at "R.V." (either Russellville or Rogersville) and Bristol, Tennessee, in November, 1863-February, 1864. Name appears on receipt rolls for clothing dated August 24 and September 17, 1864. No further records. Survived the war. [He was about 32 years of age in April, 1863.]

LAFON, ISAAC JAMES MONROE, Private

Born in Haywood County and was by occupation a farmer prior to enlisting in Haywood County at age 27, June 13, 1862, for the war. Reported present in September-October, 1862. Reported sick in hospital at Strawberry Plains, Tennessee, January-February, 1863. Died at Strawberry Plains on March 29, 1863, of "pneumonia."

LAFON, JOSHUA, Private

Born in Haywood County and was by occupation a farmer prior to enlisting in Haywood County at age 20, June 13, 1862, for the war. Reported present in September-October, 1862. Died on January 31, 1863. Place and cause of death not reported.

LAFON, JULIUS L., Private

Born in Haywood County and was by occupation a farmer prior to enlisting in Haywood County at age 30, June 13, 1862, for the war. Reported on detached service in September-October, 1862, and January-February, 1863. Rejoined the company prior to April 30, 1863. Reported present in May-June, 1863. Died, probably on June 8, 1863, probably at Strawberry Plains, Tennessee. Cause of death not reported.

LEWIS, JAMES E., Private

Enlisted at Jonesborough, Tennessee, June 8, 1863, for the war. Reported present through June 30, 1863. Reported absent without leave, "supposed to have reported to Col. Thomas in N.C.," in September-October, 1863. Reported absent due to an accidental wounding in November-December, 1863. Reported sick in hospital at Asheville in January-February, 1864. Name appears on a receipt roll for clothing datelined General Hospital, Harrisonburg, Virginia, September 20, 1864. No further records.

McDANIEL, JOSEPH E., Private
Born in Haywood County and was by occupation a farmer prior to enlisting in Haywood County at age 49, June 13, 1862, for the war. Reported present in September-October, 1862, and in January-February, 1863. Reported sick while on detached service, March-April, 1863. Rejoined the company prior to June 30, 1863. Reported absent without leave, "supposed to have reported to Col. Thomas in N.C." in September-October, 1863. Returned to duty prior to December 31, 1863. Reported present in January-February, 1864. Name appears on receipt rolls for clothing date August 18 and September 23, 1864, and on a roll showing commutation for quarters of detailed men working in the quartermaster department at Asheville, August 27-31, 1864. No further records. Survived the war.

MEASE, JOHN PINKNEY, Private
Born in Haywood County and was by occupation a farmer prior to enlisting in Haywood County age 29, June 13, 1862, for the war. Reported on detached service, September-October, 1862. Reported sick in hospital at Strawberry Plains, Tennessee, in November-December, 1862. Reported on detached service in January-February, 1863. Rejoined the company prior to April 30, 1863. Reported present, May-June, 1863. Reported absent without leave, "supposed to have reported to Col. Thomas in N.C.," in September-October, 1863. Listed as a deserter in November-December, 1863. [His surname may have been Meece.]

MEECE, MORGAN, Private
Resided in Haywood County. Place and date of enlistment not reported; probably enlisted subsequent to February 29, 1864. Deserted to the enemy in Haywood County on March 28, 1865. Confined at Knoxville, Tennessee, April 15, 1865. Took the Oath of Allegiance at Knoxville on April 17, 1865, and transferred to Chattanooga, Tennessee, the same date. Transferred to Louisville, Kentucky, and arrived there on April 27, 1865. Released at Louisville on April 28, 1865, with instructions to remain north of the Ohio River for the remainder of the war. [His surname may have been Mease.]

MILLER, JACOB, Private
Born in Haywood County and was by occupation a farmer prior to enlisting in Haywood County at age 18, June 13, 1862, for the war. Reported on detached service, September-October, 1862. Reported absent sick in hospital at Strawberry Plains, Tennessee, November-December, 1862. Reported sick in camp in January-February, 1863. Returned to duty prior to April 30, 1863. Reported present in May-June, 1863. Reported absent without leave, "supposed to have reported to Col. Thomas in N.C.," in September-October, 1863. Listed as a deserter in November-December, 1863. Name appears on receipt rolls for clothing dated August 18 and September 19, 1864. No further records.

MILLER, JOHN, Private
Born in Haywood County and was by occupation a farmer prior to enlisting in Haywood County at age 18, June 13, 1862, for the war. Reported on detached service in September-October, 1862. Rejoined the company prior to December 31, 1862. Reported present in January-June, 1863. Reported absent without leave, "supposed to have reported to Col. Thomas in N.C." in September- October, 1863. Returned to duty prior to December 31, 1863. Reported present in January-February, 1864. Reported on detail with the quartermaster department at Asheville in August, 1864. Name appears on a receipt roll for clothing dated September 17, 1864. No further records. [His middle initial may have been H.]

MILLER, L. C., Private
Resided in Haywood County. Place and date of enlistment not reported; probably enlisted subsequent to February 29, 1864. Deserted to the enemy in Haywood County on March 27, 1865. Sent to Knoxville, Tennessee, April 15, 1865. Took the Oath of Allegiance at Knoxville, Tennessee, April 17, 1865, and transferred to Chattanooga, Tennessee, the same date. Transferred to Louisville, Kentucky, and arrived there on April 27, 1865. Discharged at Louisville on April 28, 1865, with instructions to remain north of the Ohio River until the end of the war.

MILLER, PETER, Private
Born in Haywood County and was by occupation a farmer prior to enlisting in Haywood County at age 18, June 13, 1862, for the war. Reported on detached service in September-October, 1862. Rejoined the company prior to December 31, 1862. Reported present in January-June, 1863. Reported absent without leave, "supposed to have reported to Col. Thomas in N.C.," in September-October, 1863. Returned to duty prior to December 31, 1863. Reported present in January-February, 1864. Name appears on receipt rolls for clothing dated August 18 and September 17, 1864. No further records.

MOORE, GEORGE W., Private
Born in Haywood County on July 10, 1844. Was by occupation a farmer prior to enlisting in Haywood County at age 17, June 13, 1862, for the war. Reported present through October 31, 1862. Reported on detached service in November-December, 1862. Reported absent on sick furlough in January-February, 1863. Returned to duty prior to April 30, 1863. Reported present in May-June, 1863. Reported absent without leave, "supposed to have reported to Col. Thomas in N.C." in September-October, 1863. Returned to duty prior to December 31, 1863. Reported present in January-February, 1864. Wounded in the right side and left thigh and captured at Cedar Creek, Virginia, October 19, 1864. Hospitalized at Winchester, Virginia, October 22, 1864. Transferred to hospital at Baltimore, Maryland, December 10, 1864. Transferred to Point Lookout, Maryland, January 8, 1865. Hospitalized at Point Lookout on January 28, 1865. Released at Point Lookout on June 3, 1865, after taking the Oath of Allegiance.

MOORE, GOODSON M. D., Private
Born in Haywood County and was by occupation a farmer prior to enlisting in Haywood County at age 19, June 13, 1862, for the war. Reported present in September-October, 1862, and in January-June, 1863. Reported absent without leave, "supposed to have reported to Col. Thomas in N.C.," September-October, 1863. Returned to duty prior to December 31, 1863. Died at Bull's Gap, Tennessee, January 20, 1864. Cause of death not reported.

MOORE, JAMES L., Private
Enlisted at Locust Field (present-day Canton) on August 18, 1863, for the war. Reported present in November, 1863-February, 1864.

Name appears on a receipt roll for clothing dated September 1, 1864. No further records. Survived the war. [The Charlotte *Western Democrat* of October 25, 1864, states that a J. C. Moore of this company was wounded at Winchester, Virginia, September 19, 1864. It may have been this man.]

MOORE, JAMES NEWTON, Private

Born in Haywood County and was by occupation a farmer prior to enlisting in Haywood County at age 29, June 13, 1862, for the war. Reported present or accounted for in September-October, 1862, and in January-April, 1863. Reported sick in hospital at Athens, Tennessee, May-June, 1863. Returned to duty prior to June 30, 1863. Reported absent without leave in September-October, 1863. Returned to duty prior to December 31, 1863. Reported present in January-February, 1864. Captured at Winchester, Virginia, September 19, 1864. Sent to Harpers Ferry, West Virginia. Confined at Point Lookout, Maryland, September 27, 1864. Paroled at Point Lookout, probably on February 10, 1865. Received at Cox's Landing, James River, Virginia, February 14-15, 1865, for exchange. Reported present on a muster roll of paroled and exchanged prisoners at Camp Lee, near Richmond, Virginia, February 17, 1865. No further records. [The Charlotte *Western Democrat* of October 25, 1864, states that a J. C. Moore of this company was wounded at Winchester, Virginia, September 19, 1864. It may have been this man.]

MOORE, JOSEPH L., Private

Confederate gravestone records appear to indicate that he served in this company. Survived the war. [The Charlotte *Western Democrat* of October 25, 1864, states that a J. C. Moore of this company was wounded at Winchester, Virginia, September 19, 1864. It may have been this man.]

MOORE, WILLIAM HENRY, Private

Previously served as Private in Company E of this regiment. Transferred to this company in November-December, 1863. Reported present through February 29, 1864. No further records.

PARKER, CHARLES F., Private

Born in Haywood County and was by occupation a farmer prior to enlisting in Haywood County at age 26, June 13, 1862, for the war. Reported on detached service, September-October, 1862. Rejoined the company prior to December 31, 1862. Reported on detached service in January-February, 1863. Rejoined the company prior to April 30, 1863. No further records. Survived the war.

PHILLIPS, C. GUILFORD, _____

Confederate gravestone records appear to indicate that he served in this company.

PHILLIPS, CHRISENBERY B., Private

Enlisted at Locust Field (present-day Canton) at age 40, August 18, 1863, for the war. Reported absent sick on December 31, 1863. Reported absent without leave on February 29, 1864. Name appears on a receipt roll for clothing dated October 16, 1864. No further records. Survived the war.

PLEMMONS, FRANCIS, Private

Enlisted at Flat Creek, Tennessee, October 18 or October 25, 1863, for the war. Reported on detached service on October 31, 1862. Rejoined the company prior to December 31, 1862. Reported present in January-June, 1863. Reported absent without leave, "supposed to have reported to Col. Thomas in N.C.," in September-October, 1863. Returned to duty prior to December 31, 1863. Reported present in January-February, 1864. Captured at Carter's Depot, Tennessee, April 25, 1864. Sent to Nashville, Tennessee. Transferred to Louisville, Kentucky, where he arrived on May 17, 1864. Confined at Camp Morton, Indianapolis, Indiana, May 22, 1864. Paroled and transferred to Point Lookout, Maryland, on or about February 19, 1865. Exchanged prior to February 23, 1865, when he was hospitalized at Jackson Hospital, Richmond, Virginia, with frostbitten feet. Transferred to another Richmond hospital on March 15, 1865, with scabies. Furloughed for sixty days on March 31, 1865. No further records. [His surname is given erroneously as Clemmens on some prisoner of war records.]

PRESSLEY, ANDREW J., Private

Born in Haywood County and was by occupation a farmer prior to enlisting in Haywood County at age 34, June 13, 1862, for the war. Reported absent without leave in September-October, 1862. Returned to duty prior to December 31, 1862. Reported present in January-February, 1863. Reported on detached service and sick in March-April, 1863. Reported sick in hospital at Athens, Tennessee, in May-June, 1863. Reported absent without leave, "supposed to have reported to Col. Thomas in N.C.," in September-October, 1863. Returned to duty prior to December 31, 1863. Reported present in January-February, 1864. No further records.

PRESSLEY, WILLIAM W., Private

Born on July 20, 1845. Resided in Henderson County and enlisted at Locust Field (present-day Canton) at age 18, August 18, 1863, for the war. Reported present in November, 1863-February, 1864. Deserted to the enemy in Haywood County on March 27, 1865. Confined at Knoxville, Tennessee, April 16, 1865. Took the Oath of Allegiance at Knoxville, April 17, 1865. Transferred to Chattanooga, Tennessee, and Louisville, Kentucky, where he arrived on April 27, 1865. Released at Louisville on April 28, 1865, and sent north of the Ohio River with instructions to remain there until the end of the war.

REDSLEVE, JOHN G., Private

Born in Haywood County and was by occupation a farmer prior to enlisting in Haywood County at age 18, June 13, 1862, for the war. Reported present in September-October, 1862. Reported on detached service in November-December, 1862. Reported on sick furlough in January-February, 1863. Returned to duty prior to March, 30, 1863. Reported present in May-June, 1863. Reported absent without leave, "supposed to have reported to Col. Thomas who was cut off with a portion of the command in the evacuation of E[ast] T[ennessee]" in September-October, 1863. Returned to duty prior to December 31, 1863. Reported present in January-February, 1864. Captured at Piedmont, Virginia, June 5, 1864. Reported under guard at Staunton, Virginia, June 8, 1864. Confined at Camp Morton, Indianapolis, Indiana, June 21, 1864. Died at Camp Morton on February 2, 1865, of "chronic diarrhoea." [His surname may have been Redsleeve.]

REDSLEVE, MORGAMIN H., Private

Born in Haywood County and was by occupation a farmer prior to enlisting in Haywood County at age 20, June 13, 1862, for the war. Reported present in September-October, 1862. Reported on detached service in November-December, 1862. Reported on sick furlough in January-February, 1863. Returned to duty prior to April 30, 1863. Reported present in May-June, 1863. Reported absent without leave, "supposed to have reported to Col. Thomas who was cut off with a portion of the command in the evacuation in E[ast] Ten[nessee]" in September-October, 1863. Returned to duty prior to December 31, 1863. Reported present in January-February, 1864. Name appears on receipt rolls for clothing dated June 21 and September 19, 1864. No further records. [His surname may have been Redsleeve.]

REECE, LEONARD E., Private

Born in Haywood County and was by occupation a farmer prior to enlisting in Haywood County at age 27, June 13, 1862, for the war. Mustered in as Private. Appointed Musician (Drummer) prior to October 31, 1862. Reported absent on detached service in September-October, 1862, and January-February, 1863. Reduced to ranks on April 19, 1863. Rejoined the company prior to April 30, 1863. Reported present in May-June, 1863. Reported absent without leave, "supposed to have reported to Col. Thomas who was cut off with a portion of the command in the evacuation of E[ast] T[ennessee]" in September-October, 1863. Listed as a deserter on December 31, 1863. Name appears on receipt rolls for clothing dated August 18 and September 17, 1864. No further records. Survived the war.

RENO, JOHN, Private

Enlisted at Locust Field (present-day Canton) on August 18, 1863, for the war. Reported absent sick in November-December, 1863. Reported present on extra duty in January-February, 1864. Reported on extra duty as a forage master from August 15 through September 30, 1864. No further records. Survived the war. [His surname may have been Renno. He may have transferred to Company C, Walker's Battalion, prior to August, 1864, as one of the receipt rolls for his service as forage master lists him as belonging to that unit. He was probably the same man as Pvt. John Hardy Reno or Pvt. John M. Reno of this company.]

RENO, JOHN HARDY, Private

Confederate gravestone records appear to indicate that he served in this legion. Survived the war. [He may have been the same man as Pvt. John Reno of this company.]

RENO, JOHN M., Private

Confederate gravestone records appear to indicate that he served in this company. Survived the war. [He may have been the same man as Pvt. John Reno of this company.]

RENO, WILLIAM, Sergeant

Born in Haywood County in 1828. Was by occupation a farmer prior to enlisting in Haywood County at age 34, June 13, 1862, for the war. Mustered in as Private. Promoted to Sergeant on December 25, 1862. Reported present in September-December, 1862. Reported on detached service in January-February, 1863. Rejoined the company prior to April 30, 1863. Reported present in May-June, 1863. Reported absent without leave, "supposed to have reported to Col. Thomas who was cut off with a portion of the command in the in the evacuation of E[ast] Tenn[essee]" in September-October, 1863. Returned to duty prior to December 31, 1863. Reported present in January-February, 1864. No further records. Survived the war.

RIDDLE, F. B., Private

Resided in Henderson County. Place and date of enlistment not reported; probably enlisted subsequent to February 29, 1864. Deserted to the enemy in Haywood County on March 27, 1865. Sent to Knoxville, Tennessee. Transferred to Chattanooga, Tennessee, and Louisville, Kentucky. Released at Louisville on or about April 28, 1865, after taking the Oath of Allegiance.

ROBERSON, HENRY CLAY, Private

Born on February 10, 1845. Enlisted at Locust Field (present-day Canton) at age 17, January 1, 1863, for the war. Reported on detached service on February 28, 1863. Rejoined the company prior to April 30, 1863. Reported present in May-June, 1863. Reported absent without leave, "supposed to have reported to Col. Thomas in N.C.," in September-October, 1863. Returned to duty prior to December 31, 1863. Reported present in January-February, 1864. Name appears on a receipt roll for clothing dated September 17, 1864. No further records. Survived the war. [His surname may have been Robinson.]

ROBERSON, HENRY G., Private

Born in Haywood County and was by occupation a farmer prior to enlisting in Haywood County at age 27, June 13, 1862, for the war. Reported present in September-October, 1862. Reported on sick furlough in November-December, 1862. Reported on detached service in January-February, 1863. Rejoined the company prior to April 30, 1863. Reported absent without leave, "supposed to have reported to Col. Thomas in N.C.," in September-October, 1863. Returned to duty prior to December 31, 1863. Reported present on extra duty in January-February, 1864. Name appears on a receipt roll for clothing dated September 17, 1864. No further records. Survived the war. [His surname may have been Robeson or Robinson.]

ROBERSON, JAMES T., Private

Enlisted at Locust Field (present-day Canton) on March 1, 1863, for the war. Reported present through June 30, 1863. Furloughed for thirty days from hospital in Tennessee on September 1, 1863, but was "cut off from the command by evacuation of E[ast] Tenn[essee] by our army" and reported absent on October 31, 1863. Reported on detached service in November-December, 1863. Reported on sick furlough in January-February, 1864. No further records.

ROBERSON, JOHN P., Private

Enlisted at Locust Field (present-day Canton) on August 18, 1863, for the war. Reported present in November, 1863-February, 1864. Name appears on receipt rolls for clothing dated September 2 and September 17, 1864. No further records.

ROBERSON, WILLIAM M., Private

Born in Haywood County and was by occupation a farmer prior to enlisting in Haywood County at age 17, June 13, 1862, for the war. Reported present in September-October, 1862. Reported on detached service in November-December, 1862. Rejoined the company prior to February 28, 1863. Reported present in March-June, 1863. Reported absent without leave, "supposed to have reported to Col. Thomas in N.C.," in September-October, 1863. Reported "absent wounded by accident" in November-December, 1863. Reported sick in hospital in Virginia in January-February, 1864. No further records. [His surname may have been Robinson.]

SCOTT, ELISHA L., Private
Born in Haywood County and was by occupation a farmer prior to enlisting in Haywood County at age 21, June 13, 1862, for the war. Reported present in September-October, 1862, and January-June, 1863. Reported absent without leave, "supposed to have reported to Col. Thomas in N.C." in September-October, 1863. Returned to duty prior to December 31, 1863. Reported present in January-February, 1864. Wounded in the right hip at Winchester, Virginia, September 19, 1864. No further records. Survived the war.

SCOTT, GEORGE M., Private
Born in Haywood County and was by occupation a farmer prior to enlisting in Haywood County at age 18, June 13, 1862, for the war. Reported present, September-October, 1862. Reported on detached service in November-December, 1862. Rejoined the company prior to February 28, 1863. Reported present in March-June, 1863; and September, 1863-February, 1864. Name appears on receipt rolls for clothing dated June 21 and September 1, 1864. No further records. Survived the war. [North Carolina pension records indicate that he was wounded at "Lee Finn" (or "Lee Tinn," possibly a reference to Leetown), Virginia, October 15, 1864.]

SCOTT, HUMPHREY P., Private
Born in Haywood County and was by occupation a farmer prior to enlisting in Haywood County at age 32, June 13, 1862, for the war. Reported on detached service in September-October, 1862. Reported sick in hospital at Strawberry Plains, Tennessee, November-December, 1862. Died at Strawberry Plains on January 19, 1863, of "disease."

SCOTT, J. A., Private
Confederate gravestone records appear to indicate that he served in this legion. Survived the war. [He may have been the same man as Pvt. John K. Scott of this company.]

SCOTT, JOHN K., Private
Born in Haywood County and was by occupation a farmer prior to enlisting in Haywood County at age 25, June 13, 1862, for the war. Reported present in September-October, 1862; January-June, 1863; and September, 1863-February, 1864. Name appears on a receipt roll for clothing dated September 17, 1864. No further records. [He may have been the same man as Pvt. J. A. Scott of this company.]

SHARP, DAVID ALLEN, Private
Born in Haywood County where he resided as a farmer prior to enlisting in Haywood County at age 23, June 13, 1862, for the war. Reported present in September-October, 1862. Reported sick in hospital at Strawberry Plains, Tennessee, in November, 1862-February, 1863. Reported on sick furlough in March-April, 1863. Returned to duty prior to June 30, 1863. Reported absent without leave, "supposed to have reported to Col. Thomas in N.C.," in September-October, 1863. Listed as a deserter in November-December, 1863. Returned to duty on an unspecified date. Name appears on a receipt roll for clothing dated July 23, 1864. Reported on extra duty as a shoemaker in the "Mountain District of Western North Carolina" from September 9 through October 16, 1864, and in November, 1864. Deserted to the enemy in Haywood County on March 28, 1865. Confined at Knoxville, Tennessee, April 15, 1865. Transferred to Chattanooga, Tennessee, after taking the Oath of Allegiance, April 17, 1865. Transferred to Louisville, Kentucky. Released at Louisville on April 28, 1865, after affirming the Oath of Allegiance, with instructions to remain north of the Ohio River for the remainder of the war.

SHARP, EDWARD D., Private
Born in Haywood County and was by occupation a farmer prior to enlisting in Haywood County at age 22, June 13, 1862, for the war. Reported present in September-October, 1862. Reported on duty as a nurse in hospital at Strawberry Plains, Tennessee, February 14-27, 1863. Rejoined the company on February 28, 1863. Reported present in March-June, 1863. Reported absent without leave, "supposed to have reported to Col. Thomas in N.C." in September-October, 1863. Returned to duty prior to December 31, 1863. Reported present in January-February, 1864. No further records. Survived the war. [North Carolina pension records indicate that he was wounded in the head at Piedmont, Virginia, June 5, 1864.]

SHARP, J. P., _____
North Carolina pension records indicate that he served in this company. Survived the war. [He may have been the same man as Pvt. Joseph Sharp of this company.]

SHARP, JOSEPH, Private
Born in Haywood County and was by occupation a farmer prior to enlisting in Haywood County at age 17, June 13, 1862, for the war. No further records. [He may have been the same man as Pvt. J. P. Sharp of this company.]

SHARP, WINSTON, Private
Born in Virginia. Resided in Haywood County and was by occupation a farmer prior to enlisted at Locust Field (present-day Canton) at age 33, March 1, 1863, for the war. Reported present through June 30, 1863. Reported sick in hospital at White Sulphur Springs, West Virginia, September-October, 1863. Returned to duty prior to December 31, 1863. Reported present in January-February, 1864. Name appears on receipt rolls for clothing dated September 2 and September 19, 1864. No further records. Survived the war.

SHOOP, J. N., _____
Name appears on a register of Confederate officers and soldiers who were killed in battle or died of wounds or disease. Probably served either in this company or in Company C, Walker's Battalion. Died at Strawberry Plains, Tennessee, December 27, 1862. Cause of death unknown.

SMATHERS, CHARLES L., Private
Born in Haywood County and enlisted at Locust Field (present-day Canton) on January 1, 1863, for the war. Mustered in as Corporal. Reported on detached service in January-February, 1863. Rejoined the company prior to April 30, 1863. Reduced to ranks prior to April 30, 1863. Reported present in May-June, 1863. Reported absent without leave, "supposed to have reported to Col. Thomas," in September-October, 1863. Returned to duty prior to December 31, 1863. Reported present in January-February, 1864. Name appears on receipt rolls for clothing dated June 21, September 1, and September 27, 1864. No further records. Survived the war. [Records of the United Daughters of the Confederacy indicate, probably erroneously, that he served as Corporal in Company C, 29th Regiment N.C. Troops.]

SMATHERS, GEORGE A., Private
Resided in Haywood County and was by occupation a farmer prior to enlising at Locust Field (present-day Canton) at age 18, January 1, 1863, for the war. Reported on detached service in January-February, 1863. Reported on detached duty and sick in March-April, 1863. Reported sick at home in May-June and September-October, 1863. Returned to duty prior to December 31, 1863. Reported present in January-February, 1864. No further records. Survived the war.

SMATHERS, GEORGE M., Private
Born in Haywood County and was by occupation a farmer prior to enlisting in Haywood County at age 32, June 13, 1862, for the war. Reported on detached service in September-October, 1862. Reported sick in hospital at Strawberry Plains, Tennessee, November-December, 1862. Reported on detached service in January-February, 1863. Rejoined the company prior to April 30, 1863. Reported present in May-June, 1863. Reported absent without leave, "supposed to have reported to Col Thomas who was cut off with a portion of the command in the evacuation of E[ast] T[ennessee]" in September-October, 1863. Returned to duty prior to December 31, 1863. Reported present in January-February, 1864. Name appears on receipt rolls for clothing dated August 18 and September 17, 1864. No further records. Survived the war.

SMATHERS, JAMES HENRY, Private
Born in Haywood County on April 2, 1830. Was by occupation a farmer prior to enlisting in Haywood County at age 32, June 13, 1862, for the war. Reported on detached service in September-October, 1862. Reported sick in hospital at Strawberry Plains, Tennessee, November-December, 1862. Returned to duty prior to February 28, 1863. Reported present in March-April, 1863. Reported sick in hospital at Greeneville, Tennessee, in May-June, 1863. Reported absent without leave, "supposed to have reported to Col. Thomas who was cut off with a portion of the command in the evacuation of E[ast] T[ennessee]" in September-October, 1863. Returned to duty in November-December, 1863. Reported present in January-February, 1864. Wounded at Winchester, Virginia, September 19, 1864. No further records. Survived the war. [He may have served previously as Private in Company C, 29th Regiment N.C. Troops.]

SMATHERS, JESSE C., Sergeant
Born in Haywood County and was by occupation a farmer prior to enlisting in Haywood County at age 22, June 13, 1862, for the war. Mustered in as Private. Reported present in September-October, 1862. Promoted to Sergeant on December 26, 1862. Reported present in November-December, 1862, and January-February, 1863. Reported on detached service and sick in March-April, 1863. Returned to duty prior to June 30, 1863. Reported absent without leave, "supposed to have reported to Col. Thomas who was cut off with a portion of the command in the evacuation of E[ast] Tenn[essee]" in September-October, 1863. Listed as a deserter in November-December, 1863. Name appears on receipt rolls for clothing dated September 2 and September 17, 1864. No further records. Survived the war.

SMATHERS, JESSE D., Private
Born in Haywood County and was a farmer prior to enlisting in Haywood County at age 19, June 13, 1862, for the war. Reported present in September-October, 1862. Reported on detached service in November-December, 1862. Rejoined the company prior to February 28, 1863. Reported present in March-June, 1863, and September, 1863-February, 1864. Name appears on receipt rolls for clothing dated June 21 and September 1, 1864. No further records. Survived the war.

SMATHERS, MANSON, Private
Born in Haywood County and was by occupation a farmer prior to enlisting in Haywood County at age 31, June 13, 1862, for the war. Mustered in as Private. Promoted to Corporal prior to October 31, 1862. Reported present in September-October, 1862. Reported sick in camp in January-February, 1863. Reported on detached service and sick in March-April, 1863. Rejoined the company prior to June 30, 1863. Reported absent without leave, "supposed to be with Col. Thomas in N.C.," in September-October, 1863. Returned to duty prior to December 31, 1863. Reported present in January-February, 1864. Reduced to ranks prior to October 1, 1864. Reported on duty as a mechanic from September 19 through December 31, 1864. Deserted to the enemy in Haywood County on March 27, 1865. Sent to Knoxville, Tennessee. Took the Oath of Allegiance at Knoxville and transferred to Chattanooga, Tennessee, April 17, 1865. Confined at Louisville, Kentucky, April 27, 1865. Released at Louisville on April 28, 1865, after affirming the Oath of Allegiance, and sent north of the Ohio River for the remainder of the war.

SMATHERS, NELSON AMANUEL, Private
Born in Haywood County and enlisted at Locust Field (present-day Canton) at age 34, June 13, 1862, for the war. Reported on sick furlough in September-October, 1862. Reported sick in camp in January-February, 1863. Returned to duty prior to April 30, 1863. Reported present in May-June, 1863, and September-December, 1863. Reported absent without leave in January-February, 1864. Returned to duty on an unspecified date. Reported on duty as a mechanic from October 1 through October 24, 1864, and in November-December, 1864. No further records. Survived the war.

SMATHERS, NELSON N., Private
Confederate gravestone records appear to indicate that he served in this company.

SMATHERS, PHILIP, Private
Born in Haywood County and enlisted in Haywood County at age 27, June 13, 1862, for the war. Reported present in September-October, 1862. Died on January 12, 1863, of "disease." Place of death not reported.

SMATHERS, WILLIAM J., Sergeant
Born in Haywood County and was by occupation a farmer prior to enlisting in Haywood County at age 20, June 13, 1862, for the war. Mustered in as Sergeant. Reported present in September-October, 1862. Reported on detached service in November-December, 1862. Rejoined the company prior to February 28, 1863. Reported present in March-June, 1863. Reported absent without leave, "supposed to have reported to Col. Thomas who was cut off with a portion of the command in the evacuation of E[ast] Tenn[essee]," in September-October, 1863. Returned to duty prior to December 31, 1863. Reported present in January-February, 1864. Captured at Winchester, Virginia, August 17, 1864. Confined at Old Capitol Prison, Washington, D.C., August 22, 1864. Transferred to Elmira, New York, August 28, 1864. Died at Elmira on November 2, 1864, of "chronic diarrhoea." [His middle name may have been Jasper.]

SMITH, WILLIS T., Private

Reported present on a muster roll for July 19-August 31, 1862, but his name is cancelled. Probably never served in this company. Later served in Company G of this regiment.

STINES, WILLIAM A., Private

Born in Buncombe County and was by occupation a farmer prior to enlisting in Haywood County at age 29, June 13, 1862, for the war. No further records. Survived the war.

TAYLOR, G. W., Private

His name appears on a "Roll of Prisoners of War of Johnston's Army" stating that he was a Private in "Co C Thomas N.C. Infty" paroled at Greensboro on May 8, 1865. It is likely that he did not serve in this legion, as this legion was not with Johnston at Greensboro.

THOMPSON, JAMES A., Private

Previously enlisted as Private in either Company E of this regiment or in Company E, Walker's Battalion. Transferred to this company on April 11, 1863. Reported present through June 30, 1863. Reported absent without leave, "supposed to have reported to Col. Thomas in N.C.," in September-October, 1863. Listed as a deserter in November-December, 1863. Name appears on a receipt roll for clothing dated September 1, 1864. No further records.

TROY, WESLEY CLARK, Private

Confederate gravestone records appear to indicate that he served in this company. Survived the war.

TRULL, BENJAMIN R., Corporal

Born in South Carolina or Haywood County and was by occupation a farmer prior to enlisting in Haywood County at age 24, June 13, 1862, for the war. Mustered in as Corporal. Reported present in September-October, 1862, January-June, 1863, and September, 1863-February, 1864. Name appears on receipt rolls for clothing dated August 18 and September 19, 1864. No further records. Survived the war.

TRULL, BRANCH H. M., Corporal

Born in Haywood County and was by occupation a farmer prior to enlisting in Haywood County at age 31, June 13, 1862, for the war. Mustered in as Corporal. Reported present in September-October, 1862. Reported on detached service in November-December, 1862. Rejoined the company prior to February 28, 1863, when he was reported sick in camp. Returned to duty prior to April 30, 1863. Reported sick in hospital in Athens, Tennessee, May-June, 1863. Reported absent without leave, "supposed to be with Col. Thomas in N.C.," September-October, 1863. Reported captured at Warm Springs on October 9, 1863. Sent to Camp Nelson, Kentucky. Transferred to Camp Chase, Ohio, where he arrived on November 14, 1863. Transferred to Rock Island, Illinois, January 22, 1864. Paroled at Rock Island on February 25, 1865. Received at Boulware's Wharf, James River, Virginia, March 5, 1865, for exchange. Hospitalized at Richmond, Virginia, March 6, 1865, with chronic diarrhoea. Furloughed for thirty days on March 7, 1865. No further records. Survived the war.

TRULL, JAMES R., Private

Born in Haywood County and was by occupation a farmer prior to enlisting in Haywood County at age 20, June 13, 1862, for the war. Mustered in as Private. Reported present in September-October, 1862. Appointed Musician (Fifer) prior to October 31, 1862. Reported sick in hospital at Strawberry Plains, Tennessee, November-December, 1862. Reported on sick furlough in January-February, 1863. Returned to duty prior to April 30, 1863. Reported present in May-June, 1863, and September, 1863-February, 1864. Reduced to ranks on an unspecified date. Deserted to the enemy on March 27, 1865. Sent to Knoxville, Tennessee, where he arrived on April 16, 1865. Took the Oath of Allegiance at Knoxville on April 17, 1865. Transferred to Chattanooga, Tennessee, the same date. Confined at Louisville, Kentucky, on or about April 25, 1865. Took the Oath of Allegiance at Louisville on the same date. Released at Louisville on June 2, 1865, with orders to remain north of the Ohio River for the duration of the war.

TRULL, THOMAS G., Private

Previously enlisted as Private in Company E of this regiment. Transferred to this company on or about April 11, 1863. Reported present on April 30, 1863. Died at Greeneville, Tennessee, June 10, 1863. Cause of death not reported.

WADE, JOHN R., Private

Born in Haywood County and was by occupation a farmer prior to enlisting in Haywood County on June 13, 1862, for the war. Reported present through October 31, 1862. Died at Strawberry Plains, Tennessee, November 25, 1862. Cause of death not reported.

WALL, JOHN D., Private

Enlisted, probably at Strawberry Plains, Tennessee, at about age 31, January 2, 1863, for the war. Transferred to Company D of this regiment in January 10, 1863.

WATTS, DAVID, Private

Born in Haywood County and was by occupation a farmer prior to enlisting in Haywood County at age 32, June 13, 1862, for the war. Reported absent without leave in September-October, 1862. Returned to duty prior to December 31, 1862. Reported sick in hospital at Strawberry Plains, Tennessee, in January-February, 1863. Returned to duty prior to April 30, 1863. Reported sick in hospital at Athens, Tennessee, in May-June, 1863. Reported absent without leave, "supposed to have reported to Col. Thomas in N[orth] C[arolina]" in September-October, 1863. Returned to duty prior to December 31, 1863. Reported present in January-February, 1864. Name appears on receipt rolls for clothing dated August 18 and September 22, 1864. No further records. Survived the war.

WEBB, JOHN, Private

Resided in Grainger County, Tennessee. Enlisted either in this company or in Company C, Walker's Battalion, at about age 29, January 2, 1863, for the war. Probably enlisted either at Strawberry Plains, Tennessee, or at Knoxville, Tennessee. Transferred to 2nd Company D, Walker's Battalion, January 10, 1863.

WEST, JOHN S., Sergeant

Born in Haywood County and was by occupation a farmer prior to enlisting in Haywood County at age 24, June 13, 1862, for the war. Mustered in as Private. Reported present in September-October, 1862, January-June, 1863; and September, 1863-February, 1864. Promoted to Sergeant in November-December, 1863. Wounded in the left forearm at Cedar Creek, Virginia, October 19, 1864. Hospitalized at Charlottesville, Virginia, October 26, 1864. Transferred to hospital at Lynchburg, Virginia, November 5, 1864. No further records. Survived the war.

WEST, WILLIAM, Private
Enlisted in Company E of this regiment on April 11, 1863. Transferred to this company on the same date. Reported present through June 30, 1863. Reported absent without leave, "supposed to have reported to Col. Thomas in N.C." in September-October, 1863. Returned to duty prior to December 31, 1863. Reported present in January-February, 1864. Hospitalized at Charlottesville, Virginia, June 7, 1864, with acute diarrhoea. Returned to duty on June 13, 1864. Hospitalized at Richmond, Virginia, August 24, 1864. Furloughed for thirty-five days on August 26, 1864. No further records. Survived the war.

WILLIAMS, A. W., Private
Confederate gravestone records appear to indicate that he served in this company.

WILLIAMS, JAMES S., Private
Born in Haywood County and was by occupation a farmer prior to enlisting in Haywood County at age 18, June 13, 1862, for the war. Reported present in September-October, 1862, and in January-June, 1863. Reported absent without leave, "supposed to have reported to Col. Thomas in N.C.," in September-October, 1863. Returned to duty prior to December 31, 1863. Reported present in January-February, 1864. Name appears on receipt rolls for clothing dated August 18 and September 27, 1864. No further records.

WILLIAMS, JOHN A., Private
Born in Haywood County and was by occupation a farmer prior to enlisting in Haywood County at age 21, June 13, 1862, for the war. Reported on detached service, September-October, 1862. Reported absent sick in hospital at Strawberry Plains, Tennessee, November-December, 1862. Reported on detached service in January-February, 1863. Rejoined the company prior to April 30, 1863. Reported present in May-June, 1863. Reported absent without leave, "supposed to have reported to Col. Thomas in N.C." in September-October, 1863. Returned to duty prior to December 31, 1863. Reported present in January-February, 1864. Name appears on a receipt roll for clothing dated September 26, 1864. No further records. Survived the war.

WILLIAMS, R. P., Private
Resided in Haywood County. Place and date of enlistment not reported; probably enlisted subsequent to February 29, 1864. Name appears on receipt rolls for clothing dated September 2 and September 17, 1864. Deserted to the enemy in Haywood County on March 27, 1865. Confined at Knoxville, Tennessee, April 16, 1865. Took the Oath of Allegiance at Knoxville, April 17, 1865. Transferred to Chattanooga, Tennessee, the same date. Confined at Louisville, Kentucky, on or about April 25, 1865. Released at Louisville on April 28, 1865, after taking the Oath of Allegiance, with instructions "to remain North of the Ohio River during the war."

WILLIAMS, VIRGIL H., Private
Born in Haywood County and was by occupation a farmer prior to enlisting in Haywood County at age 24, June 13, 1862, for the war. Reported present, September-October, 1862. Reported on detached service, November-December, 1862. Rejoined the company prior to February 28, 1863. Reported present in March-June, 1863. Reported absent without leave, "supposed to have reported to Col. Thomas in N.C.," in September-October, 1863. Returned to duty prior to December 31, 1863. Reported present in January-February, 1864. No further records. [He may have been killed at Piedmont, Virginia, June 5, 1864.]

WILLIAMS, W. J. L., Private
Confederate gravestone records appear to indicate that he served in this company.

WINCHESTER, JAMES, Private
Confederate gravestone records appear to indicate that he served in this company.

WISE, G. W., Private
Resided in Buncombe County. Place and date of enlistment not reported; probably enlisted subsequent to February 29, 1864. Deserted to the enemy on March 28, 1865. Confined at Knoxville, Tennessee. Took the Oath of Allegiance at Knoxville, April 17, 1865. Transferred to Chattanooga, Tennessee, the same date. Confined at Louisville, Kentucky, on or about April 27, 1865. Released at Louisville on April 28, 1865, after taking the Oath of Allegiance, with instructions "to remain north of the Ohio River during the war."

WOODS, JONATHAN, Private
Resided in Haywood County where he was by occupation a farmer prior to enlisting in Haywood County at age 35, June 13, 1862, for the war. Reported present in September-October, 1862. Reported absent on detached duty from December 25, 1862, through June 30, 1863. Served as a wagoner during most or all of that period. Reported absent without leave, "supposed to have reported to Col. Thomas in N.C.," in September-October, 1863. Returned to duty prior to December 31, 1863. Reported present in January-February, 1864. No further records. Survived the war.

YOUNG, JOSEPH, Private
Resided in Haywood County where he enlisted at Locust Field (present-day Canton) on June 13, 1862, for the war. Reported present, September-October, 1862. Reported on detached service, November-December, 1862. Rejoined the company prior to February 28, 1863. Reported present in March-June, 1863. Reported absent without leave, "supposed to have reported to Col. Thomas in N.C.," September-October, 1863. Returned to duty prior to December 31, 1863. Reported present in January-February, 1864. Deserted to the enemy in Haywood County on March 27, 1865. Confined at Knoxville, Tennessee, April 16, 1865. Took the Oath of Allegiance at Knoxville, April 17, 1865. Transferred to Chattanooga, Tennessee, the same date. Confined at Louisville, Kentucky, April 27, 1865. Released at Louisville on April 28, 1865, after taking the Oath of Allegiance, and ordered "to remain North of the Ohio River during the war."

COMPANY D

This company was raised in Tennessee, in Jefferson, Knox, Grainger and Union Counties. It served previously as 2nd Company D, Walker's Battalion of this Legion. It was transferred to this regiment in late February, 1863.

The following roster was compiled in large part from company muster rolls dated January-June, 1863, September, 1863-February, 1864, and April 8, 1864. These are abstracted in the microfilm edition of the Compiled Service Records of Confederate Soldiers Who Served in Organizations from the State of North Carolina (Record Group 109, M270), National Archives, Washington, D.C. Other valuable information in the Compiled Service Records includes enlistment papers, pay vouchers, requisitions, letters of resignation, discharge certificates, and abstracts of medical and prisoner of war records.

Also utilized in this roster were *The War of the Rebellion: A Compilation of the Official Records of the Union and Confederate Armies*, the North Carolina Adjutant General's papers, state militia records, newspaper casualty lists and obituaries, wartime claims for bounty pay and allowances, postwar registers of claims for artificial limbs, Confederate pension applications filed with the states of North Carolina, Tennessee, and Florida, records of the North Carolina Confederate Soldiers' Home, and the 1860 and 1870 federal censuses of North Carolina. A search was made also for relevant letters, diaries, reminiscences, and other manuscripts in the Southern Historical Collection (University of North Carolina-Chapel Hill) and the Duke University Library Special Collections Department.

Among the secondary sources consulted were records of the North Carolina division of the United Daughters of the Confederacy, postwar rosters, regimental and county histories, marriage bond, will, and cemetery indexes, published and unpublished genealogies, biographical dictionaries, the North Carolina *County Heritage Book* series, the *Confederate Veteran*, Walter Clark's *Histories of the Several Regiments and Battalions from North Carolina in the Great War, 1861-'65*, and the North Carolina volume of the extended edition of *Confederate Military History*.

OFFICERS

CAPTAIN

LOVE, WILLIAM B.

Previously served as Captain of Company D, Walker's Battalion. Transferred to this company in late February, 1863. Reported present through April 30, 1863. Reported absent sick from May 26 through June 30, 1863. Probably returned to duty prior to July 11, 1863. Reported present in September-October, 1863. Reported on leave from December 6 through 12, 1863. Returned to duty prior to December 31, 1863. Reported present in January-February, 1864, and on April 8, 1864. Captured at Knoxville, Tennessee, May 1, 1865. Released by a civil court at Knoxville "on bond" on May 24, 1865. Took the Oath of Allegiance at Chattanooga, Tennessee, June 5, 1865. [His capture at Knoxville on May 1, 1865, indicates that he was a member of Lt. Col. William W. Stringfield's flag-of-truce party that was arrested when they refused to take the Oath of Allegiance.]

LIEUTENANTS

CARMACK, ALEXANDER R., 2nd Lieutenant

Previously served as Sergeant in 2nd Company D, Walker's Battalion. Transferred to this company in late February, 1863. Reported present until promoted to Sergeant Major of this regimen on April 1, 1863, and transferred to the Field and Staff. Appointed 2nd Lieutenant and transferred back to this company subsequent to October 5, 1864. Wounded in the left thigh and captured at Cedar Creek, Virginia, October 19, 1864. Hospitalized at Baltimore, Maryland, October 25, 1864. Confined at Point Lookout, Maryland, November 23, 1864. Confined at Old Capitol Prison, Washington, D.C., January 3, 1865. Confined at Fort Delaware, Delaware, February 4, 1865. Released at Fort Delaware on June 17, 1865, after taking the Oath of Allegiance.

JONES, WILLIAM W., 2nd Lieutenant

Previously served as Private in 2nd Company D, Walker's Battalion. Transferred to this company in late February, 1863. Reported present through April 30, 1863. Promoted to Sergeant on April 1, 1863. Appointed 3rd Lieutenant on May 9, 1863. Reported on detached service to bring in absentees, June 28-30, 1863. Reported present in September, 1863-February, 1864. Promoted to 2nd Lieutenant in March-April, 1864. Reported present on April 8, 1864. Wounded and probably captured at Winchester, Virginia, September 19, 1864, and hospitalized. Died on October 5, 1864, probably at Winchester, probably of wounds.

McBEE, GAINUM C., 1st Lieutenant

Previously served as 1st Lieutenant of 2nd Company D, Walker's Battalion. Transferred to this company in late February, 1863. Reported present through April 30, 1863. Reported on leave, June 28-30, 1863. Reported present, September, 1863-February, 1864. Resigned on March 2, 1864, because of "rheumatism." Resignation accepted on March 16, 1864. Later served as Private in Company C, 1st Regiment Tennessee Cavalry (Carter's). [His first name may have been Ganum.]

NEEDHAM, HENRY, 3rd Lieutenant

Previously served as 3rd Lieutenant in 2nd Company D, Walker's Battalion. Transferred to this company in late February, 1863. Reported present through February 28, 1863. Resigned on March 21, 1863, for "the good of the service." Resignation accepted the same day "on the grounds of incompetency." [A company muster roll dated April 8, 1864, states that he resigned and was transferred to the 1st Regiment Tennessee Cavalry; but there is no other evidence that he served in that unit.]

PECK, ADAM C., 1st Lieutenant

Previously served as 1st Sergeant in 2nd Company D, Walker's Battalion. Transferred to this company in late February, 1863. Reported present through April 30, 1863. Appointed 2nd Lieutenant on May 9, 1863. Reported present in May-June, 1863, and September, 1863-February, 1864. Promoted to 1st Lieutenant in March-April, 1864. Reported present on April 8, 1864. [Clark's *Regiments*, 3:747, indicates that he was killed at Piedmont, Virginia, June 5, 1864.]

SMART, THOMAS R., 2nd Lieutenant

Previously served as 2nd Lieutenant of 2nd Company D, Walker's Battalion. Transferred to this company in late February, 1863. Reported absent on detail to apprehend deserters on February 28, 1863. Resigned on March 19, 1863, because of rheumatism. Requested also that he be transferred as a Private to a cavalry unit. Resignation accepted on April 2, 1863, "on the grounds of incompetency." [A company muster roll dated April 8, 1864, indicates that he was transferred to the 1st Regiment Tennessee Cavalry, but there is no other evidence that he served in that unit.]

NONCOMMISSIONED OFFICERS AND PRIVATES

ALEXANDER, JESSE P., Corporal
Previously served as Private in Capt. John T. Levi's Battery. Transferred to this company March 1-April 8, 1864. Mustered in as Private. Reported present on April 8, 1864. Promoted to Corporal prior to June 4, 1864. Wounded and captured at Winchester, Virginia, September 19, 1864. Sent to Harpers Ferry, West Virginia. Transferred to Point Lookout, Maryland, September 23, 1864. Arrived at Point Lookout on September 26, 1864. Paroled at Point Lookout on March 15, 1865. Received at Boulware's Wharf, James River, Virginia, March 18, 1865, for exchange. Reported at Camp Lee, near Richmond, Virginia, March 19, 1865. Took the Oath of Allegiance at Chattanooga, Tennessee, May 21, 1865.

ALEXANDER, THOMAS, Private
Previously served as Private in 2nd Company D, Walker's Battalion. Transferred to this company in late February, 1863. Reported on duty as a teamster in the quartermaster department through June 30, 1863. Reported present in September, 1863-February, 1864, and on April 8, 1864. No further records.

ALLEN, ANDERSON, Private
Previously served as Private in 2nd Company D, Walker's Battalion. Transferred to this company in late February, 1863. Reported present through February 28, 1863. Reported in hospital at Mossy Creek, Tennessee, April 28, 1863. Hospitalized at Carter's Depot, Tennessee, June 16, 1863. Furloughed home on July 5, 1863. Failed to return to duty and was listed as a deserter in November-December, 1863.

ARMS, EDWARD, Private
Previously served as Private in 2nd Company D, Walker's Battalion. Transferred to this company in late February, 1863. Reported present on February 28, 1863. Reported on detached service at Strawberry Plains, Tennessee, from April 7, 1863, through February 29, 1864, and on April 8, 1864, serving as a teamster at least part of this time. Reported to be "getting out timber for post commissary" at Strawberry Plains on April 30, 1863. No further records.

BAILEY, JAMES W., Corporal
Previously served as Private in 2nd Company D, Walker's Battalion. Transferred to this company in late February, 1863. Mustered in as Private. Reported present through June 30, 1863. Detailed for duty at Bristol, Tennessee, October 30, 1863. Rejoined the company and was promoted to Corporal prior to December 31, 1863. Reported present in January-February, 1864, and on April 8, 1864. Hospitalized at Charlottesville, Virginia, in June, 1864, with debilitas. Signed a receipt for shoes datelined Lexington, Virginia, June 27, 1864. Name appears on a receipt roll for clothing dated July 19, 1864. No further records.

BATES, JAMES, Private
Enlisted at Strawberry Plains, Tennessee, at age 27, March 9, 1863, for the war. Reported on detached service at Strawberry Plains, Tennessee, from April 7, 1863, through April 8, 1864. Employed at least part of that period in "getting out timber for post commissary" and as a teamster in July, 1863. No further records.

BATES, JOHN, Private
Enlisted at Strawberry Plains, Tennessee, at age 25, March 9, 1863, for the war. Reported on detached service at Strawberry Plains from April 7, 1863, through April 8, 1864. Employed at least part of that period in "getting out timber for post commissary" and as a teamster in July-August, 1863. No further records.

BERRY, MICHAEL, Private
Enlisted at Carter's Depot, Tennessee, at age 47, July 1, 1863, for the war as a substitute for Pvt. James V. Walker. Deserted August 1, 1863. No further records.

BETTIS, JOSEPH E., Sergeant
Previously served as Private in 2nd Company D, Walker's Battalion. Transferred to this company in late February, 1863. Reported present but sick on February 28, 1863. Reported present in March-June, 1863. Promoted to Corporal prior to October 31, 1863, and promoted to Sergeant in November-December, 1863. Reported present in September, 1863-February, 1864, and on April 8, 1864. Hospitalized at Winchester, Virginia, July 30, 1864, with debilitas. Returned to duty on August 5, 1864. Name appears on a receipt roll for clothing dated December 14, 1864. No further records. Survived the war.

BETTIS, P. E., Sergeant
Previously served as Private in 2nd Company D, Walker's Battalion. Transferred to this company in late February, 1863. Reported sick at home on February 28, 1863. Returned to duty prior to April 30, 1863. Detailed to bring in absentees on June 28, 1863. Promoted to Corporal prior to October 31, 1863. Reported present in September-December, 1863. Promoted to Sergeant in November-December, 1863. Reported present in January-February, 1864, and on April 8, 1864. Killed at Piedmont, Virginia, June 5, 1864.

BRAZELTON, JOHN F., Private
Enlisted at Strawberry Plains, Tennessee, at age 30, March 31, 1863, for the war. Discharged on or about April 5, 1863, after providing Pvt. Manas Dawson as a substitute.

BRINDLE, J. P., Sergeant
Place and date of enlistment not reported. Promotion record not reported. Captured on May 27, 1864. Sent to Knoxville, Tennessee. Released on June 14, 1864, after taking the Oath of Allegiance.

CARTER, PEYTON, Private
Enlisted at Strawberry Plains, Tennessee, at about age 19, March 9, 1863, for the war. Reported absent sick on April 30, 1863. Reported on duty as a blacksmith at Strawberry Plains in May-June, 1863. Reported on duty as a mechanic at Strawberry Plains, August 1-31, 1863. Reported on duty as a blacksmith at Strawberry Plains, September, 1863-February, 1864; and on April 8, 1864. No further records.

CATES, JOHN H., Private
Previously served as Private in 2nd Company D, Walker's Battalion. Transferred to this company in February, 1863, while absent without leave. Reported as a deserter in March-April, 1863, and was subsequently dropped from the company rolls.

CHILDERS, J. M., Sergeant
Previously served as Private in 2nd Company D, Walker's Battalion. Transferred to this company in late February, 1863. Reported present through June 30, 1863. Promoted to Corporal in September-October, 1863. Promoted to Sergeant in November-December, 1863. Reported present in September, 1863-February, 1864, and on April 8, 1864. Name appears on receipt rolls for clothing dated June 4, July 19, and December 14, 1864. No further records.

CLARK, HUGH L., Private
Previously served as Private in Company A, Indian Battalion. Transferred to this company on February 10, 1864. Deserted at Carter's Depot, Tennessee, February 22, 1864. [He was 28 years of age in 1864.]

CLARK, JOB, Private
Previously served as Private in 2nd Company D, Walker's Battalion. Transferred to this company in late February, 1863. Reported present through April 30, 1863. Reported absent without leave on June 29, 1863. Reported on sick furlough beginning August 22, 1863. Failed to return to duty and was listed as a deserter in November-December, 1863. "Reclaimed from desertion" on February 10, 1864, and was placed under arrest. Reported present on April 8, 1864. No further records.

CLIFT, D. H., Private
Previously enlisted as Private in 2nd Company D, Walker's Battalion, but was serving in Company E, 12th Battalion Tennessee Cavalry (Day's and Phipps'), when he was captured at Murfreesboro, Tennessee, December 31, 1862. Transferred to this company in late February, 1863, while a prisoner of war. Released from prison prior to May 15, 1863, when he reported for duty with this company. Reported present through June 30, 1863. "Reclaimed" by Company E, 12th Battalion Tennessee Cavalry (Day's and Phipps's), August 15, 1863.

CLIFT, HENRY L., Private
Previously served as Private in 2nd Company D, Walker's Battalion. Transferred to this company in late February, 1863. Reported on detached service at Strawberry Plains, Tennessee, from April 7, 1863, through April 8, 1864. Reported on duty as a mechanic and "getting out timber for post commissary" during part of that period. No further records.

CLIFT, MARION, Private
Previously served as Private in 2nd Company D, Walker's Battalion. Transferred to this company in late February, 1863. Reported on detached service at Strawberry Plains, Tennessee, from April 7, 1863, through April 8, 1864. Reported on duty as a teamster and "getting out timber for post commissary" during part of that period. No further records.

COATS, JOHN H., Private
Previously enlisted as Private in 2nd Company D, Walker's Battalion. Transferred to this company in late February, 1863. Reported present through April 6, 1863. Reported on detail at Strawberry Plains, Tennessee, from April 7, 1863, through April 8, 1864. Served for at least part of that period as a teamster in the quartermaster department. No further records.

COBB, WILLIAM P., Private
Previously served as Private in 2nd Company D, Walker's Battalion. Transferred to this company in late February, 1863. Reported present through June 30, 1863, and in September-October, 1863. Reported on detached service in Bristol, Tennessee, October 30, 1863. Rejoined the company prior to December 30, 1863. Reported present in January-February, 1864, and on April 8, 1864. Wounded in the left hand at Winchester, Virginia, on or about September 19, 1864. Captured at Knoxville, Tennessee, May 1, 1865. Sent to Nashville, Tennessee. Transferred to Louisville, Kentucky, where he arrived on May 14, 1865. Released at Louisville on June 16, 1865, after taking the Oath of Allegiance. [See his Tennessee pension application No. 2456. His capture at Knoxville on May 1 indicates that he was a member of Lt. Col. Stringfield's flag-of-truce party that was arrested when they refused to take the Oath of Allegiance.]

COFFMAN, WILLIAM, Private
Previously served as Private in 2nd Company D, Walker's Battalion. Transferred to this company in late February, 1863. Reported present through February 28, 1863. Reported on detached service in the quartermaster department at Strawberry Plains, Tennessee, in March-June and August-December, 1863. Served as a teamster for at least part of that period. Rejoined the company on February 29, 1864. Reported present on April 8, 1864. Name appears on receipt rolls for clothing dated June 4 and July 19, 1864. *Southern Historical Society Papers*, 15:463, indicates that he surrendered at Appomattox Court House, Virginia, April 9, 1865, as a member of the Invalid Battalion commanded by Lt. Benjamin Bates.

COHEN, JAMES L., Private
Previously served as Private in 2nd Company D, Walker's Battalion. Transferred to this company in late February, 1863. Reported present until June 26, 1863, when he was reported absent without leave. Transferred to Capt. John T. Levi's Battery, August 1, 1863. [His surname may have been Coin.]

COKER, JAMES H., Private
Previously served as Private in 2nd Company D, Walker's Battalion. Transferred to this company in late February, 1863. Reported on detail working on a military road until May 9, 1863, when he was transferred to Company I of this regiment.

COZART, JAMES, Private
Previously served as Private in 2nd Company D, Walker's Battalion. Transferred to this company in late February, 1863. Reported present through June 30, 1863. Reported on detached service with Company A, 3rd Regiment Confederate Engineers, from August 5, 1863, through February 29, 1864. No further records.

DARROW, J. M., _____
Place and date of enlistment not reported; probably enlisted subsequent to April 8, 1864. Deserted to the enemy on an unspecified date. Took the Oath of Allegiance at Knoxville, Tennessee, December 4-16, 1864.

DAWSON, MANAS, Private
Enlisted at Strawberry Plains, Tennessee, at about age 58, April 5, 1863, for the war as a substitute for Pvt. John F. Brazelton of this company. Reported on detached service at Strawberry Plains from

April 7, 1863 through April 8, 1864. Served at least part of that time as a mechanic. No further records.

DEAN, JESSE H., Musician
Enlisted at Zollicoffer, Tennessee, at about age 16, August 22, 1863, for the war. Mustered in as Musician (Drummer). Reported present through February 29, 1864, and on April 8, 1864. Name appears on receipt rolls for clothing dated July 19 and September 1, 1864. No further records.

DEAN, T. J. R., Private
Enlisted at Zollicoffer, Tennessee, at about age 44, August 22, 1863, for the war. Deserted at Zollicoffer on August 27, 1863. [He may have served previously as Private in Company C, 29th Regiment Tennessee Infantry. His records indicate that, while a deserter from Thomas's Legion, he enlisted illegally in an unknown company of the 1st Regiment Tennessee Cavalry (Carter's); however, no surviving records of that unit confirm his service.]

DONEHEW, BENJAMIN, Private
Previously served as Private in 2nd Company D, Walker's Battalion. Transferred to this company in late February, 1863. Reported present through April 30, 1863. Promoted to Sergeant on May 22, 1863. Reported absent without leave on June 15, 1863. Returned to duty and was reduced to ranks prior to October 31, 1863. Deserted at Blain's Crossroads, Tennessee, December 5, 1863. [His surname may have been Donahew.]

DOUGLASS, ALEX J., Private
Previously served as Private in Company G, Walker's Battalion. Enlisted in this company on an unspecified date. Reported on detail as a wagon master in March-April, 1863. Reported on duty with the quartermaster department at Strawberry Plains, Tennessee, in May-June, 1863. Reported on detached service with Company A, 3rd Regiment Confederate Engineers, from August 5, 1863, through April 8, 1864. No further records.

DOUGLASS, SAMUEL N., Private
Previously served as Private in 2nd Company D, Walker's Battalion. Transferred to this company in late February, 1863. Reported on duty as a teamster in the quartermaster department through June 30, 1863. Reported on detached service with Company A, 3rd Regiment Confederate Engineers, from August 5, 1863, through April 8, 1864. No further records.

DUNN, ANDREW J., Private
Previously served as Private in 2nd Company D, Walker's Battalion. Transferred to this company in late February, 1863. Reported present through February 28, 1863. Reported on detached service at Strawberry Plains, Tennessee, in the post quartermaster department from April 7, 1863, through April 8, 1864. Served as a teamster for at least part of that period. No further records.

DYER, CASWELL, Private
Previously served as Musician (Fifer) in 2nd Company D, Walker's Battalion. Transferred to this company in late February, 1863. Reported present through June 30, 1863. Reduced to ranks in May-June, 1863. Reported present in September-October, 1863. Deserted at Blain's Crossroads, Tennessee, December 5, 1863. Went over to the enemy on an unspecified date. Took the Oath of Allegiance at Knoxville, Tennessee, January, 1864.

DYER, E. E., Private
Previously served as Private in 2nd Company D, Walker's Battalion. While absent without leave from that company, he had enlisted in Company B, 2nd Regiment Tennessee Cavalry (Ashby's) on November 4, 1862. Captured on an unspecified date. While a prisoner of war, he was transferred to this company in late February, 1863. Confined at Camp Douglas, Chicago, Illinois. Paroled at City Point, Virginia, April 6, 1863. Officially transferred to Company B, 2nd Regiment Tennessee Cavalry (Ashby's), prior to April 8, 1863.

DYER, EPHRAIM, Private
Previously served as Private in 2nd Company D, Walker's Battalion. Transferred to this company in late February, 1863. Reported present through June 30, 1863. Deserted at Zollicoffer, Tennessee, August 31, 1863. [See his Tennessee pension application No. 13610.]

DYER, HAMPTON, Private
Previously served as Private in 2nd Company D, Walker's Battalion. Transferred to this company in late February, 1863. Reported present through June 30, 1863, and in September-October, 1863. Deserted at Blain's Crossroads, Tennessee, December 5, 1863. Went over to the enemy on an unspecified date. Took the Oath of Allegiance at Knoxville, Tennessee, prior to December 16, 1863.

DYER, ISAAC, Private
Enlisted at Zollicoffer, Tennessee, at about age 17, August 22, 1863, for the war. Reported present through October 31, 1863. Deserted at Blain's Crossroads, Tennessee, December 5, 1863.

DYER, J. M., Private
Previously served as Private in 2nd Company D, Walker's Battalion. Transferred to this company in late February, 1863. Reported present through June 30, 1863, and in September-October, 1863. Deserted at Blain's Crossroads, Tennessee, December 5, 1863.

DYER, JOHN, Private
Previously served as Private in 2nd Company D, Walker's Battalion. Transferred to this company in late February, 1863. Reported present through February 28, 1863. Transferred either to Company H, 1st Regiment Tennessee Cavalry (Carter's), or Company B, 2nd Regiment Tennessee Cavalry (Ashby's), prior to April 8, 1863.

DYER, ROBERT, Private
Previously served as Private in 2nd Company D, Walker's Battalion. While absent without leave from that company, he had enlisted in Company B, 2nd Regiment Tennessee Cavalry (Ashby's), on November 4, 1862. While at home sick from that unit, he was transferred to this company in late February, 1863. Officially transferred to Company B, 2nd Regiment Tennessee Cavalry (Ashby's), prior to April 8, 1863. Returned to this company prior to October 31, 1863, probably while absent without leave from the 2nd Tennessee Cavalry. Deserted at Blain's Crossroads, Tennessee, December 5, 1863.

DYER, ROBERT, Private
Enlisted at Strawberry Plains, Tennessee, at about age 34, March 28, 1863, for the war. Reported present through April 30, 1863. Reported absent without leave on June 26, 1863. Returned to duty prior to August 31, 1863, when he deserted at Zollicoffer, Tennessee.

DYER, WILLIAM, Private

Previously served as Private in 2nd Company D, Walker's Battalion. While absent without leave from that company, he had enlisted in Company B, 2nd Regiment Tennessee Cavalry (Ashby's) on November 4, 1862. While present with that unit, he was transferred to this company in late February, 1863. Officially transferred to Company B, 2nd Regiment Tennessee Cavalry (Ashby's), prior to April 8, 1863.

ELLIS, JAMES, Private

Previously served as Private in 2nd Company D, Walker's Battalion. Transferred to this company in late February, 1863. Reported foraging as his daily duty on February 28, 1863. Reported present in March-June, 1863. Promoted to 1st Sergeant on May 9, 1863. Reported present in September-December, 1863. Reduced to ranks in November-December, 1863. Reported sick in hospital at Jonesborough, Tennessee, February 15, 1864. Captured in Sevier County, Tennessee, April 4, 1864. Sent to Nashville, Tennessee. Transferred to Louisville, Kentucky, where he arrived on April 12, 1864. Transferred to Camp Chase, Ohio, where he arrived on April 14, 1864. Paroled at Camp Chase and transferred to City Point, Virginia, February 25, 1865, for exchange. Hospitalized at Richmond, Virginia, March 7, 1865, with debilitas. Furloughed for thirty days on March 9, 1865. No further records.

ELLIS, JOHN H., Private

Enlisted at Strawberry Plains, Tennessee, at about age 17, April 19, 1863, for the war. Reported present through June 30, 1863; in September, 1863-February, 1864; and on April 8, 1864. Hospitalized at Charlottesville, Virginia, October 24, 1864, with a gunshot wound of the right side. Probably wounded at Cedar Creek, Virginia, October 19, 1864. Returned to duty on November 15, 1864. Name appears on a receipt roll for clothing dated December 14, 1864. No further records.

ESTEP, CALVIN, Private

Previously served as Private in 2nd Company D, Walker's Battalion. Transferred to this company in late February, 1863. Reported on duty as a teamster with the quartermaster department at Strawberry Plains, Tennessee, through June 30, 1863, and in August, 1863. Reported present in September-October, 1863. Deserted at Blain's Crossroads, Tennessee, December 5, 1863.

FORD, JAMES, Private

Previously served as Private in Company A, Indian Battalion. Transferred to this company on February 10, 1864. Deserted on February 22, 1864.

FRANKLIN, JOHN R., Private

Previously served as Corporal in 2nd Company D, Walker's Battalion. Transferred to this company in late February, 1863. Reported present through June 30, 1863. Promoted to Sergeant prior to October 31, 1863. Reported sick at home on July 22, 1863. Failed to return to duty and was listed as a deserter in November-December, 1863. Reduced to ranks prior to April 8, 1864. No further records.

GOFORTH, HUGH, Private

Enlisted at Strawberry Plains, Tennessee, at about age 37, March 1, 1863, for the war. Reported on duty as a ferryman on the French Broad River from March 1, 1863, through April 8, 1864. No further records.

GREEN, GEORGE W., Private

Previously served as Private in Company I, Infantry Regiment of this legion. Transferred to this company and appointed Musician (Fifer) in May-June, 1863. Deserted on October 20, 1863. Reduced to ranks on an unspecified date. No further records. [He may have been the same man as Pvt. George W. Green of Companies H and E, Walker's Battalion.]

GRIFFIN, JAMES P., Private

Previously served as Private in 2nd Company D, Walker's Battalion. Transferred to this company in late February, 1863. Reported present through February 28, 1863. Reported on duty as a teamster at Strawberry Plains, Tennessee, from April 7 through June 30, 1863, and in August, 1863. Deserted at Strawberry Plains on September 1, 1863. [Subsequently served as Private in Company K, 3rd Regiment Tennessee Infantry (Union).]

HAMMOCK, JOHN, Private

Previously served as Private in 2nd Company D, Walker's Battalion. Transferred to this company in late February, 1863. Reported present through June 30, 1863. Deserted at Zollicoffer, Tennessee, on or about September 23, 1863

HAMMOCK, WILLIAM, Private

Previously served as Private in 2nd Company D, Walker's Battalion. Transferred to this company in late February, 1863. Reported present but sick on February 28, 1863. Reported sick at home in March-April, 1863. Returned to duty in May-June, 1863. Deserted at Zollicoffer, Tennessee, August 18, 1863.

HATCHER, WILLIAM, Private

Previously served as Private in 2nd Company D, Walker's Battalion. Transferred to this company in late February, 1863. Reported present through June 30, 1863. Deserted at Carter's Depot, Tennessee, July 17, 1863. [A $240 ($30 per man) reward was issued on July 25, 1863, for the arrest of Hatcher and seven other deserters from this company. See the item from the Knoxville *Daily Chronicle* in the film jacket of Pvt. John H. Lyons of this company.]

HAYNES, ALFRED, Private

Previously served as Private in 2nd Company D, Walker's Battalion. Transferred to this company in late February, 1863. Reported present until June 15, 1863, when he was reported absent without leave. Subsequently reported as having deserted on July 1, 1863.

HAYS, JOHN W., Private

Previously served as Private in 2nd Company D, Walker's Battalion. Transferred to this company in late February, 1863. Reported present through February 28, 1863. Reported on detail as a teamster in March-June, 1863. Reported on detached service with Company A, 3rd Regiment Confederate Engineers, from August 5, 1863, through April 8, 1864. No further records.

HAYS, WILLIAM C., Private

Previously served as Private in 2nd Company D, Walker's Battalion. Transferred to this company in late February, 1863. Reported absent sick on February 28, 1863. Reported present in March-April, 1863. Died at home in Jefferson County, Tennessee, May 18, 1863. Cause of death not reported.

HIGHTOWER, W. S. A., Private
Enlisted at Carter's Depot, Tennessee, at about age 36, May 26, 1863, for the war. Reported present through June 30, 1863. Reported on detached service with Company A, 3rd Regiment Confederate Engineers, from August 5, 1863, through April 8, 1864. No further records.

HOOKER, JOHN, Private
Previously served as Private in 2nd Company D, Walker's Battalion. Was discharged from that company on February 19, 1863, after providing Joseph Hooker as a substitute, just before that company became this company. However, he was listed as a deserter from this company on August 18, 1863, possibly because his substitute deserted.

HOOKER, JOSEPH, Private
Previously served as Private in 2nd Company D, Walker's Battalion. Transferred to this company in late February, 1863. Reported present through June 30, 1863. Deserted from camp on July 22, 1863. Evidently returned to duty at an unknown date. Deserted at Zollicoffer, Tennessee, August 18, 1863. [A $240 ($30 per man) reward was issued on July 25, 1863, for the arrest of Hooker and seven other deserters from this company. See the item from the Knoxville *Daily Chronicle* in the National Archives Compiled Service Record of Pvt. John H. Lyons of this company.]

HOUSEWRIGHT, WILLIAM, Private
Previously served as Private in 2nd Company D, Walker's Battalion. While absent without leave from that company, he had enlisted in Company E, 14th Battalion Tennessee Cavalry (Carter's), on October 30, 1862. That company became Company E, 1st Regiment Tennessee Cavalry (Carter's) in November-December, 1862. While serving with that unit, he was Transferred to this company in late February, 1863. Reportedly officially transferred Company E, 1st Regiment Tennessee Cavalry (Carter's) in March-April, 1863.

HUNTER, GEORGE, Private
Previously served as Private in 2nd Company D, Walker's Battalion. Transferred to this company in late February, 1863. Reported present through February 28, 1863. Reported sick at home in March-April, 1863. Rejoined the company prior to June 30, 1863. Deserted on July 17, 1863. [A $240 ($30 per man) reward was issued on July 25, 1863, for the arrest of Hunter and seven other deserters from this company. See the item from the Knoxville *Daily Chronicle* in the National Archives Compiled Service Record of Pvt. John H. Lyons of this company.]

HUSKY, ISAAC, Private
Previously served as Private in 2nd Company D, Walker's Battalion. Transferred to this company in late February, 1863. Reported on detail working on a military road through the Smoky Mountains through April 8, 1864. Name appears on a receipt roll for clothing dated August 17, 1864. No further records.

JONES, GEORGE, Private
Previously served as Private in 2nd Company D, Walker's Battalion. Transferred to this company in late February, 1863. Reported at home sick on February 28, 1863. Returned to duty prior to April 30, 1863. Reported absent without leave on June 26, 1863. "Reclaimed by Capt. Hardy's Co[mpany], 1st Ten[nessee] Cavalry, August 15, 1863." This may refer to Company E, 12th Battalion Tennessee Cavalry (Day's), which was commanded by Capt. Leslie T. Hardy.

JONES, JOHN, Private
Previously served in a Tennessee Confederate unit, probably Company E, 1st Regiment Tennessee Cavalry (Carter's). Transferred to this company between July 1 and October 31, 1863. Reported present through February, 1864, and on April 8, 1864. Name appears on receipt rolls for clothing dated September 1 and 27 and December 14, 1864. No further records. [Was about 27 years old at time of transfer.]

KENDRICK, WILLIAM, Private
Previously served as Private in 2nd Company D, Walker's Battalion. Transferred to this company in late February, 1863. Reported on detached service working on a military road through the Smoky Mountains through April 8, 1864. No further records.

KILGORE, WILLIAM A., 1st Sergeant
Previously served as Sergeant in 2nd Company D, Walker's Battalion. Transferred to this company in late February, 1863. Reported present through June 30, 1863, and in September-October, 1863. Promoted to 1st Sergeant in November-December, 1863. Reported present in November, 1863-February, 1864, and on April 8, 1864. Wounded in the thigh and captured at Winchester, Virginia, September 19, 1864. Died in hospital at Winchester on October 1-2, 1864, of "cont[inuous] fever."

LARGE, JOSEPH, Private
Born in Grainger County, Tennessee, and resided in Jefferson County, Tennessee, where he was by occupation a farmer prior to enlisting at Strawberry Plains, Tennessee, at age 37, February 1, 1863, for the war. Reported present through April 30, 1863. Detailed for duty at Strawberry Plains on May 1, 1863. Deserted at Strawberry Plains on September 1, 1863.

LARGE, WILEY B., Private
Previously served as Private in 2nd Company D, Walker's Battalion. Transferred to this company in late February, 1863. Reported present through February 28, 1863. Reported at home sick in March-April, 1863. Reported absent without leave on June 26, 1863. Returned to duty prior to August 22, 1863, when he reportedly deserted at Jonesborough, Tennessee, while at home sick.

LAWRENCE, DAVID, Private
Previously served as Private in 2nd Company D, Walker's Battalion. Transferred to this company in late February, 1863. Reported present through June 30, 1863. Transferred to Capt. John T. Levi's Battery on July 1 or August 7, 1863.

LAWRENCE, J. CALVIN, Private
Previously served as Private in 2nd Company D, Walker's Battalion. Transferred to this company in late February, 1863. Reported present through June 30, 1863. Transferred to Capt. John T. Levi's Battery on July 1 or August 1, 1863.

LEE, JASPER C., Private
Previously served as Private in 2nd Company D, Walker's Battalion. Transferred to this company in late February, 1863. Killed at

Mossy Creek, Tennessee, February 28 or April 10, 1863, by "accidental discharge of musket." [His given name may have been C. Jasper.]

LEE, JOHN C., Private

Previously served as Private in 2nd Company D, Walker's Battalion. Transferred to this company in late February, 1863. Reported present through April 30, 1863. Reported absent without leave on June 20, 1863. Returned to duty on an unspecified date. Deserted on July 22, 1863. [A $240 ($30 per man) reward was issued on July 25, 1863, for the arrest of Lee and seven other deserters from this company. See the item from the Knoxville *Daily Chronicle* in the National Archives Compiled Service Record of Pvt. John H. Lyons of this company. He may have been the same man as Pvt. John Lee of Capt. John T. Levi's Battery. See Tennessee pension application No. 11778.]

LEE, JOSEPH C., Private

Previously served as Private in 2nd Company D, Walker's Battalion. Transferred to this company in late February, 1863. Reported present through June 30, 1863. Transferred to Capt. John T. Levi's Battery on July 1 or August 1, 1863.

LEE, WILLIAM C., Private

Previously served as Private in 2nd Company D, Walker's Battalion. Transferred to this company in late February, 1863. Reported present through June 30, 1863. Transferred to Capt. John T. Levi's Battery on July 1 or August 1, 1863.

LEWIS, MALDEN, Private

Resided in Jefferson County, Tennessee, and enlisted at Strawberry Plains, Tennessee, at about age 39, March 4, 1863, for the war. Reported present through April 30, 1863. Reported sick at home, June 12-30, 1863. Reported sick in hospital at Mossy Creek, Tennessee, from August 16, 1863, through February 29, 1864, and on April 8, 1864. No further records.

LYONS, JOHN H., Private

Previously served as Private in 2nd Company D, Walker's Battalion. Transferred to this company and promoted to Sergeant in February, 1863. Reported present through April 30, 1863. Reported absent without leave on June 26, 1863. Returned to duty on an unspecified date. Deserted from camp on July 22, 1863. Reduced to ranks on an unspecified date. Went over to the enemy on an unspecified date. Took the Oath of Allegiance at Chattanooga, Tennessee, May 12, 1865. [A $240 ($30 per man) reward was issued on July 25, 1863, for the arrest of Lyons and seven other deserters from this company, according to the Knoxville *Daily Chronicle*.]

McBEE, WILLIAM C., Private

Previously served as Private in 2nd Company D, Walker's Battalion. Transferred to this company in late February, 1863. Reported on detail in the medical department on February 28, 1863. Reported on sick furlough "1/2 mile from camp" in March-April, 1863. Discharged on June 1, 1863. Reason discharged not reported.

McDONALD, DANIEL, Private

Previously served as Private in 2nd Company D, Walker's Battalion. Transferred to this company in late February, 1863. Reported present through February 28, 1863. Reported on duty as a teamster in the quartermaster department in March-June, 1863. Was at Strawberry Plains, Tennessee, for at least part of that period. Reported absent, "supposed to have been captured on retreat from Greeneville, Tenn.," October 14-31, 1863. Subsequently listed as having deserted on October 20, 1863. Captured on October 31, 1863, and confined at Knoxville, Tennessee. Released at Knoxville on or about November 2, 1863, after taking the Oath of Allegiance. No further records.

McINTURFF, CHARLES D., Corporal

Previously served as Private in 2nd Company D, Walker's Battalion. Transferred to this company in late February, 1863. Mustered in as Private. Reported present through June 30, 1863, and in September-October, 1863. Promoted to Corporal in November-December, 1863. Reported present in November, 1863-February, 1864, and on April 8, 1864. Name appears on receipt rolls for clothing dated June 4, August 8, and December 14, 1864. No further records.

McINTURFF, RICHARD F., Corporal

Enlisted at Knoxville, Tennessee. Enlistment date reported as August 1, 1861, which indicates, if correct, that he served previously in another unit. Enlisted in or was transferred to this company subsequent to February 28, 1863. Mustered in as Private. Reported present in September, 1863-February, 1864, and on April 8, 1864. Promoted to Corporal on an unspecified date. Wounded and captured at Cedar Creek, Virginia, October 19, 1864. Hospitalized at Baltimore, Maryland, where he died on November 1, 1864, of wounds.

McMAHON, ANDREW, Private

Previously served as Private in 2nd Company D, Walker's Battalion. Transferred to this company in late February, 1863, while absent without leave. Listed as a deserter in March-April, 1863. [A company muster roll dated April 8, 1864, states that he was "reclaimed" by an unspecified unit, but this is probably an error.]

MORGAN, ABRAM H., Private

Previously served as Private in 2nd Company D, Walker's Battalion. Transferred to this company in late February, 1863. Reported present through June 30, 1863. Promoted to Corporal on May 31, 1863. Promoted to Sergeant prior to October 31, 1863. Reported present in September-October, 1863. Reduced to ranks after he deserted to the enemy at Blain's Crossroads, Tennessee, December 5, 1863. Sent to Knoxville, Tennessee. Released at Knoxville on or about December 16, 1863, after taking the Oath of Allegiance.

MORGAN, ALFRED B., Private

Previously served as Private in 2nd Company D, Walker's Battalion. Transferred to this company in late February, 1863. Reported present through April 30, 1863. Reported absent without leave on June 29, 1863. Returned to duty and was promoted to Sergeant prior to October 31, 1863. Deserted at Blain's Crossroads, Tennessee, December 5, 1863. "Reclaimed from desertion" on February 6, 1864, and was reduced to ranks. Reported present on April 8, 1864. Promoted to Sergeant on an unspecified date. Hospitalized at Charlottesville, Virginia, June 12, 1864, with acute diarrhoea. Returned to duty on June 20, 1864. Name appears on receipt rolls for clothing dated July 19, August 8, September 1, and September 27, 1864. Reduced to ranks on an unspecified date. No further records.

MORGAN, GEORGE C., Private

Previously served as Private in Company E, 1st Regiment Tennessee Cavalry (Carter's). Transferred to this company on April 7,

1863. Reported present in May-June, 1863; in September, 1863-February, 1864; and on April 8, 1864. Name appears on a receipt roll for clothing dated September 1, 1864. No further records.

MORGAN, JOHN W., Private
Previously served as Corporal in 2nd Company D, Walker's Battalion. Transferred to this company in late February, 1863. Reported present through June 30, 1863. Reduced to ranks prior to July 24-25, 1863, when he died either at home in Knox County or in hospital at Strawberry Plains, Tennessee, of "febris typhoides."

MOTT, JOHN W., Private
Enlisted at Strawberry Plains, Tennessee, at about age 17, May 1, 1863, for the war. Reported present sick through June 30, 1863. Reported on detached service as a teamster in the post quartermaster department from September 27, 1863, through February 29, 1864. Reported present on April 8, 1864. Name appears on a special requisition for clothing dated June 9, 1864, in which he notes his discharge from a hospital. Name appears on receipt rolls for clothing date July 19, September 27, and October 29, 1864. Reported in hospital at Staunton, Virginia, November 20, 1864. Paroled by Federal forces at Cumberland Gap, Tennessee, April 26, 1865.

NEWMAN, WILLIAM, Private
Enlisted at Strawberry Plains, Tennessee, at about age 17, March 9, 1863, for the war. Reported on detached service at Strawberry Plains from April 7, 1863, through April 8, 1864. He was employed in the post quartermaster department for much of that time, and was reportedly "getting out timber" during part of that time. No further records.

PACKETT, MADISON, Private
Enlisted at Strawberry Plains, Tennessee, at about age 38, March 9, 1863, for the war. Reported on detached service at Strawberry Plains from April 7, 1863, through April 8, 1864. He was detailed "getting out timber" for the post quartermaster department during part of that period. No further records.

PAGE, W. D., Private
Enlisted at Knoxville, Tennessee, at about age 37, March 25, 1863, for the war. Died at his home thirteen miles from Strawberry Plains, Tennessee, May 1, 1863. Cause of death not reported.

PATE, SAMUEL, Private
Previously served as Private in 2nd Company D, Walker's Battalion. Transferred to this company in late February, 1863. Reported present through February 28, 1863. Reported absent without leave on April 23, 1863. Deserted at Carter's Depot, Tennessee, June 26, 1863.

PEARSON, WILLIAM H., Private
Previously served as Private in 2nd Company D, Walker's Battalion. Transferred to this company in late February, 1863. Furloughed "to see sister on death bed" on April 21, 1863. Reported absent without leave on June 26, 1863. Reported as "supposed to have beeen captured on retreat from Tennessee," October 11, 1863. Subsequently listed as having deserted on October 20, 1863.

PECK, JOHN H., Private
Enlisted at Strawberry Plains, Tennessee, at about age 36, August 24, 1863, for the war. Reported sick in hospital at Abingdon, Virginia, October 31, 1863. Reported on detached service in hospital at Bristol, Tennessee, from December 12, 1863, through April 8, 1864. Detailed as a nurse in hospital at Emory, Virginia, April 28, 1864, through at least October 29, 1864. Diagnosed at the hospital at Emory on October 29, 1864, as suffering from "Mental and Physical debility," but was returned to duty. Deserted to the enemy on an unspecified date. Sent to Chattanooga, Tennessee. Took the Oath of Allegiance at Chattanooga on May 27, 1865. [He may have been promoted to Corporal in 1864.]

PIGG, RADFORD G., Private
Previously served as Private in 2nd Company D, Walker's Battalion. Transferred to this company in late February, 1863. Reported present through June 30, 1863. Deserted at Zollicoffer, Tennessee, August 24, 1863.

REED, BIRDWELL, Private
Previously served in Company E, 1st Regiment Tennessee Cavalry (Carter's). Transferred to this company on August 8, 1863, at about age 25. Reported in September-October, 1863 as absent, "supposed to have been captured on retreat from Greeneville, Tenn," October 14, 1863. Subsequently listed as having deserted on October 20, 1863. [His National Archives service records are mixed with those of Pvt. B. Reid of Levi's Battery, Thomas's Legion, to create a single service record under Birdwell Reed's name. The two do not appear to be the same man, however.]

REED, JAMES, Private
Previously served as Private in 2nd Company D, Walker's Battalion. Transferred to this company in late February, 1863. Reported present through April 30, 1863. Reported absent without leave on June 26, 1863. Returned to duty on an unspecified date. Deserted on July 22, 1863. Returned to duty prior to October 31, 1863. Deserted at Blain's Crossroads, Tennessee, December 5, 1863. Went over to the enemy on an unspecified date. Sent to Knoxville, Tennessee. Released at Knoxville on or about December 16, 1863, after taking the Oath of Allegiance. [See his Tennessee pension application No. 2716. A $240 ($30 per man) reward was issued on July 25, 1863, for the arrest of Reed and seven other deserters from this company. See the item from the Knoxville *Daily Chronicle* in the National Archives Compiled Service Record of Pvt. John H. Lyons of this company.]

REED, LEANDER, Private
Previously served as Private in 2nd Company D, Walker's Battalion. Transferred to this company in late February, 1863. Reported on detail "in search of deserters" on February 28, 1863. Rejoined the company prior to April 30, 1863. Reported present in May-June, 1863. Deserted on July 22, 1863. Returned to duty on an unspecified date. Reported present in September, 1863-February, 1864; and on April 8, 1864. Hospitalized at Winchester, Virginia, August 1, 1864, with diarrhoea. Name appears on receipt rolls for clothing dated September 1, 1864, and December 14, 1864. No further records. [A $240 ($30 per man) reward was issued on July 25, 1863, for the arrest of Reed and seven other deserters from this company. See the item from the Knoxville *Daily Chronicle* in the National Archives Compiled Service Record of Pvt. John H. Lyons of this company.]

REED, WILLIAM, Private

Previously served as Private in 2nd Company D, Walker's Battalion. Transferred to this company in late February, 1863. Reported present through June 30, 1863. Deserted at Zollicoffer, Tennessee, August 18, 1863.

SELLERS, ROBERT, Private

Previously served as Private in 2nd Company D, Walker's Battalion. Transferred to this company in late February, 1863. Reported absent sick from March 15 through June 30, 1863. Transferred to Capt. John T. Levi's Battery, July 1 or August 1, 1863.

SIMMONS, THOMAS F., Private

Previously served as Private in 2nd Company D, Walker's Battalion. Transferred to this company in late February, 1863. Reported present through April 30, 1863. Reported absent without leave June 24-30, 1863. Reported as having deserted on July 22, 1863. Transferred to Capt. John T. Levi's Battery on August 5, 1863. [A $240 ($30 per man) reward was issued on July 25, 1863, for the arrest of Simmons and seven other deserters from this company. See the item from the Knoxville *Daily Chronicle* in the National Archives Compiled Service Record of Pvt. John H. Lyons of this company.]

STANSBERRY, CAMPBELL H., Private

Previously served as Musician (Drummer) in 2nd Company D, Walker's Battalion. Transferred to this company in late February, 1863. Reported present through April 30, 1863. Reported on detail in the quartermaster department at Strawberry Plains, Tennessee, in May-August, 1863. Reduced to ranks subsequent to June 30, 1863. Deserted at Strawberry Plains on September 1, 1863.

STEWART, J. M. P., Private

Enlisted at Strawberry Plains, Tennessee, at about age 35, March 9, 1863, for the war. Reported on detached service at Strawberry Plains from April 7, 1863, through April 8, 1864. No further records.

STUBBLEFIELD, ROBERT L., Private

Previously served as Private in 2nd Company D, Walker's Battalion. Transferred to this company in late February, 1863. Reported present through June 30, 1863. Reported on detail as an artificer in Company A, 3rd Regiment Confederate Engineers, from August 5, 1863, through April 8, 1864. Transferred to that unit prior to August 31, 1864.

SUTHERLAND, AMBROSE, Private

Previously served as Private in 2nd Company D, Walker's Battalion. Transferred to this company in late February, 1863. Reported present in January-June and September-October, 1863. Promoted to Corporal in November-December, 1863. Reported present in November, 1863-February, 1864, and on April 8, 1864. Wounded at Winchester, Virginia, September 19, 1864. Reduced to ranks prior to December 14, 1864. Took the Oath of Allegiance at Chattanooga, Tennessee, May 21, 1865.

SUTHERLAND, EVAN, Private

Resided in Union County, Tennessee, and enlisted at Strawberry Plains, Tennessee, April 20, 1863, for the war. Reported present through June 30, 1863; in September, 1863-February, 1864; and on April 8, 1864. Hospitalized at Charlottesville, Virginia, June 10, 1864, with chronic bronchitis. Returned to duty on June 17, 1864. Wounded at Winchester, Virginia, September 19, 1864. Took the Oath of Allegiance at Chattanooga, Tennessee, May 21, 1864.

SUTHERLAND, WILLIAM, Private

Previously served as Private in 2nd Company D, Walker's Battalion. Transferred to this company in late February, 1863. Reported present through June 30 and in September-October, 1863. Promoted to Corporal in November-December, 1863. Reported present in November, 1863-February, 1864, and on April 8, 1864. Reduced to ranks on an unspecified date prior to July 3, 1864. Name appears on receipt rolls for clothing dated July 3 and September 1, 1864. No further records.

TROTT, JAMES, Private

Previously served as Private in 2nd Company D, Walker's Battalion. Transferred to this company in late February, 1863. Reported present through February 28, 1863. Reported on detached service in the quartermaster department at Strawberry Plains, Tennessee, from April 7, 1863, through April 8, 1864. Was "getting out timber for post commissary" for part of that period. No further records.

TROUTMAN, JONAS, Private

Previously served as Private in 2nd Company D, Walker's Battalion. Transferred to this company in late February, 1863. Reported present through February 28, 1863. Reported on detached service as a teamster in the post quartermaster department at Strawberry Plains, Tennessee, in March-June, 1863. Rejoined the company prior to October 31, 1863. Deserted at Blain's Crossroads, Tennessee, December 5, 1863.

UNDERWOOD, JESSE, Private

Previously served as Private in 2nd Company D, Walker's Battalion. Transferred to this company in late February, 1863, while absent without leave. Reported on detached service as a teamster in the post quartermaster department at Strawberry Plains, Tennessee, from April 7, 1863, through April 8, 1864. Was employed "getting out timber" for at least part of that period. No further records.

UNDERWOOD, KIRBY, Private

Enlisted at Strawberry Plains, Tennessee, at about age 25, March 9, 1863, for the war. Reported on detached service as a teamster in the post quartermaster department at Strawberry Plains, Tennessee, from April 7, 1863, through April 8, 1864. Was employed "getting out timber" for at least part of that period. No further records.

UNDERWOOD, THOMAS, Private

Previously served as Private in 2nd Company D, Walker's Battalion. Transferred to this company in late February, 1863. Reported present through February 28, 1863. Reported on detached service in the post quartermaster department at Strawberry Plains, Tennessee, from April 7, 1863, through April 8, 1864. Was employed "getting out timber" for at least part of that period. No further records.

WALKER, JAMES V., Private

Previously served as Sergeant in 2nd Company D, Walker's Battalion. Transferred to this company in late February, 1863. Reported present through June 30, 1863. Reduced to ranks on an unspecified date subsequent to June 30, 1863. Discharged prior to April 8, 1864, after providing Michael Berry as a substitute.

WALKER, JOHN D., Private
Previously served as Private in 2nd Company D, Walker's Battalion. Transferred to this company in late February, 1863. Reported present through February 28, 1863. Reported on detached duty as a teamster at the post quartermaster department at Strawberry Plains, Tennessee, from April 7, 1863, through April 8, 1864. Was employed "getting out timber" for at least part of that period. No further records.

WALKER, WILLIAM, JR., Private
Previously served as Corporal in 2nd Company D, Walker's Battalion. Transferred to this company in late February, 1863. Reduced to ranks on May 31, 1863. Reported present through June 30, 1863. Deserted at Zollicoffer, Tennessee, August 18, 1863.

WALKER, WILLIAM, SR., Private
Previously served as Private in 2nd Company D, Walker's Battalion. Transferred to this company in late February, 1863. Reported present through June 30, 1863. Reported in September-December, 1863, to be absent, "supposed to have been captured in retreat Greeneville, Tenn., October 11, 1863." Died at home in Cocke County, Tennessee, January 16, 1864. Cause of death not reported.

WALL, JOHN D., Private
Previously served as Private in Company C of this regiment. Transferred to this company, January 10, 1863. Reported present through April 30, 1863. Reported on detail in hospital at Strawberry Plains, Tennessee, May 27-June 30, 1863. Captured at Strawberry Plains, Tennessee, June 20, 1863, and paroled there the next day. Rejoined the company prior to October 31, 1863. Reported absent without leave on December 5, 1863. Went over to the enemy on an unspecified date. Took the Oath of Allegiance at Knoxville, Tennessee on or about December 16, 1863.

WALTERS, WILLIAM M., Private
Previously served as Private in 2nd Company D, Walker's Battalion. Transferred to this company in late February, 1863. Reported present through April 30, 1863. Reported on detached service to bring in absentees, June 28-30, 1863. Rejoined the company on an unspecified date. Promoted to Corporal in July-October, 1863. Promoted to Sergeant in November-December, 1863. Reported present in September, 1863-February, 1864. Name appears on receipt rolls for clothing dated June 4, July 5, July 19, September 27, and December 14, 1864. Reduced to ranks prior to December 14, 1864. No further records.

WATKINS, WILLIAM W., Private
Previously served as Private in 2nd Company D, Walker's Battalion. Transferred to this company in late February, 1863. Reported present through June 30, 1863. Deserted at Zollicoffer, Tennessee, on or about August 29, 1863.

WEBB, JOHN, Private
Previously served as Private in 2nd Company D, Walker's Battalion. Transferred to this company in late February, 1863. Reported present through June 30, 1863, and in September-October, 1863. Reported sick at home from December 5, 1863, through April 8, 1864. Name appears on receipt rolls for clothing dated July 5, August 8, and September 1, 1864. Paroled at Cumberland Gap, Kentucky, April 29, 1865.

WEEDON, WILLIAM, Private
Previously served as Private in 2nd Company D, Walker's Battalion. Transferred to this company in late February, 1863. Reported present through April 30, 1863. Furloughed home sick on June 25, 1863. Failed to return to duty and was listed as a deserter in November-December, 1863.

WELLING, G. W., Private
Enlisted at Strawberry Plains, Tennessee, at about age 17, May 1, 1863, for the war. Reported present through June 30, 1863, and in September-December, 1863. Reported absent sick near Blountville, Tennessee, in January-February, 1864. Transferred to Capt. John T. Levi's Battery, March 28, 1864.

WEST, LEONARD, Private
Place and date of enlistment not reported; probably enlisted subsequent to February 29, 1864. Captured on May 27, 1864. Sent to Knoxville, Tennessee, where he was hospitalized on June 14, 1864, with pneumonia. Discharged from hospital and was released from Federal custody on June 17, 1864, after taking the Oath of Allegiance. No further records.

WILSON, JOHN, Private
Previously served as Private in 2nd Company D, Walker's Battalion. Transferred to this company in late February, 1863. Reported on detached service as a teamster in the post quartermaster department from April 7 through June 30, 1863, and from September 1, 1863, through April 8, 1864; was stationed at Strawberry Plains, Tennessee, for all or part of that time. No further records.

WRIGHT, WILLIAM, Private
Enlisted at Strawberry Plains, Tennessee, March 9, 1863, for the war. Reported absent on detached service at Strawberry Plains from April 7, 1863, through April 8, 1864. No further records.

WYRICK, VALENTINE, Private
Previously served as Corporal in 2nd Company D, Walker's Battalion. Transferred to this company in late February, 1863. Reported present through June 30, 1863. Deserted at Zollicoffer, Tennessee, August 31, 1863, and subsequently reduced to ranks.

COMPANY E

This company was raised in Haywood County. It served previously as Company L, 16th Regiment N.C. Troops (6th Regiment N.C. Volunteers). It was transferred to this regiment on October 5, 1862. It was known as Company B as of October 31, 1862. It was redesignated Company E, probably in January, 1863.

The following roster was compiled in large part from company muster rolls dated September, 1862-June, 1863, and September, 1863-February, 1864. These are abstracted in the microfilm edition of the Compiled Service Records of Confederate Soldiers Who Served in Organizations from the State of North Carolina (Record Group 109, M270), National Archives, Washington, D.C. Other valuable information in the Compiled Service Records includes enlistment papers, pay vouchers, requisitions, letters of resignation, discharge certificates, and abstracts of medical and prisoner of war records.

Also important in compiling this roster was an account book of Company L, 16th Regiment N.C. Troops, with entries made after that company became Company E of this regiment, from the Civil War Collection, North Carolina State Archives.

Also utilized in this roster were *The War of the Rebellion: A Compilation of the Official Records of the Union and Confederate Armies*, the North Carolina Adjutant General's papers, state militia records, newspaper casualty lists and obituaries, wartime claims for bounty pay and allowances, postwar registers of claims for artificial limbs, Confederate pension applications filed with the states of North Carolina, Tennessee, and Florida, records of the North Carolina Confederate Soldiers' Home, and the 1860 and 1870 federal censuses of North Carolina. A search was made also for relevant letters, diaries, reminiscences, and other manuscripts in the Southern Historical Collection (University of North Carolina-Chapel Hill) and the Duke University Library Special Collections Department.

Among the secondary sources consulted were records of the North Carolina division of the United Daughters of the Confederacy, postwar rosters, regimental and county histories, marriage bond, will, and cemetery indexes, published and unpublished genealogies, biographical dictionaries, the North Carolina *County Heritage Book* series, the *Confederate Veteran*, Walter Clark's *Histories of the Several Regiments and Battalions from North Carolina in the Great War, 1861-'65*, and the North Carolina volume of the extended edition of *Confederate Military History*.

OFFICERS

CAPTAIN

WELCH, JULIUS M.

Previously served as Captain of Company L, 16th Regiment N.C. Troops (6th Regiment N.C. Volunteers). Appointed Captain of this company on or about October 5, 1862, to rank from September 24, 1862. Reported present sick "not yet recovered from wounds" on October 31, 1862. Reported present, November-December, 1862. Reported detailed on recruiting service in Haywood County, January-February, 1863. Rejoined the company prior to April 30, 1863. Reported on general court-martial duty at Jonesborough, Tennessee, May-June, 1863. Reported present in September-December, 1863. Name appears as a signature on a petitition dated February 25, 1864, to Gov. Zebulon B. Vance requesting assistance in reuniting Thomas's Legion and removing it from the command of Brig. Gen. Alfred E. Jackson . Reported absent on court-martial duty at Bristol, Tennessee, February 29, 1864. Killed at Piedmont, Virginia, June 5, 1864.

LIEUTENANTS

BROWN, WILLIAM CLINTON, 3rd Lieutenant

Previously served as Private in Company L, 16th Regiment N.C. Troops (6th Regiment N.C. Volunteers). Transferred to this company on October 5, 1862. Promoted to 1st Sergeant prior to October 31, 1862. Reported present through December, 1862. Reported on detail with 2nd Lt. John H. Moody of this company in January-February, 1863. Promoted to 3rd Lieutenant on March 17, 1863. Reported present or accounted for in March-June and September, 1863-February, 1864. Hospitalized at Lynchburg, Virginia, July 1, 1864. Furloughed for sixty days on August 31, 1864. Reported absent sick on September 29, 1864. No further records.

FERGUSON, THOMAS J., 1st Lieutenant

Previously served as 1st Lieutenant of Company L, 16th Regiment N.C. Troops (6th Regiment N.C. Volunteers). Transferred to this company on October 5, 1862. Mustered in as 2nd Lieutenant. Promoted to 1st Lieutenant prior to December 31, 1862. Reported present through June 30, 1863. Reported on detached duty "on recruiting service," from August 1 to November 24, 1863. Rejoined the company prior to December 31, 1863. Reported present in January-February, 1864. Captured and possibly wounded at Piedmont, Virginia, June 5, 1864. Sent to Staunton, Virginia. Transferred to Camp Morton, Indianapolis, Indiana, where he arrived on or June 21, 1864. Transferred to Johnson's Island, Ohio, where he arrived on June 23, 1864. Released at Johnson's Island on June 14, 1865, after taking the Oath of Allegiance. [According to Clark's *Regiments* 3:730, 742, he was promoted to Captain, presumably after the death of Captain Welch; if so, he was promoted in absentia while a prisoner of war and never actually served at that rank.]

MOODY, JOHN H., 2nd Lieutenant

Previously served as 2nd Lieutenant of Company L, 16th Regiment N.C. Troops (6th Regiment N.C. Volunteers). Transferred to this company on October 5, 1862. Reported present through December 31, 1862. Reported on detail at Cosby Creek, Tennessee, January-February, 1863. Rejoined the company prior to April 30, 1863. Reported present in May-June, 1863, and in September-December, 1863. Name appears as signature on a petition to Gov. Zebulon B. Vance dated February 25, 1864, requesting his assistance in reuniting Thomas's Legion and removing it from the command of Brig. Gen. Alfred E. Jackson. Reported present on February 29, 1864. Name appears on special requisitions dated August 9 and September 1 and September 27, 1864. No further records. [According to Clark's *Regiments*, 3:730, he was promoted to 1st Lieutenant, but no surviving wartime materials corroborate that claim.]

NONCOMMISSIONED OFFICERS AND PRIVATES

ABEL, GEORGE P., Private

Previously served as Private in Company L, 16th Regiment N.C. Troops (6th Regiment N.C. Volunteers). Transferred to this company on October 5, 1862. Transferred to Company C of this regiment on October 15, 1862.

ALLISON, M. S., _____

North Carolina pension records indicate that he served in this company. Survived the war.

ARRINGTON, JOSEPH GEORGE, Private

Confederate gravestone records indicate that he served in this company.

ARRINGTON, THOMAS PERY, _____

North Carolina pension records appear to indicate that he served in this company. Survived the war.

BEST, WILLIAM RODMAN, Private

Previously served as Private in Company L, 16th Regiment N.C. Troops (6th Regiment N.C. Volunteers). Transferred to this company on October 5, 1862. Reported absent sick in various Virginia hospitals through June, 1863, and in September, 1863-February, 1864. No further records.

BOLIN, WILBURN, Private
Previously served as Private in Company L, 16th Regiment N.C. Troops (6th Regiment N.C. Volunteers). Transferred to this company on October 5, 1862, while absent wounded. Reported on wounded furlough through December 31, 1862. Discharged on January 8, 1863. Reason for discharge not reported. [His surname may have been Bowlin.]

BOON, ROBERT W., Private
Previously served as Private in Company L, 16th Regiment N.C. Troops (6th Regiment N.C. Volunteers). Transferred to this company on October 5, 1862. Reported present until November 1, 1862, when he was reported absent without leave. Returned to duty prior to February 28, 1863. Reported present through June 30, 1863. Reported absent without leave in September-October, 1863. Returned to duty prior to December 31, 1863. Reported present but under arrest in January-February, 1864. No further records. Survived the war. [His surname may have been Boone.]

BOYD, DOCTOR T. J., Private
Previously served as Sergeant in Company L, 16th Regiment N.C. Troops (6th Regiment N.C. Volunteers). Transferred to this company on October 5, 1862, while on wounded furlough. Reported for duty in November-December, 1862. Discharged on January 8, 1863, presumably because of disability from wounds. Conscripted back into the company on an unspecified date. Mustered in as Private. Deserted to the enemy on an unspecified date. Confined at Knoxville, Tennessee, January 26, 1865. Transferred to Louisville, Kentucky, where he arrived on or about February 13, 1865. Released "north of the Ohio River to remain during the war" on February 14, 1865, after taking the Oath of Allegiance.

BOYD, JOHN HENRY HARRISON, Private
Previously served as Private in Company L, 16th Regiment N.C. Troops (6th Regiment N.C. Volunteers). Transferred to this company on October 5, 1862, while absent without leave. Reported for duty in November-December, 1862. Reported present in January-June, 1863. Promoted to 1st Sergeant in March-April, 1863. Reported absent without leave in September-October, 1863. Reduced to ranks prior to October 31, 1863. Returned to duty in November-December, 1863. Reported present in January-February, 1864. Captured at Carter's Depot, Tennessee, April 25, 1864. Sent to Knoxville, Tennessee. Transferred to Nashville, Tennessee, May 13, 1864. Confined at Louisville, Kentucky, May 17, 1864. Transferred to Camp Morton, Indianapolis, Indiana, where he arrived on May 22, 1864. Paroled at Camp Morton on or about March 4, 1865. Received at Boulware's Wharf, James River, Virginia, March 10-12, 1865, for exchange. Hospitalized at Richmond, Virginia, March 11, 1865. No further records.

BROWN, AARON W., Corporal
Previously served as Ordnance Sergeant in Company L, 16th Regiment N.C. Troops (6th Regiment N.C. Volunteers). Transferred to this company on October 5, 1862. Mustered in as Corporal. Reported present through April 30, 1863. No further records. Survived the war. [Born on February 24, 1841.]

BROWN, GEORGE W., Private
Confederate gravestone records indicate that he served in this company.

BROWN, HENRY C., Private
Enlisted at Waynesville on August 18, 1863, for the war. Died on December 6, 1863. Place and cause of death not reported.

BROWN, JEHU C., Private
Previously served as Private in Company L, 16th Regiment N.C. Troops (6th Regiment N.C. Volunteers). Transferred to this company on October 5, 1862. Reported present or accounted for through June, 1863, and in September-October, 1863. Reported on detail with the quartermaster department at Bristol, Tennessee, November-December, 1863, and January 15-31, 1864. Hospitalized at Charlottesville, Virginia, June 12, 1864, with diarrhoea. Returned to duty on June 17, 1864. Name appears on a receipt roll for clothing dated September 1, 1864. No further records. [Contrary to 6:101 of this series, his first name was probably Jehu rather than John.]

BROWN, WILLIAM H., Private
Previously served as Private in Company L, 16th Regiment N.C. Troops (6th Regiment N.C. Volunteers). Transferred to this company on October 5, 1862. Reported present until December 17, 1862, when he was reported absent without leave. Returned to duty prior to January 31, 1863. Reported present or accounted for in March-June, 1863. Reported present in September-December, 1863. Reported on furlough on February 29, 1864. No further records. Survived the war.

BROWNING, HARVEY, Private
Enlisted in Haywood County on April 5, 1863, for the war. Reported on hospital detail at Greeneville, Tennessee, in May-June, 1863. Reported absent without leave in September-October, 1863. Returned to duty prior to December 31, 1863. Deserted in January-February, 1864.

BURRESS, LUSCIUS P., Private
Confederate gravestone records indicate that he served in this company.

BURRIS, CHARLES, Musician
Previously served as Musician (Fifer) in Company L, 16th Regiment N.C. Troops (6th Regiment N.C. Volunteers). Transferred to this company on October 5, 1862. Reported present through December 31, 1862. Reported on detail with 2nd Lt. John H.Moody of this company at Cosby Creek, Tennessee, January-February, 1863. Rejoined the company prior to April 30, 1863. Reported present in May-June, 1863, and in September, 1863-February, 1864. Died of "cramp colic" at Saltville, Virginia, May 22, 1864.

BYERS, DILLARD H., _____
North Carolina pension records appear to indicate that he served in this company. Survived the war.

CHAMBERS, ELIHU, Musician
Previously served as Private in Company L, 16th Regiment N.C. Troops (6th Regiment N.C. Volunteers). Transferred to this company, probably on October 5, 1862. Mustered in as Musician

(Drummer). Transferred to Company C of this regiment on January 1, 1864.

CHAMBERS, JAMES R., Private

Previously served as Private in Company L, 16th Regiment N.C. Troops (6th Regiment N.C. Volunteers). Transferred to this company on October 5, 1862, while absent without leave. Reported for duty in January-February, 1863. Reported present in March-June, 1863. Reported absent without leave in September-October, 1863. Returned to duty in November-December, 1863. Reported present in January-February, 1864. Name appears on receipt rolls for clothing dated June 4, June 17, and September 1, 1864. No further records.

CHAMBERS, LEWIS, Musician

Previously served as Private in Company L, 16th Regiment N.C. Troops (6th Regiment N.C. Volunteers). Transferred to this company on October 5, 1862, while on wounded furlough. Reported for duty in November-December, 1862. Promoted to Musician (Drummer) in January-February, 1863. Reported present in January-June, 1863. Reported present in September, 1863-February, 1864. Hospitalized at Charlottesville, Virginia, June 10, 1864, with acute dysentery. Returned to duty on June 28, 1864. Deserted to the enemy on an unspecified date. Confined at Louisville, Kentucky. Released at Louisville on or about February 21, 1865, after taking the Oath of Allegiance, with instructions to remain north of the Ohio River until the end of the war.

CLARK, CARSON C., Private

Previously served as Private in Company A, 62nd Regiment N.C. Troops. Transferred to this company on May 1, 1863. Reported present in May-June, 1863, and September, 1863-February, 1864. Transferred back to Company A, 62nd Regiment N.C. Troops, subsequent to March 16, 1864.

CLARK, GEORGE M., Private

Previously served as Private in Company L, 16th Regiment N.C. Troops (6th Regiment N.C. Volunteers). Transferred to this company on October 5, 1862. Reported present through October 31, 1862. Reported absent without leave on December 20, 1862. Returned to duty prior to February 28, 1863. Reported present in March-June, 1863. Reported absent without leave in September-October, 1863. Returned to duty prior to November 29, 1863. Reported present through December 31, 1863. Name appears in a company account book for clothing issued February 16, 1864. Deserted prior to February 29, 1864. Returned to duty on an unspecified date. Name appears on receipt rolls for clothing dated August 18 and September 17, 1864. Deserted to the enemy in Haywood County on or about March 2, 1865. Sent to Knoxville, Tennessee. Transferred to Louisville, Kentucky, where he arrived on April 27, 1865. Released at Louisville on April 28, 1865, after taking the Oath of Allegiance.

CLARK, JOHN, Corporal

Previously served as Corporal in Company L, 16th Regiment N.C. Troops (6th Regiment N.C. Volunteers). Transferred to this company on October 5, 1862. Reported present through October 31, 1862. Reported absent without leave on December 20, 1862. Reduced to ranks prior to February 28, 1863, when he was reported on detail. Reported present in March-June, 1863. Promoted to Corporal in July-October, 1863. Reported present in September, 1863-February, 1864. Captured at Piedmont, Virginia, June 5, 1864. Sent to Staunton, Virginia, where he was reported under guard on June 8, 1864. Confined at Camp Morton, Indianapolis, Indiana. Paroled at Camp Morton on or about March 10, 1865, and transferred to Point Lookout, Maryland. Received at Boulware's Wharf, James River, Virginia, March 23, 1865, for exchange. No further records.

CLARK, RICHARD M., Private

Previously served as Private in Company L, 16th Regiment N.C. Troops (6th Regiment N.C. Volunteers). Transferred to this company on October 5, 1862. Reported present through October 31, 1862. Reported absent without leave on December 20, 1862. Returned to duty prior to February 28, 1863, when he was reported on detail. Reported present in March-June, 1863. Detailed to the quartermaster department as a teamster in September-December, 1863. Reported present in January-February, 1864. Reported on duty as a teamster from March 1 through March 20, 1864. Name appears on receipt rolls for clothing dated June 4 and June 17, 1864. No further records. Survived the war.

CLARK, SAMUEL C., Private

Previously served as Private in Company L, 16th Regiment N.C. Troops (6th Regiment N.C. Volunteers). Transferred to this company on October 5, 1862. Reported present through October 31, 1862. Reported on detached service in the Smoky Mountains in November-December, 1862. Reported on duty as a teamster in January-February, 1863. Reported present in March-June, 1863. Reported on detached service in September, 1863-February, 1864. Probably served in the quartermaster department as a teamster at Bristol, Tennessee, during most of that period. Name appears on receipt rolls for clothing dated June 4, June 17, and October 16, 1864. No further records. [His surname may have been Clarke.]

CLARK, WILLIAM M., 1st Sergeant

Previously served as Sergeant in Company L, 16th Regiment N.C. Troops (6th Regiment N.C. Volunteers). Transferred to this company on October 5, 1862. Mustered in as Sergeant. Reported present through October 31, 1862. Reported absent without leave on December 20, 1862. Returned to duty prior to January 31, 1863. Reduced to ranks prior to February 28, 1863. Promoted to Sergeant in March-April, 1863. Reported present in March-June, 1863. Promoted to 1st Sergeant in July-October, 1863. Reported present in September-December, 1863. Reported present but under arrest in January-February, 1864. Reason he was arrested not reported. Returned to duty prior to September 19, 1864, when he was wounded in the neck and face at Winchester, Virginia. Hospitalized at Charlottesville, Virginia, September 26, 1864. Furloughed from hospital on October 7, 1864. No further records.

CLARK, WILLIAM T., Private

Previously served as Private in Company L, 16th Regiment N.C. Troops (6th Regiment N.C. Volunteers). Transferred to this company on October 5, 1862. Reported present until December 20, 1862, when he was reported absent without leave. Returned to duty prior to February 28, 1863. Reported present in March-April, 1863. Reported on detail in May-December, 1863; was employed for most or all of that period as a tailor at Carter's Depot, Tennessee. Reported present on extra duty in January-February, 1864. Name appears in a company account book for clothing issued March 16, 1864. No further records.

CLEVENGER, WILLIAM T., Private
Previously served as Private in Company L, 16th Regiment N.C. Troops (6th Regiment N.C. Volunteers). Transferred to this company on October 5, 1862. Reported sick in hospital at Richmond, Virginia, through December 31, 1862. Reported on sick furlough in Newport, Tennessee, January-June, 1863. Reported absent without leave in September-October, 1863. Subsequently reported as having deserted on August 1, 1863.

COLDWELL, HAMILTON J., Private
Previously served as Private in Company L, 16th Regiment N.C. Troops (6th Regiment N.C. Volunteers). Transferred to this company on October 5, 1862. Reported on sick furlough through October 31, 1862. Reported absent without leave in November-December, 1862. Returned to duty in January-February, 1863. Reported present through June 30, 1863. Name appears in a company account book for shoes and clothing dated August 6 and August 8, 1863. Reported absent without leave in September-October, 1863. Returned to duty prior to November 29, 1863. Reported present through December 31, 1863. Reported present but under arrest in January-February, 1864. No further records. [His surname may have been Caldwell.]

COLDWELL, JACOB, Private
Enlisted in Haywood County on February 10, 1863, for the war. Reported present through June 30, 1863. Deserted on August 31, 1863. Returned to duty subsequent to February 29, 1864. Wounded and captured at Winchester, Virginia, September 19, 1864. Sent to Harpers Ferry, West Virginia. Transferred to Point Lookout, Maryland, where he arrived on September 26, 1864. Died at Point Lookout on May 27, 1865, of "phthisis pulmon[alis]." [His surname may have been Caldwell.]

COLDWELL, WILLIAM E., Private
Enlisted in Haywood County on February 10, 1863, for the war. Reported present through June 30, 1863. Deserted on August 31, 1863. [His surname may have been Caldwell.]

CUNNINGHAM, JOSEPH K., Private
Previously served as Private in Company L, 16th Regiment N.C. Troops (6th Regiment N.C. Volunteers). Transferred to this company on October 5, 1862. Reported present through October 31, 1862. Reported sick at home in November-December, 1862. Returned to duty prior to February 28, 1863. Reported present in May-June, 1863. Reported absent without leave in September-October, 1863. Returned to duty prior to December 31, 1863. Reported on detail with the quartermaster department at Bristol, Tennessee, in January-February, 1864. Reported on duty as a teamster at Bristol from March 1 through March 20, 1864. Captured at Piedmont, Virginia, June 5, 1864. Sent to Staunton, Virginia. Confined at Camp Morton, Indianapolis, Indiana, June 21, 1864. Paroled and transferred for exchange on February 26, 1865. No further records. Survived the war. [Born on December 17, 1840.]

DUCKETT, GREEN B., Private
Enlisted in Haywood County on August 18, 1863, for the war. Reported present in November-December, 1863. Reported absent without leave on February 29, 1864. Name appears on receipt rolls for clothing dated June 17, 1864, and September, 1864. No further records.

DUCKETT, JOHN G., Private
Enlisted in Haywood County on August 18, 1863, for the war. Reported present in November-December, 1863. Reported absent without leave on February 29, 1864. Returned to duty prior to September 19, 1864, when he was was wounded (saber cut in head) and captured at Winchester, Virginia. Hospitalized at Winchester, September 20, 1864. Transferred to hospital at Baltimore, Maryland, on or about December 10, 1864. Confined at Fort McHenry, Maryland, January 5, 1865. Transferred to Point Lookout, Maryland, February 20, 1865, for exchange. Reported in hospital at Camp Winder, Richmond, Virginia, March 3, 1865. No further records. Survived the war. [Confederate gravestone records indicate that he was born in 1832.]

ERBY, JOHN F., Private
Previously served as Private in Company L, 16th Regiment N.C. Troops (6th Regiment N.C. Volunteers). Transferred to this company on October 5, 1862. Reported present through October 31, 1862. Reported absent without leave on December 20, 1862. Transferred to Company I, 63rd Regiment Tennessee Infantry, in January-February, 1863, in exchange for Pvt. Samuel L. Love.

EVANS, FOY, Private
Confederate gravestone records appear to indicate that he served in this company.

EVANS, HENRY, Private
Previously served as Private in Company L, 16th Regiment N.C. Troops (6th Regiment N.C. Volunteers). Transferred to this company on October 5, 1862, while absent wounded. Reported absent wounded through October 31, 1862. Reported absent without leave in November-December, 1862. Reported for duty in January-February, 1863. Reported on detail at Strawberry Plains and Bristol, Tennessee, in March-June, 1863, August-December, 1863, and January 15-31, 1864. Probably served as a teamster in the quartermaster department during most of that period. Reported absent without leave on February 29, 1864. No further records.

EVANS, J. TAYLOR, _____
North Carolina pension records appear to indiacte that he served in this company.

EVANS, JACOB L., Private
Confederate gravestone records appear to indicate that he served in this company.

EVANS, JAMES, Private
Enlisted at Waynesville on August 18, 1863, for the war. Reported present or accounted for in November, 1863-February, 1864. Name appears on receipt rolls for clothing dated June 4, September 1, and October 16, 1864. No further records. Survived the war. [North Carolina pension records indicate that he was wounded in 1865.]

EVANS, JEREMIAH C., Private
Previously served as Private in Company L, 16th Regiment N.C. Troops (6th Regiment N.C. Volunteers). Transferred to this company on October 5, 1862. Reported present through December 31, 1862. Reported on detail in Haywood County in January-February,

1863. Rejoined the company prior to April 30, 1863. Reported present in May-June, 1863. Reported present in September, 1863-February, 1864. Name appears on receipt rolls for clothing dated June 4, June 17, and for the third quarter, 1864. No further records. Survived the war.

EVANS, JOSEPH, Private

Previously served as Private in Company L, 16th Regiment N.C. Troops (6th Regiment N.C. Volunteers). Transferred to this company on October 5, 1862, while absent wounded. Reported absent wounded through October 31, 1862. Reported for duty prior to December 31, 1862. Reported on detail in Haywood County in January-February, 1863. Rejoined the company prior to April 30, 1863. Reported present in May-June, 1863. Reported present or accounted for in September, 1863-February, 1864. Name appears on a receipt roll for clothing dated October 16, 1864. No further records. Survived the war.

FERGUSON, ANDREW JACKSON, Private

Previously served as Private in Company L, 16th Regiment N.C. Troops (6th Regiment N.C. Volunteers). Transferred to this company on October 5, 1862. Promoted to Sergeant on January 1, 1863. Reported present through February 28, 1863. Reported absent without leave on April 1, 1863. Reduced to ranks prior to April 30, 1863. Reported present in May-June, 1863. Reported absent without leave on October 31, 1863. Returned to duty prior to December 31, 1863. Deserted between February 16 and February 29, 1864. Returned to duty prior to March 16, 1864. Hospitalized at Charlottesville, Virginia, June 12, 1864, with acute diarrhoea. Deserted from hospital at Charlottesville on June 29, 1864. Returned to duty prior to August 6, 1864, when he was hospitalized at Richmond, Virginia. Furloughed for sixty days on August 7, 1864. No further records. Survived the war.

FERGUSON, ELBERT L., Private

Enlisted in Haywood County on August 18, 1863, for the war. Reported present in November, 1863-February, 1864. Name appears on receipt rolls for clothing dated June 4, June 17, September 1, and September 27, 1864. No further records.

FERGUSON, JOHN A., Private

Enlisted in Haywood County on August 18, 1863, for the war. Reported present in November, 1863-February, 1864. Name appears on receipt rolls for clothing dated June 4 and June 17, 1864. No further records. Survived the war. [North Carolina pension records indicate that he was wounded on June 5, 1864, probably at Piedmont, Virginia. He may have served previously as Private in Company B, 62nd Regiment N.C. Troops.]

FERGUSON, JOHN L., Private

Previously served as Private in Company L, 16th Regiment N.C. Troops (6th Regiment N.C. Volunteers). Transferred to this company on October 5, 1862. Reported absent sick on October 31, 1862. Reported sick at home on December 31, 1862. Returned to duty in January-February, 1863. Reported present in March-June, 1863. No further records.

FISHER, SPENCER, Corporal

Previously served as Private in Company L, 16th Regiment N.C. Troops (6th Regiment N.C. Volunteers). Transferred to this company on October 5, 1862. Reported present through October 31, 1862. Reported absent without leave on December 1, 1862. Returned to duty prior to January 17, 1863. Reported present or accounted for through June, 1863. Wounded at Carter's Depot, Tennessee, probably on September 21 or 22, 1863. Reported on wounded furlough on October 31, 1863. Returned to duty and was promoted to Corporal prior to December 31, 1863. Reported present in January-February, 1864. Captured at Piedmont, Virginia, June 5, 1864. Reported under guard at Staunton, Virginia, June 8, 1864. Confined at Camp Morton, Indianapolis, Indiana on or about June 21, 1864. Paroled at Camp Morton and transferred to Point Lookout, Maryland, February 19, 1865, for exchange. No further records. Survived the war.

FRANCIS, BENJAMIN F., Private

Enlisted in Haywood County on August 18, 1863, for the war. Reported present in November-December, 1863. Reported sick in hospital in Tennessee in January-February, 1864. Captured at Piedmont, Virginia, June 5, 1864. Sent to Staunton, Virginia, prior to June 8, 1864. Confined at Camp Morton, Indianapolis, Indiana, June 21, 1864. Paroled at Camp Morton on February 14, 1865. Transferred to Point Lookout, Maryland, February 19, 1865, for exchange. Hospitalized at Richmond, Virginia, February 28, 1865. No further records.

FRANCIS, NEWTON F., Private

Place and date of enlistment not reported; probably enlisted subsequent to February 29, 1864. Captured in Watauga or Haywood County on February 2-4, 1865. Sent to Knoxville, Tennessee. Transferred to Chattanooga and Nashville, Tennessee. Transferred to Louisville, Kentucky, February 19, 1865, and confined there on February 20. Transferred to Camp Chase, Ohio, March 3, 1865, and arrived there on March 5. Died at Camp Chase on May 2, 1865, of "rhubela."

FRANKLIN, GEORGE W., Sergeant

Previously served as Private in Company L, 16th Regiment N.C. Troops (6th Regiment N.C. Volunteers). Transferred to this company on October 5, 1862. Reported present through December, 1862. Reported on detail in January-February, 1863. Rejoined the company prior to April 30, 1863. Reported present and promoted to Corporal in May-June, 1863. Reported absent without leave in September-October, 1863, and reduced to ranks. Returned to duty prior to November 29, 1863. Promoted to Sergeant in January-February, 1864. Captured on April 24, 1864, probably in connection with the Federal raid on Carter's Depot, Tennessee. Sent to Knoxville, Tennessee. Transferred to Nashville, Tennessee, May 13, 1864. His name appears on receipt rolls for clothing dated June 17 and September 1, 1864, indicating that he rejoined his company. However, according to the *Asheville News* of November 3, 1864, "The brave G. W. Franklin . . . of Thomas' Legion, who was wounded in the battle of Lee Town, on the 25th Aug . . . and who on the account of the severity of his wound was left within the enemy's lines, died about two weeks after he received his wound. This information is received from two nurses from 51st Va regiment, who were left with the wounded . . . and recently made their escape through the enemy's lines."

FRANKLIN, M. DECATUR, Private

Resided in Haywood County and was by occupation a tailor prior to enlisting in Haywood County at age 33, April 5, 1863, for the war. Reported present through April 30, 1863. Transferred to Company A, 62nd Regiment N.C. Troops, May 1, 1863.

GRAHL, WOODFORD S., Private

Previously served as Private in Company L, 16th Regiment N.C. Troops (6th Regiment N.C. Volunteers). Transferred to this company on October 5, 1862. Mustered in as Private. Reported present through December 30, 1862. Promoted to Corporal in January-February, 1863. Reported present through June 30, 1863. Name appears in a company account book for shoes and clothing issued August 8, 1863. Reported absent without leave in September-October, 1863. Reduced to ranks prior to October 31, 1863. Returned to duty in November-December, 1863. Reported present in January-February, 1864. Name appears in a company account book for clothing issued March 16, 1864. Name appears on a receipt roll for clothing dated June 17, 1864. Wounded and captured at Winchester, Virginia, September 19, 1864. Sent to Harpers Ferry, West Virginia. Confined at Point Lookout, Maryland, September 26, 1864. Paroled at Point Lookout and transferred to Venus Point, Savannah River, Georgia, where he was received on November 15, 1864, for exchange. No further records. [Contrary to 6:102 of this series, his first name was probably Woodford rather than Woodard. According to the Charlotte *Western Democrat* for October 25, 1864, he was wounded at Winchester, Virginia, September 19, 1864.]

HALL, LEE W., Private

Enlisted at Carter's Depot, Tennessee, April 11, 1863, for the war. Transferred to Company C of this regiment the same date.

HAWKINS, JOHN A., Private

Enlisted at Strawberry Plains, Tennessee, March 1, 1863, for the war. Reported present through June 30, 1863. Reported absent without leave in September-October, 1863. Returned to duty prior to November 29, 1863. Reported present through December 31, 1863. Reported present but under arrest in January-February, 1864. Court-martialed on or about May 24, 1864, found guilty of absence without leave, and sentenced to be confined for fifteen days "to wear 6 pound ball attached to left leg by chain." [Letters Sent, Orders and Circulars, Dept. of E. Tenn. and Dept. of W. Va. and E. Tenn., April 1863-October, 1864, Record Group 109, Chapter II, Vol. 234, National Archives.] Name appears on receipt rolls for clothing dated June 4, June 17, and September 1, 1864. No further records.

HAYNES, D. ARCHIBALD, Private

Resided in Haywood County and was by occupation a farmer prior to enlisting in Haywood County at age 27, April 5, 1863, for the war. Reported present through June 30, 1863. No further records.

HENRY, ADOLPHUS S., Private

Resided in Haywood County and was by occupation a farmer prior to enlisting at Waynesville at age 39, April 5, 1863, for the war. Reported present through April 30, 1863. Reported absent without leave on June 28, 1863. Returned to duty prior to August 5, 1863. Reported sick in hospital at Yellow Store, Tennessee, November-December, 1863, and sick in hospital in Virginia in January-February, 1864. No further records.

HENRY, JOHN A., Private

Enlisted at Waynesville on August 18, 1863, for the war. Reported present in November, 1863-February, 1864. No further records.

HIMES, ADAM A., Private

Previously served as Private in Company L, 16th Regiment N.C. Troops (6th Regiment N.C. Volunteers). Transferred to this company on October 5, 1862, while absent wounded. Reported absent wounded through April 30, 1863. Returned to duty in May-June, 1863. Reported absent without leave in September-October, 1863. Returned to duty in November-December, 1863. Reported present in January-February, 1864. Name appears on receipt rolls for clothing dated September 1 and September 27, 1864. No further records. Survived the war.

HOGAN, DAVID ALEX, Private

Previously served as Private in Company L, 16th Regiment N.C. Troops (6th Regiment N.C. Volunteers). Transferred to this company on October 5, 1862. Reported present through June 30, 1863, and in September-December, 1863. Reported on detail at Bristol, Tennessee, from January 1, 1864, through March 20, 1864. Probably served as a teamster during most of that period. Captured in Haywood County on February 5, 1865. Sent to Knoxville, Tennessee. Transferred to Chattanooga, Tennessee, February 16, 1865. Transferred to Louisville, Kentucky. Confined at Camp Chase, Ohio, on or about March 5, 1865. Released at Camp Chase on June 13, 1865, after taking the Oath of Allegiance.

HOLLIFIELD, GEORGE W., Private

Previously served as Private in Company L, 16th Regiment N.C. Troops (6th Regiment N.C. Volunteers). Transferred to this company on October 5, 1862. Reported present through June 30, 1863. Reported present in September-December, 1863. Reported absent without leave in February, 1864. Name appears on a receipt roll for clothing dated August 18, 1864. No further records. Survived the war. [His surname may have been Holifield or Holyfield.]

HOWELL, JEREMIAH, Private

Previously served as Private in Company L, 16th Regiment N.C. Troops (6th Regiment N.C. Volunteers). Transferred to this company on October 5, 1862. Reported on sick furlough through October 31, 1862. Rejoined the company prior to December 31, 1862. Discharged on January 8, 1863. Reason discharged not reported.

HOWELL, MARCUS, Private

Served as Private in Company H, and possibly Company I, 62nd Regiment N.C. Troops. In Special Orders No. 10, March 9, 1865, Brig. Gen. James G. Martin authorized the transfers of Pvts. Daniel Seay and Riley James of this company in exchange for Pvt. Nelson Howell of Company A, 62nd Regiment N.C. Troops and Pvt. Marc Howell of Company I, 62nd Regiment N.C. Troops. It is not known if or when the transfers were carried out.

HOWELL, NELSON, Private

Served as Private in Company A, 62nd Regiment N.C. Troops. In Special Orders No. 10, March 9, 1865, Brig. Gen. James G. Martin authorized the transfers of Pvts. Daniel Seay and Riley James of this company in exchange for Pvt. Nelson Howell of Company A, 62nd Regiment N.C. Troops and Pvt. Marc Howell of Company I, 62nd Regiment N.C. Troops. It is not known if or when the transfers were carried out.

HOYLE, JOHN, _____

North Carolina pension records appear to indicate that he served in this company. Survived the war.

HOYLE, NICHOLAS, _____

North Carolina pension records appear to indicate that he served in this company. Survived the war.

HUNTER, B. JACKSON, Private

Enlisted at Waynesville on April 5, 1863, for the war. Reported present through June 30, 1863. Reported present in September, 1863-February, 1864. Hospitalized at Winchester, Virginia, on or about August 1, 1864, with remittent fever and/or chronic diarrhoea. Returned to duty on or about August 3, 1864. Captured at Harrisonburg, Virginia, September 25, 1864. Hospitalized at Winchester, Virginia, October 12, 1864, with diarrhoea. Hospitalized at Baltimore, Maryland, October 17, 1864, with chronic diarrhoea. Confined at Point Lookout, Maryland, October 18, 1864. Transferred to Venus Point, Savannah River, Georgia, October 30, 1864. Received at Venus Point on November 15, 1864, for exchange. No further records.

HYATT, H. C., _____

North Carolina pension records indicate that he served in this company.

HYATT, JESSE, Private

Enlisted at Waynesville on April 5, 1863, for the war. Reported present through June 30, 1863. Reported absent without leave in September-December, 1863. Returned to duty prior to February 16, 1864. Reported present through February 29, 1864. Name appears on a receipt roll for clothing dated June 17, 1864. No further records.

HYATT, ROBERT ALNEY LAFAYETTE, Private

Born in Haywood County on January 2, 1827. Resided in Haywood County, where he enlisted at age 36, April 5, 1863, for the war. Reported present through June 30, 1863. Reported absent without leave in September-October, 1863. Returned to duty in November-December, 1863. Reported absent without leave in January-February, 1864. Returned to duty prior to September 19, 1864, when he was wounded and captured at Winchester, Virginia. Sent to Harpers Ferry, West Virginia. Confined at Point Lookout, Maryland, September 26, 1864. Died at Point Lookout on or about January 13, 1865, of "typhoid fever."

JAMES, RILEY, Private

Previously served as Corporal in Company L, 16th Regiment N.C. Troops (6th Regiment N.C. Volunteers). Transferred to this company on October 5, 1862. Reported present through December 31, 1862. Wounded in the hand in Haywood County in January-February, 1863. Returned to duty in March-April, 1863. Reported on detail in May-June, 1863. Reduced to ranks prior to October 31, 1863, when he was reported absent without leave. Returned to duty prior to December 31, 1863. Deserted between February 16, 1864, and February 29, 1864. Name appears on receipt rolls for clothing dated August 10 and September 17, 1864. In Special Orders No. 10, March 9, 1865, Brig. Gen. James G. Martin authorized the transfers of Pvts. Daniel Seay and Riley James of this company in exchange for Pvt. Nelson Howell of Company A, 62nd Regiment N.C. Troops, and Pvt. Marc Howell of Company I, 62nd Regiment N.C. Troops. It is not known if or when the transfers were carried out. No further records.

JONES, D., _____

Name appears in a company account book for a canteen, a knapsack, and a haversack issued on March 4, 1864. No further records.

JONES, JOHN L., _____

Previously served as Corporal in Company L, 16th Regiment N.C. Troops (6th Regiment N.C. Volunteers). Transferred to this company on October 5, 1862. Name appears in a company account book for shoes and clothing issued October 24, 1862, and January 17, March 10, March 17, August 5, and September 3, 1863. No further records.

JONES, ZACHARIAH P., Private

Previously served as Private in Company L, 16th Regiment N.C. Troops (6th Regiment N.C. Volunteers). Transferred to this company on October 5, 1862. Reported absent without leave on October 31, 1862. Returned to duty prior to December 31, 1862. Reported on detail with 2nd Lt. John H. Moody of this company at Cosby Creek, Tennessee, January-February, 1863. Rejoined the company prior to April 30, 1863. Reported on detached service at Strawberry Plains, Tennessee, and Bristol, Tennessee, in May-June, 1863, and from September 1, 1863, through May 20, 1864. Probably served as a teamster in the quartermaster department during most of that period. Name appears on receipt rolls for clothing dated September 22 and 28, 1864. No further records. Survived the war.

JUSTICE, REUBEN H., Private

Previously served as Private in Company L, 16th Regiment N.C. Troops (6th Regiment N.C. Volunteers). Transferred to this company on October 5, 1862, having been recently released from Federal prison. Reported for duty prior to December 31, 1862. Reported on detail with 2nd Lt. John H. Moody of this company at Cosby Creek, Tennessee, January-February, 1863. Rejoined the company prior to April 30, 1863. Reported present in May-June, 1863. Reported absent without leave in September-October, 1863. Returned to duty prior to December 17, 1863. Detailed in the quartermaster department prior to December 31, 1863. Reported sick at home in January-February, 1864. No further records. Survived the war.

JUSTICE, WESTERN L., Private

Previously served as Private in Company L, 16th Regiment N.C. Troops (6th Regiment N.C. Volunteers). Transferred to this company on October 5, 1862. Reported absent without leave on December 20, 1862. Returned to duty prior to January 17, 1863. Reported present in March-June, 1863. Reported absent without leave in September-October, 1863. Returned to duty prior to November 29, 1863. Reported present through December 31, 1863. Reported present but under arrest in January-February, 1864. No further records. Survived the war.

JUSTICE, WILLIAM M., Private

Previously served as Private in Company L, 16th Regiment N.C. Troops (6th Regiment N.C. Volunteers). Transferred to this company on October 5, 1862. Reported present through December 31, 1862. Reported absent sick in January-February, 1863. Returned to duty prior to April 30, 1863. Reported present in May-June, 1863. Reported on detail with the commissary department in September-December, 1863. Name appears in a company account book for clothing issued February 16, 1864. No further records. Survived the war. [He was also known as "Cubby." His middle initial may have been G.]

KING, W. R., Private

Place and date of enlistment not reported; probably enlisted subsequent to February 29, 1864. Wounded in the face and captured at

Winchester, Virginia, September 19, 1864. "Deserted" or escaped from hospital at Winchester on October 8, 1864. No further records.

KIRKPATRICK, GILBERT LAWSON, Private
Previously served as Corporal in Company L, 16th Regiment N.C. Troops (6th Regiment N.C. Volunteers). Transferred to this company on October 5, 1862. Died, probably soon after November, 1862. Place, date, and cause of death not reported. [His given name may have been Lawson Gilbert.]

KIRKPATRICK, MILAS ALEXANDER, Private
Previously served as Private in Company L, 16th Regiment N.C. Troops (6th Regiment N.C. Volunteers). Transferred to this company on October 5, 1862, while absent wounded. Reported on wounded furlough through December 31, 1862. Reported for duty prior to February 28, 1863. Reported present through June 30, 1863. Reported detailed in the commissary and quartermaster departments in September-December, 1863. Reported on furlough in January-February, 1864. No further records. Survived the war. [Born on May 11, 1841.]

LEE, HENRY CULPEPPER, _____
North Carolina pension records and records of the United Daughters of the Confederacy appear to indicate that he served in this company. Survived the war.

LINER, HENRY, Private
Previously served as Private in Company L, 16th Regiment N.C. Troops (6th Regiment N.C. Volunteers). Transferred to this company on October 5, 1862. Reported present through December 31, 1862. Reported on detail with Lt. John H. Moody of this company at Cosby Creek, Tennessee, January-February, 1863. Rejoined the company prior to April 30, 1863. Reported on detail with Sgt. William J. Rogers of this company in May-June, 1863. Reported on detail as a blacksmith at Asheville from October 20, 1863, through June 30, 1864. Reported as absent without leave "since detailed as a blacksmith" in company muster rolls from September-October, 1863, through January-February, 1864. Reported on detail as a blacksmith in western North Carolina from September 9, 1864, through October 8, 1864, and in November, 1864. No further records. Survived the war. [Born on May 4, 1834.]

LINER, JEREMIAH A., Private
Born on April 23, 1822. Enlisted in Haywood County at age 41, August 18, 1863, for the war. Reported present in November, 1863-February, 1864. Name appears on a receipt roll for clothing dated October 16, 1864. Survived the war. [North Carolina pension records indicate that he was wounded in the left leg at "Cattalooche," N.C., February 3, 1865. The latter is probably a reference to either of the skirmishes that were fought about that time at Soco Gap and Soco Creek between elements of Thomas's Legion and Federal raiders under George W. Kirk. Confederate gravestone records give Liner's rank as 2nd Lieutenant; however, there is no evidence of this in company records.]

LINER, LEANDER, Private
Previously served as Private in Company A, 62nd Regiment N.C. Troops. Transferred to this company on May 1, 1863. Reported present through June 30, 1863. Reported absent without leave in September-October, 1863. Returned to duty prior to December 31, 1863. Name appears in a company account book for clothing issued February 16, 1864. Reported absent without leave on February 29, 1864. Name appears on a receipt roll for clothing dated October 16, 1864. No further records. Survived the war. [Born on November 15, 1827.]

LINER, THOMAS, Private
Previously served as Private in Company L, 16th Regiment N.C. Troops (6th Regiment N.C. Volunteers). Transferred to this company on October 5, 1862. Reported on detail through October 31, 1862. Rejoined the company prior to December 31, 1862. Reported on detail with 2nd Lt. John H. Moody of this company at Cosby Creek, Tennessee, January-February, 1863. Rejoined the company prior to April 30, 1863. Reported present in May-June, 1863. Reported absent without leave in September-October, 1863. Returned to duty prior to December 31, 1863. Reported absent under arrest at Bristol, Tennessee, January-February, 1864. Probably returned to duty prior to February 16, 1864. Captured at Piedmont, Virginia, June 5, 1864. Reported under guard at Staunton, Virginia, June 8, 1864. Confined at Camp Morton, Indianapolis, Indiana, June 21, 1864. Paroled at Camp Morton on February 26, 1865, and transferred to City Point, Virginia, for exchange. No further records. Survived the war.

LOVE, SAMUEL L., Private
Previously served in Capt. James T. Gillespie's Company of Tennessee Cavalry; Company I, Fain's Regiment of Tennessee Infantry; and Company I, 63rd Regiment Tennessee Infantry. Transferred to this company in January-February, 1863. Reported on detail with 2nd Lt. John H. Moody of this company at Cosby Creek, Tennessee, January-February, 1863. Rejoined the company prior to April 30, 1863. Appointed Surgeon of this regiment on March 14, 1863, to rank from September 27, 1862, but declined the appointment. Survived the war. [He may have served also as Private in Company E, 62nd Regiment N.C. Troops.]

LUNDY, WILLIAM ANDREW, Private
Previously served as Private in Company L, 16th Regiment N.C. Troops (6th Regiment N.C. Volunteers). Transferred to this company on October 5, 1862. Rejoined the company prior to December 29, 1862. Reported present in January-June, 1863. Captured in Kentucky or in eastern Tennessee on July 18, 1863. Sent to Cincinnati, Ohio, and confined at Kemper Barracks. Transferred to Camp Chase, Ohio, August 11, 1863. Transferred to Camp Douglas, Chicago, Illinois on an unspecified date. Released at Camp Douglas, July 16, 1865, after taking the Oath of Allegiance. [Born on February 12, 1842. According to 1904 and 1908 lists of Haywood County veterans receiving pensions, he was wounded on an unknown date. It is not known whether the wounds were received while serving with Thomas's Legion or with the 16th Regiment.]

McCRACKEN, E. ENNOS, Private
Previously served as Private in Company C, 1st Battalion N.C. Junior Reserves. Transferred to this company on an unspecified date, probably subsequent to June 30, 1864. Deserted to the enemy in Haywood County on an unspecified date. Confined at Knoxville, Tennessee, March 22, 1865. Took the Oath of Allegiance at Knoxville on March 23, 1865. Transferred to Chattanooga, Tennessee, March 25, 1865. Transferred to Louisville, Kentucky, and arrived there on April 2, 1865. Took the Oath of Allegiance at Louisville on April 8, 1865, and ordered to remain north of the Ohio River for the rest of the war.

McCRACKEN, THOMAS B., Private
Previously served as Private in Company L, 16th Regiment N.C. Troops (6th Regiment N.C. Volunteers). Transferred to this company on October 5, 1862. Promoted to Corporal prior to October 31, 1862, when he was reported sick in hospital at Danville, Virginia. Reported absent on expired sick furlough in November-December, 1862. Returned to duty and was reduced to ranks prior to February 28, 1863. Reported present in March-June, 1863. Promoted to Sergeant in July-October, 1863. Reported present in September, 1863-February, 1864. Reduced to ranks on an unspecified date. Captured at Piedmont, Virginia, June 5, 1864. Reported under guard at Staunton, Virginia, June 8, 1864. Transferred to Camp Morton, Indianapolis, Indiana, where he arrived on June 21, 1864. Paroled at Camp Morton and transferred to City Point, Virginia, February 26, 1865, for exchange. No further records. Survived the war. [Born on October 17, 1843.]

McELROY, DAVID, Private
Enlisted in Haywood County on April 5, 1863, for the war. Reported present through April 30, 1863. Reported on detail with Sgt. William J. Rogers of this company in May-June, 1863. Deserted on September 15, 1863.

McFALLS, ARTHUR, Private
Resided in Haywood County. Enlisted in Haywood County at age 35, April 5, 1863, for the war. Reported present in May-June, 1863. Deserted on August 31, 1863. Name appears on a receipt roll for clothing dated October, 1864. [North Carolina pension records indicate that he served also in Company A, 62nd Regiment N.C. Troops.]

McGEE, FRANKLIN P., Private
Previously served as Private in Company L, 16th Regiment N.C. Troops (6th Regiment N.C. Volunteers). Transferred to this company on October 5, 1862, while absent wounded. Reported absent wounded through June 30, 1863, and in September, 1863-February, 1864. No further records.

McKINNISH, WILLIAM, Private
Enlisted in Haywood County on February 10, 1863, for the war. Reported present through February 28, 1863. Deserted on April 7, 1863, at Strawberry Plains, Tennessee. Returned to duty prior to June 30, 1863. Deserted on September 15, 1863.

McNABB, DANIEL C., Private
Previously served as Private in Company L, 16th Regiment N.C. Troops (6th Regiment N.C. Volunteers). Transferred to this company on October 5, 1862. Reported absent sick in various hospitals through June 30, 1863. A company account book noted his death. Date, place, and cause of death not reported. [The Tennessee pension application for Sgt. John M. McNabb of this company seems to indicate that Daniel C. McNabb died of illness in Virginia.]

McNABB, JOHN M., Sergeant
Previously served as Private in Company L, 16th Regiment N.C. Troops (6th Regiment N.C. Volunteers). Transferred to this company on October 5, 1862. Reported present through December 31, 1862. Reported on detail with Capt. Julius M. Welch of this company in January-February, 1863. Rejoined the company prior to April 30, 1863. Reported present in May-June, 1863. Reported absent without leave in September-October, 1863. Returned to duty prior to December 31, 1863. Promoted to Sergeant in January-February, 1864. No further records. Survived the war. [Born in Cocke County, Tennessee, January 16, 1844. See his Tennessee pension application No. 15667.]

MARROW, J. L., _____
North Carolina pension records appear to indicate that he served in this company. Survived the war.

MASSEY, JAMES M., Private
Previously served as Private in Company L, 16th Regiment N.C. Troops (6th Regiment N.C. Volunteers). Transferred to this company on October 5, 1862. Reported present through October 31, 1862. Reported absent without leave on December 20, 1862. Returned to duty prior to January 17, 1863. Reported on detail with Capt. Julius M. Welch of this company in Haywood County in January-February, 1863. Reported on detail with the quartermaster department at Strawberry Plains, Tennessee, March-June, 1863. Probably served as a teamster during most of that period. Reported on detail in September, 1863-February, 1864. Probably served in the quartermaster department at Bristol, Tennessee, during most of that period. Name appears on receipt rolls for clothing dated March 12, 1864, and December 14, 1864. No further records.

MASSEY, JOHN, Private
Enlisted in Haywood County on February 27, 1863, for the war. Reported present through June 30, 1863. Deserted on September 19, 1863. Name appears on a receipt roll for clothing dated October 16, 1864. No further records.

MASSEY, LEBO, Private
Born in South Carolina. Resided in Haywood County and was by occupation a "renter" prior to enlisting in Haywood County at age 39, April 5, 1863, for the war. Reported present through April 30, 1863. Reported absent without leave on June 28, 1863. Returned to duty prior to August 5, 1863. Reported absent without leave in September-October, 1863. Returned to duty prior to December 17, 1863. Reported present in January-February, 1864. Deserted to the enemy in Haywood County on an unspecified date. Reported at Sevierville, Tennessee, May 20, 1864. Sent to Knoxville, Tennessee. Took the Oath of Allegiance at Knoxville, Tennessee, on or about May 25, 1864. Sent to Chattanooga, Tennessee, and arrived there on or about May 27, 1864. Received at Louisville, Kentucky, May 29, 1864. Discharged at Louisville on June 4, 1864, with orders to remain "North of the Ohio River for the war."

MASSEY, TILLETT L., Private
Born in South Carolina. Resided in Haywood County and was by occupation a "renter" prior to enlisting in Haywood County at age 44, February 6, 1864, for the war. Reported present on February 29, 1864. Deserted to the enemy in Haywood County on an unspecified date. Reported at Sevierville, Tennessee, May 20, 1864. Sent to Knoxville, Tennessee. Took the Oath of Allegiance at Knoxville, Tennessee, on or about May 25, 1864. Sent to Chattanooga, Tennessee, and arrived there on or about May 27, 1864. Received at Louisville, Kentucky, May 29, 1864. Discharged at Louisville on June 4, 1864, with orders to remain "North of the Ohio River for the war."

MASSEY, WILBORN, Private
Enlisted in Haywood County on February 27, 1863, for the war. Reported on detail at Strawberry Plains, Tennessee, March-June,

1863. Was probably serving as a teamster during most of that period. Reported on detail in September, 1863-February, 1864. Was probably serving in the quartermaster department at Bristol, Tennessee, during most of that period. Hospitalized at Charlottesville, Virginia, September 24, 1864. Furloughed for thirty days on September 25, 1864. No further records.

MASSEY, WILLIAM H., Private

Previously served as Private in Company L, 16th Regiment N.C. Troops (6th Regiment N.C. Volunteers). Transferred to this company on October 5, 1862, while absent wounded. Reported wounded and in hospital at Warrenton, Virginia, October 31, 1862. A company account book noted his death. Date, place, and cause of death not reported.

MASSIE, WILLIAM LEBO, _____

North Carolina pension and gravestone records and records of the United Daughters of the Confederacy appear to indicate that he served in this company. Survived the war.

MAULDIN, LEROY, Private

Previously served as Private in Company L, 16th Regiment N.C. Troops (6th Regiment N.C. Volunteers). Transferred to this company on October 5, 1862. Reported present through October 31, 1862. Reported absent without leave, December 20, 1862. Reported absent sick in Haywood County, January-February, 1863. Returned to duty prior to March 9, 1863. Reported present through June 30, 1863. Reported on detail in the brigade commissary department in September-October, 1863. Reported on furlough in November-December, 1863. Reported absent without leave in January- February, 1864. No further records. Survived the war.

MEDFORD, ELIAS, Private

Resided in Haywood County and was by occupation a farmer prior to enlisting in Haywood County at age 34, April 5, 1863, for the war. Reported present through June 30, 1863. Reported absent without leave in September-October, 1863. Returned prior to November 25, 1863. Reported present in January-February, 1864. Hospitalized at Charlottesville, Virginia, June 12, 1864, with gastritis. Returned to duty on June 17, 1864. Wounded in the face and captured at Winchester, Virginia, September 19, 1864. Hospitalized at Winchester. Transferred to Point Lookout, Maryland, November 15, 1864. Paroled at Point Lookout, March 15, 1865. Received at Boulware's Wharf, James River, Virginia, March 18, 1865, for exchange. No further records. Survived the war.

MEDFORD, JONAS, "Detail Boy"

North Carolina pension records indicate that he served in this company. Survived the war.

MEDFORD, L., _____

North Carolina pension records appear to indicate that he served in this company. Survived the war. [Was probably the same man as Lawson H. Medford or R. Lebo Medford of this company.]

MEDFORD, LAWSON H., Private

Confederate gravestone records appear to indicate that he served in this company. Survived the war. [He may have been the same man as L. Medford of this company.]

MEDFORD, LEBO, Private

Resided in Haywood County and was by occupation a farmer prior to enlisting in Haywood County at age 35, April 5, 1863, for the war. Reported present through June 30, 1863. Reported absent without leave, September-October, 1863. Returned to duty prior to December 31, 1863. Reported present in January-February, 1864. Captured in Haywood County on or about February 4, 1865. Sent to Knoxville, Tennessee. Transferred to Chattanooga, Tennessee, February 16, 1865. Transferred to Nashville, Tennessee. Confined at Louisville, Kentucky, February 20, 1865. Transferred to Camp Chase, Ohio, where he arrived on March 5, 1865. Released at Camp Chase, June 13, 1865, after taking the Oath of Allegiance. [North Carolina pension records indicate that he was wounded in the left ankle at Lynchburg, Virginia, on an unspecified date. His middle initial may have been P.]

MEDFORD, R. LEBO, _____

Confederate gravestone records appear to indicate that he served in this company. Survived the war. [He may have been the same man as L. Medford of this company.]

MEDFORD, WILLIAM LEBO, _____

Confederate gravestone records appear to indicate that he served in this company.

MESSER, ELIJAH M., Private

Previously served as Private in Company L, 16th Regiment N.C. Troops (6th Regiment N.C. Volunteers). Transferred to this company on October 5, 1862. Reported sick in hospital at Staunton, Virginia, through December 31, 1862. Returned to duty prior to February 28, 1863. Reported present in March-June, 1863. Deserted on September 8, 1863.

MESSER, GEORGE W., Private

Previously served as Private in Company L, 16th Regiment N.C. Troops (6th Regiment N.C. Volunteers). Transferred to this company on October 5, 1862, while absent without leave. Reported for duty prior to December 31, 1862. Reported present, January-February, 1863. Deserted at Strawberry Plains, Tennessee, April 7, 1863. Returned to duty on an unspecified date. Court-martialed on or about July 19, 1863. Deserted on September 15, 1863.

MESSER, RICHARD, Private

Enlisted in Haywood County on January 1, 1864, for the war. Reported present through February 29, 1864. No further records.

MESSER, SAMUEL, JR., Private

Previously served as Private in Company L, 16th Regiment N.C. Troops (6th Regiment N.C. Volunteers). Transferred to this company on October 5, 1862. Reported present through October 31, 1862. Reported absent without leave on December 20, 1862. Returned to duty prior to January 17, 1863. Reported present through February 28, 1863, and in March-June, 1863. Deserted on September 15, 1863, while absent sick. Name appears on receipt rolls for clothing dated June 4 and June 17, 1864. No further records. Survived the war.

MESSER, SAMUEL, SR., Private

Previously served as Private in Company L, 16th Regiment N.C. Troops (6th Regiment N.C. Volunteers). Transferred to this company on October 5, 1862, while absent sick in Richmond, Virginia.

Reported absent sick at home in Haywood County through February 28, 1863. Returned to duty prior to April 30, 1863. Reported present in May-June, 1863. Deserted on August 31, 1863. Returned to duty on January 13, 1864. Reported present through February 29, 1864. No further records.

MILLER, LEWIS, Private

Previously served as Private in Company L, 16th Regiment N.C. Troops (6th Regiment N.C. Volunteers). Transferred to this company on October 5, 1862, while absent wounded. Reported absent wounded through June 30, 1863, and in September, 1863-February, 1864; he was in Haywood County for at least part of that period. No further records.

MOODY, HARVEY L., Private

Previously served as Sergeant in Company L, 16th Regiment N.C. Troops (6th Regiment N.C. Volunteers). Transferred to this company on October 5, 1862. Reported present through June 30, 1863, and in September, 1863-February, 1864. Reduced to ranks in January-February, 1864. Name appears in a company account book for a canteen issued March 4 and clothing issued March 17, 1864. No further records. Survived the war.

MOODY, MILES A., Private

Previously served as Private in Company L, 16th Regiment N.C. Troops (6th Regiment N.C. Volunteers). Transferred to this company on October 5, 1862. Reported present through October 31, 1862. Reported absent without leave on December 20, 1862. Returned to duty prior to January 17, 1863. Reported on detail with 2nd Lt. John H. Moody of this company at Cosby Creek, Tennessee, January-February, 1863. Rejoined the company prior to April 30, 1863. Reported present in May-June, 1863. Reported absent without leave in September-October, 1863. Returned to duty prior to December 31, 1863. Reported present but under arrest in January-February, 1864. Name appears in a company account book for clothing issued March 16, 1864. No further records.

MOORE, WILLIAM HENRY, Private

Previously served as Private in Company L, 16th Regiment N.C. Troops (6th Regiment N.C. Volunteers). Transferred to this company on October 5, 1862. Reported present through October 31, 1862. Reported absent without leave from December 1 through 31, 1862. Returned to duty prior to February 28, 1863. Reported present in March-April, 1863. Reported on detail at Zollicoffer, Tennessee, drilling Company H of this regiment. Reported present in September-October, 1863. Transferred to Company C of this regiment in November-December, 1863.

MORRELL, JOHN L., Private

Resided in Haywood County. Place and date of enlistment not reported; probably enlisted subsequent to February 29, 1864. Captured in Haywood County on or about February 3, 1865. Sent to Knoxville, Tennessee. Transferred to Chattanooga, Tennessee,February 16, 1865. Confined at Nashville, Tennessee, prior to February 19, 1865. Transferred to Louisville, Kentucky, and confined there February 20, 1865. Confined at Camp Chase, Ohio, March 5, 1865. Released at Camp Chase on June 13, 1865, after taking the Oath of Allegiance. [His surname may have been Marr.]

MULL, JOHN HARRISON, Private

Previously served as Private in Company L, 16th Regiment N.C. Troops (6th Regiment N.C. Volunteers). Transferred to this company on October 5, 1862. Reported absent sick at Warrenton, Virginia, October 31, 1862. Reported absent without leave from December 20 through 31, 1862. Returned to duty prior to January 31, 1863. Reported present through February 28, 1863, and in March-June, 1863. Promoted to Corporal prior to October 31, 1863. Reported present in September-October, 1863. Reduced to ranks and was reported on detail in the commissary department in November-December, 1863. Reported on detail in the quartermaster department in January-February, 1864. Reported on duty as a teamster at Bristol, Tennessee, March 1-20, 1864. No further records. Survived the war.

NOLAND, ALLEN, Private

Previously served as Private in Company L, 16th Regiment N.C. Troops (6th Regiment N.C. Volunteers). Transferred to this company on October 5, 1862, while a prisoner of war. Reported sick at home in November-December, 1862. Reported for duty prior to February 28, 1863. Reported present in March-April, 1863. Reported on detached service with Sgt. William J. Rogers of this company in May-June, 1863. Reported present, September, 1863-February, 1864. Name appears in a company account book for clothing issued March 16, 1864. No further records. Survived the war.

NOLAND, JOSEPH M., Private

Previously served as Private in Company L, 16th Regiment N.C. Troops (6th Regiment N.C. Volunteers). Transferred to this company on October 5, 1862. Reported present through October 31, 1862. Reported absent without leave from December 1 through 31, 1862. Returned to duty prior to January 17, 1863. Reported present through June 30, 1863. Promoted to Corporal prior to October 31, 1863. Reported present or accounted for, September, 1863-February, 1864. Reduced to ranks on an unspecified date. Name appears on receipt rolls for clothing dated June 4 and June 17, 1864. Deserted to the enemy in Haywood County, March 18, 1865. Sent to Knoxville, Tennessee. Took the Oath of Allegiance at Knoxville, March 23, 1865. Confined at Louisville, Kentucky, April 2, 1865. Released at Louisville, April 8, 1865, after taking the Oath of Allegiance, with instructions to remain north of the Ohio River during the war.

NOLAND, TAYLOR, Private

Resided in Haywood County and enlisted at Carter's Depot, Tennessee, February 1, 1864, for the war. Reported present on February 29, 1864. Name appears on a receipt roll for clothing dated June 4, 1864. Hospitalized at Charlottesville, Virginia, June 10, 1864, with acute dysentery. Returned to duty on June 13, 1864. Deserted to the enemy in Haywood County on March 18, 1865. Sent to Knoxville, Tennessee. Took the Oath of Allegiance at Knoxville, March 23, 1865. Confined at Louisville, Kentucky, April 2, 1865. Released at Louisville on April 8, 1865, after taking the Oath of Allegiance, with instructions to remain north of the Ohio River during the war.

OWEN, DOCTOR J., Private

Previously served as Private in Company L, 16th Regiment N.C. Troops (6th Regiment N.C. Volunteers). Transferred to this company on October 5, 1862, while absent without leave. Reported for duty on an unspecified date but was again reported absent without leave on December 1, 1862. Returned to duty prior to January 17, 1863. Reported on detail with 2nd Lt. John H. Moody of this company at Cosby Creek, Tennessee, January-February, 1863. Rejoined the company prior to April 30, 1863. Reported present in May-June, 1863. Reported absent without leave in September-October, 1863.

Returned to duty prior to December 31, 1863. Reported present but under arrest in January-February, 1864. Captured at Piedmont, Virginia, June 5, 1864. Reported under guard at Staunton, Virginia, June 8, 1864. Transferred to Camp Morton, Indianapolis, Indiana, on an unspecified date. Paroled at Camp Morton on or about March 4, 1865. Received at Boulware's and Cox's Wharves, James River, Virginia, on or about March 10, 1865, for exchange. Hospitalized at Richmond, Virginia, March 11, 1865. Transferred to Camp Lee, Virginia, March 12, 1865. No further records. [Contrary to 6:105 of this series, his surname was probably Owen rather than Owens.]

OWEN, WILLIAM H., Sergeant

Previously served as Private in Company L, 16th Regiment N.C. Troops (6th Regiment N.C. Volunteers). Transferred to this company on October 5, 1862. Reported present through December 31, 1862. Reported on detail with 2nd Lt. John H. Moody of this company at Cosby Creek, Tennessee, January-February, 1863. Rejoined the company prior to April 30, 1863. Reported present in May-June, 1863. Promoted to Sergeant in July-October, 1863. Reported present in September-December, 1863, and January-February, 1864. Captured at Winchester, Virginia, September 19, 1864. Sent to Harpers Ferry, West Virginia. Confined at Point Lookout, Maryland, September 26, 1864. Paroled at Point Lookout on March 15, 1865. Received at Boulware's and Cox's Wharves, James River, Virginia, March 18, 1865, for exchange. No further records. Survived the war. [Contrary to 6:105 of this series, his surname was probably Owen rather than Owens.]

OXNER, HENRY, _____

North Carolina pension records indicate that he served in this company.

PARTON, DANIEL M., Private

Previously served as Private in Company L, 16th Regiment N.C. Troops (6th Regiment N.C. Volunteers). Transferred to this company on October 5, 1862. Reported present through October 31, 1862. Reported absent without leave on December 20, 1862. Returned to duty prior to January 31, 1863. Reported on detail with 2nd Lt. John H. Moody of this company at Cosby Creek, Tennessee, February, 1863. Rejoined the company prior to April 30, 1863. Transferred to Company A, 62nd Regiment N.C. Troops, on or about May 1, 1863.

PARTON, F. M., Private

North Carolina pension records indicate that he served in this company. Survived the war. [He may be the same man as Pvt. Marion S. Parton of this company.]

PARTON, MARION, Private

Previously served as Private in Company L, 16th Regiment N.C. Troops (6th Regiment N.C. Volunteers). Transferred to this company on October 5, 1862. Reported present through October 31, 1862. Reported absent without leave on December 20, 1862. Returned to duty prior to January 17, 1863. Reported present through June, 1863. Deserted on August 31, 1863. Returned to duty in January-February, 1864. Name appears on receipt rolls for clothing dated June 4 and June 17, 1864. No further records. Survived the war.

PARTON, MARION M., _____

North Carolina pension records indicate that he served in this company. Survived the war.

PARTON, MARION S., Private

Confederate gravestone records indicate that he served in this company. Survived the war. [He may have been the same man as Pvt. F. M. Parton of this company.]

PARTON, THOMAS, Private

Previously served as Private in Company L, 16th Regiment N.C. Troops (6th Regiment N.C. Volunteers). Transferred to this company on October 5, 1862. Reported absent sick on October 31, 1862. Reported absent without leave, December 20, 1862. Returned to duty prior to February 28, 1863. Reported present in March-June, 1863. Deserted on August 31, 1863. Returned to duty prior to February 29, 1864. Name appears on receipt rolls for clothing dated June 4 and June 17, 1864. No further records. Survived the war.

PATTERSON, JEREMIAH M., Private

Previously served as Private in Company L, 16th Regiment N.C. Troops (6th Regiment N.C. Volunteers). Transferred to this company on October 5, 1862, while absent without leave. Reported for duty prior to December 31, 1862. Reported on detail with 2nd Lt. John H. Moody of this company at Cosby Creek, Tennessee, January-February, 1863. Rejoined the company prior to April 30, 1863. Reported present in May-June, 1863. Reported absent without leave in September-October, 1863. Returned to duty prior to December 31, 1863. Reported absent without leave, February 29, 1864. Name appears in a company account book for clothing issued March 16, 1864. No further records. [His first name may have been James. Contrary to his entry in 6:105, he transferred while absent without leave, not while absent wounded.]

PLOTT, ENOS V., Private

Previously served as 3rd Lieutenant of Company A, 62nd Regiment N.C. Troops. Reduced to ranks and transferred to or enlisted illegally in this company on April 6, 1863. Transferred back to Company A, 62nd Regiment N.C. Troops, May 1, 1863, with the rank of Private. [His middle initial may have been L. Contrary to 15:45 of this series, he did not serve at any time as 3rd Lieutenant of Company E, Infantry Regiment of this legion.]

PRESNELL, WILLIAM A., Private

Previously served as Private in Company L, 16th Regiment N.C. Troops (6th Regiment N.C. Volunteers). Transferred to this company on October 5, 1862. Reported present through April 30, 1863. Reported on detail as a wagoner at Strawberry Plains, Tennessee, in May-June, 1863. Reported on detail in the quartermaster department at Bristol, Tennessee, November-December, 1863. Rejoined the company in January-February, 1864. Reported on detail as a teamster at Bristol, March 1-20, 1864. Name appears on receipt rolls for clothing dated June 4, June 17, and September 27, 1864. No further records. Survived the war.

QUEEN, SAMUEL B., Private

Resided in Haywood County. Place and date of enlistment not reported; probably enlisted subsequent to February 29, 1864. Name appears on a receipt roll for clothing dated October, 1864. Captured in Haywood County on or about February 4, 1865. Sent to Knoxville, Tennessee. Transferred to Chattanooga, Tennessee, February 6, 1865. Transferred to Nashville, Tennessee. Confined at Louisville, Kentucky, February 20, 1865. Transferred to Camp Chase, Ohio, where he arrived on March 5, 1865. Released at Camp Chase on or about June 13, 1865, after taking the Oath of Allegiance.

RATHBONE, RUSSEL MAXIL, Private

Enlisted in Haywood County on December 17, 1862, for the war. Reported present through December 31, 1862. Reported present sick in January-February, 1863. Died in hospital at Strawberry Plains, Tennessee, March 15 or June 8, 1863. Cause of death not reported.

RATHBONE, RUSSELL, Private

Resided in Haywood County and was by occupation a "renter." Enlisted in Haywood County at age 42, August 18, 1863, for the war. Reported on detail or extra duty in November, 1863-February, 1864. Served in the commissary department for at least part of that time. Name appears on receipt rolls for clothing dated June 17 and October 16, 1864. No further records. Survived the war.

REEVES, ALBERT, Private

Previously served as Private in Company L, 16th Regiment N.C. Troops (6th Regiment N.C. Volunteers). Transferred to this company on October 5, 1862, while absent wounded. Reported absent wounded through February 28, 1863. Reported for duty prior to April 30, 1863. Reported absent without leave on June 28, 1863. Returned to duty prior to August 5, 1863. Reported absent without leave in September-December, 1863. Returned to duty prior to February 16, 1864. Reported present through February 29, 1864. Name appears on a receipt roll for clothing dated June 17, 1864. No further records. Survived the war.

RHEA, JAMES A., Private

Previously served as Private in Company L, 16th Regiment N.C. Troops (6th Regiment N.C. Volunteers). Transferred to this company on October 5, 1862, while absent wounded. Reported absent wounded through October 31, 1862. Reported absent without leave, December 20, 1862. Reported for duty prior to February 28, 1863. Reported sick in hospital at Strawberry Plains, Tennessee, March-April, 1863. Returned to duty prior to June 30, 1863. Reported on detached service in September-October, 1863. Reported on detail in an unspecified Virginia hospital in November, 1863-February, 1864. Was employed for at least part of that period as a nurse. No further records.

RHEA, JOHN M., _____

Confederate gravestone records appear to indicate that he served in this company. Survived the war.

RICE, HARVEY C., Private

Resided in Haywood County. Place and date of enlistment not reported; probably enlisted subsequent to February 29, 1864. According to Federal Provost Marshal records, he served in "Co. E, Thomas' Legion;" he served either in this company or in Company E, Walker's Battalion. Captured in Haywood County on February 4, 1865. Sent to Knoxville, Tennessee. Transferred to Chattanooga, Tennessee, February 16, 1865. Transferred to Nashville, Tennessee. Confined at Louisville, Kentucky, February 20, 1865. Confined at Camp Chase, Ohio, March 5, 1865. Released at Camp Chase on June 13, 1865, after taking the Oath of Allegiance.

RICE, JAMES M., Private

Previously served as Private in Company L, 16th Regiment N.C. Troops (6th Regiment N.C. Volunteers). Transferred to this company on October 5, 1862, while absent without leave. Reported for duty prior to December 31, 1862. Reported on detail with 2nd Lt. John H. Moody of this company at Cosby Creek, Tennessee, on January-February, 1863. Reported on detail in the post quartermaster department at Strawberry Plains, Tennessee, March-June, 1863. Served as a wagon master for at least part of that period. Reported on detail, September, 1863-February, 1864. Served as a wagon master in the quartermaster department at Bristol, Tennessee, during much of that period. Name appears on a receipt roll for clothing dated June 17, 1864. No further records.

RINEHART, JAMES C., Private

Previously served as Private in Company L, 16th Regiment N.C. Troops (6th Regiment N.C. Volunteers). Transferred to this company on October 5, 1862. Reported on detail on October 31, 1862. Rejoined the company prior to December 31, 1862. Promoted to Sergeant on January 1, 1863. Reported present through June 30, 1863. Reduced to ranks prior to October 31, 1863, and reported absent without leave. Subsequently reported as having deserted on August 31, 1863. [His surname may have been Rhinehart or Rheinhart. Confederate gravestone records appear to indicate that he held the rank of Corporal, and that he may have subsequently transferred either to Company C of this regiment, Company C of Walker's Battalion, or Company C of the Indian Battalion.]

RHINEHART, THOMAS P., Private

Previously served as Private in 1st Company A of this regiment. Records of Company K, 39th Regiment N.C. Troops, indicate that he transferred to that company but did not report for duty. Transferred to this company in January, 1863. Reported present through June 30, 1863. Reported absent without leave in September-December, 1863. Returned to duty prior to February 16, 1864. Listed as a deserter on February 29, 1864. Name appears on a receipt roll for clothing dated June 17, 1864. No further records. Survived the war. [Contrary to 10:185 of this series, his surname was probably Rhinehart.]

ROBERTSON, JOHN W., Private

Previously served as Private in Company L, 16th Regiment N.C. Troops (6th Regiment N.C. Volunteers). Transferred to this company on October 5, 1862. Reported on detail through October 31, 1862. Rejoined the company prior to December 31, 1862. Reported present in January-June, 1863. Reported on sick furlough in September-December, 1863. Returned to duty prior to February 16, 1864. Reported on extra duty through February 29, 1864. Name appears on a receipt roll for clothing dated August 15, 1864. No further records.

ROGERS, SEBORN T., Private

Previously served as Musician (Drummer) in Company L, 16th Regiment N.C. Troops (6th Regiment N.C. Volunteers). Transferred to this company on October 5, 1862. Reported present through October 31, 1862. Reported absent without leave, December 1, 1862. Returned to duty and was reduced to ranks prior to February 28, 1863. Reported present in March-June, 1863. Reported absent without leave in September-October, 1863. Reported on detail in the quartermaster department at Bristol, Tennessee, in January-February, 1864. Reported on duty as a teamster at Bristol from March 1 through 20, 1864. Name appears on a receipt roll for clothing dated October 16, 1864. No further records. Survived the war.

ROGERS, WILLIAM J., Private

Previously served as Sergeant in Company L, 16th Regiment N.C. Troops (6th Regiment N.C. Volunteers). Transferred to this company on October 5, 1862. Reported present through October 31,

1862. Reported absent without leave on December 20, 1862. Returned to duty and reduced to ranks prior to January 31, 1863. Reported on detail with 2nd Lt. John H. Moody of this company at Cosby Creek, Tennessee, January-February, 1863. Rejoined the company and restored to the rank of Sergeant prior to April 30, 1863. Reported on detached service "scouting in Hawkins County, [Tennessee], for Renegades & Conscripts" in May-June, 1863. Reported absent wounded in September-October, 1863. Place and date wounded not reported. Returned to duty prior to December 31, 1863. Reduced to ranks and reported on extra duty in January-February, 1864. Name appears on a receipt roll for clothing dated June 4, 1864. No further records. Survived the war.

RUSSELL, DAVID MANSON, Private
Previously served as Private in Company L, 16th Regiment N.C. Troops (6th Regiment N.C. Volunteers). Transferred to this company on October 5, 1862, while on sick furlough. Reported on sick furlough through October 31, 1862. Reported absent without leave in November-December, 1862. Reported sick in Haywood County, January-February, 1863. Reported for duty "since [the January-February] muster & signed pay roll." Reported on sick furlough "from hospital [in] Virginia," April 30, 1863. Reported sick in Haywood County in May-June, 1863. Reported absent without leave in September-October, 1863. Returned to duty prior to December 31, 1863. Reported present in January-February, 1864. Name appears on a receipt roll for clothing dated June 4, 1864. No further records.

RUSSELL, EDWARD P., Private
Previously served as Private in Company L, 16th Regiment N.C. Troops (6th Regiment N.C. Volunteers). Transferred to this company on October 5, 1862. Reported absent sick, October 31, 1862. Reported absent without leave in November-December, 1862. Reported absent sick in Haywood County in January-February, 1863. Returned to duty on an unspecified date "since (the January-February) muster & signed pay roll." Reported absent on sick furlough "from hospital [in] Virginia," April 30, 1863. Reported absent sick in Haywood County in May-June, 1863. Reported for duty prior to October 31, 1863. Reported present in November, 1863-February, 1864. Name appears on a receipt roll for clothing dated October 16, 1864. No further records.

RUSSELL, MARION S., _____
North Carolina pension records appear to indicate that he served in this company. Survived the war. [He may have served also in Company C, 1st Battalion N.C. Junior Reserves.]

SEAY, DANIEL, Private
Previously served as Private in Company C, 25th Regiment N.C. Troops, and Company L, 16th Regiment N.C. Troops (6th Regiment N.C. Volunteers). Transferred to this company from the 16th Regiment on October 5, 1862, while absent wounded. Reported on wounded furlough through October 31, 1863. Reported for duty prior to December 31, 1863. Listed as a deserter on February 29, 1864. Name appears on a receipt roll for clothing dated October 16, 1864. In Special Orders No. 10, March 9, 1865, Brig. Gen. James G. Martin authorized the transfers of Pvts. Daniel Seay and Riley James of this company in exchange for Pvt. Nelson Howell of Company A, 62nd Regiment N.C. Troops and Pvt. Marc Howell of Company I, 62nd Regiment N.C. Troops. It is not known if or when the transfers were carried out. No further records. [Contrary to 6:106, 758, and 7:387 of this series, he is not the same soldier as Pvt. Henry D. Seay. The service record for Pvt. Daniel Seay was omitted in the rosters for the 16th and 25th Regiments N.C. Troops.]

SEAY, HENRY D., Private
Previously served as Private in Company L, 16th Regiment N.C. Troops (6th Regiment N.C. Volunteers). Transferred to this company on October 5, 1862, while absent wounded. Reported absent wounded or sick through April 30, 1863. Reported for duty prior to June 30, 1863. Reported present in September-December, 1863. Reported absent without leave in January-February, 1864. Name appears on a receipt roll for clothing dated August 18, 1864. No further records.

SEAY, THOMAS DAVID, Corporal
Previously served as Private in Company L, 16th Regiment N.C. Troops (6th Regiment N.C. Volunteers). Transferred to this company on October 5, 1862. Reported present through December 31, 1862. Reported on detail with 2nd Lt. John H. Moody of this company at Cosby Creek, Tennessee, January-February, 1863. Rejoined the company prior to April 30, 1863. Reported present in May-June, 1863. Promoted to Corporal in July-October, 1863. Reported present in September, 1863-February, 1864. Captured at Piedmont, Virginia, June 5, 1864. Reported under guard at Staunton, Virginia, June 8, 1864. Confined at Camp Morton, Indianapolis, Indiana, June 21, 1864. Paroled at Camp Morton on February 26, 1865, and transferred for exchange. No further records.

SEAY, W. P., _____
Name appears in a company account book for a canteen, a knapsack, and a haversack issued March 4, 1864. No further records.

SERRETT, SIMEON, Private
Enlisted in Haywood County on August 18, 1863, for the war. Reported present in November, 1863-February, 1864. Name appears on receipt rolls for clothing dated June 4 and June 17, 1864. No further records.

SETZER, JACOB M., Private
Born on July 30, 1827. Enlisted in Haywood County at age 35, April 5, 1863, for the war. Reported present through April 30, 1863. Reported absent without leave on June 28, 1863. Returned to duty prior to August 5, 1863. Deserted on August 31, 1863. [His surname may have been Setser.]

SMATHERS, ROLEN C., Private
Previously served as Private in Company L, 16th Regiment N.C. Troops (6th Regiment N.C. Volunteers). Transferred to this company on October 5, 1862, while absent without leave. Reported for duty prior to December 31, 1862. Promoted to Corporal on January 1, 1863. Reported present in January-June, 1863. Reported under arrest at Bristol, Tennessee, January-February, 1864. Reduced to ranks prior to February 29, 1864. Name appears on receipt rolls for clothing dated June 4 and June 17, 1864. No further records. Survived the war.

SMITH, HENRY E., Private
Previously served as Private in Company A, 62nd Regiment N.C. Troops. Transferred to this company on May 1, 1863. Reported present on June 30, 1863. Deserted on September 19, 1863.

SMITH, THOMAS B., Private
Enlisted in Haywood County on April 5, 1863, for the war. Reported present through June 30, 1863. Name appears in a company account book for shoes and clothing issued August 5 and August 8, 1863. Reported present in September-December, 1863. Reported sick in hospital at Bristol, Tennessee, in January-February, 1864. No further records.

SNIDER, DANIEL, Private
Previously served as Private in Company L, 16th Regiment N.C. Troops (6th Regiment N.C. Volunteers). Transferred to this company on October 5, 1862. Reported present through October 31, 1862. Reported on wounded furlough, November, 1862-February, 1863. [In a letter from Snider to Jefferson Davis dated April 17, 1863, Snider reported that he had been "shot through the Lungs" June 30, 1862, "in the Battle before Richmond," which would place his injury at the battle of Frayser's Farm, in which his previous unit, the 16th Regiment N.C. Troops, had participated.] Returned to duty prior to April 30, 1863. Reported present in May-June, 1863. Reported absent without leave in September-December, 1863. Returned to duty prior to February 16, 1864. Reported present through February 29, 1864. Name appears on receipt rolls for clothing dated June 4, June 17, and August 17, 1864. No further records. Survived the war.

SNYDER, R. T., _____
North Carolina pension records appear to indicate that he served in this company.

SWANGER, D. E., _____
North Carolina pension records appear to indicate that he served in this company.

SWANGER, GREEN BERRY, Private
Previously served as Private in Company L, 16th Regiment N.C. Troops (6th Regiment N.C. Volunteers). Transferred to this company on October 5, 1862, while absent wounded. Reported absent wounded through December 31, 1862. Reported for duty prior to February 28, 1863, when he was reported on detail escorting prisoners to Greeneville, Tennessee. Rejoined the company prior to April 30, 1863. Reported present in May-June, 1863. Deserted on August 31, 1863. [North Carolina pension records indicate that he was wounded in the chest at Cattaloochee, North Carolina. This may refer to either of the skirmishes that were fought about February, 1865, at Soco Gap and Soco Creek between elements of Thomas's Legion and Federal raiders under George W. Kirk. His given name may have been Greenberry.]

SWANGER, JAMES, Private
Previously served as Private in Company L, 16th Regiment N.C. Troops (6th Regiment N.C. Volunteers). Transferred to this company on October 5, 1862. Reported on sick furlough suffering from smallpox through April 30, 1863. Reported for duty prior to June 30, 1863. Deserted on August 31, 1863. [His middle initial may have been L.]

SWANGER, WILLIAM J., Private
Previously served as Private in Company L, 16th Regiment N.C. Troops (6th Regiment N.C. Volunteers). Transferred to this company on October 5, 1862. Reported present through October 31, 1862. Reported absent sick November, 1862-April, 1863. Returned to duty prior to June 30, 1863. A company account book reports that he was "killed by bushwacker." Place and date of death not reported.

TAYLOR, THOMAS B., Private
Previously served as Private in Company L, 16th Regiment N.C. Troops (6th Regiment N.C. Volunteers). Transferred to this company on October 5, 1862. Reported absent without leave through December 31, 1862. Reported for duty prior to February 28, 1863. Reported present through June 30, 1863. Reported absent without leave in September-October, 1863. Returned to duty prior to December 31, 1863. Reported under arrest at Bristol, Tennessee, January-February, 1864. Hospitalized at Winchester, Virginia, July 26, 1864, with debilitas. Returned to duty on August 1, 1864. Name appears on a receipt roll for clothing dated September 27, 1864. No further records.

TERNER, JAMES, Private
Enlisted at Carter's Depot, Tennessee, April 29, 1863, for the war. Transferred to Company I of this regiment on or about the same date. [His surname may have been Turner.]

THOMPSON, JAMES A., Private
Enlisted either in this company or in Company E, Walker's Battalion, at Carter's Depot, Tennessee, April 11, 1863, for the war. Transferred to Company C of this regiment on the same date. [He may have previously served as 1st Lieutenant in Company F, 29th Regiment N.C. Troops.]

TRULL, THOMAS G., Private
Enlisted either in this company or in Company E, Walker's Battalion, at Carter's Depot, Tennessee, April 11, 1863, for the war. Transferred to Company C of this regiment on or about the same date.

TURNER, PHILIP M., Private
Born on February 12, 1827. Enlisted in Haywood County at age 36, April 5, 1863, for the war. Reported present through June 30, 1863. Reported absent without leave in September-October, 1863. Returned to duty prior to December 31, 1863. Reported absent without leave, February 29, 1864. Name appears on a receipt roll for clothing dated October 16, 1864. No further records. Survived the war.

WELCH, JAMES L., Private
Previously served as Musician (Drum Major) in Company L, 16th Regiment N.C. Troops (6th Regiment N.C. Volunteers). Transferred to this company on October 5, 1862, while absent wounded. Reported absent wounded through October 31, 1862. A company account book reports him as discharged, but provides no date or other information.

WELCH, JOHN W., Private
Confederate gravestone records appear to indicate that he served in this company. Survived the war.

WELCH, LUCIUS M., Private
Enlisted in Haywood County on August 15, 1863, for the war. Reported on extra duty as Commissary Sergeant in September-October, 1863. Reported on detail in the commissary department in

November-December, 1863. Reported on extra duty in January-February, 1864; he probably served as Commissary Sergeant throughout this entire period. Name appears on a receipt roll for clothing dated June 4, 1864. No further records. Survived the war.

WELCH, THADDEUS D., Private
Enlisted in Haywood County on November 1, 1862, for the war. Reported present through April 30, 1863. Discharged on June 4, 1863, by reason of disability.

WEST, WILLIAM, Private
Born on November 11, 1839. Enlisted at Carter's Depot, Tennessee, at age 23, April 11, 1863, for the war. Transferred to Company C of this regiment the same date.

WILLIAMSON, WILLIAM, Private
Born in Tennessee. Resided in Haywood County and was by occupation a farmer prior to enlisting in Haywood County at age 40, August 30, 1863, for the war. Reported sick in a Virginia hospital in September-October, 1863. Rejoined the company prior to December 31, 1863. Reported present in January-February, 1864. Name appears on receipt rolls for clothing dated June 17 and October 16, 1864. No further records.

WILLIS, ISAAC, Private
Resided in Haywood County and was by occupation a farmer prior to enlisting in Haywood County at age 38, April 5, 1863, for the war. Reported present through June 30, 1863. Reported absent without leave in September-October, 1863. Returned to duty prior to December 31, 1863. No further records. Survived the war.

WOOTEN, JOHN B., Private
Previously served as Private in Company L, 16th Regiment N.C. Troops (6th Regiment N.C. Volunteers). Transferred to this company on October 5, 1862. Reported present through October 31, 1862. Reported absent without leave on December 20, 1862. Returned to duty prior to February 28, 1863. Reported present in March-June, 1863. Reported absent sick in September, 1863-February, 1864; was in hospital at Mongomery Springs, Virginia, during part of that period. Name appears on a receipt roll for clothing dated August 23, 1864. No further records. [His surname may have been Wooden.]

YARBORO, ELISHA H., Private
Previously served as Private in Company L, 16th Regiment N.C. Troops (6th Regiment N.C. Volunteers). Transferred to this company on October 5, 1862, while absent wounded. Reported for duty prior to December 31, 1862. Reported present in January-June, 1863. Deserted on September 19, 1863.

YARBORO, MINER A., Private
Previously served as Private in Company L, 16th Regiment N.C. Troops (6th Regiment N.C. Volunteers). Transferred to this company on October 5, 1862, while absent wounded. Reported absent wounded through October 31, 1862. Reported absent without leave on December 20, 1862. Reported absent sick with smallpox in Haywood County in January-February, 1863. Reported for duty prior to April 30, 1863. Reported present in May-June, 1863. Reported absent without leave in September-October, 1863. Later reported as having deserted on September 19, 1863. [His surname may have been Yarberry, Yarborough, or Yarbrough.]

COMPANY F

This company was raised in Jackson County. It was organized on July 19, 1862, at Quallatown. It was known as Company D, N.C. Cherokee Battalion, as of August 31, 1862. On September 1, 1862, a company known as Company E was split off of this company. On or about October 5, 1862, this company was designated Company F, Infantry Regiment, Thomas's Legion, and the Company E that was formed from this company was designated Company G.

The following roster was compiled in large part from company muster rolls dated July 19-October, 1862, January-June, 1863, and September, 1863-February, 1864. These are abstracted in the microfilm edition of the Compiled Service Records of Confederate Soldiers Who Served in Organizations from the State of North Carolina (Record Group 109, M270), National Archives, Washington, D.C. Other valuable information in the Compiled Service Records includes enlistment papers, pay vouchers, requisitions, letters of resignation, discharge certificates, and abstracts of medical and prisoner of war records.

Also utilized in this roster were *The War of the Rebellion: A Compilation of the Official Records of the Union and Confederate Armies*, the North Carolina Adjutant General's papers, state militia records, newspaper casualty lists and obituaries, wartime claims for bounty pay and allowances, postwar registers of claims for artificial limbs, Confederate pension applications filed with the states of North Carolina, Tennessee, and Florida, records of the North Carolina Confederate Soldiers' Home, and the 1860 and 1870 federal censuses of North Carolina. A search was made also for relevant letters, diaries, reminiscences, and other manuscripts in the Southern Historical Collection (University of North Carolina-Chapel Hill) and the Duke University Library Special Collections Department.

Among the secondary sources consulted were records of the North Carolina division of the United Daughters of the Confederacy, postwar rosters, regimental and county histories, marriage bond, will, and cemetery indexes, published and unpublished genealogies, biographical dictionaries, the North Carolina *County Heritage Book* series, the *Confederate Veteran*, Walter Clark's *Histories of the Several Regiments and Battalions from North Carolina in the Great War, 1861-'65*, and the North Carolina volume of the extended edition of *Confederate Military History*.

OFFICERS

CAPTAIN

McCONNELL, JAMES MORTIMER
Born in Macon County on March 5, 1836. Resided in Jackson County where he was by occupation a farmer prior to enlisting at Quallatown at age 26. Appointed Captain on July 19, 1862. Reported present through August 31, 1862. Reported on detached service in September-October, 1862. Reported on detail gathering up conscripts in January-February, 1863. Rejoined the company on or prior to April 30, 1863. Reported present in May-June, 1863. Reported present in September-October, 1863. Reported on detail to North Carolina to gather up absentees from this company, from on or about December 21, 1863, through January 12, 1864. Rejoined the company prior to February 25, 1864, when his name appears as a signature on a petition to Gov. Zebulon B. Vance requesting his assistance in reuniting Thomas's Legion and removing it from the command of Brig. Gen. Alfred E. Jackson. [Lt. Col. James R. Love, et al. to Vance, February 25, 1864, Governors' Papers: Zebulon Baird Vance, 1862-1865, N.C. State Archives.] Reported present on

February 29, 1864. Suffered a gunshot wound of the left knee joint at Piedmont, Virginia, June 5, 1864. Hospitalized at Charlottesville, Virginia, June 17, 1864. No further records.

LIEUTENANTS

COLLINS, DAVID KIMZEY, 3rd Lieutenant
Served as Private in this company. [See Noncommissioned Officers and Privates section below.] Clark's *Regiments*, 3:729 (picture opposite), indicates that he attained the rank of 2nd Lieutenant, but no surviving wartime records confirm this. It is more likely that he attained the rank of 3rd (Junior 2nd) Lieutenant late in the war.

CONLEY, JAMES, 2nd Lieutenant
Served as Private and probably Corporal or Sergeant in this company. [See Noncommissioned Officers and Privates' section below.] Clark's *Regiments*, 3:729 (picture opposite), indicates that he attained the rank of 2nd Lieutenant, but no surviving wartime records confirm this. If he did, it was probably subsequent to February 29, 1864.

CONLEY, ROBERT T., 1st Lieutenant
Previously served as Private in Company A, 16th Regiment N.C. Troops (6th Regiment N.C. Volunteers). Transferred to this company on September 1, 1862, and appointed 2nd Lieutenant to rank from July 19, 1862. Reported present in September-October, 1862; January-June, 1863; and September, 1863-February, 1864. Name appears on a pay record which indicates that he was present or accounted for on August 9, 1864. Clark's *Regiments*, 3: 729 (picture opposite), indicates that he attained the rank of 1st Lieutenant. He probably did so subsequent to September 19, 1864. Survived the war. [According to postwar accounts, he commanded a group of soldiers in a skirmish at White Sulphur Springs, near Waynesville, May 6, 1865, during which were fired the last shots of the war east of the Mississippi. See *Civil War History* (Extended Edition), 5:443-444, and Conley, "The Last Gun of the War," *Atlanta Constitution*, July 13, 1892.]

FISHER, DANIEL G., 3rd Lieutenant
Previously served as Private in Company A, 16th Regiment N.C. Troops (6th Regiment N.C. Volunteers). Appointed 3rd Lieutenant of this company on July 19, 1862. Promoted to Captain of Company G of this regiment on September 1, 1862.

RABY, DEMPSEY MANUEL, 2nd Lieutenant
Previously served as Private in Company A, 16th Regiment N.C. Troops (6th Regiment N.C. Volunteers). Appointed 2nd Lieutenant of this company on July 19, 1862. Reported present through August 31, 1862. Appointed 1st Lieutenant of Company G of this regiment on September 1, 1862, and transferred. [Contrary to 6:755 of this series, he did not serve as a lieutenant in the 16th Regiment, and he transferred to this company rather than Company G of this regiment, on July 19, 1862.]

WELCH, WILLIAM THOMAS, 1st Lieutenant
Born in Macon County where he resided as a farmer prior to enlisting at Quallatown at age 23. Appointed 1st Lieutenant on July 19, 1862. Reported present through October 31, 1862, and in January-June, 1863. Wounded in the thigh in battle at Henderson's Mill, Tennessee, October 11, 1863. Hospitalized at Emory and Henry, Virginia. Reported absent wounded through February 29, 1864. Returned to duty on an unspecified date. Signature appears on a pay voucher for service from October 1, 1863, through July 31, 1864. Killed at Winchester, Virginia, September 19, 1864. [Place and date of death reported in Charlotte *Western Democrat*, October 25, 1864.]

WEST, JAMES, 3rd Lieutenant
Previously served as Sergeant of Company A, 16th Regiment N.C. Troops (6th Regiment N.C. Volunteers). Transferred to this company on September 1, 1862, and appointed 3rd Lieutenant to rank from July 19, 1862. Reported present in September-October, 1862. Reported on detached service at Mossy Creek, Tennessee, January-June, 1863. Reported present in September-October, 1863. Reported sick in hospital at Rogerville, Tennessee, December 29, 1863. Returned to duty prior to February 25, 1864, when his name appears as a signature on a petition to Gov. Zebulon B. Vance requesting his assistance in reuniting Thomas's Legion and removing it from the command of Brig. Gen. Alfred E. Jackson [Lt. Col. James R. Love, et. al. to Vance, February 25, 1864, Governors' Papers: Zebulon Baird Vance, 1862-1865, N.C. State Archives.] Reported present on February 29, 1864. Hospitalized at Charlottesville, Virginia, June 10, 1864, with acute dysentery. Returned to duty on June 17, 1864. Hospitalized at Charlottesville on July 26, 1864, with debility. Transferred to hospital at Lynchburg, Virginia, the same date. Signature appears on receipt for effects of a deceased soldier on August 8, 1864. Signature appears on special requisitions dated September 18 and September 27, 1864. Reported in an unspecified hospital on October 31, 1864. No further records. [Contrary to 6:14 of this series, he was promoted and transferred to this company on September 1, 1862, rather than on October 5, 1862.]

NONCOMMISSIONED OFFICERS AND PRIVATES

ALLEN, DANIEL J., _____
Born in what later became Jackson County. Resided in Jackson County as a farmer prior to enlisting at Quallatown at age 34, July 19, 1862, for the war. Mustered in with an unspecified rank. Reported present through August 31, 1862. Elected 2nd Lieutenant of Company G of this regiment on September 1, 1862.

ALLEN, L. W., Private
Born in what later became Jackson County. Resided in Jackson County as a farmer prior to enlisting at Quallatown at age 19, July 19, 1862, for the war. Reported present through August 31, 1862. Transferred to Company G of this regiment on September 1, 1862.

ANDERSON, J. M., Private
Enlisted at Quallatown on March 5, 1863, for the war. Reported present through June 30, 1863, and in September-October, 1863. Deserted at Bean Station, Tennessee, December 8, 1863. North Carolina pension records indicate that he may have served later in Company D, 62nd Regiment N.C. Troops.

ASH, ISAAC, Private
Place and date of enlistment not reported. Killed at Cedar Creek, Virginia, October 19, 1864. [He may have been the same man as Pvt. Samuel Ash of this company.]

ASH, SAMUEL, Private
Enlisted at Quallatown on August 22, 1863, for the war. Reported present in November, 1863-February, 1864. Hospitalized at Winchester, Virginia, July 25, 1864, with a gunshot wound of the hand. Place and date wounded not reported but probably July 24, 1864, at Kernstown, Virginia. Name appears on receipt rolls for clothing dated June 18, August 27, September 1, and September 17, 1864. No further records.

ASHE, JOHN M., _____
North Carolina pension records appear to indicate that he served in this company. Survived the war.

BAILEY, WILLIAM, Private
Place and date of enlistment not reported; probably enlisted subsequent to February 29, 1864. Captured near Franklin on May 27, 1864. Sent to Knoxville, Tennessee. Transferred to Nashville, Tennessee. Transferred to Louisville, Kentucky, where he arrived on June 29, 1864. Confined at Camp Morton, Indianapolis, Indiana, July 1, 1864. Paroled at Camp Morton and transferred to City Point, Virginia, February 26, 1865, for exchange. No further records. [He may have been the same man as W. P. Bailey, whose record is in the General Miscellaneous section of this roster.]

BAIRD, A. W., Private
Born in Franklin County, Georgia, and resided in Jackson County where he was by occupation a farmer prior to enlisting at Quallatown at age 21, July 19, 1862, for the war. Reported present through August 31, 1862. Transferred to Company G of this regiment on September 1, 1862.

BAIRD, JOHN, Private
Born in Franklin County, Georgia, and resided in Jackson County where he was by occupation a farmer prior to enlisting at Quallatown at age 24, July 19, 1862, for the war. Reported present through August 31, 1862. Transferred to Company G of this regiment on September 1, 1862.

BAKER, WILLIAM H., Private
Born in Ashe County and resided in Jackson County where he was by occupation a farmer prior to enlisting at Quallatown at age 22, July 19, 1862, for the war. Reported present through October 31, 1862. Reported on extra duty as a wagoner in January-February, 1863. Reported on detached service as a teamster for the quartermaster department in March-June, 1863. Reported present in September, 1863-February, 1864. No further records.

BATTLE, A. W., Private
Reportedly enlisted at Quallatown in Jackson County on July 19, 1862, for the war; however, he was not listed in the records of this company until January-February, 1864, when he was listed as having deserted at Quallatown in December, 1863.

BATTLE, BENJAMIN F., Private
Born in Macon County where he resided as a farmer prior to enlisting at Quallatown at age 21, July 19, 1862, for the war. Reported present through October 31, 1862, and in January-February, 1863. Reported sick in hospital at Strawberry Plains, Tennessee, March-June, 1863. Reported absent without leave from August 1 through December 31, 1863. Subsequently reported as having deserted on October 20, 1863.

BATTLE, JAMES, _____
A list of veterans from the James R. Love Camp of the United Confederate Veterans in Jackson County appears to indicate that he served in this company. [He may have served instead in 2nd Company A of this regiment. He may have served also in Company D, Indian Battalion.]

BATTLE, JOHN W., Sergeant
Born in Macon County where he resided as a farmer prior to enlisting at Quallatown in Jackson County at age 24, July 19, 1862, for the war. Mustered in as Sergeant. Reported present through August 31, 1862. Reported on detached service on October 31, 1862. Reported present in January-June and September-October, 1863. Reported absent without leave on December 8, 1863. No further records.

BECK, JOHN ALVERTES, Private
Born on June 12, 1834, in Haywood County. Resided in Jackson County and was by occupation a farmer prior to enlisting at Quallatown at age 28, July 19, 1862, for the war. Reported present through August 31, 1862. Reported on detached service on October 31, 1862. Reported present in January-June, 1863, and in September, 1863-February, 1864. Name appears on receipt rolls for clothing dated June 18 and September 1, 1864. Killed at Snicker's Gap, Virginia, on an unknown date.

BECK, SAMUEL CARSON, Corporal
Born on February 3, 1839, in what later became Jackson County. Resided in Jackson County and was by occupation a farmer prior to enlisting at Quallatown at age 23, July 19, 1862, for the war. Mustered in as Corporal. Reported present or accounted for through August 31, 1862. Reported on detached service on October 31, 1862. Reported present in January-February, 1863. Reported absent on sick furlough in March-April, 1863. Returned to duty in May-June, 1863. Reported present in September, 1863-February, 1864. Name appears on receipt rolls for clothing dated June 18, September 1, and September 17, 1864. No further records.

BECK, STEPHEN JACKSON, Private
Born in Haywood County on June 21, 1836. Resided in Jackson County and was by occupation a farmer prior to enlisting at Quallatown at age 26, July 19, 1862, for the war. Mustered in as Sergeant. Reported present through October 31, 1862, and in January-February, 1863. Reported on detached service at Smoky Mountain, Tennessee, "by order of Col. Thomas" in March-June and in September-October, 1863. Reduced to ranks in September-October, 1863. Reported absent sick November, 1863-February, 1864. No further records. Survived the war.

BECK, WILLIAM ALBERT, Sergeant
Born in Haywood County on April 1, 1830. Resided in Jackson County and was by occupation a farmer prior to enlisting at Quallatown at age 32, July 19, 1862, for the war. Mustered in as Sergeant. Reported present or accounted for through August 31, 1862. Reported on detached service in September-October, 1862. Reported present in January-June, 1863, and September, 1863-February, 1864. Wounded in the fibula (compound fracture) and captured at Winchester, Virginia, September 19, 1864. Admitted to U.S. field hospital at Winchester on October 3, 1864. Leg amputated on October 4, 1864, after gangrene developed. Died in hospital at Winchester on October 26, 1864, of "pyaemia."

BELL, JOHN GAITHER, _____
North Carolina pension records appear to indicate that he served in this company. Survived the war.

BIRD, W. H., Private
Enlisted at Quallatown on December 1, 1863, for the war. Reported present on February 29, 1864. Captured at Piedmont, Virginia, June 5, 1864. Sent to Staunton, Virginia, on or about June 8, 1864. Confined at Camp Morton, Indianapolis, Indiana, June 21, 1864. Paroled at Camp Morton on or about March 4, 1865. Received at Boulware's Wharf, James River, Virginia, March 10-11, 1865, for exchange. Hospitalized at Richmond, Virginia, March 11, 1865. Captured in hospital at Richmond on April 3, 1865. No further records.

BOSWORTH, JAMES F., Private
Born in Knox County, Tennessee, where he resided as a miller prior to enlisting at Knoxville at age 23, February 4, 1863, for the war. Reported present through April 30, 1863. Reported on detail at Knoxville in May-June, 1863. Discharged at a hospital in Knoxville on August 28, 1863. Reason discharged not reported.

BRADLEY, JAMES H., Private
Born in Rutherford County and resided in Jackson County where he was by occupation a farmer prior to enlisting at Quallatown at age 28, July 19, 1862, for the war. Reported present through October 31, 1862, and in January-June, 1863. Reported missing on the retreat from Greeneville, Tennessee, September-October, 1863. Subsequently reported as absent without leave from October 14, 1863, through December 31, 1863. Returned to duty prior to February 29, 1864. Hospitalized at Charlottesville, Virginia, June 10, 1864, with acute diarrhoea. Returned to duty on June 17, 1864. Captured at Winchester, Virginia, September 19, 1864. Sent to Harpers Ferry, West Virginia. Transferred to Point Lookout, Maryland, where he arrived on September 26, 1864. Paroled at Point Lookout on March 15, 1865. Received at Boulware's Wharf, James River, Virginia, March 18, 1865, for exchange. Survived the war.

BRADLEY, OSBORN, Private
Born in Rutherford County and resided in Jackson County where he was by occupation a farmer prior to enlisting at Quallatown at age 26, July 19, 1862, for the war. Reported present through October 31, 1862, and in January-February, 1863. Died at Strawberry Plains, Tennessee, April 4, 1863, of "febris typhoides."

BRADLEY, THOMAS, Private
Enlisted at Quallatown on March 10, 1863, for the war. Reported present through June 30, 1863. Deserted near Zollicoffer, Tennessee, on or about October 14, 1863.

BRADLEY, WILLIAM, Private
Resided in Sevier County, Tennessee, and enlisted at Quallatown on March 2, 1863, for the war. Reported present through June 30, 1863. Deserted either at Webster or at Zollicoffer, Tennessee, on or about October 10, 1863. Took the Oath of Allegiance at Knoxville, Tennessee, in April, 1865.

BRADLEY, WILSON, Private
Enlisted at Quallatown on March 2, 1863, for the war. Reported present through June 30, 1863. Deserted near Greeneville, Tennessee, October 11, 1863. Returned to ranks on or prior to June 10, 1864, when he was reported hospitalized at Charlottesville, Virginia, with acute diarrhoea. Returned to duty on June 17, 1864. Reported on duty as a teamster in August-September, 1864. No further records.

BRADSHAW, JAMES A., Private
Born in Haywood County and resided in Jackson County where he was by occupation a farmer prior to enlisting at Quallatown at age 19, July 19, 1862, for the war. Reported present through October 31, 1862, and in January-February, 1863. Died at Strawberry Plains, Tennessee, on or about April 18, 1863. Cause of death not reported.

BRADSHAW, JOHN H., Private
Born in what later became Jackson County. Resided in Jackson County as a farmer prior to enlisting at Quallatown at age 20, July 19, 1862, for the war. Reported present through October 31, 1862, in January-June, 1863; and in September, 1863-February, 1864. Captured at Franklin, North Carolina, May 27, 1864. Sent to Knoxville, Tennessee. Transferred to Nashville, Tennessee, where he arrived on or about June 22, 1864. Transferred to Louisville, Kentucky, where he arrived on or prior to June 30, 1864. Confined at Camp Morton, Indianapolis, Indiana, July 1, 1864. Died at Camp Morton on December 16, 1864, of "malarial fever."

BRENDLE, HENRY P., Private
Born in Burke County on November 3, 1829. Resided in Jackson County and was by occupation a farmer prior to enlisting at Quallatown at age 32, July 19, 1862, for the war. Reported present through August 1, 1862. Transferred to Company G of this regiment on September 1, 1862. [His surname may have been Brindle.]

BRENDLE, JOHN H., Private
Born in Rutherford County and resided in Jackson County where he was by occupation a farmer prior to enlisting at Quallatown at age 21, July 19, 1862, for the war. Transferred to Company G of this regiment on September 1, 1862. [His surname may have been Brindle.]

BROOKS, I. C., Private
Born in Rutherford County and resided in Jackson County where he was by occupation a farmer prior to enlisting at Quallatown at age 33, July 19, 1862, for the war. Reported present through August 31, 1862. Transferred to Company G of this regiment on September 1, 1862.

BRYSON, GEORGE W., Private
Resided in Jackson County and was by occupation a farmer prior to enlisting at Quallatown on March 7, 1863, for the war. Mustered in as Private. Reported on detached assignment in the commissary department at Strawberry Plains, Tennessee, April 30, 1863. Rejoined the company prior to June 30, 1863. Reported present in September-October, 1863. Assigned to the Field and Staff of this regiment as Acting Ordnance Sergeant, September 1, 1863. Died near Whitesburg, Tennessee, January 1, 1864. Cause of death not reported.

BRYSON, H. BURTON, Private
Previously served as Private in Company A, 7th Battalion N.C. Cavalry. Transferred to this company on July 14, 1863. Reported absent without leave September 1-December 31, 1863. Subsequently reported as having deserted on October 20, 1863.

BUCHANAN, WILLIAM B., Private
Born in Rutherford County and resided in Jackson County where he was by occupation a farmer prior to enlisting at Quallatown at age 18, July 19, 1862, for the war. Reported present through August 31, 1862. Transferred to Company G of this regiment on September 1, 1862.

BUMGARNER, HENRY F., Private
Born in Haywood County and resided in Jackson County where he was by occupation a farmer prior to enlisting at Quallatown at age 24, July 19, 1862, for the war. Reported present through August 31, 1862. Transferred to Company G of this regiment on September 1, 1862.

BUMGARNER, JOHN, Private
Born in Haywood County and resided in Jackson County where he was by occupation a farmer prior to enlisting at Quallatown at age 25, July 19, 1862, for the war. Reported present through August 31, 1862. Transferred to Company G of this regiment on September 1, 1862.

BURNS, JOHN C. S., Private
Born in what later became Jackson County. Resided in Jackson County as a farmer prior to enlisting at Quallatown at age 21, July 19, 1862, for the war. Reported present through August 31, 1862. Transferred to Company G of this regiment on September 1, 1862.

CAGLE, EVAN HARVEY, Private
Born in Haywood County on February 10, 1839. Resided in Jackson County where he was by occupation a farmer prior to enlisting at Quallatown at age 23, July 19, 1862, for the war. Reported present through August 31, 1862. Transferred to Company G of this regiment on September 1, 1862.

CAMPBELL, L. C., Private
Enlisted at Quallatown on March 2, 1863, for the war. Reported present through June 30, 1863, and in September, 1863-February, 1864. No further records.

CARVER, BENJAMIN, Private
Born in what later became Jackson County. Resided in Jackson County as a farmer prior to enlisting at Quallatown at age 18, July 19, 1862, for the war. Reported present or accounted for through October 31, 1862, and in January-April, 1863. Died on May 24, 1863. Place and cause of death not reported.

CHAMBERLAIN, JERRY, Private
Enlisted at Strawberry Plains, Tennessee, February 13, 1863, for the war. Deserted at Carter's Depot, Tennessee, September 20, 1863.

CHAMBERS, J. ERVIN, Private
Born in what later became Jackson County. Resided in Macon County where he was by occupation a farmer prior to enlisting at Quallatown at age 18, July 19, 1862, for the war. Reported present through October 31, 1862. Reported on sick furlough in January-April, 1863. Reported in September-December, 1863, as having been absent without leave since January 1, 1863. Reported on February 29, 1864, as having deserted on October 20, 1863.

CHAMBERS, MARCUS L., Private
Born in the part of Haywood County that later became Macon County, and was by occupation a farmer prior to enlisting Quallatown at age 45, August 31, 1862, for the war. Reported absent on detached service through October 31, 1862. Reported absent without leave from December 25, 1862, through April 30, 1863. Listed as a deserter in May-June, 1863.

CLEMENTS, W. A., Private
Born in Buncombe County and resided in Jackson County where he was by occupation a farmer prior to enlisting at Strawberry Plains, Tennessee, at age 19, October 28, 1862, for the war. Reported present in January-June, 1863, and September, 1863-February, 1864. Hospitalized at Charlottesville, Virginia, June 13, 1864, with acute diarrhoea. Returned to duty on June 18, 1864. Name appears on receipt rolls for clothing dated September 1, September 17, and September 27, 1864. No further records.

CLONTS, SAMUEL W., Private
Born in Buncombe County and resided in Jackson County where he was by occupation a farmer prior to enlisting at Quallatown at age 22, July 19, 1862, for the war. Reported present through August 31, 1862. Transferred to Company G of this regiment on September 1, 1862.

COLLINS, DAVID KIMZEY, Private
Born on October 10, 1844, in Haywood County or in what later became Jackson County. Resided in Jackson County where he was by occupation a farmer prior to enlisting at Strawberry Plains, Tennessee, at age 17, June 10, 1862, for the war. Reported present in January-February, 1863. Reported on detached service at Smoky Mountain, Tennessee, March-April, 1863. Rejoined his company prior to June 30, 1863. Reported present September, 1863-February, 1864. Name appears on receipt rolls for clothing dated June 18, September 1, and September 17, 1864. According to *Confederate Veteran*, III:105, he was captured at Cedar Creek, Virginia, October [19], 1864. According to *Confederate Military History*, Extended Ed., 5:441, he escaped at Winchester three days after his capture, was later captured near Asheville, and escaped again. Survived the war. [Clark's *Regiments*, 3:729 (picture opposite), indicates that he attained the rank of 2nd Lieutenant. If he did, it was probably subsequent to September 19, 1864.]

COLLINS, JAMES M., Private
Born in Macon County where he resided as a farmer prior to enlisting at Quallatown at age 25, July 19, 1862, for the war. Reported present through October 31, 1862. No further records. Survived the war.

COLLINS, JOHN T., 1st Sergeant
Born in Haywood County and resided in Jackson County where he was by occupation a farmer prior to enlisting at Quallatown at age 27, July 19, 1862, for the war. Mustered in as 1st Sergeant. Reported present or accounted for through October 31, 1862, and in January-February, 1863. Reported on detached service at Strawberry Plains, Tennessee, March-April, 1863. Rejoined the company prior to June 30, 1863. Reported present, September, 1863-February, 1864. Wounded in the left shoulder at New Hope Church, near Staunton, Virginia, June 5, 1864. Hospitalized at Danville, Virginia, on or about June 18, 1864. Furloughed from hospital on June 19, 1864. Survived the war.

CONLEY, B. S., Private
Enlisted at Strawberry Plains, Tennessee, April 10, 1863, for the war. Reported on detached service at Strawberry Plains through April 30, 1863. Rejoined the company prior to June 30, 1863. Reported sick in September-December, 1863. Returned to duty in January-February, 1864. Name appears on a receipt roll for clothing dated June 18, 1864. No further records.

CONLEY, JAMES, Private
Previously served as 2nd Lieutenant of Company F, 29th Regiment N.C. Troops. Enlisted in this company at Quallatown on July 19, 1862, for the war. Mustered in as Private. Reported present through October 31, 1862, and in January-June, 1863. Reported on detached service in Jackson County in September-October, 1863. Rejoined the company in November-December, 1863. Reported present in January-February, 1864. Probably promoted to Corporal or Sergeant subsequent to February 29, 1864. Killed at Piedmont on June 5, 1864. [Clark's *Regiments*, 3:729 (picture opposite), indicates that he attained the rank of 2nd Lieutenant; if so, it was probably subsequent to February 29, 1864. According to an 1895 letter from David Kimzey Collins to W. W. Stringfield, Conley was a "non-Com(missioned) Officer" at the time of his death at the battle of Piedmont on June 5, 1864. D. K. Collins to W. W. Stringfield, August 17, 1895, W. W. Stringfield Papers, Western Carolina University.]

CONLEY, JASON, Private
Enlisted at Quallatown on March 7, 1863, for the war. Reported on detached service at Smoky Mountain, Tennessee, March-April, 1863. Rejoined the company prior to June 30, 1863. Reported sick in hospital in September-October, 1863. Reported absent without leave on December 8, 1863. Returned to duty prior to February 29, 1864. Name appears on a receipt roll for clothing dated June 18, 1864. No further records.

CONNER, EPHRAIM S., Private
Born in what later became Jackson County. Resided in Jackson County as a farmer prior to enlisting at Quallatown at age 18, July 19, 1862, for the war. Reported present through October 31, 1862, and in January-February, 1863. Reported on detached service at Smoky Mountain, Tennessee, March-June, 1863. Was making salt during at least part of that period. Reported present in September-October, 1863. Reported sick in hospital at Rogersville, Tennessee, November-December, 1863. Reported present in January-February, 1864. Killed near Bunker Hill, Virginia, September 5, 1864.

CONNER, MARCUS LAFAYETTE, Private
Born in Cleveland County on February 10, 1843. Resided in Jackson County where he was by occupation a farmer prior to enlisting at Quallatown at age 19, July 19, 1862, for the war. Reported present through August 31, 1862. Transferred to Company G of this regiment on September 1, 1862.

CONSTANT, JOHN J., Sergeant
Born in Roane County, Tennessee, and resided in Macon County, North Carolina, where he was by occupation a farmer prior to enlisting in Jackson County at age 28, July 19, 1862, for the war. Reported present through October 31, 1862, and in January-June, 1863. Reported on detached service in Macon County in September-October, 1863. Reported absent without leave in November-December, 1863. Returned to duty prior to February 28, 1864. Promoted to Sergeant prior to June 11, 1864, when he was hospitalized at Charlottesville, Virginia, with neuralgia. Transferred to the convalescent camp on June 19, 1864. No further records. Survived the war.

COOPER, BENJAMIN F., Private
Born in Haywood County and resided in Jackson County where he was by occupation a farmer prior to enlisting at Quallatown at age 29, July 19, 1862, for the war. Reported present through August 31, 1862. Transferred to Company G of this regiment on September 1, 1862.

COOPER, JAMES L., Sergeant
Born in Macon County and resided in Jackson County where he was by occupation a farmer prior to enlisting in Jackson County at age 31, July 19, 1862, for the war. Mustered in as Sergeant. Reported present or accounted through October 31, 1862, in January-June, 1863, and in September-October, 1863. Reported detailed to hospital in Rogersville, Tennessee, November-December, 1863. Reported present in January-February, 1864. Captured at Winchester, Virginia, September 19, 1864. Sent to Harpers Ferry, West Virginia. Confined at Point Lookout, Maryland, January 3, 1865. Died at Point Lookout on January 25-26, 1865, of "inflammation of the bowels."

COOPER, JOHN A., Private
Born in Haywood County and resided in Jackson County where he was by occupation a farmer prior to enlisting at Quallatown at age 25, July 19, 1862, for the war. Reported present through August 31, 1862. Transferred to Company G of this regiment on September 1, 1862.

CUNNINGHAM, CLINGMAN G., Private
Born in what later became Jackson County. Resided in Jackson County as a farmer prior to enlisting at Quallatown at age 19, July 19, 1862, for the war. Mustered in as Corporal. Reported present through August 31, 1862. Transferred to Company G of this regiment on September 1, 1862.

DAVIS, WILL STE, _____
North Carolina pension records appear to indicate that he served in this company. Survived the war.

DEHART, JAMES W., Private
Born in Macon County where he resided as a farmer prior to enlisting in Jackson County at age 25, July 19, 1862, for the war. Reported present through August 31, 1862. Reported on detached service in September-October, 1862. Reported sick in hospital in January-February, 1863. Returned to duty in March-April, 1863. Reported present in May-June, 1863, and in September, 1863-February, 1864. Captured at Piedmont, Virginia, June 5, 1864. Confined at Camp Morton, Indianapolis, Indiana, June 21, 1864. Paroled at Camp Morton on February 26, 1865, and transferred for exchange. No further records. Survived the war.

DEHART, JOSEPH W., Private
Enlisted in this company on October 28, 1862, but "Entry cancelled." Subsequently served as Private in Company C, 7th Battalion N.C. Cavalry, and as Brevet 2nd Lieutenant in Company D,

Indian Battalion. [His given name may have been W. Joseph. The W may have stood for Wiley.]

DILLINGHAM, J. C., Private
Enlisted at Zollicoffer, Tennessee, September 1, 1863, for the war. Reported absent without leave from about October 15, 1863, through February 29, 1864. No further records. [May have been the same man as Pvt. James Leander Dillingham, whose record is in the General Miscellaneous section of this Legion's roster.]

DILLS, ALFRED MARION, Private
Born in what later became Jackson County. Resided in Jackson County as a farmer prior to enlisting at Quallatown at age 19, July 19, 1862, for the war. Reported present through August 31, 1862. Transferred to Company G of this regiment on September 1, 1862.

DILLS, H. JASPER, Private
Born in what later became Jackson County. Resided in Jackson County as a farmer prior to enlisting at Quallatown at age 28, July 19, 1862, for the war. Reported present through October 31, 1862, and in January-February, 1863. Reported absent sick in March-April, 1863. Returned to duty in May-June, 1863. Reported sick in hospital in September-October, 1863. Reported absent without leave in December, 1863. Reported absent sick in Jackson County in January-February, 1864. No further records. Survived the war. [The Charlotte *Western Democrat*, October 25, 1864, reports the wounding of H. Dills of Company G of this regiment at Winchester, Virginia, September 19, 1864. This may refer to H. Jasper Dills.]

DILLS, JOHN, Private
Born in what later became Jackson County. Resided in Jackson County as a farmer prior to enlisting at Quallatown at age 18, July 19, 1862, for the war. Reported present through August 31, 1862. Transferred to Company G of this regiment on September 1, 1862.

DILLS, MARION, Private
Born in what later became Jackson County. Resided in Jackson County as a farmer prior to enlisting at Quallatown at age 33, July 19, 1862, for the war. Reported present through August 31, 1862. Transferred to Company G of this regiment on September 1, 1862.

ELIDGE, J. T., Private
Enlisted at Strawberry Plains, Tennessee, for the war. Enlistment date reported as April 2, 1863; however, he was not listed in the records of this company until September, 1863. Deserted at Carter's Depot, Tennessee, September 25, 1863.

ELLIDGE, T. H., Private
Enlisted at Strawberry Plains, Tennessee, February 2, 1863, for the war. Reported absent on detached service at Smoky Mountain, Tennessee, March-June, 1863. "Was paid $30 April 23, 1863, for apprehending Henderson Lewis, Rumbough's Cav. Co., as a deserter." No further records.

EMERT, D. M. J., Private
Enlisted at Strawberry Plains, Tennessee, for the war. Enlistment date reported as February 18, 1863; however, he was not listed in the records of this company until September, 1863. Deserted at Carter's Depot, Tennessee, September 25, 1863.

ENLOE, ASAPH T., Corporal
Born in what later became Jackson County. Resided in Jackson County as a farmer prior to enlisting in Jackson County at age 25, July 19, 1862, for the war. Mustered in as Private. Reported present or accounted for through October 31, 1862, and in January-February, 1863. Promoted to Corporal on April 18, 1863. Reported present in May-June, 1863, and in September, 1863-February, 1864. Name appears on a receipt roll for clothing dated May 16, 1864. No further records. Survived the war. [North Carolina pension records indicate that he was wounded in November, 1863. Place, date, and nature of wound not reported.]

ENLOE, JOHN T., Private
Born in Haywood County on December 13, 1828. Resided in Jackson County and was by occupation a farmer prior to enlisting in Jackson County at age 33, July 19, 1862, for the war. Reported absent with leave on August 31, 1862. Reported absent without leave on October 31, 1862. Returned to duty prior to February 28, 1863, when he was reported on detail. Reported on detail as a teamster in March-June, 1863. Reported present in September, 1863-February, 1864. No further records. Survived the war. [See Tennessee pension application No. 4014.]

ENLOE, SEVIER S., Corporal
Born in Haywood County and resided in Jackson County where he was by occupation a farmer prior to enlisting in Jackson County at age 19, July 19, 1862, for the war. Mustered in as Corporal. Reported present through October 31, 1862, in January-June, 1863, and in September, 1863-February, 1864. Name appears on receipt rolls for clothing dated June 18, September 1, and September 17, 1864. No further records. Survived the war. [His middle name was probably Scroop.]

ENLOE, W. AESOP, _____
North Carolina pension records indicate that he served in this company. Survived the war.

ENSLEY, WILLIAM, Private
Born in Tennessee or in what later became Jackson County, North Carolina. Resided in Jackson County as a farmer prior to enlisting at Quallatown at age 34, July 19, 1862, for the war. Reported present through August 31, 1862. Transferred to Company G of this regiment on September 1, 1862.

FARLEY, CLAYTON, Private
Born on March 25, 1840, in what later became Jackson County. Resided in Jackson County and was by occupation a farmer prior to enlisting in Jackson County at age 22, July 19, 1862, for the war. Reported present through August 31, 1862. Transferred to Company G of this regiment on September 1, 1862.

FARLEY, WILLIAM, Private
Born in what later became Jackson County. Resided in Jackson County prior to enlisting at Quallatown at age 17, July 19, 1862, for the war. Reported present through August 31, 1862. Transferred to Company G of this regiment on September 1, 1862.

FARMER, A. WESTON, Musician
Born in Haywood County and resided in Jackson County where he was by occupation a farmer prior to enlisting at Quallatown at age

31, July 19, 1862, for the war. Mustered in as Musician (Drummer). Reported present through August 31, 1862. Transferred to Company G of this regiment on September 1, 1862.

FISHER, THOMAS G., Private
Born in what later became Jackson County. Resided in Jackson County as a farmer prior to enlisting at Quallatown at age 32, July 19, 1862, for the war. Reported present through August 31, 1862. Transferred to Company G of this regiment on September 1, 1862.

GALBREATH, JOSEPH M., Private
Previously served in 2nd Company A of this regiment. Enlisted in this company at an unknown date. Reported present in September-October, 1862. Reported sick at home in Jackson County in January-April, 1863. Reported absent sick in May-June, 1863. Reported absent sick in Jackson County in September-December, 1863, "unfit for service in consequence of losing the use of one leg." Transferred to Company A, Indian Battalion of this regiment, January 1, 1864. [He seems to have been simultaneously enrolled in 2nd Company A and Company F from September, 1862, through April, 1863. It is not clear from the records whether he formally transferred to this company, was on detached service, or was illegally enrolled in both companies at the same time.]

GIBBS, JAMES F., Private
Born in what later became Jackson County. Resided in Jackson County as a farmer prior to enlisting at Quallatown at age 32, July 19, 1862, for the war. Reported present through August 31, 1862, when he transferred to Company G of this regiment.

GIBBS, WILLIAM M., Private
Enlisted at Quallatown at age 34, March 7, 1863, for the war. Reported present in May-June, 1863, and in September, 1863-February, 1864. No further records. Survived the war.

GIBBY, JAMES S., Private
Born in what later became Jackson County. Resided in Jackson County as a farmer prior to enlisting at Quallatown age 20, July 19, 1862, for the war. Reported present through October 31, 1862, and in January-February, 1863. Reported "detailed in Ast. Commissary Department at S. Plains, Tenn." Reported present in May-June, 1863, and September, 1863-February, 1864. Name appears on receipt rolls for clothing dated June 18, September 1, and September 17, and September 27, 1864. No further records. Survived the war.

GIBSON, DANIEL J., Private
Born in what later became Jackson County. Resided in Jackson County as a farmer prior to enlisting at Quallatown at age 18, July 19, 1862, for the war. Reported present through August 31, 1862. Transferred to Company G of this regiment on September 1, 1862.

GIBSON, JOHN A., Private
Previously served in 2nd Company A of this regiment. Transferred to this company, probably in November-December, 1862. Reported at home on wounded furlough in January-June, 1863, and September-October, 1863. Reported absent without leave on November 1, 1863. Reported absent sick in Jackson County in January-February, 1864. No further records. Survived the war. [North Carolina pension records indicate that he was wounded at the Holston River, Tennessee, September 30, 1863.]

GIBSON, JOHN B., Private
Born in what later became Jackson County. Resided in Jackson County as a farmer prior to enlisting at Quallatown at age 32, July 19, 1862, for the war. Reported present through October 31, 1862, and in January-February, 1863. Reported absent on sick furlough in March-June, 1863, and September, 1863-February, 1864. No further records. Survived the war.

GIBSON, MONTGOMERY, _____
Place and date of enlistment not reported. Killed at Cedar Creek, Virginia, October 19, 1864. [He may have been the same man as either Pvt. Samuel M. Gibson or Pvt. William M. Gibson of this company.]

GIBSON, SAMUEL M., Private
Born in what later became Jackson County. Resided in Jackson County as a farmer prior to enlisting at Quallatown at age 23, July 19, 1862, for the war. Reported present through October 31, 1862, and in January-February, 1863. Reported absent sick at Strawberry Plains, Tennessee, in March-April, 1863. Reported on detached duty in May-June and September-October, 1863. Reported absent without leave on November 1, 1863. Listed as a deserter on January 15, 1864.

GIBSON, WILLIAM M., Private
Previously served as Private in 2nd Company A of this regiment. Transferred to this company on or about July 19, 1862. Mustered in as Musician (Fifer). Reported present through October 31, 1862, but also listed as present with 2nd Company A in September-October, 1862. Reported present in January-June, 1863, and September, 1863-February, 1864. Reduced to ranks on an unspecified date. Hospitalized at Charlottesville, Virginia, June 15, 1864, with a gunshot wound of the right wrist. Place and date wounded not reported, but probably at Piedmont, Virginia, June 5, 1864. Returned to duty on July 10, 1864. Hospitalized at Charlottesville on August 17, 1864, with icterus. Transferred to hospital at Lynchburg, Virginia, August 18, 1864. No further records.

GRAHAM, WILLIAM E., Private
Born in Sevier County, Tennessee, and resided in Jackson County, North Carolina, where he was by occupation a farmer prior to enlisting at Strawberry Plains, Tennessee, at age 20, January 10, 1863, for the war. Reported present in January-June, 1863, and September, 1863-February, 1864. Name appears on receipt rolls for clothing dated June 18, September 1, and September 17, 1864. No further records.

GRANTE, WILLIAM H., Private
Born in Macon County where he resided as a a farmer prior to enlisting at Strawberry Plains, Tennessee, age 28, October 31, 1862, for the war. Reported present in January-June, 1863. Reported sick in hospital at White Sulphur Springs, West Virginia, in September-October, 1863. Reported absent sick in Macon County, North Carolina, November, 1863-February, 1864. No further records.

GREEN, J. MARION, _____
North Carolina pension records indicate that he served in this company.

GREEN, WILLIAM, Private
Born in what later became Jackson County. Resided in Jackson County as a farmer prior to enlisting at Quallatown on July 19, 1862,

for the war. Reported present or accounted for through October 31, 1862, and in January-February, 1863. Died at Strawberry Plains, Tennessee, April 15, 1863, of "phthisis pulmonalis" (tuberculosis).

GUNTER, GEORGE M., Sergeant
Born in what later became Jackson County. Resided in Jackson County as a farmer prior to enlisting at Quallatown at age 27, July 19, 1862, for the war. Mustered in as Sergeant. Reported present through August 31, 1862. Transferred to Company G of this regiment on September 1, 1862.

GUNTER, ROBERT LOVE, Private
Born in what later became Jackson County. Resided in Jackson County as a farmer prior to enlisting at Quallatown at age 32, July 19, 1862, for the war. Reported present through August 31, 1862. Transferred to Company G of this regiment on September 1, 1862.

GUNTER, WILLIAM HENRY, Private
Born in what later became Jackson County. Resided in Jackson County as a farmer prior to enlisting at Quallatown at age 20, July 19, 1862, for the war. Reported present through October 31, 1862. Discharged at Strawberry Plains, Tennessee, January 20, 1863, on a surgeon's certificate of disability.

GWYNN, SAMUEL H., Private
Born in Sevier County, Tennessee, where he resided as a farmer prior to enlisting in Sevier County at age 24, probably on either July 19 or July 24, 1862, for the war. Enlisted in Company I of this regiment on July 24, 1862, and his enlistment with this company was cancelled.

HALL, JOHN L. F., Private
Born in what later became Jackson County. Resided in Jackson County as a farmer prior to enlisting at Quallatown at age 24, July 19, 1862, for the war. Reported present through August 31, 1863. Reported at home sick in September-October, 1863. Rejoined the company at an unknown date. Transferred to Company G of this regiment on January 1 or February 18, 1863.

HENDERSON, JAMES, Private
Enlisted at Quallatown County on August 20, 1863, for the war. Reported present through February 29, 1864. No further records. [He may have subsequently served in either Company G of this regiment or in the Indian Battalion. See the service record for James Henderson in the Miscellaneous section of the Indian Battalion roster.]

HIGDON, WILLIAM, Private
Born in what later became Jackson County. Resided in Jackson or Macon County where he was by occupation a farmer prior to enlisting at Quallatown at age 21, July 19, 1862, for the war. Reported present through August 31, 1862. Transferred to Company G of this regiment on September 1, 1863.

HILL, ALBERT, Private
Enlisted at Quallatown on March 7, 1863, for the war. Hospitalized at Strawberry Plains, Tennessee, on an unspecified date. Discharged from hospital on April 21, 1863. Failed to return to duty, listed as a deserter and dropped from the company rolls on June 30, 1863.

HILL, JAMES W., Private
Enlisted at Quallatown on March 7, 1863, for the war. Hospitalized at Strawberry Plains, Tennessee, on an unspecified date. Discharged from hospital on April 21, 1863. Failed to return to duty, listed as a deserter and dropped from the company rolls on June 30, 1863.

HILL, JOHN F., Private
Enlisted in Jackson County at Quallatown on March 7, 1863, for the war. Hospitalized at Strawberry Plains, Tennessee, on an unspecified date. Discharged from hospital on April 21, 1863. Failed to return to duty, listed as a deserter and dropped from the company rolls on June 30, 1863.

HODGE, JESSE, Private
Born in Grainger County, Tennessee, and resided in Grainger County where he was by occupation a farmer prior to enlisting at Strawberry Plains, Tennessee, at age 36, November 18, 1862, for the war. Reported present in January-June and September-October, 1863. Deserted at Bean's Station, Tennessee, December 8, 1863. Went over to the enemy on an unspecified date. Took the Oath of Allegiance at Knoxville, Tennessee, December 16-29, 1863.

HODGE, ROBERT J., Private
Born in what later became Jackson County. Resided in Jackson County as a farmer prior to enlisting at Quallatown at age 25, July 19, 1862, for the war. Reported in jail at Webster on August 31, 1862. Reported absent without leave on October 31, 1862. Returned to duty prior to February 28, 1863. Reported on detached duty at Smoky Mountain, Tennessee, in March-April, 1863. Reported absent without leave, April 30-December 31, 1863. Subsequently reported as having deserted on October 20, 1863.

HODGE, THOMAS, Private
Born in what later became Jackson County. Resided in Jackson County as a farmer prior to enlisting at Quallatown at age 23, July 19, 1862, for the war. Reported on detached service through October 31, 1862. Rejoined the company prior to February 28, 1863. Reported present in March-April, 1863. Deserted on June 20, 1863.

HOLDER, J. A., Private
Born in Surry County and resided in Jackson County where he was by occupation a farmer prior to enlisting at Quallatown at age 25, July 19, 1862, for the war. Reported present through August 31, 1862. Transferred to Company G of this regiment on September 1, 1862.

HOOPER, WILLIAM D., Private
Resided in Jackson County where he was by occupation a farmer prior to enlisting at Quallatown at age 38, August 20, 1863, for the war. Reported present in November, 1863-February, 1864. Name appears on a receipt roll for clothing dated June 18, 1864. Name appears on a receipt roll for clothing issued in hospital at Liberty, Virginia, October 10, 1864. No further records.

HOUSE, MINER, Private
Enlisted at Quallatown on December 1, 1863, for the war. Reported present in January-February, 1864. No further records.

HOUSE, WILLIAM D., Private
Born in what later became Jackson County. Resided in Jackson County as a farmer prior to enlisting at Quallatown at age 20, July 19,

1862, for the war. Reported present through October 31, 1862, and in January-February, 1863. Died on March 2, 1863. Place and cause of death not reported.

HOWARD, NOAH J., Private
Born in Sevier County, Tennessee, and resided in Jackson County, North Carolina, where he was by occupation a farmer prior to enlisting at Quallatown at age 27, July 19, 1862, for the war. Reported present through August 31, 1862. Reported sick in hospital in September-October, 1862. Reported on detached service in January-February, 1863. Reported present in March-June, 1863. Transferred to Levi's Battery in July-August, 1863.

HUGHES, ASAPH, Private
Resided in Jackson County and was by occupation a farmer prior to enlisting at Strawberry Plains, Tennessee, at age 33, April 20, 1863, for the war. Reported on detached service at Smoky Mountain, Tennessee, through October 31, 1863. Reported absent without leave in October 20-December 31, 1863. Subsequently reported as having deserted on January 15, 1864. [His first name may have been Aesop.]

HYDE, ERVIN, Private
Enlisted in Jackson County on March 7, 1863, for the war. Reported present through June 30, 1863. No further records. [He may have been the same man as David E. Hyde of Company C, Indian Battalion.]

HYDE, WILLIAM PENDLETON, Private
Born in what later became Jackson County. Resided in Jackson County as a farmer prior to enlisting at Quallatown at age 20, July 19, 1862, for the war. Reported on detached service through October 31, 1862. Rejoined the company prior to February 23, 1863. Reported on detached service at Smoky Mountain, Tennessee, March-October, 1863. Reported absent without leave from October 20 through December 31, 1863. Reported as a deserter on January 15, 1864.

JENKINS, JAMES, Corporal
Born in Haywood County and resided in Macon County where he was by occupation a farmer prior to enlisting at Quallatown at age 34, July 19, 1862, for the war. Mustered in as Corporal. Reported present or accounted for through October 31, 1862, and in January-April, 1863. Died at Strawberry Plains, Tennessee, April 10, 1863, of "febris con[tinua] com[munis]."

JENKINS, JONAS, Sergeant
Born in what later became Jackson County. Resided in Jackson County as a farmer prior to enlisting at Quallatown at age 29, July 19, 1862, for the war. Mustered in as Private. Reported present through October 31, 1862, and in January-June, 1863. Promoted to Sergeant prior to October 31, 1863. Reported present in September, 1863-February, 1864. Name appears on a receipt roll for clothing dated October 16, 1864. No further records. Survived the war. [May have served previously as Private in Company F, 29th Regiment N.C. Troops.]

JENKINS, SAMUEL, Private
Born in what later became Jackson County. Resided in Jackson County. Was by occupation a farmer prior to enlisting at Strawberry Plains, Tennessee, at age 15, February 9, 1863, for the war. Reported present through June 30, 1863. No further records. [He may have been the same man as Pvt. S. W. Jenkins of Levi's Battery.]

JOHNSON, W. L., Private
Enlisted at Quallatown on August 20, 1863, for the war. Name appears on receipt rolls for clothing dated June 18 and September 1, 1864. No further records. Survived the war.

JONES, ANDREW, Private
Born in what later became Jackson County. Resided in Jackson County as a farmer prior to enlisting at Quallatown at age 28, July 19, 1862, for the war. Mustered in as Sergeant. Reported present through August 31, 1862. Transferred to Company G of this regiment on September 1, 1862.

JONES, CHARLES, Private
Enlisted in Jackson County on August 20, 1863, for the war. Reported present in November, 1863-February, 1864. Captured at Winchester, Virginia, September 19, 1864. Sent to Harpers Ferry, West Virginia. Transferred to Point Lookout, Maryland, where he arrived on September 26, 1864. Died at Point Lookout on February 10, 1865, of "chronic diarrhoea."

JONES, HAMILTON, Private
Born in Macon County and resided in Jackson County where he was by occupation a farmer prior to enlisting at Quallatown at age 20, July 19, 1862, for the war. Mustered in as Sergeant. Reported present through August 31, 1862. Transferred to Company G of this regiment on September 1, 1862.

JONES, JEHU, Private
Born in Macon County and resided in Jackson County where he was by occupation a farmer prior to enlisting at Quallatown at age 25, July 19, 1862, for the war. Reported present through August 31, 1862. Transferred to Company G of this regiment on September 1, 1863. [His given name may have been John.]

JONES, SAMUEL, Private
Born in what later became Jackson County. Resided in Jackson County as a farmer prior to enlisting at Quallatown at age 18, July 19, 1862, for the war. Reported present through August 31, 1862. Transferred to Company G of this regiment on September 1, 1862.

JONES, WILLIAM W., Private
Born in what later became Jackson County. Resided in Jackson County as a farmer prior to enlisting at Quallatown at age 19, July 19, 1862, for the war. Reported present through August 31, 1862. Transferred to Company G of this regiment on September 1, 1862.

KEENER, ELBERT S., Sergeant
Born in what later became Jackson County. Resided in Jackson County as a farmer prior to enlisting at Quallatown at age 19, July 19, 1862, for the war. Mustered in as Private. Reported present through October 31, 1862, in January-June, 1863, and in September, 1863-February, 1864. Promoted to Sergeant in January-February, 1864. Name appears on receipt rolls for clothing dated June 18 and September 1, 1864. No further records. Survived the war.

KEENER, THOMAS W., Private

Records of the United Confederate Veterans and North Carolina pension records indicate that he served in this legion, most likely in this company.

KIRKLAND, WILLIAM, Private

May have served previously in Company F, Walker's Battalion. Enlisted at Quallatown on March 4, 1863, for the war. Reported present through April 30, 1863. Deserted on June 10, 1863. [His materials are found in the National Archives Compiled Service Record for William Kirkland of Company F, Walker's Battalion.]

LEDFORD, MILES M., Private

Place and date of enlistment not reported; probably enlisted subsequent to February 29, 1864. Captured at Franklin on May 27, 1864. Sent to Knoxville, Tennessee. Transferred to Chattanooga, Tennessee, and Nashville, Tennessee. Confined at Louisville, Kentucky, June 29, 1864. Transferred to Camp Morton, Indianapolis, Indiana, where he arrived on July 1, 1864. Died at Camp Morton on December 18, 1864, of "inflammation of the lungs."

LEMING, G. W., Private

Born in Haywood County and resided in Jackson County where he was by occupation a farmer prior to enlisting at Quallatown at age 38, July 19, 1862, for the war. Reported present through August 31, 1862. Transferred to Company G of this regiment on September 1, 1863.

LEMING, JAMES L., Private

Born in Haywood County and resided in Jackson County where he was by occupation a farmer prior to enlisting at Quallatown at age 26, July 19, 1862, for the war. Reported on sick furlough through August 31, 1862. Transferred while on sick furlough to Company G of this regiment on September 1, 1862.

LEMING, THOMAS L., Private

Born in Cherokee County and resided in Jackson County where he was by occupation a farmer prior to enlisting at Quallatown at age 19, July 19, 1862, for the war. Reported present through August 31, 1862. Transferred to Company G of this regiment on September 1, 1862.

LEQUIRE, ISAAC W., Private

Born in Macon County and resided in Jackson County where he was by occupation a farmer prior to enlisting at Quallatown at age 22, July 19, 1862, for the war. Reported present or accounted for through October 31, 1862, and in January-February, 1863. Reported on detached service in the Smoky Mountains in Tennessee, March-April, 1863. Reported absent without leave in Macon County, May 1-December 31, 1863. Subsequently reported as having deserted on October 20, 1863.

LEQUIRE, JOSEPH, Private

Born in Macon County and resided in Jackson County where he was by occupation a farmer prior to enlisting at Quallatown at age 27, July 19, 1862, for the war. Reported present or accounted for through October 31, 1862. Reported absent sick in Jackson County, January-February, 1863. Returned to duty in March-April, 1863. Reported present in May-June, 1863. Deserted near Greeneville, Tennessee, October 11, 1863.

LEQUIRE, WILLIAM N., Private

Born in Macon County and resided in Jackson County where he was by occupation a farmer prior to enlisting at Quallatown at age 31, July 19, 1862, for the war. Reported present through August 31, 1862. Reported absent sick in Macon County in September-October, 1862, and January-April, 1863. Reported absent without leave May 1-December 31, 1863. Subsequently reported as having deserted on October 20, 1863.

LLOYD, ROBERT B., Private

Born in Grainger County, Tennessee, where he resided as a farmer prior to enlisting at Strawberry Plains, Tennessee, at age 25, August 31, 1862, for the war. Mustered in as Private. Reported present through October 31, 1862. Reported on duty as a wagon master for this regiment in January-June, 1863. Reported present in September, 1863-February, 1864. Appointed Quartermaster Sergeant subsequent to February 28, 1864, and transferred to the Field and Staff of this regiment.

LOVE, DALLAS F., Private

Enlisted at Quallatown on January 1, 1864, for the war. Reported present through February 29, 1864. Hospitalized at Winchester, Virginia, August 1, 1864, with bronchitis. Transferred to another hospital on August 3, 1864. Name appears on a receipt roll for clothing dated September 1, 1864. No further records.

LOVE, THOMAS J., Private

Born in what later became Jackson County. Resided in Jackson County as a farmer prior to enlisting at Quallatown at age 18, July 19, 1862, for the war. Reported present through October 31, 1862, and in January-June, 1863. Reported as having been sent as a courier to western North Carolina with dispatches for Brig. Gen. Robert B. Vance and Col. William H. Thomas in September-October, 1863. Rejoined the company prior to December 31, 1863. Reported present in January-February, 1864. Appointed Ensign (1st Lieutenant) to rank from October 31, 1864, and transferred to the Field and Staff of this regiment.

McCONNELL, JOSEPH JUDSON, Private

Previously served as Private in Company D, 62nd Regiment N.C. Troops. Transferred to this company in May-June, 1863. Reported present in May-June, 1863. Reported absent sick in Virginia and in Macon County in September, 1863-February, 1864. No further records. Survived the war.

McGEE, GEORGE W., Private

Born in Jefferson County, Tennessee, and resided in Grainger County, Tennessee, where he was by occupation a farmer prior to enlisting at Strawberry Plains, Tennessee, at age 35, January 10, 1863, for the war. Reported present through February 28, 1863. Reported on detached service at Mossy Creek, Tennessee, March-April, 1863. Rejoined the company prior to June 30, 1863. Reported present in September-October, 1863. Deserted at Bean's Station, Tennessee, on or about December 8, 1863.

McMAHAN, LEVI, Musician

Born in what later became Yancey County. Resided in Jackson County where he was by occupation a farmer prior to enlisting at Quallatown at age 30, July 19, 1862, for the war. Mustered in as Musician (Fifer). Reported present through August 31, 1862. Transferrred to Company G of this regiment on September 1, 1862.

MARTIN, JOHN H., Private

Born in what later became McDowell County. Resided in Jackson County and was by occupation a farmer prior to enlisting at Quallatown at age 24, July 19, 1862, for the war. Reported present through August 31, 1862. Transferred to Company G of this regiment on September 1, 1862.

MESSER, JOHN W., Private

Born in what later became Jackson County. Resided in Jackson County and was by occupation a farmer prior to enlisting at Quallatown at age 18, July 19, 1862, for the war. Reported present through August 31, 1862. Transferred to Company G of this regiment on September 1, 1862.

MESSER, REUBEN, Private

Born in what later became Jackson County. Resided in Jackson County and was by occupation a farmer prior to enlisting at Quallatown at age 15, July 19, 1862, for the war. Reported present through August 31, 1862. Transferred to Company G of this regiment on September 1, 1862.

MONTEITH, JAMES A., Private

Born in what later became Jackson County. Resided in Jackson County as a farmer prior to enlisting at Quallatown at age 22, July 19, 1862, for the war. Reported present through August 31, 1862. Transferred to Company G of this regiment on September 1, 1862.

MONTEITH, JOHN A., Private

Born in what later became Jackson County. Resided in Jackson County as a farmer prior to enlisting at Quallatown at age 21, July 19, 1862, for the war. Reported present through August 31, 1862. Transferred to Company G of this regiment on September 1, 1862.

MORGAN, BENJAMIN L., Private

Born in the part of Macon County that later became Cherokee County. Resided in Cherokee County as a farmer prior to enlisting at Quallatown at age 30, July 19, 1862, for the war. Reported present through October 31, 1862, and in January-February, 1863. Hospitalized at Strawberry Plains, Tennessee, on an unspecified date. Discharged from hospital on April 15, 1863. Failed to return to duty and was listed as a deserter on June 30, 1863.

MULL, SAMUEL JOHNSON, Private

Resided in Jackson County where he was by occupation a farmer prior to enlisting at Quallatown at age 41, March 2, 1863, for the war. Mustered in as Private. Reported present through June 30, 1863. Appointed Musician (Drummer) in May-June, 1863. Reported absent without leave, "missing in retreat from Greeneville, Tenn.," October 14, 1863. Returned to duty and was reduced to ranks in January-February, 1864. Name appears on receipt rolls for clothing dated June 18, September 1, and September 17, 1864. No further records. Survived the war.

NATIONS, ALFRED, Private

Born in what later became Jackson County. Resided in Jackson County as a farmer prior to enlisting at Quallatown at age 27, July 19, 1862, for the war. Reported on detached service through August 31, 1862. Transferred while on detached service to Company G of this regiment on September 1, 1862. [His surname may have been Nation.]

NATIONS, JAMES, Private

Born in what later became Jackson County. Resided in Jackson County as a farmer prior to enlisting at Quallatown at age 23, July 19, 1862, for the war. Reported present through August 31, 1862. Transferred to Company G of this regiment on September 1, 1862. [His surname may have been Nation.]

NATIONS, JEREMIAH, Private

Born in what later became Jackson County. Resided in Jackson County as a farmer prior to enlisting at Quallatown at age 31, July 19, 1862, for the war. Reported present through August 31, 1862. Transferred to Company G of this regiment on September 1, 1862. [His surname may have been Nation.]

NATIONS, JOHN, Private

Born in what later became Jackson County. Resided in Jackson County as a farmer prior to enlisting at Quallatown at age 34, July 19, 1862, for the war. Reported present through August 31, 1862. Transferred to Company G of this regiment on September 1, 1862. [His surname may have been Nation.]

NICHOLS, WILLIAM, Private

Born in the part of Haywood County that later became Macon County. Resided in Jackson County where he was by occupation a farmer prior to enlisting at Strawberry Plains, Tennessee, at age 38, November 18, 1862, for the war. Reported absent sick in Jackson County in January-February, 1863. Returned to duty prior to April 30, 1863. Deserted on June 15, 1863.

ODOM, JOHN A., Private

Born in Rutherford County and resided in Macon County where he was by occupation a farmer prior to enlisting at Quallatown at age 28, July 19, 1862, for the war. Reported present through August 31, 1862. Reported sick at home in September-October, 1862. Reported absent without leave, December 20, 1862-February 28, 1863; subsequently reported as "Returned & absence satisfactorily explained." Deserted on April 10, 1863, when he was discharged from hospital at Strawberry Plains, Tennessee. Federal Provost Marshal records appear to indicate that he served subsequently in the Indian Battalion.

OGLE, ISAAC B., Private

Born in Sevier County, Tennessee, and resided in Jackson County, North Carolina, where he was by occupation a farmer prior to enlisting at Quallatown at age 23, July 19, 1862, for the war. Reported on detached service through October 31, 1862. Reported present in January-February, 1863. Reported absent on detached service at Smoky Mountain, Tennessee, in March-June and September-October, 1863. Reported absent without leave from October 20 through December 31, 1863. Returned to duty prior to February 29, 1864, when he was reported present. No further records.

PARRIS, ALFRED J., Private

Born in what later became Jackson County. Resided in Jackson County as a farmer prior to enlisting at Quallatown at age 18, July 19, 1862, for the war. Reported present through August 31, 1862. Transferred to Company G of this regiment on September 1, 1862.

PARRIS, ANDREW J., Private

Born in what later became Jackson County. Resided in Jackson County and was by occupation a farmer prior to enlisting at

Quallatown at age 31, July 19, 1862, for the war. Reported present through August 31, 1862. Transferred to Company G of this regiment on September 1, 1862.

PARRIS, JAMES M., Private
Born in what later became Jackson County. Resided in Jackson County as a farmer prior to enlisting at Quallatown at age 16, July 19, 1862, for the war. Reported present through August 31, 1862. Transferred to Company G of this regiment on September 1, 1862.

PARRIS, RUFUS M., Private
Born in what later became Jackson County. Resided in Jackson County as a farmer prior to enlisting at Quallatown at age 19, July 19, 1862, for the war. Reported present through August 31, 1862. Transferred to Company G of this regiment on September 1, 1862.

PARTON, WILLIAM B., Private
Enlisted at Quallatown on March 7, 1863, for the war. Reported on detached service in the Smoky Mountains through October 31, 1863. Subsequently reported as absent without leave from October 20 through December 31, 1863. Failed to return to duty and was listed as a deserter, January-February, 1864.

PILKENTON, JAMES, Private
Born in Macon County where he resided as a famer prior to enlisting at Quallatown at age 18, July 19, 1862, for the war. Deserted from camp in the Smoky Mountains in Tennessee on August 17, 1862. Later served in Company C, Indian Battalion. [His materials in the National Archives Compiled Service Records were erroneously separated into two records, one for James Pilkenton and one for James Pilkey.]

PRESLEY, DAVID, Private
Born in Greene County, Tennessee, and resided in Jackson County, North Carolina, where he was by occupation a wheelwright prior to enlisting at Strawberry Plains, Tennessee, at age 54, November 18, 1862, for the war. Reported present in January-February, 1863. Died at Strawberry Plains on April 18-19, 1863. Cause of death not reported.

PRICE, W. T., _____
Name appears on a list of Haywood County veterans receiving pension in 1908. Recorded as a member of Company F, "69" Regiment; as there are no other records for him, it is not clear whether he served in this company or in Company F, 69th Regiment N.C. Troops (7th Regiment N.C. Cavalry).

REAGAN, JAMES H., Private
Enlisted in Jackson County on March 2, 1863, for the war. Reported present through June 30, 1863. Deserted near Zollicoffer, Tennessee, October 14, 1863.

REDMAN, JASPER, Private
Born in Henderson County and resided in Macon County where he was by occupation a farmer prior to enlisting at Quallatown at age 24, July 19, 1862, for the war. Reported present through August 31, 1862. Reported at home sick in September-October, 1862, and January-February, 1863. Returned to duty in March-April, 1863. Reported present in May-June, 1863, and September, 1863-February, 1864. No further records.

REDMAN, ROBERT M., Private
Born in Henderson County and resided in Macon County where he was by occupation a farmer prior to enlisting at Quallatown at age 22, July 19, 1862, for the war. Reported present through August 31, 1862. Reported absent sick in September-October, 1862, and January-February, 1863. Returned to duty in March-April, 1863. Reported present in May-June, 1863. Reported absent on sick furlough, September, 1863-February, 1864. Captured by the enemy in Macon County on February 3, 1864. Confined at Knoxville, Tennessee, February 7, 1864. Transferred to Nashville, Tennessee, February 25, 1864. Transferred to Louisville, Kentucky, February 28, 1864. Confined at Fort Delaware, Delaware, March 4, 1864. Died at Fort Delaware on July 28, 1864, of "intermittent fever."

RIDLEY, JOHN WILLIAM, Private
Born in Cocke County, Tennessee, and resided in Jackson County, North Carolina, where he was by occupation a farmer prior to enlisting at Quallatown at age 30, July 19, 1862, for the war. Reported present through August 31, 1862. Transferred to Company G of this regiment on September, 1862.

SAWYER, JOHN L., Private
Born in Macon County on May 7, 1833. Resided in Macon County and was by occupation a farmer prior to enlisting at Quallatown at age 29, July 19, 1862, for the war. Reported present or accounted for through October 31, 1862, and in January-February, 1863. Reported sick in hospital at Strawberry Plains, Tennessee, March-April, 1863. Reported on duty as a hospital nurse at Strawberry Plains in May-June, 1863. Captured at Strawberry Plains on June 20, 1863, and paroled there the next day. Reported absent without leave from June 21 through December 31, 1863; he was reported to be in Macon County during part of that period. Failed to return to duty and was listed as a deserter on January 15, 1864.

SAWYER, NATHAN T., Private
Born in Macon County on November 17, 1835. Resided in Macon County and was by occupation a farmer prior to enlisting at Quallatown at age 28, July 19, 1862, for the war. Reported present through October 31, 1862, and in January-February, 1863. Reported sick in hospital at Strawberry Plains, Tennessee, March-April, 1863. Reported on sick furlough in May, 1863. Reported absent without leave from June 1 through December 31, 1863. Failed to return to duty and was listed as a deserter on January 15, 1864.

SHAW, JASPER N., Private
Born in Haywood County and resided in Jackson County where he was by occupation a farmer prior to enlisting at Quallatown at age 28, July 19, 1862, for the war. Reported present through August 31, 1862. Transferred to Company G of this regiment on September 1, 1862.

SHERRELL, MOSES L., Private
Born in what later became Jackson County. Resided in Jackson County as a farmer prior to enlisting at Strawberry Plains, Tennessee, at age 47, November 18, 1862, for the war. Reported on extra duty working on a military road in January-February, 1863. Rejoined the company prior to April 30, 1863. Reported present in May-June, 1863. Transferred to Levi's Battery on July 1, 1863.

SHERRELL, RUFUS H., Private
Born in what later became Jackson County. Resided in Jackson County and was by occupation a farmer prior to enlisting at

Quallatown at age 33, July 19, 1862, for the war. Mustered in as Corporal. Reported present through October 31, 1862. Reported absent sick in January-June, 1863. Reduced to ranks in July-October, 1863. Reported absent without leave from August 1 through December 31, 1863; was reported to be in Jackson County for part of that period. Returned to duty prior to February 29, 1864. Hospitalized at Charlottesville, Virginia, June 12, 1864, with acute diarrhoea. Returned to duty on June 20, 1864. No further records. Survived the war.

SHERRILL, PHIDELA E., Private

Born in what later became Jackson County. Resided in Jackson County and was by occupation a farmer prior to enlisting at Quallatown at age 25, July 19, 1862, for the war. Reported present through October 31, 1862, and in January-February, 1863. Reported on detached service in the Smoky Mountains in Tennessee in March-April, 1863. Reported absent without leave on June 13, 1863. Returned to duty prior to October 12, 1863, when he was captured by the enemy at Jonesborough, Tennessee. Sent to Camp Nelson, Kentucky. Confined at Camp Chase, Ohio, November 14, 1863. Transferred to Rock Island, Illinois, January 14, 1864. Transferred to Point Lookout, Maryland, February 15, 1865. Exchanged prior to March 2, 1865, when he was hospitalized at Richmond, Virginia, with debilitas. Furloughed for thirty days on March 12, 1865. No further records.

SHERRILL, W. JUDSON, Private

Born in what later became Jackson County. Resided in Jackson County and was by occupation a farmer prior to enlisting at Quallatown at age 28, July 19, 1862, for the war. Reported present through October 31, 1862, and in January-February, 1863. Reported on detached service in the Smoky Mountains in Tennessee in March-April, 1863. Reported absent without leave on June 10, 1863. Returned to duty on an unknown date. Reported absent without leave, August 1-December 31, 1863. Listed as a deserter on January 15, 1864. [North Carolina pension records states that he was killed "by (Union Colonel George W.) Kirk" in February, 1865.]

SHULER, A. B., _____

North Carolina pension records indicate that he served in this company.

SHULER, PHIDELIA, Private

Enlisted at Carter's Depot, Tennessee, April 20, 1863, for the war. Reported present in April-June and September-October, 1863. Deserted at Bean's Station, Tennessee, December 8, 1863. [May have served previously as Private in Company F, 39th Regiment N.C. Troops.]

SHULER, WILLIAM LEANDER, Private

Born in Haywood County on July 4, 1845. Enlisted at Quallatown at age 18, August 20, 1863, for the war. Reported present in November, 1863-February, 1864. Name appears on receipt rolls for clothing dated June 18, September 1, and September 17, 1864. No further records. Survived the war.

STALCUP, THOMAS BELEW, Private

Born in Macon County on February 8, 1830. Resided in Jackson County and was by occupation a farmer prior to enlisting at Quallatown at age 32, July 19, 1862, for the war. Reported on detached service through August 31, 1862. Transferred to Company G of this regiment on September 1, 1862, while on detached service.

STEPHENSON, WILLIAM H., Private

Born in Haywood County and resided in Jackson County where he was by occupation a farmer prior to enlisting at Quallatown at age 20, July 19, 1862, for the war. Reported present through August 31, 1862. Transferred to Company G of this regiment on September 1, 1862.

STILES, THOMAS, Private

Born in what later became Jackson County. Resided in Macon County where he was by occupation a farmer prior to enlisting at Quallatown at age 30, July 19, 1862, for the war. Reported present through October 31, 1862, and in January-June, 1863. Reported on sick furlough in Macon County in September-October, 1863. Subsequently reported absent without leave from August 1 through December 31, 1863. Listed as a deserter on January 15, 1864. [His surname may have been Styles.]

STILLWELL, JAMES F., Corporal

Born in Macon County where he resided as a farmer prior to enlisting at Quallatown at age 23, July 19, 1862, for the war. Mustered in as Private. Reported present through October 31, 1862, and in January-June, 1863. Promoted to Corporal in July-October, 1863. Reported present or accounted for in September-October, 1863. Reported in hospital at Emory and Henry, Virginia, November-December, 1863. Returned to duty prior to December 31, 1863. Reported present in January-February, 1864. Captured at Winchester, Virginia, September 19, 1864. Sent to Harpers Ferry, West Virginia. Transferred to Point Lookout, Maryland, September 23, 1864. Paroled at Point Lookout on March 15, 1865. Received at Boulware's Wharf, James River, Virginia, March 18, 1865, for exchange. Survived the war.

STILLWELL, JOHN F., Private

Previously served as Private in Company A, 7th Battalion N.C. Cavalry. Transferred to this company on July 14, 1863. Reported present in November, 1863-February, 1864. No further records.

SUTTON, HENRY, Private

Born in what later became Jackson County. Resided in Jackson County as a farmer prior to enlisting at Quallatown at age 25, July 19, 1862, for the war. Reported on detached service through August 31, 1862. Transferred to Company G of this regiment on September 1, 1862, while on detached service.

SUTTON, JOHN, Private

Born in what later became Jackson County. Resided in Jackson County and was by occupation a farmer prior to enlisting at Quallatown at age 22, July 19, 1862, for the war. Reported present through August 31, 1862. Transferred to Company G of this regiment on September 1, 1862.

SUTTON, SOLOMON, Private

Born in what later became Jackson County. Resided in Jackson County and was by occupation a farmer prior to enlisting at Quallatown at age 26, July 19, 1862, for the war. Reported present through August 31, 1862. Transferred to Company G of this regiment on September 1, 1862.

SWEATMAN, DAVID, Private

Born in Edgefield District, South Carolina, and resided in Jackson County, North Carolina. Was by occupation a farmer prior to enlisting at Quallatown at age 29, July 19, 1862, for the war. Reported present through October 31, 1862. Reported on detached service in January-February, 1863. Rejoined the company prior to April 30, 1863. Reported present in May-June, 1863. Captured at Jonesborough, Tennessee, October 12, 1863. Sent to Camp Nelson, Kentucky. Confined at Camp Chase, Ohio, November 14, 1863. Confined at Rock Island, Illinois, January 17, 1864. Paroled at Rock Island and transferred for exchange on March 20, 1865. Received at Boulware's Wharf, James River, Virginia, March 27, 1865, for exchange. Survived the war. [North Carolina pension records indicate that he was shot in the ear at Greeneville, Tennessee, in October, 1863. He was more likely injured at Henderson's Mill, Tennessee, or Rheatown, Tennessee, October 11, 1863.]

THOMASON, W. H., Private

Enlisted at Quallatown on March 5, 1863, for the war. Reported present through June 30, 1863. Reported absent sick in Macon County in September, 1863-February, 1864. Hospitalized at Charlottesville, Virginia, June 12, 1864. Returned to duty on June 24, 1864. Name appears on a receipt roll for clothing dated September 1, 1864. No further records.

THOMASSON, J. L., _____

North Carolina pension records appear to indicate that he served in this company. Survived the war.

THOMASSON, LEMUEL LEVI, Private

Born in Macon County on February 17, 1840. Resided in Macon County and was by occupation a farmer prior to enlisting at Quallatown at age 22, July 19, 1862, for the war. Reported present through October 31, 1862, and in January-February, 1863. Reported sick in hospital at Strawberry Plains, Tennessee, March-April, 1863. Returned to duty prior to June 30, 1863. Reported present, September, 1863-February, 1864. Name appears on receipt rolls for clothing dated June 18, September 1, September 17, and September 27, 1864. No further records.

TRENTHAM, CALEB L., Musician

Born in Sevier County, Tennessee, where he resided as a farmer prior to enlisting in Jackson County, North Carolina, at age 18, July 19, 1862, for the war. Mustered in as Musician (Drummer). Reported present through October 31, 1862. No further records.

TRITT, A. W., Private

Previously served as Private in Company A, 7th Battalion N.C. Cavalry. Transferred to this company on July 14, 1863. Reported absent sick in November-December, 1863. Died in Jackson County on January 7, 1864, of disease.

TRITT, ARCHIBALD C., Private

Born in Haywood County and resided in Jackson County where he was by occupation a farmer prior to enlisting at Quallatown at age 29, July 19, 1862, for the war. Reported present through October 31, 1862, and in January-June, 1863. Reported missing on the retreat from Greeneville, Tennessee, September-December, 1863. Listed as a deserter on January 15, 1864.

WARD, GEORGE W., Private

Born in what later became Jackson County. Resided in Jackson County as a farmer prior to enlisting at Quallatown at age 22, July 19, 1862, for the war. Reported present through October 31, 1862, and in January-June, 1863. Reported sick in hospital at Emory and Henry, Virginia, October 31, 1863. Died in hospital at Emory and Henry on November 21, 1863. Cause of death not reported.

WARD, THOMAS W., Private

Previously served as Private in 2nd Company A of this regiment. Transferred to this company in September-October, 1862. Reported present on October 31, 1862, and in January-February, 1863. Reported absent sick at Strawberry Plains, Tennessee, March-April, 1863. Returned to duty prior to June 30, 1863. Reported present in September-December, 1863. Reported absent without leave on February 7, 1864. No further records. Survived the war.

WATKINS, ANDREW, Private

Born in what later became Jackson County. Resided in Jackson County as a farmer prior to enlisting at Quallatown at age 19, July 19, 1862, for the war. Reported on detached service through October 31, 1862. Rejoined the company prior to February 31, 1863. Reported sick in hospital at Strawberry Plains, Tennessee, in March-June, 1863. Reported on sick furlough in Jackson County in September-December, 1863. Failed to return to duty and was listed as a deserter on January 15, 1864.

WATKINS, DAVID, Private

Born in Wilkes County and resided in Jackson County where he was by occupation a farmer prior to enlisting at Strawberry Plains, Tennessee, at age 40, November 18, 1862, for the war. Reported absent sick in Jackson County in January-February, 1863. Reported sick in hospital at Strawberry Plains in March-June, 1863. No further records.

WATKINS, JOHN, Private

Born in Wilkes County and resided in Jackson County where he was by occupation a farmer prior to enlisting at Strawberry Plains, Tennessee, at age 33, November 18, 1862, for the war. Reported absent sick in Jackson County in January-February, 1863. Reported for or returned to duty prior to April 30, 1863. Deserted on June 10, 1863. May have returned to duty on an unspecified date, or have joined with Colonel Thomas's force in western North Carolina. Captured by the enemy near Franklin on or about May 27, 1864. Sent to Knoxville, Tennessee. Transferred to Chattanooga, Tennessee, June 22, 1864. Transferred to Nashville, Tennessee. Confined at Louisville, Kentucky, June 29, 1864. Confined at Camp Morton, Indianapolis, Indiana, July 1, 1864. Paroled at Camp Morton on February 19, 1865, and transferred to Point Lookout, Maryland, for exchange. Exchanged on an unspecified date. Furloughed on or about February 25, 1864. Hospitalized at Richmond, Virginia, with phthisis pulmonalis (tuberculosis) on or about March 3, 1865. No further records.

WEEKS, DRURY D., Private

Born in Rutherford County and resided in Jackson County. Was by occupation a farmer prior to enlisting at Quallatown at age 26, July 19, 1862, for the war. Reported on detached service through October 31, 1862. Rejoined the company prior to February 28, 1863. Reported on detached service at Smoky Mountain, Tennessee, in March-June, 1863. Reported absent without leave from October 20 through December 31, 1863. Returned to duty prior to February 29, 1864. Captured at Winchester, Virginia, September 19, 1864. Sent to Harpers Ferry, West Virginia. Transferred to Point Lookout, Maryland, September 23, 1864. Paroled at Point Lookout on March 15, 1865. Received at Boulware's Wharf, James River, Virginia, March 18, 1865, for exchange. No further records.

WELCH, ADOLPHUS H., Corporal
Resided in Macon County and enlisted at Quallatown at about age 19, March 4, 1863, for the war. Mustered in as Private. Reported sick in hospital at Strawberry Plains, Tennessee, April 30, 1863. Returned to duty prior to June 30, 1863. Reported present in September, 1863-February, 1864. Wounded in the left shoulder at Piedmont, Virginia, June 5, 1864. Hospitalized at Danville, Virginia, on or about June 18, 1864. Furloughed on June 19, 1864. Returned to duty on an unspecified date and was promoted to Corporal. Captured in Haywood County on February 5, 1865. Sent to Knoxville, Tennessee. Sent to Chattanooga, Tennessee, February 16, 1865. Sent to Nashville, Tennessee. Confined at Louisville, Kentucky, February 20, 1865. Confined at Camp Chase, Ohio, March 5, 1865. Released at Camp Chase on June 13, 1865, after taking the Oath of Allegiance.

WELCH, E. MONTRAVILLE, Private
Born in Macon County where he resided as a farmer prior to enlisting at Quallatown at age 18, July 19, 1862, for the war. Reported present through October 31, 1862, in January-June, 1863, and in September, 1863-February, 1864. Name appears on receipt rolls for clothing dated June 18 and September 1, 1864. No further records.

WELCH, J. L., Private
Enlisted at Quallatown on March 4, 1863, for the war. Reported present through June 30, 1863. Reported on detached service in hospital at White Sulfur Springs, West Virginia, in September, 1863-February, 1864. Name appears on a receipt roll for clothing dated September 27, 1864, which indicates that he was still on service at the hospital. No further records.

WELCH, JOHN W., Private
Born in Macon County where he resided as a farmer prior to enlisting at Quallatown at age 22, July 19, 1862, for the war. Reported present through October 31, 1862, and in January-April, 1863. Reported absent on sick furlough in May-June and September-October, 1863. Reported absent without leave from October 20 through December 31, 1863. Failed to return to duty and was listed as a deserter on January 15, 1864. [He probably served later in the Indian Battalion while a deserter from this company.]

WELCH, WILLIAM, Private
Resided in Macon County. Place and date of enlistment not reported; probably enlisted subsequent to February 29, 1864. Deserted to the enemy at Franklin on February 25, 1865. Confined at Knoxville, Tennessee, March 6, 1865. Took the Oath of Allegiance at Knoxville on March 6, 1865. Transferred to Louisville, Kentucky, where he arrived on March 26, 1865. Released at Louisville on March 28, 1865, after taking the Oath of Allegiance, with instructions "to remain North of the Ohio River during the war."

WEST, DAVID, Private
Born in what later became Jackson County. Resided in Jackson County and was by occupation a farmer prior to enlisting at Quallatown at age 24, July 19, 1862, for the war. Reported present through August 31, 1862. Transferred to Company G of this regiment on September 1, 1862.

WEST, ELISHA, Private
Born in Macon County where he resided as a farmer prior to enlisting at Quallatown at age 29, July 19, 1862, for the war. Reported present through August 31, 1862. Transferred to Company G of this regiment on September 1, 1862.

WEST, THOMAS M., Corporal
Tennessee pension application No. 16684 indicates that he served as Corporal in this company. Survived the war.

WHITESIDE, DAVIS, Private
Born in Rutherford County and resided in Jackson County. Was by occupation a farmer prior to enlisting at Quallatown at age 18, July 19, 1862, for the war. Reported present through August 31, 1862. Transferred to Company G of this regiment on September 1, 1862.

WIGGINS, THOMAS ALBERT, Private
Born on September 1, 1835, in the part of Macon County that later became Jackson County. Resided in Jackson County as a farmer prior to enlisting at Quallatown at age 26, July 19, 1862, for the war. Reported on detached service through October 31, 1862. Reported on detached service working on a military road in January-February, 1863, at Mossy Creek, Tennessee, March-June, 1863, and at Smoky Mountain, Tennessee, September-October, 1863. Subsequently reported absent without leave from October 20 through December 31, 1863. Listed as a deserter on January 15, 1864.

WIKE, DAVID M., Private
Born in what later became Jackson County. Resided in Jackson County as a farmer prior to enlisting at Quallatown at age 23, July 19, 1862, for the war. Reported present through October 31, 1862, and in January-June, 1863. Reported on sick furlough in Jackson County, September-October, 1863. Failed to return to duty and was reported as absent without leave from October 20 through December 31, 1863. Returned to duty prior to February 29, 1864. Deserted to the enemy at Greeneville, Tennessee, April 10, 1865. Confined at Knoxville, Tennessee, April 20, 1865. Took the Oath of Allegiance at Knoxville on April 20, 1865, and sent to Chattanooga, Tennessee.

WILSON, JEREMIAH W., Private
Place and date of enlistment not reported; probably enlisted subsequent to February 29, 1864. Captured by the enemy near Franklin on or about May 24, 1864. Sent to Knoxville, Tennessee. Transferred to Chattanooga, Tennessee, June 22, 1864. Confined at Nashville, Tennessee, prior to June 28, 1864. Confined at Louisville, Kentucky, June 29, 1864. Confined at Camp Morton, Indianapolis, Indiana, July 1, 1864. Paroled at Camp Morton on or about March 4, 1865. Received at Boulware's and Cox's Wharves, James River, Virginia, March 10-11, 1865, for exchange. Hospitalized at Richmond, Virginia, March 11, 1865, with debilitas. Furloughed for sixty days on March 15, 1865.

WILSON, NOAH B., Private
Born in Wilkes County and resided in Macon County, where he was by occupation a farmer prior to enlisting in Jackson County at age 34, July 19, 1862, for the war. Reported present through August 31,

1862. Transferred to Company G of this regiment on September 1, 1862.

WOODY, JOHN A., Private
Born in what later became Jackson County. Resided in Jackson County as a farmer prior to enlisting at Quallatown at age 33, August 31, 1862, for the war. Reported on detached service in September-October, 1862, and January-February, 1863. Reported absent without leave from March 15 through June 30, 1863. No further records. Survived the war.

COMPANY G

This company was originally known as Company E, N.C. Cherokee Battalion. It was organized at Strawberry Plains, Tennessee, September 1, 1862, being split off what was known as Company D of this regiment. The men were chiefly from Jackson County. On or about October 5, 1862, this company was designated Company G, Infantry Regiment, Thomas's Legion, and the Company D from which this company was formed was designated Company F.

The following roster was compiled in large part from a company muster and descriptive roll dated September 1, 1862, and from company muster rolls dated September, 1862-June, 1863, and September, 1863-February, 1864. These are abstracted in the microfilm edition of the Compiled Service Records of Confederate Soldiers Who Served in Organizations from the State of North Carolina (Record Group 109, M270), National Archives, Washington, D.C. Other valuable information in the Compiled Service Records includes enlistment papers, pay vouchers, requisitions, letters of resignation, discharge certificates, and abstracts of medical and prisoner of war records.

Also utilized in this roster were *The War of the Rebellion: A Compilation of the Official Records of the Union and Confederate Armies*, the North Carolina Adjutant General's papers, state militia records, newspaper casualty lists and obituaries, wartime claims for bounty pay and allowances, postwar registers of claims for artificial limbs, Confederate pension applications filed with the states of North Carolina, Tennessee, and Florida, records of the North Carolina Confederate Soldiers' Home, and the 1860 and 1870 federal censuses of North Carolina. A search was made also for relevant letters, diaries, reminiscences, and other manuscripts in the Southern Historical Collection (University of North Carolina-Chapel Hill) and the Duke University Library Special Collections Department.

Among the secondary sources consulted were records of the North Carolina division of the United Daughters of the Confederacy, postwar rosters, regimental and county histories, marriage bond, will, and cemetery indexes, published and unpublished genealogies, biographical dictionaries, the North Carolina *County Heritage Book* series, the *Confederate Veteran*, Walter Clark's *Histories of the Several Regiments and Battalions from North Carolina in the Great War, 1861-'65*, and the North Carolina volume of the extended edition of *Confederate Military History*.

OFFICERS

CAPTAIN

FISHER, DANIEL G.
Previously served as 3rd Lieutenant of Company F of this regiment. Appointed Captain of this company on September 1, 1862, and transferred. Reported present or accounted for through February 28, 1863, and in March, 1863-February, 1864. Hospitalized at Harrisonburg, Virginia, September 17, 1864, with debilitas. Hospitalized at Lynchburg, Virginia, on or about October 7, 1864, with phthisis pulmonalis (tuberculosis). No further records. Survived the war.

LIEUTENANTS

ALLEN, DANIEL J., 2nd Lieutenant
Previously served in Company F of this regiment with an unknown rank. Elected 2nd Lieutenant of this company on September 1, 1862. Reported present through October 31, 1862. Resigned on November 27, 1862, because of "ill health."

BRINKLEY, JOHN R., 3rd Lieutenant
Enlisted at Webster on March 9, 1863, for the war. Mustered in as Private. Reported present through April 30, 1863. Appointed 3rd Lieutenant in May-June, 1863. Reported present in May-June and September-October, 1863. Resigned on October 29, 1863, because of "hemor[rh]age of the lungs and cachakia [cachexia]." Resignation accepted on November 5, 1863.

RABY, DEMPSEY MANUEL, 1st Lieutenant
Previously served as 2nd Lieutenant in Company F of this regiment. Promoted to 1st Lieutenant of this company on September 1, 1862. Reported present or accounted for in September, 1862-June, 1863. Reported absent without leave from October 4, 1863, until February 24, 1864, when he was dropped from the company rolls. [Contrary to 6:755 of this series, he did not serve as a lieutenant in the 16th Regiment, and he transferred to Company F of this regiment rather than to this company, said transfer occurring on July 19, 1862.]

RABY, JOHN B., 2nd Lieutenant
Born in Macon County and resided in Jackson County where he was by occupation a farmer prior to enlisting at Quallatown at age 23. Elected 3rd Lieutenant on September 1, 1862. Promoted to 2nd Lieutenant on November 27, 1862. Reported present through February 29, 1864. Reported in hospital from August 15 through October 29, 1864. No further records. Survived the war.

NONCOMMISSIONED OFFICERS AND PRIVATES

ALLEN, L. W., Private
Previously served as Private in Company F of this regiment. Transferred to this company on September 1, 1862. Reported present through June, 1863, and in September, 1863-February, 1864. Name appears on receipt rolls for clothing dated June 17 and September 1, 1864. Survived the war.

ALLISON, WILLIAM, Private
Enlisted at Gatlinburg, Tennessee, February 22, 1863, for the war. Reported on detached service working on military roads in East Tennessee through June 30, 1863, and in September, 1863-February, 1864. No further records.

BAIRD, A. W., Private
Previously served as Private in Company F of this regiment. Transferred to this company on September 1, 1862. Reported present

through June 30, 1863, except for two days' absence without leave. Reported missing and supposed captured by the enemy from October 16, 1863, through February 29, 1864. No further records.

BAIRD, JOHN, Private

Previously served as Private in Company F of this regiment. Transferred to this regiment on September 1, 1862. Reported present through April 30, 1863, except for two days' absence without leave. Reported under arrest at Jonesborough, Tennessee, in May-June, 1863. Reported missing and supposed captured by the enemy from October 16, 1863, through February 29, 1864. No further records.

BARKER, W. A., _____

Place and date of enlistment not reported. Name appears on receipt rolls for clothing dated June 17 and September, 1864. No further records.

BENNETTE, J. M., _____

North Carolina pension records appear to indicate that he served in this company. Survived the war.

BERRY, SAMUEL, Private

Previously served as Private in Company H, 60th Regiment N.C. Troops. Enlisted in this company at Gatlinburg, Tennessee, February 22, 1863. Reported on detached duty at work on a military road and stockading through June 30, 1863, and in September, 1863-February, 1864. He was at Strawberry Plains and in Sevier County, Tennessee, during most of that period. No further records.

BLACK, REUBEN, Private

Previously served as Private in Company H, 60th Regiment N.C. Troops. Enlisted illegally in this company at Gatlinburg, Tennessee, February 22, 1863, while absent without leave from the 60th Regiment. Reported working on a military road through June 30, 1863, and in September, 1863-February, 1864. He was at Strawberry Plains and in Sevier County, Tennessee, during most of that period. No further records.

BLACK, ROYAL, Private

Previously served as Private in Company H, 60th Regiment N.C. Troops. Enlisted illegally in this company at Gatlinburg, Tennessee, February 22, 1863, while absent without leave from the 60th Regiment. Reported on detached service working on a military road through June 30, 1863, and in September, 1863-February, 1864. He was at Strawberry Plains and in Sevier County, Tennessee, during most of that period. No further records. Survived the war.

BOWMAN, B. M., Private

Enlisted at Jonesborough, Tennessee, May 24, 1863, for the war. Reported on detail as a miller in June, 1863. Reported absent without leave from June 24 through December 31, 1863. Detailed as a miller in Washington County, Tennessee, on February 10, 1864. No further records. [His middle initial may have been F or S.]

BRADLEY, W. JASPER, _____

North Carolina pension records appear to indicate that he served in this company. Survived the war.

BRENDLE, HENRY P., Private

Previously served as Private in Company F of this regiment. Transferred to this company on September 1, 1862. Reported present through June 30, 1863. Reported absent without leave, "supposed to have reported to Col. W. H. Thomas who was cut off with a portion of the command in the evacuation of E[ast] T[ennessee]," in September, 1863-February, 1864. No further records. Survived the war. [His surname may have been Brindle. North Carolina pension records and his Tennessee pension application No. 10170 indicate that he was wounded in the right hand (fingers shot off), right hip, right arm, right thigh, and back of the neck by a "bum shell" at Lynchburg, Virginia, in April, 1865. There is no other evidence to support the presence of any elements of this legion at Lynchburg at that time. Unless he was on detached service, the injuries may have been received at some engagement in the Shenandoah Valley in 1864. He also claimed in his pension application to have been captured on picket duty in the spring of 1865, and exchanged near the end of the war, although there are no extant Federal Provost Marshal records to support that claim.]

BRENDLE, JOHN H., Private

Previously served as Private in Company F of this regiment. Promoted to Corporal and transferred to this company on September 1, 1862. Reported present or accounted for through June 30, 1863. Reported absent without leave, "supposed to have reported to Col. W. H. Thomas who was cut off with a portion of the command in the evacuation of E[ast] T[ennessee]," September-February, 1864. Reduced to ranks on or prior to October 31, 1863. No further records. Survived the war. [His surname may have been Brindle.]

BROOKS, I. C., Musician

Previously served as Private in Company F of this regiment. Transferred to this company on September 1, 1862. Reported present or accounted for through February 28, 1863. Deserted on April 6, 1863. Returned to duty prior to June 30, 1863. Reported present in September-October, 1863. Appointed Musician (Fifer) on October 6, 1863. Reported sick in hospital at Rogersville, Tennessee, December 31, 1863. Returned to duty prior to February 29, 1864. Name appears on receipt rolls for clothing dated June 17 and September 1, 1864. No further records. Survived the war.

BROWN, WILLIAM, _____

North Carolina pension records indicate that he served in this company. Survived the war.

BRYSON, C. A., _____

North Carolina pension records indicate that he served in this company. Survived the war.

BUCHANAN, WILLIAM B., Corporal

Previously served as Private in Company F of this regiment. Transferred to this company on September 1, 1862. Reported present through June 30, 1863. Promoted to Corporal prior to October 31, 1863. Reported sick in hospital at Abingdon, Virginia, September, 1863-February, 1864. No further records. Survived the war.

BUMGARNER, HENRY F., Private

Previously served as Private in Company F of this regiment. Transferred to this company on September 1, 1862. Reported present through December 31, 1862. Died in hospital at Strawberry Plains, Tennessee, February 13, 1863. Cause of death not reported.

BUMGARNER, JOHN, Private

Previously served as Private in Company F of this regiment. Transferred to this company on September 1, 1862. Reported present or accounted for through April 30, 1863. Deserted on May 12, 1863. Returned to duty on an unspecified date. Reported absent without leave, "supposed to have reported to Col. W. H. Thomas who was cut off with a portion of the command following the evacuation of E[ast] T[ennessee]" in September, 1863-February, 1864. Name appears on a receipt roll for clothing dated October 16, 1864. No further records. Survived the war.

BUMGARNER, WILLIAM, 1st Sergeant
Previously served as Private in Company A, 16th Regiment N.C. Troops (6th Regiment N.C. Volunteers). Enlisted in this company at Webster on March 10, 1863, for the war. Mustered in as Private. Reported present through June 30, 1863. Promoted to 1st Sergeant prior to October 31, 1863. Reported present in September, 1863-February, 1864. Captured at Winchester, Virginia, September 19, 1864. Sent to Harpers Ferry, West Virginia. Confined at Point Lookout, Maryland, September 26, 1864. Paroled at Point Lookout on March 15, 1865. Received at Boulware's Wharf, James River, Virginia, March 18, 1865, for exchange. No further records. Survived the war.

BURNS, JOHN C. S., Private
Previously served as Private in Company F of this regiment. Transferred to this regiment on September 1, 1862. Reported present through February 28, 1863. Reported on detached service working on a military road in March-April, 1863. Captured at Strawberry Plains, Tennessee, June 20, 1863, and paroled the next day. Reported on detached service in the commissary department at Strawberry Plains on June 30, 1863, and in September, 1863-February, 1864. No further records.

CABE, JOSHUA., _____
North Carolina pension records appear to indicate that he served in this company. Survived the war.

CAGLE, EVAN HARVEY, Sergeant
Previously served as Private in Company F of this regiment. Transferred to this company on September 1, 1862. Reported present through April 30, 1863. Promoted to Corporal or Sergeant in May, 1863, but was reduced to ranks on June 1 for a brief absence without leave. Promoted to Sergeant on September 15, 1863. Reported present in September, 1863-February, 1864. Name appears on receipt rolls for clothing dated June 17, July 22, and September 20, 1864. No further records. Survived the war.

CLARK, HUGH, Private
Previously served in Company H, 60th Regiment N.C. Troops. Enlisted in this company at Gatlinburg, Tennessee, February 22, 1863, for the war. Reported on detached duty working on roads and stockading through June 30, 1863, and in September, 1863-February, 1864. He was at Strawberry Plains and Sevier County, Tennessee, through much of that period. No further records. Survived the war.

CLONTS, SAMUEL W., Private
Previously served as Private in Company F of this regiment. Transferred to this company on September 1, 1862. Reported present through June 30, 1863. Reported absent without leave, "supposed to have reported to Col. W. H. Thomas who was cut off with portion of the command in the evacuation of E[ast] T[ennessee]" in September, 1863-February, 1864. Court-martialed on May 24, 1864. Found guilty of absence without leave and sentenced to confinement for two months with "6 pound ball attached to left leg by chain" and to be fed on "bread and water alone." [Letters Sent, Orders and Circulars, Dept. of E. Tenn. and Dept. of W. Va. and E. Tenn., April 1863-October, 1864, Record Group 109, Chapter II, Vol. 234, National Archives.] Name appears on a receipt roll for clothing dated June 17, 1864. No further records.

COGDILL, JOHN, Private
Resided in Jackson County where he was by occupation a farmer prior to enlisting in Jackson County at age 27, March 10, 1863, for the war. Deserted on April 24, 1863. Returned to duty on an unspecified date. Reported absent without leave, "supposed to have reported to Col. W. H. Thomas who was cut off with a portion of the command in the evacuation of E[ast] T[ennessee]" in September, 1863-February, 1864. No further records.

CONNER, MARCUS LAFAYETTE, Private
Previously served as Private in Company F of this regiment. Transferred to this company on September 1, 1862. Reported present through October 31, 1862. Reported on sick furlough, November-December, 1863. Reported absent without leave in January-February, 1863. Returned to duty in March-April, 1863. Reported present in May-June, 1863. Reported absent without leave, "supposed to have reported to Col. W. H. Thomas who was cut off with a portion of the command in the evacuation of E[ast] Tenn[essee]," September, 1863-February, 1864. No further records. Survived the war.

COOPER, BENJAMIN F., Private
Previously served as Private in Company F of this regiment. Transferred to this company on September 1, 1862. Reported present through December 31, 1862. Reported on detached service in January-February, 1863, "detailed with Capt. J. M. McConnell after absentees." Did not return, and was reported absent without leave from March 10, 1863, through February 29, 1864. No further records.

COOPER, JOHN A., Private
Previously served as Private in Company F of this regiment. Transferred to this company on September 1, 1862. Reported on detached service in September-October, 1862. Rejoined the company prior to December 31, 1862. Reported absent without leave in January-February, 1863. Returned to duty in March-April, 1863. Reported present in May-June and September-October, 1863. Reported absent without leave from December 5, 1863, through February 29, 1864. No further records.

CRAWFORD, PHILIP J., Private
Born on January 17, 1845, in what later became Jackson County. Enlisted in Jackson County at age 18, March 10, 1863, for the war. Reported present through June 30, 1863. Reported absent without leave, "supposed to have reported to Col. W. H. Thomas, who was cut off with a portion of the command in the evacuation of E[ast] T[ennessee]" in September, 1863-February, 1864. No further records. Survived the war.

CUNNINGHAM, CLINGMAN G., Private
Previously served as Private in Company F of this regiment. Promoted to Corporal and transferred to this company on September 1, 1862. Reported present through October 31, 1862. Reported absent

without leave in November-December, 1862. Returned to duty in January-February, 1863. Reported present through June 30, 1863. Reported absent without leave, "supposed to have reported to Col. W. H. Thomas who was cut off with a portion of the command in the evacuation of E[ast] Tenn[essee]," September, 1863-February, 1864. Reduced to ranks on or prior to October 31, 1863. No further records. Survived the war.

CUNNINGHAM, JOHN, Private
Born in what later became Jackson County. Resided in Sevier County, Tennessee, where he was by occupation a farmer prior to enlisting at Strawberry Plains, Tennessee, at age 47, December 23, 1862, for the war. Reported present in January-April, 1863. Reported absent without leave from May 25 through June 30, 1863. Rejoined the company prior to October 31, 1863, when he was reported absent without leave, "supposed to have reported to Col. W. H. Thomas who was cut off with a portion of the command in the evacuation of E[ast] Tenn[essee]." Reported absent without leave, November 1863-February, 1864. No further records. Survived the war.

DALTON, C. W., Private
Enlisted at Webster on March 10, 1863, for the war. Reported present through June 30, 1863. Reported absent without leave, "supposed to have reported to Col. W. H. Thomas who was cut off with a portion of the command in the evacuation of E[ast] Tenn[essee]e" in September, 1863-February, 1864. No further records.

DIETZ, W. H., _____
North Carolina pension records appear to indicate that he served in this company. Survived the war.

DILLS, ALFRED MARION, Private
Previously served as Private in Company F of this regiment. Transferred to this company on September 1, 1862. Reported present through June 30, 1863, and in September, 1863-February, 1864. Hospitalized at Winchester, Virginia, August 1, 1864, with diarrhoea. Wounded in the right leg on September 22, 1864, probably at Fisher's Hill, Virginia. Hospitalized at Charlottesville, Virginia, September 24, 1864. Right Leg amputated. Survived the war.

DILLS, H., Private
According to the Charlotte *Western Democrat*, October 25, 1864, a man by this name, in this company, was wounded at Winchester, Virginia, September 19, 1864. However, this could refer to Pvt. John Dills of this company or Pvt. H. Jasper Dills of Company F of this regiment.

DILLS, JOHN, Private
Previously served in Company F of this regiment. Transferred to this company on September 1, 1862. Reported present through June 30, 1863, and in September, 1863-February, 1864. Captured at Winchester, Virginia, September 19, 1864. Sent to Harpers Ferry, West Virginia. Confined at Point Lookout, Maryland, September 26, 1864. Paroled at Point Lookout on March 15, 1865. Received at Boulware's Wharf, James River, Virginia, March 18, 1865, for exchange. No further records. Survived the war. [The Charlotte *Western Democrat*, October 25, 1864, reports the wounding of H. Dills of this company at Winchester on September 19, 1864. This may refer to this man.]

DILLS, MARION, Private
Previously served as Private in Company F of this regiment. Transferred to this company on September 1, 1862. Reported present through December 31, 1862. Reported absent without leave on February 12, 1863. Returned to duty in March-April, 1863. Reported present in May-June and September-December, 1863. Reported sick in hospital at Bristol, Tennessee, February 26, 1864. Name appears on a receipt roll for clothing dated September, 1864. No further records. Survived the war.

DILLS, WILLIAM, _____
North Carolina pension records indicate that he served in this company. Survived the war.

ELDERS, JOHN B., Private
Born in Wilkes County and resided in Macon County where he was by occupation a farmer prior to enlisting at Strawberry Plains, Tennessee, at age 39, January 1, 1863, for the war. Reported present through April 30, 1863. Deserted on May 12, 1863. Evidently returned to duty prior to June 30, 1863. Reported absent without leave, "supposed to have reported to Col. W. H. Thomas who was cut off with a portion of the command in the evacuation of E[ast] T[ennessee]," September, 1863-February, 1864. No further records. Survived the war.

ENSLEY, WILLIAM, Private
Previously served as Private in Company F of this regiment. Transferred to this company on September 1, 1862. Reported on detached service in September-October, 1862. Rejoined the company prior to December 31, 1863. Reported present in January-February, 1863. Deserted on April 24, 1863. Returned to duty prior to October 31, 1863, when he was reported sick in hospital at Abindgon, Virginia. Reported sick in hospitals at Abingdon and Liberty, Virginia, in November, 1863-February, 1864. No further records. Survived the war.

FARLEY, CLAYTON, Private
Previously served as Private of Company F of this regiment. Transferred to this company on September 1, 1862. Reported present through December 31, 1862. Reported absent without leave from January 25 through February 28, 1863. Reported sick in hospital at Strawberry Plains, Tennessee, from April 1, 1863, through February 29, 1864. Captured and paroled at New Market, Tennessee, June 21, 1863. No further records. Survived the war. [See Tennessee pension application No. 14935.]

FARLEY, J. L., _____
North Carolina pension records appear to indicate that he served in this company. Survived the war.

FARLEY, JAMES S., Private
Previously served as Private in 2nd Company A of this regiment. Transferred to this company in September-October, 1862. Mustered in as Corporal. Reported present or accounted for through December 31, 1862. Reported absent without leave on February 16, 1863. Returned to duty in March-April, 1863. Reported present but reduced to ranks in May-June, 1863. Reported absent without leave, "supposed to have reported to Col. W. H. Thomas was was cut off with a portion of the Command in the evacuation of E[ast] T[ennessee]," September, 1863-February, 1864. No further records. Survived the war.

FARLEY, WILLIAM, Private

Previously served as Private in Company F of this regiment. Transferred to this company on September 1, 1862. Reported present through June 30, 1863. Reported absent without leave, "supposed to have reported to Col. W.H. Thomas who was cut off with a portion of the command in the evacuation of E[ast] Tenn[essee]," September, 1863-February, 1864. Name appears in a receipt roll for clothing dated October 10, 1864. No further records.

FARMER, A. WESTON, Sergeant

Previously served as Musician (Drummer) in Company F of this regiment. Transferred to this company on September 1, 1862. Reported present through June 30, 1863, and in September, 1863-February, 1864. Promoted to Sergeant prior to September 1, 1864. Name appears on a receipt roll for clothing dated September 1, 1864. No further records. Survived the war.

FISHER, LUCIUS F., Sergeant

Enlisted at Webster on March 10, 1863, for the war. Mustered in as Private. Reported present through June 30, 1863. Promoted to Sergeant on September 15, 1863. Reported present in September, 1863-February, 1864. Name appears on a receipt roll for clothing dated June 17, 1864. No further records. Survived the war.

FISHER, THOMAS G., Private

Previously served as Private in Company F of this regiment. Transferred to this company on September 1, 1862. Reported on detached service in September-October, 1862. Rejoined the company prior to December 31, 1862. Reported present in January-June, 1863, and in September, 1863-February, 1864. Name appears on a receipt roll for clothing dated June 17, 1864. No further records. Survived the war.

FORD, JAMES, Private

Enlisted at Gatlinburg, Tennessee, February 22, 1863, for the war. Reported on detached duty working on roads and stockading at or near Strawberry Plains, Tennessee, through June 30, 1863, and in September, 1863-February, 1864. No further records.

GIBBS, JAMES F., Private

Previously served as Private in Company F of this regiment. Transferred to this company on September 1, 1862. Reported present through October 31, 1862. Reported on sick furlough in November-December, 1862. Failed to return from furlough and was reported absent without leave in January-April, 1863. Returned to duty in May-June, 1863. Reported sick in hospital at Abingdon, Virginia, in September-October, 1863. Returned to duty in November-December, 1863. Reported present in January-February, 1864. No further records. Survived the war.

GIBSON, DANIEL J., Private

Previously served as Private in Company F of this regiment. Transferred to this company on September 1, 1862. Reported present through October 31, 1862. Died in hospital at Strawberry Plains, Tennessee, November 20, 1862. Cause of death not reported.

GRANSTAFF, ISAAC, Private

Enlisted at Gatlinburg, Tennessee, February 22, 1863, for the war. Reported on detached service working on roads and stockading through June 30, 1863, and in September, 1863-February, 1864. Was probably in Sevier County, Tennessee, during most of that period. No further records.

GRIBBLE, JOHN, Private

Resided in Jackson County and was by occupation a farmer prior to enlisting at Webster at age 42, August 20, 1863, for the war. Reported sick in hospital at Rogersville, Tennessee, in November-December, 1863. Returned to duty in January-February, 1864. Reported present on February 29, 1864. Hospitalized at Richmond, Virginia, October 7, 1864, with chronic diarrhoea. Furloughed for thirty days on October 14, 1864. No further records. Survived the war.

GUNTER, GEORGE M., Private

Previously served as Sergeant in Company F of this regiment. Transferred to this company on September 1, 1862. Reported on detached service in September-October, 1862. Reported present in January-June, 1863. Reported absent without leave, "supposed to have reported to Col. W. H. Thomas who was cut off with a portion of the command in the evacuation of E[ast] T[ennessee], September, 1863-February, 1864." Reduced to ranks on or prior to October 31, 1863. No further records.

GUNTER, JOSEPH, Private

Enlisted at Strawberry Plains, Tennessee, March 2, 1863, for the war as a substitute for A. L. Davis. Reported on detached service stockading and working on a road through June 30, 1863. Reported on detached service in Sevier County, Tennessee, "manufacturing salts for government" in September, 1863-February, 1864. No further records.

GUNTER, ROBERT LOVE, Private

Previously served as Private in Company F of this regiment. Transferred to this company on September 1, 1862. Reported present through April 30, 1863. Reported on detail with Assistant. Surgeon John C. Love of this regiment at Carter's Depot, Tennessee, from April 15 through June 30, 1863. Reported absent without leave in September, 1863-February, 1864. No further records. Survived the war.

HALL, JOHN L. F., Sergeant

Previously served as Private in Company F of this regiment. Transferred to this company on January 1 or February 18, 1863. Mustered in as Private. Reported present through February 28, 1863. Reported sick in hospital at Greeneville, Tennessee, March-April, 1863. Returned to duty on or prior to June 30, 1863. Promoted to Sergeant on October 6, 1863. Reported present in September, 1863-February, 1864. No further records.

HALL, L. C., _____

North Carolina pension records indicate that he served in this company. Survived the war.

HARRELL, J. ROBERT, _____

North Carolina pension records indicate that he served in this company. Survived the war.

HARRISON, I. N., Private

Enlisted in Sevier County, Tennessee, January 1, 1863, for the war. Deserted on April 21, 1863. Returned to duty prior to June 30, 1863, and previous deserter status changed to "absent without leave." Reported absent without leave, "supposed to have reported to Col. W. H. Thomas who was cut off with a portion of the command in the evacuation of E[ast] Tenn[essee]," September, 1863-February, 1864. No further records. [He was probably the same man as Pvt. J. N. Harrison of Company I of this regiment.]

HENDERSON, BENJAMIN J. E., Private
Born in Haywood County on May 22, 1838. Enlisted at Gatlinburg, Tennessee, at age 24, February 22, 1863, for the war. Reported on detached service working on roads through June 30, 1863, and in September, 1863-February, 1864. Was in Sevier County, Tennessee, during at least part of that period. Survived the war. [According to his Tennessee pension application No. 5484, he left the army when he was granted a ten-day furlough at Mossy Creek, Tennessee, and "couldent nevr git back to my command." He remained at home and was never formally discharged from the army.]

HENDERSON, JAMES, Private
May have previously served in Company F of this regiment. Place and date of enlistment not reported. Served in this company according to a receipt for shoes dated October 24, 1864, found in the National Archives Compiled Service Record for Capt. Matthew H. Love of 2nd Company A of this regiment, and Company A, Indian Battalion.

HENDERSON, JOHN H., Private
Enlisted at Gatlinburg, Tennessee, February 22, 1863, for the war. Reported on detached service working on roads through June 30, 1863, and in September, 1863-February, 1864. Was probably at Strawberry Plains and in Sevier County, Tennessee, during most of that period. No further records.

HIGDON, WILLIAM, Private
Previously served as Private in Company F of this regiment. Transferred to this company on September 1, 1862. Reported present through June 30, 1863. Reported absent without leave, "supposed to have reported to Col. W. H. Thomas who was cut off with a portion of the command at the evacuation of E[ast] T[ennessee]," September-December, 1863. Captured by the enemy in Macon County on February 3, 1864. Confined at Knoxville, Tennessee, on February 7, 1864. Transferred to Nashville, Tennessee, where he arrived on or before February 28, 1864. Transferred to Louisville, Kentucky, where he arrived on February 29, 1864. Transferred to Fort Delaware, Delaware, where he arrived on or about March 4, 1864. Released at Fort Delaware on June 19, 1865, after taking the Oath of Allegiance.

HOLDER, J. A., Private
Previously served as Private in Company F of this regiment. Transferred to this company on September 1, 1862. Reported present through October 31, 1862. Reported on extra duty working on military road in November-December, 1862. Broke his arm in Jackson County "while on his way to join his command" on December 25, 1862. Furloughed from hospital on an unspecified date. Failed to return to duty and was reported absent without leave from January, 1863, through February, 1864. No further records.

HUGHES, F. A., Private
Enlisted in Jackson County on September 9, 1863, for the war. Reported present through October 31, 1863. Reported on leave in November-December, 1863. Rejoined the company on or prior to February 29, 1864. Reported on duty as a teamster in September, 1864. Name appears on a receipt roll for clothing dated December 14, 1864. No further records.

JOHNSON, J. G., Private
Enlisted in Jackson County on March 10, 1863, for the war. Reported "furloughed and not reported" from March 25, 1863, through February 29, 1864. Name appears on receipt rolls for clothing dated October 16, 1864. No further records. [He may have been captured at Strawberry Plains, Tennessee, June 20, 1863, and paroled the next day.]

JONES, ANDREW, Private
Previously served as Private in Company F of this regiment. Promoted to Sergeant and transferred to this company on September 1, 1862. Reported present through June 30, 1863. Reduced to ranks in July-October, 1863. Reported absent without leave, "supposed to have reported to Col. W. H. Thomas who was cut off with a portion of the command in the evacuation of E[ast] T[ennessee] in September, 1863-February, 1864. No further records.

JONES, HAMILTON, Private
Previously served as Private in Company F of this regiment. Promoted to Sergeant and transferred to this company on September 1, 1862. Reported present through October 31, 1862. Reported on sick furlough in November-December, 1862. Failed to return and was reported absent without leave in January-February, 1863. Reported sick in hospital at Strawberry Plains, Tennessee, in March-April, 1863. Returned to duty in May-June, 1863. Reported absent without leave, "supposed to have reported to Col. W. H. Thomas who was cut off with a portion of the command in the evacuation of E[ast] T[ennessee]," September-December, 1863, and reduced to ranks prior to October 31. Returned to duty prior to February 29, 1864. No further records.

JONES, JEHU, Private
Previously served as Private in Company F of this regiment. Transferred to this company on September 1, 1862. Reported present through February 28, 1863. Died at Strawberry Plains, Tennessee, April 1, 1863, of "febris con[tinua] com[munis]." [His given name may have been John.]

JONES, MARVEL, Private
Enlisted at Gatlinburg, Tennessee, February 28, 1863, for the war. Reported on detached service repairing roads and "stockading" through June 30, 1863, and in September, 1863-February, 1864. Was probably in or near Sevier County, Tennessee, during most of that period. No further records.

JONES, SAMUEL, Private
Previously served as Private in Company F of this regiment. Transferred to this company on September 1, 1862. Reported present through June 30, 1863. Reported absent without leave, "supposed to have reported to Col. W. H. Thomas who was cut off with a portion of the command in the evacuation of E[ast] T[ennessee] in September, 1863-February, 1864. Name appears on a receipt for shoes dated October 24, 1864, found in the National Archives Compiled Service Record of Capt. Matthew H. Love of 2nd Company A of this regiment, and Company A, Indian Battalion. The receipt seems to indicate that he was on duty with Company G, Indian Battalion. He was evidently absent from this company at the time the receipt was issued, as this regiment was on its way to western North Carolina from the Shenandoah Valley. Captain Love was then in command of a detachment made up of various companies of this legion, part of an expedition into eastern Tennessee under Col. John B. Palmer.

JONES, WILLIAM W., Private

Previously served as Private in Company F of this regiment. Transferred to this company on September 1, 1862. Reported present through February 28, 1863. Reported on detached service working on a road in March-April, 1863. Rejoined the company on or prior to June 30, 1863. Reported sick in hospital at Abingdon, Virginia, in September-October, 1863. Returned to duty in November-December, 1863. Reported present in January-February, 1864. Wounded in the right arm at Winchester, Virginia, September 19, 1864. Right arm amputated. Hospitalized at Charlottesville, Virginia, October 22, 1864. Transferred to hospital at Lynchburg, Virginia, October 25, 1864. No further records. Survived the war.

KIRKPATRICK, LEWIS, Private

Enlisted at Gatlinburg, Tennessee, February 22, 1863, for the war. Reported on detached service working on roads and "stockading" through February 29, 1864. Was probably in Sevier County, Tennessee, during most of that period. No further records.

LEMING, G. W., Private

Previously served as Private in Company F of this regiment. Transferred to this company on September 1, 1862. Reported present through February 28, 1863. Reported sick in hospital at Strawberry Plains, Tennessee, from April 7, 1863, through February 29, 1864. No further records.

LEMING, JAMES L., Private

Previously served as Private in Company F of this regiment. Transferred to this company while on sick furlough on September 1, 1862. Reported absent on sick furlough through October 31, 1862. Reported absent without leave in November, 1862-February, 1863. Returned to duty in March-April, 1863. Reported under arrest at Jonesborough, Tennessee, in May-June, 1863. Reported absent without leave, "[s]upposed to have reported to Col. W. H. Thomas who was cut off with a portion of the command in the evacuation of E[ast] Tenn[essee]," in September, 1863-February, 1864. No further records.

LEMING, THOMAS L., Private

Previously served as Private in Company F of this regiment. Transferred to this company on September 1, 1862. Reported present through October 31, 1862. Discharged at Strawberry Plains, Tennessee, November 21, 1862, by reason of "phthisis pulmonalis."

McMAHAN, ELI, Private

Enlisted at Gatlinburg, Tennessee, February 22, 1863, for the war. Reported on detached service working on military roads through June 30, 1863, and in September, 1863-February, 1864. Was probably in Sevier County, Tennessee, during most of that period. No further records.

McMAHAN, LEVI, Private

Previously served as Musician (Fifer) in Company F of this regiment. Transferred to this company on September 1, 1862. Reported present through December 31, 1862. Reported on sick leave in Jackson County in January-February, 1863. Failed to return to duty and was reported absent without leave on or about February 16, 1863. Reduced to ranks in July-October, 1863. Reported absent without leave through February 29, 1864. No further records. Survived the war.

MARTIN, JOHN H., Private

Previously served as Private in Company F of this regiment. Transferred to this company on September 1, 1862. Reported present through October 31, 1862. Died in hospital at Strawberry Plains, Tennessee, on or about November 5, 1862, of "measles."

MESSER, HENRY A., Private

Enlisted in Jackson County on March 10, 1863, for the war. Reported present through June 30, 1863. Reported absent without leave, "[s]upposed to have reported to Col. W. H. Thomas who was cut off with a portion of the command in E Ten[nessee]," in September, 1863-February, 1864. No further records. Survived the war.

MESSER, JOHN, Private

Enlisted at Gatlinburg, Tennessee, February 22, 1863, for the war. Reported on detached service working on roads and "stockading" through February 29, 1864. Was at Strawberry Plains, Tennessee, or in Sevier County, Tennessee, during part of that period. No further records.

MESSER, JOHN W., Private

Previously served as Private in Company F of this regiment. Transferred to this company on September 1, 1862. Reported present through June 30, 1863, and in September, 1863-February, 1864. Captured at Piedmont, Virginia, June 5, 1864. Reported under guard at Staunton, Virginia, June 8, 1864. Confined at Camp Morton, Indianapolis, Indiana, June 21, 1864. Paroled at Camp Morton on or about March 15, 1865. Received at Boulware's and Cox's Wharves, James River, Virginia, March 23, 1865, for exchange. No further records.

MESSER, JOSEPH, _____

North Carolina pension records appear to indicate that he served in this company. Survived the war.

MESSER, REUBEN, Private

Previously served as Private in Company F of this regiment. Transferred to this company on September 1, 1862. Reported present through October 31, 1862. Reported on extra duty working on a military road, November-December, 1862. Rejoined the company on or prior to February 28, 1863. Reported present in March-June, 1863, and in September, 1863-February, 1864. Captured at Piedmont, Virginia, June 5, 1864. Confined at Camp Morton, Indianapolis, Indiana, June 21, 1864. Paroled at Camp Morton on or about March 15, 1865. Received at Boulware's and Cox's Wharves, James River, Virginia, March 23, 1865, for exchange. No further records.

MESSER, ROYAL, Private

Enlisted at Gatlinburg, Tennessee, February 22, 1863, for the war. Reported on detached service working on military roads and "stockading" through June 30, 1863, and in September, 1863-February, 1864. Was at Strawberry Plains, Tennessee, or in Sevier County, Tennessee, during most of that period. No further records.

MILLER, GEORGE W., Private

Enlisted at Gatlinburg, Tennessee, February 22, 1863, for the war. Reported on detached service working on military roads and "stockading" through June 30, 1863, and in September, 1863-February, 1864. Was at Strawberry Plains, Tennessee, or in Sevier County, Tennessee, during most of that period. No further records. [He may have been the same man as Pvt. George Washington Miller of Levi's Battery.]

MILLER, ISAAC, Private
Enlisted at Gatlinburg, Tennessee, February 22, 1863, for the war. Reported on detached service working on military roads and "stockading" through June 30, 1863, and in September, 1863-February, 1864. Was at Strawberry Plains, Tennessee, or in Sevier County, Tennessee, during most of that period. No further records.

MILLER, W. F., Private
Enlisted in Jackson County on March 10, 1863, for the war. Reported absent sick in Sevier County, Tennessee, April 30, 1863. Died on May 5, 1863. Place and cause of death not reported.

MILLER, WILLIAM, Private
Enlisted at Gatlinburg, Tennessee, February 22, 1863, for the war. Reported on detached service working on military roads and "stockading" through June 30, 1863, and in September, 1863-February, 1864. Was at Strawberry Plains, Tennessee, or in Sevier County, Tennessee, during most of that period. No further records.

MILLS, J. K., _____
North Carolina pension records indicate that he served in this company. Survived the war.

MILLS, SAMUEL S, _____
North Carolina pension records appear to indicate that he served in this company. Survived the war.

MONTEITH, GEORGE W., _____
North Carolina pension records appear to indicate that he served in this company. Survived the war.

MONTEITH, JAMES A., Corporal
Previously served as Private in Company F of this regiment. Transferred to this company on September 1, 1862. Reported present through June 30, 1863. Promoted to Corporal on May 1, 1863. Reported present in September, 1863-February, 1864. Name appears on receipt rolls for clothing dated June 17 and September 1, 1864. No further records. Survived the war.

MONTEITH, JOHN A., Sergeant
Previously served as Private in Company F of this regiment. Transferred to this company on September 1, 1862. Reported present through June 30, 1863. Promoted to Sergeant on September 15, 1863. Reported present in September, 1863-February, 1864. No further records. Survived the war.

MONTEITH, THOMAS, _____
North Carolina pension records indicate that he served in this company. Survived the war.

NATIONS, ALFRED, Private
Born in what later became Jackson County. Resided in Jackson County as a farmer prior to enlisting at Quallatown at age 27, July 19, 1862, for the war. Reported present or accounted for through April 30, 1863. Deserted on May 12, 1863. Returned to duty on an unspecified date. Reported absent without leave, "supposed to have reported to Col. W. H. Thomas who was cut off with portion of the command during the evacuation of E[ast] T[ennessee]," September, 1863-February, 1864. No further records. Survived the war. [His surname may have been Nation.]

NATIONS, F. M., Private
Born in what later became Jackson County. Resided in Jackson County as a farmer prior to enlisting at Quallatown at age 32, July 19, 1862, for the war. Mustered in as Sergeant. Reported present through October 31, 1862. Reported on extra duty on work on a military road in November-December, 1862. Reported present or accounted for in January-June, 1863. Reduced to ranks in July-October, 1863. Reported absent without leave, "supposed to have reported to Col. W. H. Thomas who was cut off with a portion of the command in the evacuation of E[ast] Tenn[essee]," September, 1863-February, 1864. No further records. Survived the war. [His surname may have been Nation.]

NATIONS, JAMES, Private
Previously served as Private in Company F of this regiment. Transferred to this company on September 1, 1862. Reported present or accounted for in September, 1862-April, 1863. Deserted on May 12, 1863. Reported present in September-December, 1863. Died in hospital at Emory and Henry, Virginia, February 16, 1864. Cause of death not reported. [His surname may have been Nation.]

NATIONS, JEREMIAH, Private
Previously served as Private in Company F of this regiment. Transferred to this regiment on September 1, 1862. Reported present through February 28, 1863. Reported absent without leave in March-April, 1863. Returned to duty prior to June 30, 1863. Reported absent without leave, "supposed to have reported to Col. W. H. Thomas who was cut off with a portion of the command in the evacuation of E[ast] Tenn[essee]," September, 1863-February, 1864. No further records. Survived the war. [His surname may have been Nation.]

NATIONS, JOHN, Private
Previously served as Private in Company F of this regiment. Promoted to 1st Sergeant and transferred to this company on September 1, 1862. Reported on sick furlough in September-October, 1862. Returned to duty on or prior to December 31, 1862. Reported on sick furlough in Jackson County, January-April, 1863. Subsequently reported absent without leave from February 10 through June 30, 1863. Returned to duty prior to September 1, 1863. Reduced to ranks in July-October, 1863. Reported absent without leave in Jackson County, September 1, 1863-February 29, 1864. No further records. Survived the war. [His surname may have been Nation.]

NORMAN, DAVID S., Private
Enlisted in Jackson County on March 10, 1863, for the war. Reported present through June 30, 1863, and in September, 1863-February, 1864. Captured at Winchester, Virginia, September 19, 1864. Sent to Harpers Ferry, West Virginia. Confined at Point Lookout, Maryland, September 26, 1864. Paroled at Point Lookout on March 15, 1865. Received at Boulware's Wharf, James River, Virginia, March 18, 1865, for exchange. No further records. Survived the war.

NORTON, ELLIOTT TAYLOR, _____
North Carolina pension records indicate that he served in this company.

PARRIS, ALFRED J., Private
Previously served as Private in Company F of this regiment. Transferred to this company on September 1, 1862. Reported present through June 30, 1863, and in September, 1863-February, 1864. Name appears on a receipt roll for clothing dated June 17, 1864. No further records.

PARRIS, ANDREW J., Private
Previously served as Private in Company F of this regiment. Transferred to this company on September 1, 1862. Reported present through December 31, 1862. Reported absent without leave on January 25, 1863. Returned to duty on an unknown date. Deserted on April 24, 1863. Returned to duty on May 30, 1863. Reported absent without leave, "[s]upposed to have reported to Col. W. H. Thomas who was cut off with a portion of the command in the evacuation of E[ast] Tenn[essee]," September, 1863-February, 1864. No further records. Survived the war.

PARRIS, JAMES M., Private
Previously served as Private in Company F of this regiment. Transferred to this company on September 1, 1862. Reported present through October 31, 1862. Reported on extra duty at work on a military road in November-December, 1862. Rejoined the company prior to February 28, 1863. Reported present in March-June, 1863. Reported sick in hospital at Abingdon, Virginia, September, 1863-February 10, 1864. Returned to duty prior to February 29, 1864. Name appears on receipt rolls for clothing dated June 17, September 1, and September 27, 1864. No further records. Survived the war.

PARRIS, RUFUS M., Corporal
Previously served as Private in Company F of this regiment. Transferred to this company on September 1, 1862. Reported present through June 30, 1863. Promoted to Corporal on September 15, 1863. Reported present in September, 1863-February, 1864. Wounded in the right thigh and captured at Cedar Creek, Virginia, October 19, 1864. Hospitalized at Baltimore, Maryland. Confined at Fort McHenry, Maryland, December 9, 1864. Transferred to Point Lookout, Maryland, on or about January 1, 1865. Released at Point Lookout on June 16, 1865, after taking the Oath of Allegiance.

PARRIS, W. W., _____
North Carolina pension records appear to indicate that he served in this company. Survived the war.

QUEEN, WILLIAM HAYNES, _____
North Carolina pension records appear to indicate that he served in this company. Survived the war.

RIDLEY, JOHN WILLIAM, Private
Previously served as Private in Company F of this regiment. Transferred to this company on September 1, 1862. Reported on detached service in September-October, 1862. Reported on extra duty working on a military road in November-December, 1862. Rejoined the company prior to February 28, 1863. Reported present in March-June, 1863. Reported absent without leave in September-October, 1863. Returned to duty prior to December 31, 1863. Reported sick in hospital at Bristol, Tennessee, January 25, 1864. Name appears on a receipt roll for shoes issued October 24, 1864, as a member of "Company G, Thomas Legion;" however, from the context and time of the document it seems that he was at that time with Company G, Indian Battalion. It is not known when he transferred or enlisted in that unit. [See Tennessee pension application No. 3237.]

ROBERTS, JAMES, Private
Enlisted at Gatlinburg, Tennessee, February 22, 1863, for the war. Reported on detached service working on roads and stockading through June 30, 1863, and in September, 1863-February, 1864. Was working in the vicinity of Strawberry Plains, Tennessee, and in Sevier County, Tennessee, during most of that period. No further records.

SHAW, JASPER N., Corporal
Previously served as Private in Company F of this regiment. Promoted to Corporal and transferred to this company on September 1, 1862. Reported on detached service in September-October, 1862. Returned to duty prior to December 31, 1862. Reported present in January-June, 1863, and in September-December, 1863. Reported sick in hospital at Emory and Henry, Virginia, January 18-February 29, 1864. Hospitalized at Winchester, Virginia, August 1, 1864, with diarrhoea. Returned to duty prior to September 19, 1864, when he was wounded in the left leg and captured at Winchester. Hospitalized at Winchester. Transferred to hospital at Baltimore, Maryland, October 11, 1864. Transferred to Point Lookout, Maryland, where he arrived on October 18, 1864. Paroled at Point Lookout and transferred to Venus Point, Savannah River, Georgia, where he was received on November 15, 1864, for exchange. No further records. Survived the war.

SHERRILL, WILLIAM, _____
North Carolina pension records indicate that he served in this company. Survived the war.

SMITH, J. R., Private
Enlisted at Jonesborough, Tennessee, May 15, 1863, for the war. Reported absent without leave from May 27, 1863, through February 29, 1864. No further records.

SMITH, JOEL, Private
Enlisted at Gatlinburg, Tennessee, February 22, 1863, for the war. Reported on detached service repairing roads through June 30, 1863, and in September, 1863-February, 1864. Was probably working in the vicinity of Sevier County, Tennessee, during most of that period. No further records.

SMITH, WILLIS T., Private
Born in Sevier County, Tennessee, where he resided as a farmer prior to enlisting at Strawberry Plains, Tennessee, at age 24, October 8, 1862, for the war. Reported present through February 28, 1863. Reported "furloughed & not reported" in March-April, 1863. Returned to duty in May-June, 1863. Reported absent without leave, "supposed to have reported to Col. W. H. Thomas who was cut off with a portion of the command during the evacuation of E[ast] Tenn[essee]," September, 1863-February, 1864. No further records. [He may have briefly served in Company C of this regiment.]

STALCUP, THOMAS BELEW, Private
Previously served as Private in Company F of this regiment. Transferred to this company while on detached service on September 1, 1862. Reported on detached service through October 31, 1862.

Joined the company prior to December 31, 1862. Reported on detached service as a wagoner in January-June, 1863. Reported present in September, 1863-February, 1864. No further records. Survived the war.

STEPHENSON, WILLIAM H., Private

Previously served as Private in Company F of this regiment. Transferred to this company on September 1, 1862. Reported present through October 31, 1862. Reported absent without leave in November, 1862-February, 1863. Returned to duty prior to April 30, 1863. Deserted on May 19, 1863. Returned to duty on an unknown date. Reported absent without leave, "supposed to have reported to Col. W. H. Thomas who was cut off with a portion of the command in the evacuation of E[ast] Tenn[essee]," September, 1863-February, 1864. Died prior to November 29, 1864. Place, date, and cause of death not reported.

STILLWELL, J. S., _____

North Carolina pension records indicate that he served in this company. Survived the war.

SUTTON, HENRY, Private

Previously served as Private in Company F of this regiment. Transferred to this company while on detached service on September 1, 1862. Reported on detached service through October 31, 1862. Reported on sick furlough in November-December, 1862. Reported absent without leave in January-February, 1863. Reported for duty prior to April 30, 1863. Reported present in May-June, 1863. Reported absent without leave, "supposed to have reported to Col. W.H. Thomas who was cut off with a portion of the command in the evacuation of E[ast] Tenn[essee]," September, 1863-February, 1864. No further records.

SUTTON, JOHN, Private

Previously served as Private in Company F of this regiment. Transferred to this company on September 1, 1862. Reported present through February 28, 1863. Reported sick in hospital at Strawberry Plains, Tennessee, from April 9 until June 20, 1863, when he was captured there. Paroled the next day. Reported sick in hospital through February 29, 1864. No further records. Survived the war.

SUTTON, SOLOMON, Private

Previously served as Private in Company F of this regiment. Transferred to this company on September 1, 1862. Reported present through December 31, 1862. Reported on detached service with Capt. Daniel G. Fisher of this company in January-February, 1863. Rejoined the company prior to April 30, 1863. Reported present in May-June, 1863. Reported absent without leave, "supposed to have reported to Col. W. H. Thomas who was cut off with a portion of the Command in the evacuation of E[ast] Tenn[essee]," September, 1863-February, 1864. No further records. Survived the war.

SUTTON, WILLIAM M., Private

Previously served as Private in Company I of this regiment. Transferred to this company in March-April, 1863. Reported present through June 30, 1863. Reported absent without leave, "supposed to have reported to Col. W.H. Thomas who was cut off witha portion of the command in the evacuation of E[ast] Tenn[essee]," in September, 1863-February, 1864. No further records. Survived the war.

TAGUE, MOSES A., Private

Enlisted at Gatlinburg, Tennessee, February 22, 1863, for the war. Reported on detached service working on and repairing roads and stockading through June 30, 1863, and in September, 1863-February, 1864. Was working in the vicinity of Sevier County, Tennessee, during at least part of that period. No further records.

TAGUE, SMITH, Private

Enlisted at Gatlinburg, Tennessee, February 22, 1863, for the war. Reported on detached service working on and repairing roads and stockading through June 30, 1863, and in September, 1863-February, 1864. Was working in the vicinity of Sevier County, Tennessee, during at least part of that period. No further records.

THOMPSON, JOHN, Private

Enlisted in Jackson County on August 20, 1863, for the war. Reported present in November, 1863-February, 1864. Name appears on receipt rolls for clothing dated June 17 and September 1, 1864. No further records. Survived the war.

TURNER, WILLIAM P., Private

Enlisted at Gatlinburg, Tennessee, February 22, 1863, for the war. Reported on detached service repairing and working on a military road, and stockading through June 30, 1863, and in September, 1863-February, 1864. Was working in the vicinity of Sevier County, Tennessee, during much of that period. No further records.

WARD, A. H., _____

North Carolina pension records indicate that he served in this company. Survived the war.

WARD, HENDERSON, _____

North Carolina pension records appear to indicate that he served in this company.

WEBSTER, JOHN H., _____

North Carolina pension records appear to indicate that he served in this company. Survived the war.

WEST, DAVID, Private

Previously served as Private in Company F of this regiment. Transferred to this company on September 1, 1862. Reported present through June 30, 1863, and in September, 1863-February, 1864. Captured at Winchester, Virginia, September 19, 1864. Sent to Harpers Ferry, West Virginia. Confined at Point Lookout, Maryland, September 26, 1864. Paroled at Point Lookout on March 15, 1865. Received at Boulware's Wharf, James River, Virginia, March 18, 1865, for exchange. Hospitalized at Richmond, Virginia, the same date. No further records. Survived the war. [He may have been the same man as Pvt. David M. West of Company D, 62nd Regiment N.C. Troops.]

WEST, ELISHA, Private

Previously served as Private in Company F of this regiment. Transferred to this company on September 1, 1862. Reported present through October 31, 1862. Reported on sick furlough, November-December, 1862. Returned to duty prior to February 28, 1863. Reported present in March-April, 1863. Reported sick in hospital at Strawberry Plains, Tennessee, in May-June, 1863. Hospitalized at

Greeneville, Tennessee, on an unspecified date. Furloughed home prior to October 31, 1863. No further records.

WEST, ISAAC, Private

Enlisted at Strawberry Plains, Tennessee, April 15, 1863, for the war. Reported present through June 30, 1863. Reported absent without leave, "supposed to have reported to Col. W.H. Thomas who was cut off with a portion of the command in the evacuation of E[ast] Tenn[essee]," September, 1863-February, 1864. Name appears on receipt rolls for clothing dated June 17 and September 1, 1864. No further records.

WHITESIDE, DAVIS, Private

Previously served as Private in Company F of this regiment. Transferred to this company on September 1, 1862. Reported present through June 30, 1863. Reported absent without leave, "supposed to have reported to Col. W. H. Thomas who was cut off with a portion of the command in the evacuation of E[ast] Tenn[essee]," September, 1863-February, 1864. No further records. Survived the war.

WILSON, NOAH B., Private

Previously served as Private in Company F of this regiment. Transferred to this company on September 1, 1862. Reported present through June 30, 1863, and in September, 1863-February, 1864. Hospitalized at Winchester, Virginia, August 1, 1864, with diarrhoea and debilitas. Transferred to other hospitals on August 4 and August 8, 1864. Name appears on a receipt roll for clothing dated September 27, 1864. No further records. Survived the war.

WOOD, STRINGFIELD, _____

North Carolina pension records appear to indicate that he served in this company.

COMPANY H

This company was raised in Cherokee County. It was organized on July 23, 1862, at Fort Montgomery (present-day Robbinsville), which was in Cherokee County at the time, "for the local defense of the Carolinas, East Tennessee, South Western Virginia and the Cumberland Mountains." It was known as Company F as of August, 1862. On or about October 5, 1862, it was designated Company H, Infantry Regiment, Thomas's Legion.

The following roster was compiled in large part from a company muster and descriptive roll dated July 23, 1862, and from company muster rolls dated July 23, 1862-June, 1863, and September, 1863-February, 1864. These are abstracted in the microfilm edition of the Compiled Service Records of Confederate Soldiers Who Served in Organizations from the State of North Carolina (Record Group 109, M270), National Archives, Washington, D.C. Other valuable information in the Compiled Service Records includes enlistment papers, pay vouchers, requisitions, letters of resignation, discharge certificates, and abstracts of medical and prisoner of war records.

Also utilized in this roster were *The War of the Rebellion: A Compilation of the Official Records of the Union and Confederate Armies*, the North Carolina Adjutant General's papers, state militia records, newspaper casualty lists and obituaries, wartime claims for bounty pay and allowances, postwar registers of claims for artificial limbs, Confederate pension applications filed with the states of North Carolina, Tennessee, and Florida, records of the North Carolina Confederate Soldiers' Home, and the 1860 and 1870 federal censuses of North Carolina. A search was made also for relevant letters, diaries, reminiscences, and other manuscripts in the Southern Historical Collection (University of North Carolina-Chapel Hill) and the Duke University Library Special Collections Department.

Among the secondary sources consulted were records of the North Carolina division of the United Daughters of the Confederacy, postwar rosters, regimental and county histories, marriage bond, will, and cemetery indexes, published and unpublished genealogies, biographical dictionaries, the North Carolina *County Heritage Book* series, the *Confederate Veteran*, Walter Clark's *Histories of the Several Regiments and Battalions from North Carolina in the Great War, 1861-'65*, and the North Carolina volume of the extended edition of *Confederate Military History*.

OFFICERS

CAPTAINS

COOPER, THOMAS JEFFERSON

Born in Orangeburg District, South Carolina, on October 14, 1804. Resided in Cherokee County, North Carolina, where he was by occupation a farmer prior to enlisting at Fort Montgomery (present-day Robbinsville) at age 57, July 4, 1862, for the war. Elected Captain on July 23, 1862. Reported present through February 28, 1863. Resigned on March 14, 1863, because of "a fall from the second story of a house which renders me unfit for military duty." Resignation accepted on or about March 24, 1863.

COOPER, JAMES WARNER

Born in Haywood County on December 28, 1832, and resided in Cherokee County where he was by occupation a clerk prior to enlisting in Cherokee County at age 29. Elected 1st Lieutenant on July 23, 1862. Reported present through December 31, 1862. Detached to North Carolina to catch deserters for seven days beginning, February 6, 1863. Reported as detached in charge of prisoners to Knoxville, Tenesee, February 14-18, 1863. Rejoined the company prior to February 28, 1863. Reported present in March-June, 1863. Promoted to Captain on or before May 14, 1863, to rank from March 24, 1863. Furloughed for fifteen days on August 5, 1863. Failed to return from furlough and was reported absent without leave in November-December, 1863. Evidently arrested on February 23, 1864, "charged with disloyalty and also being absent without leave." Name appears as a signature on a petition dated February 25, 1864, of officers from Thomas's Legion asking for the reunification of the Legion and its removal from the command of Brig. Gen. Alfred E. Jackson. Court martialed at Greeneville, Tennessee, on March 15, 1864. Probably returned to duty prior to June 17, 1864. Reported in hospital on August 1, 1864. Hospitalized at Danville, Virginia, October 19, 1864, with chronic diarrhoea. Furloughed for fifteen days on October 20, 1864. No further records. Survived the war.

LIEUTENANTS

CARVER, _____, Lieutenant

Reported in a letter from Maj. W.W. Stringfield of this regiment as having recently been elected Lieutenant of this company in February, 1865, even though Stringfield described him as "a cowardly deserter." Stringfield asked Col. William Holland Thomas to disallow the rank and hold a new election. He may have been either Pvt. Azor Carver or Pvt. Lawson Carver of this company, both of whom deserted in September, 1863. Or he may have been either Pvt. Ake Carver or Pvt. William M. Carver of this company.

GEORGE, LAFAYETTE, 1st Lieutenant
Born in Blount County, Tennessee, and resided in Cherokee County where he was by occupation a farmer prior to enlisting at Fort Montgomery (present-day Robbinsville) at age 32. Elected 2nd Lieutenant on July 23, 1862. Reported present or accounted for through February 28, 1863, and in May-June, 1863. Promoted to 1st Lieutenant on May 14, 1863. Reported present in September, 1863-February, 1864. Wounded in the leg at Winchester, Virginia, September 19, 1864. Died on or about September 21, 1864, of wounds. Place of death not reported.

HYDE, JASON S., 3rd Lieutenant
Born in what later became Jackson County. Resided in Cherokee County where he was by occupation a farmer prior to enlisting at Fort Montgomery (present-day Robbinsville) at age 33, July 23, 1862, for the war. Mustered in as 1st Sergeant. Reported present through December 31, 1862. Detailed four days to escort prisoners to Knoxville, Tennessee, beginning "about the 5 February." Rejoined the company on or about February 9, 1863. Reported present on February 28, 1863, and in March-April, 1863. Elected 3rd Lieutenant on or about May 9, 1863. Reported present in May-June and September-October, 1863. Reported present in November-December, 1863. Reported on leave from February 6 through 29, 1864. Elected 1st Lieutenant of Welch's Company, Indian Battalion, prior to April 16, 1864.

INGRAM, ELI G., 2nd Lieutenant
Previously served as Private in Company A, 19th Regiment N.C. Troops (2nd Regiment N.C. Cavalry). Elected 3rd (Junior 2nd) Lieutenant of this company on July 23, 1862. Reported present through December 31, 1862. Detailed with eleven men to Cades Cove, Tennessee, to scout for four days beginning on February 1, 1863. Rejoined the company before February 28, 1863. Reported present in May-June, 1863. Probably promoted to 2nd Lieutenant on or about May 14, 1863. Reported in hospital in September-October, 1863. Returned to duty on or prior to December 31, 1863. Reported present through February 29, 1864. Reported in hospital on August 15, 1864. Reported in hospital at Staunton, Virginia, August 15, 1864. Wounded on or prior to August 25, 1864. Place of wound not reported. Reported absent wounded on October 23, 1864. No further records. Survived the war.

NONCOMMISSIONED OFFICERS AND PRIVATES

ADAMS, JOHNSON K., Corporal
Born in Sevier County, Tennessee, and resided in Macon County, North Carolina, where he was by occupation a farmer prior to enlisting in Cherokee County, North Carolina, at age 18, July 23, 1862, for the war. Mustered in as Private. Reported present through June 30, 1863. Promoted to Corporal in May-June, 1863. Reported present in September, 1863-February, 1864. Name appears on receipt rolls for clothing dated June 4 and September 17, 1864. No further records. Survived the war. [His middle initial may have been R.]

AMMONS, DAVID C., Private
Born in the part of Haywood County that later became Macon County. Resided in Cherokee County where he was by occupation a farmer prior to enlisting in Cherokee County at age 37, September 27, 1862, for the war. Reported present through December 31, 1863. Reported on detached duty arresting deserters in North Carolina in February 6-12, 1863. Rejoined the company prior to February 28, 1863. Reported on detached duty arresting deserters in Cherokee County from April 27 through 30, 1863. Rejoined the company prior to June 30, 1863. Deserted at Jonesborough, Tennessee, September 12, 1863. Went over to the enemy on an unspecified date. Released on February 13, 1864, after taking the Oath of Allegiance.

AMMONS, JOHN P., Private
Born in the part of Haywood County that later became Macon County. Resided in Cherokee County where he was by occupation a farmer prior to enlisting in Cherokee County at age 39, September 27, 1862, for the war. Reported present through December 31, 1863. Reported on detached duty arresting deserters in North Carolina, February 6-12, 1863. Reported present on February 28, 1863, in March-June, 1863, and in September, 1863-February, 1864. Captured at Winchester, Virginia, September 19, 1864. Sent to Harpers Ferry, West Virginia. Confined at Point Lookout, Maryland, September 26, 1864. Paroled at Point Lookout on or about March 15, 1865. Received at Boulware's Wharf, James River, Virginia, March 18, 1865, for exchange. Survived the war.

BARKER, HENRY W., Private
Born in Blount County, Tennessee, May 3, 1840. Resided in Cherokee County where he was by occupation a farmer prior to enlisting at Fort Montgomery (present-day Robbinsville) at age 22, July 23, 1862, for the war. Reported present through June 30, 1863, and in September, 1863-February, 1864. Hospitalized at Winchester, Virginia, August 1, 1864, with diarrhoea. Returned to duty on August 8, 1864. Captured at Winchester on August 11 or August 17, 1864. Sent to Old Capitol Prison, Washington, D.C. Transferred to Elmira, New York, where he arrived on August 29, 1864. Paroled at Elmira and transferred to the James River, Virginia, February 20, 1865, for exchange. Hospitalized at Richmond, Virginia, February 28, 1865, with an unspecified complaint. Transferred to Camp Lee, Richmond, March 1, 1865. No further records. Survived the war. [His Tennessee pension application No. 13041 indicates that he was injured at Piedmont, Virginia, probably on June 5, 1864, by a falling tree limb detached by a cannon ball.]

BARNES, JASPER, _____
Enlisted on August 19, 1863, for the war. Place of enlistment and rank not reported. Reported as transferred to Company K, 5th Regiment Tennessee Cavalry (McKenzie's), prior to February 29, 1864, "in exchange for another man;" however, there is no other evidence that he served in that unit.

BARNES, JOSEPH, _____
Enlisted on October 31, 1863, for the war. Place of enlistment and rank not reported. Reported as transferred to Company K, 5th Regiment Tennessee Cavalry (McKenzie's), prior to February 29, 1864, "in exchange for another man.;" however, there is no other evidence that he actually served with that unit.

BIRCHFIELD, NATHAN, Private
Enlisted in Blount County, Tennessee, February 19, 1863. Reported present through June 30, 1863. Deserted at Jonesborough, Tennessee, September 12, 1863.

BIRCHFIELD, WILLIAM A., Musician

Born in what later became Yancey County. Resided in Cherokee County where he was by occupation a farmer prior to enlisting in Cherokee County at age 33, July 23, 1862. Mustered in as Musician (Drummer). Reported present through June 30, 1863, and in September, 1863-February, 1864. No further records.

BRADSHAW, JAMES V., Private

Born in what later became Jackson County. Resided in Cherokee County where he was by occupation a farmer prior to enlisting in Cherokee County at age 27, July 23, 1862, for the war. Reported on sick leave through June 30, 1863, and in September, 1863-February, 1864. No further records.

BRADSHAW, JOHN T., Private

Born in what later became Jackson County. Resided in Cherokee County where he was by occupation a farmer prior to enlisting in Cherokee County at age 25, July 23, 1862, for the war. Reported present through April 30, 1863. Died in hospital at Carter's Depot, Tennessee, June 9, 1863. Cause of death not reported.

BREEDLOVE, JOHN WATKINS, Private

Previously served as Private in Company A, 7th Battalion N.C. Cavalry. Transferred to this company on September 27, 1862. Reported present through December 31, 1862. Reported absent without leave on February 28, 1863. Listed as a deserter on April 6, 1863; he deserted in Sevier County, Tennessee. Returned to duty prior to June 30, 1863. Deserted at Zollicoffer, Tennessee, August 31, 1863.

BURNET, JAMES H., Private

Transferred to this company from an unknown unit on November 8, 1863. Reported absent without leave on November 25, 1863. No further records.

CABLE, THOMAS, Private

Born in Blount County, Tennessee, and resided in Cherokee County where he was by occupation a farmer prior to enlisting in Cherokee County at age 34, July 23, 1862, for the war. Reported present through February 28, 1863. Reported on detail to "keep ferry" at Rocky Point, in Macon County, from March 3, 1863, through June 30, 1863, and in September -December, 1863. Reported absent without leave in January, 1864. Captured by Federal forces on May 2, 1864. Sent to Knoxville, Tennessee. Took the Oath of Allegiance at Knoxville on May 12, 1864.

CARPENTER, WILLIAM, Corporal

Born in what later became Watauga County. Resided in Cherokee County where he was by occupation a farmer prior to enlisting at Fort Montgomery (present-day Robbinsville) at age 31, July 23, 1862, for the war. Mustered in as Corporal. Reported present through December 31, 1862. Reported on sick leave in January-February, 1863. Returned to duty on March 2, 1863. Reported present through June 30, 1863, and in September, 1863-February, 1864. Name appears on a receipt roll for clothing dated June 4, 1864. No further records. Survived the war.

CARPENTER, WILSON, Musician

Born in Ashe County and resided in Cherokee County where he was by occupation a farmer prior to enlisting at Fort Montgomery (present-day Robbinsville) at age 27, July 23, 1862, for the war. Mustered in as Private. Reported present through June 30, 1863. Promoted to Musician (Fifer) in July-October, 1863. Reported sick in hospital in September-October, 1863. Returned to duty in November-December, 1863. Reported absent with leave from February 20 through 29, 1864. No further records. Survived the war.

CARRIER, CALVIN C., Private

Previously served as 2nd Lieutenant of Company F, 22nd Regiment N.C. Troops (12th Regiment N.C. Volunteers). Enlisted in this company at Zollicoffer, Tennessee, August 17, 1863, for the war. Deserted at Abingdon, Virginia, October 26, 1863. Returned to duty on an unspecified date, probably subsequent to February 29, 1864. Captured at Piedmont, Virginia, June 5, 1864. Reported under guard at Staunton, Virginia, June 8, 1864. Confined at Camp Morton, Indianapolis, Indiana, June 21, 1864. Took the Oath of Allegiance at Camp Morton on March 22, 1865.

CARVER, AKE, Private

Born in Blount County, Tennessee, and resided in Cherokee County, North Carolina, where he was by occupation a farmer prior to enlisting at Fort Montgomery (present-day Robbinsville) at age 22, July 23, 1862, for the war. Reported on sick leave through June 30, 1863, and in September, 1863-February, 1864. No further records. Survived the war.

CARVER, AZOR, Private

Born in Tennessee, or in what later became Yancey County, North Carolina. Resided in Cherokee County where he was by occupation a farmer prior to enlisting at Fort Montgomery (present-day Robbinsville) at age 33, July 23, 1862, for the war. Reported absent without leave until November 1, 1862, when he reported for duty. Reported present through June 30, 1863. Deserted at Greeneville, Tennessee, October 10, 1863. [May have been elected to the rank of Lieutenant in February, 1865.]

CARVER, LAWSON, Private

Born in Yancey County and resided in Cherokee County where he was by occupation a farmer prior to enlisting at Fort Montgomery (present-day Robbinsville) at age 25, July 23, 1862, for the war. Reported sick at home on October 31, 1862. Returned to duty in November-December, 1862. Reported present through June 30, 1863. Deserted at Jonesborough, Tennessee, September 12, 1863. [May have been elected to the rank of Lieutenant in February, 1865.]

CARVER, WILLIAM M., _____

Previously served as Private in Company F, Walker's Battalion. Transferred to this company on January 1, 1864, probably from Company K, 5th Regiment Tennessee Cavalry, (McKenzie's). Reported present through February 29, 1864. Name appears on receipt rolls for clothing dated June 4, September 1, and September 17, 1864. No further records.

CODY, HAMILTON, 1st Sergeant

Born in what later became Madison County. Resided in Cherokee County where he was by occupation a farmer prior to enlisting at Fort Montgomery (present-day Robbinsville) at age 25, July 23, 1862, for the war. Mustered in as Private. Reported present through June 30, 1863. Promoted to Sergeant in May-June, 1863. Promoted to 1st Sergeant on December 31, 1863. Reported present in September, 1863-February, 1864. No further records.

CODY, MILES W., Private

Enlisted in Blount County, Tennessee, March 3, 1863, for the war. Deserted at Carter's Depot, Tennessee, April 27, 1863. [May have enlisted previously in Company A, 19th Regiment N.C. Troops (2nd Regiment N.C. Cavalry) and/or Company D, 25th Regiment N.C. Troops.]

CODY, TILLMAN H., Private

Previously enlisted as Private in Company F, 39th Regiment N.C. Troops. Enlisted illegally in this company in Cherokee County at age 24, July 23, 1862, for the war, while absent without leave from the 39th Regiment. Reported present through February 28, 1863. Deserted at Carter's Depot, Tennessee, April 27, 1863. Returned to duty prior to June 30, 1863. Deserted at Zollicoffer, Tennessee, August 31, 1863. Court-martialed on or about May 24, 1864. Found guilty of absence without leave and sentenced to confinement for two months with a "6 pound ball to left leg by chain" and to be fed on "bread and water alone." [Letters Sent, Orders and Circulars, Dept. of E. Tenn. and Dept. of W. Va. and E. Tenn., April 1863-October, 1864, Record Group 109, Chapter II, Vol. 234, National Archives.] Name appears on receipt rolls for clothing dated June 4, September 1, and September 17, 1864. No further records.

COLVARD, JOHN M., Private

Born in Cherokee County where he resided as a farmer prior to enlisting Fort Montgomery (present-day Robbinsville) at age 22, July 23, 1862, for the war. Mustered in as Sergeant. Reported present through December 31, 1862. Detached for seven days to North Carolina on February 6, 1863, to catch deserters. Rejoined company prior to February 28, 1863. Reported absent sick in March-April, 1863. Reported present in May-June, 1863. Deserted at Greeneville, Tennessee, October 10, 1863. Reduced to ranks prior to October 31, 1863. [His surname may have been Calvert. He may have been the same man as Pvt. John D. Calvert of Company C, Indian Battalion.]

COLVARD, JOHN P., Private

Born in Macon County and resided in Cherokee County where he was by occupation a farmer prior to enlisting Fort Montgomery (present-day Robbinsville) at age 23, July 23, 1862, for the war. Reported present through December 31, 1862. Detached for seven days to North Carolina on February 6, 1863, to catch deserters. Rejoined the company prior to February 28, 1863. Reported present in March-June, 1863. Deserted at Jonesborough, Tennessee, September 12, 1863. [His surname may have been Calvert. He may have been the same man as Pvt. John D. Calvert of Company C, Indian Battalion.]

COOPER, GEORGE MERIDY, Private

Born in Haywood County. Resided in Cherokee County where he was by occupation a farmer prior to enlisting at Fort Montgomery (present-day Robbinsville) at age 18, July 23, 1862, for the war. Reported present through June 30, 1863. Deserted on October 10, 1863, at Greeneville, Tennessee. Returned to duty on February 22, 1864. Name appears on receipt rolls for clothing dated June 4 and September 18, 1864. No further records. Survived the war. [See Tennessee pension application No. 11834.]

COOPER, J. A., _____

North Carolina pension records appear to indicate that he served in this company. Survived the war.

COOPER, McANALLY, Private

Previously served as Musician (Bugler) in Company A, 19th Regiment N.C. Troops (2nd Regiment N.C. Cavalry). Enlisted in this company in Blount County, Tennessee, September 27, 1862, for the war. Reported present through June 30, 1863. Killed at Limestone Bridge, Tennessee, September 8, 1863.

COOPER, NATHAN F., Private

Resided in Cherokee County where he was by occupation a farmer prior to enlisting in Cherokee County at age 33, December 19, 1862, for the war. Mustered in as Private. Reported present through December, 1862. Reported as "detached after beef and water bound" in January-February, 1863. Rejoined the company on March 2, 1863. Reported present through June 30, 1863. Promoted to 1st Sergeant in May-June, 1863. Reported detailed to Cherokee County for twenty days beginning August 14, 1863, but had not rejoined the company as of October 31, 1863. Later reported absent without leave to date from September 4, 1863. Reduced to ranks in November-December, 1863. Reported absent without leave through February 29, 1864. No further records.

COOPER, W. F., _____

North Carolina pension records appear to indicate that he served in this company, and that he later served in Welch's Company, Indian Battalion. [He may also have served in Company B, Infantry Regiment and Company B, Indian Battalion.]

COOPER, WILLIAM W., Private

Born in Haywood County and resided in Cherokee County where he was by occupation a farmer prior to enlisting at Fort Montgomery (present-day Robbinsville) at age 31, July 23, 1862, for the war. Reported at home sick on October 31, 1862. Reported present, November, 1862-June, 1863. Furloughed on July 1, 1863, but reported as not having returned to duty on October 31, 1863. Reported absent without leave through February 29, 1864. No further records. Survived the war.

CRAIG, WILLIAM C., Private

Enlisted in Cherokee County on October 1, 1863, for the war. Reported present in January-February, 1864. Name appears on receipt rolls for clothing dated June 4 and September 1, 1864. No further records.

CRISP, ALEX MILLER, Private

Born in what later became Jackson County. Resided in Cherokee County where he was by occupation a farmer prior to enlisting at Fort Montgomery (present-day Robbinsville) at age 32, July 23, 1862, for the war. Mustered in as Sergeant. Reported present through June 30, 1863. Reduced to ranks in May-June, 1863. Deserted on August 31, 1863, at Zollicoffer, Tennessee. Court-martialed on or about May 24, 1864. Found guilty of absence without leave and sentenced to confinement for two months with a "6 pound ball with chain" on the left leg, and to be "fed on bread and water." [Letters Sent, Orders and Circulars, Dept. of E. Tenn. and Dept. of W. Va. and E. Tenn., April 1863-October, 1864, Record Group 109, Chapter II, Vol. 234, National Archives.] Name appears on receipt rolls for clothing dated June 4 and September 1, 1864. No further records. Survived the war.

CRISP, EZEKIEL BOWERS, Private

Born on April 8, 1832, in what later became Jackson County. Resided in Cherokee County where he was by occupation a farmer prior to enlisting at Fort Montgomery (present-day Robbinsville) at age 30, July 23, 1862, for the war. Reported present through December 31, 1862. Deserted in Sevier County, Tennessee, April 6, 1863. Court-martialed on or about May 24, 1864, for desertion. Found guilty and sentenced to be "shot to death by musketry." [Letters Sent, Orders and Circulars, Dept. of E. Tenn. and Dept. of W. Va. and E. Tenn., April 1863-October, 1864, Record Group 109, Chapter II, Vol. 234, National Archives]. However, this sentence was not carried out and he returned to duty prior to June 8, 1864. Deserted that day at Salem, Virginia. Went over to the enemy on an unspecified date. Sent to Knoxville, Tennessee, and confined there on March 6, 1865. Took the Oath of Allegiance at Knoxville on or about March 6, 1865. Transferred to Chattanooga, Tennessee, March 8, 1865. Transferred to Lousville, Kentucky, and arrived there on March 18, 1865. Released at Louisville on March 21, 1865, with instructions to remain north of the Ohio River until the end of the war.

CRISP, JAMES MANUEL, Private

Born on December 1, 1836, in what later became Jackson County. Resided in Cherokee County and was by occupation a farmer prior to enlisting at Fort Montgomery (present-day Robbinsville) at age 25, July 23, 1862, for the war. Reported at home sick on October 31, 1862. Reported present in November, 1862-February, 1863. Deserted at Carter's Depot, Tennessee, April 21, 1863.

CRISP, JOHN, Private

Born in Burke County and resided in Cherokee County where he was by occupation a farmer prior to enlisting at Fort Montgomery (present-day Robbinsville) at age 30, July 23, 1862, for the war. Reported "at home ruptured" on October 31, 1862. Reported present, November, 1862-February, 1863. Reported sick in hospital in March-April, 1863. Deserted at Mossy Creek, Tennessee, May 23, 1863.

CRISP, JOHN ALFORD, Private

Born on May 9, 1827, in what later became Jackson County. Resided in Cherokee County where he was by occupation a farmer prior to enlisting at Fort Montgomery (present-day Robbinsville) at age 35, July 23, 1862, for the war. Reported present through December 31, 1862. Reported on detached service in North Carolina for seven days beginning February 6, 1863, to catch deserters. Returned to duty prior to February 28, 1863. Reported present in March-June, 1863. Deserted at Zollicoffer, Tennessee, August 31, 1863.

CRISP, MANSEL F., Private

Born in what later became Jackson County. Resided in Cherokee County where he was by occupation a farmer prior to enlisting at Fort Montgomery (present-day Robbinsville) at age 31, July 23, 1862, for the war. Reported present through December 31, 1862. Reported absent without leave in January-February, 1863. Returned to duty on March 2, 1863. Deserted in Sevier County, Tennessee, April 6, 1863. Court-martialed on or about May 24, 1864, for desertion. Found guilty and sentenced to be "shot to death by musketry." [Letters Sent, Orders and Circulars, Dept. of E. Tenn. and Dept. of W. Va. and E. Tenn., April 1863-October, 1864, Record Group 109, Chapter II, Vol. 234, National Archives.] However, the sentence was not carried out and he returned to duty on an unspecified date. Name appears on receipt rolls for clothing dated June 4, September 1, and September 18, 1864. Captured at Winchester, Virginia, September 19, 1864. Sent to Harpers Ferry, West Virginia, on September 23, 1864. Confined at Point Lookout, Maryland, September 26, 1864. Paroled at Point Lookout on October 30, 1864. Received at Venus Point, Savannah River, Georgia, November 15, 1864, for exchange. Returned to duty, then deserted to the enemy in Cherokee County on December 15, 1864. Confined at Knoxville, Tennessee, March 6, 1865. Took the Oath of Allegiance at Knoxville, Tennessee, on or about March 6, 1865. Transferred to Chattanooga, Tennessee, March 8, 1865. Transferred to Louisville, Kentucky, and arrived there on March 18, 1865. Released at Louisville on March 21, 1865, with instructions to remain north of the Ohio River until the end of the war.

CRISP, WILLIAM, Private

Born in what later became Caldwell County. Resided in Cherokee County where he was by occupation a farmer prior to enlisting at Fort Montgomery (present-day Robbinsville) at age 29, July 23, 1862, for the war. Reported present through October 31, 1862. Reported at home sick in November-December 1862, but returned to duty prior to December 31, 1862. Deserted in January-February, 1863. Returned to duty prior to April 6, 1863, when he deserted in Sevier County, Tennessee.

CRISP, WILLIAM P., Private

Born in Macon County and resided in Cherokee County where he was by occupation a farmer prior to enlisting at Fort Montgomery (present-day Robbinsville) at age 17, July 23, 1862, for the war. Reported "at home with his foot cut" on October 31, 1862. Returned to duty prior to December 31, 1862. Deserted in January-February, 1863. Returned to duty prior to March 12, 1863, when he deserted in Sevier County, Tennessee.

DEAVER, THOMAS S., Private

Born in Blount County, Tennessee, and resided in Cherokee County where he was by occupation a farmer prior to enlisting at Fort Montgomery (present-day Robbinsville) at age 25, July 23, 1862, for the war. Reported present through December 31, 1862. Deserted in January-February, 1863. Returned to duty prior to April 6, 1863, when he deserted in Sevier County, Tennessee. Returned to duty in May-June, 1863. Reported sick in hospital in September-October, 1863. Returned to duty in November-December, 1863. Reported present in January-February, 1864. Name appears on a receipt roll for clothing dated June 4, 1864. No further records.

EDWARDS, JAMES M., Private

Born in Macon County where he resided as a farmer prior to enlisting in Blount County, Tennessee, September 1, 1862, for the war. Reported present through December 31, 1862. Reported absent sick in January-February, 1863. Deserted in Sevier County, Tennessee, April 6, 1863. Returned to duty prior to June 30, 1863. Deserted at Zollicoffer, Tennessee, August 31, 1863.

EDWARDS, JOHN R., Private

Born in Macon County where he resided as a farmer prior to enlisting in Blount County, Tennessee, at age 31, September 1, 1862, for the war. Reported present through December 31, 1862. Reported absent sick in January-February, 1863. Deserted in Sevier County, Tennessee, April 6, 1863. Returned to duty prior to June 30, 1863. Deserted at Zollicoffer, Tennessee, August 31, 1863.

ELLIS, THOMAS N., Private

Born in Iredell County and resided in Cherokee County where he was by occupation a farmer prior to enlisting at Fort Montgomery (present-day Robbinsville) at age 32, July 23, 1862, for the war. Reported at home sick on October 31, 1862. Returned to duty prior to December 31, 1862. Reported "at home crippled; a discharge necessary" in January-February, 1863. Reported absent sick in March-June, 1863, and September-December, 1863. Deserted to the enemy on an unspecified date. Sent to Knoxville, Tennessee. Released at Knoxville on February 6, 1864, after taking the Oath of Allegiance.

GEORGE, G. WASHINGTON, Sergeant
Born in Carter County, Tennessee, and resided in Cherokee County where he was by occupation a farmer prior to enlisting in Cherokee County at age 34, July 23, 1862, for the war. Mustered in as Sergeant. Reported present through December 31, 1862. Reported sick at home with measles in January-February, 1863. Reported present in March-June, 1863, and September, 1863-February, 1864. Captured at Winchester, Virginia, September 19, 1864. Sent to Harpers Ferry, West Virginia. Confined at Point Lookout, Maryland, September 26, 1864. Exchanged on October 30, 1864. No further records.

GHARLY, WILL, _____
Previously served in an unspecified unit. Transferred to this company on November 22, 1863. Reported absent without leave on January 1, 1864. No further records. [May have served previously in Company F, Walker's Battalion, and Company K, 5th Regiment Tennessee Cavalry (McKenzie's) under the name William Gorley. He may have been the same man as William G. Ghormley of Company H, 3rd Tennessee Mounted Infantry (Lillard's), or William H. Gormley of Company B, 4th Battalion Tennessee Cavalry (Branner's) and Company G, 2nd Regiment Tennesseee Cavalry (Ashby's).

GOLDEN, LOGAN R., Private
Born in Surry County and resided in Macon County where he was by occupation a farmer prior to enlisting at Fort Montgomery (present-day Robbinsville) at age 23, July 23, 1862, for the war. Reported present through June 30, 1863. Deserted at Carter's Depot, Tennessee, September 18, 1863.

GOLDEN, WILLIAM T., Private
Born in Surry County and resided in Macon County where he was by occupation a farmer prior to enlisting at Fort Montgomery (present-day Robbinsville) at age 18, July 23, 1862, for the war. Mustered in as Private. Reported present through April 30, 1863. Promoted to Corporal on April 15, 1863. Reported present in May-June, 1863. Deserted at Carter's Depot, Tennessee, September 18, 1863, and subsequently was reduced to ranks.

GOLEY, JOHN, Private
Born in Carter County, Tennessee, and resided in Cherokee County where he was by occupation a farmer prior to enlisting Fort Montgomery (present-day Robbinsville) at age 32, July 23, 1862, for the war. Reported present through October 31, 1862. Reported at home sick with fever in November-December, 1863. Returned to duty prior to December 31, 1863. Reported present in January-June, 1863. Deserted at Carter's Depot, Tennessee, September 18, 1863.

HARWOOD, PHIDELLA P., Private
Born in Buncombe County and resided in Cherokee County where he was by occupation a farmer prior to enlisting at Fort Montgomery (present-day Robbinsville) at age 28, July 23, 1862, for the war. Reported present through June 30, 1863. Deserted at Abingdon, Virginia, October 29, 1863.

HENESA, JOHN H., Private
Born in Burke County and resided in Cherokee County where he was by occupation a farmer prior to enlisting at Fort Montgomery (present-day Robbinsville) at age 33, July 23, 1862, for the war. Mustered in as Sergeant. Reported present through October 31, 1862. Detailed to Cherokee County "on business for the company" in November-December, 1862. Rejoined the company prior to December 31, 1862. Reported present in January-February, 1863. Reported on detail in Cherokee County on April 4, 1863, to arrest deserters. Rejoined the company prior to June 30, 1863. Detailed "as a guide for troops" to Cherokee County on August 15, 1863. Failed to return and reported absent without leave as of October 1, 1863. Reduced to ranks in November-December, 1863. Returned to duty on February 23, 1864. No further records. [His surname may have been Hennessee. He may have enlisted previously as Private in Company C, 39th Regiment N.C. Troops, and have enlisted illegally in this company while a deserter from that unit.]

HOGUE, JAMES L., Private
Born in what later became Caldwell County. Resided in Cherokee County where he was by occupation a farmer prior to enlisting at Fort Montgomery (present-day Robbinsville) at age 25, July 23, 1862, for the war. Reported present through December 31, 1862. Reported absent without leave in January-February, 1863. Returned to duty on March 21, 1863. Deserted in Sevier County, Tennessee, March 26, 1863.

HOOPER, ENOS M., Private
Enlisted in Blount County, Tennessee, March 3, 1863, for the war. Reported present through June 30, 1863. Deserted at Carter's Depot, Tennessee, September 18, 1863.

HOOPER, RILEY S., Private
Born in Monroe County, Tennessee, and resided in Cherokee County where he was by occupation a farmer prior to enlisting at Fort Montgomery (present-day Robbinsville) at age 34, July 23, 1862, for the war. Reported present through June 30, 1863. Sent home on detail for twenty days beginning August 10, 1863. Failed to rejoin the company and was reported absent without leave from September 1, 1863, through February 29, 1864. No further records. Survived the war.

HOOPER, THOMAS J., Private
Born in Monroe County, Tennessee, and resided in Cherokee County where he was by occupation a farmer prior to at Fort Montgomery (present-day Robbinsville) at age 32, July 23, 1862, for the war. Detailed home through October 31, 1862, "to bring a horse to act as courier." Reported sick at home in November-December, 1862. Returned to duty on or prior to December 31, 1862. Reported present through June 30, 1863, and in September, 1863-February, 1864. Hospitalized at Charlottesville, Virginia, July 25, 1864, with a gunshot wound of the right thigh. Place and date wounded not reported; but probably on July 24, 1864, at Kernstown, Virginia. Transferred to hospital at Lynchburg, Virginia, July 26, 1864. No further records.

INGRAM, ISAAC L., Private
Resided in Cherokee County. Enlisted in Blount County, Tennessee, at age 28, January 16, 1863, for the war. Reported present

through June 30, 1863. Served as a mechanic at Strawberry Plains, Tennessee, from August 1 through 31, 1863. Reported on detail as a teamster in the quartermaster's department in September-December, 1863, and from January 1 through May 20, 1864. Transferred to Company E, Walker's Battalion, on an unspecified date.

JENKINS, ABRAHAM, Private
Born in what later became Jackson County. Resided in Cherokee County where he was by occupation a farmer prior to enlisting at Fort Montgomery (present-day Robbinsville) at age 26, July 23, 1862, for the war. Reported present or accounted for through June 30, 1863, and in September-December, 1863. Reported on leave from February 20 through 28, 1863. Captured at Piedmont, Virginia, June 5, 1864. Reported under guard at Staunton, Virginia, June 8, 1864. Confined at Camp Morton, Indianapolis, Indiana, June 21, 1864. Paroled at Camp Morton and transferred for exchange on February 19, 1865. Hospitalized at Richmond, Virginia, February 28, 1865. Transferred to another hospital on March 1, 1865. No further records. Survived the war.

JENKINS, PHILIP, Private
Born in Cocke County, Tennessee, and resided in Cherokee County where he was by occupation a farmer prior to enlisting at Fort Montgomery (present-day Robbinsville) at age 25, July 23, 1862, for the war. Mustered in as Corporal. Reported present through December 31, 1862. Reported absent sick with measles in January-February, 1863. Deserted on or about April 30, 1863, and subsequently reduced to ranks.

JENKINS, WILLIAM, Private
Born in what later became Jackson County. Resided in Cherokee County where he was by occupation a farmer prior to enlisting at Fort Montgomery (present-day Robbinsville) at age 21, July 23, 1862, for the war. Reported present or accounted for through March 2, 1863. Deserted at Carter's Depot, Tennessee, April 27, 1863.

JOHNSON, DANIEL F., Corporal
Born in Yancey County and resided in Cherokee County where he was by occupation a farmer prior to enlisting at Fort Montgomery (present-day Robbinsville) at age 21, July 23, 1862, for the war. Mustered in as Corporal. Reported present through October 31, 1862. Reported at home recovering from a gunshot wound, November, 1862-February, 1863. Place, date, and circumstances of wounding not reported. Returned to duty on March 2, 1863. Deserted at Carter's Depot, Tennessee, April 27, 1863.

JOHNSON, JOHN F., Private
Born in Burke County and resided in Cherokee County where he was by occupation a farmer prior to enlisting at Fort Montgomery (present-day Robbinsville) at age 24, July 23, 1862, for the war. Reported present through February 28, 1863. Deserted at Carter's Depot, Tennessee, April 27, 1863.

JOHNSON, THOMAS M., Private
Born in Haywood County and resided in Cherokee County where he was by occupation a farmer prior to enlisting at Fort Montgomery (present-day Robbinsville) at age 32, July 23, 1862, for the war. Reported present through June 30, 1863. Deserted at Zollicoffer, Tennessee, on October 14, 1863.

KEITH, THOMAS S., Musician
Born in what later became Madison County. Resided in Cherokee County where he was by occupation a farmer prior to enlisting at Fort Montgomery (present-day Robbinsville) at age 32, July 23, 1862, for the war. Mustered in as Musician (Fifer). Reported present through June 30, 1863. Deserted at Jonesborough, Tennessee, on September 12, 1863. Went over to the enemy on an unspecified date. Sent to Knoxville, Tennessee. Released at Knoxville on February 12, 1864, after taking the Oath of Allegiance.

LAKEY, WILLIAM J., Private
Born in Buncombe County and resided in Macon County where he was by occupation a farmer prior to enlisting in Blount County, Tennessee, at age 23, September 1, 1862, for the war. Reported present through December 31, 1862. Deserted on January 9, 1863.

LONG, GREEN B., Private
Born in Burke County and resided in Cherokee County where he was by occupation a farmer prior to enlisting at Fort Montgomery (present-day Robbinsville) at age 24, July 23, 1862, for the war. Reported present through June 30, 1863. Deserted at Jonesborough, Tennessee, September 12, 1863.

LONG, THOMAS, Private
Previously served in Company E, Walker's Battalion. Transferred to this company on May 1, 1863. Deserted at Zollicoffer, Tennessee, May 26, 1863.

LOVIN, JOHN, Private
Born in what later became Caldwell County. Resided in Cherokee County where he was by occupation a farmer prior to enlisting at Fort Montgomery (present-day Robbinsville) at age 31, July 23, 1862, for the war. Reported present or accounted for through June 30, 1863, and in September, 1863-December, 1863. Reported on leave for twenty days beginning February 20, 1864. Captured in Blount County, Tennessee, February 9, 1865. Sent to Knoxville, Tennessee. Transferred to Chattanooga, Tennessee, March 10, 1865. Confined at Nashville, Tennessee, on or prior to March 22, 1865. Confined at Louisville, Kentucky, March 23, 1865. Confined at Camp Chase, Ohio, March 24, 1865. Released at Camp Chase on June 13, 1865, after taking the Oath of Allegiance. [He may have been the same man as John Lou-wan whose record is in the General Miscellaneous section of this roster.]

LOVIN, WILLIAM, Private
Born in what later became Caldwell County. Resided in Cherokee County where he was by occupation a farmer prior to enlisting at Fort Montgomery (present-day Robbinsville) at age 35, July 23, 1862, for the war. Reported present through February 28, 1863. Reported on detail as a wagoner at Strawberry Plains, Tennessee, from April 9 through 30, 1863. Rejoined the company on or prior to June 30, 1863. Reported present in September, 1863-February, 1864. No further records.

LOWEY, THOMAS S., Private
Born in South Carolina and resided in Cherokee County where he was by occupation a farmer prior to enlisting at Fort Montgomery (present-day Robbinsville) at age 18, July 23, 1862, for the war. Reported present through February 28, 1863. Deserted at Carter's Depot, Tennessee, April 27, 1863. Returned to duty prior to June 30, 1863. Deserted at Jonesborough, Tennessee, September 12, 1863.

Went over to the enemy on an unspecified date. Took the Oath of Allegiance at Knoxville, Tennessee, February 2, 1864. [See Tennessee pension application No. 14559.]

McCLAIN, G. A., Private
Name appears on a receipt roll for clothing dated October 16, 1864, as serving in Company H of this legion; he may have served in this company or in Company H of Walker's Battalion. He may have been the same man as George A. McClane, who served earlier in 1st Company D of Walker's Battalion.

McGAHY, JAMES H., Sergeant
Enlisted in Sevier County, Tennessee, April 4, 1863, for the war. Mustered in as Private. Reported present through June 30, 1863, and in September-December, 1863. Promoted to Sergeant on December 31, 1863. Reported present in January-February, 1864. Name appears on receipt rolls for clothing dated June 4, September 1, and September 18, 1864. No further records.

MARCUS, RUFUS, Private
Born in Burke County and resided in Cherokee County where he was by occupation a farmer prior to enlisting at Fort Montgomery (present-day Robbinsville) at age 30, July 23, 1862, for the war. Reported present through December 31, 1862. Listed as a deserter on February 28, 1863, but evidently returned to service at an unknown date. Deserted in Sevier County, Tennessee, April 6, 1863.

MARR, BENJAMIN FRANKLIN, Private
Enlisted in Macon County on December 22, 1862, for the war. Reported present or accounted for through June, 1863, and in September, 1863-February, 1864. Hospitalized at Charlottesville, Virginia, June 13, 1864, with intermittent fever. Returned to duty on June 26, 1864. No further records. Survived the war.

MARR, LEMUEL T., Private
Enlisted in Macon County at age 19, December 22, 1862, for the war. Reported present or accounted for through June, 1863, and in September, 1863-February, 1864. Captured at Piedmont, Virginia, June 5, 1864. Reported under guard at Staunton, Virginia, June 8, 1864. Confined at Camp Morton, Indianapolis, Indiana, June 21, 1864. Paroled at Camp Morton on March 4, 1865. Received at Boulware's and Cox's Wharves, James River, Virginia, March 10-12, 1865, for exchange. No further records. Survived the war.

MARTIN, JOSEPH W., Private
Enlisted in Blount County, Tennessee, February 14, 1863, for the war. Reported present through June 30, 1863. Deserted at Zollicoffer, Tennessee, August 31, 1863.

MATHIS, WILLIAM, Private
Born in Burke County and resided in Cherokee County where he was by occupation a farmer prior to enlisting at Fort Montgomery (present-day Robbinsville) at age 21, July 23, 1862, for the war. Reported present or accounted for through April, 1863. Reported on detail to catch "runaway mules" and afterwards detailed at Strawberry Plains, Tennessee, May-June, 1863. Deserted on July 6, 1863.

MEDLIN, LEWIS M., Private
Born in Cherokee County where he resided as a farmer prior to enlisting at Fort Montgomery (present-day Robbinsville) at age 18, July 23, 1862, for the war. Reported "at home unable for service" through October 31, 1862. Joined the company on or prior to December 31, 1862. Reported present in January-June, 1863. Reported sick in hospital from September 2 until October 31, 1863, when he was reported absent without leave. Reported absent without leave through February 29, 1864. No further records. Survived the war. [Name appears on a special order dated August 17, 1863, which states that he was transferred to Company K, 1st Regiment South Carolina Cavalry, August 17, 1863; however, no other evidence of his service in that unit was found.]

MOORE, WILLIAM D., Private
Born in Blount County, Tennessee, and resided in Cherokee County where he was by occupation a farmer prior to enlisting at Fort Montgomery (present-day Robbinsville) at age 19, July 23, 1862, for the war. Reported present or accounted for through February, 1863. Deserted on April 27, 1863.

MOOSE, BENJAMIN T., Corporal
Born in Cherokee County where he resided as a farmer prior to enlisting at Fort Montgomery (present-day Robbinsville) at age 18, July 23, 1862, for the war. Mustered in as Private. Reported present through June 30, 1863, and in September-October, 1863. Promoted to Corporal on November 1, 1863. Reported present in November, 1863-February, 1864. Name appears on receipt rolls for clothing dated June 4, September 1, September 18, and September 27, 1864. No further records. Survived the war.

MOOSE, PINKNEY A., Private
Enlisted in Blount County, Tennessee, March 3, 1863, for the war. Reported present through April 30, 1863. Died in hospital at Carter's Depot, Tennessee, May 10, 1863. Cause of death not reported.

NELSON, JAMES L., Private
Born in Haywood County and resided in Blount County, Tennessee, where he was by occupation a farmer prior to enlisting at Fort Montgomery (present-day Robbinsville) at age 29, September 27, 1862, for the war. Reported at home "unable for service," October 31, 1862. Reported for duty prior to December 31, 1862. Reported present in January-February, 1863. Reported on detail as a ferryman at Rock Point, Macon County, from March 3 through December 31, 1863. Captured in Blount County on or about January 13, 1864. Sent to Knoxville, Tennessee. Transferred to Nashville, Tennessee, and confined at the penitentiary there "for committing depredations." Confined at Louisville, Kentucky, April 27, 1864. Transferred to Camp Morton, Indianapolis, Indiana, where he arrived on May 12, 1864. Paroled at Camp Morton on March 15, 1865, and transferred for exchange. It is unclear whether he was formally exchanged; however, he is reported in records of the Federal Provost Marshal as a Confederate deserter who was confined at Knoxville on March 22, 1865. Transferred to Chattanooga, Tennessee, March 25, 1865. Released at Chattanooga on June 3, 1865, after taking the Oath of Allegiance.

OWNBY, JOSEPH C., Private
Born in Rutherford County and resided in Cherokee County where he was by occupation a farmer prior to enlisting at Fort Montgomery (present-day Robbinsville) at age 33, July 23, 1862, for the war. Reported at home unable for service through October 31, 1862. Reported for service on or prior to December 31, 1862. Reported

sick at home in January-June, 1863, and September, 1863-February, 1864. No further records. [His surname may have been Owenby.]

PACE, FLEMMING H., Private
Born in Greenville District, South Carolina, and resided in Cherokee County, North Carolina, where he was by occupation a farmer prior to enlisting at Fort Montgomery (present-day Robbinsville) at age 43, July 23, 1862, for the war. Reported present through December 31, 1862. Reported sick at home in January-April, 1863. Failed to return to duty and was listed as a deserter in May-June, 1863.

PACE, WILLIAM M., Private
Born in Cherokee County where he resided as a farmer prior to enlisting in Blount County, Tennessee, at age 18, September 27, 1862, for the war. Reported present through December 31, 1862. Deserted in Sevier County, Tennessee, April 6, 1863. Went over to the enemy on an unspecified date. Sent to Knoxville, Tennessee. Released after taking the Oath of Allegiance at Knoxville on February 6, 1864. [May have enlisted also as Private in Company F, 39th Regiment N.C. Troops.]

PHILLIPS, CHARLES H., Private
Born in Cherokee County where he resided as a farmer prior to enlisting at Fort Montgomery (present-day Robbinsville) at age 18, July 23, 1862, for the war. Reported present through October 31, 1862. Reported at home sick with measles, November, 1862-February, 1863. Reported present in March-June, 1863. Deserted at Greeneville, Tennessee, October 10, 1863. Returned to duty on an unspecified date. Reported present in January-February, 1864. Name appears on a receipt roll for clothing dated September 1, 1864. No further records. Survived the war.

PHILLIPS, THOMAS B., Private
Born in Cherokee County where he resided as a farmer prior to enlisting at Fort Montgomery (present-day Robbinsville) at age 18, September 27, 1862, for the war. Reported present through June 30, 1863. Reported detailed as a teamster in September-October, 1863. Rejoined the company on or prior to December 31, 1863. Reported present in January-February, 1864. Name appears on a receipt roll for clothing dated June 4, 1864. No further records.

PRICHARD, THOMAS, _____
Enlisted in Cherokee County on August 19, 1863, for the war. Reported absent without leave on January 15, 1864. No further records. [May have been the same man as Thomas Pritchet, who earlier served as Private in Company G, 39th Regiment N.C. Troops. If so, he enlisted illegally in this company while a deserter from that unit.]

PROCTOR, WILLIAM, Sergeant
Born in Monroe County, Tennessee, and resided in Cherokee County where he was by occupation a farmer prior to enlisting at Fort Montgomery (present-day Robbinsville) at age 32, July 23, 1862, for the war. Mustered in as Private. Reported present or accounted for through June 30, 1863. Reported sick in hospital in September-October, 1863. Promoted to Sergeant in November-December, 1863. Returned to duty prior to December 31, 1863. Reported present in January-February, 1864. Hospitalized at Charlottesville, Virginia, September 26, 1864, with pleurodynia. Transferred to hospital at Lynchburg, Virginia, September 27, 1864. No further records. Survived the war.

REAGAN, JOSEPH, Private
Born in Person County and resided in Cherokee County. Was by occupation a farmer prior to enlisting at Fort Montgomery (present-day Robbinsville) at age 28, July 23, 1862, for the war. Reported at home "unable for service" on October 31, 1862. Rejoined the company prior to December 31, 1862. Reported present in January-June, 1863, and in September-October, 1863. Deserted on December 6, 1863. [See Tennessee pension application No. 2869.]

RIDLEY, J. N., _____
A receipt roll for clothing lists him as a member of Company H, Thomas's Legion. It is not known whether he was a member of this company or of Company H, Walker's Battalion.

ROGERS, JEREMIAH S., Private
Enlisted in Blount County, Tennessee, February 21, 1863, for the war. Reported present through June 30, 1863, and in September, 1863-February, 1864. No further records.

SAWYER, ISAAC JARRET, Corporal
Born in Macon County and resided in Cherokee County where he was by occupation a farmer prior to enlisting at Fort Montgomery (present-day Robbinsville) at age 27, July 23, 1862, for the war. Mustered in as Private. Reported present or accounted for through June, 1863. Promoted to Corporal in May-June, 1863. Reported missing on the retreat to Virginia in October, 1864. No further records. Survived the war.

SCOTT, ABRAM Mc., Private
Enlisted in Blount County, Tennessee, February 21, 1863, for the war. Reported present until April 8, 1863, when he was detailed at Strawberry Plains, Tennessee. Reported on detail at Strawberry Plains through June 30, 1863. Reported on detail as a teamster in the quartermaster department, September, 1863-February, 1864. Was at Bristol, Tennessee, during at least part of that period. No further records.

SHERRELL, BENJAMIN F., Corporal
Born in what later became Jackson County. Resided in Cherokee County where he was by occupation a farmer prior to enlisting at Fort Montgomery (present-day Robbinsville) at age 22, July 18, 1862, for the war. Mustered in as Private. Reported present through June 30, 1863. Reported present in September-October, 1863. Promoted to Corporal on November 1, 1863. Reported present, November, 1863-February, 1864. Name appears on receipt rolls for clothing dated June 4, September 1, and September 27, 1864. No further records.

SHERRILL, ABRAHAM H., Sergeant
Born in Cherokee County where he resided as a farmer prior to enlisting at Fort Montgomery (present-day Robbinsville) at age 19, July 23, 1862, for the war. Mustered in as Private. Reported present through June 30, 1863, and in September-October, 1863. Promoted to Sergeant on November 1, 1863. Reported present in November, 1863-February, 1864. Name appears on receipt rolls for clothing dated June 4, September 1, September 18, and September 27, 1864. No further records.

SHERRILL, SAMUEL P., _____
Enlisted in Cherokee County on August 19, 1863, for the war. Reported present in January-February, 1864. Name appears on

receipt rolls for clothing dated June 4 and September 1, 1864. No further records. Survived the war.

SHERRILL, WILLIAM M., Private

Born in what later became Jackson County. Resided in Cherokee County where he was by occupation a farmer prior to enlisting at Fort Montgomery (present-day Robbinsville) at age 26, July 23, 1862, for the war. Reported present or accounted for through June 30, 1863. Deserted at Greeneville, Tennessee, October 10, 1863. Returned to duty on February 22, 1864. Reported present on February 29, 1864. Name appears on a receipt roll for clothing dated June 4, 1864. No further records. Survived the war. [His surname may have been Sherrell.]

SHIELDS, JONATHAN, Private

Enlisted in Blount County, Tennessee, February 19, 1863, for the war. Deserted at Iron Mountain in Blount County on February 26, 1863.

SKINNER, WILLIAM H., Private

Born in Mecklenburg County and resided in Cherokee County where he was by occupation a farmer prior to enlisting at Fort Montgomery (present-day Robbinsville) at age 25, July 23, 1862, for the war. Reported present through April 30, 1863. Deserted at Zollicoffer, Tennessee, May 26, 1863.

SMELTSER, PASCHAL, Private

Enlisted in Cherokee County on December 7, 1862, for the war. Reported present through June 30, 1863. Reported sick in hospital in September-October, 1863. Died in hospital at Emory and Henry, Virginia, November 19, 1863. Cause of death not reported.

STALCUP, CHARLES THADDEUS, Private

Born on April 28, 1836, in the part of Cherokee County that later became Clay County. Resided in Cherokee County and was by occupation a farmer prior to enlisting at Fort Montgomery (present-day Robbinsville) at age 26, July 18, 1862, for the war. Reported present or accounted for through June 30, 1863, and in September, 1863-February, 1864. Captured at Piedmont, Virginia, June 5, 1864. Reported under guard at Staunton, Virginia, June 8, 1864. Confined at Camp Morton, Indianapolis, Indiana, June 21, 1864. Paroled at Camp Morton and transferred for exchange on February 26, 1865. No further records. Survived the war. [According to his Tennessee pension application No. 10746, he was wounded slightly in the left arm by a spent ball at the battle of Piedmont.]

STALCUP, GEORGE YOUNG, Private

Born in Cherokee County on May 23, 1843. Resided in Cherokee County and was by occupation a farmer prior to enlisting at Fort Montgomery (present-day Robbinsville) at age 19, July 18, 1862, for the war. Reported present or accounted for through June, 1863, and in September, 1863-February, 1864. Name appears on a receipt roll for clothing dated September 1, 1864. No further records. Survived the war.

STUART, ARCHIBALD, Private

Enlisted in Blount County, Tennessee, February 19, 1863, for the war. Reported present on February 28, 1863. Deserted at Carter's Depot, Tennessee, April 27, 1863. [Probably served previously as a Private in Company C, Walker's Battalion.]

SUMPTER, WILLIAM H., Private

Resided in Cherokee County. Place and date of enlistment not reported; probably enlisted subsequent to February 29, 1864. Captured at Anderson, South Carolina, May 3, 1865. Paroled on or about the same date.

SWANEY, DAVID C., Private

Born in Henderson County and resided in Cherokee County where he was by occupation a farmer prior to enlisting at Fort Montgomery (present-day Robbinsville) at age 22, July 18, 1862, for the war. Reported present or accounted for through June 30, 1863. Reported sick in hospital in September-December, 1863. Subsequently reported as absent without leave, October 31, 1863-February 29, 1864. Deserted to the enemy on an unspecified date. Took the Oath of Allegiance at Knoxville, Tennessee, January 23, 1864.

WARDREP, JEREMIAH, Private

Born in Macon County and resided in Cherokee County where he was by occupation a farmer prior to enlisting at Fort Montgomery (present-day Robbinsville) at age 31, July 23, 1862, for the war. Reported present through December 31, 1862. Reported absent sick with measles in January-April, 1863. Returned to duty prior to June 30, 1863. Deserted at Carter's Depot, Tennessee, September 21, 1863.

WASHBURN, RICHARD C., Private

Born in Macon County and resided in Cherokee County where he was by occupation a farmer prior to enlisting at Fort Montgomery (present-day Robbinsville) on July 23, 1862, for the war. Reported on detail in Cherokee County to buy shoes through December 31, 1862. Reported on detail in North Carolina, January-February, 1863. Reported on detail "as salt agent for Cherokee County" from March 7, 1863, through February 29, 1864. No further records.

WASHINGTON, GEORGE, Sergeant

Place and date of enlistment not reported; probably enlisted subsequent to February 29, 1864. Promotion record not reported. Captured at Winchester, Virginia, September 19, 1864. Confined at Point Lookout, Maryland. Paroled at Point Lookout and transferred to Venus Point, Savannah River, Georgia, where he was received on November 15, 1864, for exchange. No further records.

WELCH, JOSEPH, Private

Born in Macon County and resided in Cherokee County where he was by occupation a farmer prior to enlisting at Fort Montgomery (present-day Robbinsville) at age 27, July 18, 1862, for the war. Reported present through June 30, 1863, and in September, 1863-February, 1864. Captured at Winchester, Virginia, September 19, 1864. Sent to Harpers Ferry, West Virginia. Confined at Point Lookout, Maryland, September 26, 1864. Paroled at Point Lookout on or about October 30, 1864. Received at Venus Point, Savannah River, Georgia, November 15, 1864, for exchange. No further records.

WELCH, JOSEPH W., Private

Previously served in Company D, 62nd Regiment N.C. Troops. Enlisted illegally in this company at Fort Montgomery (present-day Robbinsville) while absent without leave from the 62nd Regiment, July 18, 1862, for the war. Reported present through December 31, 1862. Reported absent sick in January-April, 1863. Reported on detached service at Strawberry Plains, Tennessee, in May-June,

1863. Reported on detail as a teamster in the post quartermaster department in September, 1863-February, 1864. Was on duty at Bristol, Tennessee, during the latter part of that period. Captured in Macon County on February 2, 1864. Confined at Knoxville, Tennessee, February 7, 1864. Sent to Nashville, Tennessee. Sent to Louisville, Kentucky, February 28, 1864. Confined at Fort Delaware, Delaware, March 7, 1864. Probably released at Fort Delaware on June 7, 1865, after taking the Oath of Allegiance. Survived the war. [He may have been serving, possibly illegally, with the Indian Battalion at the time of his capture.]

WELCH, THOMAS J., Private

Born in what later became Jackson County. Resided in Cherokee County where he was by occupation a farmer prior to enlisting at Fort Montgomery (present-day Robbinsville) at age 25, July 18, 1862, for the war. Reported present or accounted for through June 30, 1863. Reported sick in hospital, September 2-December 31, 1863. Subsequently reported as absent without leave from October 21, 1863, through February 29, 1864. No further records. Survived the war. [He may have been the same man as J. E. T. Welch, listed in the General Miscellaneous section of this roster.]

WELCH, WILLIAM L., Private

Born in Macon County and resided in Cherokee County where he was by occupation a farmer prior to enlisting at Fort Montgomery (present-day Robbinsville) at age 33, July 18, 1862, for the war. Reported present through December 31, 1862. Reported absent sick in January-February, 1863. Deserted on or about April 30, 1863.

WHITESIDE, WILLIAM F., Private

Born in Rutherford County and resided in Macon County where he was by occupation a farmer prior to enlisting at Fort Montgomery (present-day Robbinsville) at age 38, July 23, 1862, for the war. Reported present through December 31, 1862. Deserted in January-February, 1863. Returned to duty on an unspecified date. Deserted in Sevier County, Tennessee, April 6, 1863.

WIKLE, ANDREW J., Private

Previously served as Private in Company A, 7th Battalion N.C. Cavalry. Transferred to this company on September 27, 1862. Reported at home sick through December 31, 1862. Reported absent without leave in January-February, 1863. Deserted from the hospital at Strawberry Plains, Tennessee, in April, 1863. Returned to duty prior to June 30, 1863. Deserted at Zollicoffer, Tennessee, August 31, 1863. Subsequently enlisted illegally in Company C, Indian Battalion.

WILLOX, ANDREW J., Private

Born in Blount County, Tennessee, and resided in Cherokee County where he was by occupation a farmer prior to enlisting at Fort Montgomery (present-day Robbinsville) at age 28, July 18, 1862, for the war. Reported present through December 31, 1862. Reported as having deserted, but "name appears in col[umn] of names present," January-February, 1863. Deserted in Sevier County, Tennessee, April 6, 1863. [His surname may have been Willocks, Wilcox or Willcox.]

WILLOX, GRIGSBY R., Private

Born in Blount County, Tennessee, and resided in Cherokee County where he was by occupation a farmer prior to enlisting at Fort Montgomery (present-day Robbinsville) at age 36, July 18, 1862, for the war. Reported present through December 31, 1862. Reported as having deserted, but "name appears in col[umn] of names present," January-February, 1863. Deserted in Sevier County, Tennessee, April 6, 1863. [His surname may have been Willocks, Wilcox or Willcox.]

WILLOX, ROBERT M., Private

Born in Blount County, Tennessee, and resided in Cherokee County where he was by occupation a farmer prior to enlisting at Fort Montgomery (present-day Robbinsville) at age 36, July 18, 1862, for the war. Reported present through December 31, 1862. Reported as having deserted, but "name appears in col[umn] of names present," January-February, 1863. Deserted in Sevier County, Tennessee, March 26, 1863. [His surname may have been Willocks, Wilcox or Willcox.]

WILSON, THOMAS, _____

Enlisted in Cherokee County on November 8, 1863, for the war. Reported absent without leave from December 1, 1863, through February 29, 1864. No further records.

WINFREY, ISAAC B., Corporal

Born in Surry County and resided in Cherokee County where he was by occupation a farmer prior to enlisting at Fort Montgomery (present-day Robbinsville) at age 26, July 23, 1862, for the war. Mustered in as Corporal. Reported present through March-April, 1863. Transferred to Company E, Walker's Battalion, May 1, 1863.

WRIGHT, R. R., _____

Name appears on a receipt roll for clothing dated October 16, 1864, which states he served in "Co. H," Thomas's Legion; however, it is unclear whether he served in this company or in Company H, Walker's Battalion.

COMPANY I

This company was organized at Valleytown (near present-day Andrews) in Cherokee County on July 24, 1862. Its first enrollees were from Cherokee County. Many other early enrollees were from Sevier County, Tennessee, and were probably added to the company as it made its way to Strawberry Plains to join the rest of the legion. This company may have been known as Company G, N.C. Cherokee Battalion, as of August 31, 1862. On or about October 5, 1862, it was designated Company I, Infantry Regiment, Thomas's Legion.

The following roster was compiled in large part from company muster rolls dated July 24, 1862-June, 1863, and September, 1863-February, 1864. These are abstracted in the microfilm edition of the Compiled Service Records of Confederate Soldiers Who Served in Organizations from the State of North Carolina (Record Group 109, M270), National Archives, Washington, D.C. Other valuable information in the Compiled Service Records includes enlistment papers, pay vouchers, requisitions, letters of resignation, discharge certificates, and abstracts of medical and prisoner of war records.

Also utilized in this roster were *The War of the Rebellion: A Compilation of the Official Records of the Union and Confederate Armies*, the North Carolina Adjutant General's papers, state militia records, newspaper casualty lists and obituaries, wartime claims for bounty pay and allowances, postwar registers of claims for artificial limbs, Confederate pension applications filed with the states of North Carolina, Tennessee, and Florida, records of the North Carolina Confederate Soldiers' Home, and the 1860 and 1870 federal censuses of North Carolina. A search was made also for relevant letters, diaries, reminiscences, and other manuscripts in the Southern Historical Collection (University of North Carolina-Chapel Hill) and the Duke University Library Special Collections Department.

Among the secondary sources consulted were records of the North Carolina division of the United Daughters of the Confederacy, postwar rosters, regimental and county histories, marriage bond, will, and cemetery indexes, published and unpublished genealogies, biographical dictionaries, the North Carolina *County Heritage Book* series, the *Confederate Veteran*, Walter Clark's *Histories of the Several Regiments and Battalions from North Carolina in the Great War, 1861-'65*, and the North Carolina volume of the extended edition of *Confederate Military History*.

OFFICERS

CAPTAINS

PARKER, WILLIS FRANCIS

Born in the part of Haywood County that later became Macon County. Resided in Cherokee County where he was by occupation a farmer prior to enlisting in Cherokee County at age 45. Elected Captain on July 24, 1862. Reported present through October 31, 1862. Reported on detached service at the recruiting office from December 31, 1862, through April 30, 1863. Rejoined the company on or prior to June 30, 1863. Reported present in September-October, 1863. Resigned on December 20, 1863, because he was "over the conscript age and not by any means in good health." Resignation accepted on January 7, 1864.

KIMSEY, JOSEPH ANDERSON

Born in Macon County on July 26, 1836. Resided in Cherokee County where he was by occupation a farmer prior to enlisting at Valleytown at age 26. Elected 1st Lieutenant on July 24, 1862. Reported present through April 30, 1863. Reported on detached service in Cherokee County from June 6 through 30, 1863. Reported present, September, 1863-February, 1864. Signed, as 1st Lieutenant commanding the company, a petition to Gov. Zebulon B. Vance dated February 25, 1864, requesting his assistance in reuniting Thomas's Legion and removing it from the command of Brig. Gen. Alfred E. Jackson. Promoted to Captain, to rank from January 7, 1864. Name appears as signature to a pay voucher dated July 26, 1864. No further records. Survived the war.

PHILIPS, NATHANIEL GREENE

Served as 1st Lieutenant of this company. In witnessing pension applications for two men, Philips claimed that he had been captain of Company I, "Walker's Battalion." There was no Company I, Walker's Battalion, so this company was evidently intended. No wartime records confirm that he was promoted to captain.

LIEUTENANTS

GAILER, P. B., 3rd Lieutenant

Clark's *Regiments*, 3:731, states that he was elected or appointed 2nd Lieutenant of this company. He was probably elected or appointed subsequent to February 29, 1864.

IGON, SOLOMON E., 2nd Lieutenant

Born in DeKalb County, Georgia, and resided in Rabun County, Georgia, where he was by occupation a farmer prior to enlisting at Valleytown, at age 25. Elected 2nd Lieutenant on July 24, 1862. Reported present through June 30, 1863. Reported sick at Zollicoffer, Tennessee, October 20, 1863. Resigned on November 16, 1863, after being unfit for field duty for three months. The reason for his resignation was stated by a surgeon to be "partial paralysis of the tongue and left leg." Resignation accepted on December 7, 1863. [His surname may be have been Egan.]

PHILIPS, NATHANIEL GREENE, 1st Lieutenant

Born in Macon County and resided in Cherokee County where he was by occupation a farmer prior to enlisting at Valleytown at age 30. Elected 3rd Lieutenant on July 24, 1862. Reported present through February, 1863. Reported absent sick in Cherokee County from April 24 through 30, 1863. Returned to duty prior to June 30, 1863. Reported present in September-October, 1863. Reported on leave from November 2 through 24, 1863. Reported absent without leave from November 27, 1863, through January 12, 1864. Promoted to 2nd Lieutenant on an unspecified date. Returned to duty prior to February 22, 1864. Signed, as 2nd Lieutenant, a petition to Gov. Zebulon B. Vance dated February 25, 1864, requesting his assistance in reuniting Thomas's Legion and removing it from the command of Brig. Gen. Alfred E. Jackson. Promoted to 1st Lieutenant subsequent to February 25, 1864, to rank from January 7, 1864. Sent to hospital on August 1, 1864. Hospitalized at Charlottesville, Virginia, October 4, 1864, with dyspepsia. Returned to duty on October 9, 1864. No further records. Survived the war. [His surname may have been Phillips. According to Crow, *Storm in the Mountains*, 190, Company I was temporarily consolidated with Company C of this regiment under the command of Philips after the battle of Cedar Creek, Virginia. In witnessing pension applications of Joseph L. Robinson and James R. Rogers, Philips claimed to have been captain of Company I, "Walker's Battalion." Walker's Battalion had no Company I, so this company was evidently intended. No wartime records confirm that he was promoted to captain.]

STEWART, JOHN HANNIBAL, 1st Lieutenant

Served as Sergeant in this company. An 1897 letter seems to indicate that he served as 1st Lieutenant of this company. If he did, it was probably subsequent to October 9, 1864. See John H. Stewart to "Dear Otis," William Williams Stringfield Papers, Special Collections, Hunter Library, Western Carolina University.

NONCOMMISSIONED OFFICERS AND PRIVATES

ADAMS, ALFRED C., Private

Born in Haywood County and resided in Cherokee County where he was by occupation a farmer prior to enlisting at Valleytown at age 34, July 24, 1862, for the war. Reported present through October 31, 1862. Reported absent sick in Cherokee County from November 20, 1862, through October, 1863. Reportedly "deserted & joined the ranks of the enemy" in November, 1863.

ADAMS, ASA L., Private

Born in Haywood County and resided in Cherokee County where he was by occupation a farmer prior to enlisting at Valleytown at age 19, July 24, 1862, for the war. Reported absent on sick furlough on October 31, 1862. Reported absent without leave on December 31,

1862, and February 28, 1863. Reported present in March-June, 1863. Deserted at Zollicoffer, Tennessee, August 31, 1863, although "supposed to have reported to Col. Thomas." [He was probably the same man as Asaph L. Adams who was discharged for "dishonorable conduct" from Company A, 29th Regiment N.C. Troops, in May, 1862, and took the Oath of Allegiance in eastern Tennessee in January, 1864.]

ADAMS, BENJAMIN F., Private

Born in what later became Jackson County. Resided in Cherokee County where he was by occupation a farmer prior to enlisting at Valleytown at age 20, July 24, 1862, for the war. Reported present or accounted for through April, 1863. Reported "cut off by the evacuation of Tenn[essee], now supposed to be on duty with Col. Thomas in N.C." in September-October, 1863. Subsequently reported as having deserted at Zollicoffer, Tennessee, October 14, 1863. Captured by Federal forces at Knoxville, Tennessee, December 3, 1863. Refused to take the Oath of Allegiance. Transferred to Louisville, Kentucky, where he arrived on January 1, 1864. Transferred to Fort Delaware, Delaware, February 29, 1864. Arrived at Fort Delaware on March 4, 1864. Released at Fort Delaware on June 19, 1865, after taking the Oath of Allegiance.

ADAMS, FRANCIS M., Private

Born in Haywood County and resided in Cherokee County where he was by occupation a farmer prior to enlisting at Valleytown at age 30, July 24, 1862, for the war. Mustered in as Sergeant. Reported present through June 30, 1863. Reported "cut off" in the evacuation of eastern Tennessee and was "now supposed to be on duty with Col. Thomas in N.C." in September-October, 1863. Subsequently reported as having deserted at Zollicoffer, Tennessee, October 14, 1863. Reduced to ranks prior to November 1, 1863. Captured by Federal forces at Knoxville, Tennessee, December 3, 1863. Refused to take Oath of Allegiance. Transferred to Louisville, Kentucky, where he arrived on January 1, 1864. Transferred to Fort Delaware, Delaware, February 29, 1864. Arrived at Fort Delaware on March 4, 1864. Released at Fort Delaware on June 7, 1865, after taking the Oath of Allegiance.

ADAMS, JAMES, Private

Enlisted at Coker Creek, Tennessee, July 18, 1862, for the war. Deserted at Carter's Depot, Tennessee, April 24, 1863. Reported absent under arrest under sentence of general court-martial on June 30, 1863. Reported "cut off in the evacuation of East Ten[nessee], supposed to have reported to Col. Thomas," September-October, 1863. Subsequently reported as having deserted at Zollicoffer, Tennessee, October 14, 1863.

ADAMS, JOHN P., Private

Enlisted at Strawberry Plains, Tennessee, April 5, 1863, for the war. Reported present through June 30, 1863, and in September-October, 1863. Deserted on December 6, 1863.

ADAMS, RICHARD W., Private

Born in Cherokee County where he resided as a farmer prior to enlisting at Valleytown at age 8, July 24, 1862, for the war. Reported absent on sick furlough on October 31, 1862. Returned to duty prior to December 31, 1862. Reported present in January-February, 1863. Discharged at Strawberry Plains, Tennessee, April 6, 1863, by reason of being underage.

ALLMON, W. N., _____

North Carolina pension records indicate that he served in this company. Survived the war.

ANDERSON, DANIEL, Private

Born in Sevier County, Tennessee. Resided in Blount County and was by occupation a farmer prior to enlisting at Valleytown at age 34, July 24, 1862, for the war. Reported absent on sick furlough through June 30, 1863, and in September, 1863-February, 1864. No further records.

ARROWOOD, J. W., _____

North Carolina pension records indicate that he served in this company. Survived the war.

ARROWOOD, JACOB A., Private

Born in Burke County and resided in Cherokee County where he was by occupation a farmer prior to enlisting at Valleytown at age 18, July 24, 1862, for the war. Reported present through June 30, 1863, and in September-December, 1863. Reported sick in hospital in Virginia on February 29, 1864. No further records.

ASH, DANIEL P., Corporal

Previously served as Private in Company B, 40th Regiment Georgia Volunteer Infantry. Enlisted in this company at Strawberry Plains, Tennessee, February 26, 1863, for the war. Mustered in as Private. Reported present through June 30, 1863. Promoted to Corporal in July-October, 1863. Reported present in September, 1863-February, 1864. Captured at Piedmont, Virginia, June 5, 1864. Reported as a prisoner under guard at Staunton, Virginia, June 8, 1864. Confined at Camp Morton, Indianapolis, Indiana, June 21, 1864. Released at Camp Morton on June 21, 1865, after taking the Oath of Allegiance. [Born in Haywood County on December 7, 1840. See Tennessee pension application No. 1012.]

BALLARD, WILLIAM H., Private

Previously enlisted as Private in Company G, Walker's Battalion. Transferred to this company on or about September 24, 1862. Reported present in January-June, 1863. Transferred to Levi's Battery on July 1, 1863.

BARTON, ELIJAH, Private

Previously served as Private in Company H, Walker's Battalion. Transferred to this company in March-April, 1863. Mustered in as Private. Deserted at Carter's Depot, Tennessee, April 24, 1863. Reported under arrest under sentence of court-martial on June 30, 1863. Returned to duty on an unspecified date. Deserted at Carter's Depot, September 17, 1863, although "supposed to have reported to Col. Thomas." Reportedly promoted to Corporal in November-December, 1863, while still listed as a deserter, but this is probably a clerical error.

"BIG INDIAN," Private

Place and date of enlistment not reported; probably enlisted in July-September, 1863. Captured at Strawberry Plains, Tennessee, on or about September 7, 1863. Sent to Louisville, Kentucky, where he arrived on October 5, 1863. Transferred to Camp Douglas, Chicago, Illinois, October 7, 1863. No further records.

BOHANAN, JAMES, Private

Born in Sevier County, Tennessee, where he resided as a farmer prior to enlisting in Sevier County between July 24 and October 31, 1862, for the war. Reported present through December 31, 1862. Reported on duty working on a road, January-April, 1863. Reported on detached service at Strawberry Plains, Tennessee, May-June, 1863. Reported "cut off in the evacuation of East Tenn[essee] supposed to have reported to Col. Thomas," September-October, 1863. Subsequently reported as having deserted at Mossy Creek, Tennessee, October 1, 1863.

BRADY, JOHN, Private

Born in Cocke County, Tennessee, and resided in Cherokee County where he was by occupation a farmer prior to enlisting at Valleytown at age 29, July 24, 1862, for the war. Reported present through October 31, 1862. Discharged on November 30, 1862. Reason discharged not reported.

CANUP, EPPIE M., Private

Previously served as Private in Company A, 29th Regiment N.C. Troops. Enlisted illegally in this company at Strawberry Plains, Tennessee, November 15, 1862, for the war, while a deserter from the 29th Regiment. Reported present in January-June, 1863. Deserted at Zollicoffer, Tennessee, September 5, 1863. Went over to the enemy on an unspecified date. Took the Oath of Allegiance at Louisville, Kentucky, on or about December 22, 1863, and sent north of the Ohio River.

CANUP, FRANCIS M., Private

Previously served as Private in Company A, 29th Regiment N.C. Troops. Enlisted illegally in this company at Strawberry Plains, Tennessee, November 15, 1862, for the war, while a deserter from the 29th Regiment. Reported present in January-June, 1863. Deserted at Zollicoffer, Tennessee, September 6, 1863, "supposed to have reported to Col. Thomas." Went over to the enemy on an unspecified date. Took the Oath of Allegiance at Louisville, Kentucky, on or about December 22, 1863, and sent north of the Ohio River.

CARPENTER, DAVID H., _____

North Carolina pension records indicate that he served in this company. Survived the war.

CARR, JESSE, Private

Born in Blount County, Tennessee, where he resided as a farmer prior to enlisting at Valleytown at age 28, July 24, 1862, for the war. Deserted on October 29, 1862.

CARROLL, CHARLES H., Private

Previously served as Private in Company E, Walker's Battalion. Transferred to this company in May-June, 1863. Reported in hospital at Abingdon, Virginia, October 31, 1863. Died in hospital at Emory and Henry, Virginia, November 23, 1863. Cause of death not reported.

CLAUGHBAUGH, ARCHIBALD, Private

Born in Sevier County, Tennessee, where he resided as a farmer prior to enlisting in Sevier County at age 18, between July 24 and October 31, 1862, for the war. Reported on detached service through October 31, 1862. Reported absent without leave in November-December, 1862. Listed as a deserter on January 1, 1863.

CLAUGHBAUGH, JAMES, Private

Born in Sevier County, Tennessee, where he resided as a farmer prior to enlisting in Sevier County at age 23, between July 24 and October 31, 1862, for the war. Reported on detached service through October 31, 1862. Reported present on December 31, 1862. Reported on duty working on a road in January-April, 1863. Reported on detached service at Strawberry Plains, Tennesee, May-June, 1863. Reported "cut off in the evacuation of East Tenn[essee] supposed to have reported to Col Thomas" in September-October, 1863. Subsequently reported as having deserted at Mossy Creek, Tennessee, October 1, 1863.

CLAUGHBAUGH, SAMUEL, Private

Born in Sevier County, Tennessee, where he resided as a farmer prior to enlisting in Sevier County at age 18, between July 24 and October 31, 1862, for the war. Reported on detached service through October 31, 1862. Reported present on December 31, 1862. Reported on duty working on a road in January-April, 1863. Reported on detached service at Strawberry Plains, Tennessee, May-June, 1863. Reported "cut off in the evacuation of East Tenn[essee] supposed to have reported to Col. Thomas," September-October, 1863. Subsequently reported as having deserted at Mossy Creek, Tennessee, October 1, 1863.

CLINE, JOHN W., Private

Previously served as Private in 2nd Company A of this regiment. Transferred to this company on July 24, 1862. Reported on detached service through October 31, 1863. Reported on detached service working on a road on December 31, 1862. Transferred back to 2nd Company A of this regiment in January-February, 1863, because he was "dissatisfied" with Company I.

CLINE, WILLIAM R., Private

Previously served as Private in 2nd Company A of this regiment. Transferred to this company on July 24, 1862. Reported on detached service through October 31, 1862. Reported on detached service working on a road on December 31, 1862. Transferred back to 2nd Company A of this regiment in January-February, 1863, because he was "dissatisfied" with Company I.

COKER, JAMES H., Private

Previously served as Private in Company D of this regiment. Transferred to this company on May 9, 1863. No further records.

CONNER, ANDREW, Private

Born in what later became Jackson County. Resided in Sevier County, Tennessee, where he was by occupation a farmer prior to enlisting in Sevier County at age 30, between July 24 and October 31, 1862, for the war. Reported on detached service through October 31, 1862. Rejoined the company prior to December 31, 1862. Reported on duty working on a road in January-April, 1863. Reported on detached service at Strawberry Plains, Tennessee, May-June, 1863. Reported "cut off in the evacuation of East Tenn[essee] supposed to have reported to Col. Thomas" in September-October, 1863. Later reported as having deserted at Mossy Creek, Tennessee, October 1, 1863.

CRAIG, STRAWDER, Private

Resided in Haywood County. Place and date of enlistment not reported; probably enlisted subsequent to February 29, 1864. Deserted to the enemy on an unspecified date. Released after taking the Oath of Allegiance at Louisville, Kentucky, February 14, 1865, and released north of the Ohio River to remain for the duration of the war. [His given name may have been Strother. He was about age 16 in 1864.]

CUTHBERTSON, NATHAN W., Private

Born in Yancey County and resided in Blount County, Tennessee, where he was by occupation a farmer prior to enlisting at Valleytown at age 19, July 24, 1862, for the war. Reported present through June 30, 1863. Reported absent sick in September-December, 1863. Deserted to the enemy on an unspecified date. Sent to Knoxville, Tennessee. Released at Knoxville on or about February 6, 1864, after taking the Oath of Allegiance.

DERREBERRY, JOHN McCAMEY, Private

Born in 1929 in Burke County and resided in Cherokee County where he was by occupation a farmer prior to enlisting at Valleytown at age 33, July 24, 1862, for the war. Reported present through December 31, 1862. Reported on detached service as a teamster and wagoner in the quartermaster department, January-April, 1863. Rejoined the company prior to June 30, 1863. Reported absent "cut off in the evacuation of East Tenn[essee], supposed to be with Col. Thomas in N.C." in September-October, 1863. Subsequently reported as having deserted at Zollicoffer, Tennessee, October 11, 1863.

DERREBERRY, JOHN S., Musician

Born in Burke County and resided in Cherokee County where he was by occupation a mechanic prior to enlisting at Valleytown at age 50, July 24, 1862, for the war. Mustered in as Musician (Fifer). Reported present through December 31, 1862. Died in hospital at Strawberry Plains, Tennessee, January 21, 1863. Cause of death not reported.

DERREBERRY, MICHAEL ALEXANDER, Sergeant

Born in Burke County on May 27, 1836, and resided in Cherokee County. Was by occupation a farmer prior to enlisting at Valleytown at age 26, July 24, 1862, for the war. Mustered in as Sergeant. Reported present through February 28, 1863. Detailed to Cherokee County "after deserters" beginning on April 24, 1863. Rejoined the company prior to June 30, 1863. Reported present in September, 1863-February, 1864. Hospitalized at Winchester, Virginia, August 1, 1864, with debilitas. Captured at Winchester on September 19, 1864. Sent to Harpers Ferry, West Virginia. Confined at Point Lookout, Maryland, September 26, 1864. Paroled at Point Lookout on February 10, 1865. Received at Cox's Wharf, James River, Virginia, February 14-15, 1865, for exchange. Hospitalized at Richmond, Virginia, February 15, 1865, with chronic diarrhoea. Furloughed for sixty days on February 24, 1865. Survived the war.

DERREBERRY, ROBERT NEWTON, Private

Born in 1831 in Burke County and resided in Cherokee County where he was by occupation a farmer prior to enlisting at Valleytown at age 31, July 24, 1862, for the war. Reported present through April 30, 1863. Reported absent sick at Loudon, Tennessee, from May 10 through June 30, 1863. Reported in hospital at Abingdon, Virginia, in September-October, 1863. Reported on detail as a hospital nurse at Bristol, Tennessee, in November, 1863-February, 1864. No further records. Survived the war.

DERREBERRY, WILLIAM L., Private

Born in 1828 in Burke County and resided in Cherokee County where he was by occupation a farmer prior to enlisting at Valleytown at age 34, July 24, 1862, for the war. Reported present through June 30, 1863, and in September-December, 1863. Reported absent without leave in January-February, 1864. No further records. Survived the war.

DILLS, H. H., _____

North Carolina pension records indicate that he served in this company. Survived the war. [The Charlotte *Western Democrat*, October 25, 1864, reports the wounding of H. Dills of Company G of this regiment at Winchester on September 19, 1864. This might refer to this man.]

DOCKERY, DANIEL W., Private

Born in Buncombe County and resided in Cherokee County where he was by occupation a farmer prior to enlisting at Valleytown at age 28, July 24, 1862, for the war. Reported absent sick through December 31, 1862. Reported present in January-February, 1863. Deserted at Carter's Depot, Tennessee, April 24, 1863. Reported under arrest by sentence of court-martial in May-June, 1863. Reported sick in hospital at White Sulphur Springs, West Virginia, in September, 1863-February, 1864. Name appears on receipt rolls for clothing dated June 17, September 1, and September 18, 1864. No further records. Survived the war. [North Carolina pension records indicate that he was wounded on September 25, 1864. Place wounded not reported.]

DOCKERY, WILLIAM, Private

Born in Buncombe County in 1833 and resided in Cherokee County where he was by occupation a farmer prior to enlisting at Valleytown at age 29, July 24, 1862, for the war. Mustered in as Private. Reported absent sick through December 31, 1862. Reported present in January-June, 1863. Appointed Musician (Fifer) in March-April, 1863. Reported sick in hospital at Abingdon, Virginia, in September-October, 1863. Reported sick in hospital at Emory and Henry, Virginia, November, 1863-February, 1864. Reduced to ranks subsequent to February 29, 1864. Captured in Cherokee County on April 16, 1865. Sent to Knoxville, Chattanooga, and Nashville, Tennessee. Confined at Louisville, Kentucky, May 14, 1865. Released at Louisville on June 16, 1865, after taking the Oath of Allegiance.

DOUGLAS, EDWARD, Private

Born in Sevier County, Tennessee, where he resided as a farmer prior to enlisting in Sevier County at age 36, between July 24 and October 31, 1862, for the war. Reported on detached service through October 31, 1862. Rejoined the company prior to December 31, 1862. Reported on duty as a teamster in the quartermaster department in January-June, 1863. Was assigned for at least part of that time at Strawberry Plains, Tennessee. Reported on detail with Company A, 3rd Regiment Confederate Engineers, September-October, 1863. No further records.

DOUGLAS, JOHN, Private

Born in Sevier County, Tennessee, where he resided as a farmer prior to enlisting at Valleytown at age 37, July 24, 1862, for the war.

Mustered in as Corporal. Reported present through October 31, 1862. Reported on duty as a teamster in the quartermaster's department in November, 1862-June, 1863. Was at Strawberry Plains, Tennessee, for at least part of that period. Reduced to ranks in January-February, 1863. Reported on detached duty with Col. William H. Thomas in September, 1863. Subsequently reported as having deserted at Mossy Creek, Tennessee, October 1, 1863. Went over to the enemy on an unspecified date. Took the Oath of Allegiance at Knoxville, Tennessee, on or about January 10, 1864.

DRIVER, DICKEY, _____

North Carolina pension records appear to indicate that he served in this company.

DURHAM, JAMES, Private

Born in Macon County and resided in Blount County, Tennessee, where he was by occupation a farmer prior to enlisting at Valleytown at age 22, between July 24 and October 31, 1862, for the war. Reported present through December 31, 1862. Deserted on January 20, 1863.

EDWARDS, J. A. P., _____

North Carolina pension records appear to indicate that he served in this company. Survived the war.

ELY, ROBERT, Private

Previously served as Private in Company A, Walker's Battalion. Transferred to this company in March-April, 1863. Deserted at Carter's Depot, Tennessee, April 24, 1863. Reported under arrest by sentence of court-martial on June 30, 1863. Returned to duty on an unspecified date. Deserted at Carter's Depot on September 17, 1863.

EVERETT, SIGNOR, Private

Previously served as Private in Company E, 3rd Regiment Tennessee Infantry (Vaughn's). Enlisted in this company at Valleytown at age 25, July 24, 1862, for the war. Mustered in as Corporal. Reported present through December 31, 1862. Deserted on January 20, 1863, and was reduced to ranks. [Born in Sevier County, Tennessee, and resided in Blount County, Tennessee, where he was by occupation a farmer. Was age 25 at the time of his enlistment in this company. It is not clear whether he transferred to this company or left the 3rd Regiment Tennessee Infantry prior to his enlistment in this company.]

FAN, JACOB P., Private

Born in Greene County, Tennessee, and resided in Knox County, Tennessee, where he was by occupation a tailor prior to enlisting in Knox County at age 17, between July 24 and October 31, 1862, for the war. Reported on detached service on October 31, 1862; was probably with 2nd Company A of this regiment. Reported present in January-February, 1863. Reported on detail as a tailor making clothing for the army in March-June, 1863. Reported on detail as a brakeman on the East Tennessee and Virginia Railroad in September, 1863-February, 1864. No further records. [His first name may have been Joseph. His middle initial may have been T.]

FLOYD, HENRY, Private

Born in Sevier County, Tennessee, where he resided as a farmer prior to enlisting in Sevier County at age 18, between July 24 and October 31, 1862, for the war. Reported on detached service working on roads through December 31, 1862. Deserted on January 1, 1863.

FORRISTER, JOHN C., Private

Previously served in Company A, 29th Regiment N.C. Troops. Enlisted in this company at Strawberry Plains, Tennessee, November 15, 1862, for the war. Reported present in January-February, 1863. Transferred to Company H, Walker's Battalion, March 1, 1863. [His surname may have been Forester or Farrister.]

GARRISH, SAMUEL M., Private

Born in McDowell County and resided in Cherokee County where he was by occupation a farmer prior to enlisting at Valleytown at age 18, between July 24 and October 31, 1862, for the war. Mustered in as Private. Reported present through February 28, 1863. Appointed Musician (Drummer) in January-February, 1863. Reduced to ranks prior to June 30, 1863. Reported present in May-June, 1863. Reported in hospital at Abingdon, Virginia, September-October, 1863. Returned to duty in November-December, 1863. Reported in hospital at Emory and Henry, Virginia, January-February, 1864. Hospitalized at Charlottesville, Virginia, June 10, 1864, with a gunshot contusion of the left hand. Place and date wounded not reported, but probably at Piedmont, Virginia, on June 5, 1864. Returned to duty on August 5, 1864. No further records. Survived the war. [North Carolina pension records indicate that he was wounded at Rockfish Gap, Virginia, in 1864.]

GRANT, JAMES, Private

Enlisted at Strawberry Plains, Tennessee, January 11, 1863, for the war. Reported present through April 30, 1863. No further records. [A notation on his muster roll dated January-February, 1863, states that he served as 1st Sergeant from October 31, 1862, until January 11, 1863; however, his name does not appear on any muster rolls dated 1862.]

GREEN, GEORGE W., Private

Previously served as Private in Company G, Walker's Battalion. Transferred to this company on or about September 24, 1862. Reported present in January-April, 1863. Transferred to Company D of this regiment in May-June, 1863. [He may have been the same man as Pvt. George W. Green of Companies H and E, Walker's Battalion.]

GRIFFITH, JAMES A., Private

North Carolina pension records appear to indicate that he served in this company. Survived the war.

GWYNN, SAMUEL H., Private

Enlisted in Company F of this regiment, but that enlistment was cancelled when he enrolled in this company on July 24, 1862. Reported on detached service on October 31, 1862. Rejoined the company on or prior to December 31, 1862. Reported present in January-June, 1863. Transferred to Levi's Battery on July 1, 1863.

HAMPTON, HARVEY H., Private

Born in Macon County and resided in Cherokee County where he was by occupation a farmer prior to enlisting at Valleytown at age 35, July 24, 1862, for the war. Reported present through December 31, 1862. Reported "detached to Cherokee Co., N.C., after deserters

& now absent without leave" in January-February, 1863. Returned to duty in March-April, 1863. Reported present in May-June, 1863. Transferred to Company H, Walker's Battalion, July 1, 1863. [His first name or middle name may have been Henry.]

HARRIS, JAMES, Private
Previously served as Private in Company A, Walker's Battalion. Transferred to this company on April 1, 1863. Deserted at Carter's Depot, Tennessee, April 24, 1863. Reported under arrest by sentence of court-martial in May-June, 1863. Returned to duty on an unspecified date. Deserted at Carter's Depot on September 17, 1863.

HARRIS, WILLIAM F., Private
Born in Lee County, Virginia, and resided in Cherokee County where he was by occupation a farmer prior to enlisting at age 28, November 15, 1862, for the war. Reported present in January-February, 1863. Deserted at Carter's Depot, Tennessee, April 24, 1863. Reported under arrest by sentence of court-martial in May-June, 1863. Returned to duty on an unspecified date. Deserted at Carter's Depot on September 25, 1863. [He may have served previously in Company A, 29th Regiment N.C. Troops. His middle initial may have been Y.]

HARRISON, J. N., Private
Enlisted in Sevier County, Tennessee, December 1, 1862, for the war. Reported present through December 31, 1862. Reported on detached service "working & repairing road" in January-April, 1863. Reported on detached service at Strawberry Plains, Tennessee, in May-June, 1863. Reported as absent, "cut off in the evacuation of E[ast] T[ennessee] with Col. Thomas," September-October, 1863. Subsequently reported as having deserted at Mossy Creek, Tennessee, October 1, 1863. [He was probably the same man as I. N. Harrison of Company G of this regiment.]

HENDRIX, ISAAC H., Private
Born in Spartanburg District, South Carolina, and resided in Cherokee County where he was by occupation a farmer prior to enlisting at Valleytown at age 22, July 24, 1862, for the war. Reported present through December 31, 1862. Detailed to Cherokee County "after deserters" in January-February, 1863. Reported absent without leave on February 28, 1863. Returned to duty prior to April 30, 1863. Reported present in May-June, 1863. Reported absent, "cut off in the evacuation of E[ast] T[ennessee] with Col. Thomas," September-October, 1863. Subsequently reported as having deserted at Zollicoffer, Tennessee, on October 11. Returned to duty prior to February 28, 1864. Wounded at Winchester, Virginia, September 19, 1864. No further records. Survived the war. [His surname may have been Hendricks.]

HENRY, THOMAS, Private
Resided in Cherokee County and was by occupation a farmer prior to enlisting at Strawberry Plains, Tennessee, at age 27, between July 24 and October 31, 1862, for the war. Reported present in January-February, 1863. Reported on detached duty as a forage master in March-June, 1863. Was stationed at least part of that time at Strawberry Plains. Reported as absent, "cut off in the evacuation of E[ast] T[ennessee] with Col. Thomas" in September-October, 1863. Subsequently reported as having deserted at Mossy Creek, Tennessee, on October 1, 1863. He was restored to the rolls in January-February, 1864, when "official information" was received of him "being on duty with Col. Thomas" in North Carolina, and his status was officially altered to "absent on detached duty." No further records.

HOLLAND, HUGH J. L., Private
Born in Burke County and resided in Cherokee County where he was by occupation a farmer prior to enlisting Valleytown at age 18, July 24, 1862, for the war. Reported present through October 31, 1862. Discharged on November 30, 1862. Reason discharged not reported.

HUSKINS, WILLIAM, Private
Born in what later became McDowell County. Resided in Cherokee County where he was by occupation a farmer prior to enlisting at Valleytown at age 34, July 24, 1862, for the war. Reported present through April 30, 1863. Transferred or enlisted illegally in Company E, Walker's Battalion, on April 30, 1863.

HYATT, JOHN HOWELL, Private
Resided in Cherokee County and enlisted at Strawberry Plains, Tennessee, February 28, 1863, for the war. Reported present through June 30, 1863, and in September, 1863-February, 1864. Wounded at Piedmont, Virginia, June 5, 1864. Captured in Cherokee County on April 4 or April 16, 1865. Sent to Knoxville, Tennessee. Transferred to Chattanooga, Tennessee, on May 3, 1865. Transferred to Nashville, Tennessee. Transferred to Louisville, Kentucky, where he arrived on May 14, 1865. Took the Oath of Allegiance at Louisville on June 16, 1865, and released the next day.

HYATT, M. A., _____
North Carolina pension records indicate that he served in this company. Survived the war.

HYATT, NATHAN N., 1st Sergeant
Born in Macon County on January 18, 1843. Resided in Cherokee County and was by occupation a farmer prior to enlisting at Valleytown at age 19, July 24, 1862, for the war. Mustered in as Sergeant. Reported present through June 30, 1863. Promoted to 1st Sergeant prior to October 31, 1863. Reported present in September, 1863-February, 1864. Name appears on receipt rolls for clothing dated June 17 and September 1, 1864. No further records. Survived the war. [See Tennessee pension application No. 11761. May have served previously as Private in Company C, 39th Regiment N.C. Troops.]

JOHNSON, JOHN, Private
Born in Burke County and resided in Cherokee County where he was by occupation a farmer prior to enlisting at Strawberry Plains, Tennessee, at age 26, November 15, 1862, for the war. Reported present in January-February, 1863. Transferred to Company H, Walker's Battalion, March 1, 1863.

KIMSEY, WILLIAM S., Musician
Born in Union County, Georgia, and resided in Cherokee County, North Carolina, where he was by occupation a farmer prior to enlisting at Valleytown at age 18, July 24, 1862, for the war. Mustered in as Corporal. Reported present through June 30, 1863. Appointed Musician (Drummer) in July-October, 1863. Reported present in September, 1863-February, 1864. Name appears on receipt rolls for clothing dated June 17 and September 1, 18, and 27, 1864. No further records.

KING, NATHANIEL W., Private

Enlisted at Strawberry Plains, Tennessee, February 14, 1863, for the war. Reported present through February 28, 1863. Reported on detached service working on a road in March-April, 1863. Reported on detached service at Mossy Creek, Tennessee, May-June, 1863. Reported absent, "cut off in the evacuation of E[ast] T[ennnessee] with Col. Thomas in N.C.," September-October, 1863. Subsequently reported as having deserted at Mossy Creek, October 1, 1863.

KINSEY, MATTHEW R., Private

Resided in Cherokee County. Place and date of enlistment not reported; probably enlisted subsequent to February 29, 1864. Captured in Cherokee County on or about April 14, 1865. Sent to Knoxville, Tennessee. Transferred to Chattanooga, Tennessee, on May 3, 1865. Transferred to Nashville, Tennessee. Confined at Louisville, Kentucky, May 15, 1865. Released at Louisville on June 16, 1865, after taking the Oath of Allegiance. [He may have been the same man as M. R. Kimsey of Company B, Indian Battalion.]

KINSLAND, J. T., _____

North Carolina pension records appear to indicate that he served in this company. Survived the war.

LEDFORD, M. M., _____

North Carolina pension records appear to indicate that he served in this company. Survived the war. [One of his given names may have been Madison.]

LOUDERMILK, GEORGE W., Private

Previously served as Private in Company A, 29th Regiment N.C. Troops. Enlisted illegally in this company while a deserter from the 29th Regiment at Strawberry Plains, Tennessee, November 15, 1862, for the war. Reported present in January-February, 1863. Transferred to Company H, Walker's Battalion, March 1, 1863. [His surname may have been Laudermilk.]

LOUDERMILK, MADISON M., Musician

Previously served as Private in Company A, 29th Regiment N.C. Troops. Enlisted illegally in this company while a deserter from the 29th Regiment at Strawberry Plains, Tennessee, November 15, 1862, for the war. Mustered in as Private. Appointed Musician (Fifer) on January 21, 1863. Reported present in January-February, 1863. Transferred to Company H, Walker's Battalion, March 1, 1863. [His surname may have been Laudermilk.]

LOVINGGOOD, DRURY, Private

Born in Macon County and resided in Cherokee County where he was by occupation a farmer prior to enlisting at Valleytown at age 24, July 24, 1862, for the war. Mustered in as Sergeant. Reported present through December 31, 1862. Promoted to 1st Sergeant on January 11, 1863. Reported present through June 30, 1863. Deserted at Bristol, Tennessee, September 2, 1863, and reduced to ranks. Went over to the enemy on an unspecified date. Took the Oath of Allegiance at Knoxville, Tennessee, January 10, 1864. [His first name may have been Drewry.]

McCARTER, ELI, Private

Born in Sevier County, Tennessee, where he resided as a farmer prior to enlisting either in Sevier County, Tennessee, or at Strawberry Plains, Tennessee, between July 24 and October 31, 1862, for the war. Reported absent without leave on December 31, 1862. Reported on detached service working on a road in January-April, 1863. Reported on detached service at Mossy Creek, Tennessee, May-June, 1863. Reported absent, "cut off in the evacuation of E[ast] T[ennessee]," September-October, 1863. Subsequently reported as having deserted at Mossy Creek, October 1, 1863.

McCARTER, G. B., Private

Born in Sevier County, Tennessee, where he resided as a farmer prior to enlisting in either Sevier County, Tennessee or at Strawberry Plains, Tennessee at age 32, between July 24 and October 31, 1862, for the war. Reported present on December 31, 1862. Reported on duty working on a road in January-April, 1863. Reported on detached service at Mossy Creek, Tennessee, May-June, 1863. Reported absent, "cut off in the evacuation of E[ast] T[ennessee] with Col. Thomas," September-October, 1863. Subsequently reported as having deserted at Mossy Creek, October 1, 1863. [His first name may have been George.]

McCARTER, JAMES, Private

Born in Sevier County, Tennessee, where he resided as a farmer prior to enlisting either in Sevier County, Tennessee, or at Strawberry Plains, Tennessee, age 36, between July 24 and October 31, 1862, for the war. Reported on detached service "working on road in [the] charge of R. Collins" through October 31, 1862. Rejoined the company on or prior to December 31, 1862. Reported on detached service working on roads in January-April, 1863. Reported on detached service at Mossy Creek, Tennessee, May-June, 1863. Reported as absent, "cut off in the evacuation of E[ast] T[ennessee] with Col. Thomas," September-October, 1863. Subsequently reported as having deserted at Mossy Creek, Tennessee, October 1, 1863.

MAPLES, DAVID, Private

Born in Sevier County, Tennessee, where he resided as a farmer prior to enlisting in Sevier County at age 33, between July 24 and October 31, 1862, for the war. Reported on detached service through October 31, 1862. Rejoined the company prior to December 31, 1862. Reported on duty working on a road in January-April, 1863. Reported on detached service at Mossy Creek, Tennessee, May-June, 1863. Reported as absent, "cut off in the evacuation of E[ast] T[ennessee] with Col. Thomas" in September-October, 1863. Subsquently reported as having deserted at Mossy Creek on October 1, 1863.

MARONEY, BAILEY B., Private

Born in Blount County, Tennessee, and resided in Cherokee County where he was by occupation a farmer prior to enlisting at Valleytown at age 33, July 24, 1862, for the war. Provided Pvt. Joel W. Shropshire of this company as a substitute on the same day and was thus entitled to an immediate discharge. However, he was reported on sick furlough on October 31, 1862, and reported absent without leave in November, 1862-April, 1863. A muster roll dated May-June, 1863, states that he was "improperly mustered into this company" and was transferred to the 39th Regiment N.C. Troops; however, no other evidence of his service in the 39th Regiment was located.

MOONEY, SYLVANUS, Private

Born in Macon County and resided in Cherokee County where he was by occupation a farmer prior to enlisting at Valleytown at age 33, July 24, 1862, for the war. Reported absent on sick furlough on

October 31, 1862. Reported absent without leave on December 31, 1862, and in January-February, 1863. Returned to duty on or prior to April 30, 1863. Reported present in May-June and September-October, 1863. Furloughed home on December 26, 1863. Reported absent without leave from January 14 through February 29, 1864. No further records.

MOSS, A. M., _____

North Carolina pension records indicate that he served in this company. Survived the war.

NELSON, JOHN, Private

Enlisted at Strawberry Plains, Tennessee, March 9, 1863, for the war. Reported present through June 30, 1863. Reported absent, "cut off in the evacuation of E[ast] T[ennessee] with Col. Thomas" in September-October, 1863. Subsequently reported as having deserted at Carter's Depot, Tennessee, September 25, 1863.

NEWMAN, DAVID, Private

Resided in Cherokee County and was by occupation a miller prior to enlisting at Strawberry Plains, Tennessee, at age 27, March 9, 1863, for the war. Reported present through June 30, 1863. Deserted at Zollicoffer, Tennessee, September 6, 1863.

NEWMAN, JAMES, Corporal

Previously enlisted as Private in Company G, 39th Regiment N.C. Troops. Failed to report for duty with that unit. Enlisted in this company in Cherokee County on July 24, 1862, for the war. Mustered in as Musician (Drummer). Reported present through June and in September-October, 1863. Promoted to Corporal in January-February, 1863. Reported sick in hospital at Rogersville, Tennessee, in November-December, 1863. Died in hospital at Bristol, Tennessee, February 20, 1864. Cause of death not reported.

NEWMAN, TERRELL N., Private

Previously enlisted as Private in Company G, 39th Regiment N.C. Troops. Failed to report for duty with that unit. Enlisted in this company in Cherokee County on July 24, 1862, for the war. Mustered in as Private. Reported present or accounted for through June, 1863. Appointed Musician (Drummer) in March-April, 1863. Reduced to ranks in July-October, 1863. Reported present in September-October, 1863. Reported on duty as a hospital nurse near Rogersville, Tennessee, in November-December, 1863. Rejoined the company on or prior to February 29, 1864. Captured at Berryville, Virginia, August 10, 1864. Confined at Old Capitol Prison, Washington, D.C., August 17, 1864. Transferred to Elmira, New York, where he arrived on August 29, 1864. Died at Elmira on February 19, 1865, of "chro[nic] diarrh[oea]." [Contrary to 10:166 of this series, his first was probably Terrell.]

NEWMAN, WILLIAM LIVINGSTON, Private

Born on April 11, 1837, in what later became Polk County. Resided in Cherokee County where he was by occupation a farmer prior to enlisting at Valleytown at age 25, July 24, 1862, for the war. Mustered in as Private. Reported present through June, 1863. Promoted to Corporal in January-February, 1863. Reduced to ranks in July-October, 1863. Reported absent in hospital at Abingdon, Virginia, September-October, 1863. Returned to duty on or prior to December 31, 1863. Reported present in January-February, 1864. "Wounded slightly" at Piedmont, Virginia, June 5, 1864. Name appears on receipt rolls for clothing dated June 17, September 1, September 18, and September 27, 1864. No further records. Survived the war.

NEWMAN, WILLIS, Private

Resided in Cherokee County and was by occupation a farmer prior to enlisting at Strawberry Plains, Tennessee, at age 36, March 9, 1863, for the war. Reported present in May-June 30, 1863. Reported sick in hospital at Abingdon, Virginia, in September, 1863-February, 1864. No further records. Survived the war.

OGLE, ANDREW, Private

Resided in Sevier County, Tennessee, and was by occupation a farmer prior to enlisting at Strawberry Plains, Tennessee, at about age 24, February 14, 1863, for the war. Reported present on February 28, 1863. Reported on detached service working on a road in March-April, 1863. Reported on detached service at Mossy Creek, Tennessee, May-June, 1863. Reported absent, "cut off in the evacuation of East Tenn[essee] supposed to be with Col. W. H. Thomas in N.C.," September-October, 1863. Subsequently reported as having deserted at Mossy Creek on October 1, 1863.

OGLE, ARTHUR, Private

Born in Sevier County, Tennessee, where he resided as a farmer. Previously served as Private in Company A, 31st Regiment Tennessee Infantry (W. M. Bradford's). Enlisted in this company at Smoky Mountain at age 20, between July 24 and October 31, 1862, for the war, while a deserter from the 31st Tennessee. Reported on detached service repairing roads "in [the] charge of R. Collins" on October 31, 1862. Reported absent without leave on December 31, 1862, by which time he had returned to duty with his company in the 31st Tennessee. Reported on detached service from this company working on roads on February 28, 1863, although records for the 31st Tennessee indicate that he was on duty with that unit. Survived the war. [The 31st Regiment Tennessee Infantry (W. M. Bradford's) was redesignated the 39th Regiment Tennessee Infantry in June 1863 and the 39th Regiment Tennessee Mounted Infantry by the end of the year. See *Tennesseans in the Civil War*, 1:259, 263. All National Archives service record files for the unit are under the latter name.]

OGLE, BRADFORD, Private

Born in Sevier County, Tennessee, where he resided as a farmer. Previously served as Private in Company A, 31st Regiment Tennessee Infantry (W. M. Bradford's). Enlisted in this company at Smoky Mountain at age 23, between July 24 and October 31, 1862, for the war, while a deserter from the 31st Tennessee. Reported on detached service repairing roads "in [the] charge of R. Collins" on October 31, 1862. Reported absent without leave on December 31, 1862. Returned to duty on or prior to February 28, 1863, when he was reported on detached service working on roads. No further records. Survived the war. [The 31st Regiment Tennessee Infantry (W. M. Bradford's) was redesignated the 39th Regiment Tennessee Infantry in June 1863 and the 39th Regiment Tennessee Mounted Infantry by the end of the year. All National Archives service record files for the unit are under the latter name.]

OGLE, CALEB, Private

Born in Sevier County, Tennessee, where he resided as a farmer prior to enlisting at Smoky Mountain at age 32, between July 24 and October 31, 1862, for the war. Reported on detached service repairing roads "in [the] charge of R. Collins" on October 31, 1862.

Rejoined the company prior to December 31, 1862. Reported on detached service working on roads in January-April, 1863. Reported on detached service at Mossy Creek, Tennessee, May-June, 1863. Reported absent, "[c]ut off in the evacuation of E[ast] T[ennessee] with Col. W. H. Thomas," September-October, 1863. Subsequently reported as having deserted at Mossy Creek on October 1, 1863.

OGLE, CARTER, Private
Enlisted in Sevier County, Tennessee, between July 24 and October 31, 1862, for the war. Reported absent without leave on December 31, 1862. Reported on detached service working on a road in January-April, 1863. Reported on detached service at Mossy Creek, Tennessee, May-June, 1863. Reported absent, "[c]ut off in the evacuation of East Tenn[essee] supposed to be with Col. W. H. Thomas in N.C.," September-October, 1863. Subsequently reported as having deserted at Mossy Creek on October 1, 1863.

OGLE, CASWELL T., Private
Born in Sevier County, Tennessee, where he resided as a farmer. Previously served as Private in Company A, 31st Regiment Tennessee Infantry (W. M. Bradford's). Enlisted in this company at Smoky Mountain at age 20, between July 24 and October 31, 1862, for the war, while a deserter from the 31st Tennessee. Reported on detached service repairing roads "in [the] charge of R. Collins" on October 31, 1862. Reported absent without leave on December 31, 1862, by which time he had returned to duty with his company in the 31st Tennessee. Reported on detached service from this company working on roads on February 28, 1863, although records for the 31st Tennessee indicate that he was on duty with that unit. Survived the war. [The 31st Regiment Tennessee Infantry (W. M. Bradford's) was redesignated the 39th Regiment Tennessee Infantry in June 1863 and the 39th Regiment Tennessee Mounted Infantry by the end of the year. See *Tennesseans in the Civil War*, 1:259, 263. All National Archives service record files for the unit are under the latter name.]

OGLE, E. T., Private
Born in Sevier County, Tennessee, where he resided as a farmer prior to enlisting at Smoky Mountain at age 34, between July 24 and October 31, 1862, for the war. Reported on detached service repairing roads "in the charge of R. Collins" on October 31, 1862. Rejoined the company prior to December 31, 1862. Reported on duty working on roads in January-April, 1863. Reported on detached service at Mossy Creek, Tennessee, May-June, 1863. Reported absent, "[c]ut off in the evacuation of E[ast] T[ennessee] with Col.W. H. Thomas," September-October, 1863. Subsequently reported as having deserted at Mossy Creek on October 1, 1863. [His first name may have been Eli.]

OGLE, ELISHA, Private
Born in Sevier County, Tennessee, where he resided as a farmer prior to enlisting at Smoky Mountain at age 36, between July 24 and October 31, 1862, for the war. Reported on detached service repairing roads "in [the] charge of R. Collins" on October 31, 1862. Rejoined the company prior to December 31, 1862. Reported working on roads in January-April, 1863. Reported on detached service at Mossy Creek, Tennessee, May-June, 1863. Reported as absent, "[c]ut off in the evacuation of East Tenn[essee] supposed to be with Col. W. H. Thomas in N.C.," September-October, 1863. Subsequently reported as having deserted at Mossy Creek on October 1, 1863.

OGLE, GILBERT, Private
Born in Sevier County, Tennessee, where he resided as a farmer. Previously served as private in Company A, 31st Regiment Tennessee Infantry (W. M. Bradford's). Enlisted in this company at Smoky Mountain at age 22, July 24, 1862, for the war, while a deserter from the 31st Tennessee. Reported on detached service repairing roads "in the charge of R. Collins" through October 31, 1862. Reported absent without leave on December 31, 1862, by which time he had returned to duty with his company in the 31st Tennessee. Reported on detached service from this company working on roads on February 28, 1863, although records for the 31st Tennessee indicate that he was on service with that unit. No further records. [The 31st Regiment Tennessee Infantry (W. M. Bradford's) was redesignated the 39th Regiment Tennessee Infantry in June 1863 and the 39th Regiment Tennessee Mounted Infantry by the end of the year. See *Tennesseans in the Civil War*, 1:259, 263. All National Archives service record files for the unit are under the latter name. His first name may have been Silbert.]

OGLE, HENRY, Private
Resided in Sevier County, Tennessee, and was by occupation a farmer prior to enlisting in Sevier County at age 29, October 5, 1862, for the war. Reported present, December 31, 1862. Reported on duty working on roads in January-April, 1863. Reported on detached service at Mossy Creek, Tennessee, May-June, 1863. Reported absent, "[c]ut off in the evacuation of E[ast] Tenn[essee] with Col. W. H. Thomas," September-October, 1863. Subsequently reported as having deserted at Mossy Creek on October 1, 1863.

OGLE, LEVI, Private
Resided in Sevier County, Tennessee, and was by occupation a farmer prior to enlisting in Sevier County at age 28, October 5, 1862, for the war. Reported present through December 31, 1862. Reported on duty working on roads in January-April, 1863. Reported on detached service at Mossy Creek, Tennessee, May-June, 1863. Reported absent, "[c]ut off in the evacuation of E[ast] T[ennessee] with Col. W. H. Thomas." Subsequently reported as having deserted at Mossy Creek on October 1, 1863.

OGLE, PRESTON, Private
Born in Sevier County, Tennessee, where he resided as a farmer prior to enlisting at Smoky Mountain at age 37, between July 24 and October 31, 1862, for the war. Reported on detached service repairing roads "in [the] charge of R. Collins" through October 31, 1862. Rejoined the company prior to December 31, 1862. Reported on duty working on roads in January-April, 1863. Reported on detached service at Mossy Creek, Tennessee, May-June, 1863. Reported absent, "[c]ut off in the evacution of E[ast] T[ennessee] with Col. W. H. Thomas," September-October, 1863. Subsequently reported as having deserted at Mossy Creek on October 1, 1863.

OGLE, SAMUEL, Private
Born in Sevier County, Tennessee, where he resided as a farmer prior to enlisting at Smoky Mountain at age 19, between July 24 and October 31, 1862, for the war. Reported on detached service repairing roads "in [the] charge of R. Collins" through October 31, 1862. Rejoined the company prior to December 31, 1862. Reported on duty working on roads in January-February, 1863. Reported on detached service, March-April, 1863. Reported on detached service at Mossy Creek, Tennessee, May-June, 1863. Reported absent, "[c]ut off in the evacuation of East Tenn[essee] supposed to be with Col. W. H. Thomas," September-October, 1863. Subsequently reported as having deserted at Mossy Creek on October 1, 1863.

OGLE, THOMAS I., Private

Born in Sevier County, Tennessee, where he resided as a farmer. Previously served as Private in Company A, 31st Regiment Tennessee Infantry (W. M. Bradford's). Enlisted at Smoky Mountain at age 48, between July 24 and October 31, 1862, for the war, while a deserter from the 31st Tennessee. Reported on detached service repairing roads "in [the] charge of R. Collins" through October 31, 1862. Reported absent without leave on December 31, 1862. Returned to duty on or prior to February 28, 1863, when he was reported on detached service working on roads. No further records. Survived the war. [The 31st Regiment Tennessee Infantry (W. M. Bradford's) was redesignated the 39th Regiment Tennessee Infantry in June 1863 and the 39th Regiment Tennessee Mounted Infantry by the end of the year. See *Tennesseans in the Civil War*, 1:259, 263. All National Archives service record files for the unit are under the latter name.]

PACK, JOSHUA, Private

Born in Cherokee County where he resided as a farmer prior to enlisting at Strawberry Plains, Tennessee, at age 23, November 15, 1862, for the war. Reported on detached service working on roads, January-April, 1863. Reported absent sick in Cherokee County in May-June and September-October, 1863. Subsequently reported as having deserted at Mossy Creek, Tennessee, October 1, 1863.

PACK, THOMAS, Private

Previously served as Private in Company A, 29th Regiment N.C. Troops. Illegally enlisted in this company at Strawberry Plains, Tennessee, November 15, 1862, for the war, while a deserter from the 29th Regiment. Reported on detached service working on roads in January-April, 1863. Reported present in May-June, 1863, and September, 1863-February, 1864. Name appears on receipt rolls for clothing dated June 17, September 1, and September 18, 1864. No further records.

PADGETT, WILLIAM A., _____

North Carolina pension records appear to indicate that he served in this company. Survived the war.

PALMER, THOMAS, Corporal

Born in Buncombe County and resided in Cherokee County where he was by occupation a farmer prior to enlisting at Valleytown at age 34, July 24, 1862, for the war. Mustered in as Private. Reported present through December 31, 1862. Promoted to Corporal in January-February, 1863. Reported present through February 28, 1863. Reported on detail to Cherokee County after deserters, April 27-30, 1863. Returned to duty prior to June 30, 1863. Reported present in September, 1863-February, 1864. Hospitalized at Winchester, Virginia, August 1, 1864, with debilitas. Name appears on receipt rolls for clothing dated September 1 and September 18, 1864. No further records. Survived the war.

PARKER, WILLIAM, Corporal

Born in Grainger County, Tennessee, and resided in Union County, Tennessee, where he was by occupation a farmer prior to enlisting at Valleytown at age 28, July 24, 1862, for the war. Mustered in as Corporal. Reported present through December 31, 1862. Reduced to ranks in January-February, 1863. Reported present through January-April, 1863. Reported on detached service at Carter's Depot, Tennessee, May-June, 1863. Reported present in September, 1863-February, 1864. Name appears on receipt rolls for clothing dated September 1 and September 18, 1864. No further records. Survived the war.

PARKER, WILLIAM ASBERRY, Private

Born in 1834 in the part of Macon County that later became Cherokee County. Resided in Cherokee County as a farmer prior to enlisting at Valleytown at age 28, July 24, 1862, for the war. Reported on sick furlough on October 31, 1862. Rejoined the company on or prior to December 31, 1862. Discharged on January 3, 1863. Reason discharged not reported.

PETTY, MARION, Private

Born in Sevier County, Tennessee, where he resided as a farmer prior to enlisting in Sevier County at age 35, between July 24 and October 31, 1862, for the war. Reported on detached service repairing roads "in [the] charge of R. Collins," October 31, 1862. Deserted on December 15, 1862.

PRINCE, MARTIN V., Private

Previously served as Private in Company A, 29th Regiment N.C. Troops. Enlisted illegally in this company at Strawberry Plains, Tennessee, November 15, 1862, for the war, while a deserter from Company A, 29th Regiment N.C. Troops. Reported present in January-April, 1863. No further records.

PRITCHET, WILLIAM, Private

Enlisted at Carter's Depot, Tennessee, April 28, 1863, for the war. Deserted at Carter's Depot on May 1, 1863.

PRUIT, W., _____

The Charlotte *Western Democrat*, October 25, 1864, indicates that he served in this company and was captured at Winchester, Virginia, September 19, 1864. [He may have been the same man as either (W.) D. S. Puett or as Pvt. William H. Truett of this company.]

PUETT, D. S., _____

North Carolina pension records appear to indicate that he served in this company. Survived the war. [His name may have been W. D. S. Puett. He may have been the same man as W. Pruit above.]

REAGAN, JAMES, Private

Born in Sevier County, Tennessee, where he resided as a farmer prior to enlisting in Sevier County at age 19, between July 24 and October 31, 1862, for the war. Reported on detached duty repairing roads "in [the] charge of R. Collins" through October 31, 1862. Rejoined the company prior to December 31, 1862. Reported on duty working on roads, January-April, 1863. Reported on detached duty at Strawberry Plains, Tennessee, May-June, 1863. Reported as absent, "cut off in the evacuation of E[ast] T[ennessee] supposed to be with Col. Thomas," September-October, 1863. Subsequently reported as having deserted at Mossy Creek, Tennessee, October 1, 1863.

REESE, HENRY, Private

Born in Sevier County, Tennessee, where he resided as a farmer prior to enlisting in Sevier County at age 22, between July 24 and October 31, 1862, for the war. Reported present through February 28, 1863. Reported on detached service as a wagoner in the quartermaster's department, March-June, 1863. Was on duty at Strawberry

Plains, Tennessee, for at least part of that time. Reported absent, "cut off in the evacuation of E[ast] T[ennessee] supposed to be with Col. Thomas," September-October, 1863. Subsequently was erroneously reported as having deserted at Mossy Creek, Tennessee, on October 1, 1863. Restored to the rolls and reported on detached duty with Thomas in January-February, 1864. Deserted to the enemy on an unknown date. Sent to Knoxville, Tennessee. Released at Knoxville on February 27, 1864, after taking the Oath of Allegiance.

RHODARMER, W. T., Private

North Carolina pension records and records of the United Daughters of the Confederacy appear to indicate that he served in this company. Survived the war.

RICE, HENRY, Private

Enlisted at Smoky Mountain between July 24 and October 31, 1862, for the war. Reported on detached duty repairing roads "in [the] charge of R. Collins" through October 31, 1862. No further records.

ROANE, PATRICK HERN, 1st Sergeant

Previously served as Private in Company H, 16th Regiment N.C. Troops (6th Regiment N.C. Volunteers). Enlisted in this company in Knox County, Tennessee, at age 21, between July 24 and October 31, 1862, for the war. Mustered in as 1st Sergeant. Reported present or accounted for through December 31, 1862. No further records. [He may have served later as Private in Companies C and F, 62nd Regiment Tennessee Infantry.]

ROBERTS, DANIEL, Private

Born in Sevier County, Tennessee, where he resided as a farmer prior to enlisting in Sevier County at age 21, between July 24 and October 31, 1862, for the war. Reported on detached service repairing roads "in [the] charge of R. Collins" through October 31, 1862. Rejoined the company prior to December 31, 1862. Reported on duty working on roads in January-April, 1863. Reported on detached service at Strawberry Plains, Tennessee, May-June, 1863. Reported absent, "cut off in the evacuation of E[ast] T[ennessee], supposed to be with Col. Thomas," September-October, 1863. Subsequently reported as having deserted at Mossy Creek, Tennessee, October 1, 1863.

ROBERTS, JOHN, Private

Born in Sevier County, Tennessee, where he resided as a farmer prior to enlisting in Sevier County at age 35, between July 24 and October 31, 1862, for the war. Reported on detached service repairing roads "in [the] charge of R. Collins" through October 31, 1862. Rejoined the company prior to December 31, 1862. Reported on duty working on roads, January-April, 1863. Reported on detached service at Strawberry Plains, Tennessee, May-June, 1863. Reported absent, "cut off in the evacuation of E[ast] T[ennessee,] supposed to be with Col. Thomas," September-October, 1863. Deserted at Mossy Creek, Tennessee, October 1, 1863.

ROBINSON, JOSEPH L., Private

North Carolina pension records appear to indicate that he served in Company I of Walker's Battalion; however, Walker's Battalion did not have a Company I. One of the witnesses for his pension application was a Capt. N. G. Philips. Nathaniel Greene Philips was 1st Lieutenant of this company, so it is likely that he served in this company. Survived the war.

ROGERS, J. TAYLOR, Private

Resided in Haywood County. Place and date of enlistment not reported. Deserted to the enemy at Waynesville on March 15, 1865. Confined at Knoxville, Tennessee, April 1, 1865. Transferred to Chattanooga, Tennessee. Transferred to Louisville, Kentucky, where he arrived on April 10, 1865. Released at Louisville on April 13, 1865, after taking the Oath of Allegiance, with orders to remain north of the Ohio River for the remainder of the war. [He may have been the same man as John T. Rogers of Company B, Walker's Battalion.]

ROGERS, JAMES R., _____

North Carolina pension records indicate that he served in Company I of Walker's Battalion; however, Walker's Battalion did not have a Company I. One of the witnesses for his pension application was a Capt. N. G. Philips. Nathaniel Greene Philips was 1st Lieutenant of this company, so it is likely that he served in this company. Survived the war.

RUSSELL, WILLIAM, Private

Born in Sevier County, Tennessee, where he resided as a farmer prior to enlisting in Sevier County at age 36, between July 24 and October 31, 1862, for the war. Reported on detached service repairing roads "in [the] charge of R. Collins" through October 31, 1862. Reported on detached service as a cooper "making vessels for army," November, 1862-June, 1863. Reported "cut off in the evacuation of E[ast] T[ennessee] supposed to be with Col. Thomas," September-October, 1863. Subsequently reported as having deserted at Mossy Creek, Tennessee, October 1, 1863.

SEATON, WILLIAM B., Private

Enlisted at Strawberry Plains, Tennessee, October 4, 1862, for the war. Reported present in January-February, 1863. Reported on detached service working on roads in March-April, 1863. Reported on detached service at Strawberry Plains, Tennessee, May-June, 1863. Reported "cut off in the evacuation of E[ast] T[ennessee] supposed to be with Col. Thomas," September-October, 1863. Subsequently reported as having deserted at Mossy Creek, Tennessee, October 1, 1863.

SHROPSHIRE, JOEL W., Private

Born in Hawkins County, Tennessee, and resided in Cherokee County, North Carolina, where he was by occupation a farmer prior to enlisting at Valleytown on July 24, 1862, for the war as a substitute for Pvt. Bailey B. Maroney of this company. Deserted on October 29, 1862.

STEWART, JOHN HANNIBAL, Sergeant

Born in Burke County and resided in Cherokee County where he was by occupation a farmer prior to enlisting at Valleytown at age 18, July 24, 1862, for the war. Mustered in as Private. Reported on sick furlough on October 31, 1862. Returned to duty prior to December 31, 1862. Reported present in January-April, 1863; however, he is also reported absent sick at Strawberry Plains, Tennessee, March 10-June 30, 1863, in the May-June, 1863, muster roll. Captured at Strawberry Plains, Tennessee, June 20, 1863, and paroled there the next day. Reported present in September-October, 1863, and January-February, 1864. Promoted to Sergeant in March-June, 1864. Name appears on receipt rolls for clothing dated June 17, September 1, and September 18, 1864. No further records. Survived the war. [An 1897 letter seems to indicate that he served as 1st Lieutenant of this company. If he did, it was probably subsequent to October 9, 1864. See John H. Stewart to "Dear Otis," William Williams Stringfield Papers, Special Collections, Hunter Library, Western Carolina University.]

STINNETT, WILLIAM, Private
Born in Sevier County, Tennessee, where he resided as a farmer prior to enlisting in Sevier County at age 23, between July 24 and October 31, 1862, for the war. Reported on duty working on roads in January-April, 1863. Reported on detached service at Strawberry Plains, Tennessee, in May-June, 1863. Reported absent, "cut off in the evacuation of E[ast] T[ennessee] supposed to be with Col. Thomas" in September-October, 1863. Subsequently reported as having deserted at Mossy Creek, Tennessee, October 1, 1863.

STOCKTON, JAMES M., _____
North Carolina pension records indicate that he served in this company. Survived the war.

SUTTON, WILLIAM M., Private
Born in Sevier County, Tennessee, where he resided as a farmer prior to enlisting at "Smoky Mt., N.C." at age 25, between July 24 and October 31, 1862, for the war. Reported on detached service repairing roads "in [the] charge of R Collins" through December 31, 1862. Deserted on January 25, 1863. Returned to duty and was transferred to Company G of this regiment in March-April, 1863.

TERNER, JAMES, Private
Previously served as Private in Company E of this regiment. Transferred to this company on or about April 29, 1863. Reported present on April 30, 1863. No further records. [His surname may have been Turner.]

TIDWELL, REUBEN W., Private
Previously served as 1st Lieutenant in Company G, 30th Regiment Georgia Infantry. Defeated in election when that company reorganized as Company H, April 23, 1862, and retired, May 14, 1862. Enlisted in this company on July 24, 1862, for the war. Reported on detached service repairing roads "in [the] charge of R. Collins" through September 27, 1862. Appointed Assistant Commissary of Subsistence (Captain) and transferred to the Field and Staff of this regiment on or about September 27, 1862.

TOOMEY, JAMES, Private
Enlisted in Knox County, Tennessee, December 25, 1862, for the war. Reported on detached service working on roads in January-April, 1863. Reported on detached service at Strawberry Plains, Tennessee, May-June, 1863. Reported absent, "cut off in the evacuation of E[ast] T[ennessee], supposed to be with Col. Thomas," September-October, 1863. Subsequently reported as having deserted at Mossy Creek, Tennessee, October 1, 1863.

TRANTHAM, J. V., Private
Born in Sevier County, Tennessee, where he resided as a farmer prior to enlisting in Sevier County between July 24 and October 31, 1862, for the war. Reported present through December 31, 1862. Reported on detached service working on roads in January-April, 1863. Reported on detached service at Strawberry Plains, Tennessee, May-June, 1863. Reported absent, "cut off in the evacuation of E[ast] T[ennessee], supposed to be with Col. Thomas," September-October, 1863. Subsequently reported as having deserted at Mossy Creek, Tennessee, October 1, 1863. [His given name may have been Isaac. His surname may have been Trentham.]

TRUETT, CHARLES L., Private
Previously served as Private in Company B, 7th Battalion N.C. Cavalry. Transferred to this company in May-June, 1863. Reported present on June 30, 1863, and in September, 1863-February, 1864. No further records. Survived the war. [May have subsequently been appointed Lieutenant of Company B, Indian Battalion.]

TRUETT, WILLIAM H., Private
Previously served as Private in Company B, 7th Battalion N.C. Cavalry. Transferred to this company in May-June, 1863. Reported present on June 30, 1863, and in September, 1863-February, 1864. Captured at Winchester, Virginia, September 19, 1864. Sent to Harpers Ferry, West Virginia. Transferred to Point Lookout, Maryland, September 23, 1864. Released at Point Lookout on June 4, 1865, after taking the Oath of Allegiance. Admitted to a Federal hospital at Fort Monroe, Virginia, June 5, 1865, with scofula. Discharged from hospital on July 5, 1865.

VENABLE, ISAAC M., Private
Born in DeKalb County, Alabama, where he resided as a farmer prior to enlisting at Valleytown at age 21, July 24, 1862, for the war. Reported present through June 30, 1863, and in September-December, 1863; was assigned to extra duty from October 24 to October 31, 1863. Reported sick in hospital at Emory and Henry, Virginia, in January-February, 1864. Captured by the enemy on an unspecified date. Took the Oath of Allegiance at Nashville, Tennessee, May 10, 1864.

WALKER, CHARLES A., Private
Enlisted at Carter's Depot, Tennessee, January 1, 1864, for the war. Captured at Winchester, Virginia, September 19, 1864. Sent to Harpers Ferry, West Virginia. Transferred to Point Lookout, Maryland, September 23, 1864. Paroled at Point Lookout January 17, 1865. Received at Boulware's Wharf, James River, Virginia, January 21, 1865, for exchange. No further records. [He may have been the same man as Pvt. Charles Agnew Walker of Company E, Walker's Battalion.]

WATSON, DAVID, Private
Born in what later became Jackson County. Resided in Sevier County, Tennessee, where he was by occupation a farmer prior to enlisting in Sevier County at age 34, between July 24 and October 31, 1862, for the war. Reported present through December 31, 1862. Reported on duty working on roads in January-April, 1863. Reported on detached service at Strawberry Plains, Tennessee, May-June, 1863. Reported absent, "cut off in the evacuation of E[ast] T[ennessee], supposed to be with Col. Thomas" in September-October, 1863. Subsequently reported as having deserted at Mossy Creek, Tennessee, October 1, 1863.

WEAVER, JOHN W., Private
Born in Surry County and resided in Knox County, Tennessee, where he was by occupation a tailor prior to enlisting in Knox County at age 31, between July 24 and October 31, 1862, for the war. Reported absent on detached service repairing roads through October 31, 1862; he may have been attached to 2nd Company A of

this regiment at that time. Rejoined the company prior to December 31, 1862. Reported present in January-February, 1863. Reported on detached service making clothing for the army in March-June, 1863. Reported absent, "cut off in the evacuation of E[ast] T[ennessee], supposed to be with Col. Thomas," September-October, 1863. Subsequently reported as having deserted at Mossy Creek, Tennessee, October 1, 1863.

WELCH, JOHN R., Private

Enlisted at Strawberry Plains, Tennessee, March 9, 1863, for the war. Reported absent on detached service "after deserters" in Cherokee County through June 30, 1863. Reported absent, "cut off in the evacuation of E[ast] T[ennessee,] supposed to be with Col. Thomas," September-October, 1863. Subsequently reported as having deserted at Mossy Creek, Tennessee, October 1, 1863.

WHITAKER, JESSE U., Sergeant

Born in Macon County and resided in Cherokee County where he was by occupation a farmer prior to enlisting at Valleytown at age 31, July 24, 1862, for the war. Mustered in as Private. Reported on sick furlough through December 31, 1862. Promoted to Sergeant and detailed to Cherokee County "after deserters" in January-February, 1863. Rejoined the company prior to April 30, 1863. Reported present in May-June, 1863. Detailed as a nurse for "wounded brother" in hospital at White Sulphur Springs, West Virginia, October 12, 1863. Reported on hospital detail at White Sulphur Springs through February 29, 1864. [His brother was probably Pvt. James M. Whitaker of Company E, Walker's Battalion.]

WILLIAMS, JESSE, Private

Born in Blount County, Tennessee, and resided in Macon County, North Carolina, where he was by occupation a farmer prior to enlisting at Valleytown at age 33, July 24, 1862, for the war. Reported on detached service guarding ferry at Rocky Point, Tennessee, through June 30, 1863. Reported absent, "cut off in the evacuation of E[ast] T[ennessee], supposed to be with Col. Thomas," September-October, 1863. Subsequently reported as having deserted at Mossy Creek, Tennessee, October 1, 1863, but restored to the company rolls in January-February, 1864, after official information indicated that he had been on duty with Colonel Thomas during the previous period; he was again reported to be guarding the ferry at Rocky Point. No further records.

COMPANY K

This company was raised in Anderson, Roane, Morgan, and Knox Counties, Tennessee. According to a company muster roll dated April 6, 1864, the company was "originally made up during the summer of '62 of detailed men from different commands, for the purpose of scouting in Anderson, Roane and adjoining counties being more or less infested by Bushwhackers." The company was "regularly organized" on September 27, 1862, at Winter's Gap, Tennessee, and attached to this legion.

The following roster was compiled in large part from a company muster and descriptive roll dated September 27, 1862, and company muster rolls dated September 27, 1862-June, 1863, September, 1863-February, 1864, and April 6, 1864. These are abstracted in the microfilm edition of the Compiled Service Records of Confederate Soldiers Who Served in Organizations from the State of North Carolina (Record Group 109, M270), National Archives, Washington, D.C. Other valuable information in the Compiled Service Records includes enlistment papers, pay vouchers, requisitions, letters of resignation, discharge certificates, and abstracts of medical and prisoner of war records.

Also utilized in this roster were *The War of the Rebellion: A Compilation of the Official Records of the Union and Confederate Armies*, the North Carolina Adjutant General's papers, state militia records, newspaper casualty lists and obituaries, wartime claims for bounty pay and allowances, postwar registers of claims for artificial limbs, Confederate pension applications filed with the states of North Carolina, Tennessee, and Florida, records of the North Carolina Confederate Soldiers' Home, and the 1860 and 1870 federal censuses of North Carolina. A search was made also for relevant letters, diaries, reminiscences, and other manuscripts in the Southern Historical Collection (University of North Carolina-Chapel Hill) and the Duke University Library Special Collections Department.

Among the secondary sources consulted were records of the North Carolina division of the United Daughters of the Confederacy, postwar rosters, regimental and county histories, marriage bond, will, and cemetery indexes, published and unpublished genealogies, biographical dictionaries, the North Carolina *County Heritage Book* series, the *Confederate Veteran*, Walter Clark's *Histories of the Several Regiments and Battalions from North Carolina in the Great War, 1861-'65*, and the North Carolina volume of the extended edition of *Confederate Military History*.

OFFICERS

CAPTAIN

BUTLER, THOMAS A.

Born in Roane County, Tennessee, where he resided as a carpenter prior to enlisting at Winter's Gap at age 31. Appointed Captain on September 27, 1862. Reported present through April 30, 1863. Reported on leave "on business with Ordnance Department"and "to deliver cotton to men in Morgan Co., Tenn." in May-June, 1863. Reported present in September, 1863-February, 1864. Hospitalized at New Market, Virginia, October 17, 1864. Transferred to hospital at Harrisonburg, Virginia, on or about October 21, 1864. Transferred to hospital at Charlottesville, Virginia, October 24, 1864, with chronic rheumatism. Returned to duty on November 2, 1864. Captured at Knoxville, Tennessee, May 1, 1865. Released on bond by the Civil Court for Knox County, Tennessee, May 24, 1865. No further records. [May have served previously in Capt. W. C. Kain's Battery, Tennessee Light Artillery. His capture at Knoxville on May 1, 1865, indicates that he was a member of Lt. Col. William W. Stringfield's flag-of-truce party that was arrested when they refused to take the Oath of Allegiance.]

LIEUTENANTS

CROUCH, ROBERT C., 1st Lieutenant

Served previously as Private in Company B, 19th Regiment Tennessee Infantry. Reported to be 1st Lieutenant of this company on prisoner-of-war records showing that he was captured at Henderson's Mill, Tennessee, September, 1863, confined at Louisville, Kentucky, October 5, 1863, transferred to Johnson's Island, Ohio, and released at Johnson's Island on June 11, 1865, after taking the Oath of Allegiance. However, company records show that Lewis Rector was 1st Lieutenant throughout this period.

GALLAHER, DAVID HOUSTON, 3rd Lieutenant

Previously served as Private in Company B, 63rd Regiment Tennessee Infantry. Elected 3rd Lieutenant of this company on September 27, 1862. Reported present through June 30, 1863, and in September, 1863-February, 1864. Hospitalized at Winchester, Virginia, August 1, 1864, with chronic diarrhoea. Returned to duty prior to September 19, 1864, when he was wounded at Winchester. No further records.

PEAK, WILLIAM H. H., 2nd Lieutenant

Born in Anderson County, Tennessee, where he resided as a farmer prior to enlisting at Winter's Gap at age 21. Elected 2nd Lieutenant on September 27, 1862. Reported present through June 30, 1863, and in September, 1863-February, 1864. Wounded in the head at Cedar Creek, Virginia, October 19, 1864. Hospitalized at Charlottesville, Virginia, October 24, 1864. Returned to duty on November 5, 1864. No further records.

RECTOR, LEWIS, 1st Lieutenant

Born in Roane County, Tennessee, where he resided as a farmer prior to enlisting at Winter's Gap, Tennessee, at age 36. Elected 1st Lieutenant on September 27, 1862. Reported present through June 30, 1863, and in September, 1863-February, 1864. Wounded in the right hip and captured at Winchester, Virginia, September 19, 1864. Hospitalized at Winchester on the same day. Transferred to hospital at Baltimore, Maryland, October 17, 1864. Confined at Point Lookout, Maryland, October 26, 1864. Confined at Old Capitol Prison, Washington, D.C., November 3, 1864. Transferred to Fort Delaware, Delaware, December 16, 1864. Released at Fort Delaware on June 17, 1865, after taking the Oath of Allegiance.

NONCOMMISSIONED OFFICERS AND PRIVATES

ALLEY, A. S., Private

Born in Monroe County, Tennessee, and resided in Anderson County, Tennessee, where he was by occupation a farmer prior to enlisting at Winter's Gap, Tennessee, at age 35, September 27, 1862, for the war. Reported present through June 30, 1863, and in September, 1863-February, 1864. Hospitalized at Charlottesville, Virginia, June 12, 1864, with chronic diarrhoea. Returned to duty on June 17, 1864. Name appears on receipt rolls for clothing dated September 1 and December 14, 1864. No further records.

ARMS, HENRY W., Private

Born in Morgan or Knox County, Tennessee, where he resided as a farmer prior to enlisting at Winter's Gap, Tennessee, at age 25 or 36, September 27, 1862, for the war. Reported present through June 30, 1863, and in September, 1863-February, 1864. Took the Oath of Allegiance at Chattanooga, Tennessee, on May 21, 1865. [His surname may have been Armes.]

ARMS, WILLIAM P., Private

Born in Morgan County, Tennessee, where he resided as a farmer prior to enlisting at Winter's Gap, Tennessee, at age 24, September 27, 1862, for the war. Reported present through June 30, 1863, and in September, 1863-February, 1864. Name appears on receipt rolls for clothing dated June 18 and October 16, 1864. No further records. [His surname may have been Armes.]

ASHLOCK, WILLIAM H., Private

Born in Anderson County, Tennessee, where he resided as a farmer prior to enlisting at Winter's Gap at age 32, September 27, 1862, for the war. Reported present through December 31, 1863. Reported sick at home on February 28, 1863. Returned to duty prior to April 30, 1863. Reported present on June 30, 1863. A muster roll dated September-October, 1863, states that he was "cut off from the command at the evacuation of E(ast) Ten(nessee), Aug. 28, 1863." Subsequently reported as having deserted on August 5, 1863.

BRADLEY, A. JACKSON, Private

Enlisted at Winter's Gap, Tennessee, March 15, 1863, for the war. Reported present through June 30, 1863, and in September-October, 1863. Reported sick in hospital near Rogersville, Tennessee, in November-December, 1863. Returned to duty prior to February 29, 1864. Name appears on receipt rolls for clothing dated April 3, June 18, October 16, and December 14, 1864. No further records.

BRADLEY, JAMES R., Private

Born in Anderson County, Tennessee, and resided in Roane County, Tennessee, where he was by occupation a farmer prior to enlisting at Winter's Gap, Tennessee, at age 28, September 27, 1862, for the war. Reported present through June 30, 1863, and in September, 1863-February, 1864, and April 6, 1864. Hospitalized at Charlottesville, Virginia, June 10, 1864, with acute dysentery. Returned to duty on June 17, 1864. Hospitalized at Winchester, Virginia, July 25, 1864, with debilitas. Returned to duty on July 31, 1864. Captured at Winchester, Virginia, September 19, 1864. Sent to Harpers Ferry, West Virginia, and arrived there on or before September 23, 1864. Transferred to Point Lookout, Maryland, where he arrived on September 26, 1864. Paroled at Point Lookout on March 15, 1865. Received at Boulware's Wharf, James River, Virginia, March 18, 1865, for exchange. Hospitalized at Richmond, Virginia, on the same date with chronic diarrhoea. Furloughed for sixty days on March 26, 1865. Took the Oath of Allegiance at Chattanooga, Tennessee, on May 14, 1865. No further records.

BRADLEY, STEPHEN, Private

Born in Anderson County, Tennessee, and resided in Roane County, Tennessee, where he was by occupation a farmer prior to enlisting at Winter's Gap, Tennessee, at age 18, September 27, 1862, for the war. Reported present through June 30, 1863, and in September-October, 1863. Reported on duty as a nurse in hospital at Rogersville, Tennessee, in November-December, 1863. Rejoined the company in January-February, 1864. Captured at Winchester, Virginia, September 19, 1864. Sent to Harpers Ferry, West Virginia, where he arrived on or before September 23, 1864. Transferred to Point Lookout, Maryland, where he arrived on September 26, 1864. Paroled at Point Lookout on March 15, 1865. Received at Boulware's Wharf, James River, Virginia, March 18, 1865, for exchange. Name appears on a muster roll of paroled and exchanged prisoners at Camp Lee, near Richmond, Virginia, March 19, 1865. Survived the war. [See Tennessee pension application No. 4658.]

BRAY, THOMAS, Private

Born in Anderson County, Tennessee, where he resided as a farmer prior to enlisting at Winter's Gap at age 20, September 27, 1862, for the war. Reported present through December 31, 1862. Deserted on February 5, 1863. Returned to duty on April 5, 1863. Reported present through June 30, 1863, and in September-October, 1863. Deserted at Bean's Station, Tennessee, December 10, 1863. Took the Oath of Allegiance at Knoxville, Tennessee, in December, 1863.

BURUM, ABSALOM J., 1st Sergeant

Born in Blount County, Tennessee, and resided in Roane County, Tennessee, where he was by occupation a farmer prior to enlisting at Winter's Gap, Tennessee, at age 34, September 27, 1862, for the war. Mustered in as 1st Sergeant. Reported present through June 30, 1863, and in September, 1863-February, 1864. Took the Oath of Allegiance at Chattanooga, Tennessee, May 24, 1865.

BUTLER, BOLIVAR B., Corporal

Born in Morgan County, Tennessee, where he resided as a farmer prior to enlisting at Winter's Gap, Tennessee, at age 26, September 27, 1862, for the war. Mustered in as Private. Reported present through June 30, 1863. Elected Corporal on September 1, 1863. Reported sick in hospital at White Sulphur Springs, West Virginia, from October 14 through December 31, 1863. Transferred on August 5, 1864. Name appears on receipt rolls for clothing dated September 27 and December 14, 1864. No further records. Survived the war.

BUTLER, MOSES D. F., Private

Born in Roane County, Tennessee, where he resided as a farmer prior to enlisting at Winter's Gap, Tennessee, September 27, 1862, for the war. Reported present through June 30, 1863. Left leg and ankle injured near Rheatown, Tennessee, when he was accidentally bumped by a horse and knocked into a wagon wheel, probably on or about October 11, 1863. Reported sick in hospital at White Sulphur Springs, West Virginia, from October 14 through December 31, 1863. Reported on duty as a hospital nurse at White Sulphur Springs hospital in January-February, 1864, and April-September, 1864. Name appears on a receipt roll for clothing dated December 14, 1864. No further records. Survived the war. [Tennessee pension application No. 4796 states that he was born on October 6, 1830 or 1831, and was captured and paroled at Kingston, Georgia, May 12, 1865.]

BUTLER, P. K., Private

Born in Anderson County, Tennessee, and resided in Roane County, Tennessee, where he was by occupation a farmer prior to enlisting at Winter's Gap, Tennessee, at age 35, September 27, 1862, for the war. Reported present through February 28, 1863. Reported sick at home in March-June, 1863. Reported "cut off from the command at the evacuation of E[ast] Ten[nessee], Aug. 28, 1863." Subsequently reported as having deserted on August 28, 1863.

CARMICHAEL, GEORGE W., Private

Enlisted at Winter's Gap, Tennessee, March 15, 1863, for the war. Reported present through April 30, 1863. Discharged at Greeneville, Tennessee, May 12, 1863, after providing Pvt. William Henson of this company as a substitute.

CARTER, J. W., Private

Enlisted at Winter's Gap, Tennessee, December 26, 1862, for the war. Deserted prior to February 28, 1863.

CARTER, WILLIAM H., Private

Enlisted at Knoxville, Tennessee, at age 32, January 22, 1863, for the war. Transferred to this company at Winter's Gap, Tennessee, January 26, 1863. Deserted on February 5, 1863. [His given name may have been Howard W.]

CHILES, WILLIAM M., Private

Born in Anderson County, Tennessee, September 12, 1830. Enlisted at Winter's Gap, Tennessee,at age 32, February 6, 1863, for the war. Reported present through April 30, 1863. Reported absent without leave on June 5, 1863. Returned to duty prior to October 14, 1863, when he was reported as a deserter on the retreat between Zollicoffer and Bristol, Tennessee. [In his Tennessee pension application No. 4839, he claimed that he was captured in Anderson County and took the Oath of Allegiance on or about October 28, 1863.]

COLLINS, CHARLES E., Private

Born in Montgomery County, Virginia, in 1840. Enlisted at Winter's Gap, Tennessee, February 6, 1863, for the war. Reported present through June 30, 1863, and in September, 1863-February, 1864. Captured at Piedmont, Virginia, June 5, 1864. Reported under guard at Staunton, Virginia, June 8, 1864. Confined at Camp Morton, Indianapolis, Indiana, June 21, 1864. Paroled at Camp Morton on March 15, 1865. Received at Cox's Wharf, James River, Virginia, March 23, 1865, for exchange. Survived the war. [See Tennessee pension application No. 13924.]

CONNER, CALEB, Private

Enlisted at Winter's Gap, Tennessee, at about age 23, February 6, 1863, for the war. Deserted at Winter's Gap on April 9, 1863.

COX, JAMES L., Private

Born in Anderson County, Tennessee, where he resided as a farmer prior to enlisting at Winter's Gap, Tennessee, at age 27, September 27, 1862, for the war. Reported present through December 31, 1862. Deserted on February 20, 1863. Evidently returned to duty prior to April 9, 1863; reported absent without leave as of that date. Dropped from the rolls as a deserter prior to April 6, 1864.

CROZIER, SAMUEL C., Private

Born in Anderson County, Tennessee, and resided in Roane County, Tennessee, where he was by occupation a merchant prior to enlisting at Winter's Gap, Tennessee, at age 26, September 27, 1862, for the war. Reported present through June 30, 1863, and in September-December, 1863. Reported sick in hospital at Bristol, Tennessee, January-February, 1864. Hospitalized at Charlottesville, Virginia, June 12, 1864, with boils. Returned to duty on June 14, 1864. Captured at Knoxville, Tennessee, on May 1, 1865. Released by a Knox County, Tennessee, civil court on May 24, 1865. [His capture at Knoxville on May 1 indicates that he was a member of Lt. Col. William W. Stringfield's flag-of-truce party that was arrested when they refused to take the Oath of Allegiance.]

CURD, WILLIAM L., Private

Resided in Morgan County, Tennessee, and was a farm laborer prior to enlisting at Winter's Gap, Tennessee, at about age 18, January 26, 1863, for the war. Reported present through June 30, 1863. Reported sick in hospital at either White Sulphur Springs, West Virginia, or Montgomery White Sulphur Springs, Virginia, from October 14 through December 31, 1863. Reported on duty as a hospital nurse at Montgomery White Sulphur Springs, Virginia, March 9-May 31, 1864. Rejoined the company at an unspecified date. Hospitalized at Richmond, Virginia, February 16, 1865, with a gunshot wound of the left arm. Place and date wounded not reported. Furloughed for sixty days on February 21, 1865. No further records.

DANEL, L. I., _____

Born in Marion County, Tennessee, and resided in Roane County, Tennessee, where he was by occupation a farmer. Enlisted in "Ross' Regt." on April 23, 1862. Transferred to this company on September 27, 1862. No further records.

DAVIS, JAMES R., Private

Previously served as Private in Company A, Walker's Battalion. Enlisted in this company at Winter's Gap, Tennessee, February 6, 1863, for the war. Reported present through February 28, 1863. Deserted on April 9, 1863.

DAVIS, SAMUEL, ____

A company muster roll dated April 6, 1864, states that Austin L. Keith of this company enlisted on April 20, 1863, as a substitute for "Saml Davis Knox Co. Ten." There is no other evidence of Davis's service.

DICKEY, BENJAMIN, Private

Born in Knox County, Tennessee, where he resided as a farmer prior to enlisting at Winter's Gap, Tennessee, at age 22, September 27, 1862, for the war. Reported sick in camp on December 31, 1862. Reported absent sick in January-February, 1863. Sent to hospital at Strawberry Plains, Tennessee, April 15, 1863. Reported "cut off from the command at the evacuation of E(ast) Ten(nessee), Aug. 28, 1863." Subsequently reported as having deserted on August 28, 1863.

DICKEY, DAVID JACKSON, Private

Born in Knox County, Tennessee, where he resided as a farmer prior to enlisting at Winter's Gap, Tennessee, at age 20, September 27, 1862, for the war. Reported present through February 28, 1863. Reported sick at home from April 9 through June 30, 1863. Reported present in September-October, 1863. Deserted on December 10, 1863.

DONN, JOHN, Private

Born in Roane County, Tennessee, where he resided as a farmer prior to enlisting at Winter's Gap, Tennessee, at age 36, September 27, 1862, for the war. Died on November 7, 1862, of wounds received in a skirmish in Roane County.

DUNCAN, CALVIN, Private

Enlisted at Winter's Gap, Tennessee. Enlistment date reported as September 27, 1862; however, he was not listed on the rolls of this company until April 6, 1864. Hospitalized at Charlottesville, Virginia, September 26, 1864, with a gunshot wound of the back, resulting in complete paralysis below the area of the wound. Probably wounded at Harrisonburg, Virginia, September 25, 1864, but may have been wounded at Winchester, Virginia, September 19, 1864, or Fisher's Hill, Virginia, September 22, 1864. Died in hospital at Charlottesville on October 5, 1864, of wounds. [He was about 26 years of age in 1864.]

ESTES, JAMES, Private

Enlisted at Winter's Gap, Tennessee, at about age 17, February 6, 1863, for the war. Deserted on February 23, 1863. May have rejoined the company. Reported absent without leave from April 9, 1863, through April 6, 1864, and dropped from the rolls as a deserter.

FOSTER, H. KING, Private

Enlisted at Winter's Gap, Tennessee, at about age 32, November 17, 1862, for the war. Reported present through June 30, 1863. Reported absent without leave, August 14-October 31, 1863. Subsequently reported as having deserted at Carter's Depot, Tennessee, September 21, 1863.

FRAZIER, L., _____

Born in Anderson County, Tennessee, where he resided as a farmer prior to enlisting at age 27. Previously served in another unit. Transferred to this company on September 27, 1862. No further records.

FRAZIER, THOMAS J., Musician

Resided in Anderson County, Tennessee, and enlisted at Winter's Gap, Tennessee, at about age 30, September 27, 1862, for the war. Mustered in as Musician (Fifer). Reported present through June 30, 1863, and in September, 1863-December, 1863. Reported on furlough in January-February, 1864. Deserted to the enemy at Franklin, March 7, 1865. Sent to Knoxville, Tennessee, and arrived there on March 20, 1865. Took the Oath of Allegiance at Knoxville the same day. Sent to Chattanooga, Tennessee. Transferred to Louisville, Kentucky, and arrived there on March 26, 1865. Released at Louisville on March 28, 1865, "to remain North of the Ohio River during the war."

GALLAHER, ALBERT H., Private

Previously served as Private in Company F, 4th Tennessee Cavalry Battalion (Branner's) and Company F, 1st Regiment Tennessee Cavalry. Transferred to this company at Winter's Gap, Tennessee, November 12, 1862. Reported present through December 31, 1862, and in January-April, 1863. Reported on detached service as Assistant Provost Marshal at Carter's Station, Tennessee, June 18-30, 1863. Reported detailed to the commissary department of Williams' Cavalry Brigade, Ransom's Division, in September-October, 1863, and to the commissary department of Jones' Cavalry Brigade, November, 1863-February, 1864. Captured at Knoxville, Tennessee, May 1, 1865. Sent to Chattanooga, Tennessee, on May 3, 1865. Confined at Nashville, Tennessee. Transferred to Louisville, Kentucky, May 14, 1865, and confined there on or about May 15. Released after taking the Oath of Allegiance at Louisville on June 16, 1865. [His surname may have been Gallagher. The 1st Regiment Tennessee Cavalry in which he served became the 2nd Regiment Tennessee Cavalry (Ashby's) in December, 1862. It is not to be confused with the 1st Regiment Tennessee Cavalry (Carter's), an entirely different unit. His capture at Knoxville on May 1, 1865, indicates that he was a member of Lt. Col. William W. Stringfield's flag-of-truce party that was arrested when they refused to take the Oath of Allegiance.]

GALLAHER, JAMES B., _____

According to the January 13, 1864, entry in the diary of Sgt. Absalom J. Burum of this company, he served in the 26th Regiment Tennessee Infantry, was "cut off from his command, and came to our company, for the present." He was suffering from a thigh wound received at Chickamauga. [See "The Civil War Diary of Absalom J. Burum," Special Collections, Hunter Library, Western Carolina University. He was probably the same man as either Sgt. J. B. Gallaher or Pvt. James Gallaher of Company F, 26th Regiment Tennessee Infantry.]

GOBBY, JONATHAN, _____

North Carolina pension records appear to indicate that he served in this company.

GODDARD, THOMAS W., Private
Enlisted at Winter's Gap, Tennessee, at about age 24, February 6, 1863, for the war. Reported absent sick on February 28, 1863. Deserted at Winter's Gap on April 9, 1863.

GOSNEL, FRANK, Private
Born in Smith County, Tennessee, and resided in Anderson County, Tennessee, where he was by occupation a farmer prior to enlisting at Winter's Gap, Tennessee, at age 36, September 27, 1862, for the war. Reported present through February 28, 1863. Reported at home sick on April 9, 1863. Returned to duty prior to June 30, 1863. Reported in hospital at Knoxville, Tennessee, August 1-October 31, 1863. Subsequently reported as having deserted "at the evacuation of E[ast] Ten[nessee]" on August 28, 1863.

GRIFFIN, T., _____
The Charlotte *Western Democrat*, October 25, 1864, identifies him as a member of this company captured at Winchester, Virginia, September 19, 1864. He may have been the same man as Pvt. Fielder Griffith of this company.

GRIFFITH, FIELDER, Private
Born in Morgan County, Tennessee, and resided in Anderson County, Tennessee, where he was by occupation a farmer prior to enlisting at Winter's Gap, Tennessee, at age 31, September 27, 1862, for the war. Transferred to Company F, 1st Regiment Tennessee Cavalry, [later 2nd Regiment Tennessee Cavalry (Ashby's)], prior to January 1, 1863. Transferred back to this company at Zollicoffer, Tennessee, on August 1, 1863. Reported present or accounted for in September, 1863-February, 1864. Detailed as a teamster during much of that period. Name appears on receipt rolls for clothing dated June 18 and September 1, 1864. No further records. [He may have been the same man as T. Griffin of this company. His name is rendered, probably erroneously, as Fielding Gaffett, on a company muster and descriptive roll dated September 27, 1862.]

HEDRICK, WILLIAM, Private
Resided in Blount County, Tennessee. Place and date of enlistment not reported; probably enlisted subsequent to February 29, 1864. Captured at Knoxville, Tennessee, May 1, 1865. Sent to Chattanooga, Tennessee, May 3, 1865. Transferred to Nashville, Tennessee. Transferred to Louisville, Kentucky, on May 14, 1865, and arrived there on or about May 15, 1865. Released at Louisville on June 16, 1865, after taking the Oath of Allegiance. [He may have served previously in Company I, 1st Regiment Tennessee Cavalry (Rogers's). His capture at Knoxville on May 1, 1865, indicates that he was a member of Lt. Col. William W. Stringfield's flag-of-truce party that was arrested when they refused to take the Oath of Allegiance.]

HEMBREE, I. J., Private
Enlisted at Knoxville, Tennessee, at age 34, January 22, 1863, for the war. Deserted on February 5, 1863.

HENDRIX, HUGH L., Private
Resided in Anderson County, Tennessee, and was by occupation a farmer prior to enlisting at Winter's Gap, Tennessee, at about age 22 or 25, November 15, 1862, for the war. Reported present through June 30, 1863. Listed as a deserter and dropped from the company rolls on April 6, 1864.

HENLEY, WILLIAM A., Private
Resided in Roane County, Tennessee, and was by occupation a farmer prior to enlisting at Winter's Gap, Tennessee, at about age 35, November 15, 1862, for the war. Mustered in as Sergeant. Reported present through June 30, 1863, and in September, 1863-February, 1864. Reduced to ranks prior to August-September, 1864, when he was reported on duty as a teamster. No further records.

HENNINGS, A. G., Private
Enlisted at Winter's Gap, Tennessee, at about age 20, February 6, 1863, for the war. Deserted on March 3, 1863.

HENSON, WILLIAM, Private
Enlisted at Greeneville, Tennessee, at about age 29, May 12, 1863, for the war as a substitute for Pvt. George W. Carmichael of this company. Reported present through June 30, 1863. Listed as a deserter on April 6, 1864.

HOWARD, BLACK W., Private
Enlisted at Winter's Gap, Tennessee, at about age 35, November 15, 1862, for the war. Listed as a deserter on December 31, 1862. Reported for or returned to duty prior to February 28, 1863. Reported present in March-April, 1863. Deserted at Greeneville, Tennessee, May 14, 1863.

HUDSON, CALEB J., Private
Resided in Morgan County, Tennessee, and was by occupation a farmer prior to enlisting at Winter's Gap, Tennessee, at about age 29, February 6, 1863, for the war. Reported present through February 28, 1863. Deserted at Winter's Gap, April 9, 1863.

HUDSON, RUFUS, Private
Resided in Roane County, Tennessee, and enlisted at Winter's Gap, Tennessee, at about age 17, February 6, 1863, for the war. Reported present through February 28, 1863. Reported sick at home from April 9 until June 30, 1863, when he was reported absent without leave. Deserted on or about August 28, 1863.

JETT, JAMES M., Private
Born in Roane County, Tennessee, where he resided as a farmer prior to enlisting at Winter's Gap, Tennessee, at age 31, September 27, 1862, for the war. Reported present through February 28, 1863. Reported in hospital at Strawberry Plains, Tennessee, in April-June, 1863. Transferred or detailed to Company A, 3rd Regiment Confederate Engineers, prior to April 6, 1864.

JOHNSON, NOBLE, Corporal
Born in Anderson County, Tennessee, and resided in Monroe County, Tennessee, where he was by occupation a farmer prior to enlisting at Winter's Gap, Tennessee, at age 33, September 27, 1862, for the war. Mustered in as Corporal. Reported present through June 30, 1863. Reported absent without leave, "cut off from the command at the evacuation of E[ast] Tenn[essee]" from August 28, 1863, through April 6, 1864. No further records. Survived the war. [See Tennessee pension application No. 12804.]

KEITH, AUSTIN L., Private
Resided in Anderson County, Tennessee, and was by occupation a farmer prior to enlisting at Carter's Depot, Tennessee, at age 47,

April 20, 1863, for the war, as a substitute for Samuel Davis. Reported present through June 30, 1863, and in September, 1863-February, 1864. Hospitalized at Charlottesville, Virginia, June 6, 1864, with a gunshot wound. Probably wounded at Piedmont, Virginia, June 5, 1864. Transferred to hospital at Lynchburg, Virginia. Returned to duty prior to September 19, 1864, when he was captured at Winchester, Virginia. Sent to Harpers Ferry, West Virginia. Transferred on September 23, 1864, to Point Lookout, Maryland, and confined there on September 26. Paroled at Point Lookout on January 17, 1865. Received at Boulware's Wharf, James River, Virginia, January 21, 1865, for exchange. Hospitalized at Richmond, Virginia, on or about January 21, 1865, with catarrhus, chronic diarrhea, and bronchitis. Furloughed on or about January 24, 1865. No further records.

KINGTON, GEORGE F., Private

Born in Morgan County, Tennessee, and resided in Knox County, Tennessee, where he was by occupation a blacksmith prior to enlisting at Winter's Gap, Tennessee, September 27, 1862, for the war. Reported present through June 30, 1863, and in September, 1863. Reported sick in hospital at Rogersville, Tennesseee, November-December, 1863. Returned to duty on or prior to February 29, 1864. Hospitalized at Winchester, Virginia, July 25, 1864, with diarrhoea. Returned to duty prior to September 19, 1864, when he was wounded in the right hip or left leg and captured at Winchester. Transferred to hospital at Baltimore, Maryland, October 28, 1864. Transferred to Fort McHenry, Maryland, November 19, 1864. Confined at Point Lookout, Maryland, January 3, 1865. Released at Point Lookout on June 28, 1865, after taking the Oath of Allegiance. Reported to the Provost Marshal General's office in Washington, D.C., June 29, 1865, and transported to Knoxville, Tennessee.

KINGTON, JOHN L., Private

Born in Anderson County, Tennessee, where he resided as a blacksmith. Previously served in Company B, 3rd Regiment Tennessee Infantry (Vaughn's). Enlisted in this company, evidently illegally, at Winter's Gap, Tennessee, at age 30, September 27, 1862, for the war. Returned to Company B, 3rd Regiment Tennessee Infantry, prior to December 31, 1862.

KINGTON, WILLIAM M., Private

Born in Anderson County, Tennessee, where he resided as a blacksmith prior to enlisting at Winter's Gap, Tennessee, at age 28, September 27, 1862, for the war. Mustered in as Sergeant. Reported present through April 30, 1863. Wounded on or about June 5, 1863. Reported absent wounded, June 5-30, 1863. Returned to duty prior to October 31, 1863. Reduced to ranks at his own request in November-December, 1863, because of deafness. Reported present in November, 1863-February, 1864. Deserted to the enemy on an unspecified date. Confined at Knoxville, Tennessee, September 9, 1864. Took the Oath of Allegiance the same date. Sent to Chattanooga, Tennessee, September 25, 1864.

KINNEY, STEPHEN P., Private

Resided in Blount County, Tennessee. Place and date of enlistment not reported; probably enlisted subsequent to April 6, 1864. Captured at Knoxville, Tennessee, on May 1, 1865. Sent to Chattanooga, Tennessee, on May 3, 1865. Sent to Nashville, Tennessee, where he arrived on or prior to May 14, 1865. Transferred to Louisville, Kentucky, where he arrived on May 15, 1865. Released at Louisville on or about June 16, 1865, after taking the Oath of Allegiance. [His capture at Knoxville on May 1 indicates that he was a member of Lt. Col. William W. Stringfield's flag-of-truce party that was arrested when they refused to take the Oath of Allegiance.]

LEATH, W. ALEXANDER, Private

Born in Anderson County, Tennessee, where he resided as a farmer prior to enlisting at Winter's Gap, Tennessee, at age 21, September 27, 1862, for the war. Reported present through June 30, 1863, and in September-October, 1863. "Wounded and left" near Kingsport, Tennessee, in November-December, 1863. Returned to duty on or prior to February 29, 1864. Name appears on receipt rolls for clothing dated June 18, September 1, September 27, and December 14, 1864. No further records.

LEWALLEN, JOHN, Private

Resided in Morgan County, Tennessee, and was by occupation a farmer prior to enlisting at Zollicoffer, Tennessee, at about age 27, July 24, 1863, for the war. Name appears on a receipt roll for clothing dated August 15, 1863, on which he is reported as detailed. Reported on detail working in government shops at Knoxville, Tennessee, September, 1863-February, 1864; however, Knoxville was occupied by the Federals during this period. A muster roll dated April 6, 1864, indicates that he was "cut off or left in the Yankee lines," but Manuscript No. 1330, dated August, 1863 (Box 12, Entry 183: Miscellaneous Records, Manuscripts 1861-1865, Record Group 109, National Archives), indicates that he deserted at Knoxville on August 28, 1863. [His surname may have been Lewellen. He may have served previously in another unit, as his name appears on a Register of Payments on Descriptive Lists dated July 29, 1863, giving "period of service" as March 20-July 1, 1863. That document, however, describes him as a member of this company.]

LOVE, JAMES K., Private

Enlisted at Winter's Gap, Tennessee, September 27, 1862, for the war. Reported sick in camp on December 31, 1862. Reported present in January-February, 1863. Reported absent sick at Strawberry Plains, Tennessee, April 15-30, 1863. Reported on detached duty in the commissary department at Strawberry Plains from May 20 through June 30, 1863. Detailed in the commissary department at Abingdon, Virginia, October 14, 1863. Deserted to the enemy on an unspecified date. Sent to Knoxville, Tennessee. Took the Oath of Allegiance at Knoxville between December 4 and December 16, 1863, and was released.

McBEE, J. C., Private

Place and date of enlistment not reported; probably enlisted subsequent to February 29, 1864. Captured at Knoxville, Tennessee, May 1, 1865. No further records. [He may have served previously as Private in Company D, 3rd Battalion Tennessee Cavalry (Brazelton's), and Company F, 14th Battalion Tennessee Cavalry (Carter's). His capture at Knoxville on May 1 indicates that he was a member of Lt. Col. William W. Stringfield's flag-of-truce party that was arrested when they refused to take the Oath of Allegiance.]

McKAMY, ANDREW, Private

Enlisted at Winter's Gap, Tennessee, at about age 20, February 6, 1863, for the war. Reported present through February 28, 1863. Deserted at Winter's Gap on April 9, 1863. No further records.

McKAMY, JAMES M., Private

Enlisted at Winter's Gap, Tennessee, at about age 24, February 6, 1863, for the war. Reported absent without leave on February 28,

1863. Deserted at Winter's Gap on April 9, 1863. No further records.

McKAMY, WILLIAM T., Sergeant
Born in Roane County, Tennessee, and resided in Anderson County, Tennessee, where he was by occupation a farmer prior to enlisting at Winter's Gap, Tennessee, at age 22, September 27, 1862, for the war. Mustered in as Sergeant. Reported present through June 30, 1863, and in September, 1863-February, 1864. Name appears on a register of payments on descriptive lists dated September 26, 1864, for service from January 1 through April 1, 1864. Name appears on a receipt roll for clothing datelined General Hospital, Charlottesville, Virginia, July 25, 1864. No further records.

McKINNEY, JAMES M., Private
Born in Roane County, Tennessee, and resided in Anderson County, Tennessee, where he was by occupation a farmer prior to enlisting at Winter's Gap, Tennessee, at about age 29, September 27, 1862, for the war. Mustered in as Corporal. Reported present through June 30, 1863. Reduced to ranks on an unspecified date. Reported transferred or detailed to Company A, 3rd Regiment Confederate Engineers, prior to April 6, 1864, but records of that unit do not confirm his service.

McNELLY, W. R., Private
Place and date of enlistment not reported; probably enlisted subsequent to February 29, 1864. Captured at Knoxville, Tennessee, May 1, 1865. Confined at Knoxville until turned over to a civil court on June 21, 1865. [His capture at Knoxville on May 1, 1865, indicates that he was a member of Lt. Col. William W. Stringfield's flag-of-truce party that was arrested they refused to take the Oath of Allegiance.]

McPETERS, DAVID, Private
Born in Morgan or Anderson County, Tennessee. Resided in Anderson County where he was by occupation a farmer prior to enlisting at Winter's Gap, Tennessee, at age 46, January 1, 1863, for the war as a substitute for Pvt. James B. Schooler. Reported present in January-February, 1863. Reported sick at home from April 9 through 30, 1863. Returned to duty on or prior to June 30, 1863. Reported wounded and in hospital at White Sulphur Springs, West Virginia, October 12, 1863. Place and date wounded not reported, but probably at Henderson's Mill, Tennessee, October 11, 1863. Returned to duty on or prior to December 31, 1863. Reported present in January-February, 1864. Hospitalized at Charlottesville, Virginia, June 10, 1864, with acute dysentery. Returned to duty on July 16, 1864. Name appears on receipt rolls for clothing dated September 1 and December 14, 1864. Took the Oath of Allegiance at Chattanooga, Tennessee, May 21, 1865.

MANLY, ANCIL W., Private
Born in Anderson County, Tennessee, and resided in Roane County, Tennessee, where he was by occupation a farmer prior to enlisting at Winter's Gap, Tennessee, at age 51, September 27, 1862, for the war. Mustered in as Private. Promoted to Corporal on April 17, 1863. Reported present through April 30, 1863. Reported at home sick from June 5 through 30, 1863. Reported present, September, 1863-February, 1864. Reported on duty as a teamster in July, 1864. Name appears on receipt rolls for clothing dated September 1 and December 14, 1864. Reduced to ranks on an unspecified date. Took the Oath of Allegiance at Chattanooga, Tennessee, May 24, 1865.

MARTIN, JOHN W., Private
Resided in Maryville, Tennessee. Place and date of enlistment not reported; probably enlisted subsequent to February 29, 1864. Captured at Knoxville, Tennessee, May 1, 1865. Turned over to the civil courts on May 3, 1865. Sent to Nashville, Tennessee. Confined at Louisville, Kentucky, May 15, 1865. Released at Louisville on June 16, 1865, after taking the Oath of Allegiance. [His capture at Knoxville on May 1, 1865, indicates that he was a member of Lt. Col. William W. Stringfield's flag-of-truce party that was arrested when they refused to take the Oath of Allegiance.]

MARTIN, SAMUEL, Private
Born in Knox County, Tennessee, and resided in Roane County, Tennessee, where he was by occupation a farmer prior to enlisting at Winter's Gap, Tennessee, at age 44, September 27, 1862, for the war. Reported present through November 27, 1862, Reported on duty as a wagoner from that date through February 28, 1863. Reported present in March-April, 1863. Reported on leave on businss of the ordnance department in May-June, 1863. Reported absent without leave, August 18-October 31, 1863. Subsequently reported as having deserted at Jonesborough, Tennessee, September 15, 1863.

MASSENGILL, CALVIN, Private
Enlisted at Winter's Gap, Tennessee, at about age 37, February 6, 1863, for the war. Reported present through February 28, 1863. Deserted at Winter's Gap on April 9, 1863.

MORROW, W. J., _____
North Carolina pension records appear to indicate that he served in this company. Survived the war.

MOUNGER, GEORGE G., Private
Born in Anderson County, Tennessee, where he resided as a farmer prior to enlisting at Winter's Gap, Tennessee, at age 37, September 27, 1862, for the war. Reported present but sick through December 31, 1862. Reported at home sick in January-February, 1863, and April 9-June 30, 1863. Failed to return to duty and was listed as absent without leave on October 31, 1863. Subsequently reported as having deserted "at the evacuation of E[ast] Ten[nessee]" on August 28, 1863.

PARKER, GEORGE W., Private
Enlisted at Winter's Gap, Tennessee, at about age 17, February 6, 1863, for the war. Reported present through June 30, 1863. Sent to hospital at Strawberry Plains, Tennessee, August 11, 1863. Reported as such through April 6, 1864. No further records.

PEAK, LEWIS, Private
Born in what later became Scott County, Tennessee, and resided in Anderson County, Tennessee, where he was by occupation a farmer prior to enlisting at Winter's Gap, Tennessee, at age 43, September 27, 1862, for the war. Reported present through June 30, 1863. Died at Zollicoffer, Tennessee, August 8, 1863, of disease.

PEAK, LUKE, Private
Born in Morgan County, Tennessee, and resided in Anderson County, Tennessee, where he was by occupation a farmer prior to enlisting at Winter's Gap, Tennessee, at age 19, September 27, 1862, for the war. Reported present through June 30, 1863. Sent to

hospital at Strawberry Plains, Tennessee, August 10, 1863. Returned to duty on or prior to December 31, 1863. Reported present in January-February, 1864. Reported in hospital at Montgomery White Sulphur Springs, Virginia, in September, 1864. Name appears on receipt rolls for clothing dated June 18 and December 14, 1864. No further records.

PITMAN, GRANVILLE P., Private
Born in Roane or Marion County, Tennessee. Resided in Marion County and was by occupation a farmer prior to enlisting at Winter's Gap, Tennessee, at age 25, September 27, 1862, for the war. Reported present through June 30, 1863. Reported absent without leave from October 14, 1863, through April 6, 1864. No further records. Survived the war. [His surname may have been Pittman. His Tennessee pension application No. 1771 indicates that he served previously in the 26th Regiment Tennessee Infantry, but records of that unit do not confirm this.]

PITTMAN, TIMOTHY, Private
Born in Roane County, Tennessee, where he resided as a farmer prior to enlisting at Winter's Gap, Tennessee, at age 36, September 27, 1862, for the war. Reported present through April 30, 1863. Died at Zollicoffer, Tennessee, June 11, 1863. Cause of death not reported.

ROGERS, JAMES L. W., Private
Enlisted at Winter's Gap, Tennessee, at about age 28, February 6, 1863, for the war. Reported present through June 30, 1863. Reported absent without leave from August 18 through October 31, 1863. Subsequently reported as having deserted at Jonesborough, Tennessee, September 15, 1863.

SANDERS, JULE, _____
North Carolina pension records indicate that he served in this company. Survived the war.

SCHOOLER, JAMES B., Private
Born in Knox County, Tennessee, and resided in Morgan County, Tennessee, where he was by occupation a farmer prior to enlisting at Winter's Gap, Tennessee, at age 36, September 30, 1862, for the war. Reported present through December 31, 1862. Discharged on January 1, 1863, after providing Pvt. David McPeters as a substitute.

SCRIBER, J., _____
The Charlotte *Western Democrat*, October 25, 1864, states that he served in this company and was killed at Winchester, Virginia, September 19, 1864. [He may have been the same man as Pvt. Joseph Seiber of this company.]

SEIBER, ANDERSON, Private
Resided in Anderson County, Tennessee. Enlisted at Winter's Gap, Tennessee, at about age 17, February 6, 1863, for the war. Reported present through June 30, 1863, and in September, 1863-February, 1864. Name appears on receipt rolls for clothing dated June 18 and September 27, 1864. No further records.

SEIBER, F. R., Private
Resided in Anderson County, Tennessee. Enlisted at Winter's Gap, Tennessee, at about age 28, February 6, 1863, for the war. Reported present through February 28, 1863. Reported captured by "bushwhackers" in Morgan County, Tennessee, April 11, 1863; however, he was subsequently reported to have deserted at Winter's Gap on April 9, 1863. [His first name was probably Frederick.]

SEIBER, FREDERICK, JR., Private
Born in Anderson County, Tennessee, and resided in Roane County, Tennessee, where he was by occupation a farmer prior to enlisting at Winter's Gap, Tennessee, at age 18, September 27, 1862, for the war. Reported present through April 30, 1863. Deserted at Greeneville, Tennessee, on May 14, 1863. Returned to duty on June 4, 1863. Reported present in September-October, 1863. Deserted at Bean's Station, Tennessee, December 10, 1863. Went over to the enemy on an unspecified date. Sent to Knoxville, Tennessee. Released at Knoxville on or about December 29, 1863, after taking the Oath of Allegiance.

SEIBER, FREDERICK, SR., Private
Born in Anderson County, Tennessee, and resided in Roane County, Tennessee, where he was by occupation a minister prior to enlisting at Winter's Gap, Tennessee, at age 25, September 27, 1862, for the war. Reported present through June 30, 1863, and in September, 1863-February, 1864. Captured at Piedmont, Virginia, June 5, 1864. Reported under guard at Staunton, Virginia, June 8, 1864. Confined at Camp Morton, Indianapolis, Indiana, June 21, 1864. Released at Camp Morton on March 22, 1865, after taking the Oath of Allegiance. No further records.

SEIBER, GEORGE, Private
Resided in Anderson County, Tennessee. Enlisted at Winter's Gap, Tennessee, at about age 24, February 6, 1863, for the war. Reported present through February 28, 1863. Reported captured by "bushwhackers" in Morgan County, Tennessee, April 11, 1863; however, he was subsequently reported to have deserted at Winter's Gap on April 9, 1863.

SEIBER, HENRY K., Private
Resided in Roane County, Tennessee, and enlisted at Winter's Gap, Tennessee, at about age 24, February 6, 1863, for the war. Mustered in as Private. Reported present through June 30, 1863, and in September-October, 1863. Promoted to Sergeant on November 1, 1863. Reported present in November, 1863-February, 1864. Reduced to ranks prior to December 14, 1864. Deserted to the enemy on an unspecified date. Sent to Chattanooga, Tennessee. Released at Chattanooga on or about May 24, 1865, after taking the Oath of Allegiance.

SEIBER, JORDAN, Private
Resided in Anderson County, Tennessee, and was by occupation a farmer prior to enlisting at Winter's Gap, Tennessee, at about age 22, February 6, 1863, for the war. Reported present through April 30, 1863. Deserted at Greeneville, Tennessee, May 14, 1863. Returned to duty on June 4, 1863. Reported present on June 30, 1863. Listed as a deserter and dropped from the company rolls prior to April 6, 1864.

SEIBER, JOSEPH, Private
Resided in Anderson County, Tennessee, and was by occupation a farmer prior to enlisting at Winter's Gap, Tennessee, at about age 20, February 6, 1863, for the war. Reported present through June 30, 1863, and in September, 1863-February, 1864. Name appears on

receipt rolls for clothing dated June 18 and September 1, 1864. No further records. [He may have been the same man as J. Scriber of this company, in which case he was killed at Winchester, Virginia, September 19, 1864.]

SEIBER, PHILIP, Private
Resided in Anderson County, Tennessee, and was by occupation a farmer prior to enlisting at Winter's Gap, Tennessee, at about age 31, February 6, 1863, for the war. Reported present until he deserted at Greeneville, Tennessee, May 14, 1863.

SEIBER, SAMUEL, Private
Born in Anderson County, Tennessee, and resided in Roane County, Tennessee, where he was by occupation a farmer prior to enlisting at age 18, on or about September 27, 1862, for the war. No further records.

SEIBER, THOMAS, _____
Born in Anderson County, Tennessee, and resided in Roane County, Tennessee, where he was by occupation a farmer prior to enlisting at age 41, September 27, 1862, for the war. No further records.

SEYMOUR, JOSEPH, Private
Place and date of enlistment not reported; probably enlisted subsequent to February 29, 1864. Captured at Winchester, Virginia, September 19, 1864. Sent to Harpers Ferry, West Virginia. Confined at Point Lookout, Maryland, September 26, 1864. Paroled at Point Lookout on February 10, 1865. Received at Cox's Landing, James River, Virginia, February 14-15, 1865, for exchange. No further records.

SHARP, CALLOWAY, Private
Resided in Roane County, Tennessee, and was by occupation a farmer prior to enlisting at Knoxville, Tennessee, at about age 35, January 22, 1863, for the war. Deserted on February 5, 1863.

SHARP, SAMUEL, Private
Enlisted at Knoxville, Tennessee, at about age 33, January 22, 1863, for the war. Transferred from the Camp of Conscription at Knoxville and received into this company at Winter's Gap, Tennessee, January 26, 1863. Deserted on February 5, 1863.

SHAW, ROBERT L., Private
Born in Morgan County, Tennessee, and resided in Roane County, Tennessee, where he was by occupation a shoemaker prior to enlisting at Winter's Gap, Tennessee, at age 37, September 27, 1862, for the war. Reported present through April 30, 1863. Deserted at Greeneville, Tennessee, May 18, 1863.

SILVEY, JAMES M., Private
Born in Roane County, Tennessee, where he resided as a farmer prior to enlisting at Winter's Gap, Tennessee, at age 34, September 27, 1862, for the war. Mustered in as Private. Reported present through June 30, 1863. Appointed Musician (Drummer) on April 17, 1863. Hospitalized at Strawberry Plains, Tennessee, on or about August 10, 1863. Reduced to ranks prior to October 31, 1863. Reported absent without leave in November, 1863-February, 1864. Reported absent without leave and "sick in enemy's lines" on April 6, 1864. No further records.

SILVEY, PETER, Private
Resided in Roane County, Tennessee, and was by occupation a farmer prior to enlisting at Winter's Gap, Tennessee, at about age 29, November 15, 1862, for the war. Reported present through June 30, 1863. Listed as a deserter and dropped from the company rolls prior to April 6, 1864. [Served also as a Concript Camp Instructor in Tennessee.]

SILVEY, WILLIAM R., Private
Enlisted at Winter's Gap, Tennessee, at about age 22, February 27, 1863, for the war. Deserted at Winter's Gap on April 9, 1863, and joined the Federal army. Assigned to Company B, 2nd Regiment Tennessee Infantry (Union). Captured "in arms" by Confederate forces subsequent to September, 1863, and was shot for desertion on an unspecified date. [He is almost certainly the "poor fellow of Company K, a Tennesseean," who is reported in Clark's *Regiments* 3:742 as having been captured with two other Tennesseans "in the uniform of the enemy" by the forces of Brig. Gen. William E. "Grumble" Jones at Rogersville, Tennesssee, and subsequently "court-martialed and shot at the stake" in the vicinity of Blountsville, Tennessee. According to the wartime diary of Maj. William W. Stringfield of this regiment, the execution took place on November 13, 1863.]

SMITH, ANDREW THOMAS, Private
Enlisted at Winter's Gap, Tennessee, at about age 22, February 6, 1863, for the war. Deserted at Winter's Gap on April 9, 1863.

SMITH, SETH, Private
Place and date of enlistment not reported; probably enlisted subsequent to June 30, 1863. Captured in Greene County, Tennessee, September 4 or September 12, 1863. Sent to Louisville, Kentucky. Transferred to Camp Douglas, Chicago, Illinois, October 7, 1863. Died at Camp Douglas on November 1, 1864, of "dysentery."

SMITH, THOMAS A., Private
Born in Roane County, Tennessee, in 1844 and was by occupation a farmer. Enlisted at Winter's Gap, Tennessee, November 15, 1862, for the war. Reported present through April 30, 1863. Discharged on June 29, 1863, because of "scrofula" and "debility." [See Tennessee pension application No. 11166.]

STONECIPHER, JAMES H., Private
Born in Morgan County, Tennessee, and resided in Morgan or Knox County, Tennessee, where he was by occupation a farmer prior to enlisting at Winter's Gap, Tennessee, at age 23, September 27, 1862, for the war. Reported present through June 30, 1863, and in September-October, 1863. Deserted at Bean's Station, Tennessee, December 10, 1863. Name appears on a receipt roll for clothing dated December 14, 1864. Took the Oath of Allegiance at Chattanooga, Tennessee, May 21, 1865.

STONECIPHER, MARTIN, Private
Born in Morgan County, Tennessee, where he resided as a farmer prior to enlisting at Winter's Gap, Tennessee, at age 29, September 27, 1862, for the war. Mustered in as Musician (Drummer). Reported present through February 28, 1863. Reduced to ranks on March 18, 1863. Reported absent without leave on April 9, 1863. Returned to duty prior to June 30, 1863. No further records.

STONECIPHER, S. C., Private
Born in Marion County, Tennessee, and resided in Knox County, Tennessee, where he was by occupation a farmer prior to enlisting at Winter's Gap, Tennessee, at age 20, September 27, 1862, for the war. Reported present but sick in camp on December 31, 1862. No further records.

STONECIPHER, S. C., Private
Born in Morgan County, Tennessee, and resided in Anderson County, Tennessee, where he was by occupation a farmer prior to enlisting at Winter's Gap, Tennessee, at age 32, September 27, 1862, for the war. Reported present through June 30, 1863, and in September, 1863-February, 1864. No further records.

STONECIPHER, WILLIAM G., Private
Born in Morgan County, Tennessee, and resided in Knox County, Tennessee, where he was by occupation a farmer prior to enlisting at Winter's Gap, Tennessee, at age 25, September 27, 1862, for the war. "Returned to his former regiment, the 3rd Tennessee," prior to December 31, 1862. However, his name does not appear in the records of any "3rd Tennessee."

TAYLOR, JOHN D., Private
Enlisted at Winter's Gap, Tennessee, at about age 26, February 6, 1863, for the war. Deserted at Winter's Gap on April 9, 1863.

TAYLOR, SAMUEL, Private
Enlisted at Winter's Gap, Tennessee, at about age 22, September 27, 1862, for the war. Reported present through February 28, 1863. Deserted at Winter's Gap on April 9, 1863. Later served as Private in Company A, Indian Battalion.

TAYLOR, WILLIAM, Private
Place and date of enlistment not reported; probably enlisted subsequent to February 29, 1864. Captured at Knoxville, Tennessee, May 1, 1865. Sent to Chattanooga, Tennessee, "as a deserter," June 19, 1865. Took the Oath of Allegiance at Chattanooga, Tennessee, June 22, 1865. [His capture at Knoxville on May 1, 1865, indicates that he was a member of Lt. Col. William W. Stringfield's flag-of-truce party that was arrested when they refused to take the Oath of Allegiance.]

USRA, JOHN, Private
Enlisted at Winter's Gap, Tennessee, at about age 17, February 6, 1863, for the war. Deserted on March 13, 1863.

VANN, GEORGE W., Private
Enlisted at Winter's Gap, Tennessee, at about age 31, January 15, 1863, for the war. Reported present through February 28, 1863. Deserted at Winter's Gap on April 9, 1863.

WALLACE, ALFRED, Corporal
Born in Anderson County, Tennessee, and resided in Roane County, Tennessee, where he was by occupation a farmer prior to enlisting at Winter's Gap, Tennessee, at age 34, September 27, 1862, for the war. Mustered in as Corporal. Reported present through February 28, 1863. Reported "captured by bushwhackers in Morgan County," Tennessee, April 11, 1863. Subsequently reported as having deserted at Winter's Gap on April 9, 1863. Captured by the Federals at Jacksboro, Tennessee, August 27, 1863. Confined at Louisville, Kentucky, September 5, 1863. Transferred to Camp Chase, Ohio, September 9, 1863. Transferred to Rock Island, Illinois, January 22, 1864. Enlisted in the U.S. Army at Rock Island on October 15, 1864, "for frontier service" and served in the 3rd Regiment U.S. Volunteer Infantry.

WALLACE, HENRY, Private
Born in Shelby County, Alabama, and resided in Anderson County, Tennessee, where he was by occupation a farmer prior to enlisting at Winter's Gap, Tennessee, at age 42, September 27, 1862, for the war. Reported present through June 30, 1863, and in September, 1863-February, 1864. Wounded in the left leg and captured at Winchester, Virginia, September 19, 1864. Hospitalized at Baltimore, Maryland. Confined at Point Lookout, Maryland, where he arrived on January 8, 1865. Hospitalized at Point Lookout on or about January 28, 1865, possibly due to complications resulting from his leg injury. Transferred to another hospital on or about April 7, 1865. Died in hospital at Point Lookout on June 1, 1865, of "chro[nic] diarrhoea."

WALLACE, JOSEPH, Corporal
Born in Anderson County, Tennessee, and resided in Roane County, Tennessee, where he was by occupation a farmer prior to enlisting at Winter's Gap, Tennessee, at age 26, September 27, 1862, for the war. Mustered in as Corporal. Reported present through June 30, 1863. Listed as a deserter and dropped from the company rolls on April 6, 1864.

WEBB, FRANCIS, Private
Born in Morgan County, Tennessee, and resided in Anderson County, Tennessee, where he was by occupation a farmer prior to enlisting at Winter's Gap, Tennessee, at age 26, September 27, 1862, for the war. Reported present through June 30, 1863. Sent to hospital at Knoxville, Tennessee, August 1, 1863. Subsequently reported as having deserted at Zollicoffer, Tennessee, August 10, 1863.

WEBB, JACOB, Private
Born in Morgan County, Tennessee, and resided in Anderson County, Tennessee, where he was by occupation a farmer prior to enlisting at Winter's Gap, Tennessee, at age 22, September 27, 1862, for the war. Reported present through June 30, 1863. Reported absent "missing between Zollicoffer and Bristol, Tenn in a retreat," October 14, 1863. Subsequently reported as having deserted at Zollicoffer, Tennessee, October 14, 1863.

WILKINS, BENJAMIN, Private
Born in Knox County, Tennessee, where he resided as a farmer prior to enlisting at Winter's Gap, Tennessee, at age 36, September 27, 1862, for the war. Reported absent without leave on December 31, 1862. No further records.

WILKINS, CHARLES S., Sergeant
Born in Knox County, Tennessee, where he resided as a farmer prior to enlisting at Winter's Gap, Tennessee, at age 21, September 27, 1862, for the war. Mustered in as Private. Promoted to Sergeant on an unspecified date. Deserted prior to December 31, 1862.

WILLIAMS, WILLIAM H., Private
Born in Rhea County, Tennessee, and resided in Morgan County, Tennessee, where he was by occupation a farmer prior to enlisting at

Winter's Gap, Tennessee, at age 27, September 27, 1862, for the war. Reported captured by "bushwhackers" in Morgan County prior to December 31, 1862. Released or exchanged on an unspecified date. Reported absent without leave on April 9, 1863. Returned to duty prior to June 30, 1863. Listed as a deserter and dropped from the rolls prior to April 6, 1864.

WILSON, JESSE, Private
Enlisted at Whitesburg, Tennessee, January 1, 1864, for the war. Reported present in January-February, 1864. No further records. [He was a "dismounted partisan ranger" reassigned to this Legion by Maj. Gen. Robert Ransom, Jr.]

WORTHINGTON, JESSE B., Private
Born in Anderson County, Tennessee, where he resided as a farmer prior to enlisting at Winter's Gap, Tennessee, at age 22, September 27, 1862, for the war. Mustered in as Sergeant. Reported present through June 30, 1863, and in September, 1863-February, 1864. Name appears on receipt rolls for clothing dated June 17, September 27, and December 14, 1864. Reduced to ranks subsequent to September 27, 1864. No further records. Survived the war.

WRIGHT, A. JACKSON, Private
Resided in Roane County, Tennessee, and enlisted at Winter's Gap, Tennessee, at about age 21, February 6, 1863, for the war. Reported absent sick until April 9, 1863, when he was reported absent without leave. Subsequently reported as having deserted on August 28, 1863. [See Tennessee pension application No. 3474.]

WRIGHT, ALEXANDER, Musician
Born in Knox County, Tennessee, and resided in Roane County, Tennessee, where he was by occupation a farmer prior to enlisting at Winter's Gap, Tennessee, at age 20, September 27, 1862, for the war. Mustered in as Private. Reported present through June 30, 1863. Appointed Musician (Drummer) on August 1, 1863. Reported present in September, 1863-February, 1864. Name appears on receipt rolls for clothing dated June 18, September 1, and September 27, 1864. No further records.

WRIGHT, GEORGE W., Private
Born in Roane County, Tennessee, where he resided as a farmer prior to enlisting at Winter's Gap, Tennessee, at age 24, September 27, 1862, for the war. Reported present through June 30, 1863. Reported on duty as a wagoner for Brig. Gen. Alfred E. Jackson's Brigade in September-December, 1863. Reported present in January-February, 1864. Captured at Piedmont, Virginia, June 5, 1864. Reported under guard at Staunton, Virginia, June 8, 1864. Confined at Camp Morton, Indianapolis, Indiana, June 21, 1864. Died at Camp Morton on March 10, 1865, of "chronic diarrhoea." [His surname may have been Right.]

WRIGHT, GEORGE W., Private
Enlisted at Winter's Gap, Tennessee, at about age 21, September 27, 1862, for the war. Deserted prior to December 31, 1862. [His surname may have been Right.]

WRIGHT, JAMES, _____
Born in Roane County, Tennessee, where he resided as a farmer prior to enlisting at age 20, September 27, 1862, for the war. No further records.

WRIGHT, JAMES H., Private
Born in Knox County, Tennessee, and resided in Roane County, Tennessee, where he was by occupation a farmer prior to enlisting at Winter's Gap, Tennessee, at age 17, September 27, 1862, for the war. Reported present through December 31, 1862. Deserted on March 3, 1863.

WRIGHT, JOHN, _____
Born in Anderson County, Tennessee, where he resided as a farmer prior to enlisting at age 30, September 27, 1862, for the war. No further records.

WRIGHT, JOHN H., Private
Born in Anderson County, Tennessee, and resided in Roane County, Tennessee, where he was by occupation a shoemaker prior to enlisting at Winter's Gap, Tennessee, at age 30, September 27, 1862, for the war. Reported present through June 30, 1863, and in September, 1863-February, 1864. Captured at Piedmont, Virginia, June 5, 1864. Reported under guard at Staunton, Virginia, June 8, 1864. Confined at Camp Morton, Indianapolis, Indiana, June 21, 1864. Released at Camp Morton on May 23, 1865, after taking the Oath of Allegiance.

WRIGHT, LAFAYETTE, _____
Born in Anderson County, Tennessee, and resided in Morgan County, Tennessee, where he was by occupation a farmer prior to enlisting at age 28, September 27, 1862, for the war. No further records. Survived the war.

WRIGHT, REASON B., Private
Resided in Roane County, Tennessee, and was by occupation a laborer prior to enlisting at Winter's Gap, Tennessee, at about age 25, September 27, 1862, for the war. Reported present through February 28, 1863. Reported absent sick from February 9 through June 30, 1863. Died at home in Roane County on July 14, 1863, of disease. [His surname may have been Right.]

WRIGHT, STANFORD, _____
Born in Jefferson County, Tennessee, and resided in Roane County, Tennessee, where he was by occupation a farmer prior to enlisting at age 26, September 27, 1862, for the war. No further records.

WRIGHT, THOMAS CLARK, Corporal
Born in Anderson County, Tennessee, and resided in Roane or Knox County, Tennessee, where he was by occupation a farmer prior to enlisting at Winter's Gap, Tennessee, at age 24, September 27, 1862, for the war. Mustered in as Private. Reported present through February 28, 1863. Reported sick at home from April 9 through June 30, 1863. Returned to duty prior to October 31, 1863. Promoted to Corporal on August 1, 1863. Reported present through February 29, 1864. Captured at Piedmont, Virginia, June 5, 1864. Confined at Camp Morton, Indianapolis, Indiana, June 21, 1864. Released at Camp Morton on May 23, 1865, after taking the Oath of Allegiance. [See Tennessee pension application No. 4732.]

WRIGHT, WILLIAM, Private
Born in Roane County, Tennessee, where he resided as a farmer prior to enlisting at Winter's Gap, Tennessee, at age 26, September 27, 1862, for the war. Name next appears on company muster roll dated April 6, 1864, listed as a deserter.

MISCELLANEOUS

ADAMS, ELIJAH, Private
Resided in Cherokee County. Place and date of enlistment not reported. Deserted to the enemy on an unspecified date. Took the Oath of Allegiance at Chattanooga, Tennessee, May 24, 1865.

ADAMS, WILLIAM, _____
Resided in Cherokee County. Place and date of enlistment not reported. Took the Oath of Allegiance at Chattanooga, Tennessee, May 24, 1865.

ALFORD, S. A., Private
Place and date of enlistment not reported. Deserted to the enemy on an unspecified date. Confined at Knoxville, Tennessee, April 16, 1865. Transferred to Chattanooga, Tennessee, April 17, 1865. No further records.

BROBSTON, JOSEPH, Private
Place and date of enlistment not reported. Deserted to the enemy at an unspecified date. Took the Oath of Allegiance at Knoxville, Tennessee, December 29, 1863.

BRUCE, HARVEY, Private
Resided in Cherokee County. Place and date of enlistment not reported. Took the Oath of Allegiance at Chattanooga, Tennessee, May 24, 1865.

BUCHANAN, C. M., _____
North Carolina pension records appear to indicate that he served in this regiment and survived the war.

COBB, L. C., _____
Name appears on a prisoner of war record which indicates that he was captured at Knoxville, Tennessee, in March, 1865, and was sent to Chattanooga, Tennessee. No further records.

COTTER, ANDREW J., Private
Resided in Cherokee County. Took the Oath of Allegiance at Chattanooga, Tennessee, May 24, 1865. Survived the war.

GUY, G. W., _____
North Carolina pension records appear to indicate that he served in this regiment and survived the war.

HAWKINS, DAVID M., Private
Resided in Cherokee County. Place and date of enlistment not reported. Deserted to the enemy on an unspecified date. Sent to Nashville, Tennessee. Transferred to Louisville, Kentucky, on December 23, 1863, and arrived there on December 24. Released at Louisville on December 25, 1863, after taking the Oath of Allegiance, and sent north of the Ohio River.

MARTIN, WILLIAM CARROLL, _____
North Carolina pension records indicate that he served in this regiment. Survived the war.

SANDERS, THOMPSON A., _____
North Carolina pension records indicate that he served in this regiment. Survived the war.

SHROAT, B. P., _____
North Carolina pension records appear to indicate that he served in this regiment.

THOMAS, CUDGE, _____
Negro. North Carolina pension records indicate that he served in this regiment as servant to Capt., Maj. and Col. William Holland Thomas throughout the latter's service.

TIPTON, EDWARD C., Private
Resided in Washington County, Tennessee. Place and date of enlistment not reported; probably enlisted subsequent to February 29, 1864. Records of the Federal Provost Marshal appear to indicate that he served in the 1st Regiment N.C. State Troops; however, it seems more probable that he was a member of this regiment. Took the Oath of Allegiance at Chattanooga, Tennessee, May 27, 1865.

TIPTON, JACOB, Private
Resided in Bradley County, Tennessee. Place and date of enlistment not reported, probably enlisted subsequent to February 29, 1864. Took the Oath of Allegiance at Chattanooga, Tennessee, April 20, 1865.

WEST, DAVID M., Private
Previously served as Private in Company D, 62nd Regiment N.C. Troops. Enlisted in an unknown company of this regiment while absent without leave from the 62nd Regiment in September-October, 1862. No further records. [He may be the same man as Pvt. David West of Companies F and G of this regiment.]

LT. COL. WILLIAM C. WALKER'S BATTALION (LT. COL. J. A. McKAMY'S BATTALION)

FIELD AND STAFF

LIEUTENANT COLONELS

WALKER, WILLIAM CLAY

Previously served as Captain of Company B of this battalion. Elected Lieutenant Colonel on October 1, 1862, to rank from September 27, 1862, and transferred to the Field and Staff. Signature appears on payment vouchers for service from September 1 through December 31, 1862. Reported present in March-April, 1863. Name appears on a list to serve on a general court-martial on or about May 4, 1863. Signature appears on a payment voucher for service in May-June, 1863. Reported on detached duty apprehending deserters from September 29 until December 1, 1863, when he was reported absent without leave. Reported on detached service collecting absentees and deserters, December 12, 1863. "Murdered" on the night of January 3, 1864, by "bushwhackers" while at home sick. He was "a good man, a good citizen, & a good soldier" according to Lt. Col. James R. Love of the Infantry Regiment of this legion.

McKAMY, JAMES A.

Previously served as Captain of Company C of this battalion. Elected Major on August 15, 1863, and transferred to the Field and Staff. Signature appears on a payment voucher for service from October 1 through 31, 1863. Promoted to Lieutenant Colonel February 22-25, 1864, to rank from January 3-4, 1864. Name appears as signature on a petition to Gov. Zebulon B. Vance dated February 25, 1864, requesting his assistance in reuniting Thomas's Legion and removing it from the command of Brig. Gen. Alfred E. Jackson. Captured at Winchester, Virginia, September 19, 1864. Sent to Harpers Ferry, West Virginia. Confined at Fort Delaware, Delaware, September 27, 1864. Released at Fort Delaware on July 24, 1865, after taking the Oath of Allegiance.

STRINGFIELD, WILLIAM WILLIAMS

Previously served as Major of the Infantry Regiment of this legion. Transferred to this battalion with the rank of Major prior to February 21, 1865. Promoted to Lieutenant Colonel on or about March 6, 1865. Captured at Knoxville, Tennessee, May 1, 1865. Released by a civil court at Knoxville on May 24, 1865, after taking the Oath of Allegiance.

MAJOR

WHITAKER, STEPHEN

Served as Captain of Company E of this battalion, and commanded the battalion at some point in June-July, 1864. Clark's *Regiments*, 4:118, and *Confederate Military History*, Extended Ed., 5:791, indicate that he was promoted to Major of this battalion, but wartime records indicate that he was still a Captain at the time of his parole on May 12, 1865.

ADJUTANT

GASTON, PARLEY C.

Previously served as Sergeant Major of the 7th Battalion N.C. Cavalry. Assigned to this battalion as Acting Adjutant on May 20, 1863. Appointed Adjutant (1st Lieutenant), January 18, 1864, to rank from May 20, 1863. Accepted the appointment on February 25, 1864. Name appears on requisitions dated August 1 and September 1, 1864, and on a receipt roll for clothing dated August 8, 1864. No further records. Survived the war. [His given name may have been Perry.]

ASSISTANT QUARTERMASTER

JOHNSTON, THOMAS DILLARD

Previously served as 2nd Lieutenant of Company F, 14th Regiment N.C. Troops (4th Regiment N.C. Volunteers). While absent wounded from that company, he was appointed Assistant Quartermaster (Captain) of this battalion on April 11, 1863, to rank from January 13, 1863. Reported present on April 30, 1863. Signature appears on a petition to Gov. Zebulon B. Vance dated February 25, 1864, requesting his assistance in reuniting Thomas's Legion and removing it from the command of Brig. Gen. Alfred E. Jackson. Appointed Assistant Commissary of Subsistence (Captain) of this legion on November 25, 1864, to rank from November 21, 1864. No further records. Survived the war.

SURGEON

MAYFIELD, BENJAMIN

Born in 1819. Resided in Virginia. Appointed Surgeon of this battalion on February 9, 1863. Reported present in March-April, 1863. Reduced to the rank of Assistant Surgeon on February 2, 1864, to rank from May 4, 1863.

ASSISTANT SURGEONS

GREEN, CHARLES H.

Previously served as Assistant Surgeon for 5th Regiment Georgia Volunteer Infantry. Appointed Assistant Surgeon of this battalion on November 4, 1863. Name appears on receipts for forage dated August 1 and September 1, 1864, and on a receipt roll for clothing dated August 8, 1864. Reported absent on January 17, 1865. No further records.

MAYFIELD, BENJAMIN

Previously served as Surgeon of this battalion. Reduced to the rank of Assistant Surgeon on February 2, 1864, to rank from May 4, 1863. No further records. Survived the war.

SERGEANT MAJOR

WALKER, COLUMBUS F., Private

Previously served as Private in Company B of this battalion. A muster roll for that company states that he was appointed Sergeant Major on December 1, 1862. However, he is listed as a Private in that company on that roll and the company muster roll for November-December, 1862. He is listed as Sergeant Major on the Field and Staff muster roll for March-April, 1863, and a pay voucher dated May 12, 1863. Name appears on receipt rolls for clothing dated September 1 and September 27, 1864. No further records. Survived the war. [North Carolina pension records indicate that he suffered a broken left leg at Fisher's Hill, Virginia, September 22, 1864. According to a 1895 letter to Lt. Col. William W. Stringfield, his injury occurred when "(d)uring a cavalry charge made by the Feds I got one of my legs mashed." In the same letter, he stated, "When at

Green[e]ville I was taken sick of Typhoid Fever, was sent to Emly [Emory &] Henry Hospita spent night crazy and naked on the steps . . . was from there sent to White Sulpher Springs Va where I remained until in Nov (1863) - was furloughed and sent home reached home in Dec. found my father at home sick On the 3[d] night of Jany our house was surrounded father was killed. I was Captured and Carried on a horse . . . a distance of eight miles. I feigned to be almost dead was turned loose. Went back home burried father and in three weeks went back to my Command there at Zollicoffer Tenn"]

QUARTERMASTER SERGEANT

NELSON, WILLIAM N., Private

Previously served as Private in Company B of this battalion. Appointed Quartermaster Sergeant and transferred to the Field and Staff on December 1, 1862. Reported present through April 30, 1863. Name appears on payment vouchers for service from May 1 through October 31, 1863 and from November 1 through December 31, 1863. Name appears on a receipt roll for clothing dated October 16, 1864. Took the Oath of Allegiance at Chattanooga, Tennessee, May 21, 1865.

COMMISSARY SERGEANTS

HUGHES, ANDREW J.

Served as Private in Company B of this battalion. Detailed as Acting Commissary Sergeant of the battalion from March 1 through June 30 and from August 1 through September 20, 1863. Deserted at Carter's Depot, Tennessee, September 22, 1863.

McCULLOCH, THOMAS E., Private

Previously served as Private in Company C of this battalion. Detailed as Acting Commissary Sergeant in September-October, 1863, and transferred to the Field and Staff. Reported on detail with the Field and Staff through February 29, 1864. Name appears on receipt rolls for clothing dated June 22 and September 1, 1864. May have been officially appointed Commissary Sergeant. Took the Oath of Allegiance at Chattanooga, Tennessee, May 21, 1865.

ORDNANCE SERGEANT

McGEE, EDWIN P., Private

Previously served as Private in Company A of this battalion. Appointed Ordnance Sergeant and transferred to the Field and Staff on January 15, 1863. Reported present through April 30, 1863. Captured at Strawberry Plains, Tennessee, June 20, 1863, and paroled there the next day. Reported present, October 31-December 31, 1863. Name appears on receipt rolls for clothing dated March 15, September 1, and September 27, 1864. No further records. [His middle name may have been Patton. His surname may have been McGehee.]

HOSPITAL STEWARD

MAYFIELD, RANSFORD D., Private

Previously served as Private in Company A of this battalion. Appointed Hospital Steward on or about March 11, 1863, and transferred to the Field and Staff. Reported present through April 30, 1863. Reported absent without leave, May 1-October 31, 1863. Reduced to ranks and transferred back to Company A on or prior to October 31, 1863.

COMPANY A

This company was raised in Cherokee County. It was organized and mustered into Confederate service at Beaverdam on July 18, 1862, "for Local Defense of the Carolinas E Tennessee South western Virginia & the Cumberland Mountains in Ky."

The following roster was compiled in large part from company muster rolls dated July 18, 1862-April, 1863, and October 31, 1863-February, 1864. These are abstracted in the microfilm edition of the Compiled Service Records of Confederate Soldiers Who Served in Organizations from the State of North Carolina (Record Group 109, M270), National Archives, Washington, D.C. Other valuable information in the Compiled Service Records includes enlistment papers, pay vouchers, requisitions, letters of resignation, discharge certificates, and abstracts of medical and prisoner of war records.

Also utilized in this roster were *The War of the Rebellion: A Compilation of the Official Records of the Union and Confederate Armies*, the North Carolina Adjutant General's papers, state militia records, newspaper casualty lists and obituaries, wartime claims for bounty pay and allowances, postwar registers of claims for artificial limbs, Confederate pension applications filed with the states of North Carolina, Tennessee, and Florida, records of the North Carolina Confederate Soldiers' Home, and the 1860 and 1870 federal censuses of North Carolina. A search was made also for relevant letters, diaries, reminiscences, and other manuscripts in the Southern Historical Collection (University of North Carolina-Chapel Hill) and the Duke University Library Special Collections Department.

Among the secondary sources consulted were records of the North Carolina division of the United Daughters of the Confederacy, postwar rosters, regimental and county histories, marriage bond, will, and cemetery indexes, published and unpublished genealogies, biographical dictionaries, the North Carolina *County Heritage Book* series, the *Confederate Veteran*, Walter Clark's *Histories of the Several Regiments and Battalions from North Carolina in the Great War, 1861-'65*, and the North Carolina volume of the extended edition of *Confederate Military History*.

OFFICERS

CAPTAIN

BERRY, C. C.

Born in Gilmer County, Georgia, and resided in Cherokee County. Enlisted in Cherokee County. Appointed Captain on July 18, 1862. Reported present through August 31, 1862, and in November, 1862-February, 1863. Wounded accidentally in the right armpit on April 27, 1863. Sent on detached service on October 23, 1863, for twenty-five days by order of Maj. Gen. Robert Ransom, for recruitment, arrest of deserters and gathering up of absentees for return to their commands. Ordered to remain in western North Carolina by Lt. Col. William C. Walker of this battalion to operate with his collected absentees in Cherokee County. Reported absent without leave from November 20, 1863, through about February 29, 1864. Dropped from the company rolls by order of the Secretary of War on February 25, 1864, for prolonged absence without leave. An examining board appointed by the headquarters of the Mountain District of North Carolina concluded on February 20, 1865, that his absence had been due to orders, and recommended his restoration to rank. Restored to the company rolls on March 30, 1865. Survived the war. [See his Tennessee pension application No. 5857.]

LIEUTENANTS

BERRY, ANDREW C., 3rd Lieutenant

Born in Macon County in 1835 and resided in Cherokee County where he was by occupation a farmer prior to enlisting in Cherokee County at age 26. Appointed 3rd Lieutenant on July 18, 1862. Reported present through August 31, 1862, and in January-April, 1863. Reported absent without leave from about October 20, 1863, through about February 29, 1864. Dropped from the company rolls on March 23, 1864. [See his Tennessee pension application No. 11943.]

BRYSON, JAMES N., 1st Lieutenant

Born in Haywood County and resided in Cherokee County where he was by occupation a farmer prior to enlisting at Beaverdam at age 31. Appointed 1st Lieutenant on July 18, 1862, or September 30, 1862. Reported present or accounted for through August 31, 1862, in November, 1862-April, 1863, and in September, 1863-February, 1864. Name appears as signature to a special requisition dated March 15, 1864. No further records.

BURGESS, ELISHA F., 2nd Lieutenant

Born in Cherokee County where he resided as a farmer prior to enlisting at Beaverdam at age 21. Appointed 2nd Lieutenant on July 18, 1862. Reported present or accounted for through August 31, 1862; in January-May, 1863; and in July, 1863-February, 1864. Wounded at Winchester, Virginia, September 19, 1864. Hospitalized at Lynchburg, Virginia. Returned to duty on or about October 14, 1864. No further records. Survived the war.

NONCOMMISSIONED OFFICERS AND PRIVATES

ADAMS, JAMES, Private

Born in Macon County and resided in Cherokee County where he was by occupation a farmer prior to enlisting in Cherokee County at age 26, July 18, 1862, for the war. Mustered in as Private. Reported present in July-August and November-December 31, 1862. Promoted to Corporal in September-December, 1862. Reported absent with leave on February 28, 1863. Reduced to ranks in March-April, 1863. Transferred to Company H of this battalion on April 1, 1863.

ALLEN, JAMES, Private

Born in the part of Macon County that later became Cherokee County. Resided in Cherokee County as a farmer prior to enlisting in Cherokee County at age 25, July 18, 1862, for the war. Reported present through August 31, 1862. Reported absent sick on December 31, 1862. Reported present on February 28, 1863. No further records.

ALLISON, BENJAMIN, JR.

Born in Henderson County and resided in Cherokee County where he was by occupation a farmer prior to enlisting in Cherokee County at age 22, July 18, 1862, for the war. Mustered in as Corporal. Reported present through August 31, 1862. Reduced to ranks in November-December, 1862. Reported present in November, 1862-February, 1863. No further records.

ALLISON, BENJAMIN, SR., Private

Previously served as Private in Company A, 39th Regiment N.C. Troops. Deserted from that company on September 18 or December 25, 1862. Enlisted in this company on January 29, 1863, while a deserter from the 39th Regiment. Reported absent sick on February 28, 1863. Returned to duty in March-April, 1863. Reported absent without leave, June 25-October 31, 1863. Subsequenty reported as having deserted at Loudon, Tennessee, July 1, 1863.

ALLISON, ISAAC, Private

Born in Burke County and resided in Cherokee County where he was by occupation a farmer prior to enlisting in Cherokee County at age 33, August 15, 1862, for the war. Reported present through August 31, 1862, and in November-December, 1862. Reported on detached service arresting deserters on February 28, 1863. Reported absent without leave from March 6 through April 30, 1863. No further records.

ANDERSON, JAMES M., _____

May have previously served in Company G of this battalion, and possibly in Company H, 1st Regiment Tennessee Cavalry (Carter's). Name appears on a receipt roll for clothing dated October 16, 1864. According to a letter from Assistant Quartermaster Thomas D. Johnston of this battalion to Col. William H. Thomas, dated April 11, 1865, Anderson was a member of this company, and had been assisting Johnston since February 1, 1865.

BALL, JOHNSON, Private

Resided in Cherokee County and was by occupation a farmer prior to enlisting at Beaverdam at age 22, July 18, 1862, for the war. Reported present through August 31, 1862, and in November, 1862-April, 1863. Captured at Strawberry Plains, Tennessee, June 20, 1863. Paroled at Strawberry Plains on June 21, 1863. Died at Strawberry Plains on or about June 25, 1863, of "febris con[tinua] com[munis]."

BARNES, ELIJAH J., Corporal

Born in Macon County and resided in Cherokee County where he was by occupation a farmer prior to enlisting at Cherokee County at age 18, October 4, 1862, for the war. Mustered in as Private. Reported present in November-December, 1862. Reported on sick furlough on February 28, 1863. Reported present in March-April, 1863. Promoted to Corporal prior to June 20, 1863. Captured at Strawberry Plains, Tennessee, June 20, 1863, and paroled there the next day. Reported absent without leave, June 25-October 31, 1863. Subsequently reported as having deserted at Loudon, Tennessee, July 1, 1863.

BASWELL, SAMUEL, Private

Born in Spartanburg District, South Carolina, and resided in Polk County, Tennessee, where he was by occupation a farmer prior to enlisting in Cherokee County at age 52, October 1, 1862, for the war. Reported present in November, 1862-February, 1863. Reported absent sick from March 6 through April 30, 1863. Captured at Strawberry Plains, Tennessee, June 20, 1863. Paroled at Strawberry Plains on June 21, 1863. Reported sick in hospital at Abingdon, Virginia, October 27, 1863. Discharged on November 19, 1863, by reason of disability. [His surname may have been Bassell.]

BERRY, JAMES P., 1st Sergeant

Born in Macon County and resided in Cherokee County where he was by occupation a farmer prior to enlisting in Cherokee County at age 25, July 18, 1862, for the war. Mustered in as 1st Sergeant. Reported present through August 31, 1862, and in November, 1862-April, 1863. Captured at Strawberry Plains, Tennessee, June 20, 1863. Paroled at Strawberry Plains, Tennessee, June 21, 1863. Reported sick in hospital on September 14, 1863. Deserted from hospital at Emory and Henry, Virginia, October 20, 1863.

BILLINGS, GEORGE W., Private

Born in South Carolina and resided in Cherokee County where he was by occupation a farmer prior to enlisting in Cherokee County at age 26, July 18, 1862, for the war. Reported present through August 31, 1862. Deserted on December 1, 1862.

BLACKWELL, DAVID, Sergeant

Born in Buncombe County and resided in Cherokee County where he was by occupation a farmer prior to enlisting at Beaverdam at age 25, July 18, 1862, for the war. Mustered in as Private. Reported present through August 31, 1862. Promoted to Sergeant in September-December, 1862. Reported present in November, 1862-February, 1863. Detailed by Brig. Gen. Alfred E. Jackson to apprehend absentees in North Carolina in March-April, 1863. Rejoined the company on May 1, 1863. Died at Strawberry Plains, Tennessee, June 18, 1863. Cause of death not reported.

BLACKWELL, JOSIAH S., Corporal

Born in Buncombe County and resided in Cherokee County where he was by occupation a farmer prior to enlisting in Cherokee County at age 29, July 18, 1862, for the war. Mustered in as Corporal. Reported present through August 31, 1862, and in November, 1862-April, 1863. Reported absent without leave, June 25-October 31, 1863. Subsequently reported as having deserted at Strawberry Plains, Tennessee, July 1, 1863.

BOWMAN, J. W., Private

Federal Provost Marshal records indicate that he was a member of either this company or of Company A, Indian Battalion. Place and date of enlistment not reported. Captured at Knoxville, Tennessee, May 1, 1865. Released on bond by a Knox County, Tennessee, civil court May 24, 1865. [He was probably a member of Lt. Col. William W. Stringfield's flag-of-truce party that was arrested at Knoxville on May 1, 1865, when its members refused to take the Oath of Allegiance.]

BRANNON, WILLIAM, Private

Born in Tennessee and resided in Cherokee County where he was by occupation a farmer prior to enlisting at Beaverdam at age 25, July 18, 1862, for the war. Reported present through August 31, 1862, and in November, 1862-February, 1863. No further records. Survived the war.

BRYSON, JAMES, Private

Born in the part of Haywood County that later became Macon County. Resided in Cherokee County where he was by occupation a farmer prior to enlisting at Beaverdam at age 35, July 18, 1862, for the war. Reported present through August 31, 1862, and in November 1862-Apri, 1863. Reported absent without leave, June 25-October 31, 1863. Subsequently reported as having deserted at Strawberry Plains, Tennessee, July 1, 1863. Went over to the enemy on an unspecified date, probably in 1865. Confined at Nashville, Tennessee, on or prior to March 22, 1865, where he took the Oath of Allegiance on that date. Confined at Louisville, Kentucky, March 26, 1865. Released "without parole to remain north of the Ohio River during the war" on March 28, 1865. [May have also served as 1st Sgt. in Company H, 7th Regiment Tennessee Mounted Infantry (Union).]

BRYSON, JOHN, Private

Enlisted in Cherokee County on January 25, 1863, for the war. Reported present through April 30, 1863. No further records.

BUCHANAN, W. R., Private

Previously served as Private in Company B of this battalion. Transferred to this company in March-April, 1863. Reported present through April 30, 1863. Deserted at Loudon, Tennessee, on or about July 15, 1863.

BURGESS, JOHN M., Private

Born in South Carolina and resided in Cherokee County where he was by occupation a farmer prior to enlisting at Beaverdam at age 24, July 18, 1862, for the war. Reported present through August 31, 1862, and in November, 1862-April, 1863. No further records. Survived the war.

BURNETT, JAMES A., Private

Enlisted in either this company or in 2nd Company A, Infantry Regiment of this legion, October 2, 1862, in Grainger County, Tennessee, for the war. Transferred to Company C of this battalion on February 1, 1863.

CARTER, SIDNEY G., Private

Born in Halifax County, Virginia, and resided in Polk County, Tennessee, where he was by occupation a miner prior to enlisting at Beaverdam, North Carolina, at age 34, September 28, 1862, for the war. Reported present in November, 1862-February, 1863. Detailed to North Carolina "after absentees," April 12-May 1, 1863. Transferred to Company C of this battalion in July-August, 1863.

CARTER, THOMAS, Private

Born in Halifax County, Virginia, and resided in Polk County, Tennessee, where he was by occupation a farmer prior to enlisting in Cherokee County at age 36, September 28, 1862, for the war. Reported present in November, 1862-April, 1863. Transferred to Company C of this battalion in July-August, 1863.

CARVER, G. WASHINGTON, Private

Born in Carter County, Tennessee, and resided in Cherokee County where he was by occupation a farmer prior to enlisting in Cherokee County at age 36, September 12, 1862, for the war. Reported present in November, 1862-April, 1863. No further records.

CHAMBERS, BEATY F., Private

Born in Buncombe County and resided in Cherokee County where he was by occupation a farmer prior to enlisting in Cherokee County at age 38, September 12, 1862, for the war. Reported present in November, 1862-April, 1863. Captured at Strawberry Plains, Tennessee, June 20, 1863. Paroled at Strawberry Plains, June 21, 1863. Reported absent without leave from June 25 through October 31,

1863. Subsequently reported as having deserted at Loudon, Tennessee, July 1, 1863.

CLARK, CALVIN, Private
Born in the part of Macon County that later became Cherokee County. Resided in Polk County, Tennessee, where he was by occupation a farmer prior to enlisting at Beaverdam, North Carolina, at age 26, September 28, 1862, for the war. Reported absent without leave in November-December, 1862. Returned to duty in January-February, 1863. Reported present in March-April, 1863. Captured at Strawberry Plains, Tennessee, June 20, 1863. Paroled at Strawberry Plains, June 21, 1863. Reported absent without leave, June 25-October 31, 1863. Subsequently reported as having deserted at Strawberry Plains, July 1, 1863.

COLE, GOODSON M., 1st Sergeant
Born in Buncombe County and resided in Polk County, Tennessee, where he was by occupation a farmer prior to enlisting in Cherokee County at age 26, September 28, 1862, for the war. Mustered in as Sergeant. Reported present or accounted for in November, 1862-April, 1863, and September-December, 1863. Promoted to 1st Sergeant on February 1, 1864. Reported absent without leave from February 7 through 29, 1864. Captured at Winchester, Virginia, September 19, 1864. Sent to Harpers Ferry, West Virginia. Confined at Point Lookout, Maryland, on or about September 26, 1864. Paroled on or about November 1, 1864. Received at Venus Point, Savannah River, Georgia, November 15, 1864, for exchange. No further records. Survived the war.

COLE, THOMAS M., Sergeant
Born in Buncombe County and resided in Cherokee County where he was by occupation a farmer prior to enlisting at Beaverdam at age 17, October 7, 1862, for the war. Mustered in as Private. Reported present through December 31, 1862. Reported detailed "to help a sick brother home," January-Februrary, 1863. Reported present in March-April, 1863. Captured at Stawberry Plains, Tennessee, June 20, 1863, and paroled there the next day. Promoted to Sergeant on October 1, 1863. Reported present in September, 1863-February, 1864. Name appears on receipt rolls for clothing dated March 15, September 1, and September 27, 1864. No further records. Survived the war.

COLVARD, J. P., Private
Probably resided in Cherokee County. Enlisted in Jefferson County, Tennessee, April 3, 1863, for the war as a substitute for Pvt. John Lee of this company. Reported present through April 30, 1863. Reported sick in hospital on October 15, 1863. Deserted from hospital at Emory and Henry, Virginia, October 20, 1863.

COOPER, RUFUS L., Sergeant
Born in Polk County, Tennessee, and resided in Cherokee County, North Carolina. Was by occupation a miner prior to enlisting at Beaverdam at age 18, September 28, 1862, for the war. Mustered in as Private. Reported present in November, 1862-April, 1863, and October 31, 1863-February, 29, 1864. Promoted to Sergeant on February 1, 1864. Hospitalized at Winchester, Virginia, August 1, 1864, with chronic diarrhoea. Returned to duty prior to September 19, 1864, when he was captured at Winchester. Sent to Harpers Ferry, West Virginia. Confined at Point Lookout, Maryland, September 26, 1864. Paroled at Point Lookout on March 15, 1865. Received at Boulware's Wharf, James River, Virginia, March 18, 1865, for exchange. Took the Oath of Allegiance at Chattanooga, Tennessee, May 27, 1865.

CORRUTH, JAMES, _____
Born in McMinn County, Tennessee, and resided in Polk County, Tennessee, where he was by occupation a farmer prior to enlisting at age 31, September 28, 1862, for the war. Rejected by the mustering officer. Reason he was rejected not reported.

CRAIN, JOHN L., Private
Born in Cherokee County where he resided as a farmer prior to enlisting at Beaverdam at age 22, July 18, 1862, for the war. Reported present through August 31, 1862, and in November-December, 1862. Transferred to Company E of this battalion in January-February, 1863. [His surname may have been Crane.]

CRAIN, SAMUEL, Private
Resided in the part of Macon County that later became Cherokee County, and was by occupation a farmer prior to enlisting at Beaverdam at age 26, July 18, 1862, for the war. Reported present through December 31, 1862. Transferred to Company E of this battalion in January-February, 1863. [His surname may have been Crane.]

CRAIN, SPENCER, Private
Born in Wilkes County and resided in Cherokee County where he was by occupation a farmer prior to enlisting at Beaverdam at age 31, July 18, 1862, for the war. Reported present through August 31, 1862, and in November, 1862-April, 1863. No further records. [His surname may have been Crane.]

CRAWLEY, WILLIAM, Private
Enlisted either in this company or in 2nd Company A, Infantry Regiment of this legion, at about age 25, September 29, 1862, in Blount County, Tennessee. Transferred to Company C of this battalion on February 1, 1863.

CURTIS, WILLIAM J., Private
Born in Macon County and resided in Polk County, Tennessee, where he was by occupation a miner prior to enlisting at Beaverdam, North Carolina, at age 20, September 28, 1862, for the war. Reported present in November-December, 1862. Reported on detached service to arrest deserters, January-February, 1863. Reported present in March-April, 1863. Captured at Strawberry Plains, Tennessee, June 20, 1863. Paroled at Strawberry Plains, June 21, 1863. Reported absent without leave, June 25-October 31, 1863. Subsequently reported as having deserted at Strawberry Plains, Tennessee, July 1, 1863.

DAVIDSON, JOHN M., Private
Enlisted in Cherokee County on February 9, 1863, for the war. Reported present through February 28, 1863. Detailed to North Carolina on April 12, 1863, to capture absentees, and reported on this assignment on April 30, 1863. Reported absent without leave from June 20 through October 31, 1863. Subsequently reported as having deserted at Loudon, Tennessee, July 1, 1863.

DAVIS, CLEM, Private
Born in Buncombe County and resided in Cherokee County where he was by occupation a farmer prior to enlisting at Beaverdam at age

28, July 18, 1862, for the war. Reported present through August 31, 1862. Reported absent without leave in November-December, 1862. Returned to duty in January-February, 1863. No further records.

DAVIS, JACOB, Private
Born in Blount County, Tennessee, and resided in Cherokee County where he was by occupation a farmer prior to enlisting at Beaverdam at age 24, July 18, 1862, for the war. Reported present through August 31, 1862, and in November, 1862-April, 1863. Captured at Strawberry Plains, Tennessee, June 20, 1863, and paroled there the next day. Reported absent without leave, June 25-October 31, 1863. Subsequently reported as having deserted at Strawberry Plains, July 1, 1863. Went over to the enemy on an unspecified date. Took the Oath of Allegiance at Knoxville, Tennessee on or about March 13, 1865.

DAVIS, JAMES R., Private
Born in Buncombe County and resided in Cherokee County where he was by occupation a farmer prior to enlisting at Beaverdam at age 21, July 18, 1862, for the war. Was apparently mustered in as Corporal. Reported present through August 31, 1862. Reported absent without leave and was reduced to ranks prior to December 31, 1862. Returned to duty in January-February, 1863. Enlisted as Private in Company K, Infantry Regiment of this legion, February 6, 1863.

DAVIS, MITCHEL, Private
Born in Buncombe County and resided in Cherokee County where he was by occupation a farmer prior to enlisting at Beaverdam at age 28, July 18, 1862, for the war. Reported present through August 31, 1862, and in November, 1862-February, 1863. No further records.

DAVIS, WILLIAM, Private
Born in Buncombe County and resided in Cherokee County where he was by occupation a farmer prior to enlisting at Beaverdam at age 23, July 18, 1862, for the war. No further records.

DOCKERY, JACOB, Private
Born in Buncombe County and resided in Cherokee County where he was by occupation a farmer prior to enlisting at Beaverdam at age 18, July 18, 1862, for the war. Mustered in as Corporal. Reported present through August 31, 1862. Reduced to ranks on an unspecified date. Transferred to Company A, 29th Regiment N.C. Troops, in November, 1862.

EALY, ROBERT, Private
Born in Lee County, Virginia, and resided in Cherokee County, North Carolina, where he was by occupation a farmer prior to enlisting at Beaverdam at age 24. Enlistment date reported as July 18, 1862; however, he was not listed on the muster rolls of this company until March-April, 1863. Transferred to Company H of this battalion on April 1, 1863.

EARL, NOAH, Private
Resided in Macon County. Federal Provost Marshal records indicate that he was a member either of this company or of Company A, Indian Battalion. Place and date of enlistment unknown. Captured at Knoxville, Tennessee, May 1, 1865. Transferred to Nashville, Tennessee, May 3, 1865. Confined at Louisville, Kentucky, May 15, 1865. Released at Louisville on June 16, 1865, after taking the Oath of Allegiance. [His surname may have been Earles or Erles. He may have served previously in Company E, 39th Regiment N.C. Troops. His capture at Knoxville on May 1 indicates that he was a member of Lt. Col. William W. Stringfield's flag-of-truce party that was arrested when they refused to take the Oath of Allegiance.]

EDWARDS, ALONZO, Corporal
Born in Cherokee County, North Carolina, and resided in Polk County, Tennessee, where he was by occupation a miner prior to enlisting at Beaverdam, North Carolina, at age 19, October 1, 1862, for the war. Was probably mustered in as Corporal. Reported present through December 31, 1862. Reported on detached service to arrest deserters in January-February, 1863. Rejoined the company prior to April 30, 1863. Deserted prior to May 12, 1863. Was captured and returned to the battalion prior to August 13, 1863. No further records.

ELY, ROBERT, Private
Enlisted in Cherokee County on July 18, 1862, for the war. Mustered in as Sergeant. Reported present through August 31, 1862. Reduced to ranks in September-December, 1862. Reported present in November-December, 1862. Reported on detached service to catch deserters in January-February, 1863. Transferred to Company I, Infantry Regiment of this legion, March-April, 1863. [His middle initial may have been G. He may have served previously as Private in Company A, 29th Regiment N.C. Troops.]

ERWIN, GEORGE W., Private
Resided in Monroe County, Tennessee, and was by occupation a farmer prior to enlisting in Monroe County at age 40, March 4, 1863, for the war. Reported present through April 30, 1863. Reported absent without leave on June 25, 1863. Subsequently reported as having deserted at Strawberry Plains, Tennessee, July 1, 1863. Went over to the enemy on an unspecified date. Sent to Knoxville, Tennessee. Released at Knoxville on February 29, 1864, after taking the Oath of Allegiance.

ERWIN, PATRICK, Private
Resided in Monroe County, Tennessee, and was by occupation a farmer prior to enlisting in Monroe County at age 36, March 4, 1863, for the war. Reported present through April 30, 1863. Captured at Strawberry Plains, Tennessee on June 20, 1863. Paroled at Strawberry Plains on or about June 21, 1863. Reported absent without leave from June 25 through October 31, 1863. Subsequently reported as having deserted at Loudon, Tennessee, July 1, 1863.

EVANS, FRANCIS MARION, Private
Born in Marion County, Tennessee, and resided in Cherokee County, North Carolina, where he was by occupation a farmer prior to enlisting at Beaverdam at age 33, July 18, 1862, for the war. Reported present through August 31, 1862, and in November, 1862-April, 1863. No further records.

FARMER, GEORGE W., Private
Enlisted in Fannin County, Georgia, April 4, 1863, for the war. Deserted at Carter's Depot, Tennessee, on or about September 23, 1863.

FRY, CHARLES, Private
Born in Monroe County, Tennessee, where he resided as a farmer prior to enlisting at Beaverdam, North Carolina, at age 18, August 15, 1862, for the war. Reported present through August 31, 1862, and in November, 1862-April, 1863. Reported absent without leave

on June 25, 1863. Subsequently reported as having deserted at Loudon, Tennessee, July 1, 1863.

GILLESPIE, WILLIAM, Private
Born in Burke County and resided in Polk County, Tennessee, where he was by occupation a miner prior to enlisting in Polk County, Tennessee, at age 21, September 26, 1862, for the war. Reported present in November, 1862-April, 1863. Captured at Strawberry Plains, Tennessee, June 20, 1863, and paroled the next day. Reported present, October 31, 1863-February 29, 1864. Name appears on receipt rolls for clothing dated March 15, June 19, and September 18, 1864. No further records.

GREEN, CHARLES J., Private
Born in Buncombe County and resided in Cherokee County where he was by occupation a farmer prior to enlisting at Beaverdam at age 28, July 18, 1862, for the war. Illegally enlisted in Company B of this battalion on July 19, 1862. Transferred back to this company in September-December, 1862. Reported present in January-April, 1863. Captured at Strawberry Plains, Tennesse, June 20, 1863, and paroled the next day. Reported absent without leave on June 25, 1863. Subsequently reported as having deserted at Loudon, Tennessee, July 1, 1863. [His given name may have been James C. or Jasper C.]

HALL, ELISHA, Private
Born in Buncombe County and resided in Polk County, Tennessee, where he was by occupation a farmer prior to enlisting in Cherokee County at age 37, December 1, 1862, for the war. Transferred to Company E of this battalion on or about December 19, 1862. Transferred back to this company prior to December 31, 1862. Reported present in January-April, 1863. Deserted at Blountville, Tennessee, November 3, 1863. Went over to the enemy on an unspecified date. Took the Oath of Allegiance at Chattanooga, Tennessee, April 5, 1864.

HALL, HENRY B., Private
Born in the part of Pendleton District that later became Pickens District, South Carolina. Resided in Polk County, Tennessee, where he was by occupation a farmer prior to enlisting in Cherokee County at age 41, October 7, 1862, for the war. Reported present in November, 1862-April, 1863. Deserted at Blountville, Tennessee, November 3, 1863.

HALL, JOHN, Private
Enlisted in Cherokee County on January 29, 1863, for the war. Reported present through April 30, 1863. Captured at Strawberry Plains, Tennessee, June 20, 1863, and paroled the next day. Reported absent without leave on June 25, 1863. Deserted at Loudon, Tennessee, July 1, 1863.

HAMPTON, JOHN, Private
Enlisted in Cherokee County on February 1, 1863, for the war. Reported present through April 30, 1863. Captured at Strawberry Plains, Tennessee, June 20, 1863, and paroled the next day. Deserted at Loudon, Tennessee, July 1, 1863.

HARRIS, JAMES, Private
Born in Lee County, Virginia, and resided in Cherokee County, North Carolina, where he was by occupation a farmer prior to enlisting at Beaverdam at age 21, July 18, 1862, for the war. Reported present through December 31, 1862. Reported on detached service to arrest deserters in January-February, 1863. Transferred to Company I, Infantry Regiment of this legion, April 1, 1863.

HARTNESS, DOCTOR, Private
Born in Cherokee County where he resided as a farmer prior to enlisting in Cherokee County at age 18, July 18, 1862, for the war. Reported present through August 31, 1862, and in November, 1862-April, 1863. Captured at Strawberry Plains, Tennessee, June 20, 1863, and paroled the next day. Reported absent without leave from June 25 through October 31, 1863. Subsequently reported as having deserted at Strawberry Plains, July 1, 1863.

HARTNESS, MARION, Private
Born in Cherokee County where he resided as a farmer prior to enlisting at Beaverdam at age 21, July 18, 1862, for the war. Enlisted, possibly illegally, in Company B of this battalion on July 19, 1862, and served with that unit through August 31, 1862. Transferred back to this company prior to October 31, 1862. Reported present in January-April, 1863. Captured at Strawberry Plains, Tennessee, June 20, 1863, and paroled the next day. Reported absent without leave from June 25 through October 31, 1863. Subsequently reported as having deserted at Strawberry Plains on July 1, 1863.

HENDERSON, JOHN G., Private
Federal Provost Marshal records identify him as a member of either this company or Company A, Indian Battalion. Place and date of enlistment not reported. Captured at Knoxville, Tennessee, May 1, 1865. Released by a Knox County, Tennessee, civil court on May 24, 1865. [His capture at Knoxville on May 1, 1865, indicates that he was a member of Lt. Col. William W. Stringfield's flag-of-truce party that was arrested when they refused to take the Oath of Allegiance.]

HENSON, EDWARD, Private
Born in Buncombe County and resided in Cherokee County where he was by occupation a farmer prior to enlisting at Beaverdam at age 21, August 12, 1862, for the war. Reported present through August 31, 1862. Reported absent without leave in November-December, 1862. Returned to duty in January-February, 1863. No further records.

HENSON, THOMAS, Private
Born in Buncombe or Cherokee County and resided in Cherokee County where he was by occupation a farmer prior to enlisting at Beaverdam at age 21, August 12, 1862, for the war. Reported present through August 31, 1862. Transferred to 2nd Company A, Infantry Regiment of this legion, prior to December 31, 1862.

HICKEY, BRITTON, Private
Enlisted in Cherokee County on November 10, 1862, for the war. Reported absent without leave on December 31, 1862. Reported present in January-February, 1863. No further records.

HICKEY, JAMES, Private
Enlisted at Beaverdam in Cherokee County on July 18, 1862, for the war. Rejected for service by the surgeon.

HICKEY, JOHN L., Private
Enlisted in Cherokee County on November 6, 1862, for the war. Reported absent without leave on December 31, 1862. Reported present in January-February, 1863. No further records.

HILL, M. C., Private

Enlisted in Cherokee County on December 28, 1862, for the war. Reported present through April 30, 1863. Captured at Strawberry Plains on June 20, 1863, and paroled on the same date. Reported absent without leave from June 25 through October 31, 1863. Subsequently reported as having deserted at Loudon, Tennessee, on or about June 25, 1863.

HITSON, CALVIN, Private

Previously enlisted as Private in Company H, 39th Regiment N.C. Troops. Failed to report for duty with that unit. Enlisted in this company at Beaverdam at age 21, October 20, 1862, for the war. Reported present in November, 1862-April, 1863. No further records.

HOLLINGSHEAD, J. T., Corporal

Enlisted in Cherokee County on March 3, 1863, for the war. Mustered in as Private. Reported present through April 30, 1863. Promoted to Corporal subsequent to April 30, 1863. Captured at Strawberry Plains, Tennessee, June 20, 1863, and paroled the next day. Reported absent without leave from June 25 through October 31, 1863. Subsequently reported as having deserted at Strawberry Plains on July 1, 1863.

HOLLINGSHEAD, WHITTEN, Private

Resided in Cherokee County and was by occupation a farmer prior to enlisting in Cherokee County at age 18, August 22, 1862, for the war. Reported present through August 31, 1862, and in November-December, 1862. Reported on sick furlough in Cherokee County, January-April, 1863. Returned to duty prior to June 25, 1863. Reported absent without leave from June 25 through October 31, 1863. Subsequently reported as having deserted at Coker Creek, Tennessee, July 1, 1863.

HOWELL, ALNEY M., Private

Born in Haywood County and resided in Cherokee County where he was by occupation a farmer prior to enlisting at Beaverdam at age 32, July 18, 1862, for the war. Mustered in as Private. Reported present through August 31, 1862, and in November, 1862-February, 1863. Promoted to Corporal prior to April 10, 1863, when he was reported absent without leave. Returned to duty and was reduced to ranks prior to October 31, 1863. Reported present in November, 1863-December, 1863. Reported on extra duty with the battalion wagons in January-February, 1864. Reported on duty as a teamster September 3-30, 1864. No further records. Survived the war.

HOWELL, HARRISON L., Private

Previously served as Corporal in Company A, 39th Regiment N.C. Troops. Enlisted in this company in Cherokee County on January 29, 1863, for the war. Reported present through February 28, 1863. Accidentally wounded on March 29 or April 6, 1863, and reported absent sick or absent wounded in Cherokee County. Deserted at Strawberry Plains, Tennessee, July 1, 1863.

HUSKINS, WHITSON, Private

Resided in Blount County, Tennessee, and enlisted in Cherokee County, North Carolina, January 24, 1863, for the war. Reported present through April 30, 1863. Captured and paroled at Strawberry Plains, Tennessee, June 20, 1863, and paroled the next day. Reported absent without leave on June 25, 1863. Subsequently reported as having deserted at Strawberry Plains on July 1, 1863. Captured in Monroe County, Tennessee, on an unspecified date. Confined at Chattanooga, Tennessee, June 20, 1864. Took the Oath of Allegiance at Chattanooga on June 20, 1864. Transferred to Louisville, Kentucky, and arrived there on June 24, 1864. Took the Oath of Allegiance at Louisville on June 24, 1864. Discharged on June 26, 1864, "to be released North of the Ohio River."

HUTCHESON, HENRY M., Private

Born in Henderson County, North Carolina, and resided in Polk County, Tennessee, where he was by occupation a farmer prior to enlisting in Polk County at age 24, September 26, 1862, for the war. Reported present in November, 1862-April, 1863. Captured at Strawberry Plains, Tennessee, June 20, 1863, and paroled there the next day. Reported absent without leave from June 25 through October 31, 1863. Subsequently reported as having deserted at Loudon, Tennessee, July 1, 1863. Name appears on receipt rolls for clothing dated March 15, June 17, September 1, and September 27, 1864. No further records.

HYDE, JOHN AARON, Private

Enlisted in Polk County, Tennessee on February 15, 1863, for the war. Reported present through April 30, 1863. Captured at Strawberry Plains, Tennessee, June 20, 1863, and paroled there the next day. Reported absent without leave from June 25 through October 31, 1863. Subsequently reported as having deserted at Strawberry Plains on July 1, 1863.

INGRAM, ROBERT, Private

Born in Macon County and resided in Cherokee County where he was by occupation a farmer prior to enlisting at Beaverdam at age 26, July 18, 1862, for the war. Enlisted, possibly illegally, in Company B of this battalion on July 19, 1862, and served as a Corporal in that company through August 31, 1862. Transferred back to this company on an unspecified date. Reduced to ranks before or after his return to this company. Reported present in November-December, 1862, with the rank of Private. Reported absent without leave in January-February, 1863. No further records. Survived the war.

JAMES, ALBERT, Private

Born in North Carolina and resided in Cherokee County where he was by occupation a farmer prior to enlisting at Beaverdam at age 28, July 18, 1862, for the war. Reported present through August 31, 1862, and in November, 1862-April, 1863. Captured at Strawberry Plains, Tennessee, June 20, 1863, and paroled there the next day. Reported absent without leave, June 25, 1863. Subsequently reported as having deserted at Loudon, Tennessee, July 1, 1863.

JAMES, THOMAS, Private

Previously served as Private in Company H of this battalion. Transferred to this company on April 1, 1863. Reported absent without leave from June 25 through October 31, 1863. Subsequently reported as having deserted at Strawberry Plains, Tennessee, July 1, 1863.

JARVIS, T. A., _____

North Carolina pension records indicate that he served in this company. Survived the war.

JINKINS, FRANCIS F., Private

Born in Tennessee and resided in Polk County, Tennessee, where he was by occupation a farmer prior to enlisting in Cherokee County at age 15, October 28, 1862, for the war. Reported present through April 30, 1863. No further records. [His surname may have been Jenkins.]

JONES, ALFONZO J. F., Private
Born in Cherokee County where he resided as a farmer prior to enlisting in Cherokee County at age 16, October 23, 1862, for the war. Reported present through April 30, 1863. Captured at Strawberry Plains, Tennessee, June 20, 1863, and paroled the next day. Reported absent without leave from June 25 through October 31, 1863. Subsequently reported as having deserted at Loudon, Tennessee, July 1, 1863.

JONES, D. M., Private
Served either in this company or in Company A, Indian Battalion. Captured at Anderson, South Carolina, May 3, 1865. Paroled on an unspecified date.

JONES, JAMES A., Private
Cherokee Indian. Born in Cherokee County where he resided as a farmer prior to enlisting at Beaverdam at age 23 on July 18, 1862, for the war. Reportedly transferred to Company B, Infantry Regiment of this legion, on the same date, but there is no other evidence that he served in that company. Reported present with this company on August 31, 1862. Name next appears on receipt rolls for clothing dated March 15 and June 4, 1864. Hospitalized at Charlottesville, Virginia, June 12, 1864, with an abscess. Returned to duty on June 17, 1864. Reported in hospital at Harrisonburg, Virginia, September 20, 1864. Name appears on a receipt roll for clothing dated October 16, 1864. No further records.

KERKLEN, SAMUEL W., Private
Born in Haywood County and resided in Cherokee County where he was by occupation a farmer prior to enlisting at Beaverdam at age 28, July 18, 1862, for the war. Reported present through August 31, 1862, in November-December, 1862, and in March-April, 1863. No further records. [His surname may have been Kirkland.]

KERKLEN, WILLIAM A., Private
Born in Haywood County and resided in Cherokee County where he was by occupation a farmer prior to enlisting at Beaverdam at age 31, July 18, 1862, for the war. Reported present through August 31, 1862, and in November, 1862-April, 1863. No further records. [His surname may have been Kirkland.]

KIDD, JAMES C., Private
Born in Jackson County, Georgia, and resided in Cherokee County, North Carolina, where he was by occupation a farmer prior to enlisting at Beaverdam at age 16, July 18, 1862, for the war. Reported present through August 31, 1862, and in November, 1862-April, 1863. Captured at Strawberry Plains, Tennessee, June 20, 1863, and paroled there the next day. Deserted at Loudon, Tennessee, July 1, 1863. Went over to the enemy on an unspecified date. Took the Oath of Allegiance at Knoxville, Tennessee, January 23, 1864.

KIRKLIN, CALVIN, Private
Enlisted in Cherokee County on July 18, 1862, for the war; however, he was not listed in the records of this company until January-February, 1863, when he was reported present. No further records. [His surname may have been Kirkland.]

KLEPPER, JOHN M., Private
Resided in Hawkins, County, Tennessee, and was by occupation a farmer prior to enlisting either in this company or in 2nd Company A, Infantry Regiment of this legion, in Hawkins County, at about age 28, October 4, 1862, for the war. Transferred to Company C of this battalion on February 1, 1863.

LANE, J. P., Private
Name appears on a "Roll of Prisoners captured by U.S. Forces . . . and paroled at Hartwell, Ga., and Anderson and Greenville, S.C." which indicates that he served either in this company or in Company A, Indian Battalion.

LEE, JOHN, Private
Born in Jefferson County, Tennessee, and enlisted in Cherokee County on March 10, 1863, for the war. Discharged on April 3, 1863, after providing Pvt. J. P. Colvard of this company as a substitute.

LENDERMAN, AUGUSTUS, Private
Born in Wilkes County and resided in Monroe County, Tennessee, where he was by occupation a farmer prior to enlisting at Beaverdam, North Carolina, at age 17, October 20, 1862, for the war. Reported present through April 30, 1863. No further records.

LUNSFORD, MADISON M., Private
Born in Burke County and resided in Cherokee County where he was by occupation a farmer prior to enlisting at Beaverdam at age 18, July 18, 1862, for the war. Reported present through August 31, 1862, and in November-December, 1862. Reported absent sick in January-February, 1863. Reported present in March-April, 1863. Captured at Strawberry Plains, Tennessee, June 20, 1863, and paroled the next day. Reported absent without leave, June 25-October 31, 1863. Later reported as having deserted from Strawberry Plains, Tennessee, July 1, 1863.

McBEE, ELI, Private
Enlisted either in this company or in 2nd Company A, Infantry Regiment of this legion, in Grainger County, Tennessee, at about age 38, October 3, 1862, for the war. Transferred to Company C of this battalion on February 1, 1863.

McCALL, JOHN M., Private
Enlisted either in this company or in 2nd Company A, Infantry Regiment of this legion, at about age 34, January 20, 1863, for the war. Transferred to Company C of this battalion on February 1, 1863.

McDANIEL, JOHN, Private
Born in Macon County and resided in Cherokee County where he was by occupation a farmer prior to enlisting at Beaverdam at age 19, July 18, 1862, for the war. Reported present through August 31, 1862, and in November, 1862-April, 1863. Captured at Strawberry Plains, Tennessee, June 20, 1863, and paroled there the next day. Deserted at Strawberry Plains on July 1, 1863, while on sick furlough.

McDOUGAL, WILLIAM R., Corporal
Born in Rabun County, Georgia, and resided in Roane County, Tennessee, where he was by occupation a miner prior to enlisting at Beaverdam, North Carolina, at age 35, October 10, 1862, for the

war. Mustered in as Corporal. Reported present through February 28, 1863. Reported detailed by Brig. Gen. Alfred E. Jackson to North Carolina after deserters from April 12 through May 1, 1863. No further records.

McDOWELL, JOSEPH L., Private
Born in Cherokee County where he resided as a farmer prior to enlisting at Beaverdam at age 26, July 28, 1862, for the war. Reported present through August 31, 1862, and in November, 1862-February, 1863. Reported absent sick in Cherokee County from March 6 through April 30, 1863. No further records.

McGEE, EDWIN P., Private
Born in Haywood County and resided at Beaverdam where he was by occupation a farmer prior to enlisting in Cherokee County at age 30, October 7, 1862, for the war. Reported present through December 31, 1862. Promoted to Ordnance Sergeant on January 15, 1863, and transferred to the Field and Staff of this battalion. [His middle name may have been Patton. His surname may have been McGehee.]

McMILLIN, FRANK, Private
Enlisted in Cherokee County on February 1, 1863, for the war. Reported present through April 30, 1863. Reported absent without leave from June 25 through October 31, 1863. Subsequently reported as having deserted at Strawberry Plains, Tennessee, July 1, 1863.

MASHBURN, LOGAN B., Private
Born in Yancey County and resided in Cherokee County where he was by occupation a farmer prior to enlisting in Cherokee County at age 24, September 15, 1862, for the war. Reported present in November-December, 1862. Transferred to Company B of this battalion on February 1, 1863. [His surname may have been Mashbern.]

MATOY, LEVI C., Private
Cherokee Indian. Born in Cherokee County where he resided as a farmer prior to enlisting at age 19 on September 1, 1862, for the war. Place of enlistment not reported. Transferred to 2nd Company A, Infantry Regiment of this legion, September-October, 1862.

MATOY, WILLIAM R., Private
Cherokee Indian. Born in Habersham County, Georgia. Resided in Cherokee County, North Carolina, and was by occupation a farmer prior to enlisting at Quallatown at about age 42, September 1, 1862, for the war. Transferred to 2nd Company A, Infantry Regiment of this legion, September-October, 1862, to serve as an interpreter; he presumably spoke the Cherokee language.

MAYFIELD, RANSFORD D., Private
Enlisted in Polk County, Tennessee, February 28, 1863, for the war. Appointed Hospital Steward on or about March 11, 1863, and transferred to the Field and Staff of this battalion. Reduced to ranks and transferred back to this company on or prior to October 31, 1863, while absent without leave from the Field and Staff. Subsequently listed as having deserted at Loudon, Tennessee, July 1, 1863.

MILLIGAN, FRANK H., Private
Resided in Blount County, Tennessee, and enlisted either in this company or in 2nd Company A, Infantry Regiment of this legion, in Blount County at about age 20, January 21, 1863, for the war. Transferred to Company C of this battalion on February 1, 1863. [His given name may have been H. Frank.]

MOORE, WILLIAM, Private
Born in Cherokee County where he resided as a farmer prior to enlisting at Beaverdam at age 24, July 18, 1862, for the war. Reported present through August 31, 1862. Reported absent sick in November-December, 1862. Rejected for military service, probably for physical reasons, on an unspecified date. Dropped from the company rolls prior to February 28, 1863.

MORROW, AARON L., Private
Born in Union County, Georgia, and resided in Cherokee County, North Carolina, where he was by occupation a farmer prior to enlisting at Beaverdam at age 16, July 18, 1862, for the war. Reported present through August 31, 1862, and in November, 1862-February, 1863. No further records.

MORROW, GEORGE W., Private
Born in Haywood County and resided in Cherokee County where he was by occupation a farmer prior to enlisting at Beaverdam at age 20, July 18, 1862, for the war. Reported present through August 31, 1862, and in November, 1862-February, 1863. No further records.

MORROW, JAMES K., Private
Born in Haywood County and resided in Cherokee County where he was by occupation a farmer prior to enlisting at Beaverdam at age 24, July 18, 1862, for the war. Reported present or accounted for through August 31, 1862, and in November-December, 1862. Reported on leave in January-February, 1863. No further records.

MURPHY, DAVID, Private
Half Cherokee Indian. Born in the part of Haywood or Macon County that later became Cherokee County. Resided in Cherokee County as a farmer prior to enlisting at Beaverdam at age 30 or 38, August 20, 1862, for the war. Reported present through August 31, 1862. Transferred to Company B, Infantry Regiment of this legion, September 1, 1862.

MURPHY, JESSE, Private
Born in the part of Macon County that later became Cherokee County. Resided in Cherokee County as a farmer prior to enlisting at Beaverdam at age 28, August 21, 1862, for the war. Reported present through August 31, 1862, and in November, 1862-February, 1863. No further records.

MURPHY, JOHN, Private
Enlisted at Beaverdam on January 29, 1863, for the war. Reported both present and absent sick on February 28, 1863. Transferred to Company B, Infantry Regiment of this legion, April 1, 1863.

MURPHY, LEVI C., Private
Born in Cherokee County where he resided as a farmer prior to enlisting at Beaverdam at age 18, July 18, 1862, for the war. Reported present through August 31, 1862. Transferred to Company B, Infantry Regiment of this legion, prior to December 31, 1862.

MURPHY, WILLIAM, Private
Born in what later became Union County, Georgia. Resided in Cherokee County, North Carolina, where he was by occupation a farmer prior to enlisting at Beaverdam at age 46, July 18, 1862, for the war. Reported present through August 31, 1862. Transferred to Company B, Infantry Regiment of this legion, prior to December 31, 1862.

NICHOLSON, W. J., _____
North Carolina pension records appear to indicate that he served in this company. Survived the war.

NORTH, JOHN C., Private
Previously served as Private in Company H of this battalion. Transferred or was detailed to this company on March 7, 1863. Transferred back to Company H subsequent to April 30, 1863.

PATTERSON, EMERICK, Private
Born in Haywood or Macon County and resided in Cherokee County or Polk County, Tennessee, where he was by occupation a farmer prior to enlisting at Beaverdam, North Carolina, at age 33, July 18, 1862, for the war. Reported present through August 31, 1862. Transferred to Company E of this battalion on December 1, 1862. [His given name may have been Amariah or Emeriah.]

PATTERSON, JOSIAH, Private
Born in Haywood County and resided in Cherokee County where he was by occupation a farmer prior to enlisting at Beaverdam at age 29, July 18, 1862, for the war. Reported present through August 31, 1862, and November 1-December 1, 1862, when he transferred to Company E of this battalion. [His first name may have been Joseph.]

PICKELSYMER, JOHN, Private
Born in Union County, Georgia, and resided at Beaverdam, North Carolina, where he was by occupation a farmer prior to enlisting in Cherokee County at age 18, July 18, 1862, for the war. Reported present through August 31, 1862. Deserted on December 10, 1862.

PLEMMONS, JAMES M., Private
Born in the part of Macon County that later became Cherokee County. Resided in Cherokee County as a farmer prior to enlisting at Beaverdam at age 28, July 18, 1862, for the war. Reported present through August 31, 1862, and in November, 1862-April, 1863. Reported absent without leave from June 25 through October 31, 1863. Subsequently reported as having deserted at Loudon, Tennessee, July 1, 1863. [He may have briefly transferred to Company H of this battalion on March 18, 1863, but if so, he evidently returned shortly afterwards or the transfer was cancelled.]

RALSTON, WILLIAM H., Private
Enlisted either in this company or in 2nd Company A, Infantry Regiment of this legion, in Blount County, Tennessee, at about age 37, January 21, 1863, for the war. Transferred to Company C of this battalion on February 1, 1863.

RAMSEY, SAM T., _____
North Carolina pension records indicate that he served either in this company or in Company D, Indian Battalion, and survived the war.

RATLIFF, WILLIAM, Private
Born in Polk County, Tennessee, and was by occupation a farmer prior to enlisting in Polk County at age 18, September 28, 1862, for the war. Reported present in November, 1862-April, 1863. Captured at Strawberry Plains, Tennessee, June 20, 1863, and paroled there the next day. Reported absent on hospital detail, September 10-October 31, 1863. Reported sick in hospital at Rogersville, Tennessee, December 25, 1863. Reported sick in hospital in North Carolina on February 23, 1864. Name appears on a receipt roll for clothing dated March 15, 1864. No further records. [His surname may have been Ratley.]

RAY, ROBERT, Private
Enlisted in Cherokee County on January 15, 1863, for the war. Reported present on February 28, 1863. No further records.

RECTOR, JAMES, Private
Born in Cherokee County where he resided prior to enlisting at Beaverdam at age 18, September 28, 1862, for the war. Reported present in November-December, 1862. Reported absent sick in January-February, 1863. Returned to duty on or prior to April 30, 1863. Reported present on October 31, 1863, and in November, 1863-February, 1864. Name appears on receipt rolls for clothing dated March 15, June 4, September 1, September 18, and September 27, 1864. No further records.

REED, ELBERT, Private
Enlisted at Beaverdam on July 18, 1862, for the war. Deserted on July 29, 1862.

RHEA, HUGH B., Sergeant
Born in Cherokee County where he resided as a farmer prior to enlisting at Beaverdam at age 18, July 18, 1862, for the war. Mustered in as Sergeant. Reported present through August 31, 1862, and in November, 1862-April, 1863. Captured at Strawberry Plains, Tennessee, June 20, 1863, and paroled there the next day. Reported absent without leave from June 25 through October 31, 1863. Subsequently reported as having deserted at Strawberry Plains on July 1, 1863.

RHODES, JOHN J., Musician
Previously served in Company A, 39th Regiment N.C. Troops. Records of that unit indicate that he was reported to be serving in this battalion on June 28, 1863, while absent without leave from the 39th Regiment, but no surviving records of this battalion confirm his service herein.

RICHARDSON, GEORGE, Private
Enlisted in Cherokee County on February 1, 1863, for the war. Reported present through April 30, 1863, and in September, 1863-February, 1864. Name appears on receipt rolls for clothing dated March 15, June 4, September 1, and September 18, 1864. No further records.

RICHARDSON, JOHN, Private
Born in Tennessee and resided in Polk County, Tennessee, where he was by occupation a miner prior to enlisting in Cherokee County at age 48, November 27, 1862, for the war. Reported present through April 30, 1863. Captured at Strawberry Plains, Tennessee, June 20, 1863, and paroled there the next day. Reported sick in hospital on

September 6, 1863. Deserted from hospital at White Sulphur Springs, West Virginia, October 20, 1863.

RIDDLE, ISAAC M., Private
Enlisted either in this company or in 2nd Company A, Infantry Regiment of this legion, in Bradley County, Tennessee, at about age 18, September 25, 1862, for the war. Transferred to Company C of this battalion on February 1, 1863.

ROBERTS, BENJAMIN, Private
Enlisted in Cherokee County on November 6, 1862, for the war. Reported present through April 30, 1863. Captured at Strawberry Plains, Tennessee, June 20, 1863, and paroled there the next day. Reported absent without leave from June 25 through October 31, 1863. Subsequently reported as having deserted at Loudon, Tennessee, July 1, 1863.

ROBERTS, EDMOND, Private
Resided in Cherokee County and was by occupation a farmer prior to enlisting in Cherokee County at about age 33, February 15, 1863, for the war. Reported present through April 30, 1863. Died in hospital at New Market, near Strawberry Plains, Tennessee, prior to October 31, 1863. Cause of death not reported.

ROBERTS, ELISHA, Private
Born in Clarke County, Georgia, and resided in Polk County, Tennessee, where he was by occupation a farmer prior to enlisting at Beaverdam, North Carolina, at age 57, September 28, 1862, for the war. Reported present in November, 1862-April, 1863. Transferred to Company C of this battalion in May-June, 1863.

ROBERTS, JAMES D., Private
Enlisted in Cherokee County on November 6, 1862, for the war. Reported present through April 30, 1863. Reported absent without leave from June 25 through October 31, 1863. Subsequently reported as having deserted at Loudon, Tennessee, July 1, 1863.

ROBERTS, JOEL M., Private
Born in Buncombe County and resided in Cherokee County where he was by occupation a farmer prior to enlisting at Beaverdam at age 25, July 18, 1862, for the war. Reported present through August 31, 1862, and in November, 1862-April, 1863. No further records.

ROBERTS, REASON, Private
Born in Buncombe County and resided in Cherokee County where he was by occupation a farmer prior to enlisting at Beaverdam at age 40, July 18, 1862, for the war. Reported present through August 31, 1862. Reported absent without leave in November-December, 1862. Returned to duty in January-February, 1863. Reported present on February 28, 1863. No further records. Survived the war. [Later served as Private in Company D, 13th Regiment N.C. Troops (3rd Regiment N.C. Volunteers).]

ROBERTSON, WYATT, Private
Enlisted at Beaverdam on July 18, 1862, for the war. Deserted on July 29, 1862.

ROSE, JAMES, Private
Born in Cherokee County where he resided as a farmer prior to enlisting at Beaverdam at age 19, on July 18, 1862, for the war. Mustered in as Sergeant. Reported present through August 31, 1862. Reduced to ranks prior to December 31, 1862. Reported present in November, 1862-April, 1863. No further records.

ROSE, WILLIAM, Private
Born in Macon County and resided in Cherokee County where he was by occupation a farmer prior to enlisting at Beaverdam at age 18, July 28, 1862, for the war. Reported present through August 31, 1862, and in November, 1862-April, 1863. Deserted at Loudon, Tennessee, July 1, 1863. Went over to the enemy on an unspecified date. Took the Oath of Allegiance at Knoxville, Tennessee, January 23, 1864.

SCHAY, JACOB, Private
Born in Germany and resided in Cherokee County. Enlisted at Beaverdam at age 28, July 18, 1862, for the war. Reported present through August 31, 1862, and in November-December, 1862. Reported on detail as a mechanic at Tellico Plains, Tennessee, from February 15, 1863, through February 29, 1864. No further records.

SCOTT, JAMES M., Private
Born in Blount County, Tennessee, and was by occupation a farmer prior to enlisting either in this company or in 2nd Company A, Infantry Regiment of this legion, in Blount County on January 21, 1863, for the war. Transferred to Company C of this battalion on February 1, 1863.

SCULLY, WILLIAM A., Private
Resided in Jefferson County, Tennessee, and was by occupation a cabinet maker prior to enlisting either in this company or in 2nd Company A, Infantry Regiment of this legion, in Jefferson County, at about age 34, October 6, 1862, for the war. Transferred to Company C of this battalion on February 1, 1863.

SEXTON, JOSEPH W., Private
Born in Wake County and enlisted at Knoxville, Tennessee, at age 36, on November 2, 1862, for the war. Transferred either to this company or to 2nd Company A, Infantry Regiment of this legion, from the camp of instruction at Knoxville, Tennessee, January 24, 1863. Transferred to Company C of this battalion on February 1, 1863.

SEXTON, NEWTON O., Sergeant
Born in Polk County, Tennessee, where he resided as a farmer. Served previously as Private in Company D, 3rd Regiment Tennessee Infantry (Vaughn's). Enlisted at Beaverdam, North Carolina, at age 19, October 1, 1862, for the war. Promotion record not reported. Reported present in November, 1862-April, 1863. Captured at Strawberry Plains, Tennessee, June 20, 1863, and paroled there the next day. Reported absent without leave from June 25 through October 31, 1863. Subsequently reported as having deserted at Loudon, Tennessee, July 1, 1863.

SHARP, JASON, Private
Enlisted in Cherokee County on February 12, 1863, for the war. Reported on leave on February 28, 1863. Returned to duty on April 28, 1863. Reported present on April 30, 1863. Reported absent without leave from June 21 through October 31, 1863. Subsequently reported as having deserted at Strawberry Plains, Tennessee, July 1, 1863.

SIMS, JOHN M., Private

Enlisted in Cherokee County on March 8, 1863, for the war. Reported present or accounted for through April 30, 1863. Reported absent without leave from June 25 through October 31, 1863. Subsequently reported as having deserted at Strawberry Plains, Tennessee, July 1, 1863.

SMITH, CALVIN L., Private

Born in Burke County and resided in Cherokee County where he was by occupation a farmer prior to enlisting at Beaverdam at age 30, July 18, 1862, for the war. Reported present through August 31, 1862, and in November, 1862-February, 1863. No further records.

SMITH, JAMES, Private

Born in Buncombe County and resided in Monroe County, Tennessee, where he was by occupation a farmer prior to enlisting at Beaverdam, North Carolina, at age 39, October 6, 1862, for the war. Reported absent with leave in November-December, 1862. No further records.

SMITH, JAMES L., Private

Previously served as Private in Company C of this battalion. Transferred to this company on May 23, 1863. No further records.

SMITH, JONATHAN, Private

Born in Union County, Georgia, and resided in Cherokee County, North Carolina, where he was by occupation a farmer prior to enlisting at Beaverdam at age 29, July 18, 1862, for the war. Reported present through August 31, 1862, and in November-December, 1862. Reported on leave in January-February, 1863. Returned to duty prior to April 30, 1863. No further records.

SMITH, LEWIS H., Private

Enlisted in Cherokee County on May 22, 1863, for the war. Reported absent without leave from June 25 through October 31, 1863. Subsequently reported as having deserted at Strawberry Plains, Tennessee, July 1, 1863.

SMITH, NIMROD JARETT, Private

Half Cherokee Indian. Born in the part of Macon County that later became Cherokee County. Resided in Cherokee County as a farmer prior to enlisting at Beaverdam at age 24, July 18, 1862, for the war. Reported present through August 31, 1862. Transferred to Company B, Infantry Regiment of this legion, September 1, 1862. [According to Vernon Crow, *Storm in the Mountains*, his Cherokee name was Tsa la di hi.]

SMITH, WILLIAM L., Private

Born in Haywood County and resided in Cherokee County where he was by occupation a farmer prior to enlisting at Beaverdam at age 24, July 18, 1862, for the war. Reported present through August 31, 1862, and in November, 1862-February, 1863. No further records.

STEWART, JAMES G., Private

Enlisted in Cherokee County on February 7, 1863, for the war. Reported present in March-April, 1863. Reported on detail as a tanner in Polk County, Tennessee, in May, 1863-February, 1864. Surrendered at Tallahassee, Florida, May 10, 1865. Paroled at Albany, Georgia, May 22, 1865.

STEWART, JASPER H., Private

Born in Pickens District, South Carolina, and resided in Polk County, Tennessee, where he was by occupation a farmer prior to enlisting in Cherokee County, North Carolina, at age 25, September 28, 1862, for the war. Reported absent without leave in November-December, 1862. Returned to duty prior to February 28, 1863. Reported present in March-April, 1863. Captured at Strawberry Plains, Tennessee, June 20, 1863, and paroled there the next day. Deserted at Loudon, Tennessee, July 1, 1863.

STEWART, JOSEPH, Private

Enlisted in Cherokee County on January 4, 1863, for the war. Reported absent without leave on February 28, 1863. No further records. [He may have been the same man as Joseph Edmond Stewart of Company E of this battalion.]

STEWART, MARION, Private

Born in Pickens District, South Carolina, and resided in Polk County, Tennessee, where he was by occupation a farmer prior to enlisting in Cherokee County, North Carolina, at age 27, September 28, 1862, for the war. Reported absent without leave in November-December, 1862. Returned to duty prior to February 28, 1863. Reported present in March-April, 1863. Captured at Strawberry Plains, Tennessee, June 20, 1863, and paroled there the next day. Deserted at Loudon, Tennessee, July 1, 1863.

SWANN, S. C., Private

Federal Provost Marshal indicate that he served either in this company or in Company A, Indian Battalion. Place and date of enlistment not reported. Captured at Knoxville, Tennessee, May 1, 1865. Released by a Knox County, Tennessee, civil court May 24, 1865. [May have previously served in Company A, 60th Regiment N.C. Troops. He was probably a member of Lt. Col. William W. Stringfield's party that was sent to Knoxville under Brig. Gen. James Martin to find out the truth about the Johnston surrender rumors. They were jailed when they refused to take the Oath of Allegiance.]

TALLENT, JOHN, Private

Resided in Cherokee County. Enlisted at Beaverdam at age 23, July 18, 1862, for the war. Deserted on July 29, 1862. [His surname may have been Talent.]

TALLEY, JOHN, Private

Enlisted either in this company or in 2nd Company A, Infantry Regiment of this legion, in Blount County, Tennessee, at about age 16, April 9, 1863, for the war. Transferred to Company C of this battalion on the same date.

TAYLOR, BALDWIN H., Private

Resided in Cherokee County and was by occupation a farmer prior to enlisting in Cherokee County at about age 52, January 4, 1863, for the war. Reported present through April 30, 1863. Reported absent without leave from June 25 through October 31, 1863. Subsequently reported as having deserted at Strawberry Plains, July 1, 1863.

TAYLOR, LYCURGUS W., Private

Enlisted either in this company or in 2nd Company A, Infantry Regiment of this legion, at Maryville, Tennessee, at about age 16, April 15, 1863, for the war. Transferred to Company C of this battalion on or about the same date.

TAYLOR, WRIGHT, Private

Resided in Cherokee County. Enlisted in Cherokee County at age 22, August 10, 1862, for the war. Deserted on August 20, 1862.

TEDFORD, JOSEPH HOWARD, Private

Enlisted in Blount County, Tennessee, October 6, 1862, for the war, and sent to a camp of conscription. Assigned either to this company or to 2nd Company A, Infantry Regiment of this legion, January 26, 1863. Transferred to Company C of this battalion on February 6, 1863. [His given name may have been Howard Joseph.]

THOMAS, A. H., Private

Enlisted in Cherokee County on February 9, 1863, for the war. Reported present through February 29, 1863. No further records.

THOMAS, J. M., _____

Name appears on a register of effects of deceased soldiers turned over to Confederate Quartermasters in 1865, as a member of this company. No further records.

THOMPSON, ELISHA, Musician

Born in Buncombe County and resided in Cherokee County where he was by occupation a farmer prior to enlisting at Beaverdam at age 33, July 18, 1862, for the war. Mustered in as Musician (Fifer). Reported present through August 31, 1862, and in November-December, 1862. Reported absent sick in January-February, 1863. Returned to duty prior to April 30, 1863. Captured at Strawberry Plains, Tennessee, June 20, 1863, and paroled there the next day. Reported absent without leave from June 25 through October 31, 1863. Subsequently reported as having deserted at Strawberry Plains on July 1, 1863.

THOMPSON, JOHN, Private

Born in Buncombe County and resided in Cherokee County where he was by occupation a farmer prior to enlisting at Beaverdam at age 27, July 18, 1862, for the war. Reported present through August 31, 1862, and in November, 1862-April, 1863. Captured at Strawberry Plains, Tennessee, June 20, 1863, and paroled there the next day. Reported absent without leave from June 25 through October 31, 1863. Subsequently reported as having deserted at Strawberry Plains on July 1, 1863.

THOMPSON, NEHEMIAH M., Musician

Born in Buncombe County and resided in Cherokee County where he was by occupation a blacksmith prior to enlisting at Beaverdam at age 30, July 18, 1862, for the war. Mustered in as Musician (Drummer). Reported present through August 31, 1862, and in November, 1862-April, 1863. Captured at Strawberry Plains, Tennessee, June 20, 1863, and paroled there the next day. Reported absent without leave from June 25 through October 31, 1863. Subsequently reported as having deserted at Strawberry Plains, July 1, 1863.

THURMAN, JOHN M., Private

Enlisted in Cherokee County on December 28, 1862, for the war. Reported present through February 28, 1863, on October 31, 1863, and in November, 1863-February, 1864. Name appears on receipt rolls for clothing dated March 15 and June 4, 1864. No further records.

TILLEY, JAMES, Private

Born in Monroe County, Tennessee, where he resided as a farmer prior to enlisting in Cherokee County at age 20, October 6, 1862, for the war. Reported present in November, 1862-April, 1863. No further records.

TRULL, WILLIAM A., Private

Born in Henderson County and resided in Cherokee County. Was by occupation a farmer prior to enlisting at Beaverdam at age 17, October 27, 1862, for the war. Reported present through April 30, 1863, and in November-December, 1863. Sent to hospital at Emory and Henry, Virginia, February 1, 1864. Hospitalized at Charlottesville, Virginia, June 12, 1864, with typhoid fever. Returned to duty on June 17, 1864. Name appears on receipt rolls for clothing dated September 1, September 8, and September 27, 1864. No further records. Survived the war.

UNDERWOOD, SEBORN, Private

Born in Buncombe County and resided in Cherokee County. Was by occupation a farmer prior to enlisting in Cherokee County at age 27, August 10, 1862, for the war. Reported present on August 31, 1862. Reported absent without leave in November-December, 1862. Returned to duty in January-February, 1863. Reported present in March-April, 1863. No further records.

WEAVER, SOLOMON, Private

Born in Rutherford County and resided in Cherokee County. Was by occupation a farmer prior to enlisting at Beaverdam at age 24, July 18, 1862, for the war. Reported present through August 31, 1862, and in November, 1862-April, 1863. No further records.

WELCH, ALONZO L., Private

Born in Haywood County and resided in Cherokee County. Was by occupation a blacksmith prior to enlisting at Beaverdam at age 22, July 18, 1862, for the war. Reported present through August 31, 1862, and in November, 1862-February, 1863. Reported on detached service to purchase beef from April 3 through 30, 1863. Rejoined the company prior to October 31, 1863. Reported absent without leave from December 22 through 31, 1863. Returned to duty prior to February 29, 1864. Name appears on receipt rolls for clothing dated March 15 and June 19, 1864. Reported on detail as a blacksmith in September, 1864. No further records. Survived the war. [Clark's *Regiments*, 4: 117 (picture opposite), 126, indicates that he attained the rank of Sergeant; if so, it was subsequent to September 30, 1864.]

WHEELER, JORDAN, Private

Resided in Blount County and was by occupation a "tenant" prior to enlisting either in this company or in 2nd Company A, Infantry Regiment of this legion, in Rockford, Tennessee, at about age 30, September 29, 1862, for the war. Transferred to Company C of this battalion on February 1, 1863.

WHITE, ALLEN, Private

Enlisted in Cherokee County on February 15, 1863, for the war. Reported absent without leave on February 28, 1863. No further records.

WHITE, ARTHUR B., Private

Enlisted in Cherokee County on January 15, 1863, for the war. Reported absent without leave on February 28, 1863. No further records.

WHITE, DAVID L., Private

Born in what later became Caldwell County. Resided in Cherokee County where he was by occupation a farmer prior to enlisting at Beaverdam at age 24, July 18, 1862, for the war. Mustered in as Sergeant. Reported present through August 31, 1862. Reduced to ranks prior to December 31, 1862. Reported present in November, 1862-April, 1863. Promoted to Corporal in May-October, 1863. Captured at Strawberry Plains, Tennessee, June 20, 1863, and paroled there the next day. Reported on sick furlough beginning July 1, 1863. Failed to return to duty, was listed as a deserter, and reduced to ranks on December 31, 1863. Captured by the enemy at Murphy on December 9, 1863. Sent to Nashville, Tennessee. Transferred to Louisville, Kentucky, December 23, 1863. Transferred to Rock Island, Illinois, and arrived there on December 26, 1863. Paroled at Rock Island and transferred for exchange on March 2, 1865. No further records. Survived the war.

WHITE, JONAS N., Private

Born in Burke County and resided in Cherokee County where he was by occupation a farmer prior to enlisting at Beaverdam at age 20, July 18, 1862, for the war. Reported present through August 31, 1862, and in November, 1862-April, 1863. Captured at Strawberry Plains, Tennessee, June 20, 1863, and paroled there the next day. Reported on sick furlough beginning July 1, 1863. Failed to return to duty and was listed as a deserter on December 31, 1863. Captured at Murphy on December 9, 1863. Sent to Nashville, Tennessee. Transferred to Louisville, Kentucky, December 23, 1863. Transferred to Rock Island, Illinois, December 24, 1863. Died at Rock Island on February 5, 1864, of "variola."

WHITTEN, THOMAS, Private

Born in Bradley County, Tennessee, and resided in Cherokee County, North Carolina, where he was by occupation a farmer prior to enlisting at Beaverdam at age 22, July 18, 1862, for the war. Reported present through August 31, 1862. Reported absent without leave in November-December, 1862. Returned to duty prior to February 28, 1863. Reported present in March-April, 1863, and in September, 1863-February, 1864. Captured at Carter's Depot, Tennessee, April 25, 1864. Sent to Knoxville, Tennessee. Transferred to Nashville, Tennessee, May 13, 1864. Transferred to Louisville, Kentucky, and arrived there on May 17, 1864. Confined at Camp Morton, Indianapolis, Indiana, May 22, 1864. Released at Camp Morton on March 24, 1865, after joining the U.S. Army. Unit to which assigned not reported.

WILCOXSON, DANIEL, Private

Born in Wilkes County and resided in Cherokee County where he was by occupation a farmer prior to enlisting at Beaverdam at age 25, July 18, 1862, for the war. Reported present through August 31, 1862, and in November, 1862-February, 1863. Deserted at Zollicoffer, Tennessee, April 29, 1863.

WILCOXSON, SAMUEL, Private

Born in Wilkes County and resided in Cherokee County where he was by occupation a farmer prior to enlisting at Beaverdam at age 21, July 18, 1862, for the war. Reported present through August 31, 1862, and in November, 1862-February, 1863. Deserted at Zollicoffer, Tennessee, April 29, 1863. [His surname may have been Willcoxson.]

WOMBLE, JAMES P., Private

Enlisted in Cherokee County on February 9, 1863, for the war. Reported present through April 30, 1863. No further records.

WOODS, WILLIAM L. F., Private

Born in Macon County and resided in Cherokee County where he was by occupation a farmer prior to enlisting at Beaverdam at age 30, August 10, 1862, for the war. Reported present through August 31, 1862, and in November, 1862-February, 1863. Reported absent sick in Cherokee County from March 6 through April 30, 1863. No further records.

WORLEY, HENRY N., Private

Born in Buncombe County and resided in Cherokee County where he was by occupation a farmer prior to enlisting at Beaverdam at age 28, July 18, 1862, for the war. Reported present through August 31, 1862, in November, 1862-April, 1863; and October 31-December 31, 1863. Reported on furlough in January-February, 1864. Reported on duty as a teamster from August 26 through September 30, 1864; was on duty at Carter's Depot, Tennessee, for at least part of that period. No further records. Survived the war.

WRIGHT, TAYLOR, _____

Enlisted at Beaverdam on July 18, 1862, for the war. Deserted on or about the same date. [This record may refer to Pvt. Wright Taylor of this company.]

YOUNG, ELI, Private

Resided in Cherokee County and was by occupation a farmer prior to enlisting in Cherokee County at about age 40, February 5, 1863, for the war. Reported absent without leave on February 28, 1863. Reported for or returned to duty prior to April 30, 1863. Reported absent without leave from June 25 through October 31, 1863. Subsequently reported as having deserted at Strawberry Plains, Tennessee, July 1, 1863.

YOUNG, HARRISON, Private

Previously served as Private in Company H of this battalion. Transferred to this company on April 1, 1863. Reported present through April 30, 1863. Reported absent without leave from June 25 through October 31, 1863. Subsequently reported as having deserted at Strawberry Plains, Tennessee, July 1, 1863.

YOUNG, JOHN, Private

Born in Monroe County, Tennessee, and resided in Cherokee County where he was by occupation a farmer prior to enlisting Beaverdam at age 19, July 18, 1862, for the war. Reported present through August 31, 1862, and in November, 1862-April, 1863. No further records. Survived the war.

YOUNG, WILLIAM H. H., Private

Enlisted in Cherokee County on January 5, 1863, for the war. Reported absent without leave on February 28, 1863. Returned to duty on an unspecified date. Captured at Strawberry Plains, Tennessee, June 20, 1863, and paroled there the next day. No further records. Survived the war.

COMPANY B

This company was raised in Cherokee County. It was organized on July 19, 1862.

The following roster was compiled in large part from a company muster and descriptive roll dated October 31, 1862, and company muster rolls dated July 19-August 31, 1862, and November, 1862-February, 1864. These are abstracted in the microfilm edition of the Compiled Service Records of Confederate Soldiers Who Served in Organizations from the State of North Carolina (Record Group 109, M270), National Archives, Washington, D.C. Other valuable information in the Compiled Service Records includes enlistment papers, pay vouchers, requisitions, letters of resignation, discharge certificates, and abstracts of medical and prisoner of war records.

Also utilized in this roster were *The War of the Rebellion: A Compilation of the Official Records of the Union and Confederate Armies*, the North Carolina Adjutant General's papers, state militia records, newspaper casualty lists and obituaries, wartime claims for bounty pay and allowances, postwar registers of claims for artificial limbs, Confederate pension applications filed with the states of North Carolina, Tennessee, and Florida, records of the North Carolina Confederate Soldiers' Home, and the 1860 and 1870 federal censuses of North Carolina. A search was made also for relevant letters, diaries, reminiscences, and other manuscripts in the Southern Historical Collection (University of North Carolina-Chapel Hill) and the Duke University Library Special Collections Department.

Among the secondary sources consulted were records of the North Carolina division of the United Daughters of the Confederacy, postwar rosters, regimental and county histories, marriage bond, will, and cemetery indexes, published and unpublished genealogies, biographical dictionaries, the North Carolina *County Heritage Book* series, the *Confederate Veteran*, Walter Clark's *Histories of the Several Regiments and Battalions from North Carolina in the Great War, 1861-'65*, and the North Carolina volume of the extended edition of *Confederate Military History*.

OFFICERS

CAPTAINS

WALKER, WILLIAM CLAY
Previously served as Lieutenant Colonel of the 29th Regiment N.C. Troops. Elected Captain of this company on July 19, 1862. Signed company muster roll as Captain and Inspector & Mustering Officer, August 31, 1862. Signature appears on a payment voucher for service from September 1 through October 31, 1862. Elected Lieutenant Colonel on October 1, 1862, to rank from September 27, 1862, and transferred to the Field and Staff of this battalion.

NELSON, WILLIAM BUTLER
Previously served as 1st Lieutenant of Company A, 29th Regiment N.C. Troops. Appointed 1st Lieutenant of this company on July 19, 1862. Reported present through August 31, 1862. Promoted to Captain on October 1, 1862, to rank from September 27, 1862. Name appears on a payment voucher for service from September 1 through October 31, 1862. Signature appears on company muster roll for November-December, 1862. Reported present in January, 1863-June 30, 1863. Reported absent with leave for twenty-five days on recruiting service and to arrest deserters in North Carolina beginning October 23, 1863. Reported absent without leave on November 25, 1863. According to Maj. James A. McKamy of this battalion, "I am informed by officers of this command, that he has abandoned the service and says he will not return to his command" [Maj. James A. McKamy to Confederate Adjutant and Inspector General Samuel Cooper, February 22, 1864, Item No. 124N 1864, Letters Received: C.S.A. Adjutant and Inspector General's Office, Microfilm M474: Roll #133, National Archives]. Dropped from the company rolls on April 2, 1864. Survived the war.

LIEUTENANTS

FOWLER, MATHEW C., 2nd Lieutenant
Born in Forsyth County, Georgia, and resided in Cherokee County, North Carolina, where he was by occupation a farmer prior to enlisting in Cherokee County at age 23, July 19, 1862, for the war. Mustered in as Private. Reported present through August 31, 1862. Promoted to Corporal with a Brevet rank of 2nd Lieutenant prior to October 31, 1862, possibly on October 1, 1862. Reported present or accounted for in November, 1862. Reported present in March-April, 1863. Promoted to 2nd Lieutenant on March 5, 1863, possibly to rank from September 27, 1862. Reported on detached service in Cherokee County in May-June, 1863. Rejoined the company prior to October 31, 1863. Reported present, November, 1863-February, 1864. Signature appears on a pay voucher dated July 6, 1864. Reported in hospital at Winchester, Virginia, August 5, 1864, suffering from debilitas. No further records.

KIRKLAND, JOHN H., 2nd Lieutenant
Served as Sergeant in this company. According to Clark's *Regiments,* 4:118, he was elected or appointed 2nd Lieutenant of this company. He may have been appointed 3rd (Junior 2nd) Lieutenant late in the war, but there is no wartime evidence of this.

LOUDERMILK, GARNER N., 3rd Lieutenant
Born in Knox County, Tennessee, and resided in Cherokee County where he was by occupation a farmer prior to enlisting in Cherokee County at age 42. Appointed 3rd Lieutenant on July 19, 1862. Signature appears on a payment voucher for service from July 19 through August 31, 1862. Reported present in January-February, 1863. Elected Captain of Company H of this battalion on March 5, 1863, and transferred.

McREE, WILLIAM J., 1st Lieutenant
Born in Mecklenburg County and resided in Cherokee County where he was by occupation a farmer prior to enlisting at age 31. Appointed 2nd Lieutenant on July 19, 1862. Promoted to 1st Lieutenant on October 1, 1862, to rank from September 27, 1862. Reported present in January, 1863-February, 1864. Reported absent without leave from April 10 through 20, 1864. Sent to hospital on August 15, 1864. Signature appears on a special requisition for clothing dated September 1, 1864. Reported in hospital at Harrisonburg, Virginia, September 30, 1864. No further records. [Clark's *Regiments* 4:118 incorrectly gives his surname as McGehee.]

PHILLIPS, WILLIAM H., 3rd Lieutenant
Born in North Carolina and resided in Cherokee County where he was by occupation a farmer prior to enlisting in Cherokee County at age 29, July 19, 1862, for the war. Mustered in as Sergeant. Reported present through August 31, 1862, and in November, 1862-February, 1863. Reported on detached service with Capt. Garner N. Loudermilk of Company H of this battalion in Cherokee County, April 12-May 2, 1863. Elected or appointed 3rd Lieutenant on May 2, 1863. Reported present, May 2-June 30, 1863. Detailed to Cherokee County on July 18, 1863. Did not return to duty and was reported absent without leave from August 18, 1863, through February 29, 1864. Reported on March 4, 1864, as "dropped from the rolls by order of Secty. of War for long absense." Survived the war. [His surname may have been Philips.]

SIMS, BLUFORD M., 2nd Lieutenant

Previously enlisted as Private in Company H, 39th Regiment N.C. Troops. Failed to report for duty with that unit. Enlisted in this company in Cherokee County on October 4, 1862, for the war. Mustered in as Private. Reported present through December 31, 1862. Detailed as a sutler on January 1, 1863. Reported absent without leave in January-February, 1863. Reported to duty prior to April 30, 1863, when he was reported on detail at Atlanta, Georgia, "to purchase clothing [presumably for his company]" in March-April, 1863. Reported absent with leave, May 1-November 15, 1863. Detailed as a sutler during most of that period. Reported present, December 31, 1863, and in January-February, 1864. Appointed 2nd Lieutenant on March 20, 1864. Name appears on a payment voucher for service from March 29 through April 30, 1864. Reported in hospital at Lynchburg, Virginia, on or about June 21, 1864. Captured at Winchester, Virginia, September 19, 1864. Escaped from the enemy at Winchester on an unspecified date [See *Asheville News*, November 3, 1864]. Hospitalized at Harrisonburg, Virginia, October 7, 1864, with debilitas. Hospitalized at Lynchburg on or about October 31, 1864, with chronic diarrhoea. Surrendered to the enemy on May 8, 1865. Released after taking the Oath of Allegiance at Nashville, Tennessee, May 22, 1865. [He may have served as a 3rd (Junior 2nd) Lieutenant rather than a Senior 2nd Lieutenant.]

NONCOMMISSIONED OFFICERS AND PRIVATES

AKIN, ROBERT A., Private

Born in Greenville District, South Carolina, and resided in Polk County, Tennessee, where he was by occupation a merchant. Enlisted in Cherokee County, North Carolina, at age 24, October 4, 1862, for the war. Reported present through February 28, 1863. Elected 1st Lieutenant of Company H of this battalion on March 5, 1863, and transferred. [His surname may have been Aiken.]

BAILY, JOHN M., Private

Enlisted in Cherokee County on February 11, 1863, for the war. Reported present through June 30, 1863. Deserted at Carter's Depot, Tennessee, August 31, 1863.

BOWERS, GEORGE A., Private

Born in Hall County, Georgia, and resided in Cherokee County, North Carolina, where he was by occupation a mail carrier prior to enlisting in Cherokee County at age 19, September 30, 1862, for the war. Reported present in November, 1862-February, 1863. No further records.

BRANNON, SAMPSON, Private

Enlisted in Cherokee County on March 6, 1863, for the war. Reported present through April 30, 1863. Captured and paroled at Lenoir Station, Tennessee, June 19, 1863. Deserted at Carter's Depot, Tennessee, August 31, 1863.

BRANOM, EDWARD, Private

Enlisted in Cherokee County on January 1, 1863, for the war. Reported present through June 30, 1863. No further records. [His surname may have been Branum.]

BRANOM, JAMES, Private

Enlisted in Cherokee County on January 5, 1863, for the war. Reported absent with leave on February 28, 1863. Reported present in March-June, 1863. Deserted on or about July 9, 1863. [His surname may have been Branum.]

BRANOM, JULIUS, Private

Enlisted in Cherokee County on December 28, 1862, for the war. Reported present or accounted for through June 30, 1863. Deserted on or about July 9, 1863. [His surname may have been Branham or Branum.]

BRANOM, MARTIN, Private

Born in Kentucky and resided in Cherokee County where he was by occupation a farmer prior to enlisting in Cherokee County at age 36, October 2, 1862, for the war. Reported present or accounted for in November, 1862-June, 1863. Deserted on or about July 9, 1863. [His surname may have been Branum.]

BROWN, JAMES, Private

Born in Henderson County and resided in Cherokee County where he was by occupation a farmer prior to enlisting in Cherokee County at age 24, July 19, 1862, for the war. Reported present through August 31, 1862. Transferred to Company E of this battalion on December 1, 1862.

BROWN, LEONARD C., Private

Born in the part of Buncombe County that later became Henderson County. Resided in Fannin County, Georgia, where he was by occupation a farmer prior to enlisting in Blount County, Tennessee, at age 29 or 30, October 11, 1862, for the war. Transferred to Company E of this battalion on December 1, 1862.

BROWN, WILLIAM L., Private

Born in Laurens County, Georgia, where he resided as a farmer prior to enlisting in Cherokee County, North Carolina, at age 18, October 30, 1862, for the war. Reported absent without leave in November, 1862-February, 1863. Returned to duty in March-April, 1863. Reported present in May-June, 1863. Transferred to Company B, 65th Regiment Georgia Infantry, July-August, 1863, in exchange for Pvt. William F. Shope.

BUCHANAN, W. R., Private

Enlisted in Cherokee County on February 20, 1863, for the war. Reported absent with leave through February 28, 1863. Transferred to Company A of this battalion prior to April 30, 1863.

BURNETT, J. P., _____

North Carolina pension records appear to indicate that he served in this company. Survived the war. [He may have served also in Barr's Virginia Battery.]

BURNS, HASSEL H., Sergeant

Enlisted in Cherokee County on November 17, 1862, for the war. Mustered in as Private. Reported present through June 30, 1863. Promoted to Sergeant on September 22, 1863. Reported deserted or missing on the retreat from Greeneville, Tennessee, October 11, 1863. Captured by Federal forces on or about November 2, 1863. Sent to Knoxville, Tennessee. Released on November 17, 1863, after taking the Oath of Allegiance.

BURNS, WILLIAM H. H., Private

Born in Forsyth County, Georgia, and resided in Cherokee County, North Carolina. Was by occupation a farmer prior to enlisting in

Cherokee County at age 21, August 21, 1862, for the war. Reported present through August 31, 1862, and in November, 1862-April, 1863. Furloughed from hospital at Loudon, Tennessee, June 16, 1863. Reason hospitalized not reported. Reported absent without leave on July 11, 1863. Returned to duty on November 11, 1863. Reported present through February 29, 1864. Captured at Cedar Creek, Virginia, October 19, 1864. Sent to Harpers Ferry, West Virginia. Confined at Point Lookout, Maryland, on or about October 28, 1864. Transferred to hospital at Point Lookout on January 27, 1865. Died in hospital at Point Lookout on February 19, 1865, of "chronic diarrhoea."

CARROLL, JAMES, Private

Born in Cherokee County where he resided as a farmer prior to enlisting in Cherokee County at age 18. Place and date of enlistment not reported. Transferred to Company E of this battalion on December 1, 1862.

CARTER, BENJAMIN F., Private

Previously served as Private in Company A, 29th Regiment N.C. Troops. Enlisted in this company in Cherokee County on July 19, 1862, for the war. Reported present through August 31, 1862, and in November, 1862-June, 1863. Deserted at Carter's Depot, Tennessee, October 11, 1863.

CARTER, BERRY, Private

Enlisted in Cherokee County on an unspecified date. Deserted prior to February 28, 1863.

CLARK, JAMES W., Private

Enlisted in Cherokee County on December 28, 1862, for the war. Reported present through December 31, 1862. Reported on leave in January-February, 1863. Reported present in March-April, 1863. Reported absent sick in May-June, 1863. Deserted at Carter's Depot, Tennessee, August 31, 1863.

COLE, THOMAS R., Private

Enlisted in Cherokee County on February 1, 1863, for the war. Reported present through February 28, 1863. Reported absent sick from March 6 through April 30, 1863. Reported as a deserter in May-June, 1863. Apparently rejoined the company prior to August 31, 1863, when he reportedly deserted at Carter's Depot, Tennessee.

COLEMAN, LORENZO, Private

Born in Monroe County, Tennessee, and resided in Cherokee County, North Carolina, where he was by occupation a farmer prior to enlisting in Cherokee County at age 26, July 19, 1862, for the war. Reported present or accounted for through August 31, 1862, and in November, 1862-May, 1863. Furloughed from hospital at Loudon, Tennessee, June 28, 1863. Failed to return to duty and was listed as a deserter in January-February, 1864.

COLEMAN, WILLIAM R., Private

Born in Monroe County, Tennessee, in 1845. Enlisted in Cherokee County, North Carolina, February 1, 1863, for the war. Reported present through April 30, 1863. Deserted prior to June 30, 1863. [See his Tennessee pension application number 8651.]

COLLIS, JAMES M., Private

Born in Yancey County and resided in Fannin County, Georgia, where he was by occupation a farmer prior to enlisting in Cherokee County, North Carolina, at age 25, August 22, 1862, for the war. Reported present on August 31, 1862, and in November, 1862-February, 1863. Deserted at Mossy Creek, Tennessee, April 6, 1863.

COLLIS, STEPHEN M., Private

Born in Yancey County and resided in Fannin County, Georgia, where he was by occupation a farmer prior to enlisting in Cherokee County, North Carolina, at age 23, August 26, 1862, for the war. Reported present on August 31, 1862, and in November, 1862-February, 1863. Deserted on April 6, 1863.

CRAWFORD, GEORGE W., Private

Born in Monroe County, Tennessee, and resided in Fannin County, Georgia, where he was by occupation an "officer" prior to enlisting in Cherokee County, North Carolina, at age 30, August 21, 1862, for the war. Reported present on August 31, 1862, and in November, 1862-April, 1863. Reported absent without leave on June 15, 1863. No further records.

CROSS, MARTIN, Private

Born in Blount County, Tennessee, and resided in Tennessee where he was by occupation a farmer prior to enlisting in Cherokee County, North Carolina, at age 48, between July 19 and November 30, 1862. Transferred to Company E of this battalion on December 1, 1862.

DAVIS, JOHN, Private

Resided in Cherokee County and was by occupation a farmer prior to enlisting in Cherokee County at age 16, December 1, 1862, for the war. Transferred to Company E of this battalion on December 16, 1864. [May have served previously as Private in Company F, 39th Regiment N.C. Troops, in which case he enlisted in this company while absent without leave from that unit.]

DAVIS, MARTIN V. B., Private

Enlisted in Cherokee County on February 11, 1863, for the war. Reported present through June 30, 1863. Failed to return from a leave of absence and was listed as a deserter on October 31, 1863. [His middle name was probably Van Buren.]

DEAVER, THOMAS S., Private

Born in Monroe County, Tennessee, and resided in Cherokee County, North Carolina, where he was by occupation a farmer prior to enlisting in Cherokee County at age 27, July 19, 1862, for the war. Reported present through August 31, 1862. Transferred to Company E of this battalion on December 1, 1862.

DEAVER, WILLIAM H., Private

Born in Buncombe County and resided in Cherokee County where he was by occupation a farmer prior to enlisting in Cherokee County at age 34, July 19, 1862, for the war. Reported present through August 31, 1862. Transferred to Company E of this battalion on December 1, 1862.

DECKER, ALEXANDER, Private

Born in what later became Alexander County. Resided in Cherokee County where he was by occupation a farmer prior to enlisting in Cherokee County at age 17, July 19, 1862, for the war. Reported present through August 31, 1862, and in November, 1862-April, 1863. Reported absent sick in May-June, 1863. Furloughed from hospital at Loudon, Tennessee, June 16, 1863. Failed to return to duty and was listed as a deserter in January-February, 1864.

DEWEESE, GARRET A., Private

Born in North Carolina and resided in Cherokee County where he was by occupation a smith prior to enlisting in Cherokee County at age 33, July 19, 1862, for the war. Reported present through August 31, 1862, and in November, 1862-February, 1863. Sent home sick from Coker Creek, Tennessee, March 6, 1863. Failed to return and was listed as a deserter in January-February, 1864.

DIXON, SIMON A., Private

Born in Indiana on March 6, 1832. Enlisted in Cherokee County at age 30, January 5, 1863, for the war. Reported present or accounted for through June 30, 1863. Deserted at Carter's Depot, Tennessee, in October, 1863. [See Tennessee pension application No. 10792.]

DIXON, WILLIAM A., Private

Enlisted in Cherokee County on January 5, 1863, for the war. Reported present or accounted for through June 30, 1863. Name appears on a quartermaster department requisition for clothing dated August 25, 1863. Deserted at Carter's Depot, Tennessee, in October, 1863.

DOBKINS, WILLIAM, Private

Born in Sevier County, Tennessee, and resided in Cherokee County, North Carolina, where he was by occupation a farmer prior to enlisting in Cherokee County at age 34, July 19, 1862, for the war. Reported present through August 31, 1862, and in November, 1862-February, 1863. Transferred to Company H of this battalion on March 5, 1863.

FARREL, JAMES, Private

Resided in Cherokee County where he enlisted on July 19, 1862, for the war. Reported present through August 31, 1862, and in November-December, 1862. Reported absent sick in January-February, 1863. Discharged on March 25, 1863. Reason discharged not reported. Apparently reenlisted in the company, probably subsequent to February 29, 1864. Deserted to the enemy on an unspecified date. Sent to Chattanooga, Tennessee, where he arrived on or about March 15, 1865. Took the Oath of Allegiance at Chattanooga on March 15, 1865. Transferred to Louisville, Kentucky, where he arrived on March 18, 1865. Released at Louisville on March 21, 1865, with instructions "to remain north of the Ohio River during the war."

FLEMING, JAMES A., Private

Born in the part of Surry County that later became Yadkin County. Resided in Cherokee County where he was by occupation a farmer prior to enlisting in Cherokee County at age 18, July 19, 1862, for the war. Reported present through August 31, 1862, and from November 1 through December 30, 1862. Reported absent sick from December 31, 1862, through December 31, 1863. Listed as a deserter on February 29, 1864.

FRANKLIN, JAMES H., Private

Born in Henderson County and resided in Fannin County, Georgia, where he was by occupation a farmer prior to enlisting in Cherokee County, North Carolina, at age 16, August 22, 1862, for the war. Reported absent without leave in November-December, 1862. Listed as a deserter in January-February, 1863. Returned to duty in March-April, 1863. Reported present in May, 1863-February, 1864. Captured at Piedmont, Virginia, June 5, 1864. Sent to Staunton, Virginia on or prior to June 8, 1864. Confined at Camp Morton, Indianapolis, Indiana, June 21, 1864. Died at Camp Morton on January 27, 1865, of "inflammation of the lungs."

FRANKLIN, OVERTON E., Private

Born in Cherokee County where he resided as a farmer prior to enlisting in Cherokee County at age 21, July 19, 1862, for the war. Reported present through August 31, 1862. Reported absent without leave in November-December, 1862. Listed as a deserter in January-February, 1863.

FRANKLIN, SYLVESTER, Private

Born in Buncombe County and resided in Cherokee County where he was by occupation a farmer prior to enlisting in Cherokee County at age 26, July 19, 1862, for the war. Reported present through August 31, 1862. Reported absent without leave in November-December, 1862. Listed as a deserter in January-February, 1863.

GOINS, HUGH, Private

Enlisted in Cherokee County on December 28, 1862, for the war. Reported present through December 31, 1862. Reported on leave, January-February, 1863. Returned to duty prior to April 30, 1863. Reported present, May-June, 1863. Deserted at Carter's Depot, Tennessee, August 31, 1863.

GOINS, JOHN, Private

Born in Bradley County, Tennessee, and enlisted in Cherokee County on March 6, 1863, for the war. Deserted on April 5, 1863. Returned to duty prior to June 30, 1863. Failed to return from a furlough on July 9, 1863. Listed as a deserter on October 31, 1863. [See his Tennessee pension application No. 10879.]

GOINS, JOHN W., Corporal

Enlisted in Cherokee County on March 6, 1863, for the war. Mustered in as Corporal. Reported present through June 30, 1863. Failed to return from a furlough on July 9, 1863, and was listed as a deserter on October 31, 1863.

GOINS, WILLIAM, Private

Resided in Cherokee County and was by occupation a carpenter prior to enlisting in Cherokee County at about age 48, January 5, 1863, for the war. Reported absent with leave on February 28, 1863. Listed as a deserter on April 5, 1863. Returned to duty prior to June 30, 1863. Deserted at Carter's Depot, Tennessee, August 31, 1863.

GREEN, CHARLES J., Private

Enlisted illegally in this company on July 19, 1862, after enlisting in Company A of this battalion on the previous day. Reported present through August 31, 1862. Transferred back to Company A in September-December, 1862. [His given name may have been James C. or Jasper C.]

GREEN, MARVILLE, Private

Born in Yancey County and resided in Cherokee County where he was by occupation a farmer prior to enlisting in Cherokee County at age 28, July 19, 1862, for the war. Reported present through August 31, 1862, and in November, 1862-February, 1863. Transferred to Company A, 29th Regiment N.C. Troops, March 1, 1863. [His first name may have been Marvil.]

GREEN, WILLIAM E., Private
Born in Tennessee and resided in Cherokee County where he was by occupation a farmer prior to enlisting in Cherokee County at age 22, July 19, 1862, for the war. Reported present through August 31, 1862, and in November, 1862-June, 1863. No further records.

HALL, BURTON KIMSEY, Private
Born in Macon County on May 26, 1840, and resided in Cherokee County where he was by occupation a farmer prior to enlisting in Cherokee County at age 22, July 19, 1862, for the war. Mustered in as Private. Reported present through August 31, 1862. Promoted to Corporal prior to September 22, 1862, when he deserted at Carter's Depot, Tennessee. Returned to duty prior to December 31, 1862. Reported present in January-April, 1863. Captured and paroled at Strawberry Plains, Tennessee, June 20, 1863. Returned to duty prior to June 30, 1863. Reduced to ranks on an unspecified date. Captured in Cherokee County on February 18, 1864. Sent to Nashville, Tennessee. Transferred to Louisville, Kentucky, February 27, 1864. Transferred to Fort Delaware, Delaware, February 29, 1864. Arrived at Fort Delaware on March 4 or March 7 , 1864. Released at Fort Delaware on June 19, 1865, after taking the Oath of Allegiance.

HALL, DANIEL, Private
Records of the Federal Provost Marshal indicate that he served either in this company or in Company B, Indian Battalion. Place and date of enlistment not reported. Captured by the enemy in Lee County, Virginia, January 26, 1865. Sent to Knoxville, Tennessee. Transferred to Chattanooga, Tennessee, February 16, 1865. No further records.

HALL, MERRIMAN M., Private
Born in Macon County and resided in Cherokee County where he was by occupation a farmer prior to enlisting in Cherokee County at age 24, July 19, 1862, for the war. Reported present through August 31, 1862, and in November, 1862-June, 1863. Deserted at Carter's Depot, Tennessee, September 22, 1863. Captured by the enemy in Cherokee County on February 18, 1864. Sent to Nashville, Tennessee. Transferred to Louisville, Kentucky, where he arrived on February 27, 1864. Transferred to Fort Delaware, Delaware, February 29, 1864. Arrived at Fort Delaware on March 4 or March 7 , 1864. Died at Fort Delaware on March 31, 1864, of "smallpox."

HALL, MOSES IRVIN, Private
Born on January 8, 1833. Resided in Cherokee County and was by occupation a farmer prior to enlisting in Cherokee County at age 29, July 19, 1862, for the war. Mustered in as Sergeant. Reported present through August 31, 1862. Reduced to ranks prior to February 28, 1863. Reported absent sick from February 15 through December 31, 1863. Listed as a deserter on February 29, 1864.

HALL, ROBERT PATTON, Sergeant
Born in Macon County on July 14, 1831, and resided in Cherokee County where he was by occupation a farmer prior to enlisting in Cherokee County at age 30, July 19, 1862, for the war. Mustered in as Private. Reported present through August 31, 1862. Promoted to Sergeant prior to October 31, 1862. Reported present in November, 1862-June, 1863. Sent to hospital at Emory and Henry, Virginia, September 22, 1863. Failed to return to duty and was listed as a deserter on February 29, 1864. Survived the war.

HAMILTON, _____, Private
Born in Monroe County, Tennessee, and resided in Polk County, Tennessee, where he was by occupation a trader prior to enlisting at age 22, October 11, 1862, for the war. No further records.

HAMPTON, DAVID W., Private
Born in Washington County, Tennessee, and resided in Fannin County, Georgia, where he was by occupation a farmer prior to enlisting in Cherokee County, North Carolina, at age 26, July 19, 1862, for the war. Reported present through August 31, 1862. Reported absent sick in November-December, 1862. Returned to duty in January-February, 1863. Reported present in March-June, 1863. Deserted at Carter's Depot, Tennessee, August 31, 1863.

HANCOCK, GEORGE W., Private
Enlisted in Cherokee County on February 20, 1863, for the war. Reported on leave on February 28, 1863. Deserted on March 22, 1863.

HARRIS, BENJAMIN W., Private
Born in Iredell County and resided in Cherokee County where he was by occupation a farmer prior to enlisting in Cherokee County at age 33, July 19, 1862, for the war. Reported present through August 31, 1862, and in November, 1862-February, 1863. Transferred to Company H of this battalion March 1 or April 11, 1863.

HARRIS, WILLIAM C., Private
Born in Iredell County and resided in Cherokee County where he was by occupation a farmer prior to enlisting in Cherokee County at age 31, July 19, 1862, for the war. Reported present through August 31, 1862, and in November, 1862-February, 1863. Transferred to Company H of this battalion in March-April, 1863.

HARRISON, DANIEL J., Private
Born in Rutherford County and resided in Georgia where he was by occupation a farmer prior to enlisting in Cherokee County at age 21, August 22, 1862, for the war. Reported absent sick in November-December, 1862. Briefly returned to duty but was reported absent sick from February 10 through December 31, 1863. Listed as a deserter on February 29, 1864.

HARTNESS, CADAMUS, Private
Born in Macon County and resided in Cherokee County where he was by occupation a farmer prior to enlisting in Cherokee County at age 25 or 33, July 19, 1862, for the war. Reported absent without leave on August 31, 1862. Transferred to Company E of this battalion on December 1, 1862. [His given name may have been Cadmus.]

HARTNESS, MARION, Private
Enlisted in this company, possibly illegally, on July 19, 1862, after having enlisted in Company A of this battalion on July 18, 1862. Reported "absent without leave at the time of signing the Rolls," but was reported present on August 31, 1862. Transferred back to Company A, probably prior to October 31, 1862.

HATCHEL, JOHN S., Private

Born in Orange County and resided in Cherokee County where he was by occupation a farmer prior to enlisting in Cherokee County at age 34, July 19, 1862, for the war. Reported present through August 31, 1862, and in November-December, 1862. Reported absent sick in January-February, 1863. Returned to duty prior to April 30, 1863. Reported present in May-June, 1863. Deserted at Carter's Depot, Tennessee, September 22, 1863. [His surname may have been Hatchett.]

HIBBERT, CORNELIUS, Private

Born in Haywood County and resided in Cherokee County where he was by occupation a farmer prior to enlisting in Cherokee County at age 23, July 19, 1862, for the war. Reported present through August 31, 1862, and in November, 1862-February, 1863. Transferred to Company H of this battalion on March 1 or April 1, 1863. [His surname may have been Hibberts.]

HICE, ROMULOUS A., Private

Enlisted in Cherokee County on February 11, 1863, for the war. Reported present in March-June, 1863. Wounded at Henderson's Depot, Tennessee, October 11, 1863. Reported absent wounded through February 29, 1864. No further records.

HOOPER, JAMES W., Private

Born in Lincoln County and resided in Cherokee County where he was by occupation a farmer prior to enlisting in Cherokee County at age 26, July 19, 1862, for the war. Reported present through August 31, 1862, and in November, 1862-February, 1863. Transferred to Company H of this battalion on March 1 or April 1, 1863.

HUGHES, ANDREW JACKSON, Private

Born on May 16, 1834, in the part of Orange County that later became Alamance County. Resided in Cherokee County where he was by occupation a farmer prior to enlisting in Cherokee County at age 28, August 2, 1862, for the war. Reported present through August 31, 1862, and in November-December, 1862. Reported on leave in January-February, 1863. Rejoined the company prior to March 1, 1863. Reported present in March-June, 1863. Served as Acting Commissary Sergeant of the battalion from March 1 through June 30, 1863, and from August 1 through September 20, 1863. Deserted at Carter's Depot, Tennessee, September 22, 1863.

HUGHES, THOMAS J., Private

Previously served as Private in Company E, 65th Regiment Georgia Volunteer Infantry. Transferred to this company on April 26, 1863, apparently in exchange for another man. Reported present through June 30, 1863. Deserted at Carter's Depot, Tennessee, September 22, 1863.

HUSSEY, H. F., Private

Place and date of enlistment not reported. Captured in Lee County, Virginia, January 26, 1865. Sent to Knoxville, Tennessee. Transferred to Chattanooga, Tennessee, February 16, 1865. No further records.

INGRAM, JOHN A., Private

Born in Buncombe County. Resided in Cherokee County and was by occupation a farmer prior to enlisting in Cherokee County at age 28, July 19, 1862, for the war. Reported present through December 31, 1862. Reported absent sick from February 28 through December 31, 1863. Listed as a deserter on February 29, 1864.

INGRAM, ROBERT, Corporal

Born in Macon County. Resided in Cherokee County and was by occupation a farmer prior to enlisting in this company, possibly illegally, at age 23, July 19, 1862, after having enlisted in Company A of this battalion on July 18, 1862. Served as Corporal through August 31, 1862. Transferred back to Company A prior to December 31, 1862. Reduced to ranks before or after his return to Company A.

IRONS, ALVIN J., Private

Enlisted in Cherokee County on July 28, 1863, for the war. Reported absent without leave, "cut off from below London, Tenn.," until December 31, 1863, when he was listed as a deserter.

JOHNSON, JAMES, Private

Enlisted in Cherokee County on January 5, 1863, for the war. Reported on leave on February 28, 1863. Rejoined the company on or prior to April 30, 1863. Reported present in May-June, 1863. Deserted on July 9, 1863, while on leave.

JOHNSON, JASON L., Private

Born in what later became Fannin County, Georgia. Resided in Cherokee County, North Carolina, where he was by occupation a farmer prior to enlisting in Cherokee County at age 24, July 19, 1862, for the war. Reported present through August 31, 1862. Transferred to Company E of this battalion on December 1, 1862.

JOHNSON, JOHN, Private

Enlisted in Cherokee County on January 5, 1863, for the war. Reported on leave on February 28, 1863. Returned to duty on or prior to April 30, 1863. Reported present in May-June, 1863. Deserted on July 9, 1863, while on leave.

JOHNSON, JOHN M., Private

Enlisted in Cherokee County on February 1, 1863, for the war. Reported present through April 30, 1863. Reported absent sick in May-June, 1863. Furloughed from a hospital in Loudon, Tennessee, July 10, 1863. Reported absent sick through December 31, 1863. Failed to return to duty and was listed as a deserter on February 29, 1864.

JOHNSON, SAMUEL, Private

Enlisted in Cherokee County on January 5, 1863, for the war. Reported absent without leave on February 28, 1863. Returned to duty on or prior to April 30, 1863. Reported absent sick in May-June, 1863, and December 8-31, 1863. Returned to duty on or prior to February 29, 1864. Name appears on a receipt roll for clothing dated September 1, 1864. No further records.

JONES, JOHN W., Private

Born in Macon County and resided in Cherokee County where he was by occupation a farmer prior to enlisting in Cherokee County at age 21, July 19, 1862, for the war. Reported present through August 31, 1862, and in November, 1862-February, 1863. Deserted at Zollicoffer, Tennessee, April 22, 1863. Reported in hospital in Virginia on October 31, 1863. Returned to duty on or prior to

December 31, 1863. Reported present in January-February, 1864. Captured at Piedmont, Virginia, June 5, 1864. Reported under guard at Staunton, Virginia on June 8, 1864. Confined at Camp Morton, Indianapolis, Indiana, June 21, 1864. Died at Camp Morton on September 4, 1864, of "typho malarial fever."

KEY, JAMES A., Private
Born in Georgia and resided in Cherokee County, Georgia, where he was by occupation a farmer prior to enlisting in Cherokee County, North Carolina, at age 22, July 19, 1862, for the war. Mustered in as Private. Reported present through August 31, 1862. Promoted to Corporal in September-December, 1862. Reported present in November, 1862-February, 1863. Deserted at Zollicoffer, Tennessee, April 22, 1863. Reduced to ranks prior to April 30, 1863. Returned to duty on November 3, 1863. Reported present through February 29, 1864. Reported on duty as a teamster in July-September, 1864. No further records. Survived the war.

KEY, JOHN F., Private
Born in Georgia and resided in Cherokee County, North Carolina, where he was by occupation a farmer prior to enlisting in Cherokee County at age 34, July 19, 1862, for the war. Reported present through August 31, 1862, and in November, 1862-December, 1862. Reported absent sick in January-February, 1863. Deserted at Zollicoffer, Tennessee, April 22, 1863.

KEY, WILLIAM A., Private
Born in Georgia and resided in Cherokee County, North Carolina, where he was by occupation a farmer prior to enlisting in Cherokee County at age 26, July 19, 1862, for the war. Reported present through August 31, 1862, and in November-December, 1862. Reported absent sick from December 31, 1862, through April 30, 1863. Listed as a deserter in May-June, 1863.

KIRKLAND, JAMES A., Private
Born in Rhea County, Tennessee, and resided in Cherokee County where he was by occupation a farmer prior to enlisting at age 20, July 26, 1862, for the war. Reported present through August 31, 1862, and in November, 1862-April, 1863. Listed as a deserter in May-June, 1863. Evidently returned to duty prior to October 11, 1863, when he deserted from Carter's Station, Tennessee.

KIRKLAND, JOHN H., Sergeant
Born in Macon County and resided in Cherokee County where he was by occupation a farmer prior to enlisting in Cherokee County at age 26, July 19, 1862, for the war. Mustered in as Sergeant. Reported present through August 31, 1862. Reduced to ranks in September-December, 1862. Reported present or accounted for in November, 1862-February, 1863. Reported on detached service with Capt. Garner N. Loudermilk of Company H of this battalion in Cherokee County, April 12-30, 1863. Rejoined the company prior to June 30, 1863. Promoted to Sergeant on February 10, 1864. Reported present through February 29, 1864. Captured at Carter's Depot, Tennessee, April 25, 1864. Sent to Knoxville, Tennessee. Transferred to Nashville, Tennessee on May 13, 1864. Confined at Louisville, Kentucky, May 17, 1864. Confined at Camp Morton, Indianapolis, Indiana, May 22, 1864. Paroled at Camp Morton on or about March 4, 1865. Received at Boulware's and Cox's Wharves, James River, Virginia, March 10-11, 1865, for exchange. Hospitalized at Richmond, Virginia, March 11, 1865. Transferred to Camp Lee on March 12, 1865. Survived the war. [According to Clark's *Regiments* 4:118, he was elected or appointed 2nd Lieutenant of this company. It is possible that he was made either a Brevet or Junior 2nd Lieutenant in the final days of the war, but there is no wartime evidence of this.]

KIRKLAND, JOHNSON C., Musician
Born in Jackson County. Resided in Cherokee County, or in Monroe County, Tennessee, and was by occupation a farmer prior to enlisting in Cherokee County at age 14 or 15, August 15, 1862, for the war. Mustered in as Private. Reported present through August 31, 1862, and in November, 1862-February, 1863. Appointed Musician (Drummer) and transferred to Company H of this battalion on March 5, 1863. Detailed back to this company on March 23, 1863. Reported absent without leave on June 1, 1863. Returned to duty with Company H on July 25, 1863. [His surname may have been Kirklin.]

LEDFORD, ELIJAH, _____
Place and date of enlistment not reported. An undated company muster and descriptive roll indicates that he transferred from this company to Company E of this battalion on December 1, 1862.

LEDFORD, JAMES M., Private
Born in Macon County and resided in Cherokee County where he was by occupation a farmer prior to enlisting in Cherokee County at age 25, July 19, 1862, for the war. Reported present through August 31, 1862, and in November, 1862-February, 1863. Transferred to Company H of this battalion on March 5, 1863.

LEDFORD, JOHN, _____
Place and date of enlistment not reported. An undated company muster and descriptive roll indicates that he transferred from this company to Company E of this battalion on December 1, 1862.

LORANCE, JAMES P., Musician
Born in Yancey County and resided in Cherokee County where he was by occupation a farmer prior to enlisting in Cherokee County at age 16, August 15, 1862, for the war. Mustered in as Private. Reported present through August 31, 1862, and in November, 1862-February, 1863. Elected Musician (Fifer) on March 5, 1863. Transferred to Company H of this battalion on March 5 or April 1, 1863.

LORANCE, JOSEPH, Private
Born in Cocke County, Tennessee, and resided in Cherokee County, North Carolina, where he was by occupation a farmer prior to enlisting in Cherokee County at age 20, July 19, 1862, for the war. Reported present or accounted for through August 31, 1862, and in November-December, 1862. Reported absent sick in January-February, 1863. Transferred to Company H of this battalion on March 1 or April 1, 1863, although Company H records reported him on detached service with this company in March-April, 1863.

LOUDERMILK, HUGH W., Corporal
Born in Monroe County, Georgia, and resided in Cherokee County, North Carolina, where he was by occupation a farmer prior to enlisting in Cherokee County at age 26, July 19, 1862, for the war. Mustered in as Corporal. Reported present or accounted for through August 31, 1862, and in November-December, 1862. Reported absent sick in January-February, 1863. Transferred to Company H

of this battalion on March 1 or April 1, 1863. [His surname may have been Lowdermilk.]

LYLES, AMOS, Private
Born in Ashe County and resided in Cherokee County where he was by occupation a farmer prior to enlisting in Cherokee County at age 22, July 19, 1862, for the war. Reported present through August 31, 1862, and in November, 1862-February, 1864. Name appears on a receipt roll for clothing dated September 1, 1864. No further records.

McALISTER, FRANCIS, Private
Enlisted in Cherokee County on March 6, 1863, for the war. Deserted on April 5, 1863.

McTAGGART, JAMES FLETCHER, Private
Born in what later became McDowell County. Resided in Cherokee County where he was by occupation a farmer prior to enlisting at age 30, July 19, 1862, for the war. Reported present through August 31, 1862, and in November, 1862-April, 1863. Reported absent sick in May-June, 1863. Died at Athens, Tennessee, July 15, 1863, of "fever" and/or "measles."

MALONE, THOMAS J., Private
Enlisted in Cherokee County on November 19, 1862, for the war. Reported present in January-June, 1863. Furloughed from hospital at Loudon, Tennessee, July 1, 1863. Failed to return to duty and was listed as a deserter in January-February, 1864.

MALONE, WILLIAM T., Private
Enlisted in Cherokee County on November 19, 1862, for the war. Reported present in January-April, 1863. No further records.

MASHBURN, DAVID, Private
Born in Buncombe County and resided in Cherokee County where he was by occupation a farmer prior to enlisting in Cherokee County at age 21, July 19, 1862, for the war. Reported present through August 31, 1862, and in November, 1862-February, 1864. Captured at Piedmont, Virginia, June 5, 1864. Confined at Camp Morton, Indianapolis, Indiana, June 21, 1864. Paroled at Camp Morton on or about March 4, 1865. Received at Boulware's and Cox's Wharf, James River, Virginia, March 10-12, 1865, for exchange. No further records.

MASHBURN, JOSHUA C., Private
Resided in Cherokee County. Enlisted in Cherokee County at age 18, February 1, 1863, for the war. Reported present until March 2, 1863, when he was reported absent without leave. Returned to duty on June 25, 1863. Reported present on June 30, 1863. No further records.

MASHBURN, LOGAN B., Private
Previously served as Private in Company A of this battalion. Transferred to this company on February 1, 1863. Reported absent without leave on March 2, 1863. Returned to duty on June 25, 1863. Reported present on June 30, 1863. No further records. Survived the war.

MASHBURN, WILLIAM, Private
Born in Yancey County and resided in Cherokee County where he was by occupation a farmer prior to enlisting in Cherokee County at age 19, July 19, 1862, for the war. Reported present through August 31, 1862, and in November, 1862-June, 1863. Sent to hospital at Abingdon, Virginia, October 20, 1863. Returned to duty on or prior to December 31, 1863. Reported present in January-February, 1864. No further records.

MASHBURN, WILLIAM N., Musician
Born in Yancey County and resided in Cherokee County where he was by occupation a farmer prior to enlisting in Cherokee County at age 20, July 19, 1862, for the war. Mustered in as Musician (Drummer). Reported present through August 31, 1862, and in November, 1862-June, 1863. Deserted at Zollicoffer, Tennessee, October 14, 1863.

MASON, GOLDMON, Private
Born in the part of Macon County that later became Cherokee County. Resided in Cherokee County as a farmer prior to enlisting in Cherokee County at age 27, July 19, 1862, for the war. Mustered in as 1st Sergeant. Reported present through August 31, 1862. Reduced to ranks in September-December, 1862. Reported present in November, 1862-April, 1863. Deserted at Loudon, Tennessee, July 1, 1863. Name appears on a receipt roll for clothing dated October 16, 1864. No further records.

MASON, PETER A., Private
Born in Cherokee County where he resided as a farmer prior to enlisting in Cherokee County at age 18, July 19, 1862, for the war. Reported present through August 31, 1862, and in November, 1862-April, 1863. Reported absent sick in May-June, 1863. Furloughed from hospital at Loudon, Tennessee, June 28, 1863. Failed to return to duty and was listed as a deserter in January-February, 1864. No further records.

MILES, JOHN H., Corporal
Resided in Fannin County, Georgia, and was by occupation a farmer prior to enlisting in Cherokee County, North Carolina, at age 23, August 22, 1863, for the war. Mustered in as Private. Reported present through August 31, 1862, and in November, 1862-February, 1863. Promoted to Corporal in January-February, 1863. Promoted to 1st Sergeant and transferred to Company H of this battalion on March 5, 1863.

MILLS, ANDREW H., Private
Born in what later became Fannin County, Georgia. Resided in Cherokee County, North Carolina, where he was by occupation a farmer prior to enlisting in Cherokee County at age 34, July 19, 1862, for the war. Reported present through June 30, 1863. Died prior to January 1, 1864. Place, date and cause of death not reported.

MOORE, LEMUEL J., 1st Sergeant
Born in Monroe County, Tennessee, December 20, 1842. Resided at Cartersville, Georgia, and was by occupation a farmer prior to enlisting in Cherokee County, North Carolina, at age 19, July 19, 1862, for the war. Mustered in as Private. Reported present through August 31, 1862. Reported absent without leave in November-December, 1862. Returned to duty on or prior to February 28, 1863. Reported present in March-October, 1863. Promoted to Sergeant on September 2, 1863. Promoted to 1st Sergeant on September 22, 1863. Reported present in November, 1863-February, 1864. Captured at Piedmont, Virginia, June 5, 1864. Reported under guard at Staunton, Virginia, June 8, 1864. Confined at Camp

Morton, Indianapolis, Indiana, June 21, 1864. Released at Camp Morton on or about May 22, 1865, after taking the Oath of Allegiance. [See Tennessee pension application No. 9019.]

MOORE, THOMAS ANDREW, Private
Born in Buncombe County and resided in Fannin County, Georgia, where he was by occupation a farmer prior to enlisting in Cherokee County, North Carolina, at age 23, August 24, 1862, for the war. Reported present on August 31, 1862. Reported absent without leave on December 31, 1862. Returned to duty on or prior to February 28, 1863. Reported present in March-April, 1863. Reported absent sick in May-June, 1863. Sent to hospital at Greeneville, Tennessee, July 23, 1863. Transferred to a Virginia hospital on July 25, 1863. Reported absent sick until he was listed as a deserter on February 29, 1864. Went over to the enemy on an unspecified date. Confined at Chattanooga, Tennessee. Took the Oath of Allegiance at Chattanooga on February 18, 1864. [His given name may have been Andrew Thomas.]

MORGAN, HENRY, Private
Resided in Cherokee County and was by occupation a farmer prior to enlisting in Cherokee County at age 27, July 19, 1862, for the war. Reported present through August 31, 1862, and in November, 1862-February, 1863. Transferred to Company H of this battalion on April 1, 1863.

MORRIS, JAMES, Private
Enlisted in Cherokee County on February 11, 1863, for the war. Reported present in March-June, 1863. No further records.

MULKY, JACOB B., Private
Born in what later became Fannin County, Georgia. Resided in Fannin County as a farmer prior to enlisting in Cherokee County at age 21, August 18, 1862, for the war. Reported present through August 31, 1862, and in November, 1862-April, 1863. No further records.

MULL, MARSHALL R., Private
Born in North Carolina and resided in Fannin County, Georgia, where he was by occupation a farmer prior to enlisting in Cherokee County at age 22, July 19, 1862, for the war. Reported present through August 31, 1862, and in January-June, 1863. Deserted at Carter's Depot, Tennessee, August 31, 1863.

NELSON, ELBERT E., Private
Born in Tennessee and resided in Fannin County, Georgia, where he was by occupation a farmer prior to enlisting in Cherokee County, North Carolina, at age 26, July 19, 1862, for the war. Reported present through August 31, 1862, and in November, 1862-February, 1863. Reported absent sick from March 1 through December 31, 1863. Listed as a deserter in January-February, 1864.

NELSON, WILLIAM N., Private
Born in Polk County, Tennessee, and resided in Cherokee County, North Carolina, where he was by occupation a farmer prior to enlisting in Cherokee County at age 18, July 19, 1862, for the war. Reported present through August 31, 1862. Appointed Quartermaster Sergeant on December 1, 1862, and transferred to the Field and Staff of this battalion.

NEWTON, BENJAMIN C., Private
Born in Macon County and resided in Cherokee County where he was by occupation a farmer prior to enlisting in Cherokee County at age 16, July 19, 1862, for the war. Reported present through August 31, 1862, and in November-December, 1862. Deserted in January-February, 1863.

NEWTON, JESSE C., Private
Born in Haywood County and resided in Fannin County, Georgia, where he was by occupation a farmer prior to enlisting in Cherokee County, North Carolina, at age 24, July 19, 1862, for the war. Reported present through August 31, 1862, and in November, 1862-June, 1863. Deserted at Carter's Depot, Tennessee, October 11, 1863.

NICHOLSON, WILLIAM A., Private
Born in Surry County and resided in Cherokee County where he was by occupation a farmer prior to enlisting in Cherokee County at age 33, July 19, 1862, for the war. Reported present through August 31, 1862, and in November, 1862-February, 1863. Deserted on April 25, 1863.

ORTON, JAMES, Private
Enlisted in Cherokee County on February 28, 1863, for the war. Deserted on April 6, 1863.[He may have been the same man as Pvt. James Orton of Company H of this battalion.]

PARSONS, DAVID, Private
Enlisted in Cherokee County on January 5, 1863, for the war. Reported on leave on February 28, 1863. Joined or rejoined the company on or before April 30, 1863. Reported present through February 29, 1864. Name appears on receipt rolls for clothing dated September 1 and September 27, 1864. No further records.

PATE, JESSE. Private
Born in what later became Yancey County. Resided in Cherokee County where he was by occupation a farmer prior to enlisting in Cherokee County at age 46, July 30, 1862, for the war. Reported present through August 31, 1862, and in November-December, 1862. Reported on leave in January-February, 1863. Returned to duty on or prior to April 30, 1863. Reported present in May-October, 1863. Furloughed on December 20, 1863. Reported absent without leave on January 19, 1864. Reported on duty as a wagon and forage master, September 10-30, 1864. No further records.

PATTON, NOAH, Private
Enlisted at Knoxville, Tennessee, June 23, 1862, for the war. Transferred to "Capt. Gholson's Cavalry Co [at] Loudon," Tennessee, in July, 1863.

PAYNE, RUSSELL, Private
Born in Cherokee County where he resided as a farmer prior to enlisting in Cherokee County at age 16. Place and date of enlistment not reported; probably enlisted subsequent to August 31, 1862. Transferred to Company E of this battalion on December 1, 1862.

PIERCE, WILLIAM M., Private
Born in Union County, Georgia, and resided in Fannin County, Georgia, where he was by occupation a farmer prior to enlisting in

Cherokee County, North Carolina, at age 15, September 21, 1862, for the war. Reported present through December 31, 1862. Listed as a deserter on February 28, 1863.

PIRKINS, DAVID J., Private
Enlisted in Cherokee County on March 6, 1863, for the war. Enlisted, probably illegally, in Company H of this battalion on March 7, 1863, but reported to this company prior to April 30, 1863. Reported present through that date. Deserted prior to June 30, 1863.

POSTELL, JAMES W., Private
Born in Macon County and resided in Cherokee County where he was by occupation a farmer prior to enlisting in Cherokee County at age 29, July 19, 1862, for the war. Reported present through August 31, 1862, and in November 1862-April, 1863. Reported absent sick from May 20 through December 31, 1863. Failed to return to duty and was listed as a deserter on February 29, 1864.

PRICE, JAMES W., Private
Born in the part of Macon County that later became Cherokee County. Resided in Cherokee County as a farmer prior to enlisting in Cherokee County at age 25, July 19, 1862, for the war. Mustered in as Corporal. Reported present through August 31, 1862. Reduced to ranks in September-December, 1862. Reported present in November, 1862-June, 1863. Deserted at Jonesborough, Tennessee, September 17, 1863.

QUINN, ASHFORD T., 1st Sergeant
Born in Habersham County, Georgia, and resided in Hall County, Georgia, where he was by occupation a stonemason prior to enlisting in Cherokee County, North Carolina, at age 24, September 20, 1862, for the war. Mustered in as Private. Promoted to 1st Sergeant prior to December 31, 1862. Reported present in November, 1862-June, 1863. Deserted at Carter's Depot, Tennessee, September 21, 1863.

QUINN, JOHN MARSHELL, Private
Enlisted in Cherokee County on March 1, 1863, for the war. Enlisted illegally in Company H of this battalion on March 7, 1863, but reported to Company B prior to April 30, 1863. Reported present through June 30, 1863. Deserted at Carter's Depot, Tennessee, September 21, 1863.

QUINN, TILMON S., Corporal
Born in Habersham County, Georgia, and resided in Cherokee County, North Carolina, where he was by occupation a farmer prior to enlisting in Cherokee County at age 33, July 19, 1862, for the war. Mustered in as Private. Reported present through August 31, 1862, and in November, 1862-February, 1863. Reported on detached service with Capt. Garner N. Loudermilk of Company H of this battalion from April 12 through 30, 1863. Rejoined the company on or prior to June 30, 1863. Promoted to Corporal prior to August 31, 1863, when he deserted at Carter's Depot, Tennessee.

RAINS, JOHN W., Corporal
Born in Sevier County, Tennessee. Resided in Cherokee County, North Carolina, and was by occupation a farmer prior to enlisting in Cherokee County at about age 33, February 11, 1863, for the war. Mustered in as Private. Reported on leave on February 28, 1863. Reported for duty or rejoined the company on or prior to April 30, 1863. Reported present in May-June, 1863. Promoted to Corporal prior to October 11, 1863, when he deserted at Carter's Depot, Tennessee.

REED, JEHU, Private
Born in Cherokee County, where he resided as a farmer prior to enlisting in Cherokee County at age 23, reportedly on July 19, 1862; however, he was not listed in the records of this company until January-February, 1863, when he was reported present. No further records.

REYNOLDS, SIMON H.
Born in the part of Surry County that later became Yadkin County. Resided in Cherokee County where he was by occupation a farmer prior to enlisting in Cherokee County at age 20, July 19, 1862, for the war. Reported present through August 31, 1862. Enlisted in Company A, 29th Regiment N.C. Troops, in November, 1862.

REYNOLDS, WILLIAM K., Corporal
Born in Sullivan County, Tennessee, and resided in Fannin County, Georgia, where he was by occupation a farmer prior to enlisting in Cherokee County, North Carolina, at age 24, July 19, 1862, for the war. Mustered in as Private. Reported present through August 31, 1862, and in November-December, 1862. Reported on leave in January-February, 1863. Rejoined the company on or prior to April 30, 1863. Promoted to Corporal in March-April, 1863. Reported present in May-June, 1863. No further records.

RICE, ISAAC R., Private
Born in Buncombe County and resided in Cherokee County where he was by occupation a farmer prior to enlisting in Cherokee County at age 30, July 19, 1862, for the war. Reported present through August 31, 1862, and in November, 1862-June, 1863. Detailed for duty in Cherokee County with Lt. William H. Philips of this company on July 18, 1863. Listed as a deserter on December 31, 1863.

RICE, JESSE, Private
Born in what later became Madison County. Resided in Cherokee County where he was by occupation a farmer prior to enlisting in Cherokee County at age 24, July 19, 1862, for the war. Reported absent without leave on August 31, 1862. Listed as a deserter on December 31, 1862.

RICE, JOSEPH M., Private
Born in what later became Madison County. Resided in Cherokee County, Enlisted in Cherokee County at age 19, June 20, 1863, for the war. Reported present through June 30, 1863. Deserted at Carter's Depot, Tennessee, August 31, 1863.

RICE, SPENCER, Private
Born in what later became Madison County. Resided in Madison or Cherokee County where he was by occupation a farmer prior to enlisting in Cherokee County at age 20, July 19, 1862, for the war. Reported absent without leave on August 31, 1862. Reported for duty in November-December, 1862. Reported present through June 30, 1863. Deserted at Carter's Depot, Tennessee, August 31, 1863. Went over to the enemy on an unspecified date. Took the Oath of Allegiance at Nashville, Tennessee, January 13, 1864.

ROBINSON, W. A., _____
North Carolina pension records indicate that he served in this company. Survived the war.

ROGERS, GEORGE W., Private

Born in Randolph County, Alabama, and resided in Cherokee County, North Carolina, where he was by occupation a farmer prior to enlisting in Cherokee County at age 23, July 19, 1862, for the war. Reported present through August 31, 1862, and in November, 1862-February, 1864. Captured at Piedmont, Virginia, June 5, 1864. Reported under guard at Staunton, Virginia, June 8, 1864. Confined at Camp Morton, Indianapolis, Indiana, June 21, 1864. Paroled at Camp Morton on or about March 4, 1865. Received at Boulware's and Cox's Wharves, James River, Virginia, March 10-11, 1865, for exchange. Hospitalized at Richmond, Virginia, March 11, 1865. Transferred to Camp Lee, near Richmond, March 12, 1865. Apparently returned to duty and then deserted to the enemy on an unknown date. Took the Oath of Allegiance at Chattanooga, Tennessee, May 13, 1865.

ROGERS, HOUSTON, Private

Previously served as Private in Company A, 29th Regiment N.C. Troops. Enlisted in this company on or about March 20, 1863, while a deserter from Company A, 29th Regiment N.C.Troops, although his transfer may have been legitimated later. Reported present in May-June, 1863. Detached for duty in Cherokee County on July 18, 1863, with Lt. William H. Philips of this company. Listed as a deserter on December 31, 1863. [Probably served later in Company D, 3rd Tennessee Mounted Infantry (Union) and/or Company E, 11th Tennessee Cavalry (Union). His surname may have been Rodgers.]

ROGERS, JOHN T., Private

Previously served as Private in Company A, 29th Regiment N.C. Troops. Transferred to this company on December 1, 1862. Reported present in January-February, 1862. Reported on detached service in Cherokee County with Capt. Garner N. Loudermilk of this company, April 12-30, 1863. Rejoined the company on or about April 30, 1863. Reported present in May-June, 1863. Detached for duty in Cherokee County on July 15, 1863. Failed to return and was listed as a deserter on December 31, 1863. [He may have been the same man as J. Taylor Rogers of Company I, Infantry Regiment of this legion.]

ROGERS, JONATHAN K., Private

Previously served as Private in Company A, 29th Regiment N.C. Troops. Enlisted in this company in Cherokee County on November 15, 1862, for the war. Mustered in as Private. Reported present in January-April, 1863. Promoted to Sergeant in May-June, 1863. Reported present in May, 1863-February, 1864. Reduced to ranks in January-February, 1864. Deserted to the enemy on an unspecified date. Took the Oath of Allegiance at Chattanooga, Tennessee, May 21, 1865.

ROGERS, JOSEPH, Private

Born in Cherokee County where he resided as an "iron maker" prior to enlisting in Cherokee County at age 20, July 22, 1862, for the war. Reported present through August 31, 1862, and in November, 1862-June, 1863. Deserted at Carter's Depot, Tennessee, August 31, 1863.

SCARBOROUGH, HUGH, Private

Previously enlisted in Company H of this battalion. Enlisted in this company in Cherokee County on March 6, 1863, for the war. Reported present through June 30, 1863. Furloughed on an unspecified date. Failed to return to duty and was listed as a deserter on July 9, 1863.

SHIELDS, WILLIAM L., Private

Born in Tennessee and resided in Cherokee County, North Carolina, where he was by occupation a physician prior to enlisting in Cherokee County at age 23, August 5, 1862, for the war. Reported present through August 31, 1862, and in November-December, 1862. No further records.

SHOPE, WILLIAM F., Private

Previously served as Private in Company B, 65th Regiment Georgia Infantry. Transferred to this company in July-August, 1863, in exchange for Pvt. William L. Brown. Deserted prior to October 31, 1863.

SLUDER, PRESTON V., Private

Born in Lincoln County, Kentucky and resided in Fannin County, Georgia, where he was by occupation a farmer prior to enlisting in Cherokee County, North Carolina, at age 31, October 11, 1862, for the war. Transferred to Company E of this battalion on December 1, 1862.

SPRINKLE, GEORGE F., Corporal

Born in the part of Surry County that later became Yadkin County. Resided in Cherokee County where he was by occupation a farmer prior to enlisting in Cherokee County at age 25, July 19, 1862, for the war. Mustered in as Corporal. Reported present through August 31, 1862. Transferred to Company E of this battalion on December 1, 1862.

STANDRIDGE, JOHN W., Private

Born in the part of Haywood County that later became Macon County. Resided in Cherokee County where he was by occupation a farmer prior to enlisting in Cherokee County at age 37. Probably enlisted on or about July 19, 1862. Transferred to Company E of this battalion on December 1, 1862.

STANLY, SAMUEL, Private

Enlisted in Cherokee County on February 1, 1863, for the war. Detailed to go home for clothing, presumably for the company, on April 1, 1863, and failed to return. Subsequently listed as having deserted on April 1 or May 1, 1863.

STANLY, WILLIAM, Private

Resided in Cherokee County and was by occupation a farm laborer prior to enlisting in Cherokee County at about age 20, February 11, 1863, for the war. Reported present through June 30, 1863. No further records.

STILES, JESSE A., Private

Born in Haywood County and resided in Cherokee County where he was by occupation a farmer prior to enlisting in Cherokee County at age 23, July 19, 1862, for the war. Reported present through August 31, 1862, and in November-December, 1862. Reported absent without leave in January-February, 1863. Reported absent sick in March-April, 1863. Furloughed from hospital at Loudon, Tennessee, June 16, 1863. Failed to return to duty and was listed as a deserter on February 29, 1864.

STILES, JOHN R., Private

Born in Haywood County and resided in Cherokee County where he was by occupation a farmer prior to enlisting in Cherokee County at age 28, July 25, 1862, for the war. Reported present through August 31, 1862, and in November-December, 1862. Reported absent without leave in January-February, 1863. Returned to duty prior to April, 1863. Furloughed from hospital at Loudon, Tennessee, June 16, 1863. Failed to return to duty and was listed as a deserter on February 29, 1864.

TALLENT, EPHRAIM, Private

Born in Burke County. Resided in Cherokee County, where he enlisted at age 26, September 25 or September 29, 1862, for the war. Deserted prior to December 31, 1862. Went over to the enemy on an unspecified date. Admitted to a Federal hospital at Nashville, Tennessee, December 22, 1863, with pneumonia. Transferred to another hospital on January 27, 1864. No further records. [His surname was erroneously rendered as Tolbert on a Company Muster and Descriptive roll.]

TILSON, JESSE A., Private

Born in Washington County, Tennessee, and resided in Cherokee County, North Carolina, where he was by occupation a farmer prior to enlisting in Cherokee County at age 33, July 19, 1862, for the war. Mustered in as Musician (Fifer). Reported present through August 31, 1862, and in November-December, 1862. Reported absent sick in January-February, 1863. Reported absent sick at home on March 2, 1863. Reduced to ranks prior to April 30, 1863. Failed to return to duty and was listed as a deserter in January-February, 1864. Went over to the enemy on an unspecified date. Sent to Nashville, Tennessee. Released at Nashville on January 13, 1864, after taking the Oath of Allegiance.

TIPTON, WILEY, Private

Born in Yancey County and resided in Fanin County, Georgia, where he was by occupation a farmer prior to enlisting in Cherokee County, North Carolina, at age 28, July 19, 1862, for the war. Reported present through August 31, 1862. Reported absent without leave in November-December, 1862. Returned to duty prior to February 28, 1863. Reported present in March-June, 1863. Deserted at Carter's Depot, Tennessee, August 31, 1863.

VINCENT, HOWELL, Private

Enlisted at Knoxville, Tennessee, June 11, 1863, for the war. Sent to hospital at Greeneville, Tennessee, August 28, 1863. Failed to return to duty, was listed as a deserter and dropped from the company rolls on February 29, 1864.

WADKINS, WARREN W., Private

Enlisted in Cherokee County on February 11, 1863, for the war. Reported present through February 28, 1863. Detailed to go home for clothing, presumably for the company, on April 1, 1863, and failed to return. Listed as a deserter on or about April 30, 1863.

WALKER, COLUMBUS F., Private

Born in Cherokee County where he resided as a farmer prior to enlisting in Cherokee County at age 17, July 22, 1862, for the war. Reported present through August 31, 1862, and in November, 1862-February, 1863. A company muster roll dated November-December, 1862, states that he was appointed Sergeant Major on December 1, 1862, however, he is listed as a Private in this company on that roll and the muster roll for January-February, 1863. He is listed as Sergeant Major on the Field & Staff muster roll for March-April, 1863, and a pay voucher dated May 12, 1863. [Clark's *Regiments*, 117-118, 128, gives his name as "Dr. Chas. F. Walker." It also identifies a "D.C.F. Walker" as 2nd Lieutenant of this company, presumably the same man, although in the two places where "Dr. Walker" is referred to he is referred to as Sergeant Major (117, 118), and no explicit identification is made between the two. There is no wartime evidence that Walker became a Lieutenant in this company.]

WALKER, MEMORY, Private

Enlisted in Cherokee County. Place and date of enlistment not reported. First listed in the records of this company when he was reported present in January-February, 1863. No further records.

WALLIS, MORGAN E., Private

Born in what later became Alexander County. Resided in Cherokee County where he was by occupation a farmer prior to enlisting in Cherokee County at age 25, July 19, 1862, for the war. Reported present through August 31, 1862, and in November, 1862-February, 1863. Transferred to Company H of this battalion on March 1 or April 1, 1863.

WELCH, THOMAS K., Private

Born in Cherokee County where he resided as a farmer prior to enlisting in Cherokee County at age 21, July 19, 1862, for the war. Reported present through August 31, 1862, and in November, 1862-June, 1863. No further records. Survived the war.

WELCH, WILLIAM W., Corporal

Born in the part of Macon County that later became Cherokee County. Resided in Cherokee County as a farmer prior to enlisting in Cherokee County at age 24, July 19, 1862, for the war. Mustered in as Private. Reported present through August 31, 1862, and in November, 1862-February, 1863. Promoted to Corporal in March-April, 1863. Reported present in March-June, 1863. Reported on detail in Cherokee County on July 13-October 31, 1863. Listed as a deserter in November-December, 1863.

WEST, JESSE, Private

Born in Macon County on September 17, 1830. Resided in Cherokee County and was by occupation a farmer prior to enlisting in Cherokee County at age 31, July 19, 1862, for the war. Reported present through August 31, 1862, and in November-December, 1862. Deserted in January-February, 1863. Returned to duty prior to June 30, 1863. Survived the war. [See his Tennessee pension application No. 6774.]

WEST, JOHN W., Private

Born in Macon County and resided in Cherokee County where he was by occupation a farmer prior to enlisting in Cherokee County at age 34, July 19, 1862, for the war. Reported present through August 31, 1862. Reported absent sick from December 24, 1862, through December 31, 1863. Listed in January-February, 1864, as "not returned, not reported." No further records. Survived the war.

WILKERSON, LAWSON H., Private

Born in Polk County, Tennessee, and resided in Cherokee County, North Carolina. Was by occupation a farmer prior to enlisting in

Cherokee County at age 17, August 26, 1862, for the war. Reported present through August 31, 1862, and in November, 1862-June, 1863. Detailed for duty with Lt. William H. Phillips of this company in Cherokee County on July 18, 1863. Failed to rejoin the company and was listed as a deserter, December 31, 1863.

WILKINSON, GUILFORD P., Sergeant

Born in Polk County, Tennessee, and resided in Cherokee County where he was by occupation a farmer prior to enlisting in Cherokee County at age 19, July 22, 1862, for the war. Mustered in as Private. Reported present through August 31, 1862. Promoted to Sergeant in September-December, 1862. Reported present in November, 1862-June, 1863. Reported on detail in Cherokee County from July 18 through October 31, 1863. Failed to rejoin the company and was listed as a deserter on December 31, 1863.

WILSON, CALEB J., Private

Born in North Carolina and resided in Cherokee County where he was by occupation a farmer prior to enlisting in Cherokee County at age 24, July 19, 1862, for the war. Reported absent with leave on August 31 and November-December, 1862. Returned to duty prior to February 28, 1863. Reported present in May-June, 1863. North Carolina pension records indicate that he died at home on August 20, 1863, of fever.

WILSON, SAMUEL P., Sergeant

Born in Burke County and resided in Cherokee County where he was by occupation a farmer prior to enlisting in Cherokee County at age 31, July 19, 1862, for the war. Mustered in as Sergeant. Reported present through August 31, 1862, and in November, 1862-June, 1863. Deserted at Carter's Depot, Tennessee, August 31, 1863.

WOODRING, D., Private

Born in Haywood County and resided in Towns County, Georgia, where he was by occupation a farmer prior to enlisting at age 28, October 20, 1862, for the war. His name was cancelled on his company muster and descriptive roll, indicating that he was never mustered into this company. [May have served later as Private in Infantry Battalion, Col. Sumner J. Smith's Georgia Legion, and in Company G, 65th Regiment Georgia Volunteer Infantry.]

WRIGHT, CHARLES A., Private

Born in Union County, Georgia, and resided in Fannin County, Georgia, where he was by occupation a farmer prior to enlisting in Cherokee County, North Carolina, at age 18, October 28, 1862, for the war. Deserted prior to December 31, 1862. [His given name may have been Andon C.]

ZIMMERMAN, JOHN, _____

Place and date of enlistment not reported. Transferred to Company E of this battalion on December 1, 1862.

COMPANY C

This company was raised in Blount County, Tennessee. It was organized at Maryville, Tennessee, September 29, 1862.

The following roster was compiled in large part from a company muster and descriptive roll dated September 29, 1862, and company muster rolls dated September 29-October 31, 1862, and January-June, 1863, September, 1863-February, 1864, and April 7, 1864. These are abstracted in the microfilm edition of the Compiled Service Records of Confederate Soldiers Who Served in Organizations from the State of North Carolina (Record Group 109, M270), National Archives, Washington, D.C. Other valuable information in the Compiled Service Records includes enlistment papers, pay vouchers, requisitions, letters of resignation, discharge certificates, and abstracts of medical and prisoner of war records.

Also utilized in this roster were *The War of the Rebellion: A Compilation of the Official Records of the Union and Confederate Armies*, the North Carolina Adjutant General's papers, state militia records, newspaper casualty lists and obituaries, wartime claims for bounty pay and allowances, postwar registers of claims for artificial limbs, Confederate pension applications filed with the states of North Carolina, Tennessee, and Florida, and the 1860 and 1870 federal censuses of Tennessee. A search was made also for relevant letters, diaries, reminiscences, and other manuscripts in the Southern Historical Collection (University of North Carolina-Chapel Hill) and the Duke University Library Special Collections Department.

Among the secondary sources consulted were records of the North Carolina division of the United Daughters of the Confederacy, postwar rosters, regimental and county histories, marriage bond, will, and cemetery indexes, published and unpublished genealogies, biographical dictionaries, the North Carolina *County Heritage Book* series, the *Confederate Veteran*, Walter Clark's *Histories of the Several Regiments and Battalions from North Carolina in the Great War, 1861-'65*, and the North Carolina volume of the extended edition of *Confederate Military History*.

OFFICERS

CAPTAINS

McKAMY, JAMES A.

Born in Blount County, Tennessee, where he resided as a merchant. Served previously as Captain of Company E, 3rd Regiment Tennessee Infantry (Vaughn's). Enlisted in this company at age 36 at Maryville, Tennessee. Appointed Captain on September 29, 1862. Reported present through October 31, 1862, and in January-June, 1863. Signature appears on a payment voucher for service from July 1 through 31, 1863. Elected Major of this battalion on August 15, 1863, and transferred to the Field and Staff.

SINGLETON, JAMES M.

Born in Blount County, Tennessee, where he resided as a farmer. Previously served as Private and Corporal in Company E, 3rd Regiment Tennessee Infantry (Vaughn's). Enlisted in this company at Maryville, Tennessee, September 10, 1862, for the war. Appointed 1st Lieutenant on September 29, 1862. Reported present through October 31, 1862, and in January-June, 1863. Promoted to Captain on August 15, 1863. Reported present in September, 1863-February, 1864. Captured at Winchester, Virginia, September 19, 1864. Sent to Harpers Ferry, West Virginia. Confined at Fort Delaware, Delaware, September 27, 1864. Released at Fort Delaware on June 17, 1865, after taking the Oath of Allegiance.

LIEUTENANTS

ASHLEY, WILLIAM, 1st Lieutenant

Born in Chester, England, and resided in Blount County, Tennessee, where he was by occupation a clerk prior to enlisting at Maryville, Tennessee, at age 35. Appointed 2nd Lieutenant on September 29, 1862. Reported present through October 31, 1862, and in January-

June, 1863. Promoted to 1st Lieutenant on August 15, 1863. Reported present in September, 1863-February, 1864. Name appears on a receipt roll for clothing dated August 8, 1864. No further records.

McKAMY, JOHN W., 2nd Lieutenant
Previously served in Company F of this battalion. Transferred to this company on September 29, 1862. Mustered in as Private. Reported present through October 31, 1862. Reported absent on detached service in January-February, 1863. Rejoined the company on or prior to April 30, 1863. Reported present in May-June, 1863. Promoted to 1st Sergeant on September 1, 1863. Reported present in September-December, 1863. Elected 2nd Lieutenant on February 8, 1864, and was commissioned as such on February 25, 1864. Reported present through February 29, 1864. Reported present on April 7, 1864. Name appears on a payment voucher dated September 27, 1864. Signed, as commanding the battalion, a requisition for clothing dated September 27, 1864. No further records.

McNUTT, HUGH L., 3rd Lieutenant
Served as 1st Sergeant of this company. Elected 3rd Lieutenant, probably on August 15, 1863, while detailed as a recruiting officer in Blount County, Tennessee. Failed to return to duty and was reported absent without leave from September 6 through December 31, 1863. Reduced to ranks in January-February, 1864; it was reported at this time that his election as 3rd Lieutenant was never confirmed due to his absence without leave. Listed on April 7, 1864, as having deserted at Carter's Depot, Tennessee, September 6, 1863.

PAUL, JAMES A., 2nd Lieutenant
Born in Blount County, Tennessee, and where he resided as a farmer prior to enlisting at Maryville, Tennessee, at age 30, September 10, 1862, for the war. Appointed 3rd (Junior 2nd) Lieutenant on September 29, 1862. Reported present through October 31, 1862. Name appears on a payment voucher for service from November 1 through December 31, 1862. Reported absent sick from February 25 through 28, 1863. Returned to duy on or prior to April 30, 1863. Reported present in May-June, 1863. Sent to hospital at Knoxville, Tennessee, July 28, 1863. Probably promoted to 2nd Lieutenant on August 15, 1863. Reported absent without leave on September 1, 1863. Dropped from the company rolls on February 1, 1864, presumably for absence without leave.

YOUNG, LEWIS R., 3rd Lieutenant
Born in McMinn County, Tennessee, and resided in Blount County, Tennessee, where he was by occupation a carpenter prior to enlisting at Maryville, Tennessee, at age 26, September 18, 1862, for the war. Mustered in as Sergeant. Reported present through October 31, 1862, in January-June, 1863; and in September, 1863-February, 1864. Elected 3rd (Junior 2nd) Lieutenant on or about February 24, 1864. Signature appears on a pay voucher for service from February 24 through March 31, 1864. Captured at Winchester, Virginia, September 19, 1864. Sent to Harpers Ferry, West Virginia. Confined at Fort Delaware, Delaware, September 27, 1864. Released at Fort Delaware on June 17, 1865, after taking the Oath of Allegiance.

NONCOMMISSIONED OFFICERS AND PRIVATES

ALEXANDER, THOMAS, Private
Born in Jefferson County, Tennessee, and resided in Hawkins County, Tennessee, where he was by occupation a farmer prior to enlisting at Morristown, Tennessee, at age 35, October 1, 1862, for the war. Transferred to 2nd Company D of this battalion on December 15, 1862.

ALLEN, ANDERSON, Private
Resided in Grainger County, Tennessee, and enlisted either in this company or in Company C, Infantry Regiment of this legion, probably either at Strawberry Plains, Tennessee, or at Knoxville, Tennessee, January 2, 1863, for the war. Transferred on January 10, 1863, to 2nd Company D of this battalion.

ARMSTRONG, WILLIAM J., Private
Born in Blount County, Tennessee, where he resided as a laborer prior to enlisting at Maryville, Tennessee, at age 16, September 29, 1862, for the war. Reported present through October 31, 1862. Deserted at Knoxville, Tennessee, January 10, 1863.

BADGETT, AUGUSTINE, Private
Resided in Blount County, Tennessee, and was by occupation a farmer prior to enlisting at Rockford, Tennessee, at age 40, January 13, 1863, for the war. Discharged on January 18, 1863, after providing a substitute, probably Pvt. William Payne. [His first name may have been Augustus.]

BADGETT, JOSIAH R., Private
Previously served as Private in 1st Company D of this battalion. Transferred to this company prior to October 31, 1862. Reported present in January-April, 1863. Reported absent without leave in May-June, 1863. Returned to duty prior to October 31, 1863. Reported present in November, 1863-February, 1864. Captured at Piedmont, Virginia, June 5, 1864. Confined at Camp Morton, Indianapolis, Indiana, June 21, 1864. Transferred to City Point, Virginia, February 26, 1865, for exchange. No further records. [His middle name may have been Romulus.]

BALLINGER, JOSEPH, Private
Born in Blount County, Tennessee, where he resided as a farmer prior to enlisting at Maryville, Tennessee, at age 32, September 24, 1862, for the war. Reported present through October 31, 1862. Deserted at Maryville on November 24, 1862.

BARKER, JAMES M., Private
Born in Blount County, Tennessee, where he resided as a laborer prior to enlisting at Maryville, Tennessee, at age 17, September 15, 1862, for the war. Reported present through October 31, 1862, and in January-June, 1863. Deserted near Jonesborough, Tennessee, September 16, 1863.

BASTIAN, J. S., Private
Place and date of enlistment not reported. Name appears on a list of Confederate prisoners under guard by Federal forces at Staunton, Virginia, June 8, 1864. Place and date captured not reported, but was most likely at Piedmont, Virginia, June 5, 1864. Transferred to Wheeling, West Virginia, in July, 1864. No further records.

BELT, WILLIAM W., Private
Born in Blount County, Tennessee, where he resided as a farmer prior to enlisting at Maryville, Tennessee, at age 35, September 23, 1862, for the war. Rejected for service on November 4, 1862, after an examination by a surgeon.

BLAIR, SAMUEL, Corporal
Born in Blount County, Tennessee, where he resided as a farmer prior to enlisting at Maryville, Tennessee, at age 34, September 8, 1862, for the war. Mustered in as Corporal. Reported present or accounted for through October 31, 1862, and in January-April, 1863. Reported absent sick in May-June, 1863. Returned to duty in July-October, 1863. Reported present through February, 1864. Captured at Piedmont, Virginia, June 5, 1864. Sent to Staunton, Virginia. Confined at Camp Morton, Indianapolis, Indiana, June 21, 1864. Released at Camp Morton on June 12, 1865, after taking the Oath of Allegiance.

BOGLE, R. HUGH, Private
Born in Blount County, Tennessee, where he resided as a farmer. Served previously in Company E, 31st Regiment Tennessee Infantry (A. H. Bradford's). Enlisted in this company at Maryville, Tennessee, at age 30, September 20, 1862, for the war, while a deserter from the 31st Tennessee. Rejected for service on November 4, 1862, after an examination by the surgeon.

BOND, ISAAC H., Private
Enlisted in an unspecified unit in Knox County, Tennessee, October 4, 1862, for the war. Transferred to this company in March-April, 1863. Reported present in May-June, 1863. Reported on duty as a hospital steward in September-October, 1863. Deserted at Bull's Gap, Tennessee, January 1, 1864. Returned to duty on an unspecified date. Captured at Winchester, Virginia, September 19, 1864. Sent to Harpers Ferry, West Virginia. Transferred to Point Lookout, Maryland, September 23, 1864. No further records.

BOREN, ABSALOM, Private
Born in Blount County, Tennessee, where he resided as a carpenter prior to enlisting at Maryville, Tennessee, at age 33, September 29, 1862, for the war. Reported present through October 31, 1862. Deserted at Maryville on November 23, 1863.

BULLYERS, J. L., Private
Place and date of enlistment not reported; probably enlisted subsequent to April 7, 1864. Name appears on a Federal prisoner of war record which states that he was under guard at Staunton, Virginia, June 8, 1864. Place and date of capture not reported, but probably at Piedmont, Virginia, June 5, 1864. No further records.

BURNETT, JAMES A., Private
Previously served as Private either in Company A of this battalion or in 2nd Company A, Infantry Regiment of this legion. Transferred to this company on February 1, 1863. Reported absent sick on February 28, 1863. Deserted at Strawberry Plains, Tennessee, on or about April 7, 1863.

CALDWELL, HUGH D., Private
Enlisted at Knoxville, Tennessee, at about age 52, March 18, 1863, for the war as a substitute for Pvt. George W. Henry of this battalion. Reported present through June 30, 1863. Reported sick in hospital at Knoxville from July 19, 1863, through February 29, 1864. No further records. [He may have served later in Company A, 10th Regiment Tennessee Infantry.]

CALDWELL, JOSEPH A., Corporal
Born in Blount County, Tennessee, June 26, 1843. Resided in Blount County and was by occupation a farmer prior to enlisting at Maryville, Tennessee, at age 19, September 12, 1862, for the war. Mustered in as Private. Reported present through October 31, 1862, and in January-February, 1863. Promoted to Corporal on March 1, 1863. Reported present in March-June, 1863, and in September, 1863-February, 1864. Paroled at Franklin on May 12, 1865. [See his Tennessee pension application No. 4068.]

CARTER, SIDNEY G., Private
Previously served as Private in Company A of this battalion. Transferred to this company in July-August, 1863. Deserted at Carter's Depot, Tennessee, September 19, 1863.

CARTER, THOMAS, Private
Previously served as Private in Company A of this battalion. Transferred to this company in July-August, 1863. Detailed for hospital duty on September 10, 1863. Reported present in November-December, 1863. Reported on furlough in January-February, 1864. Name appears on receipt rolls for clothing dated June 22, September 1, and December 14, 1864. No further records.

CARTER, WILLIAM C., Private
Enlisted at Loudon, Tennessee, at about age 21, June 15, 1863, for the war. Deserted at Knoxville, Tennessee on July 19, 1863.

CHARLES, SAMUEL L., Private
Born in North Carolina and resided in Blount County, Tennessee, where he was by occupation a farmer prior to enlisting at Maryville, Tennessee, at age 51, September 14, 1862, for the war. Reported present through October 31, 1862. Reported sick in Blount County from November 24, 1862, through April 30, 1863. Reported sick in May-June, 1863. No further records.

COX, CYRUS S., Private
Born in Blount County, Tennessee, where he resided as a farmer prior to enlisting at Maryville, Tennessee, at about age 30, September 16, 1862, for the war. Reported present through October 31, 1862. Rejected for service after examination by a surgeon on November 6, 1862, and was discharged.

COZART, JAMES, Private
Born in Hawkins County, Tennessee, and resided in Jackson County, Tennessee, where he was by occupation a farmer prior to enlisting at Morristown, Tennessee, at age 25, October 1, 1862, for the war. Transferred to 2nd Company D of this battalion on December 15, 1862.

CRAIGMILES, JOHN H., Private
Enlisted at Loudon, Tennessee, June 1, 1863, for the war. Discharged at Loudon on June 10, 1863, after providing Pvt. John Pressley of this battalion as a substitute.

CRAWLEY, WILLIAM, Private
Previously served as Private either in Company A of this battalion or in 2nd Company A, Infantry Regiment of this legion. Transferred to this company on February 1, 1863. Deserted at Knoxville, Tennessee, February 8, 1863.

DAILY, PLEASANT, Private
Born in Blount County, Tennessee, where he resided as a farmer prior to enlisting at Maryville, Tennessee, at age 19, September 25,

1862, for the war. Reported present through October 31, 1862. Deserted at Maryville on November 24, 1862.

DAVIS, GEORGE T., Private

Born in Blount County, Tennessee, where he resided as a farmer prior to enlisting at Maryville, Tennessee, at age 30, September 29, 1862, for the war. Reported present through October 31, 1862, and in January-April, 1863. Reported absent without leave in May-June, 1863. Returned to duty prior to September 19, 1863, when he deserted at Carter's Depot, Tennessee.

DUNCAN, RICHARD C., Private

Born in Blount County, Tennessee, where he resided as a farmer prior to enlisting at Maryville, Tennessee, at age 37, September 29, 1862, for the war. Reported present through October 31, 1862. Rejected for military service on November 4, 1862, after an examination by a surgeon.

DYCHE, WILLIAM H., Private

Enlisted at Knoxville, Tennessee, at about age 16, January 17, 1863, for the war. Reported present through June 30, 1863. Deserted at Carter's Depot, Tennessee, September 1, 1863.

DYER, MARTIN, Private

Born in Burke County and resided in Blount County, Tennessee, where he was by occupation a laborer prior to enlisting at Maryville, Tennessee, at age 20, September 24, 1862, for the war. Reported present through October 31, 1862. Reported absent sick in Blount County on November 24, 1862. Returned to duty on May 9, 1863. Reported present through June 30, 1863. Deserted at either Jonesborough, Tennessee, or Carter's Depot, Tennessee, September 16, 1863.

EARLY, ANDREW HOWARD, Private

Resided in Blounty County. Enlisted at Maryville, Tennessee, at about age 36, January 7, 1863, for the war. Reported present through April 30, 1863. Discharged at Loudon, Tennessee, May 22, 1863, after providing Pvt. James L. Smith as a substitute.

GIBBS, GEORGE W., Private

Born in Blount County, Tennessee, where he resided as a farmer prior to enlisting at Maryville, Tennessee, at age 23, September 28, 1862, for the war. Reported through October 31, 1862, and in January-April, 1863. Reported on detached service as a teamster at Loudon, Tennessee, May-June, 1863. Rejoined the company prior to October 31, 1863. Reported present, November, 1863-February, 1864. Name appears on a receipt roll for clothing dated June 4, 1864. No further records.

GIBBS, LEVI, Private

Enlisted at Knoxville, Tennessee, at about age 45, December 18, 1862, for the war, probably as a substitute for Pvt. William Hamilton Thompson. Reported present or accounted for in January-April, 1863. Reported on detached service as a teamster at Loudon, Tennessee, May-June, 1863. Reported absent sick from September 3, 1863, through April 7, 1864. No further records.

GIBBS, MONTGOMERY H., Private

Born in Blount County, Tennessee, where he resided as a farmer prior to enlisting at Maryville, Tennessee, at age 17, September 12, 1862, for the war. Reported present through October 31, 1862. Reported on detached service in January-February, 1863. Rejoined the company prior to April 30, 1863. Reported present in May-June, 1863. A company muster roll dated April 7, 1864, states that he was transferred to the "1st Tennessee Cavalry" on August 12, 1863; however, there is no other evidence that he served in any Tennessee unit. No further records.

GIBBS, ZACHARY T., Private

Born in Blount County, Tennessee, where he resided as a farmer prior to enlisting at Maryville, Tennessee, at age 16, September 12, 1862, for the war. Reported present through October 31, 1862. Reported sick in hospital in January-February, 1863. Died in Blount County on March 24, 1863, of disease.

GILLESPIE, WILLIAM D., 1st Sergeant

Born in Blount County, Tennessee, where he resided as a farmer prior to enlisting at Maryville, Tennessee, at age 34, September 29, 1862, for the war. Mustered in as 1st Sergeant. Reported present through October 31, 1862. Reported sick at home from February 20 through 27, 1863. Died in Blount County on February 27, 1863, of disease.

GOODEN, JAMES, Private

Born in Hawkins County, Tennessee, and resided in Blount County, Tennessee, where he was by occupation a shoemaker prior to enlisting at Maryville, Tennessee, at age 33, September 18, 1862, for the war. Rejected for service after examination by a surgeon on November 4, 1862, and dropped from the company rolls. Reported absent without leave on September 23, 1863. No further records.

GOURLEY, JOHN C., Private

Born in Tennessee. Enlisted in Blount County, Tennessee, at about age 35, September 29, 1862, for the war. Discharged at Knoxville, Tennessee, February 18, 1863, after providing Pvt. Jackson Sims as a substitute.

GRASTEN, JOHN S., Private

Born in Blount County, Tennessee, where he resided as a farmer prior to enlisting at Maryville, Tennessee, at age 21, September 29, 1862, for the war. Reported present or accounted for in October, 1862; in January-June, 1863; and in September, 1863-February, 1864. Captured at Piedmont, Virginia, June 5, 1864. Confined at Camp Morton, Indianapolis, Indiana, June 21, 1864. Transferred to Point Lookout, Maryland, February 19, 1865, for exchange. Hospitalized at Richmond, Virginia, February 28, 1865. Transferred on March 1, 1865, to Camp Lee, Richmond. No further records.

HAFLEY, WINSTON C., Private

Born in McMinn County, Tennessee, and resided in Blount County, Tennessee, where he was by occupation a farmer prior to enlisting at Maryville, Tennessee, at age 23, September 29, 1862, for the war. Reported present through October 31, 1862, and in January-April, 1863. Reported absent without leave in May-June, 1863. Returned to duty prior to October 31, 1863. Deserted to the enemy at Blain's Crossroads, Tennessee, December 6, 1863. Took the Oath of Allegiance at Knoxville, Tennessee, December 16, 1863.

HARRIS, DANIEL M., Private

Born in Blount County, Tennessee, and was by occupation a farmer prior to enlisting at Rockford, Tennessee, at age 17, January 18,

1863, for the war. Died in hospital at Knoxville, Tennessee, February 27, 1863, of disease. [He may have been the same man as Melmouth D. Harris, whose record is in the General Miscellaneous section of this roster; if so, he served previously in Company G, 39th Regiment N.C. Troops.]

HARRIS, JAMES M., Private
Born in Blount County, Tennessee, May 26, 1841. Resided in Blount County and was by occupation a farmer prior to enlisting at Maryville, Tennessee, at age 21, September 12, 1862, for the war. Reported present through October 31, 1862. Reported on detached service as a teamster and mechanic at Strawberry Plains, Tennessee, from December 22, 1862, through April 7, 1864. Rejoined the company prior to June 5, 1864, when he was captured at Piedmont, Virginia. Reported under guard at Staunton, Virginia, June 8, 1864. Confined at Camp Morton, Indianapolis, Indiana, June 21, 1864. Transferred to Point Lookout, Maryland, February 19, 1865, for exchange. Hospitalized at Richmond, Virginia, February 28, 1865, with phthisis pulmonalis. Transferred on March 1, 1865. Took the Oath of Allegiance at Chattanooga, Tennessee, May 21, 1865. [See his Tennessee pension application No. 12642.]

HENRY, GEORGE W., Private
Resided in Blount County, Tennessee, and was by occupation a farmer prior to enlisting in Blount County at about age 35, March 5, 1863, for the war. Discharged at Knoxville, Tennessee, March 18, 1863, after providing Pvt. Hugh D. Caldwell as a substitute.

HENRY, SAMUEL H., Private
Probably resided in Blounty County. Enlisted at Loudon, Tennessee, at about age 40, June 4, 1863, for the war. Discharged on the same date after providing Pvt. Thomas Lane as a substitute.

HIX, MOSES, Private
Born in Haywood County and resided in Clay County where he was by occupation a farmer prior to enlisting in Clay County at age 38, September 25, 1862, for the war. Reported present in January-April, 1863. Died in hospital at Greeneville, Tennessee, August 26, 1863, of unknown causes. [His surname may have been Hicks.]

HUTCHINSON, W. P., Private
Enlisted at Knoxville, Tennessee, at about age 31, January 17, 1863, for the war. Deserted at Knoxville on February 24, 1863.

JOHNSON, L. F., Private
Previously served in an unspecified unit. Transferred to this company on June 15, 1863. Failed to report for duty and was dropped from the rolls as a deserter on or about April 7, 1864. [He was 32 years of age in April, 1864.]

JOHNSON, ROBERT E., Private
Born in Blount County, Tennessee, June 17, 1843. Enlisted at Carter's Depot, Tennessee, at age 20, August 15, 1863, for the war. Reported present through October 31, 1863. Deserted at Blain's Crossroads, Tennessee, December 6, 1863. [See his Tennessee pension application No. 11728.]

KELLER, JOHN H., Private
Born in Hawkins County, Tennessee, in 1845. Resided in Blount County, Tennessee, and was a farmer prior to enlisting at Maryville, Tennessee, at age 17, September 22, 1862, for the war. Reported present through October 31, 1862. Reported on detached service in January-February, 1863. Rejoined the company on or prior to April 30, 1863. Reported present in May-June, 1863, and September, 1863-February, 1864. Captured at Piedmont, Virginia, June 5, 1864. Reported under guard at Staunton, Virginia, June 8, 1864. Confined at Camp Morton, Indianapolis, Indiana, June 21, 1864. Released at Camp Morton on May 22, 1865, after taking the Oath of Allegiance. [See his Tennessee pension application No. 8737.]

KELLY, JOSEPH, Private
Resided in Blount County, Tennessee, and was by occupation a laborer prior to enlisting at Maryville, Tennessee, at age 32, March 9, 1863, for the war. Reported present through June 30, 1863, and in September, 1863-February, 1864. Name appears on receipt rolls for clothing date June 22, September 1, and September 27, 1864. No further records.

KLEPPER, CORNELIUS, Private
Resided in Hawkins County, Tennessee. Enlisted in Hawkins County, Tennessee, at about age 20, October 10, 1862, for the war. Died in hospital at Knoxville, Tennessee, on or about February 12, 1863, of disease.

KLEPPER, JOHN M., Private
Previously served as Private in either Company A of this battalion or in 2nd Company A, Infantry Regiment of this legion. Transferred to this company on February 1, 1863. Reported present through April 30, 1863. Reported absent sick in May-June, 1863. Reported detached on hospital service from September 10 through October 31, 1863. Reported sick at home near Rogersville, Tennessee, from December 29, 1863, through April 7, 1864. No further records.

LAND, RUFUS A., Private
Born in Blount County, Tennessee, where he resided as a farmer prior to enlisting at Maryville, Tennessee, September 29, 1862, for the war. Reported present through October 31, 1862. Deserted at Maryville on November 24, 1862.

LANE, THOMAS, Private
Enlisted at Loudon, Tennessee, at about age 49, June 4, 1863, for the war as a substitute for Pvt. Samuel H. Henry. Deserted at Carter's Depot, Tennessee, September 1, 1863.

LEBOW, LAFAYETTE, Private
Born in Blount County, Tennessee, where he resided as a farmer prior to enlisting at Maryville, Tennessee, at age 18, September 29, 1862, for the war. Reported absent with leave on October 31, 1862. Deserted at Maryville on November 24, 1862.

LOGAN, JAMES H., Sergeant
Born in Blount County, Tennessee, where he resided as a farmer prior to enlisting at Maryville, Tennessee, at age 22, September 25, 1862, for the war. Mustered in as Private. Reported present through October 31, 1862. Promoted to Sergeant prior to February 28, 1863. Reported present in January-June, 1863. Reportedly transferred to Company G, 5th Regiment Tennessee Cavalry, on August 12, 1863; however, no other evidence of his service in that unit was located.

LOGAN, JOHN A., Private

Born in Blount County, Tennessee, where he resided as a farmer prior to enlisting at Maryville, Tennessee, at age 20, September 25, 1862, for the war. Reported present through October 31, 1862, and in January-June, 1863. Reportedly transferred to Company G, 5th Regiment Tennessee Cavalry, August 12, 1863; however, no other evidence of his service in that unit was located.

LOGAN, SAMUEL A., Private

Born in Blount County, Tennessee, where he resided as a farmer prior to enlisting at Maryville, Tennessee, at age 26, September 25, 1862, for the war. Reported present through October 31, 1862, and in January-February, 1863. Deserted at Knoxville, Tennessee, March 10, 1863.

LONG, A. RILEY, Private

Born in Blount County, Tennessee, where he resided as a farmer prior to enlisting at Maryville, Tennessee, at age 20, September 24, 1862, for the war. Reported absent with leave on October 31, 1862. Deserted at Maryville on or about November 24, 1862.

LONG, ANDREW C., Private

Born in Blount County, Tennessee, in 1839. Resided in Blount County and was by occupation a farmer prior to enlisting at Maryville, Tennessee, at age 23, September 19, 1862, for the war. Reported present through October 31, 1862, and in January-April, 1863. Captured and paroled at Lenoir's Station, Tennessee, June 19, 1863. Returned to duty prior to October 31, 1863. Reported present in November, 1863-February, 1864. Survived the war. [According to his Tennessee pension application No. 9299, he surrendered at Franklin in 1865, probably on May 12 when the battalion officially surrendered.]

LONG, JAMES, Private

Born in Blount County, Tennessee, where he resided as a farmer prior to enlisting at Maryville, Tennessee, at age 23, September 24, 1862, for the war. Reported present through October 31, 1862. Reported on detached service in January-February, 1863. Rejoined the company on or prior to April 30, 1863. Reported on detached service in May-June, 1863. Reported absent without leave from July 10, 1863, through April 7, 1864. No further records.

LONG, JOHN, Private

Probably resided in Blount County, Tennessee. Transferred to this company at about age 28, August 5, 1863, probably from the Conscript Camp of Instruction at Knoxville, Tennessee. Reported present in September, 1863-February, 1864. Name appears on receipt rolls for clothing dated June 22, September 1, and December 14, 1864. No further records. Survived the war.

LONG, WILLIAM H., Private

Born in Blount County, Tennessee, where he resided as a farmer prior to enlisting at Maryville, Tennessee, at age 27, September 24, 1862, for the war. Reported present through October 31, 1862. Died in hospital at Knoxville, Tennessee, February 24, 1863, of disease.

McBEE, ELI, Private

Previously served as Private either in Company A of this battalion or in 2nd Company A, Infantry Regiment of this legion. Transferred to this company on February 1, 1863. Reported present through June 30, 1863, and in September, 1863-February, 1864. Hospitalized at Winchester, Virginia, July 26, 1864, with a gunshot wound of the thigh. Place and date wounded not reported. No further records.

McCALL, JOHN M., Private

Previously served as Private either in Company A of this battalion or in 2nd Company A, Infantry Regiment of this legion. Transferred to this company on February 1, 1863. Reported present through February 28, 1863. Deserted at Strawberry Plains, Tennessee, on or about April 7, 1863.

McCULLOCH, THOMAS E., Private

Born in Blount County, Tennessee, where he resided as a farmer prior to enlisting at Maryville, Tennessee, at age 36, September 29, 1862, for the war. Reported present through October 31, 1862. Rejected by the battalion surgeon in January-February, 1863, for unspecified physical disabilities but rejoined the company after a second examination on April 12, 1863. Reported present through June 30, 1863. Detailed as Acting Commissary Sergeant in September-October, 1863, and transferred to the Field and Staff of this battalion.

McCULLOUGH, JOSHUA J., Sergeant

Resided in Blount County, Tennessee, and enlisted at Maryville, Tennessee, at about age 23, September 29, 1862, for the war. Mustered in as Private. Reported present through October 31, 1862. Reported on detached service in January-February, 1863. Rejoined the company on or prior to April 30, 1863. Reported absent without leave in May-June, 1863. Returned to duty prior to September 1, 1863, when he was elected Sergeant. Reported present in September, 1863-February, 1864. Reported on duty as a teamster in July-September, 1864. Deserted to the enemy at Franklin on March 1, 1865. Confined at Knoxville, Tennessee, March 7, 1865. Released on bond at Knoxville on March 8, 1865, after taking the Oath of Allegiance.

McLAIN, JOHN E., Private

Born in Blount County, Tennessee, where he resided as a farmer prior to enlisting at Maryville, Tennessee, at age 18, September 10, 1862, for the war. Mustered in as Corporal. Reported present through October 31, 1862, and in January-June, 1863. Reported absent sick in Blount County from July 25 through December 31, 1863. Reported absent without leave in January-February, 1864. Reduced to ranks prior to April 7, 1864, when he was listed as a deserter.

McNUTT, HUGH L., Private

Born in Blount County, Tennessee, where he resided as a farmer prior to enlisting at Maryville, Tennessee, at age 30, September 29, 1862, for the war. He may have enlisted illegally in 1st Company D of this battalion, September 30, 1862, or may have enlisted in that company first and transferred to this company. Mustered in as Corporal. Reported present through October 31, 1862, and in January-February, 1863. Promoted to 1st Sergeant on March 1, 1863. Reported present in March-June, 1863. Detailed on August 6, 1863, for thirty days as a recruiting officer in Blount County, Tennessee. Elected 3rd Lieutenant, probably on August 15, 1863, while on detail. Failed to return to duty and was reported absent without leave September 6-December 31, 1863. Reduced to ranks in January-February, 1864; it was reported at this time that his election as 3rd

Lieutenant was never officially confirmed due to his absence without leave. Listed on April 7, 1864, as having deserted at Carter's Depot, Tennessee, September 6, 1863.

MALCOLM, JAMES P., Private
Born in Blount County, Tennessee, where he resided as a farmer prior to enlisting at Maryville, Tennessee, at age 18, September 29, 1862, for the war. Reported present through October 31, 1862. Reported absent without leave, "supposed to be in Blount Co., Ten," from November 24, 1862, through June 30, 1863. No further records.

MANN, JOSEPH H., Private
Enlisted at Maryville, Tennessee, at about age 23, September 29, 1862, for the war. Reported present through October 31, 1862. Reported on detached service in January-February, 1863. Rejoined the company on or prior to April 30, 1863. Reported present in May-June, 1863, and in September, 1863-February, 1864. Captured at Winchester, Virginia, September 19, 1864. Sent to Harpers Ferry, West Virginia. Confined at Point Lookout, Maryland, September 26, 1864. Died at Point Lookout on January 21, 1865, of "chronic dysentery."

MEANS, ROBERT A., Corporal
Born in Blount County, Tennessee, where he resided as a farmer prior to enlisting at Maryville, Tennessee, at age 19, September 8, 1862, for the war. Mustered in as Private. Reported present through October 31, 1862. Severely injured his back in a fall on February 14, 1863. Furloughed on or about February 25, 1863. Returned to duty or prior to April 30, 1863. Reported present in May-June, 1863, and in September, 1863-February, 1864. Promoted to Corporal prior to April 7, 1864. Name appears on receipt rolls for clothing dated June 4, June 22, September 1, and December 14, 1864. No further records. Survived the war.

MILLIGAN, FRANK H., Private
Previously served as Private in either Company A of this battalion or in 2nd Company A, Infantry Regiment. Transferred to this company on February 1, 1863. Reported absent without leave on February 28, 1863. Returned to duty prior to April 30, 1863. Reported absent without leave in May-June, 1863. Returned to duty on an unspecified date. Reported present in September-October, 1863. Deserted to the enemy near Blain's Crossroads, Tennessee, December 6, 1863. Confined at Knoxville, Tennessee. Released at Knoxville on or about December 16, 1863, after taking the Oath of Allegiance. [His given name may have been H. Frank.]

MYERS, JOHN, Private
Born in Blount County, Tennessee, where he resided as a farmer prior to enlisting at Maryville, Tennessee, on or about September 16, 1862, for the war. Reported absent with leave through October 31, 1862. Reported on detached service in January-February, 1863. Reported on detached service in the government blacksmith shop at Knoxville, Tennessee, in March-June, 1863. No further records.

NEAL, THOMAS, Private
Born in Monroe County, Tennessee, and resided in Blount County, Tennessee, where he was by occupation a farmer prior to enlisting at Maryville, Tennessee, at age 29, September 15, 1862, for the war. Reported present through October 31, 1862. Deserted at Knoxville, Tennessee, December 1, 1862.

PARKS, THOMAS A., Private
Born in Blount County, Tennessee, where he resided as a farmer prior to enlisting at Maryville, Tennessee, at age 21, September 10, 1862, for the war. Reported present through October 31, 1862. Deserted at Maryville or Rockford, Tennessee, November 24, 1862.

PAYNE, WILLIAM, Private
Resided in Blount County and was by occupation a farmer prior to enlisting at Rockford, Tennessee, at about age 47, January 18, 1863, for the war as a substitute for Pvt. Augustine Badgett of this company. Reported absent sick on February 28, 1863. Reported for duty or rejoined the company on or before April 30, 1863. Reported absent without leave in May-June, 1863, but returned to duty prior to June 30, 1863. Reported present in September-October, 1863. Reported absent without leave from November 10, 1863, through February 29, 1864. No further records.

PRESSLEY, JOHN, Private
Enlisted at Loudon, Tennessee, at about age 46, June 10, 1863, for the war as a substitute for Pvt. John H. Craigmiles of this company. Reported present through June 30, 1863. Reported absent on detached service at Loudon from July 10, 1863, through April 7, 1864. No further records.

PRIVETT, MATTHEW T., Private
Born in what later became Marshall County, Tennessee. Resided in Blount County, Tennessee, where he was by occupation a farmer prior to enlisting at Maryville, Tennessee, at age 29, September 11, 1862, for the war. Mustered in as Musician. Reported present through October 31, 1862, and in January-April, 1863. Reported sick in hospital at Loudon, Tennessee, in May-June, 1863. Reported present in September, 1863-February, 1864. Hospitalized at Bristol, Tennessee, March 21, 1864. Name appears on a register of payments for service from March 1 through August 31, 1864. Reduced to ranks on an unspecified date. Took the Oath of Allegiance at Chattanooga, Tennessee, May 24, 1865.

PUGH, JAMES T., Sergeant
Born in Blount County, Tennessee, where he resided as a farmer prior to enlisting at Maryville, Tennessee, at age 27, September 27, 1862, for the war. Mustered in as Sergeant. Died in Blount County on November 27, 1862, of disease.

RALSTON, PHILIP N., Private
Born in Blount County, Tennessee, where he resided as a farmer prior to enlisting at Maryville, Tennessee, at age 33, September 12, 1862, for the war. Reported present through October 31, 1862. Reported on detached service in January-February, 1863. Rejoined the company on or prior to April 30, 1863. Reported present in May-June, 1863. Deserted at Carter's Depot, Tennessee, September 1, 1863.

RALSTON, WILLIAM H., Private
Previously served as Private either in Company A of this battalion or in 2nd Company A, Infantry Regiment of this legion. Transferred to this company on February 1, 1863. Reported present until March 9, 1863, when he was reported absent sick in Blount County, Tennessee. Failed to return to duty and reported absent without leave in May-June and September-October, 1863. Listed as a deserter on December 31, 1863.

RENO, JOHN, Private
Served as Private in Company C, Infantry Regiment of this legion. May have transferred to this battalion between March 1, 1864, and July 31, 1864.

RIDDLE, ISAAC M., Private
Previously served as Private either in Company A of this battalion or in 2nd Company A, Infantry Regiment of this legion. Transferred to this company on February 1, 1863. Reported on detached service as a teamster at Knoxville, Tennessee, from February 10, 1863, through April 7, 1864. No further records.

ROBERTS, ELISHA, Private
Previously served as Private in Company A of this battalion. Transferred to this company in May-June, 1863. Reported sick in hospital at Loudon, Tennessee, June 30, 1863. Died on July 8, 1863, of disease. Place of death not reported.

ROBERTS, PETER, Private
Born in Blount County, Tennessee, where he resided as a farmer prior to enlisting at Maryville, Tennessee, at age 17, September 29, 1862, for the war. Reported present through October 31, 1862, and in January-April, 1863. Reported on leave in May-June, 1863. Reported present in September, 1863-February, 1864. Hospitalized at Winchester, Virginia, August 1, 1864, with remittent fever. Returned to duty prior to September 19, 1864, when he was captured at Winchester, Virginia. Sent to Harpers Ferry, West Virginia. Transferred to Point Lookout, Maryland, September 23, 1864. Paroled at Point Lookout on February 13, 1865. Received at Cox's Wharf, James River, Virginia, February 14-15, 1865, for exchange. Name appears on a list of paroled and exchanged prisoners at Camp Lee, near Richmond, Virginia, February 18, 1865. No further records.

RODDY, HOLSTON, Private
Born in Blount County, Tennessee, July 23, 1839. Resided in Blount County and was by occupation a farmer prior to enlisting at Maryville, Tennessee, at age 23, September 29, 1862, for the war. Reported present through October 31, 1862, and in January-June, 1863. Detached as a teamster on September 28, 1863. Rejoined the company prior to October 31, 1863. Reported present in November, 1863-February, 1864. Captured at Winchester, Virginia, September 19, 1864. Sent to Harpers Ferry, West Virginia. Confined at Point Lookout, Maryland, September 26, 1864. Paroled at Point Lookout on March 15, 1865. Received at Boulware's Wharf, James River, Virginia, March 18, 1865, for exchange. Name appears on a list of paroled and exchanged prisoners at Camp Lee, near Richmond, Virginia, March 19, 1865. Survived the war. [See his Tennessee pension application No. 12272.]

ROWLETT, CHARLES W., Private
Born in Blount County, Tennessee, where he resided as a farmer prior to enlisting at Maryville, Tennessee, at age 22, September 29, 1862, for the war. Reported present through October 31, 1862. Reported absent without leave in Blount County, Tennessee, February 26, 1863. Returned to duty on or prior to April 30, 1863. Deserted at Jonesborough, Tennessee, September 15, 1863.

RUSSELL, JAMES G., Private
Resided in Blount County, Tennessee, and was by occupation a farmer prior to enlisting at Knoxville, Tennessee, at about age 39, December 10, 1862, for the war. Reported present in January-June, 1863, and in September, 1863-February, 1864. Captured at Winchester, Virginia, September 19, 1864. Sent to Harpers Ferry, West Virginia. Transferred to Point Lookout, Maryland, September 23, 1864. Paroled at Point Lookout on March 15, 1865. Received at Boulware's Wharf, James River, Virginia, March 18, 1865, for exchange. Name appears on a list of paroled and exchanged prisoners at Camp Lee, near Richmond, Virginia, March 19, 1865. No further records.

SCOTT, JAMES M., Private
Previously served as Private either in Company A of this battalion or in 2nd Company A, Infantry Regiment of this legion. Transferred to this company on February 1, 1863. Discharged on March 21, 1863, by reason of "chronic rheumatism" He was 35 years of age at the time he was discharged.

SCRIVENER, JAMES HENRY, Private
Born in Blount County, Tennessee, March 4, 1844. Resided in Blount County and was by occupation a farmer prior to enlisting at Maryville, Tennessee, at age 18, September 12, 1862, for the war. Reported present through October 31, 1862, and in January-April, 1863. Reported on leave in May-June, 1863. Reported sick at home in September-October, 1863. Failed to return to duty and was subsequently reported as absent without leave from July 15, 1863, through April 7, 1864. No further records. Survived the war. [His surname may have been Scribner or Scrivner. His Tennessee pension application No. 14815 indicates that he served previously in the 3rd Regiment Tennessee Infantry (Vaughn's), but there is no known wartime evidence of his service in that unit.]

SCULLY, WILLIAM A., Private
Previously served as Private either in Company A of this battalion or in 2nd Company A, Infantry Regiment of this legion. Transferred to this company on February 1, 1863. Reported present through February 29, 1863. Reported absent without leave from April 15 through 30, 1863. Returned to duty prior to June 30, 1863. Reported on detached duty with the engineer corps at Knoxville, Tennessee, from August 7, 1863, through April 7, 1864. No further records.

SEXTON, JOSEPH W., Private
Previously served as Private either in Company A of this battalion or in 2nd Company A, Infantry Regiment of this legion. Transferred to this company on February 1, 1863. Died in hospital at Knoxville, Tennessee, February 2, 1863, of disease.

SHAVER, BARTLEY C., Private
Born in Blount County, Tennessee, where he resided as a farmer prior to enlisting at Maryville, Tennessee, at age 22, September 29, 1862, for the war. Reported present through October 31, 1862, and in January-June, 1863. Deserted at Jonesborough, Tennessee, September 15, 1863.

SHAVER, JAMES H., Private
Born in Blount County, Tennessee, where he resided as a farmer prior to enlisting at Maryville, Tennessee, at age 25, September 29, 1862, for the war. Reported present through October 31, 1862. Reported absent sick in Blount County, Tennessee, from February 9 through 28, 1863. Returned to duty prior to April 30, 1863. Reported present in May-June, 1863. Deserted at Jonesborough, Tennessee, September 15, 1863.

SHOOP, J. N., _____
Name appears on a register of Confederate officers and soldiers who were killed in battle or died of wounds or disease. Probably served either in this company or in Company C, Infantry Regiment of this legion. Died at Strawberry Plains, Tennessee, December 27, 1862. Cause of death unknown.

SIMMERLEY, HAMILTON, Private
Born in Blount County, Tennessee, where he resided as a farmer prior to enlisting at Maryville, Tennessee, at age 28, September 24, 1862, for the war. Reported present through October 31, 1862. Deserted at Maryville on November 24, 1862.

SIMS, JACKSON, Private
Enlisted at Knoxville, Tennessee, at about age 39, February 18, 1863, for the war as a substitute for Pvt. John C. Gourley. Reported present through April 30, 1863. Subsequently reported as having deserted at Greeneville, Tennessee, March 20, 1863. No further records. [His surname may have been Simms.]

SINGLETON, JAMES, 1st Sergeant
Born in Blount County, Tennessee, where he resided as a farmer prior to enlisting at Maryville, Tennessee, at age 40, September 24, 1862, for the war. Mustered in as Private. Reported present through October 31, 1862, in January-June, 1863, and in September, 1863-February, 1864. Promoted to 1st Sergeant on February 1, 1864. Captured at Piedmont, Virginia, June 5, 1864. Reported under guard at Staunton, Virginia, June 8, 1864. Confined at Camp Morton, Indianapolis, Indiana, June 21, 1864. Died at Camp Morton on July 6, 1864, of "pneumonia."

SMITH, JAMES L., Private
Enlisted at Loudon, Tennessee, at about age 19, May 22, 1863, for the war as a substitute for Pvt. Andrew Howard Early. Transferred to Company A of this battalion on May 23, 1863.

SMITH, JAMES M., Sergeant
Born in Kentucky and resided in Blount County, Tennessee, where he was by occupation a farmer prior to enlisting at Maryville, Tennessee, at age 19, September 9, 1862, for the war. Mustered in as Sergeant. Reported present through October 31, 1862. Reported absent without leave in Blount County, Tennessee, February 20, 1863. Returned to duty prior to April 30, 1863. Reported present in September, 1863-February, 1864. Hospitalized at Winchester, Virginia, August 1, 1864, with rheumatism. Transferred to another hospital on August 3, 1864. Name appears on a receipt roll for clothing dated September 27, 1864. No further records.

SMITH, JOSEPH, Private
Enlisted at Carter's Depot, Tennessee, at about age 18, July 28, 1863, for the war. Reported present in September, 1863-February, 1864. Name appears on receipt rolls for clothing dated June 4, June 22, and September 1, 1864. No further records.

SNEED, JOHN T., Private
Born in Blount County, Tennessee, where he resided as a farmer prior to enlisting at Maryville, Tennessee, at age 17, September 29, 1862, for the war. Reported present through October 31, 1862. Reported on detached service in January-February, 1863. Rejoined the company prior to April 30, 1863. Reported present in May-June, 1863, and in September, 1863-February, 1864. Captured at Piedmont, Virginia, June 5, 1864. Sent to Staunton, Virginia. Confined at Camp Morton, Indianapolis, Indiana, June 21, 1864. Paroled at Camp Morton on February 19, 1865, and transferred for exchange. No further records.

STEWART, THOMAS, Private
Born in Blount County, Tennessee, where he resided as a farmer prior to enlisting at Maryville, Tennessee, at age 28, September 29, 1862, for the war. Reported present through October 31, 1862, and in January-April, 1863. Reported absent without leave in May-June, 1863. Returned to duty prior to October 31, 1863. Reported present in November, 1863-February, 1864. Name appears on receipt rolls for clothing dated June 22 and September 1, 1864. No further records.

STRANGE, FRANK M., Private
Born in Georgia and resided in Blount County, Tennessee, where he was by occupation a farmer prior to enlisting at Maryville, Tennessee, at age 26, September 15, 1862, for the war. Reported present through October 31, 1862. Rejected for service by a surgeon on November 6, 1862. Reason he was rejected not reported.

STUART, ARCHIBALD, Private
Born in Blount County, Tennessee, where he resided as a farmer prior to enlisting at Maryville, Tennessee, at age 33, September 29, 1862, for the war. Reported present through October 31, 1862. Deserted at Knoxville, Tennessee, December 29, 1862. Probably enlisted subsequently as a Private in Company H, Infantry Regiment in this legion.

TALLEY, JOHN, Private
Previously served as Private either in Company A of this battalion or in 2nd Company A, Infantry Regiment of this legion. Transferred to this company on April 9, 1863. Reported present through June 30, 1863. Reported in hospital at Greeneville, Tennessee, in September-October, 1863. Returned to duty prior to October 31, 1863. Reported in hospital at Bristol, Tennessee, from November 28, 1863, through February 29, 1864. Deserted to the enemy on March 11, 1864. Sent to Knoxville, Tennessee. Hospitalized at Knoxville on March 12, 1864, with rheumatism. Died in hospital at Knoxville on April 4, 1864. Cause of death not reported.

TAYLOR, ANDREW J., Private
Born in Blount County, Tennessee, where he resided as a farmer prior to enlisting at Maryville, Tennessee, at age 21, September 29, 1862, for the war. Reported present or accounted for through October 31, 1862, in January-June, 1863, and September-October, 1863. Reported on detached duty as brigade wagoner from November 1, 1863, through April 7, 1864. No further records.

TAYLOR, DANIEL R., Private
Born in Blount County, Tennessee, where he resided as a farmer prior to enlisting at Maryville, Tennessee, at age 32, September 29, 1862, for the war. Rejected for service by a surgeon on November 6, 1862. Reason he was rejected not reported.

TAYLOR, LYCURGUS W., Private
Previously served as Private either in Company A of this battalion or in 2nd Company A, Infantry Regiment of this legion. Transferred to

this company on April 15, 1863. Reported present through June 30, 1863, and in September, 1863-February, 1864. Captured at Cedar Creek, Virginia, October 19, 1864. Hospitalized at Baltimore, Maryland, October 25, 1864. Confined at Point Lookout, Maryland, October 28, 1864. Paroled at Point Lookout on October 30, 1864. Received at Venus Point, Savannah River, Georgia, November 15, 1864, for exchange. Name appears on a receipt roll for clothing dated November 22, 1864, where he is reported to be a paroled prisoner. No further records.

TAYLOR, THOMAS D., Private

Born in Grainger County, Tennessee, June 9, 1844. Resided in Blount County, Tennessee, and was by occupation a farmer prior to enlisting at Maryville, Tennessee, at age 18, September 29, 1862, for the war. Reported present through October 31, 1862, in January-June, 1863, and in September, 1863-February, 1864. Captured at Piedmont, Virginia, June 5, 1864. Reported under guard at Staunton, Virginia, June 8, 1864. Confined at Camp Morton, Indianapolis, Indiana, June 21, 1864. Paroled at Camp Morton on February 14, 1865, and transferred for exchange. No further records. Survived the war. [See his Tennessee pension application No. 8320. Contrary to 15:47 of this series, he is probably not the same man as Pvt. Thomas D. Taylor of Company A, 62nd Regiment N.C. Troops.]

TAYLOR, WILLIAM B., Corporal

Born in Blount County, Tennessee, where he resided as a farmer prior to enlisting at Maryville, Tennessee, at age 31, September 29, 1862, for the war. Mustered in as Corporal. Reported present through October 31, 1862; in January-June, 1863; and in September, 1863-February, 1864. Name appears on receipt rolls for clothing dated June 4 and June 22, 1864. Took the Oath of Allegiance at Chattanooga, Tennessee, June 22, 1865.

TEDFORD, JOSEPH HOWARD, Private

Previously served as Private in either Company A of this battalion or in 2nd Company A, Infantry Regiment of this legion. Transferred to this company on February 6, 1863. Reported absent sick on February 28, 1863. Returned to duty on an unknown date. Sent to a hospital on April 18, 1863; however, he never reported and subsequently was listed as a deserter. [His given name may have been Howard Joseph.]

TEEFETELLER, JOSEPH H., Private

Born in 1825 in Blount or Monroe County, Tennessee, and resided in Blount County where he was by occupation a farmer prior to enlisting at Maryville, Tennessee, at age 30, September 29, 1862, for the war. Reported present through October 31, 1862. Reported absent without leave in Blount County on February 20, 1863. Returned to duty prior to April 30, 1863. Reported present in May-June and September-October, 1863. Deserted to the enemy near Blain's Crossroads, Tennessee, December 6, 1863. Sent to Knoxville, Tennessee. Released at Knoxville on or about December 16, 1863, after taking the Oath of Allegiance. [His surname may have been Teffeteller. His Tennessee pension application No. 8092 states that he injured his left leg and suffered a rupture in his left side in a fall off a bluff near the railroad bridge at Zollicoffer, Tennessee, or Carter's Depot, Tennessee.]

THOMAS, NOAH, Private

Born in Blount County, Tennessee, where he resided as a farmer prior to enlisting at Maryville, Tennessee, at age 20, September 29, 1862, for the war. Reported present through October 31, 1862. Deserted at Rockford, Tennessee, November 25, 1862.

THOMPSON, HAMILTON WILLIAM, Private

Born in Blount County, Tennessee, where he resided as a farmer prior to enlisting at Maryville, Tennessee, at age 37, September 29, 1862, for the war. Discharged on December 18, 1862, after providing a substitute, probably Pvt. Levi Gibbs.

WEAR, DAVID H., Sergeant

Born in Blount County, Tennessee, where he resided as a farmer prior to enlisting at Maryville, Tennessee, at age 22, September 10, 1862, for the war. Mustered in as Sergeant. Reported present through October 31, 1862. Reported absent sick in Blount County from January 13 through April 30, 1863. Returned to duty prior to June 30, 1863. Reported present in September, 1863-February, 1864. Name appears on receipt rolls for clothing dated June 22, September 1, September 27, and December 14, 1864. No further records.

WEAR, ROBERT A., Private

Born in Blount County, Tennessee, where he resided as a farmer prior to enlisting at Maryville, Tennessee, at age 35, September 28, 1862, for the war. Reported present through October 31, 1862. Reported absent sick in Blount County from January 23 through February 28, 1863. Returned to duty prior to April 30, 1863. Reported on detached duty as a teamster at Loudon, Tennessee, in May-June, 1863. Rejoined the company prior to October 31, 1863. Reported present, November, 1863-February, 1864. Name appears on a receipt roll for clothing dated June 4, 1864. No further records.

WEBB, JOHN, Private

Enlisted either in this company or in Company C, Infantry Regiment of this legion, at about age 29, January 2, 1863, for the war. He probably enlisted either at Strawberry Plains, Tennessee, or at Knoxville, Tennessee. Transferred to 2nd Company D, Walker's Battalion, January 10, 1863.

WELLS, LEONIDAS, Private

Born in Blount County, Tennessee, where he resided as a farmer prior to enlisting at Maryville, Tennessee, at age 22, September 27, 1862, for the war. Reported absent without leave on October 31, 1862. Subsequently reported as having deserted at Maryville on or about November 23, 1862.

WEST, ALFRED, Private

Born in Blount County, Tennessee, where he resided as a farmer prior to enlisting at Maryville, Tennessee, at age 26, September 23, 1862, for the war. Rejected for service by a surgeon on November 4, 1862.

WHEELER, JORDAN, Private

Previously served as Private either in Company A of this battalion or in 2nd Company A, Infantry Regiment of this legion. Transferred to this company on February 1, 1863. Deserted at Knoxville, Tennessee, February 8, 1863.

WHITE, WILLIAM, Private

Born in Blount County, Tennessee, where he resided as a farmer prior to enlisting at Maryville, Tennessee, at age 38, September 29,

1862, for the war. Reported present through October 31, 1862. Reported absent without leave from November 24, 1862, through October 31, 1863. Listed as a deserter in November-December, 1863.

WHITEHEAD, MATTHIAS, Private
Born in Carter County, Tennessee, and resided in Blount County, Tennessee, where he was by occupation a farmer prior to enlisting at Maryville, Tennessee, at age 39, September 12, 1862, for the war. Reported present through October 31, 1862. Deserted at Maryville, Tennessee, November 23, 1862.

WIMBERLEY, HOUSTON, Private
Born in Blount County, Tennessee, where he resided as a farmer prior to enlisting at Maryville, Tennessee, at age 20, September 25, 1862, for the war. Deserted at Maryville on November 24, 1862.

WRINKLE, JACOB L., Private
Born in Blount County, Tennessee, where he resided as a farmer prior to enlisting at Maryville, Tennessee, at age 28, September 28, 1862, for the war. Reported present through October 31, 1862. Reported on detached service in January-February, 1863. Reported absent without leave from March 20 through June 30, 1863. No further records.

1st COMPANY D

This cavalry company was raised in Blount County, Tennessee. It was organized at Maryville, Tennessee, September 25-28, 1862. On November 14, 1862, it was transferred to the 1st Regiment Tennessee Cavalry (Carter's) and designated Company I of that regiment.

The following roster was compiled in large part from a company muster and descriptive roll dated September 28, 1862. It is abstracted in the microfilm edition of the Compiled Service Records of Confederate Soldiers Who Served in Organizations from the State of North Carolina (Record Group 109, M270), National Archives, Washington, D.C. Other valuable information in the Compiled Service Records includes enlistment papers, pay vouchers, requisitions, letters of resignation, discharge certificates, and abstracts of medical and prisoner of war records.

Also utilized in this roster were *The War of the Rebellion: A Compilation of the Official Records of the Union and Confederate Armies*, the North Carolina Adjutant General's papers, state militia records, newspaper casualty lists and obituaries, wartime claims for bounty pay and allowances, postwar registers of claims for artificial limbs, Confederate pension applications filed with the states of North Carolina, Tennessee, and Florida, and the 1860 and 1870 federal censuses of Tennessee. A search was made also for relevant letters, diaries, reminiscences, and other manuscripts in the Southern Historical Collection (University of North Carolina-Chapel Hill) and the Duke University Library Special Collections Department.

Among the secondary sources consulted were records of the North Carolina division of the United Daughters of the Confederacy, postwar rosters, regimental and county histories, marriage bond, will, and cemetery indexes, published and unpublished genealogies, biographical dictionaries, the North Carolina *County Heritage Book* series, the *Confederate Veteran*, Walter Clark's *Histories of the Several Regiments and Battalions from North Carolina in the Great War, 1861-'65*, and the North Carolina volume of the extended edition of *Confederate Military History*.

OFFICERS

CAPTAIN

WALLACE, WILLIAM C.
Born in Blount County, Tennessee, where he resided as a merchant prior to enlisting on September 1, 1862, at age 34. Appointed Captain on September 28, 1862. Transferred to Company I, 1st Regiment Tennessee Cavalry (Carter's), November 14, 1862.

LIEUTENANTS

CARNES, JAMES, 1st Lieutenant
Born in Knox County, Tennessee, and resided in Blount County, Tennessee, where he was by occupation a wagon maker prior to enlisting, probably in Blount County, at age 28. Appointed 1st Lieutenant on September 28, 1862. Transferred to Company I, 1st Regiment Tennessee Cavalry (Carter's), November 14, 1862.

HARDIN, JOSEPH, 3rd Lieutenant
Born in Blount County, Tennessee, and resided in Monroe County, Tennessee, where he was by occupation a farmer prior to enlisting, probably in Blount County, at age 24, September 25, 1862, for the war. Appointed 3rd Lieutenant on or about September 28, 1862. Transferred to Company I, 1st Regiment Tennessee Cavalry (Carter's), November 14, 1862. [His surname may have been Harden.]

LANTER, FRANCIS M., 2nd Lieutenant
Born in Wythe County, Virginia, and resided in Blount County, Tennessee, where he was by occupation a farmer. Previously served as 1st Lieutenant in Capt. S. J. McReynolds' Company, 1st East Tennessee Rifle Regiment; Company I, 7th Regiment Tennessee Infantry; and Company I, 37th Regiment Tennessee Infantry (all designations for the same company and regiment at different stages of organization). Dropped from the rolls at the regimental reorganization on May 10, 1862, presumably because he either did not stand for reelection, or was defeated. Enlisted in this company at age 36, probably in Blount County. Appointed 2nd Lieutenant on or about September 28, 1862. Transferred to Company I, 1st Regiment Tennessee Cavalry (Carter's), November 14, 1862. [His surname may have been Lauter.]

NONCOMMISSIONED OFFICERS AND PRIVATES

AMBURN, JOSEPH, Private
Previously served in Company F of this battalion. Transferred to this company on September 24-25, 1862. Transferred to Company I, 1st Regiment Tennessee Cavalry (Carter's), November 14, 1862.

ANDERSON, A. L., Private
Born in Blount County, Tennessee, where he resided as a farmer prior to enlisting, probably in Blount County, at age 19, September 25, 1862, for the war. Transferred to Company I, 1st Regiment Tennessee Cavalry (Carter's), November 14, 1862.

BADGETT, B. F., Private
Born in Knox County, Tennessee, where he resided as a farmer prior to enlisting, probably in Blount County, Tennessee, at age 33, on

September 28, 1862, for the war. Transferred to Company I, 1st Regiment Tennessee Cavalry (Carter's), November 14, 1862. [His surname may have been Bagett.]

BADGETT, JOSIAH R., Private
Born in Knox County, Tennessee, and resided in Blount County, Tennessee, where he was by occupation a farmer prior to enlisting in Blount County, at age 26, September 29, 1862, for the war. Transferred to Company C of this battalion prior to October 31, 1862.

BADGITT, RANSON, Private
Born in Blount County, Tennessee, where he resided as a farmer prior to enlisting, probably in Blount County, at age 37, on or about September 28, 1862, for the war. Transferred to Company I, 1st Regiment Tennessee Cavalry (Carter's), November 14, 1862.

BAKER, SAMUEL, Private
Born in Blount County, Tennessee, where he resided as a cooper prior to enlisting, probably in Blount County, at age 21, September 25, 1862, for the war. Transferred to Company I, 1st Regiment Tennessee Cavalry (Carter's), November 14, 1862.

BLOUNT, JAMES J., Private
Born in Blount County, Tennessee, where he resided as a wagoner prior to enlisting, probably in Blount County, at age 27, September 25, 1862, for the war. Transferred to Company I, 1st Regiment Tennessee Cavalry (Carter's), November 14, 1862.

BOWEN, ALEXANDER B., Private
Born in Blount County, Tennessee, where he resided as a farmer prior to enlisting, probably in Blount County, at age 18, September 29, 1862, for the war. Transferred to Company I, 1st Regiment Tennessee Cavalry (Carter's), November 14, 1862.

BRYANT, W. R., Private
Born in Blount County, Tennessee, where he resided as a farmer prior to enlisting, probably in Blount County, at age 34, on or about September 28, 1862, for the war. Transferred to Company I, 1st Regiment Tennessee Cavalry (Carter's), November 14, 1862.

CLEMONS, SAMUEL H., Private
Born in Blount County, Tennessee, where he resided as a farmer prior to enlisting, probably in Blount County, at age 30 on or about September 28, 1862, for the war. Transferred to Company I, 1st Regiment Tennessee Cavalry (Carter's), November 14, 1862.

COLLINS, R. A., Private
Born in South Carolina and resided in Blount County, Tennessee, where he was by occupation a farmer prior to enlisting, probably in Blount County, at age 23, September 27, 1862, for the war. Transferred to Company I, 1st Regiment Tennessee Cavalry (Carter's), November 14, 1862.

COSTON, WILLIAM T., Sergeant
Born in Blount County, Tennessee, where he resided as a farmer prior to enlisting, probably in Blount County, at age 26, September 25, 1862, for the war. Mustered in as Sergeant. Transferred to Company I, 1st Regiment Tennessee Cavalry (Carter's), November 14, 1862.

CRAIG, HUGH H., Private
Born in Blount County, Tennessee, where he resided as a farmer prior to enlisting, probably in Blount County, at age 27, September 28, 1862, for the war. Transferred to Company I, 1st Regiment Tennessee Cavalry (Carter's), November 14, 1862.

DAVIS, CALVIN B., Private
Born in Blount County, Tennessee, where he resided as a farmer prior to enlisting, probably in Blount County, at age 24, September 25, 1862, for the war. Transferred to Company I, 1st Regiment Tennessee Cavalry (Carter's), November 14, 1862.

DAVIS, H. J., Corporal
Born in Blount County, Tennessee, where he resided as a farmer prior to enlisting, probably in Blount County, at age 23, September 28, 1862, for the war. Mustered in as Corporal. Transferred to Company I, 1st Regiment Tennessee Cavalry (Carter's), November 14, 1862.

ESTERDAY, JACOB, Private
Born in Germany and resided in Blount County, Tennessee, where he was by occupation a wagoner prior to enlisting, probably in Blount County, at age 36, September 25, 1862, for the war. Transferred to Company I, 1st Regiment Tennessee Cavalry (Carter's), November 14, 1862. [His surname may have been Easterday.]

EVERETT, ISAAC C., Corporal
Born in Blount County, Tennessee, where he resided as a farmer prior to enlisting, probably in Blount County, at age 20, September 25, 1862, for the war. Mustered in as Corporal. Transferred to Company I, 1st Regiment Tennessee Cavalry (Carter's), November 14, 1862.

EVERETT, WILLIAM A., Private
Born in Blount County, Tennessee, where he resided as a farmer prior to enlisting, probably in Blount County, at age 25, September 26, 1862, for the war. Transferred to Company I, 1st Regiment Tennessee Cavalry (Carter's), November 14, 1862.

FRENCH, JAMES W., Private
Born in Blount County, Tennessee, where he resided as a farmer prior to enlisting, probably in Blount County, at age 32, September 29, 1862, for the war. Transferred to Company I, 1st Regiment Tennessee Cavalry (Carter's), November 14, 1862.

FURGESON, W. W., Private
Born in Blount County, Tennessee, where he resided as a farmer prior to enlisting, probably in Blount County, at age 28, September 26, 1862, for the war. Transferred to Company I, 1st Regiment Tennessee Cavalry (Carter's), November 14, 1862.

GENTRY, P. B., Private
Born in Monroe County, Tennessee, where he resided as a farmer prior to enlisting, probably in Blount County, Tennessee, at age 18, September 28, 1862, for the war. Transferred to Company I, 1st Regiment Tennessee Cavalry (Carter's), November 14, 1862.

GRAY, JOHN, Private
Born in Blount County, Tennessee, and resided in Monroe County, Tennessee, where he was by occupation a farmer prior to enlisting,

probably in Blount County, at age 23, September 28, 1862, for the war. Transferred to Company I, 1st Regiment Tennessee Cavalry (Carter's), November 14, 1862.

GRAY, RUFUS F., Private
Born in Monroe County, Tennessee, where he resided as a farmer prior to enlisting, probably in Blount County, Tennessee, at age 27, September 28, 1862, for the war. Transferred to Company I, 1st Regiment Tennessee Cavalry (Carter's), November 14, 1862.

GRAY, WILLIAM M., Private
Probably born in Sevier County, Tennessee. Resided in Monroe County, Tennessee, where he was by occupation a farmer prior to enlisting, probably in Blount County, Tennessee, at age 21, September 28, 1862, for the war. Transferred to Company I, 1st Regiment Tennessee Cavalry (Carter's), November 14, 1862.

HALL, THOMAS T., Private
Born in Blount County, Tennessee, where he resided as a farmer prior to enlisting at age 26, September 30, 1862, for the war. Transferred to Company I, 1st Regiment Tennessee Cavalry (Carter's), November 14, 1862.

HENRY, SAMUEL, Corporal
Born in Blount County, Tennessee, where he resided as a farmer. Previously served in Capt. W. T. Goss' Company, Brazelton's Battalion Tennessee Cavalry; Company C, 3rd Battalion Tennessee Cavalry (Brazelton's); and Company E, 3rd Battalion Tennessee Cavalry/14th Battalion Tennessee Cavalry (Carter's) (all designations for the same company and battalion at different stages of organization). Transferred to or enlisted in this company, probably in Blount County, at age 27, September 28, 1862, for the war. Mustered in as Corporal. Transferred to Company I, 1st Regiment Tennessee Cavalry (Carter's), November 14, 1862.

INGRAHAM, WILLIAM, Private
Born in what later became Yancey County. Resided in Blount County, Tennessee, where he was by occupation a wagoner prior to enlisting, probably in Blount County, at age 36, September 25, 1862, for the war. Transferred to Company I, 1st Regiment Tennessee Cavalry (Carter's), November 14, 1862.

JAMES, ELIJAH, Private
Born in Jefferson County, Tennessee, and resided in Blount County, Tennessee, where he was by occupation a farmer prior to enlisting, probably in Blount County, at age 23, September 26, 1862, for the war. Transferred to Company I, 1st Regiment Tennessee Cavalry (Carter's), November 14, 1862.

JAMES, WILLIAM, Private
Born in Greene County, Tennessee, and resided in Blount County, Tennessee, where he was by occupation a farmer prior to enlisting, probably in Blount County, at age 27, September 28, 1862, for the war. Transferred to Company I, 1st Regiment Tennessee Cavalry (Carter's), November 14, 1862.

KEITH, G. P., Private
Born in Buncombe County and resided in Blount County, Tennessee, where he was by occupation a farmer prior to enlisting, probably in Blount County, at age 23, September 28, 1862, for the war. Transferred to Company I, 1st Regiment Tennessee Cavalry (Carter's), November 14, 1862.

KENNEDY, ANDREW, Private
Born in Blount County, Tennessee, where he resided as a farmer prior to enlisting, probably in Blount County, at age 25 on or about September 28, 1862, for the war. Transferred to Company I, 1st Regiment Tennessee Cavalry (Carter's), November 14, 1862.

KERR, WILLIAM R., Private
Born in Blount County, Tennessee, where he resided as a farmer prior to enlisting, probably in Blount County, at age 25, September 30, 1862, for the war. Transferred to Company I, 1st Regiment Tennessee Cavalry (Carter's), November 14, 1862.

KITH, EDNON, Private
Born in Blount County, Tennessee, where he resided as a farmer prior to enlisting, probably in Blount County, at age 34, September 30, 1862, for the war. Transferred to Company I, 1st Regiment Tennessee Cavalry (Carter's), November 14, 1862.

McCLANE, GEORGE A., Private
Born in Blount County, Tennessee, where he resided as a "soldier." Previously served as Musician (Fifer) in Capt. John E. Toole's Company of Tennessee Volunteers; Company B, Bradford's Regiment of Tennessee Volunteers; and Company B, 31st Regiment Tennessee Infantry (W. M. Bradford's) (all designations for the same unit at different stages of organization). Enlisted illegally in this company at age 15, October 31, 1862, for the war, while absent without leave from the 31st Regiment Tennessee Infantry (W. M. Bradford's). Transferred to Company I, 1st Regiment Tennessee Cavalry (Carter's), November 14, 1862. [He may been the same man as G. A. McClain, who served later either in Company H of this battalion or Company H, Infantry Regiment of this legion.]

McCOLLUM, BURTON, Private
Born in Blount County, Tennessee, where he resided as a farmer prior to enlisting, probably in Blount County, at age 32, September 25, 1862, for the war. Transferred to Company I, 1st Regiment Tennessee Cavalry (Carter's), November 14, 1862. [His first name may have been Birton.]

McCOLLUM, HARVEY, Private
Born in Blount County, Tennessee, where he resided as a farmer prior to enlisting, probably in Blount County, at age 30, September 25, 1862, for the war. Transferred to Company I, 1st Regiment Tennessee Cavalry (Carter's), November 14, 1862.

McCOLLUM, JAMES, Private
Born in Blount County, Tennessee, where he resided as a farmer prior to enlisting, probably in Blount County, at age 24, September 25, 1862, for the war. Transferred to Company I, 1st Regiment Tennessee Cavalry (Carter's), November 14, 1862.

McGINLEY, JACOB, Private
Born in Blount County, Tennessee, where he resided as a farmer prior to enlisting, probably in Blount County, at age 32, September 20, 1862, for the war. Transferred to Company I, 1st Regiment Tennessee Cavalry (Carter's), November 14, 1862.

MALCOMB, SAMUEL N., Private
Born in Blount County, Tennessee, where he resided as a farmer prior to enlisting, probably in Blount County, at age 32, September 28, 1862, for the war. Transferred to Company I, 1st Regiment Tennessee Cavalry (Carter's), November 14, 1862.

MARTIN, JOSEPH L., Private
Born in Blount County, Tennessee, where he resided as a farmer prior to enlisting, probably in Blount County, at age 23, September 28, 1862, for the war. Transferred to Company I, 1st Regiment Tennessee Cavalry (Carter's), November 14, 1862.

MORROW, GEORGE H., Private
Born in Blount County, Tennessee, where he resided as a farmer prior to enlisting, probably in Blount County, at age 28, September 28, 1862, for the war. Transferred to Company I, 1st Regiment Tennessee Cavalry (Carter's), November 14, 1862.

MOXLEY, WILLIAM, Private
Born in Maryland and resided in Blount County, Tennessee, where he was by occupation a farmer prior to enlisting, probably in Blount County, at age 33, September 29, 1862, for the war. Transferred to Company I, 1st Regiment Tennessee Cavalry (Carter's), November 14, 1862.

MYERS,WAYNE W., Private
Born in Blount County, Tennessee, where he resided as a farmer prior to enlisting, probably in Blount County, at age 21, September 28, 1862, for the war. Transferred to Company I, 1st Regiment Tennessee Cavalry (Carter's), November 14, 1862.

PAGE, WILLIAM J., Private
Born in Blount County, Tennessee, where he resided as a farmer prior to enlisting, probably in Blount County, at age 26, September 25, 1862, for the war. Transferred to Company I, 1st Regiment Tennessee Cavalry (Carter's), November 14, 1862.

PARSONS, HOLDEN R., Sergeant
Born in Blount County, Tennessee, where he resided as a farmer prior to enlisting at age 36, probably in Blount County, September 25, 1862, for the war. Mustered in as Sergeant. Transferred to Company I, 1st Regiment Tennessee Cavalry (Carter's), November 14, 1862.

PLEMONS, JAMES H., Private
Born in Blount County, Tennessee, where he resided as a farmer prior to enlisting, probably in Blount County, at age 23, September 28, 1862, for the war. Transferred to Company I, 1st Regiment Tennessee Cavalry (Carter's), November 14, 1862.

RHEA, SAMUEL, Private
Born in Blount County, Tennessee, where he resided as a farmer prior to enlisting, probably in Blount County, at age 22, September 25, 1862, for the war. Transferred to Company I, 1st Regiment Tennessee Cavalry (Carter's), November 14, 1862.

RODDY, PRESTON, Private
Born in Blount County, Tennessee, where he resided as a farmer. Enlisted, probably in Blount County, at age 23, September 28, 1862, for the war. Transferred to Company I, 1st Regiment Tennessee Cavalry (Carter's), November 14, 1862.

SHERRILL, WILLIAM, Private
Born in Blount County, Tennessee, where he resided as a farmer prior to enlisting, probably in Blount County, at age 32, September 27, 1862, for the war. Transferred to Company I, 1st Regiment Tennessee Cavalry (Carter's), November 14, 1862.

SMITH, ANDREW J., Private
Born in Blount County, Tennessee, where he resided as a farmer prior to enlisting, probably in Blount County, at age 26, September 25, 1862, for the war. Transferred to Company I, 1st Regiment Tennessee Cavalry (Carter's), November 14, 1862.

SMITH, SAMUEL, Private
Born in Alabama and resided in Blount County, Tennessee, where he was by occupation a farmer prior to enlisting, probably in Blount County, at age 22, September 30, 1862, for the war. Transferred to Company I, 1st Regiment Tennessee Cavalry (Carter's), November 14, 1862.

SPRADLAN, THOMAS M., Private
Born in Blount County, Tennessee, where he resided as a farmer prior to enlisting, probably in Blount County, at age 32, September 30, 1862, for the war. Transferred to Company I, 1st Regiment Tennessee Cavalry (Carter's), November 14, 1862.

SPRADLING, DAVID, Private
Born in Blount County, Tennessee, where he resided as a farmer prior to enlisting, probably in Blount County, at age 28, September 25, 1862, for the war. Transferred to Company I, 1st Regiment Tennessee Cavalry (Carter's), November 14, 1862.

STEELE, B. F., Private
Born in Monroe County, Tennessee, where he resided as a farmer prior to enlisting, probably in Blount County, Tennessee, at age 20, September 27, 1862, for the war. Transferred to Company I, 1st Regiment Tennessee Cavalry (Carter's), November 14, 1862.

STEELE, JAMES, Private
Born in Buncombe County and resided in Blount County, Tennessee, where he was by occupation a farmer prior to enlisting, probably in Blount County, at age 31, September 27, 1862, for the war. Transferred to Company I, 1st Regiment Tennessee Cavalry (Carter's), November 14, 1862.

STEELE, JOSEPH, Corporal
Born in North Carolina and resided in Blount County, Tennessee, where he was by occupation a farmer prior to enlisting, probably in Blount County, at age 30, September 28, 1862, for the war. Mustered in as Corporal. Transferred to Company I, 1st Regiment Tennessee Cavalry (Carter's), November 14, 1862.

TEMPLE, J. DOBSON, Private
Born in Greene County, Tennessee, and resided in Blount County, Tennessee, where he was by occupation a farmer prior to enlisting, probably in Blount County, at age 22, September 25, 1862, for the war. Transferred to Company I, 1st Regiment Tennessee Cavalry

(Carter's), November 14, 1862. [His first name may have been James.]

TEMPLE, R. H., Private
Born in Greene County, Tennessee, and resided in Blount County, Tennessee, where he was by occupation a carpenter prior to enlisting, probably in Blount County, at age 26, September 25, 1862, for the war. Transferred to Company I, 1st Regiment Tennessee Cavalry (Carter's), November 14, 1862. [His first name may have been Robert]

TEMPLE, WILLIAM M., Private
Born in Greene County, Tennessee, and resided in Blount County, Tennessee, where he was by occupation a farmer prior to enlisting, probably in Blount County, at age 19, September 25, 1862, for the war. Transferred to Company I, 1st Regiment Tennessee Cavalry (Carter's), November 14, 1862.

THOMAS, DAVID, Private
Born in Blount County, Tennessee, where he resided as a farmer prior to enlisting, probably in Blount County, at age 26, September 28, 1862, for the war. Transferred to Company I, 1st Regiment Tennessee Cavalry (Carter's), November 14, 1862.

THOMPSON, ALEX N. B., Private
Born in Blount County, Tennessee, where he resided as a farmer prior to enlisting, probably in Blount County, at age 32, on or about September 28, 1862, for the war. Transferred to Company I, 1st Regiment Tennessee Cavalry (Carter's), November 14, 1862.

THOMPSON, DAVID, Sergeant
Born in Blount County, Tennessee, where he resided as a farmer prior to enlisting, probably in Blount County, at age 32, September 25, 1862, for the war. Mustered in as Sergeant. Transferred to Company I, 1st Regiment Tennessee Cavalry (Carter's), November 14, 1862.

THOMPSON, L. W., Private
Born in Blount County, Tennessee, where he resided as a farmer prior to enlisting, probably in Blount County, at age 25, September 28, 1862, for the war. Transferred to Company I, 1st Regiment Tennessee Cavalry (Carter's), November 14, 1862.

WALLACE, ABRAM, Private
Born in Blount County, Tennessee, where he resided as a farmer prior to enlisting, probably in Blount County, at age 28, September 28, 1862, for the war. Transferred to Company I, 1st Regiment Tennessee Cavalry (Carter's), November 14, 1862.

WALLACE, SAMUEL H., Private
Born in Blount County, Tennessee, where he resided as a "soldier" prior to enlisting, probably in Blount County, at age 26, September 28, 1862, for the war. Transferred to Company I, 1st Regiment Tennessee Cavalry (Carter's), November 14, 1862.

WATERS, WILLIAM P., Sergeant
Born in Blount County, Tennessee, where he resided as a farmer prior to enlisting, probably in Blount County, at age 25, September 25, 1862, for the war. Mustered in as Sergeant. Transferred to Company I, 1st Regiment Tennessee Cavalry (Carter's), November 14, 1862. [His middle initial may have been M.]

WILLBURN, JOHN, Private
Born in Monroe County, Tennessee, and resided in Blount County, Tennessee, where he was by occupation a blacksmith prior to enlisting, probably in Blount County, at age 24, September 25, 1862, for the war. Transferred to Company I, 1st Regiment Tennessee Cavalry (Carter's), November 14, 1862.

WILLBURN, WILLIAM, Private
Born in Monroe County, Tennessee, and resided in Blount County, Tennessee, where he was by occupation a blacksmith prior to enlisting, probably in Blount County, at age 26, September 25, 1862, for the war. Transferred to Company I, 1st Regiment Tennessee Cavalry (Carter's), November 14, 1862.

WRIGHT, WILLS E., Private
Born in Blount County, Tennessee, where he resided as a farmer prior to enlisting, probably in Blount County, at age 27, September 30, 1862, for the war. Transferred to Company I, 1st Regiment Tennessee Cavalry (Carter's), November 14, 1862.

2nd COMPANY D

This company was raised in Tennessee, in Jefferson, Knox, Grainger and Union Counties. It was organized at Strawberry Plains, Tennessee, September 30, 1862. It may have been known originally as Company E or Company H. It was known as Company D after 1st Company D transferred to the 1st Regiment Tennessee Cavalry (Carter's) on November 14, 1862. In late February, 1863, this company was transferred to the Infantry Regiment of this legion and was designated Company D of that regiment.

The following roster was compiled in large part from an undated company muster and descriptive roll, and company muster rolls dated September 30-December, 1862. These are abstracted in the microfilm edition of the Compiled Service Records of Confederate Soldiers Who Served in Organizations from the State of North Carolina (Record Group 109, M270), National Archives, Washington, D.C. Other valuable information in the Compiled Service Records includes enlistment papers, pay vouchers, requisitions, letters of resignation, discharge certificates, and abstracts of medical and prisoner of war records.

Also utilized in this roster were *The War of the Rebellion: A Compilation of the Official Records of the Union and Confederate Armies*, the North Carolina Adjutant General's papers, state militia records, newspaper casualty lists and obituaries, wartime claims for bounty pay and allowances, postwar registers of claims for artificial limbs, Confederate pension applications filed with the states of North Carolina, Tennessee, and Florida, and the 1860 and 1870 federal censuses of Tennessee. A search was made also for relevant letters, diaries, reminiscences, and other manuscripts in the Southern Historical Collection (University of North Carolina-Chapel Hill) and the Duke University Library Special Collections Department.

Among the secondary sources consulted were records of the North Carolina division of the United Daughters of the Confederacy, postwar rosters, regimental and county histories, marriage bond, will, and cemetery indexes, published and unpublished genealogies, biographical dictionaries, the North Carolina *County Heritage Book* series, the *Confederate Veteran*, Walter Clark's *Histories of the Several Regiments and Battalions from North Carolina in the Great War, 1861-'65*, and the North Carolina volume of the extended edition of *Confederate Military History*.

OFFICERS

CAPTAIN

LOVE, WILLIAM B.

Born in what later became Jackson County. Resided in Jefferson County, Tennessee, where he was by occupation a farmer prior to enlisting at Strawberry Plains, Tennessee, at age 32. Elected Captain on September 30, 1862. Reported present through December 31, 1862. Transferred to Company D, Infantry Regiment of this legion, in late February, 1863.

LIEUTENANTS

McBEE, GAINUM C., 1st Lieutenant

Born in Knox County, Tennessee, where he resided as a farmer prior to enlisting at Strawberry Plains, Tennessee, at age 22. Elected 1st Lieutenant on September 30, 1862. Reported present through December 31, 1862. Transferred to Company D, Infantry Regiment of this legion, in late February, 1863. [May have served previously as Private in Company D, 3rd Battalion Tennessee Cavalry (Brazelton's), and Company F, 14th Battalion Tennessee Cavalry (Carter's), (the same company and battalion at different stages of organization).]

NEEDHAM, HENRY, 3rd Lieutenant

Appointed 3rd Lieutenant of this company on September 30, 1862. Transferred to Company D, Infantry Regiment of this legion, in late February, 1863.

SMART, THOMAS R., 2nd Lieutenant

Born in Knox County, Tennessee, where he resided as a farmer prior to enlisting at age 26. Appointed 2nd Lieutenant on September 30, 1862. Reported present through October 31, 1862. Reported sick at home in November-December, 1862. Transferred to Company D, Infantry Regiment of this legion, in February, 1863.

NONCOMMISSIONED OFFICERS AND PRIVATES

ALEXANDER, THOMAS, Private

Previously served as Private in Company C of this battalion. Transferred to this company on December 15, 1862. Reported present through December 31, 1862. Reported on duty as a teamster in the quartermaster department, January-February 1863. Transferred to Company D, Infantry Regiment of this legion, in late February, 1863.

ALLEN, ANDERSON, Private

Previously served either in Company C of this battalion or in Company C, Infantry Regiment of this legion. Transferred to this company on January 10, 1863. Transferred to Company D, Infantry Regiment of this legion, in late February, 1863.

ARMS, EDWARD, Private

Born in Jefferson County, Tennessee, and resided in Knox County, Tennessee, where he was by occupation a farmer prior to enlisting at Strawberry Plains, Tennessee, at age 17, September 30, 1862, for the war. Reported on detached service repairing road through October 31, 1862. Reported present in November-December, 1862. Transferred to Company D, Infantry Regiment of this legion, in late February, 1863.

BAILEY, JAMES W., Private

Born in Carter County, Tennessee, and resided in Knox County, Tennessee, where he was by occupation a farmer prior to enlisting at Strawberry Plains, Tennessee, at age 18, September 30, 1862, for the war. Reported present through October 31, 1862. Reported absent sick in November-December, 1862. Transferred to Company D, Infantry Regiment of this legion, in late February, 1863.

BETTIS, JOSEPH E., Private

Born in Jefferson County, Tennessee, where he resided as a farmer prior to enlisting at Strawberry Plains, Tennessee, at age 23, September 30, 1862, for the war. Reported present through October 31, 1862. Reported absent due to illness of father on December 31, 1862. Transferred to Company D, Infantry Regiment of this legion, in late February, 1863.

BETTIS, P. E. Private

Born in Jefferson County, Tennessee, where he resided as a farmer prior to enlisting at Strawberry Plains, Tennessee, at age 29, September 30, 1862, for the war. Reported present through December 31, 1862. Transferred to Company D, Infantry Regiment of this legion, in late February, 1863.

BYERLY, MARTIN, Private

Born in Knox County, Tennessee, and resided in Grainger County, Tennessee, where he was by occupation a farmer prior to enlisting at Strawberry Plains, Tennessee, at age 30, September 30, 1862, for the war. Reported on detached service repairing a road through October 31, 1863. Reported absent sick in November-December, 1862. Deserted on January 10, 1863.

CARMACK, ALEXANDER R., Sergeant

Born in Tennessee or Pennsylvania and resided in Knox County, Tennessee, where he was by occupation a farmer prior to enlisting at Strawberry Plains, Tennessee, at age 31, September 30, 1862, for the war. Mustered in as Sergeant. Reported present through January, 1863. Transferred to Company D, Infantry Regiment of this legion, in late February, 1863.

CATES, JOHN H., Private

Born in Sevier County, Tennessee, where he resided as a farmer prior to enlisting at Strawberry Plains, Tennessee, at age 35, September 30, 1862, for the war. Reported present through October 31, 1862. Reported absent without leave in November-December, 1862. Transferred to Company D, Infantry Regiment of this legion, in February, 1863, while absent without leave.

CHILDERS, J. M., Private

Born in Williamson County, Illinois, where he resided as a farmer prior to enlisting at Strawberry Plains, Tennessee, at age 22, on

September 30, 1862, for the war. Reported present through December 30, 1862. Transferred to Company D, Infantry Regiment of this legion, in late February, 1863.

CLARK, JOB, Private
Born in Washington County, Virginia, and resided in Jefferson County, Tennessee, where he was by occupation a farmer prior to enlisting at Strawberry Plains, Tennessee, at age 37, February 19, 1863, for the war. Transferred to Company D, Infantry Regiment of this legion, in February 1863.

CLIFT, D. H., Private
Born in Knox County, Tennessee, where he resided as a farmer prior to enlisting at Strawberry Plains, Tennessee, at age 20, September 30, 1862, for the war. Sent on detached service repairing roads through October 31, 1862. Reported absent without leave in November, 1862-February, 1863. During this period he served with Company E, 12th Battalion Tennessee Cavalry (Day's and Phipps'), from September 30 until he was captured at Murfreesboro, Tennessee, December 31, 1862. Transferred to Company D, Infantry Regiment of this legion, in February, 1863, while a prisoner of war.

CLIFT, HENRY L., Private
Born in Knox County, Tennessee, where he resided as a farmer prior to enlisting at Strawberry Plains, Tennessee, at age 24, September 30, 1862, for the war. Reported present until Transferred to Company D, Infantry Regiment of this legion, in late February, 1863.

CLIFT, MARION, Private
Born in Knox County, Tennessee, where he resided as a farmer prior to enlisting at Strawberry Plains, Tennessee, at age 23, September 30, 1862, for the war. Reported present until Transferred to Company D, Infantry Regiment of this legion, in late February, 1863.

COATS, JOHN H., Private
Born in Grainger County, Tennessee, where he resided as a laborer prior to enlisting at Strawberry Plains, Tennessee, at age 35, September 30, 1862, for the war. Reported on detached service through October 31, 1862, repairing roads. Reported present, November, 1862-February, 1863. Transferred to Company D, Infantry Regiment of this legion, in late February, 1863.

COBB, WILLIAM P., Private
Born in Knox County, Tennessee, June 10, 1841. Resided in Knox County and was by occupation a farmer prior to enlisting at Strawberry Plains, Tennessee, at age 20, September 30, 1862, for the war. Mustered in as Private. Promoted to Sergeant prior to October 31, 1862. Reduced to ranks in November-December, 1862. Reported present until Transferred to Company D, Infantry Regiment of this legion, in late February, 1863.

COFFMAN, WILLIAM, Private
Born in Indiana and resided in Knox County, Tennessee, where he was by occupation a farmer prior to enlisting at Strawberry Plains, Tennessee, at age 27, September 30, 1862, for the war. Reported absent sick in November-December, 1862. Reported present in January-February, 1863. Transferred to Company D, Infantry Regiment of this legion, in late February, 1863.

COHEN, JAMES L., Private
Born in Grainger County, Tennessee, and resided in Knox County, Tennessee, where he was by occupation a farmer prior to enlisting at Strawberry Plains, Tennessee, at age 27, on or about November 15, 1862, for the war. Reported present until Transferred to Company D, Infantry Regiment of this legion, in late February, 1863. [His surname may have been Coin.]

COKER, JAMES H., Private
Born in Knox County, Tennessee, where he resided as a farmer prior to enlisting at Strawberry Plains, Tennessee, at age 32, September 30, 1862, for the war. Reported present through October 31, 1862. Reported on detail working on military road in November, 1862-February, 1863. Transferred to Company D, Infantry Regiment of this legion, in late February, 1863.

COZART, JAMES, Private
Previously served as Private in Company C of this battalion. Transferred to this company on December 15, 1862. Reported present until Transferred to Company D, Infantry Regiment of this legion, in late February, 1863.

DONEHEW, BENJAMIN, Private
Born in Knox County, Tennessee, and resided in Union County, Tennessee, where he was by occupation a farmer prior to enlisting at Strawberry Plains, Tennessee, at about age 31, September 30, 1862, for the war. Reported present until Transferred to Company D, Infantry Regiment of this legion, in late February, 1863. [His surname may have been Donahew.]

DOUGLASS, SAMUEL N., Private
Born in Sevier County, Tennessee, where he resided as a farmer prior to enlisting at Strawberry Plains, Tennessee, at age 24, September 30, 1862, for the war. Reported present through December 31, 1862. Transferred to Company D, Infantry Regiment of this legion, in late February, 1863.

DUNN, ANDREW J., Private
Previously served as a Private in Company C, Infantry Regiment of this legion. Transferred to this company on December 7, 1862. Reported present through December 31, 1862. Transferred to Company D, Infantry Regiment of this legion, in late February, 1863.

DYER, CASWELL, Private
Born in Grainger County, Tennessee, and resided in Union County, Tennessee, where he was by occupation a farmer prior to enlisting at Strawberry Plains, Tennessee, at age 17, September 30, 1862, for the war. Mustered in as Musician (Fifer). Reported present until Transferred to Company D, Infantry Regiment of this legion, in late February, 1863.

DYER, E. E., Private
Born in Grainger County, Tennessee, and resided in Union County, Tennessee, where he was by occupation a farmer prior to enlisting at Strawberry Plains, Tennessee, at age 19, September 30, 1862, for the war. Reported on detached service repairing roads through October 31, 1862. Reported absent without leave in November-December, 1862. While absent without leave he enlisted in Company B, 2nd Regiment Tennessee Cavalry (Ashby's) on November 4, 1862. Captured at Murfreesboro on December 31,

1862, during the battle of Stone's River, while serving with Ashby's Cavalry. Sent to Nashville, Tennessee. Sent to Camp Douglas, Illinois, where he arrived on January 7, 1863. Transferred to Company D, Infantry Regiment of this legion, in February, 1863, while a prisoner of war.

DYER, EPHRAIM, Private.
Born in Grainger County, Tennessee, July 15, 1833. Resided in Union County, Tennessee, and was by occupation a farmer prior to enlisting at Strawberry Plains, Tennessee, at age 29, September 30, 1862, for the war. Reported present until Transferred to Company D, Infantry Regiment of this legion, in late February, 1863.

DYER, HAMPTON, Private
Born in Grainger County, Tennessee, and resided in Union County, Tennessee, where he was by occupation a farmer prior to enlisting at Strawberry Plains, Tennessee, at age 25, September 30, 1862, for the war. Reported present through October 31, 1862. Reported "detached to take a deserter in Union County" on December 30, 1862. Rejoined the company prior to his transfer to Company D, Infantry Regiment of this legion, in late February, 1863.

DYER, J. M., Private
Born in Grainger County, Tennessee, and resided in Union County, Tennessee, where he was by occupation a farmer prior to enlisting at Strawberry Plains, Tennessee, at age 21, September 30, 1862, for the war. Reported present until Transferred to Company D, Infantry Regiment of this legion, in late February, 1863.

DYER, JOHN, Private
Born in Grainger County, Tennessee, where he resided as a farmer. Previously served in Company C, 5th Battalion Tennesee Cavalry (McClellan's), and Company B, 1st Regiment Tennessee Cavalry. He was reported absent without leave from the latter unit on July 27, 1862, and was probably still absent from that unit when he enlisted in this company at Strawberry Plains, Tennessee, at age 21, September 30, 1862, for the war. Reported present in November-December, 1862. Transferred to Company D, Infantry Regiment of this legion, in late February, 1863.

DYER, ROBERT, Private
Born in Grainger County, Tennessee, and resided in Union County, Tennessee, where he was by occupation a farmer prior to enlisting at Strawberry Plains, Tennessee, at age 21, September 30, 1862, for the war. Reported absent without leave through December 31, 1862. While absent without leave he enlisted in Company B, 2nd Regiment Tennessee Cavalry (Ashby's) on November 4, 1862. While reported at home sick from that unit, he was transferred from this company to Company D, Infantry Regiment of this legion, in late February, 1863.

DYER, WILLIAM, Private
Born in Grainger County, Tennessee, and resided in Union County, Tennessee, where he was by occupation a farmer prior to enlisting at Strawberry Plains, Tennessee, at age 25, September 30, 1862, for the war. Reported on detached service repairing roads on October 31, 1862. Reported absent without leave in November-December, 1862. While absent without leave he enlisted in Company B, 2nd Regiment Tennessee Cavalry (Ashby's) on November 4, 1862. While reported present with that unit, he was transferred from this company to Company D, Infantry Regiment of this legion, in late February, 1863.

ELLIS, JAMES, Private
Born in Sevier County, Tennessee, where he resided as a farmer prior to enlisting at Strawberry Plains, Tennessee, at age 27, September 30, 1862, for the war. Reported on detached service guarding a ferry on October 31, 1862. Reported present in November-December, 1862. Transferred to Company D, Infantry Regiment of this legion, in late February, 1863.

ESTEP, CALVIN, Private
Born in the part of Rowan County that later became Davie County. Resided in Jefferson County, Tennessee, where he was by occupation a farmer prior to enlisting at Strawberry Plains, Tennessee, at age 30, September 30, 1862, for the war. Reported present through December 31, 1862. Transferred to Company D, Infantry Regiment of this legion, in late February, 1863.

FRANKLIN, JOHN R., Corporal
Born in Jefferson County, Tennessee, where he resided as a farmer prior to enlisting at Strawberry Plains, Tennessee, at age 38, September 30, 1862, for the war. Mustered in as Corporal. Reported on detached service repairing roads through October 31, 1862. Reported on December 31, 1862, to have gone home to sick family. Transferred to Company D, Infantry Regiment of this legion, in late February, 1863.

GRIFFIN, JAMES P., Private
Born in Grainger County or Jefferson County, Tennessee. Resided as a farmer in Grainger County prior to enlisting at Strawberry Plains, Tennessee, at age 28, September 30, 1862, for the war. Reported present until Transferred to Company D, Infantry Regiment of this legion, in late February, 1863.

HAMMOCK, JOHN, Private
Born in Grainger County, Tennessee, where he resided as a wheelwright prior to enlisting at Strawberry Plains, Tennessee, at age 25, September 30, 1862, for the war. Reported present through October 31, 1862, and in January-February, 1863. Transferred to Company D, Infantry Regiment of this legion, in late February, 1863.

HAMMOCK, WILLIAM, Private
Born in Grainger County, Tennessee, where he resided as a farmer prior to enlisting at Strawberry Plains, Tennessee, at age 28, September 30, 1862, for the war. Reported present through October 31, 1862. Reported absent sick in November-December, 1862. Transferred while sick in camp to Company D, Infantry Regiment of this legion, in late February, 1863.

HATCHER, WILLIAM, Private
Born in Greenville District, South Carolina, and resided in Jefferson County, Tennessee, where he was by occupation a farmer prior to enlisting at Strawberry Plains, Tennessee, at age 22, October 18, 1862, for the war. Reported present in November-December, 1862. Transferred to Company D, Infantry Regiment of this legion, in late February, 1863.

HAYNES, ALFRED, Private
Born in Greene County, Tennessee, and resided in Sevier County, Tennessee, where he was by occupation a shoemaker prior to enlisting at Strawberry Plains, Tennessee, at age 27, September 30, 1862, for the war. Reported on detached service repairing road through

October 31, 1862. Reported absent sick in November-December, 1862. Transferred to Company D, Infantry Regiment of this legion, in late February, 1863.

HAYS, JOHN W., Private
Born in Jefferson County, Tennessee, and resided in Sevier County, Tennessee, where he was a farmer prior to enlisting at Strawberry Plains, Tennessee, at age 31, September 30, 1862, for the war. Reported present through December 31, 1862. Transferred to Company D, Infantry Regiment of this legion, in late February, 1863.

HAYS, WILLIAM C., Private
Born in Guilford County and resided in Jefferson County, Tennessee, where he was by occupation a farmer prior to enlisting at Strawberry Plains, Tennessee, at age 38, September 30, 1862, for the war. Reported present through December 31, 1862. Transferred to Company D, Infantry Regiment of this legion, in late February, 1863.

HODGES, C. B. C., Private
Born in Jefferson County, Tennessee, where he resided as a farmer prior to enlisting at Strawberry Plains, Tennessee, at age 19, September 30, 1862, for the war. Discharged on the same date after providing Pvt. Samuel Pate as a substitute.

HODGES, JOSEPH C. H., Sergeant
Born in Jefferson County, Tennessee, where he resided as a farmer prior to enlisting at Strawberry Plains, Tennessee, at age 17, September 30, 1862, for the war. Mustered in as Sergeant. Reported present through December 31, 1862. Discharged on January 3, 1863, after providing Pvt. Alfred B. Morgan as a substitute.

HOOKER, JOHN, Private
Born in Jefferson County, Tennessee, and resided in Union County, Tennessee, where he was by occupation a farmer prior to enlisting at Strawberry Plains, Tennessee, at age 21, February 14, 1863, for the war. Discharged on February 19, 1863, after providing Joseph Hooker as a substitute.

HOOKER, JOSEPH, Private
Born in Buncombe County and resided in Union County, Tennessee, where he was by occupation a farmer prior to enlisting at Strawberry Plains, Tennessee, at age 46, February 19, 1863, for the war as a substitute for Pvt. John Hooker. Transferred to Company D, Infantry Regiment of this legion, in late February, 1863.

HOUSEWRIGHT, WILLIAM, Private
Born in Virginia and resided in Grainger County, Tennessee, where he was by occupation a farmer prior to enlisting at age 25, September 30, 1862, for the war. Reported on detached service through October 31, 1862. Reported absent without leave in November-December, 1862. Enlisted illegally in Company E, 14th Battalion Tennessee Cavalry (Carter's) at Tazewell, Tennessee, October 30, 1862. He appears to have been with that company after it became Company E, 1st Regiment Tennessee Cavalry (Carter's) in November-December, 1862. Transferred to Company D, Infantry Regiment of this legion, in late February, 1863.

HOWELL, HOWARD, Private
Enlisted at Strawberry Plains, Tennessee, September 30, 1862, for the war. Reported on detached service as a ferry guard on October 31, 1862. No further records.

HUNTER, GEORGE, Private
Born in Claiborne County, Tennessee, where he resided as a farmer prior to enlisting at Strawberry Plains, Tennessee, at age 26, September 30, 1862, for the war. Reported present or accounted for through October 31, 1862. "Detailed to take a deserter in Union Co." on December 30, 1862. Transferred to Company D, Infantry Regiment of this legion, in late February, 1863.

HUSKY, ISAAC, Private
Born in Sevier County, Tennessee, where he resided as a farmer prior to enlisting at Strawberry Plains, Tennessee, at age 29, September 30, 1862, for the war. Reported on detail working on a military road through the Smoky Mountains until late February, 1863, when he was transferred to Company D, Infantry Regiment of this legion.

JONES, GEORGE, Private
Born in Pittsylvania County, Virginia, and resided in Grainger County, Tennessee, where he was by occupation a farmer prior to enlisting at Strawberry Plains, Tennessee, at age 28, September 30, 1862, for the war. Reported present through December 31, 1862. Transferred to Company D, Infantry Regiment of this legion, in late February, 1863.

JONES, WILLIAM W., Private
Born in Alleghany County, Virginia, and resided in Jefferson County, Tennessee, where he was by occupation a farmer prior to enlisting at Strawberry Plains, Tennessee, at age 36, September 30, 1862, for the war. Reported present through December 31, 1862. Transferred to Company D, Infantry Regiment of this legion, in late February, 1863.

KENDRICK, WILLIAM, Private
Born in Sevier County, Tennessee, and resided in Jefferson County, Tennessee, where he was by occupation a farmer prior to enlisting at Strawberry Plains, Tennessee, at age 26, September 30, 1862, for the war. Reported on detached service working on roads through December 31, 1862. Transferred to Company D, Infantry Regiment of this legion, in late February, 1863, while on detached service.

KILGORE, WILLIAM A., Sergeant
Born in Jefferson County, Tennessee, where he resided as a shoemaker prior to enlisting at Strawberry Plains, Tennessee, at age 33, September 30, 1862, for the war. Mustered in as Sergeant. Reported present through December 31, 1862. Transferred to Company D, Infantry Regiment of this legion, in late February, 1863.

LARGE, WILEY B., Private
Born in Jefferson County, Tennessee, where he resided as a farmer prior to enlisting at Strawberry Plains, Tennessee, at age 25, September 30, 1862, for the war. Reported present through December 31, 1862. Transferred to Company D, Infantry Regiment of this legion, in late February, 1863.

LAWRENCE, DAVID, Private
Born in Jefferson County, Tennessee, where he resided as a farmer prior to enlisting at age 29, September 30, 1862, for the war. Reported present through December 31, 1862. Transferred to Company D, Infantry Regiment of this legion, in late February, 1863.

LAWRENCE, J. CALVIN, Private

Previously served as Private in Company B, Infantry Regiment of this legion. Transferred to this company on November 1, 1862. Reported present until Transferred to Company D, Infantry Regiment of this legion, in late February, 1863.

LEE, JASPER C., Private

Born in Jefferson County, Tennessee, where he resided as a farmer prior to enlisting at Strawberry Plains, Tennessee, at age 26, September 30, 1862, for the war. Reported present through December 31, 1862. Transferred to Company D, Infantry Regiment of this legion, in late February, 1863. [His given name may have been C. Jasper.]

LEE, JOHN C., Privatee

Born in Jefferson County, Tennessee, where he resided as a farmer prior to enlisting at Strawberry Plains, Tennessee, at age 24, September 30, 1862, for the war. Reported present through December 31, 1862. Transferred to Company D, Infantry Regiment of this legion, in late February, 1863.

LEE, JOSEPH C., Private

Born in Knox County, Tennessee, where he resided as a farmer prior to enlisting at Strawberry Plains, Tennessee, at age 17, September 30, 1862, for the war. Mustered in as Private. Promoted to Corporal in September-October, 1862. Reduced to ranks in November-December, 1862. Reported present until Transferred to Company D, Infantry Regiment of this legion, in late February, 1863.

LEE, WILLIAM C., Private

Born in Jefferson County, Tennessee, where he resided as a farmer prior to enlisting at Strawberry Plains, Tennessee, at age 20, September 30, 1862, for the war. Reported present through December 31, 1862. Transferred to Company D, Infantry Regiment of this legion, in late February, 1863.

LYONS, JOHN H., Private

Born in DeKalb County, Alabama, and resided in Knox County, Tennessee, where he was by occupation a farmer prior to enlisting at Strawberry Plains, Tennessee, at age 26, September 30, 1862, for the war. Reported present through December 31, 1862. Transferred to Company D, Infantry Regiment of this legion, in late February, 1863.

McBEE, WILLIAM C., Private

Born in Knox County, Tennessee, where he resided as a farmer prior to enlisting at Strawberry Plains, Tennessee, at age 38, September 30, 1862, for the war. Reported present through December 31, 1862. Transferred to Company D, Infantry Regiment of this legion, in late February, 1863.

McDONALD, DANIEL, Private

Born in Knox County, Tennessee, where he resided as a farmer prior to enlisting at Strawberry Plains, Tennessee, at age 17, February 9, 1863, for the war. Transferred to Company D, Infantry Regiment of this legion, in late February, 1863.

McINTURFF, CHARLES D., Private

Born in Jefferson County, Tennessee, and resided in Knox County, Tennessee, where he was by occupation a farmer prior to enlisting at Strawberry Plains, Tennessee, at age 22, September 30, 1862, for the war. Reported present through October 31, 1862. Reported sick in November-December, 1862. Transferred to Company D, Infantry Regiment of this legion, in late February, 1863.

McMAHAN, ANDERSON, Private

Born in Tennessee and resided in Union County, Tennessee, where he was by occupation a farmer. Was absent without leave from Company I, 59th Regiment Tennessee Infantry, at the time that he illegally enlisted in this company at Strawberry Plains, Tennessee, at age 23, September 30, 1862, for the war. Reported present through October, 31, 1862. "Reclaimed" by Capt. W. H. Smith of Company I, 59th Regiment Tennessee Infantry, December 31, 1862.

McMAHAN, ANDREW, Private

Born in Grainger County, Tennessee, where he resided as a farmer prior to enlisting at Strawberry Plains, Tennessee, at age 38, September 30, 1862, for the war. Reported present through October 31, 1862. Reported absent without leave in November-December, 1862. Transferred to Company D, Infantry Regiment of this legion, in late February, 1863, while absent without leave.

MORGAN, ABRAM H., Private

Born in Union County, Illinois, where he resided as a farmer prior to enlisting at Strawberry Plains, Tennessee, at age 20, September 30, 1862, for the war. Reported present until Transferred to Company D, Infantry Regiment of this legion, in late February, 1863.

MORGAN, ALFRED B., Private

Enlisted at Strawberry Plains, Tennessee, at about age 46, January 3, 1863, for the war as a substitute for Sgt. Joseph C. H. Hodges. Transferred to Company D, Infantry Regiment of this legion, in late February, 1863.

MORGAN, JOHN W., Corporal

Born in Knox County, Tennessee, where he resided as a farmer prior to enlisting at age 18, September 30, 1862, for the war. Mustered in as Corporal. Reported present through December 31, 1862. Transferred to Company D, Infantry Regiment of this legion, in late February, 1863.

NELSON, ROBERT, Private

Born in Union District, South Carolina, and resided in Sevier County, Tennessee, where he was by occupation a farmer prior to enlisting at Strawberry Plains, Tennessee, at age 19, September 30, 1862, for the war. Deserted at Strawberry Plains on or about December 29, 1862.

PATE, SAMUEL, Private

Born in Sevier County, Tennessee, where he resided as a farmer prior to enlisting at Strawberry Plains, Tennessee, at age 46, September 30, 1862, for the war as a substitute for Pvt. C. B. C. Hodges. Reported present through October 31, 1862. Reported detailed as a courier to the Smoky Mountains in November-December, 1862. Rejoined the company in January-February, 1863. Transferred to Company D, Infantry Regiment of this legion, in late February, 1863.

PEARSON, JOHN T., Private

Born in Knox County, Tennessee, where he resided as a farmer prior to enlisting at Strawberry Plains, Tennessee, at age 24, November

15, 1862, for the war. Reported present through December 31, 1862. Deserted at Strawberry Plains, Tennessee on or about January 26, 1863.

PEARSON, WILLIAM H., Private
Born in Jefferson County, Tennessee, where he resided as a farmer prior to enlisting at Strawberry Plains, Tennessee, at age 22, September 30, 1862, for the war. Reported present through December 31, 1862. Transferred to Company D, Infantry Regiment of this legion, in late February, 1863.

PECK, ADAM C., 1st Sergeant
Born in Tennessee and resided in Jefferson County, Tennessee, where he was by occupation a farmer prior to enlisting at Strawberry Plains, Tennessee, at age 48, September 30, 1862, for the war. Mustered in as 1st Sergeant. Reported present through December 31, 1862. Transferred to Company D, Infantry Regiment of this legion, in late February, 1863.

PIGG, RADFORD G., Private
Born in Knox County, Tennessee, where he resided as a farmer prior to enlisting at Strawberry Plains, Tennessee, at age 19, September 30, 1862, for the war. Reported present through December 31, 1862. Transferred to Company D, Infantry Regiment of this legion, in late February, 1863.

REED, JAMES, Private
Born in Knox County, Tennessee, October 19, 1828. Resided in Knox County and was by occupation a farmer prior to enlisting at Strawberry Plains, Tennessee, at age 32, September 30, 1862, for the war. Reported present through December 31, 1862. Transferred to Company D, Infantry Regiment of this legion, in late February, 1863.

REED, LEANDER, Private
Born in Knox County, Tennessee, where he resided as a farmer prior to enlisting at Strawberry Plains, Tennessee, at age 21, September 30, 1862, for the war. Reported present through October 31, 1863. Reported at home sick in November-December, 1862. Returned to duty prior to being Transferred to Company D, Infantry Regiment of this legion, in late February, 1863.

REED, WILLIAM, Private
Born in Knox County, Tennessee, where he resided as a farmer prior to enlisting at Strawberry Plains, Tennessee, at age 26, September 30, 1862, for the war. Reported present through December 31, 1862. Transferred to Company D, Infantry Regiment of this legion, in late February, 1863.

SELLERS, ROBERT, Private
Born in Jefferson County, Tennessee, where he resided as a farmer prior to enlisting at Strawberry Plains, Tennessee, at age 39, February 19, 1863, for the war. Transferred to Company D, Infantry Regiment of this legion, in late February, 1863.

SIMMONS, THOMAS F., Private
Born in Jefferson County, Tennessee, where he resided as a farmer prior to enlisting at Strawberry Plains, Tennessee, at age 37, on September 30, 1862, for the war. Reported on detached service repairing roads on October 31, 1862. Rejoined the company in November-December, 1862. Transferred to Company D, Infantry Regiment of this legion, in late February, 1863.

SMITH, JABEY, Private
Born in Grainger County, Tennessee, where he resided as a farmer prior to enlisting in Grainger County at age 27, October 8, 1862, for the war. Transferred to this company from Camp of Instruction on December 13, 1862. Deserted at Strawberry Plains, Tennessee, December 15, 1862. [His first name may have been Jabez.]

STANSBERRY, CAMPBELL H., Musician
Born in Sevier County, Tennessee, and resided in Jefferson County, Tennessee, where he was by occupation a farmer prior to enlisting at Strawberry Plains, Tennessee, at age 22, September 30, 1862, for the war. Mustered in as Musician (Drummer). Reported present or accounted for through December 31, 1862. Transferred to Company D, Infantry Regiment of this legion, in late February, 1863.

STUBBLEFIELD, ROBERT L., Private
Previously served as Private in 2nd Company A, Infantry Regiment of this legion. Transferred to this company on December 15, 1862. Reported present on December 31, 1862. Transferred to Company D, Infantry Regiment of this legion, in late February, 1863.

SUTHERLAND, AMBROSE, Private
Born in Jefferson County, Tennessee, and resided in Union County, Tennessee, where he was by occupation a farmer prior to enlisting at Strawberry Plains, Tennessee, at age 36, February 14, 1863, for the war. Transferred to Company D, Infantry Regiment of this legion, in late February, 1863.

SUTHERLAND, WILLIAM, Private
Born in Jefferson County, Tennessee, and resided in Union County, Tennessee, where he was by occupation a farmer prior to enlisting at Strawberry Plains, Tennessee, at age 38, February 14, 1863, for the war. Transferred to Company D, Infantry Regiment of this legion, in late February, 1863.

TROTT, JAMES, Private
Born in Jefferson County, Tennessee, and resided in Knox County, Tennessee, where he was by occupation a farmer prior to enlisting at Strawberry Plains, Tennessee, at age 24, September 30, 1862, for the war. Reported on detached service repairing roads on October 31, 1862. Rejoined the company prior to December 31, 1862. Transferred to Company D, Infantry Regiment of this legion, in late February, 1863.

TROUTMAN, JONAS, Private
Born in Iredell County and resided in Jefferson County, Tennessee, where he was by occupation a farmer prior to enlisting at Strawberry Plains, Tennessee, at age 21, September 30, 1862, for the war. Reported present through December 31, 1862. Transferred to Company D, Infantry Regiment of this legion, in late February, 1863.

UNDERWOOD, JESSE, Private
Born in Knox County, Tennessee, where he resided as a farmer prior to enlisting at Strawberry Plains, Tennessee, at age 29, November 15, 1862, for the war. Reported present through December 31, 1862.

Reported absent without leave on February 1, 1863. Transferred to Company D, Infantry Regiment of this legion, in late February, 1863, while absent without leave.

UNDERWOOD, THOMAS, Private
Born in Knox County, Tennessee, where he resided as a farmer prior to enlisting at Strawberry Plains, Tennessee, at age 29, September 30, for the war. Reported on detached service repairing a road through October 31, 1862. Rejoined the company prior to December 31, 1862. Reported present until Transferred to Company D, Infantry Regiment of this legion, in late February, 1863.

WALKER, JAMES V., Sergeant
Born in Tennessee and resided in Knox County, Tennessee, where he was by occupation a farmer prior to enlisting at Strawberry Plains, Tennessee, at age 30, September 30, 1862, for the war. Mustered in as Sergeant. Reported present through December 31, 1862. Transferred to Company D, Infantry Regiment of this legion, in late February, 1863.

WALKER, JOHN D., Private
Born in Knox County, Tennessee, where he resided as a farmer prior to enlisting at Strawberry Plains, Tennessee, at age 28, September 30, 1862, for the war. Reported present through December 31, 1862. Transferred to Company D, Infantry Regiment of this legion, in late February, 1863.

WALKER, WILLIAM, JR., Corporal
Born in Knox County, Tennessee, where he resided as a farmer prior to enlisting at Strawberry Plains, Tennessee, at age 22, September 30, 1862, for the war. Mustered in as Corporal. Reduced to ranks prior to October 31, 1862. Promoted to Corporal prior to December 31, 1862. Reported present through December 31, 1862. Transferred to Company D, Infantry Regiment of this legion, in late February, 1863.

WALKER, WILLIAM, SR., Private
Born in Jefferson County, Tennessee, where he resided as a farmer prior to enlisting at Strawberry Plains, Tennessee, at age 26, September 30, 1862, for the war. Reported present through December 31, 1862. Transferred to Company D, Infantry Regiment of this legion, in late February, 1863.

WALTERS, WILLIAM M., Private
Born in Knox County, Tennessee, and resided in Jefferson County, Tennessee, where he was by occupation a farmer prior to enlisting at Strawberry Plains, Tennessee, at age 35, February 9, 1863, for the war. Transferred to Company D, Infantry Regiment of this legion, in late February, 1863.

WATKINS, WILLIAM W., Private
Previously enlisted as Private in 2nd Company A, Infantry Regiment. Transferred to this company on December 14, 1862. Transferred to Company D, Infantry Regiment of this legion, in late February, 1863.

WEBB, JOHN, Private
Previously served as Private either in Company C of this battalion or Company C, Infantry Regiment of this legion.Transferred to this company on January 10, 1863. Transferred to Company D, Infantry Regiment of this legion, in late February, 1863.

WEEDON, WILLIAM, Private
Born in Grainger County, Tennessee, and resided in Jefferson County, Tennessee, where he was by occupation a farmer prior to enlisting at Strawberry Plains, Tennessee, at age 17, February 16, 1863, for the war. Transferred to Company D, Infantry Regiment of this legion, in late February, 1863.

WILSON, JOHN, Private
Born in Jefferson County, Tennessee, where he resided as a farmer prior to enlisting at Strawberry Plains, Tennessee, at age 21, September 30, 1862, for the war. Reported on detached service working on a road on October 31, 1862. Reported absent, "absence explained," November-December, 1862. Transferred to Company D, Infantry Regiment of this legion, in late February, 1863.

WYRICK, VALENTINE, Corporal
Born in Knox County, Tennessee, and resided in Union County, Tennessee, where he was by occupation a farmer prior to enlisting at Strawberry Plains, Tennessee, at age 34, September 30, 1862, for the war. Mustered in as Corporal. Reported on detached service repairing roads through October 31, 1862. Rejoined the company prior to December 31, 1862. Transferred to Company D, Infantry Regiment of this legion, in late February, 1863.

COMPANY E

This company was raised in Cherokee and Clay Counties. "Organized with a captain and reported with forty men" on September 30, 1862. "Organized into a company with company officers" on November 29, 1862.

The following roster was compiled in large part from an undated company muster and descriptive roll, and company muster rolls dated January-April, 1863, and September, 1863-February, 1864. These are abstracted in the microfilm edition of the Compiled Service Records of Confederate Soldiers Who Served in Organizations from the State of North Carolina (Record Group 109, M270), National Archives, Washington, D.C. Other valuable information in the Compiled Service Records includes enlistment papers, pay vouchers, requisitions, letters of resignation, discharge certificates, and abstracts of medical and prisoner of war records. Another important source for this roster is a parole roll for this company dated May 12, 1865, in the Stephen Whitaker Papers, N.C. State Archives.

Also utilized in this roster were *The War of the Rebellion: A Compilation of the Official Records of the Union and Confederate Armies*, the North Carolina Adjutant General's papers, state militia records, newspaper casualty lists and obituaries, wartime claims for bounty pay and allowances, postwar registers of claims for artificial limbs, Confederate pension applications filed with the states of North Carolina, Tennessee, and Florida, records of the North Carolina Confederate Soldiers' Home, and the 1860 and 1870 federal censuses of North Carolina. A search was made also for relevant letters, diaries, reminiscences, and other manuscripts in the Southern Historical Collection (University of North Carolina-Chapel Hill) and the Duke University Library Special Collections Department.

Among the secondary sources consulted were records of the North Carolina division of the United Daughters of the Confederacy, postwar rosters, regimental and county histories, marriage bond, will, and cemetery indexes, published and unpublished genealogies, biographical dictionaries, the North Carolina *County Heritage Book* series, the *Confederate Veteran*, Walter Clark's *Histories of the Several Regiments and Battalions from North Carolina in the Great War, 1861-'65*, and the North Carolina volume of the extended edition of *Confederate Military History*.

OFFICERS

CAPTAIN

WHITAKER, STEPHEN

Born in Buncombe County on February 9, 1814. Resided in Cherokee County where he was by occupation a farmer prior to enlisting at age 48. Appointed Captain on November 29, 1862, to rank from September 8, 1862. Reported present in January-April, 1863. Signature appears on a pay voucher for service in May-June, 1863. Detached to Cherokee County, October 26, 1863, to gather up deserters and absentees and return within twenty-five days. Received new orders from Col. William H. Thomas assigning him to duty in Cherokee County. These orders were not regarded as valid by Brig. Gen. Alfred E. Jackson, commander of the brigade of which Thomas's Legion was a part. Whitaker was therefore reported absent without leave from November 21 through December 31, 1863. Returned to duty prior to February 25, 1864, when his name appears as signature on a petition to Gov. Zebulon B. Vance requesting his assistance in reuniting Thomas's Legion and removing it from the command of General Jackson. Dropped from the rolls by special order of the Confederate Adjutant & Inspector General's Office, February 25, 1864, for prolonged absence without leave, although reported present on a company muster roll dated February 29, 1864. Cleared of wrongdoing by a board of court martial and returned to command subsequent to June 18, 1864. Commanded this battalion at some point in June-July, 1864. Hospitalized at Mount Jackson, Virginia, and Staunton, Virginia, between July 30 and August 1, 1864. Hospitalized at Charlottesville, Virginia, August 1, 1864, with acute dysentery. Transferred to hospital in North Carolina on August 6, 1864. Paroled at Franklin, May 12, 1865. [Clark's *Regiments*: 4:118, and *Confederate Military History*, Extended Ed., 5:791, indicate that he was promoted to Major of this Battalion, but wartime records indicate that he was still a Captain at the time of his parole on May 12, 1865. See excerpt from Special Orders No. 5, District of South West Virginia and Eastern Tennessee, October 25, 1863; Office of Provost Marshal, Department of Eastern Tennessee, No. 460: Permission Issued to Captain Stephen Whitaker to visit Raleigh, October 26, 1863; Special Orders No. 46, Adjutant and Inspector General's Office February 25, 1864 (copy also in Confederate Adjutant and Inspector General's Office Records: Vol. 16, Ch. 1, RG 109, National Archives); Capts. Eli(sha C.) Johnson, John C. Summers, and L(uther). C. May to Capt. B. G. Manard, June 18, 1864; Stephen Whitaker to James Whitaker, [August, 1864]; Stephen Whitaker to James Whitaker, August 5, 1864; and parole roll for Company E, Walker's Battalion, Thomas's Legion, all in Stephen Whitaker Papers, N.C. State Archives; Capt. James W. Terrell to Col. William Holland Thomas, March 12, 1864, William Holland Thomas Papers, Special Collections, Perkins Library, Duke University; Lt. Col. James R. Love, et al., to Vance, February 25, 1864, Governors' Papers: Zebulon Baird Vance, 1862-1865.]

LIEUTENANTS

ROBINSON, JOHN A., 1st Lieutenant

Born in Burke County and resided in Clay County where he was by occupation a farmer prior to enlisting in Clay County at age 44, September 25, 1862, for the war. Mustered in as Private. Elected 1st Lieutenant on November 29, 1862. Name appears on an officer's pay account for service December 28-31, 1862. Reported present in January-April, 1863, and September, 1863-July, 1864. Name appears on special requisitions for clothing dated September 18, 1864. Paroled at Franklin on May 12, 1865. [His surname may have been Roberson. According to Clark's *Regiments* 4:118, he was promoted to Captain. However, parole records for this company confirm that he was still 1st Lieutenant at the war's end.]

TATHAM, WILLIAM CLINTON, 2nd Lieutenant

Born in Macon County on March 23, 1833. Resided in Cherokee County where he was by occupation a farmer prior to enlisting in Cherokee County at age 29, September 25, 1862, for the war. Mustered in as Private. Elected 2nd Lieutenant on November 29, 1862. Reported present in January-April, 1863. Captured at Strawberry Plains, Tennessee, June 20, 1863, and paroled there the next day. Reported present in September-December, 1863. Reported absent sick in January-February, 1864. Subsequently reported absent without leave from February 5 through April 20, 1864. Returned to duty on an unknown date. Furloughed for fifty days on August 20, 1864. Paroled at Franklin on May 12, 1865. [According to Clark's *Regiments* 4:118, he was promoted to 1st Lieutenant. However, parole records for this company confirm that Tatham was still 2nd Lieutenant at the war's end.]

WIGGINS, WILLIAM ALEXANDER, 3rd Lieutenant

Born in Burke County and resided in Clay County where he was by occupation a farmer prior to enlisting in Clay County at age 39, September 25, 1862, for the war. Mustered in as Private. Elected 3rd Lieutenant on November 29, 1862. Signature appears on a pay voucher for service from November 29 through December 31, 1862. Reported present in January-April, 1863. Signature appears on a pay voucher for service from June 1 through November 30, 1863. Reported present, September, 1863-February, 1864. Hospitalized at Gordonsville, Virginia, July 28, 1864, with rheumatism. Reported in hospital through September 29, 1864. Paroled at Franklin on May 12, 1865. [According to Clark's *Regiments* 4:118, he was promoted to 2nd Lieutenant. However, parole records for this company confirm that Wiggins was still 3rd Lieutenant at the war's end.]

NONCOMMISSIONED OFFICERS AND PRIVATES

ADAMS, NELSON, Private

Enlisted in Company H of this battalion. Served on detail with this company from March 5 through June 30, 1863, and in September, 1863, until his desertion on September 18, 1863.

AGNEW, _____, Private

Records of the United Daughters of the Confederacy indicate that he served in this company.

ALLMAN, NELSON, _____

North Carolina pension records indicate that he served in this company.

ANDERSON, ELISHA, Private
Born in Burke County. Resided in Cherokee County. Enlisted in Cherokee County at age 23, February 22, 1863, for the war. Reported present through April 30, 1863. Deserted on June 20, 1863, at Strawberry Plains, Tennessee, in the confusion surrounding the Federal capture of that place.

ANDERSON, THOMAS F., Private
Enlisted in Clay County on February 24, 1863, for the war. Reported absent sick on April 30, 1863. North Carolina pension records indicate that he died at Loudon, Tennessee, July 8, 1863. Cause of death not reported.

ARNOLD, WILLIAM, Private
Born in Johnson County, Tennessee, and resided in Cherokee County where he was by occupation a farmer prior to enlisting in Cherokee County at age 17, December 22, 1862, for the war. Reported absent without leave from enlistment through April 30, 1863. No further records.

AXLEY, JAMES CAMPBELL., Private
Born in Sevier County, Tennessee, in 1831. Resided in Cherokee County and was by occupation a farmer prior to enlisting in Cherokee County at about age 31, February 27, 1863, for the war. Reported on detached service on April 30, 1863. Reported present in September-October, 1863. Reported on furlough on December 31, 1863. Reported absent without leave from January 20 through February 29, 1864. Reported on duty as a teamster from September 3 through 30, 1864. Paroled at Franklin on May 12, 1865.

BAKER, JAMES M., Private
Born in Ashe County and resided in Cherokee County where he was by occupation a farmer prior to enlisting in Clay County at age 17, September 25, 1862, for the war. Reported present in January-April, 1863. Deserted at Carter's Depot, Tennessee, September 18, 1863. Captured by the enemy in Cherokee County on or about February 19, 1864. Sent to Nashville, Tennessee. Transferred to Louisville, Kentucky. Transferred to Fort Delaware, Delaware, February 29, 1864. Arrived at Fort Delaware on March 4 or March 7, 1864. Release at Fort Delaware on June 19, 1865, after taking the Oath of Allegiance. [His first name may have been Jeremiah.]

BAKER, RILEY, Private
Born in Ashe County and resided in Clay County where he was by occupation a farmer prior to enlisting in Clay County at age 29, December 18, 1862, for the war. Mustered in as Sergeant. Reported present in January-April, 1863. Deserted at Carter's Depot, Tennessee, September 18, 1863.

BATTLE, M. E., _____
North Carolina pension records indicate that he served in this company.

BEDFORD, B. R., Private
Enlisted in Cherokee County on an unspecified date. Reported absent without leave in March-April, 1863. No further records.

BELL, ROBERT, Private
Resided in Clay County where he enlisted on February 1, 1863, for the war. Reported present through April 30, 1863. Reported absent without leave from June 20, 1863, through February 29, 1864. Went over to the enemy on an unspecified date. Took the Oath of Allegiance at Chattanooga, Tennessee, February 14, 1864. [He probably deserted in the confusion surrounding the capture of Strawberry Plains on June 20, 1863.]

BIRD, ROBERT, Private
Born in Macon County and resided in Cherokee County where he was by occupation a farmer. Probably served previously as Sergeant in Company D, 25th Regiment N.C. Troops. Enlisted in Cherokee County at age 24, September 25, 1862, for the war. Mustered in as 1st Sergeant. Reported present in January-April, 1863. Reduced to ranks in September-October, 1863, and was reported on detached duty in North Carolina. Deserted at Cherokee on November 1, 1863.

BISHOP, JOHN CALVIN, _____
Born in Spartanburg District, South Carolina, and enlisted in Clay County on February 1, 1863, for the war. Reported present through April 30, 1863. Deserted from camp near Jonesborough, Tennessee, September 15, 1863. [In his Tennessee Civil War Veteran's Questionnaire (No. 420) he states that he was "sent home" from hospital at Strawberry Plains, Tennessee, in 1864 because his left hand was "badly mangled" with "three fingers gone at palm."]

BORING, NICHOLAS, Private
Enlisted at Monroe, Tennessee, March 25, 1863, for the war. Reported absent without leave on or about June 20, 1863. No further records.

BRADLEY, THORNTON M., Private
Enlisted in Fannin County, Georgia, March 2, 1863, for the war as a substitute for Pvt. Alen B. Dickey. Reported on detached duty on April 30, 1863. Rejoined the company on an unspecified date. Captured at Strawberry Plains on June 20, 1863. Paroled at Strawberry Plains, June 21, 1863. Deserted on or about the same date.

BRIDGES, MARTIN C., Private
Born in Rutherford County and was by occupation a farmer prior to enlisting in Cherokee County on February 24, 1863, for the war. Reported present in March-April, 1863. Transferred to Company H of this battalion prior to June 30, 1863. [He had probably enlisted in Company H on February 23, 1863, one day before he enlisted in this company. His enlistment in this company therefore would have been illegal, requiring the transfer to Company H.]

BRITTAIN, PHILIP VANCE, Private
Born in Haywood County on May 16, 1823. Resided in Cherokee County and was by occupation a farmer prior to enlisting in Cherokee County at age 39, February 24, 1863, for the war. Mustered in as Private. Reported sick at home on February 28, 1863. Reported present in March-April, 1863. Promoted to Corporal prior to October 31, 1863. Reported present in September, 1863-February, 1864. Reduced to ranks in January-February, 1864. Paroled at Franklin on May 12, 1865.

BROWN, HENRY T., Private
Enlisted in Clay County on February 1, 1863, for the war. Reported present through April 30, 1863. Died in hospital at Strawberry Plains, Tennessee, June 17, 1863, of "rubeola."

BROWN, JAMES, Private
Previously served as Private in Company B of this battalion. Transferred to this company on December 1, 1862. No further records.

BROWN, LEONARD C., Private
Previously served as Private in Company B of this battalion. Transferred to this company on December 1, 1862. Reported on detached service in March-April, 1863. No further records.

BRYSON, JOSEPH H., Private
Born in Haywood County and resided in Cherokee County where he was by occupation a farmer prior to enlisting in Cherokee County at age 22, September 25, 1862, for the war. Mustered in as Sergeant. Reported present in January-February, 1863. Reported absent without leave in March-April, 1863. Reduced to ranks on an unspecified date. Captured at Strawberry Plains, Tennessee on June 20, 1863. Paroled at Strawberry Plains on June 21, 1863. Deserted on or about the same date.

CARROLL, CHARLES H., Private
Enlisted in Clay County on February 20, 1863, for the war. Reported present through April 30, 1863. Transferred to Company I, Infantry Regiment of this legion, in May-June, 1863.

CARROLL, JAMES, Private
Previously served as Private in Company B of this battalion. Transferred to this company on December 1, 1862. Reported present in January-April, 1863. Captured at Mossy Creek, Tennessee, June 21, 1863, and paroled the same day. Failed to return to duty and was listed as a deserter on December 31, 1863.

CHAMBERS, LEVI D., Private
Born in Greene County, Tennessee, and resided in Cherokee County where he was by occupation a farmer prior to enlisting in Cherokee County at age 35, September 25, 1862, for the war. Mustered in as Corporal. Reduced to ranks prior to March 1, 1863. Reported on detached duty in January-February, 1863. Rejoined the company, probably on March 1, 1863. Reported present through April 30, 1863. No further records.

COLLETT, HUGH MACK, Sergeant
Born in Burke County on July 13, 1826, and resided in Cherokee County. Was by occupation a farmer prior to enlisting in Cherokee County at age 36, September 25, 1862, for the war. Mustered in as Corporal. Reported present in January-April, 1863. Promoted to Sergeant in May-October, 1863. Reported absent sick in September, 1863-February, 1864. Paroled at Franklin on May 12, 1865.

COTHRIEN, WILLIAM L., Private
Born in Georgia and resided in Clay County, North Carolina, where he was by occupation a farmer prior to enlisting at age 19, September 25, 1862, for the war. No further records.

CRAIN, JOHN L., Private
Previously served as Private in Company A of this battalion. Enlisted in this company in Cherokee County on December 1, 1862, while still a member of Company A. Transferred to this company in January-February, 1863. Reported absent with leave in January-April, 1863. No further records. Survived the war. [His surname may have been Crane.]

CRAIN, SAMUEL, Private
Previously served as Private in Company A of this battalion. Enlisted in this company in Cherokee County on December 1, 1862, while still a member of Company A. Transferred to this company in January-February, 1863. Reported present through April 30, 1863. Deserted at Strawberry Plains, Tennessee, June 20, 1863, in the confusion surrounding the Federal capture of that place. [His surname may have been Crane.]

CRAWFORD, CALVIN W., Private
Previously served as Private in Company G, 39th Regiment N.C. Troops. Enlisted in this company in Cherokee County on February 23, 1863, while absent without leave from the 39th Regiment. Rejoined Company G, 39th Regiment, in March-April, 1863.

CRAWFORD, JAMES H., Private
Previously served as Private in Company G, 39th Regiment N.C. Troops. Enlisted in this company in Cherokee County on February 23, 1863, while absent without leave from the 39th Regiment. Rejoined Company G, 39th Regiment, prior to May 14, 1863.

CROMWELL, WILLIAM O., Private
Previously served as Private in Company A, 29th Regiment N.C. Troops. Enlisted in this company in Cherokee County on September 25, 1862, for the war. Reported present in January-April, 1863. Deserted on July 6, 1863. [Contrary to 8:240 of this series, his occupation may have been shoemaker rather than farmer.]

CROSS, MARTIN, Private
Previously served as Private in Company B of this battalion. Transferred to this company on December 1, 1862. Reported present or accounted for in January-April, 1863. No further records.

CRUSE, CALEB W., Private
Born in Cherokee County where he resided as a farmer prior to enlisting in Cherokee County at age 17, September 25, 1862, for the war. Mustered in as Corporal. Reported present in January-April, 1863. Reduced to ranks in May-October, 1863. Captured at Strawberry Plains, Tennessee, June 20, 1863, and paroled there the next day. Failed to return to duty and was listed as a deserter in January-February, 1864.

CRUSE, WILLIAM, Sergeant
Born in Hawkins County, Tennessee, and resided in Cherokee County where he was by occupation a farmer prior to enlisting in Cherokee County at age 47, September 25, 1862, for the war. Mustered in as Sergeant. Reported present in January-April, 1863. Captured at Strawberry Plains, Tennessee, June 20, 1863, and paroled there the next day. North Carolina pension records indicate that he died in hospital at Strawberry Plains in June, 1863, of measles.

CURTIS, AMOS W., Private
Enlisted in Clay County on February 24, 1863, for the war. Reported present through April 30, 1863, and in September, 1863-February, 1864. Name appears on a receipt roll for clothing dated June 4, 1864. Reported sick on September 1, 1864. Deserted to the enemy on an unspecified date. Confined at Knoxville, Tennessee, on or about September 28, 1864. Took the Oath of Allegiance at Knoxville, September 29, 1864. Sent to Chattanooga, Tennessee, September 30, 1864. Name appears on a list of men paroled at Franklin on May 12, 1865.

DAILEY, BRYANT D., Private

Born in Georgia and resided in Clay County, North Carolina, where he was by occupation a farmer prior to enlisting in Clay County at age 35, September 25, 1862, for the war. Reported present or accounted for through April 30, 1863. Deserted at Strawberry Plains, Tennessee, on or about June 21, 1863.

DAVENPORT, MARTIN, _____

Name appears on an undated muster and descriptive Roll indicating that he served in this company.

DAVIS, JOHN, Private

Previously served as Private in Company B of this battalion. Transferred to this company on December 16, 1862. Reported on leave "with sick family" in January-February, 1864. Reported absent without leave in March-April, 1864. No further records.

DEAVER, THOMAS S., Private

Previously served as Private in Company B of this battalion. Transferred to this company on December 1, 1862. Reported sick at home on February 28, 1863. Reported absent without leave in March-April, 1863. No further records.

DEAVER, WILLIAM H., Private

Previously served as Private in Company B of this battalion. Transferred to this company on December 1, 1862. Reported absent sick through December 31, 1863. Failed to return to duty and subsequently reported as having deserted in Cherokee County on June 20, 1863.

DICKEY, ALEN B., Private

Enlisted in Cherokee County on February 15, 1863, for the war. Reported present on February 28, 1863. Discharged on or about March 2, 1863, after providing Pvt. Thornton M. Bradley as a substitute. [His first name may have been Allen.]

DICKEY, JOSHUA B., Private

Enlisted in Cherokee County on February 15, 1863, for the war. Reported present on February 28, 1863. Discharged on or about March 2, 1863, after providing Pvt. Thomas J. Ellis as a substitute.

ELLIS, THOMAS J., Private

Born in North Carolina. Resided in Fannin County, Georgia, and was by occupation a farm hand prior to enlisting in Fannin County at age 32, on or about March 2, 1863, for the war as a substitute for Pvt. Joshua B. Dickey. Deserted on September 28, 1863.

FARMER, BAAL, _____

According to a letter to Gov. Zebulon Baird Vance dated March 28, 1863, he served in this company. [Governors' Papers, N.C. State Archives.]

FERGUSON, GEORGE W., Private

Previously served as Sergeant in Company A, 39th Regiment N.C. Troops. Transferred to this company in August, 1862, with the rank of Private. Reported present in January-April, 1863. Deserted at Strawberry Plains, Tennessee, on or about June 21, 1863.

FERGUSON, WILLIAM R., _____

Born in Haywood County and resided in Cherokee County where he was by occupation a farmer prior to enlisting in Cherokee County at age 24, December 18, 1862, for the war. No further records. [Probably served previously and subsequently as Private in Company A, 39th Regiment N.C. Troops.]

FLETCHER, WILLIAM J., Private

Enlisted in Cherokee County on February 14, 1863, for the war. Reported present through February 28, 1863. Reported absent without leave in March-April, 1863. No further records.

FLOWERS, ANDREW R., Private

Enlisted in Cherokee County on February 14, 1863, for the war. Reported present through April 30, 1863. Captured and paroled, probably at or near Strawberry Plains, Tennessee, on or about June 20, 1863. Failed to return to duty and was reported absent without leave in November, 1863-February, 1864. No further records.

FLOWERS, JAMES W., Private

Enlisted in Cherokee County on February 14, 1863, for the war. Reported present through February 28, 1863. Reported absent without leave in March-April, 1863. No further records.

FLOWERS, PETER C., Private

Enlisted in Cherokee County on February 14, 1863, for the war. Reported present through April 30, 1863. Captured at Strawberry Plains, Tennessee, June 20, 1863, and was paroled there the next day. Reported absent sick through October 31, 1863. Failed to return to duty and was reported absent without leave in November, 1863-February, 1864. No further records.

GADD, JOHN D., Private

Resided in Monroe County, Tennessee, and was by occupation a laborer prior to enlisting in Monroe County at about age 18, March 10, 1863, for the war. Reported absent without leave on March 31, 1863. No further records. [He probably served earlier in Capt. E. E. Hankins' Company, 1st East Tennessee Rifle Regiment; Company G, 7th Regiment Tennessee Infantry; and Company G, 37th Regiment Tennessee Infantry. These designations refer to the same company at different times. If he was the same man as J. D. Gadd of the 37th Regiment Tennessee Infantry, he subsequently deserted to the enemy, was confined at Knoxville, Tennessee on August 3, 1864, took the Oath of Allegiance on August 5, 1864, and was released.]

GARRISON, ELAM N., Private

Born in Burke County and resided in Clay County. Was by occupation a farmer prior to enlisting in Clay County at age 26, September 25, 1862, for the war. Reported present in January-April, 1863. Reported absent without leave on June 20, 1863. Failed to return to duty and was listed as a deserter in January-February, 1864. [He probably deserted in the confusion surrounding the Federal capture of Strawberry Plains on June 20, 1863.]

GARRISON, WILLIAM A., Private

Enlisted in Clay County on January 5, 1863, for the war. Deserted on February 8, 1863. Returned to duty in March-April, 1863. Reported present on April 30, 1863. No further records. [His middle initial may have been S. He may have served previously in Company E, 39th Regiment N.C. Troops, and Company A, 43rd Regiment Tennessee Infantry.]

GENTRY, JOHN N., Private

Born in 1845. Enlisted in Cherokee County on February 19, 1863, for the war. Reported present through February 28, 1863. Reported on detached service in March-April, 1863. Rejoined the company on or prior to April 30, 1863. Captured at Strawberry Plains, Tennessee, June 20, 1863, and paroled the next day. Failed to return to duty and was listed as a deserter on December 31, 1863. [According to *The Heritage of Cherokee County*, 1:198-199, he and his father and brother were captured and shot by Confederate soldiers on September 11, 1864, for bushwhacking and/or pro-Union activities.]

GIPSON, JOSEPH L., Private

Enlisted in Clay County on February 19, 1863, for the war. Reported present in January-April, 1863. Captured and paroled, probably at or near Strawberry Plains, Tennessee, on or about June 20, 1863. Failed to return to duty and reported absent without leave in November, 1863-February, 1864. [His surname may have been Gibson. According to two letters from Capt. George G. Bristol, Company E, 39th Regiment N.C. Troops, to Capt. Stephen Whitaker of this company, dated November 17 and 23, 1863, Gipson deserted from this company, burglarized the home of a Mrs. Baker, and was arrested and jailed in Dahlonega, Georgia. He was then sent under orders by Bristol to the Provost Marshal in Atlanta, for transfer back to Whitaker. The paperwork was lost, and as Gipson did not want to return to Whitaker's company, Bristol allowed him to serve with his company instead. In response to Whitaker's demand that Bristol return Gipson, Bristol in effect proposed a swap: in exchange for allowing Gipson to continue serving under Bristol, Whitaker could keep any of Bristol's men who were absent without leave in Whitaker's area of service and who did not wish to return to Georgia. Joseph L. Gipson would thus appear to be the same soldier recorded as Joseph L. Gibson in the rosters of Company E, 39th Regiment, whose record is in Volume 10:152 of this series. In the second of Bristol's letters, it is reported that the exchange would involve Joseph L. Perry of Company E, 39th Regiment, who had deserted in May, 1863. Perry's father approached Whitaker about the possibility of a swap. While Bristol cheerfully agreed, there is no evidence that Perry actually ever served in the Legion. (Stephen Whitaker Papers, N.C. State Archives.)]

GRAHAM, LEVI S., Private

Enlisted in Cherokee County on December 18, 1862, for the war. Reported present in January-April, 1863. Captured at Strawberry Plains, Tennessee, June 20, 1863, and paroled the next day. Deserted at Jonesborough, Tennessee, September 18, 1863. Name appears on a list of men paroled at Franklin on May 12, 1865.

GREEN, ANDREW J., Private

Enlisted in Clay County on February 24, 1863, for the war. Reported present in January-February, 1863. Reported absent sick in March-April and September-October, 1863. Failed to return to duty and was listed as absent without leave from June 20, 1863, through February 29, 1864. Federal provost marshal records indicate that he was captured in Clay County on December 10, 1863. Confined at Nashville, Tennessee. Transferred for exchange to Louisville, Kentucky, December 23, 1863, and arrived there on December 24. Transferred from Louisville to Rock Island, Illinois, December 24, 1863. Returned to Louisville on January 1, 1864, with unspecified charges. Hospitalized at Louisville on January 19, 1864, with smallpox. Reported in various hospitals at Lousiville from February 5 to April 26, 1864, with smallpox. Transferred to Camp Chase, Ohio, August 10, 1864. Paroled at Camp Chase and transferred on March 4, 1865, for exchange. Received at Boulware's and Cox's Wharves, James River, Virginia, March 10-12, 1865, for exchange. No further records. Survived the war.

GREEN, GEORGE W., Private

Served in Company H of this battalion. Reported on detail with this company from March 5-June 30, 1863. [He may have been the same man as Pvt. George W. Green of Company G of this battalion and Companies I and D, Infantry Regiment of this legion.]

GREEN, WILLIAM J., Private

Enlisted in Clay County on February 24, 1863, for the war. Reported present on February 28, 1863. Reported absent without leave in March-April, 1863. No further records.

GREENWOOD, WILLIAM H. A., Private

Enlisted in Cherokee County on July 9, 1863, for the war. Reported absent without leave through February 29, 1864. Hospitalized at Charlottesville, Virginia, August 17, 1864, with acute diarrhoea. Returned to duty on September 21, 1864. Paroled at Franklin on May 12, 1865.

HALL, ELISHA, Private

Previously served as Private in Company A of this battalion. Transferred to this company on or about December 19, 1862. Transferred back to Company A prior to December 31, 1862.

HAMON, JOHN, _____

Born in Buncombe County and resided in Cherokee County where he was by occupation a farmer prior to enlisting at age 38, September 25, 1862, for the war. No further records.

HANEY, SAMUEL T., Private

Born in Cherokee County and resided in Clay County where he was by occupation a farmer prior to enlisting in Clay County at age 16, January 5, 1863, for the war. Reported absent without leave on February 28, 1863. No further records. [May have served later as Private in Company F, 65th Regiment N.C. Troops (6th Regiment N.C. Cavalry).]

HARTNESS, CADAMUS, Private

Previously served as Private in Company B of this battalion. Transferred to this company on December 1, 1862. Reported present in January-February, 1863. Reported absent without leave in March-April, 1863. No further records. [His given name may have been Cadmus.]

HAWKINS, JACKSON, Private

Previously served as Private in Company K, 62nd Regiment Tennessee Infantry. Enlisted in this company in Monroe County, Tennessee, March 10, 1863, for the war, while absent without leave from the 62nd Tennessee. Reported present through April 30, 1863. Deserted at Strawberry Plains, Tennessee, June 20, 1863, in the confusion surrounding the Federal capture of that place.

HAWKINS, MARION, Private

Previosuly served as Private in Company K, 62nd Regiment Tennessee Infantry. Enlisted in this company in Monroe County, Tennessee, March 10, 1863, for the war, while absent without leave from the 62nd Tennessee. Reported present through April 30, 1863.

Deserted at Strawberry Plains, Tennessee, June 20, 1863, in the confusion surrounding the Federal capture of that place.

HENRY, WILLIAM L., Private

Enlisted in Cherokee County at age 17, May 19, 1863, for the war. Reported present in September, 1863-February, 1864. Name appears on receipt rolls for clothing dated June 22 and October 16, 1864. [According to a letter written by Capt. Stephen Whitaker, he fell out of the ranks and died from fatigue between Salem and Staunton, Virginia, during Lt. Gen. Jubal A. Early's march toward Washington, the dates of which were June 22 to 27, 1864. North Carolina pension records indicate that he died in Virginia on July 1, 1864, of disease.]

HOLLAND, W. L., _____

North Carolina pension records appear to indicate that he served in this company. [He was known also as Tom Holland. He may have served also in the 39th Regiment N.C. Troops.]

HUGHES, DILLON A., Private

Born in the part of Haywood County that later became Macon County. Resided in Cherokee County where he was by occupation a farmer prior to enlisting in Cherokee County at age 39, December 18, 1862, for the war. Reported present in January-April, 1863. Reported absent sick in September, 1863-February, 1864. Captured in Cherokee County on October 9, 1864. Sent to Knoxville, Tennessee. Transferred to Chattanooga, Tennessee, October 11, 1864. Transferred to Nashville, Tennessee, where he arrived on or about October 20, 1864. Transferred to Louisville, Kentucky, where he arrived on October 22, 1864. Confined at Camp Chase, Ohio, October 24, 1864. Died at Camp Chase on or about December 15, 1864, of "diarrhoea chr[onica]."

HUNT, WILLIAM, Private

Resided in Monroe County, Tennessee, where he enlisted on March 10, 1863, for the war. Reported present through April 30, 1863. Although he was reported as having deserted at Strawberry Plains, Tennessee, June 20, 1863, he was in fact captured at Flat Creek, Tennessee, June 17, 1863. Took the Oath of Allegiance at Knoxville, Tennessee, July 11, 1864. "Allowed to go to his home on recommendation of Jos. Givins Asst. Pro[vost] Ma[rsha]l of Monroe Co. Tenn."

HUSKINS, JOHN, _____

Tennessee pension application No. 14058 indicates that he served in this company. Survived the war.

HUSKINS, WILLIAM, Private

Previously served as Private in Company I, Infantry Regiment of this legion. Transferred to, or enlisted illegally in, this company on April 30, 1863. Deserted near Jonesborough, Tennessee, September 16, 1863.

HYATT, EPHRAIM J., Private

Previously served as Private in Company G, 39th Regiment N.C. Troops. Enlisted in Cherokee County on February 24, 1863, while absent without leave from the 39th Regiment. Reported on leave through March 2, 1863. Joined the company on or prior to April 30, 1863. Captured at Strawberry Plains, Tennessee, June 20, 1863, and paroled there the next day. Failed to return to duty and was listed as a deserter in November-December, 1863.

HYATT, JASON S., Private

Enlisted in Cherokee County on February 24, 1863, for the war. Reported absent sick since enlistment in September-October, 1863. Listed as having deserted in Cherokee County in November-December, 1863.

INGRAM, ISAAC L., Private

Previously served as Private in Company H, Infantry Regiment of this legion. Transferred to this company subsequent to May 20, 1864. Paroled at Franklin on May 12, 1865.

JOHNSON, B. F., Private

Place and date of enlistment not reported; probably enlisted subsequent to February 28, 1864. Paroled at Franklin on May 12, 1865.

JOHNSON, JAMES B., Private

Born in Georgia and resided in Clay County, North Carolina, where he was by occupation a farmer prior to enlisting in Clay County at age 17, January 5, 1863, for the war. Reported present through April 30, 1863. Captured at Strawberry Plains, Tennessee, June 20, 1863, and paroled the next day. No further records.

JOHNSON, JASON L., Private

Previously served as Private in Company B of this battalion. Transferred to this company on December 1, 1862. Reported present in January-February, 1863. Reported on detached service in March-April, 1863. Rejoined the company on or prior to April 30, 1863. Deserted at Strawberry Plains, Tennessee, June 20, 1863, in the confusion surrounding the Federal of that place.

LEATHERWOOD, SAMUEL M., Private

Enlisted illegally in this company on September 25, 1862, while serving in Company E, 39th Regiment N.C. Troops. Reported absent sick in January-April, 1863, and September, 1863-February, 1864; he was probably in Clay County for most or all of that period. No further records. Survived the war.

LEATHERWOOD, THOMAS W., Private

Born in Cherokee County and resided in Clay County where he was by occupation a farmer prior to enlisting in Clay County at age 18, September 25, 1862, for the war. Reported present in January-April, 1863. No further records.

LEATHERWOOD, WILLIAM, Private

Born in the part of Cherokee County that later became Clay County. Resided in Clay County as a farmer prior to enlisting in Clay County at age 17, September 25, 1862, for the war. Reported present in January-February, 1863. Reported absent without leave in March-April, 1863. No further records.

LEDFORD, DAVID A., Private

Previously enlisted in Company E, 39th Regiment N.C. Troops, November 6, 1861. Illegally enlisted in Company B, 7th Battalion N.C. Cavalry, July 5, 1862, although there is no evidence that he actually served with that unit at that time. Illegally enlisted in this company in Clay County on September 25, 1862, for the war. Reported captured in Kentucky, October 15, 1862, as a member of Company E, 39th Regiment N.C. Troops; his record for that unit was amended in November to report him as absent without leave, and in January- February, 1863, as "deserted according to Gen. Bragg's order." Reported "absent without leave; conscript & carried to Ga" from this company in January-February, 1863. [He later enlisted in Company A, 16th Battalion Georgia Partisan Rangers (Cavalry), on February 23, 1863. He deserted from that unit on February 24, 1863. Records from Company E, 39th Regiment N.C. Troops, subsequently report his return to that unit on February 28, 1863. Simultanously, he reenlisted in Company B, 7th Battalion N.C. Cavalry, February 28, 1863. He was reported absent without leave from the 7th Battalion on July 13, 1863, and as a deserter from the 39th on August 1, 1863. He was reported as absent without leave when Company B, 7th Battalion N.C. Cavalry became Company F, 65th Regiment N.C. Troops (6th Regiment N.C. Cavalry), and was reported as a deserter in September-October, 1863. Subsequently, he returned to the 39th Regiment, where he was court-martialed in February, 1864. His entry at 2:527 of this series indicates that he served continuously in that unit from July 5, 1862, but the actual muster rolls are scanty and do not document most of the period involved; furthermore, the records seem to indicate that he enlisted on two different occasions in that unit. The information regarding his court martial was omitted from 10:154 of this series. It would appear that Pvt. Ledford was a bounty jumper. See also the records of Pvts. Eli Center Ledford and Elijah Ledford of this company.]

LEDFORD, ELI CENTER, Private
Resided in Clay County where he was by occupation a farmer. Previously enlisted in Company E, 39th Regiment N.C.Troops, and was reported as a deserter from that company from October 15, 1862. Illegally enlisted in Company B, 7th Battalion N.C. Cavalry, under the name Sentre Ledford, July 5, 1862, although there is no evidence that he actually served in that unit at that time. Illegally enlisted in this company as Center Ledford in Clay County at age 26, September 25, 1862, for the war. Reported captured in Kentucky, October 15, 1862, as a member of Company E, 39th Regiment N.C. Troops; his record for that unit was amended in November to report him as absent without leave, and in January-February, 1863, as "deserted according to Gen. Bragg's order." Reported "absent without leave; conscript & carried to Ga" from this unit in January-February, 1863. [His National Archives Compiled Service Records for Thomas's Legion records are filed under the name Center Ledford. According to other records, he illegally enlisted for the war as Center Ledford in Company A, 16th Battalion Georgia Partisan Rangers (Cavalry), at Dahlonega, Georgia, February 23, 1863. He deserted from that unit on February 24, 1863. Records of Company E, 39th Regiment N.C. Troops, report his subsequent return to that unit on February 28, 1863. Simultaneously, he reenlisted as Center Ledford in Company B, 7th Battalion N.C Cavalry on February 28, 1863. He was reported as having deserted from the 39th Regiment on May 13, 1863, and as absent without leave from the 7th Battalion on July 13. He was reported as absent without leave when Company B, 7th Battalion N.C. Cavalry became Company F, 65th Regiment N.C. Troops (6th Regiment N.C. Cavalry), where he was reported as a deserter in September-October, 1863. Subsequently, he returned to the 39th Regiment, where he was court martialed in February, 1864. His entry at 2:526 of this series indicates that he served continuously in that unit from July 5, 1862, but the actual muster rolls are scanty and do not document most of the period involved; furthermore, the records seem to indicate that he enlisted on two different occasions in that unit. The information regarding his court martial was omitted from his entry at 10:154 of this series. It would appear that Pvt. Ledford was a bounty jumper. See also the records for Pvts. David A. Ledford and Elijah Ledford of this company.]

LEDFORD, ELIJAH, _____
An undated company muster and descriptive roll indicates that he transferred from Company B of this battalion to this company on December 1, 1862. No further records. [He may have been the same man as E. Mc. Ledford or Elisha Mc. Leford who subsequently served with David A. Ledford and Eli C. Ledford in Company A, 16th Battalion Georgia Partisans (Cavalry), and in Company B, 7th Battalion N. C. Cavalry.]

LEDFORD, JOHN, _____
An undated company muster and descriptive roll indicates that he transferred from Company B of this battalion to this company on December 1, 1862. No further records.

LEFEVER, ALEXANDER, Private
Born in Burke County and resided in Cherokee County where he was by occupation a farmer prior to enlisting in Cherokee County at age 38, December 17, 1862, for the war. Mustered in as Corporal. Reduced to ranks on or prior to February 28, 1863. Reported present in January-April, 1863. Reported absent sick in September, 1863. Reported absent without leave from October 2, 1863, through February 29, 1864. No further records. Survived the war.

LEWIS, MATHEW M., Musician
Born in Burke County and resided in Cherokee County where he was by occupation a farmer prior to enlisting in Cherokee County at age 36, December 18, 1862, for the war. Mustered in as Private. Appointed Musician (Drummer) prior to February 28, 1863. Reported present in January-April, 1863. Reported sick in hospital in September-October, 1863. Subsequently reported absent without leave from October 2, 1863, through February 29, 1864. Deserted to the enemy on an unspecified date. Confined at Knoxville, Tennessee, May 22, 1864. Release at Knoxville on May 23, 1864, after taking the Oath of Allegiance.

LONG, THOMAS, Private
Enlisted in Clay County on February 24, 1863, for the war. Reported present through April 30, 1863. Transferred to Company H, Infantry Regiment of this legion, May 1, 1863.

LOYD, GEORGE W., Private
Resided in Clay County where he enlisted at age 23, April 30, 1863, for the war. Deserted at Strawberry Plains, Tennessee, June 20, 1863, in the confusion surrounding the Federal capture of that place. Went over to the enemy on an unspecified date. Took the Oath of Allegiance at Chattanooga, Tennessee, March 22, 1864.

LOYD, JAMES M., Private
Born in Macon County and resided in Clay County where he was by occupation a farmer prior to enlisting in Clay County at age 37, September 25, 1862, for the war. Mustered in as Corporal. Reported present in January-February, 1863. Reported on detached service in March-April, 1863. Rejoined the company on May 1, 1863. Deserted at Strawberry Plains, Tennessee, June 20, 1863, in the confusion surrounding the Federal capture of that place.. Reduced to ranks prior to October 31, 1863. Went over to the enemy on an unspecified date. Took the Oath of Allegiance at Chattanooga, Tennessee, March 22, 1864.

McCARSON, WILLIAM J., _____

Born in Buncombe County and resided in Cherokee County where he was by occupation a farmer prior to enlisting at age 40. Enlisted illegally in this company on September 29, 1862, while serving as a member of Company E, 39th Regiment N.C. Troops. It appears that he was never mustered into this company.

McCONKEY, JAMES, Private

Enlisted in Monroe County, Tennessee, March 25, 1863, for the war. Captured at Strawberry Plains, Tennessee, June 20, 1863, and paroled there the next day. Failed to return to duty and was listed as a deserter in January-February, 1864.

McGALLEARD, THOMAS, Private

Enlisted in Macon County on March 3, 1863, for the war. Reported absent without leave on April 30, 1863. Returned to duty on or prior to June 20, 1863, when he was captured at Strawberry Plains, Tennessee, and paroled the next day. Failed to return to duty and was listed as a deserter in November-December, 1863. Paroled at Franklin on May 12, 1865. [His surname may have been McGalliard.]

McGUIRE, WILLIAM, Private

Previously served as Private in Company A, 39th Regiment N.C. Troops. Transferred to this company in August, 1862. Reported present in January-April, 1863. Deserted at Strawberry Plains, Tennessee on or about June 20, 1863, probably in the confusion surrounding the Federal capture of that place.

McLELLAND, GEORGE L. D., Private

Born in Cherokee County, where he resided prior to enlisting in Cherokee County at age 18, February 23, 1863, for the war. Reported present through April 30, 1863. No further records.

McLELLAND, NEWTON R., 1st Sergeant

Resided in Cherokee County and was by occupation a farmer prior to enlisting in Cherokee County at age 17, January 12, 1863, for the war. Mustered in as Corporal. Reported present through April 30, 1863. Captured at Strawberry Plains, Tennessee, June 20, 1863, and paroled there the next day. Promoted to 1st Sergeant prior to October 31, 1863. Reported present in September, 1863-February, 1864. Captured at Winchester, Virginia, September 19, 1864. Sent to Harpers Ferry, West Virginia. Confined at Point Lookout, Maryland, September 26, 1864. Paroled at Point Lookout on February 13, 1865. Received at Cox's Wharf, James River, Virginia, February 14-15, 1865, for exchange. Reported present with other paroled and exchanged prisoners at Camp Lee near Richmond, Virginia, February 18, 1865. Paroled at Franklin on May 12, 1865.

MARRISON, JAVAN, Private

Enlisted in Cherokee County on February 20, 1863, for the war. Reported present through April 30, 1863. Deserted at Strawberry Plains, Tennessee, June 20, 1863, in the confusion surrounding the Federal capture of that place. [His surname may have been Morrison.]

MARSHALL, GEORGE W., Private

Born in Lincoln County and resided in Cherokee County where he was by occupation a farmer prior to enlisting in Cherokee County at age 38, September 25, 1862, for the war. Reported present in January-February, 1863. Reported absent sick in March-April, 1863. Died at or near Carter's Depot, Tennessee, probably in late August, 1863. Cause of death not reported.

MARTIN, ADEN C., Musician

Born in McDowell County and resided in Clay County where he was by occupation a farmer prior to enlisting in Clay County at age 18, September 25, 1862, for the war. Mustered in as Musician (Fifer). Reported present in January-April, 1863. Captured at Strawberry Plains, Tennessee, June 20, 1863, and paroled there the next day. Reported absent sick in Clay County in September-October, 1863. Failed to return to duty and reported as absent without leave in November, 1863-February, 1864. Paroled at Franklin on May 12, 1865.

MARTIN, CALVIN, Private

Born in North Carolina and resided in Clay County where he was by occupation a farmer prior to enlisting in Clay County at age 23, September 25, 1862, for the war. Reported absent without leave from December 29, 1862, through April 30, 1863. No further records.

MARTIN, HENRY K., Private

Enlisted illegally in this company in Clay County on February 18, 1863, for the war, while a deserter from Company E, 39th Regiment N.C. Troops. Reported present through April 30, 1863. Deserted at Strawberry Plains, Tennessee, June 20, 1863, in the confusion surrounding the Federal capture of that place.

MATHISON, JOHN L., Private

Enlisted in Clay County on February 19, 1863, for the war. Reported present through April 30, 1863. Captured at Strawberry Plains, Tennessee, June 20, 1863, and paroled there the next day. Returned to duty on an unspecified date. Reported present in September-December, 1863. Reported absent sick in January-February, 1864. A list of Confederate burials at Emory, Virginia, indicates that he died on February 23, 1864. Cause of death not reported.

MEADOWS, WILLIAM F., Private

Enlisted in Cherokee County on February 25, 1863, for the war. Reported present through April 30, 1863. Deserted at Carter's Depot, Tennessee, September 28, 1863. Returned to duty on November 20, 1863. Reported present in January-February, 1864. Captured at Piedmont, Virginia, June 5, 1864. Reported under guard at Staunton, Virginia, June 8, 1864. Confined at Camp Morton, Indianapolis, Indiana, June 21, 1864. Paroled at Camp Morton on or about March 4, 1865. Received at Boulware's and Cox's Wharves, James River, Virginia, March 10-12, 1865, for exchange. No further records.

MELTON, COLUMBUS B., Private

Enlisted in Clay County on February 24, 1863, for the war. Reported present on February 28, 1863. Reported absent without leave on April 30, 1863. No further records. Survived the war.

MINGUS, JOHN, Private

Born in Burke County and resided in Cherokee County where he was by occupation a carpenter prior to enlisting in Clay County at age 46, September 29, 1862, for the war. Reported absent without leave from December 29, 1862, through April 30, 1863. No further records. Survived the war. [May have served also as Private in

Company D, 25th Regiment N.C. Troops, and Company E, 64th Regiment N.C. Troops.]

MOORE, ALEXANDER CONSTINE, Private
Resided in Cherokee County. Enlisted in Cherokee County at about age 18, January 1, 1864, for the war. Reported present through February 29, 1864. Hospitalized at Winchester, Virginia, August 3, 1864, with diarrhoea. Returned to duty on August 4, 1864. Name appears on a receipt roll for clothing dated September 18, 1864. Paroled at Franklin on May 12, 1865. [His middle name may have been Constantine.]

MURPHY, JOHN N., Private
Enlisted in Monroe County, Tennessee, March 10, 1863, for the war. Reported present through April 30, 1863. Captured in hospital at Strawberry Plains, Tennessee, June 20, 1863, and paroled there the next day. Failed to return to duty and was listed as a deserter in January-February, 1864.

NELSON, BERRY, Private
Born in Haywood County and resided in Clay County where he was by occupation a farmer prior to enlisting in Clay County at age 35, September 25, 1862, for the war. Reported present in January-April, 1863. Deserted at Strawberry Plains, Tennessee, June 20, 1863, in the confusion surrounding the Federal capture of that place. Went over to the enemy on an unspecified date. Sent to Knoxville, Tennessee. Released at Knoxville on January 28, 1864, after taking the Oath of Allegiance.

NICHOLS, ENOCH, Private
Born in Surry County and resided in Cherokee County where he was by occupation a blacksmith prior to enlisting in Cherokee County at age 35, September 25, 1862, for the war. Reported present in January-April, 1863. Deserted near Jonesborough, Tennessee, September 16, 1863.

OWENBY, JOHN, Private
Born in Rutherford County and resided in Cherokee County where he was by occupation a farmer prior to enlisting in Cherokee County at age 39, September 29, 1862, for the war. Reported present in January-February, 1863. Reported absent sick in March-April, 1863. Deserted near Jonesborough, Tennessee, September 15, 1863.

PASSMORE, ELIJAH, Private
Born in Macon County. Resided in Clay County, where he enlisted at about age 18, February 24, 1863, for the war. Reported present through April 30, 1863. Captured in hospital at Strawberry Plains, Tennessee, June 20, 1863, and paroled there the next day. Reported absent sick in September, 1863-February, 1864. Paroled at Franklin on May 12, 1865.

PASSMORE, HARDIN, Private
Born in Wilkes County. Resided in Clay County and was by occupation a farmer prior to enlisting in Clay County at about age 32, February 24, 1863, for the war. Reported present through April 30, 1863. No further records.

PASSMORE, LEANDER H., Private
Born in Macon County. Resided in Clay County, where he enlisted at about age 20, February 26, 1863, for the war. Reported present through February 28, 1863. Reported absent without leave in March-April, 1863. No further records.

PASSMORE, WASHINGTON K., Private
Enlisted in Clay County on February 26, 1863, for the war. Reported present through April 30, 1863. Deserted on an unknown date. Apprehended on or about May 15, 1863. Reported on detached service in a hospital, September-October, 1863. Rejoined the company on or prior to December 31, 1863. Deserted in Greene County, Tennessee, January 15, 1864.

PATTERSON, EMERICK, Private
Previously served as Private in Company A of this battalion. Transferred to this company on December 1, 1862. Reported present through February 28, 1863. Reported on detached service in March-April, 1863. Rejoined the company on or prior to April 30, 1863. Deserted at Strawberry Plains, Tennessee, June 20, 1863, in the confusion surrounding the Federal capture of that place. [His given name may have been Amariah or Emeriah.]

PATTERSON, JOSIAH, Private
Previously served as Private in Company A of this battalion. Transferred to this company on December 1, 1862. Reported present in January-April, 1863. Deserted at Carter's Depot, Tennessee, September 18, 1863. [His first name may have been Joseph or Joberes.]

PAYNE, RUSSELL, Private
Previously served as Private in Company B of this battalion. Transferred to this company on December 1, 1862. Reported present in January-February, 1863. Reported absent without leave in March-April, 1863. No further records.

PRINCE, JOHN, Private
Enlisted in Company H of this battalion on February 19, 1863. Detailed to serve in this company on March 5, 1863, and was permitted to go home for clothing on the same date. Reported absent without leave on April 30, 1863. No further records. [He may have enlisted illegally in this company before he was detailed from Company H to serve in it, as he is reported present on the muster roll for this company on February 28, 1863.]

REED, BAXTER, Private
Resided in Clay County and was by occupation a farmer prior to enlisting in Clay County at age 37, September 25, 1862, for the war. Reported present in January-April, 1863. Captured at Strawberry Plains, Tennessee, June 20, 1863, and paroled there the next day. Failed to return to duty and was listed as a deserter in January-February, 1864.

RICE, HARVEY C., Private
Resided in Haywood County. Place and date of enlistment not reported; probably enlisted subsequent to February 29, 1864. According to Federal Provost Marshal records, he served in "Co. E, Thomas' Legion;" he served either in this company or in Company E, Infantry Regiment of this legion. Captured in Haywood County on February 4, 1865. Sent to Knoxville, Tennessee. Transferred to Chattanooga, Tennessee, February 16, 1865. Transferred to Nashville, Tennessee. Confined at Louisville, Kentucky, February 20, 1865. Confined at Camp Chase, Ohio, March 5, 1865. Released at Camp Chase on June 13, 1865, after taking the Oath of Allegiance.

RIDER, ALEXANDER, Private

Resided in Monroe County, Tennessee, and was by occupation a farmer prior to enlisting in Monroe County at age 24, March 9, 1863, for the war. Reported present through April 30, 1863. Captured at Strawberry Plains, Tennessee, June 20, 1863, and paroled there the next day. Failed to return to duty and was listed as a deserter in January-February, 1864.

RIDER, SAMUEL R., Private

Born in Monroe County, Tennessee, in 1828. Resided in Monroe County and was by occupation a farmer prior to enlisting in Monroe County on March 9, 1863, for the war. Reported present through April 30, 1863. Deserted at Carter's Depot, Tennessee, September 18, 1863. [See his Tennessee pension application No. 8994.]

ROBERDS, MARTIN, Private

Enlisted in Monroe County, Tennessee, March 10, 1863, for the war. Reported present through April 30, 1863. Captured at Strawberry Plains, Tennessee, June 20, 1863, and paroled there the next day. Failed to return to duty and was listed as a deserter in January-February, 1864. [His surname may have been Roberts.]

ROBERTS, WILLIAM, Private

Enlisted in Monroe County, Tennessee, March 10, 1863, for the war. Reported absent without leave on April 30, 1863. No further records.

ROBERTSON, JOHN L, Private

Place and date of enlistment unknown; probably enlisted subsequent to February 29, 1864. Reported on extra duty as a teamster in October-December, 1864. Paroled at Franklin on May 12, 1865. [His surname may have been Roberson.]

ROBINSON, JOSEPH LEANDER, Sergeant

Born in the part of Haywood County that later became Macon County. Resided in Clay County where he was by occupation a farmer prior to enlisting in Clay County at age 39, September 25, 1862, for the war. Mustered in as Sergeant. Reported present in January-April, 1863, and September, 1863-February, 1864. Captured at Piedmont, Virginia, June 5, 1864. Sent to Staunton, Virginia. Confined at Camp Morton, Indianapolis, Indiana, June 21, 1864. Paroled at Camp Morton on or about March 4, 1865. Received at Boulware's and Cox's Wharves, James River, Virginia, March 10-12, 1865, for exchange. No further records. [His surname may have been Roberson or Robeson.]

ROBINSON, LEE, ____

Tennessee pension application No. 10861 indicates that he served in this company. Survived the war.

ROGERS, BARNEY, Private

Born in the part of Haywood County that later became Macon County. Resided in Cherokee County where he was by occupation a farmer prior to enlisting in Cherokee County at age 35, September 25, 1862, for the war. Reported present in January-April, 1863. Deserted at Loudon, Tennessee, July 6, 1863. Paroled at Franklin on May 12, 1865.

SHEARER, HENRY C., Private

Enlisted illegally in this company in Cherokee County on February 24, 1863, for the war, while a member of Company H of this battalion. Reported in the records of Company H as on detail with this company from March 5 through June 30, 1863; however, he was reported as absent without leave from this company from April 24 to December 31, 1863. Subsequently reported as having deserted at Coco Creek, Tennessee, April 24, 1863. [His surname may have been Sherrer.]

SHEARER, JAMES W., Private

Born in Union County, Georgia. Resided in Clay County, North Carolina, where he enlisted at about age 24, February 19, 1863, for the war. Reported present or accounted for through April 30, 1863. Captured at Strawberry Plains, Tennessee, June 20, 1863, and paroled there the next day. Failed to return to duty and was listed as a deserter in January-February, 1864. [May have served previously as 3rd Lieutenant of Company E, 39th Regiment N.C. Troops.]

SHEARER, JOHN H., Private

Previously served as Private in Company E, 39th Regiment N.C. Troops. Transferred to this company on or about March 1, 1863. Reported present through April 30, 1863. Captured at Strawberry Plains, Tennessee, June 20, 1863, and paroled there the next day. Failed to return to duty and was listed as a deserter in January-February, 1864. [Contrary to 10:156 of this series, he served in this company rather than Company H of this battalion.]

SIMONS, WILLIAM, Private

Resided in Clay County where he enlisted on February 19, 1863, for the war. Reported present through February 28, 1863. Reported absent without leave in March-April, 1863. Deserted to the enemy on an unknown date. Sent to Chattanooga, Tennessee, where he took the Oath of Allegiance on June 24, 1864. Confined at Louisville, Kentucky, June 26, 1864. Took the Oath of Allegiance at Louisville on or about June 30, 1864, and sent north of the Ohio River for the remainder of the war.

SLUDER, PRESTON V., Private

Previously served as Private in Company B of this battalion. Transferred to this company on December 1, 1862. Reported present in January-February, 1863. Reported absent sick in March-April, 1863. No further records.

SMITH, CATLETT, Private

Born in Cherokee County and resided in Clay County where he was by occupation a farmer prior to enlisting in Clay County at age 18, September 25, 1862, for the war. Reported present in January-April, 1863. Captured in hospital at Strawberry Plains, Tennessee, June 20, 1863, and paroled there the next day. Reported absent without leave in October-December, 1863. Reported absent sick in January-February, 1864. Paroled at Franklin on May 12, 1865.

SMITH, ELIJAH M., Private

Enlisted in Clay County on February 24, 1863, for the war. Reported present through April 30, 1863. Paroled at Franklin on May 12, 1865.

SNIDER, FRANCIS M., Private

Born in North Carolina and resided in Cherokee County where he enlisted on January 19, 1863, for the war. Reported present through April 30, 1863. Captured at Strawberry Plains, Tennessee, June 20, 1863, and paroled there the next day. Returned to duty prior to October 31, 1863. Reported present in November, 1863-February, 1864.

Name appears on receipt rolls for clothing dated June 4, September 1, and October 16, 1864. Paroled at Franklin on May 12, 1865. [Was 20 years old at time of parole. He may have been the man whose pension records indicate served in Company C, 25th Regiment N.C. Troops.]

SNIDER, JESSE E., Private

Born in Buncombe County and resided in Cherokee County where he was by occupation a farmer prior to enlisting in Cherokee County at age 36, January 1, 1863, for the war. Reported present through April 30, 1863. Captured at Strawberry Plains, Tennessee, June 20, 1863, and paroled there the next day. Returned to duty prior to October 31, 1863. Reported present in November, 1863-February, 1864. Captured at Winchester, Virginia, September 19, 1864. Sent to Harpers Ferry, West Virginia. Confined at Point Lookout, Maryland, September 26, 1864. Released at Point Lookout on June 3, 1865, after taking the Oath of Allegiance.

SPARKS, M. H., _____

North Carolina pension records appear to indicate that he served in this company. Survived the war.

SPRINKLE, GEORGE F., Private

Previously served as Corporal in Company B of this battalion. Transferred to this company on December 1, 1862. Reduced to ranks on or about the same date. Reported absent sick through February 29, 1864. Paroled at Franklin on May 12, 1865.

STANDRIDGE, JOHN W., Private

Previously served as Private in Company B of this battalion. Transferred to this company on December 1, 1862. Reported present in January-February, 1863. Reported absent without leave in March-April, 1863. No further records.

STARNES, WILLIAM B., Private

Resided in Cherokee County and was by occupation a farm hand prior to enlisting in Cherokee County at age 32, March 4, 1863, for the war. Reported present through April 30, 1863. Deserted at Carter's Depot, Tennessee, September 18, 1863.

STEWART, JOSEPH EDMOND, _____

North Carolina pension records indicate that he served in this company. Survived the war. [He may have been the same man as Joseph Stewart of Company A of this battalion.]

STILLWELL, PETER, Private

Enlisted in Clay County on February 26, 1863, for the war. Reported absent without leave "and since returned to duty" in March-April, 1863. No further records.

TATHAM, PINKNEY BENTON, Private

Born in Macon County on February 6, 1835. Resided in Cherokee County where he was by occupation a farmer prior to enlisting at Valleytown at age 27, September 25, 1862, for the war. Mustered in as Private. Promoted to Sergeant on November 29, 1862. Reported absent sick in January-February, 1863. Returned to duty prior to April 30, 1863. Captured at Strawberry Plains, Tennessee, June 20, 1863, and paroled there the next day. Deserted from camp near Jonesborough, Tennessee on September 16, 1863. Reduced to ranks prior to October 31, 1863.

TERRY, JOHN, Private

Enlisted in Monroe County, Tennessee, on February 24, 1863, for the war. Reported present on February 28, 1863. Reported absent sick from April 24, 1863, through February 29, 1864. No further records.

THOMAS, JOHN, Private

Enlisted in Monroe County, Tennessee, March 10, 1863, for the war. Deserted at Strawberry Plains, Tennessee on or about June 21, 1863.

THOMPSON, JAMES A., Private

Enlisted either in this company or in Company E, Infantry Regiment of this legion, at Carter's Depot, Tennessee, April 11, 1863, for the war. Transferred to Company C, Infantry Regiment of this legion, on the same date. [May have previously served as 1st Lieutenant in Company F, 29th Regiment N.C. Troops.]

TIPTON, WILLIAM, Private

Born in what later became Yancey County. Resided in Clay County where he was by occupation a farmer prior to enlisting in Clay County at age 35, September 25, 1862, for the war. Reported present in January-February, 1863. Reported absent without leave in March-April, 1863. Court-martialed on May 24, 1864, for desertion. Found guilty and sentenced to be transferred to regular service "shot to death with musketry." [Letters Sent, Orders and Circulars, Dept. of E. Tenn. and Dept. of W. Va. and E. Tenn., April 1863-October, 1864, Record Group 109, Chapter II, Vol. 234, National Archives.] The sentence was remitted and he returned to duty. Reported on September 1, 1864, as sick for several days. Deserted to the enemy at Harrisonburg, Virginia, October 7, 1864. Sent to Knoxville, Tennessee. Released at Knoxville on December 2, 1864, after taking the Oath of Allegiance.

TRUITT, JOHN R., Private

Born in Buncombe County and resided in Cherokee County where he was by occupation a farmer prior to enlisting in Cherokee County at age 36, December 18, 1862, for the war. Reported absent sick in January-April, 1863. Deserted at Montgomery White Sulphur Springs, Virginia, on or about October 2, 1863. Paroled at Franklin on May 12, 1865. [His surname may have been Truett. May have served also in Company C, 7th Battalion N.C. Cavalry, and Company A, Indian Battalion.]

TRULL, THOMAS G., Private

Enlisted either in this company or in Company E, Infantry Regiment of this legion, at Carter's Depot, Tennessee, April 11, 1863, for the war. Transferred to Company C, Infantry Regiment of this legion, on or about the same date.

TURNER, WILLIAM M., Private

Born in Burke County and resided in Clay County where he was by occupation a farmer prior to enlisting in Clay County at age 35, December 18, 1862, for the war. Reported present or accounted for in January-April, 1863, and September, 1863-February, 1864. No further records.

WAKEFIELD, SAMUEL, _____

North Carolina pension records indicate that he served in this company. Survived the war.

WALKER, CHARLES AGNEW, Private

Born in Cherokee County. Resided in Cherokee County prior to enlisting in Cherokee County at about age 18, January 1, 1864, for the war. Reported absent without leave from February 25 through 29, 1864. No further records. Survived the war. [He may have been the same man as Charles A. Walker of Company I, Infantry Regiment of this legion.]

WEATHERMAN, HENRY H., Private

Born in Surry County and resided in Cherokee County where he was by occupation a farmer prior to enlisting in Cherokee County at age 48, September 25, 1862, for the war. Reported present in January-April, 1863. Reported sick in hospital in Virginia in September-October, 1863. Reported absent sick, November-December, 1863. Subsequently reported absent without leave from October 2, 1863, through February 29, 1864. No further records. Survived the war.

WHITAKER, JAMES M., Private

Born in Macon County and resided in Cherokee County where he was by occupation a farmer prior to enlisting in Cherokee County at age 26, December 18, 1862, for the war. Reported present in January-April, 1863. Wounded in the breast at Henderson's Mill, Tennessee, October 11, 1863. Reported absent wounded through February 29, 1864. Paroled at Franklin on May 12, 1865.

WHITAKER, JAMES MAXADENT, Sergeant

Born in 1846. Resided in Cherokee County. Enlisted in Cherokee County at age 17, November 1, 1863, for the war. Mustered in as Private. Promoted to Sergeant on December 1, 1863. Reported present in January-February, 1864. Hospitalized at Mount Jackson, Staunton, and Charlottesville, Virginia, prior to August 1, 1864. Name appears on receipt roll for clothing issued in hospital at Harrisonburg, Virginia, September 20, 1864. Paroled at Franklin on May 12, 1865.

WINFREY, ISAAC B., Private

Previously served as Corporal in Company H, Infantry Regiment of this legion. Transferred to this company at Greeneville, Tennessee, May 1, 1863. Mustered in as Corporal. Captured at Strawberry Plains, Tennessee, June 20, 1863, and paroled there the next day. Failed to return to duty and was reduced to ranks prior to October 31, 1863. Listed as a deserter in January-February, 1864.

WORLEY, WILLIAM J., Private

Born in Georgia and resided in Clay County, North Carolina, where he was by occupation a farmer prior to enlisting in Clay County at age 38, September 25, 1862, for the war. Reported present in January-April, 1863. Deserted at Strawberry Plains, Tennessee, on or about June 20, 1863, probably in the confusion surrounding the Federal capture of that place.

YOUNG, JOSHUA A., Private

Born in the part of Surry County that later became Yadkin County. Resided in Cherokee County where he was by occupation a blacksmith prior to enlisting in Cherokee County at age 35, September 25, 1862, for the war. Reported sick at home in January-February, 1863. Returned to duty prior to April 30, 1863. Captured at Strawberry Plains, Tennessee, June 20, 1863, and paroled there the next day. Died at home on July 29, 1863, of "fever."

ZIMMERMAN, JOHN, _____

Previously enlisted in Company B of this battalion. Transferred to this company on December 1, 1862. No further records.

COMPANY F

The predecessor to this cavalry company was raised in Blount County, Tennessee. It was organized at Maryville, Tennessee, on June 15 or July 4, 1862, as Capt. D. C. Ghormley's Company of Marshal Guards for the counties of Monroe, Blount and Sevier. It was also known as Capt. Ghormley's Company, Provost Guard. It was reorganized as Company F of this battalion at Maryville on September 24, 1862. On December 16, 1862, it was transferred to the 5th Regiment Tennessee Cavalry (McKenzie's), where it became Company K. There is some evidence to indicate that all or part of this company returned to North Carolina under Captain Ghormley in late 1863 and served thereafter as part Col. William H. Thomas's new battalion, possibly unofficially, as there are no records to indicate that it formally transferred from the 5th Regiment Tennessee Cavalry. See the company history accompanying the roster for Company G, Indian Battalion, Thomas's Legion, in this volume.

The following roster was compiled in large part from a company muster and descriptive roll dated September 24, 1862, and a company muster roll dated July 4-September 24, 1862. These are abstracted in the microfilm edition of the Compiled Service Records of Confederate Soldiers Who Served in Organizations from the State of North Carolina (Record Group 109, M270), National Archives, Washington, D.C. Other valuable information in the Compiled Service Records includes enlistment papers, pay vouchers, requisitions, letters of resignation, discharge certificates, and abstracts of medical and prisoner of war records.

Also utilized in this roster were *The War of the Rebellion: A Compilation of the Official Records of the Union and Confederate Armies*, the North Carolina Adjutant General's papers, state militia records, newspaper casualty lists and obituaries, wartime claims for bounty pay and allowances, postwar registers of claims for artificial limbs, Confederate pension applications filed with the states of North Carolina, Tennessee, and Florida, and the 1860 and 1870 federal censuses of Tennessee. A search was made also for relevant letters, diaries, reminiscences, and other manuscripts in the Southern Historical Collection (University of North Carolina-Chapel Hill) and the Duke University Library Special Collections Department.

Among the secondary sources consulted were records of the North Carolina division of the United Daughters of the Confederacy, postwar rosters, regimental and county histories, marriage bond, will, and cemetery indexes, published and unpublished genealogies, biographical dictionaries, the North Carolina *County Heritage Book* series, the *Confederate Veteran*, Walter Clark's *Histories of the Several Regiments and Battalions from North Carolina in the Great War, 1861-'65*, and the North Carolina volume of the extended edition of *Confederate Military History*.

OFFICERS

CAPTAIN

GHORMLEY, DeWITT C.

Born in Blount County, Tennessee, where he resided as a farmer. He previously served as 2nd Lieutenant of Company E, 3rd Regiment Tennessee Volunteer Cavalry and Company E, 3rd Regiment

Tennessee Infantry (Vaughn's). Appointed Captain of this company on September 29, 1862, to rank from September 24, 1862. Transferred to Company K, 5th Regiment Tennessee Cavalry (McKenzie's), on December 16, 1862. [Both he and part of his company seem to have returned later to serve with this legion in some capacity. In November, 1863, Col. William Holland Thomas wrote that "[S]uch of Capt[.] G[h]ormley's men as are at home will report to him and hold themselves in readiness to serve when called on. I design getting his company permanently attached to the Legion, and fill up the company with such men as want to mount themselves." A letter to Colonel Thomas in April, 1864, reports that Ghormley had made arrangements to consolidate his company with that of a Captain Everett. Everett seems to be the man referred to as Captain E. P. Everett in the Civil War memoirs of Lieutenant Colonel William Williams Stringfield of the Legion, and as Captain E. Everett in *CMH* 5:479; he is also apparently the same man whose wartime records are under the name of 2nd Lt. Eppie Everett of Company E, 3rd Regiment Tennessee Infantry (Vaughn's), P.A.C.S., a company in which Ghormley had also served earlier in the war, and as Private Eppy Everett of Company A, Thomas's Legion (see Everett's record in the General Miscellaneous section of this roster, and accompanying notes). In Clark's *Regiments*, Stringfield refers to "Ghormley and Everett's Cavalry" and assigned their unit to Walker's Battalion in the Legion. A special requisition dated October 16, 1864, in Ghormley's filmjacket for the 5th Regiment Tennessee Cavalry (McKenzie's) is signed by Lieutenant Colonel B. G. McDowell of the 62nd North Carolina Troops; McDowell was acting in command of that part of the Legion with Thomas in western N.C. at a time when Thomas himself was absent, so his signature would seem to indicate some sort of formal or informal relationship between Ghormley's and Thomas's respective commands. Ghormley is noted in this document as being at Johnathon's Creek, which is located in Haywood County, one of Thomas' main areas of operations, and also as in command of "Co. G," which may be the letter by which his company was known as part of Thomas's command. Survived the war. See Colonel William Holland Thomas To Lieutenant Colonel William C. Walker, November 8, 1863, Stephen Whitaker Papers, NCDAH; W. H. Parker, P.A.C.S., to Colonel William Holland Thomas, April 17, 1864, 1860-1864 Correspondence folder, William Holland Thomas Papers, Special Collections, Perkins Library, Duke University; Crow, *Storm in the Mountains*, 132, 136, 220, 260 n. 56; Special Requistion, October 16, 1864, filmjacket for D. C. Ghormley, Company K, 5th Regiment Tennessee Cavalry (McKenzie's), NA-MC268-23; Stringfield, "Memoirs of the Civil War," unpublished typescript, McClung Library, Knoxville (photocopy in the William Williams Stringfield Papers, Special Collections, Hunter Library, Western Carolina University), 23, 34-35; Clark's *Regiments*, 3: 758, 4:128.]

LIEUTENANTS

GRANT, JOHN, 1st Lieutenant
Born in Blount County, Tennessee, and resided in Cherokee County where he was by occupation a farmer prior to enlisting at age 32, July 21, 1862, for the war. Mustered in as Private. Appointed 1st Lieutenant on September 24, 1862. Signature appears on a forage voucher dated December 11, 1862. Transferred to Company K, 5th Regiment Tennessee Cavalry (McKenzie's), December 16, 1862.

NELSON, ELIJAH R., 2nd Lieutenant
Born in Blount County, Tennessee, where he resided as a farmer prior to enlisting at age 28. Appointed 2nd Lieutenant on September 24, 1862. Name appears on a payment voucher for service from that date through October 31, 1862. Transferred to Company K, 5th Regiment Tennessee Cavalry (McKenzie's), December 16, 1862.

NUCHOLS, DAVID T., 3rd Lieutenant
Born in Blount County, Tennessee, where he resided as a farmer prior to enlisting at age 26. Appointed 3rd Lieutenant on or about September 24, 1862. Transferred to Company K, 5th Regiment Tennessee Cavalry (McKenzie's), December 16, 1862. [His surname may have been Knickolds or something similar.]

NONCOMMISSIONED OFFICERS AND PRIVATES

ALFORD, CHARLES N., Private
Born in Sevier County, Tennessee, and resided in Blount County, Tennessee, where he was by occupation a farmer prior to enlisting at Maryville, Tennessee, September 24, 1862, for the war. Transferred to Company K, 5th Regiment Tennessee Cavalry (McKenzie's), December 16, 1862.

AMBURN, JOSEPH, Private
Born in Blount County, Tennessee, where he resided as a farmer prior to enlisting at Maryville, Tennessee, at age 20, July 14, 1862, for the war. Transferred to 1st Company D of this battalion on September 24-25, 1862.

AMBURN, WILLIAM, _____
Place and date of enlistment not reported. Name appears on a list of members of Capt. D. C. Ghormley's Company, Tennessee Provost Guard for Monroe, Blount, and Sevier Counties dated August 1, 1862. No further records. [He may have later served as Private in Capt. William H. Burrough's Company, Tennessee Light Artillery.]

AUTREY, WILLIAM, Private
Born in Blount County, Tennessee, where he resided as a blacksmith prior to enlisting at age 29, September 24, 1862, for the war. No further records. [He is probably the same man as William Anthony who later served in Company K, 5th Regiment Tennessee Cavalry (McKenzie's).]

BRADFORD, BENNETT B., Private
Born in Jefferson County, Tennessee, where he resided as a farmer prior to enlisting at Maryville, Tennessee, at age 36, September 24, 1862, for the war. Transferred to Company K, 5th Regiment Tennessee Cavalry (McKenzie's), December 16, 1862.

BRADSHAW, JOHN H., Private
Born in Haywood County and resided in Macon County where he was by occupation a farmer prior to enlisting at Maryville at age 24, August 27, 1862, for the war. Transferred to Company K, 5th Regiment Tennessee Cavalry (McKenzie's), December 16, 1862.

BREWER, JOHN, Private
Born in Blount County, Tennessee, and resided in Cherokee County, North Carolina, where he was by occupation a farmer prior to enlisting at Maryville, Tennessee, at age 26, July 21, 1862, for the war. Transferred to Company K, 5th Regiment Tennessee Cavalry (McKenzie's), December 16, 1862.

BROWN, ELIJAH, Private
Born in Sevier County, Tennessee, where he resided as a farmer prior to enlisting at Maryville, Tennessee, September 24, 1862, for the war. Reported absent without leave on October 24, 1862. Transferred to Company K, 5th Regiment Tennessee Cavalry (McKenzie's), December 16, 1862, while absent without leave.

BROWN, SAMUEL C., Private
Born in Blount County, Tennessee, and resided in Sevier County, Tennessee, where he was by occupation a farmer prior to enlisting at Maryville, Tennessee, at age 25, September 24, 1862, for the war. Transferred to Company K, 5th Regiment Tennessee Cavalry (McKenzie's), December 16, 1862. He may have transferred to or illegally reenlisted in this legion at a later date, and may have been the same man as S. C. Brown, whose service record is in the General Miscellaneous section of this roster.

BURNES, WILLIAM, Private
Born in Sevier County, Tennessee, where he resided as a farmer prior to enlisting at Maryville, Tennessee, at age 24, September 24, 1862, for the war. Reported absent without leave on November 5, 1862. Transferred to Company K, 5th Regiment Tennessee Cavalry (McKenzie's), December 16, 1862. [His surname may have been Burns.]

CABLE, ADAM, Private
Born in Blount County, Tennessee, and resided in Cherokee County, North Carolina, where he was by occupation a farmer prior to enlisting Maryville, Tennessee, at age 36, August 27, 1862, for the war. Transferred to Company K, 5th Regiment Tennessee Cavalry (McKenzie's), December 16, 1862.

CABLE, WILLIAM, Private
Born in Blount County, Tennessee, and resided in Cherokee County, North Carolina, where he was by occupation a farmer prior to enlisting at Maryville, Tennessee, at age 22, September 7, 1862, for the war. Transferred to Company K, 5th Regiment Tennessee Cavalry (McKenzie's), December 16, 1862.

CAMPBELL, WILLIAM, Private
Enlisted at Maryville, Tennessee, September 24, 1862, for the war, as a substitute for Pvt. William R. Hooper. Transferred to Company K, 5th Regiment Tennessee Cavalry (McKenzie's), December 16, 1862.

CARINGER, FRANCIS MARION, Private
Born in Cherokee County where he resided as a farmer prior to enlisting at Maryville, Tennessee, at age 20, July 21, 1862, for the war. Transferred to Company K, 5th Regiment Tennessee Cavalry (McKenzie's), December 16, 1862. [His surname may have been Carringer.]

CARRINGER, WESTLY, Private
Born in the part of Macon County that later became Cherokee County. Resided in Cherokee County as a farmer prior to enlisting at Maryville, Tennessee, at age 26, September 24, 1862, for the war. Reported absent sick on surgeon's certificate, November 15, 1862. Transferred to Company K, 5th Regiment Tennessee Cavalry (McKenzie's), December 16, 1862, while absent sick. [His first name may have been Wesley.]

CARRINGER, WILLIAM H., Private
Previously served as Private in Company A, 29th Regiment N.C. Troops. Enlisted in this company at Maryville, Tennessee, September 24, 1862, for the war. Transferred to Company K, 5th Regiment Tennessee Cavalry (McKenzie's), December 16, 1862. [His surname may have been Caringer.]

CARVER, REUBEN, Private
Born in Blount County, Tennessee, and resided in Cherokee County, North Carolina, where he was by occupation a farmer prior to enlisting Maryville, Tennessee, at age 27, July 4, 1862, for the war. Transferred to Company K, 5th Regiment Tennessee Cavalry (McKenzie's), December 16, 1862. Later served as Private in Company H of this battalion.

CARVER, THOMAS, Corporal
Enlisted at Maryville, Tennessee, July 28, 1862, for the war. Mustered in as a Private. Promoted to Corporal on August 20, 1862. Discharged on account of disability on October 1, 1862.

CARVER, WILLIAM M., Private
Born in Cherokee County where he resided as a farmer prior to enlisting at Maryville, Tennessee, at age 21, July 4, 1862, for the war. Transferred to Company K, 5th Regiment Tennessee Cavalry (McKenzie's), December 16, 1862. Later served in Company H, Infantry Regiment of this legion.

CHAMBERS, JASPER J., _____
Place and date of enlistment not reported. Name appears on a list of members of this company dated August 1, 1862. No further records.

CHAMBERS, PHILLIP, _____
Place and date of enlistment not reported. Name appears on a list of members of this company dated August 1, 1862. No further records.

CHAMBERS, THOMAS B., Private
Born in Macon County where he resided as a farmer prior to enlisting at age 21, July 29, 1862, for the war. Transferred to Company K, 5th Regiment Tennessee Cavalry (McKenzie's), December 16, 1862.

COLTER, ROBERT B., Private
Born in Blount County, Tennessee, where he resided prior to enlisting at Maryville, Tennessee, at age 29, September 24, 1862, for the war. Transferred to Company K, 5th Regiment Tennessee Cavalry (McKenzie's), December 16, 1862.

COLVIN, LEANDER, Private
Born in Cherokee County where he resided as a farmer prior to enlisting at Maryville, Tennessee, at age 18, September 24, 1862, for the war. Transferred to Company K, 5th Regiment Tennessee Cavalry (McKenzie's), December 16, 1862.

COOK, ALEXANDER, Private
Born in Blount County, Tennessee, and resided in Polk County, Tennessee, where he was by occupation a farmer prior to enlisting at Maryville, Tennessee, at age 27, September 24, 1862, for the war. Discharged on November 4, 1862, after providing Pvt. James C. Wright as a substitute.

CRUSE, WILLIAM, Private
Born in Blount County, Tennessee, where he resided as a farmer prior to enlisting at age 26, September 24, 1862, for the war. Transferred to Company K, 5th Regiment Tennessee Cavalry (McKenzie's), December 16, 1862.

DAVIS, ALFRED, Private
Born in Blount County, Tennessee, where he resided as a farmer prior to enlisting at Maryville, Tennessee, at age 19, September 24, 1862, for the war. Deserted November 20, 1862.

DAVIS, CHARLES, Private
Born in Union County, Tennessee, where he resided as a farmer prior to enlisting at Maryville, Tennessee, at age 19, September 24, 1862, for the war. Killed Pvt. William McEldry of this company on November 18, 1862. Transferred to Company K, 5th Regiment Tennessee Cavalry (McKenzie's), December 16, 1862. [In records of the 5th Regiment Tennessee Cavalry (McKenzie's), he was reported imprisoned for this crime at Knoxville, January-April, 1863.]

DAVIS, JOHN HARVY., Private
Born in Yancey County and resided in Cherokee County where he was by occupation a farmer prior to enlisting at Maryville, Tennessee, at age 27, September 1, 1862, for the war. Reported absent sick on December 1, 1862. Transferred to Company K, 5th Regiment Tennessee Cavalry (McKenzie's), December 16, 1862, while absent sick.

DEAVER, GEORGE W., Private
Born in the part of Macon County that later became Cherokee County where he resided as a farmer prior to enlisting at Maryville, Tennessee, at age 27, July 4, 1862, for the war. Transferred to Company K, 5th Regiment Tennessee Cavalry (McKenzie's), December 16, 1862.

DITMORE, JOHN H., Private
Born in South Carolina. Resided in McMinn County, Tennessee, and was by occupation a farmer prior to enlisting at Maryville, Tennessee, at age 50, November 1, 1862, for the war as a substitute for Pvt. James W. Everett. Transferred to Company K, 5th Regiment Tennessee Cavalry (McKenzie's), December 16, 1862.

DYRE, MARTIN B., Private
Enlisted on July 4, 1862, for the war. No further records. [His surname may have been Dyer. His middle initial my have been S.]

ELLEGE, WILLIAM, _____
Place and date of enlistment not reported. Name appears on a list of members of this company dated August 1, 1862. No further records.

EVERETT, JAMES W., Private
Enlisted at Maryville, Tennessee, October 1, 1862, for the war. Discharged on November 1, 1862, after providing Pvt. John H. Ditmore as a substitute.

FARMER, JOHN, Private
Born in Blount County, Tennessee, where he resided as a farmer prior to enlisting at Maryville, Tennessee, at age 22, August 1, 1862, for the war. Transferred to Company K, 5th Regiment Tennessee Cavalry (McKenzie's), December 16, 1862.

FARR, JOHN, Private
Born in Blount County, Tennessee, and resided in Cherokee County where he was by occupation a farmer prior to enlisting Maryville, Tennessee, at age 40, September 24, 1862, for the war. Transferred to Company K, 5th Regiment Tennessee Cavalry (McKenzie's), December 16, 1862.

FARR, LEWIS, Private
Born in Blount County, Tennessee, and resided in Cherokee County where he was by occupation a farmer prior to enlisting Maryville, Tennessee, at age 29, August 20, 1862, for the war. Transferred to Company K, 5th Regiment Tennessee Cavalry (McKenzie's), December 16, 1862.

FISHER, ISAAC, Private
Born in Blount County, Tennessee, where he resided as a farmer prior to enlisting at Maryville, Tennessee, at age 19, September 24, 1862, for the war. Transferred to Company K, 5th Regiment Tennessee Cavalry (McKenzie's), December 16, 1862.

GILLESPIE, MATHEW H., Private
Born in Blount County, Tennessee, where he resided as a farmer prior to enlisting at Maryville, Tennessee, at age 24, September 24, 1862, for the war. Transferred to Company K, 5th Regiment Tennessee Cavalry (McKenzie's), December 16, 1862. [His surname may have been Galaspy.]

GLADDEN, THOMAS H., Private
Born in Monroe County, Tennessee, and resided in Cherokee County, North Carolina, where he was by occupation a farmer prior to enlisting at Maryville, Tennessee, at age 21, July 21, 1862, for the war. Transferred to Company K, 5th Regiment Tennessee Cavalry (McKenzie's), December 16, 1862.

GLADDEN, WILLIAM, Private
Born in Monroe County, Tennessee, and resided in Cherokee County, North Carolina, where he was by occupation a farmer prior to enlisting at Maryville, Tennessee, at age 23, July 21, 1862, for the war. Transferred to Company K, 5th Regiment Tennessee Cavalry (McKenzie's), December 16, 1862.

GORLEY, WILLIAM, Private
Born in Blount County, Tennessee, and resided in Cherokee County, North Carolina, where he was by occupation a blacksmith prior to enlisting at Maryville, Tennessee, at age 33, July 4, 1862, for the war. Transferred to Company K, 5th Regiment Tennessee Cavalry (McKenzie's), December 16, 1862. [His surname may have been Gorely. He may have been the same man as Will Gharly of Company H, Infantry Regiment of this legion.]

GREGORY, CHARLES, Private
Born in Blount County, Tennessee, where he resided as a farmer prior to enlisting at Maryville, Tennessee, at age 39, September 24, 1862, for the war. Transferred to Company K, 5th Regiment Tennessee Cavalry (McKenzie's), December 16, 1862.

GREGORY, JAMES H., Private
Born in Blount County, Tennessee, where he resided as a farmer prior to enlisting at Maryville, Tennessee, at age 19, September 28,

1862, for the war. Transferred to Company K, 5th Regiment Tennessee Cavalry (McKenzie's), December 16, 1862.

HARDEN, THOMAS, Corporal

Resided in Blount County, Tennessee, and was by occupation a farmer prior to enlisting at Maryville, Tennessee, at age 29, September 24, 1862, for the war. Discharged on or about the same day after providing Charles C. Person as a substitute.

HEDRICK, DANIEL LEBON T., Private

Born in Blount County, Tennessee, where he resided as a farmer prior to enlisting at Maryville, Tennessee, at age 18, September 24, 1862, for the war. Tranferred to Company K, 5th Regiment Tennessee Cavalry (McKenzie's), December 16, 1862. [His surname may have been Headrick.]

HEDRICK, JOHN, Private

Born in Blount County, Tennessee, where he resided as a farmer prior to enlisting at age 22, September 24, 1862, for the war. Transferred to Company K, 5th Regiment Tennessee Cavalry (McKenzie's), December 16, 1862. [His middle initial may have been S. His surname may have been Headrick. He may have served previously in Company E, 1st Regiment (East) Tennessee Cavalry (Roger's); Company E, 2nd Regiment Tennessee Cavalry (McLinn's); and Company F, 2nd Battalion Tennessee Cavalry/13th Battalion Tennessee Cavalry (McKenzie's), with the ranks of Private and Sergeant. These are the same company under different organizations.]

HERRIN, THOMAS, Private

Born in Blount County, Tennessee, where he resided as a farmer prior to enlisting at Maryville, Tennessee, at age 27, September 24, 1862, for the war. Transferred to Company K, 5th Regiment Tennessee Cavalry (McKenzie's), December 16, 1862.

HICKS, THOMAS, Private

Resided in Blount County, Tennessee, and was by occupation a laborer prior to enlisting at Maryville, Tennessee, at age 27, September 24, 1862, for the war. Transferred to Company B, 31st Regiment Tennessee Infantry (W.M. Bradford's), November 17, 1862 (later known as the 39th Regiment Tennessee Mounted Infantry, under which its service records are filed at the National Archives). [His surname may have been Hix. His records for the 31st Regiment Tennessee Infantry (W. M. Bradford's) indicates that he transferred on November 1, 1862.]

HOOPER, THOMAS W., Private

Born in DeKalb County, Georgia, and resided in Fulton County, Georgia, where he was by occupation a sawyer prior to enlisting at Maryville, Tennessee, at age 22, August 15, 1862, for the war. Transferred to Company K, 5th Regiment Tennessee Cavalry (McKenzie's), December 16, 1862. [He may have been the same man as Pvt. William Hooper of this company.]

HOOPER, WILLIAM, Private

Enlisted on September 1, 1862, for the war. No further records. [He may have been the same man as Pvt. Thomas W. Hooper of this company.]

HOOPER, WILLIAM R., Corporal

Born in DeKalb County, Georgia, where he resided as a sawyer prior to enlisting at Maryville, Tennessee, at age 24, September 1, 1862, for the war. Discharged on September 24, 1862, after furnishing Pvt. William Campbell as a substitute.

JOHNSON, JEFFERSON, Private

Born in Rutherford County and resided in Cherokee County where he was by occupation a farmer prior to enlisting at Maryville, Tennessee, at age 28, August 20, 1862, for the war. Transferred to Company K, 5th Regiment Tennessee Cavalry (McKenzie's), December 16, 1862.

JOHNSON, JOHN, Private

Born in Rutherford County and resided in Cherokee County where he was by occupation a farmer prior to enlisting at Maryville, Tennessee, at age 26, August 20, 1862, for the war. Transferred to Company K, 5th Regiment Tennessee Cavalry (McKenzie's), December 16, 1862.

JOHNSON, PERRY, Corporal

Born in Knox County, Tennessee, and resided in Cherokee County where he was by occupation a farmer prior to enlisting at Maryville, Tennesssee, at age 38, September 24, 1862, for the war. Mustered in as Corporal. Transferred to Company K, 5th Regiment Tennessee Cavalry (McKenzie's), December 16, 1862.

JOHNSON, WILBURN, Private

Previously served as Private in Company A, 29th Regiment N.C. Troops. Enlisted in this company at Maryville, Tennessee, on September 24, 1862, for the war. Transferred to Company K, 5th Regiment Tennessee Cavalry (McKenzie's), December 16, 1862. [Contrary to 8:241 of this series, his given name was probably Wilburn rather than Wilborn.]

JONES, ALEXANDER, Private

Born in Cherokee County where he resided as a farmer prior to enlisting at Maryville, Tennessee, at age 18, September 24, 1862, for the war. Transferred to Company K, 5th Regiment Tennessee Cavalry (McKenzie's), December 16, 1862.

KINNAMON, JOHN, Private

Born in Blount County, Tennessee, where he resided as a farmer prior to enlisting at Maryville, Tennessee, at age 20, September 24, 1862, for the war. Transferred to Company K, 5th Regiment Tennessee Cavalry (McKenzie's), December 16, 1862.

KIRKLAND, GEORGE W., Private

Born in Rhea County, Tennessee, and resided in Blount County, Tennessee, where he was by occupation a farmer prior to enlisting at Maryville, Tennessee, at age 22, July 21, 1862, for the war. Transferred to Company K, 5th Regiment Tennessee Cavalry (McKenzie's), December 16, 1862. [His surname may have been Kerklind. Later served as Private in Captain Marshall's Company Confederate Artillery (Brown Horse Artillery).]

KIRKLAND, THOMAS, Private

Enlisted at Maryville, Tennessee, July 4 or 21, 1862, for the war. Discharged due to disability on October 1, 1862.

KIRKLAND, WILLIAM T., Private
Enlisted August 1, 1862, for the war. Place of enlistment not reported. Transferred to Company K, 5th Regiment Tennessee Cavalry (McKenzie's), December 16, 1862. [His surname may have been Kirklin. He may have served later in Company F, Infantry Regiment of this legion.]

McANNILLY, WILLIAM R., Private
Born in Sevier County, Tennessee, where he resided as a farmer prior to enlisting at Maryville, Tennessee, at age 18, September 24, 1862, for the war. Transferred to Company K, 5th Regiment Tennessee Cavalry (McKenzie's), December 16, 1862. [His surname may have been McNelley. He may have later served in Company K, Infantry Regiment of this legion.]

McCLAIN, ANDREW, _____
Place and date of enlistment not reported. Name appears on a list of members of this company dated August 1, 1862. No further records.

McKAMY, JOHN W., Private
Born in Blount County, Tennessee, and where he resided as a farmer prior to enlisting at Maryville, Tennessee, at age 31, August 1 or 14, 1862, for the war. Transferred to Company C of this battalion on September 29, 1862. [His middle initial may have been A.]

McKELDRY, WILLIAM, Private
Born in Blount County, Tennessee, where he resided as a farmer prior to enlisting at age 27, September 24, 1862, for the war. Killed on November 18, 1862, by Pvt. Charles Davis of this company. [His surname may have been McEldry.]

MOORE, WILLIAM, _____
Enlisted on August 1, 1862, for the war. Place of enlistment not reported. No further records.

MORRISON, WILLIAM A., Private
Born in Blount County, Tennessee, where he resided as a farmer prior to enlisting at Maryville, Tennessee, at age 19, September 24, 1862, for the war. Transferred to Company K, 5th Regiment Tennessee Cavalry (McKenzie's), December 16, 1862. [His surname may have been Morison.]

MULLENDORE, ABRAM L., Sergeant
Born in Sevier County, Tennessee, where he resided as a farmer prior to enlisting at Maryville, Tennessee, at age 31, September 24, 1862, for the war. Mustered in as Sergeant. Transferred to Company K, 5th Regiment Tennessee Cavalry (McKenzie's), December 16, 1862.

MULLENDORE, ROBERT B., Private
Born in Sevier County, Tennessee, where he resided as a farmer prior to enlisting at Maryville, Tennessee, at age 24, September 24, 1862, for the war. Transferred to Company K, 5th Regiment Tennessee Cavalry (McKenzie's), December 16, 1862.

NELSON, JAMES W., Private
Born in Blount County, Tennessee, where he resided as a farmer prior to enlisting at Maryville, Tennessee, at age 18, September 24, 1862, for the war. Transferred to Company K, 5th Regiment Tennessee Cavalry (McKenzie's), December 16, 1862.

NORWOOD, JOHN H., Private
Resided in Blounty County, Tennessee and was by occupation a farmer prior to enlisting at Maryville, Tennessee, at age 34, December 1, 1862, for the war. Transferred to Company K, 5th Regiment Tennessee Cavalry (McKenzie's), December 16, 1862.

NUCHOLS, ISAAC F., Private
Born in Blount County, Tennessee, where he resided as a farmer prior to enlisting Maryville, Tennessee, at age 21, September 24, 1862, for the war. Transferred to Company K, 5th Regiment Tennessee Cavalry (McKenzie's), December 16, 1862. [His middle initial may have been T. His surname may have been Knuckols or something similar.]

NUCHOLS, JAMES W., Private
Born in Blount County, Tennessee, where he resided as a farmer prior to enlisting Maryville, Tennessee, at age 18, September 24, 1862, for the war. Transferred to Company K, 5th Regiment Tennessee Cavalry (McKenzie's), December 16, 1862. [His surname may have been Knickols or something similar.]

OLIVER, WILLIAM, Private
Born in Blount County, Tennessee, where he resided as a farmer prior to enlisting at Maryville, Tennessee, at age 25, September 24, 1862, for the war. Transferred to Company K, 5th Regiment Tennessee Cavalry (McKenzie's), December 16, 1862.

PAYNE, WESTLEY, Private
Born in Blount County, Tennessee, where he resided as a farmer prior to enlisting at Maryville, Tennessee, at age 21, September 24, 1862, for the war. Transferred to Company K, 5th Regiment Tennessee Cavalry (McKenzie's), December 16, 1862. [His given name may have been Wesley.]

PERSON, CHARLES C., Corporal
Born in Rutherford County and resided in Blount County, Tennessee, where he was by occupation a farmer prior to enlisting at Maryville, Tennessee, at age 54, September 24, 1862, for the war as a substitute for Corpl. Thomas Harden. Mustered in as Corporal. Transferred to Company K, 5th Regiment Tennessee Cavalry (McKenzie's), December 16, 1862. [His surname may have been Pearson or Pierson.]

PORTER, ANDREW J., Private
Enlisted at Maryville, Tennessee, September 24, 1862, for the war. Transferred to Company K, 5th Regiment Tennessee Cavalry (McKenzie's), December 16, 1862.

PORTER, STEPHEN, 1st Sergeant
Born in Monroe County, Tennessee, and resided in Blount County, Tennessee, where he was by occupation a farmer prior to enlisting at Maryville, Tennessee, at age 21, July 4, 1862, for the war. Mustered in as Sergeant. Promoted to 1st Sergeant prior to September 24, 1862. Transferred to Company K, 5th Regiment Tennessee Cavalry (McKenzie's), December 16, 1862.

RICE, GABRIEL P., Private
Born in Buncombe County and resided in Cherokee County where he was by occupation a farmer prior to enlisting at Maryville, Tennessee, at age 25, July 4, 1862, for the war. Transferred to Company K, 5th Regiment Tennessee Cavalry (McKenzie's), December 16, 1862.

RODDY, HENDERSON, Private
Born in Monroe County, Tennessee, where he resided as a farmer prior to enlisting at Maryville, Tennessee, at age 19, September 24, 1862, for the war. Transferred to Company K, 5th Regiment Tennessee Cavalry (McKenzie's), December 16, 1862.

RORIX, JAMES ADAM, Private
Born in Blount County, Tennessee, where he resided as a farmer prior to enlisting at Maryville, Tennessee, at age 24, September 24, 1862, for the war. Transferred to Company K, 5th Regiment Tennessee Cavalry (McKenzie's), in December 16, 1862. Evidently later served as a member of Company F, Indian Battalion.

ROSE, ISAAC T., Private
Born in Blount County, Tennessee, and resided in Cherokee County, North Carolina, where he was by occupation a farmer prior to enlisting at Maryville, Tennessee, at age 32, August 23, 1862, for the war. Transferred to Company K, 5th Regiment Tennessee Cavalry (McKenzie's), December 16, 1862.

SEATON, PLEASANT PINCKNEY, Private
Born in Sevier County, Tennessee, where he resided as a farmer prior to enlisting at Maryville, Tennessee, at age 23, September 24, 1862, for the war. No further records. [His given name may have been Pinckney Pleasant.]

SHERRILL, JAMES H., Private
Born in Blount County, Tennessee, where he resided as a doctor prior to enlisting at Maryville, Tennessee, at age 23, September 24, 1862, for the war. Reported absent sick on November 15, 1862. Transferred to Company K, 5th Regiment Tennessee Cavalry (McKenzie's), December 16, 1862, while absent sick.

SPARKS, JAMES A., Private
Born in Blount County, Tennessee, where he resided as a farmer prior to enlisting at Maryville, Tennessee, at age 24, September 24, 1862, for the war. Transferred to Company K, 5th Regiment Tennessee Cavalry (McKenzie's), December 16, 1862.

TAYLOR, DANIEL A., Sergeant
Born in Blount County, Tennessee, and resided in Macon County, North Carolina, where he was by occupation a farmer prior to enlisting at Maryville, Tennessee, at age 20, July 4, 1862, for the war. Mustered in as Private. Name appears on a list of members of this company dated August 1, 1862. Promoted to or elected Sergeant on or prior to September 24, 1862. Transferred to Company K, 5th Regiment Tennessee Cavalry (McKenzie's), December 16, 1862.

WALLACE, ABRAM L., Private
Born in Blount County, Tennessee, where he resided as a farmer prior to enlisting at Maryville, Tennessee, at age 23, September 24, 1862, for the war. Transferred to Company K, 5th Regiment Tennessee Cavalry (McKenzie's), in December, 1862.

WHITE, ISAAC A., Private
Born in Blount County, Tennessee, where he resided as a farmer prior to enlisting at Maryville, Tennessee, at age 29, September 24, 1862, for the war. Transferred to Company K, 5th Regiment Tennessee Cavalry (McKenzie's), December 16, 1862.

WILLIAMS, JAMES, Sergeant
Born in Blount County, Tennessee, and resided in Cherokee County where he was by occupation a farmer prior to enlisting at Maryville, Tennessee, at age 27, July 4, 1862, for the war. Probably mustered in as Private. Promoted to Sergeant prior to September 24, 1862. Transferred to Company K, 5th Regiment Tennessee Cavalry (McKenzie's), December 16, 1862.

WILLIAMS, SAMUEL J., Corporal
Born in Blount County, Tennessee, where he resided as a farmer prior to enlisting at Maryville, Tennessee, at age 32, September 24, 1862, for the war. Mustered in as Corporal. Transferred to Company K, 5th Regiment Tennessee Cavalry (McKenzie's), in December, 1862.

WILLIAMS, WILLIAM H., 1st Sergeant
Born in Blount County, Tennessee, where he resided as a teacher prior to enlisting at Maryville, Tennessee, at age 27, September 24, 1862, for the war. Mustered in as 1st Sergeant. Transferred to Company K, 5th Regiment Tennessee Cavalry (McKenzie's), December 16, 1862. [His middle initial may have been A.]

WRIGHT, JAMES C., Private
Enlisted at Maryville, Tennessee, November 4, 1862, as a substitute for Pvt. Alexander Cook. Transferred to Company K, 5th Regiment Tennesssee Cavalry (McKenzie's), December 16, 1862.

COMPANY G

This cavalry company was raised in Tennessee, in Jefferson and Cocke Counties. It was organized at Dandridge, Tennessee, September 24, 1862. On or about November 14, 1862, it was transferred to the 1st Regiment Tennessee Cavalry (Carter's), and designated Company H.

The following roster was compiled in large part from an undated company muster and descriptive roll. It is abstracted in the microfilm edition of the Compiled Service Records of Confederate Soldiers Who Served in Organizations from the State of North Carolina (Record Group 109, M270), National Archives, Washington, D.C. Other valuable information in the Compiled Service Records includes enlistment papers, pay vouchers, requisitions, letters of resignation, discharge certificates, and abstracts of medical and prisoner of war records.

Also utilized in this roster were *The War of the Rebellion: A Compilation of the Official Records of the Union and Confederate Armies*, the North Carolina Adjutant General's papers, state militia records, newspaper casualty lists and obituaries, wartime claims for bounty pay and allowances, postwar registers of claims for artificial limbs, Confederate pension applications filed with the states of North Carolina, Tennessee, and Florida, and the 1860 and 1870 federal censuses of Tennessee. A search was made also for relevant letters, diaries, reminiscences, and other manuscripts in the Southern Historical Collection (University of North Carolina-Chapel Hill) and the Duke University Library Special Collections Department.

Among the secondary sources consulted were records of the North Carolina division of the United Daughters of the Confederacy, postwar rosters, regimental and county histories, marriage bond, will, and cemetery indexes, published and unpublished genealogies, biographical dictionaries, the North Carolina *County Heritage Book* series, the *Confederate Veteran*, Walter Clark's *Histories of the Several Regiments and Battalions from North Carolina in the Great War, 1861-'65*, and the North Carolina volume of the extended edition of *Confederate Military History*.

OFFICERS

CAPTAIN

NEFF, DAVID
Born in Shenandoah County, Virginia, and resided in Jefferson County, Tennessee, where he was by occupation a farmer prior to enlisting at Dandridge, Tennessee, at age 53. Appointed Captain on September 24, 1862. Transferred to Company H, 1st Regiment Tennessee Cavalry (Carter's), in November, 1862.

LIEUTENANTS

COURSEY, JAMES F., 1st Lieutenant
Born in Augusta County, Virginia, and resided in Jefferson County, Tennessee, where he was by occupation a carpenter prior to enlisting at Dandridge, Tennessee, at age 23. Appointed 1st Lieutenant on September 24, 1862. Transferred to Company H, 1st Regiment Tennessee Cavalry (Carter's), in November, 1862.

COWAN, WILLIAM W., 3rd Lieutenant
Born in Jefferson County, Tennessee, where he resided as a farmer prior to enlisting at Dandridge, Tennessee, at age 22. Appointed 3rd Lieutenant on September 24, 1862. Transferred to Company H, 1st Regiment Tennessee Cavalry (Carter's), in November, 1862.

WARD, BENJAMIN F., 2nd Lieutenant
Born in Greenville District, South Carolina, and resided in Jefferson County, Tennessee, where he was by occupation a blacksmith prior to enlisting at Dandridge, Tennessee, at age 29. Appointed 2nd Lieutenant on September 24, 1862. Transferred to Company H, 1st Regiment Tennessee Cavalry (Carter's), in November, 1862.

NONCOMMISSIONED OFFICERS AND PRIVATES

ALLMAN, OLIVER, Private
Born in Cocke County, Tennessee, where he resided as a farmer prior to enlisting at Dandridge, Tennessee, September 24, 1862, for the war. Transferred to Company H, 1st Regiment Tennessee Cavalry (Carter's), in November, 1862.

ANDERSON, JAMES, Private
Born in Cocke County, Tennessee, where he resided as a farmer prior to enlisting at Dandridge, Tennessee, September 24, 1862, for the war. May have transferred to Company H, 1st Regiment Tennessee Cavalry (Carter's), in November, 1862, although there is no record for him in that unit. He may have served later in Company A, Walker's Battalion.

BAKER, JACOB, Private
Born in Jefferson County, Tennessee, and resided in Greene County, Tennessee, where he was by occupation a farmer prior to enlisting at Dandridge, Tennessee, at age 21, September 24, 1862, for the war. Transferred to Company H, 1st Regiment Tennessee Cavalry (Carter's), in November, 1862.

BALEY, JOSEPH, Private
Born in Jefferson County, Tennessee, where he resided as a farmer prior to enlisting at Dandridge, Tennessee, at age 26, September 24, 1862, for the war. Transferred to Company H, 1st Regiment Tennessee Cavalry (Carter's), in November, 1862.

BALEY, SAMUEL M., Private
Born in Jefferson County, Tennessee, where he resided as a farmer prior to enlisting at Dandridge, Tennessee, at age 29, September 24, 1862, for the war. Transferred to Company H, 1st Regiment Tennessee Cavalry (Carter's), in November, 1862. [His surname may have been Baily.]

BALLARD, WILLIAM H., Private
Born in Sevier County, Tennessee, where he resided as a farmer prior to enlisting at Strawberry Plains, Tennessee, at age 21, September 24, 1862, for the war. Transferred to Company I, Infantry Regiment of this legion on or about the same date.

BETTIS, BRALEY, Private
Born in Jefferson County, Tennessee, where he resided as a farmer prior to enlisting at Dandridge, Tennessee, at age 22, September 24, 1862. Transferred to Company H, 1st Regiment Tennessee Cavalry (Carter's), in November, 1862.

BROWN, JAMES, Private
Born in Sevier County, Tennessee, and resided in Cocke County, Tennessee, where he was by occupation a farmer prior to enlisting at at Dandridge, Tennessee, at age 29, September 24, 1862, for the war. Transferred to Company H, 1st Regiment Tennessee Cavalry (Carter's), in November, 1862.

CARVILE, WILLIAM Z., Private
Born in Jefferson County, Tennessee, where he resided as a farmer prior to enlisting at Dandridge, Tennessee, at age 30, September 24, 1862, for the war. Transferred to Company H, 1st Regiment Tennessee Cavalry (Carter's), in November, 1862.

CASEY, HENRY, Private
Born in Cocke County, Tennessee, where he resided as a farmer prior to enlisting at Dandridge, Tennessee, at age 31, September 24, 1862, for the war. Transferred to Company H, 1st Regiment Tennessee Cavalry (Carter's), in November, 1862.

CLARK, WILLIAM M., Private
Born in Cocke County, Tennessee, where he resided as a farmer prior to enlisting at Dandridge, Tennessee, at age 19, September 24, 1862, for the war. Transferred to Company H, 1st Regiment Tennessee Cavalry (Carter's), in November, 1862.

COOPER, ISAAC, Private
Born in Cocke County, Tennessee, and resided in Jefferson County, Tennessee, where he was by occupation a farmer prior to enlisting at

Dandridge, Tennessee, at age 24, September 24, 1862, for the war. Transferred to Company H, 1st Regiment Tennessee Cavalry (Carter's), in November, 1862.

COOPER, THOMAS, Private
Born in Cocke County, Tennessee, and resided in Jefferson County, Tennessee, where he was by occupation a farmer prior to enlisting at Dandridge, Tennessee, at age 18, September 24, 1862, for the war. Transferred to Company H, 1st Regiment Tennessee Cavalry (Carter's), in November, 1862.

COWAN, JOHN P., Private
Born in Jefferson County, Tennessee, where he resided as a farmer prior to enlisting at Dandridge, Tennessee, at age 21, September 24, 1862, for the war. Transferred to Company H, 1st Regiment Tennessee Cavalry (Carter's), in November, 1862.

CROOKSHANKS, GEORGE C., Private
Born in Cocke County, Tennessee, and resided in Jefferson County, Tennessee, where he was by occupation a merchant prior to enlisting at Dandridge, Tennessee, at age 26, September 24, 1862, for the war. Transferred to Company H, 1st Regiment Tennessee Cavalry (Carter's), in November, 1862.

DENTON, RICE D., Private
Born in Augusta County, Virginia, and resided in Jefferson County, Tennessee, where he was by occupation a farmer prior to enlisting at Dandridge, Tennessee, at age 19, September 24, 1862, for the war. No further records.

DOUGLASS, ALEX J., Private
Born in Sevier County, Tennessee, where he resided as a farmer prior to enlisting at Strawberry Plains, Tennessee, at age 29, September 24, 1862, for the war. Later served as Private in Company D, Infantry Regiment of this legion. [He may have served previously in another unit.]

DRINNING, WILLES L., Private
Born in Jefferson County, Tennessee, where he resided as a farmer prior to enlisting at Dandridge, Tennessee, at age 21, September 24, 1862, for the war. Transferred to Company H, 1st Regiment Tennessee Cavalry (Carter's), in November, 1862. Later served in Capt. W. R. Marshall's Company, Brown Horse Artillery. [His surname may have been Drennin.]

DUNWODY, THOMAS M., Private
Born in Greene County, Tennessee, and resided in Jefferson County, Tennessee, where he was by occupation a farmer prior to enlisting at Dandridge, Tennessee, at age 33, September 24, 1862, for the war. Transferred to Company H, 1st Regiment Tennessee Cavalry (Carter's), in November, 1862. [His surname may have been Dunwoody.]

DUNWODY, WILLIAM M., Private
Born in Jefferson County, Tennessee, where he resided as a farmer prior to enlisting at Dandridge, Tennessee, at age 26, September 24, 1862, for the war. Transferred to Company H, 1st Regiment Tennessee Cavalry (Carter's), in November, 1862. [His surname may have been Dunwoody.]

ECKEL, ALEXANDER, Private
Born in Jefferson County, Tennessee, where he resided as a farmer prior to enlisting at Dandridge, Tennessee, at age 20, September 24, 1862, for the war. Transferred to Company H, 1st Regiment Tennessee Cavalry (Carter's), in November, 1862.

ELKINS, WILLIAM, Private
Born in Cocke County, Tennessee, where he resided as a farmer prior to enlisting at Dandridge, Tennessee, at age 28, September 24, 1862, for the war. Transferred to Company H, 1st Regiment Tennessee Cavalry (Carter's), in November, 1862.

EMERY, OLIVER, Private
Born in Cocke County, Tennessee, and resided in Jefferson County, Tennessee, where he was by occupation a farmer prior to enlisting at Dandridge, Tennessee, at age 36, September 24, 1862, for the war. Transferred to Company H, 1st Regiment Tennessee Cavalry (Carter's), in November, 1862. Later served in Capt. W. R. Marshall's Company, Brown Horse Artillery. [His surname may have been Emory.]

ENDALEY, GEORGE A., Private
Born in Jefferson County, Tennessee, where he resided as a farmer prior to enlisting at Dandridge, Tennessee, at age 20, September 24, 1862, for the war. Transferred to Company H, 1st Regiment Tennessee Cavalry (Carter's), in November, 1862. Later served in Capt. W. R. Marshall's Company, Brown Horse Artillery. [His surname may have been Eudaly.]

ESTES, MELVIN, Private
Born in Grainger County, Tennessee, and resided in Greene County, Tennessee, where he was by occupation a farmer prior to enlisting at Dandridge, Tennessee, at age 23, September 24, 1862, for the war. Transferred to Company H, 1st Regiment Tennessee Cavalry (Carter's), in November, 1862.

FINCHURN, ELIJA, Private
Born in Cocke County, Tennessee, where he resided as a farmer prior to enlisting at Dandridge, Tennessee, at age 24, September 24, 1862, for the war. Transferred to Company H, 1st Regiment Tennessee Cavalry (Carter's), in November, 1862.

FINCHURN, JOHN, Private
Born in Cocke County, Tennessee, where he resided as a farmer prior to enlisting Dandridge, Tennessee, at age 19, September 24, 1862, for the war. Transferred to Company H, 1st Regiment Tennessee Cavalry (Carter's), in November, 1862.

FINE, STEPHEN V., Private
Born in Rhea County, Tennessee, and resided in Cocke County, Tennessee, where he was by occupation a gunsmith prior to enlisting at Dandridge, Tennessee, at age 35, September 24, 1862, for the war. Transferred to Company H, 1st Regiment Tennessee Cavalry (Carter's), in November, 1862.

FOLAND, GEORGE H., Private
Born in Rockingham County, Virginia, and resided in Jefferson County, Tennessee, where he was by occupation a blacksmith prior to enlisting at Dandridge, Tennessee, at age 25, September 24, 1862,

for the war. Transferred to Company H, 1st Regiment Tennessee Cavalry (Carter's), in November, 1862. [His surname may have been Folden.]

FOX, TENN D., Private
Born in Sevier County, Tennessee, and resided in Jefferson County, Tennessee, where he was by occupation a lawyer prior to enlisting at Dandridge, Tennessee, at age 28, September 24, 1862, for the war. Transferred to Company H, 1st Regiment Tennessee Cavalry (Carter's), in November, 1862.

GIVENS, PETER H., Private
Born in Jefferson County, Tennessee, where he resided as a farmer prior to enlisting at Dandridge, Tennessee, at age 26, September 24, 1862, for the war. Transferred to Company H, 1st Regiment Tennessee Cavalry (Carter's), in November, 1862.

GOIN, OLIVER R., Private
Born in Jefferson County, Tennessee, where he resided as a farmer prior to enlisting at Dandridge, Tennessee, at age 20, September 24, 1862, for the war. Transferred to Company H, 1st Regiment Tennessee Cavalry (Carter's), in November, 1862.

GORMAN, BENJAMIN F., Private
Born in McMinn County, Tennessee, and resided in Cocke County, Tennessee, where he was by occupation farmer prior to enlisting at Dandridge, Tennessee, at age 25, September 24, 1862, for the war. Transferred to Company H, 1st Regiment Tennessee Cavalry (Carter's), in November, 1862.

GREEN, GEORGE W., Private
Born in Haywood County and resided in Sevier County, Tennessee, where he was by occupation a farmer prior to enlisting at Strawberry Plains, Tennessee, at age 21, September 24, 1862, for the war. Transferred to Company I, Infantry Regiment of this legion, on or about the same date. [He may have been the same man as Pvt. George W. Green of Companies H and E of this battalion.]

GREENLEE, DOUGLASS, Private
Born in Grainger County, Tennessee, and resided in Sevier County, Tennessee, where he was by occupation a farmer prior to enlisting at Dandridge, Tennessee, at age 23, September 24, 1862, for the war. Transferred to Company H, 1st Regiment Tennessee Cavalry (Carter's) in November, 1862. [His given name may have been L. Douglas.]

GRIFFIN, HENRY W. H., Private
Born in what later became Cleveland County. Resided in Jefferson County, Tennessee, where he was by occupation a farmer prior to enlisting at Dandridge, Tennessee, at age 22, September 24, 1862, for the war. Transferred to Company H, 1st Regiment Tennessee Cavalry (Carter's), in November, 1862.

HAGOOD, ARDEN S., Private
Born in Hawkins County, Tennessee, and resided in Jefferson County, Tennessee, where he was by occupation a farmer prior to enlisting at Dandridge, Tennessee, at age 23, September 24, 1862, for the war. Transferred to Company H, 1st Regiment Tennessee Cavalry (Carter's), in November, 1862.

HAGOOD, BENJAMIN R., Private
Born in Hawkins County, Tennessee, and resided in Jefferson County, Tennessee, where he was by occupation a farmer prior to enlisting at Dandridge, Tennessee, at age 19, September 24, 1862, for the war. Transferred to Company H, 1st Regiment Tennessee Cavalry (Carter's), in November, 1862.

HAGOOD, JOHN R., Private
Born in Hawkins County, Tennessee, and resided in Jefferson County, Tennessee, where he was by occupation a farmer prior to enlisting at Dandridge, Tennessee, at age 21, September 24, 1862, for the war. Transferred to Company H, 1st Regiment Tennessee Cavalry (Carter's), in November, 1862.

HALESAUSER, ALEXANDER, Private
Born in Rowan County and resided in Jefferson County, Tennessee, where he was by occupation a carpenter prior to enlisting at Dandridge, Tennessee, at age 28, September 24, 1862, for the war. Possibly transferred to Company H, 1st Regiment Tennessee Cavalry (Carter's), in November, 1862; however, records of that unit do not indicate that he served therein. [His surname may have been Holshouser.]

HALL, JOHN A., Private
Born in Cocke County, Tennessee, and resided in Jefferson County, Tennessee, where he was by occupation a carpenter prior to enlisting at Dandridge, Tennessee, at age 24, September 24, 1862, for the war. Transferred to Company H, 1st Regiment Tennessee Cavalry (Carter's), in November, 1862.

HALL, PHILIP, Private
Born in Cocke County, Tennessee, and resided in Jefferson County, Tennessee, where he was by occupation a carpenter prior to enlisting at Dandridge, Tennessee, at age 26, September 24, 1862, for the war. Transferred to Company H, 1st Regiment Tennessee Cavalry (Carter's), in November, 1862.

HAMMOND, JAMES W., Private
Born in Jefferson County, Tennessee, where he resided as a farmer prior to enlisting at Dandridge, Tennessee, at age 25, September 24, 1862, for the war. Transferred to Company H, 1st Regiment Tennessee Cavalry (Carter's), in November, 1862.

HAMPTON, DAVID, Private
Born in Washington County, Tennessee, and resided in Cocke County, Tennessee, where he was by occupation a farmer prior to enlisting at Dandridge, Tennessee, at age 20, September 24, 1862, for the war. Transferred to Company H, 1st Regiment Tennessee Cavalry (Carter's), in November, 1862.

HAMPTON, EZEKIEL, Private
Born in what later became Yancey County. Resided in Cocke County, Tennessee, where he was by occupation a farmer prior to enlisting at Dandridge, Tennessee, at age 33, September 24, 1862, for the war. Transferred to Company H, 1st Regiment Tennessee Cavalry (Carter's), in November, 1862.

HANCE, SAMUEL, Private
Born in Cocke County, Tennessee, where he resided as a farmer prior to enlisting at Dandridge, Tennessee, at age 33, September 24,

1862, for the war. Transferred to Company H, 1st Regiment Tennessee Cavalry (Carter's), in November, 1862.

HEDRICK, CHARLES H., Private
Born in Jefferson County, Tennessee, where he resided as a farmer prior to enlisting at Dandridge, Tennessee, at age 20, September 24, 1862, for the war. Transferred to Company H, 1st Regiment Tennessee Cavalry (Carter's), in November, 1862.

HEDRICK, LEONIDAS, Private
Born in Jefferson County, Tennessee, where he resided as a farmer prior to enlisting at Dandridge, Tennessee, at age 36, September 24, 1862, for the war. Transferred to Company H, 1st Regiment Tennessee Cavalry (Carter's), in November, 1862.

HENRY, CICERO, Private
Born in Cocke County, Tennessee, where he resided as a farmer prior to enlisting at Dandridge, Tennessee, at age 28, September 24, 1862, for the war. Transferred to Company H, 1st Regiment Tennessee Cavalry (Carter's), in November, 1862.

HENRY, PATRICK, Private
Born in Cocke County, Tennessee, where he resided as a farmer prior to enlisting at Dandridge, Tennessee, at age 31, September 24, 1862, for the war. Transferred to Company H, 1st Regiment Tennessee Cavalry (Carter's), in November, 1862.

HOLT, WILLIAM, Private
Born in Grainger County, Tennessee, and resided in Jefferson County, Tennessee, where he was by occupation a farmer prior to enlisting at Dandridge, Tennessee, at age 26, September 24, 1862, for the war. Transferred to Company H, 1st Regiment Tennessee Cavalry (Carter's), in November, 1862.

HOWELL, ISAAC B., Private
Born in Jefferson County, Tennessee, where he resided as a farmer prior to enlisting at Dandridge, Tennessee, at age 25, September 24, 1862, for the war. Transferred to Company H, 1st Regiment Tennessee Cavalry (Carter's), in November, 1862.

HOWELL, JOHN S., Private
Born in Grainger County, Tennessee, where he resided as a farmer prior to enlisting at Dandridge, Tennessee, at age 22, September 24, 1862, for the war. Transferred to Company H, 1st Regiment Tennessee Cavalry (Carter's), in November, 1862.

HUFFACRE, ALEX H., Private
Born in Knox County, Tennessee, where he resided as a farmer prior to enlisting at Dandridge, Tennessee, at age 17, September 24, 1862, for the war. Transferred to Company H, 1st Regiment Tennessee Cavalry (Carter's), in November, 1862.

HUTCHISON, JAMES H., Private
Born in Jefferson County, Tennessee, where he resided as a farmer prior to enlisting at Dandridge, Tennessee, at age 24, September 24, 1862, for the war. Transferred to Company H, 1st Regiment Tennessee Cavalry (Carter's), in November, 1862.

INMAN, ABRAM T., Private
Born in Jefferson County, Tennessee, where he resided as a farmer prior to enlisting at Dandridge, Tennessee, at age 27, September 24, 1862, for the war. Transferred to Company H, 1st Regiment Tennessee Cavalry (Carter's), in November, 1862.

INMAN, WILLIAM, Private
Born in Sevier County, Tennessee, and resided in Jefferson County, Tennessee, where he was by occupation a farmer prior to enlisting at Dandridge, Tennessee, at age 23, September 24, 1862, for the war. Transferred to Company H, 1st Regiment Tennessee Cavalry (Carter's), in November, 1862.

LANDRUM, RUFUS, Private
Born in Jefferson County, Tennessee, where he resided as a farmer prior to enlisting at Dandridge, Tennessee, at age 19, September 24, 1862, for the war. Transferred to Company H, 1st Regiment Tennessee Cavalry (Carter's), in November, 1862.

LANE, LEWIS, Private
Born in Cocke County, Tennessee, where he resided as a farmer prior to enlisting at Dandridge, Tennessee, at age 37, September 24, 1862, for the war. Transferred to Company H, 1st Regiment Tennessee Cavalry (Carter's), in November, 1862.

LAREMORE, JOSEPH C., Private
Born in Jefferson County, Tennessee, where he resided as a farmer prior to enlisting at Dandridge, Tennessee, at age 18, September 24, 1862, for the war. Transferred to Company H, 1st Regiment Tennessee Cavalry (Carter's), in November, 1862.

LEE, CLAY C., Private
Born in Grainger County, Tennessee, and resided in Jefferson County, Tennessee, where he was by occupation a farmer prior to enlisting at Dandridge, Tennessee, at age 24, September 24, 1862, for the war. Transferred to Company H, 1st Regiment Tennessee Cavalry (Carter's), in November, 1862.

LEE, WILLIAM L., Private
Born in Grainger County, Tennessee, and resided in Knox County, Tennessee, where he was by occupation a farmer prior to enlisting at Dandridge, Tennessee, at age 21, September 24, 1862, for the war. Transferred to Company H, 1st Regiment Tennessee Cavalry (Carter's), in November, 1862.

McPHADDEN, JOSEPH, Private
Born in Rutherford County and resided in Jefferson County, Tennessee, where he was by occupation a farmer prior to enlisting at Dandridge, Tennessee, at age 25, September 24, 1862, for the war. Transferred to Company H, 1st Regiment Tennessee Cavalry (Carter's), in November, 1862.

MANNING, CHRIST C., Private
Born in Cocke County, Tennessee, where he resided as a farmer prior to enlisting at Dandridge, Tennessee, at age 16, September 24, 1862, for the war. Transferred to Company H, 1st Regiment Tennessee Cavalry (Carter's), in November, 1862.

MOORE, ADOLPHUS, Private
Born in Burke County and resided in Cocke County, Tennessee, where he was by occupation a farmer prior to enlisting at Dandridge, Tennessee, at age 23, September 24, 1862, for the war. Transferred to Company H, 1st Regiment Tennessee Cavalry (Carter's), in November, 1862.

MOORE, PETER O., Private
Born in Washington County, Tennessee, and resided in Cocke County, Tennessee, where he was by occupation a farmer prior to enlisting at at Dandridge, Tennessee, at age 23, September 24, 1862, for the war. Transferred to Company H, 1st Regiment Tennessee Cavalry (Carter's), in November, 1862.

MORGAN, JAMES, Private
Born in York District, South Carolina, and resided in Cocke County, Tennessee, where he was by occupation as farmer prior to enlisting at Dandridge, Tennessee, at age 22, September 24, 1862, for the war. Transferred to Company H, 1st Regiment Tennessee Cavalry (Carter's), in November, 1862.

MOSS, ALEXANDER, Private
Born in Spartanburg District, South Carolina, and resided in Cocke County, Tennessee, where he was by occupation a farmer prior to enlisting at Dandridge, Tennessee, at age 24, September 24, 1862, for the war. Transferred to Company H, 1st Regiment Tennessee Cavalry (Carter's), in November, 1862.

MUNSEY, WILLIAM A., Private
Born in Giles County, Virginia, and resided in Jefferson County, Tennessee, where he was by occupation a farmer prior to enlisting at Dandridge, Tennessee, at age 28, September 24, 1862, for the war. Transferred to Company H, 1st Regiment Tennessee Cavalry (Carter's), in November, 1862.

NEFF, JOHN A., Private
Born in Shenandoah County, Virginia, and resided in Jefferson County, Tennessee, where he was by occupation a carpenter prior to enlisting at Dandridge, Tennessee, at age 28, September 24, 1862, for the war. Transferred to Company H, 1st Regiment Tennessee Cavalry (Carter's), in November, 1862.

NEWMAN, JASPER A., Private
Born in Jefferson County, Tennessee, where he resided as a farmer prior to enlisting at Dandridge, Tennessee, at age 31, September 24, 1862, for the war. Transferred to Company H, 1st Regiment Tennessee Cavalry (Carter's), in November, 1862.

NORTH, JAMES, Private
Born in what later became Marshall County, Alabama. Resided in Jefferson County, Tennessee, where he was by occupation a farmer prior to enlisting at Dandridge, Tennessee, at age 28, September 24, 1862, for the war. Transferred to Company H, 1st Regiment Tennessee Cavalry (Carter's), in November, 1862.

ODEL, FRANCIS M., Private
Born in Cocke County, Tennessee, and resided in Jefferson County, Tennessee, where he was by occupation a farmer prior to enlisting at Dandridge, Tennessee, at age 21, September 24, 1862, for the war. Transferred to Company H, 1st Regiment Tennessee Cavalry (Carter's), in November, 1862.

ODEL, JAMES P., Private
Born in Cocke County, Tennessee, and resided in Jefferson County, Tennessee, where he was by occupation a farmer prior to enlisting at Dandridge, Tennessee, at age 25, September 24, 1862, for the war. Transferred to Company H, 1st Regiment Tennessee Cavalry (Carter's), in November, 1862.

ODEL, LEWIS M., Private
Born in Cocke County, Tennessee, and resided in Jefferson County, Tennessee, where he was by occupation a farmer prior to enlisting at Dandridge, Tennessee, at age 20, September 24, 1862, for the war. Transferred to Company H, 1st Regiment Tennessee Cavalry (Carter's), in November, 1862.

PINION, JOEL, Private
Born in what later became Alexander County. Resided in Cocke County, Tennessee, where he was by occupation a farmer prior to enlisting at Dandridge, Tennessee, at age 26, September 24, 1862, for the war. Transferred to Company H, 1st Regiment Tennessee Cavalry (Carter's), in November, 1862.

PITTILLO, JAMES, Private
Born in Jefferson County, Tennessee, where he resided as a farmer prior to enlisting at Dandridge, Tennessee, at age 24, September 24, 1862, for the war. Transferred to Company H, 1st Regiment Tennessee Cavalry (Carter's), in November, 1862. [His surname may have been Pitillo.]

PITTILLO, SAMUEL, Private
Born in Jefferson County, Tennessee, where he resided as a farmer prior to enlisting at Dandridge, Tennessee, at age 18, September 24, 1862, for the war. Transferred to Company H, 1st Regiment Tennessee Cavalry (Carter's), in November, 1862. [His surname may have been Pitillo.]

QUAREL, NATHEN W., Private
Born in Jefferson County, Tennessee, where he resided as a farmer prior to enlisting at Dandridge, Tennessee, at age 24, September 24, 1862, for the war. Transferred to Company H, 1st Regiment Tennessee Cavalry (Carter's), in November, 1862.

QUARL, WILLIAM, Private
Born in Jefferson County, Tennessee, where he resided as a farmer prior to enlisting at Dandridge, Tennessee, at age 20, September 24, 1862, for the war. Reportedly transferred to Company H, 1st Regiment Tennessee Cavalry (Carter's), in November, 1862. However, his name does not appear in the records of that company.

ROACH, AGENAN, Private
Born in Grainger County, Tennessee, and resided in Jefferson County, Tennessee, where he was by occupation a farmer prior to enlisting at Dandridge, Tennessee, at age 34, September 24, 1862, for the war. Transferred to Company H, 1st Regiment Tennessee Cavalry (Carter's), in November, 1862. No further records.

SAMPELS, FIELDING S., Private
Born in Sevier County, Tennessee, and resided in Jefferson County, Tennessee, where he was by occupation a farmer prior to enlisting at Dandridge, Tennessee, at age 30, September 24, 1862, for the war. Transferred to Company H, 1st Regiment Tennessee Cavalry (Carter's), in November, 1862.

SARTIN, HENRY, Private

Born in Jefferson County, Tennessee, where he resided as a farmer prior to enlisting at Dandridge, Tennessee, at age 35, September 24, 1862, for the war. Transferred to Company H, 1st Regiment Tennessee Cavalry (Carter's), in November, 1862.

SARTIN, WILLIAM N., Private

Born in Jefferson County, Tennessee, where he resided as a farmer prior to enlisting at Dandridge, Tennessee, at age 33, September 24, 1862, for the war. Transferred to Company H or K, 1st Regiment Tennessee Cavalry (Carter's), in November, 1862. [His middle initial may have been A.]

SATTERFIELD, BENJAMIN C., Private

Born in Jefferson County, Tennessee, where he resided as a farmer prior to enlisting at Dandridge, Tennessee, at age 26, September 24, 1862, for the war. Transferred to Company H, 1st Regiment Tennessee Cavalry (Carter's), in November, 1862.

SCOTT, MARCUS, Private

Born in North Carolina and resided in Cocke County, Tennessee, where he was by occupation a farmer prior to enlisting at Dandridge, Tennessee, at age 29, September 24, 1862, for the war. Transferred to Company H, 1st Regiment Tennessee Cavalry (Carter's), in November, 1862.

SEAHORN, JACOB W., Private

Born in Jefferson County, Tennessee, where he resided as a farmer prior to enlisting at Dandridge, Tennessee, at age 21, September 24, 1862, for the war. Transferred to Company H, 1st Regiment Tennessee Cavalry (Carter's), in November, 1862. [His surname may have been Sehorn.]

SEAHORN, SAMUEL L., Private

Born in Jefferson County, Tennessee, where he resided as a farmer prior to enlisting at Dandridge, Tennessee, at age 20, September 24, 1862, for the war. Transferred to Company H, 1st Regiment Tennessee Cavalry (Carter's), in November, 1862. [His surname may have been Sehorn.]

SEAHORN, WILLIAM H., Private

Born in Jefferson County, Tennessee, where he resided as a farmer prior to enlisting at Dandridge, Tennessee, at age 30, September 24, 1862, for the war. Transferred to Company H, 1st Regiment Tennessee Cavalry (Carter's), in November, 1862. [His surname may have been Sehorn.]

SEBOLT, GEORGE W., Private

Born in Knox County, Tennessee, and resided in Jefferson County, Tennessee, where he was by occupation a brick mason prior to enlisting at Dandridge, Tennessee, at age 27, September 24, 1862, for the war. Transferred to Company H, 1st Regiment Tennessee Cavalry (Carter's), in November, 1862.

SHADDAN, JOSEPH T., Private

Born in Jefferson County, Tennessee, where he resided as a farmer prior to enlisting at Dandridge, Tennessee, at age 18, September 24, 1862, for the war. Transferred to Company H, 1st Regiment Tennessee Cavalry (Carter's), in November, 1862.

SOARD, JOHN, Private

Born in Knox County, Tennessee, and resided in Jefferson County, Tennessee, where he was by occupation a brick mason prior to enlisting at Dandridge, Tennessee, at age 34, September 24, 1862, for the war. Transferred to Company H, 1st Regiment Tennessee Cavalry (Carter's), in November, 1862.

STRANGE, WILLIAM H., Private

Born in Cocke County, Tennessee, where he resided as a farmer prior to enlisting at Dandridge, Tennessee, at age 19, September 24, 1862, for the war. Transferred to Company H, 1st Regiment Tennessee Cavalry (Carter's), in November, 1862.

TALLEY, BENJAMIN D., Private

Born in Jefferson County, Tennessee, where he resided as a farmer prior to enlisting at Dandridge, Tennessee, at age 29, September 24, 1862, for the war. Transferred to Company H, 1st Regiment Tennessee Cavalry (Carter's), in November, 1862.

TALLY, DANIEL F., Private

Born in Jefferson County, Tennessee, where he resided as a farmer prior to enlisting at Dandridge, Tennessee, at age 22, September 24, 1862, for the war. Transferred to Company H, 1st Regiment Tennessee Cavalry (Carter's), in November, 1862.

TALLY, DUDLEY C., Private

Born in Jefferson County, Tennessee, and resided in Cocke County, Tennessee, where he was by occupation a farmer prior to enlisting at Dandridge, Tennessee, at age 31, September 24, 1862, for the war. Transferred to Company H, 1st Regiment Tennessee Cavalry (Carter's), in November, 1862.

TAYLOR, HENRY, Private

Born in Cocke County, Tennessee, where he resided as a farmer prior to enlisting at Dandridge, Tennessee, at age 34, September 24, 1862, for the war. Transferred to Company H, 1st Regiment Tennessee Cavalry (Carter's), in November, 1862.

THOMAS, MABERY C., Private

Born in Cleveland County and resided in Jefferson County, Tennessee, where he was by occupation a farmer prior to enlisting at Dandridge, Tennessee, at age 17, September 24, 1862, for the war. Transferred to Company H, 1st Regiment Tennessee Cavalry (Carter's), in November, 1862.

TROUTMAN, JAMES W., Private

Born in Iredell County and enlisted in Jefferson County, Tennessee, where he was by occupation a farmer prior to enlisting at Dandridge, Tennessee, at age 21, September 24, 1862, for the war. Transferred to Company H, 1st Regiment Tennessee Cavalry (Carter's), in November, 1862.

WALKER, SAMUEL, Private

Born in Jefferson County, Tennessee, where he resided as a farmer prior to enlisting at Dandridge, Tennessee, at age 27, September 24, 1862, for the war. Transferred to Company H, 1st Regiment Tennessee Cavalry (Carter's), in November, 1862.

WALKER, THOMAS C., Private

Born in Jefferson County, Tennessee, where he resided as a farmer prior to enlisting at Dandridge, Tennessee, at age 24, September 24,

1862, for the war. Transferred to Company H, 1st Regiment Tennessee Cavalry (Carter's), in November, 1862.

WARD, JOSEPH K., Private
Born in Greenville District, South Carolina, and resided in Jefferson County, Tennessee, where he was by occupation a farmer prior to enlisting at Dandridge, Tennessee, at age 23, September 24, 1862, for the war. Transferred to Company H, 1st Regiment Tennessee Cavalry (Carter's), in November, 1862.

WELLING, DAVID, Private
Born in Sullivan County, Tennessee, and resided in Jefferson County, Tennessee, where he was by occupation a farmer prior to enlisting at Dandridge, Tennessee, at age 27, September 24, 1862, for the war. Transferred to Company H, 1st Regiment Tennessee Cavalry (Carter's), in November, 1862.

WHALIN, GARDNER J., Private
Born in Jefferson County, Tennessee, where he resided as a farmer prior to enlisting at Dandridge, Tennessee, at age 28, September 24, 1862, for the war. Transferred to Company H, 1st Regiment Tennessee Cavalry (Carter's), in November, 1862. [His surname may have been Whalen.]

WHALIN, RUSSEL B., Private
Born in Jefferson County, Tennessee, where he resided as a farmer prior to enlisting at Dandridge, Tennessee, at age 25, September 24, 1862, for the war. Transferred to Company H, 1st Regiment Tennessee Cavalry (Carter's), in November, 1862. [His surname may have been Whalen.]

WHALIN, SOLOMON, Private
Born in Jefferson County, Tennessee, where he resided as a farmer prior to enlisting at Dandridge, Tennessee, at age 21, September 24, 1862, for the war. Transferred to Company H, 1st Regiment Tennessee Cavalry (Carter's), in November, 1862. [His surname may have been Whalen.]

WRIGHT, POWELL H., Private
Born in Jefferson County, Tennessee, where he resided as a farmer prior to enlisting at Dandridge, Tennessee, at age 22, September 24, 1862, for the war. Transferred to Company H, 1st Regiment Tennessee Cavalry (Carter's), in November, 1862.

COMPANY H

This company was raised in Cherokee County, North Carolina, and Monroe County, Tennessee. It was organized at Coker Creek, Tennessee, March 5, 1863, and mustered into service on March 7, 1863.

The following roster was compiled in large part from company muster rolls dated March 5-June, 1863, and October 31, 1863-February, 1864. These are abstracted in the microfilm edition of the Compiled Service Records of Confederate Soldiers Who Served in Organizations from the State of North Carolina (Record Group 109, M270), National Archives, Washington, D.C. Other valuable information in the Compiled Service Records includes enlistment papers, pay vouchers, requisitions, letters of resignation, discharge certificates, and abstracts of medical and prisoner of war records.

Also utilized in this roster were *The War of the Rebellion: A Compilation of the Official Records of the Union and Confederate Armies*, the North Carolina Adjutant General's papers, state militia records, newspaper casualty lists and obituaries, wartime claims for bounty pay and allowances, postwar registers of claims for artificial limbs, Confederate pension applications filed with the states of North Carolina, Tennessee, and Florida, records of the North Carolina Confederate Soldiers' Home, and the 1860 and 1870 federal censuses of North Carolina and Tennessee. A search was made also for relevant letters, diaries, reminiscences, and other manuscripts in the Southern Historical Collection (University of North Carolina-Chapel Hill) and the Duke University Library Special Collections Department.

Among the secondary sources consulted were records of the North Carolina division of the United Daughters of the Confederacy, postwar rosters, regimental and county histories, marriage bond, will, and cemetery indexes, published and unpublished genealogies, biographical dictionaries, the North Carolina *County Heritage Book* series, the *Confederate Veteran*, Walter Clark's *Histories of the Several Regiments and Battalions from North Carolina in the Great War, 1861-'65*, and the North Carolina volume of the extended edition of *Confederate Military History*.

OFFICERS

CAPTAINS

LOUDERMILK, GARNER N.
Previously served as 2nd Lieutenant of Company B of this battalion. Elected Captain of this company on March 5, 1863. Reported present on March 7, 1863. Reported on detached service on April 30, 1863. Rejoined the company on or prior to June 30, 1863. Signature appears on a payment voucher dated July 11, 1863. Reported absent without leave from October 11, 1863, through February 29, 1864. Deserted to the enemy on an unspecified date. Took the Oath of Allegiance at Chattanooga, Tennessee, February 14, 1864. [His surname may have been Lowdermilk.]

AKIN, ROBERT A.
Previously served as Private in Company B of this battalion. Elected 1st Lieutenant of this company on March 5, 1863. Reported present through June 30, 1863. Reported on detached service on August 14, 1863. Reported absent without leave from September 15 through December 31, 1863, but was apparently acting under orders during at least part of that period. Returned to duty and evidently accounted satisfactorily for his absence. Reported present and in command of the company in January-February, 1864, and May 23, 1864. Wounded at Piedmont, Virginia, June 5, 1864. Wounded at or near Winchester, Virginia on August 13, 1864. Reported on medical furlough, probably due to wound, September 18, 1864. According to Clark's *Regiments* 4:118-119, he was promoted to Captain, presumably after September 18, 1864. No further records. Survived the war. [His surname may have been Aiken.]

LIEUTENANTS

HIBBERTS, JOHN, 3rd Lieutenant
Enlisted in Cherokee County on February 26, 1863, for the war. Mustered in as Private. Elected 3rd Lieutenant of this battalion on

March 5 or March 11, 1863. Reported present through June 30, 1863. Obtained a 24-hour leave on August 5, 1863, but failed to return to duty. Reported absent without leave from August 27, 1863, until February 24, 1864, when he was dropped from the company rolls for prolonged absence without leave.

LEDFORD, HIRAM, 1st Lieutenant
Born in Cherokee County. Resided in Cherokee County. Enlisted in Cherokee County at age 28, March 5, 1863, for the war. Mustered in as Private. Elected 2nd Lieutenant on March 5 or 11, 1863. Reported present through June 30, 1863, and in September-December, 1863. Reported absent without leave in January-February, 1864; he may have been with Colonel Thomas in western North Carolina at that time. Returned to duty with this company on an unspecified date. Name appears on a receipt for pay for February 1 through 29, 1864. Name appears on a receipt roll for payment dated August 20, 1864. Name appears on a special requisition for clothing dated September 1, 1864. Wounded in the leg and/or ankle and captured at Winchester, Virginia, September 19, 1864. Hospitalized at Winchester, September 24, 1864. Transferred to hospital at Baltimore, Maryland, where he arrived on November 10, 1864. Confined at Fort Delaware, Delaware, January 11, 1865. Paroled and transferred to City Point, Virginia, February 27, 1865, for exchange. Clark's *Regiments* 4: 119, reports that he was promoted to 1st Lieutenant, presumably subsequent to his return from prison and as a result of the supposed promotion of 1st Lt. Robert A. Akin to Captain. No further records.

NONCOMMISSIONED OFFICERS AND PRIVATES

ADAMS, JAMES, Private
Previously served as Private in Company A of this battalion. Transferred to this company on April 1, 1863. No further records.

ADAMS, NELSON, Private
Resided in Cherokee County. Enlisted in Cherokee County at about age 18, February 23, 1863 for the war. Reported on detail with Company E of this battalion from March 5 through June 30, 1863, and in September, 1863. Deserted at Carter's Station, Tennessee, September 18, 1863.

ALLEN, DAVID L. "WARREN," Private
Born in Towns County, Georgia, in 1829. Enlisted in Cherokee County on February 13, 1863, for the war. Allowed to return home for clothing on March 5, 1863, with orders to report to Strawberry Plains, Tennessee. Reported on detail working on a forge in Cherokee County from March 5 through June 30, 1863, and from October 31, 1863, through February 29, 1864. No further records. Survived the war.

BARTON, ELIJAH, Private
Enlisted in Cherokee County on February 19, 1863, for the war. Reported present on March 7, 1863. Transferred to Company I, Infantry Regiment of this legion, prior to April 30, 1863.

BOWERS, JASPER J., Private
Enlisted in Cherokee County on March 5, 1863, for the war. Reported present on March 7, 1863. No further records. [May have served also as Private in Company F, 29th Regiment N.C. Troops.]

BRIDGES, CROWDER, Private
Enlisted in Cherokee County on February 23, 1863, for the war. Reported on detached duty with Company E of this battalion from March 5 through April 30, 1863. No further records.

BRIDGES, MARTIN C., Private
Previously served as Private in Company E of this battalion. Transferred to this company in May-June, 1863. Reported present on June 30, 1863. Discharged on August 15, 1863, by reason of being under age. Discharge certificate gives his age as 17. [He had probably enlisted in this company on February 23, 1863, one day before he enlisted in Company E. His enlistment and service in Company E therefore would have been illegal, requiring his transfer to this company.]

BROWN, SAMUEL, Private
Enlisted in Monroe County, Tennessee, March 5, 1863, for the war. Reported present on March 7, 1863. No further records. [A receipt roll for clothing dated October 16, 1864, lists the name S. P. Brown; he may have been this man.]

BRYANT, JOHNSON A., Private
Enlisted in Monroe County, Tennessee, February 15, 1863, for the war. Mustered in as Corporal. Reported present through June 30, 1863. Reduced to ranks prior to October 31, 1863. Reported on detail with Company A, 3rd Regiment Confederate Engineers, from August 4, 1863, through February 29, 1864. Records of that company indicate that he was in a hospital in Georgia from September 25, 1863-August 31, 1864. No further records.

BUCHANAN, R., Private
Enlisted in Monroe County, Tennessee, March 5, 1863, for the war. Reported present on March 7, 1863. No further records.

CANNON, ELI, Private
Enlisted in Monroe County, Tennessee, March 5, 1863, for the war. Reported absent without leave from April 5 through 30, 1863. No further records.

CARVER, REUBEN, Private
Previously served as Private in Company K, 5th Regiment Tennessee Cavalry (McKenzie's). Transferred to this company on November 22, 1863. Reported present in January-February, 1864. Name appears on a receipt roll for clothing dated September 1, 1864. No further records.

COALMAN, CALVIN, Private
Enlisted in Monroe County, Tennessee, March 5, 1863, for the war. Reported absent without leave from April 6 through 30, 1863. No further records. [His surname may have been Coleman.]

CUNNINGHAM, CALVIN C., Sergeant
Resided in Monroe County, Tennessee, and was by occupation a farmer prior to enlisting in Cherokee County, North Carolina, at about age 36, February 13, 1863, for the war. Mustered in as Private. Reported present through June 30, 1863. Promoted to Sergeant in November-December, 1863. Reported present from October 31, 1863, through February 29, 1864. Name appears on receipt rolls for clothing dated June 22 and September 1, 1864. No further records. [His surname may have been Cuningham.]

CUNNINGHAM, CHRISTOPHER, Private
Resided in Monroe County, Tennessee, and was by occupation a laborer prior to enlisting in Cherokee County, North Carolina, at about age 23, February 20, 1863, for the war. Mustered in as Corporal. Reported present through June 30, 1863. Reduced to ranks in November-December, 1863. Reported absent without leave from August 31, 1863, through February 29, 1864. No further records.

CUNNINGHAM, MATHEW, Private
Resided in Monroe County, Tennessee, and was by occupation a farmer prior to enlisting in Monroe County at age 33, March 5, 1863, for the war. Reported present through June 30, 1863. Reported present from October 31, 1863, through February 29, 1864. Captured at Piedmont, Virginia, June 5, 1864. Sent to Staunton, Virginia, on or prior to June 8, 1864. Confined at Camp Morton, Indianapolis, Indiana, June 21, 1864. Died at Camp Morton on February 10, 1865, of "inflammation of the lungs."

CUNNINGHAM, THOMAS M., 1st Sergeant
Resided in Monroe County, Tennessee, and was by occupation a laborer prior to enlisting in Cherokee County, North Carolina, at about age 21, February 26, 1863, for the war. Mustered in as Sergeant. Reported present through June 30, 1863. Promoted to 1st Sergeant on September 1, 1863. Reported present from October 31, 1863, through February 29, 1864. Name appears on receipt rolls for clothing dated June 22, September 1, and September 18, 1864. No further records.

DEHART, JAMES, Private
Resided in Monroe County, Tennessee, and was by occupation a laborer prior to enlisting in Monroe County at age 33, March 5, 1863, for the war. Reported present through June 30, 1863. No further records. [His surname may have been Dehort.]

DEHART, WILLIAM J., Private
Resided in Monroe County, Tennessee, and was by occupation a laborer prior to enlisting in Monroe County at age 21, March 5, 1863, for the war. Reported present through April 30, 1863. Reported sick in hospital June 10-30, 1863. No further records. [His surname may have been Dehort.]

DOBKINS, WILLIAM, Sergeant
Previously served as Private in Company B of this battalion. Promoted to Sergeant and transferred to this company on March 5, 1863. Reported present through April 30, 1863. Reported absent without leave on May 25, 1863. Survived the war. [Name appears with the rank of Private on a receipt roll for clothing dated June 21, 1864, for "Company C." He may have transferred to Company C of this battalion, of the Infantry Regiment of this legion, or of the Indian Battalion.]

DODSON, AMBER, Private
Enlisted in Monroe County, Tennessee, March 5, 1863, for the war. Reported present through June 30, 1863. No further records.

EALY, ROBERT, Private
Previously served as Private in Company A of this battalion. Transferred to this company on April 1, 1863. No further records.

EDWARDS, OSSIMY, Private
Enlisted in Monroe County, Tennessee, March 1, 1863, for the war. Reported present through April 30, 1863. Furloughed home sick on June 16, 1863. Reported absent without leave from August 31, 1863, through February 29, 1864. No further records.

ELLIS, CALVIN, Private
Born in Iredell County. Resided in Cherokee County and was by occupation a farmer prior to enlisting in Cherokee County at about age 31, February 19, 1863, for the war. Permitted to go home for clothing on March 5, 1863, with orders to report at Strawberry Plains, Tennessee. Later reported on duty in Cherokee County working in a forge from March 5, 1863, through February 29, 1864. No further records.

FARMER, ENOCH, Private
Born in Yadkin County. Resided in Cherokee County and was by occupation a carpenter prior to enlisting in Cherokee County at about age 36, February 23, 1863, for the war. Permitted to go home for clothing on March 5, 1863, with orders to report at Strawberry Plains, Tennessee. No further records.

FARMER, MADISON, Private
Enlisted in Cherokee County on February 23, 1863, for the war. Permitted to go home for clothing on March 5, 1863, with orders to report at Strawberry Plains, Tennessee. No further records.

FORRISTER, JOHN C., Private
Previously served as Private in Company I, Infantry Regiment of this legion. Transferred to this company on March 1, 1863. Reported present or accounted for through June 30, 1863. Reported absent without leave from August 31, 1863, through February 29, 1864. No further records. [His surname may have been Forester or Farrister.]

GARLAND, JESSE, Private
Enlisted in Cherokee County on February 15, 1863, for the war. Mustered in as Corporal. Reported present in March-April, 1863. Detailed to Cherokee County "for guns" on June 20, 1863. Reported absent without leave from July 8 through October 31, 1863. Reduced to ranks on or prior to October 31, 1863. Name appears on a roll of Confederate deserters which states that he took the Oath of Allegiance at Chattanooga, Tennessee, May 21, 1865.

GOODEN, MOSES, Private
Enlisted in Cherokee County on February 13, 1863, for the war. Permitted to go home for clothing on March 5, 1863, with orders to report at Strawberry Plains, Tennessee. No further records.

GOWIN, J. W., Private
Enlisted in Monroe County, Tennessee, March 5, 1863, for the war. Reported present on March 7, 1863. No further records.

GRAY, GEORGE W., Private
Enlisted in Cherokee County on March 5, 1863, for the war. Permitted to go home for clothing on March 5, 1863, with orders to report at Strawberry Plains, Tennessee. Reported at home sick on surgeon's certificate in May-June, 1863, to date from March 5, 1863.

Failed to return duty and listed as absent without leave in November-December, 1863.

GREEN, GEORGE W., Private

Enlisted in Cherokee County on February 24, 1863, for the war. Permitted to go home for clothing on March 5, 1863, with orders to report at Strawberry Plains, Tennessee. Reported on detail with Capt. Stephen Whitaker of Company E of this battalion from March 5 through June 30, 1863. No further records. [He may have been the same man as Pvt. George W. Green of Company G of this battalion and of Companies I and D of the Infantry Regiment of this legion.]

HALL, JOSHUA M., Private

Enlisted in Monroe County, Tennessee, March 5, 1863, for the war. Reported present through June 30, 1863. Reported absent without leave from August 31, 1863, through February 29, 1864. No further records.

HAMBY, RUBIN, Private

Enlisted in Monroe County, Tennessee, March 5, 1863, for the war. Reported absent without leave from June 4 through 30, 1863. No further records.

HAMPTON, HARVEY H., Private

Previously served as Private in Company I, Infantry Regiment of this legion. Transferred to this company on July 1, 1863. Reported absent without leave from July 10, 1863, through February 29, 1864. Went over to the enemy on an unspecified date. Took the Oath of Allegiance at Chattanooga, Tennessee, April 13, 1864. [His first name or his middle name may have been Henry.]

HARRIS, BENJAMIN W., Corporal

Previously served as Private in Company B of this battalion. Transferred to this company in March-April, 1863. Mustered in as Private. Reported present in May-June, 1863. Promoted to Corporal on September 1, 1863. Reported present in November-December, 1863. Reported absent without leave on February 7, 1864. Went over to the enemy. Took the Oath of Allegiance at Chattanooga, Tennessee, February 14, 1864.

HARRIS, WILLIAM C., Private

Previously served as Private in Company B of this battalion. Transferred to this company in March-April, 1863. Reported present in May-June, 1863. Reported absent without leave from July 10, 1863, through February 29, 1864. No further records.

HAWKINS, MARTIN, Private

Born in Hall County, Georgia. Resided in Cherokee County, North Carolina, and was by occupation a farmer prior to enlisting in Cherokee County at about age 30, February 21, 1863, for the war. Reported absent without leave on March 27, 1863. Name appears on a receipt roll for clothing dated November 25, 1863. Reported as having rejoined the company on January 14, 1864. Reported absent without leave on February 10, 1864. No further records. Survived the war.

HAWKINS, NEWTON, Private

Born in Hall County, Georgia. Resided in Cherokee County, North Carolina, where he was by occupation a farmer prior to enlisting in Cherokee County at age 28, March 2, 1863, for the war. Permitted to go home for clothing on March 5, 1863, with orders to report at Strawberry Plains, Tennessee. Failed to return to duty and was reported absent without leave on April 30, 1863.

HEFFNER, JOHN, Private

Enlisted in Cherokee County on February 13, 1863, for the war. Reported present until June 4, 1863, when he was reported absent without leave. Returned to duty on June 27, 1863. Reported absent without leave from August 31, 1863, through February 29, 1864. No further records.

HIBBERT, CORNELIUS, Private

Previously served as Private in Company B of this battalion. Transferred to this company on March 1 or April 1, 1863. Reported present through June, 1863, and in September, 1863-February, 1864. Captured at Winchester, Virginia, September 19, 1864. Sent to Harpers Ferry, West Virginia. Transferred to Point Lookout, Maryland on September 23, 1864. Arrived at Point Lookout on September 26, 1864. Died at Point Lookout on February 14, 1865, of "pneumonia." [His surname may have been Hibberts.]

HOOPER, JAMES W., Private

Previously served as Private in Company B of this battalion. Transferred to this company on March 1 or April 1, 1863. Mustered in as Private. Promoted to 1st Sergeant on April 23, 1863. Reported present through June 30, 1863. Reported absent without leave from August 31, 1863, through February 29, 1864. Reduced to ranks in November-December, 1863. No further records. [His first name may have been John.]

HUGHES, JOHN E., Private

Enlisted in Monroe County, Tennessee, March 1, 1863, for the war. Reported present on March 7, 1863. No further records.

IRONS, JAMES, Private

Enlisted in Monroe County, Tennessee, March 5, 1863, for the war. Reported present on March 7, 1863. Reported absent without leave from April 5 through 30, 1863. No further records.

JAMES, THOMAS, Private

Enlisted in Cherokee County on March 3, 1862, for the war. Reported present through March 7, 1863. Transferred to Company A of this battalion on April 1, 1863.

JOHNSON, JOHN, Private

Previously served as Private in Company I, Infantry Regiment of this legion. Transferred to this company on March 1, 1863. Reported on detached duty with Capt. Garner N. Loudermilk of this company from April 12 through 30, 1863. Rejoined the company on or prior to June 30, 1863. Promoted to Corporal on September 1, 1863. Reported present in September-October, 1863. Reduced to ranks in November-December, 1863. Reported present in November, 1863-February, 1864. No further records.

KICHERSIDE, THOMAS O., Private

Enlisted in Cherokee County on February 18, 1863, for the war. Reported on detail with Company E of this battalion from March 5 through June 30, 1863. Reported absent sick in Cherokee County,

September-December, 1863; according to the January-February, 1864, muster for Company E, however, he deserted at Loudon, Tennessee, July 6, 1863.

KING, GEORGE H., Private
Born in Buncombe County. Resided in Cherokee County and was by occupation a farmer prior to enlisting in Cherokee County at age 37, March 5, 1863, for the war. Reported present in May-June, 1863. Reported absent without leave from September 20, 1863, through February 29, 1864. No further records.

KIRKLAND, JOHNSON C., Musician
Previously served as Private in Company B of this battalion. Appointed Musician (Drummer) and transferred to this company on March 5, 1863. Detailed to serve in Company B on March 23, 1863. Rejoined this company on July 25, 1863, following a period of absence without leave from Company B. Reported present through February 29, 1864. Deserted to the enemy on an unspecified date. Took the Oath of Allegiance at Chattanooga, Tennessee, May 21, 1865. [See his Tennessee pension application No. 4598.]

LAND, ISAAC S., Private
Resided in Monroe County, Tennessee, and was by occupation a farmer prior to enlisting in Monroe County at about age 27, March 5, 1863, for the war. Reported present through June 30, 1863. Reported absent without leave from August 31, 1863, through February 29, 1864. No further records.

LAND, JAMES N., Private
Resided in Monroe County, Tennessee, and was by occupation a laborer prior to enlisting in Monroe County at about age 24, March 5, 1863, for the war. Reported present through June 30, 1863. Reported absent without leave from August 31, 1863, through February 29, 1864. No further records.

LAND, JOHN, Private
Resided in Monroe County, Tennessee, and was by occupation a farmer prior to enlisting in Monroe County at about age 27, March 5, 1863, for the war. Reported present through April 30, 1863. Reported absent sick at home from June 15 through October 31, 1863. Listed as absent without leave from November, 1863, through February, 1864. No further records.

LEDFORD, ALEXANDER R., Private
Previously served as Private in Company G, 39th Regiment N.C. Troops. Transferred to this company on or about July 23, 1863. Mustered in as Musician (Fifer). Reported absent without leave from October 11 through December 31, 1863. Reduced to ranks in November-December, 1863. No further records. Survived the war. [Contrary to 10:165 of this series, he was transferred from the 39th Regiment to this company rather than to Company H, Infantry Regiment of this legion.]

LEDFORD, B. R., _____
North Carolina pension records indicate that he served in this company.

LEDFORD, JAMES M., Private
Previously served as Private in Company B of this battalion. Transferred to this company on March 5, 1863, and was elected Sergeant the same date. Reported present through June 30, 1863. Reported absent without leave on August 31, 1863. Reduced to ranks in November-December, 1863. Reported absent without leave through February 29, 1864. No further records.

LEDFORD, JEFFERSON R., Private
Enlisted in Monroe County, Tennessee, March 5, 1863, for the war. Reported present through June 30, 1863. No further records.

LEDFORD, RUSSEL, Private
Enlisted in Cherokee County on May 5, 1863, for the war. Detailed to attend government stock on May 10, 1863. No further records. [A company muster roll dated May-June, 1863, states that he was transferred from "Capt. Morris co May 5." Company E, 64th Regiment N.C. Troops, was under the captaincy of Beverly T. Morris, but there is no other evidence that Pvt. Ledford served in that company.]

LORANCE, JAMES P., Private
Previously served as Private in Company B of this battalion. Transferred to this company on March 5 or April 1, 1863. Mustered in as Musician (Fifer). Reported present through June 30, 1863. Reported absent without leave from July 20 through December 31, 1863. Reduced to ranks prior to December 31, 1863. Went over to the enemy on an unknown date. Took the Oath of Allegiance at Knoxville, Tennessee on January 23, 1864.

LORANCE, JOSEPH, Private
Previously served as Private in Company B of this battalion. Transferred to this company on either March 1 or April 1, 1863, although Company H records report him as on detached service with Company B in March-April. Reported present in May-June, 1863. Reported absent without leave from August 31, 1863, through February 29, 1864. No further records.

LOUDERMILK, GEORGE W., Corporal
Previously served as Private in Company I, Infantry Regiment of this legion. Transferred to this company on March 1, 1863. Reported on detached service with Capt. Garner N. Loudermilk of this company in Cherokee County, April 12-30, 1863. Rejoined the company on or prior to June 30, 1863. Promoted to Corporal in July-August, 1863. Reported killed in battle at Limestone Bridge, Tennessee, September 1, 1863. [His surname may have been Laudermilk. His date of death may have been September 8, 1863, as this legion fought at Limestone Bridge on that date.]

LOUDERMILK, HUGH W., Private
Previously served as Corporal in Company B of this battalion. Transferred to this company on March 1 or April 1, 1863, although Company H records report him as on detached service with Company B in March-April. Mustered in as Private. Reported on surgeon's furlough from hospital from June 20 through 30 and from July 8 until October 31, 1863. He was later variously reported as absent without leave from August 31through December 31, 1863, or from July 10, 1863 to February 29, 1864. No further records. Survived the war. [His surname may have been Lowdermilk.]

LOUDERMILK, MADISON M., Private
Previously served as Musician (Fifer) in Company I, Infantry Regiment of this legion. Transferred to this company on March 1, 1863. Mustered in as Private. Reported present through June 30, 1863.

Promoted to Sergeant on May 29, 1863. Reported absent without leave from August 31 through December 31, 1863. Reduced to ranks in November-December, 1863. Deserted to the enemy on an unspecified date. Took the Oath of Allegiance at Chattanooga, Tennessee, February 14, 1864. [His surname may have been Laudermilk.]

McALISTER, FRANKLIN, Private

Enlisted in Monroe County, Tennessee, March 5, 1863, for the war. Reported present on March 7, 1863. No further records.

McCLAIN, G. A., Private

Name appears on a receipt roll for clothing dated October 16, 1864, as serving in Company H of this legion; he may have served in this company or in Company H, Infantry Regiment of this legion. He may have been the same man as George A. McClane, who served earlier in 1st Company D of this battalion.

McCORMICK, WILLIAM, Private

Resided at Covington, Kentucky, and enlisted in Monroe County, Tennessee, March 5, 1863, for the war. Reported present through March 7, 1863. Reported sick in hospital at Strawberry Plains, Tennessee, March 17-April 30, 1863. Reported present in May-June, 1863. Took the Oath of Allegiance at Charleston, South Carolina, May 8, 1865. No further records.

McMILLEN, WILLIAM M., Private

Enlisted in Monroe County, Tennessee, March 5, 1863, for the war. Reported present through June 30, 1863. No further records. [His surname may have been McMillan. May have served previously as Private in Company F, 39th Regiment N.C. Troops, in which case he enlisted illegally in this company while absent without leave. Contrary to 10:161 of this series, he served in this company rather than Company A of this battalion.]

MARR, WILLIAM, Private

Resided in Cherokee County and was by occupation a farmer prior to enlisting in Cherokee County at about age 46, February 19, 1863, for the war. Reported present through June 30, 1863, and in September, 1863-February, 1864. No further records. [May have served previously as Private in Company H, 39th Regiment N.C. Troops.]

MASHBURN, CALAWAY, Private

Resided in Cherokee County where he enlisted on February 15, 1863, for the war. Reported present through June 30, 1863, and in September-December, 1863. Reported absent without leave on February 10, 1864. Name appears on receipt rolls for clothing dated June 22 and September 1, 1864. Took the Oath of Allegiance at Chattanooga, Tennessee, May 21, 1865. [His given name may have been Calloway.]

MICHAEL, DAVID, Private

Enlisted in Monroe County, Tennessee, March 5, 1863, for the war. Reported present through April 30, 1863. No further records.

MILES, JOHN H., 1st Sergeant

Previously served as Corporal in Company B of this battalion. Transferred to this company on March 5, 1863. Mustered in as 1st Sergeant. Died at Zollicoffer, Tennessee, April 20, 1863. Cause of death not reported.

MONDAY, JAMES C., Private

Enlisted in Cherokee County on February 10, 1863, for the war. Permitted to go home for clothing on March 5, 1863, with orders to report at Strawberry Plains, Tennessee. Reported on detached duty working in a forge in Cherokee County from March 5 through June 30, 1863. No further records.

MONTGOMERY, JOHN, Private

Born in Hall County, Georgia, where he resided as a farmer prior to enlisting in Cherokee County, North Carolina, at age18, September 20, 1862, for the war. Reported present in November, 1862-June, 1863. Reported absent sick from July 9 through December 31, 1863. Returned to duty prior to February 29, 1864. No further records.

MORGAN, HENRY, Private

Previously served as Private in Company B of this battalion. Transferred to this company on April 1, 1863. Reported present through June 30, 1863. Reported absent without leave from August 31, 1863, through February 29, 1864. No further records.

MORRIS, WILLIAM S., Private

Enlisted in Cherokee County on February 19, 1863, for the war. Permitted to go home for clothing on March 5, 1863, with orders to report at Strawberry Plains, Tennessee. No further records.

NEWMAN, JAMES M., Private

Enlisted in Cherokee County on February 15, 1863, for the war. Reported present through June 30, 1863. Reported absent without leave from August 31, 1863, through February 29, 1864. No further records.

NORTH, JOHN C., Private

Resided in Monroe County, Tennessee, and was by occupation a laborer prior to enlisting in Monroe County at about age 22, February 11, 1863, for the war. Reported present through March 7, 1863. Transferred or was placed on detached service with Company A of this battalion, March 7, 1863. Transferred back or returned to this company subsequent to April 30, 1863. Hospitalized at Greeneville, Tennessee, May 15, 1863. Reported absent without leave from August 31, 1863, through February 29, 1864. No further records.

ORTON, JAMES, Private

Enlisted in Monroe County, Tennessee, February 11, 1863, for the war. Reported present through March 7, 1863. No further records. [He may have been the same man as Pvt. James Orton of Company B of this battalion.]

PARKER, ALEXANDER, Private

Born in Macon County. Resided in Cherokee County and was by occupation a farmer prior to enlisting in Cherokee County at about age 35, February 19, 1863, for the war. Reported present through April 30, 1863. Reported absent without leave from June 4, 1863, through February 29, 1864. No further records. Survived the war.

PAYNE, ALEXANDER, Private

Enlisted in Cherokee County on June 23, 1863, for the war. Reported present through June 30, 1863. Deserted at Carter's Depot, Tennessee, September 22, 1863.

PAYNE, JEFFERSON, Private
Enlisted at Loudon, Tennessee, July 25, 1863, for the war. Deserted at Carter's Depot, Tennessee, September 22, 1863.

PIRKINS, DAVID J., Private
Enlisted in Company B of this battalion on March 6, 1863. Enlisted illegally in this company in Monroe County, Tennessee, March 7, 1863. Ordered to report to Company B prior to April 30, 1863.

POSTELL, JACOB, Private
Enlisted in Cherokee County at age 36, February 15, 1863, for the war. Mustered in as Corporal. Reported present, March 5-April 30, 1863. Put on medical furlough on June 10, 1863. Reported absent without leave from July 10, 1863, to February 29, 1864, and reduced to ranks in November-December, 1863. No further records. Survived the war.

PRINCE, JOHN, Private
Born in Polk County, Tennessee. Resided in Cherokee County, North Carolina, and was by occupation a farmer prior to enlisting in Cherokee County at about age 27, February 19, 1863, for the war. Permitted to go home for clothing on March 5, 1863, with orders to report at Strawberry Plains, Tennessee. Detailed to serve in Company E of this battalion on the same date. [He may have enlisted illegally in Company E before he was detailed from this company to serve in it, as he is reported present in the muster roll for Company E on February 28, 1863.]

QUINN, MARSHELL, Private
Enlisted in Monroe County, Tennessee, March 5, 1863, for the war. Reported present on March 7, 1863. No further records.

RAY, WILLIAM, Private
Enlisted at Lenoir's Station, Tennessee, July 1, 1863, for the war. Reported absent without leave from September 12, 1863, through February 29, 1864. No further records.

RICH, JAMES M., Private
Enlisted in Cherokee County on February 15, 1863, for the war. Mustered in as Sergeant. Reported present through April 30, 1863. Furloughed home from hospital on June 11, 1863. Reported absent without leave from July 10 or August 31, 1863, through February 29, 1864. Reduced to ranks in November-December, 1863. No further records.

RIDLEY, J. N., _____
A receipt roll for clothing lists him as a member of "Co H," Thomas' Legion. He probably served either in this company or in Company H, Infantry Regiment of this legion.

ROGERS, MITCHELL M., Private
Resided in Cherokee County where he enlisted on February 19, 1863, for the war. Furloughed home to obtain clothing on March 5, 1863. Reported absent without leave on April 6, 1863. Apprehended by Confederate authorities on an unknown date. Returned to duty on June 20, 1863. Reported absent without leave on August 31, 1863. Went over to the enemy on an unspecified date. Sent to Nashville, Tennessee. Transferred to Louisville, Kentucky, where he arrived on December 24, 1863. Released at Louisville on December 25, 1863, after taking the Oath of Allegiance. [See Account of Sgt. Maj. C. F. Walker, Walker's Battalion, "For Expenses incurred in apprehending and delivering" Rogers and other deserters from Walker's Battalion, August 13, 1863, Record Group 109, Miscellaneous Records: Manuscripts: 1861-1865, Entry 183, Box 19, Item 1951, National Archives.]

ROSS, GEORGE H., Private
Resided in Polk County, Tennessee. Enlisted in Monroe County, Tennessee, at about age 20, February 17, 1863, for the war. Reported present through June 30, 1863. Reported on detached service with a Lieutenant Green from September 10 through October 31, 1863. Returned to duty on or prior to December 31, 1863. Reported present in January-February, 1864. Hospitalized at Winchester, Virginia, August 3, 1864, with dysentery. Hospitalized at Charlottesville, Virginia, September 1, 1864. Furloughed from hospital on November 8, 1864. Deserted to the enemy in Charlotte County, Virginia, at an unknown date. Sent to Knoxville, Tennessee. Released at Knoxville on March 23, 1865, after taking the Oath of Allegiance. [Federal Provost Marshal records report that he deserted on August 12, 1864, but this is evidently erroneous.]

ROY, JONATHAN, Private
Resided in Monroe County, Tennessee, and was by occupation a farmer prior to enlisting in Monroe County at about age 33, March 5, 1863, for the war. Furloughed home to obtain clothing on the same date with orders to report to Strawberry Plains, Tennessee. Reported absent without leave on March 12, 1863. No further records.

ROY, JOSEPH, Private
Resided in Monroe County, Tennessee, and was by occupation a farmer prior to enlisting in Monroe County at about age 36, March 5, 1863, for the war. Furloughed home to obtain clothing on the same date with orders to report to Strawberry Plains, Tennessee. Reported to duty on an unknown date. Detailed with Capt. Garner N. Loudermilk of this company to go to Cherokee County, North Carolina, after absent enlisted men. Reported absent without leave on March 12, 1863. No further records.

SCARBOROUGH, HUGH, Private
Enlisted in Monroe County, Tennessee, March 5, 1863, for the war. Enlisted in Company B of this battalion on March 6, 1863, and never returned to this company.

SHEARER, HENRY C., Private
Resided in Cherokee County. Enlisted in Cherokee County at about age 18, February 23, 1863, for the war. Enlisted illegally in Company E of this battalion on February 24, 1863. Permitted to go home for clothing on March 5, 1863, with orders to report at Strawberry Plains, Tennessee. Reported on duty with Company E of this battalion from March 5 through June 30, 1863. [His surname may have been Sherrer.]

SHULER, JOHN F., Private
Previously served as Private in Company F, 29th Regiment N.C. Troops. Either transferred to this company on March 1, 1863, or enlisted illegally in this company on that date, while a deserter from the 29th Regiment. Reported present through June 30, 1863. Reported on detail with an engineer company from August 4, 1863, through February, 1864. Federal Provost Marshal records indicate that he was serving with Company C, Indian Battalion, when he was captured in Jackson County on February 2, 1864.

SIMS, JOSEPH, Private

Enlisted in Monroe County, Tennessee, March 5, 1863, for the war. Reported present through June 30, 1863, and in September, 1863-February, 1864. Admitted to hospital at Charlottsville, Virginia, with acute diarrhea on June 12, 1864. Returned to duty on June 17, 1864. Name appears on receipt rolls for clothing dated June 22 and September 1, 1864. No further records. [His medical records are misfiled in the National Archives Compiled Service Record for Pvt. Jackson Sims of Company C of this battalion.]

SPURRLAND, DANIEL E. L., Private

Born in Fentress County, Tennessee, and was by occupation a farmer prior to enlisting in Monroe County, Tennessee, at about age 22, March 5, 1863, for the war. Hospitalized at Strawberry Plains, Tennessee, prior to March 31, 1863. Reported sick in hospital at Strawberry Plains on April 30, 1863. Discharged at Loudon, Tennessee, May 27, 1863, by reason of "pulmonary consumption." [His surname may have been Spurlin.]

SPURRLAND, HICKS, Private

Enlisted in Monroe County, Tennessee, March 5, 1863, for the war. Reported present through June 30, 1863. No further records. [His surname may have been Spurlin.]

STILES, JAMES, Private

Enlisted in Cherokee County on February 14, 1863, for the war. Permitted to go home for clothing on March 5, 1863, with orders to report at Strawberry Plains, Tennessee. Reported on detail in Cherokee County working in a forge from March 5, 1863, through February 29, 1864. No further records. [May have served previously as Private in Company A, 29th Regiment N.C. Troops.]

STILES, JOHN L., Private

Enlisted in Cherokee County on February 23, 1863, for the war. Reported present on March 7, 1863. Reported absent without leave from March 27 through April 30, 1863. No further records. Survived the war.

STOW, WILLIAM H., Private

Enlisted in Cherokee County on February 23, 1863, for the war. Reported present on March 7, 1863. Reported absent without leave from March 27 through April 30, 1863. Returned to duty prior to June 30, 1863. No further records.

TAYLOR, ABIGAH, Private

Enlisted in Cherokee County on February 14, 1863, for the war. Permitted to go home for clothing on March 5, 1863, with orders to report at Strawberry Plains, Tennessee. Detailed to work in forge in Cherokee County from March 5, 1863, through February 29, 1864. No further records. Survived the war. [His given name may have been Abijah or Abiyah.]

TAYLOR, ALBERT, Private

Enlisted in Cherokee County on February 27, 1863, for the war. Reported present through February 27, 1863. Reported absent without leave from March 27 through April 30, 1863. No further records.

TAYLOR, JESSE, Private

Resided in Cherokee County where he enlisted on March 2, 1863, for the war. Reported absent without leave on March 27, 1863. Returned to duty on June 20, 1863. May have deserted again, as his name is not on company muster rolls for September-December, 1863, but it does appear on a receipt roll for clothing dated November 25, 1863. Returned to duty on January 14, 1864. Reported absent without leave on February 10, 1864. Name appears on receipt rolls for clothing dated September 1 and September 18, 1864. Went over to the enemy on an unspecified date. Sent to Chattanooga, Tennessee, where he took the Oath of Allegiance on March 15, 1865. Transferred to Louisville, Kentucky. Discharged from Louisville on March 21, 1865, with instructions to remain north of the Ohio River for the remainder of the war. [See Account of Sgt. Maj. C. F. Walker, Walker's Battalion, "For Expenses incurred in apprehending and delivering" Taylor and other deserters from Walker's Battalion, August 13, 1863, Record Group 109, Miscellaneous Records: Manuscripts: 1861-1865, Entry 183, Box 19, Item 1951, National Archives. North Carolina pension records indicate that he was wounded in the stomach at Winchester, Virginia, presumably on September 19, 1864.]

TAYLOR, MONROE, Private

Born in Tennessee. Enlisted in Cherokee County at age 33, February 14, 1863, for the war. Permitted to go home for clothing on March 5, 1863, with orders to report at Strawberry Plains, Tennessee. Detailed to work in a forge in Cherokee County from March 5, 1863, through February 29, 1864. No further records. Survived the war.

TAYLOR, WOODSON, Private

Resided in Monroe County, Tennessee, and was by occupation a merchant prior to enlisting in Monroe County at about age 27, March 7, 1863, for the war. Reported present through April 30, 1863. No further records.

TIPTON, SAMUEL, Private

Born in Yancey County. Resided in Cherokee County and was by occupation a farmer prior to enlisting in Cherokee County at about age 27, February 19, 1863, for the war. Reported present from March 5 through April 30, 1863. Reported absent without leave from May 29 through June 30, 1863. No further records.

TRADERHOPF, G. N., _____

Name appears as signature to a muster roll of this company dated November-December, 1863, as "commanding the company." There is no other evidence of his service. This is probably a poor rendering of G. N. Loudermilk (who was absent at the time) or a false name.

VEST, CALVIN C., Private

Enlisted in Cherokee County on February 15, 1863, for the war. Permitted to go home for clothing on March 5, 1863, with orders to report at Strawberry Plains, Tennessee. Detailed to work in a forge in Cherokee County from March 5, 1863, through February 29, 1864. No further records.

VEST, WILLIAM T., Private

Born in Tennessee. Enlisted in Cherokee County at age 36, February 15, 1863, for the war. Permitted to go home for clothing on March 5, 1863, with orders to report at Strawberry Plains, Tennessee. Detailed to work in a forge in Cherokee County from March 5, 1863, through February 29, 1864. No further records. Survived the war.

WALLIS, MORGAN E., Private

Previously served as Private in Company B of this battalion. Transferred to this company on March 1 or on April 1, 1863. Reported present through June 30, 1863. Reported absent without leave from July 10, 1863, through February 29, 1864. No further records. Survived the war. [North Carolina pension records indicate that he was wounded in the shoulder in Tennessee on an unspecified date.]

WILLIS, BENJAMIN F., Private
Enlisted in Monroe County, Tennessee, February 12, 1863, for the war. Reported absent without leave on March 23, 1863. No further records.

WRIGHT, R. R., _____
Name appears on a receipt roll for clothing dated October 16, 1864, which states he served in "Co. H," Thomas' Legion; he probably served either in this company or in Company H, Infantry Regiment of this legion.

YOUNG, HARRISON, Private
Enlisted in Monroe County, Tennessee, February 10, 1863, for the war. Reported present on March 7, 1963. Transferred to Company A of this battalion on April 1, 1863.

MISCELLANEOUS

BUCHANAN, JAMES., _____
Name appears on a list of deserters recaptured and returned to Walker's Battalion, dated August 13, 1863. [See Account of Sgt. Maj. C. F. Walker, Walker's Battalion, "For Expenses incurred in apprehending and delivering" Buchanan and other deserters from Walker's Battalion, August 13, 1863, Record Group 109, Miscellaneous Records: Manuscripts: 1861-1865, Entry 183, Box 19, Item 1951, National Archives.]

HOLLAND, DANIEL L., _____
North Carolina pension records indicate that he served in this battalion. Survived the war.

MORRISETTE, JOHNSTON, _____
Records of the United Daughters of the Confederacy appear to indicate that he served in this battalion.

NICHOLS, W. P., _____
Place and date of enlistment and company of service not reported. Records of the Federal Provost Marshal indicate that he was captured and paroled at Anderson, South Carolina, on an unspecified date in 1865. No further records.

ROBERTS, D., _____
Name appears in a list of deserters recaptured and returned to this battalion, dated August 13, 1863. No further records. [See Account of Sgt. Maj. C. F. Walker, Walker's Battalion, "For Expenses incurred in apprehending and delivering" Roberts and other deserters from Walker's Battalion, August 13, 1863, Record Group 109, Miscellaneous Records: Manuscripts: 1861-1865, Entry 183, Box 19, Item 1951, National Archives.]

CAPT. JOHN T. LEVI'S BATTERY LIGHT ARTILLERY

This company was raised in Virginia. It was organized on April 1, 1863, at Wytheville, Virginia. Many of the first enrollees had previously served in Company A, Jackson's Battalion Light Artillery, Virginia State Line, which had disbanded. This company was transferred out of this legion on August 17, 1864, and was thereafter known as Capt. John W. Barr's Battery, Virginia Light Artillery.

The following roster was compiled in large part from company muster rolls dated April 1, 1863-February 29, 1864. These are abstracted in the microfilm edition of the Compiled Service Records of Confederate Soldiers Who Served in Organizations from the State of North Carolina (Record Group 109, M270), National Archives, Washington, D.C. Other valuable information in the Compiled Service Records includes enlistment papers, pay vouchers, requisitions, letters of resignation, discharge certificates, and abstracts of medical and prisoner of war records.

Also utilized in this roster were *The War of the Rebellion: A Compilation of the Official Records of the Union and Confederate Armies*, the North Carolina Adjutant General's papers, state militia records, newspaper casualty lists and obituaries, wartime claims for bounty pay and allowances, postwar registers of claims for artificial limbs, Confederate pension applications filed with the states of North Carolina, Tennessee, and Florida, records of the North Carolina Confederate Soldiers' Home, and the 1860 and 1870 federal censuses of North Carolina. A search was made also for relevant letters, diaries, reminiscences, and other manuscripts in the Southern Historical Collection (University of North Carolina-Chapel Hill) and the Duke University Library Special Collections Department.

Among the secondary sources consulted were records of the North Carolina division of the United Daughters of the Confederacy, postwar rosters, regimental and county histories, marriage bond, will, and cemetery indexes, published and unpublished genealogies, biographical dictionaries, the North Carolina *County Heritage Book* series, the *Confederate Veteran*, Walter Clark's *Histories of the Several Regiments and Battalions from North Carolina in the Great War, 1861-'65*, and the North Carolina volume of the extended edition of *Confederate Military History*.

OFFICERS

CAPTAINS

LEVI, JOHN T.

Previously served as 2nd Lieutenant of Company A, Jackson's Battalion Light Artillery, Virginia State Line. Appointed Captain of this company on April 1, 1863. Reported present in July through November 10, 1863. Name appears on a special requisition for supplies dated November, 16, 1863. Name appears as a signature on a petition to Gov. Zebulon B. Vance dated February 25, 1864, requesting his assistance in reuniting Thomas's Legion and removing it from the command of Brig. Gen. Alfred E. Jackson [Lt. Col. James R. Love, Jr., et al., to Vance, February 25, 1864, Governors' Papers: Zebulon Baird Vance, 1862-1865, N.C. State Archives]. Reported as "absent captured" on February 29, 1864, although other materials indicate that he was court-martialed on or about that date and cashiered soon thereafter. No further records. [His age is given as 25 on an undated muster roll for Capt. Horace B. Balfour's Company Virginia Mounted Rifleman, which later became Company A, Jackson's Battalion Light Artillery. A letter from Lt. Col. James R. Love of the Infantry Regiment of this legion, to Colonel Thomas dated February 28, 1864, reports that "Capt Levi is . . . under arrest and being tried" (William Holland Thomas Papers, Duke University). Clark's *Regiments*, 4:119, has the notation "Louisiana Tigers" after Levi's name, and further states that there were "50 from Virginia and Louisiana in the battery." These are the only known references to Levi or his men having a connection to that state or its units, and are probably a the result of a misunderstanding.]

BARR, JOHN W.

Previously served as Private in Capt. Robert M. Anderson's Company, Virginia Light Artillery, and 1st Lieutenant of Howitzer Battery, Jackson's Battalion Light Artillery, Virginia State Line. Enlisted in this company at Wytheville, Virginia, April 1, 1863, for the war. Mustered in as Private. Elected 1st Lieutenant on May 15, 1863. Reported present through November 10, 1863. Reported on detached service as Assistant Inspector General for Brig. Gen. Alfred E. Jackson's Brigade beginning on November 16, 1863. Promoted to Inspector General (Captain) of General Jackson's Brigade prior to January 12, 1864. Appointed Captain of this company on March 22, 1864. Name appears as signature to a pay voucher for service from February 1 through March 1, 1864. Serving as Assistant Inspector General for General Jackson's Brigade on April 20, 1864. Transferred to Capt. John W. Barr's Battery, Virginia Light Artillery, August 17, 1864. [Information in his service file for a Confederate and General Staff Officer indicate that in 1862 he also served as a Private in the President's Guard (Company B, 28th Battalion [Tabb's] Virginia Volunteers), probably on detailed duty to the Tredegar Iron Works.]

LIEUTENANTS

SEARCEY, REUBEN C., 3rd Lieutenant

Previously served as Private in Company A, Jackson's Battalion Light Artillery, Virginia State Line. Enlisted in this company at Wytheville, Virginia, April 1, 1863, for the war. Mustered in as Private. Reported present through August 31, 1863. Elected 3rd Lieutenant on August 26, 1863. Transferred to Capt. John W. Barr's Battery, Virginia Light Artillery, August 17, 1864. [His age is given as 25 on an undated muster roll for Capt. Horace B. Balfour's Company Virginia Mounted Rifleman, which later became Company A, Jackson's Battalion Light Artillery.]

SHIPP, J. M., 2nd Lieutenant

Enlisted at Wytheville, Virginia, April 1, 1863, for the war. Mustered in as Private. Elected 2nd Lieutenant on May 15, 1863. Reported present through August 31, 1863. Reported sick in hospital at Abingdon, Virginia, September-October, 1863. Court-martialed on or about August 2, 1864, for "selling government property without a proper order . . . and embezzling the same." Found guilty and sentenced to be dismissed from service, the particulars of the events to "be published in newspaper" and "it be deemed scandalous to associate with him." [Letters Sent, Orders and Circulars, Dept. of E. Tenn. and Dept. of W. Va. and E. Tenn., April 1863-October, 1864, Record Group 109, Chapter II, Vol. 234, National Archives.]

NONCOMMISSIONED OFFICERS AND PRIVATES

ALEXANDER, ISAAC W., Private

Enlisted at Strawberry Plains, Tennessee, July 20, 1863, for the war. Reported present on August 31 and November 10, 1863. Reported captured in eastern Tennessee on December 10, 1863, but no Federal records document his capture or imprisonment. Reported transferred to Capt. John W. Barr's Battery, Virginia Light Artillery, August 17, 1864.

ALEXANDER, JESSE P., Private
Resided in Knox County, Tennessee, and enlisted at Strawberry Plains, Tennessee, at about age 43, July 20, 1863, for the war. Reported present through November 10, 1863. Reported absent on furlough on February 29, 1864. Transferred to Company D, Infantry Regiment of this legion, prior to April 8, 1864.

ALEXANDER, WILLIAM B., Private
Enlisted at Strawberry Plains, Tennessee, May 15, 1863, for the war. Reported present through August, 1863. Reported captured in eastern Tennessee on December 10, 1863, but no Federal records document his capture or imprisonment. Reported transferred to Capt. John W. Barr's Battery, Virginia Light Artillery, August 17, 1864, while a prisoner of war.

ALLISON, JAMES H., Private
Enlisted at Bristol, Tennessee, December 31, 1863, for the war. Reported present through February 29, 1864. Transferred to Capt. John W. Barr's Battery, Virginia Light Artillery, August 17, 1864.

ALLISON, MARTIN VAN BUREN, Private
Born on March 4, 1843, in the part of Ashe County that later became Alleghany County. Enlisted at Bristol, Tennessee, at age 20, December 31, 1863, for the war. Reported present through February 29, 1864. Transferred to Capt. John W. Barr's Battery, Virginia Light Artillery, August 17, 1864.

ANDERSON, DAVID, Private
Enlisted at Zollicoffer, Tennessee, October 1, 1863, for the war. Reported present through October 31, 1863. Deserted prior to February 29, 1864.

BALLARD, WILLIAM H., Private
Previously served as Private in Company I, Infantry Regiment of this legion. Transferred to this company on July 1, 1863. Reported present through August 31, 1863. Reported captured on October 10, 1863, but no Federal records document his capture or imprisonment. Reported absent sick at Emory and Henry, Virginia, February 29, 1864. No further records.

BARBARY, JAMES, Private
Enlisted at Strawberry Plains, Tennessee, May 15, 1863, for the war. Reported present until transferred to Capt. Thomas Ellett's Battery, Virginia Light Artillery, July 1, 1863.

BARLOW, M. G., Private
Previously served as Sergeant in Company A, Jackson's Battalion Light Artillery, Virginia State Line. Enlisted as Private in this company at Wytheville, Virginia, April 1, 1863, for the war. Reported present through June 30, 1863. Transferred to another unit on July 24, 1863.

BARR, H. C., Private
Enlisted at Strawberry Plains, Tennessee, August 1, 1863, for the war. Reported present through November 10, 1863. Served on extra duty as Quartermaster Sergeant during part of that period. Reported on detached duty on February 29, 1864. Transferred to Capt. John W. Barr's Battery, Virginia Light Artillery, August 17, 1864.

BARTLEY, JOHN, Private
Enlisted at Blountsville, Tennessee, November 2, 1863, for the war. Reported under arrest at Carter's Depot, Tennessee, February 29, 1864. Court-martialed on or about May 24, 1864, for "conduct to the prejudice of the good order and military discipline." Found guilty and sentenced to ten days in the guard house, to be fed on "bread and water alone." [Letters Sent, Orders and Circulars, Dept. of E. Tenn. and Dept. of W. Va. and E. Tenn., April 1863-October, 1864, Record Group 109, Chapter II, Vol. 234, National Archives.] Transferred to Capt. John W. Barr's Battery, Virginia Light Artillery, August 17, 1864.

BATTLE, B. F., _____
North Carolina pension records indicate that he served in this company.

BENNETT, T., Private
Enlisted at Wytheville, Virginia, April 1, 1863, for the war. Reported present through August 31, 1863. Died on September 9, 1863. Place and cause of death not reported.

BISHOP, J. J., Private
Enlisted at Strawberry Plains, Tennessee, August 1, 1863, for the war. Reported present through October 31, 1863. Reported absent without leave in November, 1863-February, 1864. Later served as Lieutenant in Capt. John W. Barr's Battery, Virginia Light Artillery.

BISHOP, MARTIN H., Private
Enlisted at Strawberry Plains, Tennessee, August 1, 1863, for the war. Reported on detail in the quartermaster department in September-October, 1863. Reported present on November 10, 1863. On detail at Abingdon, Virginia, February 29, 1864, and from July 15 through December 31, 1864. Served as a "yard master" during most of that period. Transferred to Capt. John W. Barr's Battery, Virginia Light Artillery, August 17, 1864.

BLUFF, HARRY, Private
Enlisted at Wytheville, Virginia, April 1, 1863, for the war. Reported under arrest from June 10 through June 30, 1863. Court-martialed on or about August 4, 1863, probably for desertion. Reported under arrest at Jonesborough, Tennessee, August 31, 1863. Name appears on a jailer's report as charged with either desertion or drunkenness on September 11, 1863. Confined for five days in the county jail, Washington County, Virginia. Hospitalized at Richmond, Virginia, on or about September 17, 1863, with syphilis. Imprisoned in Richmond on September 28, 1863. Reported in prison at Richmond through November 10, 1863. Returned to duty prior to February 29, 1864. No further records.

BOWLES, JOHN, Private
Enlisted at Wytheville, Virginia, April 1, 1863, for the war. Reported present through June 30, 1863. Transferred to an unspecified unit on July 1, 1863.

BOYD, WILLIAM, _____
North Carolina pension records indicate that he served in this company.

BUTLER, JOHN, Corporal
Enlisted at Wytheville, Virginia, April 1, 1863, for the war. Mustered in as Private. Reported present through August 31, 1863. Promoted to Corporal on September 1, 1863. Reported present in September, 1863-February, 1864. Transferred to Capt. John W. Barr's Battery, Virginia Light Artillery, August 17, 1864.

CALVERT, W. M., Private
Enlisted at Strawberry Plains, Tennessee, June 15, 1863, for the war. Reported present until transferred to an unspecified unit on July 1, 1863.

CAMPBELL, W. F., Sergeant
Enlisted at Strawberry Plains, Tennessee, August 1, 1863, for the war. Mustered in as Private. Promoted to Corporal on September 1, 1863. Reported present through November 10, 1863. Promoted to Sergeant in November, 1863-February, 1864. Reported sick at home during the same period. Transferred to Capt. John W. Barr's Battery, Virginia Light Artillery, August 17, 1864.

CARR, JOHN H., Private
Enlisted at Zollicoffer, Tennessee, October 1, 1863, for the war. Confined for thirty days on November 1, 1863, at the county jail, Washington County, Virginia, on charges of desertion. Confined there again on December 1, 1863. Deserted prior to February 29, 1864. [See Miscellaneous Records: Manuscripts, 1861-1865, Entry 183, Box 13, Items 1386 and 1387, Record Group 109, National Archives.]

CHAUVIN, ALFRED F., 1st Sergeant
Previously served as Sergeant in Company A, Jackson's Battalion Light Artillery, Virginia State Line. Enlisted at Wytheville, Virginia, April 1, 1863, for the war. Mustered in as 1st Sergeant. Reported present through February 29, 1864. Transferred to Capt. John W. Barr's Battery, Virginia Light Artillery, August 17, 1864.

CLAY, JOHN, _____
Name appears as a member of this company on a roster of prisoners at the county jail, Washington County, Virginia, charged with desertion and confined, November 1, 1863, for eleven days. Does not appear in this company's records, however. [He may have served also or instead in McClung's Company, Tennessee Light Artillery.]

COHEN, JAMES L., Private
Previously served as Private in Company D, Infantry Regiment of this legion. Transferred to this company on August 1, 1863. Reported present through February 29, 1864. Transferred to Capt. John W. Barr's Battery, Virginia Light Artillery, August 17, 1864. [His surname may have been Coin.]

COLLEY, JOHN, Private
Resided in Washington County, Virginia, and was by occupation a farmer. Place and date of enlistment not reported. Reported present in November, 1863-February, 1864. No further records.

CONWAY, M., Private
Enlisted at Wytheville, Virginia, April 1, 1863, for the war. Reported present through June 30, 1863. Deserted on August 1, 1863.

CORBITT, WILLIAM, Private
Previously served in as Private in Company A, Jackson's Battalion Light Artillery, Virginia State Line. Enlisted in this company at Wytheville, Virginia, April 1, 1863, for the war. Deserted on June 10, 1863. [His age is given as 42 on an undated muster roll for Capt. Horace B. Balfour's Company Virginia Mounted Riflemen, which later became Company A, Jackson's Battalion Light Artillery.]

CUNNINGHAM, H. A., _____
North Carolina pension records indicate that he served in this company and survived the war.

DALEY, JOHN, Private
Previously served as Private in Company A, Jackson's Battalion Light Artillery, Virginia State Line. Enlisted in this company at Wytheville, Virginia, April 1, 1863, for the war. Captured at Strawberry Plains, Tennessee, June 20, 1863, and paroled there the next day. Reported present through October 31, 1863, and from November 11, 1863, through February 29, 1864. No further records. [His age is given as 22 on an undated muster roll for Capt. Horace B. Balfour's Company Virginia Mounted Riflemen, which later became Company A, Jackson's Battalion Light Artillery.]

DAVIS, JAMES, Private
Enlisted at Wytheville, Virginia, April 1, 1863, for the war. Captured at Strawberry Plains, Tennessee, June 20, 1863. Paroled at Strawberry Plains on June 21, 1863. Returned to duty prior to June 30, 1863. Reported present through August 31, 1863. Reported captured in eastern Tennessee on October 10, 1863, but no Federal records document his capture or imprisonment. Reported transferred to Capt. John W. Barr's Battery, Virginia Light Artillery, presumably on August 17, 1864.

DAVIS, JOHN, Private
Enlisted at Wytheville, Virginia, April 1, 1863, for the war. Captured at Strawberry Plains, Tennessee, June 20, 1863. Paroled at Strawberry Plains, June 21, 1863. Returned to duty prior to June 30, 1863. Deserted on August 1, 1863. Returned to duty in September-October, 1863. Deserted prior to February 29, 1864.

FORD, JOHN H., Private
Enlisted at Strawberry Plains, Tennessee, August 1, 1863, for the war. Reported present until he deserted on September 2, 1863.

GENETT, CHARLES, Private
Enlisted at Abingdon, Virginia, October 15, 1863, for the war. Reported present through October 31, 1863. Deserted prior to February 29, 1864.

GUYNN, SAMUEL H., Private
Previously served as Private in Company I, Infantry Regiment of this legion. Transferred to this company on July 1, 1863. Reported present through August 31, 1863. Reported absent sick in September, 1863-February, 1864, but records of Capt. John W. Barr's Battery, to which he was to be transferred, indicate that he deserted at Strawberry Plains, Tennessee, on September 1, 1863. [His surname may have been Gwynn.]

HAHN, JOHN S., Private
Enlisted at Wytheville, Virginia, April 1, 1863, for the war. Reported present through August 31, 1863. Deserted on September

3, 1863. Confined at the county jail, Washington County, Virginia, January 31, 1864, for fifty days, probably for desertion. Reported present on February 29, 1864, but "name canceled." No further records. [His surname may have been Hand. He may have served previously as Private in Company A, Jackson's Battalion Light Artillery, Virginia State Line.]

HAMPTON, JACOB, Private
Enlisted at Wytheville, Virginia, April 1, 1863, for the war. Reported present through August 31, 1863. Reported captured in eastern Tennessee on September 1, 1863, but no Federal records document his capture or imprisonment. Reported transferred to Capt. John W. Barr's Battery, Virginia Light Artillery, August 17, 1864. [May have served previously in Company B, 2nd Regiment Tennessee Cavalry (McLinn's), Company B, 13th (2nd) Battalion Tennessee Cavalry, and Company C, 5th Regiment Tennessee Cavalry (McKenzie's); these are designations for the same company during successive phases of its service.]

HARE, THOMAS, Private
Enlisted at Wytheville, Virginia, April 1, 1863, for the war. Reported under arrest at Jonesborough, Tennessee, June 10, 1863. Returned to duty in July-August, 1863. Reported sick in hospital at Emory and Henry, Virginia, in September-October, 1863, and through November 10. Listed as a deserter from November 11, 1863, through February 29, 1864.

HOBBS, JAMES A., Private
Previously served as Private in Company A, Jackson's Battalion Light Artillery, Virginia State Line. Enlisted in this company at Wytheville, Virginia, April 1, 1863, for the war. Reported present through October 31, 1863. Deserted prior to February 29, 1864. [His age is given as 18 in an undated muster roll for Capt. Horace B. Balfour's Co. Virginia Mounted Riflemen, which later became Company A, Jackson's Battalion Light Artillery.]

HOLMES, V. J., Private
Enlisted at Wytheville, Virginia, April 1, 1863, for the war. Reported under arrest at Jonesborough, Tennessee, June 7, 1863. Returned to duty in July-August, 1863. Reported present in September, 1863-February, 1864. Transferred to Capt. John W. Barr's Battery, Virginia Light Artillery, August 17, 1864.

HOWARD, NOAH J., Private
Previously served as Private in Company F, Infantry Regiment of this legion. Transferred to this company in July-August, 1863. Reported present through October 31 and on November 10, 1863. Deserted between that date and February 29, 1864.

HUSSEY, T., Private
Enlisted at Wytheville, Virginia, April 1, 1863, for the war. Reported present through August 30, 1863. Reported in prison at Abingdon, Virginia, from October 25 through November 10, 1863. Reported absent without leave on February 29, 1864. No further records. [He may have been the same man as H.F. Hussey, whose record is in the General Miscellaneous section of this roster.]

HYDE, ANSON E., Private
Enlisted at Strawberry Plains, Tennessee, July 1, 1863, for the war. Reported absent without leave from July 15 through November 10, 1863. Dropped from the company rolls, presumably as a deserter, subsequent to the latter date. Went over to the enemy. Confined at Knoxville, Tennessee, July 3, 1864. Took the Oath of Allegiance at Knoxville on July 5, 1864. Transferred to Louisville, Kentucky, where he arrived on July 14, 1864. Took the Oath of Allegiance at Lousiville on July 16, 1864, and released, probably at Jeffersonville, Indiana, with instruction to remain north of the Ohio River.

JACO, ANDREW JACKSON, Private
Previously served as Private in Company A, Jackson's Battalion Light Artillery, Virginia State Line. Enlisted in this company at Wytheville, Virginia, April 1, 1863, for the war. Reported present through February 29, 1864. Transferred to Capt. John W. Barr's Battery, Virginia Light Artillery, August 17, 1864. [His age is given as 21 on an undated muster roll for Capt. Horace B. Balfour's Company Virginia Mounted Rifleman, which later became Company A, Jackson's Battalion Light Artillery.]

JACO, JOHN J., Private
Enlisted at Wytheville, Virginia, April 1, 1863, for the war. Reported present through February 29, 1864. Transferred to Capt. John W. Barr's Battery, Virginia Light Artillery, August 17, 1864.

JENKINS, FRANCIS M., Private
Previously served as Private in Company F, 29th Regiment N.C. Troops. Enlisted in this company while a deserter from the 29th Regiment, at Wytheville, Virginia, April 1, 1863, for the war. Reported present through February 29, 1864. Transferred to Capt. John W. Barr's Battery, Virginia Light Artillery, August 17, 1864.

JENKINS, J., Private
Enlisted at Wytheville, Virginia, April 1, 1863, for the war. Reported absent without leave from June 21 through November 10, 1863. He probably deserted at Strawberry Plains, Tennessee, in the confusion caused by the Federal capture of that post on June 20, 1863.

JENKINS, S. W., Private
Enlisted at Strawberry Plains, Tennessee, July 1, 1863, for the war. Reported present through October 31, 1863. Reported on furlough on February 29, 1864. No further records. [He may have been the same man as Pvt. Samuel Jenkins of Company F, Infantry Regiment of this legion.]

JOHNSTON, JOHN, Private
Enlisted at Strawberry Plains, Tennessee, August 1, 1863, for the war. Reported present through November 10, 1863. Reported captured in eastern Tennessee on December 10, 1863, but no Federal records document his capture or imprisonment. Reported transferred to Capt. John W. Barr's Battery, Virginia Light Artillery, August 17, 1864.

JONES, PETER, Private
Enlisted at Wytheville, Virginia, April 1, 1863, for the war. Deserted on June 21, 1863. He probably deserted at Strawberry Plains, Tennessee, in the confusion caused by the Federal capture of that post on June 20, 1863.

KELLEY, JAMES, Private
Enlisted at Wytheville, Virginia, April 1, 1863, for the war. Reported present until he deserted on September 5, 1863. Reported in jail at Abingdon, Virginia, on an unspecified date in 1863.

KELLEY, JOHN, Private
Enlisted at Wytheville, Virginia, April 1, 1863, for the war. Deserted on July 26, 1863.

KING, THOMAS, Private
Enlisted at Strawberry Plains, Tennessee, June 20, 1863, for the war. Reported present through August 30, 1863. Reported absent without leave in September-October, 1863, and on November 10, 1863. No further records.

LAWRENCE, DAVID, Private
Previously served as Private in Company D, Infantry Regiment of this legion. Transferred to this company on July 1 or August 7, 1863. Deserted on September 5, 1863.

LAWRENCE, J. CALVIN, Private
Previously served as Private in Company D, Infantry Regiment of this legion. Transferred to this company on July 1 or August 1, 1863. Reported present through August 31, 1863. Reported captured in eastern Tennessee on October 10, 1863, but no Federal records document his capture or imprisonment. Reported transferred to Capt. John W. Barr's Battery, Virginia Light Artillery, August 17, 1864.

LEE, JOHN, Private
Enlisted at Strawberry Plains, Tennessee, July 1, 1863, for the war. Reported present through August 31, 1863. Deserted on September 1, 1863. Went over to the enemy on an unspecified date. Sent to Knoxville, Tennessee. Released at Knoxville on February 8, 1864, after taking the Oath of Allegiance. [He may have been the same man as Pvt. John C. Lee of 2nd Company D, Walker's Battalion, and Company D, Infantry Regiment of this legion.]

LEE, JOSEPH C., Private
Previously served as Private in Company D, Infantry Regiment of this legion. Transferred to this company on July 1 or August 1, 1863. Reported present through February 29, 1864. Transferred to Capt. John W. Barr's Battery, Virginia Light Artillery, August 17, 1864.

LEE, WILLIAM C., Private
Previously served as Private in Company D, Infantry Regiment of this legion. Transferred to this company in July-August, 1863. Reported present through February 29, 1864.Transferred to Capt. John W. Barr's Battery, Virginia Light Artillery, August 17, 1864.

LIGON, WILLIAM, Corporal
Enlisted at Wytheville, Virginia, April 1, 1863, for the war. Mustered in as Private. Captured at Strawberry Plains, Tennessee, June 20, 1863, and paroled there the next day. Reported present in July-August, 1863. Promoted to Corporal on September 1, 1863. Reported present from September 1 through November 10, 1863. Reported captured in eastern Tennessee on December 10, 1863, but no Federal records document his capture or imprisonment. Reported transferred to Capt. John W. Barr's Battery, Virginia Light Artillery, August 17, 1864.

LOLLIS, E. B., Private
Enlisted, probably at Wytheville, Virginia, April 1, 1863, for the war. Reported absent without leave through November 10, 1863. No further records.

LOMBARD, CAMILE, Private
Previously served as Private in Company A, Jackson's Battalion Light Artillery, Virginia State Line. Enlisted in this company at Wytheville, Virginia, April 1, 1863, for the war. Reported present through November 10, 1863. Reported absent without leave on February 29, 1864. Transferred to Capt. John W. Barr's Battery, Virginia Light Artillery, August 17, 1864. [His age is given as 27 on an undated muster roll for Capt. Horace B. Balfour's Company Virginia Mounted Riflemen, which later became Company A, Jackson's Battalion Light Artillery.]

LONG, J. P., Private
Enlisted at Strawberry Plains, Tennessee, August 1, 1863, for the war. Deserted on August 15, 1863.

McLANE, PAT H., Private
Previously served as Private in Company A, Jackson's Battalion Light Artillery, Virginia State Line. Enlisted in this company at Wytheville, Virginia, April 1, 1863, for the war. Reported present through November 10, 1863. Reported absent without leave on February 29, 1864. Court-martialed on or about July 15, 1864. Found guilty of absence without leave and sentenced to be confined for one month wearing a "12 pound ball" on his "left leg with chain." Transferred to Capt. John W. Barr's Battery, Virginia Light Artillery, August 17, 1864.

MALONEY, PATRICK, Private
Enlisted at Strawberry Plains, Tennessee, June 1, 1863, for the war. Captured at Strawberry Plains, Tennessee, June 20, 1863, and paroled there the next day. Reported present in July-October, 1863. Reported absent sick at Bristol, Tennessee, February 29, 1864. Transferred to Capt. John W. Barr's Battery, Virginia Light Artillery, August 17, 1864.

MAY, W. A., Private
Enlisted at Zollicoffer, Tennessee, October 1, 1863, for the war. Reported present through October 31, 1863. Deserted prior to February 29, 1864.

MAYS, J. F., Sergeant
Enlisted at Wytheville, Virginia, April 1, 1863, for the war. Mustered in as Sergeant. Reported present through February 29, 1864. Transferred to Capt. John W. Barr's Battery, Virginia Light Artillery, August 17, 1864.

MAYS, S. H., Private
Enlisted at Wytheville, Virginia, April 1, 1863, for the war. Mustered in as Corporal. Reported present through August 31, 1863. Reduced to ranks on September 1, 1863. Reported present in September, 1863-February, 1864. Transferred to Capt. John W. Barr's Battery, Virginia Light Artillery, August 17, 1864.

MAYS, W. K., Private
Enlisted at Wytheville, Virginia, April 1, 1863, for the war. Mustered in as Corporal. Reported present through August 31, 1863. Reported absent without leave in September-October, 1863. Reduced to ranks on September 1, 1863. No further records.

MILLER, GEORGE WASHINGTON, Private
Enlisted, probably at Wytheville, Virginia, on April 1, 1863, for the war. Reported absent without leave from June 21 through

November 10, 1863. No further records. [He may have been the same man as Pvt. George W. Miller of Company G, Infantry Regiment of this legion.]

MOORE, JESSE H., Sergeant
Enlisted, probably at Wytheville, Virginia, April 1, 1863, for the war. Mustered in as Sergeant. Captured at Strawberry Plains, Tennessee, June 20, 1863, and paroled there the next day. Reported present, June 30, 1863-February, 1864. Transferred to Capt. John W. Barr's Battery, Virginia Light Artillery, August 17, 1864.

MORRAND, A. C., Private
Enlisted at Strawberry Plains, Tennessee, July 1, 1863, for the war. Transferred to an unspecified unit on August 14, 1863.

NEWTON, WILLIAM M., Private
Enlisted, probably at Wytheville, Virginia, April 1, 1863, for the war. Reported absent without leave from June 21 through November 10, 1863. No further records. [He probably deserted at Strawberry Plains, Tennessee, in the confusion caused by the Federal capture of that post on June 20, 1863.]

NUGENT, WILLIAM, Private
Enlisted, probably at Wytheville, Virginia, April 1, 1863, for the war. Reported present until captured at Strawberry Plains, Tennessee, on June 20, 1863, and paroled there the next day. Returned to duty and was reported present through February 29, 1864. No further records. [An item in the September-October, 1863, muster roll referring to his death appears to be incorrect.]

O'DONALD, JOHN, Private
Enlisted at Strawberry Plains, Tennessee, July 1, 1863, for the war. Reported present through August 31, 1863. Reported sick in hospital at Emory and Henry, Virginia, in September-October, 1863, and on November 10, 1863. Reported absent on furlough on February 29, 1864. No further records.

PHILLIPS, MOSES, Private
Enlisted at Zollicoffer, Tennessee, September 10, 1863, for the war. Reported present through February 29, 1864. Transferred to Capt. John W. Barr's Battery, Virginia Light Artillery, August 17, 1864.

POWERS, JOHN, _____
Name appears as a member of this company on a roster of prisoners at the county jail in Washington County, Virginia, charged with desertion and confined on November 1, 1863, for eleven days. He does not appear in the records of this company, however.

PRATHER, WILLIAM, Private
Enlisted at Zollicoffer, Tennessee, September 10, 1863, for the war. Reported present through October 31, 1863. Reported on detail in the conscript department subsequent to October 31, 1863. Rejoined the company prior to November 10, 1863. Reported absent sick at Emory and Henry, Virginia, February 29, 1864. Reported on extra duty at the office of committee of conscripts from May 3 through June 1, 1864. Transferred to Capt. John W. Barr's Battery, Virginia Light Artillery, August 17, 1864.

REID, B. Private
Enlisted at Strawberry Plains, Tennessee, May 1, 1863, for the war. Reported present through June 21, 1863, when he deserted. [He probably deserted at Strawberry Plains in the confusion caused by the Federal capture of that post on June 20, 1863. His National Archives service records are mixed with those of Private Birdwell Reed of Company D, Infantry Regiment, Thomas's Legion, to create a single filmjacket under Birdwell Reed's name. The two do not appear to be the same man, however.]

REID, WILLIAM, Private
Enlisted at Strawberry Plains, Tennessee, May 1, 1863, for the war. Reported present through October 31, 1863. Reported captured in eastern Tennessee on December 10, 1863, but no Federal records document his capture or imprisonment. Reported transferred to Capt. John W. Barr's Battery, Virginia Light Artillery, on August 17, 1864.

REYNOLDS, ROBERT H., Private
Previously served as Private in Company A, Jackson's Battalion Light Artillery, Virginia State Line. Enlisted in this company at Wytheville, Virginia, April 1, 1863, for the war. Mustered in as Corporal. Reported present through August 31, 1863. Reduced to ranks on September 1, 1863. Name appears in a jailer's report as charged with desertion and/or drunkenness on September 11, 1863; confined for five days in the county jail, Washington County, Virginia. Reported in prison at Richmond, Virginia, from September 15 through November 10, 1863. Returned to duty prior to February 29, 1864, when he was reported present. Transferred to Capt. John W. Barr's Battery, Virginia Light Artillery, August 17, 1864. [His age is given as 29 in an undated muster roll for Capt. Horace B. Balfour's Company Viginia Mounted Riflemen, which later became Company A, Jackson's Battalion Light Artillery.]

RILEY, JOHN, Private
Enlisted at Wytheville, Virginia, April 1, 1863, for the war. Reported under arrest at Jonesborough, Tennessee, June 10-30, 1863. Deserted on August 1, 1863.

ROBARDS, D. L., Private
Enlisted, probably at Wytheville, Virginia, April 1, 1863, for the war. Reported absent without leave on June 21, 1863. Transferred to an unspecified unit on July 1, 1863. Returned to duty on July 12, 1863, with "absence satisfactorily accounted for." No further records.

ROBERTS, JOHN J., Private
Enlisted at Strawberry Plains, Tennessee, May 20, 1863, for the war. Deserted on June 10, 1863.

ROBERTSON, J. R., Private
Enlisted at Strawberry Plains, Tennessee, July 21, 1863, for the war. Reported present through October 31, 1863. Reported absent without leave on February 29, 1864. Subsequently reported in the records of Capt. John W. Barr's Battery, Virginia Light Artillery, of having deserted at Bristol, Tennessee, on December 15, 1863.

ROBERTSON, R. T., Private
Enlisted at Strawberry Plains, Tennessee, July 21, 1863, for the war. Reported present through November 10, 1863. Reported absent without leave on February 29, 1864. Transferred to Capt. John W. Barr's Battery, Virginia Light Artillery, August 17, 1864. [The name "R. Robinson" appears as a member of Levi's Battery on a roster of prisoners at the Washington County, Virginia jail, charged

with desertion and confined, October 19, 1863, for thirty days; it may have been this man. See Miscellaneous Records: Manuscripts, 1861-1865, Entry 183, Box 13, Item 1387, Record Group 109, National Archives.]

ROBINSON, JOHN, Private
Enlisted at Wytheville, Virginia, April 1, 1863, for the war. Reported present until he was captured and paroled at Mossy Creek, Tennessee, June 21, 1863. Returned to duty on or prior to June 30, 1863. Reported present through February 29, 1864; however, name appears on a jailer's report as charged with desertion on September 11, 1863, and confined for five days in the county jail, Washington County, Virginia. Transferred to Capt. John W. Barr's Battery, Virginia Light Artillery, August 17, 1864. [May have previously served as Private in Company A, Jackson's Battalion Light Artillery, Virginia State Line.]

ROBINSON, OSCAR, Private
Enlisted at Strawberry Plains, Tennessee, August 15, 1863, for the war. Reported present through October 31, 1863. Reported absent sick in Washington County, Virginia, November 10, 1863. Reported absent without leave on February 29, 1864. Transferred to Capt. John W. Barr's Battery, Virginia Light Artillery, August 17, 1864. [His records for Barr's Battery show that he was present, October 31, 1864; it is not know if he returned to duty before or after his transfer, however.]

RODGERS, FRANCIS M., Private
Enlisted at Wytheville, Virginia, April 1, 1863, for the war. Reported present until he was captured at Strawberry Plains, Tennessee, June 20, 1863, and paroled there the next day. Transferred to Captain Jackson's Company (2nd Organization), Virginia Horse Artillery, July 1, 1863.

ROSE, QUILLAN L., Private
Previously served as Private in Company F, 29th Regiment N.C. Troops. Enlisted at Strawberry Plains, Tennessee, August 1, 1863, while a deserter from the 29th Regiment. Reported present through February, 1864. Transferred to Capt. John W. Barr's Battery, Virginia Light Artillery, August 17, 1864. [May have served also in Company K, 9th Regiment N.C. Troops (1st Regiment N.C. Cavalry).]

ROYSTER, HUNTER, Private
Previously served as Private in Company A, Jackson's Battalion Light Artillery, Virginia State Line. Enlisted in this company at Wytheville, Virginia, April 1, 1863, for the war. Reported present until he was captured at Strawberry Plains, Tennessee, June 20, 1863, and paroled there the next day. Returned to duty prior to June 30, 1863. Reported present in July-October, 1863, and on November 10, 1863. Reported present through February 29, 1864. No further records. [His age is given as 16 on an undated muster roll for Capt. Horace B. Balfour's Company Virginia Mounted Riflemen, which later became Company A, Jackson's Battalion Light Artillery.]

RYAN, PATRICK, Private
Enlisted at Strawberry Plains, Tennessee, July 1, 1863, for the war. Reported present through February 29, 1864. Transferred to Capt. John W. Barr's Battery, Virginia Light Artillery, August 17, 1864. [Probably served previously in Company D, 3rd Regiment Confederate Engineers.]

SAWYER, JOHN H. SITTON, _____
Name appears as a member of this company on a roster of prisoners at the county jail, Washington County, Virginia, charged with desertion and confined on November 1, 1863, for eleven days. He does not appear in the records of this company, however.

SCOTT, WILLIAM M., Corporal
Enlisted at Wytheville, Virginia, April 1, 1863, for the war. Mustered in as Private. Reported sick in hospital at Strawberry Plains, Tennessee, June 30, 1863. Returned to duty prior to August 31, 1863. Promoted to Corporal on September 1, 1863. Reported present in September, 1863-February, 1864. Transferred to Capt. John W. Barr's Battery, Virginia Light Artillery, August 17, 1864.

SELLERS, ROBERT, Private
Previously served as Private in Company D, Infantry Regiment of this legion. Transferred to this company on July 1 or August 1, 1863. Deserted September 2, 1863.

SHEPHERD, THOMAS C., Private
Enlisted at Abingdon, Virginia, October 15, 1863, for the war. Reported present though November 10, 1863. Reported under arrest at Carter's Depot, Tennessee, February 29, 1864. Court-martialed on May 24, 1864, for "conduct to the prejudice of good order and military discipline." Found guilty and sentenced to ten days in the guard house, to be fed on "bread and water alone." [Letters Sent, Orders and Circulars, Dept. of E. Tenn. and Dept. of W. Va. and E. Tenn., April 1863-October, 1864, Record Group 109, Chapter II, Vol. 234, National Archives.] Transferred to Capt. John W. Barr's Battery, Virginia Light Artillery, August 17, 1864.

SHERRELL, MOSES L., Private
Previously served as Private in Company F, Infantry Regiment of this legion. Transferred to this company on July 1, 1863. Reported absent without leave on July 15, 1863. No further records.

SHULAR, JOHN A., _____
Born in 1844 in the part of Macon County that later became Jackson County. Tennessee pension application No. 12184 indicates that he enlisted in Levi's Battery in early 1864; however, he does not appear on any muster rolls or other wartime records for this company or its successor, Capt. John W. Barr's Battery Virginia Light Artillery. Survived the war.

SHULER, D. M., Private
Enlisted at Wytheville, Virginia, April 1, 1863, for the war. Reported present in July-October, 1863, and November 10, 1863, through February 29, 1864. No further records. [May have previously served in Company F, 29th Regiment N.C. Troops.]

SHULER, THOMAS J., Private
Previously served as Private in Company F, 29th Regiment N.C. Troops. Enlisted illegally in this company at Wytheville, Virginia, April 1, 1863, for the war, while a deserter from the 29th Regiment. Reported absent without leave from June 21 through 30, 1863. Returned to duty prior to August 31, 1863. Reported present in

September-October, 1863. Reported present from November 10, 1863, through February 29, 1864. No further records. Survived the war.

SHULER, WILLIAM P., Private
Previously served as Private in Company F, 29th Regiment N.C. Troops. Illegally enlisted in this company at Wytheville, Virginia, April 1, 1863, for the war, while a deserter from the 29th Regiment. Reported absent without leave from June 21 through 30, 1863. Returned to duty prior to August 31, 1863. Reported present in September, 1863-February, 1864. Transferred to Capt. John W. Barr's Battery, Virginia Light Artillery, August 17, 1864.

SIMMONS, THOMAS F., Private
Previously served as Private in Company D, Infantry Regiment of this legion. Transferred to this company on August 5, 1863. Deserted on September 2, 1863.

SMITH, BENJAMIN F., Private
Previously served as Private in Company A, Jackson's Battalion Light Artillery, Virginia State Line. Enlisted in this company at Wytheville, Virginia, April 1, 1863, for the war. Mustered in as Sergeant. Reported present through October 31, 1863, and on November 10, 1863. Reduced to ranks on an unspecified date. Reported captured in eastern Tennessee on December 10, 1863, but no Federal records document his capture or imprisonment. Reported transferred to Capt. John W. Barr's Battery, Virginia Light Artillery.

SMITH, PETER, Private
Enlisted at Wytheville, Virginia, April 1, 1863, for the war. Reported present until he was captured at Strawberry Plains, Tennessee, June 20, 1863, and paroled there the next day. Reported present in July-August, 1863. Reported in prison at Abingdon, Virginia, October 29, 1863. Reason he was confined not reported. Confined for thirty days on November 1, 1863, at the county jail, Washington County, Virginia, on charges of desertion. Confined there again on December 1, 1863. Listed as a deserter, February 29, 1864.

SPEAKER, GEORGE, Private
Enlisted at Wytheville, Virginia, April 1, 1863, for the war. Mustered in as Corporal. Reported present through August 31, 1863. Reported captured on September 1, 1863, but no Federal records document his capture or imprisonment. Reduced to ranks the same date. Reported transferred to Capt. John W. Barr's Battery, Virginia Light Artillery.

SPENCER, F., Private
Enlisted at Strawberry Plains, Tennessee, July 1, 1863, for the war. Reported present through February 29, 1864. Transferred to Capt. John W. Barr's Battery, Virginia Light Artillery, August 17, 1864.

STANBERRY, WILLIAM P., Private
Previously served in Company F, 29th Regiment N.C. Troops. Enlisted illegally in this company at Wytheville, Virginia, April 1, 1863, for the war, while a deserter from the 29th Regiment. Reported present through June 30, 1863. Reported absent without leave in July-October, 1863. No further records. Survived the war. [His surname may have been Stansberry.]

STOUT, JOHN, Private
Enlisted at Strawberry Plains, Tennessee, May 15, 1863, for the war. Reported present through June 30, 1863. No further records.

TAYLOR, JOHN, Private
Enlisted at Bristol, Tennessee, December 31, 1863, for the war. Reported present but sick on February 29, 1864. No further records.

THOMPSON, J. H., Private
Enlisted at Strawberry Plains, Tennessee, August 1, 1863, for the war. Reported present through February 29, 1864. Name appears on a receipt roll for clothing dated June 21, 1864. Transferred to Capt. John W. Barr's Battery, Virginia Light Artillery, August 17, 1864.

WALLACE, WILLIAM F., Sergeant
Previously served as Private in Company A, Jackson's Battalion Light Artillery, Virginia State Line. Enlisted in this company at Wytheville, Virginia, April 1, 1863, for the war. Mustered in as Sergeant. Reported present through February 29, 1864. Transferred to Capt. John W. Barr's Battery, Virginia Light Artillery, August 17, 1864. [His age is given as 22 on an undated muster roll for Capt. Horace B. Balfour's Company Virginia Mounted Riflemen, which later became Company A, Jackson's Battalion Light Artillery.]

WELLING, G. W., Private
Previously served as Private in Company D, Infantry Regiment of this legion. Transferred to this company on March 28, 1864. No further records.

WIGGINS, ANDREW C., Private
Previously served as Private in Company F, 29th Regiment N.C. Troops. Enlisted illegally in this company at Wytheville, Virginia, April 1, 1863, for the war, while absent without leave from the 29th Regiment. Reported absent without leave on June 21, 1863. Returned to duty on July 12, 1863, with "absence satisfactorily accounted for." Reported present through August 31, 1863. Reported present from November 11, 1863, through February 29, 1864. No further records.

WIGGINS, JOHN, _____
North Carolina pension records indicate that he transferred from Company D, Indian Battalion, to this company in September-October, 1864. However, the battery was known by that time as Barr's Battery. It had become physically detached from the Legion in May, 1864, and as no longer considered a formal part of the Legion by the Richmond authorities beginning in August, 1864. Survived the war.

WIGGINS, MOSES L., Private
Previously served as Private in Company F, 29th Regiment N.C. Troops. Enlisted illegally in this company at Wytheville, Virginia, April 1, 1863, for the war, while absent without leave from the 29th Regiment. Reported absent without leave from June 21, 1863, through November 10, 1863. No further records. [He probably deserted in the confusion surrounding the Federal capture of Strawberry Plains on June 20, 1863.]

WILBAR, G. H., Private
Enlisted at Strawberry Plains, Tennessee, August 1, 1863, for the war. Reported present through October 31, 1863. Reported on detached service on February 29, 1864. No further records.

WILLIAMS, GEORGE M., Private
Enlisted, probably at Wytheville, Virginia, April 1, 1863, for the war. Reported present through November 10, 1863. Reported absent without leave on February 29, 1864. Transferred to Capt. John W. Barr's Battery, Virginia Light Artillery, August 17, 1864.

WILLIAMS, H. G., Private
Enlisted at Strawberry Plains, Tennessee, July 21, 1863, for the war. Reported present through November 10, 1863. Reported absent without leave on February 29, 1864. Transferred to Capt. John W. Barr's Battery, Virginia Light Artillery, August 17, 1864.

YOUNG, THOMAS, Private
Enlisted at Strawberry Plains, Tennessee, July 15, 1863, for the war. Reported present through August 31, 1863. Reported captured on October 10, 1863, but no Federal records document his capture or imprisonment. Returned to duty, probably in November, 1863. Reported present through February 29, 1864. Transferred to Capt. John W. Barr's Battery, Virginia Light Artillery, August 17, 1864.

INDIAN BATTALION

The so-called "Indian Battalion" is the most problematic unit of Thomas's Legion. In many ways, the title is a bit of a misnomer, and it might in fact be more accurate to describe the command under the rubric of Western North Carolina Battalion or Second Battalion, Thomas's Legion. However, Thomas's original intent was to use the original Indian companies from the Infantry Regiment as a nucleus around which to raise more Cherokee companies. Although the evidence indicates that Thomas also raised new companies made up of whites as well, offical inspection report abstracts indicate that Thomas officially commanded only three to four companies of Indians throughout the period September, 1863-November, 1864. With a formal reorganization near the war's end, Thomas evidently separated the Indian companies from all other units, so the title "Indian Battalion" has stuck.

The evolution of this unit is complex, however, and due to the ambiguous and incomplete information on the exact nature of the command, some explanations are necessary. On September 2, 1863, Colonel Thomas withdrew from Strawberry Plains, Tennessee, for the mountains of western North Carolina. He was accompanied by the original Cherokee Indian companies, 2nd Company A and Company B of the Infantry Regiment. Thomas claimed that he was acting under orders from Maj. Gen. Simon Bolivar Buckner. According to Thomas, he was subsequently authorized by General Braxton Bragg to begin raising more Indian companies. He also attempted to organize absentees from Thomas's Legion into companies, often under their own company commanders. This was particularly true in the case of several companies of Walker's Battalion. At this time, the rest of Thomas's Legion was stationed in eastern Tennessee and (some times with other units) was known officially as Jackson's Brigade, commanded by Alfred E. Jackson. It was Jackson who had dispatched the company officers in the fall of 1863 to gather up their deserters and absentees; Thomas, who did not acknowledge Jackson's authority over the Legion, either persuaded or pressured the company officers and their men to remain with him in western N.C.

Over the next few months, Thomas also organized one or two companies made up of deserters from other units (especially cavalry regiments). There is also evidence that part or all of Company K, 5th Regiment Tennessee Cavalry (McKenzie's), formerly Company F, Walker's Battalion, joined Thomas by the spring of 1864 and consolidated with another company which is otherwise undocumented. Finally, there are vague references to a number of other units (some of which were possibly Home Guard or militia units) that are mentioned in the correspondence of Thomas as either under his authoroity or as acting in cooperation with him. There were seven companies in all by April, 1864, four of which were primarily made up of Cherokee Indians.

Thomas's efforts to, in effect, recreate the Legion in absentia by organizing the absentees into counterparts of their actual units seems to have quickly floundered, in part due to the murder of Lt. Col. William C. Walker of Walker's Battalion in January, 1864. This was followed by the prosecution by Jackson of many of the company officers who had stayed with Thomas, forcing them to return to Tennessee to defend themselves and get their ranks restored. In addition, Lt. Col. James R. Love, Jr., of the Infantry Regiment, who was otherwise sympathetic to Thomas's goals of reuniting the Legion under Thomas's own command, bombarded his erstwhile commander with missives both requesting and demanding that Thomas return the men to Tennessee. It is not known for certain how Thomas organized those absentees who refused to return to Tennessee and continued to serve with him; they were probably put into some of the other companies in the command.

The rest of the Legion returned to western North Carolina from the Shenandoah Valley in December, 1864. At this time, the Legion was in a fairly disorganized shape, including as it did the remnants of the Infantry Regiment, Walker's [McKamy's] Battalion, and the companies Thomas had already with him. Those men with Thomas who were absentees from other units of the Legion probably returned to their old companies at this time. Thomas seems to have gathered the Indian companies together separately by February 1865. He received authorization to formally organize them into a battalion on April 9, 1865, the anniversary of the enlistment of the original Indian companies in 1862 and the date that they would be required to re-enlist for the war. [Thomas to Love, March 31, 1865, William H. Thomas Papers, Western Carolina University]. Due to the beginning of the final campaign in western North Carolina at about that time, it is not known if he completed this task. What happened to the other three companies made up of whites that had been serving with them, and how they fit into the overall organization of the final version of Thomas's Legion, is uncertain. Information contained in an estimate of funds for the Department of Western North Carolina seems to indicate that two of the companies went to the Infantry Regiment, while the third went to McKamy's Battalion. [Consolidated Estimate of Funds Required for the Pay of the Troops in the Department of Western North Carolina for the Months of March and April 1865, March 11, 1865, Thomas Legion, Battalion Field and Staff File #1, Muster and Pay Rolls, Chapter 1: Entry 18, Box 826, RG 109, NA.]

The exact size of Thomas's western North Carolina command, and both the nature of its organization and precisely how it evolved, seems now impossible to fully straighten out. Early historians of Thomas's Legion, such as the authors of the unit histories in Clark's *Regiments*, did nothing to really untangle the issue, perhaps because they did not truly understand the situation themselves. Further complications arose as a result of the efforts of the author of the history of Walker's Battalion in Clark's *Regiments* to retroactively increase the size of his unit from a battalion to a regiment (the "80th N.C. Regiment"); in order to accomplish this, he added Thomas's two later Indian companies to the organization of Walker's Battalion. In the process, he may have mixed up or incorrectly assigned which officers belonged to which company. The often vaguely-worded Provost Marshall records for soldiers captured from Thomas's mountain command have added to the confusion, as they often identify the soldiers by company letter only. When the National Archives transcribers began creating service jackets for soldiers, they automatically identified men from the Legion with a company letter only as belonging to companies in the Infantry Regiment; however, in some cases, the date and location of capture clearly identify these men as having been with Thomas. In the cases of some men who were apparently AWOL from other companies of the Legion, some of these men have two different company designations in their records: the identifiable company letter of their actual company in either the Infantry Regiment or Walker's Battalion, and a different company letter designation, which is presumed to be the letter of the company they were serving under in western North Carolina. Finally, other documents ranging from Thomas's wartime correspondence to pension records introduce the names of a number of company officers and enlisted men who are often difficult or impossible to identify fully, as are their units.

The organization of the battalion in the following roster represents the seven-company structure that is known to have existed by April 1864, and which lasted until the end of that year or early 1865, when Thomas separated the Indian companies. There is also a place for one more company which Thomas attempted to organize in August-September 1864, but which was probably never completed. As no formal rosters exist for any of the companies of this battalion survive, the following reconstruction is based on a variety of sources.

Many of the identifications of officers and soldiers with particular companies remain tentative at best; decisions to their placement were made based on careful consideration of a number of factors.

FIELD AND STAFF

COLONEL

THOMAS, WILLIAM HOLLAND

Previously served as Colonel of the Infantry Regiment of this legion. According to Thomas and others, either Maj. Gen. Simon Bolivar Buckner, then commander of the Department of East Tennessee, or General Braxton Bragg, commander of the Department of Tennessee (to whom Buckner at that time answered), or both, officially ordered him at this time to take 2nd Company A and Company B of this regiment to guard the mountain passes running from eastern Tennessee to western North Carolina. Under this arrangement, Thomas was supposed to answer directly to Buckner, rather than to Brig. Gen. Alfred E. Jackson, Thomas's immediate superior. [James Wharrey Terrell to Governor Zebulon Baird Vance, February 22, 1864, Governors' Papers: Zebulon Baird Vance, 1862-1865, N.C. State Archives; William Holland Thomas to "General" (Samuel Cooper), July 8, 1864, unbound letterbook pages, William Holland Thomas Papers, Special Collections, Perkins Library, Duke University; William Holland Thomas, remarks written on Special Requisition No. 40, September 3, 1864, Compiled Service Records for Col. William H. Thomas, National Archives.] No official papers directly documenting this assignment have so far surfaced. Thomas is known to have departed with the Indian companies from Strawberry Plains, Tennessee, on September 2, 1863. [Mollie Stringfield to William Williams Stringfield, September 3, 1863, William Williams Stringfield Papers, N.C. State Archives.] Although the companies were still considered officially to be a part of the Infantry Regiment, Thomas soon began organizing other companies which he lettered successively in order after the companies he already had; Companies C and D are documented. This informally marks the beginning of what became known as the Indian Battalion, although it was not officially organized until 1865. From September, 1863, until December, 1864, when the remnants of the legion returned to North Carolina from the Shenandoah Valley, Thomas had direct command only of these companies, although he both claimed and attempted to exercise direct authority over the rest of the legion. At the time Thomas departed Strawberry Plains with the Indian companies, he was officially reported absent under arrest from August 15, 1863, on three inspection reports dated November 24 and December 12, 1863, and January 12, 1864, as well as a fourth report which is undated. Reason he was considered under arrest is not reported, but it appears that it was due to "some alleged disobedience of orders." Thomas had been sent to Knoxville, Tennessee, for trial but the trial had evidently been cancelled or postponed indefinitely [Terrell to Vance, February 22, 1864, Governors' Papers: Zebulon Baird Vance, near Morganton, N.C. State Archives. Terrell misdates the arrest to June.] According to Capt. Stephen Whitaker of Company E, Walker's Battalion, Thomas had been restored to duty by August 25, 1863, prior to his assignment with the Indian companies. [Stephen Whitaker to James Whitaker, August 25, 1863, Stephen Whitaker Papers, N.C. State Archives.] Why he was considered under arrest for so long is not known, but the charges were originally instituted by Brig. Gen. Alfred E. Jackson, and it is possible that he considered Thomas's restoration to command only a temporary expediency in the face of military necessity. Regardless, the charges seem to have been subsequently dropped on an unknown date. Signature appears on a list of receipts for issuances to the army, December 12, 1863. Name appears on a pay voucher dated November 19, 1864, for service in July-October, 1864. Signature appears on a special requisition for corn dated September 3, 1864. Signature appears on a special requisition for horse forage, September 12, 1864. Court martialed in Goldsboro, North Carolina, prior to October 22, 1864, on charges of "recruiting and enlisting deserters," "conduct unbecoming an officer and a gentleman," and "conduct to the prejudice of good order and military discipline." Found not guilty on twenty-one of twenty-two specifications of the first count, on both specifications of the second count, and the second of three specifications of the third count. Found guilty on the twenty-second specification of the first count and the first and third specifications of the third count. Sentenced "to be reprimanded in orders from Department Head Quarters," but ordered "to resume his sword." [See Charges and Specifications Against Colonel William H. Thomas of Thomas N.C. Legion, May 11, 1864, microfilm 284-03-01, William Holland Thomas Papers, Special Collections, Perkins Library, Duke University (original in the William Holland Thomas Papers, Special Collections, Hunter Library, Western Carolina University); Court Martial Proceedings Against Colonel William Holland Thomas' N.C. Legion, October 22, 1864, published in General Orders No. 63, Department of North Carolina and South Virginia, Entry 68, Box 2, RG 109, National Archives.] Resumed command of the entirety of Thomas's Legion in December, 1864.

LIEUTENANT COLONEL

McDOWELL, BRYAN GIBBS

Served as Lieutenant Colonel of the 62nd Regiment N.C. Troops. Appointed acting commander of that section of this legion operating in western North Carolina on an unknown date between August 8 and October 16, 1864, during a period when Colonel Thomas was absent. No further records. [See Special Requisition dated October 16, 1864, in which he signs hmself "Lt Col Comdg," compiled service record for Captain D.C. Ghormley, 5th Regiment Tennessee Cavalry (McKenzie's); Special Requisition dated October 17, 1864, in which McDowell signs himself as "Lt Col Comdg Thomas's Legion," with his headquarters in Asheville, compiled service record for Lt. Col. Bryan Gibbs McDowell, 62nd N.C. Troops. He may have also temporarily acted in command of the Infantry Regiment during early 1865 due to the illness of Lieutenant Colonel Love. See Clark's *Regiments*, 3:756; Crow, *Storm in the Mountains*, 112-113, 150.]

ASSISTANT QUARTERMASTER

TERRELL, WILLIAM STUART

Previously served as 1st Lieutenant in Company A of this battalion. According to a letter dated July 7, 1864, from Colonel Thomas to Maj. R. W. Memminger, Assistant Adjutant General of the District of Western North Carolina, Terrell was "my Acting A.Q.M." [Thomas to Memminger, July 7, 1864, unbound pages, Thomas Letterbook, 1860-1864 Correspondence Folder, William Holland Thomas Papers, Special Collections, Perkins Library, Duke University.] Date and duration of this appointment is unknown. No further records. Survived the war.

COMPANY A

This company, raised in Jackson County and composed primarily of Cherokee Indians, served previously as (2nd) Company A, Infantry Regiment of this legion. In April, 1865, it formally became Company A, Indian Battalion of this legion. However, the Indian Battalion had been informally organized in late 1863. For the purposes of these rosters, September 2, 1863, will be used for separating materials for members of 2nd Company A, Infantry Regiment, from those of Company A, Indian Battalion. It was on that date that Col. William H. Thomas left Strawberry Plains, Tennessee, with this company and Company B of the Infantry Regiment, marched into the Smoky Mountains, and began recruiting a third Indian company. These companies were never reintegrated into the structure of the Infantry Regiment again, even after the Legion was reunited in western North Carolina in December, 1864.

No muster rolls survive for this company. Valuable information was obtained from the microfilm edition of the Compiled Service Records of Confederate Soldiers Who Served in Organizations from the State of North Carolina (Record Group 109, M270), National Archives, Washington, D.C. The Compiled Service Records series includes enlistment papers, pay vouchers, requisitions, letters of resignation, discharge certificates, and abstracts of medical and prisoner of war returns.

Also utilized in this roster were *The War of the Rebellion: A Compilation of the Official Records of the Union and Confederate Armies*, the North Carolina Adjutant General's papers, state militia records, newspaper casualty lists and obituaries, wartime claims for bounty pay and allowances, postwar registers of claims for artificial limbs, Confederate pension applications filed with the states of North Carolina, Tennessee, and Florida, records of the North Carolina Confederate Soldiers' Home, and the 1860 and 1870 federal censuses of North Carolina. A search was made also for relevant letters, diaries, reminiscences, and other manuscripts in the Southern Historical Collection (University of North Carolina-Chapel Hill) and the Duke University Library Special Collections Department.

Among the secondary sources consulted were records of the North Carolina division of the United Daughters of the Confederacy, postwar rosters, regimental and county histories, marriage bond, will, and cemetery indexes, published and unpublished genealogies, biographical dictionaries, the North Carolina *County Heritage Book* series, the *Confederate Veteran*, Walter Clark's *Histories of the Several Regiments and Battalions from North Carolina in the Great War, 1861-'65*, and the North Carolina volume of the extended edition of *Confederate Military History*.

OFFICERS

CAPTAIN

LOVE, MATTHEW HALE

Previously served as Captain of 2nd Company A, Infantry Regiment of this legion. Transferred to this company on an unspecified date. Signature appears on requisitions and receipts for shoes dated October 16, 20, and 24, 1864. No further records. Survived the war. [The special requisitions for shoes dated October 24, 1864, designate him as "Com[man]d[ing] Thomas Legion." At the time, Love was in command of a detachment of men from different companies in this legion that was part of an expedition under Colonel John B. Palmer into eastern Tennessee. See the history of Thomas's Legion in this volume, as well as Crow's *Storm in the Mountains*, and the sources cited within both. The October 16, 1864 requisition refers to Love as "Com[man]d[ing] Detachment Thomas Legion." According to Clark's *Regiments* 3: 760, he was part of the flag-of-truce party under Lieutenant Colonel William Williams Stringfield of Walker's Battalion which was captured and imprisoned by Federal authorities on May 1, 1865, when they refused to take the Oath of Allegiance; however, unlike other members of that party, there are no surviving Federal Provost Marshal records for Love to indicate that he was actually captured at that time. Although Stringfield again recalled Love's presence in his "Memoirs of the Civil War," 34-35, it is more likely that he surrendered with his company and Colonel Thomas at Waynesville on May 9, 1865.]

LIEUTENANTS

COLLINS, JOSEPH A, 2nd Lieutenant

Previously served as Private in Company B, 25th Regiment N.C. Troops. Transferred to or enlisted in this company on an unknown date, probably illegally while absent without leave from the 25th Regiment. [Allen, *Annals of Haywood County*, 455. According to Allen, Joseph A. Collins was in command of the company at the end of the war.]

TERRELL, WILLIAM STUART, 1st Lieutenant

Previously served as 1st Lieutenant of 2nd Company A, Infantry Regiment of this legion. Transferred to this company on an unspecified date. Later served as Acting Assistant Quartermaster of this battalion.

WHITAKER, DAVID LAFAYETTE, 3rd Lieutenant

Served as 3rd Lieutenant of 2nd Company A, Infantry Regiment of this legion. May have served later in this company.

NONCOMMISSIONED OFFICERS AND PRIVATES

AMMONS, SAM, _____

North Carolina pension records appear to indicate that he served in this company. Survived the war.

ARMACHAIN, SEVIER, _____

Cherokee Indian. North Carolina pension records appear to indicate that he served in 2nd Company A, Infantry Regiment of this legion. He may have served later in this company. [His name was also rendered as Severe Armachan.]

ARQUETAGE, JR., Private

Cherokee Indian. Served as Private in 2nd Company A, Infantry Regiment of this legion. May have served later in this company.

ARQUETAGE, SR., Private

Cherokee Indian. Served as Private in 2nd Company A, Infantry Regiment of this legion. May have served later in this company.

BATTLE, JAMES F., _____

North Carolina pension records appear to indicate that he served in 2nd Company A, Infantry Regiment of this legion. He may have served later in this company.

BIRD, SQUINEY, _____

Cherokee Indian. North Carolina pension records appear to indicate that he served in 2nd Company A, Infantry Regiment of this legion. He may have served later in this company. [His name was also rendered as Squanci Bird.]

BOWMAN, J. W., Private

Federal Provost Marshal records indicate that he was either a member of this company or of Company A, Walker's Battalion. Place and date of enlistment not reported. Captured at Knoxville, Tennessee, May 1, 1865. Released on bond by a Knox County, Tennessee, civil court on May 24, 1865. [His capture at Knoxville on May 1, 1865, indicates that he was a member of Lt. Col. William W. Stringfield's flag-of-truce party that was arrested when they refused to take the Oath of Allegiance.]

BRADLEY, WILLIAM M., _____

North Carolina pension records appear to indicate that he served in 2nd Company A, Infantry Regiment of this legion. He may have served later in this company.

BRANNER, JOSEPH A., Private

Served as Private in 2nd Company A, Infantry Regiment of this legion. He may have served later in this company.

CAH HAH, Private

Cherokee Indian. Served as Private in 2nd Company A, Infantry Regiment of this legion. He may have served later in this company. [He was also known as Wild Cat.]

CHAR CHU, Private

Cherokee Indian. Served as Private in 2nd Company A, Infantry Regiment of this legion. May have served later in this company. [His name may have been Charche or Charchee.]

CHELETOOHSKIH, Corporal

Cherokee Indian. Previously served as Corporal in 2nd Company A, Infantry Regiment of this legion. Transferred to this company on an unspecified date. Name appears on a receipt roll for clothing dated October 16, 1864. No further records. Survived the war. [Name also rendered as Chee-le-tos-Key, Chee-lee-tos-Key, and Chiltosk.]

CHELLEE, Private

Cherokee Indian. Served in 2nd Company A, Infantry Regiment of this legion. May have served later in this company.

CHILDERS, GEORGE, Private

Previously served in 2nd Company A, Infantry Regiment of this legion. Transferred to this company on an unspecified date. Captured at Jonesborough, Tennessee, September 4, 1863. Sent to Louisville, Kentucky, where he arrived on October 5, 1863. Transferred to Camp Douglas, Chicago, Illinois, October 7, 1863. Arrived at Camp Douglas on an unspecified date. No further records.

CHONAH, Private

Cherokee Indian. Served as Private in 2nd Company A, Infantry Regiment of this legion. May have served later in this company. [His name was also rendered as Tso:na.]

CHOWISHKEH, Private

Cherokee Indian. Served as Private in 2nd Company A, Infantry Regiment of this legion. May have served later in this company.

CHUCHOLETEH, Private

Cherokee Indian. Served as Private in 2nd Company A, Infantry Regiment of this legion. May have served later in this company.

CHULOTATAGEH, Private

Cherokee Indian. Served as Private in 2nd Company A, Infantry Regiment of this legion. May have served later in this company.

CHUNOILEGAH, Private

Cherokee Indian. Served as Private in 2nd Company A, Infantry Regiment of this legion. May have served later in this company.

CHUWHALOOKEEH, Private

Cherokee Indian. Served as Private in 2nd Company A, Infantry Regiment of this legion. May have served later in this company. [His name was also rendered as Chu-wa-lookeh.]

CLANTEESTEH, Private

Cherokee Indian. Served as Private in 2nd Company A, Infantry Regiment of this legion. May have served later in this company. [His name was also rendered as Chlantees-teh and Clantechee. He was also known as Pheasant.]

CLARK, HUGH L., Private

Probably previously served as Private in 2nd Company A, Infantry Regiment of this legion. Transferred to this company on an unspecified date. Transferred to Company D of the Infantry Regiment on February 10, 1864.

CLINE, ALFRED, 1st Sergeant

Served as 1st Sergeant of Company A, Infantry Regiment of this legion. May have served later in this company.

CLINE, JOHN W., Private

Previously served as Private in 2nd Company A, Infantry Regiment of this legion. North Carolina pension records appear to indicate that he subsequently served in this company as well. Survived the war. [North Carolina pension records indicate that he was "shot six times . . . in left arm" at the Little River, Tennessee, in July, 1864.]

CLINE, WILLIAM R., Private

Served as Private in 2nd Company A, Infantry Regiment of this legion. May have served later in this company.

COHGOH, Private

Cherokee Indian. Served as Private in 2nd Company A, Infantry Regiment of this legion. May have served later in this company. [His name is also rendered as Cohgah. He was also known as Wesley Crow.]

COLA CHUSTEE, Private

Cherokee Indian. Previously served as Private in 2nd Company A, Infantry Regiment of this legion. Transferred to this company on an unspecified date. Captured on or about February 25, 1864. Confined at Knoxville, Tennessee, the same date. Released on March 10, 1864, after taking the Oath of Allegiance. [His name may have been Chustee Cola. He was probably one of the party of fifteen Indians who surrendered to the Federals at Motley's Ford, Tennessee, February 22, 1864.]

COMMONIH, Private

Cherokee Indian. Served as Private in 2nd Company A, Infantry Regiment of this legion. May have served later in this company. [His name is also rendered as Com-mnih. He was also known as Ross Cucumber.]

CONNER, J. S., _____

North Carolina pension records appear to indicate that he served in this company following prior service in 2nd Company A, Infantry Regiment of this legion. Survived the war. [North Carolina pension records indicate that he was wounded by a bullet in his left calf and injured in the right hip by a saber at Sweetwater, Tennessee, in 1864.]

COWWHEELEH, JOHNSON, Musician

Cherokee Indian. Served as Musician in 2nd Company A, Infantry Regiment of this legion. May have served later in this company.

DO:TSULE':HNV, _____

Cherokee Indian. Served either in 2nd Company A or in Company B, Infantry Regiment of this legion. If he served in 2nd Company A, he may have served later in this company.

EARL, NOAH, Private

Resided in Macon County. Federal Provost Marshal records indicate that he served either in this company or in Company A, Walker's Battalion. Place and date of enlistment not reported. Captured at Knoxville, Tennessee, May 1, 1865. Transferred to Nashville, Tennessee, May 3, 1865. Confined at Louisville, Kentucky, May 15, 1865. Released at Lousville on June 16, 1865, after taking the Oath of Allegiance. [If he served in this company, he may have previously served in 2nd Company A, Infantry Regiment. His surname may have been Earles or Erles. He may have served previously in Company E, 39th Regiment N.C.Troops. His capture at Knoxville on May 1, 1865, indicates that he was a member of Lt. Col. William W. Stringfield's flag-of-truce party that was arrested when they refused to take the Oath of Allegiance.]

ECOOEH, JOHN, Private

Cherokee Indian. Served as Private in 2nd Company A, Infantry Regiment of this legion. May have served later in this company.

ESSICKEH, GOOTAGEESKIH, Private

Cherokee Indian. Served as Private in 2nd Company A, Infantry Regiment of this legion. May have served later in this company.

FORD, JAMES, Private

Enlisted in this company at about age 21, on an unspecified date. Transferred to Company D, Infantry Regiment of this legion, February 10, 1864. [May have served previously in 2nd Company A, Infantry Regiment of this legion.]

FORESTER, WILLIAM C., _____

Served as Private in Company C, 7th Battalion N.C. Cavalry. Reported absent without leave from that company at the time of its transfer to the 65th Regiment N.C. Troops (6th Regiment N.C. Cavalry), where it became Company C and, later, 2nd Company G. Enlisted illegally in this company between September, 1863, and April, 1864. Survived the war. [His surname may have been Forister, Forrester, or Forster.]

GALBREATH, JOSEPH M., Private

Previously served in Company F, Infantry Regiment of this legion. Transferred to this company on January 1, 1864.

GE:DINI, _____

Cherokee Indian. Served either in 2nd Company A or Company B, Infantry Regiment of this legion. If he served in 2nd Company A, he may have served later in this company.

GIBBS, H. F., Private

Served as Private in 2nd Company A, Infantry Regiment of this legion. May have served later in this company.

GIBSON, E. P., _____

North Carolina pension records appear to indicate that he served in this company. Later served as 2nd Lieutenant of Company D of this battalion.

GREYBEARD, EZEKIEL, Private

Cherokee Indian. Served as Private in 2nd Company A, Infantry Regiment of this legion. May have served later in this company. [His surname may have been Graybeard.]

HENDERSON, JOHN G., Private

Federal Provost Marshal records indicate that he served either in this company or in Company A, Walker's Battalion. Place and date of enlistment not reported. Captured at Knoxville, Tennessee, May 1, 1865. Released by a Knox County, Tennessee, civil court on May 24, 1865. [If he served in this company, he may have previously served in 2nd Company A, Infantry Regiment of this legion. His capture at Knoxville on May 1 indicates that he was a member of Lt. Col. William W. Stringfield's flag-of-truce party that was arrested when they refused to take the Oath of Allegiance. In his history of the Infantry Regiment, former Lieutenant Colonel Stringfield gives Henderson's rank as "Captain" at the time of his arrest; see Clark's *Regiments*, 3:760. In his "Memoirs of the Civil War," p. 35, Stringfield gives Henderson's rank as Lieutenant. Rank is Pvt on P.O.W. record.]

HENSON, THOMAS, Private

Served as Private in 2nd Company A, Infantry Regiment of this legion. May have served later in this company.

HOWEENEETE, Private

Cherokee Indian. Served as Private in 2nd Company A, Infantry Regiment of this legion. May have served later in this company. [His name is also rendered as Howaneete and Howee-neo-ta. He was also known as James D. Walkingstick. Later served in Company D, 3rd N. C. Mounted Infantry (Union).]

IYAHANEH, Sergeant

Cherokee Indian. Served as Sergeant in 2nd Company A, Infantry Regiment of this legion. May have served later in this company. [His name was also rendered as Iyo-ha-ne. He was also known as Swimmer Fox.]

JACKSON, JOHN, _____

Cherokee Indian. North Carolina pension records seem to indicate that he served in 2nd Company A, Infantry Regiment of this legion. If he did, he may have served later in this company.

JASSAN, Private

Cherokee Indian. Served as Private in 2nd Company A, Infantry Regiment of this legion. May have served later in this company. [His name was also rendered as Jessan, Jasson, and Jess Ann.]

JENKINS, JOHN _____

North Carolina pension records appear to indicate that he served in 2nd Company A, Infantry Regiment of this legion. He may have served later in this company.

JENKINS, THOMAS, _____

North Carolina pension records appear to indicate that he served in this company.

JONES, D. M., Private

Served either in this company or in Company A, Walker's Battalion. Captured at Anderson, South Carolina, May 3, 1865. Paroled on an unspecified date.

JUNALUSKEE, Musician

Cherokee Indian. Served as Musician in 2nd Company A, Infantry Regiment of this legion. May have served later in this company.

KUNTISKEE, Private

Cherokee Indian. Previously served as Private in 2nd Company A, Infantry Regiment of this legion. Transferred to this company on an unspecified date. Captured on or about February 25, 1864. Confined at Knoxville, Tennessee, February 25, 1864. Released at Knoxville on March 10, 1864, after taking the Oath of Allegiance. Later served in Company D, 3rd Regiment N.C. Mounted Infantry (Union) [Name also rendered as Keen-tis-kee. Also known as John Igotpa. He was probably one of the party of fifteen Indians who surrendered to the Federals at Motley's Ford, Tennessee, on February 22, 1864.]

LANE, J. P., Private

Name appears on a "Roll of Prisoners captured by U.S. Forces . . . and paroled at Hartwell, Ga., and Anderson and Greenville, S.C." which indicates that he served either in this company or in Company A, Walker's Battalion.

LOSSIH, JOHN, Private

Cherokee Indian. Served as Private in 2nd Company A, Infantry Regiment of this legion. May have served later in this company. [His name was also rendered as Tsa:n(i)lo:si. His name is rendered, probably erroneously, as Lossih John in the National Archives Compiled Service Records.]

LOWSINNEH, Private

Cherokee Indian. Served as Private in 2nd Company A, Infantry Regiment of this legion. May have served later in this company. [His name was also rendered as La:hw(i)sini.]

MATOY, LEVI C., Private

Cherokee Indian. Served as Private in 2nd Company A, Infantry Regiment of this legion. May have served later in this company.

MATOY, WILLIAM R., "Interpreter"

Cherokee Indian. Served as Interpreter in 2nd Company A, Infantry Regiment of this legion. May have served later in this company.

MAY, PATRICK H., Private

Previously served as Private in Company B, Infantry Regiment of this legion. Transferred to a "Company A" of this legion, probably this company, on an unspecified date. Captured at Knoxville, Tennessee, May 1, 1865. Sent to Chattanooga, Tennessee, and Nashville, Tennessee. Confined at Louisville, Kentucky, May 15, 1865. Released at Louisville on or about June 16, 1865, after taking the Oath of Allegiance. [His capture at Knoxville on May 1, 1865, indicates that he was a member of Lt. Col.William W. Stringfield's flag-of-truce party that was arrested when they refused to take the Oath of Allegiance.]

NINNETOOYEH, Private

Cherokee Indian. Served as Private in 2nd Company A, Infantry Regiment of this legion. May have served later in this company.

ONOKATA, _____

Cherokee Indian. Place and date of enlistment not reported; probably enlisted subsequent to February 29, 1864. Name appears on a receipt roll for clothing dated October 16, 1864. No further records. Survived the war.

OODAHNEETAHDEE, _____

Cherokee Indian. North Carolina pension records indicate that he served in 2nd Company A, Infantry Regiment of this legion. He may have served later in this company.

OOLASTIEH, Private

Cherokee Indian. Served as Private in 2nd Company A, Infantry Regiment of this legion. May have served later in this company. [His name was also rendered as Oo-lassta-eh. He was also known as Joe Lowin.]

OOLONUSTEESKIH, Corporal

Cherokee Indian. Previously served as Corporal in 2nd Company A, Infantry Regiment of this legion. Transferred to this company on an unspecified date. Name appears on a receipt roll for clothing dated October 16, 1864. No further records. Survived the war. [His name may have been Ooloanustiskee.]

OOLSECOGATE, Corporal

Cherokee Indian. Served as Corporal in 2nd Company A, Infantry Regiment of this legion. He may have served later in this company.

OOLSTOOIH, Private

Cherokee Indian. Served as Private in 2nd Company A, Infantry Regiment of this legion. May have served later in this company. [He was also known as John Wagoola, John Daboo, and John Brown. Subsequently deserted to the enemy and served in Company D, 3rd Regiment N.C. Mounted Infantry (Union).]

OOLSTOOIH, Private

Cherokee Indian ("Essicheeh's son"). Served as Private in 2nd Company A, Infantry Regiment of this legion. May have served later in this company.

OONOHLEE, Private

Cherokee Indian. Served as Private in 2nd Company A, Infantry Regiment of this legion. May have served later in this company.

OOSOWIH, Private

Cherokee Indian. Served as Private in 2nd Company A, Infantry Regiment of this legion. May have served later in this company. [His name was also rendered as John Uosowii. He may have been the same man as Tso:wah of this company.]

OOSTENACOO, Private

Cherokee Indian. Served as Private in 2nd Company A, Infantry Regiment of this legion. May have served later in this company. [His name was also rendered as Oo-ste-na-coo. He was also known as John Taylor. Subsequently deserted to the enemy and served in Company D, 3rd Regiment N.C. Mounted Infantry (Union).]

OOTALKIH, Private

Cherokee Indian. Served as Private in 2nd Company A, Infantry Regiment of this legion. May have served later in this company.

OOTEELTEGEESKIH, WALLESKIH, Private

Cherokee Indian. Served as Private in 2nd Company A, Infantry Regiment of this legion. May have served later in this company. [His name was also rendered as Oo-teet-geeskih Wallaski.]

OOTEETTIGEESKIH, TECOLUGEESKIH, Private

Cherokee Indian. Served as Private in 2nd Company A, Infantry Regiment of this legion. May have served later in this company.

OOYOSKEE, TOM, Private

Cherokee Indian. Served as Private in 2nd Company A, Infantry Regiment of this legion. May have served later in this company.

OTTER, NOWEYOUTEEH, Private

Cherokee Indian. Served as Private in 2nd Company A, Infantry Regiment of this legion. May have served later in this company. [His name was also rendered as Otter Now-eyontieh. He was also known as Thomas Otter and Tom Otter. Later deserted to the enemy and served in Company D, 3rd Regiment N.C. Mounted Infantry (Union).]

OWKWATAGA, _____

Cherokee Indian. Place and date of enlistment not reported. Deserted to the enemy on an unknown date. Subsequently served in Company D, 3rd Regiment N. C. Mounted Infantry (Union). [Name also rendered as Okwataga. May have served previously in 2nd Company A, Infantry Regiment of this legion.]

PANTHER, S. C., _____

North Carolina pension records appear to indicate that he served in 2nd Company A, Infantry Regiment of this legion. May have served later in this company.

QUENNA IYANTOOGA, Private

Cherokee Indian. Served as Private in 2nd Company A, Infantry Regiment of this legion. May have served later in this company.

RECKLEY, MASON, Private

Half Cherokee Indian. Previously served as Private in 2nd Company A, Infantry Regiment of this legion. Transferred to this company on an unspecified date. Captured on or about February 7, 1864, probably in the Federal raid on Colonel Thomas's camp at Deep Creek, near Quallatown, February 2, 1864. Confined at Knoxville, Tennessee. Reported as having been "[s]ent out as scout by order [of] the Genl Comd Dept of the Ohio." Returned to Knoxville on March 8, 1864. Released at Knoxville on March 10, 1864, after taking the Oath of Allegiance. Later served in Company D, 3rd Regiment N.C. Mounted Infantry (Union). [His surname may have been Ratley or Ratliff.]

REED, JESSE, Private

Three-quarters Cherokee Indian. Served as Private in 2nd Company A, Infantry Regiment of this legion. May have served later in this company. [He may have been the same man as Pvt. Jesse whose record appears in the miscellaneous section of this roster.]

RICE, WILLIAM E., Private

Previously served as Private in 2nd Company A, Infantry Regiment of this legion. Transferred to this company on an unspecified date. Deserted to the enemy on an unspecified date. Confined at Knoxville, Tennessee, January 26, 1865. Transferred to Louisville, Kentucky, where he arrived on February 13, 1865. Took the Oath of Allegiance and was released at Louisville on February 14, 1865, with instructions to remain north of the Ohio River during the war.

SAMMIH, NEDDA., Private

Cherokee Indian. Previously served as Private in 2nd Company A, Infantry Regiment of this legion. Transferred to this company on an unspecified date. Name appears on a receipt roll for clothing dated October 16, 1864. No further records. Survived the war. [His name may have been Samuel Nedda or Needa. He may also have been known as Samrrinreth. He may have been the same man as Ne:di who served in Company C of this battalion.]

SANDERS, JOHN, Private

Cherokee Indian. Served as Private in 2nd Company A, Infantry Regiment of this legion. May have served later in this company. [According to an 1892 U.S. Extra Census Bulletin, he deserted to the enemy and served in an unspecified Federal unit.]

SANTONEH, Private

Cherokee Indian. Served as Private in 2nd Company A, Infantry Regiment of this legion. May have served later in this company. [His name was also rendered as San-to-neh. He was also known as James Kegg.]

SANTOOLA, Private

Cherokee Indian. Served as Private in 2nd Company A, Infantry Regiment of this legion. May have served later in this company.

SEGILLEH, HOWETEIYEH, Private
Cherokee Indian. Served as Private in 2nd Company A, Infantry Regiment of this legion. May have served later in this company.

SEKETYAKNCH., _____
Cherokee Indian. Place and date of enlistment not reported; probably enlisted subsequent to December 31, 1863. Name appears on a receipt roll for clothing dated October 16, 1864. No further records. [The receipt roll information is misfiled in the National Archives Compiled Service Record for Pvt. Scacheloskee of 2nd Company A, Infantry Regiment of this legion.]

SEQUOYEH, STANDING WOLF, Private
Cherokee Indian. Served as Private in 2nd Company A, Infantry Regiment of this legion. May have served later in this company. [His name may have been Sequoyeh Standing Wolf.]

SHULER, JOSEPH, Private
Served as Private in 2nd Company A, Infantry Regiment of this legion. May have served later in this company.

SIHKIH, Private
Cherokee Indian. Served as Private in 2nd Company A, Infantry Regiment of this legion. May have served later in this company. [He may have been the same man as Selkonie, also known as John Seke, whose record appears in the miscellaneous section of this roster.]

SKITTEH, MIKEE, Private
Cherokee Indian. Served as Private in 2nd Company A, Infantry Regiment of this legion. May have served later in this company. [His name was also rendered as Mickee Skittes and Skitteh Mikee. He may have served later in Company D, 3rd Regiment N.C. Mounted Infantry (Union).]

SMILEY, J. M., _____
North Carolina pension records appear to indicate that he served in this company. Survived the war.

SOLOLANETA, BIRD, _____
Cherokee Indian. North Carolina pension records indicate that he served in 2nd Company A, Infantry Regiment of this legion. May have served later in this company. [His name was also rendered as Bird Solanuta and Sololaneeta Bird.]

SOOQUECHEE, Private
Cherokee Indian. Served as Private in 2nd Company A, Infantry Regiment of this legion. May have served later in this company. [His name was also rendered as Soo-quechee.]

SQUENSEH, Private
Cherokee Indian. Served as Private in 2nd Company A, Infantry Regiment of this legion. May have served later in this company.

STEAH, WILL, Private
Cherokee Indian. Served as Private in 2nd Company A, Infantry Regiment of this legion. May have served later in this company.

STEE, SKILLE, Private
Cherokee Indian. Served as Private in 2nd Company A, Infantry Regiment of this legion. May have served later in this company.

SUNKEE, _____
Cherokee Indian. North Carolina pension records indicate that he served in 2nd Company A, Infantry Regiment of this legion. May have served later in this company.

SUQUEYEH, Private
Cherokee Indian. Served as Private in 2nd Company A, Infantry Regiment of this legion. May have served later in this company. [His name was also rendered as Suque-yeh.]

SUTAGAH, _____
Cherokee Indian. North Carolina pension records appear to indicate that he served in 2nd Company A, Infantry Regiment of this legion. May have served later in this company.

SWANN, S. C., Private
Reported in Federal Provost Marshal records to be a member of "Co. A, Thomas Legion." He served either in this company or in Company A, Walker's Battalion. Place and date of enlistment not reported. Captured at Knoxville, Tennessee, May 1, 1865. Released by a Knox County, Tennessee, civil court on May 24, 1865. [May have previously served in Company A, 60th Regiment N.C. Troops. His capture at Knoxville on May 1, 1865, indicates that he was a member of Lt. Col. William W. Stringfield's flag-of-truce party that was arrested when they refused to take the Oath of Allegiance.]

SWATEH, Sergeant
Cherokee Indian. Served as Sergeant in 2nd Company A, Infantry Regiment of this legion. May have served later in this company. [His name was also rendered as Suateh, Swa-tah, Suate Owl, Swatie Owl, Sou Ate, Sou-ate-Owle, and Sui-ate Owl.]

TABOR, JOHN D., _____
North Carolina pension records appear to indicate that he served in this company. Survived the war.

TACHANOWIETA, _____
Cherokee Indian. Place and date of enlistment not reported. A receipt roll for clothing dated October 16, 1864, indicates that he served in this company. [This information is misfiled in the National Archives Compiled Service Record for Pvt. Arquetage Tahsekeyahgee of 2nd Company A, Infantry Regiment of this legion.]

TAHKEHYEH, Private
Cherokee Indian. Served as Private in 2nd Company A, Infantry Regiment of this legion. May have served later in this company. [His name was also rendered as Tahguyeh and Tahgeeyeh.]

TAHNOHLEE, Private
Cherokee Indian. Served as Private in 2nd Company A, Infantry Regiment of this legion. May have served later in this company.

TAHSEKEYAHGEE, STOOGATOGEH, Private
Cherokee Indian. Served as Private in 2nd Company A, Infantry Regiment of this legion. May have served later in this company. [He

may have been the same man as Sdugi:gado:ga of Company C of this battalion.]

TALAGEESKIH, Sergeant
Cherokee Indian. Served as Sergeant in 2nd Company A, Infantry Regiment of this legion. May have served later in this company.

TALANOSTEH, TAGENTEH, Private
Cherokee Indian. Served as Private in 2nd Company A, Infantry Regiment of this legion. May have served later in this company.

TALASKASKEE, Private
Cherokee Indian. Served as Private in 2nd Company A, Infantry Regiment of this legion. May have served later in this company.

TALUNOSTEH, NICKOJACK, Private
Cherokee Indian. Served as Private in 2nd Company A, Infantry Regiment of this legion. May have served later in this company.

TAYLOR, SAMUEL, Private
Previously served as Private in Company K, Infantry Regiment of this legion, and deserted from that unit at Winter's Gap on April 9, 1863. Name appears on a receipt roll for clothing dated October 16, 1864, as a member of "Co. A," Thomas's Legion. While it is possible that he returned to the ranks of Company K of the Infantry Regiment and legitimately transferred to Company A, Walker's Battalion, it is more likely that he served in this company.

TECOLAGEESKIH, Private
Cherokee Indian. Served as Private in 2nd Company A, Infantry Regiment of this legion. May have served later in this company.

TEEGEESKEE, JESS, _____
Cherokee Indian. North Carolina pension records indicate that he served in 2nd Company A, Infantry Regiment of this legion. May have served later in this company.

TEGAHHOOGEESKIH, Private
Cherokee Indian. Served as Private in 2nd Company A, Infantry Regiment of this legion. May have served later in this company.

TEHEE, JONNY, Private
Cherokee Indian. Served as Private in 2nd Company A, Infantry Regiment of this legion. May have served later in this company.

TELAHLAH, Private
Cherokee Indian. Served as Private in 2nd Company A, Infantry Regiment of this legion. May have served later in this company.

TEQUEEESKIH, Sergeant
Cherokee Indian. Previously served as Sergeant in 2nd Company A, Infantry Regiment of this legion. Transferred to this company on an unspecified date. [Name also rendered as Teque-eeskih. Also known as John Bigwitch.]

TESEEKEE, Private
Cherokee Indian. Served as Private in 2nd Company A, Infantry Regiment of this legion. May have served later in this company.

TESEEYOGIH, Private
Cherokee Indian. Served as Private in 2nd Company A, Infantry Regiment of this legion. May have served later in this company.

TESESKIH, Private
Cherokee Indian. Served as Private in 2nd Company A, Infantry Regiment of this legion. May have served later in this company. [His name was also rendered as Te-ses-kih. He may have been the same man as Pvt. Teseteskih of this company.]

TESETESKIH, Private
Cherokee Indian. Served as Private in 2nd Company A, Infantry Regiment of this legion. May have served later in this company. [He may have been the same man as Pvt. Teseskih of this company.]

TEWYEH, NICKOJACK, Private
Cherokee Indian. Served as Private in 2nd Company A, Infantry Regiment of this legion. May have served later in this company.

THOMPSON, IYANTOOGA, Private
Cherokee Indian. Previously served as Private in 2nd Company A, Infantry Regiment of this legion. Transferred to this company on an unspecified date. Captured on or about February 25, 1864. Confined at Knoxville, Tennessee, February 25, 1864. Released at Knoxville on March 10, 1864, after taking the Oath of Allegiance. No further records. [He was probably one of the party of fifteen Indians who surrendered to the Federals at Motley's Ford, Tennessee, February 22, 1864.]

THOMPSON, OOLIYOIH, Private
Cherokee Indian. Served as Private in 2nd Company A, Infantry Regiment of this legion. May have served later in this company.

TOONIGHYEH, Private
Cherokee Indian. Served as Private in 2nd Company A, Infantry Regiment of this legion. May have served later in this company.

TOYANEETE, Corporal
Cherokee Indian. Served as Corporal in 2nd Company A, Infantry Regiment of this legion. May have served later in this company. [His name was also rendered Toya Neta, Toy-a-ne-teh and Toi-neeta.]

TRUITT, JOHN, _____
Served as Private in Company C, 7th Battalion N.C. Cavalry. Reported absent without leave from that company at the time of its transfer to the 65th Regiment N.C. Troops (6th Regiment N.C. Cavalry) where it became Company C and, later, 2nd Company G. North Carolina pension records indicate that he transferred to "Co. A," Thomas's Legion, "on or about July or August 1864." While it is possible that he served in Company A, Walker's Battalion, it is more likely that he served in this company. [His surname may have been Truett. He may be the same man as Pvt. John R. Truitt of Company E, Walker's Battalion.]

TSE:GH(I)SINI, _____
Cherokee Indian. Served either in 2nd Company A or in Company B, Infantry Regiment of this legion. If he served in 2nd Company A, he may have served later in this company.

TSO:WA, _____

Cherokee Indian. Served either in 2nd Company A or in Company B, Infantry Regiment of this legion. If he served in 2nd Company A, he may have served later in this company. [He may have been the same man as Pvt. Oosowih of this company.]

TSUMI, _____

Cherokee Indian. Served either in 2nd Company A or in Company B, Infantry Regiment of this legion. If he served in 2nd Company A, he may have served later in this company.

UNDERWOOD, ROBERT TAYLOR, _____

North Carolina pension records and his personal reminiscences indicate that he served in this company. Survived the war. [R. T. Underwood Reminiscences, Special Collections, Perkins Library, Duke University.]

WAHGACOO, Private

Cherokee Indian. Served as Private in 2nd Company A, Infantry Regiment of this legion. May have served later in this company.

WAHHAHOO, MOSES, Private

Cherokee Indian. Served as Private in 2nd Company A, Infantry Regiment of this legion. May have served later in this company.

WAHLANEETEH, Private

Cherokee Indian. Served as Private in 2nd Company A, Infantry Regiment of this legion. May have served later in this company.

WAHTASUTTEH, Private

Cherokee Indian. Served as Private in 2nd Company A, Infantry Regiment of this legion. May have served later in this company.

WAHWAHSEETEH, Private

Cherokee Indian. Served as Private in 2nd Company A, Infantry Regiment of this legion. May have served later in this company.

WAHYELOSSIH, Private

Cherokee Indian. Served as Private in 2nd Company A, Infantry Regiment of this legion. May have served later in this company.

WASHINGTON, JIM, Private

Cherokee Indian. Served as Private in 2nd Company A, Infantry Regiment of this legion. May have served later in this company.

WELCH, JOE, Private

Cherokee Indian ("Willogeeskih's son"). Served as Private in 2nd Company A, Infantry Regiment of this legion. May have served later in this company.

WILLEGIH, Private

Cherokee Indian. Served as Private in 2nd Company A, Infantry Regiment of this legion. May have served later in this company. [His name was also rendered as Wi:ligi.]

WILLSOEH, Private

Cherokee Indian. Served as Private in 2nd Company A, Infantry Regiment of this legion. May have served later in this company.

WILNOTY, LOUTY, _____

Cherokee Indian. North Carolina pension records indicate that he served in 2nd Company A, Infantry Regiment of this legion. May have served later in this company.

WOHHOHTIH, Private

Cherokee Indian. Served as Private in 2nd Company A, Infantry Regiment of this legion. May have served later in this company.

COMPANY B

This company was raised in Jackson and Cherokee Counties and was composed primarily of Cherokee Indians. It served previously as Company B, Infantry Regiment of this legion. In April, 1865, it formally became Company B, Indian Battalion of this legion. However, the Indian Battalion had been informally organized in late 1863. For the purposes of these rosters, September 2, 1863, will be used for separating materials for members of Company B, Infantry Regiment, from those of Company B, Indian Battalion. It was on that date that Col. William H. Thomas left Strawberry Plains, Tennessee, with this company and 2nd Company A of the Infantry Regiment, marched into the Smoky Mountains, and began recruiting a third Indian company. These companies were never reintegrated into the structure of the Infantry Regiment again, even after the Legion was reunited in western North Carolina in December, 1864.

There are no surviving muster rolls for this company. Valuable information was obtained from the microfilm edition of the Compiled Service Records of Confederate Soldiers Who Served in Organizations from the State of North Carolina (Record Group 109, M270), National Archives, Washington, D.C. The Compiled Service Records series includes enlistment papers, pay vouchers, requisitions, letters of resignation, discharge certificates, and abstracts of medical and prisoner of war returns.

Also utilized in this roster were *The War of the Rebellion: A Compilation of the Official Records of the Union and Confederate Armies*, the North Carolina Adjutant General's papers, state militia records, newspaper casualty lists and obituaries, wartime claims for bounty pay and allowances, postwar registers of claims for artificial limbs, Confederate pension applications filed with the states of North Carolina, Tennessee, and Florida, records of the North Carolina Confederate Soldiers' Home, and the 1860 and 1870 federal censuses of North Carolina. A search was made also for relevant letters, diaries, reminiscences, and other manuscripts in the Southern Historical Collection (University of North Carolina-Chapel Hill) and the Duke University Library Special Collections Department.

Among the secondary sources consulted were records of the North Carolina division of the United Daughters of the Confederacy, postwar rosters, regimental and county histories, marriage bond, will, and cemetery indexes, published and unpublished genealogies, biographical dictionaries, the North Carolina *County Heritage Book* series, the *Confederate Veteran*, Walter Clark's *Histories of the Several Regiments and Battalions from North Carolina in the Great War, 1861-'65*, and the North Carolina volume of the extended edition of *Confederate Military History*.

OFFICERS

CAPTAINS

HANKS, GIDEON M.

Previously served as Captain of Company B, Infantry Regiment of this legion. Transferred to this company on an unspecified date. According to Vernon Crow, *Storm in the Mountains*, p. 104, he was "Killed late in 1863." Place of death not reported.

TAYLOR, JAMES MADISON

Part Cherokee Indian. Previously served as 1st Lieutenant of Company B, Infantry Regiment of this legion. Transferred to this company on an unspecified date. Signature appears on a receipt for issues to the army dated November 15, 1863. Signature appears on a forage requisition dated December 11, 1863. Promoted to Captain between December 11, 1863, and April 16, 1864, following the death of Captain Hanks. Captured either in Cherokee County or in Monroe County, Tennessee, October 9, 1864. Sent to Knoxville, Tennessee. Transferred to Chattanooga, Tennessee, on October 11, 1864. Transferred to Nashville, Tennessee. Confined at Louisville, Kentucky, October 21, 1864. Transferred to Johnson's Island, Ohio, October 23, 1864. Released at Johnson's Island on May 13, 1865, after taking the Oath of Allegiance.

LIEUTENANTS

POWELL, MARCUS L., _____ Lieutenant

Previously served as Brevet 2nd Lieutenant, and/or probably 3rd Lieutenant of Company B, Infantry Regiment of this legion. Transferred to this company on an unspecified date. Reported on April 16, 1864, to bear the rank of Lieutenant, and to be in command of this company in the absence of Captain Taylor. No further records. Survived the war.

TAYLOR, CAMPBELL HARRISON, 2nd Lieutenant

Part Cherokee Indian. Previously served as 2nd Lieutenant of Company B, Infantry Regiment of this legion. According to Clark's *Regiments*, 4: 119, 126, he subsequently served as 1st Lieutenant of "Company I, 80th Regiment," by which was meant Company C of this battalion. It is possible that he was promoted to that rank while a member of this company. He subsequently became Captain of Company C of this battalion.

TRUETT, CHARLES L., _____ Lieutenant

Previously served as Private in Company I, Infantry Regiment of this legion. May have transferred to this company on an unknown date subsequent to February 29, 1864, and promoted to the rank of Lieutenant, grade unknown. Capt. James Taylor of this company wrote on August 10, 1864, to Colonel Thomas, "I have sent Lt. C. L. Truett with 78 men to aid the Home Guards in protecting the citizens and their property against the robbers until otherwise ordered by you." Survived the war.

NONCOMMISSIONED OFFICERS AND PRIVATES

AH LEE CHEE, Private

Cherokee Indian. Served as Private in Company B, Infantry Regiment of this legion. May have served later in this company.

AHMASCOSITY, Private

Cherokee Indian. Served as Private in Company B, Infantry Regiment of this legion. May have served later in this company.

AH TO HEE, Private

Cherokee Indian. Served as Private in Company B, Infantry Regiment of this legion. May have served later in this company. [His name may have been Ground Squirrel Atowhee or Ahtohee Ground Squirrel].

AH TOW EH, Private

Cherokee Indian. Served as Private in Company B, Infantry Regiment of this legion. May have served later in this company. [His name was also rendered as Ahtowih, Ahtowee and Ahtowhee.]

ALLENEH, Private

Cherokee Indian. Served as Private in Company B, Infantry Regiment of this legion. A pay voucher appears to indicate he served also in this company, through at the earliest December 31, 1863. No further records.

ALLISON, JULIUS J., _____

Confederate gravestone records indicate that he served in Company B, Infantry Regiment of this legion. He may have served later in this company.

ARCHEE, Musician

Cherokee Indian. Served as Musician in Company B, Infantry Regiment of this legion. May have served later in this company.

ARCHEE, JR., Private

Cherokee Indian ("Owl's son"). Served as Private in Company B, Infantry Regiment of this legion. May have served later in this company.

ARROWOOD, WILLIAM H., _____

North Carolina pension records indicate that he served in Company B, Infantry Regiment of this legion. He may have served later in this company.

ATAHHEE, Private

Cherokee Indian. Served as Private in Company B, Infantry Regiment of this legion. May have served later in this company. [His name was also rendered as Ahtahhee.]

AX, WILSON, Sergeant

Served as Sergeant in Company B, Infantry Regiment of this legion. A pay voucher appears to indicate he served also in this company through at the earliest December 31, 1863. No further records. Survived the war.

BIGMEAT, LACEY, Private

Cherokee Indian. Served as Private in Company B, Infantry Regiment of this legion. May have served later in this company. [His first name may have been Lazy.]

BIGMEAT, SEGILLEH, Private

Cherokee Indian. Served as Private in Company B, Infantry Regiment of this legion. May have served later in this company.

[His name was also rendered as Sekilla Bigmeat and Bigmeat Segilleh.]

BUSHEYHEAD, GEORGE W., Sergeant

Cherokee Indian. Previously served as Sergeant in Company B, Infantry Regiment of this legion. Transferred to this company on an unspecified date. Name appears on pay vouchers for service from September 1 through December 31, 1863. Transferred to Company D of this battalion on or prior to February 29, 1864.

CALHOUN, JOHN, Private

Cherokee Indian. Served as Private in Company B, Infantry Regiment of this legion. May have served later in this company.

CASSEE, Private

Cherokee Indian. Served as Private in Company B, Infantry Regiment of this legion. May have served later in this company.

CHARLESTOWN, Private

Cherokee Indian. Served as Private in Company B, Infantry Regiment of this legion. May have served later in this company.

CHEESQUAHNEETE, Private

Cherokee Indian. Served as Private in Company B, Infantry Regiment of this legion. May have served later in this company.

CHEOIH, JIM, Private

Cherokee Indian. Previously served as Private in Company B, Infantry Regiment of this legion. Transferred to this company on an unspecified date. Captured, probably at Deep Creek, near Quallatown, February 2, 1864. Confined at Knoxville, Tennessee, on February 7, 1864. Released at Knoxville on March 10, 1864, after taking the Oath of Allegiance. [He may have been the same man as Tso:wa of this company. He may have subsequently served as Corporal in Company D, 3rd Regiment N.C. Mounted Infantry (Union).]

CHESQUANOLLA, Private

Cherokee Indian. Served as Private in Company B, Infantry Regiment of this legion. May have served later in this company.

CHICK A LE LEE, Private

Cherokee Indian. Served as Private in Company B, Infantry Regiment of this legion. May have served later in this company. [His name was also rendered as Chickalela, Chickalila, and Chigilili.]

CHONOH, Private

Cherokee Indian (son of Da wa seh). Served as Private in Company B, Infantry Regiment of this legion. May have served later in this company.

CHUTAH SOCK TEH, Private

Cherokee Indian. Served as Private in Company B, Infantry Regiment of this legion. May have served later in this company.

CHUWANNASKEE, Sergeant

Cherokee Indian. Served as Sergeant in Company B, Infantry Regiment of this legion. May have served later in this company.

COLARCHEE, Private

Cherokee Indian. Served as Private in Company B, Infantry Regiment of this legion. May have served later in this company.

COLLOWAHESKEE, Private

Cherokee Indian. Served as Private in Company B, Infantry Regiment of this legion. May have served later in this company.

CONNOHHALAKAH, Private

Cherokee Indian. Served as Private in Company B, Infantry Regiment of this legion. May have served later in this company. [He was also known as Hunter Reed.]

CONNOSKEESKEE, Private

Cherokee Indian. Served as Private in Company B, Infantry Regiment of this legion. May have served later in this company. [His name was also rendered as Connoskeeskih.]

CONNOSKEESKEE, DEVIR, Private

Cherokee Indian. Served as Private in Company B, Infantry Regiment of this legion. May have served later in this company. [His given name was also rendered as Dever. His surname was also rendered as Cannos-kees-kih or Cannos-kees-kit. He was also known as Armstrong Cornsilk.]

CONNOSTEAH, Private

Cherokee Indian. Served as Private in Company B, Infantry Regiment of this legion. May have served later in this company.

COOK, ROBERT, Private

Served as Private in Company B, Infantry Regiment of this legion. May have served later in this company.

DANELAH, Private

Cherokee Indian. Served as Private in Company B, Infantry Regiment of this legion. May have served later in this company.

DARROW, ROBERT, _____

Enlisted at an unknown place and date, possibly when this company was still Company B, Infantry Regiment of this legion. Deserted to the enemy on an unspecified date. Took the Oath of Allegiance at Knoxville, Tennessee, December 4-16, 1864.

DAVIS, JOHN, _____

Cherokee Indian. Place and date of enlistment not reported. Survived the war. [See the Eleventh Census of the United States, *Extra Census Bulletin. Indians. Eastern Band of Cherokees of North Carolina* (Washington, D.C.: 1892), 21.]

DICKAGEESKIH, JESS, Private

Cherokee Indian. Served as Private in Company B, Infantry Regiment of this legion. May have served later in this company. [His name was also rendered as Dick-a-geeskee and Di:ghyui:sgi.]

DO:TSULE':HNV, _____

Cherokee Indian. Served either in 2nd Company A or in Company B, Infantry Regiment of this legion. If he served in Company B, he may have served later in this company.

ECHULEHAH, Private
Cherokee Indian. Served as Private in Company B, Infantry Regiment of this legion. May have served later in this company. [His name was also rendered as Echu-le-hah. He was also known as Steve Johnson. Later deserted to the enemy and served as Private in Company D, 3rd Regiment N.C. Mounted Infantry (Union).]

ENELOSSIH, Private
Cherokee Indian. Served as Private in Company B, Infantry Regiment of this legion. May have served later in this company.

GE:DINI, _____
Cherokee Indian. Served either in 2nd Company A or Company B, Infantry Regiment of this legion. If he served in Company B, he may have served later in this company.

GOOLOWIH, Corporal
Cherokee Indian. Served as Corporal in Company B, Infantry Regiment of this legion. May have served later in this company.

HAWKINS, JOSEPH, Sergeant
Cherokee Indian. Served as Sergeant in Company B, Infantry Regiment of this legion. May have served later in this company.

HOWEE, AQUAH, Corporal
Cherokee Indian. Served as Corporal in Company B, Infantry Regiment of this legion. May have served later in this company.

JOHNSON, BLYTHE, Private
Cherokee Indian. Served as Private in Company B, Infantry Regiment of this legion. May have served later in this company.

JONAS, JIM, Private
Cherokee Indian. Served as Private in Company B, Infantry Regiment of this legion. May have served later in this company.

KALOUXEH, Private
Cherokee Indian. Served as Private in Company B, Infantry Regiment of this legion. May have served later in this company.

KANE, SWAGA, Private
Cherokee Indian. Previously served as Private in Company B, Infantry Regiment of this legion. Transferred to this company. Captured reportedly on February 1, 1864, but more likely in the Federal raid on Colonel Thomas' camp at Deep Creek, near Quallatown, February 2, 1864. Confined at Knoxville, Tennessee, February 7, 1864. Released at Knoxville on March 10, 1864, after taking the Oath of Allegiance.

KANTZ, WILLIAM H., Private
Previously served as Private in Company B, Infantry Regiment of this legion. Transferred to this company on an unspecified date. Name appears on requisitions for forage dated July 11 and 19 and August 3, 1864. No further records.

KENETEH, Private
Cherokee Indian. Served as Private in Company B, Infantry Regiment of this legion. May have served later in this company.

KILCHULEE, JOHN, Private
Half Cherokee Indian. Served as Private in Company B, Infantry Regiment of this legion. May have served later in this company.

KIMSEY, M. R., _____
North Carolina pension records indicate that he served in Company B, Infantry Regiment of this legion. He may have served later in this company. [He may have been the same man as Matthew R. Kinsey of Company I, Infantry Regiment of this legion.]

KOOE, SKOOE, Private
Cherokee Indian. Served as Private in Company B, Infantry Regiment of this legion. May have served later in this company. [His name was also rendered as Kooe-Skooe. He was also known as Ross Cochran.]

KYHULEGA, Private
Cherokee Indian. Served as Private in Company B, Infantry Regiment of this legion. May have served later in this company.

LARCHEE, Private
Cherokee Indian. Served as Private in Company B, Infantry Regiment of this legion. May have served later in this company.

LOCUST, ALFRED, Corporal
Cherokee Indian. Served as Corporal in Company B, Infantry Regiment of this legion. May have served later in this company.

LOCUST, JOHNSON, Private
Cherokee Indian. Served as Private in Company B, Infantry Regiment of this legion. May have served later in this company.

McCARTY, WILLIAM T., Private
Served as Private in Company B, Infantry Regiment of this legion. May have served later in this company.

MARTIN, HENRY C., Private
Served as Private in Company B, Infantry Regiment of this legion. May have served later in this company.

MURPHY, DAVID, Private
Half Cherokee Indian. Served as Private in Company B, Infantry Regiment of this legion. May have served later in this company.

MURPHY, JOHN, Private
Served as Private in Company B, Infantry Regiment of this legion. May have served later in this company.

MURPHY, LEVI C., Private
Served as Private in Company B, Infantry Regiment of this legion. May have served later in this company.

MURPHY, WILLIAM, Private
Served as Private in Company B, Infantry Regiment of this legion. May have served later in this company.

NEWETOWIH, ISAAC, Corporal
Cherokee Indian. Served as Corporal in Company B, Infantry Regiment of this legion. May have served later in this company.

OBEDIAH, Private
Cherokee Indian. Served as Private in Company B, Infantry Regiment of this legion. May have served later in this company.

OGATUTLEE, JOE, Private
Cherokee Indian. Served as Private in Company B, Infantry Regiment of this legion. May have served later in this company.

OKUNIYEH, Private
Cherokee Indian. Served as Private in Company B, Infantry Regiment of this legion. May have served later in this company. [His name was also rendered as Okieniyeh and Okunnieh.

OKUNIYEH, Private
Cherokee Indian ("Kunaseen's son"). Served as Private in Company B, Infantry Regiment of this legion. May have served later in this company.

OLETASTIEH, Private
Cherokee Indian. Served as Private in Company B, Infantry Regiment of this legion. May have served later in this company.

OOCHELOOTEH, Private
Cherokee Indian. Served as Private in Company B, Infantry Regiment of this legion. May have served later in this company.

OOCHUNTEH, Private
Cherokee Indian. Served as Private in Company B, Infantry Regiment of this legion. May have served later in this company. [Name also rendered as Oo-chum-teh. He was also known as Comeback Wolf.]

OOCUMMUH, Private
Cherokee Indian. Served as Private in Company B, Infantry Regiment of this legion. May have served later in this company. [His name was also rendered as U:gama.]

OOLETASTICH, _____
Cherokee Indian. Served as Private in Company B, Infantry Regiment of this legion. May have served later in this company. [He was also known as Jake Consuna.]

OOLTLOHNANEH, Private
Cherokee Indian. Served as Private in Company B, Infantry Regiment of this legion. May have served later in this company.

OOTELUKEH, Private
Cherokee Indian. Served as Private in Company B, Infantry Regiment of this legion. May have served later in this company.

OSSAKILLEH, Private
Cherokee Indian. Previously served as Private in Company B, Infantry Regiment of this legion. Transferred to this company on an unspecified date. Reportedly captured on or about February 7, 1864, probably in the Federal raid on Colonel Thomas's camp at Deep Creek, near Quallatown, February 2, 1864. Confined at Knoxville, Tennessee, February 7, 1864. Released at Knoxville on March 20, 1864, after taking the Oath of Allegiance.

OTTER, JIM, Private
Cherokee Indian. Previously served as Private in Company B, Infantry Regiment of this legion. Transferred to this company on an unspecified date. Captured on or about February 25, 1864. Confined at Knoxville, Tennessee, February 25, 1864. Released at Knoxville on March 10, 1864, after taking the Oath of Allegiance. Subsequently served in Company D, 3rd Regiment N. C. Mounted Infantry (Union). [He was also known as James Otter. He was probably one of the party of fifteen Indians who surrendered to the Federals at Motley's Ford, Tennessee, on February 22, 1864.]

PARTRIDGE, DAVID, Private
Cherokee Indian. Served as Private in Company B, Infantry Regiment of this legion. May have served later in this company. Deserted either from the Infantry Regiment or from this company. Later served in Company D, 3rd Regiment N.C. Mounted Infantry (Union). [He may have been the same man as Dave, whose record appears in the miscellaneous section of this battalion roster.]

QUILL, SCACHEE, Private
Cherokee Indian. Served as Private in Company B, Infantry Regiment of this legion. May have served later in this company.

ROSS, JESSE, Private
Cherokee Indian. Served as Private in Company B, Infantry Regiment of this legion. May have served later in this company. [He may have been the same man as Pvt. Jesse, whose record appears in the miscellaneous section of this battalion roster.]

ROSS, JOHN, Sergeant
Cherokee Indian. Served as Sergeant in Company B, Infantry Regiment of this legion. May have served later in this company. [He may have served also as Chaplain in Thomas's Legion.]

SAHGEYAH, Private
Cherokee Indian. Served as Private in Company B, Infantry Regiment of this legion. May have served later in this company.

SCACHEE, OONANOOTEH, Private
Cherokee Indian. Served as Private in Company B, Infantry Regiment of this legion. May have served later in this company.

SELLALEESEH, NICKEE, Private
Cherokee Indian. Served as Private in Company B, Infantry Regiment of this legion. May have served later in this company.

SELLALEESEH, SEQUOYEH, Private
Cherokee Indian. Served as Private in Company B, Infantry Regiment of this legion. May have served later in this company. [His name was also rendered as Se-qua-yah and as Sequo-yo Sell-alle-seh.]

SELLALEESEH, WAHTEH, Private
Cherokee Indian. Served as Private in Company B, Infantry Regiment of this legion. May have served later in this company. [Name also rendered as Wah-tee and as Watteh Sell-alle-seh.]

SINECOOYEH, Private
Cherokee Indian. Served as Private in Company B, Infantry Regiment of this legion. May have served later in this company.

SMITH, GEORGE, Private
Served as Private in Company B, Infantry Regiment of this legion. May have served later in this company.

SMITH, NIMROD JARETT, 1st Sergeant
Half Cherokee Indian. Served as 1st Sergeant of Company B, Infantry Regiment of this legion. May have served later in this company. [After the war he became principal chief of the Eastern Band of Cherokees. According to Vernon Crow, *Storm in the Mountains*, his Cherokee name was Tsaladihi.]

TAHGENSEH, Private
Cherokee Indian. Served as Private in Company B, Infantry Regiment of this legion. May have served later in this company.

TAHLEE, Private
Cherokee Indian ("Catalstas's son"). Served as Private in Company B, Infantry Regiment of this legion. May have served later in this company. [He was also known as Tah-lee Casabsta, Ca-tol-ster, and Charley Catolster.]

TAHLEE, Private
Cherokee Indian. Served as Private in Company B, Infantry Regiment of this legion. May have served later in this company.

TAHNEENTEH, Private
Cherokee Indian. Served as Private in Company B, Infantry Regiment of this legion. May have served later in this company.

TAWASKILLEH, Private
Cherokee Indian. Served as Private in Company B, Infantry Regiment of this legion. May have served later in this company. [His name was also rendered as Tawaskilles.]

TAYLOR, ANDREW J., Private
Served as Private in Company B, Infantry Regiment of this legion. May have served later in this company.

TESATESKIH, Private
Cherokee Indian. Served as Private in Company B, Infantry Regiment of this legion. May have served later in this company.

TESATESKIH, Private
Cherokee Indian ("Owl's son"). Served as Private in Company B, Infantry Regiment of this legion. May have served later in this company.

TETALETOGAH, Private
Cherokee Indian. Served as Private in Company B, Infantry Regiment of this legion. May have served later in this company.

TEYULETOHHEE, JIM, Private
Cherokee Indian. Served as Private in Company B, Infantry Regiment of this legion. May have served later in this company.

TICKANEESKEH, JOE, Private
Cherokee Indian. Served as Private in Company B, Infantry Regiment of this legion. May have served later in this company.

TOHHEESKIH, Private
Cherokee Indian. Served as Private in Company B, Infantry Regiment of this legion. May have served later in this company. [His name was also rendered as Tohesky.]

TOOCHEESTEH, Private
Cherokee Indian. Served as Private in Company B, Infantry Regiment of this legion. May have served later in this company. [He was also known as Aleck Tiyonehala.]

TOONOWIH, Private
Cherokee Indian. Served as Private in Company B, Infantry Regiment of this legion. May have served later in this company.

TOOSTOO, Private
Cherokee Indian. Served as Private in Company B, Infantry Regiment of this legion. May have served later in this company.

TOWIH, JOHN, Private
Cherokee Indian. Served as Private in Company B, Infantry Regiment of this legion. May have served later in this company.

TSE:GH(I)SINI, _____
Cherokee Indian. Served either in 2nd Company A or in Company B, Infantry Regiment of this legion. If he served in Company B, he may have served later in this company.

TSO:WA, _____
Cherokee Indian. Served either in 2nd Company A or in Company B, Infantry Regiment of this legion. If he served in Company B, he may have served later in this company. [He may have been the same man as Pvt. Jim Cheoih of this company.]

TSUMI, _____
Cherokee Indian. Served either in 2nd Company A or in Company B, Infantry Regiment of this legion. If he served in Company B, he may have served later in this company.

ULLATEESKIH, Private
Cherokee Indian. Served as Private in Company B, Infantry Regiment of this legion. May have served later in this company. [He was also known as Jesse Leteske.]

WAHHOSSEH, Private
Cherokee Indian. Served as Private in Company B, Infantry Regiment of this legion. May have served later in this company. [His name was also rendered as Wah-has-eh. He was also known as Tom Skitty.]

WAHYACALOONEH, Private
Cherokee Indian. Served as Private in Company B, Infantry Regiment of this legion. May have served later in this company.

WAHYAHNEETE, JOHN, Musician
Cherokee Indian. Served as Musician in Company B, Infantry Regiment of this legion. May have served later in this company. [His surname was also rendered as Wah-ye-neete, Wah-hah-neeta, and Wahhaneeta.]

WAHYANEETE, SICATOWIH, Private
Cherokee Indian. Served as Private in Company B, Infantry Regiment of this legion. May have served later in this company.

WELCH, DAVID, Private
Cherokee Indian. Served as Private in Company B, Infantry Regiment of this legion. May have served later in this company.

WELCH, EDWARD, Private
One-quarter Cherokee Indian.. Served as Private in Company B, Infantry Regiment of this legion. May have served later in this company.

WILLESTE, Private
Cherokee Indian. Served as Private in Company B, Infantry Regiment of this legion. May have served later in this company.

WILSONEH, Private
Cherokee Indian. Served as Private in Company B, Infantry Regiment of this legion. May have served later in this company.

WOLF, MOSES, Private
Cherokee Indian. Served as Private in Company B, Infantry Regiment of this legion. May have served later in this company.

COMPANY C

This company was organized in December, 1863, and was composed primarily of Cherokee Indians.

There are no surviving muster rolls for this company. The following roster was compiled in large part from a list for clothing issued February 13, 1865, and lists of soldiers who were killed or who died of disease and whose orphans received clothing on February 14, 1865. Valuable information was also obtained from the microfilm edition of the Compiled Service Records of Confederate Soldiers Who Served in Organizations from the State of North Carolina (Record Group 109, M270), National Archives, Washington, D.C. The Compiled Service Records series includes enlistment papers, pay vouchers, requisitions, letters of resignation, discharge certificates, and abstracts of medical and prisoner of war returns.

Also utilized in this roster were *The War of the Rebellion: A Compilation of the Official Records of the Union and Confederate Armies*, the North Carolina Adjutant General's papers, state militia records, newspaper casualty lists and obituaries, wartime claims for bounty pay and allowances, postwar registers of claims for artificial limbs, Confederate pension applications filed with the states of North Carolina, Tennessee, and Florida, records of the North Carolina Confederate Soldiers' Home, and the 1860 and 1870 federal censuses of North Carolina. A search was made also for relevant letters, diaries, reminiscences, and other manuscripts in the Southern Historical Collection (University of North Carolina-Chapel Hill) and the Duke University Library Special Collections Department.

Among the secondary sources consulted were records of the North Carolina division of the United Daughters of the Confederacy, postwar rosters, regimental and county histories, marriage bond, will, and cemetery indexes, published and unpublished genealogies, biographical dictionaries, the North Carolina *County Heritage Book* series, the *Confederate Veteran*, Walter Clark's *Histories of the Several Regiments and Battalions from North Carolina in the Great War, 1861-'65*, and the North Carolina volume of the extended edition of *Confederate Military History*. See Anna Gritts Kilpatrick and Jack Frederick Kilpatrick, "Chronicles of Wolftown: Social Documents of the North Carolina Cherokees, 1850-1862," *Smithsonian Instution Bureau of American Ethnology Bulletin* 196, Anthropological Papers No. 75 (1966), 65, 105, MS in "The Inoli Letters," MS No. 2236, Folder 1, Bureau of American Ethnology, Smithsonian Institute, Washington, D.C., translated and published in Jack Frederick Kilpatrick and Anna Gritts Kilpatrick, translators and editors, *The Shadow of Sequoyah: Social Documents of the Cherokees* (Norman: University of Oklahoma Press, 1965), 13.] MS in "Inali Formulae," Bureau of American Ethnology, Smithsonian Instituton, Washington, D.C., translated and published in Jack Frederick Kilpatrick and Anna Gritts Kilpatrick, translators and editors, *The Shadow of Sequoyah: Social Documents of the Cherokees* (Norman: University of Oklahoma Press, 1965), 16.]

OFFICERS

CAPTAINS

TAYLOR, CAMPBELL HARRISON
Part Cherokee Indian. Previously served as 2nd Lieutenant of Company B of this battalion. According to Clark's *Regiments* 4:119, he served as 1st Lieutenant of Company I of the "Eightieth Regiment (Walker's Regiment of Thomas' Legion)," by which was meant Company C of this battalion. It is possible that he was promoted to that rank while still a member of Company B of this battalion. Promoted to Captain on an unknown date. Resigned his Captaincy on June 27, 1864, because as "a native of the (Indian) nation" he was "not willing to serve in the Capacity of an officer. proffere [prefer] a privates position." (Taylor to Col. William H. Thomas, June 27, 1864, William Holland Thomas Papers, Special Collections, Perkins Library, Duke University); this document also confirms that Taylor, not Welch, was commander of Company C. It is probable that Thomas refused Taylor's resignation. An abstract from a Federal Provost Marshal roll of prisoners in Taylor's National Archives Compiled Service Record reports him as captured at Hartwell, Georgia, on May 10, 1865; he is identified therein as "Capt Co C Thomas Legion." However, information in Kilpatrick and Kilpatrick, *The Shadow of Sequoyah*, 13 and 13 n. 3, indicates that Company C was the company commanded in the latter part of the war by Inoli (Black Fox). It is possible that Welch originally commanded this company, followed by Taylor and then Inoli; or that Taylor commanded first and was succeeded by Inoli. The latter scenario seems the most likely.

INOLI
Cherokee Indian. Previously served with the rank of Sergeant in either 2nd Company A or Company B, Infantry Regiment of this legion, and/or in either Company A, Company B, or Company C of

this battalion. He is identified in Kilpatrick and Kilpatrick, *The Shadow of Sequoyah*, 13 and 13, n.3, as the commander of Company C of this battalion. Date of promotion or election to Captain unknown, but it was subsequent to the resignation of Capt. Campbell H. Taylor of this company on June 27, 1864. [His name is also rendered as I:no:li, I-Na-Li and Enola. He was known also as Black Fox. According to Clark's *Regiments* 4:119, he served as Captain of Company K of the "Eightieth Regiment (Walker's Regiment of Thomas' Legion)," by which was meant Company D of this battalion. It appears that the personnel of this company and Company D, and probably others in this battalion, were mixed together in the account in Clark's *Regiments*. He is probably the man identified as "Blackhawk" in some Federal Provost Marshal records for men captured as members of "Blackhawk's Company"; see, for example, the record of Pvt. Eunitteni below. According to various sources, Inoli was both a shaman and a Methodist preacher (Crow, *Storm in the Mountains*, 233; Finger, *Eastern Band of Cherokees*, 64; Kilpatrick and Kilpatrick, 5, n.8).]

WELCH, JAMES

According to Clark's *Regiments* 4:119, he served as Captain of Company I of the "Eightieth Regiment (Walker's Regiment of Thomas' Legion)," by which was meant Company C of this battalion. However, wartime correspondence indicates that Welch and Campbell H. Taylor were commanders of different companies at the same time (W. H. Parker to Col. William H. Thomas, April 16, 1864, Microfilm 284-03-01, William Holland Thomas Papers, Special Collections, Perkins Library, Duke University [original in William Holland Thomas Papers, Special Collections, Hunter Library, Western Carolina University]). Welch may have briefly served as Captain of this company before becoming Captain of the company listed in this roster as Welch's Company of this battalion.

LIEUTENANT

DALE, JOHN H., 2nd Lieutenant

Previously served as Private in Company K, 22nd Regiment N.C. Troops (12th Regiment N.C. Volunteers). Appointed 2nd Lieutenant of this company, probably subsequent to February 29, 1864. Captured in Cherokee County on or about October 9, 1864. Transferred to Nashville, Tennessee. Confined at Louisville, Kentucky, October 21, 1864. Transferred to Johnson's Island, Ohio, where he arrived on October 25, 1864. Released at Johnson's Island on May 13, 1865, after taking the Oath of Allegiance.

NONCOMMISSIONED OFFICERS AND PRIVATES

A?HW(I)GADO:GA, _____

Cherokee Indian. Place and date of enlistment not reported. Name appears on a list for clothing issued February 13, 1865.

A:MATSV:NA, _____

Cherokee Indian. Place and date of enlistment not reported. Name appears on a list for clothing issued February 13, 1865.

AMA:Y(I)GADO:GA, _____

Cherokee Indian. Place and date of enlistment not reported. Name appears on a list of soldiers who died of disease and whose orphans received clothing on February 14, 1865. Date and place of death unknown.

ANIDO':NA?, _____

Cherokee Indian. Place and date of enlistment not reported. Name appears on a list of soldiers killed, whose orphans received clothing on February 14, 1865. Place and date of death unknown.

BOWERS, GEORGE W., Private

Resided in Jackson County. Place and date of enlistment not reported. Captured in Jackson County, probably at Deep Creek, near Quallatown, February 2, 1864. Sent to Knoxville, Tennessee, where he arrived on Februrary 7, 1864. Transferred to Nashville, Tennessee, where he arrived on or about February 25, 1864. Transferred to Louisville, Kentucky, where he arrived on February 28, 1864. Transferred from Louisville to Fort Delaware, Delaware, where he arrived on or about March 4, 1864. Released at Fort Delaware on or about June 7, 1865, after taking the Oath of Allegiance.

CALVERT, JOHN D., Private

Place and date of enlistment not reported. Captured in Jackson County, probably at Deep Creek, near Quallatown, February 2, 1864. Confined at Knoxville, Tennessee, February 7, 1864. Sent to Nashville, Tennessee. Transferred to Louisville, Kentucky, where he arrived on February 28, 1864. Transferred to Fort Delaware, Delaware, where he arrived on or about March 4, 1864. Paroled at Fort Delaware on October 30, 1864. Received at Venus Point, Savannah River, Georgia, November 15, 1864, for exchange. No further records. [He may have been the same man as either Pvt. John M. Colvard or Pvt. John P. Colvard, both of Company H, Infantry Regiment of this legion.]

DA:DHLVDA, _____

Cherokee Indian. Place and date of enlistment not reported. Name appears on a list for clothing issued February 13, 1865.

DA:HW(I)SINI, _____

Cherokee Indian. Place and date of enlistment not reported. Name appears on a list of soldiers who died of disease and whose orphans received clothing on February 14, 1865. Date and place of death unknown.

DASGI:GIDI:HI, _____

Cherokee Indian. Place and date of enlistment not reported. Died of disease, June 23, 1864. Place of death unknown.

DA:TSVDA, _____

Cherokee Indian. Place and date of enlistment not reported. Name appears on a list of residents of Wolftown who died in October, 1865; with the indication that he had served in this company.

DIDA:LIDO':GI, _____

Cherokee Indian. Place and date of enlistment not reported. Name appears on a list for clothing issued February 13, 1865.

DI:GINI, _____

Cherokee Indian. Place and date of enlistment not reported. Name appears on a list for clothing issued February 13, 1865.

DIGV:GI:SGI, _____

Cherokee Indian. Place and date of enlistment not reported. Name appears on a list of soldiers who died of disease and whose orphans received clothing on February 14, 1865. Place and date of death not reported.

DIWO:SGI, _____

Cherokee Indian. Place and date of enlistment not reported. Name appears on a list of soldiers who died of disease and whose orphans received clothing on February 14, 1865. Place and date of death not reported.

DI:YE:LIDO':HI, _____

Cherokee Indian. Place and date of enlistment not reported. Name appears on a list of soldiers killed, whose orphans received clothing on February 14, 1865. Place and date of death not reported.

DO:SAGAYA:SDI, _____

Cherokee Indian. Place and date of enlistment not reported. Name appears on a list of soldiers who died of disease and whose orphans received clothing on February 14, 1865. Place and date of death not reported.

DVNI:GISI, _____

Cherokee Indian. Place and date of enlistment not reported. Name appears on a list of soldiers who died of disease and whose orphans received clothing on February 14, 1865. Place and date of death not reported.

EUNITTENI, Private

Cherokee Indian. Place and date of enlistment not reported. Captured in Haywood County on February 5, 1865. Sent to Knoxville, Tennessee. Hospitalized at Knoxville on February 12, 1865. Died in hospital at Knoxville on February 21, 1865, of "tetanus" resulting from "inflammation [of] finger." [Some materials in his National Archives Compiled Service Record place him in Company E, Infantry Regiment of this legion, but two cards list him as a member of "Blackhawk's Company." As Blackhawk is otherwise unknown, it is likely that Black Fox (i.e., Inoli) is meant.]

GA:GAMA, _____

Cherokee Indian. Place and date of enlistment not reported. Name appears on a list for clothing issued February 13, 1865.

GAHU:NI, _____

Cherokee Indian. Place and date of enlistment not reported. Name appears on a list for clothing issued February 13, 1865.

GALU:SADI:HI, _____

Cherokee Indian. Place and date of enlistment not reported. Name appears on a list for clothing issued February 13, 1865.

GA:YANI, _____

Cherokee Indian. Place and date of enlistment not reported. Name appears on a list of soldiers who died of disease and whose orphans received clothing on February 14, 1865. Place and date of death not reported.

GODAGWA:SGI, _____

Cherokee Indian. Place and date of enlistment not reported. Name appears on a list of soldiers who died of disease and whose orphans received clothing on February 14, 1865. Place and date of death not reported.

GRANT, JOHN P., Private

Place and date of enlistment not reported. Captured in Jackson County, probably at Deep Creek, near Quallatown, February 2, 1864. Confined at Knoxville, Tennessee, February 7, 1864. Transferred to Nashville, Tennessee, February 25, 1864. Transferred to Louisville, Kentucky, February 28, 1864. Transferred from Louisville to Fort Delaware, Delaware, February 29, 1864. Arrived at Fort Delaware on or about March 4, 1864. Paroled at Fort Delaware on September 14, 1864. Received at Varina, Virginia, September 22, 1864, for exchange. Hospitalized at Richmond, Virginia. Furloughed from hospital to Walhalla, South Carolina, September 28, 1864. No further records. Survived the war.

GREEN, JESSE N., Private

Resided in Jackson County. Place and date of enlistment not reported. Captured at Deep Creek, near Quallatown, February 2, 1864. Confined at Knoxville, Tennessee, February 7, 1864. Sent to hospital sick. Transferred to Nashville, Tennessee, February 25, 1864. Transferred to Louisville, Kentucky, February 28, 1864. Transferred from Louisville to Fort Delaware, Delaware, February 29, 1864. Arrived at Fort Delaware on or about March 4, 1864. Released at Fort Delaware on June 19, 1865, after taking the Oath of Allegiance.

GV:HNIDV, _____

Cherokee Indian. Place and date of enlistment not reported. Name appears on a list of soldiers killed, whose orphans received clothing on February 14, 1865. Place and date of death not reported.

GV:NA, _____

Cherokee Indian. Place and date of enlistment not reported. Name appears on a list of soldiers killed, whose orphans received clothing on February 14, 1865. Place and date of death not reported.

GWE:NI, _____

Cherokee Indian. Place and date of enlistment not reported. Name appears on a list for clothing issued February 13, 1865.

HA:LI, _____

Cherokee Indian. Place and date of enlistment not reported. Name appears on a list of soldiers who died of disease and whose orphans received clothing on February 14, 1865. Place and date of death not reported.

HYDE, DAVID E., _____

North Carolina pension records appear to indicate that he served in this company. Survived the war. [He may have been the same man as Pvt. Ervin Hyde of Company F, Infantry Regiment of this legion.]

I:NADV, _____

Cherokee Indian. Place and date of enlistment not reported. Name appears on a list of soldiers who died of disease and whose orphans received clothing on February 14, 1865. Place and date of death not reported.

NE:DI, _____

Cherokee Indian. Place and date of enlistment not reported. Name appears on a list for clothing issued February 13, 1865. [He may have been the same man as Pvt. Nedda Sammih of 2nd Company A, Infantry Regiment of this legion, and Company A of this battalion.]

NEWTON, ELBERT S., Private

Place and date of enlistment not reported; probably enlisted subsequent to December 31, 1863. Captured in Jackson County on February 2, 1864. Confined at Knoxville, Tennessee, February 7, 1864. Transferred to Camp Chase, Ohio, February 25, 1864. Paroled on February 27, 1864. Confined at Nashville, Tennessee, on or about February 28, 1864. Confined at Louisville, Kentucky, February 29, 1864. Confined at Fort Delaware, Delaware, on or about March 4, 1864. Name appears on an undated roll of prisoners forwarded to City Point, Virginia, for exchange. No further records. Survived the war. [His first name may have been Albert. North Carolina pension records indicate that he was wounded in the back of the head in North Carolina on December 15, 1863.]

NI:GI, _____

Cherokee Indian. Place and date of enlistment not reported. Name appears on a list of soldiers killed, whose orphans received clothing on February 14, 1865. Place and date of death not reported.

OGA?HNAWA, _____

Cherokee Indian. Place and date of enlistment not reported. Name appears on a list of soldiers who died of disease and whose orphans received clothing on February 14, 1865. Place and date of death not reported.

PILKENTON, JAMES, Private

Previously served in Company F, Infantry Regiment of this legion. Enlisted in this company at an unknown date and place, probably illegally while a deserter from Company F, Infantry Regiment. Captured in Jackson County, probably at Deep Creek, near Quallatown, February 2, 1864. Confined at Knoxville, Tennessee, February 7, 1864. Transferred to Nashville, Tennessee. Confined at Louisville, Kentucky, February 28, 1864. Transferred to Fort Delaware, Delaware, where he arrived on or about March 7, 1864. Died at Fort Delaware on September 3, 1864, of "inf[lammation] of bowels."

SDUGI:GADO:GA, _____

Cherokee Indian. Place and date of enlistment not reported. Name appears on a list of soldiers killed, whose orphans received clothing on February 14, 1865. Place and date of death not reported. [He may have been the same man as Pvt. Stoogatogeh Tahsekeyahgee of 2nd Company A, Infantry Regiment of this legion.]

SELKONIE, Private

Cherokee Indian. Resided in Jackson County. Place and date of enlistment not reported. Captured in Haywood County on February 4, 1865. Sent to Knoxville, Tennessee. Hospitalized at Knoxville on February 12, 1865, with a gunshot wound of the shoulder. Place and date wounded not reported. Transferred to Chattanooga, Tennessee, on or about June 6, 1865. Transferred to Nashville, Tennessee. Confined at Louisville, Kentucky, June 11, 1865. Released at Louisville on June 17, 1865, after taking the Oath of Allegiance. [Also known as John Seke. He may be the same man as Pvt. Sihkih of 2nd Company A, Infantry Regiment of this legion.]

SE:LUWA:YA, _____

Cherokee Indian. Place and date of enlistment not reported. Name appears on a list for clothing issued February 13, 1865.

SGALI:LO:SGI, _____

Cherokee Indian. Place and date of enlistment not reported. Name appears on a list of soldiers who died of disease and whose orphans received clothing on February 14, 1865. Place and date of death not reported.

SHERRILL, ASAPH W., Private

Place and date of enlistment not reported; probably enlisted subsequent to December 31, 1863. Captured in Jackson County, probably at Deep Creek, near Quallatown, February 2, 1864. Confined at Knoxville, Tennessee, February 7, 1864. Transferred to Nashville, Tennessee. Transferred to Louisville, Kentucky, February 28, 1864. Confined at Fort Delaware, Delaware, March 4, 1864. Died at Fort Delaware on March 2, 1865, of "ac[ute] dysentery."

SHULER, JOHN F., Private

Served as Private in Company H, Walker's Battalion. Reported on detail with an engineer company from August 4, 1863, until February, 1864; however, Federal Provost Marshal records indicate that he was serving with Company C of this battalion by February 2, 1864, when he was captured in Jackson County, probably at Deep Creek, near Quallatown. Confined at Knoxville, Tennessee, February 7, 1864. Transferred to Nashville, Tennessee. Transferred to Louisville, Kentucky, February 28, 1864. Confined at Fort Delaware, Delaware, on March 4, 1864. Paroled at Fort Delaware on September 28, 1864. Received at Varina, Virginia, October 5, 1864, for exchange. Reported in hospital at Richmond, Virginia, October 10, 1864. Rejoined or transferred back to Company F, 29th Regiment N.C. Troops, prior to February 1, 1865.

SI?DUWE:GI, _____

Cherokee Indian. Place and date of enlistment not reported. Name appears on a list of soldiers who died of disease and whose orphans received clothing on February 14, 1865. Place and date of death not reported.

TSADHA:G(A)NIHYV:GA, _____

Cherokee Indian. Place and date of enlistment not reported. Name appears on a list of residents of Wolftown who died in October, 1865, with the indication that he had served in this company.

TSA:LI, _____

Cherokee Indian. Place and date of enlistment not reported. Name appears on a list of soldiers killed, whose orphans received clothing on February 14, 1865. Place and date of death not reported.

TSA:N(I)LA:TSI, _____

Cherokee Indian. Place and date of enlistment not reported. Name appears on a list for clothing issued February 13, 1865. [He may have been the same man as Pvt. John Lossih of 2nd Company A, Infantry Regiment of this legion, and possibly also of Company A of this battalion.]

TSA:TS(I), _____

Cherokee Indian. Place and date of enlistment not reported. Name appears on a list of soldiers killed, whose orphans received clothing on February 14, 1865. Place and date of death not reported.

TSE:GWADI:HI, _____
Cherokee Indian. Place and date of enlistment not reported. Name appears on a list for clothing issued February 13, 1865.

TS(I)SGILI, _____
Cherokee Indian. Place and date of enlistment not reported. Name appears on a list for clothing issued February 13, 1865.

TSUDA:SODI, _____
Cherokee Indian. Place and date of enlistment not reported. Name appears on a list of soldiers killed, whose orphans received clothing on February 14, 1865. Place and date of death not reported.

TSU:HLA, _____
Cherokee Indian. Place and date of enlistment not reported. Name appears on a list for clothing issued February 13, 1865.

TSUMI, _____
Cherokee Indian. Place and date of enlistment not reported. Name appears on a list of soldiers who died of disease and whose orphans received clothing on February 14, 1865. Place and date of death not reported. [May have served previously in the Infantry Regiment of this legion.]

TSUTSO:LADHA, _____
Cherokee Indian. Place and date of enlistment not reported. Name appears on a list for clothing issued February 13, 1865.

U:DAN(I)DHU:DA, _____
Cherokee Indian. Place and date of enlistment not reported. Name appears on a list of soldiers killed, whose orphans received clothing on February 14, 1865. Place and date of death not reported.

U:DHLVNA:DA, _____
Cherokee Indian. Place and date of enlistment not reported. Name appears on a list for clothing issued February 13, 1865.

ULE:NA:HI, _____
Cherokee Indian. Place and date of enlistment not reported. Name appears on a list of soldiers who died of disease and whose orphans received clothing on February 14, 1865. Place and date of death not reported.

ULE:YOE, _____
Cherokee Indian. Place and date of enlistment not reported. Name appears on a list of residents of Wolftown who died in October, 1865, with the indication that he had served in this company.

ULI:DA:SDI, _____
Cherokee Indian. Place and date of enlistment not reported. Name appears on a list of soldiers who died of disease and whose orphans received clothing on February 14, 1865. Place and date of death not reported.

U:L(I)SDU:HI, _____
Cherokee Indian. Place and date of enlistment not reported. Name appears on a list for clothing issued February 13, 1865.

WAHHYANI:DA, _____
Cherokee Indian. Place and date of enlistment not reported. Name appears on a list of soldiers who died of disease and whose orphans received clothing on February 14, 1865. Place and date of death not reported.

WA:SIDA?NI, _____
Cherokee Indian. Place and date of enlistment not reported. Name appears on a list for clothing issued February 13, 1865.

WIKLE, ANDREW J., Private
Previously served as Private in Company H, Infantry Regiment of this legion. Enlisted illegally in this company, probably subsequent to October 31, 1863, while a deserter from the Infantry Regiment. Captured by the enemy in Jackson County, probably at Deep Creek, near Quallatown, February 2, 1864. Confined at Knoxville, Tennessee, February 7, 1864. Transferred to Nashville, Tennessee. Confined at Louisville, Kentucky, February 28, 1864. Confined at Fort Delaware, Delaware, on or about March 7, 1864. Died at Fort Delaware on or about March 15, 1865, of "ch[ronic] diarrhoea."

WO:YIGVGI:SGI, _____
Cherokee Indian. Place and date of enlistment not reported. Name appears on a list for clothing issued February 13, 1865.

COMPANY D

This company seems to have had its origins in western North Carolina in late 1863 or early 1864. It may have been organized informally as a partisan company under the command of John D. Berry, a former Private in the 19th Regiment N.C. Troops (2nd Regiment N.C. Cavalry). Based on information in a letter written by John S. Smiley, the 1st Sergeant of the company, it was active scouting at the time of a Federal raid in early 1864, at which time Smiley joined it. The raid in question was probably the operation that included the attack on Thomas's camp at Deep Creek near Quallatown on February 2, 1864. Some prisoners captured at that time were identified as members of "Co. D, Thomas' Legion," so apparently the company was already understood to be a component of Thomas's informal Indian Battalion. However, a letter from a Confederate officer named W. H. Parker to Colonel Thomas dated April 16, 1864, indicates that the company was not formally organized until shortly before the latter date. This is supported by Smiley, who noted that he "took to Scouting with Capt Berry and his boys" at the time of the Federal raid, but added that "when his (Co) was organised I was put in as a first Sergt.," indicating that the formal organization occurred some time after "Capt Berry and his boys" had been operating. [J. S. Smiley to Colonel William Holland Thomas, January 10, 1865 (the "5" in 1865 has been written over by someone with a "4," but it is clear from the context that the letter does indeed belong to 1865, not 1864), William Holland Thomas Papers, Special Collections, Perkins Library, Duke University; W. H. Parker to Thomas, April 16, 1864, microfilm 214-03-01 (original letter in William Holland Thomas Papers, Special Collections, Hunter Library, Duke University), William Holland Thomas Papers, Duke.]

It has been traditionally assumed that Company D was under the command of an Indian known as Black Fox and (due to lack of other evidence) was organized by the summer of 1864 at the latest. [Crow,

Storm in the Mountains, 104, 233]. This is partly due to the history of Walker's Battalion written by R. A. Aiken for Clark's *Regiments*. Aiken, for reasons that are not entirely clear, "raised" Walker's Battalion into a hitherto unknown regiment, the 80th Regiment N.C. Troops, by adding several unattached or otherwise organized companies to the roster of the battalion. These included two Indian companies misidentified by Aiken as Companies I and K; Black Fox's was supposedly Company K [Clark's *Regiments*, 4:119]. Vernon Crow read the evidence to indicate that "Company I" of Walker's Battalion was Company C of Thomas's Indian Battalion, while Black Fox's "Company K" was in fact Company D of the Indian Battalion. However, this is not necessarily the case, as Parker's April 16 letter indicates that Thomas had as many as six companies operating in western North Carolina at that time. Black Fox's company may have been Berry's Company D, or it may have been a different unit altogether. For the present, however, with a lack of firm evidence to the contrary, it will be assumed that Black Fox's company was Company D, although what time he took command is unknown. [It is possible that Black Fox commanded Company C, rather than Company D, of the Indian Battalion, following the resignation of Capt. Campbell Taylor of that unit.Again, however, this is speculation only, prompted by the fact that there was a command vacancy in that company which had to have been filled by someone, whether Black Fox or not. See also the company histories for Company C and for Welch's Company in this battalion roster, as well as the history of Thomas's Legion in this volume.]

The Parker letter indicates that the company was organized at the mouth of the Tuckaseegee River, where Thomas's North Carolina forces were evidently based at the time. There is no known muster roll or other roster of this company. There is a list of an Indian company dated May 28, 1865, that Crow identifies as being Black Fox's company. The original list identifies the unit as being "Enola's Company"; as Black Fox in phonetic Cherokee is i-na-li, this would indeed appear to be the case [Crow, *Storm in the Mountains*, 260 n. 71; List of Indians Present, Enola's Company, May 28, 1865, William Holland Thomas Papers, Duke; online English-Cherokee Dictionary, http://wehali.com/tsalgi/index.cfm?B]. It is not known for what purpose the May, 1865, list was compiled; it was written in the Cherokee syllabary.

Some information was obtained from the microfilm edition of the Compiled Service Records of Confederate Soldiers Who Served in Organizations from the State of North Carolina (Record Group 109, M270), National Archives, Washington, D.C. The Compiled Service Records series includes enlistment papers, pay vouchers, requisitions, letters of resignation, discharge certificates, and abstracts of medical and prisoner of war returns.

Also utilized in this roster were *The War of the Rebellion: A Compilation of the Official Records of the Union and Confederate Armies*, the North Carolina Adjutant General's papers, state militia records, newspaper casualty lists and obituaries, wartime claims for bounty pay and allowances, postwar registers of claims for artificial limbs, Confederate pension applications filed with the states of North Carolina, Tennessee, and Florida, records of the North Carolina Confederate Soldiers' Home, and the 1860 and 1870 federal censuses of North Carolina.

Among the secondary sources consulted were records of the North Carolina division of the United Daughters of the Confederacy, postwar rosters, regimental and county histories, marriage bond, will, and cemetery indexes, published and unpublished genealogies, biographical dictionaries, the North Carolina *County Heritage Book* series, the *Confederate Veteran*, Walter Clark's *Histories of the Several Regiments and Battalions from North Carolina in the Great War, 1861-'65*, and the North Carolina volume of the extended edition of *Confederate Military History*.

OFFICERS

CAPTAINS

BERRY, JOHN D.

Previously served as Private in Company A, 19th Regiment N.C. Troops (2nd Regiment N.C. Cavalry). Enlisted in Col. William H. Thomas's force in western North Carolina at an unknown date. Led this company as some sort of informal command as early as January-February, 1864. Elected Captain when the company was formally organized shortly before April 16, 1864. No further records.

INOLI

Cherokee Indian. Previously served as Sergeant in either 2nd Company A or Company B, Infantry Regiment of this legion, and/or in either Company A, Company B, or Company C of this battalion. According to Clark's *Regiments* 4:119, he served as Captain of Company K of the "Eightieth Regiment (Walker's Regiment of Thomas' Legion)," by which was meant Company D of this battalion. However, Inoli is identified in Kilpatrick and Kilpatrick, *The Shadow of Sequoyah*, 13 and 13 n. 3 as the commander of Company C of this battalion, which is more likely. It appears that the personnel of these two companies, and probably others in this battalion, were mixed together in the account in Clark. [His name is also rendered as I:no:li, I-Na-Li and Enola. He was known also as Black Fox. It is possible that he is the same man as Pvt. Oonohlee of 2nd Company A, Infantry Regiment of this battalion, although evidence in Inoli's personal papers tends to suggest that he was at home in western North Carolina until at least the fall of 1863 (see Kilpatrick and Kilpatrick, 4-13). He is probably the man identified as "Blackhawk" in some Federal Provost Marshal records for men captured as members of "Blackhawk's Company". According to various sources, Inoli was both a shaman and a Methodist preacher (Crow, *Storm in the Mountains*, 233; Finger, *Eastern Band of Cherokees*, 64; Kilpatrick and Kilpatrick, 5 n. 8).

LIEUTENANTS

BUCHANAN, JAMES M., 1st Lieutenant

Resided in Baltimore County, Maryland. Place and date of appointment as 1st Lieutenant not reported. Captured in Jackson County, probably at Deep Creek, near Quallatown, February 2, 1864. Confined at Knoxville, Tennessee, on February 7, 1864. Confined at Nashville, Tennessee, where he arrived on or before February 25, 1864. Confined at Louisville, Kentucky, where he arrived on or about February 29, 1864. Confined at Camp Chase, Ohio, where he arrived on March 2, 1864. Transferred to Fort Delaware, Delaware, where he arrived on March 27, 1864. Took the Oath of Allegiance on June 10, 1865. Released at Fort Delaware on June 16, 1865.

COLVARD, PEYTON S., 3rd Lieutenant

Previously served as Private in Company A, 19th Regiment N.C. Troops (2nd Regiment N.C. Cavalry). Appointed 3rd Lieutenant of this company on an unspecified date. Captured in Jackson County, probably at Deep Creek, near Quallatown, February 2, 1864. Confined at Knoxville, Tennessee, February 7, 1864. Sent to Nashville, Tennessee. Transferred to Louisville, Kentucky, where he arrived on February 28, 1864. Transferred to Camp Chase, Ohio, where he arrived on March 2, 1864. Transferred to Fort Delaware,

Delaware, where he arrived on March 27, 1864. Released at Fort Delaware on June 16, 1865, after taking the Oath of Allegiance. [His surname may have been Calvert.]

COLVARD, WILLIAM P., 2nd Lieutenant
Previously served as Private in Company A, 19th Regiment N.C. Troops (2nd Regiment N.C. Cavalry). Appointed 2nd Lieutenant of this company on an unspecified date. Captured in Jackson County, probably at Deep Creek, near Quallatown, February 2, 1864. Confined at Knoxville, Tennessee, February 7, 1864. Sent to Nashville, Tennessee. Transferred to Louisville, Kentucky, where he arrived on February 28, 1864. Transferred to Camp Chase, Ohio, where he arrived on March 2, 1864. Transferred to Fort Delaware, Delaware, where he arrived on March 27, 1864. Released at Fort Delaware on June 16, 1865, after taking the Oath of Allegiance. [His surname may have been Calvert.]

DeHART, DALLAS, 1st Lieutenant
Place of enlistment not reported. Elected 1st Lieutenant shortly before April 16, 1864. Survived the war. [A North Carolina pension application for S. C. Panther of 2nd Company A, Infantry Regiment of this legion, indicates that DeHart may have previously served in that company, and probably also in Company A of this battalion.]

DEHART, JOSEPH W., Brevet 2nd Lieutenant
Previously enlisted as Private in Company F, Infantry Regiment of this legion, but did not serve therein (entry cancelled). Served as Private in Company C, 7th Battalion N.C. Cavalry. Enlisted illegally in this company while absent without leave from the 7th Battalion between September, 1863, and April, 1864. Elected or appointed Brevet 2nd Lieutenant shortly before April 16, 1864. No further records. [His given name may have been W. Joseph. His first name may have been Wiley.]

GIBSON, E. P., 2nd Lieutenant
North Carolina pension records appear to indicate that he served in Company A of this battalion. Enlisted in or transferred into this company at an unknown date and place. Elected 2nd Lieutenant shortly before April 16, 1864. Survived the war. [North Carolina pension records appear to indicate that he also served in the Infantry Regiment of this legion, possibly in 2nd Company A or Company F.]

NONCOMMISSIONED OFFICERS AND PRIVATES

BAIN, W. S., Private
North Carolina pension records indicate that he served in this company. Survived the war.

BATTLE, JAMES, Private
Place and date of enlistment not reported. He served in this company, according to a receipt for shoes dated October 24, 1864, filed in the National Archives Compiled Service Record of Capt. Matthew H. Love of Company A of this battalion. [He may have served also in either 2nd Company A or Company F, Infantry Regiment of this legion.]

BUSHEYHEAD, GEORGE W., Sergeant
Cherokee Indian. Previously served as Sergeant in Company B of this battalion. Transferred to this company on or prior to February 29, 1864. Name appears as signature to a pay voucher dated March 15, 1864, for service from January 1 through February 29, 1864. No further records. Survived the war.

CABE, W. R., Private
Place and date of enlistment not reported. He served in this company, according to a receipt for shoes dated October 24, 1864, filed in the National Archives Compiled Service Record of Capt. Matthew H. Love of Company A of this battalion. Survived the war. [North Carolina pension records indicate that he may have served also in Company A of this battalion or Company A, Walker's Battalion.]

COLLINS, JOHN S., _____
North Carolina pension records appear to indicate that he served in this company. Survived the war.

OWEN, W. P., _____
Born in Macon County in 1847. Tennessee pension application No. 15630 indicates that he served in this company. Survived the war.

QUEEN, WILLIAM, Private
Place and date of enlisted not reported; probably enlisted subsequent to February 29, 1864. Captured on May 27, 1864. Sent to Knoxville, Tennessee. Released at Knoxville on June 14, 1864, after taking the Oath of Allegiance.

RAMSEY, SAM T., _____
North Carolina pension records indicate that he served either in this company or in Company A, Walker's Battalion, and survived the war.

ROANE, WILBER, Private
Place and date of enlistment not reported. Transferred to Company E, 65th Regiment N.C. Troops (6th Regiment N.C. Cavalry), September 11, 1864, in exchange for Pvt. William H. Shepherd.

SHEPHERD, WILLIAM H., Private
Previously served as Private in Company A, 7th Battalion North Carolina Cavalry, and was reported as absent without leave from that company when it became Company E, 65th Regiment N.C. Troops (6th North Carolina Cavalry) on August 3, 1863. Enlisted illegally in an unknown company of this Legion between September, 1863, and April, 1864, while absent without leave from Company E, 65th N.C. Troops (6th Regiment N.C. Cavalry). Transferred to this company on September 11, 1864, in exchange for Pvt. Wilber Roane.

SMILEY, JOHN S, Sergeant
Previously served as Private and Musician in Company E, 39th Regiment N.C. Troops, and was last reported as absent on furlough from that unit in January-February, 1864. His letter to Col. William H. Thomas dated January 10, 1865, indicates that while he was home on his furlough begun on January 27, 1864, Federal raiders entered the area (probably on the raid that included the attack on Thomas's camp at Deep Creek, near Quallatown, February 2, 1864).

Smiley "had no time to rest on my furlough but took up my gun and went to Scouting with Capt Berry and his boys and when his [company] was organised I was put in as first Sergt." Smiley identified this company as Company D. He claimed that his former captain from the 39th Regiment never asked for his return. By early 1865, Smiley asked Colonel Thomas permission to raise his own company, but there is no evidence that he was ever allowed to do so. Survived the war. [William Holland Thomas Papers, Special Collections, Perkins Library, Duke University.]

TALLEY, JONAS, Private
Place and date of enlistment not reported. Captured in Cherokee County on May 27, 1864. Sent to Knoxville, Tennessee, where he was hospitalized on June 17, 1864, with intermittent fever. Transferred to Chattanooga, Tennessee, October 11, 1864. Confined at Camp Chase, Ohio, October 24, 1864. Died at Camp Chase on November 21, 1864, probably of diarrhoea.

WIGGINS, JOHN, _____
North Carolina pension records indicate that enlisted in this company, at about age 16, on March 1, 1864. Transferred either to Levi's Battery, or to Capt. John W. Barr's Battery, Virginia Light Artillery, in September or October, 1864.

CAPT. JAMES WELCH'S COMPANY
(PROBABLY COMPANY E)

This company was active in western North Carolina as early as April, 1864. It may have begun as a Home Guard company, as it was recorded as such in the North Carolina pension application of A. T. Crisp, who claimed to have served in it; however, in this case "Home Guard" may reflect confusion on Crisp's part about the nature of his unit, given the mission of the Legion companies in North Carolina as defined by Col. William Holland Thomas. It has been traditionally assumed that Welch's Company was Company C of this battalion. [Crow, *Storm in the Mountains*, 104, 131, 233]. This is partly due to the history of Walker's Battalion written by Robert A. Akin (Aiken) for Clark's *Regiments*. Akin, for reasons that are not entirely clear, "raised" Walker's Battalion into a hitherto unknown regiment, the 80th Regiment N.C. Troops, by adding several unattached or otherwise organized companies to the roster of the battalion. These included two Indian companies misidentified by Akin as Companies I and K; Welch's company was referred to as "Company I." Campbell Taylor was listed as 1st Lieutenant of the company. [Clark's *Regiments*, 4:119]. It is known that Taylor was captain of an Indian company at some point in 1864; in his letter of resignation in June of that year, he identified his command as "the third Indian Co. of Col. Thomas' Legion," which would indicate that he commanded Company C of the Indian Battalion [C. H. Taylor to Colonel William Holland Thomas, June 27, 1864, William Holland Thomas Papers, Special Collections, Perkins Library, Duke University]. Attempting to reconcile the material in Akin with that in Taylor's letter, Vernon Crow concluded that Taylor originally commanded Company C, and was replaced upon his resignation by Welch. However, an April, 1864 letter to Colonel Thomas from a Confederate officer named W. H. Parker indicates that Welch and Parker were captains in command of two separate companies at that time [W. H. Parker, P.A.C.S. to Thomas, April 16, 1864, microfilm 284-03-01 (original letter in William Holland Thomas Papers, Special Collections, Hunter Library, Western Carolina University), William Holland Thomas Papers, Duke University]. The letter designation of this company is unknown.

There is no known muster roll or other roster of this company. The identities of the officers are based largely on the letter from Confederate officer W. H. Parker to Col. William H. Thomas dated April 16, 1864, William Holland Thomas Papers, Hunter Library, Western Carolina University. The identities of other members of the company are based on North Carolina pension applications, and records of the Federal Provost Marshal.

OFFICERS

CAPTAIN

WELCH, JAMES
May have served previously as Captain of Company C of this battalion. Reported in April, 1864, with the rank of Captain in command of a company operating with Col. William H. Thomas of this battalion in April, 1864. No official letter designation for this company has been found. Elected Captain prior to April 16, 1864. (W. H. Parker to Col. William H. Thomas, April 16, 1864, Microfilm 284-03-01, William Holland Thomas Papers, Special Collections, Perkins Library, Duke University [original in William Holland Thomas Papers, Special Collections, Hunter Library, Western Carolina University]). It has been speculated that Welch later was appointed or elected to command Company C of this battalion following the resignation of Capt. Campbell H. Taylor of that company in June, 1864; however, Thomas may have refused Taylor's resignation, as Federal Provost Marshal records indicate that he was still in command of Company C at the end of the war.

LIEUTENANTS

CALVERT, N., 2nd Lieutenant
Elected 2nd Lieutenant prior to April 16, 1864. No further records.

HAWKINS, JOSEPH, 3rd Lieutenant
Elected 3rd Lieutenant prior to April 16, 1864. No further records.

HYDE, JASON S., 1st Lieutenant
Previously served as 2nd Lieutenant in Company H, Infantry Regiment of this legion. Elected 1st Lieutenant of this company prior to April 16, 1864. No further records. Survived the war.

NONCOMMISSIONED OFFICERS AND PRIVATES

CAMPBELL, A. H., _____
Cherokee Indian. North Carolina pension records indicate that he served in this company. Survived the war.

COOPER, A. L., _____
North Carolina pension records indicate that he served in this company. Survived the war.

COOPER, W. F., _____
North Carolina pension records appear to indicate that he served in this company after having served in Company H, Infantry Regiment

of this legion. Survived the war. [He may have served also in Company B, Infantry Regiment of this legion, and/or Company B of this battalion.]

CRISP, A. T., _____

North Carolina pension records appear to indicate that he served in this company. Survived the war.

HARDIN, WILLIAM H., Private

Resided in Cherokee County. Place and date of enlistment not reported; probably enlisted subsequent to February 29, 1864. North Carolina pension record indicate that he served in this company. Records of the Federal Provost Marshal indicate that he was a "boy" who deserted in Cherokee County on November 4, 1864, and was captured in Blount County, Tennessee, November 7, 1864. Took the Oath of Allegiance at Knoxville, Tennessee, and was released on November 12, 1864, "on statement of his father." Survived the war.

PARKER, W. B., _____

North Carolina pension records appear to indicate that he served in this company. Survived the war.

CAPT. A. L. HICKS'S COMPANY (PROBABLY COMPANY F)

This company was evidently acting as an ad hoc organization in early 1864. It consisted of a mixture of men whom Col. John B. Palmer had ordered to report to Col. William Holland Thomas's camp at the mouth of the Tuckasegee River, together with other men who had enlisted in Thomas's command but were not formally attached to any particular company (the latter may have included men who were absent without leave from the rest of Thomas's Legion in eastern Tennessee). These men acted under the command of a man named Albert. L. Hicks, a deserter from Company C, 7th Battalion N.C. Cavalry/2nd Company G, 65th Regiment N.C. Troops (6th Regiment N.C. Cavalry), who held some grade of lieutenancy. W. H. Parker, P.A.C.S., an otherwise unidentified Confederate officer whom Thomas had sent to inspect his companies and report on their organizational status, informed these men that they had to organize formally and elect company officers. An election was held some time before Parker reported to Thomas in writing on April 16, 1864. Parker commented that "[t]he formation of this company is subject to approval or Disapproval." It is not known whether Thomas approved the organization of this company, or whether was also officially accepted by the Confederate authorities. It may have been consolidated with one of Thomas's other companies, or disbanded and its men placed into other companies. No roster of this company has been found. [W. H. Parker, P.A.C.S. to Col. William Holland Thomas, microfilm 284-03-01 (original letter in William Holland Thomas Papers, Special Collections, Hunter Library, Western Carolina University), William Holland Thomas Papers, Special Collections, Perkins Library, Duke University].

OFFICERS

CAPTAIN

HICKS, ALBERT L.

Served as Private in Company C, 7th Battalion N.C. Cavalry, and was reported absent without leave from that unit at the time of its transfer to the 65th Regiment N.C. Troops (6th Regiment N.C. Cavalry), where it became Company C (later 2nd Company G). Enlisted illegally in this company between September, 1863, and April, 1864, while absent without leave from the 65th Regiment. Appointed Lieutenant, grade of lieutenancy unknown, and commanded this company prior to April, 1864. Elected Captain when the company was formally organized shortly before April 16, 1864. No further records.

LIEUTENANTS

MEHAFFEY, D. F., 3rd Lieutenant

Elected 3rd Lieutenant prior to April 16, 1864. No further records.

WILLIAMS, J. K., 1st Lieutenant

Elected 1st Lieutenant prior to April 16, 1864. No further records.

YOUNG, W. G., 2nd Lieutenant

Elected 2nd Lieutenant prior to April 16, 1864. No further records.

NONCOMMISSIONED OFFICERS AND PRIVATES

RIDLEY, NATHAN B., _____

North Carolina pension records indicate that he enlisted in this legion in September, 1863. He served in this company, according to a receipt for shoes dated October 24, 1864, filed in the National Archives Compiled Service Record of Capt. Matthew H. Love of Company A of this battalion. [May have served previously as Private in Company A, 20th Regiment South Carolina Infantry.]

RORIX, JAMES ADAM, Private

Previously served in Company F, Walker's Battalion, and Company K, 5th Regiment Tennessee Cavalry (McKenzie's). He served in this company, according to a receipt for shoes dated October 24, 1864, filed in the National Archives Compiled Service Record of Capt. Matthew H. Love of Company A of this battalion. No further records. [His surname may have been Rorax.]

COMPANY G (GHORMLEY'S AND EVERETT'S CONSOLIDATED COMPANY)

Consisting of all or elements of the company which was formerly Company F, Walker's Battalion, Thomas's Legion, and Company K, 5th Regiment Tennessee Cavalry (McKenzie's), consolidated with an otherwise unknown company commanded by "Captain" Eppa (Eppie) Everett. Beyond Ghormley himself, it is not known for certain how many men from F-WB-TL and K-5TennCav served in this unit, as no muster rolls are available. See also the company history accompanying the roster for Company F, Walker's Battalion.

There is some evidence to indicate that all or part of Company K, 5th Regiment Tennessee Cavalry (McKenzie's) (formerly Company F, Walker's Battalion, Thomas's Legion) returned to North Carolina under Captain Ghormley in late 1863 and served thereafter as part of Col. William H. Thomas's new battalion, possibly unofficially, as there are no records to indicate that it formally transferred from the 5th Regiment Tennessee Cavalry. On November 8, 1863, Thomas wrote to Lt. Col. William C. Walker that "such of Capt Gormley's men as are at home will report to him and hold themselves in readiness to serve when called on. I design getting his company permanently attached to the Legion, and fill up the company with such men as want to mount themselves." [Stephen Whitaker Papers, N.C. Office of Archives and Records.] W. H. Parker, a Confederate officer who traveled to Thomas's camp at the mouth of the Tuckasegee River to inspect his companies and enroll some newer ones, wrote in April 1864 that "Capt G[h]ormley had reported. He informs me that he has made an arrangment with Capt Everett to consolidate their commands." [W. H. Parker, P.A.C.S. to Colonel William Holland Thomas, April 17, 1864, 1860-1864 Correspondence folder, William Holland Thomas Papers, Special Collections, Perkins Library, Duke University.] Captain Everett appears to be Eppa [Eppie] Everett, former 2nd Lieutenant of Company E, 3rd Regiment Tennessee Infantry (Vaughn's), P.A.C.S. Postwar sources report that Everett became a conscription officer in Tennessee with the rank of Captain, and that he subsequently commanded a company in Thomas's Legion. [*CMH* 5: 479.] Former Lt. Col. William Williams Stringfield of the Legion, who commanded Walker's Battalion at the end of the war, referred to "Ghormley's and Everett's Cavalry" of Walker's Battalion in his history of the Legion in Clark's *Regiments*, and mentioned a "Captain E. P. Everett, of my command," in his unpublished Civil War memoirs [Clark's *Regiments*, 3:758; Stringfield, "Memoirs of the Civil War," typescript, McClung Collection, Lawson-McGhee Library, Knoxville, Tennessee (copy in William Williams Stringfield Papers, Special Collections, Hunter Library, Western Carolina University), p. 34].

The above information has led some to assume that this consolidated company automatically resumed the place of Company F in Walker's Battalion [Crow, *Storm in the Mountains*, 136, 220]; however, as it was connected with Thomas's battalion in western North Carolina until at least late 1864, when Walker's Battalion finally returned to the area, this is by no means certain. Furthermore, the nature of Everett's company before its supposed consolidation with this company is unknown. Crow, *Storm in the Mountains*, refers to the company as "Captain Eppa Everett's Company, Third Tennessee Cavalry" (220), but there is no wartime evidence that Everett ever served with the 3rd Regiment Tennessee Cavalry. The reference is probably the result of information in Everett's service file for the 3rd Regiment Tennessee Infantry (Vaughn's), P.A.C.S. That regiment originally mustered in to Tennessee service as the 3rd Regiment Tennessee Volunteer Cavalry. For some reason (probably due to a lack of mounts) it became an infantry regiment at the time or soon after it was accepted into Confederate service in June 1861. Although the unit became a mounted infantry regiment later in the war (and was some times erroneously referred to as a cavalry regiment as a result), the latter change occurred long after Everett's departure.

As Everett left Vaughn's 3rd Regiment Tennessee Infantry with the rank of 2nd Lieutenant, and as far as can be told had no further association with it, the organization and affiliation of Everett's company in April 1864 remains unknown. Further, it is difficult to discern in the records which man commanded the consolidated company. Ghormley seems to have been in western North Carolina through October 1864, based on a requisition form signed by Lt. Col. Bryan Gibbs McDowell of the 62nd Regiment N.C. Troops, at that time acting commander of Thomas's battalion. The requisition gives refers to Ghormley as commander of Company G, indicating its position in the organization of Thomas's battalion. [Service record file of D. C. Ghormley, 5th Regiment Tennessee Cavalry (McKenzie's), NA-MC268-23.] Everett is referred to in some of Stringfield's postwar writings about the last day of the war. Furthermore, when Everett was captured at Knoxville on May 1, 1865, as part of Stringfield's flag-of-truce party, he was reported by his captors as "Private Eppie Everett" of "Co. A, Thomas' Legion," and is recorded as a deserter. Thus, full information regarding this company's later service with Thomas and the details of its consolidation with Everett's company, whatever its nature, remain unknown. [See also the biographical sketch of Sergeant Stephen Porter of Company F, Walker's Battalion, in *CMH* 5: 698. It claims that Porter organized and was elected captain of Company K of Thomas's Legion (not the 5th Tennessee Cavalry, although that unit is clearly intended), and after serving as part of "the forces of General Vaughn" (which included the 5th Tennessee Cavalry), operated in western North Carolina along the Tuckasegee River and at Asheville, only to surrender and receive parole at Franklin. This implies again that at least some elements of this company were with Thomas, although it is documented that Ghormley, not Porter, originally raised it. As Porter's rank of captain is also not documented, it is not known how he would fit into the already confused command structure involving captains Ghormley and Everett.]

OFFICERS

CAPTAINS

EVERETT, EPPA

Previously served as 2nd Lieutenant in Company E, 3rd Regiment Tennessee Infantry (Vaughn's), and resigned from that unit in December 1861. Apparently enlisted in this legion in April 1864. One source indicates that he was in command of an unnamed cavalry company operating in western North Carolina. This company seems to have consolidated in April 1864 with all or a part of Capt. DeWitt C. Ghormley's Company K, 5th Regiment Tennessee Cavalry (McKenzie's), formerly known as Company F, Walker's Battalion. Other sources indicate that this consolidated company operated as a part of Thomas's western North Carolina command during the spring of 1864 and beyond, and that it functioned as Company G of Thomas's force. Some sources assign Everett with the rank of Captain and place him in command of this consolidated cavalry company, although it appears that he was actually ranked by Ghormley. Everett was captured at Knoxville, Tennessee, May 1, 1865. Reported as a Private in Company A, Thomas's Legion, at the time of his capture. As Thomas had evidently reassigned the three white companies from his western North Carolina battalion when he separated the four Indian companies, It is unclear whether Everett was supposed to have been a member of Company A, Infantry Regiment, Company A, Walker's (McKamy's) Battalion, or Company A, Indian Battalion, or under what circumstances he may have been reassigned and demoted. Transferred to Chattanooga, Tennessee, June 19, 1865, "as a deserter." No further records. Survived the war. [His first name may be Eppie or Eppy. According to *Confederate Military History*, V:479, "he was detailed for enlistment service in Blount county" in May 1863, with the rank of Captain, and became Captain of an unnamed company in this legion in August,1863. In April 1864, a Confederate officer inspecting Thomas's companies wrote that "Capt Gormley had reported. He informs me that he has made an arrangement with Capt Everett to consolidate their commands" (William Holland Thomas Papers, Special Collections, Perkins Library, Duke University). Former Lt. Col. William W. Stringfield of this legion wrote in his history of the Infantry Regiment of "Ghormley's and Everett's Cavalry" of Walker's Battalion operating late in the war (Clark's *Regiments*, 3:758), and in his unpublished Civil War memoir referred to "Captain E. P. Everett, of my command" (Walker's Battalion) as a member of his flag-of-truce party which was arrested at Knoxville on May 1, 1865. See W. H.

Parker, P.A.C.S. to Colonel William Holland Thomas, April 17, 1864, 1860-1864 Correspondence folder, William Holland Thomas Papers, Special Collections, Perkins Library, Duke University; Clark's *Regiments*, 3:758; Stringfield, "Memoirs of the Civil War," typescript, McClung Collection, Lawson-McGhee Library, Knoxville, Tennessee (copy in William Williams Stringfield Papers, Special Collections, Hunter Library, Western Carolina University), p. 34. The reasons why Everett was referred to as a Private and a deserter in his prisoner-of-war records remain unclear. The nature of his company, the manner of its supposed consolidation with Ghormley's company, and its exact connection to Thomas's Legion all remain uncertain, as do Everett's actual rank and whether he or Ghormley was its actual commander.]

GHORMLEY, DeWITT C.
Previously served as Captain of Company F, Walker's Battalion, and Company K, 5th Regiment Tennessee Cavalry (McKenzie's). In November 1863, Col. William H. Thomas wrote of Ghormley's presence in western North Carolina to Lt. Col. William C. Walker, noting that Ghormley had been ordered to gather up those of his men who were in the mountains for service with Thomas. A letter to Colonel Thomas in April 1864 reports that Ghormley had made arrangements to consolidate his company with that of a Captain Everett. Everett was Eppa (Eppie) Everett, former 2nd lieutenant of Company E, 3rd Regiment Tennessee Infantry (Vaughn's), a company in which Ghormley had also served earlier in the war. In Clark's *Regiments*, Stringfield refers to "Ghormley and Everett's Cavalry." Ghormley's signature appears on a special requisition dated October 16, 1864, and signed by Lt. Col. B. G. McDowell of the 62nd Regiment N.C. Troops. As McDowell was acting in command of the portion of the Legion that was in western N.C. at a time when Thomas was absent, his signature indicates that Ghormley's company was a part of Thomas's battalion. Ghormley is noted in this document as being at Jonathan's Creek, in Haywood County, one of Thomas's main areas of operations, and also as in command of "Co. G," which identifies the letter by which his company was known as a part of Thomas's command. No further records. Survived the war. [See Col. William H. Thomas To Lt. Col. William C. Walker, November 8, 1863, Stephen Whitaker Papers, N.C. Office of Archives and History; W. H. Parker, P.A.C.S., to Col. William H. Thomas, April 17, 1864, 1860-1864 Correspondence folder, William Holland Thomas Papers, Special Collections, Perkins Library, Duke University; Crow, *Storm in the Mountains*, 132, 136, 220, 260 n. 56; Special Requisition, October 16, 1864, National Archives Compiled Service Record for D. C. Ghormley, Company K, 5th Regiment Tennessee Cavalry (McKenzie's), NA-MC268-23; Stringfield, "Memoirs of the Civil War," unpublished typescript, McClung Library, Knoxville (photocopy in the William Williams Stringfield Papers, Special Collections, Hunter Library, Western Carolina University), 23, 34-35; Clark's *Regiments*, 3: 758, 4:128.]

NONCOMMISSIONED OFFICERS AND PRIVATES

HENDERSON, JAMES, Private
He served in this company, according to a receipt for shoes dated October 24, 1864, filed in the National Archives Compiled Service Record of Capt. Matthew H. Love of Company A of this battalion. No further records. [He may have served also in Company F, Infantry Regiment of this legion.]

JONES, SAMUEL, Private
Previously served as Private in Company G, Infantry Regiment of this legion. Enlisted in or transferred to this company on an unknown date, possibly while absent without leave from Company G, Infantry Regiment. He served in this company, according to a receipt for shoes dated October 24, 1864, filed in the National Archives Compiled Service Record of Capt. Matthew H. Love of Company A of this battalion. No further records.

RIDLEY, JOHN WILLIAM, Private
Previously served as Private in Company G, Infantry Regiment of this legion. Last reported as a member of that company while sick in hospital at Bristol, Tennessee, January 25, 1864. He served in this company and was serving on an expedition into eastern Tennessee, according to a receipt for shoes dated October 24, 1864, filed in the National Archives Compiled Service Record of Capt. Matthew H. Love of Company A of this battalion. Paroled at Franklin on May 9, 1865. [His Tennessee pension application No. 3237 contains a copy of a thirty-day medical furlough issued at a hospital in Emory, Virginia, on February 24, 1864.]

CAPT. JOHN TILLERY'S COMPANY

On August 19, 1864, Colonel Thomas authorized a former lieutenant of the 1st Regiment Tennessee Cavalry (Carter's) and the 8th Regiment Tennessee Cavalry (Baxter Smith's) named John Tillery to organize a company for Thomas's Legion among East Tennessean Confederates who were behind Federal lines. The company, which would be organized "subject to the approval of the Superior authorities," would "operate within East Tennessee and elsewhere" and would act as scouts. It is not known whether Tillery was successful in organizing the company; whether it was formally accepted into service by the proper authorities, whether it became a part of Thomas's Legion as intended, or operated as an independent company. If organized, it is presumed that Tillery was the captain, but this is not certain. There is no other record of the company's existence, and there is a strong likelihood that the organization was never completed due to Tillery's capture in September 1864. [Thomas to Lt. John Tellery, August 19, 1864, unbound letterbook, 1860-1864 Correspondence folder, William Holland Thomas Papers, Special Collections, Perkins Library, Duke University].

There is no known roster of this company.

CAPTAIN

TILLERY, JOHN
Resided in Knox County, Tennessee. Previously served as 1st Lieutenant of Company L, 8th Regiment Tennessee Cavalry (Baxter Smith's). Resigned from the latter unit due to a desire "to promote the good of the public service.... [b]elieving that I can best promote the cause of my country in an other capacity." Resignation from the latter unit accepted on June 4 or July 1, 1864. Authorized by Col. William H. Thomas on August 19, 1864, to organize a mounted infantry company among East Tennesseans behind Federal lines for service in Thomas's Legion, "subject to the approval of the Superior authorities." Captured in Knox County on an unknown date. Received at the military prison at Louisville, Kentucky, on September 25, 1864. Took the Oath of Allegiance on September 26, 1864. Discharged with orders to remain north of the Ohio River for

the rest of the war. [May have also served as 2nd Lieutenant in an unknown company of the 1st Regiment Tennessee Cavalry (Carter's). His surname may have been Tellery, as given in Colonel Thomas's letter of August 19, 1864. In his letter, Thomas refers to Tillery's most recent unit as the "4th Tennessee Cavalry." Tillery did not serve in the unit known officially as the 4th Regiment Tennessee Cavalry (Starnes'-McLemore's), but in the 8th Regiment Tennessee Cavalry (Baxter Smith's), which was often informally referred to as the 4th Regiment Tennessee Cavalry because it was in part a successor to an earlier unit known as the 4th Regiment Tennessee Cavalry (Murray's). See *Tennesseans in the Civil War*, 1: 59-60, 62, 71.]

MISCELLANEOUS

Information relating to the men who had served in Company E, 65th Regiment N.C. Troops (6th Regiment N.C. Cavalry) and enlisted illegally in this legion, most likely in this battalion, comes from "Charges and Specifications Against Col. William H. Thomas of Thomas' N.C. Legion," May 11, 1864, microfilm 284-03-01, William Holland Thomas Papers, Special Collections, Perkins Library, Duke University (original in the William Holland Thomas Collection, Special Collections, Hunter Library, Western Carolina University).

BASSETT, _____, Sergeant
On July 8, 1864, Col. William H. Thomas sent a provision return to a Sergeant Bassett at Webster, so that Bassett would supply Thomas's command in western North Carolina. It is unclear from the context of the letter whether or not Bassett is a member of the part of Thomas's Legion that was in western North Carolina, or of another unit serving in the area, or a member of the department staff. [William H. Thomas to Sergeant Bassett, July 8, 1864, unbound letterbook, William Holland Thomas Papers, Special Collections, Perkins Library, Duke University.]

BEARD, _____, Sergeant
On August 20, 1864, Col. William H. Thomas sent instructions to a Sergeant Beard regarding the collection of cattle in Macon County. It is unclear from the context of the letter whether or not Beard was a member of this legion, of another unit serving in the area, or of the department staff. [William H. Thomas to Sergeant Beard, August 20, 1864, unbound letterbook, William Holland Thomas Papers, Special Collections, Perkins Library, Duke University.]

BRACKETT, WILLIAM, Private
Served in Company E, 65th Regiment N.C. Troops (6th Regiment N.C. Cavalry). Enlisted illegally in this legion, most likely in this battalion, between September, 1863, and April, 1864. No further records.

BROWN, _____, Sergeant
On August 26, 1864, Col. William H. Thomas ordered a Sergeant Brown to "move the men with you" to watch the roads leading south of "Mount Starlin" (probably Mount Sterling in Haywood County). It is not known whether Sergeant Brown was serving in this battalion or another unit stationed in the area; he may have been a non-commissioned officer in a Home Guard company cooperating with Thomas. [William H. Thomas to Sergeant Brown, August 26, 1864, unbound letterbook, William Holland Thomas Papers, Special Collections, Perkins Library, Duke University.]

BUCHANAN, WILLIAM O., Private
Served in Company E, 65th Regiment N.C. Troops (6th Regiment N.C. Cavalry). Enlisted illegally in this legion, most likely in this battalion, between September, 1863, and April, 1864. He returned to the 65th Regiment prior to October 31, 1864.

BURNETT, ENOCH J. A., Private
Served in Company A, 7th Battalion N.C. Cavalry and was absent without leave from that company when it became Company E, 65th N.C. Troops (6th Regiment N.C. Cavalry), August 3, 1863. Enlisted illegally in this legion, most likely in this battalion, between September, 1863, and April, 1864. No further records.

BURNETT, HENRY C., Private
Served in 2nd Company G, 65th Regiment N.C. Troops (6th Regiment N.C. Cavalry). Enlisted illegally in this legion, most likely in this battalion, between September, 1863, and April, 1864. No further records.

CATLANI, Private
Cherokee Indian. Federal Provost Marshal records indicate that he served in this battalion and was captured on or about February 25, 1864, and was released at Knoxville, Tennessee, March 10, 1864, after taking the Oath of Allegiance. [He was probably one of the party of fifteen Indians who surrendered to the Federals at Motley's Ford, Tennessee, February 22, 1864.]

CHILDERS, ALLEN, Private
Served in Company E, 65th Regiment N.C. Troops (6th Regiment N.C. Cavalry). Enlisted illegally in this legion, most likely in this battalion, between September, 1863, and April, 1864. He returned to the 65th Regiment prior to October 31, 1864.

CUNNINGHAM, DEWIT C., Farrier
Previously served as Private in Company E, 65th Regiment N.C. Troops (6th Regiment N.C. Cavalry). Transferred to this legion, most likely this battalion, on September 11, 1864, possibly in exchange for Pvt. Thomas W. Owens. No further records. [W. E. McDowell to Colonel Thomas, October 9, 1864, microfilm 284-03-1, William Holland Thomas Papers, Special Collections, Perkins Library, Duke University.]

DAVE, _____
Cherokee Indian. Place and date of enlistment not reported. Captured on or about February 25, 1864. Confined at Knoxville, Tennessee. Released at Knoxville on or about March 10, 1864, after taking the Oath of Allegiance. [He was probably one of the party of fifteen Indians who surrendered to the Federals at Motley's Ford, Tennessee, on February 22, 1864. He may have been the same man as Pvt. David Partridge of Company B, Infantry Regiment of this legion, who deserted to the Federals on an unknown date and subsequently served in Company D, 3rd Regiment N.C. Mounted Infantry (Union); if so, he was probably serving in Company B of this battalion at the time of his desertion.]

DUVALL, BENJAMIN F., Private
Served in Company E, 65th Regiment N.C. Troops (6th Regiment N.C. Cavalry). Enlisted illegally in this legion, most likely in this battalion, between September, 1863, and April, 1864. No further records.

DUVALL, JOHN R., Private

Served in Company E, 65th Regiment N.C. Troops (6th Regiment N.C. Cavalry). Enlisted illegally in this legion, most likely in this battalion, between September, 1863, and April, 1864. He returned to service with the 65th Regiment by August 31, 1864.

ELLIOTT, CASH, Private

Cherokee Indian. Place and date of enlistment not reported. Reportedly captured on February 7, 1864, and confined at Knoxville, Tennessee, on the same date. Released at Knoxville on March 10, 1864, after taking the Oath of Allegiance. [He was probably captured in the Federal raid on Thomas's camp at Deep Creek, near Quallatown, February 2, 1864.]

FORESTER, JAMES M., Private

Served as Private in Company C, 7th Battalion N.C. Cavalry, and was reported absent without leave from that unit at the time of its transfer to the 65th Regiment N.C. Troops (6th Regiment N.C. Cavalry), where it became Company C (later 2nd Company G). Enlisted illegally in this legion, most likely in this battalion, between September, 1863, and April, 1864. No further records.

GIPSON, JAMES G., Private

Served as Private in Company C, 7th Battalion N.C. Cavalry, and was reported absent without leave from that unit at the time of its transfer to the 65th Regiment N.C. Troops (6th Regiment N.C. Cavalry), where it became Company C (later 2nd Company G). Enlisted illegally in this legion, most likely in this battalion, between September, 1863, and April, 1864. He was probably still serving with this battalion when he went over to the enemy prior to June 30, 1864, although Federal Provost Marshal records show him as a member of the 65th Regiment.

GIPSON, WALTON A., Private

Served as Private in Company C, 7th Battalion N.C. Cavalry, and reported as absent without leave from that unit at the time of its transfer to the 65th Regiment N.C. Troops (6th Regiment N.C. Cavalry), where it became Company C (later 2nd Company G). Enlisted illegally in this legion, most likely in this battalion, between September, 1863, and April, 1864. No further records.

GRANT, HENRY B., Private

Served as Private in Company E, 65th Regiment N.C. Troops (6th Regiment N.C. Cavalry). Enlisted illegally in this legion, most likely in this battalion, between September, 1863, and April, 1864, while absent without leave from the 65th Regiment. No further records.

HALL, RUFUS H., _____

Served as Sergeant in Company E, 65th Regiment N.C. Troops (6th Regiment N.C. Cavalry). Enlisted illegally in this legion, most likely in this battalion, between September, 1863, and April, 1864, while absent without leave from the 65th Regiment. No further records.

HENRY, THOMAS, Private

Served as Private in Company I, Infantry Regiment of this legion. Reported to be "on duty with Col. Thomas" in North Carolina on the January-February, 1864, muster roll of that company.

HOLLAND, JAMES W., Private

Served as Private in Company C, 7th Battalion N.C. Cavalry, and reported as absent without leave from that unit at the time of its transfer to the 65th Regiment N.C. Troops (6th Regiment N.C. Cavalry), where it became Company C (later 2nd Company G). Enlisted illegally in this legion, most likely in this battalion, between September, 1863, and April, 1864. No further records.

JACKSON, Private

Cherokee Indian. Place and date of enlistment not reported. Reportedly captured on February 7, 1864. Confined at Knoxville, Tennessee, the same date. Released at Knoxville on March 10, 1864, after taking the Oath of Allegiance. [He was probably captured in the Federal raid on Colonel Thomas's camp at Deep Creek, near Quallatown, February 2, 1864.]

JESSE, Private

Cherokee Indian. Place and date of enlistment not reported. Captured on or about February 7, 1864. Confined at Knoxville, Tennessee, on February 7, 1864. Released at Knoxville on March 22, 1864, after taking the Oath of Allegiance. [He was probably captured in the Federal raid on Colonel Thomas's camp at Deep Creek, near Quallatown, February 2, 1864. He may have been the same man as either Pvt. Jesse Reed of 2nd Company A, Infantry Regiment of this legion, or Pvt. Jesse Ross of Company B, Infantry Regiment of this legion.]

JIMMY, Private

Cherokee Indian. Place and date of enlistment not reported. Captured on or about February 25, 1864. Confined at Knoxville, Tennessee, on February 25, 1864. Released at Knoxville on March 10, 1864, after taking the Oath of Allegiance. [He was probably one of the party of fifteen Indians who surrendered to the Federals at Motley's Ford, Tennessee, on February 22, 1864.]

JOHNNY, Private

Cherokee Indian. Place and date of enlistment not reported. Captured on or about February 25, 1864. Sent to Knoxville, Tennessee. Released at Knoxville on March 10, 1864, after taking the Oath of Allegiance. [He was probably one of the party of fifteen Indians who surrendered to the Federals at Motley's Ford, Tennessee, on February 22, 1864.]

KIRKLAND, JOHN, _____

Described by Col. William H. Thomas as one "of my secret agents," and referred to in a letter to Col. John B. Palmer as "a man you have Some Knowledge of." May have served in this battalion. Reported in August, 1864, as spying on Federal and Unionist activities in eastern Tennessee for Thomas. [Thomas to Palmer, August 24, 1864, unbound letterbook, William Holland Thomas Papers, Special Collections, Perkins Library, Duke University.]

LAKEY, JOHN E., Private

Served as Private in Company E, 65th Regiment N.C. Troops (6th Regiment N.C. Cavalry). Enlisted illegally in this legion, most likely in this battalion, between September, 1863, and April, 1864, while absent without leave from the 65th Regiment. No further records.

LOW, SAMUEL., _____

Place and date of enlistment not reported. Served in an unknown company of this battalion, or with its Field & Staff. Appointed in August, 1864, to assist with the collection of cattle in Macon County. No further records. [Col. William H. Thomas to Sgt. Beard, August 20, 1864, William Holland Thomas Papers, Special Collections, Perkins Library, Duke University.]

McCOY, WILLIAM, Private

Resided in Macon County. Place and date of enlistment not reported; probably enlisted subsequent to February 29, 1864. Deserted to the enemy at Franklin on June 3, 1864. Confined at Knoxville, Tennessee, June 30, 1864. Transferred to Louisville, Kentucky, where he arrived on July 14, 1864. Took the Oath of Allegiance at Louisville on July 16, 1864, and sent to Jeffersonville, Indiana, with instructions to remain north of the Ohio River.

MATTOCK, JOHN H., Private

Served as Private in Company E, 65th Regiment N.C. Troops (6th Regiment N.C. Cavalry). Enlisted illegally in this legion, most likely in this battalion, between September, 1863, and April, 1864, while absent without leave from the 65th Regiment. Returned to the 65th Regiment on June 13, 1864.

MEADOWS, DANIEL J., Private

Served as Private in Company E, 65th Regiment N.C. Troops (6th Regiment N.C. Cavalry). Enlisted illegally in this legion, most likely in this battalion, between September, 1863, and April, 1864, while absent without leave from the 65th Regiment. No further records.

MORRISON, JOSEPH, Private

Served as Private in Company E, 65th Regiment N.C. Troops (6th Regiment N.C. Cavalry). Enlisted illegally in this legion, most likely in this battalion, between September, 1863, and April, 1864, while absent without leave from the 65th Regiment. No further records.

NORTON, E. R., Sergeant

Place and date of enlistment not reported. Reported as "leading a scout" near the South Carolina border in September, 1864. His base of operations at this time was at a place called Horse Cove, North Carolina, probably the Horse Cove in Macon County. [See Sgt. E.R. Norton to Gov. Zebulon B. Vance, September 27, 1864, Governors' Papers: Vance, 1862-1865, Box 13, September 25-27, 1864; N.C. State Archives.]

ODOM, JOHN A., Private

Served previously as a Private in Company F, Infantry Regiment of this legion. Federal Provost Marshal records seem to indicate that he served illegally with this battalion following his desertion from the Infantry Regiment on April 10, 1863. Captured on or about February 7, 1864. Confined at Knoxville, Tennessee, February 7, 1864. Released at Knoxville on February 13, 1864, after taking the Oath of Allegiance. [He was probably captured on February 2, 1864, in the Federal raid on Thomas's camp at Deep Creek, near Quallatown.]

OWENS, THOMAS W., Private

Place and date of enlistment not reported. Transferred to Company E, 65th Regiment N.C. Troops (6th Regiment North Carolina Cavalry) on September 11, 1864. [It is presumed that Owens served in the Indian Battalion because he evidently had immediate access to Col. William H. Thomas just prior to his transfer. According to a letter to Thomas from Capt. William E. McDowell of Company E, 65th Regiment, Owens may have been exchanged, perhaps illegally, for Farrier Dewit C. Cunningham of McDowell's company: "I received your note by T W Owen It is all right with [Lt.] Col [Alfred Hunter] Baird [of the 65th Regiment] you may consider D Cunningham belonging to your command" W. E. McDowell to Colonel Thomas, October 9, 1864, microfilm 284-03-1 (original in the William Holland Thomas Papers, Special Collections, Hunter Library, Western Carolina University), William Holland Thomas Papers, Special Collections, Perkins Library, Duke University.]

PARKER, MORTON, Private

Place and date of enlistment not reported; probably enlisted subsequent to December 31, 1863. Captured at Murphy on or about February 18, 1864. Sent to Nashville, Tennessee. Transferred to Louisville, Kentucky, where he arrived on February 27, 1864. Transferred to Fort Delaware, Delaware, where he arrived on March 4, 1864. Paroled at Fort Delaware on September 14, 1864. Received at Aiken's Landing, James River, Virginia, September 18, 1864, for exchange. Hospitalized at Richmond, Virginia. Furloughed to Walhalla, South Carolina, September 26, 1864. No further records. [His given name may have been Martin. He is variously reported in records of the Federal Provost Marshal to have served in Companies A and C, Thomas's Legion, while his Confederate hospital records report him as a member of Company E, Thomas's Legion; The date and place of his capture indicate that he served in the Indian Battalion.]

PATTERSON, _____, Captain

Reported in command of a company within Colonel Thomas's area of operations in western North Carolina in August, 1864. In a letter to a local citizen, Thomas gave instructions to secure beef to feed Patterson's company. This company may have been part of the Indian Battalion, or Patterson may have commanded a local Home Guard unit or militia company that was cooperating with Thomas at the time. [Col. William H. Thomas to Mr. F. Erwin Rice, August 18, 1864, unbound letterbook, William Holland Thomas Papers, Special Collections, Perkins Library, Duke University.]

PATTERSON, WILLIAM T., Private

Place and date of enlistment not reported. Captured in Cherokee County on November 4, 1864. Sent to Knoxville, Tennessee. Transferred to Chattanooga, Tennessee, December 31, 1864. Transferred to Nashville, Tennessee. Confined at Louisville, Kentucky, January 8, 1865. Transferred to Camp Chase, Ohio, where he arrived on January 15, 1865. Died at Camp Chase on February 14, 1865, of "pneumonia." [His gravestone marker indicates that he served in "Company F, Thomas' Legion," without specifying whether or not he served in Company F, Infantry Regiment, or Company F, Indian Battalion, which most likely would be either Welch's Company or Hick's Company, or perhaps another company yet undocumented. The place and date of his capture, as well as his obscurity in the records, seem to indicate that he served in the Indian Battalion.]

PLEMMONS, DANIEL S., _____

Served as Assistant Commissary of Subsistence of the 29th Regiment N.C. Troops; last reported in the records of that unit on April 15, 1863. Directed by Col. William H. Thomas in August,

1864, to assist with the collection of cattle in Macon County. He may have been serving with this battalion. [Col. William H. Thomas to Sgt. Beard, August 20, 1864, unbound letterbook, William Holland Thomas Papers, Special Collections, Perkins Library, Duke University]

RATLER, STEPHEN, Private

Cherokee Indian. Place and date of enlistment not reported; probably enlisted subsequent to December 31, 1863. Reported captured on or about February 7, 1864. Confined at Knoxville, Tennessee, February 7, 1864. Released at Knoxville on March 10, 1864, after taking the Oath of Allegiance. [He was probably captured in the Federal raid on Thomas's camp at Deep Creek, near Quallatown, February 2, 1864.]

ROUND, JOE, Private

Cherokee Indian. Place and date of enlistment not reported; probably enlisted subsequent to December 31, 1863. Reportedly captured on or about February 7, 1864. Confined at Knoxville, Tennessee, February 7, 1864. Sent to hospital sick on February 22, 1864. Released at Knoxville on March 10, 1864, after taking the Oath of Allegiance. [He was probably captured in the Federal raid on Thomas's camp at Deep Creek, near Quallatown, February 2, 1864.]

RUSE, JOHN, Private

Cherokee Indian. Place and date of enlistment not reported; probably enlisted subsequent to December 31, 1863. Reportedly captured on or about February 7, 1864. Confined at Knoxville, Tennessee, February 7, 1864. Released at Knoxville on March 10, 1864, after taking the Oath of Allegiance. [He was probably captured in the Federal raid on Thomas's camp at Deep Creek, near Quallatown, February 2, 1864.]

SCHIRSKA, Private

Cherokee Indian. Place and date of enlistment not reported; probably enlisted subsequent to December 31, 1863. Captured on or about February 25, 1864. Confined at Knoxville, Tennessee, February 25, 1864. Released at Knoxville on March 10, 1864, after taking the Oath of Allegiance. [He was probably one of the party of fifteen Indians who surrendered to the Federals at Motley's Ford, Tennessee, on February 22, 1864.]

SELOLA, Private

Cherokee Indian. Place and date of enlistment not reported; probably enlisted subsequent to December 31, 1863. Captured on or about February 25, 1864. Sent to Knoxville, Tennessee. Released at Knoxville on March 10, 1864, after taking the Oath of Allegiance. [He was probably one of the party of fifteen Indians who surrendered to the Federals at Motley's Ford, Tennessee, on February 22, 1864.]

SHEPHERD, THOMAS P., Private

Served as Private in Company E, 65th Regiment N.C. Troops (6th Regiment N.C. Cavalry). Enlisted illegally in this legion, most likely in this battalion, between September, 1863, and April, 1864, while absent without leave from the 65th Regiment. Returned to the 65th Regiment prior to August 31, 1864.

SMOKE, _____

Cherokee Indian. Place and date of enlistment not reported; probably enlisted subsequent to December 31, 1863. Reportedly captured on or about February 7, 1864. Sent to Knoxville, Tennessee. Sent to hospital on February 22, 1864. Returned to prison on March 9, 1864. Released at Knoxville on March 10, 1864, after taking the Oath of Allegiance. [He was probably captured in the Federal raid on Thomas's camp at Deep Creek, near Quallatown, February 2, 1864.]

SOUND, Private

Cherokee Indian. Place and date of enlistment not reported; probably enlisted subsequent to December 31, 1863. Reportedly captured on or about February 7, 1864. Sent to Knoxville, Tennessee. Released at Knoxville on March 10, 1864, after taking the Oath of Allegiance. Hospitalized at Richmond, Virginia, August 17, 1864, with an unspecified complaint. Transferred to another hospital on August 18, 1864. No further records. [He was probably captured in the Federal raid on Thomas's camp at Deep Creek, near Quallatown, February 2, 1864.]

STOMPER, _____

Cherokee Indian. Reportedly captured on or about February 7, 1864. Confined at Knoxville, Tennessee, February 7, 1864. Released at Knoxville on March 10, 1864, after taking the Oath of Allegiance. [He was probably captured in the Federal raid on Thomas's camp at Deep Creek, near Quallatown, February 2, 1864.]

TAKASKA, Private

Cherokee Indian. Place and date of enlistment not reported. Captured on or about February 25, 1864. Sent to Knoxville, Tennessee. Released at Knoxville on March 10, 1864, after taking the Oath of Allegiance. [He was probably one of the party of fifteen Indians who surrendered to the Federals at Motley's Ford, Tennessee, February 22, 1864.]

TAKE, J. W., Private

Cherokee Indian. Place and date of enlistment not reported. Reportedly captured on or about February 7, 1864. Sent to Knoxville, Tennessee. Hospitalized on February 22, 1864. Released at Knoxville on March 10, 1864, after taking the Oath of Allegiance. [He was probably captured in the Federal raid on Thomas's camp at Deep Creek, near Quallatown, February 2, 1864.]

TEEETLADAHHEE, JIM, _____

Cherokee Indian. North Carolina pension records appear to indicate that he served in this legion, probably in this battalion. Survived the war. [Also known as Jim Driver. He claimed to have served in a unit known as "Capt. Hugg's Co.," otherwise unidentified.]

THAYER, JOHN, Private

Place and date of enlistment not reported. Reportedly captured on or about February 7, 1864. Confined at Knoxville, Tennessee, February 7, 1864. Released at Knoxville on March 10, 1864, after taking the Oath of Allegiance. [He was probably captured in the Federal raid on Thomas's camp at Deep Creek, near Quallatown, February 2, 1864.]

TISTOSKA, Private

Cherokee Indian. Place and date of enlistment not reported; probably enlisted subsequent to December 31, 1863. Captured on or about February 25, 1864. Confined at Knoxville, Tennessee, February 25, 1864. Released at Knoxville on March 10, 1864, after taking the Oath of Allegiance. [He was probably one of the party of fifteen Indians who surrendered to the Federals at Motley's Ford, Tennessee, February 22, 1864.]

WALLACE, _____, Private
Cherokee Indian. Place and date of enlistment not reported; probably enlisted subsequent to December 31, 1863. Reportedly captured on or about February 7, 1864. Confined at Knoxville, Tennessee, February 7, 1864. Sent to hospital sick on an unknown date. Discharged and returned to prison, February 20, 1864. Released at Knoxville on March 10, 1864, after taking the Oath of Allegiance. [He was probably captured in the Federal raid on Thomas's camp at Deep Creek, near Quallatown, February 2, 1864.]

WASHA, _____, Private
Cherokee Indian. Place and date of enlistment not reported; probably enlisted subsequent to December 31, 1863. Reportedly captured on or about February 7, 1864. Confined at Knoxville, Tennessee, February 7, 1864. Released at Knoxville on March 10, 1864, after taking the Oath of Allegiance. [He was probably captured in the Federal raid on Thomas's camp at Deep Creek, near Quallatown, February 2, 1864.]

WELCH, JOHN W., Private
Previously served as Private in Company F, Infantry Regiment of this legion. Federal Provost Marshal records appear to indicate that he served with this battalion following his desertion from the Infantry Regiment. Captured in Macon or Jackson County on February 2, 1864, probably during the Federal raid on Thomas's camp at Deep Creek, near Quallatown. Confined at Fort Delaware, Delaware, on an unknown date. Died at Fort Delaware on July 1, 1864, after being stabbed "in a contest with one of his comrades."

WELCH, JOSEPH W., Private
Served as Private in Company H, Infantry Regiment of this legion. He was captured in Macon County on February 2, 1864. He may have been serving, possibly illegally, with this battalion at the time of his capture. He may have been captured during the Federal raid on Colonel Thomas's camp at Deep Creek, near Quallatown. Confined at Knoxville, Tennessee, February 7, 1864. Sent to Nashville, Tennessee. Sent to Louisville, Kentucky, February 28, 1864. Confined at Fort Delaware, Delaware, March 7, 1864. Probably released at Fort Delaware on June 7, 1865, after taking the Oath of Allegiance. Survived the war.

WHITTIER, _____
Described by Col. William H. Thomas as one "of my secret agents," and reported in August, 1864, as spying on Federal troop movements near Strawberry Plains, Tennessee. He may have been serving with this battalion. [Col. William H. Thomas to Col. John B. Palmer, August 24, 1864, unbound letterbook, 1860-1864 Correspondence Folder, William Holland Thomas Papers, Special Collections, Perkins Library, Duke University.]

WILLIE, _____, Private
Cherokee Indian. Place and date of enlistment not reported; probably enlisted subsequent to December 31, 1863. Captured on or about February 25, 1864. Confined at Knoxville, Tennessee, February 25, 1865. Released at Knoxville on March 10, 1864, after taking the Oath of Allegiance. [He was probably one of the party of fifteen Indians who surrendered to the Federals at Motley's Ford, Tennessee, on February 22, 1864.]

WOLDER, MOSS, Private
Cherokee Indian. Place and date of enlistment not reported; probably enlisted subsequent to December 31, 1863. Reportedly captured on or about February 7, 1864. Confined at Knoxville, Tennessee, February 7, 1864. Released at Knoxville on March 10, 1864, after taking the Oath of Allegiance. [He was probably captured in the Federal raid on Thomas's camp at Deep Creek, near Quallatown, February 2, 1864.]

GENERAL MISCELLANEOUS

The following soldiers served in the Thomas's Legion. However, it is unknown whether they served in the Infantry Regiment, Walker's Battalion or the Indian Battalion. A number of these names come from an undated (ca. 1900) list of living Confederate Cherokees, found in the William W. Stringfield Papers at Western Carolina Univerity.

ALLISON, JULIUS J., Captain
Confederate gravestone records indicate that he served as Captain in this legion. Survived the war.

ANDREWS, MARSH, _____
North Carolina pension records appear to indicate that he served in this legion. Survived the war.

ANGEL, L. M., _____
North Carolina pension records indicate that he served in this legion. Survived the war.

BAILEY, LEE J., _____
North Carolina pension records indicate that he served in this legion. Survived the war.

BAILEY, W. P., _____
North Carolina pension records indicate that he served in this legion. Survived the war. [May have been the same man as William Bailey who served in Company F, Infantry Regiment of this legion.]

BATTLE, ASA H., _____
He filed a North Carolina pension application claiming to have served in this legion. He had previously filed an application claiming to have served in the 65th Regiment N.C. Troops (6th Regiment N.C. Cavalry) and received a wound at Plymouth. He was probably the same man as Pvt. Asaph H. Battle of 2nd Company G, 65th Regiment. He probably did not serve in Thomas's Legion, which was never at Plymouth.

BIRD, TAW-HEESKA, _____
Enlisted at Strawberry Plains, Tennessee, on an unknown date. Survived the war. [His given name was also rendered as Tah-heeska, Tohesha, and Ta heeskee.]

BRINSON, DANIEL J., _____
North Carolina pension records indicate that he served in this legion. Survived the war.

BROCK, GEORGE F., _____
North Carolina pension records indicate that he served in this legion. Survived the war.

BROWN, S. C., _____
A prisoner-of-war record indicates that he served in "Co. M., 1 Regt Thomas Legion." and was captured at Knoxville, Tennessee, May 1, 1865. There was no Company M in this legion. He may have been the same man as Pvt. Samuel C. Brown of Company F, Walker's Battalion.

BRYSON, THAD G., _____
North Carolina pension records indicate that he served in this legion. Survived the war.

BUCHANAN, JOHN P., Private
Confederate gravestone records appear to indicate that he served in this legion.

BURCHFIELD, J. L., Private
Confederate gravestone records appear to indicate that he served in this legion.

CANIPE, JOHN, _____
North Carolina pension records appear to indicate that he served in this legion. Survived the war.

CARVER, ISAAC, _____
North Carolina pension records appear to indicate that he served in this legion.

CATHEY, WILLIAM B., _____
In what appears to be a petition dated March 1, 1865, this man is identified as a member of this legion and is reported on detail "as a miller to keep the mills of Col Joseph Cathey engaged in grinding for the troops belonging to the Confederate Service and the citizens of Haywood County, N C." [William Holland Thomas Papers, Perkins Library, Duke University.]

CHARAL, C. H., _____
Confederate gravestone records appear to indicate that he served in this legion.

CLARK, E. L., _____
North Carolina pension records indicate that he served in this legion. Survived the war.

COALOSKA, JOHN, Private
Served as Private in Company F, 39th Regiment N.C. Troops. Records of that company indicate that he served also in this legion; however, records of this legion do not indicate that he served herein.

COCKRAN, A., _____
North Carolina pension records indicate that he served in this legion. Survived the war.

COLEMAN, CALVIN, _____
North Carolina pension records indicate that he served in this legion. Survived the war.

COLVER, ALBERT, _____
A list of paroled Confederates captured in Tennessee in June, 1863, by cavalry raiders led by Col. William P. Sanders indicates that this man was a member of this legion, was captured at Strawberry Plains, Tennessee, June 20, 1863, and paroled there the next day. [File 7069, National Archives]

CONSEEN, JAKE, _____
Cherokee Indian. Name appears on an undated (ca. 1900) list of living Confederate Cherokees. Probably served in this legion.

CONSEEN, OGANI, _____
Cherokee Indian. Name appears on an undated (ca. 1900) list of living Confederate Cherokees. Probably served in this legion.

COOPER, W., _____
North Carolina pension records appear to indicate that he served in this legion.

COPE, A. J., _____
North Carolina pension records appear to indicate that he served in this legion. Survived the war.

COPE, GEORGE, _____
North Carolina pension records appear to indicate that he served in this legion. Survived the war.

CRISP, JOAB A., _____
North Carolina pension records indicate that he served in this legion. Survived the war.

CRYMES, JOHN E., Private
Confederate gravestone records appear to indicate that he served in this legion.

DAVES, J. M., _____
North Carolina pension records indicate that he served in this legion. Survived the war. [He may have served previously in Company A, 7th Battalion N.C. Cavalry, and Company E, 65th Regiment N.C. Troops (6th Regiment N.C. Cavalry).]

DAVES, ROBERT W., _____
North Carolina pension records indicate that he served in this legion.

DILLINGHAM, JAMES LEANDER., Private
Records of the United Daughters of the Confederacy indicate that he served in this legion. Survived the war. [He may have been the same man as Pvt. J. C. Dillingham of Company F, Infantry Regiment of this legion.]

ELK, CASA, Private
Cherokee Indian. Served as Private in Company F, 39th Regiment N.C. Troops. Records of that company indicate that he enlisted in this legion; however, no other records of his service in this legion were located.

ENGLAND, S. A., _____
Records of the United Daughters of the Confederacy indicate that he served in this legion. Survived the war.

FISHER, RUFUS, _____
North Carolina pension records indicate that he served in this legion.

FLIPPIN, JOHN M., _____
North Carolina pension records appear to indicate that he served in this legion.

FLOYD, R. G., _____
Place and date of enlistment in this legion not reported. Lost both legs during his military service. No further records. Survived the war. [See Civil War Collection, Box 41, North Carolina State Archives, Raleigh.]

FORESTER, EDWARD, Private
Served as Private in Company A, 29th Regiment N.C. Troops. Records of that company indicate that he was transferred to this legion in March, 1863; however, there are no other records of his service in this legion.

FOUTE, OBEDIAH BOAZ, _____
Records of the United Daughters of the Confederacy appear to indicate that he served in this legion.

FOWLER, SAMPSON, _____
North Carolina pension records indicate that he served in this legion.

FRADY, JOHN S., _____
North Carolina pension records appear to indicate that he served in this legion. Survived the war.

FULTNER, GEORGE, Private
Served as Private in Company F, 39th Regiment N.C. Troops. Records of that regiment indicate that he was transferred to this legion prior to December 1, 1862; however, there are no other records of his service in this legion.

GARRISON, HENRY T., _____
North Carolina pension records indicate that he served in this legion.

GIBSON, J. S. , _____
A list of paroled Confederates captured in Tennessee in June, 1863, by cavalry raiders led by Col. William P. Sanders indicates that this man was a member of this legion, was captured at Strawberry Plains, Tennessee, June 20, 1863, and paroled there the next day. [File 7069, National Archives]

GOLDSMITH, E. B., Private
Records of the United Daughters of the Confederacy appear to indicate that he served in this legion.

GRANT, E. J., _____
North Carolina pension records indicate that he served in this legion.

GREEN, R. W., _____
North Carolina pension records appear to indicate that he served in this legion. Survived the war.

GUDGER, S. R., _____
North Carolina pension records appear to indicate that he served in this legion. Survived the war.

HARRIS, MELMOUTH D., Private
Served as Private in Company G, 39th Regiment N.C. Troops. Records of that company indicate that he enlisted in this legion; however, no other records of his service in this legion were located. [He may have been the same man as Pvt. Daniel M. Harris of Company A, Walker's Battalion.]

HARRIS, W. N., _____
North Carolina pension records appear to indicate that he served in this legion. Survived the war.

HAWKINS, ALLEN D., Private
Records of the Federal Provost Marshal indicate that he served in this legion. Resided in Macon County. Place and date of enlistment not reported. Deserted to the enemy on an unspecified date. Sent to Chattanooga, Tennessee. Transferred to Louisville, Kentucky. Took the Oath of Allegiance at Louisville on June 14, 1864, to be released north of the Ohio River on the same date and to remain north of the river for the duration of the war. [May have served previously as Private in Company I, 39th Regiment N.C.Troops.]

HAYES, HARRY, _____
A list of paroled Confederates captured in Tennessee in June, 1863, by cavalry raiders led by Col. William P. Sanders indicates that this man served in this legion, was captured at Strawberry Plains, Tennessee, June 20, 1863, and paroled there the next day. [File 7069, National Archives]

HEDGECOCK, DAVID, Private
Served as Private in Company F, 39th Regiment N.C. Troops. Records of that company indicate that he enlisted in this legion; however, no other evidence of his service in this legion were located.

HENDRIX, H. M., _____
North Carolina pension records appear to indicate that he served in this legion. Survived the war.

HENRY, WILLIAM L., _____
North Carolina pension and state auditor records appear to indicate that he served in this legion. Survived the war.

HILL, K. G., _____
A list of paroled Confederates captured in Tennessee in June, 1863, by cavalry raiders led by Col. William P. Sanders indicates that this man served in this legion, was captured at Strawberry Plains, Tennessee, June 20, 1863, and paroled there the next day. [File 7069, National Archives]

HILL, RICHARD, _____
North Carolina pension records appear to indicate that he served in this legion. Survived the war.

HIPPS, LEVI C., _____
Previously served as Private in Company E, 29th Regiment N.C. Troops. Enlisted in this legion on an unspecified date, probably subsequent to February 29, 1864. No further records. Survived the war.

HOGSED, JACK, _____
North Carolina pension records appear to indicate that he served in this legion.

HOYLE, JOHN, _____
North Carolina pension records appear to indicate that he served in this legion.

HOYLE, JOHN B., _____
North Carolina pension records indicate that he served in this legion.

HUDSON, BENJAMIN, Private
Resided in Pickens District, South Carolina. Recorded in both receipt roll records and Federal Provost Marshal records as having served in a Company A of this legion; however, it is not reported which Company A. Name appears on a receipt roll for clothing dated October 16, 1864. Deserted to the enemy in Jackson County on December 11, 1864. Sent to Knoxville, Tennessee. Released at Knoxville on December 28, 1864, after taking the Oath of Allegiance.

HUGHES, JOHN E., _____
North Carolina pension records indicate that he served in a Company A of this legion. Survived the war.

HURST, THOMAS N., 3rd Lieutenant
Served as Private in Company E, 65th Regiment N.C. Troops (6th Regiment N.C. Cavalry). Records of the 65th Regiment indicate that he was appointed 3rd Lieutenant and ordered to report for duty with Company F, Walker's Battalion, February 8, 1865. No other evidence of his service in that company was located. [It is possible that this Company F, Walker's Battalion, commanded by a Capt. W. S. Singleton, was one of the three white companies that had served in Thomas's western North Carolina battalion in 1864. An estimate for funding for the units in the Department of Western North Carolina for early 1865 would seem to indicate that Thomas had sent two of those companies to the Infantry Regiment and one to McKamy's (Walker's) Battalion, based on the number of captains given for the regiment and the battalion and the fact that the four Indian companies from the western North Carolina battalion had been separated from their white counterparts. See Consolidated Estimate of Funds Required for the Pay of the Troops in the Department of Western North Carolina for the Months of March and April 1865, March 11, 1865, Thomas Legion, Battalion Field and Staff File #1, Muster and Pay Rolls, Chapter 1: Entry 18, Box 826, RG 109, NA. If this is correct, it is not known which of the three white companies went to Walker's old battalion. It may have been Company K, 5th Regiment Tennessee Cavalry (McKenzie's), which had originally been Company F of Walker's Battalion and had served in Thomas's western North Carolina battalion as Company G (see the company history accompanying the roster for Company G, Indian Battalion, in this volume). At the same time, it is possible that Singleton's company was not connected with Thomas's Legion at all. The company was near Clayton, Georgia, far from Thomas's normal range of operations (but not necessarily impossible, given his concerns for his supply line to South Carolina). Secondly, it seems likelier that Walker's Battalion would be known formally as McKamy's Battalion or Stringfield's Battalion at this point in the war, or as the 1st Battalion, Thomas's Legion. Thus, the connection of Singleton's company to this legion, and Hurst's possible service with it, is tentative at best.]

HYATT, WILLIAM, Private
Confederate gravestone records appear to indicate that he served in a Company E of this legion.

ISRAEL, W. L., _____
North Carolina pension records indicate that he served in this legion.

JACKSON, JOHN, _____
North Carolina pension records appear to indicate that he served in this legion. [He may be the same man as John Jackson of 2nd Company A, Infantry Regiment of this legion.]

JACOBS, W. B., _____
North Carolina pension records indicate that he served in this legion.

JIM, BIG, _____
Cherokee Indian. Name appears on an undated (ca. 1900) list of living Confederate Cherokees. Probably served in this legion.

JUSTUS, EDMOND, _____
North Carolina pension records indicate that he served in this legion. Survived the war.

KINTEEHEE, CHARLES, Private
Cherokee Indian. Served as Private in Company F, 39th Regiment N.C. Troops. Records of that unit indicate that he enlisted in this legion prior to February 28, 1863, while absent without leave from the 39th Regiment; however, no other records of his service in this legion were located.

KIRBY, J. B., _____
North Carolina pension records indicate that he served in this legion. Survived the war.

LANE, THOMAS P., 1st Lieutenant
Place and date of enlistment not reported. Captured at Hartwell, Georgia, May 18, 1865. Paroled, probably at Hartwell on the same date. [He may have served previously as 2nd Lieutenant of Company H, 25th Regiment N.C. Troops.]

LEATHERWOOD, J. C., _____
North Carolina pension records appear to indicate that he served in this legion. Survived the war.

LEAVELL, GEORGE C., _____
Florida pension application AO3474 indicates that he served in this legion.

LEDBETTER, WILLIAM, _____
North Carolina pension records appear to indicate that he served in this legion. Survived the war.

LEDFORD, GEORGE W., _____
North Carolina pension records indicate that he served in this legion. Survived the war.

LEDFORD, MILTON McELROY, _____
North Carolina pension records and records of the United Daughters of the Confederacy appear to indicate that he served in this legion. Survived the war. [He may have been the same man as the Milton M. Ledford whose name appears on a receipt roll for clothing dated March 18, 1864, as an unassigned conscript.]

LOMINAC, J. W., _____
North Carolina pension records appear to indicate that he served in this legion.

LONG, JOHN _____
Cherokee Indian. Name appears on an undated (ca. 1900) list of living Confederate Cherokees. Probably served in this legion. [May have been the same man as Pvt. John Long of Company C, Walker's Battalion.]

LOOTII, _____
Cherokee Indian. Name appears on an undated (ca. 1900) list of living Confederate Cherokees. Probably served in this legion.

LOU-WAN, JOHN, _____
Cherokee Indian. Name appears on an undated (ca. 1900) list of living Confederate Cherokees. Probably served in this legion. [May have been the same man as Pvt. John Lovin of Company H, Infantry Regiment of this legion.]

McCRACKEN, JOHN L., Lieutenant
Confederate gravestone records appear to indicate that he served in this legion.

McINTYRE, CHARLES, Private
Resided in Knox County, Tennessee. Place and date of enlistment not reported. Took the Oath of Allegiance at Chattanooga, Tennessee, May 21, 1865.

McMAHAN, G. W., _____
Born in Sevier County, Tennessee, in 1842. Served in Company L, 8th Regiment Tennessee Cavalry. Tennessee pension application No. 13926 indicates that he was cut off from his command while on special assignment after the battle of Atlanta and later served with this legion until the end of the war. Survived the war.

MARROW, ANDREW JACKSON, _____
North Carolina pension records indicate that he served in this legion. Survived the war.

MARTIN, A. J., _____
North Carolina pension records indicate that he served in this legion. Survived the war.

MARTIN, W. B., _____
North Carolina pension records indicate that he served in this legion. Survived the war.

MASNER, EDWARD, Private
Place and date of enlistment not reported. Records of the Federal Provost Marshal indicate that he was a "boy" who was "not

enlisted," presumably meaning that he was serving illegally in this legion, when he was captured at Chickamauga, Georgia, September 4, 1863. Sent to Louisville, Kentucky. Transferred to Camp Morton, Indianapolis, Indiana, November 4, 1863. Paroled at Camp Morton on or about March 10, 1865. Received at Boulware's and Cox's Wharves, James River, Virginia, March 23, 1865, for exchange. No further records.

MASON, ISIE, _____
North Carolina pension records indicate that he served in this legion.

MASSIE, WILLIAM M., Private
Confederate Gravestone Records appear to indicate that he served in this legion. Survived the war.

MATHES, J. K, Lieutenant
Two cards misfiled with the National Archive records of Pvt. John L. Mathison of Company E, Walker's Battalion, indicate that he was a Lieutenant in "Love's Command," either the Infantry Regiment of this legion, or all of the elements of the legion present in the Shenandoah Valley in 1864, as Lt. Col. James R. Love, Jr. was in command of the entire contingent. Wounded at Piedmont, Virginia, June 5, 1864. No further records. [His surname may have been Mathus.]

MATHIS, DANIEL LEVI, _____
North Carolina pension records appear to indicate that he served in this legion. Survived the war.

MERRELL, SAMUEL A., _____
North Carolina pension records appear to indicate that he served in this legion. Survived the war.

MESSER, SAMUEL, Private
Confederate Gravestone Records appear to indicate that he served in this legion. According to those records, he served as a Federal scout during the most of the war but enlisted in the Confederate army on May 1, 1865.

MESSER, W. J. _____
North Carolina pension records indicate that he served in this legion. Survived the war.

MILLER, CLARENCE W., _____
North Carolina pension records indicate that he served in this legion. Survived the war.

MILLER, DAVID L., _____
Resided in Macon County. Place and date of enlistment not reported; probably enlisted subsequent to February 29, 1864. Deserted to the enemy at Franklin on an unspecified date. Confined at Knoxville, Tennessee, June 30, 1864. Transferred to Louisville, Kentucky, where he arrived on July 14, 1864. Released at Louisville on July 16, 1864, after taking the Oath of Allegiance, and sent to Jeffersonville, Indiana with instructions to remain north of the Ohio River for the war.

MILLER, J. WESLEY, Private
Confederate Gravestone Records appear to indicate that he served in this legion. Survived the war.

MILLER, JACOB F., Private
Confederate Gravestone Records appear to indicate that he served in this legion.

MILLER, LEWIN, Private
Confederate Gravestone Records appear to indicate that he served in this legion. Survived the war.

MILLER, LEWIN F., Private
Confederate Gravestone Records appear to indicate that he served in this legion. Survived the war.

MILLER, MARCUS HENRY, Private
Confederate Gravestone Records appear to indicate that he served in this legion. Survived the war.

MINK, _____
Cherokee Indian. Name appears on an undated (ca. 1900) list of living Confederate Cherokees. Probably served in this legion.

MOORE, J. D. _____
North Carolina pension records appear to indicate that he served in this legion. Survived the war.

MOORE, T. B., _____
North Carolina pension records appear to indicate that he served in this legion.

MURRAY, M. M., Corporal
Confederate Gravestone Records appear to indicate that he served in this legion. Survived the war.

NORMAN, J. I., _____
North Carolina pension records indicate that he served in this legion.

ORR, W. B., _____
North Carolina pension records indicate that he served in this legion. Survived the war.

OWEN, M. A., _____
North Carolina pension records indicate that he served in this legion.

PALMER, LAFAYETTE L., _____
North Carolina pension records appear to indicate that he served in this legion.

PATTERSON, J. R., _____
Name appears on a receipt roll for clothing dated October 16, 1864, as a member of "Co M," Thomas's Legion.

PEASLEY, CHARLES, Private
Resided at Richmond, Virginia. Place and date of enlistment not reported; probably enlisted subsequent to February 29, 1864. Deserted to the enemy on an unspecified date. Sent to Chattanooga, Tennessee. Took the Oath of Allegiance at Chattanooga on May 26, 1865.

PENLEY, W. D., _____
North Carolina pension records indicate that he served in this legion. Survived the war.

PENTON, FRANCIS, Private
Place and date of enlistment not reported; probably enlisted subsequent to December 31, 1863. Captured in Haywood County on February 5, 1865. Sent to Knoxville, Tennessee. No further records.

PHILLIPS, J. M., _____
North Carolina pension records indicate that he served in this legion.

PHILLIPS, JOE, _____
North Carolina pension records indicate that he served in this legion. Survived the war.

PRESLEY, M. C., _____
North Carolina pension records indicate that he served in this legion. Survived the war.

PURUCHER, JOHN WILLIAM, Sergeant
Records of the United Daughters of the Confederacy appear to indicate that he served either in this legion or in the 69th Regiment N.C. Troops (7th Regiment N.C. Cavalry). Also served in the Armory Guard Battalion.

QUEEN, LUKE, _____
Name appears on a list of Confederate veterans from Jackson County. Survived the war.

RAPER, JOHN A., Private
Served with the 39th Regiment N.C. Troops. Records of that unit indicate that he served in this legion prior to his transfer to the 39th Regiment.

REED, DAVID C., _____
North Carolina pension records appear to indicate that he served in this legion.

REYNOLDS, D. W., _____
North Carolina pension records indicate that he served in this legion. Survived the war.

RHEA, WILLIAM MADISON, _____
Records of the United Daughters of the Confederacy indicate that he served in this legion.

RHODARMER, JOHN L., Private
Confederate Gravestone Records appear to indicate that he served in this legion.

RHODARMER, R. JOHN, Private
Confederate Gravestone Records appear to indicate that he served in this legion.

RHODARMER, WILLIAM K., Private
Confederate Gravestone Records appear to indicate that he served in this legion. Survived the war.

RICE, JOHN S., _____
North Carolina pension records indicate that he served in this legion. Survived the war.

RICH, J. C., _____
North Carolina pension records appear to indicate that he served in this legion. Survived the war.

RICH, JOHN _____
Name appears on a receipt roll for clothing dated October 16, 1864, as a member of "Co. M," Thomas's Legion.

ROBINSON, J. A.., Private
Confederate Gravestone Records appear to indicate that he served in this legion. Survived the war.

ROGERS, T. J. M., _____
North Carolina pension records indicate that he served in "Captain Teague's Company" of Thomas's Legion; however, none of the companies in this legion appear to have been commanded by a captain named Teague.

ROPER, WILLIAM E. _____
North Carolina pension records indicate that he served in this legion. Survived the war.

ROWLAND, JOHN WESLEY, _____
North Carolina pension records appear to indicate that he served in this legion. Survived the war.

SAWYER, CLINGMAN, _____
North Carolina pension records indicate that he served in this legion. Survived the war.

SHOPE, PHILIP, _____
North Carolina pension records appear to indicate that he served in this legion. Survived the war.

SHULER, GEORGE WASHINGTON, _____
North Carolina pension records appear to indicate that he served in this legion. Survived the war.

SHULER, WILLIAM G., _____

North Carolina pension records indicate that he served in this legion.

SINGLETON, W. S., Captain

According to the records of Pvt. Thomas N. Hurst of Company E, 65th Regiment N.C. Troops (6th Regiment N.C. Cavalry), Singleton was in command of "Company F, Walker's Battalion," described as part of this legion, in February, 1865. [It is possible that Singleton's company was one of the three white companies that had served in Thomas's western North Carolina battalion in 1864. An estimate for funding for the units in the Department of Western North Carolina for early 1865 would seem to indicate that Thomas had sent two of those companies to the Infantry Regiment and one to McKamy's (Walker's) Battalion, based on the number of captains given for the regiment and the battalion and the fact that the four Indian companies from the western North Carolina battalion had been separated from their white counterparts. See Consolidated Estimate of Funds Required for the Pay of the Troops in the Department of Western North Carolina for the Months of March and April 1865, March 11, 1865, Thomas Legion, Battalion Field and Staff File #1, Muster and Pay Rolls, Chapter 1: Entry 18, Box 826, RG 109, NA. If this is correct, it is not known which of the three white companies went to Walker's old battalion. It may have been Company K, 5th Regiment Tennessee Cavalry (McKenzie's), which had originally been Company F of Walker's Battalion and had served in Thomas's western North Carolina battalion as Company G (see the company history accompanying the roster for Company G, Indian Battalion, in this volume); however, W. S. Singleton has no known connection to that unit. At the same time, it is possible that Singleton's company was not connected with Thomas's Legion at all. The company was near Clayton, Georgia, far from Thomas's normal range of operations (but not necessarily impossible, given his concerns for his supply line to South Carolina). Secondly, it seems likelier that Walker's Battalion would be known formally as McKamy's Battalion or Stringfield's Battalion at this point in the war, or as the 1st Battalion, Thomas's Legion. Thus, the connection of Singleton's company to this legion is tentative at best.]

SKITTY, SEVIER S., _____

North Carolina pension records indicate that he served in this legion. Survived the war. [His surname may have been Kitty. May have been a Cherokee Indian.]

SLEAVER, JAMES H., _____

Confederate Gravestone Records indicate that he served in this legion.

SMITH, W. B., _____

Born in Haywood County on February 20, 1847. Tennessee pension application No. 13650 indicates that he served in this legion. Survived the war.

SNIDER, THOMAS L., Sergeant

Served as Sergeant in Company C, 25th Regiment N.C. Troops. Last reported absent wounded in February, 1865, following the loss of his left foot in action at or near Globe Tavern, Virginia, in August, 1864; however, he claimed after the war that "as soon as he could walk joined Thomas's Legion, where he remained until the surrender." ["Our Reunion: The True and Tried Who Followed the Banner of the 'Lost Cause' in Camps!" (undated newspaper account of a reunion of Haywood County veterans), Civil War Collection, North Carolina State Archives. His surname may have been Snyder.]

STAMEY, ELISHA STANFORD, _____

North Carolina pension records indicate that he served in this legion. Survived the war.

STEELMAN, JOHN MARION, _____

A Tennessee "Civil War Veteran's Questionnaire" indicates that he served in this legion.

STEPP, JOSEPH F., _____

North Carolina pension records appear to indicate that he served in this legion. Survived the war.

TABOR, J. S., _____

North Carolina pension records indicate that he served in this legion.

TAYLOR, HENRY, _____

North Carolina pension records indicate that he may have served in this legion. Survived the war.

TAYLOR, WILLIAM, Private

Resided in Polk County, Tennessee. Place and date of enlistment not reported. Took the Oath of Allegiance at Nashville, Tennessee, January 7, 1864.

THOMAS, CUDGE, _____

Negro. North Carolina pension records indicate that he served as servant to Col. William Holland Thomas throughout the latter's service. *The* (Sylva) *Ruralite* of June 28, 1932, describes him as one of nine surviving Jackson County Civil War veterans. [His given name may have been Gudge.]

THOMAS, WILLIAM, Sergeant

Confederate Gravestone Records appear to indicate that he served in this legion, after having served in Company B, 6th Regiment South Carolina Infantry. [There is no record of Sgt. Thomas's service in Company B, 6th South Carolina. There was a Pvt. W. L. Thomas who served briefly in 2nd Company F of that unit, but it is not certain that they were the same man.]

TIDWELL, ROBERT S., Captain

Tennessee pension application No. 13015 indicates that he served as a Captain in this legion, but his service is doubtful. Survived the war.

TIPPETT, W. D., _____

North Carolina pension records appear to indicate that he served in this legion. Survived the war.

TRIPLET, ROSS, Private

Resided in Macon County or in Lawrence County, Kentucky. Place and date of enlistment not reported; probably enlisted subsequent to February 29, 1864. Deserted on an unknown date. Captured by the enemy in Lawrence County, Kentucky, on an unknown date. Sent to

Chattanooga, Tennessee. Took the Oath of Allegiance at Chattanooga on June 11, 1864. Transferred to Louisville, Kentucky, where he arrived on June 14, 1864. Took (affirmed) the Oath of Allegiance at Louisville on June 14, 1864. Released at Louisville on June 15, 1864, with orders to remain north of the Ohio River for the remainder of the war.

TURPIN, DAVID W., _____
North Carolina pension records indicate that he served in this legion.

UNDERWOOD, JAMES P., _____
North Carolina pension records indicate that he served in this legion. Survived the war.

WA-ATTI, _____
Cherokee Indian. Name appears on an undated (ca. 1900) list of living Confederate Cherokees. Probably served in this legion.

WALDROP, ANDERSON, Private
Served as Private in Companies A and F, 39th Regiment N.C. Troops. Records of Company F indicate that he enlisted in this legion on an unspecified date; however, there is no other evidence that he served in this legion.

WALLACE, MATTHEW C., Private
Served as Private in Company G, 39th Regiment N.C. Troops. Records of that company indicate that he was transferred to this legion on an unspecified date; however, there is no other evidence that he served in this legion.

WARREN, WALLACE, _____
North Carolina pension records indicate that he served in this legion.

WATSON, GEORGE W., Private
Confederate gravestone records appear to indicate that he served in this legion. Survived the war.

WELCH, J. E. T., _____
North Carolina pension records appear to indicate that he served in this legion and survived the war. [May have been the same man as Pvt. Thomas J. Welch of Company H, Infantry Regiment of this legion.]

WEST, A. B., _____
North Carolina pension records indicate that he served in this legion. Survived the war.

WEST, ANDY, _____
North Carolina pension records indicate that he served in this legion. Survived the war.

WEST, WILL, _____
Cherokee Indian. North Carolina pension records indicate that he served in this legion. Survived the war.

WHITE, MANSON J., Private
Confederate Gravestone Records appear to indicate that he served in this legion. Survived the war.

WIGGINS, JAMES NEWTON, _____
North Carolina pension records indicate that he served in this legion. Survived the war.

WIKE, JOHN T., _____
North Carolina pension records appear to indicate that he served in this legion. Survived the war.

WILSON, JAMES M., _____
North Carolina pension records indicate that he served in this legion. Survived the war.

WILSON, WILLIAM JOHNSON, _____
North Carolina pension records indicate that he served in this legion. Survived the war.

WOLFE, JOHN, _____
Cherokee Indian. Name appears on an undated list (ca. 1900) of living Cherokee Confederates. Probably served in this legion.

WYATT, J. B., _____
North Carolina pension records appear to indicate that he served in this legion. Survived the war.

YOUNG, JOSEPH, _____
Confederate Gravestone Records appear to indicate that he served in this legion.

INDEX

This index contains citations for soldiers and principals of substitutes listed in the foregoing rosters and for a variety of entries, including all persons, places, regiments, and battalions mentioned in the regimental histories. Alternate spellings of some surnames are cross-referenced. Because this index is composed primarily of personal names, a modified form of the word-by-word method of alphabetization has been employed whereby each entry is *initially* alphabetized to the point where the first comma appears; words that follow the first comma are alphabetized separately as a *secondary* category. That method permits the placement of entries such as "Franklin Rifles" at the end, rather than awkwardly in the middle, of the Franklin surname section. Place names are placed *after* identical surnames; for example, an entry for Franklin, North Carolina, would follow all entries for men whose surname was Franklin. Military units are listed under entries in which the word "units" is preceded by the name of the state of origin. Numbered units are listed first, in numerical order, followed by other units, in alphabetical order.

D

E

G

T

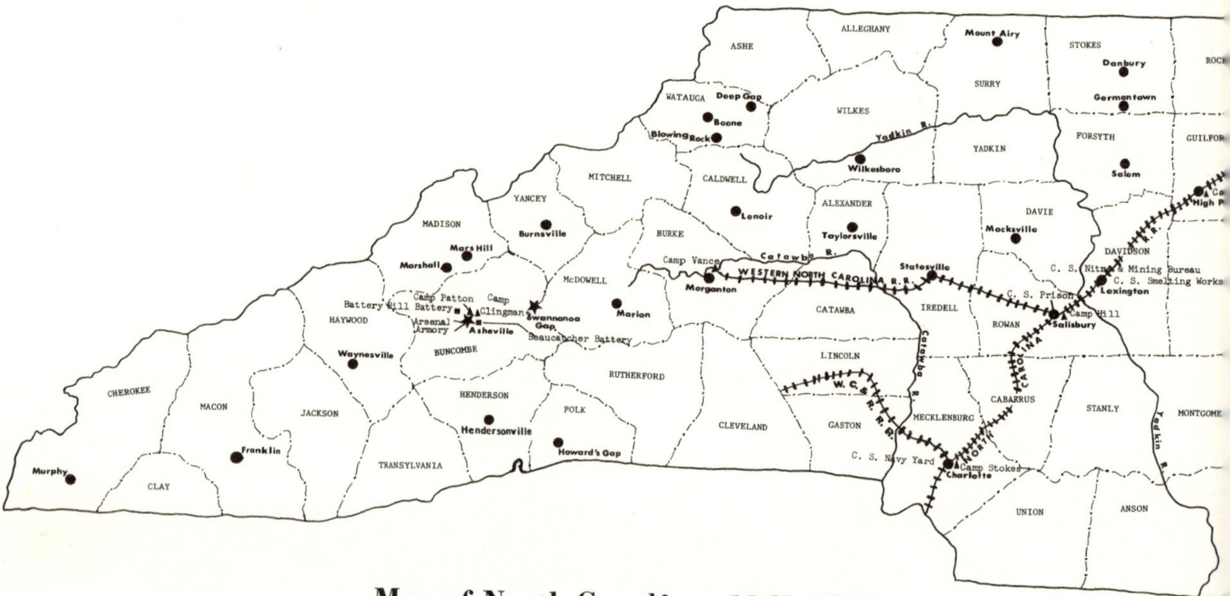

Map of North Carolina, 1861-1865

Drawn by James R. Vogt

This map locates the principal camps, forts, towns, railroads, and engagements fought in the state during the Civil War.

LEGEND

- ● — **Towns**
- ■ — **Forts and batteries**
- ▲ — **Camps of instruct**
- ★ — **Engagements**
- ╫ — **Railroads**